NATIVE TREES, SHRUBS, AND VINES for URBAN and RURAL AMERICA

NATIVE TREES, SHRUBS, AND VINES for URBAN and RURAL AMERICA

A Planting Design Manual for Environmental Designers

Gary L. Hightshoe
Professor of Landscape Architecture
Iowa State University

VNR VAN NOSTRAND REINHOLD
—————————————— New York

Van Nostrand Reinhold
115 Fifth Avenue
New York, New York 10003

Van Nostrand Reinhold (International) Limited
11 New Fetter Lane
London EC4P 4EE, England

Van Nostrand Reinhold
480 La Trobe Street
Melbourne, Victoria 3000, Australia

Macmillan of Canada
Division of Canada Publishing Corporation
164 Commander Boulevard
Agincourt, Ontario M1S 3C7, Canada

16   15   14   13   12   11   10   9   8   7   6   5   4   3   2

Library of Congress Cataloging-in-Publication Data

Hightshoe, Gary L.
  Native trees, shrubs, and vines for urban and
rural America.

  Bibliography: p.
  Includes index.
  1. Ornamental woody plants—United States.
2. Woody plants—United States. I. Title.
SB435.5.H54   1987   715'.0973   87-18911
ISBN 0-442-23274-8

To my respected colleague Robert W. Dyas, Professor of Landscape Architecture, Iowa State University, Ames, Iowa, whose genuine love of native plants and stewardship for natural landscapes have influenced many.

And to my students, who have roamed with me through woods, marsh, and prairie; who, with their enthusiastic and sincere questions, have kept me awake to the very great variety and beauty of our natural landscape heritage and to the challenge of managing it for the use and enjoyment of future generations.

CONTENTS

PART I
NATIVE TREES

CONTENTS

LIST OF TABLES AND FIGURES

INTRODUCTION

Survey of Plant Literature

Studies of the trees and shrubs that might be used by the designer have been well documented by writers over a long period of time. Most have treated the subject from a strictly professional viewpoint. The botanist's principal concern focused upon the proper identification of plant materials in the field, emphasizing important identification characteristics including twig, bud, leaf, flower, and fruit differences. Horticultural publications concentrated on proper plant culture. This included plant adaptability and hardiness, preparation of plant root environments, identification and treatment of biological disorders, and propagation techniques. Foresters traditionally stressed the identification and classification of plant community types and floristic composition. Emphasis was on plant tolerances, as these related to forest productivity and yield. The potential uses of plant materials in the designed landscape have been largely explored in the literature of landscape gardeners, horticulturists, and more recently landscape architects. Visual aspects of plants (including qualities of form, texture, color, and seasonal change) have generally been discussed in a broad theoretical sense with infrequent or incomplete reference to specific examples.

Environmental Designer Defined

It is a measure of our progress today that we are in the midst of a dynamic movement to restore, protect and preserve our environment and to plan for the most effective use of our environmental resources. The principal objective of this awakening is to provide a better quality of life for ourselves and for future generations. We have learned that our past cultural progress was often achieved at an environmental cost which despoiled our air, water, vegetation, and land.

The attitude of today's society toward plants is changing. As a result, the various contemporary professional disciplines together with a knowledgeable citizenry are rallying behind a collective mission which attempts to safeguard future environmental quality. The gardenesque approach (which carried over from earlier periods and stressed the value of plants to enhance architecture, beautify a site, or improve aesthetic qualities of an area) will continue to be popular. However, it is the challenge of contemporary environmental designers and planners to make provisions for the use of native plants and natural systems in large scale planning, policy, and management.

Jens Jensen, one of America's foremost landscape architects was deeply impressed by the subtle beauties of the prairie landscape of the midwest and tried to re-create the artistic form and spirit of prairie in his landscape designs. In his book *Siftings* he states,

> To me it is stupid to transplant trees into an environment they dislike and in which their length of life will be shortened and their beauty never revealed. Nature is not to be copied — man cannot copy God's out-of-doors. He can interpret its message in a composition of living tones. The real worth of the landscaper lies in his ability to give to humanity the blessing of nature's spiritual values as they are interpreted in his art.

In "A Designer Looks at the Garden", Robert W. Dyas, Professor of Landscape Architecture at Iowa State University, includes the following evaluation

> The landscape architect designs for people, but his design is of the land - a particular place within the continuum of time and space. The spirit of this place has resulted from the interaction of all elements and activities throughout its history. The **new landscape design** is a continuation of these activities and interactions. If the designer is to preserve and provide for others the spirit or essence of this place, he must treat it with understanding and compassion. If he does, the potential values of the site will be experienced and enjoyed by all who use it. It will express beauty and utility through its own integrity and individuality.

He concludes that the site design

> must honestly express its continuity with the greater landscape of which it is a part. This is often attained by preserving and emphasizing its natural topography, vegetation, water features, and sometimes by preserving significant

buildings and other manmade features. These elements remain as integral parts of the greater landscape permitting the designer and the user to claim and experience the qualities and strength of the whole.

American Environmental Design Tradition

Traditionally urban landscape architecture in America has stressed the importance of planted open space as an integral part of the city. There is also a strong tradition relating the urban fabric to the surrounding landscape region as mirrored in the use of natural features and indigenous plant material.

Frederick Law Olmstead (1822-1903), the first to call himself a landscape architect, is generally considered our most comprehensive environmental planner and designer. His design approach was based on his understanding of the social needs of persons living in the city and of the responsibility to aesthetic and ecological principles. Dr. Albert Fein, Director of the Urban Studies Program at the Brooklyn Center of Long Island University, in his book *Frederick Law Olmstead and the American Environmental Tradition* reviews Olmstead's major design legacy

> The two major urban accomplishments that mark the start and the conclusion of Olmstead's career as an environmental planner — Central Park in New York and the Chicago World's Fair — present two different sharply contrasting environmental forms. Central Park is romantic in style, oriented to the land, and small-scale detail; the Fair landscape is classical in style, dominated by structures, and monumentally scaled.

Both designs reflect Olmstead's concept that the ecological context must be given precedence over social, political, architectural, managerial, and commercial factors which influence design form and material selection. It was Olmstead's contention that if ecological laws were violated, there was little hope for social planning or other types of planning.

> Nothing was more disturbing to Olmstead in the 1880's than the increased use of exotic plant materials for decorative purposes. The need for public education in sound ecological principles and "natural" gardening motivated Olmstead to join with the noted horticulturist and botanist Charles Sprague Sargent in the planning and design of the Arnold Arboretum (Fein 1972).

The Contemporary Challenge

Olmstead articulated for his generation and ours a philosophy and a set of working principles for the creation of urban and rural landscapes. The type of planning that considers cities as separated from regions and unrelated to considerations of ecology cannot hope to succeed. All environmental planning must proceed with the awareness that any alterations of ecological processes have deep implications which threaten the health and survivability of both the immediate site area and the larger landscape region. The contemporary challenge to environmental design and planning remains sociological, ecological, and aesthetic, as it was in Olmstead's day (Fein 1972).

> We have noticed an increasing use of native plant materials, especially in the application of whole associations or formations of plants, such as the prairie restorations we are experiencing in the midwest. Along with this, we expect to see an increasing reliance upon methods of management, utilizing natural systems, such as fire and natural predators. Plants will be more closely related to the site as a habitat, where climate, aspect, and soils will be more sensitively considered. We anticipate a trend away from landscape designs dependent upon irrigation, special seasonal protection, and constant mechanical control of diseases and pests (Dyas 1975).

The Need — An Environmental Design Tool

Plant materials offer a richness of vocabulary, a wealth of palette not surpassed by the material range of any other sort of creative work. Plants are living organisms which change in complex patterned response to the influences of climate, soils, topography, wind, animals, other plants, and man. The potential for richness and variety of expression in the rural and urban landscapes through the use of plant materials is all but overwhelming (Eckbo 1950). This variety proposes a problem of discipline in selection of those materials. The key to successful use of plant materials in the designed landscape expression is adequate communication. The dilemma of the environmental designer is the immediate need to develop a system which would:

1) present a basic language which would facilitate communication between layman, student, and professional regarding plant analysis, selection, and synthesis.

2) classify ecological relationships as well as cultural requirements and visual characteristics.

3) combine the many popular literary efforts and scientific information into one comprehensive planting design source and tool.

4) organize critical plant information and vocabulary into a standarized format to facilitate efficient economic analysis and comparison of the complex of relationships (plant to design program, plant to plant, and plant to environment). This articulated framework could be transferred to other regional analysis systems, e.g. computer retrieval system. It is not unrealistic to project for the near future a plant resource memory system of scientific and environmental information for every floristic region in North America. Such a comprehensive tool would prove invaluable to the designer, with environmental landscape quality more assured for future generations.

The intent of this publication is to provide the layman, student, and professional with text and tool to clarify complex plant interrelationships and comparisons. Clarification enables the designer to select, with greater confidence and understanding, plant materials which not only satisfy design program directives but, more importantly, maximize plant health and survivability through regional environmental fit.

Part I of this volume offers a classification format and text that identifies, categorizes, and theorizes about the benefits and uses of indigenous trees.

How to Use Part I

Part I is divided into two principal parts: an **ELIMINATION KEY** section followed by a **MASTER PLATES** section.

ELIMINATION KEY

Tree selection is based on definite classifiable characteristics. No two trees exhibit all the same characteristics. If the list of plant performance criteria is expanded it becomes possible to narrow the selection field to a few suitable species by eliminating the unsuitable from consideration. This is done simply and quickly in this book by employing the elimination key format.

Plants that exhibit similar design characteristics are grouped together in plant lists. These plant lists are organized and classified according to various design attributes under three primary categories which include visual characteristics, cultural requirements, and ecological relationships. When choosing a suitable tree for a specific design criteria (for example, trees with colorful white bark), the process would be to 1) consult the general category (bark coloration), 2) identify the specific color feature (white) and 3) review the corresponding plant list. Such plant lists facilitate efficient comparison between plants exhibiting similar design characteristics. Trees within each category are listed in alphabetical order according to their botanic or scientific names, genus first, followed by the species name. Preferred common names are included in parenthesis. Important botanic nomenclature is quickly learned through repeated association with the more familiar preferred common name.

The **ELIMINATION KEY** section presents basic classification terminology and descriptions used in this book. The principle advantage of the **ELIMINATION KEY** is that the designer need be familiar only with the plant performance criteria. Prior knowledge regarding specific plant species, although helpful, is not necessary. The plants under consideration can be explored in greater written and illustrated detail by consulting the **MASTER PLATE** section.

MASTER PLATES

This section brings together all the design information for any given tree. If the designer is familiar with the specific plant under consideration, consulting directly the **MASTER PLATE** text and illustrations would be the next step in determining the plant's suitability in the design program. If the botanic or preferred common name is known, it is not necessary to consult the key, and the **MASTER PLATE** can be consulted directly by using the index in the back of the book. At the heading of each **MASTER PLATE** the botanical name (left page) and the preferred common name (right page) are given.

Text: The format of the **MASTER PLATE** text offers the designer a classification system which facilitates efficient plant comparison and the analysis and synthesis of important design criteria. The classification system employed in this manual establishes a rational hierarchy showing relationships among and between categories. This hierarchy is organized as follows:

> *GENERAL CHARACTERISTIC GROUP,* all plant information is organized into three areas of designer concern, e.g. *VISUAL CHARACTERISTICS, ECOLOGICAL RELATIONSHIPS,* and *CULTURAL REQUIREMENTS.*
>
> **PRIMARY CHARACTERISTIC CLASS,** e.g. **FORM, BRANCHING, FOLIAGE, FLOWER, FRUIT.** (Identified by bold face caps.)
>
> Secondary Characteristic Class, e.g. Size, Spread, Mass, Twig, Bud, Bark. (Identified by medium face, first letter caps.)
>
> **specific design data, e.g. large canopy, wide, open.** (Identified by bold face, lower case. These are key words which are cross-referenced to the plant lists presented in the **ELIMINATION KEY** section.)
>
> specific design data, e.g. 15 to 22.5 m (50 to 75 ft), usually 2/3 that of mature height. (Identified by medium face, lower case. This is additional text presented for clarity and designer review. This information is not of key word importance and is not reflected in the **ELIMINATION KEY** section.)

The classification system as it appears in the **MASTER PLATE** text is summarized below and the major categories are identified.

```
                    ──────────── PRIMARY CHARACTERISTIC CLASS
                  ┌────────────
   FORM:   ovoid to globular
 ( Size:   large canopy - 22.5 to 30 m (75 to 100 ft) )─────── GENERAL CHARACTERISTIC
   Spread:   wide - 15 to 22.5 m (50 to 75 ft)                 GROUP-VISUAL
   Mass:   extremely dense
      │                    │
      │          └────────── specific design data
      │                     (with key word in bold face)
      └──────────── Secondary Characteristic Class
```

Metric and Standard Measure: The metric system has been used throughout. The following table of approximate equivalents will clarify the measurements for the reader who is not familiar with metric measure. In the text all metric measurements are followed by the American Standard Equivalent in parentheses. It was felt that by repeatedly seeing both systems of measure side by side the reader would quickly become familiar with the metric equivalent through association.

Common metric conversion factors
- 1 cm = 0.3937 inch
- 1 inch = 2.54 cm = 25.4 mm
- 1 meter = 3.281 feet
- 1 foot = 0.3048 meter

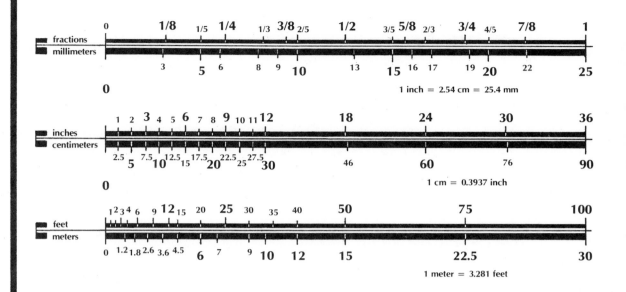

Symbols: For convenience and quick cross reference between sections, a system of abstract pictorial symbols is used in the margins of both the **ELIMINATION KEY** section and the **MASTER PLATE** section opposite the corresponding written characteristics description.

Range Map: The natural range of each native tree is mapped showing geographic distribution by county. The use of geographic distribution maps as general guides to the conservation, preservation, and restoration of historic natural landscapes is encouraged. Even though a species is not recorded for a certain county, its proved occurrence in an adjacent county or within the same floristic region may be taken to mean that its adaptability is possible (providing suitable habitat exists).

Drawings: For the designer an accurate visual image of the plant (with its typical form, structure, mass, size, and detail) is essential. Text description alone is rarely sufficient and then only if the designer has seen and become familiar with the plant in the field. Photographs, often used for this purpose, rarely give proper prominence to plant qualities of most critical importance to the designer. The undiscriminating camera eye captures detail more attractive to the botanist but often confusing to the designer. Separation of plant form and structure from competing background images is often difficult. Light direction (front light, back light, side light) and intensity frequently alter or destroy perception of important plant qualities. Freehand line drawings are most successful in capturing attributes of designer importance providing the drawings are sensitively and compassionately labored. Over 300 freehand drawings successfully capture the visual spirit of 122 native trees.

The artwork is intended to visually assist the layman, student, and professional in the selection of tree species that fulfill the design program. Tree crown sketches portray mature adult open field plants. A metric scale documents adult canopy height (vertical scale) and spread (horizontal scale).

Freehand illustrations of important plant details (for example, twig, bud, foliage, flower, fruit, and armament) are also included for reference and clarification. The majority of the detail illustrations of twig and leaf were drawn from fresh specimens; a few were made from photographic records and herbarium specimens. All of the tree crown illustrations were sketched from slides or from pencil sketches in the field.

Region of Use: The region of application and use of this manual includes southeastern and south central Canada; north central, northeastern, central and east central United States.

ACKNOWLEDGMENTS

Many persons have been involved in the preparation and review of part I. The author wishes to recognize and thank the many students, colleagues, professionals, and laypersons whose suggestions and encouragement were vital to its completion. Those persons who carried a major share of the responsibility are:

William C. Boon, colleague and good friend, for the many excellent illustrative sketches drawn especially for this part.

Gregg A. Coyle, Landscape Architect, Houston, Texas, for the endless hours spent in drawing all the tree crowns. His skill and artistic talent capture so well the detailed spirit of the native trees.

Harlen D. Groe, Landscape Architect, for creating and producing the design format and graphic and copy layout.

Gretchen F. Harshbarger, Landscape Architect, Iowa City, Iowa, for generously offering some 35 original illustrations sketched in 1935 and an equal number completed specifically for this part. Her artistic skills and enthusiasm were greatly appreciated.

John A. Harrington, for designing and drafting the range maps, which were patterned after those presented in *Atlas of United States Trees*, volumes 1 and 3, authored by E.L. Little, Jr., Forest Service, U.S.D.A.

Tina M. Herzog, for typing the many early drafts of the manuscript and plant lists.

A special thank you to my wife, Joan, and daughter Kate for their patience and support during the years this part has been in preparation.

Finally, we acknowledge our great debt to the many botanists, horticulturists, foresters, landscape architects, and landscape gardeners past and present, whose popular writings and teachings form the background upon which we have relied. The author, of course, accepts full responsibility for any inaccuracies or misrepresentation of the information herein.

TREE
ELIMINATION KEY

NOMENCLATURE:

The scientific and common names used in this book are given in *Standardized Plant Names*. The trees are listed alphabetically according to their scientific or botanical name. *Standardized Plant Names*, current edition, is the most complete single reference available and is approved by the American Committee on Horticultural Nomenclature and the American Society of Landscape Architects. Botanical nomenclature has several principal advantages: it is understood in all countries, is based on natural relationships of plants and is consistent in form. Common names, however, were not originated with these features in mind. Many common names for the same plant are encountered and reflect local usage. Many plants also share the same common names. The plants used in landscape design can be designated by using the generic and specific name. Generic names (genus) distinguish groups of plants such as oaks and maples. Specific names (species) are used to distinguish variables within a genus, and are geneally descriptive of some visual or physiological aspect such as leaf size, shape, color, texture and surface, or geographical aspect (virginiana, canadensis, americana).

FORM:

Each species of trees has a characteristic shape when grown in an open field under favorable environmental conditions. The shape of a particular tree refers to the outline of the crown as perceived in silhouette. Volumetric description best expresses the adult crown form for each species. Six basic crown forms for natural, open grown trees are classified.

GLOBULAR:
rounded circular form, vertical and horizontal axis about equal,
indicator—*Quercus macrocarpa* (Bur Oak)

Acer nigrum   (Black Maple)
Acer pensylvanicum   (Striped Maple)
Acer rubrum   (Red Maple)
Acer saccharinum   (Silver Maple)
Acer saccharum   (Sugar Maple)
Alnus rugosa   (Hazel Alder)
Amelanchier canadensis   (Shadblow Serviceberry)
Amelanchier laevis   (Allegany Serviceberry)
Betula lenta   (Sweet Birch)
Betula lutea   (Yellow Birch)
Betula papyrifera   (Paper Birch)
Carpinus caroliniana   (American Hornbeam)
Carya cordiformis   (Bitternut Hickory)
Carya illinoensis   (Pecan)
Castanea dentata   (American Chestnut)
Celtis occidentalis   (Common Hackberry)
Cercis canadensis   (Eastern Redbud)
Cladrastis lutea   (American Yellowwood)
Cornus florida   (Flowering Dogwood)
Crataegus crusgalli   (Cockspur Hawthorn)
Crataegus mollis   (Downy Hawthorn)
Crataegus nitida   (Glossy Hawthorn)
Crataegus pruinosa   (Frosted Hawthorn)

Crataegus punctata   (Dotted Hawthorn)
Euonymus atropurpureus   (Eastern Wahoo)
Gleditsia triacanthos   (Common Honeylocust)
Halesia carolina   (Carolina Silverbell)
Hamamelis virginiana   (Common Witchhazel)
Maclura pomifera   (Osageorange)
Malus ioensis   (Prairie Crabapple)
Morus rubra   (Red Mulberry)
Pinus rigida   (Pitch Pine)
Platanus occidentalis   (American Planetree)
Populus deltoides   (Eastern Poplar)
Prunus americana   (American Plum)
Quercus alba   (White Oak)
Quercus borealis   (Northern Red Oak)
Quercus coccinea   (Scarlet Oak)
Quercus macrocarpa   (Bur Oak)
Quercus montana   (Chestnut Oak)
Quercus muhlenbergi   (Chinkapin Oak)
Quercus stellata   (Post Oak)
Quercus velutina   (Black Oak)
Ulmus americana   (American Elm)
Viburnum rufidulum   (Rusty Blackhaw Viburnum)

Form (cont.)

OVOID:

elliptic to egg-shaped, broadest at base, vertical axis exceeding horizontal by 2 to 1 ratio, indicator—*Acer saccharum* (Sugar Maple)

Acer nigrum   (Black Maple)
Acer rubrum   (Red Maple)
Acer saccharum   (Sugar Maple)
Betula lutea   (Yellow Birch)
Carya ovata   (Shagbark Hickory)
Carya tomentosa   (Mockernut Hickory)
Cornus alternifolia   (Pagoda Dogwood)
Crataegus phaenopyrum   (Washington Hawthorn)
Diospyros virginiana   (Common Persimmon)
Fagus grandifolia   (American Beech)
Fraxinus americana   (White Ash)
Fraxinus pennsylvanica   (Green Ash)
Liquidambar styraciflua   (American Sweetgum)
Magnolia acuminata   (Cucumbertree Magnolia)

Oxydendrum arboreum   (Sourwood)
Pinus flexilis   (Limber Pine)
Pinus ponderosa   (Ponderosa Pine)
Pinus resinosa   (Red Pine)
Pinus strobus   (Eastern White Pine)
Prunus pensylvanica   (Pin Cherry)
Prunus serotina   (Black Cherry)
Quercus bicolor   (Swamp White Oak)
Quercus borealis   (Northern Red Oak)
Quercus ellipsoidalis   (Northern Pin Oak)
Quercus marilandica   (Blackjack Oak)
Quercus velutina   (Black Oak)
Sorbus decora   (Showy Mountainash)
Tilia americana   (American Linden)

OBOVOID:

elliptic to egg-shaped, broadest at crown apex, vertical axis exceeding horizontal by 2 to 1 ratio, indicator—*Amelanchier laevis* (Allegany Serviceberry)

Acer negundo   (Boxelder)
Acer pensylvanicum   (Striped Maple)
Acer spicatum   (Mountain Maple)
Amelanchier canadensis   (Shadblow Serviceberry)
Amelanchier laevis   (Allegany Serviceberry)
Carpinus caroliniana   (American Hornbeam)
Carya glabra   (Pignut Hickory)
Carya ovata   (Shagbark Hickory)
Carya tomentosa   (Mockernut Hickory)
Chionanthus virginicus   (White Fringetree)
Cotinus americanus   (Cockspur Hawthorn)
Crataegus phaenopyrum   (Washington Hawthorn)

Halesia carolina   (Carolina Silverbell)
Hamamelis virginiana   (Common Witchhazel)
Populus deltoides   (Eastern Poplar)
Prunus virginiana   (Common Chokecherry)
Rhododendron maximum   (Rosebay Rhododendron)
Rhus copallina   (Flameleaf Sumac)
Rhus glabra   (Smooth Sumac)
Rhus typhina   (Staghorn Sumac)
Viburnum lentago   (Nannyberry Viburnum)
Viburnum prunifolium   (Blackhaw Viburnum)
Viburnum rufidulum   (Rusty Blackhaw Viburnum)
Zanthoxylum americanum   (Common Pricklyash)

CONICAL:

approaching triangular in outline, broadest at base, indicator—*Picea pungens* (Colorado Spruce)

Abies balsamea   (Balsam Fir)
Abies concolor   (White Fir)
Abies lasiocarpa   (Alpine Fir)
Catalpa speciosa   (Northern Catalpa)
Fagus grandifolia   (American Beech)
Franklinia alatamaha   (Franklinia)
Juniperus virginiana   (Eastern Redcedar)
Larix laricina   (Eastern Larch)
Liquidambar styraciflua   (American Sweetgum)
Nyssa sylvatica   (Black Tupelo)
Ostrya virginiana   (American Hophornbeam)
Oxydendrum arboreum   (Sourwood)
Picea engelmanni   (Engelmann Spruce)
Picea glauca   (White Spruce)
Picea glauca densata   (BlackHills White Spruce)

Picea mariana   (Black Spruce)
Picea pungens   (Colorado Spruce)
Pinus banksiana   (Jack Pine)
Pinus flexilis   (Limber Pine)
Pinus ponderosa   (Ponderosa Pine)
Pinus resinosa   (Red Pine)
Pinus strobus   (Eastern White Pine)
Pseudotsuga taxifolia   (Common Douglasfir)
Quercus imbricaria   (Shingle Oak)
Quercus palustris   (Pin Oak)
Sassafras albidum   (Common Sassafras)
Taxodium distichum   (Common Baldcypress)
Thuja occidentalis   (Eastern Arborvitae)
Tsuga canadensis   (Canada Hemlock)

COLUMNAR:

cylindrical, vertical axis much exceeding horizontal, indicator—*Populus tremuloides* (Quaking Aspen)

Betula nigra   (River Birch)

Betula populifolia   (Gray Birch)

Chionanthus virginicus   (White Fringetree)
Liriodendron tulipifera   (Tuliptree)
Populus grandidentata   (Bigtooth Aspen)
Populus tremuloides   (Quaking Aspen)
Prunus pensylvanica   (Pin Cherry)
Prunus serotina   (Black Cherry)

Robinia pseudoacacia   (Black Locust)
Salix amygdaloides   (Peachleaf Willow)
Salix bebbiana   (Bebb Willow)
Salix discolor   (Pussy Willow)
Salix nigra   (Black Willow)
Taxodium distichum   (Common Baldcypress)

IRREGULAR:
   assymetrical, uneven outline,
   indicator—*Acer negundo* (Boxelder)

Acer negundo   (Boxelder)
Acer saccharinum   (Silver Maple)
Acer spicatum   (Mountain Maple)
Aesculus glabra   (Ohio Buckeye)
Aesculus octandra   (Yellow Buckeye)
Aralia spinosa   (Devils-Walkingstick)
Asimina triloba   (Common Pawpaw)
Carya glabra   (Pignut Hickory)
Carya ovata   (Shagbark Hickory)
Carya tomentosa   (Mockernut Hickory)
Catalpa speciosa   (Northern Catalpa)
Cotinus americanus   (American Smoketree)
Fraxinus americana   (White Ash)
Fraxinus nigra   (Black Ash)
Fraxinus pennsylvanica   (Green Ash)
Fraxinus quadrangulata   (Blue Ash)

Gleditsia triacanthos   (Common Honeylocust)
Gymnocladus dioicus   (Kentucky Coffeetree)
Juglans cinerea   (Butternut)
Juglans nigra   (Eastern Black Walnut)
Pinus banksiana   (Jack Pine)
Pinus rigida   (Pitch Pine)
Ptelea trifoliata   (Common Hoptree)
Quercus muhlenbergi   (Chinkapin Oak)
Rhododendron maximum   (Rosebay Rhododendron)
Rhus copallina   (Flameleaf Sumac)
Rhus glabra   (Smooth Sumac)
Rhus typhina   (Staghorn Sumac)
Robinia pseudoacacia   (Black Locust)
Sassafras albidum   (Common Sassafras)
Zanthoxylum americanum   (Common Pricklyash)

SIZE:

The compatibility of the dimensional measure of a selected plant crown with the designed program function is essential. Designer knowledge of the relative mature height and spread is especially critical where spacial limitations exist. Failure to recognize the potential adult size of a plant results in spatial overcrowding and often necessitates severe and unsightly maintenance, which alters the natural form of the plant and consequently the designer's intent. Knowledge of mature crown size is demanded if proper scale and proportion are to be achieved in the designed landscape expression.

HEIGHT: Four strata of relative mature tree height are classified.

LARGE CANOPY:
   22.5 to 30 meters or more (75 to 100 feet plus),
   indicator—*Acer saccharinum* (Silver Maple)

Abies concolor   (White Fir)
Abies lasiocarpa   (Alpine Fir)
Acer nigrum   (Black Maple)
Acer rubrum   (Red Maple)
Acer saccharinum   (Silver Maple)
Acer saccharum   (Sugar Maple)
Carya cordiformis   (Bitternut Hickory)
Carya glabra   (Pignut Hickory)
Carya illinoensis   (Pecan)
Carya ovata   (Shagbark Hickory)
Carya tomentosa   (Mockernut Hickory)

Catalpa speciosa   (Northern Catalpa)
Celtis occidentalis   (Common Hackberry)
Fagus grandifolia   (American Beech)
Fraxinus americana   (White Ash)
Gymnocladus dioicus   (Kentucky Coffeetree)
Juglans nigra   (Eastern Black Walnut)
Liquidambar styraciflua   (American Sweetgum)
Liriodendron tulipifera   (Tuliptree)
Magnolia acuminata   (Cucumbertree Magnolia)
Picea engelmanni   (Engelmann Spruce)
Picea pungens   (Colorado Spruce)

Height (cont.)

Pinus ponderosa   (Ponderosa Pine)
Pinus resinosa   (Red Pine)
Pinus strobus   (Eastern White Pine)
Platanus occidentalis   (American Planetree)
Populus deltoides   (Eastern Poplar)
Pseudotsuga taxifolia   (Common Douglasfir)
Quercus alba   (White Oak)
Quercus bicolor   (Swamp White Oak)

Quercus borealis   (Northern Red Oak)
Quercus macrocarpa   (Bur Oak)
Quercus velutina   (Black Oak)
Taxodium distichum   (Common Baldcypress)
Tilia americana   (American Linden)
Tsuga canadensis   (Canada Hemlock)
Ulmus americana   (American Elm)

SMALL CANOPY:
   15 to 22.5 meters (50 to 75 feet),
   indicator—*Betula papyrifera* (Paper Birch)

Abies balsamea   (Balsam Fir)
Aesculus octandra   (Yellow Buckeye)
Betula lenta   (Sweet Birch)
Betula lutea   (Yellow Birch)
Betula nigra   (River Birch)
Betula papyrifera   (Paper Birch)
Castanea dentata   (American Chestnut)
Cladrastis lutea   (American Yellowwood)
Diospyros virginiana   (Common Persimmon)
Fraxinus nigra   (Black Ash)
Fraxinus pennsylvanica   (Green Ash)
Fraxinus quadrangulata   (Blue Ash)
Gleditsia triacanthos   (Common Honeylocust)
Juglans cinerea   (Butternut)
Juniperus virginiana   (Eastern Redcedar)
Larix laricina   (Eastern Larch)

Nyssa sylvatica   (Black Tupelo)
Picea glauca   (White Spruce)
Picea glauca densata   (BlackHills White Spruce)
Picea mariana   (Black Spruce)
Pinus banksiana   (Jack Pine)
Pinus flexilis   (Limber Pine)
Pinus rigida   (Pitch Pine)
Populus grandidentata   (Bigtooth Aspen)
Prunus serotina   (Black Cherry)
Quercus coccinea   (Scarlet Oak)
Quercus ellipsoidalis   (Northern Pin Oak)
Quercus montana   (Chestnut Oak)
Quercus palustris   (Pin Oak)
Robinia pseudoacacia   (Black Locust)
Thuja occidentalis   (Eastern Arborvitae)

LARGE UNDERSTORY:
   10 to 15 meters (35 to 50 feet),
   indicator—*Maclura pomifera* (Osageorange)

Acer pensylvanicum   (Striped Maple)
Acer negundo   (Boxelder)
Aesculus glabra   (Ohio Buckeye)
Amelanchier canadensis   (Shadblow Serviceberry)
Aralia spinosa   (Devils-Walkingstick)
Betula populifolia   (Gray Birch)
Carpinus caroliniana   (American Hornbeam)
Cornus florida   (Flowering Dogwood)
Crataegus mollis   (Downy Hawthorn)
Maclura pomifera   (Osageorange)
Morus rubra   (Red Mulberry)
Ostrya virginiana   (American Hophornbeam)

Oxydendrum arboreum   (Sourwood)
Populus tremuloides   (Quaking Aspen)
Prunus virginiana   (Common Chokecherry)
Quercus imbricaria   (Shingle Oak)
Quercus marilandica   (Blackjack Oak)
Quercus muhlenbergi   (Chinkapin Oak)
Quercus stellata   (Post Oak)
Rhus typhina   (Staghorn Sumac)
Salix amygdaloides   (Peachleaf Willow)
Salix nigra   (Black Willow)
Sassafras albidum   (Common Sassafras)

SMALL UNDERSTORY:
   6 to 10 meters (20 to 35 feet),
   indicator—*Cercis canadensis* (Eastern Redbud)

Acer spicatum   (Mountain Maple)
Alnus rugosa   (Hazel Alder)
Amelanchier laevis   (Allegany Serviceberry)
Asimina triloba   (Common Pawpaw)
Cercis canadensis   (Eastern Redbud)
Chionanthus virginicus   (White Fringetree)
Cornus alternifolia   (Pagoda Dogwood)
Cotinus americanus   (American Smoketree)
Crataegus crusgalli   (Cockspur Hawthorn)
Crataegus nitida   (Glossy Hawthorn)

Crataegus phaenopyrum   (Washington Hawthorn)
Crataegus pruinosa   (Frosted Hawthorn)
Crataegus punctata   (Dotted Hawthorn)
Euonymus atropurpureus   (Eastern Wahoo)
Franklinia alatamaha   (Franklinia)
Halesia carolina   (Carolina Silverbell)
Hamamelis virginiana   (Common Witchhazel)
Malus ioensis   (Prairie Crabapple)
Prunus americana   (American Plum)
Prunus pensylvanica   (Pin Cherry)

Ptelea trifoliata   (Common Hoptree)
Rhododendron maximum   (Rosebay Rhododendron)
Rhus copallina   (Flameleaf Sumac)
Rhus glabra   (Smooth Sumac)
Salix bebbiana   (Bebb Willow)
Salix discolor   (Pussy Willow)

Sorbus decora   (Showy Mountainash)
Viburnum lentago   (Nannyberry Viburnum)
Viburnum prunifolium   (Blackhaw Viburnum)
Viburnum rufidulum   (Rusty Blackhaw Viburnum)
Zanthoxylum americanum   (Common Pricklyash)

SPREAD: Four categories of mature crown width are classified.

VERY WIDE:
   22.5 meters and more (75 feet plus),
      indicator—*Acer saccharinum* (Silver Maple)

Acer saccharinum   (Silver Maple)
Carya cordiformis   (Bitternut Hickory)
Carya illinoensis   (Pecan)
Celtis occidentalis   (Common Hackberry)
Juglans nigra   (Eastern Black Walnut)
Platanus occidentalis   (American Planetree)
Populus deltoides   (Eastern Poplar)

Quercus alba   (White Oak)
Quercus borealis   (Northern Red Oak)
Quercus macrocarpa   (Bur Oak)
Quercus montana   (Chestnut Oak)
Quercus velutina   (Black Oak)
Ulmus americana   (American Elm)

WIDE:
   15 to 22.5 meters (50 to 75 feet),
      indicator—*Gleditsia triacanthos* (Common Honeylocust)

Acer nigrum   (Black Maple)
Acer rubrum   (Red Maple)
Acer saccharum   (Sugar Maple)
Castanea dentata   (American Chestnut)
Cladrastis lutea   (American Yellowwood)
Fagus grandifolia   (American Beech)
Fraxinus americana   (White Ash)
Gleditsia triacanthos   (Common Honeylocust)
Gymnocladus dioicus   (Kentucky Coffeetree)
Juglans cinerea   (Butternut)

Liquidambar styraciflua   (American Sweetgum)
Pinus ponderosa   (Ponderosa Pine)
Pinus resinosa   (Red Pine)
Pinus rigida   (Pitch Pine)
Pinus strobus   (Eastern White Pine)
Quercus bicolor   (Swamp White Oak)
Quercus coccinea   (Scarlet Oak)
Quercus ellipsoidalis   (Northern Pin Oak)
Quercus palustris   (Pin Oak)
Tilia americana   (American Linden)

INTERMEDIATE:
   10 to 15 meters (35 to 50 feet),
      indicator—*Fraxinus pennsylvanica* (Green Ash)

Acer negundo   (Boxelder)
Aesculus octandra   (Yellow Buckeye)
Amelanchier canadensis   (Shadblow Serviceberry)
Betula lenta   (Sweet Birch)
Betula lutea   (Yellow Birch)
Betula nigra   (River Birch)
Betula papyrifera   (Paper Birch)
Carpinus caroliniana   (American Hornbeam)
Carya glabra   (Pignut Hickory)
Carya ovata   (Shagbark Hickory)
Carya tomentosa   (Mockernut Hickory)
Catalpa speciosa   (Northern Catalpa)
Cornus florida   (Flowering Dogwood)
Crataegus mollis   (Downy Hawthorn)
Diospyros virginiana   (Common Persimmon)
Fraxinus nigra   (Black Ash)
Fraxinus pennsylvanica   (Green Ash)
Fraxinus quadrangulata   (Blue Ash)
Juniperus virginiana   (Eastern Redcedar)

Larix laricina   (Eastern Larch)
Liriodendron tulipifera   (Tuliptree)
Maclura pomifera   (Osageorange)
Magnolia acuminata   (Cucumbertree Magnolia)
Morus rubra   (Red Mulberry)
Nyssa sylvatica   (Black Tupelo)
Pinus flexilis   (Limber Pine)
Prunus serotina   (Black Cherry)
Quercus imbricaria   (Shingle Oak)
Quercus marilandica   (Blackjack Oak)
Quercus muhlenbergi   (Chinkapin Oak)
Quercus stellata   (Post Oak)
Rhus typhina   (Staghorn Sumac)
Robinia pseudoacacia   (Black Locust)
Salix amygdaloides   (Peachleaf Willow)
Sassafras albidum   (Common Sassafras)
Thuja occidentalis   (Eastern Arborvitae)
Tsuga canadensis   (Canada Hemlock)

Spread (cont.)

NARROW:
    6 to 10 meters (20 to 35 feet),
      indicator—*Abies concolor* (White Fir)

*Abies balsamea** (Balsam Fir)
Abies concolor (White Fir)
Abies lasiocarpa (Alpine Fir)
Acer pensylvanicum (Striped Maple)
*Acer spicatum** (Mountain Maple)
Aesculus glabra (Ohio Buckeye)
Alnus rugosa (Hazel Alder)
Amelanchier laevis (Allegany Serviceberry)
Aralia spinosa (Devils-Walkingstick)
Asimina triloba (Common Pawpaw)
Betula populifolia (Gray Birch)
Cercis canadensis (Eastern Redbud)
*Chionanthus virginicus** (White Fringetree)
*Cornus alternifolia** (Pagoda Dogwood)
*Cotinus americanus** (American Smoketree)
Crataegus crusgalli (Cockspur Hawthorn)
Crataegus nitida (Glossy Hawthorn)
Crataegus phaenopyrum (Washington Hawthorn)
Crataegus pruinosa (Frosted Hawthorn)
Crataegus punctata (Dotted Hawthorn)
*Euonymus atropurpureus** (Eastern Wahoo)
*Franklinia alatamaha** (Franklinia)
Halesia carolina (Carolina Silverbell)
Hamamelis virginiana (Common Witchhazel)
Malus ioensis (Prairie Crabapple)
Ostrya virginiana (American Hophornbeam)

Oxydendrum arboreum (Sourwood)
Picea engelmanni (Engelmann Spruce)
Picea glauca (White Spruce)
Picea glauca densata (BlackHills White Spruce)
*Picea mariana** (Black Spruce)
Picea pungens (Colorado Spruce)
Pinus banksiana (Jack Pine)
Populus grandidentata (Bigtooth Aspen)
Populus tremuloides (Quaking Aspen)
Prunus americana (American Plum)
Prunus pensylvanica (Pin Cherry)
Prunus virginiana (Common Chokecherry)
Pseudotsuga taxifolia (Common Douglasfir)
*Ptelea trifoliata** (Common Hoptree)
Rhododendron maximum (Rosebay Rhododendron)
Rhus copallina (Flameleaf Sumac)
*Rhus glabra** (Smooth Sumac)
*Salix bebbiana** (Bebb Willow)
*Salix discolor** (Pussy Willow)
Salix nigra (Black Willow)
*Sorbus decora** (Showy Mountainash)
Taxodium distichum (Common Baldcypress)
*Viburnum lentago** (Nannyberry Viburnum)
*Viburnum prunifolium** (Blackhaw Viburnum)
*Viburnum rufidulum** (Rusty Blackhaw Viburnum)
Zanthoxylum americanum (Common Pricklyash)

Commonly very narrow; less than 6 meters (20 feet) in width

MASS:

The complexity of foliage and branching which is controlled by the genetic code of each species produces a predictable density which can be measured and quantified. Density can be measured as a ratio of positive to negative space within the plant crown. Positive space includes branching, foliage, and other plant parts perceived as line and mass in two-dimensional silhouette.

Negative space is the illusory space between the branching and foliage perceived as sky or background. This space determines the degree of opacity, translucency, or transparency for each species. Three categories of crown mass are classified:

DENSE:
    extremely well developed branching system, heavily clothed with foliage, negative space minimal or absent,
    indicator—*Fagus grandifolia* (American Beech)

Abies balsamea (Balsam Fir)
Abies concolor (White Fir)
Abies lasiocarpa (Alpine Fir)
Acer nigrum (Black Maple)
Acer saccharum (Sugar Maple)
Amelanchier canadensis (Shadblow Serviceberry)
Amelanchier laevis (Allegany Serviceberry)

Carpinus caroliniana (American Hornbeam)
Castanea dentata (American Chestnut)
Cornus florida (Flowering Dogwood)
Crataegus crusgalli (Cockspur Hawthorn)
Crataegus mollis (Downy Hawthorn)
Crataegus nitida (Glossy Hawthorn)
Crataegus phaenopyrum (Washington Hawthorn)

Crataegus pruinosa   (Frosted Hawthorn)
Crataegus punctata   (Dotted Hawthorn)
Fagus grandifolia   (American Beech)
Halesia carolina   (Carolina Silverbell)
Hamamelis virginiana   (Common Witchhazel)
Juniperus virginiana   (Eastern Redcedar)
Liquidambar styraciflua   (American Sweetgum)
Maclura pomifera   (Osageorange)
Malus ioensis   (Prairie Crabapple)
Morus rubra   (Red Mulberry)
Nyssa sylvatica   (Black Tupelo)
Ostrya virginiana   (American Hophornbeam)
Picea engelmanni   (Engelmann Spruce)

Picea glauca   (White Spruce)
Picea glauca densata   (BlackHills White Spruce)
Picea mariana   (Black Spruce)
Picea pungens   (Colorado Spruce)
Prunus americana   (American Plum)
Pseudotsuga taxifolia   (Common Douglasfir)
Quercus borealis   (Northern Red Oak)
Thuja occidentalis   (Eastern Arborvitae)
Tilia americana   (American Linden)
Tsuga canadensis   (Canada Hemlock)
Viburnum lentago   (Nannyberry Viburnum)
Viburnum prunifolium   (Blackhaw Viburnum)
Viburnum rufidulum   (Rusty Blackhaw Viburnum)

MODERATE:
   branching and foliage of intermediate density, positive to negative space ratio ranging between 2 to 1 and 1 to 1,
   indicator—*Quercus alba* (White Oak)

Acer rubrum   (Red Maple)
Acer spicatum   (Mountain Maple)
Aesculus glabra   (Ohio Buckeye)
Aesculus octandra   (Yellow Buckeye)
Betula lenta   (Sweet Birch)
Betula lutea   (Yellow Birch)
Betula papyrifera   (Paper Birch)
Carya cordiformis   (Bitternut Hickory)
Celtis occidentalis   (Common Hackberry)
Cercis canadensis   (Eastern Redbud)
Chionanthus virginicus   (White Fringetree)
Cladrastis lutea   (American Yellowwood)
Euonymus atropurpureus   (Eastern Wahoo)
Fraxinus americana   (White Ash)
Fraxinus nigra   (Black Ash)
Fraxinus pennsylvanica   (Green Ash)
Fraxinus quadrangulata   (Blue Ash)

Liriodendron tulipifera   (Tuliptree)
Magnolia acuminata   (Cucumbertree Magnolia)
Oxydendrum arboreum   (Sourwood)
Pinus resinosa   (Red Pine)
Pinus strobus   (Eastern White Pine)
Prunus virginiana   (Common Chokecherry)
Quercus alba   (White Oak)
Quercus bicolor   (Swamp White Oak)
Quercus coccinea   (Scarlet Oak)
Quercus ellipsoidalis   (Northern Pin Oak)
Quercus marilandica   (Blackjack Oak)
Quercus montana   (Chestnut Oak)
Quercus palustris   (Pin Oak)
Quercus velutina   (Black Oak)
Salix bebbiana   (Bebb Willow)
Salix discolor   (Pussy Willow)
Ulmus americana   (American Elm)

OPEN:
   sparse branching, clothed with relatively small quantity of foliage, high percentage of negative space visible,
   indicator—*Salix nigra* (Black Willow)

Acer negundo   (Boxelder)
Acer pensylvanicum   (Striped Maple)
Acer saccharinum   (Silver Maple)
Alnus rugosa   (Hazel Alder)
Aralia spinosa   (Devils-Walkingstick)
Asimina triloba   (Common Pawpaw)
Betula nigra   (River Branch)
Betula populifolia   (Gray Birch)
Carya glabra   (Pignut Hickory)
Carya illinoensis   (Pecan)
Carya ovata   (Shagbark Hickory)
Carya tomentosa   (Mockernut Hickory)
Catalpa speciosa   (Northern Catalpa)
Cornus alternifolia   (Pagoda Dogwood)
Cotinus americanus   (American Smoketree)
Diospyros virginiana   (Common Persimmon)
Franklinia alatamaha   (Franklinia)
Gleditsia triacanthos   (Common Honeylocust)
Gymnocladus dioicus   (Kentucky Coffeetree)
Juglans cinerea   (Butternut)

Juglans nigra   (Eastern Black Walnut)
Larix laricina   (Eastern Larch)
Pinus banksiana   (Jack Pine)
Pinus flexilis   (Limber Pine)
Pinus ponderosa   (Ponderosa Pine)
Pinus rigida   (Pitch Pine)
Platanus occidentalis   (American Planetree)
Populus deltoides   (Eastern Poplar)
Populus grandidentata   (Bigtooth Aspen)
Populus tremuloides   (Quaking Aspen)
Prunus pensylvanica   (Pin Cherry)
Prunus serotina   (Black Cherry)
Ptelea trifoliata   (Common Hoptree)
Quercus imbricaria   (Shingle Oak)
Quercus macrocarpa   (Bur Oak)
Quercus muhlenbergi   (Chinkapin Oak)
Quercus stellata   (Post Oak)
Rhododendron maximum   (Rosebay Rhododendron)
Rhus copallina   (Flameleaf Sumac)
Rhus glabra   (Smooth Sumac)

Mass (cont.)

Rhus typhina (Staghorn Sumac)	*Sassafras albidum* (Common Sassafras)
Robina pseudoacacia (Black Locust)	*Sorbus decora* (Showy Mountainash)
Salix amygdaloides (Peachleaf Willow)	*Taxodium distichum* (Common Baldcypress)
Salix nigra (Black Willow)	*Zanthoxylum americanum* (Common Pricklyash)

BRANCHING CHARACTER:

The shape or form of a plant is greatly affected by the structure of the main trunk and primary branches. The following structural arrangements may occur within almost any volumetric plant form.

UPRIGHT:
main branches stiffly vertical or diverging at a slight angle from vertical,
indicator—*Cladrastis lutea* (American Yellowwood)

Acer pensylvanicum (Striped Maple)	*Euonymus atropurpureus* (Eastern Wahoo)
Acer spicatum (Mountain Maple)	*Franklinia alatamaha* (Franklinia)
Alnus rugosa (Hazel Alder)	*Populus deltoides* (Eastern Poplar)
Amelanchier canadensis (Shadblow Serviceberry)	*Rhododendron maximum* (Rosebay Rhododendron)
Amelanchier laevis (Allegany Serviceberry)	*Salix amygdaloides* (Peachleaf Willow)
Asimina triloba (Common Pawpaw)	*Salix bebbiana* (Bebb Willow)
Celtis occidentalis (Common Hackberry)	*Salix discolor* (Pussy Willow)
Cladrastis lutea (American Yellowwood)	*Sorbus decora* (Showy Mountainash)
Cotinus americanus (American Smoketree)	*Ulmus americana* (American Elm)
Crataegus pruinosa (Frosted Hawthorn)	*Viburnum lentago* (Nannyberry Viburnum)

ASCENDING:
main branches diverging at near 45 degree angle from the vertical,
indicator—*Acer nigrum* (Black Maple)

Acer negundo (Boxelder)	*Liquidambar styraciflua* (American Sweetgum)
Acer nigrum (Black Maple)	*Liriodendron tulipifera* (Tuliptree)
Acer rubrum (Red Maple)	*Morus rubra* (Red Mulberry)
Acer saccharinum (Silver Maple)	*Oxydendrum arboreum* (Sourwood)
Acer saccharum (Sugar Maple)	*Prunus pensylvanica* (Pin Cherry)
Betula lenta (Sweet Birch)	*Prunus serotina* (Black Cherry)
Betula lutea (Yellow Birch)	*Prunus virginiana* (Common Chokecherry)
Betula nigra (River Birch)	*Ptelea trifoliata* (Common Hoptree)
Betula papyrifera (Paper Birch)	*Quercus borealis* (Northern Red Oak)
Carya cordiformis (Bitternut Hickory)	*Quercus coccinea* (Scarlet Oak)
Carya glabra (Pignut Hickory)	*Quercus montana* (Chestnut Oak)
Carya illinoensis (Pecan)	*Quercus muhlenbergi* (Chinkapin Oak)
Carya ovata (Shagbark Hickory)	*Quercus velutina* (Black Oak)
Carya tomentosa (Mockernut Hickory)	*Robinia pseudoacacia* (Black Locust)
Chionanthus virginicus (White Fringetree)	*Salix amygdaloides* (Peachleaf Willow)
Halesia carolina (Carolina Silverbell)	*Salix nigra* (Black Willow)
Juglans cinerea (Butternut)	*Sorbus decora* (Showy Mountainash)
Juglans nigra (Eastern Black Walnut)	

HORIZONTAL:

possessed of main branches predominantly oriented at near 90 degree angle to the trunk (vertical), indicator—*Crataegus crusgalli* (Cockspur Hawthorn)

Abies balsamea   (Balsam Fir)
Abies concolor   (White Fir)
Abies lasiocarpa   (Alpine Fir)
Betula populifolia   (Gray Birch)
Carpinus caroliniana   (American Hornbeam)
Castanea dentata   (American Chestnut)
Cercis canadensis   (Eastern Redbud)
Cornus alternifolia   (Pagoda Dogwood)
Cornus florida   (Flowering Dogwood)
Crataegus crusgalli   (Cockspur Hawthorn)
Crataegus mollis   (Downy Hawthorn)
Crataegus nitida   (Glossy Hawthorn)
Crataegus phaenopyrum   (Washington Hawthorn)
Crataegus punctata   (Dotted Hawthorn)
Fagus grandifolia   (American Beech)
Gleditsia triacanthos   (Common Honeylocust)
Hamamelis virginiana   (Common Witchhazel)
Juniperus virginiana   (Eastern Redcedar)
Larix laricina   (Eastern Larch)
Malus ioensis   (Prairie Crabapple)

Nyssa sylvatica   (Black Tupelo)
Ostrya virginiana   (American Hophornbeam)
Pinus flexilis   (Limber Pine)
Pinus ponderosa   (Ponderosa Pine)
Pinus resinosa   (Red Pine)
Pinus strobus   (Eastern White Pine)
Platanus occidentalis   (American Planetree)
Prunus americana   (American Plum)
Pseudotsuga taxifolia   (Common Douglasfir)
Quercus alba   (White Oak)
Quercus imbricaria   (Shingle Oak)
Quercus macrocarpa   (Bur Oak)
Quercus marilandica   (Blackjack Oak)
Quercus stellata   (Post Oak)
Sassafras albidum   (Common Sassafras)
Taxodium distichum   (Common Baldcypress)
Thuja occidentalis   (Eastern Arborvitae)
Tsuga canadensis   (Canada Hemlock)
Viburnum prunifolium   (Blackhaw Viburnum)
Viburnum rufidulum   (Rusty Blackhaw Viburnum)

RECURVING:

main branches arching at near 45 degree angle from the bole becoming descending to recurving ascending at the branch tips, indicator—*Fraxinus pennsylvanica* (Green Ash)

Aesculus glabra   (Ohio Buckeye)
Aesculus octandra   (Yellow Buckeye)
Fraxinus americana   (White Ash)
Fraxinus nigra   (Black Ash)
Fraxinus pennsylvanica   (Green Ash)
Fraxinus quadrangulata   (Blue Ash)

Maclura pomifera   (Osageorange)
Magnolia acuminata   (Cucumbertree Magnolia)
Pinus banksiana   (Jack Pine)
Pinus rigida   (Pitch Pine)
Tilia americana   (American Linden)

DESCENDING:

main branches diverging from the bole at an angle below the horizontal, indicator—*Quercus palustris* (Pin Oak)

Picea engelmanni   (Engelmann Spruce)
Picea glauca   (White Spruce)
Picea glauca densata   (BlackHills White Spruce)
Picea mariana   (Black Spruce)
Picea pungens   (Colorado Spruce)

Quercus bicolor   (Swamp White Oak)
Quercus ellipsoidalis   (Northern Pin Oak)
Quercus imbricaria   (Shingle Oak)
Quercus palustris   (Pin Oak)

BRANCHING APPEARANCE IS FURTHER MODIFIED IN SEVERAL WAYS:

LEGGY:

multiple stemmed plant devoid of foliage below, frequently observed in shade intolerant pioneer species spreading into large colonies by vegetative root propogation, indicator—*Rhus typhina* (Staghorn Sumac)

Alnus rugosa   (Hazel Alder)
Amalanchier canadensis   (Shadblow Serviceberry)
Amalanchier laevis   (Allegany Serviceberry)

Aralia spinosa   (Devils-Walkingstick)
Diospyros virginiana   (Common Persimmon)
Populus grandidentata   (Bigtooth Aspen)

Branching character (cont.)

Populus tremuloides   (Quaking Aspen)
Prunus virginiana   (Common Chokecherry)
Rhus copallina   (Flameleaf Sumac)

Rhus glabra   (Smooth Sumac)
Rhus typhina   (Staghorn Sumac)
Salix bebbiana   (Bebb Willow)
Salix discolor   (Pussy Willow)

PICTURESQUE:
   naturally irregular or contorted branching occurring occasionally in most species but common to rapid growing species,
   indicator—*Gymnocladus dioicus* (Kentucky Coffeetree)

Aesculus glabra   (Ohio Buckeye)
Aesculus octandra   (Yellow Buckeye)
Alnus rugosa   (Hazel Alder)
Carpinus caroliniana   (American Hornbeam)
Carya cordiformis   (Bitternut Hickory)
Carya glabra   (Pignut Hickory)
Carya ovata   (Shagbark Hickory)
Carya tomentosa   (Mockernut Hickory)
Catalpa speciosa   (Northern Catalpa)
Cercis canadensis   (Eastern Redbud)
Diospyros virginiana   (Common Persimmon)
Gleditsia triacanthos   (Common Honeylocust)

Gymnocladus dioicus   (Kentucky Coffeetree)
Hamamelis virginiana   (Common Witchhazel)
Nyssa sylvatica   (Black Tupelo)
Platanus occidentalis   (American Planetree)
Populus grandidentata   (Bigtooth Aspen)
Populus tremuloides   (Quaking Aspen)
Quercus alba   (White Oak)
Quercus macrocarpa   (Bur Oak)
Quercus marilandica   (Blackjack Oak)
Querus stellata   (Post Oak)
Rhododendron maximum   (Rosebay Rhododendron)
Sassafras albidum   (Common Sassafras)

WEEPING:
   secondary branchlets or tertiary branch tips and twigs pendant,
   indicator—*Prunus serotina* (Black Cherry)

Betula lenta   (Sweet Birch)
Betula lutea   (Yellow Birch)
Betula nigra   (River Birch)
Betula papyrifera   (Paper Birch)
Betula populifolia   (Gray Birch)
Carpinus caroliniana   (American Hornbeam) slightly

Larix laricina   (Eastern Larch)
Ostrya virginiana   (American Hophornbeam) slightly
Oxydendrum arboreum   (Sourwood)
Prunus serotina   (Black Cherry)
Taxodium distichum   (Common Baldcypress)
Tsuga canadensis   (Canada Hemlock)

BRANCHING TEXTURE:

Texture in the landscape is the result of the detailed structure of plant growth or of the total plant mass, influenced by the distance from which the scene is viewed. In the winter landscape, texture in deciduous plants is a product of the size, surface, spacing, disposition, grouping and attitude of twigs and branches, persisting seeds and dried leaves. Every species exhibits its own characteristic branching personality which produces a consistent texture within a limited range. Some plants are coarse, medium or fine the year around. Others are fine or medium in summer and coarser in winter. The following textural categories (winter) are considered.

COARSE:
   large prominent branches and twigs, spacing open,
   indicator—*Catalpa speciosa* (Northern Catalpa)

Acer negundo   (Boxelder)
Acer pensylvanicum   (Striped Maple)
Acer saccharinum   (Silver Maple)
Aesculus glabra   (Ohio Buckeye)
Aesculus octandra   (Yellow Buckeye)

Alnus rugosa   (Hazel Alder)
Aralia spinosa   (Devils-Walkingstick)
Asimina triloba   (Common Pawpaw)
Carya glabra   (Pignut Hickory)
Carya illinoensis   (Pecan)

Carya ovata   (Shagbark Hickory)
Carya tomentosa   (Mockernut Hickory)
Castanea dentata   (American Chestnut)
Catalpa speciosa   (Northern Catalpa)
Cotinus americanus   (American Smoketree)
Crataegus mollis   (Downy Hawthorn)
Franklinia alatamaha   (Franklinia)
Fraxinus americana   (White Ash)
Fraxinus nigra   (Black Ash)
Fraxinus pennsylvanica   (Green Ash)
Fraxinus quadrangulata   (Blue Ash)
Gleditsia triacanthos   (Common Honeylocust)
Gymnocladus dioicus   (Kentucky Coffeetree)
Juglans cinerea   (Butternut)
Juglans nigra   (Eastern Black Walnut)
Maclura pomifera   (Osageorange)
Magnolia acuminata   (Cucumbertree Magnolia)
Morus rubra   (Red Mulberry)
Pinus banksiana   (Jack Pine)

Pinus flexilis   (Limber Pine)
Pinus ponderosa   (Ponderosa Pine)
Pinus rigida   (Pitch Pine)
Platanus occidentalis   (American Planetree)
Populus deltoides   (Eastern Poplar)
Populus grandidentata   (Bigtooth Aspen)
Populus tremuloides   (Quaking Aspen)
Quercus alba   (White Oak)
Quercus macrocarpa   (Bur Oak)
Quercus marilandica   (Blackjack Oak)
Quercus montana   (Chestnut Oak)
Quercus stellata   (Post Oak)
Rhododendron maximum   (Rosebay Rhododendron)
Rhus copallina   (Flameleaf Sumac)
Rhus glabra   (Smooth Sumac)
Rhus typhina   (Staghorn Sumac)
Robinia pseudoacacia   (Black Locust)
Zanthoxylum americanum   (Common Pricklyash)

MEDIUM:
>   branches and twigs of intermediate diameter and spacing,
>   indicator—*Celtis occidentalis* (Common Hackberry)

Abies balsamea   (Balsam Fir)
Abies concolor   (White Fir)
Abies lasiocarpa   (Alpine Fir)
Acer nigrum   (Black Maple)
Acer rubrum   (Red Maple)
Acer saccharum   (Sugar Maple)
Acer spicatum   (Mountain Maple)
Carya cordiformis   (Bitternut Hickory)
Celtis occidentalis   (Common Hackberry)
Cercis canadensis   (Eastern Redbud)
Chionanthus virginicus   (White Fringetree)
Cladrastis lutea   (American Yellowwood)
Cornus alternifolia   (Pagoda Dogwood)
Cornus florida   (Flowering Dogwood)
Crataegus crusgalli   (Cockspur Hawthorn)
Crataegus nitida   (Glossy Hawthorn)
Crataegus phaenopyrum   (Washington Hawthorn)
Crataegus pruinosa   (Frosted Hawthorn)
Crataegus punctata   (Dotted Hawthorn)
Diospyros virginiana   (Common Persimmon)
Euonymus atropurpureus   (Eastern Wahoo)
Halesia carolina   (Carolina Silverbell)
Hamamelis virginiana   (Common Witchhazel)
Juniperus virginiana   (Eastern Redcedar)
Liquidambar styraciflua   (American Sweetgum)
Liriodendron tulipifera   (Tuliptree)
Malus ioensis   (Prairie Crabapple)
Nyssa sylvatica   (Black Tupelo)
Oxydendrum arboreum   (Sourwood)

Picea engelmanni   (Engelmann Spruce)
Picea glauca   (White Spruce)
Picea glauca densata   (BlackHills White Spruce)
Picea mariana   (Black Spruce)
Picea pungens   (Colorado Spruce)
Pinus resinosa   (Red Pine)
Pinus strobus   (Eastern White Pine)
Prunus americana   (American Plum)
Prunus virginiana   (Common Chokecherry)
Pseudotsuga taxifolia   (Common Douglasfir)
Ptelea trifoliata   (Common Hoptree)
Quercus bicolor   (Swamp White Oak)
Quercus borealis   (Northern Red Oak)
Quercus coccinea   (Scarlet Oak)
Quercus ellipsoidalis   (Northern Pin Oak)
Quercus imbricaria   (Shingle Oak)
Quercus muhlenbergi   (Chinkapin Oak)
Quercus palustris   (Pin Oak)
Quercus velutina   (Black Oak)
Sassafras albidum   (Common Sassafras)
Sorbus decora   (Showy Mountainash)
Thuja occidentalis   (Eastern Arborvitae)
Tilia americana   (American Linden)
Tsuga canadensis   (Canada Hemlock)
Ulmus americana   (American Elm)
Viburnum lentago   (Nannyberry Viburnum)
Viburnum prunifolium   (Blackhaw Viburnum)
Viburnum rufidulum   (Rusty Blackhaw Viburnum)

FINE:
>   branches and twigs conspicuously slender, spacing closed,
>   indicator—*Betula papyrifera* (Paper Birch)

Amelanchier canadensis   (Shadblow Serviceberry)
Amelanchier laevis   (Allegany Serviceberry)
Betula lenta   (Sweet Birch)
Betula lutea   (Yellow Birch)
Betula nigra   (River Birch)

Betula papyrifera   (Paper Birch)
Betula populifolia   (Gray Birch)
Carpinus caroliniana   (American Hornbeam)
Fagus grandifolia   (American Beech)
Larix laricina   (Eastern Larch)

Branching texture -fine (cont.)

Ostrya virginiana   (American Hophornbeam)
Prunus pensylvanica   (Pin Cherry)
Prunus serotina   (Black Cherry)
Salix amygdaloides   (Peachleaf Willow)

Salix bebbiana   (Bebb Willow)
Salix discolor   (Pussy Willow)
Salix nigra   (Black Willow)
Taxodium distichum   (Common Baldcypress)

TWIG AND BUD:

Twigs and buds may be distinctive in color, size and shape. Buds of many plants are naked, scaly, gummy, hairy or smooth. Some twigs frequently are marked with large leaf scars while others are smooth or covered with hair. Although unusual twig and bud characteristics exhibit greatest visual impact in the winter landscape, it is the subtle discovery of this detail in other seasons which produces a richer environmental perception of the design.

TWIG CHARACTER:

LARGE LEAF-SCARS:

Acer negundo   (Boxelder)
Aralia spinosa   (Devils-Walkingstick)
Catalpa speciosa   (Northern Catalpa)
Cornus alternifolia   (Pagoda Dogwood)
Cornus florida   (Flowering Dogwood)
Franklinia alatamaha   (Franklinia)
Fraxinus americana   (White Ash)
Fraxinus nigra   (Black Ash)

Fraxinus pennsylvanica   (Green Ash)
Fraxinus quadrangulata   (Blue Ash)
Gymnocladus dioicus   (Kentucky Coffeetree)
Juglans cinerea   (Butternut)
Juglans nigra   (Eastern Black Walnut)
Rhus copallina   (Flameleaf Sumac)
Rhus glabra   (Smooth Sumac)
Rhus typhina   (Staghorn Sumac)

POWDERY BLOOM:

Acer negundo   (Boxelder)
Rhus glabra   (Smooth Sumac)

VELVETY:

Acer spicatum   (Mountain Maple)
Carya tomentosa   (Mockernut Hickory)
Chionanthus virginicus   (White Fringetree)
Juglans cinerea   (Butternut)

Juglans nigra   (Eastern Black Walnut)
Quercus stellata   (Post Oak)
Rhus typhina   (Staghorn Sumac)
Viburnum rufidulum   (Rusty Blackhaw Viburnum)

WINGED LINES:

Asimina triloba   (Common Pawpaw)
Euonymus atropurpureus   (Eastern Wahoo)
Fraxinus quadrangulata   (Blue Ash)

Liquidambar styraciflua   (American Sweetgum)
Quercus macrocarpa   (Bur Oak) young
Robinia pseudoacacia   (Black Locust)

FLAKY:

Acer rubrum   (Red Maple)
Acer saccharinum   (Silver Maple)
Crataegus crusgalli   (Cockspur Hawthorn)
Crataegus mollis   (Downy Hawthorn)

Crataegus nitida   (Glossy Hawthorn)
Crataegus phaenopyrum   (Washington Hawthorn)
Crataegus pruniosa   (Frosted Hawthorn)
Crataegus punctata   (Dotted Hawthorn)

Malus ioensis (Prairie Crabapple)
Nyssa sylvatica (Black Tupelo)
Prunus americana (American Plum)

Prunus pensylvanica (Pin Cherry)
Sorbus decora (Showy Mountainash)
Tilia americana (American Linden)

ZIGZAG:

Alnus rugosa (Hazel Alder)
Carpinus caroliniana (American Hornbeam)
Celtis occidentalis (Common Hackberry)
Cercis canadensis (Eastern Redbud)
Diospyros virginiana (Common Persimmon)
Fagus grandifolia (American Beech)

Gleditsia triacanthos (Common Honeylocust)
Maclura pomifera (Osageorange)
Ostrya virginiana (American Hophornbeam)
Platanus occidentalis (American Planetree)
Robinia pseudoacacia (Black Locust)
Ulmus americana (American Elm) slightly

TWIG COLORATION:

GRAY:

Amelanchier canadensis (Shadblow Serviceberry)
Amelanchier laevis (Allegany Serviceberry)
Fagus grandifolia (American Beech)
Liquidambar styraciflua (American Sweetgum)

Nyssa sylvatica (Black Tupelo)
Pinus flexilis (Limber Pine)
Pinus strobus (Eastern White Pine)

GREEN-GRAY:

Abies balsamea (Balsam Fir)
Salix bebbiana (Bebb Willow)

Thuja occidentalis (Eastern Arborvitae)

GREEN:

Acer negundo (Boxelder)
Acer spicatum (Mountain Maple)
Cornus alternifolia (Pagoda Dogwood)
Cornus florida (Flowering Dogwood)
Euonymus atropurpureus (Eastern Wahoo)
Juniperus virginiana (Eastern Redcedar)
Oxydendrum arboreum (Sourwood)

Pinus strobus (Eastern White Pine)
Quercus imbricaria (Shingle Oak)
Quercus palustris (Pin Oak)
Salix discolor (Pussy Willow)
Sassafras albidum (Common Sassafras)
Taxodium distichum (Common Baldcypress)

GREEN-YELLOW:

Abies concolor (White Fir)
Abies lasiocarpa (Alpine Fir)
Aralia spinosa (Devils-Walkingstick)
Larix laricina (Eastern Larch)

Pinus resinosa (Red Pine)
Salix nigra (Black Willow)
Sassafras albidum (Common Sassafras)
Thuja occidentalis (Eastern Arborvitae)

YELLOW:

Salix amygdaloides (Peachleaf Willow)
Sassafras albidum (Common Sassafras)

YELLOW-BRONZE:

Betula lutea (Yellow Birch)
Sorbus decora (Showy Mountainash)

Twig coloration (cont.)

GRAY-BROWN:

Carya cordiformis   (Bitternut Hickory)
Carya glabra   (Pignut Hickory)
Carya illinoensis   (Pecan)
Carya ovata   (Shagbark Hickory)
Carya tomentosa   (Mockernut Hickory)
Crataegus mollis   (Downy Hawthorn)
Diospyros virginiana   (Common Persimmon)

Populus grandidentata   (Bigtooth Aspen)
Populus tremuloides   (Quaking Aspen)
Pseudotsuga taxifolia   (Common Douglasfir)
Quercus muhlenbergi   (Chinkapin Oak)
Viburnum lentago   (Nannyberry Viburnum)
Viburnum prunifolium   (Blackhaw Viburnum)

GREEN-BROWN:

Celtis occidentalis   (Common Hackberry)
Chionanthus virginicus   (White Fringetree)

Quercus imbricaria   (Shingle Oak)

YELLOW-BROWN:

Acer nigrum   (Black Maple)
Fraxinus americana   (White Ash)
Fraxinus nigra   (Black Ash)
Fraxinus pennsylvanica   (Green Ash)
Fraxinus quadrangulata   (Blue Ash)
Hamamelis virginiana   (Common Witchhazel)
Picea engelmanni   (Engelmann Spruce)

Picea glauca   (White Spruce)
Picea glauca densata   (BlackHills White Spruce)
Picea mariana   (Black Spruce)
Populus deltoides   (Eastern Poplar)
Quercus macrocarpa   (Bur Oak)
Tsuga canadensis   (Canada Hemlock)

TAN-BROWN:

Juglans cinerea   (Butternut)
Juglans nigra   (Eastern Black Walnut)

BROWN:

Acer saccharum   (Silver Maple)
Aesculus glabra   (Ohio Buckeye)
Aesculus octandra   (Yellow Buckeye)
Asimina triloba   (Common Pawpaw)

Cotinus americanus   (American Smoketree)
Gymnocladus dioicus   (Kentucky Coffeetree)
Halesia carolina   (Carolina Silverbell)

RED-BROWN:

Acer saccharinum   (Silver Maple)
Alnus rugosa   (Hazel Alder)
Betula lenta   (Sweet Birch)
Betula nigra   (River Birch)
Betula papyrifera   (Paper Birch)
Betula populifolia   (Gray Birch)
Carpinus caroliniana   (American Hornbeam)
Castanea dentata   (American Chestnut)
Catalpa speciosa   (Northern Catalpa)
Cercis canadensis   (Eastern Redbud)
Cladrastis lutea   (American Yellowwood)
Crataegus crusgalli   (Cockspur Hawthorn)
Crataegus nitida   (Glossy Hawthorn)
Crataegus phaenopyrum   (Washington Hawthorn)
Crataegus pruinosa   (Frosted Hawthorn)
Franklinia alatamaha   (Franklinia)
Gleditsia triacanthos   (Common Honeylocust)
Liriodendron tulipifera   (Tuliptree)
Magnolia acminata   (Cucumbertree Magnolia)
Malus ioensis   (Prairie Crabapple)

Ostrya virginiana   (American Hophornbeam)
Pinus banksiana   (Jack Pine)
Prunus americana   (American Plum)
Prunus serotina   (Black Cherry)
Prunus virginiana   (Common Chokecherry)
Ptelea trifoliata   (Common Hoptree)
Quercus bicolor   (Swamp White Oak)
Quercus borealis   (Northern Red Oak)
Quercus coccinea   (Scarlet Oak)
Quercus ellipsoidalis   (Northern Pin Oak)
Quercus marilandica   (Blackjack Oak)
Quercus montana   (Chestnut Oak)
Quercus palustris   (Pin Oak)
Quercus velutina   (Black Oak)
Rhododendron maximum   (Rosebay Rhododendron)
Rhus typhina   (Staghorn Sumac)
Robinia pseudoacacia   (Black Locust)
Sorbus decora   (Showy Mountainash)
Ulmus americana   (American Elm)
Viburnum rufidulum   (Rusty Blackhaw Viburnum)

ORANGE-BROWN:

Crataegus punctata   (Dotted Hawthorn)
Maclura pomifera   (Osageorange)
Morus rubra   (Red Mulberry)
Picea pungens   (Colorado Spruce)

Pinus ponderosa   (Ponderosa Pine)
Pinus rigida   (Pitch Pine)
Platanus occidentalis   (American Planetree)

ORANGE:

Quercus stellata   (Post Oak)
Salix amygdaloides   (Peachleaf Willow)

RED:

Acer pensylvanicum   (Striped Maple)
Acer rubrum   (Red Maple)
Acer saccharinum   (Silver Maple)
Acer spicatum   (Mountain Maple)
Cornus alternifolia   (Pagoda Dogwood)
Cornus florida   (Flowering Dogwood)
Prunus pensylvanica   (Pin Cherry)

Quercus alba   (White Oak)
Quercus stellata   (Post Oak)
Rhus copallina   (Flameleaf Sumac)
Rhus glabra   (Smooth Sumac)
Salix discolor   (Pussy Willow)
Tilia americana   (American Linden)
Zanthoxylum americanum   (Common Pricklyash)

PURPLE:

Acer negundo   (Boxelder)
Cornus alternifolia   (Pagoda Dogwood)

Cornus florida   (Flowering Dogwood)
Cotinus americanus   (American Smoketree)

BUD CHARACTER:

NAKED:

Asimina triloba   (Common Pawpaw)
Carya cordiformis   (Bitternut Hickory)
Carya illinoensis   (Pecan)
Fraxinus americana   (White Ash)
Fraxinus nigra   (Black Ash)
Fraxinus pennsylvanica   (Green Ash)
Fraxinus quadrangulata   (Blue Ash)

Hamamelis virginiana   (Common Witchhazel)
Juglans cinerea   (Butternut)
Juglans nigra   (Eastern Black Walnut)
Magnolia acuminata   (Cucumbertree Magnolia)
Viburnum lentago   (Nannyberry Viburnum)
Viburnum prunifolium   (Blackhaw Viburnum)
Viburnum rufidulum   (Rusty Blackhaw Viburnum)

RESINOUS:

Abies balsamea   (Balsam Fir)
Abies concolor   (White Fir)
Abies lasiocarpa   (Alpine Fir)
Betula papyrifera   (Paper Birch)
Betula populifolia   (Gray Birch)
Pinus banksiana   (Jack Pine)

Pinus ponderosa   (Ponderosa Pine)
Pinus resinosa   (Red Pine)
Pinus rigida   (Pitch Pine)
Pinus strobus   (Eastern White Pine)
Populus deltoides   (Eastern Poplar)
Sorbus decora   (Showy Mountainash)

WOOLY:

Acer negundo   (Boxelder)
Asimina triloba   (Common Pawpaw)
Carya tomentosa   (Mockernut Hickory)
Juglans cinerea   (Butternut)
Juglans nigra   (Eastern Black Walnut)
Magnolia acuminata   (Cucumbertree Magnolia)
Populus grandidentata   (Bigtooth Aspen)

Ptelea trifoliata   (Common Hoptree)
Quercus velutina   (Black Oak)
Rhus copallina   (Flameleaf Sumac)
Rhus typhina   (Staghorn Sumac)
Viburnum rufidulum   (Rusty Blackhaw Viburnum)
Zanthoxylum americanum   (Common Pricklyash)

Bud character (cont.)

STALKED:

Acer pensylvanicum   (Striped Maple)
Acer spicatum   (Mountain Maple)
Alnus rugosa   (Hazel Alder)
Betula lenta   (Sweet Birch)
Betula lutea   (Yellow Birch)
Betula nigra   (River Birch)

Betula papyrifera   (Paper Birch)
Betula populifolia   (Gray Birch)
Cornus florida   (Flowering Dogwood)
Hamamelis virginiana   (Common Witchhazel)
Larix laricina   (Eastern Larch)
Sorbus decora   (Showy Mountainash)

ONE/TWO SCALED:

Acer pensylvanicum   (Striped Maple)
Acer spicatum   (Mountain Maple)
Alnus rugosa   (Hazel Alder)
Castanea dentata   (American Chestnut)
Diospyros virginiana   (Common Persimmon)
Liriodendron tulipifera   (Tuliptree)

Salix amygdaloides   (Peachleaf Willow)
Salix bebbiana   (Bebb Willow)
Salix discolor   (Pussy Willow)
Salix nigra   (Black Willow)
Tilia americana   (American Linden)

LARGE PAPERY:

Aesculus glabra   (Ohio Buckeye)
Aesculus octandra   (Yellow Buckeye)
Carya glabra   (Pignut Hickory)

Carya ovata   (Shagbark Hickory)
Carya tomentosa   (Mockernut Hickory)
Rhododendron maximum   (Rosebay Rhododendron)

ONION:

Asimina triloba   (Common Pawpaw)
Cornus florida   (Flowering Dogwood)

NARROW, LONG POINTED:

Amelanchier canadensis   (Shadblow Serviceberry)
Amelanchier laevis   (Allegany Serviceberry)

Fagus grandifolia   (American Beech)
Viburnum lentago   (Nannyberry Viburnum)

CLUSTERED, SHARP POINTED:

Acer nigrum   (Black Maple)
Acer saccharum   (Sugar Maple)
Castanea dentata   (American Chestnut)
Populus deltoides   (Eastern Poplar)
Populus grandidentata   (Bigtooth Aspen)
Populus tremuloides   (Quaking Aspen)
Prunus americana   (American Plum)
Prunus pensylvanica   (Pin Cherry)

Prunus virginiana   (Common Chokecherry)
Quercus borealis   (Northern Red Oak)
Quercus ellipsoidalis   (Northern Pin Oak)
Quercus marilandica   (Blackjack Oak)
Quercus montana   (Chestnut Oak)
Quercus muhlenbergi   (Chinkapin Oak)
Quercus palustris   (Pin Oak)
Quercus velutina   (Black Oak)

CLUSTERED, BLUNT ROUNDED:

Abies balsamea   (Balsam Fir)
Abies concolor   (White Fir)
Abies lasiocarpa   (Alpine Fir)
Acer rubrum   (Red Maple)
Acer saccharinum   (Silver Maple)
Quercus alba   (White Oak)

Quercus bicolor   (Swamp White Oak)
Quercus coccinea   (Scarlet Oak)
Quercus imbricaria   (Shingle Oak)
Quercus macrocarpa   (Bur Oak)
Quercus stellata   (Post Oak)

DOME SHAPED, SURROUNDED BY LEAFSCAR:

Cladrastis lutea   (American Yellowwood)
Platanus occidentalis   (American Planetree)

Ptelea trifoliata   (Common Hoptree)
Rhus glabra   (Smooth Sumac)

BUD COLORATION:

YELLOW:

Carya cordiformis   (Bitternut Hickory)
Carya illinoensis   (Pecan)

Hamamelis virginiana   (Common Witchhazel)

YELLOW-BROWN:

Abies concolor   (White Fir)
Abies lasiocarpa   (Alpine Fir)

Populus deltoides   (Eastern Poplar)
Salix nigra   (Black Willow) orange

CHOCOLATE-BROWN:

Fraxinus americana   (White Ash)
Fraxinus nigra   (Black Ash) black
Fraxinus pennsylvanica   (Green Ash)

Fraxinus quadrangulata   (Blue Ash)
Viburnum rufidulum   (Rusty Blackhaw Viburnum)

RED:

Acer pensylvanicum   (Striped Maple)
Acer rubrum   (Red Maple)
Acer saccharinum   (Silver Maple)
Acer spicatum   (Mountain Maple)
Alnus rugosa   (Hazel Alder)
Asimina triloba   (Common Pawpaw) brown
Crataegus crusgalli   (Cockspur Hawthorn)
Crataegus mollis   (Downy Hawthorn)
Crataegus nitida   (Glossy Hawthorn)
Crataegus phaenopyrum   (Washington Hawthorn)
Crataegus pruinosa   (Frosted Hawthorn)

Crataegus punctata   (Dotted Hawthorn)
Liriodendron tulipifera   (Tuliptree)
Malus ioensis   (Prairie Crabapple)
Populus deltoides   (Eastern Poplar)
Populus tremuloides   (Quaking Aspen)
Prunus pensylvanica   (Pin Cherry)
Pseudotsuga taxifolia   (Common Douglasfir)
Salix discolor   (Pussy Willow)
Sorbus decora   (Showy Mountainash)
Tilia americana   (American Linden)
Zanthoxylum americanum   (Common Pricklyash)

PINK:

Cornus florida   (Flowering Dogwood)
Viburnum lentago   (Nannyberry Viburnum)

Viburnum prunifolium   (Blackhaw Viburnum)

GREEN:

Euonymus atropurpureus   (Eastern Wahoo)
Magnolia acuminata   (Cucumbertree Magnolia)

Salix discolor   (Pussy Willow) purplish
Sassafras albidum   (Common Sassafras)

SILVERY:

Acer negundo   (Boxelder)
Carya tomentosa   (Mockernut Hickory)

Magnolia acuminata   (Cucumbertree Magnolia)

BARK CHARACTER:

The distinctive textural characteristics of tree bark is most interesting, especially on deciduous trees during the winter season. The surface on trunks and lower limbs changes for many species with the advance of maturity. The bark of a young linden is smooth while that of the venerable forest monarch becomes divided into long parallel longitudinal ridges and fissures. Many species are valued primarily for their ornamental bark. The knowledgeable designer appreciates the palette of bark variation and shows this to best advantage. Seven categories of bark character are recognized.

SMOOTH:
> having a continuous even surface with a minimum of fissures,
> indicator—*Fagus grandifolia* (American Beech)

Abies balsamea   (Balsam Fir)
Abies concolor   (White Fir)
Abies lasiocarpa   (Alpine Fir)
Acer pensylvanicum   (Striped Maple)
Acer saccharinum   (Silver Maple)
Acer spicatum   (Mountain Maple)
Alnus rugosa   (Hazel Alder)
Amelanchier canadensis   (Shadblow Serviceberry)
Amelanchier laevis   (Allegany Serviceberry)
Asimina triloba   (Common Pawpaw)
Betula populifolia   (Gray Birch)
Carpinus caroliniana   (American Hornbeam)
Carya cordiformis   (Bitternut Hickory)
Carya illinoensis   (Pecan)
Cladrastis lutea   (American Yellowwood)
Cornus alternifolia   (Pagoda Dogwood)
Euonymus atropurpureus   (Eastern Wahoo)
Fagus grandifolia   (American Beech)

Franklinia alatamaha   (Franklinia)
Halesia carolina   (Carolina Silverbell)
Hamamelis virginiana   (Common Witchhazel)
Populus grandidentata   (Bigtooth Aspen)
Populus tremuloides   (Quaking Aspen)
Prunus pensylvanica   (Pin Cherry)
Prunus virginiana   (Common Chokecherry)
Ptelea trifoliata   (Common Hoptree)
Quercus coccinea   (Scarlet Oak)
Quercus ellipsoidalis   (Northern Pin Oak)
Quercus palustris   (Pin Oak)
Rhus copallina   (Flameleaf Sumac)
Rhus glabra   (Smooth Sumac)
Rhus typhina   (Staghorn Sumac)
Salix bebbiana   (Bebb Willow)
Salix discolor   (Pussy Willow)
Sorbus decora   (Showy Mountainash)
Zanthoxylum americanum   (Common Pricklyash)

SCALY:
> regular thin papery flakes separated by a mesh pattern of fine shallow vertical and horizontal fissures,
> indicator—*Ostrya virginiana* (Eastern Hophornbeam)

Aesculus glabra   (Ohio Buckeye)
Aesculus octandra   (Yellow Buckeye)
Betula lenta   (Sweet Birch)
Cercis canadensis   (Eastern Redbud)
Chionanthus virginicus   (White Fringetree)
Cotinus americanus   (American Smoketree)
Crataegus crusgalli   (Cockspur Hawthorn)
Crataegus mollis   (Downy Hawthorn)
Crataegus nitida   (Glossy Hawthorn)
Crataegus phaenopyrum   (Washington Hawthorn)
Crataegus pruinosa   (Frosted Hawthorn)
Crataegus punctata   (Dotted Hawthorn)
Fraxinus nigra   (Black Ash)
Fraxinus quadrangulata   (Blue Ash)
Gymnocladus dioicus   (Kentucky Coffeetree)
Larix laricina   (Eastern Larch)

Malus ioensis   (Prairie Crabapple)
Ostrya virginiana   (American Hophornbeam)
Picea engelmanni   (Engelmann Spruce)
Picea glauca   (White Spruce)
Picea glauca densata   (BlackHills White Spruce)
Picea mariana   (Black Spruce)
Picea pungens   (Colorado Spruce)
Pinus banksiana   (Jack Pine)
Pinus flexilis   (Limber Pine)
Prunus americana   (American Plum)
Prunus serotina   (Black Cherry)
Quercus alba   (White Oak)
Quercus imbricaria   (Shingle Oak)
Quercus muhlenbergi   (Chinkapin Oak)
Rhododendron maximum   (Rosebay Rhododendron)

EXFOLIATING:
> thin or coarse strips or sheets peeling either vertically, horizontally or into irregular mottled patches,
> indicator—*Betula nigra* (River Birch)

VERTICAL:

Acer rubrum   (Red Maple)
Acer saccharinum   (Silver Maple)
Carya ovata   (Shagbark Hickory)

Juniperus virginiana   (Eastern Redcedar)
Taxodium distichum   (Common Baldcypress)
Thuja occidentalis   (Eastern Arborvitae)

HORIZONTAL:

Betula lutea (Yellow Birch)
Betula nigra (River Birch)

Betula papyrifera (Paper Birch)

PATCHY:

Aesculus octandra (Yellow Buckeye)
Platanus occidentalis (American Planetree)

BLOCKY:

short knobby, warty, flat-topped squarish plates or ridges,
indicator—*Diospyros virginiana* (Common Persimmon)

Acer negundo (Boxelder)
Celtis occidentalis (Common Hackberry)
Cornus florida (Flowering Dogwood)
Diospyros virginiana (Common Persimmon)
Nyssa sylvatica (Black Tupelo)

Quercus marilandica (Blackjack Oak)
Viburnum lentago (Nannyberry Viburnum)
Viburnum prunifolium (Blackhaw Viburnum)
Viburnum rufidulum (Rusty Blackhaw Viburnum)

SHALLOW-FURROWED:

grooved by shallow longitudinal cracks with narrow to wide rounded or flattened ridges becoming
checked across into elongated rectangular platy segments,
indicator wide—*Juglans cinerea* (Butternut);
indicator narrow—*Liriodendron tulipifera* (Tuliptree)

NARROW:

Abies balsamea (Balsam Fir)
Abies concolor (White Fir)
Abies lasiocarpa (Alpine Fir)
Aralia spinosa (Devils-Walkingstick)
Carya cordiformis (Bitternut Hickory)
Carya glabra (Pignut Hickory)
Carya illinoensis (Pecan)
Carya tomentosa (Mockernut Hickory)
Catalpa speciosa (Northern Catalpa)

Fraxinus americana (White Ash)
Fraxinus pennsylvanica (Green Ash)
Gymnocladus dioicus (Kentucky Coffeetree)
Liriodendron tulipifera (Tuliptree)
Magnolia acuminata (Cucumbertree Magnolia)
Quercus alba (White Oak)
Quercus velutina (Black Oak)
Tilia americana (American Linden)
Ulmus americana (American Elm)

WIDE:

Castanea dentata (American Chestnut) upper trunk
Gleditsia triacanthos (Common Honeylocust)
Juglans cinerea (Butternut)
Pinus ponderosa (Ponderosa Pine)
Pinus resinosa (Red Pine)

Pinus rigida (Pitch Pine)
Quercus borealis (Northern Red Oak)
Quercus velutina (Black Oak)
Salix amygdaloides (Peachleaf Willow)

DEEP-FURROWED:

grooved by coarse deep longitudinal cracks with narrow to wide rounded or flattened ridges
becoming checked across into rectangular segments,
indicator—*Populus deltoides* (Eastern Poplar)

Acer nigrum (Black Maple)
Acer saccharum (Sugar Maple)
Juglans nigra (Eastern Black Walnut)
Liquidambar styraciflua (American Sweetgum)
Maclura pomifera (Osageorange)
Morus rubra (Red Mulberry)
Oxydendrum arboreum (Sourwood)
Pinus strobus (Eastern White Pine)
Populus deltoides (Eastern Poplar)
Pseudotsuga taxifolia (Common Douglasfir)

Quercus bicolor (Swamp White Oak)
Quercus macrocarpa (Bur Oak)
Quercus montana (Chestnut Oak)
Quercus stellata (Post Oak)
Robinia pseudoacacia (Black Locust)
Salix amygdaloides (Peachleaf Willow)
Salix nigra (Black Willow)
Sassafras albidum (Common Sassafras)
Tsuga canadensis (Canada Hemlock)
Ulmus americana (American Elm)

BARK COLORATION:

The vast palette of color in plants is a basic aesthetic consideration in their use. The use of dynamic bark coloration achieves emphasis, accent, decoration, attraction, and organization in the landscape. Bark character and color form one of the most interesting visual features of the winter landscape when contrasted with the white background of snow or the green background of evergreens. Eight classes represent the basic bark color possibilities.

WHITE:

Betula papyrifera   (Paper Birch)
Betula populifolia   (Gray Birch)
Platanus occidentalis   (American Planetree)
Populus tremuloides   (Quaking Aspen)

GRAY:

Abies concolor   (White Fir)
Abies lasiocarpa   (Alpine Fir)
Acer rubrum   (Red Maple)
Acer saccharinum   (Silver Maple)
Amelanchier canadensis   (Shadblow Serviceberry)
Amelanchier laevis   (Allegany Serviceberry)
Carpinus caroliniana   (American Hornbeam)
Carya cordiformis   (Bitternut Hickory)
Carya glabra   (Pignut Hickory)
Carya illinoensis   (Pecan)
Carya ovata   (Shagbark Hickory)
Carya tomentosa   (Mockernut Hickory)
Celtis occidentalis   (Common Hackberry)
Cladrastis lutea   (American Yellowwood)
Cornus florida   (Flowering Dogwood)
Crataegus crusgalli   (Cockspur Hawthorn)
Crataegus mollis   (Downy Hawthorn)
Crataegus nitida   (Glossy Hawthorn)
Crataegus phaenopyrum   (Washington Hawthorn)
Crataegus pruinosa   (Frosted Hawthorn)
Crataegus punctata   (Dotted Hawthorn)
Euonymus atropurpureus   (Eastern Wahoo)
Fagus grandifolia   (American Beech)

Fraxinus americana   (White Ash)
Fraxinus nigra   (Black Ash)
Fraxinus pennsylvanica   (Green Ash)
Fraxinus quadrangulata   (Blue Ash)
Halesia caroliniana   (Carolina Silverbell)
Juglans cinerea   (Butternut)
Liquidambar styraciflua   (American Sweetgum)
Liriodendron tulipifera   (Tuliptree)
Malus ioensis   (Prairie Crabapple)
Oxydendrum arboreum   (Sourwood) reddish
Picea glauca   (White Spruce)
Picea glauca densata   (BlackHills White Spruce)
Picea mariana   (Black Spruce)
Picea pungens   (Colorado Spruce)
Pinus flexilis   (Limber Pine)
Pinus resinosa   (Red Pine) reddish
Prunus virginiana   (Common Chokecherry)
Quercus alba   (White Oak)
Quercus muhlenbergi   (Chinkapin Oak)
Quercus stellata   (Post Oak)
Rhus copallina   (Flameleaf Sumac)
Rhus glabra   (Smooth Sumac)
Rhus typhina   (Staghorn Sumac)

YELLOW-ORANGE:

Betula lutea   (Yellow Birch)
Betula nigra   (River Birch)
Maclura pomifera   (Osageorange)
Morus rubra   (Red Mulberry)
Pinus banksiana   (Jack Pine)

Pinus ponderosa   (Ponderosa Pine)
Populus grandidentata   (Bigtooth Aspen)
Prunus pensylvanica   (Pin Cherry)
Sorbus decora   (Showy Mountainash)

GREEN:

Acer pensylvanicum   (Striped Maple)
Acer spicatum   (Mountain Maple)

Cornus alternifolia   (Pagoda Dogwood)
Salix bebbiana   (Bebb Willow)

MAROON-PURPLE

Acer spicatum   (Mountain Maple)
Cercis canadensis   (Eastern Redbud)

Cornus alternifolia   (Pagoda Dogwood)
Salix bebbiana   (Bebb Willow)

RED-BROWN:

Abies balsamea (Balsam Fir)
Acer spicatum (Mountain Maple)
Alnus rugosa (Hazel Alder)
Chionanthus virginicus (White Fringetree)
Juniperus virginiana (Eastern Redcedar)
Larix laricina (Eastern Larch)
Picea engelmanni (Engelmann Spruce)
Pinus rigida (Pitch Pine)
Prunus pensylvanica (Pin Cherry)
Pseudotsuga taxifolia (Common Douglasfir)

Ptelea trifoliata (Common Hoptree)
Quercus stellata (Post Oak)
Rhododendron maximum (Rosebay Rhododendron)
Robinia pseudoacacia (Black Locust)
Salix amygdaloides (Peachleaf Willow)
Salix discolor (Pussy Willow)
Taxodium distichum (Common Baldcypress)
Thuja occidentalis (Eastern Arborvitae)
Tsuga canadensis (Canada Hemlock)
Zanthoxylum americanum (Common Pricklyash)

GRAY-BROWN:

Acer negundo (Boxelder)
Aralia spinosa (Devils-Walkingstick)
Asimina triloba (Common Pawpaw)
Castanea dentata (American Chestnut)
Catalpa speciosa (Northern Catalpa)
Cotinus americanus (American Smoketree)
Franklinia alatamaha (Franklinia)
Gymnocladus dioicus (Kentucky Coffeetree)
Hamamelis virginiana (Common Witchhazel)
Magnolia acuminata (Cucumbertree Magnolia)

Ostrya virginiana (American Hophornbeam)
Populus deltoides (Eastern Poplar)
Quercus bicolor (Swamp White Oak)
Quercus imbricaria (Shingle Oak)
Quercus macrocarpa (Bur Oak)
Salix nigra (Black Willow)
Sassafras albidum (Common Sassafras)
Tilia americana (American Linden)
Ulmus americanum (American Elm)

BROWN-BLACK:

Acer nigrum (Black Maple)
Acer saccharum (Sugar Maple)
Aesculus glabra (Ohio Buckeye)
Aesculus octandra (Yellow Buckeye)
Alnus rugosa (Hazel Alder)
Betula lenta (Sweet Birch)
Diospyros virginiana (Common Persimmon)
Gleditsia triacanthos (Common Honeylocust)
Juglans nigra (Eastern Black Walnut)
Nyssa sylvatica (Black Tupelo)
Pinus strobus (Eastern White Pine)
Prunus americana (American Plum)

Prunus serotina (Black Cherry)
Quercus borealis (Northern Red Oak)
Quercus coccinea (Scarlet Oak)
Quercus ellipsoidalis (Northern Pin Oak)
Quercus marilandica (Blackjack Oak)
Quercus montana (Chestnut Oak)
Quercus palustris (Pin Oak)
Quercus velutina (Black Oak)
Salix nigra (Black Willow)
Viburnum lentago (Nannyberry Viburnum)
Viburnum prunifolium (Blackhaw Viburnum)
Viburnum rufidulum (Rusty Blackhaw Viburnum)

ARMAMENT:

Many plant species have ornamental prickles, spines, true thorns or sharp modified twigs which contribute special color and textural beauty in the landscape. Where personal injury liability is a real concern, use of these species should be limited. However, in many design situations, species with ornamental armament add interest and dimension not afforded by other plants.

indicator—*Crataegus mollis* (Downy Hawthorn)

Aralia spinosa (Devils-Walkingstick)
Crataegus crusgalli (Cockspur Hawthorn)
Crataegus mollis (Downy Hawthorn)

Crataegus nitida (Glossy Hawthorn)
Crataegus phaenopyrum (Washington Hawthorn)
Crataegus pruinosa (Frosted Hawthorn)

Armament (cont.)

Crataegus punctata   (Dotted Hawthorn)
Gleditsia triacanthos   (Common Honeylocust)
Maclura pomifera   (Osageorange)
Malus ioensis   (Prairie Crabapple)
Nyssa sylvatica   (Black Tupelo)

Prunus americana   (American Plum)
Robinia pseudoacacia   (Black Locust)
Viburnum prunifolium   (Blackhaw Viburnum)
Viburnum rufidulum   (Rusty Blackhaw Viburnum)
Zanthoxylum americanum   (Common Pricklyash)

FOLIAGE DURATION:

As we travel through the forest or savanna landscape and look about us, it soon becomes apparent that there are two predominant races of trees visually quite different from each other. The first includes species of maple, oak, birch, and others with large spreading leaves that fall each autumn (deciduous). Species of fir, hemlock, spruce and pine represent the second great group. Narrow needle-like leaves remain for many years (evergreen). The evergreen species are considered masculine in gender and are symbols of constancy and endurance while the feminine moods of the deciduous trees change in patterned response to the influence of season, day and hour. This dynamic contrast must be considered one of the most enriching landscape experiences perceived by man.

DECIDUOUS:
leaves shed annually in early to mid autumn,
indicator—*Celtis occidentalis* (Common Hackberry)

Acer negundo   (Boxelder)
Acer nigrum   (Black Maple)
Acer pensylvanicum   (Striped Maple)
Acer rubrum   (Red Maple)
Acer saccharinum   (Silver Maple)
Acer saccharum   (Sugar Maple)
Acer spicatum   (Mountain Maple)
Aesculus glabra   (Ohio Buckeye)
Aesculus octandra   (Yellow Buckeye)
Alnus rugosa   (Hazel Alder)
Amelanchier canadensis   (Shadblow Serviceberry)
Amelanchier laevis   (Allegany Serviceberry)
Aralia spinosa   (Devils-Walkingstick)
Asimina triloba   (Common Pawpaw)
Betula lenta   (Sweet Birch)
Betula lutea   (Yellow Birch)
Betula nigra   (River Birch)
Betula papyrifera   (Paper Birch)
Betula populifolia   (Gray Birch)
Carpinus caroliniana   (American Hornbeam)
Carya cordiformis   (Bitternut Hickory)
Carya glabra   (Pignut Hickory)
Carya illinoensis   (Pecan)
Carya ovata   (Shagbark Hickory)
Carya tomentosa   (Mockernut Hickory)
Castanea dentata   (American Chestnut)
Catalpa speciosa   (Northern Catalpa)
Celtis occidentalis   (Common Hackberry)
Cercis canadensis   (Eastern Redbud)
Chionanthus virginicus   (White Fringetree)
Cladrastis lutea   (American Yellowwood)
Cornus alternifolia   (Pagoda Dogwood)
Cornus florida   (Flowering Dogwood)
Cotinus americanus   (American Smoketree)
Crataegus crusgalli   (Cockspur Hawthorn)
Crataegus mollis   (Downy Hawthorn)
Crataegus nitida   (Glossy Hawthorn)
Crataegus phaenopyrum   (Washington Hawthorn)

Crataegus pruinosa   (Frosted Hawthorn)
Crataegus punctata   (Dotted Hawthorn)
Diospyros virginiana   (Common Persimmon)
Euonymus atropurpureus   (Eastern Wahoo)
Franklinia alatamaha   (Franklinia)
Fraxinus americana   (White Ash)
Fraxinus nigra   (Black Ash)
Fraxinus pennsylvanica   (Green Ash)
Fraxinus quadrangulata   (Blue Ash)
Gleditsia triacanthos   (Common Honeylocust)
Gymnocladus dioicus   (Kentucky Coffeetree)
Halesia carolina   (Carolina Silverbell)
Hamamelis virginiana   (Common Witchhazel)
Juglans cinerea   (Butternut)
Juglans nigra   (Eastern Black Walnut)
Larix laricina   (Eastern Larch)
Liquidambar styraciflua   (American Sweetgum)
Liriodendron tulipifera   (Tuliptree)
Maclura pomifera   (Osageorange)
Magnolia acuminata   (Cucumbertree Magnolia)
Malus ioensis   (Prairie Crabapple)
Morus rubra   (Red Mulberry)
Nyssa sylvatica   (Black Tupelo)
Oxydendrum arboreum   (Sourwood)
Platanus occidentalis   (American Planetree)
Populus deltoides   (Eastern Poplar)
Populus grandidentata   (Bigtooth Aspen)
Populus tremuloides   (Quaking Aspen)
Prunus americana   (American Plum)
Prunus pensylvanica   (Pin Cherry)
Prunus serotina   (Black Cherry)
Prunus virginiana   (Common Chokecherry)
Ptelea trifoliata   (Common Hoptree)
Quercus bicolor   (Swamp White Oak)
Quercus borealis   (Northern Red Oak)
Quercus coccinea   (Scarlet Oak)
Quercus macrocarpa   (Bur Oak)
Quercus marilandica   (Blackjack Oak)

Quercus montana (Chestnut Oak)
Quercus muhlenbergi (Chinkapin Oak)
Quercus stellata (Post Oak)
Rhus copallina (Flameleaf Sumac)
Rhus glabra (Smooth Sumac)
Rhus typhina (Staghorn Sumac)
Robinia pseudoacacia (Black Locust)
Salix amygdaloides (Peachleaf Willow)
Salix bebbiana (Bebb Willow)
Salix discolor (Pussy Willow)

Salix nigra (Black Willow)
Sassafras albidum (Common Sassafras)
Sorbus decora (Showy Mountainash)
Taxodium distichum (Common Baldcypress)
Tilia americana (American Linden)
Ulmus americana (American Elm)
Viburnum lentago (Nannyberry Viburnum)
Viburnum prunifolium (Blackhaw Viburnum)
Viburnum rufidulum (Rusty Blackhaw Viburnum)
Zanthoxylum americanum (Common Pricklyash)

EVERGREEN:
> coniferous or broadleaved trees whose leaves remain throughout the year and are continually dropping and being replaced by new springtime growth,
> indicator—*Pinus resinosa* (Red Pine)

Abies balsamea (Balsam Fir)
Abies concolor (White Fir)
Abies lasiocarpa (Alpine Fir)
Juniperus virginiana (Eastern Redcedar)
Picea engelmanni (Engelmann Spruce)
Picea glauca (White Spruce)
Picea glauca densata (BlackHills White Spruce)
Picea mariana (Black Spruce)
Picea pungens (Colorado Spruce)
Pinus banksiana (Jack Pine)

Pinus flexilis (Limber Pine)
Pinus ponderosa (Ponderosa Pine)
Pinus resinosa (Red Pine)
Pinus rigida (Pitch Pine)
Pinus strobus (Eastern White Pine)
Pseudotsuga taxifolia (Common Douglasfir)
Rhododendron maximum (Rosebay Rhododendron)
Thuja occidentalis (Eastern Arborvitae)
Tsuga canadensis (Canada Hemlock)

PERSISTENT:
> leaves losing summer color in autumn but with a significant percentage persisting into winter or early spring,
> indicator—*Quercus imbricaria* (Shingle Oak)

Fagus grandifolia (American Beech)
Ostrya virginiana (American Hophornbeam)
Platanus occidentalis (American Planetree)
Quercus alba (White Oak)
Quercus ellipsoidalis (Northern Pin Oak)

Quercus imbricaria (Shingle Oak)
Quercus marilandica (Blackjack Oak)
Quercus palustris (Pin Oak)
Quercus velutina (Black Oak)

FOLIAGE STRUCTURE:

Relatively few trees in this region exhibit ornamentally colorful flowers, fruit, or foliage during the summer season. Leaves, with their variety of structure and shape are the most important visual interest in the summer landscape. Four basic leaf structures are recognized.

SIMPLE:
> leaf having only one blade in which the midrib is unbranched and is united continuously along the blade margin,
> indicator—*Fagus grandifolia* (American Beech)

Acer nigrum (Black Maple)
Acer pensylvanicum (Striped Maple)
Acer rubrum (Red Maple)

Acer Saccharinum (Silver Maple)
Acer saccharum (Sugar Maple)
Acer spicatum (Mountain Maple)

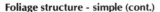

Foliage structure - simple (cont.)

Alnus rugosa   (Hazel Alder)
Amelanchier canadensis   (Shadblow Serviceberry)
Amelanchier laevis   (Allegany Serviceberry)
Asimina triloba   (Common Pawpaw)
Betula lenta   (Sweet Birch)
Betula lutea   (Yellow Birch)
Betula nigra   (River Birch)
Betula papyrifera   (Paper Birch)
Betula populifolia   (Gray Birch)
Carpinus caroliniana   (American Hornbeam)
Castanea dentata   (American Chestnut)
Catalpa speciosa   (Northern Catalpa)
Celtis occidentalis   (Common Hackberry)
Cercis canadensis   (Eastern Redbud)
Chionanthus virginicus   (White Fringetree)
Cornus alternifolia   (Pagoda Dogwood)
Cornus florida   (Flowering Dogwood)
Cotinus americanus   (American Smoketree)
Crataegus crusgalli   (Cockspur Hawthorn)
Crataegus mollis   (Downy Hawthorn)
Crataegus nitida   (Glossy Hawthorn)
Crataegus phaenopyrum   (Washington Hawthorn)
Crataegus pruinosa   (Frosted Hawthorn)
Crataegus punctata   (Dotted Hawthorn)
Diospyros virginiana   (Common Persimmon)
Euonymus atropurpureus   (Eastern Wahoo)
Fagus grandifolia   (American Beech)
Franklinia alatamaha   (Franklinia)
Halesia carolina   (Carolina Silverbell)
Hamamelis virginiana   (Common Witchhazel)
Liquidambar styraciflua   (American Sweetgum)
Liriodendron tulipifera   (Tuliptree)
Maclura pomifera   (Osageorange)
Magnolia acuminata   (Cucumbertree Magnolia)
Malus ioensis   (Prairie Crabapple)
Morus rubra   (Red Mulberry)

Nyssa sylvatica   (Black Tupelo)
Ostrya virginiana   (American Hophornbeam)
Oxydendrum arboreum   (Sourwood)
Platanus occidentalis   (American Planetree)
Populus deltoides   (Eastern Poplar)
Populus grandidentata   (Bigtooth Aspen)
Populus tremuloides   (Quaking Aspen)
Prunus americana   (American Plum)
Prunus pensylvanica   (Pin Cherry)
Prunus serotina   (Black Cherry)
Prunus virginiana   (Common Chokecherry)
Quercus alba   (White Oak)
Quercus bicolor   (Swamp White Oak)
Quercus borealis   (Northern Red Oak)
Quercus coccinea   (Scarlet Oak)
Quercus ellipsoidalis   (Northern Pin Oak)
Quercus imbricaria   (Shingle Oak)
Quercus macrocarpa   (Bur Oak)
Quercus marilandica   (Blackjack Oak)
Quercus montana   (Chestnut Oak)
Quercus muhlenbergi   (Chinkapin Oak)
Quercus palustris   (Pin Oak)
Quercus stellata   (Post Oak)
Quercus velutina   (Black Oak)
Rhododendron maximum   (Rosebay Rhododendron)
Salix amygdaloides   (Peachleaf Willow)
Salix bebbiana   (Bebb Willow)
Salix discolor   (Pussy Willow)
Salix nigra   (Black Willow)
Sassafras albidum   (Common Sassafras)
Tilia americana   (American Linden)
Ulmus americana   (American Elm)
Viburnum lentago   (Nannyberry Viburnum)
Viburnum prunifolium   (Blackhaw Viburnum)
Viburnum rufidulum   (Rusty Blackhaw Viburnum)

PINNATELY COMPOUND:
several individual leaflets of a once compound leaf arranged along each side of a common unbranched axis (rachis), resembling the pattern of a feather,
indicator—*Fraxinus pennsylvanica* (Green Ash)

Acer negundo   (Boxelder)
Carya cordiformis   (Bitternut Hickory)
Carya glabra   (Pignut Hickory)
Carya illinoensis   (Pecan)
Carya ovata   (Shagbark Hickory)
Carya tomentosa   (Mockernut Hickory)
Cladrastis lutea   (American Yellowwood)
Fraxinus americana   (White Ash)
Fraxinus nigra   (Black Ash)
Fraxinus pennsylvanica   (Green Ash)

Fraxinus quadrangulata   (Blue Ash)
Gleditsia triacanthos   (Common Honeylocust)
Juglans cinerea   (Butternut)
Juglans nigra   (Eastern Black Walnut)
Rhus copallina   (Flameleaf Sumac)
Rhus glabra   (Smooth Sumac)
Rhus typhina   (Staghorn Sumac)
Robinia pseudoacacia   (Black Locust)
Sorbus decora   (Showy Mountainash)
Zanthoxylum americanum   (Common Pricklyash)

PALMATELY COMPOUND:
several individual leaflets of a compound leaf radiating from a single point at the apex of the petiole,
indicator—*Aesculus glabra* (Ohio Buckeye)

Aesculus glabra   (Ohio Buckeye)
Aesculus octandra   (Yellow Buckeye)

Ptelea trifoliata   (Common Hoptree)

BIPINNATELY COMPOUND:
>
> several individual leaflets of a twice compound leaf arranged along each side of a branched axis, indicator—*Gymnocladus dioicus* (Kentucky Coffeetree)

Aralia spinosa   (Devils-Walkingstick)   *Gymnocladus dioicus*   (Kentucky Coffeetree)
Gleditsia triacanthos   (Common Honeylocust)   *Taxodium distichum*   (Common Baldcypress)

LEAF SHAPE:

The most conspicuous feature of foliage is leaf shape. The shape of a leaf or leaflet is usually characteristic of a species. The following shape terminology has the authority of precedence and of wide usage (Preston 1948, Sargent 1949, Watts 1944).

SCALE:
>
> small, short leaves resembling scales and overlapping one another like the shingles on a roof, indicator—*Thuja occidentalis* (Eastern Arborvitae)

Juniperus virginiana   (Eastern Redcedar)
Thuja occidentalis   (Eastern Arborvitae)

ACICULAR:
>
> needle-like, very slender, long and pointed, indicator—*Pinus rigida* (Pitch Pine)

Abies balsamea   (Balsam Fir)   *Picea pungens*   (Colorado Spruce)
Abies concolor   (White Fir)   *Pinus banksiana*   (Jack Pine)
Abies lasiocarpa   (Alpine Fir)   *Pinus flexilis*   (Limber Pine)
Larix laricina   (Eastern Larch)   *Pinus ponderosa*   (Ponderosa Pine)
Picea engelmanni   (Engelmann Spruce)   *Pinus resinosa*   (Red Pine)
Picea glauca   (White Spruce)   *Pinus rigida*   (Pitch Pine)
Picea glauca densata   (BlackHills White Spruce)   *Pinus strobus*   (Eastern White Pine)
Picea mariana   (Black Spruce)   *Pseudotsuga taxifolia*   (Common Douglasfir)

LINEAR:
>
> much longer than wide, with nearly parallel margins, indicator—*Tsuga canadensis* (Eastern Hemlock)

Taxodium distichum   (Common Baldcypress)
Tsuga canadensis   (Canada Hemlock)

LANCEOLATE-OBLONG LANCEOLATE:
>
> about 4 times as long as wide, widest near stem end, lance shaped, indicator—*Fraxinus pennsylvanica* (Green Ash)

Carya illinoensis   (Pecan)   *Oxydendrum arboreum*   (Sourwood)
Castanea dentata   (American Chestnut)   *Prunus pensylvanica*   (Pin Cherry)
Fagus grandifolia   (American Beech)   *Prunus serotina*   (Black Cherry)
Fraxinus americana   (White Ash)   *Rhus copallina*   (Flameleaf Sumac)
Fraxinus nigra   (Black Ash)   *Rhus glabra*   (Smooth Sumac)
Fraxinus pennsylvanica   (Green Ash)   *Rhus typhina*   (Staghorn Sumac)
Fraxinus quadrangulata   (Blue Ash)   *Salix amygdaloides*   (Peachleaf Willow)
Juglans cinerea   (Butternut)   *Salix nigra*   (Black Willow)
Juglans nigra   (Eastern Black Walnut)   *Sorbus decora*   (Showy Mountainash)

39

Leaf shape (cont.)

OVATE LANCEOLATE:
about 3 times as long as wide, widest near stem end,
indicator—*Celtis occidentalis* (Common Hackberry)

Acer negundo   (Boxelder)
Carya cordiformis   (Bitternut Hickory)
Carya illinoensis   (Pecan)

Celtis occidentalis   (Common Hackberry)
Zanthoxylum americanum   (Common Pricklyash)

OBLANCEOLATE:
about 4 times as long as wide, widest near tip end,
indicator—*Carya ovata* (Shagbark Hickory)

Aesculus glabra   (Ohio Buckeye)
Aesculus octandra   (Yellow Buckeye)
Carya glabra   (Pignut Hickory)

Carya ovata   (Shagbark Hickory)
Carya tomentosa   (Mockernut Hickory)

ELLIPTIC-OVAL:
twice as long as broad, widest at middle, both ends rounded,
indicator—*Cornus florida* (Flowering Dogwood)

Alnus rugosa   (Hazel Alder)
Amelanchier canadensis   (Shadblow Serviceberry)
Amelanchier laevis   (Allegany Serviceberry)
Carpinus caroliniana   (American Hornbeam)
Cornus florida   (Flowering Dogwood)
Cotinus americanus   (American Smoketree)
Crataegus pruinosa   (Frosted Hawthorn)
Diospyros virginiana   (Common Persimmon)
Fagus grandifolia   (American Beech)
Gleditsia triacanthos   (Common Honeylocust)

Halesia caroliniana   (Carolina Silverbell)
Magnolia acuminata   (Cucumbertree Magnolia)
Ostrya virginiana   (American Hophornbeam)
Prunus americana   (American Plum)
Quercus imbricaria   (Shingle Oak)
Robinia pseudoacacia   (Black Locust)
Salix discolor   (Pussy Willow)
Viburnum prunifolium   (Blackhaw Viburnum)
Viburnum rufidulum   (Rusty Blackhaw Viburnum)

OVATE-OBLONG OVATE:
egg shaped, widest near stem end,
indicator—*Betula lutea* (Yellow Birch)

Alnus rugosa   (Hazel Alder)
Aralia spinosa   (Devils-Walkingstick)
Betula lenta   (Sweet Birch)
Betula lutea   (Yellow Birch)
Betula papyrifera   (Paper Birch)
Celtis occidentalis   (Common Hackberry)
Chionanthus virginicus   (White Fringetree)
Cornus alternifolia   (Pagoda Dogwood)
Crataegus mollis   (Downy Hawthorn)

Euonymus atropurpureus   (Eastern Wahoo)
Gymnocladus dioicus   (Kentucky Coffeetree)
Maclura pomifera   (Osageorange)
Populus grandidentata   (Bigtooth Aspen)
Ptelea trifoliata   (Common Hoptree)
Sassafras albidum   (Common Sassafras)
Viburnum lentago   (Nannyberry Viburnum)

OBOVATE-OBLONG OBOVATE:
egg shaped, widest near tip end,
indicator—*Asimina triloba* (Common Pawpaw)

Asimina triloba   (Common Pawpaw)
Cladrastis lutea   (American Yellowwood)
Crataegus crusgalli   (Cockspur Hawthorn)
Crataegus nitida   (Glossy Hawthorn)
Crataegus punctata   (Dotted Hawthorn)
Franklinia alatamaha   (Franklinia)
Hamamelis virginiana   (Common Witchhazel)
Nyssa sylvatica   (Black Tupelo)
Populus grandidentata   (Bigtooth Aspen)

Prunus americana   (American Plum)
Prunus virginiana   (Common Chokecherry)
Quercus bicolor   (Swamp White Oak)
Quercus marilandica   (Blackjack Oak)
Quercus montana   (Chestnut Oak)
Quercus muhlenbergi   (Chinkapin Oak)
Rhododendron maximum   (Rosebay Rhododendron)
Salix bebbiana   (Bebb Willow)
Ulmus americana   (American Elm)

CORDATE:
> heart shaped,
> indicator—*Cercis canadensis* (Eastern Redbud)

Catalpa speciosa   (Northern Catalpa)
Cercis canadensis   (Eastern Redbud)
Morus rubra   (Red Mulberry)

Populus tremuloides   (Quaking Aspen)
Tilia americana   (American Linden)

DELTOID-WEDGE:
> triangular,
> indicator—*Populus deltoides* (Eastern Poplar)

Betula nigra   (River Birch)
Betula populifolia   (Gray Birch)
Crataegus phaenopyrum   (Washington Hawthorn)

Malus ioensis   (Prairie Crabapple)
Populus deltoides   (Eastern Poplar)

PALMATELY LOBED:
> major lobes (sinuses) radiating from central point at leaf base, fan lobed,
> indicator—*Acer rubrum* (Red Maple)

Acer nigrum   (Black Maple)
Acer pensylvanicum   (Striped Maple)
Acer rubrum   (Red Maple)
Acer saccharinum   (Silver Maple)
Acer saccharum   (Sugar Maple)

Acer spicatum   (Mountain Maple)
Liquidambar styraciflua   (American Sweetgum)
Liriodendron tulipifera   (Tuliptree)
Platanus occidentalis   (American Planetree)
Sassafras albidum   (Common Sassafras)

PINNATELY LOBED:
> lobes at more or less right angles along parallel leaf margins,
> indicator—*Quercus alba* (White Oak)

Morus rubra   (Red Mulberry) occasionally
Quercus alba   (White Oak)
Quercus bicolor   (Swamp White Oak)
Quercus borealis   (Northern Red Oak)
Quercus coccinea   (Scarlet Oak)

Quercus ellipsoidalis   (Northern Pin Oak)
Quercus macrocarpa   (Bur Oak)
Quercus palustris   (Pin Oak)
Quercus stellata   (Post Oak)
Quercus velutina   (Black Oak)

FOLIAGE TEXTURE:

Texture in the summer landscape is due essentially to different foliage patterns. Texture appears coarse or medium or fine because of leaf size which is a function primarily of leaf length and width. Texture is more subtly influenced by spacing of leaves, shape and division of leaves, surface quality of leaves or by length and stiffness of petioles. Coarse textures, for example, are found in linden and catalpa. Since linden leaves are spaced closer together and denser, the effect is somewhat less coarse than catalpa. Fineness, like coarseness, may be more apparent when leaves are more widely spaced or sparser. Fine textures are represented by Eastern Red Cedar and Eastern Arborvitae, yet red cedar appears finer. Flattened leaf petioles of Eastern Poplar flutter in the most modest breeze. Light passing through the crown is refracted and reflected giving the crown a dancing quality in the landscape. Five foliage texture categories are classified.

Foliage texture (cont.)

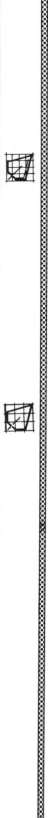

COARSE:

deciduous—leaf blades expansive, greater than 100 square centimeters (15 square inches) in total leaf surface area,
indicator—*Platanus occidentalis* (American Planetree)
conifers—leaf blades greater than 16 centimeters (6 inches) long,
indicator—*Pinus ponderosa* (Ponderosa Pine)

Asimina triloba   (Common Pawpaw)
Castanea dentata   (American Chestnut)
Catalpa speciosa   (Northern Catalpa)
Franklinia alatamaha   (Franklinia)
Magnolia acuminata   (Cucumbertree Magnolia)

Pinus ponderosa   (Ponderosa Pine)
Platanus occidentalis   (American Planetree)
Quercus macrocarpa   (Bur Oak)
Quercus marilandica   (Blackjack Oak)
Rhododendron maximum   (Rosebay Rhododendron)

MEDIUM COARSE:

deciduous—leaf blades between 60 and 100 square centimeters (9 and 15 square inches) in total leaf surface area,
indicator—*Acer saccharum* (Sugar Maple)
conifers—leaf blades between 10 and 16 centimeters (4 and 6 inches) long,
indicator—*Pinus rigida* (Pitch Pine)

Acer nigrum   (Black Maple)
Acer pensylvanicum   (Striped Maple)
Acer saccharum   (Sugar Maple)
Carya ovata   (Shagbark Hickory)
Cercis canadensis   (Eastern Redbud)
Chionanthus virginicus   (White Fringetree)
Crataegus mollis   (Downy Hawthorn)
Fagus grandifolia   (American Beech)
Hamamelis virginiana   (Common Witchhazel)
Liriodendron tulipifera   (Tuliptree)

Morus rubra   (Red Mulberry)
Oxydendrum arboreum   (Sourwood)
Pinus rigida   (Pitch Pine)
Quercus bicolor   (Swamp White Oak)
Quercus borealis   (Northern Red Oak)
Quercus montana   (Chestnut Oak)
Quercus stellata   (Post Oak)
Quercus velutina   (Black Oak)
Tilia americana   (American Linden)
Viburnum lentago   (Nannyberry Viburnum)

MEDIUM:

deciduous—leaf blades between 20 and 60 square centimeters (3 and 9 square inches) in total leaf surface area,
indicator—*Ulmus americana* (American Elm)
conifers—leaf blades between 5 and 10 centimeters (2 and 4 inches) long,
indicator—*Pinus resinosa* (Red Pine)

Acer spicatum   (Mountain Maple)
Aesculus glabra   (Ohio Buckeye)
Aesculus octandra   (Yellow Buckeye)
Alnus rugosa   (Hazel Alder)
Aralia spinosa   (Devils-Walkingstick)
Betula lenta   (Sweet Birch)
Betula lutea   (Yellow Birch)
Betula papyrifera   (Paper Birch)
Carya cordiformis   (Bitternut Hickory)
Carya glabra   (Pignut Hickory)
Carya illinoensis   (Pecan)
Carya tomentosa   (Mockernut Hickory)
Cladrastis lutea   (American Yellowwood)
Cornus florida   (Flowering Dogwood)
Diospyros virginiana   (Common Persimmon)
Euonymus atropurpureus   (Eastern Wahoo)
Fraxinus nigra   (Black Ash)
Fraxinus pennsylvanica   (Green Ash)
Fraxinus quadrangulata   (Blue Ash)
Halesia carolina   (Carolina Silverbell)

Juglans cinerea   (Butternut)
Liquidambar styraciflua   (American Sweetgum)
Maclura pomifera   (Osageorange)
Nyssa sylvatica   (Black Tupelo)
Ostrya virginiana   (American Hophornbeam)
Pinus resinosa   (Red Pine)
Pinus strobus   (Eastern White Pine)
Prunus americana   (American Plum)
Prunus pensylvanica   (Pin Cherry)
Prunus serotina   (Black Cherry)
Prunus virginiana   (Common Chokecherry)
Quercus alba   (White Oak)
Quercus coccinea   (Scarlet Oak)
Quercus ellipsoidalis   (Northern Pin Oak)
Quercus imbricaria   (Shingle Oak)
Quercus muhlenbergi   (Chinkapin Oak)
Rhus typhina   (Staghorn Sumac)
Salix amygdaloides   (Peachleaf Willow)
Salix discolor   (Pussy Willow)
Ulmus americana   (American Elm)

MEDIUM FINE:

> deciduous—leaf blades between 6 and 20 square centimeters (1 and 3 square inches) in total leaf surface area,
> indicator—*Amelanchier canadensis* (Shadblow Serviceberry)
> conifers—leaf blades between 2.5 and 5 centimeters (1 and 2 inches) long,
> indicator—*Pinus banksiana* (Jack Pine)

Acer negundo (Boxelder)
Acer rubrum (Red Maple)
Acer saccharinum (Silver Maple)
Amelanchier canadensis (Shadblow Serviceberry)
Amelanchier laevis (Allegany Serviceberry)
Betula nigra (River Birch)
Betula populifolia (Gray Birch)
Carpinus caroliniana (American Hornbeam)
Celtis occidentalis (Common Hackberry)
Cornus alternifolia (Pagoda Dogwood)
Cotinus americana (American Smoketree)
Crataegus crusgalli (Cockspur Hawthorn)
Crataegus nitida (Glossy Hawthorn)
Crataegus phaenopyrum (Washington Hawthorn)
Crataegus pruinosa (Frosted Hawthorn)
Crataegus punctata (Dotted Hawthorn)
Fraxinus americana (White Ash)
Gymnocladus dioicus (Kentucky Coffeetree)

Juglans nigra (Eastern Black Walnut)
Malus ioensis (Prairie Crabapple)
Picea pungens (Colorado Spruce)
Pinus banksiana (Jack Pine)
Pinus flexilis (Limber Pine)
Populus deltoides (Eastern Poplar)
Populus grandidentata (Bigtooth Aspen)
Populus tremuloides (Quaking Aspen)
Ptelea trifoliata (Common Hoptree)
Quercus palustris (Pin Oak)
Rhus copallina (Flameleaf Sumac)
Rhus glabra (Smooth Sumac)
Salix bebbiana (Bebb Willow)
Salix nigra (Black Willow)
Sassafras albidum (Common Sassafras)
Viburnum prunifolium (Blackhaw Viburnum)
Viburnum rufidulum (Rusty Blackhaw Viburnum)
Zanthoxylum americanum (Common Pricklyash)

FINE:

> deciduous—leaf blades compact or divided, less than 6 square centimeters (one square inch) in total leaf surface area,
> indicator—*Gleditsia triacanthos* (Common Honeylocust)
> conifers—leaf blades less than 2.5 centimeters (1 inch) long,
> indicator—*Picea glauca* (White Spruce)

Abies balsamea (Balsam Fir)
Abies concolor (White Fir)
Abies lasiocarpa (Alpine Fir)
Gledistisa triacanthos (Common Honeylocust)
Juniperus virginiana (Eastern Redcedar)
Larix laricina (Eastern Larch)
Picea engelmanni (Engelmann Spruce)
Picea glauca (White Spruce)

Picea glauca densata (BlackHills White Spruce)
Picea mariana (Black Spruce)
Pseudotsuga taxifolia (Common Douglasfir)
Robinia pseudoacacia (Black Locust)
Sorbus decora (Showy Mountainash)
Taxodium distichum (Common Baldcypress)
Thuja occidentalis (Eastern Arborvitae)
Tsuga canadensis (Canada Hemlock)

FOLIAGE COLORATION:

The tremendous palette of foliage colors with a wide selection of hues, intensities and values provides the designer with a color spectrum which changes with the season. Through the judicious selection of vegetation species, designers can provide spots or splashes of color in either the natural or the cultural landscape in much the same manner that an artist uses paints on canvas. Although the leaves of most deciduous woody plants are of little tonal contrast during the summer growing season, most species have leaves which are differently colored at other seasons. Leaves are green because they contain chlorophyll which is continually manufactured during the growing season by the plant under the heat and light of day. Seasonal coloration is determined by the amount of two general groups of coloring pigments in the leaf which mask the chlorophyll. These pigments are the carotins (yellow-producing pigments) and the anthocyanins (red-producing pigments). These pigments become most pronounced during the autumn season when most of the chlorophyll is destroyed in many deciduous plants. The coloration of new spring foliage can be as beautiful as that in autumn but is usually more subtle and does not last as long. As the spring season progresses and more and more chlorophyll is manufactured, most deciduous plants produce sufficient chlorophyll to completely mask any coloration exhibited at leaf emergence. Coniferous

Foliage Coloration: Table I

	Winter									Spring									Summer									Autumn								
	silver gray	light green	med. green	dark green	blue green	yellow green	or-red green	maroon green	tan brown	silver gray	light green	med. green	dark green	blue green	yellow green	or-red green	maroon-purple	tan brown	silver gray	light green	med. green	dark green	blue green	yellow green	or-red green	maroon green	tan brown	silver gray	med. green	dark green	blue green	yellow green	yellow	orange-red	maroon-purple	tan brown
Abies balsamea				■						■												■								■						
Abies concolor				■						■			■									■								■						
Abies lasiocarpa				■						■			■									■								■						
Acer negundo															■									■								■				
Acer nigrum																								■											■	
Acer pensylvanicum													■																					■		
Acer rubrum											■																							■		
Acer saccharinum											■													■									■			
Acer saccharum											■											■												■		
Acer spicatum											■											■		■									■			
Aesculus glabra											■													■						■						
Aesculus octandra											■													■						■						
Alnus rugosa												■										■								■						
Amelanchier canadensis										■												■												■		
Amelanchier laevis															■															■						
Aralia spinosa													■									■										■		■		
Asimina triloba											■										■												■			
Betula lenta											■											■											■			
Betula lutea											■											■											■			
Betula nigra															■									■								■				
Betula papyrifera													■									■										■				
Betula populifolia																						■										■				
Carpinus caroliniana																■						■											■			
Carya cordiformis															■																	■				■
Carya glabra													■									■														■
Carya illinoensis												■												■								■				

44

Foliage Coloration: Table I

	Winter									Spring									Summer									Autumn								
	silver gray	light green	med. green	dark green	blue green	yellow green	or-red green	maroon green	tan brown	silver gray	light green	med. green	dark green	blue green	yellow green	or-red green	maroon-purple	tan brown	silver gray	light green	med. green	dark green	blue green	yellow green	or-red green	maroon green	tan brown	silver gray	med. green	dark green	blue green	yellow green	yellow	orange-red	maroon-purple	tan brown
Carya ovata															■									■									■			■
Carya tomentosa															■									■									■			■
Castanea dentata															■									■									■			■
Catalpa speciosa																																				
Celtis occidentalis											■											■											■			
Cercis canadensis																																				
Chionanthus virginicus																						■											■			
Cladrastis lutea																																				
Cornus alternifolia										■												■													■	
Cornus florida																						■											■			
Cotinus americanus																	■					■											■			
Crataegus crusgalli												■										■											■			
Crataegus mollis															■									■									■		■	
Crataegus nitida																						■											■			
Crataegus phaenopyrum											■											■											■			
Crataegus pruinosa													■									■											■			
Crataegus punctata										■												■											■			
Diospyros virginiana											■											■								■						
Euonymus atropurpureus																																				
Fagus grandifolia									■													■														■
Franklinia alatamaha																					■											■				
Fraxinus americana																						■													■	
Fraxinus nigra																						■													■	
Fraxinus pennsylvanica																						■											■			
Fraxinus quadrangulata															■							■														
Gleditsia triacanthos																																				

45

Foliage Coloration: Table I

	Winter									Spring									Summer									Autumn								
	silver gray	light green	med. green	dark green	blue green	yellow green	or-red green	maroon green	tan brown	silver gray	light green	med. green	dark green	blue green	yellow green	or-red green	maroon-purple	tan brown	silver gray	light green	med. green	dark green	blue green	yellow green	or-red green	maroon green	tan brown	silver gray	med. green	dark green	blue green	yellow green	yellow	orange-red	maroon-purple	tan brown
Gymnocladus dioicus																	■					■											■			
Halesia carolina											■										■															
Hamamelis virginiana											■										■												■			
Juglans cinerea															■								■													
Juglans nigra															■								■													
Juniperus virginiana								■					■									■								■						
Larix laricina											■										■												■			
Liquidambar styraciflua											■										■													■	■	
Liriodendron tulipifera											■										■												■			
Maclura pomifera											■										■												■			
Magnolia acuminata											■										■											■				
Malus ioensis																■	■				■															
Morus rubra											■										■												■			
Nyssa sylvatica											■											■													■	
Ostrya virginiana					■								■										■									■				
Oxydendrum arboreum											■										■															
Picea engelmanni					■						■											■								■						
Picea glauca					■									■								■									■					
Picea glauca densata					■									■	■						■											■				
Picea mariana					■								■									■									■					
Picea pungens					■									■									■								■					
Pinus banksiana						■									■						■											■				
Pinus flexilis					■									■									■								■					
Pinus ponderosa				■																	■									■						
Pinus resinosa			■																											■						
Pinus rigida						■									■						■											■				

Foliage Coloration: Table I

Species	Winter									Spring									Summer									Autumn								
	silver gray	light green	med. green	dark green	blue green	yellow green	or-red green	maroon green	tan brown	silver gray	light green	med. green	dark green	blue green	yellow green	or-red green	maroon-purple	tan brown	silver gray	light green	med. green	dark green	blue green	yellow green	or-red green.	maroon green	tan brown	silver gray	med. green	dark green	blue green	yellow green	yellow	orange-red	maroon-purple	tan brown
Pinus strobus			█								█										█								█							
Platanus occidentalis									█		█										█															█
Populus deltoides											█										█													█		
Populus grandidentata											█										█												█			
Populus tremuloides											█												█										█			
Prunus americana											█											█												█		
Prunus pensylvanica															█							█												█		
Prunus serotina																█	█					█												█		
Prunus virginiana															█							█												█		
Pseudotsuga taxifolia				█	█								█	█								█								█	█					
Ptelea trifoliata																						█								█						
Quercus alba									█		█										█															█
Quercus bicolor														█							█															█
Quercus borealis											█										█															█
Quercus coccinea												█									█													█		
Quercus ellipsoidalis									█				█								█													█		
Quercus imbricaria									█						█						█									█						
Quercus macrocarpa															█						█													█		
Quercus marilandica									█													█										█				█
Quercus muhlenbergi															█						█												█			
Quercus palustris													█								█													█		█
Quercus montana									█				█									█										█		█		
Quercus stellata															█						█												█			
Quercus velutina												█									█															█
Rhododendron maximum				█							█										█									█						
Rhus copallina													█								█													█		█

47

Foliage Coloration: Table I

Color columns per season:
- **Winter / Summer:** silver gray, light green, med. green, dark green, blue green, yellow green, or-red green, maroon green, tan brown
- **Spring:** silver gray, light green, med. green, dark green, blue green, yellow green, or-red green, maroon-purple, tan brown
- **Autumn:** silver gray, med. green, dark green, blue green, yellow green, yellow, orange-red, maroon-purple, tan brown

Species	Winter	Spring	Summer	Autumn
Rhus glabra		med. green	dark green	orange-red
Rhus typhina		yellow green	dark green	yellow green
Robinia pseudoacacia		dark green	dark green	yellow green
Salix amygdaloides		light green	light green	yellow green
Salix bebbiana		silver gray	dark green	dark green
Salix discolor			dark green	
Salix nigra		light green	dark green	
Sassafras albidum	silver gray	med. green	yellow green	orange-red, maroon-purple, tan brown
Sorbus decora		light green	dark green	orange-red, maroon-purple
Taxodium distichum			dark green	tan brown
Thuja occidentalis	yellow green		yellow green	yellow green, maroon-purple
Tilia americana			dark green	
Tsuga canadensis	dark green	dark green	dark green	dark green
Ulmus americana		light green		
Viburnum lentago				maroon-purple, tan brown
Viburnum prunifolium		light green	yellow green	
Viburnum rufidulum			dark green	maroon-purple, tan brown
Zanthoxylum americanum		light green	dark green	yellow green

and broadleaf evergreens along with a few deciduous plants with persisting leaves offer foliage coloration throughout the winter landscape and are strongly contrasted with the defoliated crowns of other species. Table 1 correlates foliage color variation of plants for quick cross reference, comparison, and evaluation. This table can be used as a foliage color tool to assist designers in making decisions concerning intraseasonal and interseasonal landscape color composition.

FOLIAGE SURFACE:

Glossy leaves or leaves that are very light on either upper or lower surface (such as Pin Oak) tend to appear fine textured because there is more sparkle and reflected light. The resultant appearance is that there are many small leaves. Foliage which is noticeably light or silvery on the underside (such as Silver Maple) assumes a lightened dancing ornamental quality when whipped by summer breezes. Such ephemeral qualities strongly contrast the normal reflective foliage values on breezeless days. Three leaf surface categories indicate the amount of light reflected or absorbed.

GLOSSY:
one or both blade surfaces lustrous, often thick leathery appearance,
indicator—*Quercus palustris* (Pin Oak)

Abies balsamea   (Balsam Fir)
Betula nigra   (River Birch)
Betula populifolia   (Gray Birch)
Chionanthus virginicus   (White Fringetree)
Crataegus crusgalli   (Cockspur Hawthorn)
Crataegus nitida   (Glossy Hawthorn)
Crataegus phaenopyrum   (Washington Hawthorn)
Diospyros virginiana   (Common Persimmon)
Franklinia alatamaha   (Franklinia)
Fraxinus pennsylvanica   (Green Ash)
Larix laricina   (Eastern Larch)
Liquidambar styraciflua   (American Sweetgum)
Liriodendron tulipifera   (Tuliptree)
Maclura pomifera   (Osageorange)
Nyssa sylvatica   (Black Tupelo)
Oxydendrum arboreum   (Sourwood)
Pinus resinosa   (Red Pine)
Pinus strobus   (Eastern White Pine)
Populus deltoides   (Eastern Poplar)
Populus tremuloides   (Quaking Aspen)
Prunus pensylvanica   (Pin Cherry)

Prunus serotina   (Black Cherry)
Ptelea trifoliata   (Common Hoptree)
Quercus coccinea   (Scarlet Oak)
Quercus ellipsoidalis   (Northern Pin Oak)
Quercus imbricaria   (Shingle Oak)
Quercus macrocarpa   (Bur Oak)
Quercus marilandica   (Blackjack Oak)
Quercus montana   (Chestnut Oak)
Quercus palustris   (Pin Oak)
Quercus stellata   (Post Oak)
Quercus velutina   (Black Oak)
Rhododendron maximum   (Rosebay Rhododendron)
Rhus copallina   (Flameleaf Sumac)
Rhus glabra   (Smooth Sumac)
Salix amygdaloides   (Peachleaf Willow)
Salix nigra   (Black Willow)
Tsuga canadensis   (Canada Hemlock)
Ulmus americana   (American Elm)
Viburnum lentago   (Nannyberry Viburnum)
Viburnum rufidulum   (Rusty Blackhaw Viburnum)
Zanthoxylum americanum   (Common Pricklyash)

DULL:
both blade surfaces lacking luster,
indicator—*Acer saccharum* (Sugar Maple)

Abies concolor   (White Fir)
Abies lasiocarpa   (Alpine Fir)
Acer negundo   (Boxelder)
Acer nigrum   (Black Maple)
Acer pensylvanicum   (Striped Maple)
Acer rubrum   (Red Maple)
Acer saccharinum   (Silver Maple)
Acer saccharum   (Sugar Maple)

Acer spicatum   (Mountain Maple)
Aesculus glabra   (Ohio Buckeye)
Aesculus octandra   (Yellow Buckeye)
Alnus rugosa   (Hazel Alder)
Amelanchier canadensis   (Shadblow Serviceberry)
Amelanchier laevis   (Allegany Serviceberry)
Aralia spinosa   (Devils-Walkingstick)
Asimina triloba   (Common Pawpaw)

Foliage surface (cont.)

Betula lenta   (Sweet Birch)
Betula lutea   (Yellow Birch)
Betula papyrifera   (Paper Birch)
Carpinus caroliniana   (American Hornbeam)
Carya cordiformis   (Bitternut Hickory)
Carya glabra   (Pignut Hickory)
Carya illinoensis   (Pecan)
Carya ovata   (Shagbark Hickory)
Carya tomentosa   (Mockernut Hickory)
Castanea dentata   (American Chestnut)
Catalpa speciosa   (Northern Catalpa)
Celtis occidentalis   (Common Hackberry)
Cercis canadensis   (Eastern Redbud)
Cladrastis lutea   (American Yellowwood)
Cornus alternifolia   (Pagoda Dogwood)
Cornus florida   (Flowering Dogwood)
Cotinus americanus   (American Smoketree)
Crataegus pruinosa   (Frosted Hawthorn)
Crataegus punctata   (Dotted Hawthorn)
Euonymus atropurpureus   (Eastern Wahoo)
Fagus grandifolia   (American Beech)
Fraxinus americana   (White Ash)
Fraxinus nigra   (Black Ash)
Fraxinus quadrangulata   (Blue Ash)
Gleditsia triacanthos   (Common Honeylocust)
Gymnocladus dioicus   (Kentucky Coffeetree)
Halesia carolina   (Carolina Silverbell)
Juglans cinerea   (Butternut)
Juglans nigra   (Eastern Black Walnut)
Juniperus virginiana   (Eastern Redceder)
Magnolia acuminata   (Cucumbertree Magnolia)

Morus rubra   (Red Mulberry)
Ostrya virginiana   (American Hophornbeam)
Picea engelmanni   (Engelmann Spruce)
Picea glauca   (White Spruce)
Picea glauca densata   (BlackHills White Spruce)
Picea mariana   (Black Spruce)
Picea pungens   (Colorado Spruce)
Pinus banksiana   (Jack Pine)
Pinus flexilis   (Limber Pine)
Pinus ponderosa   (Ponderosa Pine)
Pinus rigida   (Pitch Pine)
Platanus occidentalis   (American Planetree)
Populus grandidentata   (Bigtooth Aspen)
Prunus americana   (American Plum)
Prunus virginiana   (Common Chokecherry)
Pseudotsuga taxifolia   (Common Douglasfir)
Quercus alba   (White Oak)
Quercus bicolor   (Swamp White Oak)
Quercus borealis   (Northern Red Oak)
Quercus muhlenbergi   (Chinkapin Oak)
Rhus typhina   (Staghorn Sumac)
Robinia pseudoacacia   (Black Locust)
Salix bebbiana   (Bebb Willow)
Salix discolor   (Pussy Willow)
Sassafras albidum   (Common Sassafras)
Sorbus decora   (Showy Mountainash)
Taxodium distichum   (Common Baldcypress)
Thuja occidentalis   (Eastern Arborvitae)
Tilia americana   (American Linden)
Ulmus americana   (American Elm)
Viburnum prunifolium   (Blackhaw Viburnum)

TOMENTOSE:
blade covered on one or both surfaces by woolly hairlike fibers,
indicator—*Crataegus mollis* (Downy Hawthorn)

Acer nigrum   (Black Maple)
Alnus rugosa   (Hazel Alder)
Crataegus mollis   (Downy Hawthorn)
Crataegus pruinosa   (Frosted Hawthorn)
Hamamelis virginiana   (Common Witchhazel)
Juglans cinerea   (Butternut)

Malus ioensis   (Prairie Crabapple)
Morus rubra   (Red Mulberry)
Quercus stellata   (Post Oak)
Rhus typhina   (Staghorn Sumac)
Viburnum rufidulum   (Rusty Blackhaw Viburnum)

FLOWER STRUCTURE:

One of a child's first consciousness of plant characteristics is the bright colors and fragile form of flowers. The diversity of shape and arrangement of parts is captivating. Flower qualities are one of the most popular design criteria influencing plant selection. There is a corresponding great amount of published research and literature available in this area for public and professional review. Seven structural arrangements are considered:

CONE:
small staminate and pistillate flowers clustered into tight cylindrical cones (conifers),
Note: The reproductive organs of conifers are not considered true flowers. They are not accom-

panied by the greenish sepals and colorful petals of a normal flower, but by minute bodies borne on scales and placed very close to one another to form a structure called a cone.
indicator—*Pinus banksiana* (Jack Pine)

Abies balsamea   (Balsam Fir)
Abies concolor   (White Fir)
Abies lasiocarpa   (Alpine Fir)
Juniperus virginiana   (Eastern Redcedar)
Larix laricina   (Eastern Larch)
Picea engelmanni   (Engelmann Spruce)
Picea glauca   (White Spruce)
Picea glauca densata   (BlackHills White Spruce)
Picea mariana   (Black Spruce)
Picea pungens   (Colorado Spruce)

Pinus banksiana   (Jack Pine)
Pinus flexilis   (Limber Pine)
Pinus ponderosa   (Ponderosa Pine)
Pinus resinosa   (Red Pine)
Pinus rigida   (Pitch Pine)
Pinus strobus   (Eastern White Pine)
Pseudotsuga taxifolia   (Common Douglasfir)
Taxodium distichum   (Common Baldcypress)
Thuja occidentalis   (Eastern Arborvitae)
Tsuga canadensis   (Canada Hemlock)

SMALL CLUSTERS:
flowers mostly in small clusters along the stems,
indicator—*Acer saccharinum* (Silver Maple)

Acer negundo   (Boxelder)
Acer nigrum   (Black Maple)
Acer rubrum   (Red Maple)
Acer saccharinum   (Silver Maple)
Acer saccharum   (Sugar Maple)
Celtis occidentalis   (Common Hackberry)
Cercis canadensis   (Eastern Redbud)
Euonymus atropurpureus   (Eastern Wahoo)
Fagus grandifolia   (American Beech)
Fraxinus americana   (White Ash)
Fraxinus nigra   (Black Ash)

Fraxinus pennsylvanica   (Green Ash)
Fraxinus quadrangulata   (Blue Ash)
Hamamelis virginiana   (Common Witchhazel)
Liquidambar styraciflua   (American Sweetgum)
Maclura pomifera   (Osageorange)
Nyssa sylvatica   (Black Tupelo)
Platanus occidentalis   (American Planetree)
Sassafras albidum   (Common Sassasfras)
Ulmus americana   (American Elm)
Zanthoxylum americanum   (Common Pricklyash)

PYRAMIDAL SPIKE:
flowers in elongated pyramidal or cylindrical clusters mostly at the ends of twigs,
indicator—*Prunus serotina* (Black Cherry)

Acer pensylvanicum   (Striped Maple)
Acer spicatum   (Mountain Maple)
Aesculus glabra   (Ohio Buckeye)
Aesculus octandra   (Yellow Buckeye)
Amelanchier canadensis   (Shadblow Serviceberry)
Amelanchier laevis   (Allegany Serviceberry)
Aralia spinosa   (Devils-Walkingstick)
Castanea dentata   (American Chestnut)
Chionanthus virginicus   (White Fringetree)
Cladrastus lutea   (American Yellowwood)

Cotinus americanus   (American Smoketree)
Gleditsia triacanthos   (Common Honeylocust)
Gymnocladus dioicus   (Kentucky Coffeetree)
Prunus serotina   (Black Cherry)
Prunus virginiana   (Common Chokecherry)
Rhus copallina   (Flameleaf Sumac)
Rhus glabra   (Smooth Sumac)
Rhus typhina   (Staghorn Sumac)
Robinia pseudoacacia   (Black Locust)

CATKIN:
flowers in the form of slender elongated catkins,
indicator—*Quercus macrocarpa* (Bur Oak)

Alnus rugosa   (Hazel Alder)
Betula lenta   (Sweet Birch)
Betula lutea   (Yellow Birch)
Betula nigra   (River Birch)
Betula papyrifera   (Paper Birch)
Betula populifolia   (Gray Birch)
Carpinus caroliniana   (American Hornbeam)
Carya cordiformis   (Bitternut Hickory)
Carya glabra   (Pignut Hickory)
Carya illinoensis   (Pecan)
Carya ovata   (Shagbark Hickory)
Carya tomentosa   (Mockernut Hickory)

Juglans cinerea   (Butternut)
Juglans nigra   (Eastern Black Walnut)
Morus rubra   (Red Mulberry)
Ostrya virginiana   (American Hophornbeam)
Populus deltoides   (Eastern Poplar)
Populus grandidentata   (Bigtooth Aspen)
Populus tremuloides   (Quaking Aspen)
Quercus alba   (White Oak)
Quercus bicolor   (Swamp White Oak)
Quercus borealis   (Northern Red Oak)
Quercus coccinea   (Scarlet Oak)
Quercus ellipsoidalis   (Northern Pin Oak)

Flower structure - catkin (cont.)

Quercus imbricaria   (Shingle Oak)
Quercus macrocarpa   (Bur Oak)
Quercus marilandica   (Blackjack Oak)
Quercus montana   (Chestnut Oak)
Quercus muhlenbergi   (Chinkapin Oak)
Quercus palustris   (Pin Oak)

Quercus stellata   (Post Oak)
Quercus velutina   (Black Oak)
Salix amygdaloides   (Peachleaf Willow)
Salix bebbiana   (Bebb Willow)
Salix discolor   (Pussy Willow)
Salix nigra   (Black Willow)

FLAT TOP:
small flowers in rounded or flat-topped clusters mostly at the ends of twigs,
indicator—*Viburnum lentago* (Nannyberry Viburnum)

Cornus alternifolia   (Pagoda Dogwood)
Crataegus crusgalli   (Cockspur Hawthorn)
Crataegus mollis   (Downy Hawthorn)
Crataegus nitida   (Glossy Hawthorn)
Crataegus phaenopyrum   (Washington Hawthorn)
Crataegus pruinosa   (Frosted Hawthorn)
Crataegus punctata   (Dotted Hawthorn)
Prunus americana   (American Plum)

Prunus pensylvanica   (Pin Cherry)
Ptelea trifoliata   (Common Hoptree)
Sorbus decora   (Showy Mountainash)
Tilia americana   (American Linden)
Viburnum lentago   (Nannyberry Viburnum)
Viburnum prunifolium   (Blackhaw Viburnum)
Viburnum rufidulum   (Rusty Blackhaw Viburnum)

LARGE SINGLE:
flowers widely open with conspicuous distinct petals
indicator—*Malus ioensis* (Prairie Crabapple)

Asimina triloba   (Common Pawpaw)
Cornus florida   (Flowering Dogwood) bracts
Franklinia alatamaha   (Franklinia)

Liriodendron tulipifera   (Tuliptree)
Magnolia acuminata   (Cucumbertree Magnolia)
Malus ioensis   (Prairie Crabapple)

BELL:
bell-shaped and cup-like, or tubular trumpet shaped,
indicator—*Halesia carolina* (Carolina Silverbell)

Catalpa speciosa   (Northern Catalpa)
Diospyros virginiana   (Common Persimmon)
Halesia carolina   (Carolina Silverbell)

Oxydendrum arboreum   (Sourwood)
Rhododendron maximum   (Rosebay Rhododendron)

FLOWER COLOR:

The flowers of many trees contribute a pageant of color which brightens the landscape. After the long winter season, the silvery gray blossoms of Quaking Aspen and the bright red blooms of Red Maple become the harbingers of spring. Although the majority of species flower during the spring season, a few bloom in late summer and autumn. The great spectrum of brilliant flower hues and the dramatic visual impact achieved by mass plantings has an arresting power that has long been appealing to the designer. A range of nine color classes is used. Where appropriate, symbols distinguish between pistillate (*) and staminate (+) flowers.

WHITE:

Amelanchier canadensis   (Shadblow Serviceberry)
Amelanchier laevis   (Allegany Serviceberry)
Aralia spinosa   (Devils-Walkingstick)

Catalpa speciosa   (Northern Catalpa)
Chionanthus virginicus   (White Fringetree)
Cladrastis lutea   (American Yellowwood)

Cornus alternifolia (Pagoda Dogwood)
Cornus florida (Flowering Dogwood)
Crataegus crusgalli (Cockspur Hawthorn)
Crataegus mollis (Downy Hawthorn)
Crataegus nitida (Glossy Hawthorn)
Crataegus phaenopyrum (Washington Hawthorn)
Crataegus pruinosa (Frosted Hawthorn)
Crataegus punctata (Dotted Hawthorn)
Franklinia alatamaha (Franklinia)
Halesia carolina (Carolina Silverbell)
Nyssa sylvatica (Black Tupelo)

Oxydendrum arboreum (Sourwood)
Prunus americana (American Plum)
Prunus pensylvanica (Pin Cherry)
Prunus serotina (Black Cherry)
Prunus virginiana (Common Chokecherry)
Robinia pseudoacacia (Black Locust)
Sorbus decora (Showy Mountainash)
Viburnum lentago (Nannyberry Viburnum)
Viburnum prunifolium (Blackhaw Viburnum)
Viburnum rufidulum (Rusty Blackhaw Viburnum)

SILVER-GRAY:

Populus grandidentata (Bigtooth Aspen)
Populus tremuloides (Quaking Aspen)

Salix discolor (Pussy Willow)

YELLOW-GREEN:

Acer negundo (Boxelder)
Acer nigrum (Black Maple)
Acer saccharum (Sugar Maple)
Acer spicatum (Mountain Maple)
Betula lenta (Sweet Birch)
Betula lutea (Yellow Birch)
Betula nigra (River Birch)
Betula papyrifera (Paper Birch)
Betula populifolia (Gray Birch)
Carya cordiformis (Bitternut Hickory)
Carya glabra (Pignut Hickory)
Carya illinoensis (Pecan)
Carya ovata (Shagbark Hickory)
Carya tomentosa (Mockernut Hickory)
Celtis occidentalis (Common Hackberry)
Cotinus americanus (American Smoketree)
Fagus grandifolia (American Beech)
Gleditsia triacanthos (Common Honeylocust)
Gymnocladus dioicus (Kentucky Coffeetree)
Juglans cinerea (Butternut)
Juglans nigra (Eastern Black Walnut)
Liquidambar styraciflua (American Sweetgum)
Liriodendron tulipifera (Tuliptree)
Maclura pomifera (Osageorange)

Magnolia acuminata (Cucumbertree Magnolia)
Morus rubra (Red Mulberry)
Platanus occidentalis (American Planetree)
Ptelea trifoliata (Common Hoptree)
Quercus alba (White Oak)
Quercus bicolor (Swamp White Oak)
Quercus borealis (Northern Red Oak)
Quercus coccinea (Scarlet Oak)
Quercus ellipsoidalis (Northern Pin Oak)
Quercus imbricaria (Shingle Oak)
Quercus macrocarpa (Bur Oak)
Quercus marilandica (Blackjack Oak)
Quercus montana (Chestnut Oak)
Quercus muhlenbergi (Chinkapin Oak)
Quercus palustris (Pin Oak)
Quercus stellata (Post Oak)
Quercus velutina (Black Oak)
Rhus copallina (Flameleaf Sumac)
Rhus glabra (Smooth Sumac)
Rhus typhina (Staghorn Sumac)
Salix amygdaloides (Peachleaf Willow)
Salix bebbiana (Bebb Willow)
Salix nigra (Black Willow)
Zanthoxylum americanum (Common Pricklyash)

YELLOW:

Acer pensylvanicum (Striped Maple)
Acer saccharinum (Silver Maple) +
Aesculus glabra (Ohio Buckeye)
Aesculus octandra (Yellow Buckeye)
Castanea dentata (American Chestnut)

Diospyros virginiana (Common Persimmon)
Hamamelis virginiana (Common Witchhazel)
Sassafras albidum (Common Sassafras)
Tilia americana (American Linden)
Tsuga canadensis (Canada Hemlock) +

PINK-LAVENDER

Cercis canadensis (Eastern Redbud)
Malus ioensis (Prairie Crabapple) pink

Rhododendron maximum (Rosebay Rhododendron)

RED:

Abies concolor (White Fir) +
Acer rubrum (Red Maple) *+
Acer saccharinum (Silver Maple) *

Carpinus caroliniana (American Hornbeam)
Populus deltoides (Eastern Poplar)
Pseudotsuga taxifolia (Common Douglasfir) *+

Flower color (cont.)

RED-PURPLE:

Abies lasiocarpa   (Alpine Fir)
Alnus rugosa   (Hazel Alder)
Euonymus atropurpureus   (Eastern Wahoo)
Juniperus virginiana   (Eastern Redcedar) *
Larix laricina   (Eastern Larch) *
Picea engelmanni   (Engelmann Spruce) *+
Picea glauca   (White Spruce) *+
Picea glauca densata   (BlackHills White Spruce) *+

Picea mariana   (Black Spruce) *+
Picea pungens   (Colorado Spruce) *+
Pinus flexilis   (Limber Pine) *+
Pinus ponderosa   (Ponderosa Pine) *
Pinus resinosa   (Red Pine) *+
Pinus rigida   (Pitch Pine) *
Pinus strobus   (Eastern White Pine) *

PURPLE:

Abies balsamea   (Balsam Fir) *+
Abies lasiocarpa   (Alpine Fir) *+
Fraxinus americana   (White Ash)
Fraxinus nigra   (Black Ash)

Fraxinus pennsylvanica   (Green Ash)
Fraxinus quadrangulata   (Blue Ash)
Pinus banksiana   (Jack Pine) *
Taxodium distichum   (Common Baldcypress) *

RED-BROWN:

Asimina triloba   (Common Pawpaw)
Ostrya virginiana   (American Hophornbeam)

Thuja occidentalis   (Eastern Arborvitae) *+
Ulmus americana   (American Elm)

PLANT SEX:

Most trees have both staminate (male) and pistillate (female) flowers on the same plant allowing self-fertilization. Some groups of plants are dioecious and bear staminate flowers on one plant and pistillate flowers on another. The selection of a staminate plant might be desirable where seed becomes a nuisance maintenance problem. Of course the pistillate plant will not bear heavy fruit crops unless the pollen-bearing staminate plant is located in close proximity. The following species are frequently dioecious.

indicator—*Juniperus virginiana*   (Eastern Redcedar)

Acer negundo   (Boxelder)
Acer nigrum   (Black Maple)
Acer rubrum   (Red Maple)
Acer saccharinum   (Silver Maple)
Acer saccharum   (Sugar Maple)
Cercis canadensis   (Eastern Redbud)
Chionanthus virginicus   (White Fringetree)
Cotinus americanus   (American Smoketree)
Diospyros virginiana   (Common Persimmon)
Fraxinus americana   (White Ash)
Fraxinus nigra   (Black Ash)
Fraxinus pennsylvanica   (Green Ash)
Gleditsia triacanthos   (Common Honeylocust)
Juniperus virginiana   (Eastern Redcedar)
Liriodendron tulipifera   (Tuliptree)
Maclura pomifera   (Osageorange)

Morus rubra   (Red Mulberry)
Nyssa sylvatica   (Black Tupelo)
Populus deltoides   (Eastern Poplar)
Populus grandidentata   (Bigtooth Aspen)
Populus tremuloides   (Quaking Aspen)
Rhus copallina   (Flameleaf Sumac)
Rhus glabra   (Smooth Sumac)
Rhus typhina   (Staghorn Sumac)
Robinia pseudoacacia   (Black Locust)
Salix amygdaloides   (Peachleaf Willow)
Salix bebbiana   (Bebb Willow)
Salix discolor   (Pussy Willow)
Salix nigra   (Black Willow)
Sassafras albidum   (Common Sassafras)
Zanthoxylum americanum   (Common Pricklyash)

FLOWER FRAGRANCE:

The flowers and foliage of certain plants create pleasant scents. The spicy blossoms of viburnums and lindens are plants which exude pleasant scents. Plants with olfactory values should be studied and used by environmental designers to enrich the sensual dimension of the rural and urbanized landscape. Plants with fragrant flowers include:

indicator—*Prunus americana* (American Plum)

Asimina triloba   (Common Pawpaw)
Castanea dentata   (American Chestnut)
Chionanthus virginicus   (White Fringetree)
Cladrastis lutea   (American Yellowwood) slightly
Cornus alternifolia   (Pagoda Dogwood)
Franklinia alatamaha   (Franklinia)
Liriodendron tulipifera   (Tuliptree)
Magnolia acuminata   (Cucumbertree Magnolia)
Malus ioensis   (Prairie Crabapple)
Oxydendrum arboreum   (Sourwood)
Prunus americana   (American Plum)

Prunus pensylvanica   (Pin Cherry)
Prunus serotina   (Black Cherry)
Prunus virginiana   (Common Chokecherry)
Robinia pseudoacacia   (Black Locust)
Sassafras albidum   (Common Sassafras)
Sorbus decora   (Showy Mountainash)
Tilia americana   (American Linden)
Viburnum lentago   (Nannyberry Viburnum)
Viburnum prunifolium   (Blackhaw Viburnum)
Viburnum rufidulum   (Rusty Blackhaw Viburnum)

FRUIT STRUCTURE:

The array of ornamental fruits that hold tree seeds are often as interesting as the flowers they follow. Some, like the American Hornbeam's bright red winged samaras, cling to the branches until late autumn. The multiple ball-like fruits of American Planetree and American Sweetgum hang like Christmas ornaments throughout much of the winter season. A few, such as Common Witchhazel, exhibit fuzzy woody capsules year round: remain on the tree through winter, mature in summer, open when the tree is in bloom, and clusters of empty capsules persist into another year. Nine categories of fruit structure are distinguished for designer consideration:

BERRY:
   fruits with soft fleshy covering over the seed,
   indicator—*Sorbus decora* (Showy Mountainash)

Amelanchier canadensis   (Shadblow Serviceberry)
Amelanchier laevis   (Allegany Serviceberry)
Aralia spinosa   (Devils-Walkingstick)
Asimina triloba   (Common Pawpaw)
Celtis occidentalis   (Common Hackberry)
Chionanthus virginicus   (White Fringetree)
Cornus alternifolia   (Pagoda Dogwood)
Cornus florida   (Flowering Dogwood)
Cotinus americanus   (American Smoketree)
Crataegus crusgalli   (Cockspur Hawthorn)
Crataegus mollis   (Downy Hawthorn)
Crataegus nitida   (Glossy Hawthorn)
Crataegus phaenopyrum   (Washington Hawthorn)
Crataegus pruinosa   (Frosted Hawthorn)
Crataegus punctata   (Dotted Hawthorn)
Diospyros virginiana   (Common Persimmon)
Juniperus virginiana   (Eastern Redcedar)

Malus ioensis   (Prairie Crabapple)
Morus rubra   (Red Mulberry)
Nyssa sylvatica   (Black Tupelo)
Prunus americana   (American Plum)
Prunus pensylvanica   (Pin Cherry)
Prunus serotina   (Black Cherry)
Prunus virginiana   (Common Chokecherry)
Rhus copallina   (Flameleaf Sumac)
Rhus glabra   (Smooth Sumac)
Rhus typhina   (Staghorn Sumac)
Sassafras albidum   (Common Sassafras)
Sorbus decora   (Showy Mountainash)
Viburnum lentago   (Nannyberry Viburnum)
Viburnum prunifolium   (Blackhaw Viburnum)
Viburnum rufidulum   (Rusty Blackhaw Viburnum)
Zanthoxylum americanum   (Common Pricklyash)

Fruit structure (cont.)

NUT OR ACORN:

nut partially or wholly enclosed in a husk which may be papery, woody, leafy, or spiney in character, indicator—*Juglans nigra* (Eastern Black Walnut)

Aesculus glabra (Ohio Buckeye)
Aesculus octandra (Yellow Buckeye)
Carya cordiformis (Bitternut Hickory)
Carya glabra (Pignut Hickory)
Carya illinoensis (Pecan)
Carya ovata (Shagbark Hickory)
Carya tomentosa (Mockernut Hickory)
Castanea dentata (American Chestnut)
Fagus grandifolia (American Beech)
Juglans cinerea (Butternut)
Juglans nigra (Eastern Black Walnut)
Quercus alba (White Oak)

Quercus bicolor (Swamp White Oak)
Quercus borealis (Northern Red Oak)
Quercus coccinea (Scarlet Oak)
Quercus ellipsoidalis (Northern Pin Oak)
Quercus imbricaria (Shingle Oak)
Quercus macrocarpa (Bur Oak)
Quercus marilandica (Blackjack Oak)
Quercus montana (Chestnut Oak)
Quercus muhlenbergi (Chinkapin Oak)
Quercus palustris (Pin Oak)
Quercus stellata (Post Oak)
Quercus velutina (Black Oak)

LEGUME:

elongated bean like pod splitting open along two seams at maturity, indicator—*Gleditsia triacanthos* (Common Honeylocust)

Catalpa speciosa (Northern Catalpa)
Cercis canadensis (Eastern Redbud)
Cladrastis lutea (American Yellowwood)

Gleditsia triacanthos (Common Honeylocust)
Gymnocladus dioicus (Kentucky Coffeetree)
Robinia pseudoacacia (Black Locust)

SAMARA:

seeds with thin membranous wing, indicator—*Fraxinus americana* (White Ash)

Acer negundo (Boxelder)
Acer nigrum (Black Maple)
Acer pensylvanicum (Striped Maple)
Acer rubrum (Red Maple)
Acer saccharinum (Silver Maple)
Acer saccharum (Sugar Maple)
Acer spicatum (Mountain Maple)
Carpinus caroliniana (American Hornbeam)
Fraxinus americana (White Ash)

Fraxinus nigra (Black Ash)
Fraxinus pennsylvanica (Green Ash)
Fraxinus quadrangulata (Blue Ash)
Halesia carolina (Carolina Silverbell)
Liriodendron tulipifera (Tuliptree)
Ostrya virginiana (American Hophornbeam) sack-like
Ptelea trifoliata (Common Hoptree)
Tilia americana (American Linden)
Ulmus americana (American Elm)

CONE:

woody fruit primarily of coniferous plants having stiff overlapping scales which support naked seeds, indicator—*Pinus resinosa* (Red Pine)

Abies balsamea (Balsam Fir)
Abies concolor (White Fir)
Abies lasiocarpa (Alpine Fir)
Larix laricina (Eastern Larch)
Picea engelmanni (Engelmann Spruce)
Picea glauca (White Spruce)
Picea glauca densata (BlackHills White Spruce)
Picea mariana (Black Spruce)
Picea pungens (Colorado Spruce)
Pinus banksiana (Jack Pine)

Pinus flexilis (Limber Pine)
Pinus ponderosa (Ponderosa Pine)
Pinus resinosa (Red Pine)
Pinus rigida (Pitch Pine)
Pinus strobus (Eastern White Pine)
Pseudotsuga taxifolia (Common Douglasfir)
Taxodium distichum (Common Baldcypress)
Thuja occidentalis (Eastern Arborvitae)
Tsuga canadensis (Canada Hemlock)

MULTIPLE:

small unwinged but sometimes plumed, one celled, one seeded fruit compounded to form a globose or ball-like head, indicator—*Platanus occidentalis* (American Planetree)

Liquidambar styraciflua (American Sweetgum)
Maclura pomifera (Osageorange)

Platanus occidentalis (American Planetree)

CAPSULE:
fruit of more than one chamber usually splitting lengthwise along multiple seams from one end, indicator—*Hamamelis virginiana* (Common Witchhazel)

Euonymus atropurpureus　(Eastern Wahoo)
Franklinia alatamaha　(Franklinia)
Hamamelis virginiana　(Common Witchhazel)
Oxydendrum arboreum　(Sourwood)

Populus deltoides　(Eastern Poplar)
Populus grandidentata　(Bigtooth Aspen)
Populus tremuloides　(Quaking Aspen)
Rhododendron maximum　(Rosebay Rhododendron)

STROBILE:
slender pendant and erect catkin-like or cone-like fruit with papery overlapping seeds, indicator—*Betula lenta* (Sweet Birch)

Alnus rugosa　(Hazel Alder)
Betula lenta　(Sweet Birch)
Betula lutea　(Yellow Birch)
Betula nigra　(River Birch)
Betula papyrifera　(Paper Birch)

Betula populifolia　(Gray Birch)
Salix amygdaloides　(Peachleaf Willow)
Salix bebbiana　(Bebb Willow)
Salix discolor　(Pussy Willow)
Salix nigra　(Black Willow)

FOLLICLE:
aggregate of small fleshy pods on stout short erect stems resembling a cucumber, indicator—*Magnolia acuminata*　(Cucumbertree Magnolia)

Magnolia acuminata　(Cucumbertree Magnolia)

FRUIT COLORATION:

Fruit colors frequently afford beauty in the landscape in much the same manner as flowers, foliage, and bark. Species with conspicuous early fruit production are a welcome contrast against the summer background of green leaves. Others hold significant quantities of fruit which brightly decorate the winter landscape. Fruit coloration is considered for the period during which the ripe fruits remain ornamentally effective. Eight color classes are presented for designer consideration:

GREEN-YELLOW:

Juglans nigra　(Eastern Black Walnut)
Maclura pomifera　(Osageorange)
Malus ioensis　(Prairie Crabapple)
Populus deltoides　(Eastern Poplar)
Populus grandidentalis　(Bigtooth Aspen)

Populus tremuloides　(Quaking Aspen)
Salix amygdaloides　(Peachleaf Willow)
Salix bebbiana　(Bebb Willow)
Salix discolor　(Pussy Willow)
Salix nigra　(Black Willow)

YELLOW-ORANGE:

Asimina triloba　(Common Pawpaw) to brown
Crataegus pruinosa　(Frosted Hawthorn)

Diospyros virginiana　(Common Persimmon)
Sorbus decora　(Showy Mountainash)

RED:

Acer pensylvanicum　(Striped Maple)
Acer rubrum　(Red Maple)
Acer spicatum　(Mountain Maple)

Carpinus caroliniana　(American Hornbeam)
Cornus florida　(Pagoda Dogwood)
Cotinus americanus　(American Smoketree)

Fruit coloration - red (cont.)

Crataegus crusgalli   (Cockspur Hawthorn)
Crataegus mollis   (Downy Hawthorn)
Crataegus nitida   (Glossy Hawthorn)
Crataegus phaenopyrum   (Washington Hawthorn)
Crataegus punctata   (Dotted Hawthorn)
Euonymus atropurpureus   (Eastern Wahoo)
Magnolia acuminata   (Cucumbertree Magnolia)

Prunus pensylvanica   (Pin Cherry)
Rhus copallina   (Flameleaf Sumac)
Rhus glabra   (Smooth Sumac)
Rhus typhina   (Staghorn Sumac)
Sorbus decora   (Showy Mountainash)
Zanthoxylum americanum   (Common Pricklyash)

RED-PURPLE:

Amelanchier canadensis   (Shadblow Serviceberry)
Amelanchier laevis   (Allegany Serviceberry)

Morus rubra   (Red Mulberry)
Prunus americana   (American Plum)

PURPLE-BROWN:

Abies balsamea   (Balsam Fir)
Abies concolor   (White Fir)
Abies lasiocarpa   (Alpine Fir)
Celtis occidentalis   (Common Hackberry)
Cercis canadensis   (Eastern Redbud)

Cornus alternifolia   (Pagoda Dogwood)
Gleditsia triacanthos   (Common Honeylocust)
Gymnocladus dioicus   (Kentucky Coffeetree)
Taxodium distichum   (Common Baldcypress)

TAN-BROWN:

Acer negundo   (Boxelder)
Acer nigrum   (Black Maple)
Acer pensylvanicum   (Striped Maple)
Acer saccharinum   (Silver Maple)
Acer saccharum   (Sugar Maple)
Aesculus glabra   (Ohio Buckeye)
Aesculus octandra   (Yellow Buckeye)
Betula lenta   (Sweet Birch)
Betula lutea   (Yellow Birch)
Betula nigra   (River Birch)
Betula papyrifera   (Paper Birch)
Betula populifolia   (Gray Birch)
Castanea dentata   (American Chestnut)
Catalpa speciosa   (Northern Catalpa)
Cladrastis lutea   (American Yellowwood)
Fagus grandifolia   (American Beech)
Franklinia alatamaha   (Franklinia)
Fraxinus americana   (White Ash)
Fraxinus nigra   (Black Ash)
Fraxinus pennsylvanica   (Green Ash)
Fraxinus quadrangulata   (Blue Ash)
Halesia carolina   (Carolina Silverbell)
Hamamelis virginiana   (Common Witchhazel)
Juglans cinerea   (Butternut)
Larix laricina   (Eastern Larch)
Liquidambar styraciflua   (American Sweetgum)
Liriodendron tulipifera   (Tuliptree)
Ostrya virginiana   (American Hophornbeam)
Oxydendrum arboreum   (Sourwood)
Picea engelmanni   (Engelmann Spruce)
Picea glauca   (White Spruce)

Picea glauca densata   (BlackHills White Spruce)
Picea mariana   (Black Spruce)
Picea pungens   (Colorado Spruce)
Pinus banksiana   (Jack Pine)
Pinus flexilis   (Limber Pine)
Pinus ponderosa   (Ponderosa Pine)
Pinus resinosa   (Red Pine)
Pinus rigida   (Pitch Pine)
Pinus strobus   (Eastern White Pine)
Platanus occidentalis   (American Planetree)
Pseudotsuga taxifolia   (Common Douglasfir)
Ptelea trifoliata   (Common Hoptree)
Quercus alba   (White Oak)
Quercus bicolor   (Swamp White Oak)
Quercus borealis   (Northern Red Oak)
Quercus coccinea   (Scarlet Oak)
Quercus ellipsoidalis   (Northern Pin Oak)
Quercus imbricaria   (Shingle Oak)
Quercus macrocarpa   (Bur Oak)
Quercus marilandica   (Blackjack Oak)
Quercus montana   (Chestnut Oak)
Quercus muhlenbergi   (Chinkapin Oak)
Quercus palustris   (Pin Oak)
Quercus stellata   (Post Oak)
Quercus velutina   (Black Oak)
Rhododendron maximum   (Rosebay Rhododendron)
Robinia pseudoacacia   (Black Locust)
Thuja occidentalis   (Eastern Arborvitae)
Tilia americana   (American Linden)
Tsuga canadensis   (Canada Hemlock)
Ulmus americana   (American Elm)

BLUE:

Chionanthus virginicus   (White Fringetree)
Juniperus virginiana   (Eastern Redcedar)
Nyssa sylvatica   (Black Tupelo)
Sassafras albidum   (Common Sassafras)

Viburnum lentago   (Nannyberry Viburnum)
Viburnum prunifolium   (Blackhaw Viburnum)
Viburnum rufidulum   (Rusty Blackhaw Viburnum)

BLACK:

Alnus rugosa (Hazel Alder)
Aralia spinosa (Devils-Walkingstick)
Carya cordiformis (Bitternut Hickory)
Carya glabra (Pignut Hickory)
Carya illinoensis (Pecan)
Carya ovata (Shagbark Hickory)

Carya tomentosa (Mockernut Hickory)
Prunus serotina (Black Cherry)
Prunus virginiana (Common Chokecherry)
Viburnum lentago (Nannyberry Viburnum)
Viburnum prunifolium (Blackhaw Viburnum)
Viburnum rufidulum (Rusty Blackhaw Viburnum)

WILDLIFE VALUE:

Food is one of the primary necessities of all life forms, and for wild animals cover is also a vital requirement. Survival in critical periods—during inclement weather, during spring and summer rearing of young, or when subjected to attack by enemies—depends largely on these fundamental factors of food and cover (Martin, Zim, Nelson 1961). These factors dominate the welfare of all kinds of wildlife and determine to a large degree the increase or decrease of animal populations.

Although grass and shrub species constitute the bulk of plants used for food and cover, many tree species provide fruits, seeds, leaves, twigs, bark, stems and roots for many kinds of wildlife.

Wildlife biologists have been alarmed at the rapid decrease in wildlife habitat within the last decade. Prime habitat has been lost to expanded agriculture, forestry, and urbanization. For example, methods of seeding, harvesting and the size of machinery have necessitated the farming of large acreages. Fencerows and shelterbelts are destroyed because woody pioneer plants compete with agronomic crops for available soil moisture at distances up to 12.5 meters (40 feet) from the row, reducing crop yield.

Animal food use information can aid the environmental designer in planning wildlife habitat developments for forests, marshlands, grazing ranges, wildlife refuges, farms, and residential areas. Food-habits data collected and published on more than 300 species of birds and mammals makes it possible to project and approximate the extent to which some 250 different genera of plants have been used by wildlife (Martin, Zim, Nelson 1961). The following classification reflects the relative attractiveness values for different plant genera as wildlife food sources in the northeast and midwest regions. Five categories are considered.

VERY HIGH: 50 wildlife users or more

Acer negundo (Boxelder)
Acer nigrum (Black Maple)
Acer pensylvanicum (Striped Maple)
Acer rubrum (Red Maple)
Acer saccharinum (Silver Maple)
Acer saccharum (Sugar Maple)
Acer spicatum (Mountain Maple)
Betula lenta (Sweet Birch)
Betula lutea (Yellow Birch)
Betula nigra (River Birch)
Betula papyrifera (Paper Birch)
Betula populifolia (Gray Birch)
Celtis occidentalis (Common Hackberry)
Cornus alternifolia (Pagoda Dogwood)
Cornus florida (Flowering Dogwood)
Juniperus virginiana (Eastern Redcedar)
Pinus banksiana (Jack Pine)
Pinus flexilis (Limber Pine)
Pinus ponderosa (Ponderosa Pine)

Pinus resinosa (Red Pine)
Pinus rigida (Pitch Pine)
Pinus strobus (Eastern White Pine)
Prunus pensylvanica (Pin Cherry)
Prunus serotina (Black Cherry)
Prunus virginiana (Common Chokecherry)
Quercus alba (White Oak)
Quercus bicolor (Swamp White Oak)
Quercus borealis (Northern Red Oak)
Quercus coccinea (Scarlet Oak)
Quercus ellipsoidalis (Northern Pin Oak)
Quercus imbricaria (Shingle Oak)
Quercus macrocarpa (Bur Oak)
Quercus marilandica (Blackjack Oak)
Quercus montana (Chestnut Oak)
Quercus muhlenbergi (Chinkapin Oak)
Quercus palustris (Pin Oak)
Quercus stellata (Post Oak)
Quercus velutina (Black Oak)

Wildlife value (cont.)

HIGH: 25 to 49 wildlife users

Abies balsamea   (Balsam Fir)
Abies concolor   (White Fir)
Abies lasiocarpa   (Alpine Fir)
Alnus rugosa   (Hazel Alder)
Amelanchier canadensis   (Shadblow Serviceberry)
Amelanchier laevis   (Allegany Serviceberry)
Aralia spinosa   (Devils-Walkingstick)
Diospyros virginiana   (Common Persimmon)
Fagus grandifolia   (American Beech)
Morus rubra   (Red Mulberry)
Picea engelmanni   (Engelmann Spruce)
Picea glauca   (White Spruce)
Picea glauca densata   (BlackHills White Spruce)
Picea mariana   (Black Spruce)
Picea pungens   (Colorado Spruce)

Populus deltoides   (Eastern Poplar)
Populus grandidentata   (Bigtooth Aspen)
Populus tremuloides   (Quaking Aspen)
Pseudotsuga taxifolia   (Common Douglasfir)
Rhus copallina   (Flameleaf Sumac)
Rhus glabra   (Smooth Sumac)
Rhus typhina   (Staghorn Sumac)
Salix amygdaloides   (Peachleaf Willow)
Salix bebbiana   (Bebb Willow)
Salix discolor   (Pussy Willow)
Salix nigra   (Black Willow)
Viburnum lentago   (Nannyberry Viburnum)
Viburnum prunifolium   (Blackhaw Viburnum)
Viburnum rufidulum   (Rusty Blackhaw Viburnum)
Zanthoxylum americanum   (Common Pricklyash)

INTERMEDIATE: 15 to 24 wildlife users

Carya cordiformis   (Bitternut Hickory)
Carya glabra   (Pignut Hickory)
Carya illinoensis   (Pecan)
Carya ovata   (Shagbark Hickory)
Carya tomentosa   (Mockernut Hickory)
Chionanthus virginicus   (White Fringetree)
Crataegus crusgalli   (Cockspur Hawthorn)
Crataegus mollis   (Downy Hawthorn)
Crataegus nitida   (Glossy Hawthorn)
Crataegus phaenopyrum   (Washington Hawthorn)

Crataegus pruinosa   (Frosted Hawthorn)
Crataegus punctata   (Dotted Hawthorn)
Larix laricina   (Eastern Larch)
Malus ioensis   (Prairie Crabapple)
Nyssa sylvatica   (Black Tupelo)
Ptelea trifoliata   (Common Hoptree)
Sorbus decora   (Showy Mountainash)
Tsuga canadensis   (Canada Hemlock)
Ulmus americana   (American Elm)

LOW: 5 to 14 wildlife users

Franklinia alatamaha   (Franklinia)
Fraxinus americana   (White Ash)
Fraxinus nigra   (Black Ash)
Fraxinus pennsylvanica   (Green Ash)
Fraxinus quadrangulata   (Blue Ash)
Hamamelis virginiana   (Common Witchhazel)
Juglans cinerea   (Butternut)

Juglans nigra   (Eastern Black Walnut)
Liquidambar styraciflua   (American Sweetgum)
Liriodendron tulipifera   (Tuliptree)
Ostrya virginiana   (American Hophornbeam)
Oxydendrum arboreum   (Sourwood)
Sassafras albidum   (Common Sassafras)
Thuja occidentalis   (Eastern Arborvitae)

VERY LOW: less than 5 wildlife users

Aesculus glabra   (Ohio Buckeye)
Aesculus octandra   (Yellow Buckeye)
Asimina triloba   (Common Pawpaw)
Carpinus caroliniana   (American Hornbeam)
Castanea dentata   (American Chestnut)
Catalpa speciosa   (Northern Catalpa)
Cercis canadensis   (Eastern Redbud)
Cladrastis lutea   (American Yellowwood)
Cotinus americanus   (American Smoketree)
Euonymus atropurpureus   (Eastern Wahoo)
Gleditsia triacanthos   (Common Honeylocust)

Gymnocladus dioicus   (Kentucky Coffeetree)
Halesia carolina   (Carolina Silverbell)
Maclura pomifera   (Osageorange)
Magnolia acuminata   (Cucumbertree Magnolia)
Platanus occidentalis   (American Planetree)
Prunus americana   (American Plum)
Rhododendron maximum   (Rosebay Rhododendron)
Robinia pseudoacacia   (Black Locust)
Taxodium distichum   (Common Baldcypress)
Tilia americana   (American Linden)

PHENOLOGICAL CALENDAR:

As rain, snow, fog, and seasonal change alter human perception of the composite of plant qualities, the plant is viewed as a dynamic changeable element. Plants are the most dynamic materials used by the designer. Phenological observations (records) document the patterned response of plants to seasonal change. This patterned response is correlated primarily with seasonal variation in temperature. Phenological phases considered include calendar dates for leaf emergence, flowering, fruiting, fruit ripeness, fruit dissemination, autumn coloration, and leaf drop.

The actual calendar day which a certain plant initiates a particular phenophase varies from year to year in response to unpredictability of optimum temperature and moisture conditions. Similarly the length of phenophase duration or the amount of time that particular visual plant character remains ornamentally effective varies with annual weather fluctuations. However, observations suggest that certain species always coincide in phenophase periods and that the progressive sequencing between other species can be forecast. For example, Eastern Redbud and Shadblow Serviceberry consistently bloom at the same time. These species are followed several weeks later by American Plum. The sequence is the same, only the actual dates vary annually.

Another important factor causing a variance in the specific phenophase dates is the geographic distribution of the species. Sugar Maple blooms up to six weeks earlier in the southern latitude of its natural range than along the northern limits. Differences in phenophase dates at higher altitudes is also apparent. Flowering Dogwood leafs out many days later in the higher elevations of the Boston mountains of Arkansas than they do in the surrounding valleys.

Plant phenophases have been annually monitored by professional groups and respected individuals for most areas of the United States and southern Canada. The phenological calendar presented in Table II plots the normal phenophase periods for trees in our area (latitude 45° north). These can easily be adjusted for other regions where the same tree is hardy. Once the normal phenophase periods for several key indicator trees can be established in other areas and correlated with the calendar herein, the corresponding periods for all other species can be projected.

Phenological calendars of this type are tools which enable the designer to compare, organize, explore, and evaluate the complex of possible plant to plant and plant to man relationships. It remains the challenge of the designer to develop a viable program which demonstrates this understanding.

Phenological Calendar: Table II

	Winter			Spring			Summer			Autumn		
flower / foliage / fruit	Jan.	Feb.	Mar.	Apr.	May	June	July	Aug.	Sept.	Oct.	Nov.	Dec.
Abies balsamea												
Abies concolor												
Abies lasiocarpa												
Acer negundo												
Acer nigrum												
Acer pensylvanicum												
Acer rubrum												
Acer saccharinum												
Acer saccharum												
Acer spicatum												
Aesculus glabra												
Aesculus octandra												
Alnus rugosa												
Amelanchier canadensis												
Amelanchier laevis												
Aralia spinosa												
Asimina triloba												
Betula lenta												
Betula lutea												
Betula nigra												

Phenological Calendar: Table II

	flower / foliage / fruit	Winter			Spring			Summer			Autumn		
		Jan.	Feb.	Mar.	Apr.	May	June	July	Aug.	Sept.	Oct.	Nov.	Dec.
Betula papyrifera						flower/foliage/fruit							
Betula populifolia													
Carpinus caroliniana													
Carya cordiformis													
Carya glabra													
Carya illinoensis													
Carya ovata													
Carya tomentosa													
Castanea dentata													
Catalpa speciosa													
Celtis occidentalis													
Cercis canadensis													
Chionanthus virginicus													
Cladrastis lutea													
Cornus alternifolia													
Cornus florida													
Cotinus americanus													
Crataegus crusgalli													
Crataegus mollis													
Crataegus nitida													

Phenological Calendar: Table II

	Winter			Spring			Summer			Autumn		
flower / foliage / fruit	Jan.	Feb.	Mar.	Apr.	May	June	July	Aug.	Sept.	Oct.	Nov.	Dec.
Crataegus phaenopyrum												
Crataegus pruinosa												
Crataegus punctata												
Diospyros virginiana												
Euonymus atropurpureus												
Fagus grandifolia												
Franklinia alatamaha												
Fraxinus americana												
Fraxinus nigra												
Fraxinus pennsylvanica												
Fraxinus quadrangulata												
Gleditsia triacanthos												
Gymnocladus dioicus												
Halesia carolina												
Hamamelis virginiana												
Juglans cinerea												
Juglans nigra												
Juniperus virginiana												
Larix laricina												
Liquidambar styraciflua												

64

flower ░ foliage ▓ fruit ▒	Winter			Spring			Summer			Autumn		
	Jan.	Feb.	Mar.	Apr.	May	June	July	Aug.	Sept.	Oct.	Nov.	Dec.
Liriodendron tulipifera												
Maclura pomifera												
Magnolia acuminata												
Malus ioensis												
Morus rubra												
Nyssa sylvatica												
Ostrya virginiana												
Oxydendrum arboreum												
Picea engelmanni												
Picea glauca												
Picea glauca densata												
Picea mariana												
Picea pungens												
Pinus banksiana												
Pinus flexilis												
Pinus ponderosa												
Pinus resinosa												
Pinus rigida												
Pinus strobus												
Platanus occidentalis												

Phenological Calendar: Table II

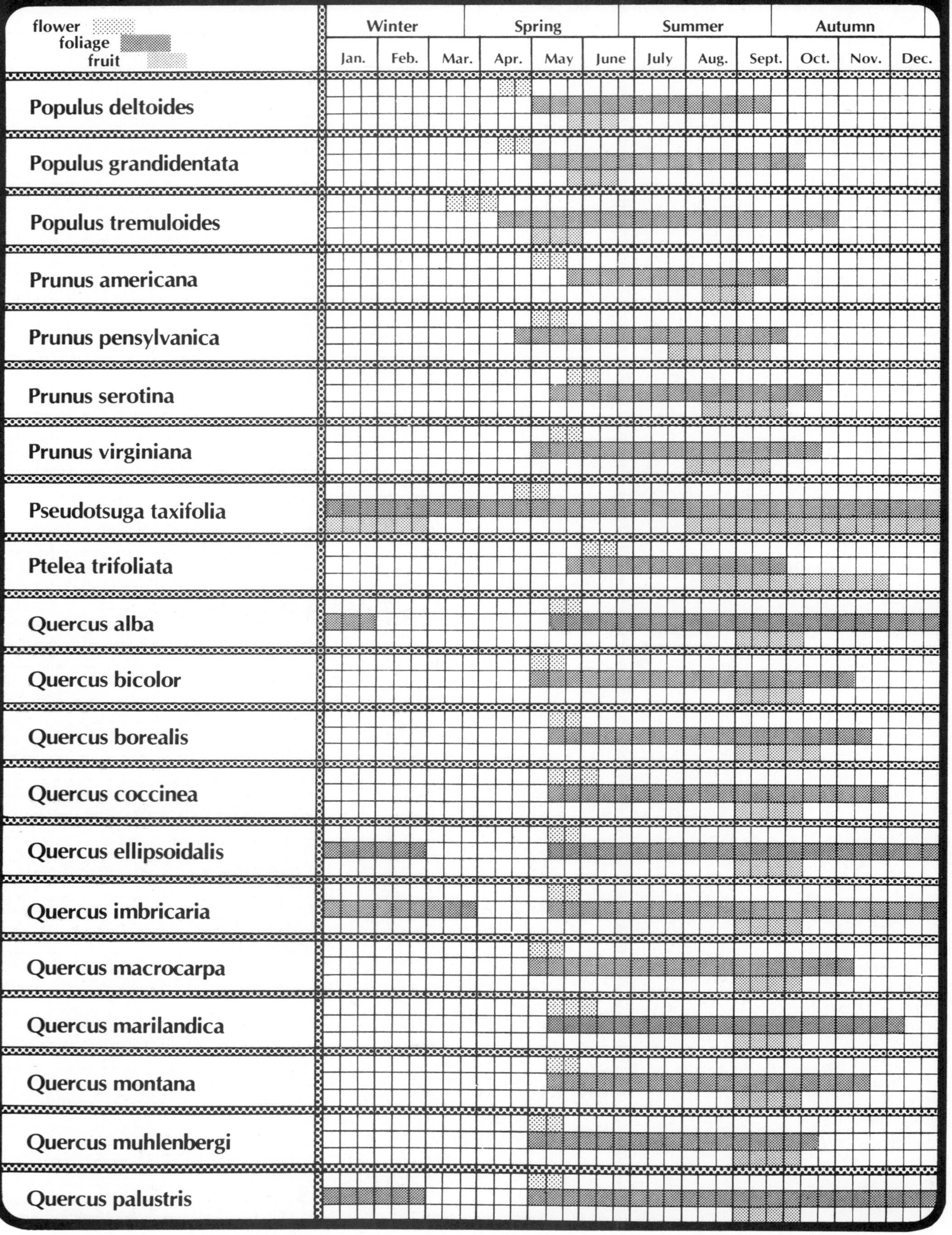

flower
foliage
fruit
Winter
Spring
Summer
Autumn
Jan.
Feb.
Mar.
Apr.
May
June
July
Aug.
Sept.
Oct.
Nov.
Dec.
Populus deltoides
Populus grandidentata
Populus tremuloides
Prunus americana
Prunus pensylvanica
Prunus serotina
Prunus virginiana
Pseudotsuga taxifolia
Ptelea trifoliata
Quercus alba
Quercus bicolor
Quercus borealis
Quercus coccinea
Quercus ellipsoidalis
Quercus imbricaria
Quercus macrocarpa
Quercus marilandica
Quercus montana
Quercus muhlenbergi
Quercus palustris

Phenological Calendar:

Legend:
- flower (light stipple)
- foliage (dark solid)
- fruit (medium gray)

Species	Jan.	Feb.	Mar.	Apr.	May	June	July	Aug.	Sept.	Oct.	Nov.	Dec.
		Winter			Spring			Summer			Autumn	
Quercus stellata					flower	foliage	foliage	foliage	foliage	fruit		
Quercus velutina					flower	foliage	foliage	foliage	foliage	fruit		
Rhododendron maximum	foliage	foliage	foliage	foliage	flower/foliage	foliage	foliage	foliage	foliage	foliage	foliage	foliage
Rhus copallina	fruit	fruit	fruit	fruit	foliage	foliage	flower	foliage	foliage	fruit	fruit	fruit
Rhus glabra	fruit	fruit	fruit	foliage	foliage	flower	foliage	foliage	fruit	fruit	fruit	fruit
Rhus typhina	fruit	fruit	fruit	foliage	foliage	flower	foliage	foliage	fruit	fruit	fruit	fruit
Robinia pseudoacacia				foliage	foliage	flower	foliage	foliage	fruit			
Salix amygdaloides			flower	foliage	foliage	foliage	foliage	foliage	foliage	fruit		
Salix bebbiana				flower	foliage	foliage	foliage	foliage	foliage	fruit		
Salix discolor			flower	foliage	foliage	foliage	foliage	foliage	foliage	fruit		
Salix nigra				flower	foliage	foliage	foliage	foliage	foliage	fruit		
Sassafras albidum					flower	foliage	foliage	foliage	fruit			
Sorbus decora					flower	foliage	foliage	foliage	fruit	fruit		
Taxodium distichum				flower	foliage	foliage	foliage	foliage	fruit			
Thuja occidentalis	foliage	foliage	foliage	foliage	flower	foliage	foliage	foliage	fruit			
Tilia americana					foliage	flower	foliage	foliage	fruit			
Tsuga canadensis	foliage	foliage	foliage	foliage	flower	foliage	foliage	foliage	foliage	foliage	foliage	foliage
Ulmus americana			flower	foliage	foliage	foliage	foliage	foliage	fruit			
Viburnum lentago					flower	foliage	foliage	foliage	fruit			
Viburnum prunifolium					flower	foliage	foliage	foliage	fruit			

Phenological Calendar: Table II

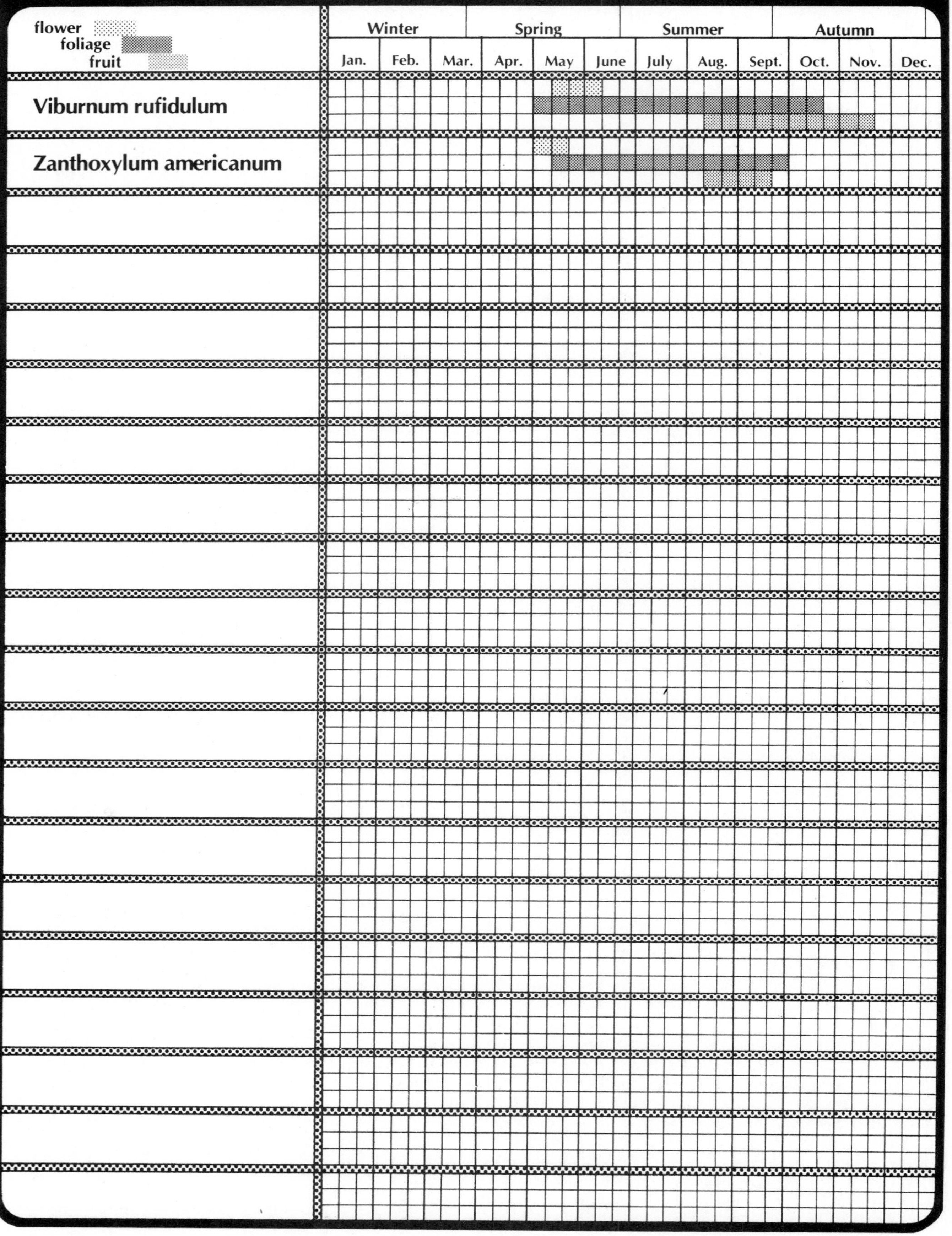
flower
foliage
fruit
Winter
Spring
Summer
Autumn
Jan.
Feb.
Mar.
Apr.
May
June
July
Aug.
Sept.
Oct.
Nov.
Dec.
Viburnum rufidulum
Zanthoxylum americanum

MOST SUITABLE HABITAT:

A plant community is basically an aggregation of individual species having mutual relationships with their physical environment or habitat (Oosting 1956). Environmental factors include those of climate, such as various measures of light, radiation, humidity, precipitation and air movement. Plant distribution is also influenced by soil characteristics such as texture, structure and depth, moisture capacity and drainage, nutrient content, and topographic position. Species vary in their ability to survive and reproduce in different habitats. Some survive extreme heat, others extreme cold. Many require much continuous moisture, others small amounts periodically. Some species such as Bur Oak have a wide ecologic amplitude and are found over much wider ranges of climate and site. Other species, like Eastern Hemlock, have a narrow amplitude with limited geographic distribution and specific habitat preference. Within any given region where habitat is held in dynamic equilibrium, tree stands of fairly homogeneous composition consistently recur. This integral relationship of plant and habitat represents the maximum utilization of available environmental resources.

The first step in the recognition of the major habitat types for general landscape use is to identify the broad vegetational cover differences present in eastern and central United States (Fig. 1). The major portion of the vegetation can be divided into three formation types:

 FOREST:
> greater than 50 percent tree crown cover, successional or climax trees forming closed stands.

 SAVANNA:
> 5 to 50 percent tree crown cover, grasslands with scattered trees, forest openings and forest-prairie transitions where a mosaic of irregular patches and groves of forest are intermingled with grassland or cultivated farmlands, pioneer species colonizing open disturbed areas where prolonged exposure, extreme daily temperature fluctuations, rapid changes in water supply, and lack of soil stability exist, including wooded pasture, abandoned fields, roadsides, exposed ridges, and steep rocky land.

 GRASSLAND:
> less than 5 percent tree crown cover, essentially treeless grasslands including; short, mid height and tall grass prairie landscapes, pasture lands, and cultivated landscapes of the midwest. Trees are planted as windbreaks around farmsteads, shelterbelts, for shade in towns and occur naturally in linear patches along stream bottoms.

A further separation is made which subdivides the forest and savanna vegetational formations (Fig. 1) into three floristic regions:

NORTHERN:
> transitional region between the northern coniferous forest (boreal) of Canada and the eastern deciduous forest of the United States. The landscape character is of glacial origin dotted with many lakes and bogs.

CENTRAL:
> primarily temperate deciduous forest with some coniferous stands occurring locally throughout.

SOUTHERN:
> mixed forest of broadleaf deciduous, broadleaf evergreen and coniferous evergreen species. Since this text considers only native trees hardy farther north, this floristic region is not included.

The over-riding environmental factor determining the disposition of plant communities is plant available soil moisture. The assembled plant species are placed under selective stress along the moisture and topographic gradients of the landscape. Topographic gradient is commonly divided into two series, lowland and upland. Five soil moisture and topographic gradient segments are delineated:

 LOWLAND WET:
> river margin and streamside floodplain depressions, areas subject to frequent and violent inundation due to cyclic flooding in late winter and spring, high water tables, lake margin and swamp, slow draining flats and depressions, sluggish streams, areas of poor internal or surface drainage supporting standing water much of the time, cool areas with high humidity and high water table.

 LOWLAND WET-MESIC:
> alluvial bottomlands and elevated terraces of major streams, where soil moisture supply is in excess of that falling as rain, areas of intermittent yearly flooding of short duration, characterized by excess surface wetness in winter and spring to nearly xeric conditions during midsummer low water stages.

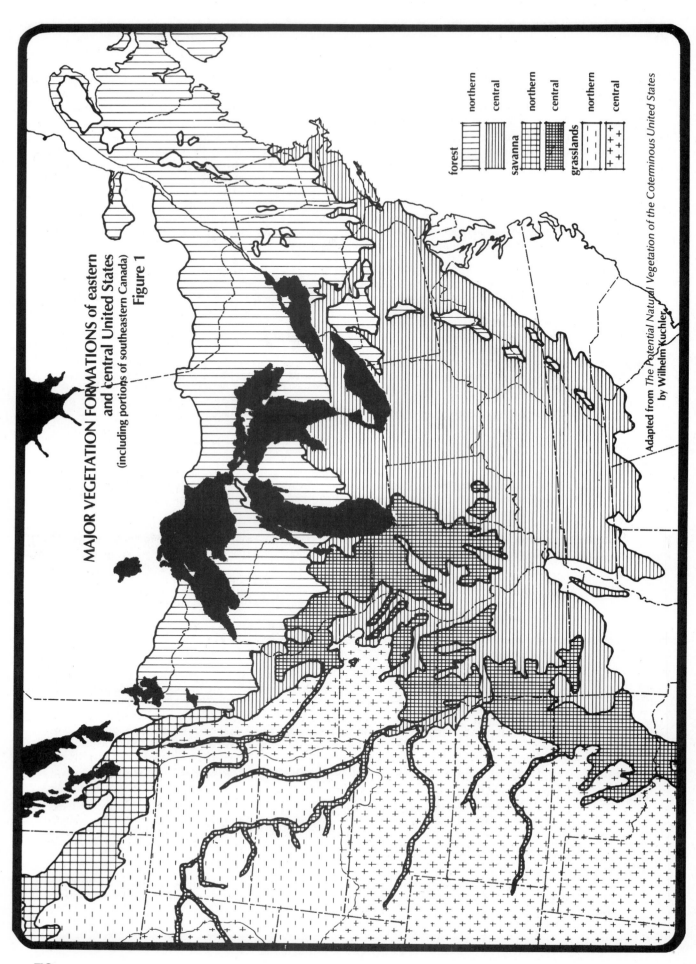

MAJOR VEGETATION FORMATIONS of eastern and central United States (including portions of southeastern Canada)

Figure 1

forest
northern
central

savanna
northern
central

grasslands
northern
central

Adapted from *The Potential Natural Vegetation of the Coterminous United States* by Wilhelm Kuchler.

70

UPLAND MESIC:
>
> wet ravines and sheltered coves, moist but well drained slopes and uplands, generally north and east facing slope aspects, protection from direct sun exposure and to prevailing dry winds together with cool air drainage into these areas maintains a regime of greater available soil moisture, reduced evaporation stress and stable temperature near the ground.

UPLAND MESIC-DRY:
>
> dry slopes and upland flats, generally warmer south and west facing slope aspects, upland ridges and ravines, direct sun exposure accelerates evaporation stress, reduces available soil moisture and greatly increases temperature near the ground.

UPLAND DRY:
>
> high banks, calcareous waterworn cliffs, steep rocky land, excessively drained sandy soils or shallow stoney soils over rock outcrop.

Table III synthesizes the habitat classification format. By multiplying the five moisture gradient segments (wet to dry) with the two vegetational formations of forest and savanna and the two floristic regions (Northern and Central) a sum of 20 major habitat situations can be described.

Red Maple, for example, is common to a variety of habitat situations. This species is found in the glaciated Northern Forest Region on soil moisture and topographic gradient extremes—either lowland wet or upland dry. In the mountain country it is common on the drier ridges and on south and west exposures of upper slopes. It is also frequent in swampy areas, on slow draining flats and along sluggish streams. In the Central Forest Region, Red Maple is a wet-mesic bottomland species occupying river valleys and alluvial flats.

"The environmental designer works with the land, the surface of the earth; his decisions deal with the arrangement of the land and the elements on it for man's use and enjoyment. His challenge is to improve man's relationship with his environment. The disposition of plants is his inescapable responsibility, since plants are integral parts of that physical environment." (Dyas 1970)

Table III provides rapid assessment of the most suitable habitat conditions available to the native tree species.

FLOOD TOLERANCE:

At present only a very limited amount of research regarding the tolerance of woody plant materials to periodic and permanent flooding has been published. Hall and Smith (1955) reported tolerance data for 40 native species flooded by the Kentucky Reservoir on the Tennessee River over an 8 year period from 1944 through 1952. Although reservoir construction has progressed at a rapid pace since, the work published by Hall and Smith unfortunately is still the most significant contribution in this area. More complete information is critically needed to ensure sound vegetation management planning and policy.

The observation of natural systems and specific habitats has enabled the professional to confidently extrapolate a more complete picture regarding the effects of flooding on woody plants. Trees vary greatly in their ability to withstand root suffocation by prolonged inundations.

Along rivers and streams (lowland wet habitats) throughout the region, bands of vegetation consistently recur in a successional pattern generally paralleling the present channel and maintaining a uniform species to species relationship. This pattern directly correlates with the flood tolerance of each species. As one moves away from streamside the following order of zonation is observed; Sandbar Willow, Black Willow, Eastern Poplar, and Silver Maple. Field observation logically suggests that Sandbar Willow is more tolerant than Black Willow which in turn is more tolerant than Eastern Poplar and so on. Studies by Hall and Smith concur.

Similarly American Elm, a common floodplain (lowland wet-mesic) species, is observed to be more tolerant than American Beech (upland mesic) which invades the floodplain only on elevated mounds and high terraces.

Black Cherry, a common upland-dry species, was found by Hall and Smith to be the most intolerant species they studied.

Table III assists in the development of a viable vegetation management policy where frequent and prolonged inundation are a concern. Five classes of tolerance are considered by projecting the survival data for each species against the percent of time flooded during the growing season (Hall and Smith). Attention is focused on the growing season because periodic winter flooding is of little significance in the survival of woody plants. Flooding during the growing season is mainly responsible for the death and injury observed.

VERY TOLERANT:
>   generally lowland wet species surviving when flooded more than 40 percent of the growing season.

TOLERANT:
>   generally lowland wet species surviving when flooded more than 30 percent of the growing season but less than 40 percent.

INTERMEDIATE:
>   generally lowland wet-mesic species surviving occasional inundation, between 20 and 30 percent of the growing season.

INTOLERANT:
>   generally upland mesic and mesic dry species rarely inundated for periods of short duration, between 5 and 20 percent of the growing season (mesic-xeric species commonly dying after 10 percent of growing season).

VERY INTOLERANT:
>   generally upland dry species exhibiting immediate and rapid decline frequently culminating in death if inundated more than 5 percent of the growing season.

SHADE TOLERANCE:

Most plants do well in full sun exposure. Where plants are being considered for shaded or partially shaded site conditions however, it becomes important to know which will perform best and how much shade each will tolerate. An attempt has been made to quantify shade tolerance for native species using a method outlined by Samuel A. Graham, University of Michigan. The method involved rating a sample of each tree species numerically according to various tolerance indicators. The highest rating any species may have is a 10, the lowest a 0. (Table III)

Usually the less shade tolerant plant materials of our native hardwood forests have a lighter foliage pattern and permit more light to reach the forest floor. Consequently the oak-hickory type, for example, has a greater amount of light reaching the forest floor for somewhat less tolerant species to survive than does a maple-linden forest. The reverse is also true—that the more shade tolerant species require the more stable environment provided by shade of the parent canopy in order to grow, and consequently are not naturally invaders of more open sites. Five classes of shade tolerance have been delineated.

VERY TOLERANT:
>   trees that will grow and survive in a state of health and vigor beneath dense shade; shade tolerance index range (Graham)—8.0 to 10.0,
>   indicator—Sugar Maple 10.0

TOLERANT
>   trees that will grow and survive in a state of health and vigor beneath moderately dense shade, shade tolerance index range 6.0 to 7.9,
>   indicator—Northern Red Oak 7.8

INTERMEDIATE:
>   trees that will grow and survive in a state of health and vigor beneath moderate shade, shade tolerance index range 4.0 to 5.9,
>   indicator—Eastern White Pine 4.4

Most Suitable Habitat: Table III

	Land Position									Flood Tolerance					Shade Tolerance				
	forest	savanna	northern	central	wet	wet-mesic	mesic	mesic-dry	dry	very intolerant	intolerant	intermediate	tolerant	very tolerant	very intolerant	intolerant	intermediate	tolerant	very tolerant
Abies balsamea	■		■	■	■			■					■						■
Abies concolor	■							■			■		■						■
Abies lasiocarpa	■							■											■
Acer negundo	■		■	■		■	■					■			■				
Acer nigrum	■			■		■		■				■						■	
Acer pensylvanicum	■		■				■					■						■	
Acer rubrum	■	■	■	■	■	■	■	■			■		■				■		
Acer saccharinum	■		■	■	■								■				■		
Acer saccharum	■		■	■		■	■					■							■
Acer spicatum	■		■				■					■							■
Aesculus glabra		■		■		■	■					■					■		
Aesculus octandra	■			■		■	■					■					■		
Alnus rugosa		■	■		■								■	■				■	
Amelanchier canadensis	■	■	■	■		■	■	■			■					■			
Amelanchier laevis	■	■	■	■		■	■	■			■					■			
Aralia spinosa	■	■		■	■	■	■	■	■		■				■				
Asimina triloba	■			■		■	■	■				■						■	
Betula lenta	■		■	■			■	■			■					■			
Betula lutea	■	■	■			■	■				■							■	
Betula nigra	■			■	■								■			■			
Betula papyrifera		■	■	■			■	■			■				■				
Betula populifolia	■	■	■				■	■			■				■				
Carpinus caroliniana	■			■		■	■					■							■
Carya cordiformis	■			■		■	■	■				■				■			
Carya glabra	■			■			■	■				■						■	
Carya illinoensis	■			■	■		■					■			■				

73

	Land Position									Flood Tolerance					Shade Tolerance				
	forest	savanna	northern	central	wet	wet-mesic	mesic	mesic-dry	dry	very intolerant	intolerant	intermediate	tolerant	very tolerant	very intolerant	intolerant	intermediate	tolerant	very tolerant
Carya ovata	■			■				■			■							■	
Carya tomentosa	■			■					■	■						■			
Castanea dentata	■			■			■	■		■							■		
Catalpa speciosa	■			■		■							■			■			
Celtis occidentalis	■			■		■		■				■					■		
Cercis canadensis	■			■			■		■			■						■	
Chionanthus virginicus	■			■				■			■						■		
Cladrastis lutea	■			■			■				■							■	
Cornus alternifolia			■			■		■			■						■		
Cornus florida				■			■	■			■						■		
Cotinus americanus	■	■							■		■						■		
Crataegus crusgalli	■		■			■		■			■	■				■			
Crataegus mollis	■		■			■		■			■	■				■			
Crataegus nitida	■		■			■		■			■	■				■			
Crataegus phaenopyrum	■		■			■		■			■	■				■			
Crataegus pruinosa	■		■			■		■			■	■				■			
Crataegus punctata *dotted*	■		■			■		■			■	■				■			
Diospyros virginiana	■			■		■		■			■					■			
Euonymus atropurpureus	■			■		■					■							■	
Fagus grandifolia	■		■				■			■								■	
Franklinia alatamaha				■		■					■					■			
Fraxinus americana	■		■				■				■						■		
Fraxinus nigra			■		■	■						■					■		
Fraxinus pennsylvanica	■			■		■						■					■		
Fraxinus quadrangulata	■			■			■		■		■							■	
Gleditsia triacanthos	■			■		■		■				■				■			

Redbud

Hawthorn / Smoketree

Blue Ash

Table III

Most Suitable Habitat:

	Land Position									Flood Tolerance					Shade Tolerance				
	forest	savanna	northern	central	wet	wet-mesic	mesic	mesic-dry	dry	very intolerant	intolerant	intermediate	tolerant	very tolerant	very intolerant	intolerant	intermediate	tolerant	very tolerant
Gymnocladus dioicus	■			■		■						■				■			
Halesia carolina	■						■				■							■	
Hamamelis virginiana				■			■				■							■	
Juglans cinerea				■		■	■				■						■		
Juglans nigra				■			■				■						■		
Juniperus virginiana		■		■					■				■			■			
Larix laricina	■		■		■									■		■			
Liquidambar styraciflua				■	■								■					■	
Liriodendron tulipifera	■			■			■			■						■			
Maclura pomifera		■		■				■					■			■			
Magnolia acuminata				■			■					■						■	
Malus ioensis		■						■				■				■			
Morus rubra				■			■					■					■		
Nyssa sylvatica				■	■	■	■						■					■	
Ostrya virginiana			■	■			■	■				■							■
Oxydendrum arboreum				■				■				■						■	
Picea engelmanni			■	■									■					■	
Picea glauca			■	■			■						■				■		
Picea glauca densata			■								■						■		
Picea mariana			■		■									■					■
Picea pungens			■				■						■				■		
Pinus banksiana			■						■							■			
Pinus flexilis									■				■			■			
Pinus ponderosa		■							■				■					■	
Pinus resinosa	■		■						■		■							■	
Pinus rigida				■					■							■	■		

	Land Position									Flood Tolerance					Shade Tolerance				
	forest	savanna	northern	central	wet	wet-mesic	mesic	mesic-dry	dry	very intolerant	intolerant	intermediate	tolerant	very tolerant	very intolerant	intolerant	intermediate	tolerant	very tolerant
Pinus strobus	■		■	■			■				■						■		
Platanus occidentalis	■			■				■			■						■		
Populus deltoides	■	■		■		■							■		■				
Populus grandidentata			■	■			■	■	■		■				■				
Populus tremuloides			■	■				■	■		■				■				
Prunus americana				■			■				■					■			
Prunus pensylvanica			■	■				■			■				■				
Prunus serotina	■		■	■			■	■			■						■		
Prunus virginiana			■	■			■	■			■						■		
Pseudotsuga taxifolia	■			■				■			■						■		
Ptelea trifoliata				■			■				■							■	
Quercus alba			■	■			■	■	■		■						■		
Quercus bicolor				■	■	■							■				■		
Quercus borealis			■	■			■	■			■							■	
Quercus coccinea				■				■	■		■						■		
Quercus ellipsoidalis		■		■				■	■		■				■				
Quercus imbricaria	■		■	■			■	■			■					■			
Quercus macrocarpa	■	■	■	■			■	■			■						■		
Quercus marilandica		■		■				■	■		■				■				
Quercus montana			■	■			■	■			■						■		
Quercus muhlenbergi		■		■			■	■			■						■		
Quercus palustris				■	■	■							■				■		
Quercus stellata		■		■				■	■		■				■				
Quercus velutina	■		■	■			■	■			■						■		
Rhododendron maximum	■			■			■						■				■		■
Rhus copallina		■		■				■	■		■				■				

76

Table III

Most Suitable Habitat:

	Land Position									Flood Tolerance					Shade Tolerance				
	forest	savanna	northern	central	wet	wet-mesic	mesic	mesic-dry	dry	very intolerant	intolerant	intermediate	tolerant	very tolerant	very intolerant	intolerant	intermediate	tolerant	very tolerant
Rhus glabra		█	█						█	█	█				█				
Rhus typhina		█	█	█					█	█					█				
Robinia pseudoacacia	█			█					█	█						█			
Salix amygdaloides		█	█	█	█	█								█	█				
Salix bebbiana		█	█	█	█	█								█	█				
Salix discolor		█	█	█	█	█								█	█				
Salix nigra		█	█	█	█	█								█	█				
Sassafras albidum	█	█		█			█	█			█					█			
Sorbus decora		█	█		█		█	█					█		█				
Taxodium distichum		█	█	█	█	█								█			█		
Thuja occidentalis		█	█	█	█	█							█		█				
Tilia americana	█		█	█			█					█					█	█	
Tsuga canadensis	█		█	█		█	█			█					█				
Ulmus americana	█		█	█	█	█						█	█		█				
Viburnum lentago	█	█	█	█			█	█		█					█				
Viburnum prunifolium		█	█	█							█				█				
Viburnum rufidulum		█	█	█					█		█	█			█				
Zanthoxylum americanum	█	█	█	█				█			█	█			█				

INTOLERANT:
> trees that will grow and survive in a state of health and vigor beneath light shade, shade tolerance index range 2.0 to 3.9,
> indicator—Black Cherry 2.4

VERY INTOLERANT:
> trees that become suppressed in shade and therefore demand full sun exposure for best growth and survival, shade tolerance index range 0. to 1.9,
> indicator—Quaking Aspen 1.0

SOIL TEXTURE:

Texture refers to the size of soil particles. Soil particles are classified in three general sizes: sand, silt and clay.

Few soils contain only one particle size. Nearly all soils have a certain proportion of sand, silt and clay. Soil texture can be estimated in the field by rubbing a small amount of moist soil between the thumb and forefinger. Sand particles can be seen easily and feel gritty. Silt particles can be seen with a magnifying lense, and when dry they feel like flour. When wet they have a smooth, floury feel with little evidence of stickiness. Clay particles are very fine. Clay is sticky and plastic when wet and can be molded; it will dry into a hard mass.

Textural class for the surface layer is always a part of the soil type name; for example, Muscatine silty clay loam. Textural class for subsoil and parent material is given in profile descriptions which are a part of all survey reports.

Texture is a permanent soil property that greatly influences root growth and plant health and vigor. Soils with a high proportion of coarse particles (sandy soils) have rather low productivity. Likewise, soils with a high proportion of fine particles (high clay soils) are often low in productivity. Sandy soils do not hold enough water for good plant growth and they are poor storehouses for plant nutrients. They must receive frequent additions of water and nutrients to be productive. The main problem with high clay soils is their slow permeability and poor internal drainage, which are the result of their large number of very small pores. This means that soils high in clay will often be so wet that root development is hindered.

The most productive soils are usually medium to moderately fine in texture. Examples are loams, silt loams and silty clay loams. Such soils are good storehouses for plant nutrients and are capable of storing a high proportion of water available to plants. Conditions are generally very favorable for root growth.

SOIL DRAINAGE:

Drainage refers to the frequency and duration of periods of saturation or partial saturation during soil formation. Six classes of natural soil drainage (Table IV) are recognized:

EXCESSIVELY DRAINED:
> water is removed from the soil very rapidly. Excessively drained soils are commonly very coarse textures, rocky, or shallow. Some are so steep that much of the water they receive is lost as runoff. All are free of the mottling* due to wetness.

WELL DRAINED:
> water is removed from the soil readily, but not rapidly. It is available to plants throughout most of the growing season, and wetness does not inhibit growth of roots for significant periods during

most growing seasons. Well drained soils are commonly medium textured. They are mainly free of mottling.*

MODERATELY WELL DRAINED:
water is removed from the soil somewhat slowly during some periods. Moderately well drained soils are wet for only a short time during the growing season. They commonly have a slowly pervious layer within or directly below the solum, or periodically receive high rainfall, or both. Most trees attain their best development on moderate to well-drained sites.

SOMEWHAT POORLY DRAINED:
water is removed slowly enough that the soil is wet for significant periods during the growing season. Somewhat poorly drained soils commonly have a slowly pervious layer, a high water table, additional water from seepage, nearly continuous rainfall, or a combination of these.

POORLY DRAINED:
water is removed so slowly that the soil is saturated periodically during the growing season or remains wet for long periods. Free water is commonly at or near the surface for brief periods during the growing season. The soil is not continuously saturated in layers directly below. Poor drainage results from a high water table, a slowly pervious layer within the profile, seepage, nearly continuous rainfall, or a combination of these.

VERY POORLY DRAINED:
water is removed from the soil so slowly that free water remains at or on the surface during most of the growing season. Very poorly drained soils are commonly level or depressed and are frequently ponded. Yet, where rainfall is high and nearly continuous, they can have moderate or high slope gradients, as for example in "hillpeats" and "climatic moors." Wet sites have cold soils which results in a much shorter growing season.

*Mottling, soil: Irregular spots of different colors that vary in number and size. Mottling generally indicates poor aeration and impeded drainage. Descriptive terms are as follows: abundance—few, common, and many; size—fine, medium, and coarse; and contrast—faint, distinct, and prominent.

AVAILABLE SOIL MOISTURE CAPACITY:

Available moisture capacity refers to the capacity of soils to hold water available for use by most plants (Table IV). It is commonly defined as the difference between the amount of soil water at field moisture capacity and the amount at wilting point. Field moisture capacity is the moisture content of a soil held between the soil particles by surface tension after the gravitational, or free, water has drained away 2 or 3 days after a soaking rain; also called normal field capacity, normal moisture capacity, or capillary capacity. It is commonly expressed as inches of water per given depth of soil. The capacity, in inches, in a 150 centimeter (60-inch) profile or to a limiting layer is expressed as:

VERY LOW (droughty): 0 to 7.5 cm (0 to 3 inches)
LOW (dry): 7.5 to 15 cm (3 to 6 inches)
MODERATE (average): 15 to 22.5 cm (6 to 9 inches)
HIGH (moist): 22.5 to 30 cm (9 to 12 inches)
VERY HIGH (wet): more than 30 cm (12 inches)

SOIL REACTION:

Soils can be divided into 7 classes based on measurable differences in chemical reaction (Table IV). The degree of acidity or alkalinity of a soil is expressed in pH values. A soil that tests to pH 7.0 is described

	Texture					Drainage						Moisture					Reaction-pH				
	coarse	mod. coarse	medium	mod. fine	fine	very poor	poor	mod. poor	mod. well	well	excessive	wet	moist	average	dry	droughty	4.0-5.0	5.1-6.0	6.1-6.5	6.6-7.5	7.6-8.5
Abies balsamea		■	■			■	■	■	■			■	■				■	■	■		
Abies concolor		■	■		■		■	■	■				■	■			■	■	■	■	
Abies lasiocarpa		■	■	■				■	■				■	■			■	■	■	■	
Acer negundo	■	■	■				■	■	■			■	■	■				■	■	■	■
Acer nigrum	■	■	■		■		■	■	■				■	■	■				■	■	
Acer pensylvanicum	■	■	■		■			■	■				■	■	■		■	■			
Acer rubrum	■	■	■	■	■		■	■	■	■		■	■	■	■		■	■		■	
Acer saccharinum	■	■	■			■	■	■	■			■	■	■				■	■	■	
Acer saccharum	■	■	■					■	■				■	■	■			■	■	■	
Acer spicatum	■	■	■					■	■				■	■	■		■	■	■		
Aesculus glabra	■	■	■				■	■	■				■	■					■	■	
Aesculus octandra	■	■	■					■	■				■	■					■	■	
Alnus rugosa	■	■	■				■	■	■			■	■					■	■		
Amelanchier canadensis	■	■	■					■	■				■	■			■	■	■		
Amelanchier laevis	■	■	■					■	■				■	■			■	■	■		
Aralia spinosa	■	■	■					■	■				■	■				■	■		
Asimina triloba		■	■				■	■	■				■	■				■	■		
Betula lenta	■	■	■					■	■				■	■			■	■	■		
Betula lutea	■	■	■					■	■				■	■			■	■	■	■	
Betula nigra	■	■	■				■	■	■			■	■	■			■	■			
Betula papyrifera	■	■	■					■	■				■	■			■	■	■		
Betula populifolia	■	■	■					■	■				■	■			■	■			
Carpinus caroliniana		■	■				■	■	■				■	■				■	■		
Carya cordiformis	■	■	■					■	■				■	■					■	■	
Carya glabra		■	■					■	■				■	■	■				■	■	
Carya illinoensis	■	■	■					■	■				■	■					■	■	

Table IV

Soil Correlations:

	Texture					Drainage						Moisture					Reaction-pH				
	coarse	mod. coarse	medium	mod. fine	fine	very poor	poor	mod. poor	mod. well	well	excessive	wet	moist	average	dry	droughty	4.0-5.0	5.1-6.0	6.1-6.5	6.6-7.5	7.6-8.5
Carya ovata			■	■	■			■	■			■	■	■					■		
Carya tomentosa	■	■	■	■					■	■	■			■	■			■	■	■	
Castanea dentata	■	■	■					■	■					■	■	■	■	■			
Catalpa speciosa	■	■	■	■				■	■				■	■	■				■	■	■
Celtis occidentalis	■	■	■	■				■	■				■	■	■				■	■	■
Cercis canadensis	■	■	■	■				■	■				■	■	■				■	■	■
Chionanthus virginicus	■	■	■	■				■	■				■	■			■	■	■		
Cladrastis lutea	■	■	■	■	■				■	■				■	■			■	■	■	
Cornus alternifolia	■	■	■	■				■	■	■			■	■			■	■	■		■
Cornus florida	■	■	■	■				■	■	■			■	■			■	■	■		
Cotinus americanus	■	■	■					■	■	■	■			■	■	■		■	■	■	■
Crataegus crusgalli	■	■	■	■				■	■	■			■	■	■			■	■	■	■
Crataegus mollis	■	■	■	■				■	■	■			■	■	■			■	■	■	■
Crataegus nitida	■	■	■	■				■	■	■			■	■	■			■	■	■	■
Crataegus phaenopyrum	■	■	■	■				■	■	■			■	■	■			■	■	■	■
Crataegus pruinosa	■	■	■	■				■	■	■			■	■	■			■	■	■	■
Crataegus punctata	■	■	■	■				■	■	■			■	■	■			■	■	■	■
Diospyros virginiana	■		■	■		■	■	■	■				■	■	■			■	■	■	■
Euonymus atropurpureus	■	■	■	■				■	■				■	■	■		■	■		■	■
Fagus grandifolia	■	■	■	■				■	■				■	■			■	■	■		
Franklinia alatamaha	■	■	■	■				■	■	■			■	■			■	■	■		
Fraxinus americana	■	■	■	■				■	■				■	■				■	■	■	
Fraxinus nigra	■	■	■			■	■	■	■			■	■	■			■	■	■		
Fraxinus pennsylvanica	■	■	■		■	■	■	■	■			■	■	■				■	■	■	
Fraxinus quadrangulata	■	■	■		■			■	■				■	■	■			■	■	■	■
Gleditsia triacanthos	■	■	■	■			■	■	■		■		■	■	■			■	■	■	■

Soil Correlations: Table IV

Species	Texture					Drainage						Moisture					Reaction-pH				
	coarse	mod. coarse	medium	mod. fine	fine	very poor	poor	mod. poor	mod. well	well	excessive	wet	moist	average	dry	droughty	4.0-5.0	5.1-6.0	6.1-6.5	6.6-7.5	7.6-8.5
Gymnocladus dioicus		■	■	■				■	■	■		■	■	■						■	
Halesia carolina	■	■	■	■				■	■	■			■	■			■	■	■		
Hamamelis virginiana	■	■	■	■				■	■	■			■	■	■			■	■	■	
Juglans cinerea		■	■	■				■	■	■			■	■				■	■	■	
Juglans nigra		■	■	■				■	■	■			■	■				■	■	■	
Juniperus virginiana	■	■	■	■				■	■	■	■		■	■	■			■	■	■	■
Larix laricina	■	■	■	■		■	■	■				■	■			■	■	■	■		■
Liquidambar styraciflua		■	■	■			■	■	■	■		■	■	■			■	■	■		
Liriodendron tulipifera		■	■	■	■			■	■	■			■	■			■	■	■		
Maclura pomifera		■	■	■	■		■	■	■	■		■	■	■	■		■	■	■	■	
Magnolia acuminata		■	■	■				■	■	■			■	■			■	■	■		
Malus ioensis		■	■	■	■			■	■	■			■	■	■		■	■	■	■	
Morus rubra		■	■	■	■			■	■	■			■	■	■					■	■
Nyssa sylvatica	■	■	■	■			■	■	■	■		■	■	■			■	■	■		
Ostrya virginiana	■	■	■	■				■	■	■			■	■	■			■	■	■	
Oxydendrum arboreum	■	■	■	■				■	■	■			■	■	■		■	■	■		
Picea engelmanni		■	■	■				■	■	■			■	■			■	■	■		
Picea glauca		■	■	■				■	■	■			■	■			■	■	■		
Picea glauca densata	■	■	■	■				■	■	■			■	■	■		■	■	■		
Picea mariana	■	■	■	■		■	■	■				■	■				■	■	■		
Picea pungens	■	■	■	■				■	■	■			■	■			■	■	■		
Pinus banksiana	■	■						■	■	■	■		■	■	■	■	■	■	■		
Pinus flexilis	■	■	■					■	■	■	■			■	■	■	■	■	■		
Pinus ponderosa	■	■	■					■	■	■	■			■	■	■	■	■	■		
Pinus resinosa	■	■	■					■	■	■	■			■	■	■	■	■	■		
Pinus rigida	■	■						■	■	■	■			■	■	■	■	■	■		

	Texture					Drainage						Moisture					Reaction-pH				
	coarse	mod. coarse	medium	mod. fine	fine	very poor	poor	mod. poor	mod. well	well	excessive	wet	moist	average	dry	droughty	4.0-5.0	5.1-6.0	6.1-6.5	6.6-7.5	7.6-8.5
Pinus strobus	■	■	■	■				■	■	■			■	■			■	■			
Platanus occidentalis	■	■	■		■		■	■	■	■			■	■	■				■	■	
Populus deltoides	■	■	■	■	■		■	■	■	■		■	■	■					■	■	
Populus grandidentata	■	■			■				■	■	■		■	■	■		■	■			
Populus tremuloides	■	■	■	■	■			■	■	■		■	■	■			■	■	■	■	■
Prunus americana		■	■	■					■	■			■	■	■			■	■	■	
Prunus pensylvanica	■	■	■	■					■	■	■		■	■	■		■	■	■		
Prunus serotina	■	■	■	■					■	■	■		■	■	■		■	■	■	■	
Prunus virginiana	■	■	■	■					■	■	■		■	■	■			■	■	■	
Pseudotsuga taxifolia	■	■	■	■					■	■			■	■	■		■	■	■		
Ptelea trifoliata	■	■	■	■				■	■	■			■	■	■			■	■	■	
Quercus alba	■	■	■	■				■	■	■			■	■	■		■	■	■	■	
Quercus bicolor		■	■			■	■	■	■			■	■	■			■	■	■	■	
Quercus borealis	■	■	■	■				■	■	■			■	■	■		■	■	■		
Quercus coccinea	■	■	■	■					■	■	■			■	■		■	■	■		
Quercus ellipsoidalis	■	■	■	■					■	■	■			■	■		■	■	■		
Quercus imbricaria		■	■	■				■	■	■			■	■					■	■	
Quercus macrocarpa	■	■	■	■				■	■	■			■	■	■			■	■	■	
Quercus marilandica	■	■			■			■	■	■				■	■		■	■			
Quercus montana	■	■	■	■				■	■	■				■	■		■	■	■		
Quercus muhlenbergi	■	■	■	■	■			■	■	■			■	■	■				■	■	■
Quercus palustris	■	■	■	■			■	■	■			■	■	■			■	■	■	■	
Quercus stellata	■	■	■	■				■	■	■				■	■		■	■	■		
Quercus velutina	■	■	■	■					■	■	■			■	■		■	■	■		
Rhododendron maximum	■	■	■	■				■	■	■			■	■			■	■			
Rhus copallina	■	■	■	■					■	■	■			■	■		■	■	■	■	

Soil Correlations:

Table IV

	Texture					Drainage						Moisture					Reaction-pH				
	coarse	mod. coarse	medium	mod. fine	fine	very poor	poor	mod. poor	mod. well	well	excessive	wet	moist	average	dry	droughty	4.0-5.0	5.1-6.0	6.1-6.5	6.6-7.5	7.6-8.5
Rhus glabra	■	■	■	■					■	■	■			■	■	■			■	■	■
Rhus typhina	■	■	■	■					■	■	■			■	■	■			■	■	■
Robinia pseudoacacia	■	■	■		■				■	■	■			■	■					■	■
Salix amygdaloides	■	■	■			■	■	■	■			■	■	■						■	■
Salix bebbiana	■	■	■			■	■	■	■			■	■	■						■	■
Salix discolor	■	■	■			■	■	■	■			■	■	■						■	■
Salix nigra	■	■	■			■	■	■	■			■	■	■						■	■
Sassafras albidum		■	■	■				■	■	■			■	■	■			■	■	■	
Sorbus decora	■	■	■					■	■	■	■		■	■	■			■	■	■	
Taxodium distichum	■		■					■	■			■	■	■			■	■	■		
Thuja occidentalis	■	■	■			■	■	■	■			■	■	■						■	■
Tilia americana	■	■	■	■				■	■	■			■	■	■			■	■	■	
Tsuga canadensis	■	■	■					■	■	■			■	■	■		■	■	■		
Ulmus americana	■	■	■	■			■	■	■	■			■	■	■			■	■	■	■
Viburnum lentago	■	■	■	■			■	■	■	■			■	■	■			■	■	■	
Viburnum prunifolium	■	■	■	■				■	■	■			■	■	■			■	■	■	
Viburnum rufidulum	■	■	■	■				■	■	■			■	■	■				■	■	■
Zanthoxylum americanum	■	■	■	■				■	■	■			■	■	■			■	■	■	

as precisely neutral in reaction because it is neither acid nor alkaline. The degree of acidity or alkalinity is expressed as:

SLIGHTLY ACID: 6.1 to 6.5

MODERATELY ACID: 5.1 to 6.0   NEUTRAL: 6.6 to 7.5

STRONGLY ACID: 4.1 to 5.0   ALKALINE: 7.6 to 8.5

EXTREMELY ACID*: Below 4.0   STRONGLY ALKALINE*: 8.6 and higher

* Plant growth is severely restricted due to hostile soil chemistry. These classes are not included in Table IV and must be modified if plant growth and survival is to be possible. Soil pH can be modified toward neutrality by the introduction of lime to acidic soils. Sulphur, aluminum sulfate or calcium sulfate lowers pH. The most appropriate planting is that which is best suited to local existing conditions. Trees already growing on the site and in surrounding areas should be utilized as a guide in plant selection.

HARDINESS:

Although the combined effects of many environmental factors determine true plant adaptability, winter hardiness is the most important single governing factor according to many contemporary authors. The United States Department of Agriculture publishes a hardiness map which shows the average annual minimum temperatures for most of North America. Each zone delineated on the USDA map includes 10 degree increments and is split into an *a* and *b* area with the lower temperature occurring in the *a* zone. Temperatures of adjacent zones become increasingly similar near their boundaries. A plant species that flourishes in one part of a given zone is likely to be adaptable in other parts of the same zone or in a warmer zone. Other factors of the physical environment must also be relatively comparable.

USDA Hardiness Zones mapped in figure 2:

Zone 2 .... -50 to -40F
Zone 3a .... -40 to -35F
Zone 3b .... -35 to -30F
Zone 4a .... -30 to -25F
Zone 4b .... -25 to -20F
Zone 5a .... -20 to -15F
Zone 5b .... -15 to -10F
Zone 6 .... -10 to   0F

ZONE 2:

Abies balsamea   (Balsam Fir)
Abies lasiocarpa   (Alpine Fir)
Acer negundo   (Boxelder)
Acer spicatum   (Mountain Maple)
Alnus rugosa   (Hazel Alder)
Betula papyrifera   (Paper Birch)
Carpinus caroliniana   (American Hornbeam)
Fraxinus nigra   (Black Ash)
Fraxinus pennsylvanica   (Green Ash)
Larix laricina   (Eastern Larch)
Malus ioensis   (Prairie Crabapple)
Picea engelmanni   (Engelmann Spruce)
Picea glauca   (White Spruce)
Picea glauca densata   (BlackHills White Spruce)
Picea mariana   (Black Spruce)

Picea pungens   (Colorado Spruce)
Pinus banksiana   (Jack Pine)
Pinus flexilis   (Limber Pine)
Pinus resinosa   (Red Pine)
Populus tremuloides   (Quaking Aspen)
Prunus pensylvanica   (Pin Cherry)
Prunus virginiana   (Common Chokecherry)
Quercus macrocarpa   (Bur Oak)
Rhus glabra   (Smooth Sumac)
Salix bebbiana   (Bebb Willow)
Salix discolor   (Pussy Willow)
Sorbus decora   (Showy Mountainash)
Thuja occidentalis   (Eastern Arborvitae)
Ulmus americana   (American Elm)
Viburnum lentago   (Nannyberry Viburnum)

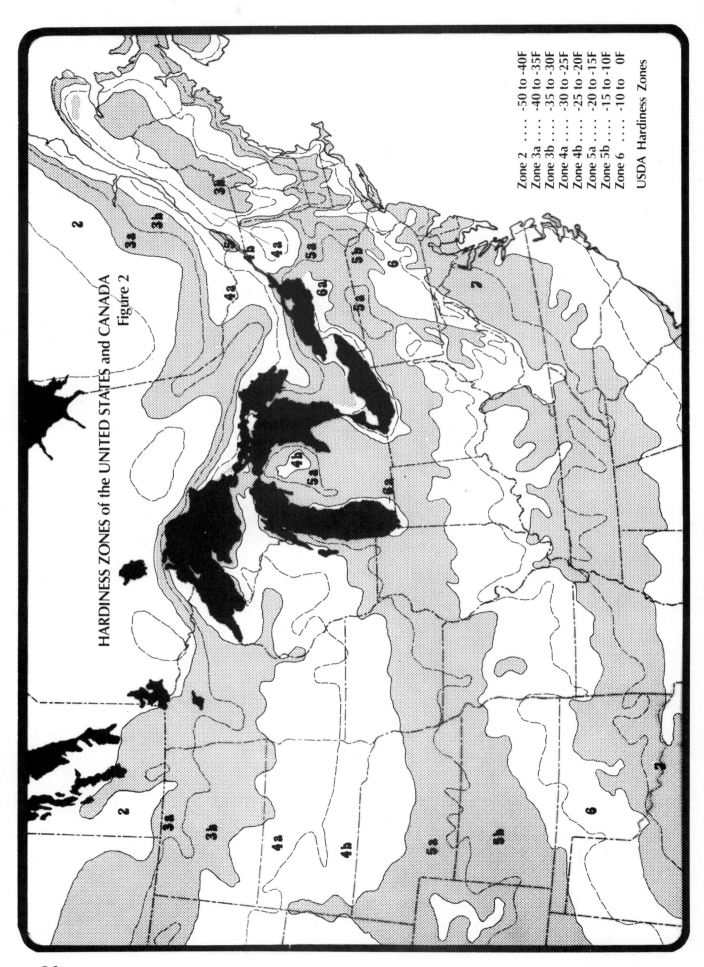

HARDINESS ZONES of the UNITED STATES and CANADA
Figure 2

USDA Hardiness Zones

Zone 2 ..... -50 to -40F
Zone 3a ..... -40 to -35F
Zone 3b ..... -35 to -30F
Zone 4a ..... -30 to -25F
Zone 4b ..... -25 to -20F
Zone 5a ..... -20 to -15F
Zone 5b ..... -15 to -10F
Zone 6 ..... -10 to 0F

ZONE 3a:

Acer rubrum   (Red Maple)
Acer saccharum   (Sugar Maple)
Amelanchier canadensis   (Shadblow Serviceberry)
Amelanchier laevis   (Allegany Serviceberry)
Betula lutea   (Yellow Birch)
Celtis occidentalis   (Common Hackberry)
Crataegus pruinosa   (Frosted Hawthorn)
Juniperus virginiana   (Eastern Redcedar)
Pinus strobus   (Eastern White Pine)

Populus grandidentata   (Bigtooth Aspen)
Prunus americana   (American Plum)
Quercus borealis   (Northern Red Oak)
Rhus typhina   (Staghorn Sumac)
Salix amygdaloides   (Peachleaf Willow)
Salix nigra   (Black Willow)
Tilia americana   (American Linden)
Zanthoxylum americanum   (Common Pricklyash)

ZONE 3b:

Acer nigrum   (Black Maple)
Acer pensylvanicum   (Striped Maple)
Acer saccharinum   (Silver Maple)
Betula lenta   (Sweet Birch)
Cladrastis lutea   (American Yellowwood)
Cornus alternifolia   (Pagoda Dogwood)
Crataegus mollis   (Downy Hawthorn)
Fagus grandifolia   (American Beech)
Fraxinus americana   (White Ash)

Juglans cinerea   (Butternut)
Populus deltoides   (Eastern Poplar)
Prunus serotina   (Black Cherry)
Quercus ellipsoidalis   (Northern Pin Oak)
Rhododendron maximum   (Rosebay Rhododendron)
Robinia pseudoacacia   (Black Locust)
Tsuga canadensis   (Canada Hemlock)
Viburnum prunifolium   (Blackhaw Viburnum)

ZONE 4a:

Abies concolor   (White Fir)
Aesculus glabra   (Ohio Buckeye)
Aesculus octandra   (Yellow Buckeye)
Betula populifolia   (Gray Birch)
Carya cordiformis   (Bitternut Hickory)

Carya ovata   (Shagbark Hickory)
Platanus occidentalis   (American Planetree)
Quercus alba   (White Oak)
Quercus bicolor   (Swamp White Oak)

ZONE 4b:

Crataegus crusgalli   (Cockspur Hawthorn)
Crataegus punctata   (Dotted Hawthorn)
Euonymus atropurpureus   (Eastern Wahoo)
Gleditsia triacanthos   (Common Honeylocust)

Juglans nigra   (Eastern Black Walnut)
Pinus ponderosa   (Ponderosa Pine)
Quercus muhlenbergi   (Chinkapin Oak)
Quercus velutina   (Black Oak)

ZONE 5a:

Aralia spinosa   (Devils-Walkingstick)
Betula nigra   (River Birch)
Carya glabra   (Pignut Hickory)
Castanea dentata   (American Chestnut)
Catalpa speciosa   (Northern Catalpa)
Cercis canadensis   (Eastern Redbud)
Crataegus nitida   (Glossy Hawthorn)
Crataegus phaenopyrum   (Washington Hawthorn)
Diospyros virginiana   (Common Persimmon)
Fraxinus quadrangulata   (Blue Ash)
Gymnocladus dioicus   (Kentucky Coffeetree)
Hamamelis virginiana   (Common Witchhazel)
Liriodendron tulipifera   (Tuliptree)
Maclura pomifera   (Osageorange)

Magnolia acuminata   (Cucumbertree Magnolia)
Morus rubra   (Red Mulberry)
Nyssa sylvatica   (Black Tupelo)
Ostrya virginiana   (American Hophornbeam)
Pinus rigida   (Pitch Pine)
Pseudotsuga taxifolia   (Common Douglasfir)
Ptelea trifoliata   (Common Hoptree)
Quercus coccinea   (Scarlet Oak)
Quercus imbricaria   (Shingle Oak)
Quercus montana   (Chestnut Oak)
Quercus palustris   (Pin Oak)
Rhus copallina   (Flameleaf Sumac)
Taxodium distichum   (Common Baldcypress)
Viburnum rufidulum   (Rusty Blackhaw Viburnum)

Hardiness (cont.)

ZONE 5b:

Asimina triloba   (Common Pawpaw)
Carya tomentosa   (Mockernut Hickory)
Chionanthus virginicus   (White Fringetree)
Cornus florida   (Flowering Dogwood)

Halesia carolina   (Carolina Silverbell)
Quercus marilandica   (Blackjack Oak)
Quercus stellata   (Post Oak)
Sassafras albidum   (Common Sassafras)

ZONE 6:

Carya illinoensis   (Pecan)
Cotinus americanus   (American Smoketree)
Franklinia alatamaha   (Franklinia)

Liquidambar styraciflua   (American Sweetgum)
Oxydendrum arboreum   (Sourwood)

GROWTH RATE:

The measured vertical increase in height during one growing season determines the rate of plant growth. Different species have correspondingly varying rates of growth. Rate is also influenced by numerous variables such as age and factors of the plant's physical environment. Generally, young trees grow rapidly, adding a great deal of height before slowing with maturity. Three classes are designated, (Table V)

SLOW:
having an annual leader increment of 30 centimeters (12 inches) or less,
indicator—Quercus alba (White Oak)

MEDIUM:
between 30 and 60 centimeters (12 to 24 inches) per year,
indicator—Acer saccharum (Sugar Maple)

FAST:
possessed of the potential to produce 60 centimeters (24 inches) or more of leader growth annually,
indicator—Larix laricina (Eastern Larch)

LONGEVITY:

Longevity refers to length of time a selected plant can be expected to live where environmental conditions are favorable. (Table V)

SHORT LIVED:
100 years or less, possessed of a relatively short life expectancy due to genetic constitution,
indicator—Salix nigra (Black Willow)

MEDIUM LIVED:
100 to 200 years,
indicator—Celtis occidentalis (Common Hackberry)

LONG LIVED:
200 years or more, having the potential to endure for centuries before the onset of decadence,
indicator—Quercus macrocarpa (Bur Oak)

Silvical Characteristics: Table V

	Growth			Longevity			Physiol.		Disease		Insect		Wind-Ice	
	slow	medium	fast	short	medium	long	infrequent	frequent	infrequent	frequent	infrequent	frequent	infrequent	frequent
Abies balsamea	■				■		■		■			■		■
Abies concolor	■					■	■		■		■		■	
Abies lasiocarpa		■			■		■		■		■			■
Acer negundo			■	■				■		■		■		■
Acer nigrum		■				■		■		■	■		■	
Acer pensylvanicum		■		■				■	■		■		■	
Acer rubrum		■				■	■			■		■	■	
Acer saccharinum			■		■			■		■		■		■
Acer saccharum	■					■	■			■		■	■	
Acer spicatum		■		■				■	■		■		■	
Aesculus glabra	■				■			■		■	■		■	
Aesculus octandra	■					■	■			■	■		■	
Alnus rugosa		■		■				■		■		■	■	
Amelanchier canadensis		■			■			■	■		■		■	
Amelanchier laevis		■			■			■	■		■		■	
Aralia spinosa			■	■				■	■		■			■
Asimina triloba	■				■			■	■		■		■	
Betula lenta			■			■		■	■			■		■
Betula lutea	■					■	■			■		■		■
Betula nigra			■		■			■		■		■		■
Betula papyrifera		■			■			■		■		■		■
Betula populifolia			■	■				■		■		■		■
Carpinus caroliniana	■				■			■	■		■		■	
Carya cordiformis	■					■		■		■		■	■	
Carya glabra	■					■		■		■		■	■	
Carya illinoensis		■				■		■		■		■		■

89

Table V

Silvical Characteristics:

	Growth			Longevity			Physiol.		Disease		Insect		Wind-Ice	
	slow	medium	fast	short	medium	long	infrequent	frequent	infrequent	frequent	infrequent	frequent	infrequent	frequent
Carya ovata	■					■		■	■		■		■	
Carya tomentosa	■					■		■	■		■			■
Castanea dentata			■		■		■			■	■		■	
Catalpa speciosa		■			■		■			■		■		■
Celtis occidentalis		■				■		■		■		■		■
Cercis canadensis	■				■			■		■	■		■	
Chionanthus virginicus	■				■		■			■	■		■	
Cladrastis lutea	■				■		■			■	■		■	
Cornus alternifolia	■				■		■		■		■		■	
Cornus florida	■				■			■		■		■	■	
Cotinus americanus	■			■			■			■	■		■	
Crataegus crusgalli	■				■		■			■	■			■
Crataegus mollis	■				■		■			■		■		■
Crataegus nitida	■				■		■			■		■		■
Crataegus phaenopyrum	■				■		■			■		■		■
Crataegus pruinosa	■				■		■			■		■		■
Crataegus punctata	■				■		■			■		■		■
Diospyros virginiana	■				■		■		■		■		■	
Euonymus atropurpureus			■		■		■			■	■		■	
Fagus grandifolia	■					■		■	■			■		■
Franklinia alatamaha		■		■			■			■	■		■	
Fraxinus americana		■				■		■		■		■		■
Fraxinus nigra			■		■			■		■		■	■	
Fraxinus pennsylvanica			■		■			■		■		■		■
Fraxinus quadrangulata		■			■			■		■	■			■
Gleditsia triacanthos			■		■			■		■		■		■

Silvical Characteristics: Table V

	Growth			Longevity			Physiol.		Disease		Insect		Wind-Ice	
	slow	medium	fast	short	medium	long	infrequent	frequent	infrequent	frequent	infrequent	frequent	infrequent	frequent
Gymnocladus dioicus		X			X		X		X		X		X	
Halesia carolina		X			X			X	X		X		X	
Hamamelis virginiana		X			X			X	X		X		X	
Juglans cinerea		X	X	X				X		X	X		X	
Juglans nigra		X				X		X		X		X	X	
Juniperus virginiana	X	X				X		X		X	X		X	
Larix laricina			X		X		X			X		X		X
Liquidambar styraciflua		X				X		X		X		X		X
Liriodendron tulipifera		X	X			X		X		X	X		X	
Maclura pomifera		X			X		X		X			X	X	
Magnolia acuminata		X			X		X		X			X		X
Malus ioensis		X		X				X		X		X	X	
Morus rubra		X		X			X			X		X	X	
Nyssa sylvatica	X					X	X			X		X	X	
Ostrya virginiana	X					X	X		X		X		X	
Oxydendrum arboreum	X				X		X		X		X		X	
Picea engelmanni	X					X	X			X		X	X	
Picea glauca		X				X	X			X		X	X	
Picea glauca densata		X				X	X			X		X	X	
Picea mariana	X					X	X			X		X	X	
Picea pungens	X					X	X			X		X	X	
Pinus banksiana			X		X			X		X		X	X	
Pinus flexilis	X					X	X		X		X		X	
Pinus ponderosa		X				X		X		X		X	X	
Pinus resinosa		X				X		X		X		X		X
Pinus rigida			X		X			X		X		X	X	

91

	Growth			Longevity			Physiol.		Disease		Insect		Wind-Ice	
	slow	medium	fast	short	medium	long	infrequent	frequent	infrequent	frequent	infrequent	frequent	infrequent	frequent
Pinus strobus		■				■		■	■		■		■	
Platanus occidentalis			■			■		■		■	■			■
Populus deltoides			■		■			■		■		■	■	
Populus grandidentata		■			■			■		■		■		■
Populus tremuloides		■			■			■		■		■	■	
Prunus americana		■			■			■		■		■	■	
Prunus pensylvanica		■		■				■		■		■	■	
Prunus serotina			■			■		■		■		■	■	
Prunus virginiana		■			■			■		■		■	■	
Pseudotsuga taxifolia		■				■		■	■		■		■	
Ptelea trifoliata	■				■		■		■		■		■	
Quercus alba	■					■		■	■			■	■	
Quercus bicolor		■				■	■		■		■		■	
Quercus borealis		■				■		■		■		■	■	
Quercus coccinea		■				■		■		■		■	■	
Quercus ellipsoidalis	■					■		■		■		■	■	
Quercus imbricaria	■				■			■		■	■		■	
Quercus macrocarpa	■					■		■	■		■		■	
Quercus marilandica	■				■			■		■	■		■	
Quercus montana	■					■		■		■		■	■	
Quercus muhlenbergi	■					■		■	■		■		■	
Quercus palustris		■				■	■			■		■	■	
Quercus stellata	■					■		■		■		■	■	
Quercus velutina	■					■		■		■		■	■	
Rhododendron maximum		■				■	■			■	■		■	
Rhus copallina			■		■		■		■		■		■	

Silvical Characteristics: Table V

	Growth			Longevity			Physiol.		Disease		Insect		Wind-Ice	
	slow	medium	fast	short	medium	long	infrequent	frequent	infrequent	frequent	infrequent	frequent	infrequent	frequent
Rhus glabra			X	X			X		X		X		X	
Rhus typhina			X	X			X		X		X		X	
Robinia pseudoacacia			X		X		X			X		X	X	
Salix amygdaloides			X	X			X			X		X		X
Salix bebbiana			X	X			X			X		X		X
Salix discolor			X	X			X			X		X		X
Salix nigra			X	X			X			X		X		X
Sassafras albidum		X		X			X			X		X	X	
Sorbus decora		X		X			X			X		X	X	
Taxodium distichum	X					X	X		X		X		X	
Thuja occidentalis		X				X	X			X		X	X	
Tilia americana		X			X		X			X		X		X
Tsuga canadensis	X					X	X		X		X			X
Ulmus americana		X			X		X			X		X		X
Viburnum lentago		X		X			X			X		X	X	
Viburnum prunifolium	X			X			X			X		X	X	
Viburnum rufidulum		X		X			X		X			X	X	
Zanthoxylum americanum			X	X			X		X		X		X	

BIOLOGICAL DISORDERS:

Most kinds of trees are subject to one or more biological disorders. Most of these cause little noticeable damage to the trees. Others, by severely injuring leaves, twigs, branches, or roots, cause stunting, decadence and eventual death of the infected tree. Plant health is affected by the severity of disease, insect, and physiological factors. The most virulent disorders are: chestnut blight, dutch elm disease and oak wilt (disease); gypsy moth and mimosa webworm (insect); and oak chlorosis (physiological). These usually cause rapid decline. Susceptibility is magnified in species (commonly fast growing pioneer species such as Black Willow, Silver Maple, and Quaking Aspen) which suffer frequent breakage as the result of wind and ice storms (Table V).

The value of individual trees and collective stands for shade and ornamental purposes on lawns or in recreation areas, for windbreaks, for wildlife habitat, and for forestry purposes can be greatly reduced or destroyed by these disorders. The removal of dead trees and subsequent replacement may be very costly to home owners, park districts, forest preserve districts or municipal governments (Carter 1964).

Most biological disorders that are of frequent, widespread or destructive nature are outlined in the master plates for each species. The reader is referred to county extension service expertise and publications for information on identification, prevention and control. Two categories of plant susceptibility are presented (Table V).

FREQUENT:
    species whose visual appearance, health and survivability are noticeably threatened

INFREQUENT:
    species hosting only occasional or minor disorders which do not significantly alter visual appearance, threaten health and survivability

URBAN CONDITIONS:

Where urban vegetation exists it modifies and enhances the urban environment, making it more enjoyable and livable. Nowhere is there a greater need for plant material. Vegetation in parks and plazas, along street and river corridors, or in scattered forest preserves must grow and survive the hostile conditions of environment common to many metropolitan landscapes. The more hostile the environment, the more limited the selection of plants able to withstand it. Limiting factors include air pollution, too little soil moisture, improper drainage, compacted soils, infertile soils, high heat albedos, night lighting, and salt spray. High maintenance costs due to extensive tree mortality must be avoided in favor of species that are biologically and functionally adapted.

A guide to the selection of suitable native trees for the urban environment is included in Table VI. Trees are ranked in three general categories (resistant, intermediate, sensitive) according to their tolerance. Table VI is based upon extensive review of popular literature and recent research in some areas. The designer is encouraged to frequently update the table as new information becomes available. Finally, the designer must use the night lighting tolerance data with caution. Pioneering research in this area is very incomplete with preliminary experimental results inconclusive.

SELECTION OF TREES TOLERANT OF ATMOSPHERIC POLLUTANTS:

The emission trends of numerous air pollutants have been increasing in the recent past and the total national cost of air pollution in 1968, with much of this damage concentrated in urban areas, was estimated to be in excess of 16 billion dollars. Air quality considerations in metropolitan areas are especially critical because of the tremendous aggregation of people and machines. In addition, urban regions cover impressively large areas. By the year 2000 the total urban-suburban land area may exceed 300 million acres, with approximately 85 percent of the U.S. population residing in urban communities (Smith and Dochinger 1976).

There is considerable research evidence indicating that trees in urban environments have considerable potential to remove both particulate and gaseous pollutants from the atmosphere. The primary way vegetation removes gases from the atmosphere is by uptake through leaf stomates. The processes of transpiration and photosynthesis require that plants exchange gases with the ambient atmosphere through leaf, branch, and stem pores. Contaminant gases present in the atmosphere in the vicinity of a plant are absorbed when the stomates or lenticels are open (Smith and Dochinger, 1976).

Species vary in their efficiency as particle collectors. Coniferous species retaining their foliage year-round may appropriately be more efficient than deciduous species. The atmospheric burden of both particulates and gases is generally higher in winter than in summer for most urban areas. It is important, therefore, to have maximum plant surface available for absorption and adsorption during the winter months. Because evergreen foliage persists longer than deciduous foliage, the opportunity for pollutant removal is correspondingly longer. Petioles are especially efficient particle receptors, species with long petioles (for example, ash, aspen, maple) are more efficient. Surface hairiness on plant parts (leaves, twigs, petioles, buds) may be especially effective for retention of particles. Those species possessing these hairs (for example, oak, birch, hawthorn, mulberry, sumac) should be considered. Species with small branches and twigs (for example, beech, hornbeam, birch) may be selected over species with large branches or twigs as the former are more efficient particle collectors (Smith and Dochinger, 1976).

Information is inadequate to document the ability of trees to remove meaningful quantities of pollutants from actual urban atmospheres. Trees have yet to be shown capable of reducing a particular air contaminant to acceptable standards for urban areas (Smith and Dochinger 1977).

Trees selected or bred to provide this amenity function must be tolerant of the acute adverse influences of air pollution. Clearly, if the tree is severely damaged or killed by one or an interaction of air contaminants, its utility will be short-lived. Godzik (1968) observed that the greatest amount of sulfur was absorbed by leaves of a Betula species, which is resistant to SO_2, and the least by a Picea species, which is susceptible to SO_2. He concluded that the susceptibility of species is not governed by the amount of pollutant absorbed. In addition to air-pollution tolerance, suitable tree varieties should be capable of withstanding other urban stresses such as poor soil aeration and drought, nutrient deficiencies, and microclimatic extremes. A suitable species should be capable of more than mere persistence in the urban environment. It should be able to grow vigorously (Smith and Dochinger 1976).

The principal air pollutants injurious to plant tissues may be grouped as oxidants or non-oxidants. The oxidants reviewed here include: sulfur dioxide (SO_2); ozone (O_3); oxides of nitrogen (NOx); and peroxyacetyl nitrate (PAN). The principal non-oxidants considered include: hydrogen fluoride; chlorine; ammonia; and ethylene. The oxidants generally, and ozone in particular, are the principal constituents of the photochemical smog generated in most of our large cities and on our highways. Most oxidants originate as by-products of combustion of organic matter or hydrocarbons; SO_2 results from burning of fossil fuels, such as coal, while O_3, NOx and PAN result primarily from photo-oxidation of automobile exhaust, arising from combustion of hydrocarbon-based fuels.

Sulfur dioxide and ozone are probably responsible for more air-pollution injury to woody plants than all other air pollutants combined. Sulfur dioxide wastes are being emitted from industrial complexes. Sulfur dioxide originates from the combustion of nearly every fuel, but especially from coal and oil and from the heating of sulfide ores in the smelting process. The burning of coal accounts for nearly 60 percent of the sulfur dioxide released annually in the United States. Upon burning, the sulfur in the coal is converted to sulfur dioxide; thus, the higher the sulfur content of the coal, the more sulfur dioxide released. The production, refining, and utilization of petroleum and natural gas adds another 20 percent to the sulfur dioxide emission. Ore smelting and refining (principally iron, zinc, copper, and nickel) produce 7 percent of the sulfur dioxide emissions. The remaining sulfur dioxide in the atmosphere originates mainly from industries that manufacture or use sulfuric acid and sulfur (Davis and Gerhold 1976).

Ozone—the major pollutant in smog—is common to densely populated metropolitan areas; however, ozone damage has been spotted up to 100 miles away from any metropolitan source. Along with the combustion of automobile and industrial fuels, ozone probably causes more injury to plants than any other aerial toxicant in the United States. Hydrocarbons and oxides of nitrogen are emitted into the atmosphere from automotive exhaust. Once in the atmosphere, these compounds undergo photochemical reactions in the presence of sunlight, producing ozone along with a variety of other compounds (Davis and Gerhold, 1976).

Industries and communities both discharge gaseous and particulate flourides in the atmosphere from the smelting of nonferrous ores, steel, aluminum, combustion of coal; manufacture of brick, ceramics, cement, glass, and phosphate fertilizers; production and use of hydrofluoric acid; and use of fluorides as oxidizing agents in rocket fuel. Fluorides are more damaging to vegetation than equivalent concentrations from other air pollutants. Fluorides frequently cause extensive tree damage around large point sources such as smelters or fertilizer plants, but are probably not as significant as sulfur dioxide and ozone. Ethylene, ammonia, chlorine, hydrogen chloride, particulate dusts, and heavy metals are also capable of injuring woody plants to some extent (Davis and Gerhold 1976).

Approximately 125 million tons of air pollutants are emitted into the air in the United States every year from five major sources (Fig. 3). The pollutants arising from these sources may be categorized arbitrarily as general (all air pollutants) and those that injure plants (phytotoxic pollutants). Transportation is a significant source for both categories. Transportation, industry, and the generation of electricity represent the major sources of phytotoxic air pollutants (Davis and Gerhold 1976).

Figure 3. Sources of general air pollutants and phytotoxic air pollutants

Source	All major pollutants	Phytotoxic pollutants
	Percent	Percent
Transportation	60	28
Industry	18	30
Generation of electricity	14	26
Space heating	5	9
Refuse disposal	3	7

Foliage injury is often one of the early manifestations of pollutants that precedes other effects. It is an obvious symptom, fairly easy to estimate or measure. Gaseous pollutants are taken into the plant leaf through the stomata along with the normal constituents of the air. Once inside the leaf, the toxic chemical reacts with cells, causing injury or death of tissues. The resulting symptoms may be classified as chronic or acute depending upon the severity of injury. Chronic symptoms usually imply tissue injury but not death, while acute injury signifies tissue death. Chronic symptoms often result from exposure of a plant to low levels of pollution for a long time, or occur when a plant is fairly resistant to a pollutant. Acute injury is observed after a short-term high level exposure to pollution, or when a plant is very sensitive (Davis and Gerhold 1976).

Home and professional gardeners, horticulturists, landscape architects, arborists, and foresters should be aware of the information available on the relationship between trees and air pollution. In seeking pollution-resistant trees, one must first acquire a listing of the phytotoxic air pollutants prevalent in his area. The following lists, Table VI, representing the personal observations and reports of many professionals, are a compilation of the known responses by both hardwoods and softwoods to various pollutants. Check these lists before planting. (Table VI should not be taken as an absolute basis for assessing the responses of trees to pollutants. Considerable local variation must be anticipated, because of genetic and environmental factors.) Control of emissions may reduce or stabilize the levels of certain air pollutants in the most severely affected areas, but in the foreseeable future we will continue to have an appreciable spread in the amount of pollution will continue. Air quality standards are being set at levels that safeguard the health of humans, but not always the most sensitive plants. Evaluation for susceptibility of tree species to any specific pollutant are incomplete and are not conclusive. Further research is necessary (Davis and Gerhold, 1976).

SELECTION OF TREES TOLERANT OF EXTENDED PHOTOPERIODS CAUSED BY NIGHT LIGHTING:

At present there are some 12.5 million street and highway lights in service in the contiguous United States. Mercury vapour (Hg) lamps dominate the total with 75 percent, followed by incandescent (INC) lamps at 20 percent; and high-pressure sodium (HPS) vapour, metal halide (MH), fluorescent (F), and miscellaneous lights make up the other 5 percent. One of the changes that is occurring in the outdoor environment is increased installation of lighting for outdoor activities and security. High-intensity-discharge (HID) sources of light make possible acceptable visibility with less use of electricity than incandescent (INC) filament lamps. Illumination levels in outdoor lighting now are from about ½ foot-candle (ft-c) to 5 ft-c along roadways, walkways in parks, and building surroundings. Both the amount of light per unit area (ft-c) and the total area lighted have increased. The HID lamps provide up to 6 times as much visible light as incandescent lamps for equal use of electricity. In addition to emission quantity, the quality of radiant energy (wavelength) also varies by source of filament or ionized gas. They also differ in color, providing a range from blue to yellow-orange (Andresen 1976).

Three types of HID lamps are in use: mercury (Hg), metal-halide (MH), and high-pressure sodium (HPS). The Hg lamp, up until recently, has been the standard for vision-lighting at night. Hg lamps emit radiation that appears blue over all surfaces and distorts color values. It also attracts large numbers of night-flying insects because of the high incidence of blue in the radiation. Metal-halide lamps emit radiation that appears white or slightly green. They are more efficient than Hg and the color distortion of plants is less apparent than with Hg and HPS. MH is intermediate between Hg and HPS in attractiveness to insects. High pressure sodium vapour lamps emit radiation that appears intense yellow-orange. They are more efficient than the other HID lamps. HPS lamps emit only traces of blue light, thus attract insects minimally. Yellow light distorts colors of green plants under all circumstances and is objectionable where esthetics are important. The yellow-orange peak of the HPS is near the maximum sensitivity for human vision. The preference for HPS over MH or Hg is based on efficiency and visibility, with less regard for the color values of the objects that are lighted, the insect attractiveness of the lamps themselves, or for their relative effects on plant growth. A trend toward HPS began with the invention of Lucalox in 1966. A number of major cities in the United States began installing large numbers of HPS about 1970. The Chicago Department of Streets and Sanitation installed some 40,000 HPS lamps. Today about 3 percent of our large city street lights are HPS (Andresen 1976).

Research demonstrates that outdoor night lighting at an intensity of 1 ft-c or more, dusk to dawn, has adverse effects on the growth of plants in the landscape that border lighted areas. Outdoor area lighting exerts its greatest effect in photoperiodically extending the growth of many plants and dormancy of many species was delayed. Manipulation of photoperiod and favorable temperatures can produce continuous growth in such species as *Liriodendron tulipifera* and *Robinia pseudoacacia*; but *Pinus sylvestris, Acer pseudoplatanus,* and *Phellodendron amurense* assumed varying forms of winter dormancy (Wareing 1956). Wareing also tabulated some 60 species of 31 woody genera that were photoperiodically sensitive in producing extended growth. In general, short photoperiods induce dormancy, long days (natural or artificial) prolong periods of vegetative growth, and long days can break the dormancy induced by short photoperiods. The order of effectiveness for controlling photoperiodic responses of plants, when compared was INC > HPS > F = MH > Hg. The order for photoperiodic effectiveness on plants is determined by the quantity of red-far-red wave lengths of the light source (Andresen 1976).

During normal periods of daylight, urban trees are exposed to direct and reflected radiant energy. When natural light falls upon the leaf during long days, radiant energy of far-red wave lengths is converted to photosynthetic processes and plant growth. Light controls the growth period of both evergreen and deciduous plants, i.e. growth stops when the daylight is less than 12 to 16 hours depending upon the plant. Incandescent light has its radiation primarily in the same region as the sun. Those lighted all night with an INC light were always taller than corresponding plants lighted with either HPS, F, MH, or Hg. High-pressure sodium (HPS) was second in effectiveness in extending photoperiodic responses in plants. Mercury was relatively inactive, except on catalpa and sycamore. Red radiant energy emitted by fluorescent lamps inhibited flowering of short-day plants and promoted flowering of long-day plants. If the leaf pigment remained predominantly in the red-absorbing form for an appreciable time during each dark period, woody plants stopped growth and became dormant, because the amount of the active form of the pigment, the far-red form, was inadequate.

Alternative light sources should be considered for some locations. High-pressure sodium lamps could be used in parking lots, streets, and malls in which nonsensitive plants would be used. Lighting of parks and buildings that are landscaped with green plants could be done with MH lamps. Although less efficient than HPS lamps, MH lamps are much less active photoperiodically than HPS, but still are an efficient HID light source. MH has good color rendition of plants, buildings, and people, but emits some blue light, which is attractive to night-flying insects. Incandescent lamps for lighting the landscape should be avoided under all circumstances; they actively regulate the growth of most plant species and can prolong growth through the later summer and fall thereby maximizing the chance of plant injury from autumn frosts. Alternatives should be considered to reduce effects of existing light sources. One way would be to use improved shielded luminaires to direct the light onto the pedestrians and the vehicular traffic and away from the plants (Andresen 1976).

The selection of plants for use in the landscape becomes more critical when one takes into account the possibility of growth-regulating effects from lighting. The landscape architect should avoid placing extremely photo-responsive plants such as *Betula* and *Platanus* in locations where artificial light levels are high. Other species such as *Pinus* and *Acer* appear to be much more suitable for planting in such areas. In nature, the plant's age, its site, and its maintenance would affect profoundly its sensitivity to light. Many of our street trees at maturity become dormant by midsummer, thus are not vulnerable to artificial light at night. The responsiveness of the plants is complicated further by the intensity of the light and the ambient night temperature. When combined with the site and maintenance, an extremely complex environmental situation is created. Detailed studies in the urban environment are needed to determine which species of plants are affected under which circumstances.

In general and under urban conditions there probably is a strong linkage in trees between resistance to post-dormancy response to artifical light and low-temperature hardiness. Preliminary experiments with woody plants indicate that temperature and light operate independently. However low night temperatures may prevent the long-day effect from being exhibited. Wareing (1956) reported that when European ecotypes of *Salix*, *Betula*, *Populus*, *Ribes*, and *Vaccinium* were introduced from southern latitudes to regions of high latitude, they suffered from autumn frosts because of extended growth under laboratory conditions. Particular attention should be given to species that possess extensive latitudinal range, such as the North American *Acer saccharum*, *A. rubrum*, *Carpinus caroliniana*, *Ostrya virginiana*, *Betula nigra*, and *Fagus grandifolia*. Of these, *A. rubrum* appears to be especially responsive to photoperiods (Andresen, 1976).

SELECTION OF TREES TOLERANT OF DROUGHT AND HEAT:

Temperature is the best documented component of meteorological differences between urban and rural landscapes. Urban conditions produce a consistently higher temperature by 2 to 5 degrees C than that of rural areas. City-scapes contribute to thermal accretion in several ways: (1) additive surface area of buildings with large horizontal and vertical faces, and paving for vehicular and pedestrian circulation traffics provides suitable conditions for substantial exchanges of energy with high conductivities, heat capacities, and albedos; (2) cities generate supplemental heat because of human metabolism, traffic, industrial activities, domestic heating, and air-conditioning condensers; and (3) impervious surfaces of the city structure lead to a rapid drain of rain and snow, fundamentally altering moisture and heat budgets. Infrared radiation reaching trees from adjacent emitters heats the surfaces, especially of bark, to temperatures similar to the source. If tree tissues are already under moisture stress, such temperatures have a damaging, sometimes lethal, effect (Andresen 1976).

For this discussion of the capacity of trees and shrubs to resist detrimental effects from heat and drought of metropolitan centers, the terms thermotolerance and thermoavoidance are helpful.

Thermotolerance, a synonym for heat resistance or thermoresistance, is the ability of trees, shrubs, and other woody plants to survive heat stress on internal tissues. Thermoavoidance or heat avoidance, on the other hand, suggests the ability to adjust to or resist lethal or injurious external infrared radiation. Heat avoidance can occur through (1) insulation, (2) respiration, (3) reflection of radiant energy, and (4) transpiration cooling. The last two have the most importance. Glabrous leaves and white-colored bark seem most effective in reflecting radiation of 775 to 1100 nm (infrared wavelengths). Transmissibility also plays a role in decreased absorption; that is, thin, pale-green leaves transmit more radiant energy than thick, dark-green leaves (Andresen 1976).

In general and under urban conditions there is a strong linkage in trees between heat resistance and drought resistance. The dehydration of trees results from high transpiration rates or slow absorption of water from dry, poorly aerated or cold soils or, more commonly, from both high transpiration and relatively low absorption rates. Temporary water deficits and leaf-wilting often occur in the afternoon because of excess transpiration over absorption. This is not serious if the soil is well watered because the leaves rehydrate and recover turgidity at night when absorption exceeds transpiration. However, as soil dries over a period of days, temporary water deficits in trees tend to persist longer each successive day because leaves are less likely to recover turgidity at night. Water deficits in trees affect virtually all important physiological processes, including stomatal closure, photosynthesis, metabolism, mineral relations, and growth (Andresen 1976).

The closure of stomatal pores is a very early response to drought. As the guard cells lose water and turgidity decreases, the stomatal pores close. The dehydration of trees is controlled somewhat by earlier closure of stomata during each day of a developing drought and by temporary closure of stomata during the day. As leaves dehydrate and lose water they eventually wilt. Wilting varies in degree and may be classified as (1) incipient, (2) temporary, or (3) permanent. Incipient wilting does not cause drooping of leaves. Temporary wilting involves drooping of leaves during the day and recovery from wilting during the night. During a sustained drought, plants temporarily wilted may become permanently wilted. Such plants do not recover from wilting at night. Recovery from permanent wilting requires rewetting of the soil. Trees that stay in a state of permanent wilting for an extended period often die. Various tissues and organs of trees often are injured or killed by drought without necessarily killing the tree. Leaf responses to drought include curling, scorching, marginal browning, early autumn coloration, and premature leaf fall. Leaf drying often causes considerable winter injury to evergreens. During winter or early spring days, the air may warm and cause considerable transpiration at a time when water cannot be absorbed by roots from cold or frozen soil. They may cause the leaves to dry out and turn brown (Kozlowski 1976).

Drought avoidance is much more important in enabling trees to survive under conditions of aridity accelerated by high temperatures. The most important drought-avoiding adaptations of roots are capacity for extensive root growth (high root-shoot ratios). Because water in soil not penetrated by roots is largely unavailable to plants, trees with deeply penetrating and branching root systems absorb water most efficiently and prevent or postpone drought injury. There are many examples of the importance of a high root-shoot ratio, relatively high water-absorbing capacity and relatively low transpiration capacity (wet and wet-mesic species) to survival of trees under drought conditions. Planting of mesic tree species that have shallow-moisture demanding adventitious root systems should be limited (Kozlowski 1976).

Wide variations occur among species in stomatal responses to atmospheric factors (for example, high temperature, high light intensity, low humidity, and wind) which induce water deficits in trees. For example, experiments were conducted on species that occur along an ecological gradient from xeric to mesic. These included *Quercus macrocarpa*, *Q. velutina*, *Q. alba*, *Q. rubra*, and *Acer saccharum*. All species showed an increase in transpiration with increased leaf temperature. The rate of increase of transpiration resistance with rise in leaf temperature was greatest for *Q. velutina*, intermediate for *Q. macrocarpa* and *Q. rubra*, and least for *Q. alba* and *Acer saccharum*. Water use efficiency (the ratio of transpiration to photosynthesis) increased with leaf temperature up to 35 degrees C and decreased at higher temperatures. Water use efficiency was greatest in *Quercus velutina*, intermediate in *Q. macrocarpa*, *Q. rubra*, and *Q. alba*, and least in *Acer saccharum*. At 40 degrees C, water use efficiency of *Q. velutina* declined only slightly, but in the other four species it decreased greatly. These experiments showed that stomatal resistance decreased along the gradient from xerophytic to meophytic species. In particular it emphasized that *Q. velutina* had the highest water-use efficiency and was the most drought-resistant species studied. It fixed CO_2 rapidly while losing little water and therefore was successful on hot and dry sites (Kozlowski 1976).

SELECTION OF TREES TOLERANT OF MINE SPOILS:

Mining of a wide variety of metals, industrial minerals and coal takes place in midwestern and eastern North America. The largest amount of environmental disruption has been caused by the surface mining of coal, iron, base metals (copper, lead and zinc) and gypsum. Deposited on the landscape are mine spoils in the United States which vary greatly in their physical characteristics from one region to another and even within regions depending on mining procedures. The demand for surface mined materials continues to increase. Continued growth in electrical power requirements of the nation dictates, for example, the need for new coal sources and electrical generating plants. The dependence of the United States on foreign oil imports and accompanying oil price hikes, experienced in the early 1970's, encourages the development of coal as an alternate energy source because of its relatively low cost of mining and extensive minable deposits. Consequently, coal production in many of the major producing states of the east and west is accelerating every year, and projections are for greater expansions in production to continue for the next several decades. The rate of land disturbance for many purposes has increased rapidly during the past few years. The public demands that disturbed areas be returned to beneficial uses, that environmenal quality be maintained or improved, and that reclaimed areas are aesthetically pleasing. The demands of present-day society are expressed in recent reclamation laws of many states to stabilize the soil, to reduce sediment and runoff to adjacent land and downstream areas, to enhance natural beauty, and to return the land to some useful purpose are the objectives of such legislation. ·

The major soil limitations for vegetative purposes are droughtiness, coarse textures, claypan soils, wetness, salinity, alkalinity, acidity, shallow depth, and toxicity, or severe nutrient imbalance. Slope, stoniness, degree of erosion, and the amount of surface materials available for reclamation, are also important within the climatic range of adaptation of each species.

Water is perhaps the most important raw material used in tree growth, at least with regard to quantity for survival and growth. Most mine spoils contain a large amount of coarse fragments (2mm in diameter), some as much as 80% by volume. This results in low water holding capacity. The normal condition of spoil banks (steep slopes, slaty shale surfaces and excessively exposed sites) makes them poor interceptors and conservers of rainwater. Excessive runoff and erosion are major adverse effects of surface mining. Surface mining can greatly affect streamflow, sediment load, and water quality of streams. Problems with stormflow, erosion and sedimentation usually are more serious with contour stripping than with area type surface mining. Erosion and subsequent sedimentation destroy aquatic life in the streams below mined watersheds. Even after several years of successful establishment and growth, trees are often washed out.

The second single most important problem and the most difficult to solve is that of low pH and factors associated with it. The rock wastes from metal mining are generally coarse with little sand-size material. The coal mining wastes are largely shales which have weathered to a gravel. The tailings wastes from the processing of iron and base metal ores are fine grained materials. Chemically all the wastes are low in nutrients and vary in pH from highly acid to alkaline. The more acid contain toxic amounts of heavy metals and sulphate. The base metal mine tailings high in sulphides (pyrite) have a pH below 4 and sometimes near 2. In these wastes dissolved heavy metal content and sulphate ions can reach 10,000 ppm. Plants cannot survive in such toxic conditions. Some species can be grown in the tailings from the iron metal and base metal mines where the sulphide content is low and pH neutral.

The oxidation of coal seams and coal waste piles causes an acid condition in the soil and water. When oxidation of this material is complete, no new acid is formed. Erosion exposes unoxidized material which then oxidizes large amounts of acid drainage to adjoining areas. The cause of the extreme acidity often found on coal-spoil banks has interested several investigators (Croxton 1928, Einspahr 1955, Kohnke 1950). Croxton noted that the oxidation of iron pyrites in coal-spoil materials in Illinois was the cause of the acidity found in his studies. Kohnke observed that roof coal and other strata of carboniferous age contained pyrites and other forms of iron sulphide and that the oxidation of these compounds, with the production of sulphuric acid, led to extremely acid conditions. Limstrom and Merz (1949) observed that spoils with pH 4.0 and lower were toxic to most trees.

The waste from gypsum operations is an unconsolidated overburden of glacial origin. It is the only type of mining where broken or finely crushed rock is not part of the mining waste. The pH of mined overburden remains essentially unchanged from that of the original soil. A wider variety of native plants grow on the gypsum wastes where adequate soil moisture regimes are found.

More recently, researchers have shown that the acidity and toxicity can be reduced or alleviated with various amendments. Adding lime or gypsum to acid spoils reduces the solubility of the toxic elements and usually helps to provide a suitable balance of calcium and magnesium for optimum plant growth. Covering acid spoil with topsoil is receiving popular support from many people. More research is needed to identify the problems and benefits of topsoiling before it is required by law as a standard reclamation practice in the United States.

Most of the early research was concerned with the forestation of spoils in the relatively gentle terrain in the midwest. Formal or designed reforestation research was conducted primarily by the Central States and Northeastern Forest Experiment Stations of the U. S. Forest Service. Tree planting experiments were made also by several of the State Agricultural Experiment Stations including Ohio, Indiana, Iowa, Pennsylvania, and West Virginia, and by a few individuals at other colleges. These reforestation studies identified species of planted trees that survived and grew best on a variety of surface mine spoils. This early research resulted in the publishing of lists of recommended species and tree planting guides in several of the mining states. These guides have been used in the planting of thousands of acres of mine spoil. Many of the recently published planting and revegetation guides still are based largely upon those earlier research publications. Unfortunately, most of the older tree planting experiments have not been reevaluated in recent years.

SELECTION OF TREES TOLERANT OF SALT SPRAY:

The extensive use of deicing salts in urban environments in northern states has created a synthetic saline environment frequently resulting in significant plant injury. Approximately 12 million tons of salt are applied to northeastern U.S. highways per year. In severe winters, Chicago freeways reportedly received as much as 80 tons per lane mile. On 6 lane freeways the amounts total 480 tons per mile. Metropolitan areas receive the greatest quantities of salts: in Illinois approximately 272 metric tons (300,000 tons) were applied to state maintained roads during the winter of 1969-70, and Chicago freeways received about 20 percent of this. Along Chicago freeways plant injury was evident as far as 150 to 200 feet from the pavement's edge. The two principal deicing salts are sodium chloride (NaCl) and calcium chloride ($CaCl_2$).

Plants growing along highways, on lawns, and along sidewalks exhibit stem dieback, and many are killed. The salts are deposited by aerial drift on dormant buds and twigs of deciduous trees and on twigs, buds, and foliage of evergreen species or by excess accumulation of salts that leach into the root zone. Most authorities attributed the greatest percentage of injury to aerial deposition. General injury patterns are most severe on the side of the plant facing the road. Plants appear one sided due to branch dieback. Na and Cl ions are aerially deposited on plants, penetrating the stems, buds, and leaves. The basis for plant resistance to salt spray is not known. Dirr (1977) suggests that the degree of salt tolerance among woody plants depends on their ability to preclude Cl, and possibly Na, from entering cells and tissues. He speculated that the salt tolerance of Common Honeylocust under highway conditions was attributable to the inability of the Na and Cl ions to penetrate the waxy branches and partially embedded buds in the stem of dormant trees. Plants with naked buds (lacking scales) were observed to be highly susceptible to salt spray. Lumis and others (1973) noted that increased amounts of wax (bloom) on spruce needles added to their protection, because the bluer the spruce the more resistant it was found to be (Dirr, 1976).

Several woody species exhibit resistance to abnormal salt levels. The plants identified in Table VI have been reported to be salt-tolerant by various authorities. Such a list should significantly assist the environmental planner and ensure success for municipal programs which depend on plants tolerant to salt and other pollutants. Trees with the highest degree of tolerance should be used in the most exposed areas and those of moderate tolerance in low salt areas. Sensitive species should be restricted to areas where salts are not a problem.

SELECTION OF TREES TOLERANT OF SOIL COMPACTION:

Soils are very complex, naturally formed entities that vary widely with the natural landscape. The principal mineral fractions are sand, silt and clay. These three fractions combined form roughly 45 percent of a hypothetical "ideal" soil for plant growth. The remaining 55 percent is composed of 5 percent organic matter (decaying and decayed plant parts, organisms, etc.), 25 percent air space (N_2 forming 79.2 percent of the soil atmosphere, O_2 20.6 percent and CO_2 0.2 percent), and 25 percent water or moisture. Pore space, ideally 50 percent composed of equal amounts of air and water space, fluctuates widely depending upon rainfall, humidity, temperature, soil structure and compaction or use (Patterson 1976).

Generally sands and loamy sand have a range of available water from 7.5 to 40 percent, moderate-textured soils from 10 to 18 percent, and clay loam to clayey soils from 11 to 14 percent (Peterson and others 1968).

In areas of intensive human use, the soil characteristic that seems to be the best single barometer of soil conditions is bulk density. Bulk density has been used as the index of compaction. Pore space is the portion of the soil matrix that is directly and adversely affected by heavy use. Pore size and distribution does not remain constant, but is altered by compaction, cultivation, aggregation, fertilization, etc. Good permeabilities for water and air occur with a variety and continuity of pore space. Pores initially affected by compaction were the very large macropores, $150\text{-}50\mu$. With a reduction of macropores, there is an increase in number of pores less than 10μ—pores that provide very low permeabilities for water and air. Total pore space can be calculated when the bulk density (BD) and particle densities (PD) are known: (100 - BD/PD) x 100 = total percent pore space (Patterson 1976).

As bulk density increases, the maximum aeration decreases and becomes the most limiting factor to root elongation. Root elongation and root penetration into soils of high bulk densities is restricted to the naturally occurring cracks rather than within the soil matrix. When the compaction is severe enough to reduce air space to less than 15 percent, root growth becomes restricted; and less than 2 percent air space results in essentially no root growth. 20 percent air space is needed for adequate gaseous exchange between the soil and the atmosphere (Patterson 1976).

Oxygen in the soil profile is the key to regulating plant growth. When the oxygen content of soil drops below 10 percent by volume, growth of Scotch Pine and Norway Spruce seedlings is drastically reduced. When the oxygen concentration drops below 10 percent, Lodgepole Pine growth was severely limited. He observed that oxygen was required for root extension in these plants. Similarly, containerized plantings commonly used in urban areas require adequate soil aeration.

Within the soil profile the principal movement of oxygen and carbon dioxide is through diffusion. An inverse relationship exists between concentrations of oxygen and carbon dioxide in the soil. In the surface soil, oxygen will generally predominate over carbon dioxide. With increased depth in the soil profile, the relationship is altered so that carbon dioxide begins to predominate over oxygen. Yelenosky (1963, 1964) found that, under poor aeration the oxygen concentration drops to as low as 1 percent, while the carbon dioxide content rises to 10 percent or higher. Soil aeration can be reduced by a layer of fill clay over existing soil, by compaction (as from heavy use or heavy construction impact), or by a paving operation. Under those treatments the soil atmosphere changes from aerobic to anaerobic, and the change can, seemingly, occur within a growing season. Once an area becomes compacted, recreation of an aerobic soil condition is difficult. Pavements cause the soil atmosphere to change from aerobic to anaerobic, thereby reducing the vigor of plants. Pavements prevent gaseous exchange with the atmosphere, and a general anaerobic condition occurs beneath pavements. Normal gaseous exchange between the soil and the atmosphere is necessary for tree roots and microbes to respire. This exchange can be interrupted by pavements and compaction, thus retarding root growth essential to tree vigor (Patterson 1976).

Soil compaction and anaerobic conditions caused by paving, heavy use, and grade change due to soil addition do cause an unfavorable rooting environment for most trees. Differences exist in the tolerance of tree species and of individuals within species to compacted conditions. Plants most suited to such conditions have undergone some selection simply through survival of adapted species. The most significant research data on soil compaction to date is related to flood studies which evaluates flood tolerances of native woody species (Hall and Smith 1955). Air pore space becomes 100 percent saturated which terminates gaseous exchange between soil and atmosphere. For example, in a controlled study, Tuliptree seedlings were not adversely affected by flooding for 14 days during the dormant season, but mortality occurred after 4 days of flooding in May or 3 days in June. In contrast, Green Ash and Sweetgum seedlings were not affected by up to 14 days of flooding during any month, and the short term flooding seemed beneficial rather than detrimental to their growth. Data on bulk density and pore space in these samples verified the inadequate pore space for air exchange. However, much research still needs to be done as a basis for selecting suitable species or cultivars (Patterson 1976).

High bulk density and low amount of pore space seem to exist in most urban soils examined and probably form the most restrictive characteristic of urban soils for plant growth (Patterson 1977). Other characteristics observed by Patterson as common in urban soils are extreme heterogeneity from area to area, variability in percentages of organic matter with profile depth, unoriented coarse fragments (rock and stones), highly variable fertility and pH, a wide variation in textural distribution (percent of sand, silt and clay) with depth of profile, and a tendency for the compacted soils to repel moisture. Patterson (1977) conducted an experiment to determine "urban soils density." Four commonly used construction materials were tested: cinder block, brick, asphalt, and concrete. The data revealed that most urban soils are indeed as dense as concrete! Soil renovation is difficult once trees are established—because of the predominance of roots in the surface A_1 and A_2 soil horizons.

Soil compaction imposes severe stress upon urban vegetation. Treatments tested by the Ecological Services Laboratory of the National Capital Parks have produced a significant reduction in soil compaction as measured by bulk density. Lightweight aggregates rotary-tilled into plots reduced soil compaction, even though the area was continually used. Composts of leaves, wood chips, and sewage sludge help to reduce compaction of urban soils and also increase their fertility and content of organic matter. Wood chips, when used on heavily compacted soils in shaded areas, reduce damage to soil and to tree roots from continued heavy use. Such applications of organic materials aid the development of a "natural" soil profile. Soil amendments in order of effectiveness (Patterson 1977) used in recent National Park studies included sintered fly-ash (a light weight aggregate with about 70% pore space), expanded slate (a heat expanded slate with about 50 percent pore space), coarse construction sand, and digested sewage sludge. The best treatment gave an increase of 7 percent for pore space in the rooting zone over a four year period under continued heavy use. Some work has been done in an attempt to reduce the adverse effect of high bulk densities through application of gypsum. Gypsum increases aggregation and porosity while reducing the bulk density of the surface soil (Patterson 1976).

Effective soil amendments offer only a partial solution for alleviating some of the deleterious effects of compaction. Although there are means available to help recreate an aerobic soil atmosphere, prevention of poor aeration by the forecasting of potential compaction situations and taking proper protective measures during construction and use insures the longevity of aerobic soil conditions. This should be the measure of all environmental designers to insure quality landscape health and richer landscape experience (Patterson, 1976).

ROOT STRUCTURE:

The roots of a plant perform two primary functions. The vertical taproot and the network of lateral roots branching from it anchor and brace the crown. Root tips and root hairs filter and draw in a steady supply of oxygen, water, and minerals which nourishes the growth of the crown structure overhead. Generally trees have a tendency to develop root structure arrangements of three types (Table VI).

SHALLOW LATERAL:
dividing and redividing, the lateral roots form a fibrous mat up to four feet in depth and from 1½ to 3 times the reach of the crown. In general, shallow rooted trees like Black Maple are relatively fast growing and easily transplanted. In the midwest, during periods of low precipitation or low available moisture in upper soil layers, shallow rooted plants suffer early injury. Prolonged drought can result in the eventual death of many individuals. Similarly, extensive damage results when soil is compacted forming an impermeable crust which greatly reduces oxygen and moisture in upper soil layers.

Plants Suitable for Urban Environments — Table VI

Legend: ● sensitive ◐ intermediate ○ resistant (▓ = filled root-pattern bar)

	Atmospheric Pollutants									Other Factors				Root Pattern			
	Sulfur dioxide	Ozone	Oxides of nitrogen	Peroxyacetyl nitrate	Hydrogen fluoride	Hydrogen chloride	Ethylane	Particulates	2,4-D	Light	Heat-drought	Mine spoils	Salt	Soil compaction	Shallow lateral	Deep lateral	Taproot
Abies balsamea	◐	○				○					●	◐	●	○	▓		
Abies concolor	◐	◐									◐	◐	◐	●	▓		
Abies lasiocarpa											◐	◐	◐	●	▓		
Acer negundo	◐	◐			●	●			●	●	○	○	◐	○		▓	
Acer nigrum	○	○				○				◐	●	●	●	●	▓		
Acer pensylvanicum											●	●	●	●	▓		
Acer rubrum	◐	○				○				●	○	◐	●	○	▓		
Acer saccharinum	○	●			◐	○					○	○	◐	◐		▓	
Acer saccharum	○	○		○		●				◐	●	●	●	●	▓		
Acer spicatum	○										●	●	●	●	▓		
Aesculus glabra										◐	◐			◐			▓
Aesculus octandra											●	●		◐			▓
Alnus rugosa											●		●	○	▓		
Amelanchier canadensis	●	●			◐						●	●	○	●	▓		
Amelanchier laevis	●	●			◐						●	●	●	●	▓		
Aralia spinosa										○	○			◐	▓		
Asimina triloba											●	◐	●	●		▓	
Betula lenta	●	○				○			●	●	●	◐	◐	●	▓		
Betula lutea	●	○				○			●	●	●	●	●	●	▓		
Betula nigra									●	●	○		○	○	▓		
Betula papyrifera	●	○			○	○			●	●	◐	◐	○	●	▓		
Betula populifolia	●	○				○			●	●	◐	○	○	○	▓		
Carpinus caroliniana	○		●		◐					●	●	●		●		▓	
Carya cordiformis									●		◐	●	●	◐			▓
Carya glabra									●		○	○	●	●			▓

104

Plants Suitable for Urban Environments — Table VI

Legend: ● sensitive, ◐ intermediate, ○ resistant

	Atmospheric Pollutants									Other Factors				Root Pattern			
	Sulfur dioxide	Ozone	Oxides of nitrogen	Peroxyacetyl nitrate	Hydrogen fluoride	Hydrogen chloride	Ethylane	Particulates	2,4-D	Light	Heat-drought	Mine spoils	Salt	Soil compaction	Shallow lateral	Deep lateral	Taproot
Carya illinoensis									●		◐	◐	●	◐			▓
Carya ovata									●		○	◐	●	◐			▓
Carya tomentosa									●		○	○	●	●			▓
Castanea dentata					◐						◐	◐		●			▓
Catalpa speciosa	●	●								●	○	○	◐	○			
Celtis occidentalis											○	○	○	◐	▓	▓	
Cercis canadensis		●									○	○	●	◐	▓	▓	
Chionanthus virginicus											●	●		●		▓	
Cladrastis lutea									●		●	●		●		▓	
Cornus alternifolia									●		●	●		◐	▓		
Cornus florida	○	○			○				●	●	◐	◐		●	▓		
Cotinus americanus											○	○		●			▓
Crataegus crusgalli	○										○	○	○	◐		▓	
Crataegus mollis	○										○	○	●	◐		▓	
Crataegus nitida	○										○	○	●	◐		▓	
Crataegus phaenopyrum	○										○	○	●	◐		▓	
Crataegus pruinosa	○										○	○	●	◐		▓	
Crataegus punctata	○										○	○	●	◐		▓	
Diospyros virginiana											○	○		◐			▓
Euonymus atropurpureus											◐	◐		○	▓		
Fagus grandifolia	○	○								●	●	●	●	●			
Franklinia alatamaha																▓	
Fraxinus americana		●							○	○	◐	◐	◐	◐	▓		
Fraxinus nigra									○	○	○	○	◐	○	▓		
Fraxinus pennsylvanica	●	●			◐				○	○	○	○	○	○	▓		

Plants Suitable for Urban Environments — Table VI

Legend: ● sensitive ◐ intermediate ○ resistant (▓ = root pattern present)

	Atmospheric Pollutants									Other Factors				Root Pattern			
	Sulfur dioxide	Ozone	Oxides of nitrogen	Peroxyacetyl nitrate	Hydrogen fluoride	Hydrogen chloride	Ethylane	Particulates	2,4-D	Light	Heat-drought	Mine spoils	Salt	Soil compaction	Shallow lateral	Deep lateral	Taproot
Fraxinus quadrangulata									○	○	○	○	◐	◐	▓		
Gleditsia triacanthos		●									○	○	○	○	▓	▓	▓
Gymnocladus dioicus											○	○				▓	
Halesia carolina											●	●	●	●			
Hamamelis virginiana											●	●	●	●			
Juglans cinerea											◐	●	●	◐			
Juglans nigra		○			◐						○	○	●	◐			▓
Juniperus virginiana	○	○			○						○	○	○	●			
Larix laricina	●	●			●	●					○	○	○	◐	▓		
Liquidambar styraciflua		◐				●			◐	◐	◐			○	▓	▓	
Liriodendron tulipifera	○	●		●						●	●	◐		●	▓		
Maclura pomifera											○	○		●			
Magnolia acuminata											●	●	●	●	▓		
Malus ioensis	●					●		●			○	○	◐	◐	▓		
Morus rubra	●	●			◐			◐			○	○	○	◐	▓		▓
Nyssa sylvatica	○	○				◐					○	○	○	◐			▓
Ostrya virginiana										◐	◐			●			▓
Oxydendrum arboreum	○									◐	◐			●			
Picea engelmanni	●									○	●	●		●	▓		
Picea glauca	◐	○	●	○	◐					○	◐	◐	○	◐	▓		
Picea glauca densata		○								○	○	○	○	●	▓		
Picea mariana										○	○	○		○	▓		
Picea pungens	○	○	●	○	●				◐	○	●	●	◐	●	▓		
Pinus banksiana	●	●			○	◐				○	○	○	○	●	▓		
Pinus flexilis	○									○	○	○	○	●			

Plants Suitable for Urban Environments — Table VI

Legend: ● sensitive · ◐ intermediate · ○ resistant

	Atmospheric Pollutants									Other Factors				Root Pattern			
	Sulfur dioxide	Ozone	Oxides of nitrogen	Peroxyacetyl nitrate	Hydrogen fluoride	Hydrogen chloride	Ethylane	Particulates	2,4-D	Light	Heat-drought	Mine spoils	Salt	Soil compaction	Shallow lateral	Deep lateral	Taproot
Pinus ponderosa	●		●		●					○	○	○	◐	●			■
Pinus resinosa		○								○	◐	◐	●	●		■	
Pinus rigida		●			○					○	○	○	○	●			■
Pinus strobus	●	●	●	●	○	●	●			○	●	◐	●	●			■
Platanus occidentalis	○	●			○				●	●	○	○		○	■		
Populus deltoides	○									●	○	○	○	○	■	■	
Populus grandidentata	◐										◐	○	◐	●	■	■	
Populus tremuloides	●	●			◐					●	◐	○	○	●		■	
Prunus americana						●					○	○	○	●		■	
Prunus pensylvanica						●					○	○	○	●		■	
Prunus serotina						◐					○	○	○	●		■	■
Prunus virginiana	◐				◐	●					○	○	○	●		■	
Pseudotsuga taxifolia	◐	○		○	◐						◐	●	◐	●		■	
Ptelea trifoliata											○	○	○	●		■	
Quercus alba	◐	●			◐	○				◐	○	◐	○	●		■	
Quercus bicolor											○	◐		○	■	■	
Quercus borealis	○	○			◐	○			◐	◐	◐	●	○	●		■	
Quercus coccinea		◐			◐						○	○		●		■	
Quercus ellipsoidalis											○	○		●		■	
Quercus imbricaria		○			◐	○					○	○		◐		■	
Quercus macrocarpa		○			◐	○					○	○	○	●			■
Quercus marilandica											○	○	○	●		■	
Quercus montana										◐	○	◐	○	●		■	
Quercus muhlenbergi											○	○		●	■		■
Quercus palustris	○	◐			◐	●			◐		○	◐		○	■	■	

107

Plants Suitable for Urban Environments — Table VI

Legend: ● sensitive · ◐ intermediate · ○ resistant (root-type columns: ■ indicates root pattern)

	Atmospheric Pollutants									Other Factors				Root Pattern			
	Sulfur dioxide	Ozone	Oxides of nitrogen	Peroxyacetyl nitrate	Hydrogen fluoride	Hydrogen chloride	Ethylane	Particulates	2,4-D	Light	Heat-drought	Mine spoils	Salt	Soil compaction	Shallow lateral	Deep lateral	Taproot
Quercus stellata										◐	○	○		●			■
Quercus velutina		◐			◐				●		○	○		●		■	■
Rhododendron maximum					◐						●	●		●			
Rhus copallina										●	○	○	○	●			
Rhus glabra	○				◐					●	○	○	○	●			
Rhus typhina	●				◐					●	○	○	○	●			
Robinia pseudoacacia	○	●	●		◐					●	○	○	○	●			
Salix amygdaloides	●	●			◐						○	○	○	○	■		
Salix bebbiana	●	●			○						○	○	○	○	■		
Salix discolor	●	●			○						○	○	○	○	■		
Salix nigra	●	●			○						○	○	◐	○	■		
Sassafras albidum							●				○	○		○			■
Sorbus decora	●	●			○						○	○	◐	◐			
Taxodium distichum														○	■		
Thuja occidentalis	○	○			◐	○	●			○	○	○	◐	○			
Tilia americana	◐	○	◐		○				●	●	●	●		●		■	
Tsuga canadensis		●		○		○			◐	●	●	●	●	●	■	■	
Ulmus americana	●				○					●	○	○	◐	◐	■	■	
Viburnum lentago											○	○	●	●			
Viburnum prunifolium										○	○	○	●	●			
Viburnum rufidulum											○	○	●	●			
Zanthoxylum americanum											○	○		●			

DEEP LATERAL:

in many species, like Eastern Poplar, the taproot of a youthful sapling soon stops growing when intermediate to deep penetrating lateral roots are large enough to take over. Since these roots are often voracious, use near open tile fields, irrigation systems, etc. is not recommended.

TAPROOT:

trees whose deep carrot-like taproot may grow to a depth of 15 feet or more. Plants having deep tap or lateral root systems are considerably more tolerant of drought because root penetration is to a depth where moisture is available from ground water sources. Die back is not so soon affected by soil compaction or drought. Transplanting of wild trees such as Shagbark Hickory is very difficult and limited to small saplings where sufficient root structure can be retained.

ASSOCIATE SPECIES:

Each assemblage of vegetation that is homogeneous and differs from adjacent vegetation assemblages constitutes a *stand*. All stands in which the dominant species are essentially the same comprise an *association* (Daubenmire 1968). It is important to recognize that although no two stands grouped into one association are identical, they do exhibit a high degree of similarity. This similarity is quantifiable and can be classified. A plant association then is a kind of plant community of definite composition presenting a uniform appearance and growing in uniform suitable habitat conditions.

The association concept is a useful guide to the environmental planner. After a series of habitat types have been inventoried within the project area, each can be managed in complimentary fashion to utilize the landscape resource most efficiently. A habitat type is not equally favorable for all plant associations. Growth and survivability for a particular association vary significantly from one habitat type to another. Plant associations likewise can be used as indicators to confirm potential habitat, since the vegetation community and its environment are inseparable.

As a rule, the random distribution of a single species has little fundamental significance in determining habitat. Where two or more species exhibit similar distribution patterns, however, the designer may suspect intrinsic differences in environmental tolerance. Optimal management demands recognition of all habitat types in an area. Conscientious land use policy must reflect these unique environmental potentialities. Knowing the correlation between specific associations and their specific habitat tolerances is essential.

The common associates are cross referenced with each tree species catalogued in the master plates. As previously discussed the forest, savanna, and grassland biomes of eastern and central North America have been divided further into northern and central regions because of difference in floristic composition and most suitable habitat. Red Maple, for example, is common to both forest regions. In the glaciated northern forest region it is commonly associated with Black Ash, Gray, Yellow and Paper Birch, Pin Cherry, American Elm, White Pine and Red Spruce. Throughout the central region common associates include Sugar and Black Maple, American Beech, Northern Red Oak and American Linden.

SIMILAR SPECIES:

The designer, landscape contractor and nurseryman are frequently faced with the task of proposing a comparable substitute when difficulties with nursery availability of the selected plant are incurred. Too often substitutes are suggested whose performance is perceivably incompatible with the original program intent. Such changes in a viable program function are unacceptable to the environmental designer. Substitute species whose genetic or ornamental properties and physiographic requirements most closely resembling those of the selected plant are presented for designer consideration. Critical differences are also reviewed.

SPECIES CULTIVARS:

Several of the more popular contemporary hybrids developed from the native trees are listed and principal variations outlined for expanded designer consideration in special performance situations.

TREE
MASTER PLATES

Abies balsamea

FORM: **conical,** spire-like
Size: **small canopy** - 15 to 22.5 m (50 to 75 ft)
Spread: **narrow** - 6 to 10 m (20 to 35 ft), commonly 3 to 6 m, 1/8 to 1/5 the height
Mass: very **dense**

BRANCHING: central trunk, stiff **horizontal,** branched to ground, **medium** texture
Twig: moderately stout, conspicuous resin blisters, circular leaf scar, tomentose, **green gray**
Bud: **clustered, blunt rounded,** commonly in 3's, **resinous,** yellow brown
Bark: juvenile **smooth** with resin blisters, **shallow furrowed** with **narrow** horny ridges at maturity; **red brown**

FOLIAGE: spirally arranged, **acicular,** flat, blunt rounded at tip, crowded along upper sides of twig, **fine** texture
Surface: **glossy,** with white stomatic bands beneath, aromatic balsam odor
Color: spring - **light green;** summer, autumn, winter - **dark green**
Season: coniferous **evergreen**

FLOWER: erect **cone,** borne in very top of crown
Color: female - red **purple,** male - **yellow**
Season: mid through late **May**
Sex: monoecious

FRUIT: resinous erect **cone,** 5 to 10 cm (2 to 4 in) tall, scales shed on tree leaving central stalk
Color: dark violet when young, **purple brown** at maturity
Season: mid **July through** mid **October**
Wildlife Value: **high;** songbirds, small mammals, hoofed browsers

HABITAT: formation - **forest;** region - **northern;** gradient - **lowland wet, wet mesic and upland mesic;** swamp, bog, mesic
north and east slope aspects, moist steep rocky land, areas of cool air drainage
Shade Tolerance: **very tolerant;** index range 8.0 to 10.0, most shade tolerant fir
Flood Tolerance: **tolerant**

SOIL; Texture: **coarse to moderately fine;** gravels and sands, loamy sands, loams, silt loam, clay loam
Drainage: **very poor to well**
Moisture: demands **wet to moist**
Reaction: **strongly acid to slightly acid,** pH 4.0 to 6.5

HARDINESS: **zone 2**
Rate: **slow** - 10 to 15 cm (4 to 6 in) a year
Longevity: **medium** - maturity reached at 125 to 175 years

SUSCEPTIBILITY; Physiological: **infrequent**
Disease: **infrequent** - several canker diseases
Insect: **infrequent** - spruce budworm, woolly aphid cause problems
Wind-Ice: **frequent** - subject to windfall in shallow soils

URBAN TOLERANCE; Pollution: **intermediate** - SO$_2$; **resistant** - O$_3$, HCl, Cl
Lighting: Drought-Heat: **sensitive** Mine Spoils: **sensitive**
Salt: most **sensitive** fir Soil Compaction: **resistant**
Root Pattern: **shallow,** lateral spreading; transplants readily B&B as small tree in early spring

SPECIES; Associate: pure stands, lowland-Black Spruce, Eastern Arborvitae, Black Ash, American Larch; upland-Eastern
White Pine, Striped, Mountain, Red and Sugar Maples, Showy Mountain Ash, Quaking Aspen, Paper Birch
Similar: Canada Hemlock (not tolerant of poor soil drainage)
Cultivars: none available commercially

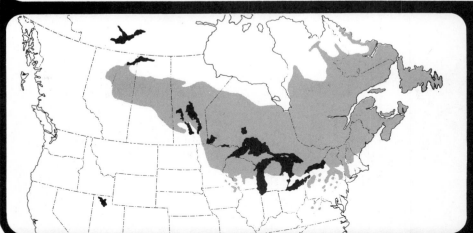

Balsam Fir

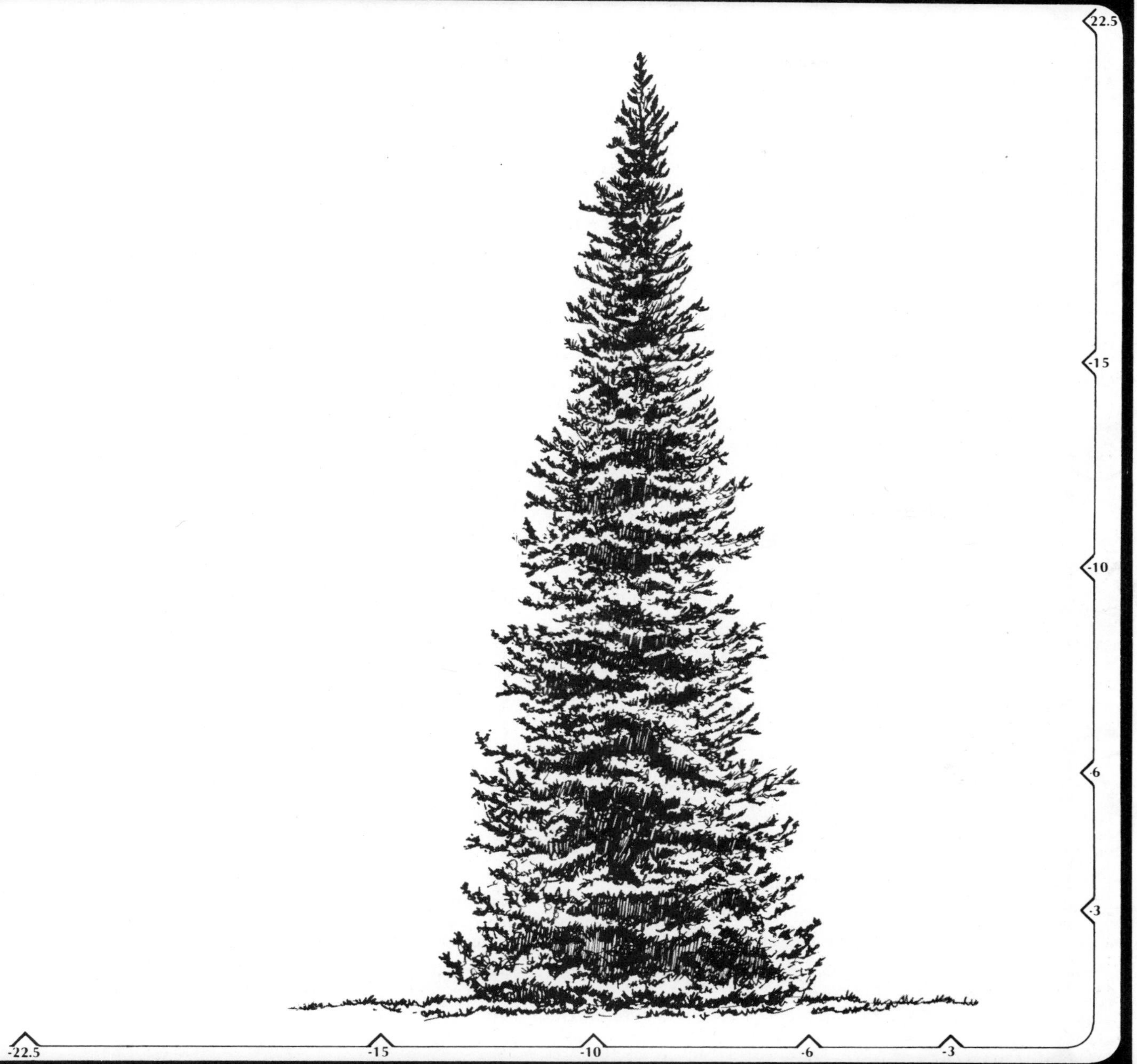

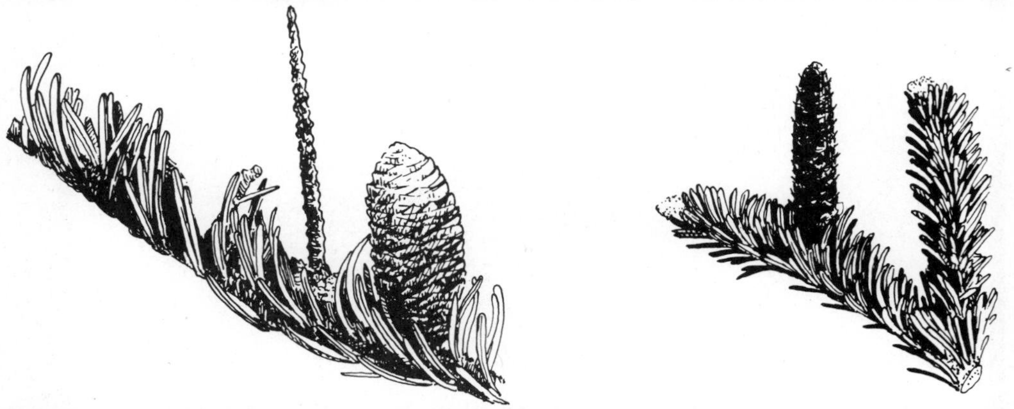

Abies concolor

FORM: conical
Size: **large canopy** - 22.5 to 30 m (75 to 100 ft)
Spread: **narrow** - 6 to 10 m (20 to 35 ft), 1/4 to 1/3 the height
Mass: very **dense**

BRANCHING: central trunk, stiff **horizontal**, branched to the ground, **medium** texture
Twig: moderately stout, conspicuous resin blisters, circular leaf scar, **green yellow**
Bud: **clustered, blunt rounded,** commonly in 3's, **resinous, yellow brown**
Bark: juvenile **smooth** with resin blisters, **shallow furrowed** with **narrow** horny flattened ridges at maturity; ashy **gray**

FOLIAGE: spirally arranged, **acicular,** flat, blunt rounded at tip, crowded along upper sides of twigs, **fine** texture
Surface: **dull**, aromatic
Color: all seasons - silvery **blue green** on both surfaces, yellow tip discoloration in winter, spring growth **silvery gray**
Season: coniferous **evergreen**

FLOWER: erect **cone,** born in very top of crown
Color: female - rose **red**
Season: mid through late **May**
Sex: monoecious

FRUIT: cylindrical erect **cone,** 7.5 to 12.5 cm (3 to 5 in) tall, scales shed on tree leaving central stalk
Color: olive green becoming **purple brown**
Season: mid **July through** mid **October**
Wildlife Value: **high;** songbirds, small mammals, hoofed browsers

HABITAT: formation - **forest** (mountain); region - western; gradient - **upland mesic dry;** moist to dry rocky slopes, along rocky streams, areas of cool air drainage
Shade Tolerance: **tolerant;** index range 6.0-7.9
Flood Tolerance: **intolerant**

SOIL; Texture: **moderately coarse to moderately fine;** gravelly and sandy loams, medium loams, does poorly on clays
Drainage: prefers **well,** tolerates **moderately poor**
Moisture: **moist to dry,** requires less moisture than other firs
Reaction: prefers **acidic;** pH 4.0-6.5

HARDINESS: **zone 4a**
Rate: **slow -** 10 to 15 cm (4 to 6 in) a year
Longevity: **long -** maturity at 300 years

SUSCEPTIBILITY; Physiological: **infrequent**
Disease: **infrequent** - few problems
Insect: **infrequent**
Wind-Ice: **frequent** - subject to windfall

URBAN TOLERANCE; Pollution: **intermediate** - SO_2, O_3
Lighting: Drought-Heat: **intermediate**   Mine Spoils: **intermediate**
Salt: **intermediate**   Soil Compaction: **sensitive**
Root Pattern: **shallow, lateral** spreading; transplants readily B&B as small tree in early spring

SPECIES; Associate: Ponderosa Pine, Limber Pine, Douglasfir, Quaking Aspen, Alpine Fir, occasionally with Engelmann and Colorado Spruce
Similar: Alpine Fir, Colorado Spruce and hybrids, Douglasfir
Cultivars: commercially available but not significantly different from species

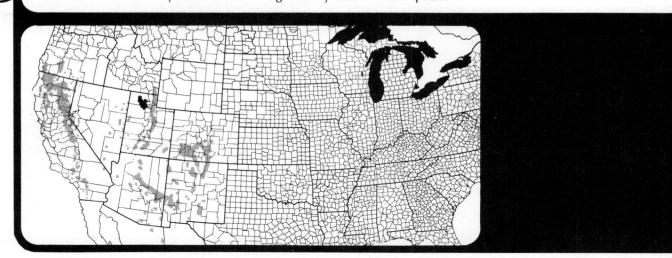

Abies lasiocarpa

FORM: **conical**, narrow spire-like
Size: **large canopy** - 22.5 to 30 m (75 to 100 ft)
Spread: **narrow** - 6 to 10 m (20 to 35 ft), 1/5 to 1/3 the height
Mass: very **dense**

BRANCHING: central trunk, stiff **horizontal**, branched to the ground, **medium** texture
Twig: moderately stout, conspicuous resin blisters, circular leaf scar, **green yellow**
Bud: **clustered, blunt rounded,** commonly in 3's, **resinous, yellow brown**
Bark: juvenile **smooth** with resin blisters, **shallow** furrowed with **narrow** horny ridges; ashy **gray**

FOLIAGE: spirally arranged, **acicular,** flat, blunt rounded at tip, crowded along upper side of twigs, **fine** texture
Surface: **dull,** aromatic
Color: all seasons - pale **bluish green** on both surfaces, new spring growth **silvery gray**
Season: coniferous **evergreen**

FLOWER: upright **cone,** born in very top of crown
Color: both sexes - **red purple,** male commonly indigo blue
Season: mid through late **May**
Sex: monoecious

FRUIT: cylindrical erect **cone,** 7.5 to 10 cm (3 to 4 in) tall, scales shed on tree leaving central stalk
Color: **purple brown**
Season: mid **July through** mid **October**
Wildlife Value: **high;** songbirds, small and large mammals, hoofed browsers

HABITAT: formation - **forest** (mountain); region - **western;** gradient - **upland mesic dry;** steep rocky land, along rocky
streams, areas of cool air drainage
Shade Tolerance: **very tolerant;** index range 8.0 to 10.0
Flood Tolerance: **intolerant**

SOIL; Texture: **moderately coarse to medium;** gravelly or sandy loams, medium loams, and silt loams
Drainage: **moderately poor to well**
Moisture: **moist to dry,** requires less moisture than most other fir species
Reaction: **acid;** pH ranges from 4.0-6.5

HARDINESS: zone 2 - 3a
Rate: **intermediate to slow** - 23 to 38 cm (9 to 15 in) per year for first 80 years in native habitat
Longevity: **long** - 200 years, trees over 250 years are common

SUSCEPTIBILITY; Physiological: **infrequent**
Disease: **infrequent** - Balsam Fir rust, several root rots
Insect: **infrequent** - spruce budworm, black headed budworm
Wind-Ice: **frequent** - subject to windfall

URBAN TOLERANCE; Pollution: **intermediate** - SO_2
Lighting: Drought-Heat: **intermediate** Mine Spoils: **intermediate**
Salt: **intermediate** Soil Compaction: **sensitive**
Root Pattern: **shallow** spreading or shallow taproot; transplants readily if moved as small tree B&B in early spring

SPECIES; Associate: Engelmann Spruce, White Spruce, Colorado Spruce, Quaking Aspen, Douglasfir, western
species of larch and pine
Similar: White Fir, Douglasfir, Colorado Spruce are most similar
Cultivars: none commerically available

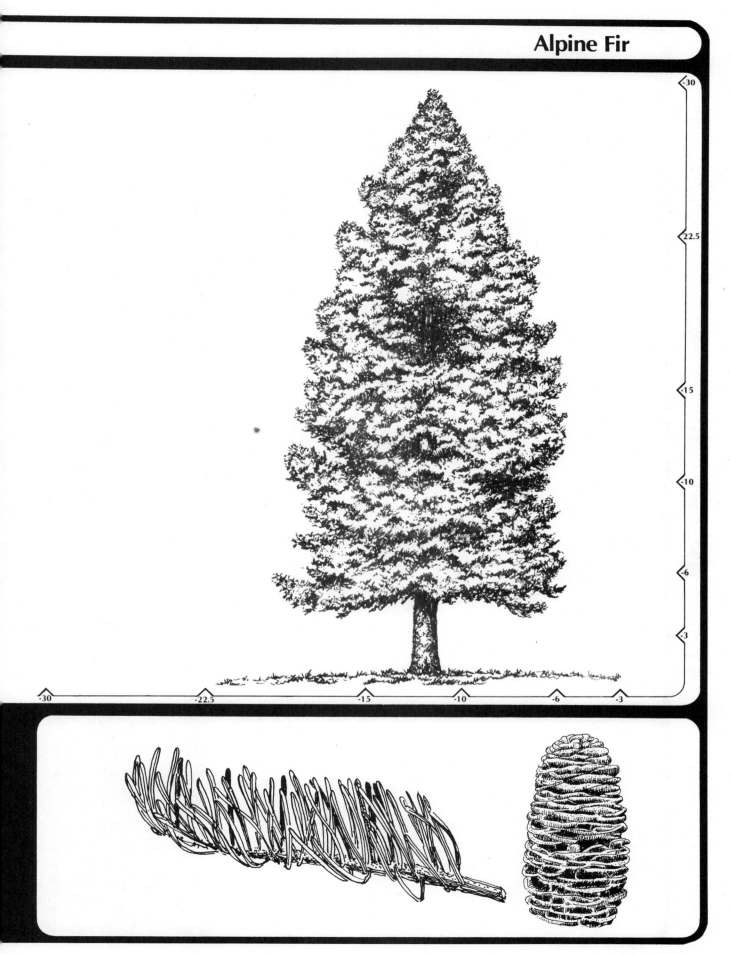

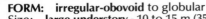

Acer negundo

FORM: **irregular-obovoid** to globular
Size: **large understory** - 10 to 15 m (35 to 50 ft), commonly about 15 m
Spread: **intermediate** - 10 to 15 m (35 to 50 ft), as wide or wider than height
Mass: moderate, becoming **open** at maturity

BRANCHING: short trunk dividing near ground into several stout **ascending** limbs, **coarse** texture
Twig: stout smooth, **large leaf scars** encircle twig, bright **green** to **purple** with bluish **bloom**
Bud: terminal bud blunt, 3 mm (1/8 in) long, scales minutely **woolly**, **silvery** coloration
Bark: **blocky**, mature trunks furrowed into irregular bumpy or warty ridges, yellowish tan or **gray brown**

FOLIAGE: opposite, **pinnately compound**, 3-5 leaflets, **ovate lanceolate, medium-fine** texture
Surface: **dull**, often **tomentose** below
Color: spring - light **yellow green**; summer - **yellow green**; autumn - **yellow green** to pale yellow
Season: **deciduous**; emergence - late **April or** early **May**, drop - late **September**

FLOWER: **small clusters**, blooms born on slender pendulous wire-like filaments (female)
Color: **yellow green** to lime green
Season: early or mid **April**, before or with the leaves
Sex: **dioecious**

FRUIT: paired **samaras**, 38 to 50 mm (1 1/2 to 2 in) long, in dense terminal clusters
Color: green becoming **tan brown** at maturity
Season: mid **July through September**, often **persistent through** late **February**
Wildlife Value: **very high**; songbirds, waterbirds, small mammals, hoofed browsers

HABITAT: formation - **forest, savanna**; region - **central**; gradient - **lowland wet, wet-mesic**; river channel, lake margin,
floodplain depressions, wet ravines, midwest windbreaks
Shade Tolerance: **very intolerant**; index 1.8, least tolerant of the maples
Flood Tolerance: **tolerant**; most tolerant maple

SOIL; Texture: **moderately coarse** sandy loams **to fine** sandy or silty clays, porous droughty granular soils
Drainage: **poor** internal drainage **to excessive**
Moisture: **wet to droughty** soils, high water table
Reaction: prefers **neutral** pH 6.5-7.5, tolerates **acid** pH 5.0-6.5

HARDINESS: **zone 2**
Rate: very **fast** - 4.5 to 6 m (15 to 20 ft) in 5 year period
Longevity: **short** - reaching maturity at 50 to 75 years, rarely survives 100 years

SUSCEPTIBILITY; Physiological: **infrequent** - occasional leaf scorch
Disease: **frequent** - Anthracnose, powdery mildew; several canker diseases
Insect: **frequent** - boxelder bug, striped maple worm, many species of borers
Wind-Ice: **frequent** - weak wooded, often severe damage

URBAN TOLERANCE; Pollution: **sensitive** - HFl, HCl, Cl, 2,4-D; **intermediate** - SO_2, O_3
Lighting: **sensitive**   Drought-Heat: **very resistant**   Mine Spoils: **resistant**
Salt: **intermediate**   Soil Compaction: **resistant**
Root Pattern: several coarse moderately **deep** and spreading **laterals**; easily transplanted any season B&B or BR

SPECIES; Associate: wet - Sandbar, Black and Peachleaf Willows, Silver Maple, Eastern Poplar, American Elm,
Red Mulberry, Green Ash; wet mesic - Cockspur Hawthorn, Butternut, Black Walnut, Pin, Swamp White and
Bur Oaks, American Planetree
Similar: Green Ash attains greater size at maturity
Cultivars: 'Auratum' - woolly yellow leaves, 'Variegatum' - white marginal leaves

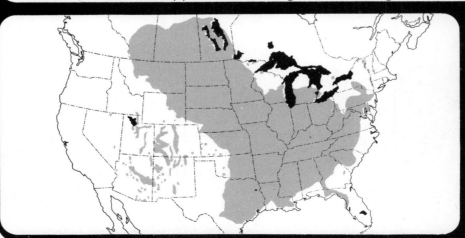

Acer nigrum

FORM: ovoid to globular
Size: **large canopy -** 22.5 to 30 m (75 to 100 ft)
Spread: **wide -** 15 to 22.5 m (50 to 75 ft), usually 2/3 that of mature height
Mass: extremely **dense**

BRANCHING: **ascending,** symmetrical, candelabra branching, **medium** texture
Twig: marked by conspicuous lenticels, glossy, **yellow brown** to gray brown
Bud: mostly covered by leaf petiole,**clustered sharp pointed,** 6 mm (1/4 in) long, black
Bark: variable, **deeply furrowed** into hard scaly ridges; dark **brown black,** ridges often chalky white

FOLIAGE: opposite, **simple, palmately** 3 **lobed -** shallow, toothless, edges tend to droop, **medium coarse** texture
Surface: thick, **dull** above, **tomentose** beneath
Color: spring - **light green;** summer - **yellow green;** autumn - **golden yellow, orange to red**
Season: **deciduous;** emergence - early **May,** drop - late **September** or early October

FLOWER: small clusters, 5 mm (1/5 in) bell shaped blooms, born on slender pendulous stringy filaments
Color: light or pale **yellow green**
Season: late **April or** early **May** before or with the leaves
Sex: monoecious or **dioecious**

FRUIT: paired **samaras,** 25 mm (1 in) long, loose terminal clusters
Color: green becoming **tan brown** at maturity
Season: late summer maturing in **September**
Wildlife Value: **very high;** songbirds, upland ground birds, large and small mammals

HABITAT: formation - **forest;** region - **central;** gradient - **upland mesic;** mesic ravines, coves, north and east slope aspects, floodplain knolls, areas of cool air drainage
Shade Tolerance: **very tolerant;** index 9.7, protect from wind exposure
Flood Tolerance: **intolerant**

SOIL; Texture: **coarse** loamy sands **to medium** loams and silt loams, soils with better aeration
Drainage: **moderately well to well**
Moisture: demands **moist** soils **to average** conditions
Reaction: **slightly acid to neutral,** pH 6.0-7.5

HARDINESS: zone 3b
Rate: **medium to slow -** 7.5 m (25 ft) in 18 to 20 year period, less than 15 cm (6 in) after first 50 years
Longevity: **medium -** 150 years, commonly to 200 before decadence

SUSCEPTIBILITY; Physiological: **infrequent -** leaf scorch common during dry seasons
Disease: **frequent -** Verticillium wilt, Anthracnose, various canker disorders
Insect: **frequent -** maple leaf cutter, sugar maple and other borers
Wind-Ice: **infrequent**

URBAN TOLERANCE; Pollution: **resistant -** SO_2, O_3, HCl, Cl
Lighting: **intermediate**   Drought-Heat: **sensitive**   Mine Spoils: **sensitive**
Salt: **sensitive**   Soil Compaction: **sensitive**
Root Pattern: **shallow spreading,** fibrous; easily transplanted in early spring B&B

SPECIES; Associate: American Linden, Sugar Maple, American Beech, American Hophornbeam, White Ash, American Hornbeam, Cucumbertree Magnolia, Tuliptree, Yellow Buckeye, White Oak, Northern Red Oak
Similar: Sugar and Norway Maples, American Linden
Cultivars: 'Slavins upright' - columnar form, faster growing than upright varieties of Acer saccharum

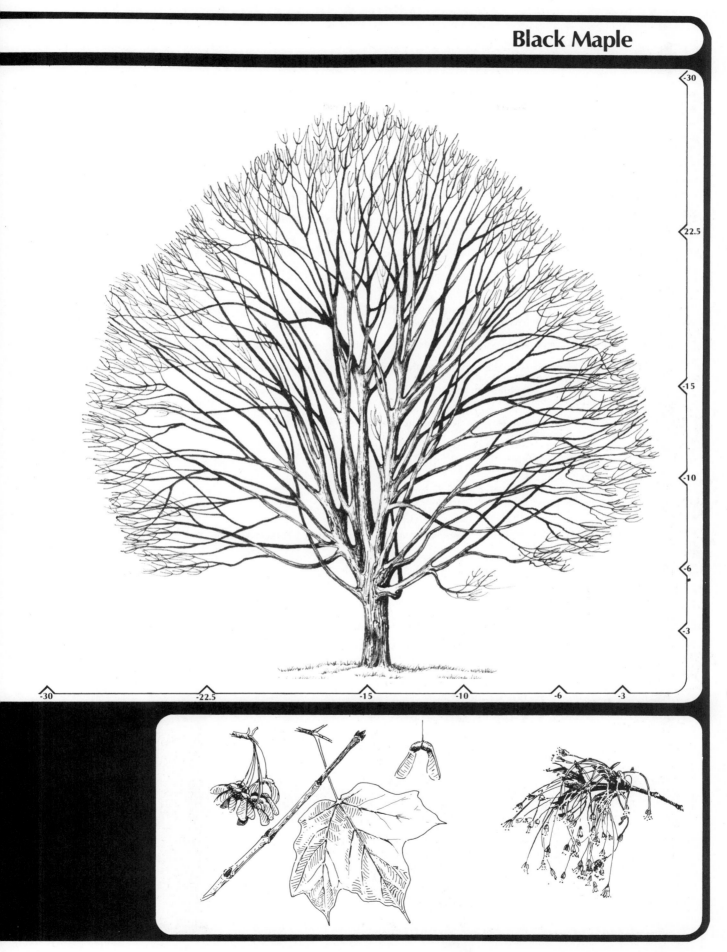

-30

-22.5

-15

-10

-6

-3

-30   -22.5   -15   -10   -6   -3

121

Acer pensylvanicum

FORM: obovoid to broad **globular**
Size: **large understory** - 10 to 15 m (35 to 50 ft)
Spread: **narrow** - 6 to 10 m (10 to 35 ft), usually less than, but can be equal to height
Mass: **open**

BRANCHING: short trunk, **upright** becoming arching, **coarse** texture
Twig: stout, smooth, leaf scars almost encircle twig, young twigs mostly greenish or **reddish**
Bud: **stalked,** with **two scales,** somewhat flattened, bright **red**
Bark: **smooth** with longitudinal stripes on trunk and branches; bright **green** with white stripes

FOLIAGE: opposite, **simple, palmately 3 lobed** with shallow notches, sharp pointed, **medium coarse** texture
Surface: **dull**
Color: spring - pale **red;** summer - **light green;** autumn - **lemon yellow**
Season: **deciduous;** emergence - early **May,** drop - late **September**

FLOWER: **pyramidal clusters,** 10 to 15 cm (4 to 6 in) long, each flower 13 mm (1/2 in) diameter, pendulous
Color: pale **yellow**
Season: late **May to** early **June,** after the leaves
Sex: monoecious

FRUIT: paired **samaras,** 5 cm (2 in) in elongated pendant clusters
Color: pale **red** becoming **tan brown** at maturity
Season: **July through September**
Wildlife Value: **very high;** songbirds, upland ground birds, small mammals, hoofed browsers

HABITAT: formation - **forest;** region - **northern;** gradient - **upland mesic;** cool moist soils on northern slopes,
steep ravines, protected valleys
Shade Tolerance: **very tolerant;** index 10, demands shade, protect from sun, wind
Flood Tolerance: **intolerant**

SOIL; Texture: **coarse** loamy sands **to medium** sandy loams and loams
Drainage: **moderately well to well**
Moisture: demands **moist to average**
Reaction: **strong acid** preference, pH 4.0-5.0

HARDINESS: zone 3b
Rate: **slow** - 15 to 23 cm (6 to 9 in) in a year
Longevity: **medium**

SUSCEPTIBILITY; Physiological: **frequent** - extensive leaf scorch, protect from sun
Disease: **infrequent**
Insect: **infrequent**
Wind-Ice: **frequent** - weak wooded, requires sheltered location

URBAN TOLERANCE; Pollution:
Lighting: Drought-Heat: **sensitive**   Mine Spoils: **sensitive**
Salt: **sensitive**   Soil Compaction: **sensitive**
Root Pattern: **shallow** fibrous; transplanting moderately difficult, best season - early spring B&B

SPECIES; Associate: American Beech, Canada Hemlock, Yellow and Sweet Birches, Mountain Maple, Sugar Maple,
Eastern White Pine, American Hornbeam, American Linden, Common Witch-hazel, Shadblow Serviceberry
Similar: Mountain Maple has darker unstriped bark, several oriental maples; A. capillipes, A. davidii
Cultivars: 'Erythrocladum' - bright red winter twigs

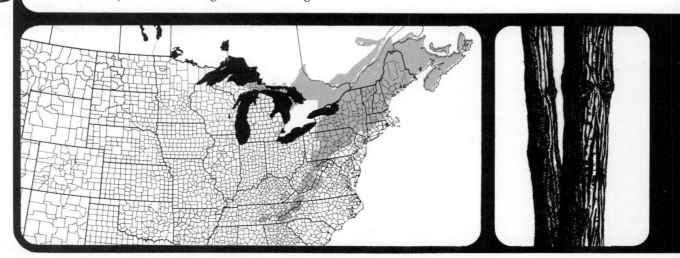

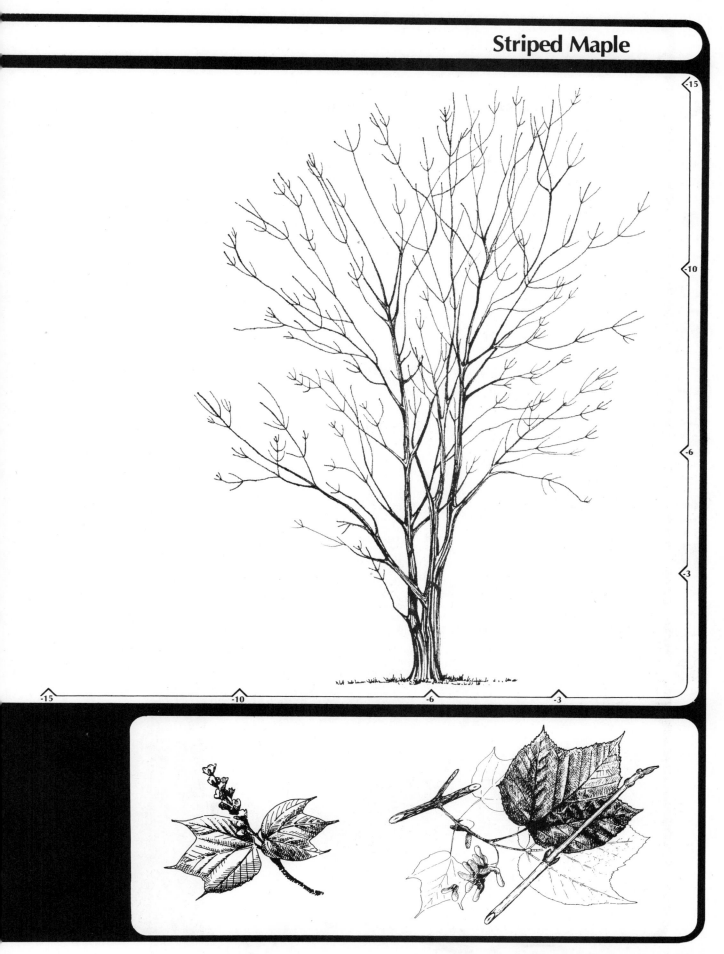

Acer rubrum

FORM: **ovoid to globular**, young trees often conical to elliptic
Size: **large canopy** - 22.5 to 30 m (75 to 100 ft)
Spread: **wide** - 15 to 22.5 m (50 to 75 ft), commonly 3/4 the height
Mass: **moderate**

BRANCHING: strong **ascending**, less regular than Sugar and Black Maples, **medium** texture
Twig: slender, smooth becoming **flaky**, green-red becoming bright **red** in winter
Bud: flower buds **clustered, blunt rounded**, bright **red**, 5 mm (1/5 in) long
Bark: smooth breaking into scaly plates **exfoliating** at ends; silvery **gray** with occasional orangish patches

FOLIAGE: opposite, **simple**, usually **palmately 3 lobed**, v-shaped sinuses, **medium fine** to medium texture
Surface: upper **dull**, lower light silvery gray
Color: spring - **red green**; summer - **light green**; autumn - varies, usually crimson **red**
Season: **deciduous**; emergence - mid to late **April**, drop - late **September**

FLOWER: **small** local **clusters**, 5 to 10 mm (1/5 to 2/5 in) long, short spider-like filaments
Color: both male and female bright **red**
Season: late **March or** early **April**, several weeks before the leaves
Sex: monoecious or **dioecious**

FRUIT: paired **samaras**, keys 19 to 32 mm (3/4 to 1 1/4 in) long, in heavy terminal clusters
Color: usually bright **red** maturing to red brown, rarely yellowish
Season: late **April** to mid **June**, appearing with new leaves
Wildlife Value: **very high**; songbirds, waterbirds, small mammals, hoofed browsers

HABITAT: formation - **forest**: region - **northern, central**; gradients - **lowland wet, wet-mesic, and upland dry**;
   north - cool low wet areas, high humidity, also steep rocky land; central - mesic ravines; south - floodplain
Shade Tolerance: **tolerant**; index range 6.0-7.9
Flood Tolerance: **tolerant**

SOIL; Texture: **coarse** sands and sandy loams **to fine** silty clays and clays, common on poorly aerated soils
Drainage: **very poor to well**
Moisture: demands **wet to average**
Reaction: prefers **acid**, pH 4.5-6.5

HARDINESS: **zone 3a**
Rate: **medium to fast** - 5.5 to 7.5 m (18 to 25 ft) in 10 year period
Longevity: **medium** - seldom living longer than 150 years

SUSCEPTIBILITY; Physiological: **frequent** - manganese chlorosis in calcareous soils
Disease: **frequent** - rot causing fungi, canker injuries, Verticillium wilt
Insect: **frequent** - leaf hoppers, many borers and scale
Wind-Ice: **frequent** - weak wooded

URBAN TOLERANCE; Pollution: **resistant** - O_3, HCl, Cl; **intermediate** - SO_2
Lighting: **sensitive**   Drought-Heat: **intermediate**   Mine Spoils: **intermediate**
Salt: **sensitive**   Soil Compaction: **resistant**
Root Pattern: very **shallow**, widespreading fibrous; easily transplanted in early spring B&B or BR if small

SPECIES; Associate: north - Gray Birch, Paper Birch, Black Spruce, Balsam Fir, Quaking Aspen, Black Ash; central - Black
   and Sugar Maple, Yellow Buckeye, American Beech; south - River Birch, Baldcypress, American Sweetgum
Similar: Silver Maple exhibits more massive irregular form, yellow green autumn coloration
Cultivars: 'Columnare' - narrow upright form, 'Armstrong' - fastigiate, 'October Glory' - retains leaves late

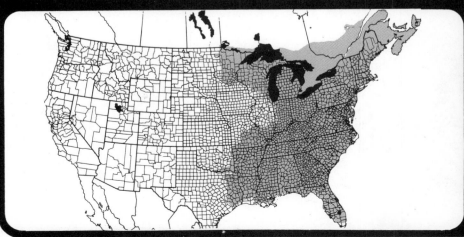

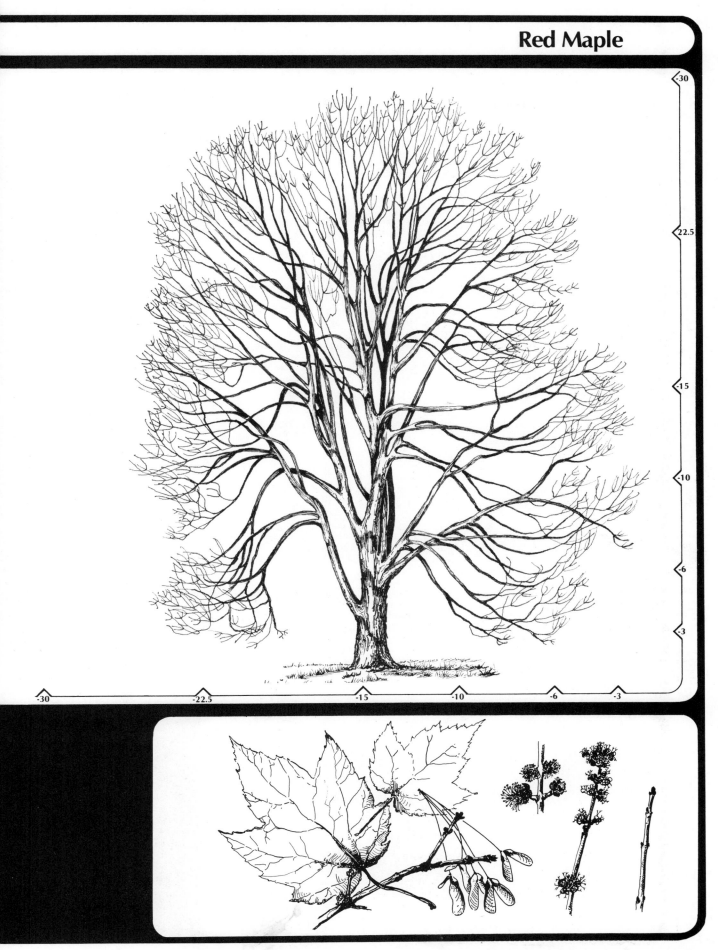

Acer saccharinum

FORM: irregular-globular
Size: **large canopy -** 22.5 to 30 m (75 to 100 ft) plus
Spread: **very wide -** 22.5 to 30 m (75 to 100 ft) plus, frequently wider than tall
Mass: **open**

BRANCHING: dividing near ground, massive **ascending** limbs, branchlets recurving with upturned ends, **coarse** texture
Twig: smooth becoming **flaky, red brown,** winter twig bright **red**
Bud: flower buds **clustered, blunt rounded,** bright **red**
Bark: young - **smooth,** becoming scaly, **exfoliating** at ends; silvery **gray** with occasional orangish patches

FOLIAGE: opposite, **simple, palmately 5 lobed,** deep narrow sinuses, **medium fine** texture
Surface: **dull,** lower whitened sometimes hairy, gives silvery appearance in summer
Color: spring - **light green;** summer - **light green;** autumn - **yellow green** to pale yellow, rarely red
Season: **deciduous;** emergence - early to mid **April,** drop - varies, late **October,** last maple to defoliate

FLOWER: **small clusters,** 13 mm (1/2 in) long, short spider-like filaments
Color: female - bright **red;** male - **yellowish** to silvery
Season: **March,** several weeks before leaves
Sex: **dioecious** or monoecious, trees with predominately female branches, other branches largely male

FRUIT: paired **samaras,** 19 to 32 mm (3/4 to 1 1/4 in) long, in terminal clusters
Color: greenish to bright red becoming **tan brown** at maturity
Season: **April-May,** appearing with leaves
Wildlife Value: **very high;** songbirds, waterbirds, waterfowl, small mammals, hoofed browsers

HABITAT: formation - **forest, savanna;** region - **central;** gradient - **lowland wet, wet-mesic;** alluvial floodplain, streamside, low lakeshore and swamp, midwest windbreak and farmstead plantings
Shade Tolerance: **intermediate;** index 5.8
Flood Tolerance: **tolerant;** can withstand temporary flooding but susceptible to prolonged inundation

SOIL; Texture: **moderately coarse** sandy loams **to fine** sandy and silty clays
Drainage: **poor to well**
Moisture: prefers very **wet** but tolerates **dry**
Reaction: **acid** soils of pH 5.5 to 6.5 preferred

HARDINESS: zone 3b
Rate: very **fast -** between 60 to 90 cm (24 to 36 in) per year, 7.5 to 10.5 m (25 to 35 ft) in 10 year period
Longevity: **short -** reaching maturity at 50 to 75 years, rarely beyond 125 years

SUSCEPTIBILITY; Physiological: **frequent -** manganese cholorsis in calcareous or high pH soils
Disease: **frequent -** Anthracnose, Verticillium wilt, Nectria canker
Insect: **frequent -** ocellate leaf gall, cottony maple scale, borers, other scale
Wind-Ice: **frequent -** very weak, brittle branches

URBAN TOLERANCE; Pollution: **resistant -** SO$_2$, HCl, Cl; **intermediate -** HFl; **sensitive -** O$_3$
Lighting: Drought-Heat: **very resistant**   Mine Spoils: **resistant**
Salt: **intermediate**   Soil Compaction: **resistant**
Root Pattern: **shallow** very widespreading, fibrous; easily transplanted any season B&B or BR if small

SPECIES; Associate: American Elm, American Sweetgum, Eastern Poplar, Red Maple, Swamp White Oak, American Planetree, Black Walnut, Green Ash, River Birch, Common Hackberry, Pin Oak, Eastern Wahoo
Similar: Red Maple with more regular symmetric form, red autumn coloration, commonly hybridize
Cultivars: 'Pyramidal' - broadly columnar habit, 'Silver Queen' - fruitless, 'Weiri' - branches pendulous

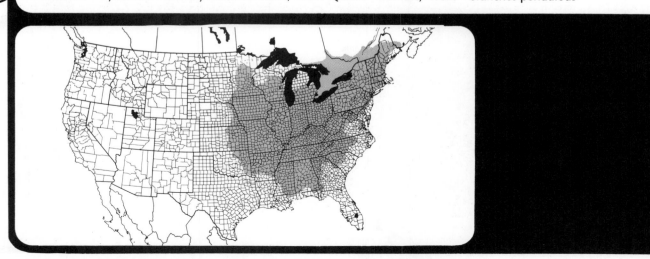

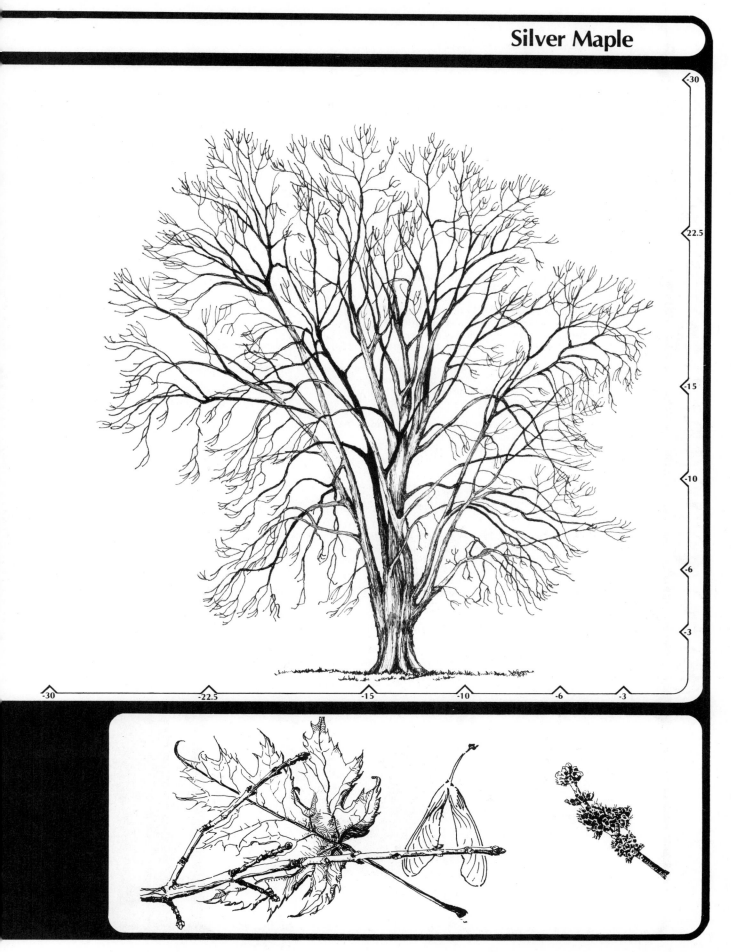

-30
-22.5
-15
-10
-6
-3

-30 -22.5 -15 -10 -6 -3

Acer saccharum

FORM: ovoid to globular
Size: **large canopy -** 22.5 to 30 m (75 to 100 ft)
Spread: **wide -** 15 to 22.5 m (50 to 75 ft), 2/3 or equal to height
Mass: very **dense**

BRANCHING: mostly **ascending,** compact and regular, **medium** texture
Twig: lenticels not as conspicuous as Black Maple, glossy, **brown**
Bud: not hidden by leaf petiole in comparison with Black Maple, slender, **clustered sharp pointed**
Bark: variable, **deeply furrowed** into hard scaly ridges; **brown black,** major limbs black

FOLIAGE: opposite, **simple, palmately 5 lobed,** moderately deep sinuses, edges not drooping, **medium coarse** texture
Surface: **dull,** paler green beneath, usually hairless, thin
Color: spring - **light green;** summer - **medium green;** autumn - **golden yellow, orange and red**
Season: **deciduous;** emergence - early **May,** drop - mid **October,** approx. 2 weeks after Black Maple

FLOWER: **small clusters,** 5 mm (1/5 in) bell shaped blossoms, born on slender pendulous stringy filaments
Color: pale **yellow green**
Season: late **April or** early **May,** before leaf emergence
Sex: monoecious or **dioecious**

FRUIT: paired **samaras,** keys 2.5 cm (1 in) long, in loose terminal clusters
Color: green becoming **tan brown** at maturity
Season: late summer maturing in **September**
Wildlife Value: **very high;** songbirds, upland ground birds, small mammals, hoofed browsers

HABITAT: formation - **forest;** region - **northern, central;** gradient - **upland mesic;** mesic ravines, coves, north and east facing
slopes, floodplain knobs, areas of cool air drainage
Shade Tolerance: **very tolerant;** index 10, most tolerant maple
Flood Tolerance: **intolerant**

SOIL; Texture: **coarse to medium;** loamy sands, sandy loams, loams and occasionally silt-loams
Drainage: demands **moderately well to well**
Moisture: demands **moist to average** soils, more demanding than Black Maple
Reaction: common on soils having pH 6.0-7.5, best development on **slightly acid to neutral** soils

HARDINESS: **zone 3a**
Rate: **slow,** medium in youth - 18 m (60 ft) in 100 years
Longevity: **medium -** 75 to 150 years, frequently reaching 200

SUSCEPTIBILITY; Physiological: **infrequent -** occasional leaf scorch during dry years
Disease: **frequent -** Verticillium wilt, Ceratacystis wilt - common in southeastern states, Anthracnose
Insect: **frequent -** sugar maple borer, maple phenacoccus scale
Wind-Ice: **infrequent -** very strong

URBAN TOLERANCE; Pollution: **resistant -** SO$_2$, O$_3$, PAN; **sensitive -** HCl, Cl
Lighting: **intermediate** Drought-Heat: **sensitive** Mine Spoils: **sensitive**
Salt: **sensitive** Soil Compaction: **sensitive**
Root Pattern: **shallow** to moderately deep, widespreading, fibrous; easily transplanted in early spring B&B

SPECIES; Associate: northern - American Linden, American Beech, American Hophornbeam, Yellow Birch, Canada Hem-
lock, Red Spruce; central - American Linden, American Beech, Yellow Buckeye, White Oak, Cucumbertree Magnolia
Similar: Black Maple, Norway Maple (European), American Linden
Cultivars: 'Monumentale' - narrow 40x12 feet, 'Temples Upright' - pyramidal at maturity, 'Caddo' - drought resistant

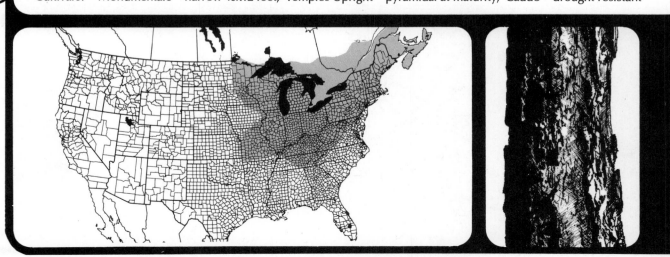

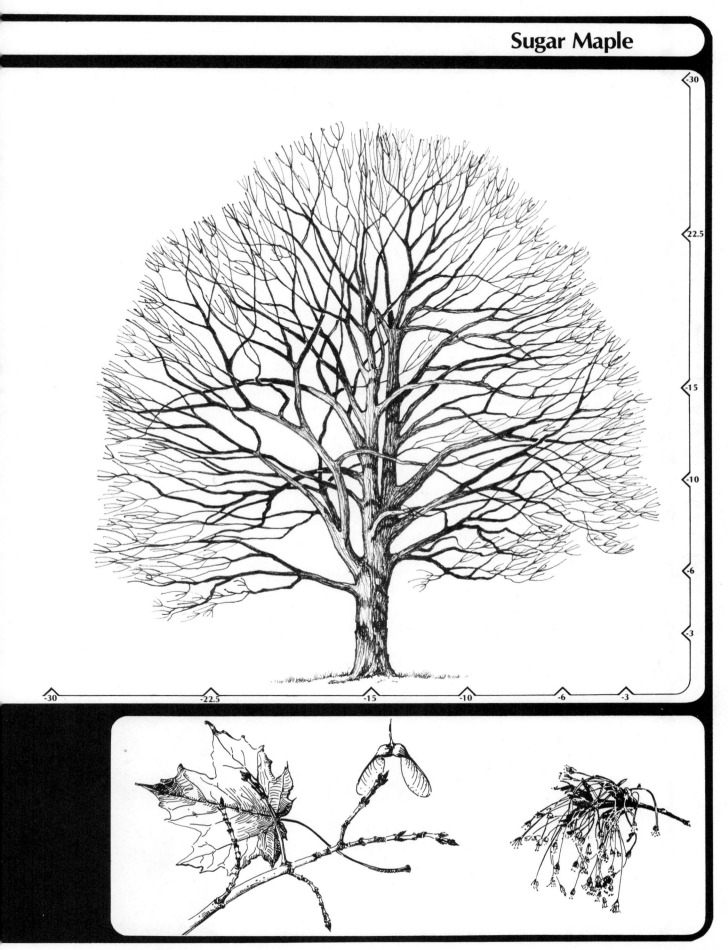

Acer spicatum

FORM: **irregular-obovoid** to broad globular
Size: **small understory** - 6 to 10 m (20 to 35 ft)
Spread: **narrow** - 6 to 10 m (20 to 35 ft), commonly less than 6 m
Mass: **moderate**

BRANCHING: short multiple trunks, stiffly **upright** becoming arching, **medium** texture
Twig: **velvety** hairy twigs, bright **red or greenish**
Bud: appearing **stalked**, with **2 scales**, bright **red**
Bark: **smooth** or slightly furrowed, thin; **greenish**, often **maroon purple** to **red brown**

FOLIAGE: opposite, **simple**, usually **palmately** 3 **lobed** with shallow notches, coarse-toothed, **medium** texture
Surface: **dull**
Color: spring - **light green**; summer - **bright green to yellow green**; autumn - **orange to** bright **red**
Season: **deciduous**; emergence - early **May**, drop - early **October**

FLOWER: **pyramidal clusters**, 10 to 15 cm (4 to 6 in) long, borne in erect terminal spikes
Color: **yellow green** to yellow
Season: late **May** - early **June**, after the leaves
Sex: monoecious

FRUIT: paired **samaras**, approximately 19 mm (3/4 in) long, in terminal clusters
Color: bright **red** or yellow becoming tan-brown at maturity
Season: mid **July through** mid **September**
Wildlife Value: **very high**; songbirds, upland ground birds, small mammals, hoofed browsers

HABITAT: formation - **forest**; region - **northern**; gradient - **upland mesic**; cool rich woods, moist rocky slopes and flats, along small streams
Shade Tolerance: **very tolerant**; index 10, demands shade, protect from sun, wind
Flood Tolerance: **intolerant**

SOIL; Texture: **coarse** loamy sands **to medium** sandy loams and loams
Drainage: **moderately well to well**
Moisture: demands **moist to average**
Reaction: **strong acid** preference, pH 4.0-5.0

HARDINESS: **zone 2**
Rate: **slow** - 15 to 20 cm (6 to 8 in) per year average
Longevity: **short**

SUSCEPTIBILITY; Physiological: **frequent** - leaf scorch, protect from sun exposure
Disease: **infrequent**
Insect: **infrequent**
Wind-Ice: **frequent** - weak wooded, requires sheltered locations

URBAN TOLERANCE; Pollution: **resistant** - SO_2
Lighting: Drought-Heat: **sensitive**   Mine Spoils: **sensitive**
Salt: **sensitive**   Soil Compaction: **sensitive**
Root Pattern: **shallow**; moderately difficult, transplant B&B in early spring

SPECIES; Associate: Red, Striped, and Sugar Maple, Paper Birch, Yellow Birch, Eastern White Pine, American Linden, Common Witch-hazel, Shadblow Serviceberry, Mountain Laurel
Similar: Striped Maple has striped bark and yellow autumn coloration, Cranberrybush Viburnum somewhat smaller
Cultivars: none available commercially

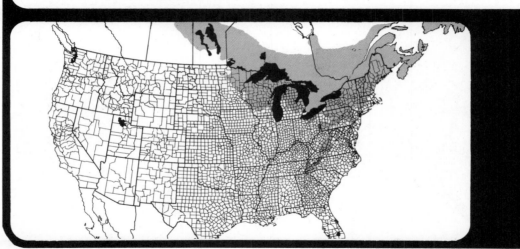

Aesculus glabra

FORM: **irregular**-ovoid
Size: **large understory** - 10 to 15 m (35 to 50 ft), commonly larger
Spread: **narrow** - 6 to 10 m (20 to 35 ft), 1/2 the height
Mass: **moderate**

BRANCHING: stout, **recurving, picturesque,** frequently sweeping the ground, very **coarse** texture
Twig: smooth, **brown** to black
Bud: **large papery,** 17 to 25 mm (2/3 to 1 in) long, scales exfoliating, red brown
Bark: separating into thin irregular **scales; brown black,** major limbs coal black

FOLIAGE: opposite, **palmately compound,** 5 leaflets, **oblanceolate, medium** texture
Surface: **dull,** smooth above, pale beneath
Color: spring - **light** to lime **green;** summer - **dark yellow green;** autumn - **orange to red**
Season: **deciduous;** emergence - mid **April,** drop - late **September**

FLOWER: born in erect **pyramidal** terminal **spikes,** individual trumpet shaped, 13 mm (1/2 in) long
Color: **yellow**
Season: mid to late **May,** after leaves are fully grown
Sex: monoecious

FRUIT: smooth glossy **nut** enclosed by 2.5 to 5 cm (1 to 2 in) long prickly partitioned husk
Color: husk **tan brown,** nut red brown
Season: late **June through** late **September**
Wildlife Value: **very low,** poisonous; small mammals occasionally

HABITAT: formation - **forest;** region - **central;** gradient - **lowland wet-mesic, upland mesic-dry;** elevated floodplain terrace
and knobs, dry warm south and west facing upland slopes
Shade Tolerance: **intermediate;** index range 4.0-5.9
Flood Tolerance: **intermediate**

SOIL; Texture: **coarse** loamy sands, sandy loams **to medium** loams and silt loams, poor growth on clayey soils
Drainage: **well to moderately poor**
Moisture: prefers **wet,** tolerates **dry**
Reaction: **slightly acid,** pH 6.1-6.5

HARDINESS: **zone 4a**
Rate: **slow** - 2.4 to 3 m (8 to 10 ft) in 10 year period
Longevity: **medium** - 100 to 150 years, up to 200

SUSCEPTIBILITY; Physiological: **frequent** - leafscorch (browning along margin), protect from wind
Disease: **frequent** - leaf blotch, powdery mildew, Anthracnose
Insect: **infrequent** - comstock mealybug, Japanese beetle, bagworm
Wind-Ice: **infrequent**

URBAN TOLERANCE; Pollution:
Lighting: Drought-Heat: **intermediate**   Mine Spoils: **intermediate**
Salt: Soil Compaction: **intermediate**
Root Pattern: **taproot;** moderately difficult, transplant in early spring B&B

SPECIES; Associate: lowland wet-mesic - Common Hackberry, American Elm, Black Walnut, Red Mulberry, Kentucky
Coffeetree; upland mesic-dry - Bur Oak, White Oak, Chinkapin Oak, Shagbark Hickory
Similar: Yellow Buckeye attains greater size, more demanding of moist well drained site
Cultivars: none available commercially

Ohio Buckeye

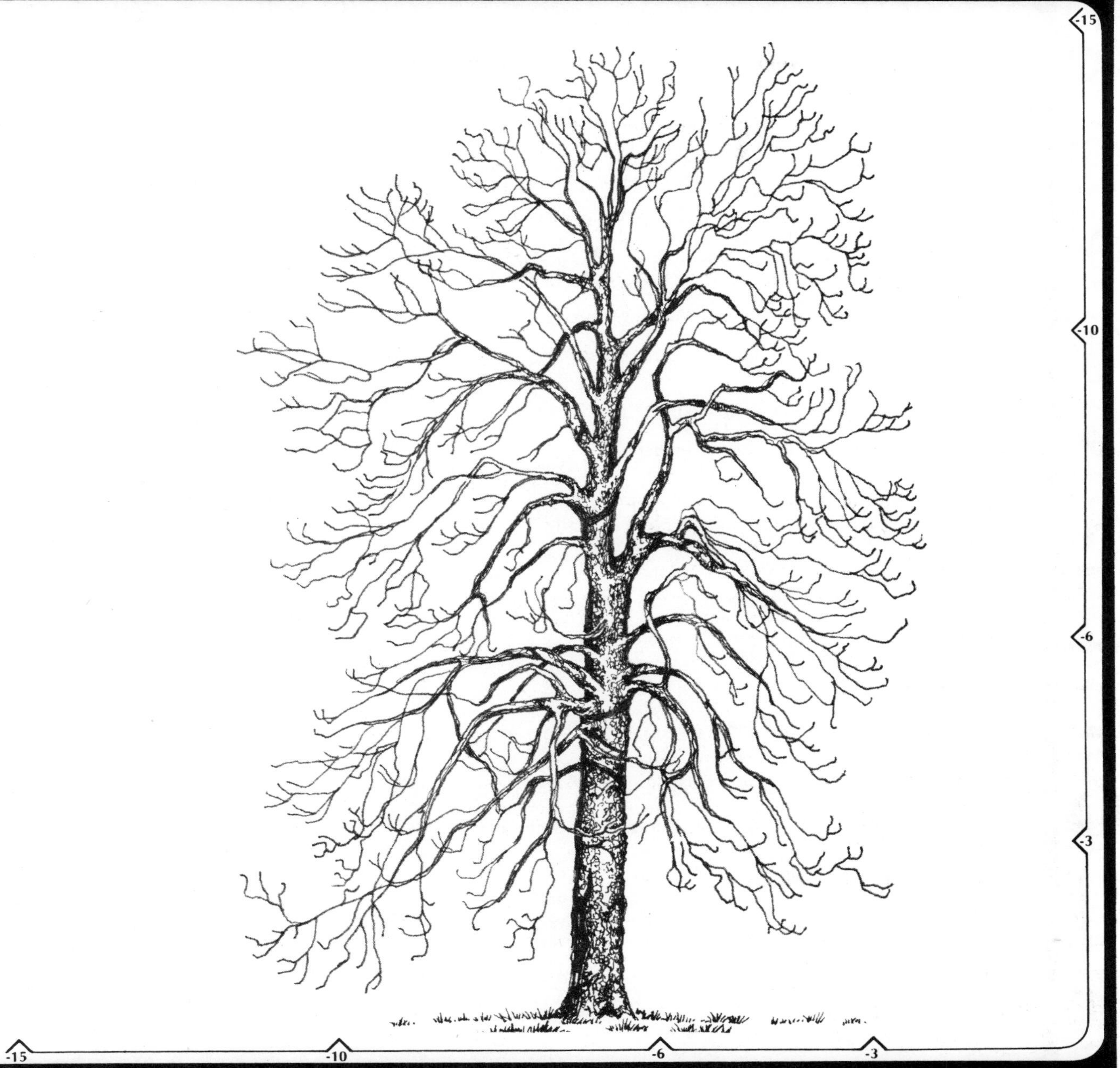

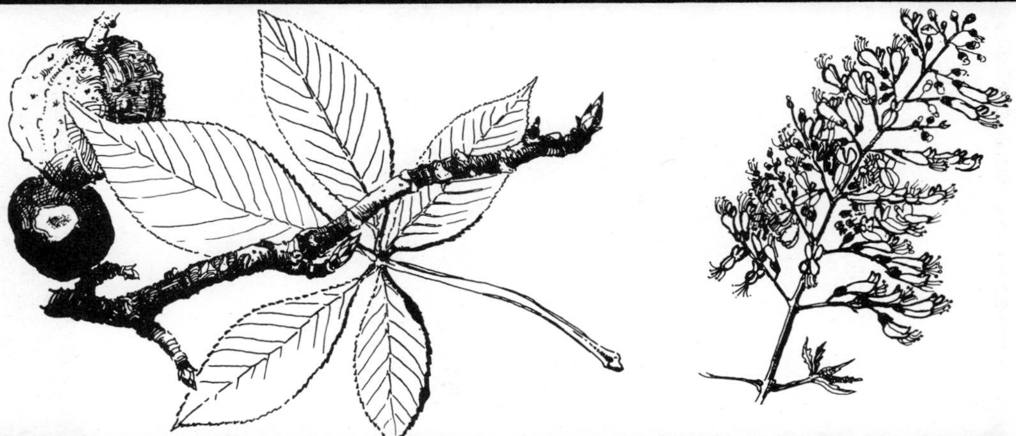

Aesculus octandra

FORM: irregular-ovoid
Size: **small canopy** - 15 to 22.5 cm (50 to 75 ft)
Spread: **intermediate** - 10 to 15 m (30 to 50 ft), 1/2 the height
Mass: **moderate**

BRANCHING: stout, **recurving, picturesque,** commonly sweeping the ground, very **coarse** texture
Twig: smooth, **brown** to black
Bud: **large papery**, scales exfoliating, 17 to 25 mm (2/3 to 1 in) long, red brown
Bark: variable, trunk and major limbs **scaly** or with mottled **patchy exfoliating** sheets; dark **brown black**

FOLIAGE: opposite, **palmately compound**, 5 leaflets, **oblanceolate, medium** texture
Surface: **dull**, smooth above, pale beneath
Color: spring - **light green;** summer - dark **yellow green;** autumn - **orange to red**
Season: **deciduous;** emergence - late **April**, drop - late **September**

FLOWER: clustered in erect **pyramidal** terminal **spikes**, individual trumpet shaped, 13 mm (1/2 in) long
Color: **yellow**
Season: late **May through** early **June,** after leaves have fully developed
Sex: monoecious

FRUIT: smooth glossy **nut** enclosed by 5 to 7.5 cm (2 to 3 in) smooth partitioned husk
Color: husk **tan brown**, nut red brown
Season: early **July through** late **September**
Wildlife Value: **very low**, poisonous; small mammals occasionally

HABITAT: formation - **forest;** region - **central;** gradient - **upland mesic;** mesic coves, northern slopes, high cool
mountainous slopes, a bottomland tree in northern part of range
Shade Tolerance: **tolerant;** index range 6.0 to 7.9
Flood Tolerance: **intermediate**

SOIL; Texture: **coarse** loamy sands, sandy loams **to medium** loams and occasionally silt loams
Drainage: **moderately poor to well**
Moisture: **wet to moist** preferred, tolerates **dry**
Reaction: prefers **slightly acid;** pH 6.1 to 7.0

HARDINESS: **zone 4a**
Rate: **slow** - 2.4 to 3.6 m (8 to 12 ft) in 10 year period
Longevity: **medium** - 150 to 200 years, up to 250 common

SUSCEPTIBILITY; Physiological: **frequent** - leaf scorch, protect from wind
Disease: **frequent** - leaf blotch is most severe, powdery mildew, leaf spot, Anthracnose
Insect: **frequent** - buckeye lacebug, walnut scale, white-marked tussock moth, oystershell scale
Wind-Ice: **infrequent**

URBAN TOLERANCE; Pollution:
Lighting: Drought-Heat **sensitive** Mine Spoils: **sensitive**
Salt: Soil Compaction: **intermediate**
Root Pattern: **taproot;** moderately difficult, transplant in early spring B&B

SPECIES; Associate: Sugar and Black Maples, Yellow Birch, American Beech, American Linden, White Ash,
Northern Red Oak, White Oak, Beetree Linden, Allegany Serviceberry, Carolina Silverbell, Tuliptree
Similar: Ohio Buckeye, European Horsechestnut has white flowers, lacks showy autumn coloration
Cultivars: none available commercially

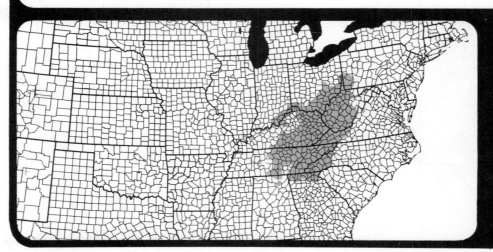

Alnus rugosa

FORM: **globular**
Size: **small understory** - 6 to 10 m (20 to 35 ft)
Spread: **narrow** - 6 to 10 m (20 to 35 ft), as wide as tall
Mass: **open**

BRANCHING: multiple crooked **leggy** trunks, bent in wide curve at base becoming **upright, picturesque, coarse** texture
Twig: **zig zag**, moderately slender, **red brown**
Bud: **stalked, two** bud **scales**, purplish **red**
Bark: **smooth**, roughened by wart-like lenticels; **red brown** to **brown black** with bright orange lenticels

FOLIAGE: alternate, **simple, elliptic-oval to oblong ovate**, doubly serrate margin, prominant veins, **medium** texture
Surface: **dull**, leathery, grayish **tomentose** beneath, orange colored petioles
Color: spring - **medium green**; summer - **dark green**; autumn - **dark green**
Season: **deciduous**; emergence - mid **April**, drop - mid **October**

FLOWER: **catkin** (male), 10 to 12.5 cm (4 to 5 in) long at peak bloom, formed previous fall
Color: **purplish red** with bright red stems
Season: late **March through** early **April**, before leaf emergence
Sex: monoecious

FRUIT: **strobile**, resembles small woody cone, 19 mm (3/4 in) long by 10 mm (3/8 in) wide
Color: purplish becoming **black** on bright orange stems
Season: early **August** persisting **through** winter until **February**
Wildlife Value: **high**; songbirds, waterbirds, small mammals, hoofed browsers

HABITAT: formation - **forest**; region - **northern**; gradient - **lowland wet**; streamside, openings in low wet woods, open
floodplain, low alluvial flats, swamp, lake margin
Shade Tolerance: **very intolerant**; index range 0-1.9
Flood Tolerance: **very tolerant**

SOIL; Texture: varying from **coarse** gravel or sand **to fine** clay, prefers deep silt loams or loamy sands
Drainage: **very poor to moderately poor,** more prevalent on soils of restricted internal drainage
Moisture: demands **wet to moist**
Reaction: **neutral,** pH 6.6-7.0

HARDINESS: **zone 2**
Rate: **fast** - 76 to 90 cm (30 to 36 in) a year average
Longevity: **short** - old at 30 years, seldom survives 40 years

SUSCEPTIBILITY; physiological: **infrequent**
Disease: **infrequent** - occasional heart rot in overmature trees
Insect: **frequent** - several borers, alder bark beetle, tent caterpillar
Wind-Ice: **frequent** - root system gives little wind support especially in wet spongy soils, weak wooded

URBAN TOLERANCE; Pollution: **sensitive** - O_3
Lighting: Drought-Heat: **sensitive**   Mine Spoils: **sensitive**
Salt: **intermediate**   Soil Compaction: **resistant**
Root Pattern: very **shallow** narrow spreading; transplants readily B&B or BR spring or fall

SPECIES; Associate: Black Ash, Red Maple, Gray Birch, American Larch, Eastern Arborvitae,
Black Spruce, Balsam Fir, American Elm, Nannyberry Viburnum, rhododendron, willow
Similar: Common Buttonbush is large shrub with larger leaves
Cutlivars: none commercially obtainable

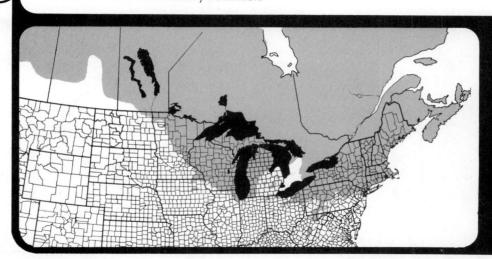

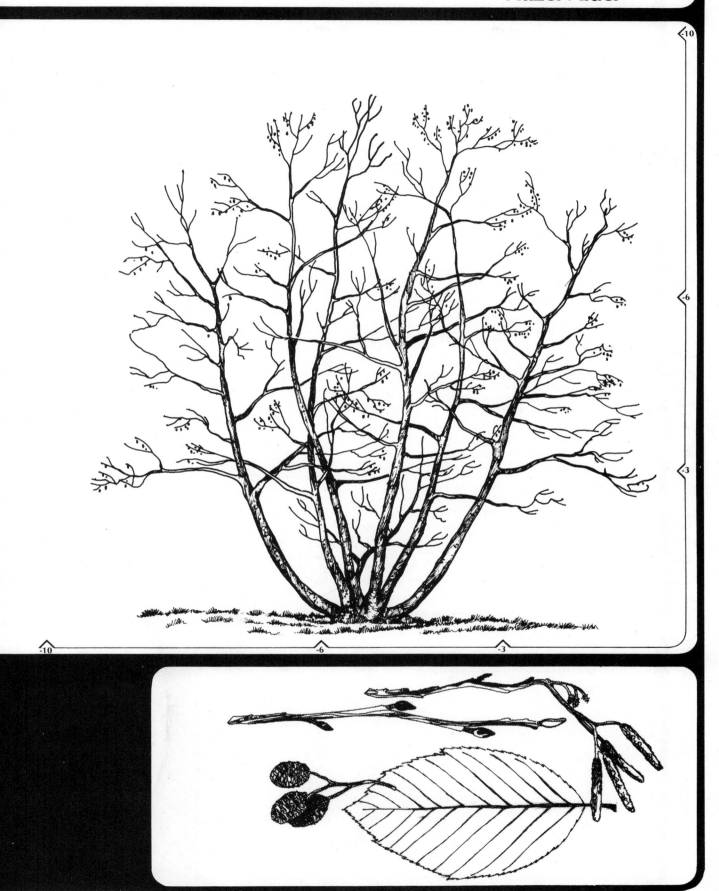

Amelanchier canadensis

FORM: globular or obovoid
Size: **large understory** - 10 to 15 m (35 to 50 ft)
Spread: **intermediate** - 10 to 15 m (35 to 50 ft), 2/3 to equal the height
Mass: **dense**

BRANCHING: slender **leggy multiple trunks**, **upright** undulating habit, **fine** texture
Twig: very slender, **gray** with silvery gray exfoliating scales
Bud: **narrow, long pointed**, cigar shaped, chestnut brown with silvery hairs extending beyond bud scales
Bark: **smooth** with vertical slightly twisting, line-like stripes; ashy **gray** with whitish lines

FOLIAGE: alternate, **simple, elliptic-oval,** finely serrate margin, **medium fine** texture
Surface: young leaves thickly woolly, mature **dull,** paler below
Color: spring - **silvery gray;** summer - **blue green;** autumn - **orange to** dull **red**
Season: **deciduous;** emergence - early **May,** drop - mid **October**

FLOWER: nodding **pyramidal spike,** 7.5 cm (3 in) long, individual blooms 5 to 8 mm (1/5 to 1/3 in) long
Color: **white**
Season: mid through late **April,** before leaf emergence
Sex: monoecious

FRUIT: globular **berry,** 6 mm (1/4 in) diameter, in open drooping pyramidal clusters
Color: sequence from **red** to maroon **purple** when ripe becoming bluish at drop
Season: mid **June through** mid **July**
Wildlife Value: **high;** man, songbirds, small mammals

HABITAT: formation - **forest;** regions - **northern, central;** gradient - **upland mesic;** mesic slopes along western limits of
    range, most common along shoulder of north and east slope aspects
Shade Tolerance: **very tolerant;** index range 8.0 to 10.0
Flood Tolerance: **intolerant**

SOIL; Texture: **coarse** loamy sands, sandy loams **to medium** loams
Drainage: demands **well to moderately well**
Moisture: demands **moist to average**
Reaction: **slight acid** preference, pH 6.1-6.5

HARDINESS: zone 3a
Rate: **medium** - 76 cm (30 in) per year
Longevity: **medium**

SUSCEPTIBILITY; Physiological: **infrequent**
Disease: **infrequent** - cedar serviceberry rust, powdery mildew, fire blight
Insect: **infrequent** - leaf minor, borers, pear slug sawfly, pear leaf blister mite
Wind-Ice: **infrequent**

URBAN TOLERANCE; Pollution: **sensitive** - SO_2 O_3; **intermediate** - HFl
Lighting: Drought-Heat: **sensitive**   Mine Spoils: **sensitive**
Salt: **resistant**   Soil Compaction: **sensitive**
Root Pattern: **shallow** fibrous, widespreading; transplants moderately easy in early spring or fall B&B

SPECIES; Associate: Sugar and Black Maples, American Linden, White Ash, American Hophornbeam, Northern Red Oak,
    Pagoda Dogwood, Leatherwood, American Hornbeam, Common Witch-hazel
Similar: American Hornbeam, Common Chokecherry, Allegany Serviceberry, Red and Purple Chokeberry are shrubbier
Cultivars: none available commercially

Shadblow Serviceberry

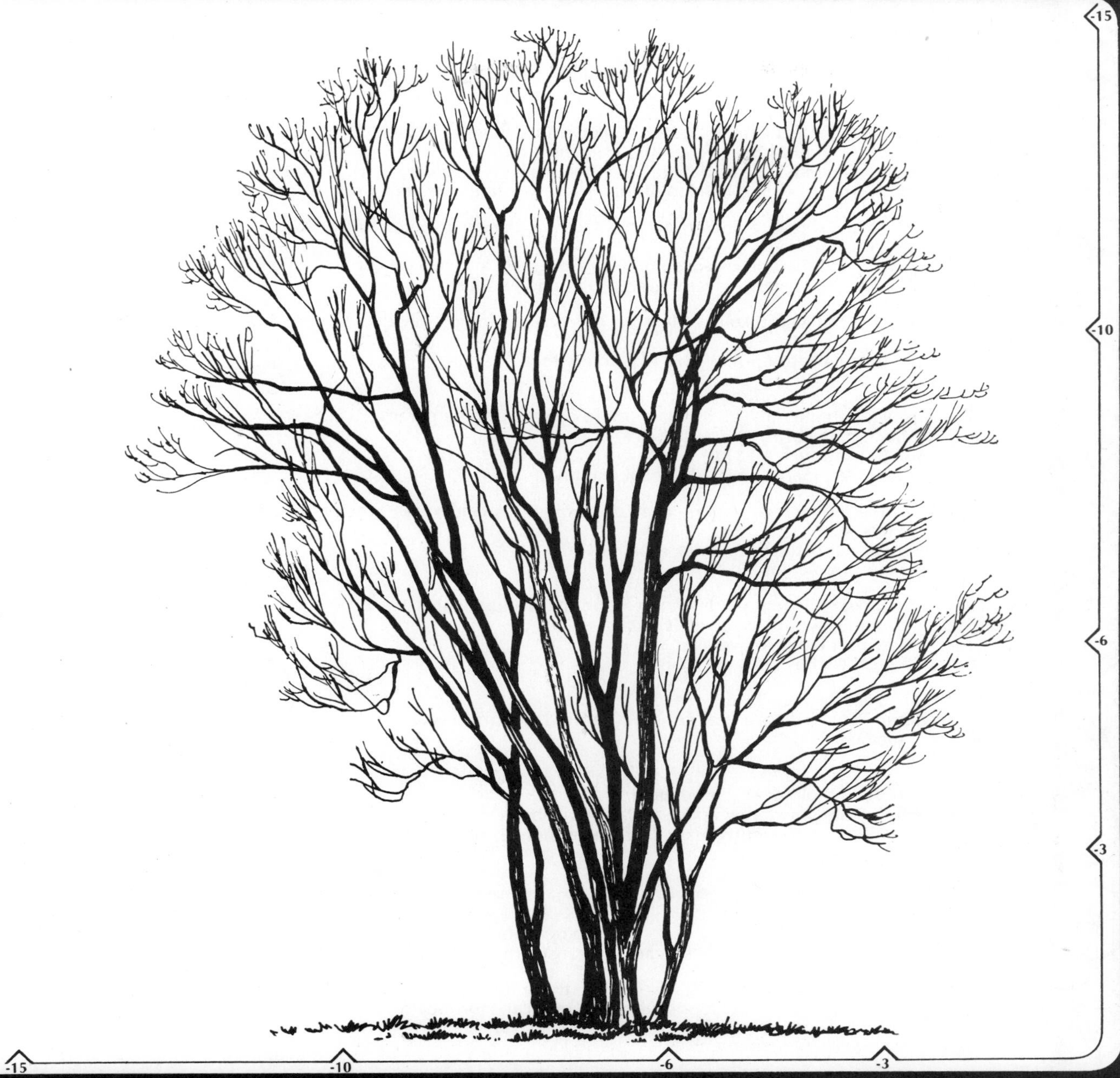

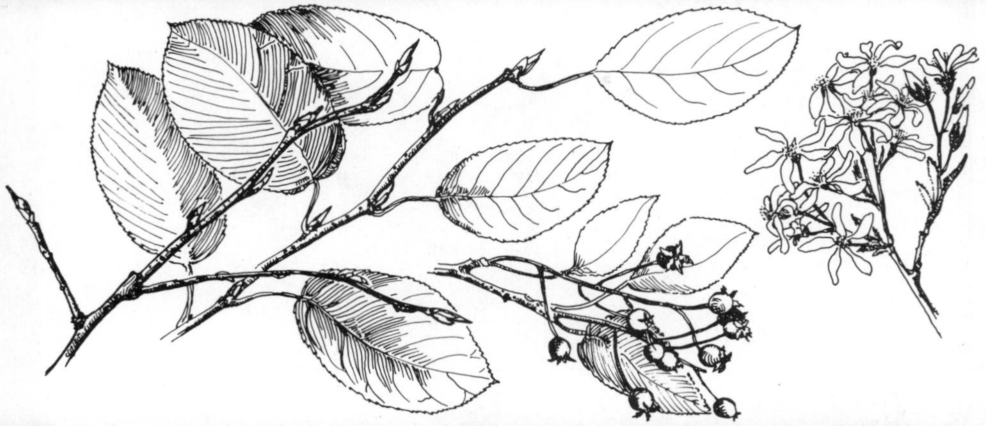

Amelanchier laevis

FORM: **globular or obovoid**
Size: **small understory** - 6 to 10 m (25 to 25 ft)
Spread: **narrow** - 6 to 10 m (25 to 35 ft), 2/3 to 3/4 the height
Mass: **dense**

BRANCHING: slender **leggy** multiple trunks, **upright** undulating branches, **fine** texture
Twig: very slender, **gray** with silvery gray exfoliating scales
Bud: **narrow, long pointed,** cigar shaped, chestnut brown with silvery hairs extending beyond bud scales
Bark: **smooth** with narrow line-like longitudinal stripes; slate **gray** with white stripes

FOLIAGE: alternate, **simple, elliptic-oval,** finely serrate margin, **medium fine** texture
Surface: **dull,** paler beneath
Color: spring - **red** to **maroon green;** summer - **blue green;** autumn - **orange to** dull **red**
Season: **deciduous;** emergence - early **May,** drop - mid **October**

FLOWER: erect **pyramidal spike**-like clusters, 7.5 cm (3 in) long, individual blooms 8 mm (1/3 in) long
Color: **white**
Season: mid through late **April,** before leaf emergence
Sex: monoecious

FRUIT: globular **berry,** 8 mm (1/3 in) diameter in open drooping pyramidal clusters
Color: **red** becoming **purple** or nearly black
Season: mid **June through** mid **July**
Wildlife Value: **high;** man, songbirds, small mammals

HABITAT: formation - **forest;** region - **central;** gradient - **upland mesic;** mesic coves, north and east slope aspects, cool rich woods
Shade Tolerance: **very tolerant;** index range 8.0-10.0
Flood Tolerance: **intolerant**

SOIL; Texture: **coarse** loamy sands, sandy loams, **to medium** loams
Drainage: demands **well to moderately well**
Moisture: demands **moist to average**
Reaction: prefers **slightly acid,** pH 6.1-6.5

HARDINESS: **zone 3a**
Rate: **medium** - 76 cm (30 in) a year generally, 4.5 m (15 ft) in 10 year period
Longevity: **medium**

SUSCEPTIBILITY; Physiological: **infrequent**
Disease: **infrequent** - powdery mildew, cedar serviceberry rust, leaf blight, fire blight
Insect: **infrequent** - willow scurfy scale, leaf minor, borers, pear leaf blister mite
Wind-Ice: **infrequent**

URBAN TOLERANCE; Pollution: **sensitive** - SO_2, O_3; **intermediate** - HFl
Lighting: Drought-Heat: **sensitive**   Mine Spoils: **sensitive**
Salt: **sensitive**   Soil Compaction: **sensitive**
Root Pattern: **shallow** fibrous wide spreading; transplants moderately easily in early spring or fall B&B

SPECIES; Associate: Sugar and Black Maples, Northern Red and White Oaks, Pagoda and Flowering Dogwoods, American Linden, American Hophornbeam, American Hornbeam
Similar: Shadblow Serviceberry, Common Chokecherry, American Hornbeam lacks showy white flowers
Cultivars: none available commercially

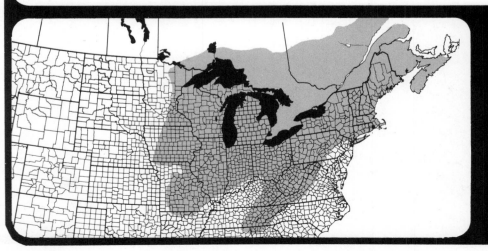

Allegany Serviceberry

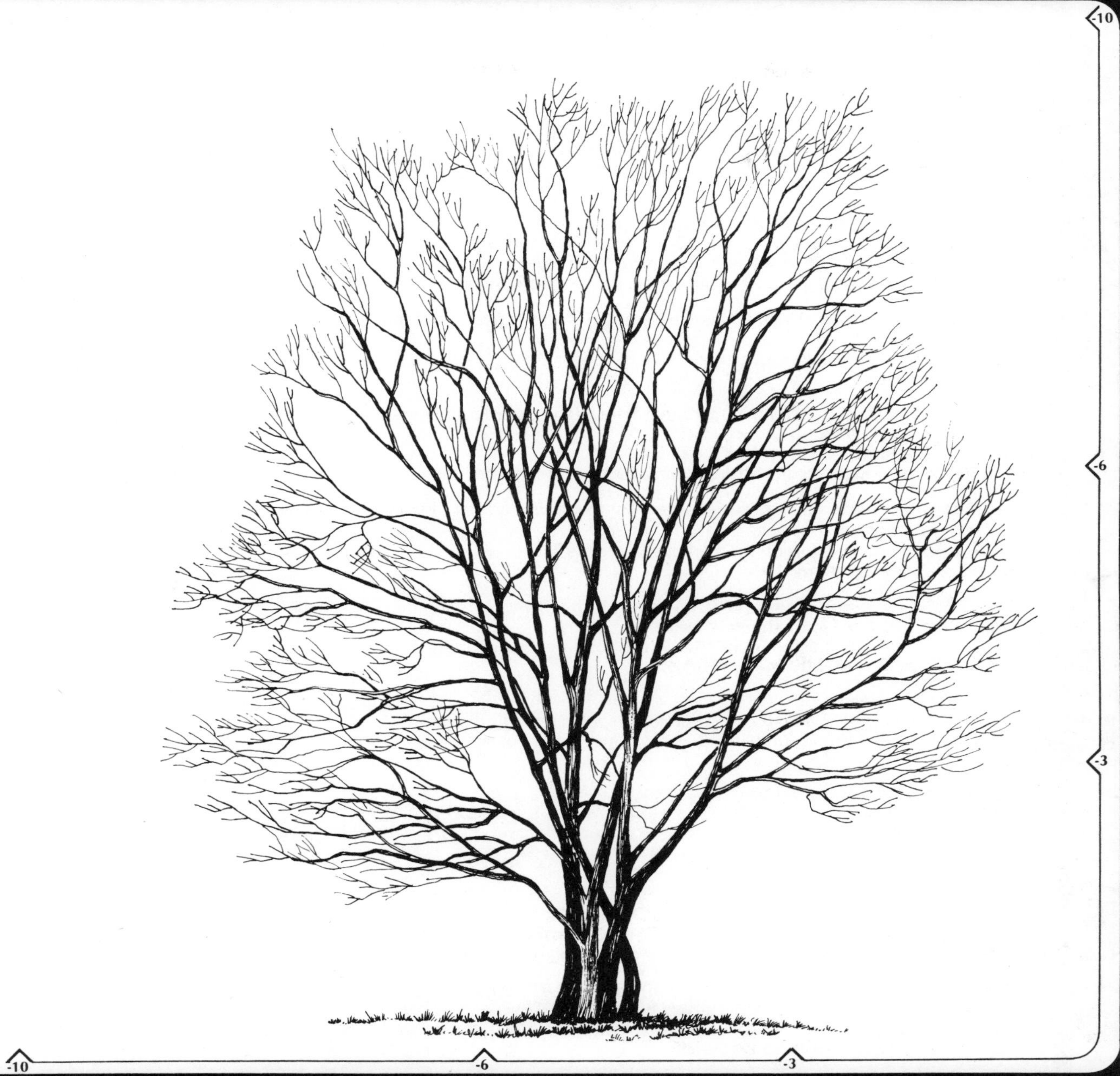

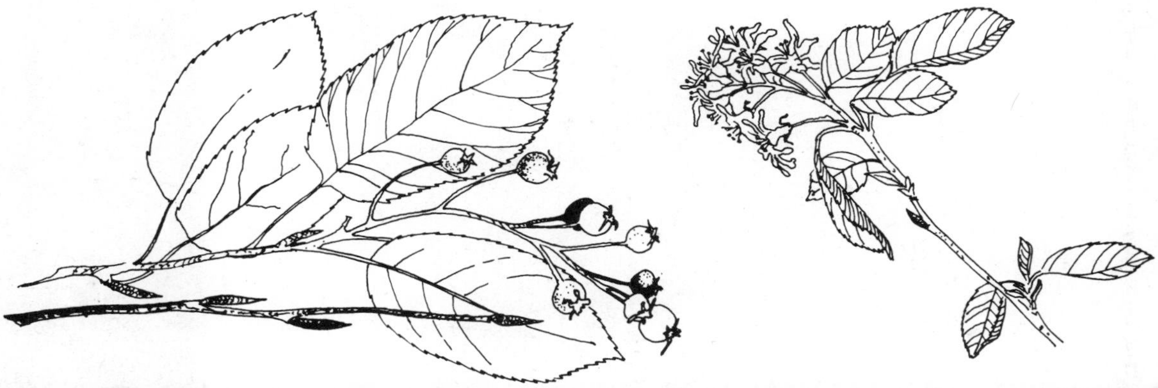

Aralia spinosa

FORM: **irregular**
Size: **large understory** - 10 to 15 m (35 to 50 ft)
Spread: **narrow** - 6 to 10 m (20 to 35 ft)
Mass: **open**

BRANCHING: **leggy** multiple trunks, several stout upright branches, forms thickets, very **coarse** texture
Twig: **large leaf scars, green yellow; armed** with orange colored scattered prickles on branches and foliage
Bud: terminal conical, 19 mm (3/4 in) long, chestnut brown
Bark: divided into **shallow narrow fissures** with wide rounded irregularly broken ridges; **gray brown**

FOLIAGE: alternate, **bipinnately compound,** 13 leaflets, **ovate-oblong ovate,** clustered at branch ends, **medium** texture
Surface: **dull** or lustrous, pale beneath, rachis armed with slender prickles
Color: spring - glossy **maroon green;** summer - **dark green;** autumn - pale **yellow to purplish**
Season: **deciduous;** emergence - early **June,** drop - late **September**

FLOWER: small globular many flowered clusters in open **pyramidal spikes**
Color: **white**
Season: late **July through** early **August**
Sex: monoecious

FRUIT: globular **berries,** 8 mm (1/3 in) diameter, tight globular clusters in open pyramidal spikes
Color: **black**
Season: late **August through** mid **October**
Wildlife Value: **high;** songbirds, upland gamebirds, small mammals

HABITAT: formation - **forest, savanna;** region - **central;** gradient - **lowland wet-mesic and upland dry;** floodplain, rocky
pastures, border of woods, dry rocky open woods
Shade Tolerance: **intolerant;** index range 2.0 to 3.9
Flood Tolerance: **intermediate**

SOIL; Texture: **coarse** sands and sandy loams **to fine** silty clays and clays, rocky land
Drainage: **very poor to moderately well**
Moisture: performs best in **moist to average,** tolerates **dry** droughty conditions
Reaction: prefers **slightly acid,** pH 6.1-6.5

HARDINESS: zone 5a
Rate: very **fast** - especially from sucker shoots, old wood growth slow
Longevity: **short** - rarely surviving 50 years, long lived root system perpetuates colony

SUSCEPTIBILITY; physiological: **infrequent**
Disease: **infrequent** - none serious
Insect: **infrequent** - none serious
Wind-Ice: **infrequent**

URBAN TOLERANCE; Pollution:
Lighting: Drought-Heat: **resistant**   Mine Spoils: **resistant**
Salt: Soil Compaction: **intermediate**
Root Pattern: **deep** coarse **lateral** spreading; transplants readily in all seasons with care, BR

SPECIES; Associate: Common Prickly Ash, Sassafras, Common Persimmon, Eastern Redcedar, Osageorange,
Common Pawpaw, Common Chokecherry, Black Cherry, sumac, hawthorn, crabapple
Similiar: Aralia elata is related; Common Prickly Ash; Bristly locust and Bristly Sarsaparilla are smaller and bristly
Cultivars: none available commercially

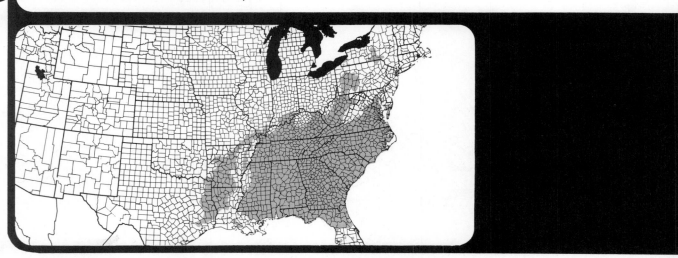

Devils-Walkingstick

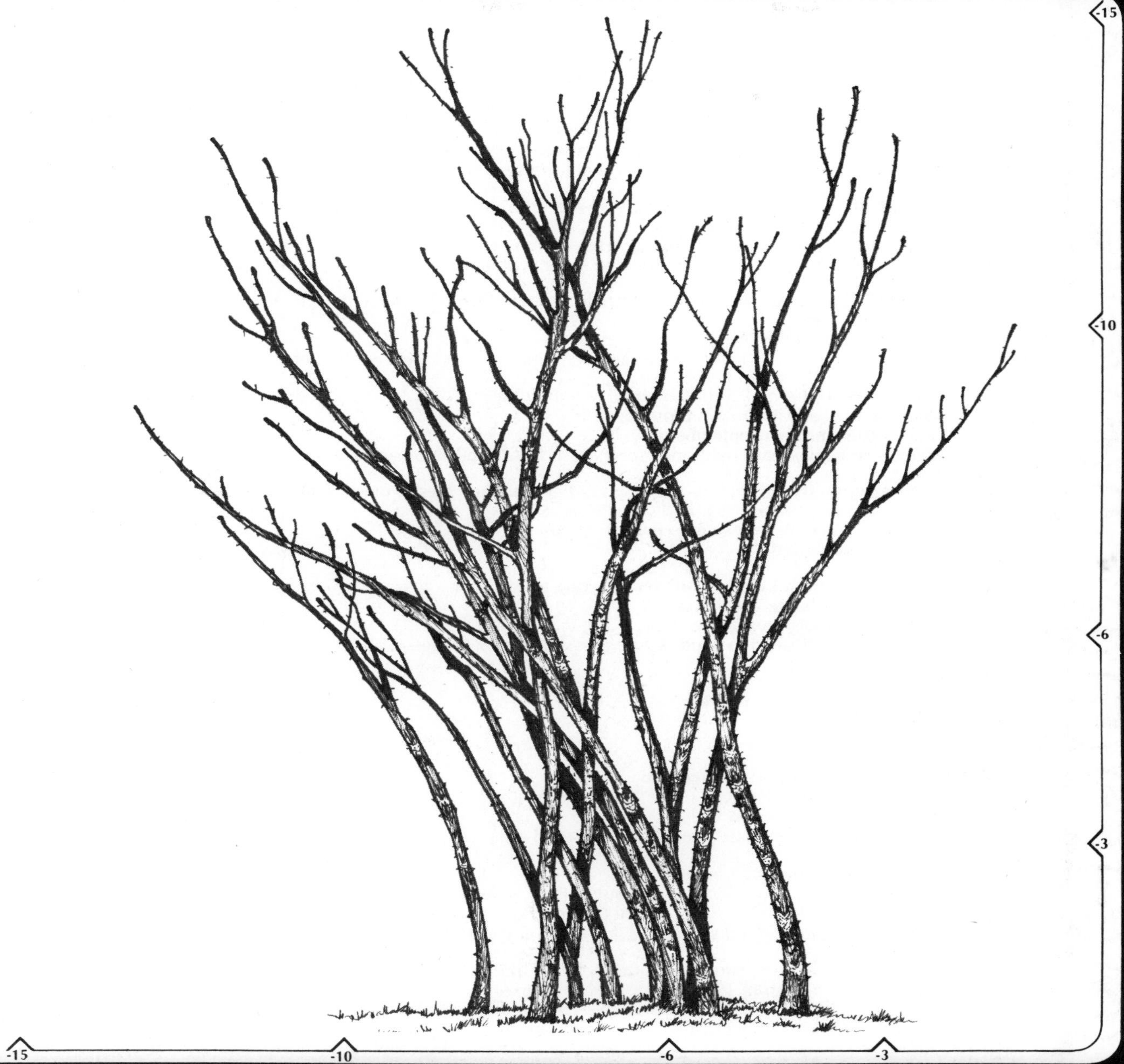

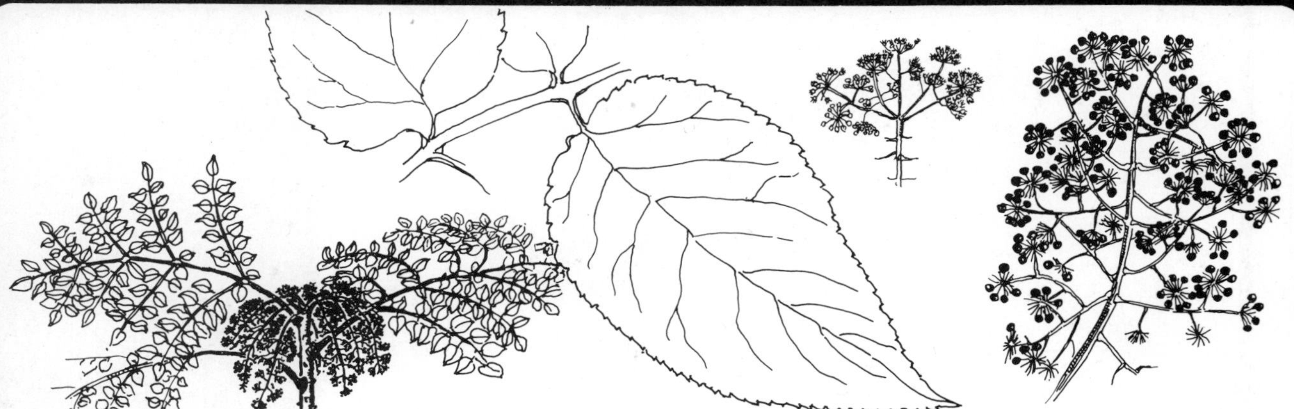

Asimina triloba

FORM: irregular
Size: **small understory** - 6 to 10 m (20 to 35 ft)
Spread: **narrow** - 6 to 10 m (20 to 35 ft)
Mass: **open**

BRANCHING: stiffly **upright**, forming open thickets, **coarse** texture
Twig: **winged lines**, hairy, conspicuous lenticels, **brown**
Bud: flower buds along stem **onion**-like, **naked**, covered with rusty **red** hairs, **woolly**
Bark: **smooth**, blotchy with warty appearance due to raised lenticels; **gray brown** with light ash colored blotches

FOLIAGE: alternate, **simple, obovate-oblong obovate**, entire margin, coarse texture
Surface: **dull**, smooth, paler beneath
Color: spring - **light green;** summer - **light green;** autumn - **pale yellow**
Season: **deciduous;** emergence - mid **May**, drop - late **September**

FLOWER: **large** 6 petaled **solitary** leathery wrinkled blooms, 25 to 38 mm (1 to 1 1/2 in) diameter
Color: **red brown**
Season: early through mid **May**, appearing before the new leaves
Sex: **monoecious**   **Fragrant:** odor similar to fermenting grapes

FRUIT: cylindric fleshy **berry**, 7.5 to 12.5 cm (3 to 5 in) long
Color: **yellowish orange** with brown blotches
Season: mid **August through September**
Wildlife Value: **very low;** man, small mammals, flesh taste similar to banana

HABITAT: formation - **forest;** region - **central;** gradient - **upland mesic;** mesic slope, lake margin, stream borders, base of slope, occasional in abandoned fields, waste areas
Shade Tolerance: **tolerant;** index range 6.0-7.9
Flood Tolerance: **intolerant**

SOIL; Texture: **moderately coarse to moderately fine** sandy loams, loams, shallow soils over limestone
Drainage: prefers **moderately well to well**
Moisture: demands **moist to average**
Reaction: prefers **slightly acid to neutral,** tolerates **alkaline,** pH range 6.1-8.0

HARDINESS: zone 5b
Rate: **slow** - 3.6 m (12 ft) in 15 years
Longevity: **medium**

SUSCEPTIBILITY; Physiological: **infrequent**
Disease: **infrequent** - none serious
Insect: **infrequent** - none serious
Wind-Ice: **frequent** - weak wooded, locate in sheltered area

URBAN TOLERANCE; Pollution:
Lighting: Drought-Heat: **sensitive**   Mine Spoils: **sensitive**
Salt: **sensitive**   Soil Compaction: **sensitive**
Root Pattern: **deep** coarse **lateral** spreading; transplanting difficult, move small trees B&B in early spring

SPECIES; Associate: Tuliptree, American Linden, Sugar and Black Maple, American Beech, Northern Red Oak, White Ash, Bitternut Hickory, Sassafras
Similar: several species of magnolia have similar bark and leathery foliage, Star Magnolia has white flowers
Cultivars: none available commercially

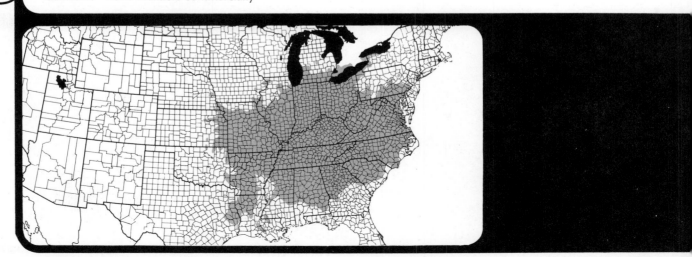

Common Pawpaw

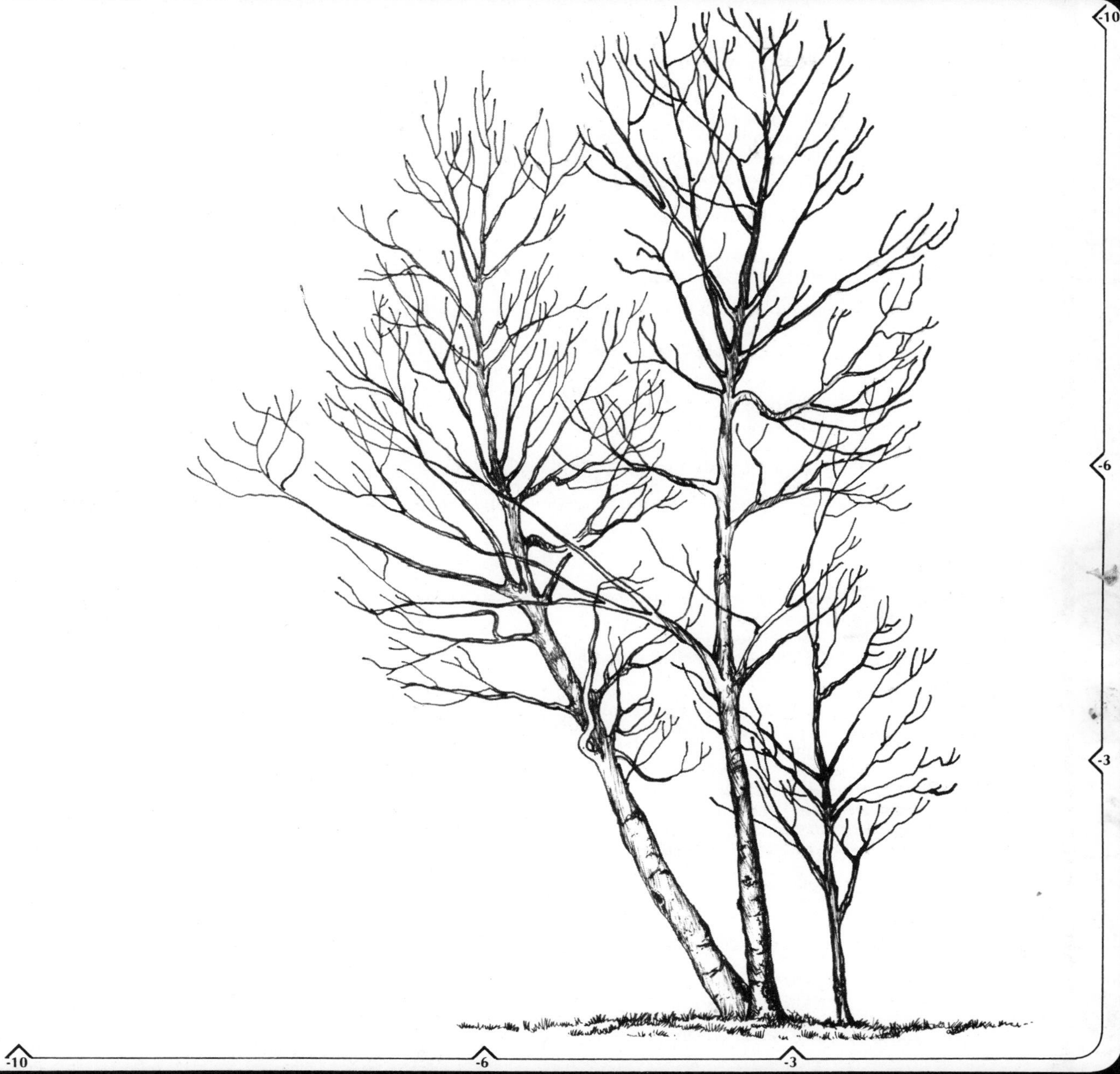

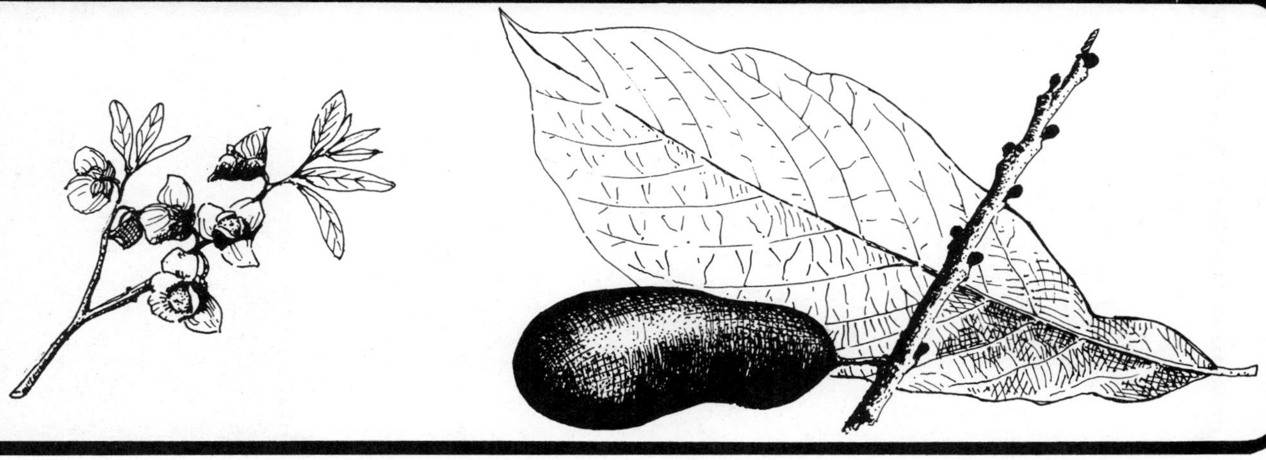

Betula lenta

FORM: **ovoid to globular** at maturity, conical in youth
Size: **small canopy** - 15 to 22.5 m (50 to 75 ft)
Spread: **intermediate** - 10 to 15 m (35 to 50 ft), 2/3 the height commonly
Mass: **moderate**

BRANCHING: many stout **ascending** limbs, slightly **pendulous** branchlets, **fine** texture
Twig: slender, glossy, **reddish brown,** crushed twig with wintergreen aroma
Bud: **stalked,** terminal absent, glossy, 6 mm (1/4 in) conical sharp pointed, chestnut brown
Bark: prominent horizontal lenticels, large thin irregular **scaly** plates; **brown** becoming **black,** cherry-like

FOLIAGE: alternate, **simple, ovate-oblong ovate,** fine toothed, **medium** texture
Surface: **dull**
Color: spring - **light green;** summer - **dark green;** autumn - clear lemon to golden **yellow**
Season: **deciduous;** emergence - late **April,** drop - early **October**

FLOWER: male clustered in slender pendant pencil-like **catkins,** 2.5 to 5 cm (1 to 2 in)
Color: light green to **yellow green**
Season: mid **April** appearing before leaves, male formed previous autumn
Sex: monoecious

FRUIT: erect **strobiles,** 25 to 38 mm (1 to 1 1/2 in) long
Color: medium green becoming **tan brown** at maturity
Season: **August through November**
Wildlife Value: **very high;** songbirds, upland ground birds, small mammals, hoofed browsers

HABITAT: formation - **forest;** region - **northern;** gradient - **upland mesic and mesic dry;** cool north and east slope aspects,
steep rocky land, lower slopes
Shade Tolerance: **intermediate;** index range 4.0-5.9
Flood Tolerance: **intolerant;** does not tolerate poor drainage sites

SOIL: Texture: **coarse** sands, loamy sands, gravels, prefers **moderately fine** sandy loams, silt loams and silts
Drainage: **moderately well to well**
Moisture: prefers **moist,** tolerant of **dry**
Reaction: narrow pH amplitude, **strongly acid,** pH 4.5-5.0

HARDINESS: **zone 3b**
Rate: **slow -** about 30 cm (1 ft) per year generally
Longevity: **medium -** maturity reached at about 150 to 175 years

SUSCEPTIBILITY; Physiological: **infrequent**
Disease: **frequent -** white trunk rot, yellow cap fungus, Nectria canker
Insect: **frequent -** bronze birch borer, witch-hazel leaf gall aphid, seed mite, birch skeletonizer
Wind-Ice: **infrequent -** moderately strong

URBAN TOLERANCE; Pollution: **sensitive -** SO$_2$, 2,4-D; **resistant -** O$_3$, HCl, Cl
Lighting: **sensitive**   Drought-Heat: **intermediate**   Mine Spoils: **intermediate**
Salt: **intermediate**   Soil Compaction: **sensitive**
Root Pattern: **deep** coarse spreading **lateral;** somewhat difficult to transplant, B&B in early spring

SPECIES; Associate: Eastern White Pine, Northern Red Oak, White Ash, Canada Hemlock, Yellow Birch, Sugar Maple,
American Beech, American Linden, Paper Birch, American Hornbeam, Pagoda Dogwood
Similar: Black Cherry, major differences in fruit and flower, Yellow Birch - young bark dissimilar
Cultivars: none available commercially

22.5

15

10

6

-3

-22.5   -15   -10   -6   -3

Betula lutea

FORM: ovoid to globular, conical in youth
Size: **small canopy** - 15 to 22.5 m (50 to 75 ft), largest of our native birch species
Spread: **intermediate** - 10 to 15 m (35 to 50 ft), 2/3 the height
Mass: **moderate**

BRANCHING: central stem well defined, stout **ascending** limbs, slightly **pendulous** branchlets, **fine** texture
Twig: slender, smooth, **yellowish** brown to **bronze**, crushed twig with wintergreen aroma
Bud: **stalked,** terminal bud absent, laterals 6 mm (1/4 in) sharp pointed, chestnut brown
Bark: **exfoliating horizontally** into thin papery curls, glossy horizontal lenticels; **yellow orange,** old trunks black

FOLIAGE: alternate, **simple, ovate-oblong ovate,** sharp pointed, doubly serrate, **medium** texture
Surface: **dull** above, pale yellow green beneath
Color: spring - **light green;** summer - **medium green;** autumn - clear lemon to golden **yellow**
Season: **deciduous;** emergence - late **April,** drop - early **October**

FLOWER: slender drooping pencil-like **catkins,** 5 to 7.5 cm (2 to 3) long
Color: greenish to **yellow green**
Season: female appearing before leaves in mid **April,** male formed preceding autumn
Sex: monoecious

FRUIT: small papery erect **strobiles,** 2.5 cm (1 in) long
Color: light green becoming **tan brown** at maturity
Season: late **July through** mid **October**
Wildlife Value: **very high;** songbirds, small mammals, hoofed browsers

HABITAT: formation - **forest;** region - **northern;** gradient - **lowland wet mesic and upland mesic;** elevated floodplain
  terrace and knobs, lower slopes, cool north and east slopes
Shade Tolerance: **tolerant;** index 6.3, most tolerant of the birches
Flood Tolerance: **intolerant**

SOIL; Texture: grows best on **moderately coarse** sandy loams, common on **moderately fine** clay and sandy clay loams
Drainage; somewhat **poor to well**
Moisture: prefers **moist to average**
Reaction: wide pH amplitude, **strongly acid to alkaline,** pH 4.5-8.0, common on calcareous soils

HARDINESS: zone 3a
Rate: **medium** - 9 m (30 ft) over 20 year period
Longevity: **medium** - maturity reached at about 150 years, not as long lived as Sweet Birch

SUSCEPTIBILITY; Physiological: **infrequent**
Disease: **frequent** - heart rots, stem canker, other canker decay, leaf spot, blister leaf
Insect: **frequent** - bronze birch borer, birch skeletonizer, gypsy moth
Wind-Ice: **infrequent**

URBAN TOLERANCE; Pollution: **sensitive** - SO_2, 2,4-D; **resistant** - O_3, HCl, Cl
Lighting: **sensitive**   Drought-Heat: **sensitive**   Mine Spoils: **sensitive**
Salt: **intermediate**   Soil Compaction: **sensitive**
Root Pattern: moderately **deep laterals;** moderately difficult to transplant, root pruned trees move well B&B in early spring

SPECIES; Associate: Paper, Gray and Sweet Birches, Red, Striped, Mountain, and Sugar Maples, Eastern White Pine,
  Red Spruce, American Linden, Northern Red Oak, Canada Hemlock, White Ash, Pagoda Dogwood,
  Rosebay Rhododendron
Similar: Sweet Birch - young tree bark dissimilar
Cultivars: none available commercially

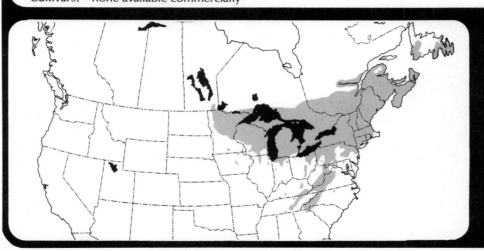

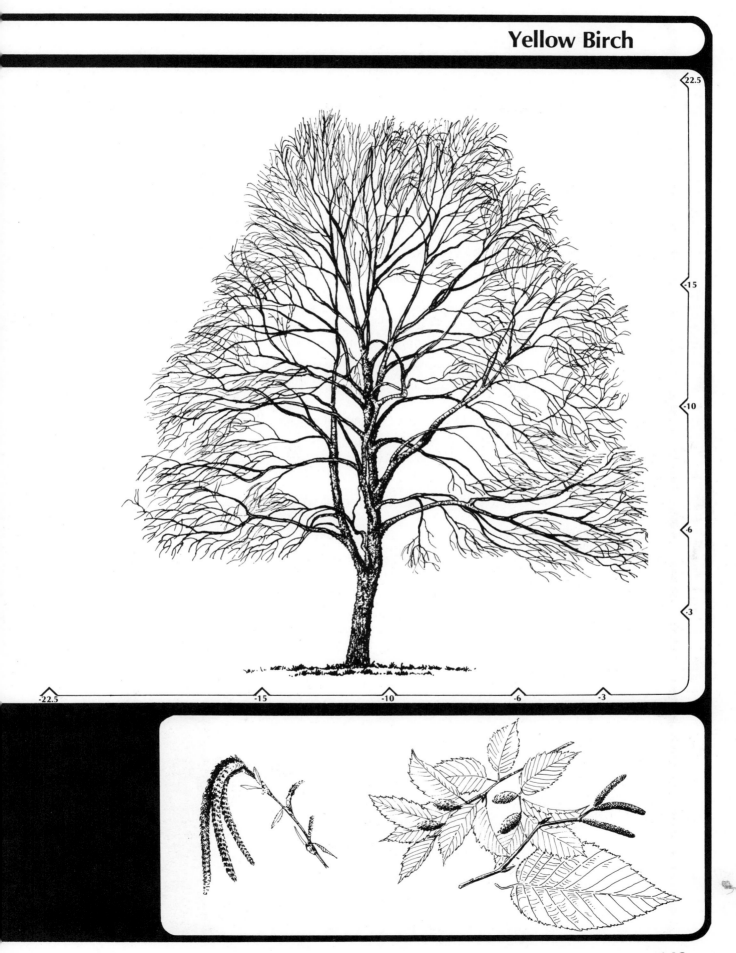

Betula nigra

FORM: **columnar** in youth, adult trees commonly globular
Size: **small canopy** - 15 to 22.5 m (50 to 75 ft)
Spread: **intermediate** - 10 to 15 m (35 to 50 ft), 1/3 the height in youth, equal to height at maturity
Mass: **open**

BRANCHING: single or multiple trunks, **ascending** slightly **pendulous** ends, adult with stout arching limbs, **fine** texture
Twig: cherry-like with conspicuous horizontal striped lenticels, glossy, **red-brown** to maroon
Bud: **stalked,** woolly through summer, small, less than 15 mm (1/5 in), light chestnut brown
Bark: papery **horizontal exfoliation,** blocky scales at base; whitish pink to **salmon orange,** adult trunks red brown to black

FOLIAGE: alternate, **simple, deltoid to wedge** shape, sharp pointed, doubly serrate, **medium fine** texture
Surface: **glossy,** whitish beneath
Color: spring - bright **yellow green;** summer - light green to **yellow green;** autumn - clear **yellow**
Season: **deciduous;** emergence - early **May,** drop - late **October,** often earlier

FLOWER: male in slender drooping **catkins,** 5 to 7.5 cm (2 to 3 in) long
Color: light green to pale **yellow green**
Season: late **April through** early **May;** appearing before leaves, male formed previous autumn
Sex: monoecious

FRUIT: oblong elliptic **strobiles,** 25 to 38 mm (1 to 1 1/2 in) long, erect
Color: medium green becoming **tan-brown** at maturity
Season: earliest birch to seed; **June, July, and** early **August**
Wildlife Value: **very high;** songbirds, waterfowl, small mammals, hoofed browsers

HABITAT: formation - **forest;** region - **central;** gradient - **lowland wet and wet mesic;** floodplain depression, ox-bows, swampy bottomlands, low open sites of recent disturbance along streamside
Shade Tolerance: **intolerant;** pioneer species, index range 2.0-3.9
Flood Tolerance: **tolerant**

SOIL; Texture: **coarse to fine;** adaptable to most soil textures including fine heavy clays
Drainage: **poor to moderately well**
Moisture: prefers **wet to average,** survives **dry** summer-autumn seasons, perhaps best birch for hot-dry climates
Reaction: prefers **acid** soils, pH 6.5 or less

HARDINESS: zone 5a
Rate: **fast** - 9 to 12 m (30 to 40 ft) in 20 year period
Longevity: **short** - mature at 50 to 75 years, rarely survives 125 years

SUSCEPTIBILITY; Physiological: **infrequent**
Disease: **infrequent** - leaf spot in wet years
Insect: **infrequent** - unlike other birch species not susceptible to bronze birch borer
Wind-Ice: **frequent** - weak wooded

URBAN TOLERANCE; Pollution: **sensitive** - 2,4-D
Lighting: **sensitive**   Drought-Heat: **resistant**   Mine Spoils: **resistant**
Salt: Soil Compaction: **resistant**
Root Pattern: **shallow** fibrous widespreading; transplants easily B&B in early spring or late autumn

SPECIES; Associate: pure stands - American Sweetgum, Black Willow, Eastern Poplar, Boxelder, American Planetree, Pin Oak, Swamp White Oak, Black Ash, Silver Maple
Similar: Paperbark Maple (Asiatic) exhibits similar bark character, color, leaf texture and autumn coloration
Cultivars: none available commercially

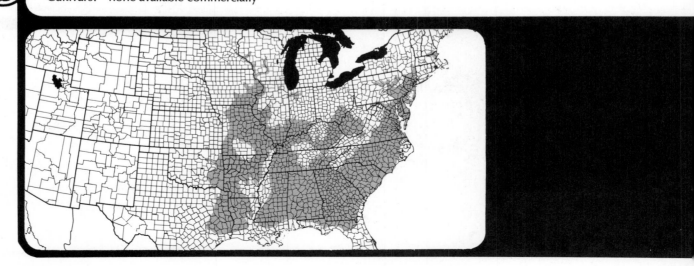

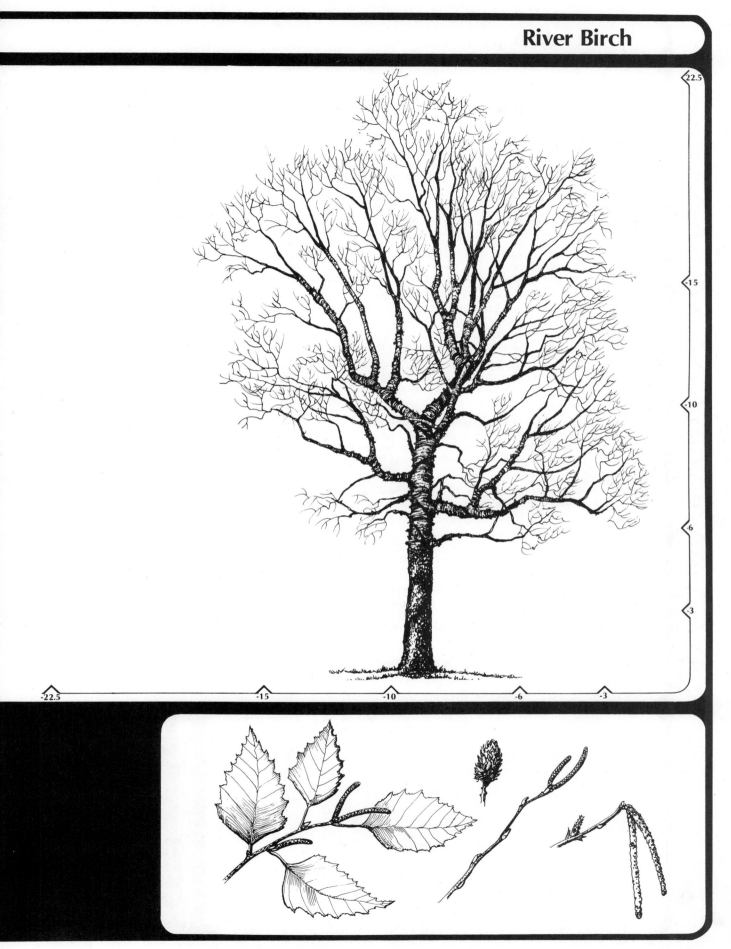

22.5

15

10

6

3

-22.5   -15   -10   -6   -3

Betula papyrifera

FORM: adult crown **globular,** young trees loosely conical
Size: **small canopy -** 15 to 22.5 m (50 to 75 ft)
Spread: **intermediate -** 10 to 15 m (35 to 50 ft), 1/2 to 2/3 the height
Mass: **moderate**

BRANCHING: single or multiple trunks, several stout **ascending** branches, slightly **pendulous** branchlets, **fine** texture
Twig: smooth, shiny, **reddish brown** to maroon, speckled with whitish lenticels
Bud: **stalked, resinous,** terminal lacking, laterals sharp pointed, 6 mm (1/4 in) long, brown-black
Bark: **exfoliating horizontal** papery strips, horizontal lenticels, chalky **white,** lenticels black; old trunks black

FOLIAGE: alternate, **simple, ovate-oblong ovate,** sharp pointed, doubly serrate, **medium** texture
Surface: **dull,** thin, smooth, paler beneath
Color: spring - **bright green;** summer - **medium green;** autumn - clear lemon **yellow**
Season: **deciduous;** emergence - late **April,** drop - mid **October**

FLOWER: slender drooping pencil-like **catkins,** 17 mm (2/3 in) long
Color: light **yellow-green**
Season: late **April through** early **May,** female appearing with the leaves, male formed previous autumn
Sex: monoecious

FRUIT: pendant cylindrical **strobiles,** 2.5 cm (1 in) long
Color: light green becoming **tan brown** at maturity
Season: **August through** early **October**
Wildlife Value: **very high;** songbirds, upland ground birds, small mammals, hoofed browsers

HABITAT: formation - **forest;** region - **northern;** gradients - **upland mesic and mesic dry;** cool north and east slope aspects
      along southern range limits, steep rocky land
Shade Tolerance: **very intolerant;** index 1.0
Flood Tolerance: **intolerant**

SOIL; Texture: **coarse to moderately fine,** best growth on stony to sandy loams, glacial tills and outwash terraces
Drainage: **poor to well,** seldom found on wet poorly drained soils
Moisture: **moist to dry,** somewhat more abundant on soils slightly dryer than average
Reaction: **moderately acid to alkaline,** common on soils with pH 5.0-8.0, tolerates highly calcareous soils

HARDINESS: **zone 2**
Rate: **medium -** 46 to 60 cm (18 to 24 in) a year over a 20 year period
Longevity: **short -** trees mature in about 60 to 75 years, rarely survive 125 years

SUSCEPTIBILITY; Physiological: **infrequent**
Disease: **frequent -** canker, mildew
Insect: **frequent -** bronze birch borer, leaf minor, birch skeletonizer, dieback
Wind-Ice: **infrequent -** strong wooded

URBAN TOLERANCE; Pollution: **sensitive -** SO_2, 2,4-D; **resistant -** O_3, HFl, HCl, Cl
Lighting: **sensitive**   Drought-Heat: **intermediate**   Mine Spoils: **intermediate**
Salt: **resistant**   Soil Compaction: **sensitive**
Root Pattern: **deep** coarse **lateral** system; somewhat difficult to transplant, move small root pruned trees B&B in
      early spring

SPECIES; Associate: Balsam Fir, Black Spruce, Quaking Aspen, Yellow and Sweet Birches, Red Pine, Eastern White Pine,
      Pin Cherry, Eastern Arborvitae, Red Maple, Mountain Maple, American Hornbeam
Similar: Quaking Aspen plus 4 species of birch have white bark; European White, Gray, European Weeping, Blue Leaf
Cultivars: none available commercially

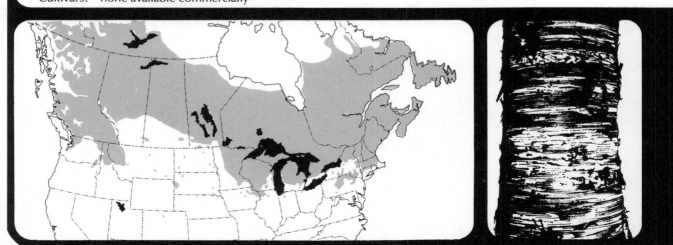

22.5

-15

-10

-6

-3

-22.5   -15   -10   -6   -3

Betula populifolia

FORM: narrow **columnar**
Size: **large understory** - 10 to 15 m (35 to 50 ft)
Spread: **narrow** - 6 to 10 m (20 to 35 ft), 1/2 the height
Mass: **open**

BRANCHING: single or multiple trunks, slender **horizontal** with somewhat **pendulous** branchlets, very **fine** texture
Twig: with roughened warty resinous glands, very slender, glossy, **reddish brown** or grayish
Bud: small, **stalked,** somewhat **resinous,** sharp pointed laterals, terminal lacking, chestnut brown
Bark: **smooth,** not peeling, black triangular patches where branches intersect trunk; chalky **white,** old trunks black

FOLIAGE: alternate, **simple, wedge** shape, long pointed at apex, coarse doubly serrate, **medium fine** texture
Surface: **glossy**
Color: spring - **light green;** summer - **light green;** autumn - clear **yellow**
Season: **deciduous;** emergence - mid **April,** drop - late **September**

FLOWER: male in slender **catkin,** 5 to 9 cm (2 to 3 1/2 in) long, solitary at end of twigs
Color: light green to **yellow green**
Season: early to mid **April,** appearing before the leaves, male formed previous autumn
Sex: monoecious

FRUIT: drooping **strobile,** 19 mm (3/4 in) long
Color: medium green becoming **tan brown** at maturity
Season: **September through** mid **December**
Wildlife Value: **very high;** songbirds, waterbirds, small mammals, hoofed browsers

HABITAT: formation - **forest, savanna;** region - **northern;** gradients - **lowland wet and upland dry;** common along swamp
and low lake margin, dry steep rocky land
Shade Tolerance: **very intolerant;** index 1.0
Flood Tolerancy: **very tolerant**

SOIL; Texture: **coarse** sands and gravels **to moderately fine** poorly aerated clay loams and silty clay loams
Drainage: **poor to excessive**
Moisture: tolerates **wet and dry** soils, tolerates poor sterile soils
Reaction: **moderately acid to neutral,** common on soils ranging from pH 5.0 to 7.5

HARDINESS: zone 4a
Rate: **fast** - 60 to 76 cm (24 to 30 in) annually in first 10 years
Longevity: **short** - rarely exceeding 50 years, commonly 15 to 30 years

SUSCEPTIBILITY; Physiological: **infrequent**
Disease: **frequent** - various canker disorders
Insect: **infrequent** - resistant to bronze birch borer, occasional leaf minor damage
Wind-Ice: **frequent** - weak wooded

URBAN TOLERANCE; Pollution: **sensitive** - SO_2, 2,4-D; **resistant** - O_3, HCl, Cl
Lighting: **sensitive**   Drought-Heat: **resistant**   Mine Spoils: **resistant**
Salt: **resistant**   Soil Compaction: **resistant**
Root Pattern: **shallow** fibrous widespreading, moderately **deep** on dry sites; transplants well B&B in early spring

SPECIES; Associate: Paper Birch, Red Maple, American Larch, Black Ash, Black Spruce, Eastern Arborvitae,
Showy Mountain Ash, Boxelder, Hazel Alder
Similar: Quaking and Bigtooth Aspen, Paper Birch has exfoliating bark, Blue Leaf Birch
Cultivars: none commercially available

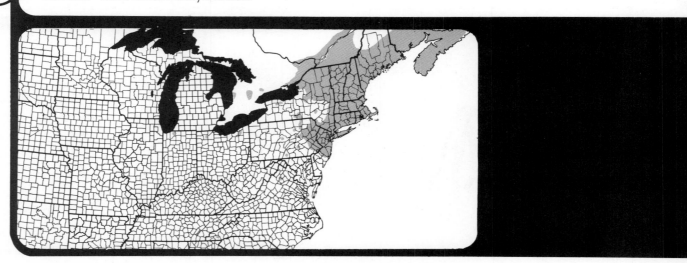

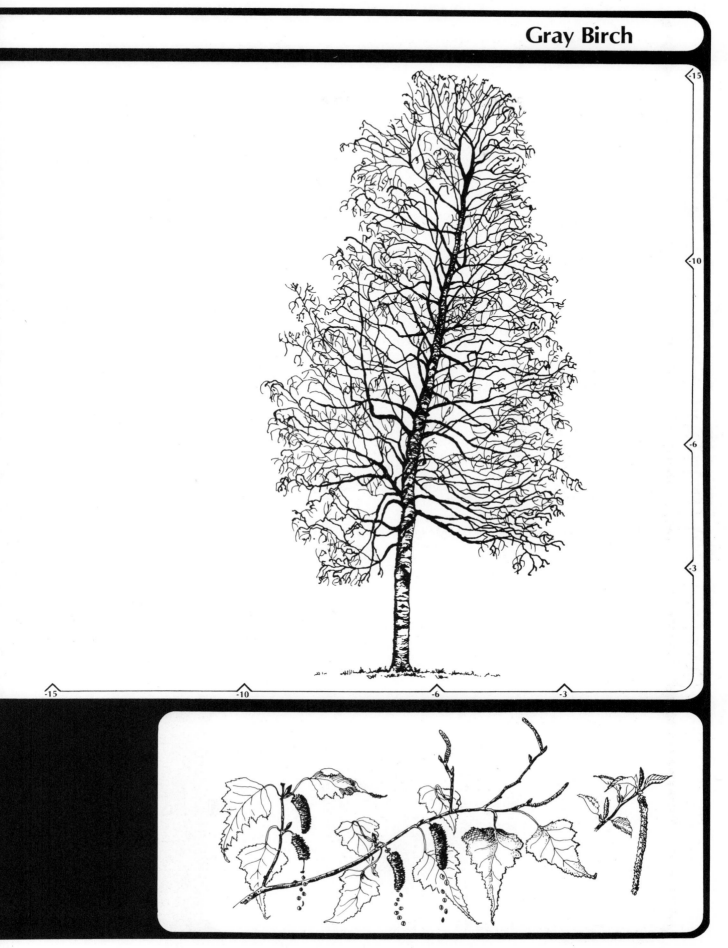

Carpinus caroliniana

FORM: obovoid to globular
Size: **large understory -** 10 to 15 m (35 to 50 ft)
Spread: **intermediate -** 10 to 15 m (35 to 50 ft), 2/3 or equal to height
Mass: very **dense**

BRANCHING: multiple trunks, low branched, **horizontal, picturesque,** slightly **pendulous, fine** texture
Twig: very slender, slightly **zig zag, red brown**
Bud: 3 mm (1/8 in) long, chestnut brown, scales with white margins
Bark: **smooth,** irregularly fluted with sinewy muscle-like character, thin longitudinal stripes; dark **gray**

FOLIAGE: alternate, **simple, elliptic-oval,** doubly serrate margin, **medium fine** texture
Surface: **dull** above, pale beneath
Color: spring - orange to **reddish green;** summer - **blue green;** autumn - **orange to** deep **red**
Season: **deciduous;** emergence - late **April,** drop - early **October**

FLOWER: male **catkins** 2.5 to 5 cm (1 to 2 in) long
Color: **red** or reddish green
Season: late **April through** early **May,** with the new leaves
Sex: monoecious

FRUIT: 3 lobed winged **samara** in drooping clusters, seeds exposed
Color: orange to scarlet **red**
Season: mid **June to** late **October**
Wildlife Value: **very low;** songbirds, waterfowl

HABITAT: formation - **forest;** region - **northern, central;** gradient - **lowland wet mesic, upland mesic;** elevated floodplain
     terrace and knobs, lower slopes, cool north and east slopes
Shade Tolerance: **very tolerant;** index range 8.0 to 10.0
Floor Tolerance: **intolerant**

SOIL; Texture: **medium** loams **to fine** sandy loams and silt loams
Drainage: **poor to excessive**
Moisture: demands **moist to average** soils
Reaction: **slightly acid to neutral,** pH 6.1-7.5

HARDINESS: zone 2
Rate: **slow -** 20 cm (8 in) in a year on better sites, 9 to 10.5 m (30 to 35 ft) in 40 year period
Longevity: **medium -** maturity reached at about 150 years

SUSCEPTIBILITY; Physiological: **infrequent**
Disease: **infrequent -** occasional leaf spot, cankers, twig blight
Insect: **infrequent -** occasional maple phenococcus scale, not serious
Wind-Ice: **infrequent**

URBAN TOLERANCE; Pollution: **sensitive -** NOx; **intermediate -** HFl; **resistant -** SO$_2$
Lighting: **sensitive**   Drought-Heat: **sensitive**   Mine Spoils: **sensitive**
Salt: Soil Compaction: **sensitive**
Root Pattern: **deep** coarse **lateral** spreading; difficult to transplant, move root pruned trees B&B in early spring

SPECIES; Associate: Black and Sugar Maple, American Beech, American Linden, Common Witch-hazel, Northern Red
     Oak, Pagoda Dogwood, Shadblow Serviceberry, Eastern Wahoo, American Hophornbeam
Similar: Carpinus betulus (European) is related, Allegheny, Shadblow Serviceberry, Common Chokecherry, chokeberry
Cultivars: none available commercially

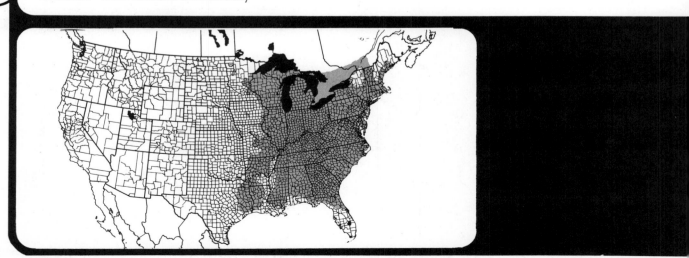

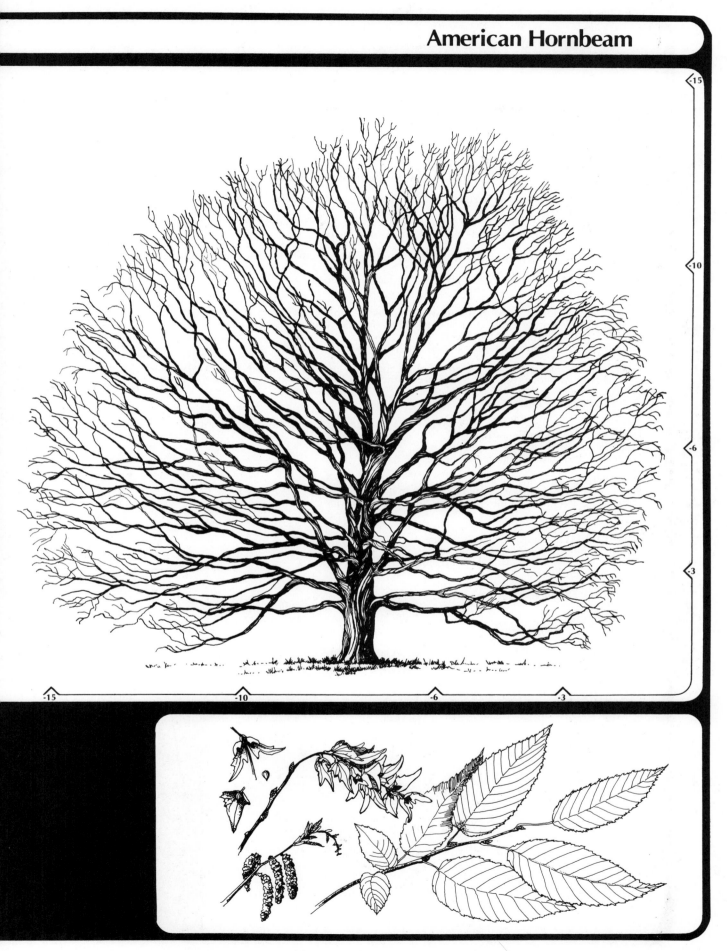

Carya cordiformis

FORM: **globular**
Size: **large canopy** - 22.5 to 30 m (75 to 100 ft)
Spread: **very wide** - 22.5 to 30 m (75 to 100 ft), as wide as tall, commonly much narrower
Mass: **moderate**

BRANCHING: straight trunk, slender **ascending picturesque** branches, slightly drooping branchlets, **medium** texture
Twig: smooth, **gray brown**
Bud: **naked,** bright sulfur **yellow**
Bark: young trees **smooth** becoming **shallow furrowed** with **narrow** line-like ridges; slate **gray,** major limbs black

FOLIAGE: alternate, **pinnately compound,** 7-11 leaflets, **ovate-lanceolate,** terminal leaflet largest, **medium** texture
Surface: **dull**
Color: spring - light **yellow green;** summer - dark **yellow green;** autumn - golden **yellow brown**
Season: **deciduous;** emergence - mid **May,** drop - mid **October**

FLOWER: male **catkins** in 3's at base of new growth, 7.5 to 10 cm (3 to 4 in) long, pendulous
Color: **yellow green**
Season: mid **May,** appear with or shortly after leaf emergence
Sex: monoecious

FRUIT: round **nut** enclosed by a four winged husk splitting about to the middle, 2.5 cm (1 in) diameter
Color: husk yellow green becoming **black** when ripe, brown nut
Season: late **August to** mid **October**
Wildlife Value: **intermediate;** songbirds, small mammals

HABITAT: formation - **forest;** region - **central;** gradient - **lowland wet-mesic, upland mesic and mesic dry;** floodplain,
moist or dry slopes and uplands, more restricted to moist sites in southern part of range
Shade Tolerance: **intermediate;** index 5.8
Flood Tolerance: **intermediate**

SOIL; Texture: **coarse** loamy sands, loams and silt loams preferred, common on **moderately fine** silty or sandy clays
Drainage: **moderately poor to well**
Moisture: **wet,** moist, average **to dry**
Reaction: **moderately acid to alkaline,** pH 5.6-8.0

HARDINESS: zone 4a
Rate: **slow** to medium - 7.5 to 9 m (25 to 30 ft) in 50 year period, commonly less
Longevity: **long** to medium - maximum age around 200 years, shortest lived hickory

SUSCEPTIBILITY; Physiological: **infrequent**
Disease: **infrequent** - Anthracnose, scab
Insect: **infrequent** - occasional bark beetles in drought years
Wind-Ice: **infrequent**

URBAN TOLERANCE; Pollution: **sensitive** - 2,4-D
Lighting: Drought-Heat: **intermediate**   Mine Spoils: **intermediate**
Salt: **sensitive**   Soil Compaction: **intermediate**
Root Pattern: deep **taproot;** transplants somewhat easier than other hickories, move B&B in early spring

SPECIES; Associate: White and Northern Red Oaks, White Ash, Tuliptree, American Elm, Sugar and Black Maples,
Butternut, American Beech, American Sweetgum, Shagbark Hickory
Similar: Pecan attains greater size at maturity, Green Ash exhibits similar form and foliage character
Cultivars: none available commercially

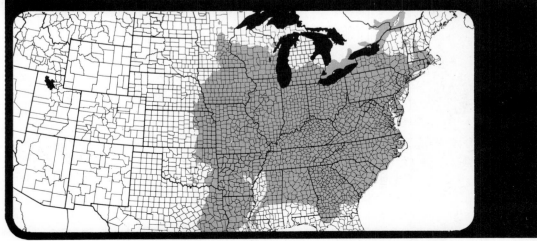

Carya glabra

FORM: irregular-obovoid
Size: **large canopy** - 22.5 to 30 m (75 to 100 ft)
Spread: **intermediate** - 10 to 15 m (35 to 50 ft), commonly narrower
Mass: **open**

BRANCHING: short **picturesque ascending** branches, lower branchlets and branch tips drooping, **coarse** texture
Twig: stout, **gray brown**
Bud: **large papery,** exfoliating scales
Bark: **shallow furrowed** with **narrow** flat cross-checked ridges; slate **gray,** major limbs coal black

FOLIAGE: alternate, **pinnately compound,** usually 7 leaflets, **oblanceolate,** terminal leaflet largest, **medium** texture
Surface: **dull,** paler beneath
Color: spring - **maroon green;** summer - dark **yellow green;** autumn - golden **yellow brown**
Season: **deciduous;** emergence - mid **May,** drop - late **October**

FLOWER: male **catkins** in groups of 3, 7.5 to 10 cm (3 to 4 in) long, pendulous
Color: **yellow green**
Season: mid **May,** appear with leaf emergence or after leaves are partly grown
Sex: monoecious

FRUIT: pear shaped **nut** enclosed in four ridged husk, 38 mm (1 1/2 in) long
Color: yellow green husk becoming **black** at maturity, brown nut
Season: early **September** to late **October**
Wildlife Value: **intermediate;** songbirds, small mammals

HABITAT: formation - **forest;** region - **central;** gradient - **upland dry;** steep rocky land, sandy hills, upland ridges and
ravines, warm south facing slopes
Shade Tolerance: **intermediate;** index range 4.0-5.9, most tolerant hickory
Flood Tolerance: **very intolerant;** most intolerant hickory

SOIL; Texture: **medium to fine;** heavy soils, sandy and silty clays, clays
Drainage: **well** drained **to moderately well**
Moisture: **average,** tolerates **droughty**
Reaction: **slightly acid to neutral,** pH 6.1-7.5

HARDINESS: **zone 5a**
Rate: **slow** - 15 cm (6 in) of growth per year generally, more rapid than Shagbark Hickory
Longevity: **long** - mature at 200 years, many survive 300 years

SUSCEPTIBILITY; Physiological: **frequent** - easily damaged by frost
Disease: **frequent** - leaf blotch, Anthracnose, scab, cankers, Phomopsis tumor
Insect: **frequent** - hickory bark beetle, twig girdler, gall insects
Wind-Ice: **infrequent**

URBAN TOLERANCE; Pollution: **sensitive** - 2,4-D
Lighting: Drought-Heat: **resistant**   Mine Spoils: **resistant**
Salt: **sensitive**   Soil Compaction: **sensitive**
Root Pattern: deep **taproot,** difficult to transplant; move as small tree B&B in early spring

SPECIES; Associate: Post, Black, Blackjack, Scarlet, Shingle, Chinkapin, and White Oaks, Shagbark, and Mockernut
Hickories, Black Tupelo, Sourwood, Eastern Redcedar, Flowering Dogwood
Similar: Mockernut Hickory, Ohio Buckeye has orange autumn color and scaly bark
Cultivars: none available commercially

160

Pignut Hickory

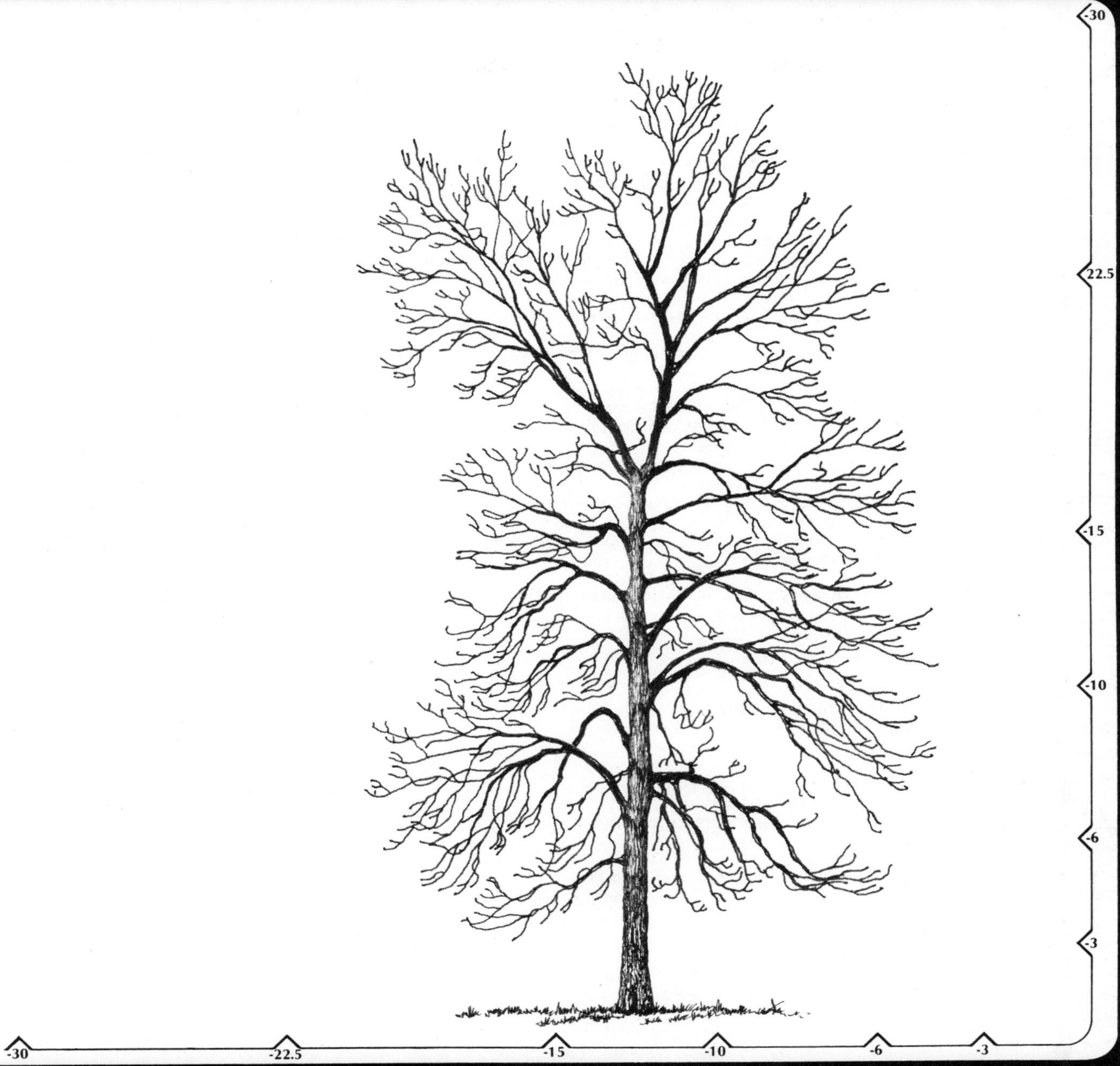

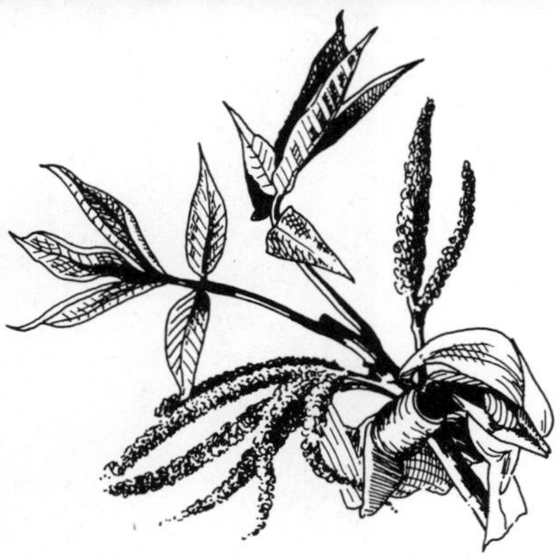

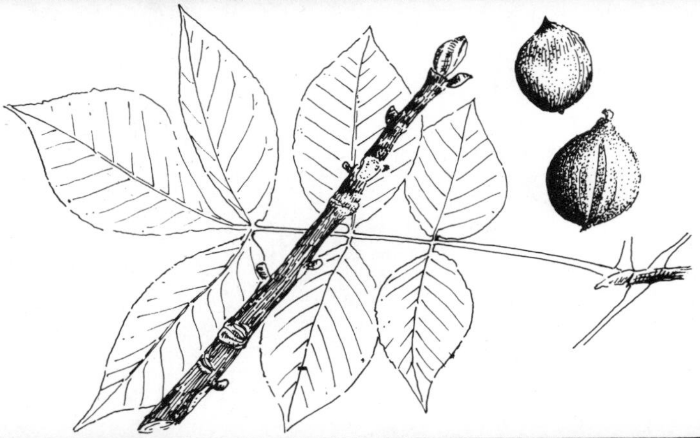

Carya illinoensis

FORM: globular
Size: **large canopy -** 22.5 to 30 m (75 to 100 ft)
Spread: **very wide -** 22.5 to 30 m (75 to 100 ft), commonly 3/4 or equal to height
Mass: **open**

BRANCHING: massive trunk, stout symmetrical **ascending** branches, **coarse** texture
Twig: smooth **gray brown**
Bud: **naked,** sulfur **yellow** to yellow brown
Bark: remaining **smooth** for years, old trees **shallow furrowed** with long flat **narrow** ridges; slate **gray**

FOLIAGE: alternate, **pinnately compound,** 9-13 leaflets, **ovate-lanceolate,** scythe shaped, **medium** texture
Surface: **dull,** paler beneath
Color: spring - **medium green;** summer - dark **yellow green;** autumn - golden **yellow brown**
Season: **deciduous;** emergence - early **May,** drop - mid **October**

FLOWER: male **catkins** in 3's, 7.5 to 10 cm (3 to 4 in) long, pendulous
Color: **yellow green**
Season: early **May,** appear with or shortly after leaf emergence
Sex: monoecious

FRUIT: cylindric **nut** enclosed by a thin 4 sectioned winged husk, 4 to 5 cm (1 1/2 to 2 in) long
Color: green husk becoming **black** when ripe, light brown nut
Season: late **August** to early **October**
Wildlife Value: **intermediate;** man, songbirds, small mammals

HABITAT: formation - **forest;** region - **central;** gradient - **lowland wet-mesic;** river bottoms, low terraces, very low land
which is subject to overflow
Shade Tolerance: **intolerant;** index range 2.0-3.9, most intolerant hickory
Flood Tolerance: **intermediate**

SOIL; Texture: **moderately coarse** sandy loams **to moderately fine** sandy or silty clays
Drainage: **poor to moderately well**
Moisture: demands **moist**
Reaction: **neutral,** pH 6.6-7.5

HARDINESS: **zone 6**
Rate: **slow** to medium - 20 cm (8 in) per year, 30 m (75 ft) in 80 years, most rapid hickory
Longevity: **long -** commonly survives 300 years

SUSCEPTIBILITY: Physiological: **infrequent**
Disease: **infrequent -** none serious
Insect: **infrequent -** pecan carpenterworm, twig girdler, obscure scale are of local importance
Wind-Ice: **infrequent**

URBAN TOLERANCE; Pollution: **sensitive -** 2,4-D
Lighting: Drought-Heat: **intermediate** Mine Spoils: **intermediate**
Salt: **sensitive** Soil Compaction: **intermediate**
Root Pattern: **taproot;** difficult to transplant, move as small B&B tree in early spring

SPECIES; Associate: American Elm, Eastern Poplar, Green Ash, American Planetree, Black Willow, Pin Oak,
Black Tupelo, American Sweetgum
Similar: Bitternut Hickory is similar
Cultivars: 'Gormely' - dense foliage; 'San Saba' - small crown, open; 'Western' - rapid growth; others

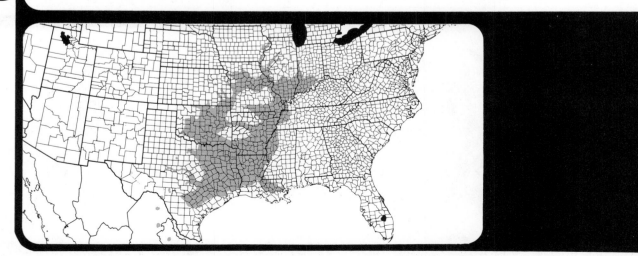

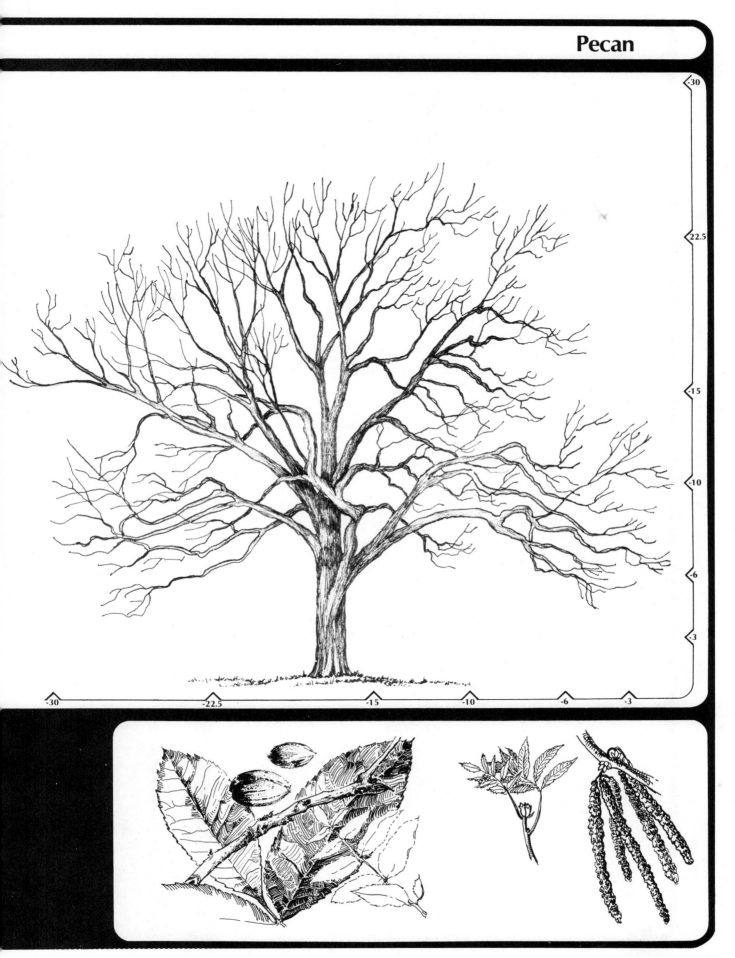

Carya ovata

FORM: **irregular-ovoid** and **obovoid**
Size: **large canopy** - 22.5 to 30 m (75 to 100 ft)
Spread: **intermediate** - 10 to 15 m (35 to 50 ft), 1/2 the height
Mass: **open**

BRANCHING: short stout **picturesque ascending** and spreading, lower branchlets often drooping, **coarse** texture
Twig: stout, shiny, **gray-brown**
Bud: **large papery**, exfoliating scales
Bark: **vertical exfoliating** plates, curl outward at ends, shaggy appearance; slate **gray**, major limbs coal black

FOLIAGE: alternate, **pinnately compound**, 5 leaflets, **oblanceolate**, terminal leaflet largest, **medium coarse** texture
Surface: **dull**, paler beneath
Color: spring - light **yellow green**; summer - dark **yellow green**; autumn - golden **yellow brown**
Season: **deciduous;** emergence - mid **May**, drop - mid **October**

FLOWER: pendulous **catkins** in loose stringy clusters, 7.5 to 10 cm (3 to 4 in) long
Color: **yellow green**
Season: mid **May**, appearing with or shortly after leaf emergence
Sex: monoecious

FRUIT: globular **nut** encased by a thick 4 sectioned husk, 4 cm (1 1/2 in) diameter
Color: green husk becoming **black** when ripe, brown nut
Season: early **September** to mid **October**
Wildlife Value: **intermediate;** man, songbirds, small mammals

HABITAT: formation - **forest, savanna;** region - **central;** gradient - **upland mesic-dry;** dry south and west facing slopes, occasional on alluvial land in southern part of range
Shade Tolerance: **intermediate;** index 5.4
Flood Tolerance: **intolerant**

SOIL; Texture: **medium to fine;** loams, fine silty clays, sandy clays and clay; occasional on alluvial soils
Drainage: **moderately poor to well drained**
Moisture: **wet to** porous **droughty** granular soils
Reaction: **slightly acid,** pH 6.1-6.5

HARDINESS: **zone 4a**
Rate: **slow** - 15 cm (6 in) per year, slower than White Oak
Longevity: **long -** mature at 150 to 200 years, many surviving 250 years

SUSCEPTIBILITY; Physiological: **infrequent**
Disease: **infrequent -** occasional leaf blotch, heart rot fungi, Anthracnose
Insect: **frequent -** hickory bark beetle
Wind-Ice: **infrequent**

URBAN TOLERANCE; Pollution: **sensitive** - 2,4-D
Lighting: Drought-Heat: **resistant**   Mine Spoils: **resistant**
Salt: **sensitive**   Soil Compaction: **intermediate**
Root Pattern: deep **taproot;** difficult to transplant, move as small tree B&B in early spring

SPECIES; Associate: White, Black, Shumard, Bur and Chestnut Oaks, Mockernut, Bitternut, and Pignut Hickories, Black Cherry, Flowering Dogwood, Tuliptree, White Ash, American Linden, Ohio Buckeye
Similar: Shellbark Hickory is very close
Cultivars: none available commercially

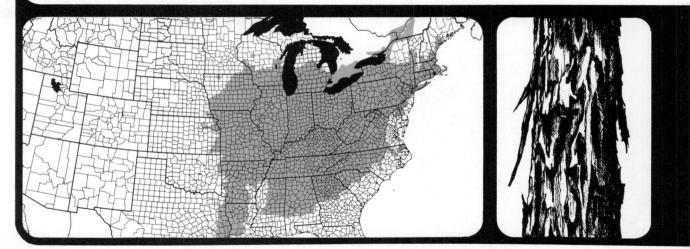

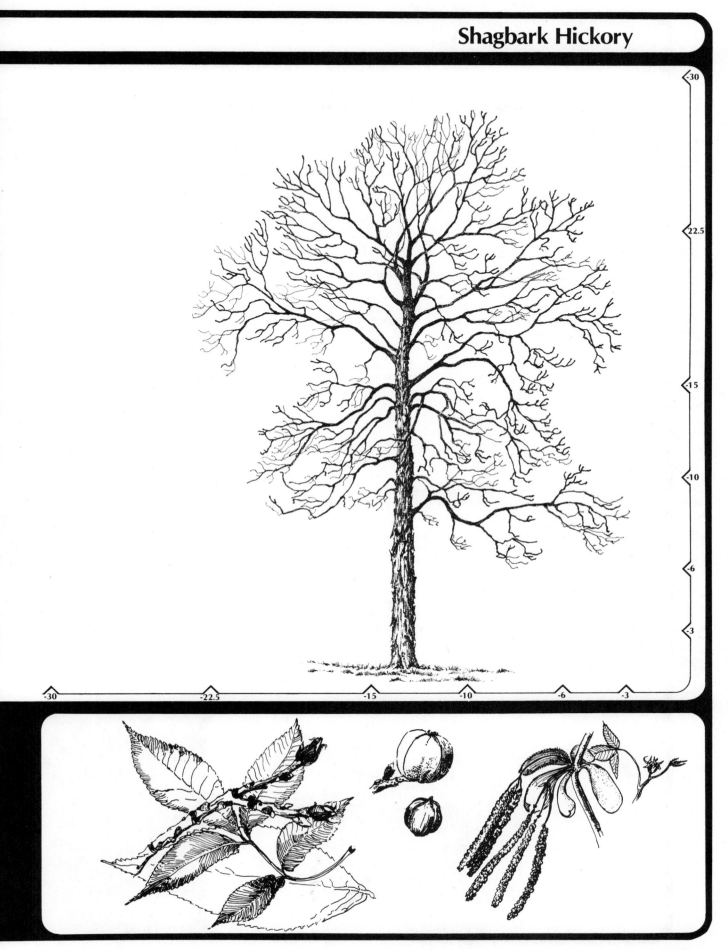

Carya tomentosa

FORM: irregular-obovoid
Size: **large canopy -** 22.5 to 30 m (75 to 100 ft)
Spread: **intermediate -** 10 to 15 m (35 to 50 ft), 1/2 the height
Mass: **open**

BRANCHING: short stout **picturesque ascending** branches, lower branchlets and branch tips drooping, **coarse** texture
Twig: stout, matted **velvety, gray brown**
Bud: **large papery,** winter buds **woolly, silvery**
Bark: **shallow furrowed** with **narrow** flat cross-checked ridges; dark **gray,** major limbs coal black

FOLIAGE: alternate, **pinnately compound,** 7 to 9 leaflets, **oblanceolate,** terminal leaflet largest, **medium** texture
Surface: **dull,** paler beneath
Color: spring - light **yellow green;** summer - dark **yellow green;** autumn - golden **yellow brown**
Season: **deciduous;** emergence - mid **May,** drop - mid **October**

FLOWER: male **catkins** in groups of 3, 7.5 to 10 cm (3 to 4 in) long, pendulous
Color: **yellow green**
Season: mid **May,** appear with or shortly after leaf emergence
Sex: monoecious

FRUIT: globular **nut** encased by a thick 4 sectioned husk, 3 to 5 cm (1 1/2 to 2 in) diameter
Color: green husk becoming **black** when ripe, brown nut
Season: early **September to** mid **October**
Wildlife Value: **intermediate;** man, songbirds, small mammals

HABITAT: formation - **forest;** region - **central;** gradient - **upland mesic-dry and dry;** dry ridgetops and ravines, sandy
terraces, warm south and west facing slope aspects
Shade Tolerance: **intolerant;** index range 2.0 to 3.9
Flood Tolerance: **very intolerant**

SOIL; Texture: **coarse** sands and sandy loams **to fine** silty clays and clays, common on poorly aerated soils
Drainage: **moderately well,** tolerates **excessive**
Moisture: **average,** tolerates **droughty** conditions
Reaction: **slightly acid,** pH 6.1-6.5

HARDINESS: **zone 5b**
Rate: **slow -** approximately 15 cm (6 in) in a year
Longevity: **long -** mature at 150 years, trees 250 years are common, shorter lived than Shagbark or Pignut

SUSCEPTIBILITY; Physiological: **infrequent**
Disease: **infrequent -** occasional leaf blotch, Anthracnose, scab
Insect: **infrequent -** hickory spiral borer, hickory bark beetle, pecan carpenterworm
Wind-Ice: **infrequent**

URBAN TOLERANCE; Pollution: **sensitive -** 2,4-D
Lighting: Drought-Heat: **resistant**   Mine Spoils: **resistant**
Salt: **sensitive**   Soil Compaction: **sensitive**
Root Pattern: **strong deep taproot;** difficult to transplant, move as small tree B&B in early spring

SPECIES; Associate: Shumard, Post, Black and Blackjack Oaks, Shagbark and Pignut Hickory, Flowering Dogwood,
Pitch Pine, Sassafras, Ohio Buckeye
Similar: Pignut Hickory, perhaps Ohio Buckeye
Cultivars: none commercially available

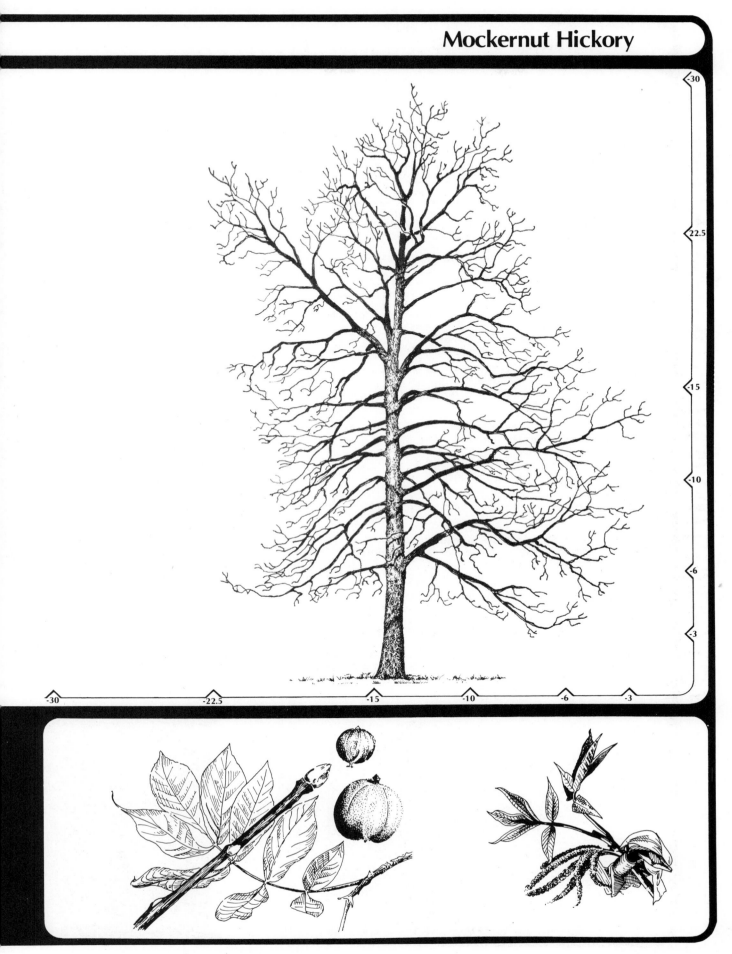

Castanea dentata

FORM: globular
Size: **small canopy** - 15 to 22.5 m (50 to 75 ft)
Spread: **wide** - 15 to 22.5 m (50 to 75 ft), as wide as tall
Mass: **dense**

BRANCHING: short trunk divided into 3 or 4 massive **horizontal** limbs, broad low crown, **coarse** texture
Twig: stout glossy, **red brown**
Bud: **clustered, sharp pointed, 2 scales,** terminal bud lacking, laterals chestnut brown
Bark: **shallow furrows** with **wide** flat-topped platy ridges, old trunks deeply furrowed; **gray brown,** plates ashy gray

FOLIAGE: alternate, **simple, lanceolate-oblong lanceolate,** coarsely toothed margin, bristly tipped, **coarse** texture
Surface: **dull,** smooth above, paler beneath, thin
Color: spring - **yellow green;** summer - dark **yellow green;** autumn - bright clear **yellow to** golden **yellow brown**
Season: **deciduous;** emergence - mid **May,** drop - mid **October**

FLOWER: long slender pencil-thin **pyramidal spike,** 15 to 20 cm (6 to 8 in) long
Color: **yellow**
Season: early through mid **July,** after leaves are fully grown
Sex: monoecious   **Fragrant:** strong

FRUIT: **nut** encased in a spiny bur-like husk, 5 cm (2 in) diameter, husk interior densely woolly
Color: husk light **tan brown,** nut reddish brown
Season: late **August through** late **November**
Wildlife Value **very low;** man, small mammals

HABITAT: formation - **forest;** region - **central;** gradient - **upland mesic** and **mesic-dry;** best development in rich mesic
sites common on dry ridges and rocky slopes
Shade Tolerance: **intermediate;** index range 4.0-5.9, more tolerant than oak or hickory associates
Flood Tolerance: **intolerant**

SOIL; Texture: **moderately coarse to fine;** loams, fine silty clays, sandy clays and heavy clay
Drainage: **moderately poor to well**
Moisture: **moist to dry**
Reaction: **strong acid** preference, pH 4.0-6.0

HARDINESS: **zone 5a**
Rate: **medium to fast** - 6 m (20 ft) in 10 year period
Longevity: **long** - trees 200 years or more were common, chestnut blight reduces expectancy to short

SUSCEPTIBILITY; Physiological: **infrequent**
Disease: **frequent** - chestnut blight has all but eliminated the species from its former range
Insect: **infrequent**
Wind-Ice: **frequent** - weak wooded, easily broken

URBAN TOLERANCE; Pollution: **intermediate** - HFl
Lighting: Drought-Heat: **intermediate**   Mine Spoils: **intermediate**
Salt: Soil Compaction: **sensitive**
Root Pattern: stout, perpendicular **taproot;** difficult to transplant, move as a small tree B&B in early spring

SPECIES; Associate: Scarlet Oak, Chestnut Oak, Northern Red Oak, White Oak, Tuliptree, Flowering Dogwood,
American Hophornbeam, Sugar Maple, Red Maple, hickory species
Similar: Chinese Chestnut is smaller, but is resistant to chestnut blight
Cultivars: none grown commercially

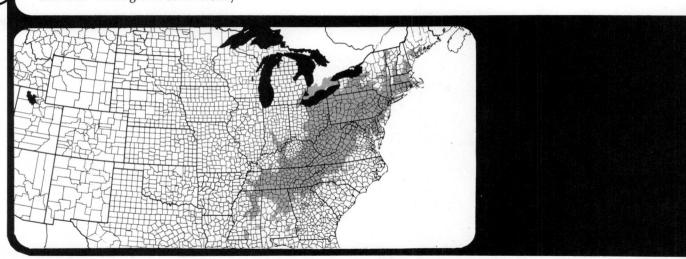

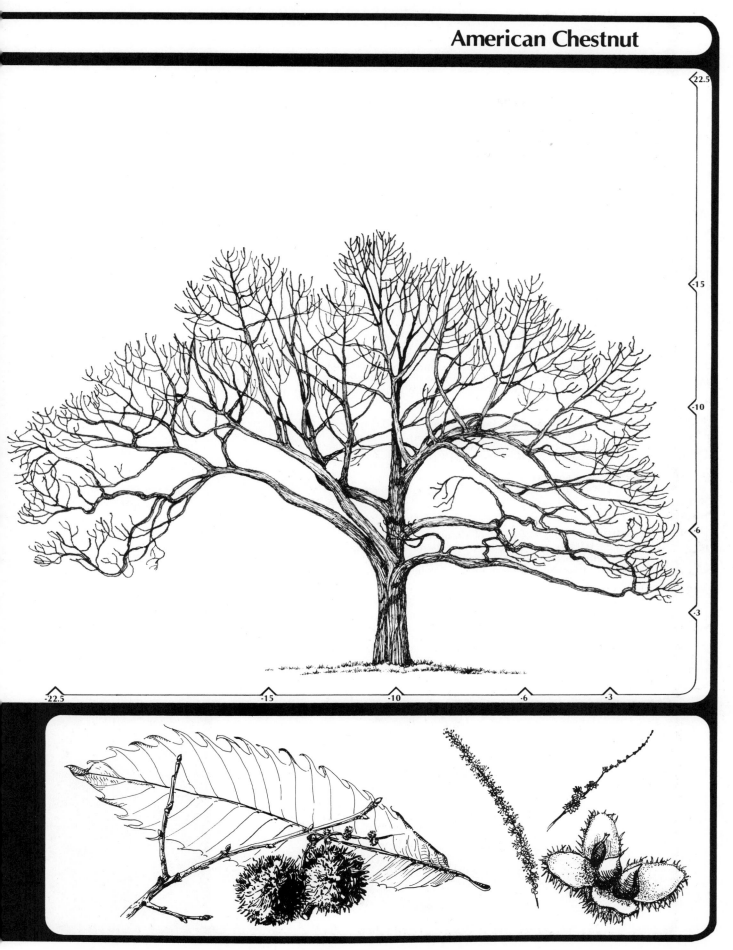

22.5

-15

-10

-6

-3

-22.5   -15   -10   -6   -3

Catalpa speciosa

FORM: irregular-conical
Size: **large canopy** - 22.5 to 30 m (75 to 100 ft)
Spread: **intermediate** - 10 to 15 m (35 to 50 ft), 1/2 the height
Mass: **open**

BRANCHING: ascending, **picturesque** gnarled twisting contorted habit, very **coarse** texture
Twig: stout, **large leaf scars,** conspicuous lenticels appear swollen at nodes, **red brown**
Bud: small red brown (inconspicuous)
Bark: **shallow furrowed, narrow** irregular scaly ridges, often twisting character; pale **gray brown**

FOLIAGE: whorled and opposite, **simple, cordate,** entire margin, very **coarse** texture
Surface: **dull** upper, tomentose beneath
Color: spring - **yellow green;** summer - **yellow green;** autumn - **yellow green** turning black
Season: **deciduous;** emergence - early **June,** drop - mid **October**

FLOWER: large **bell-shaped,** orchid-like, 5 cm (2 in) diameter in open 15 cm (6 in) snowball shaped clusters
Color: **white** with purplish and yellow spots or streaks over the lower lobe and inner tube
Season: mid through late **June**
Sex: monoecious

FRUIT: **legume,** long linear pencil thin curved pod, 20 to 50 cm (8 to 20 in) long
Color: **tan brown**
Season: throughout winter into spring, **October through April**
Wildlife Value: **very low**

HABITAT: formation - **forest;** region - **central;** gradient - **lowland wet-mesic;** streamside alluvial bottomlands, upper
    terrace and lower slope, midwest windbreak and farmstead plantings
Shade Tolerance: **intolerant;** index range 2.0-3.9
Flood Tolerance: **tolerant**

SOIL; Texture: **medium to moderately fine** silt and clay loams
Drainage: **well to poor** internal drainage
Moisture: **wet** soils **to** porous **droughty** granular soils
Reaction: **slightly acid to alkaline,** pH 6.1-8.0

HARDINESS: **zone 5a**
Rate: **fast** - forestry plots at Morton Arboretum averaged 60 to 76 cm (24 to 30 in) for 16 year period
Longevity: **short** - generally mature between 50 and 75 years, rarely survives 125 years

SUSCEPTIBILITY; Physiological: **infrequent**
Disease: **infrequent** - leaf spots, powdery mildew, Verticillium wilt, root rot
Insect: **infrequent** - catalpa midge and catalpa sphinx, comstock mealy bug
Wind-Ice: **frequent** - brittle branches, small branches frequently injured by storm

URBAN TOLERANCE; Pollution: **sensitive** - SO_2, O_3
Lighting: **sensitive**   Drought-Heat: **resistant**   Mine Spoils: **resistant**
Salt: **intermediate**   Soil Compaction: **resistant**
Root Pattern: **taproot** or **deep** coarse **laterals;** transplant as small tree B&B in early spring

Species; Associate: American Sweetgum, Black Willow, River Birch, Boxelder, Red Maple, False Indigo (shrub),
    chokeberry, Common Hackberry, American Planetree, Green and Blue Ash, Black Tupelo
Similar: Southern Catalpa is related, Royal Paulownia - flowers are pale violet
Cultivars: 'Aurea' - summer leaves golden yellow, 'Nana' - dwarf to 1.5 m (5 ft)

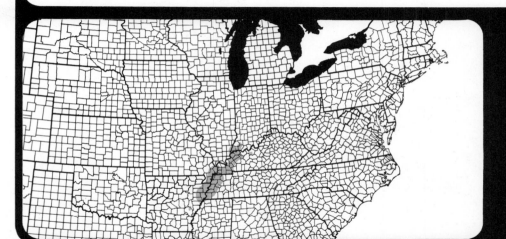

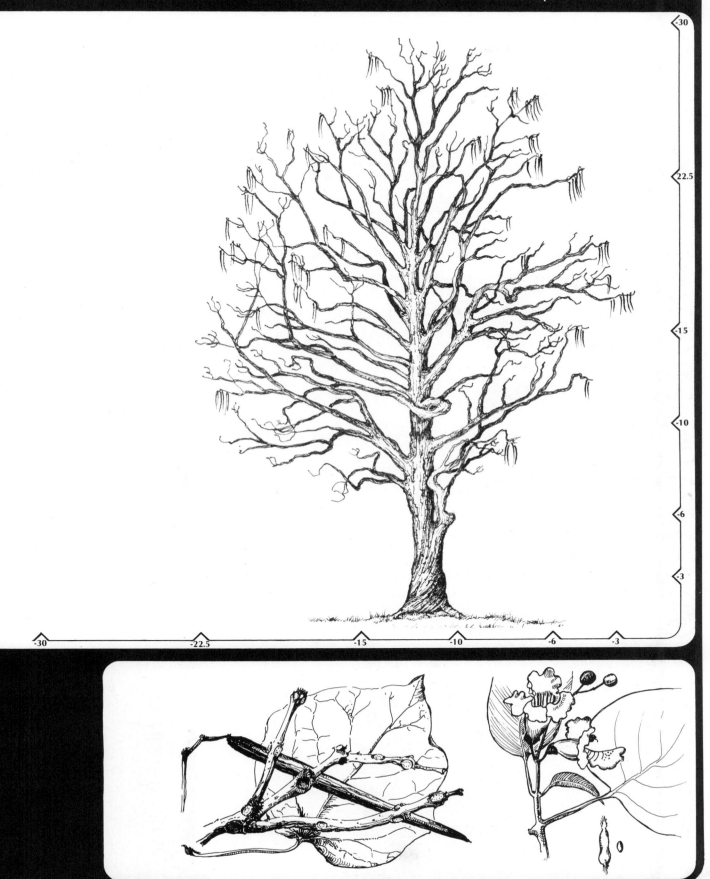

Celtis occidentalis

FORM: **globular**
Size: **large canopy** - 22.5 to 30 m (75 to 100 ft)
Spread: **very wide** - 22.5 to 30 m (75 to 100 ft), as wide as tall
Mass: **moderate**

BRANCHING: long clear trunk, abruptly **upright** limbs becoming arching, high umbrella crown, **medium** texture
Twig: **zig zag, green brown**
Bud: inconspicuous, egg shaped, light brown
Bark: **blocky,** young trees with short narrow knobby cork-like ridges; light **gray**

FOLIAGE: alternate, **simple, ovate, oblong ovate** to **ovate-lanceolate,** long tapered tip, uneven base, **medium fine** texture
Surface: **dull** and rough, young leaves densely woolly
Color: spring - **light green;** summer - light **blue green;** autumn - pale lemon **yellow**
Season: **deciduous;** emergence - late **April,** drop - early **November**

FLOWER: **small clusters,** individual 3 mm (1/8 in) across
Color: **yellowish green** with brown tint
Season: late **April through** early **May,** with the leaves
Sex: monoecious

FRUIT: singular thin fleshy **berry,** 8 mm (1/3 in) diameter, on slender 19 mm (3/4 in) stem
Color: **purple brown**
Season: **September-October, persisting** on tree most of winter **through February**
Wildlife Value: **very high;** man, songbirds, small mammals

HABITAT: formation - **forest, savanna;** region - **central;** gradient - **lowland wet-mesic and upland mesic dry;** drainage
  basins, mature floodplains, also wooded slopes or on high rocky limestone bluffs bordering streams, windbreak
Shade Tolerance: **intermediate;** index range 4.0-5.9
Flood Tolerance: **intermediate** - sites with permanent high water table harmful

SOIL; Texture: **moderately coarse** sandy loams, silty clays **to moderately fine** sandy loams
Drainage: **well to moderately poor**
Moisture: from **wet to dry**
Reaction: **neutral to alkaline,** pH 6.6-8.0, common on limestone soils and rock outcrops

HARDINESS: **zone 3a**
Rate: **medium** to fast - 56 to 76 cm (22 to 30 in) annually, 6 to 9 m (20 to 30 ft) in 20 year period
Longevity: medium to **long** - mature at 100 years, commonly surviving 200 years

SUSCEPTIBILITY; Physiological: **infrequent**
Disease: **frequent** - witches' broom, powdery mildew, leaf spots
Insect: **frequent** - hackberry nipple gall, morning cloak butterfly, scales
Wind-Ice: **infrequent**

URBAN TOLERANCE; Pollution:
Lighting: Drought-Heat: **resistant**   Mine spoils: **resistant**
Salt: **resistant**   Soil Compaction: **intermediate**
Root Pattern: **deep** coarse widespreading **laterals;** easily transplanted B&B or BR in spring or fall with care

SPECIES; Associate: Sugarberry, American Elm, White Ash, Green Ash, Silver Maple, Red Mulberry, Black Walnut,
  Common Honeylocust, Eastern Wahoo, American Planetree, hawthorn species
Similar: American Elm, Japanese Zelkova (Asiatic) exhibits finer texture, Sugarberry is more southern
Cultivars: 'Prairie Prince' - resistant to witches' broom, uniform shape

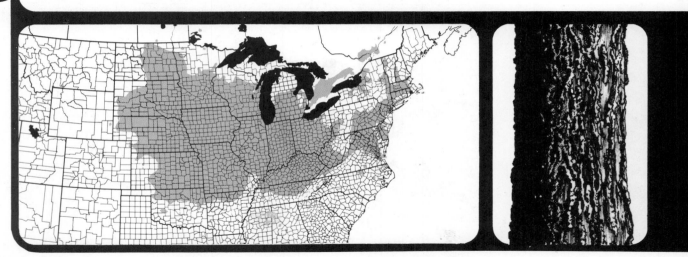

Cercis canadensis

FORM: broad **globular**
Size: **small understory** - 6 to 10 m (20 to 35 ft)
Spread: **narrow** - 6 to 10 m (20 to 35 ft), as wide or wider than tall
Mass: **moderate**

BRANCHING: several picturesque trunks, **horizontal picturesque** branching, high umbrella-like crown, **medium** texture
Twig: **zig zag** pattern, **red brown** to black coloration
Bud: small globular, glossy, black
Bark: thin squarish **scaly** plates, easily exfoliated under hand pressure; trunk **maroon purple**

FOLIAGE: alternate, **simple, cordate,** entire margin, **medium coarse** texture
Surface: **dull** above, pale beneath
Color: spring - **light green;** summer - **blue green;** autumn - **golden yellow**
Season: **deciduous;** emergence - mid **May,** drop - mid **October**

FLOWER: **small clusters** of 4 to 10 pea-like blooms, frequent on older branches and trunk
Color: carmen **pink to lavender**
Season: mid **April through** early **May,** before the new leaves
Sex: **dioecious**

FRUIT: **leguminous** bean-like pods, 5 cm (2 in) long, flattened and papery
Color: **purple brown**
Season: mid **July** persisting **through** late **December**
Wildlife Value: **very low**

HABITAT: formation - **forest;** region - **central;** gradient - **lowland wet-mesic and upland dry;** alluvial soils along streams
but absent from low alluvial flats, in southern part of range common to dry slopes and ravines, limestone bluffs
Shade Tolerance: **tolerant;** index range 6.0-7.9
Flood Tolerance: **intermediate**

SOIL; Texture: **moderately coarse** sandy loams **to moderately fine** sandy and silty clays
Drainage: **well to moderately well**
Moisture: prefers **moist,** tolerates **dry**
Reaction: **slightly acid to alkaline,** pH 6.1-8.0

HARDINESS: zone 5a
Rate: **slow** - generally about 30 cm (1 ft) per year
Longevity: **short** - maturity reached between 40 and 80 years

SUSCEPTIBILITY; Physiological: **infrequent**
Disease: **infrequent** - canker can be locally severe, occasional Verticillium wilt
Insect: **infrequent** - caterpillars, leaf hoppers, various scales cause some damage
Wind-Ice: **frequent**

URBAN TOLERANCE; Pollution: **sensitive** - O$_3$
Lighting: Drought-Heat: **resistant** Mine Spoils: **resistant**
Salt: very **sensitive** Soil Compaction: **intermediate**
Root Pattern: **shallow** fibrous becoming deep spreading on drier sites; transplants well B&B in spring or autumn

SPECIES; Associate: Flowering Dogwood, American Hophornbeam, Red Mulberry, Blackhaw Viburnum, American Elm,
Shagbark Hickory, Post, Bur, Blackjack, White, Black and Shumard Oaks
Similar: Chinese Redbud is related, many pink flowering crabapples
Cultivars: 'Alba' - has white flowers, 'Withers Pink Charm' - without purplish tint of species

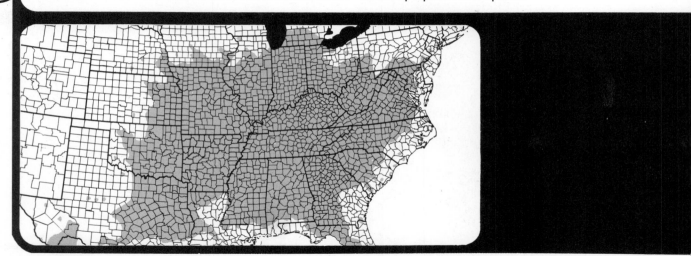

-10

-6

-3

-10   -6   -3

Chionanthus virginicus

FORM: columnar to obovoid
Size: **small understory** - 6 to 10 m (20 to 35 ft)
Spread: **narrow** - 6 to 10 m (20 to 35 ft), commonly 3 to 6 m (10 to 20 ft)
Mass: **moderate**

BRANCHING: short trunk, several moderately stout thick **ascending** branches, **medium** texture
Twig: **velvety**, slightly angular, conspicuous lenticels, **green brown**
Bud: angular, 3 mm (1/8 in), scaly
Bark: irregular thick flaky **scales,** larger limbs smooth with conspicuous dot-like lenticels; **red brown**

FOLIAGE: opposite, **simple, ovate-oblong ovate,** entire margin, **medium course** texture
Surface: **glossy above,** pale beneath
Color: spring - glossy **yellow green**; summer - **dark green**; autumn - bright **yellow**
Season: **deciduous;** emergence - late **May** or early **June,** drop - late **September**

FLOWER: in drooping feathery **pyramidal spike,** 10 to 15 cm (4 to 8 in) long
Color: **white,** profuse
Season: late **May through** early **June,** with new leaves
Sex: **dioecious**   Fragrant: slight agreeable odor

FRUIT: oval grape-like **berry,** 1 cm (1/2 in) wide, in loose drooping spikes
Color: dark **blue** to black
Season: mid **September through** mid **October**
Wildlife Value: **intermediate;** songbirds

HABITAT: formation - **forest;** region - **central;** gradient - **upland mesic-dry and dry;** upland slope and ravines,
    oak openings, high calcareous ridges, ledges on sandstone or limestone bluffs
Shade Tolerance: **very tolerant;** index range 8.0 to 10.0
Flood Tolerance: **intolerant**

SOIL; Texture: **moderately coarse** sandy and gravelly loams, medium loams, **to fine** clays
Drainage: **poor to excessive**
Moisture: demands **moist to average** soils
Reaction: **strongly acid to slightly acid,** pH 4.6-6.5

HARDINESS: zone 5b
Rate: **slow** - 10 to 15 cm (4 to 6 in) per year generally
Longevity: **medium**

SUSCEPTIBILITY; Physiological: **infrequent**
Disease: **infrequent** - none serious, powdery mildew, canker
Insect: **infrequent** - occasional scale problems
Wind-Ice: **infrequent**

URBAN TOLERANCE; Pollution:
Lighting: Drought-Heat: **sensitive**   Mine Spoils: **sensitive**
Salt: Soil Compaction: **sensitive**
Root Pattern: **deep** coarse **laterals;** somewhat difficult to transplant, move as small tree B&B in early spring

SPECIES; Associate: White, Scarlet, Chinkapin, Black and Chestnut Oaks, American
    Chestnut, Tuliptree, Pignut and Mockernut Hickories, Cucumbertree Magnolia
Similar: C. retusus (Asiatic) is related, Shadblow and Allegany Serviceberry, Common Chokecherry
Cultivars: none commercially available

White Fringetree

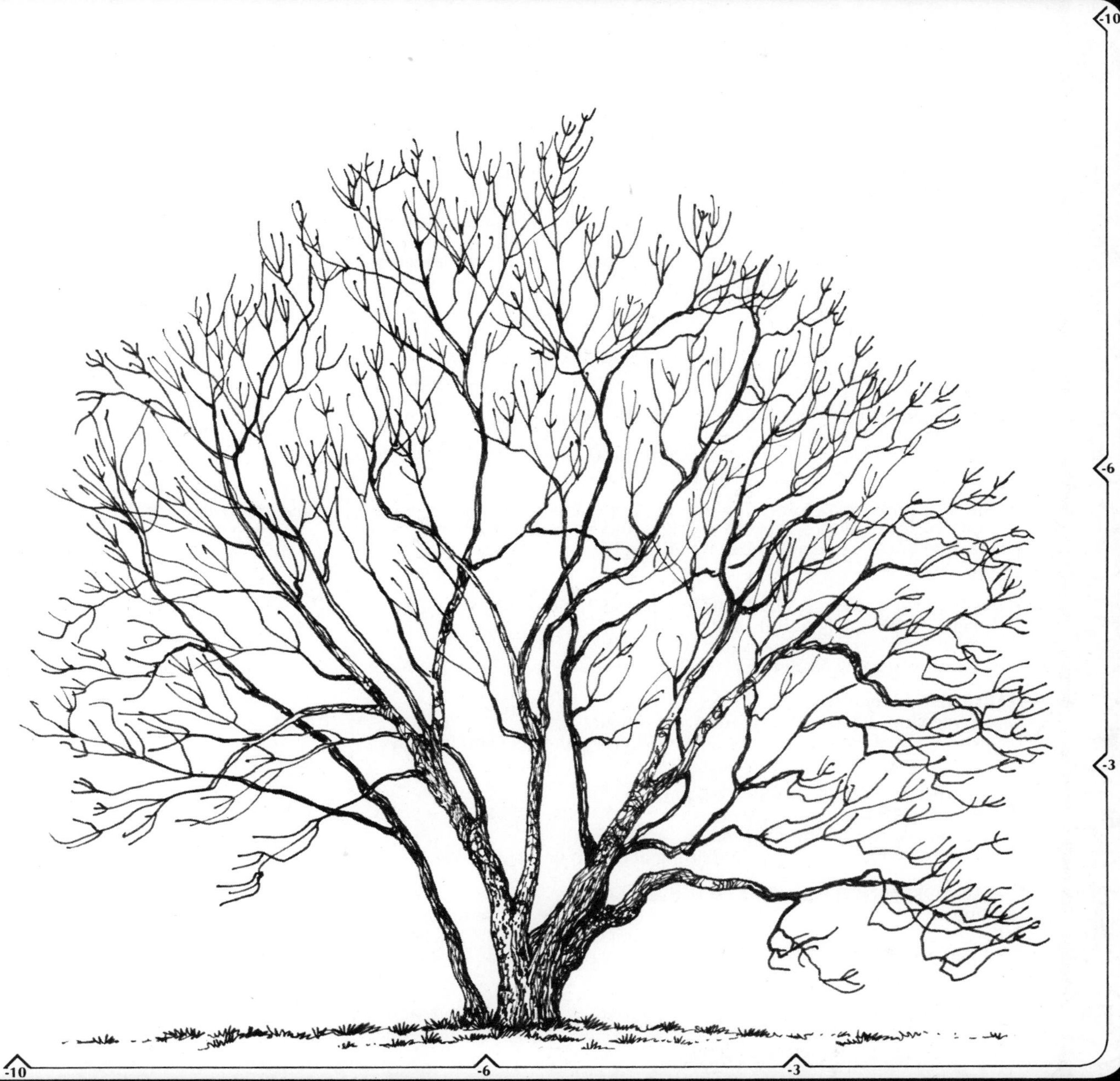

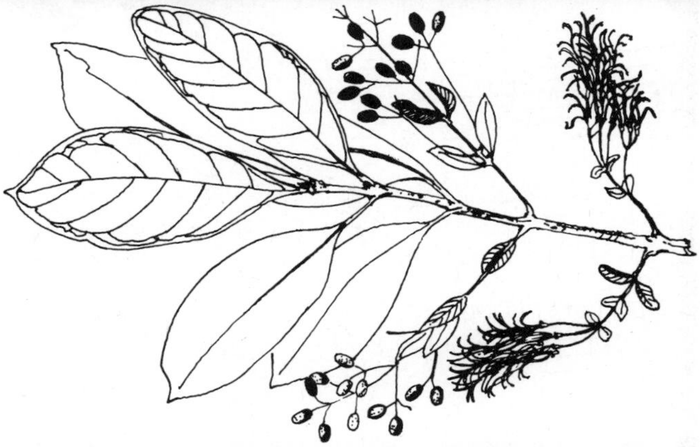

Cladrastis lutea

FORM: **globular**
Size: **small canopy** - 15 to 22.5 m (50 to 75 ft)
Spread: **wide** - 15 to 22.5 m (50 to 75 ft), 3/4 or equal to height
Mass: **moderate**

BRANCHING: trunk dividing near ground into several noticeably **upright** branches, **medium** texture
Twig: prominent dark colored lenticels, smooth, glossy, **red brown**
Bud: **dome shaped, surrounded by leaf scar**
Bark: **smooth,** similar to that of beech; ashy **gray**

FOLIAGE: alternate, **pinnately compound,** 7 to 11 leaflets, **obovate-oblong obovate,** entire margin, **medium** texture
Surface: **dull** above, paler beneath
Color: spring - **light green;** summer - **blue green;** autumn - pale lemon **yellow**
Season: **deciduous;** emergence - mid **May,** drop - early **October**

FLOWER: large broad pendant **pyramidal spikes,** 30 to 35 cm (12 to 14 in) long, pea-like individual bloom
Color: **white** or creamy white
Season: late **May through** early **June,** after new leaves unfold
Sex: monoecious   **Fragrant:** slight agreeable

FRUIT: **legume,** long narrow flattened pod, in broad loose open pyramidal clusters
Color: light **tan brown**
Season: mid **August through** winter season until late February or **March**
Wildlife Value: **very low**

HABITAT: formation - **forest;** region - **central;** gradient - **lowland wet-mesic, upland mesic;** mesic coves and ravines, river
valleys, lower slopes, limestone ridges and slopes overhanging streams
Shade Tolerance: **tolerant;** index range 6.0-7.9
Flood Tolerance: **intolerant**

SOIL; Texture: **coarse** loamy sands **to moderately fine** sandy loams and loams
Drainage: **moderately well to well**
Moisture: prefers **wet to average**
Reaction: **neutral to alkaline,** pH 6.6-8.0

HARDINESS: zone **3b**
Rate: **medium** - 30 to 60 cm (12 to 24 in) annually
Longevity: **medium** - commonly 120 to 160 years, shorter lived in midwest

SUSCEPTIBILITY; Physiological: **infrequent**
Disease: **infrequent** - none serious
Insect: **infrequent** - none serious
Wind-Ice: **frequent** - commonly splitting at crotch of major limbs

URBAN TOLERANCE; Pollution: **sensitive** - 2,4-D
Lighting: Drought-Heat: **sensitive**   Mine Spoils: **sensitive**
Salt: Soil Compaction: **sensitive**
Root Pattern: **deep** coarse **lateral** system; transplants well as small tree B&B in early spring

SPECIES; Associate: American Smoketree, American Chestnut, American Beech, Carolina Silverbell, American Sweetgum,
Tuliptree, Cucumbertree Magnolia, Sourwood, Sugar and Red Maple, Yellow Buckeye, White Oak
Similar: American Beech has similar bark, size and form, cultural requirements
Cultivars: none commercially obtainable

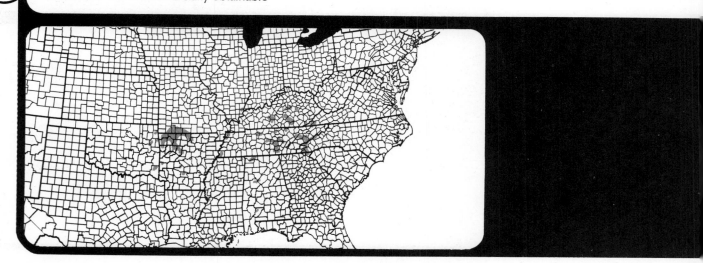

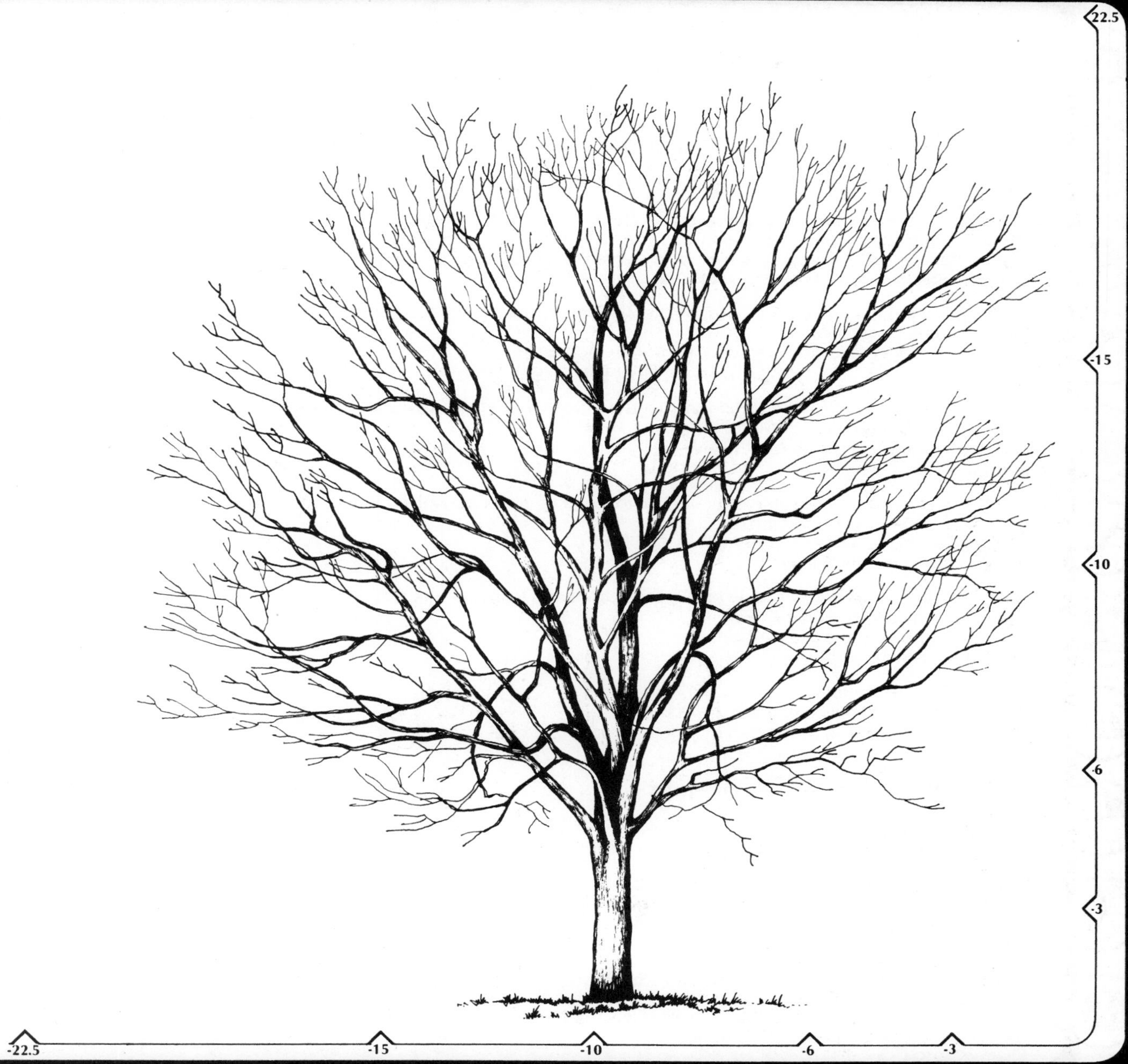
22.5
-15
-10
-6
-3
-22.5
-15
-10
-6
-3

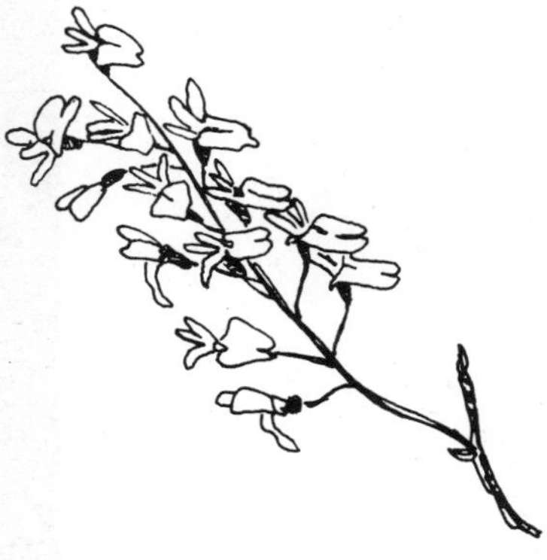

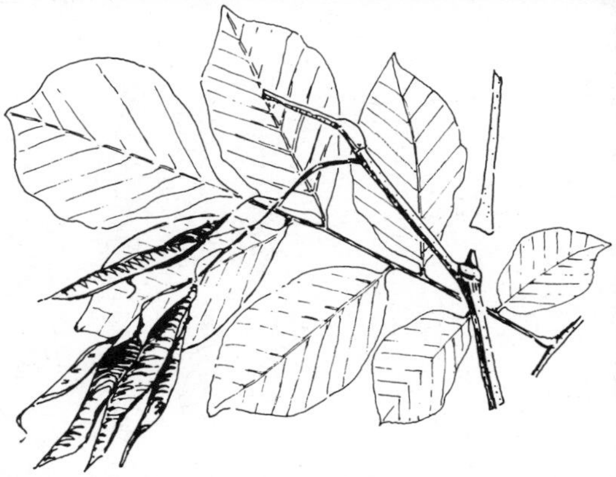

Cornus alternifolia

FORM: ovoid
Size: **small understory** - 6 to 10 m (20 to 35 ft)
Spread: **narrow** - 6 to 10 m (20 to 35 ft), commonly much narrower, 2/3 the height
Mass: **open**

BRANCHING: decidedly **horizontal** tiered with ends of branches and lateral twigs turning upwards, **medium** texture
Twig: **conspicuous leaf scar** encircles twig giving segmented appearance, lustrous, slender, **green to red or purple**
Bud: small, pointed, red brown
Bark: **smooth** on young trees becoming slightly fissured at base; **green or maroon purple**

FOLIAGE: alternate, **simple, ovate-oblong ovate**, entire margin, parallel veination, **medium fine** texture
Surface: **dull** above, whitish beneath
Color: spring - **silvery gray**; summer - **bright green to dark green**; autumn - dull **maroon purple**
Season: **deciduous**; emergence - **mid May**, drop - **mid October**

FLOWER: wide **flat topped**, 5 to 7.5 cm (2 to 3 in), many flowered clusters borne erect along twigs above leaves
Color: **white** or creamy
Season: late **May through** early **June**, after leaf emergence
Sex: monoecious   **Fragrant:** slight agreeable

FRUIT: globular **berry**, 8 mm (1/3 in) diameter, in loose flat-topped clusters, 7.5 cm (3 in) diameter
Color: dark blue or **red purple** on bright red stems
Season: early **July through** mid **August**
Wildlife Value: **very high;** upland ground birds, songbirds, waterbirds, large and small mammals, hoofed browsers

HABITAT: formation - **forest**; region - **northern, central**; gradient - **upland mesic**; elevated floodplain knobs and terraces, mesic ravines, sheltered coves
Shade Tolerance: **very tolerant;** index range 8.0-10.0
Flood Tolerance: **intermediate**

SOIL; Texture: **moderately coarse** loamy sands, medium loams **to moderately fine** silt loams
Drainage: **moderately poor to well**
Moisture: prefers **moist to average**
Reaction: **neutral,** pH 6.6-7.5

HARDINESS: zone 3b
Rate: **slow** - about 30 cm (1 ft) in a year
Longevity: **medium**

SUSCEPTIBILITY; Physiological: **infrequent**
Disease: **infrequent**
Insect: **infrequent**
Wind-Ice: **frequent** - windthrow, requires protection from wind, somewhat weak wooded

URBAN TOLERANCE; Pollution: **sensitive** - 2,4-D
Lighting: Drought-Heat: **sensitive**   Mine Spoils: **sensitive**
Salt: Soil Compaction: **intermediate**
Root Pattern: **shallow** fibrous, widespreading; transplants easily, slow recovery period, move B&B in early spring

SPECIES; Associate: American Hornbeam, Sugar, Black, Striped, and Mountain Maples, American Beech, Yellow and Sweet Birches, American Linden, Shadblow Serviceberry, Flowering Dogwood
Similar: very unique - Flowering Dogwood has similar form and branching habit, perhaps Crataegus douglasi
Cultivars: 'Argentea' - variegated foliage

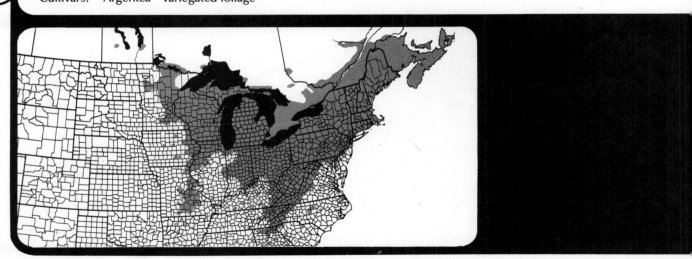

Pagoda Dogwood

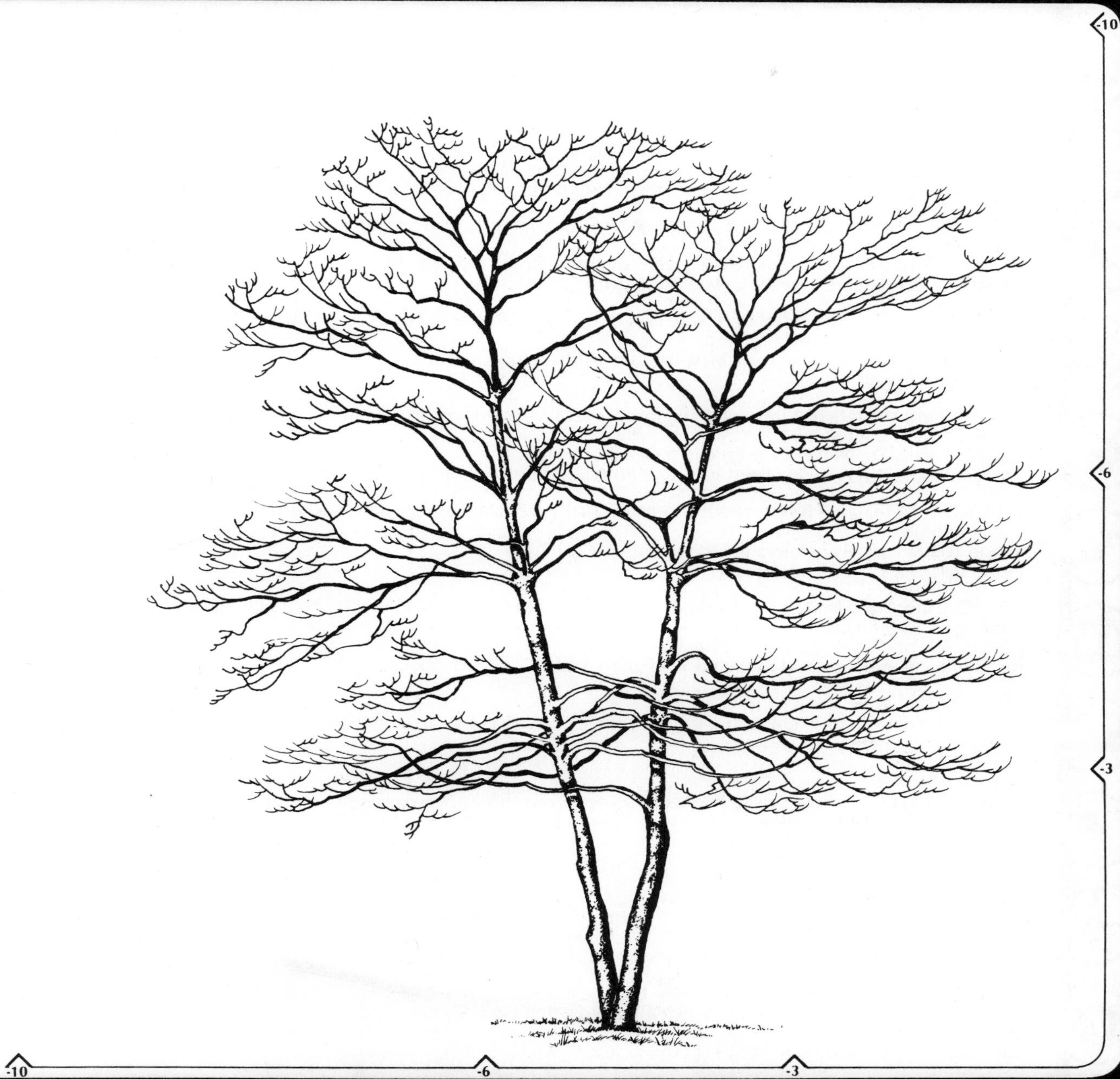

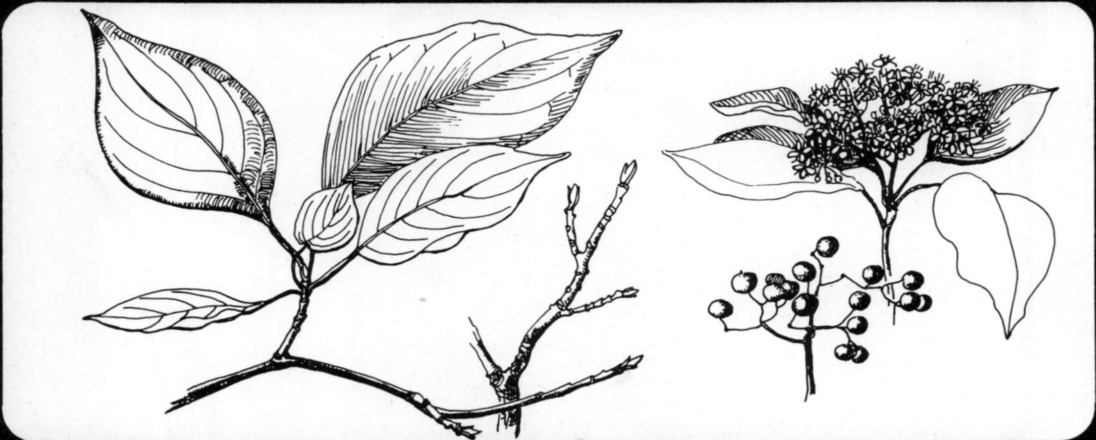

Cornus florida

FORM: **globular**
Size: **large understory** - 10 to 15 m (35 to 50 ft)
Spread: **intermediate** - 10 to 15 m (35 to 50 ft), as wide as tall
Mass: **dense**

BRANCHING: **horizontal** tiered appearance, branchlet tips upturned at ends, flat-topped crown, **medium** texture
Twig: **conspicuous leaf scar** encircles twig, smooth, **green or red** to purple, dull
Bud: **stalked, onion** shaped terminal flower bud, sitting upright along twigs, flesh **pink**
Bark: **blocky,** broken into roundish or squarish grid-like segments; **gray**

FOLIAGE: opposite, **simple,** broad **elliptic-oval,** entire margin, parallel veination, **medium** texture
Surface: thick **dull** above, pale whitish beneath
Color: spring - **light green or yellow green;** summer - **bright green;** autumn - **scarlet red**
Season: **deciduous;** emergence - late **April,** drop - late **October**

FLOWER: small, surrounded by 4 large bracts, give appearance of **large single** flower, 7.5 to 10 cm
Color: bracts **white,** flowers yellow
Season: late **April through** early **May,** when new leaves unfold
Sex: monoecious

FRUIT: tight clusters of 13 mm (1/2 in) glossy football shaped **berries,** 4 to 8 fruits per cluster
Color: bright scarlet **red**
Season: early **September through** mid **November**
Wildlife Value: **very high;** waterbirds, upland ground birds, songbirds, large and small mammals, hoofed browsers

HABITAT: formation - **forest;** region - **central;** gradient - **upland mesic and mesic-dry;** wooded slopes, ravines
and bluffs
Shade Tolerance: **very tolerant;** index range 8.0-10.0
Flood Tolerance: **very intolerant**

SOIL; Texture: **moderately coarse** sandy loams, loams **to fine** sandy clays, silty clay, clays; sandstone, limestone
Drainage: **well to poor**
Moisture: prefers **moist,** tolerates **dry** conditions
Reaction: **moderately acid to slightly acid,** pH 5.5-6.5

HARDINESS: zone 5b
Rate: **medium** - 30 to 46 cm (1 to 1 1/2 ft) a year for first 25 years, slowing thereafter
Longevity: **medium**

SUSCEPTIBILITY; Physiological: **frequent** - severe crown die back in droughty seasons
Disease: **infrequent** - weakened trees very susceptible to borers
Insect: **infrequent** - none serious
Wind-Ice: **infrequent**

URBAN TOLERANCE; Pollution: **sensitive** - 2,4-D; **resistant** - SO_2, O_3, HFl
Lighting: **sensitive**   Drought-Heat: **intermediate**   Mine Spoils: **intermediate**
Salt: Soil Compaction: **sensitive**
Root Pattern: **deep** coarse **lateral;** somewhat difficult to transplant, move root pruned trees B&B in early spring

SPECIES; Associate: Scarlet, White, Post, Blackjack, Chinkapin, Chestnut and Black Oaks, Pignut, Shagbark, Mockernut
Hickories, Tuliptree, White Ash, Black Tupelo, Pitch Pine, Black Locust, Eastern Redbud
Similar: Japanese Dogwood
Cultivars: 'Apple Blossom' - flowers pink fading to white in center, 'New Hampshire' - hardier flower buds; several others

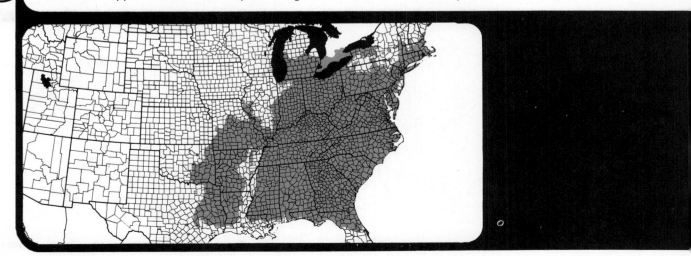

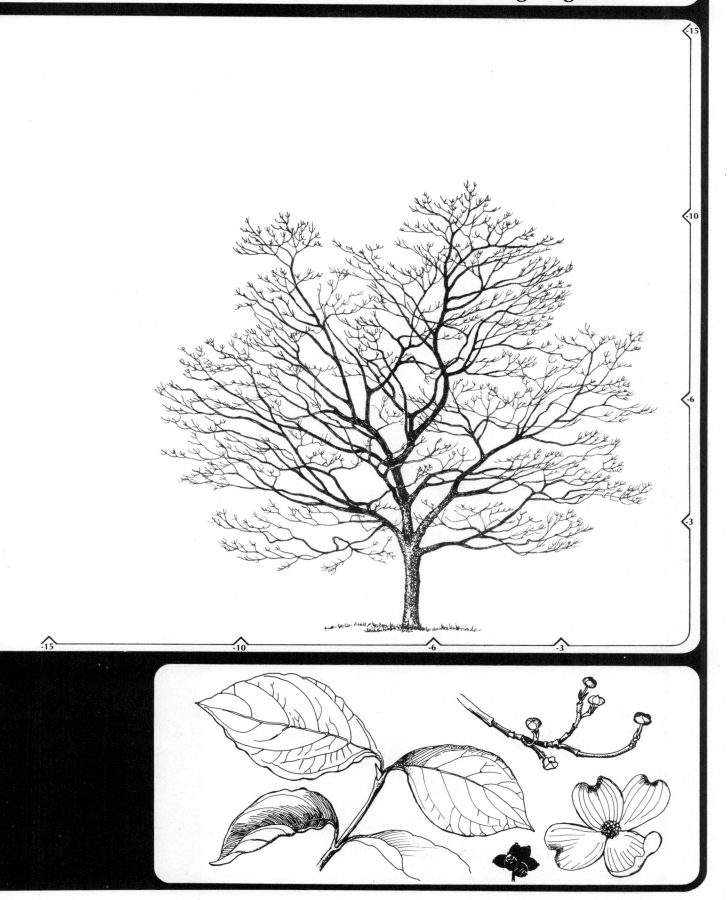

Cotinus americanus

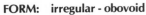

FORM: irregular - obovoid
Size: **small understory** - 6 to 10 m (20 to 35 ft)
Spread: **narrow** - 6 to 10 m (20 to 35 ft), commonly 3 to 6 m (10 to 20 ft)
Mass: **open**

BRANCHING: upright erect stems, coarse stout clustered lateral branches widely spaced along limbs, **coarse** texture
Twig: stout, **purple or brown**
Bud: small, 3 mm (1/8 in), scaly, red brown
Bark: broken on the surface into thin oblong **scaly** flakes; **gray brown**

FOLIAGE: alternate, simple, elliptic-oval, entire margin, crowded towards ends of twigs, **medium fine** texture
Surface: **dull** above, pale beneath
Color: spring - **maroon green;** summer - dark **blue green;** autumn - **orange red**
Season: **deciduous;** emergence - early **June,** drop - early **November**

FLOWER: terminal pyramidal spikes, 12.5 to 15 cm (5 to 6 in) long, feathery fine texture
Color: greenish to **yellow green**
Season: mid **June through** early **July,** after the leaves are fully grown
Sex: **dioecious**

FRUIT: berry, 3 mm (1/8 in), produced sparingly, almost sterile, stems with conspicuous feathery hair-like covering
Color: sterile stems with pinkish gray "smoke-like" appearance, berries **red** - infrequent
Season: early **August through September**
Wildlife Value: **very low**

HABITAT: formation - savanna; region - **central;** gradient - **upland dry;** high calcareous bluffs, steep rocky land
upland ridges
Shade Tolerance: **intolerant;** index range 2.0-3.9
Flood Tolerance: **very intolerant**

SOIL; Texture: **coarse** gravels and sands, shallow soils over sandstone or limestone **to moderately fine** sandy loam
Drainage: **moderately well,** tolerates **excessive**
Moisture: **moist,** tolerates **droughty** conditions
Reaction: **neutral to alkaline,** pH 6.6-8.0

HARDINESS: zone 6
Rate: **slow** - 15 to 30 cm (6 to 12 in) per year
Longevity: **short**

SUSCEPTIBILITY; Physiological: **infrequent**
Disease: **infrequent** - some rust, leaf spot, not serious
Insect: **infrequent** - San Jose scale, leaf rollers attack occasionally
Wind-Ice: **infrequent**

URBAN TOLERANCE; Pollution:
Lighting: Drought-Heat: **resistant**   Mine Spoils: **resistant**
Salt: Soil Compaction: **sensitive**
Root Pattern: **shallow** fibrous; transplants readily B&B in early spring

SPECIES; Associate: Blackhaw and Rusty Blackhaw Viburnum, Common Prickly Ash, Eastern Redcedar,
Blackjack, Chinkapin, and Post Oak, American Yellowwood, Common Hackberry, Eastern Redbud, Sassafras,
hawthorn species
Similar: European Smoketree is related
Cultivars: none commercially available

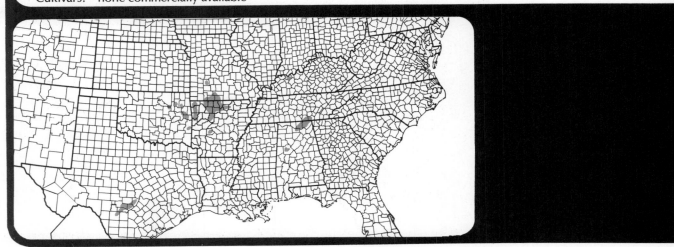

Crataegus crusgalli

FORM: globular
Size: **small understory** - 6 to 10 m (20 to 35 ft)
Spread: **narrow** - 6 to 10 m (20 to 35 ft), wider than tall
Mass: very **dense**

BRANCHING: short trunk, decidedly **horizontal,** branching usually sweeping ground, **medium** texture
Twig: **flaky** exfoliating patches along glossy **red brown** twigs; **armed** with dense hooked red brown slender thorns
Bud: small, dome shaped, **red**
Bark: shredding rectilinear **scales,** shaggy exfoliation along top and bottom margins; silvery **gray**

FOLIAGE: alternate, **simple, obovate,** entire toward base, leaves clustered at ends of twigs, **medium fine** texture
Surface: very **glossy,** paler beneath, thick
Color: spring - **bright green;** summer - **dark green;** autumn - bright **orange to** scarlet **red,** late
Season: **deciduous;** emergence - mid **May,** drop - mid **November**

FLOWER: dense **flat topped clusters,** 7.5 cm (3 in) diameter, individual 17 mm (2/3 in) diameter
Color: **white,** profuse
Season: late **May through** mid **June,** when leaves are half grown
Sex: monoecious

FRUIT: apple-like **berry,** 13 mm (1/2 in), in dense 5 to 7.5 cm (2 to 3 in) diameter flat-topped drooping clusters
Color: dull brick **red**
Season: mid **August** persistent **until January**
Wildlife Value: **intermediate;** songbirds, upland ground birds, large and small mammals

HABITAT: formation - **forest, savanna;** region - **central;** gradient - **lowland wet mesic, upland dry;** floodplain, rocky
pastures, border of woods, dry rocky open woods
Shade Tolerance: **intolerant;** index range 2.0 to 3.9
Flood Tolerance: **intermediate**

SOIL; Texture: moderately coarse sandy or gravelly loams, medium loams, **to fine** loamy silts and heavy clay
Drainage: **moderately poor to excessive**
Moisture: prefers **moist,** tolerates **droughty** conditions
Reaction: **slightly acid to alkaline,** pH 6.1-8.0

HARDINESS: zone 4b
Rate: **slow** - 15 to 30 cm (6 to 12 in) in a year, 6 m (20 ft) in 25 year period
Longevity: **short** - 75 to 100 years commonly

SUSCEPTIBILITY; Physiological: infrequent
Disease: **frequent** - fire blight, several species of rust, powdery mildew, scab
Insect: **frequent** - aphids, borers, apple leaf blotch miner, lace bugs
Wind-Ice: **infrequent**

URBAN TOLERANCE; Pollution: resistant - SO$_2$
Lighting: Drought-Heat: **resistant**   Mine Spoils: **resistant**
Salt: **sensitive**   Soil Compaction: **intermediate**
Root Pattern: **taproot;** transplant as small tree B&B in early spring or autumn

SPECIES; Associate: Common Prickly Ash, Eastern Redcedar, American Plum, Red Mulberry, viburnum, sumac, cherry,
crabapple species, other hawthorns, filbert, dogwood
Similar: several species of hawthorn (specifically Lavalle Hawthorn), Blackhaw Viburnum, crabapple species
Cultivars: 'Inermis' - thornless, 'Splendens' - very glossy foliage

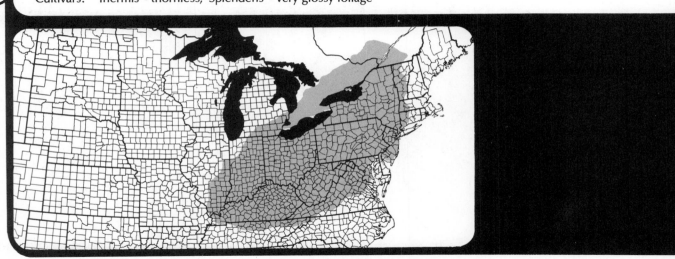

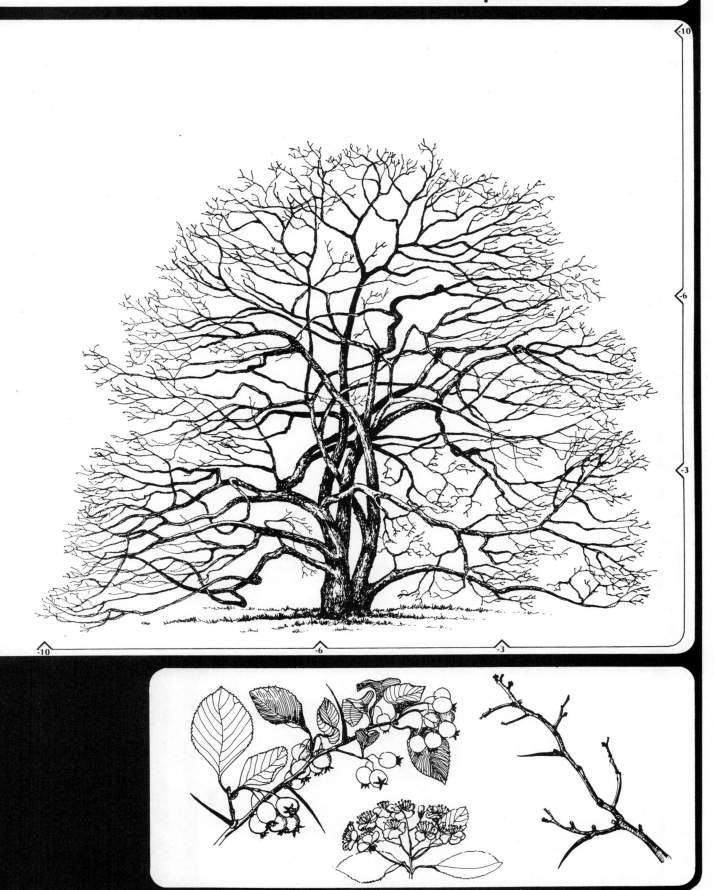

Crataegus mollis

FORM: **globular**
Size: **large understory** - 10 to 15 m (35 to 50 ft)
Spread: **intermediate** - 10 to 15 m (35 to 50 ft), wider than tall
Mass: very **dense**

BRANCHING: strong **horizontal**, rounded or flat-topped symmetrical high crown, **coarse** texture
Twig: **flaky**, exfoliating patches, dull **gray brown; armed** with occasional chestnut brown glossy thorns
Bud: dome shaped, dull, **reddish**
Bark: twisting, rectilinear flaky **scales**, peeling along top and bottom margin, shaggy appearance; silvery **gray**

FOLIAGE: alternate, **simple, ovate-oblong ovate,** coarse doubly serrate margin, **medium coarse** texture
Surface: **tomentose,** dull above, paler beneath
Color: spring - **yellow green;** summer - **yellow green;** autumn - golden **yellow brown**
Season: **deciduous;** emergence - mid **May,** drop - mid to late **September,** commonly as early as late August

FLOWER: broad open **flat-topped clusters,** 7.5 to 10 cm (3 to 4 in), individual bloom 18 mm (3/4 in) diameter
Color: **white**
Season: late **May through** early **June,** first hawthorn to bloom when the new leaves are half grown
Sex: monoecious

FRUIT: globular apple-like **berry,** 2 to 2.5 cm (3/4 to 1 in) diameter, in drooping few fruited open clusters
Color: dull **red**
Season: late **August through** mid or late **September**
Wildlife Value: **intermediate;** man, songbirds, upland ground birds, large and small mammals, hoofed browsers

HABITAT: formation - **forest, savanna;** region - **central;** gradient - **lowland wet-mesic, upland dry;** low open alluvial
woods, rocky hillsides and hilltops, woods edge, open pasture
Shade Tolerance: **intolerant;** index range 2.0-3.9
Flood Tolerance: **intermediate**

SOIL; Texture: **moderately coarse** sandy and gravelly loams, medium loams, **to fine** silty clay loams and clay
Drainage: **moderately poor to excessive**
Moisture: prefers **moist,** tolerates **droughty** conditions
Reaction: **slightly acid to alkaline,** pH 6.1-8.0

HARDINESS: zone **3b**
Rate: **slow** - 23 to 30 cm (9 to 12 in) per year
Longevity: **short** - commonly 75 to 100 years

SUSCEPTIBILITY; Physiological: **infrequent**
Disease: **frequent** - fire blight, cedar apple rust, other rusts, leaf spots, powdery mildew
Insect: **frequent** - borers, western tent caterpillar, apple and thorn skeletonizer, scales
Wind-Ice: **infrequent**

URBAN TOLERANCE; Pollution: **resistant - SO$_2$**
Lighting: Drought-Heat: **resistant** Mine Spoils: **resistant**
Salt: **sensitive** Soil Compaction: **intermediate**
Root Pattern: **taproot;** somewhat difficult to transplant, move small trees B&B in early spring or autumn

SPECIES; Associate: dry - Eastern Redcedar, Common Honeylocust, Black Cherry, American Plum, Common Chokecherry,
viburnum, crabapple; wet mesic - Black Walnut, Common Hackberry, Silver Maple, American Elm, Eastern Poplar
Similar: several species of hawthorn or crabapple
Cultivars: none available commercially

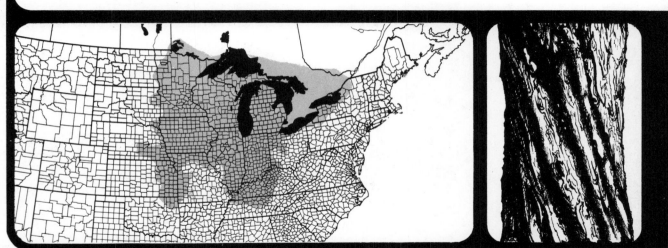

-15

-10

-6

-3

-15

-10

-6

-3

Crataegus nitida

FORM: globular
Size: **small understory -** 6 to 10 m (20 to 35 ft)
Spread: **narrow -** 6 to 10 m (20 to 35 ft), wider than tall
Mass: **dense**

BRANCHING: stout **horizontal** lower, upper erect, broad irregular open crown, low sweeping limbs, **medium** texture
Twig: **flaky,** exfoliating silvery patches along **red brown** twigs; **armed** with straight slender glossy thorns
Bud: small, dome-like, **reddish**
Bark: close tight knit in rectangular **scales,** shredding along upper and lower margin; silvery **gray**

FOLIAGE: alternate, **simple, oblong-obovate,** doubly serrate margin, **medium fine** texture
Surface: very **glossy** above, pale beneath
Color: spring - **light green;** summer - **dark green;** autumn - bright **orange to orange red,** late
Season: **deciduous;** emergence - mid **May,** drop - mid **October**

FLOWER: flat-topped cluster, individual bloom 19 mm (3/4 in) in diameter
Color: **white**
Season: late **May through** early **June,** when leaves nearly full grown
Sex: monoecious

FRUIT: small apple-like **berry,** 9 mm (3/8 in) diameter, in many fruited drooping clusters
Color: orange to **red**
Season: **September** persistent **until January**
Wildlife Value: **intermediate;** songbirds, upland ground birds, large and small mammals

HABITAT: formation - **forest, savanna;** region - **central;** gradient - **lowland wet-mesic, upland dry;** usually on low ground, creek banks, floodplains or low pastures
Shade Tolerance: **intolerant;** index range 2.0-3.9
Flood Tolerance: **intermediate**

SOIL; Texture: moderately coarse sandy or gravelly loams, medium loams, **to fine** silt loams and heavy clays
Drainage: **moderately poor to excessive**
Moisture: prefers **moist,** tolerates **droughty** conditions
Reaction: **slightly acid to alkaline,** pH 6.1-8.0

HARDINESS: zone 5a
Rate: **slow -** 15 to 30 cm (6 to 12 in) in a year, 3 m (10 ft) in 12 to 14 years
Longevity: **short -** between 50 and 100 years

SUSCEPTIBILITY; Physiological: infrequent
Disease: **frequent -** fire blight, powdery mildew, several rusts, scab, leaf spots, cedar hawthorn rust
Insect: **frequent -** plant hopper, two spotted mite, borers, apple and thorn skeletonizer
Wind-Ice: **infrequent**

URBAN TOLERANCE; Pollution: resistant - SO_2
Lighting: Drought-Heat: **resistant**   Mine Spoils: **resistant**
Salt: **sensitive**   Soil Compaction: **intermediate**
Root Pattern: **taproot;** somewhat difficult to transplant, move B&B in early spring or late autumn

SPECIES; Associate: dry - Sassafras, Common Persimmon, Common Pawpaw, Devils-Walkingstick, Common Prickly Ash, Red Mulberry, Osageorange, crabapple, cherries, other hawthorns
Similar: substitutes include other hawthorns (especially Green Hawthorn) and crabs
Cultivars: none commercially obtainable

Glossy Hawthorn

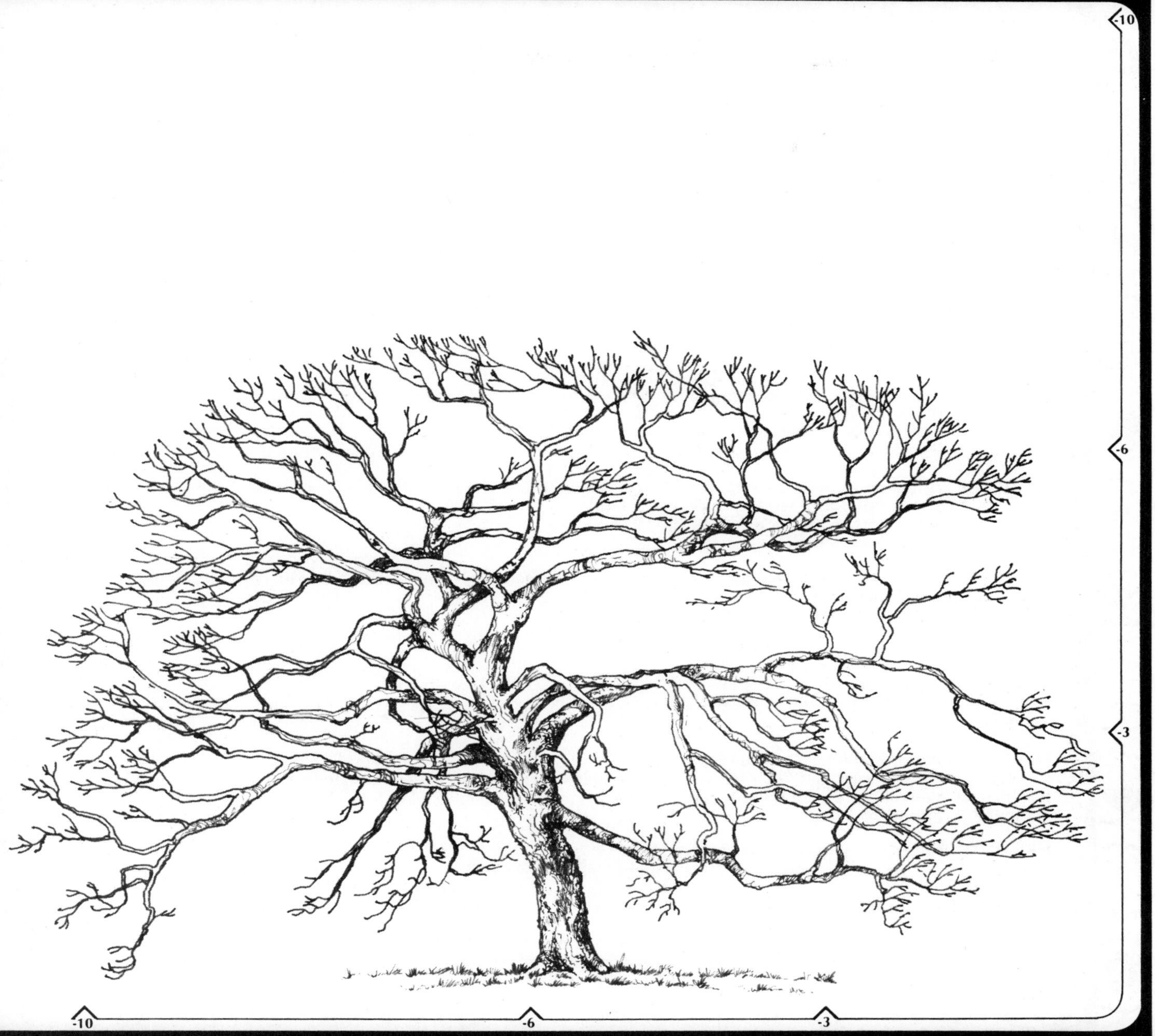

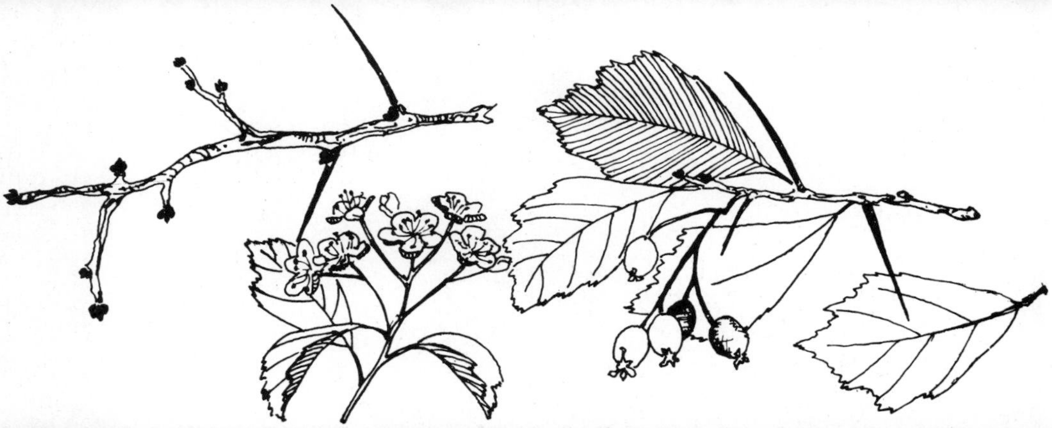

Crataegus phaenopyrum

FORM: ovoid to globular
Size: **small understory -** 6 to 10 m (20 to 35 ft)
Spread: **narrow -** 6 to 10 m (20 to 35 ft), commonly less, 2/3 the height
Mass: very **dense**

BRANCHING: generally dividing 1.2 or 1.5 m (4 or 5 ft) above ground into slender **horizontal** branches, **medium** texture
Twig: **flaky** exfoliating scales, glossy, zig zag, **red brown; armed** with straight slender thorns
Bud: dome shaped, glossy, **red**
Bark: thin narrow vertical rectilinear **scales** peeling away along top and bottom margins; silvery **gray**

FOLIAGE: alternate, **simple, deltoid-wedge,** 3-5 lobed, terminal elongated, doubly serrate margin, **medium fine** texture
Surface: **glossy,** smooth, thin but firm, pale beneath
Color: spring - lustrous **light green;** summer - **dark green;** autumn - **orange to** scarlet **red,** late
Season: **deciduous;** emergence - late **May,** drop - early **November**

FLOWER: many flowered broad **flat topped clusters,** individual blooms 13 mm (1/2 in) wide
Color: **white**
Season: early through mid **June,** after leaves are full grown
Sex: monoecious

FRUIT: globular glossy apple-like **berry,** 6 mm (1/4 in) diameter, born in loose flattened clusters
Color: bright orange **red**
Season: late **September** persisting throughout winter season **until** mid **March**
Wildlife Value: **intermediate;** man, songbirds, upland ground birds, small mammals, hoofed browsers

HABITAT: formation - **forest, savanna;** region - **central;** gradient - **lowland wet-mesic, upland dry;** banks of streams, open
  alluvial woods, margin of woods, open rocky land
Shade Tolerance: **intolerant;** index range 2.0-3.9
Flood Tolerance: **intermediate**

SOIL; Texture: **moderately coarse** sandy or gravelly loams, medium loams, **to fine** silt loams and heavy clays
Drainage: **moderately poor to excessive**
Moisture: prefers **moist,** tolerates **droughty** conditions
Reaction: **slightly acid to alkaline,** pH 6.1-8.0

HARDINESS: zone 5a
Rate: **slow -** 15 to 30 cm (6 to 12 in) per year
Longevity: **short -** 50 to 100 years

SUSCEPTIBILITY; Physiological: **infrequent**
Disease: **frequent -** fire blight, markedly less susceptible to rust than many other hawthorns
Insect: **frequent -** borers, lace bugs, scale, two spotted mite, leaf blight, leaf spots
Wind-Ice: **infrequent**

URBAN TOLERANCE; Pollution: **resistant -** SO_2
Lighting: Drought-Heat: **resistant**   Mine Spoils: **resistant**
Salt: **sensitive**   Soil Compaction: **intermediate**
Root Pattern: **taproot;** transplants well as small tree B&B in early spring or late autumn

SPECIES; Associate: dry - Sassafras, Common Persimmon, Eastern Redcedar, Osageorange, Red Mulberry,
  Common Prickly Ash, sumac, viburnum, dogwood, crabapple, filbert, other hawthorns
Similar: other hawthorns especially Green and Glossy Hawthorns
Cultivars: 'Clarke' - heavy fruiting, 'Fastigiata' - columnar form

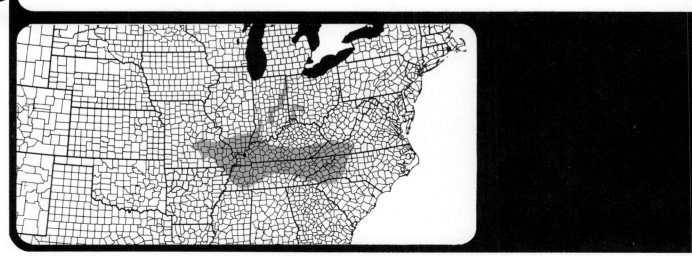

192

-10

-6

-3

-10

-6

-3

Crataegus pruinosa

FORM: globular
Size: **small understory** - 6 to 10 (20 to 35 ft), commonly 3 to 6 m (10 to 20 ft)
Spread: **narrow** - 6 to 10 m (20 to 35 ft), commonly to 15 m, usually 2/3 the height
Mass: very **dense**

BRANCHING: short multiple trunk, **upright** and ascending, shrub-like character, **medium** texture
Twig: thin **flaky** exfoliating silvery patches along dark **red brown** twigs; **armed** with slender thorns
Bud: small, dome shaped, **reddish**
Bark: shredding rectilinear **scales**, shaggy exfoliation along horizontal margins of scales; silvery **gray**

FOLIAGE: alternate, **simple, elliptic-oval,** doubly serrate, bright red petiole, **medium fine** texture
Surface: **dull, tomentose**
Color: spring - **blue green;** summer - dark **blue green;** autumn - dull **orange to reddish**
Season: **deciduous;** emergence - mid **May,** drop - early **October**

FLOWER: borne in loose **flat-topped clusters,** individual 19 mm (3/4 in) diameter
Color: **white**
Season: late **May through** early **June,** after leaves are fully grown
Sex: monoecious

FRUIT: small globular apple-like **berry,** 9 mm (3/8 in) diameter in few fruited drooping cluster
Color: glossy **yellow orange**
Season: late **August through** mid **October**
Wildlife Value: **intermediate;** songbirds, upland ground birds, small mammals, hoofed browsers

HABITAT: formation - **forest, savanna;** region - **central;** gradient - **lowland wet-mesic, upland dry;** rocky open woods,
   margin of woods, open hillsides, open pasture, open alluvial woods
Shade Tolerance: **intolerant;** index range 2.0-3.9
Flood Tolerance: **intermediate**

SOIL; Texture: **moderately coarse** gravelly or sandy loams, medium loams, **to fine** silty clay loams and clay
Drainage: **moderately poor to excessive**
Moisture: prefers **moist,** tolerates **droughty** conditions
Reaction: **slightly acid to alkaline,** pH 6.1-8.0

HARDINESS: zone 3a
Rate: **slow** - 15 to 30 cm (6 to 12 in) per year
Longevity: **short** - 60 to 100 years commonly

SUSCEPTIBILITY; Physiological: **infrequent**
Disease: **frequent** - cedar hawthorn rust, other rusts, fire blight, leaf spot, scab
Insect: **frequent** - apple leaf blotch miner, aphids, borers, apple and thorn skeletonizer
Wind-Ice: **infrequent**

URBAN TOLERANCE; Pollution: **resistant** - SO$_2$
Lighting: Drought-Heat: **resistant**   Mine Spoils: **resistant**
Salt: **sensitive**   Soil Compaction: **intermediate**
Root Pattern: **taproot;** somewhat difficult to transplant, move B&B in early spring or late autumn

SPECIES; Associate: dry - Eastern Redcedar, Osageorange, Common Prickly Ash, Gray Dogwood, American Filbert,
   Bur Oak, Northern Pin Oak, American Plum, Pin Cherry, hawthorns, sumac, crabapple
Similar: American Plum, Blackhaw Viburnum, other hawthorns
Cultivars: none commercially obtainable

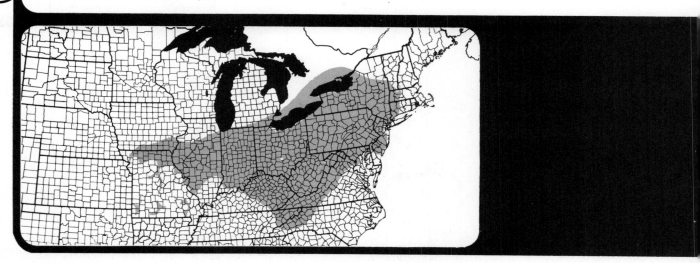

Crataegus punctata

FORM: globular
Size: **small understory** - 6 to 10 m (20 to 35 ft)
Spread: **narrow** - 6 to 10 m (20 to 35 ft), up to twice as wide as tall
Mass: very **dense**

BRANCHING: high clear trunk, stout **horizontal**, forming high widespreading flat-topped crown, **medium** texture
Twig: **flaky** sheet-like exfoliating silvery patches, light **orange brown; armed** with straight slender thorns
Bud: lustrous, dome shaped, **red**
Bark: thin narrow shredding rectilinear **scales**, shaggy exfoliation along top and bottom margins; silvery **gray**

FOLIAGE: alternate, **simple, obovate,** fine doubly serrate above the middle, deep veins, **medium fine** texture
Surface: **dull** smooth above, pale beneath, thick
Color: spring - **silvery gray;** summer - **blue green;** autumn - **orange and red**
Season: **deciduous;** emergence - mid **May,** drop - mid **October**

FLOWER: many flowered broad **flat-topped clusters,** 5 to 7.5 cm (2 to 3 in) wide
Color: **white**
Season: late **May through** early **June,** after leaves are half grown
Sex: monoecious

FRUIT: oval apple-like **berry,** 19 mm (3/4 in) diameter, among the largest of the native haws, in drooping clusters
Color: dull orange to **red,** conspicuous white dots
Season: mid **August through** mid **October**
Wildlife Value: **intermediate;** man, songbirds, upland ground birds, large and small mammals

HABITAT: formation - **forest, savanna;** region - **central;** gradient - **lowland wet-mesic, upland dry;** border of streams in rich moist soil, open hillsides, margin of woods usually in rocky ground, open areas of grazed pastures
Shade Tolerance: **intolerant;** index range 2.0-3.9
Flood Tolerance: **intermediate**

SOIL; Texture: moderately coarse gravelly or sandy loams, loamy sands, **to fine** silty loams and heavy clay
Drainage: **moderately poor to excessive**
Moisture: prefers **moist,** tolerates **droughty** conditions
Reaction: **slightly acid to alkaline,** pH 6.1-8.0

HARDINESS: zone **4b**
Rate: **slow** - 22.5 to 30 cm (9 to 12 in) per year, 6 m (20 ft) in 25 to 30 years on good sites
Longevity: **short** - 50 to 100 years at maturity

SUSCEPTIBILITY; Physiological: infrequent
Disease: **frequent** - cedar hawthorn rust is particularly bad, fire blight
Insect: **frequent** - apple leaf blotch miner, lacebugs, leaf hopper, scale
Wind-Ice: **infrequent**

URBAN TOLERANCE; Pollution: resistant - SO_2
Lighting: Drought-Heat: **resistant** Mine Spoils: **resistant**
Salt: **sensitive** Soil Compaction: **intermediate**
Root Pattern: **taproot;** somewhat difficult to transplant, move as small tree B&B in early spring or autumn

SPECIES; Associate: dry - Eastern Redcedar, American Plum, Sassafras, Common Persimmon, Common Prickly Ash, Prairie Crabapple, other hawthorns
Similar: other native and exotic hawthorns, many crabs as well
Cultivars: 'Ohio Pioneer' - essentially thornless

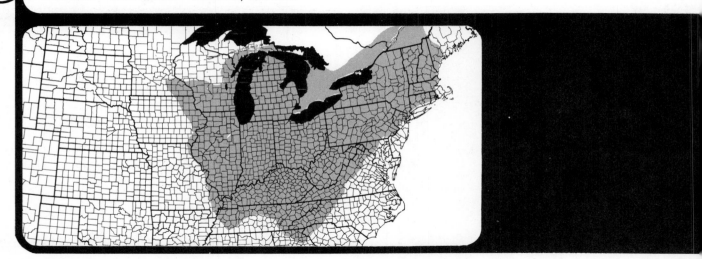

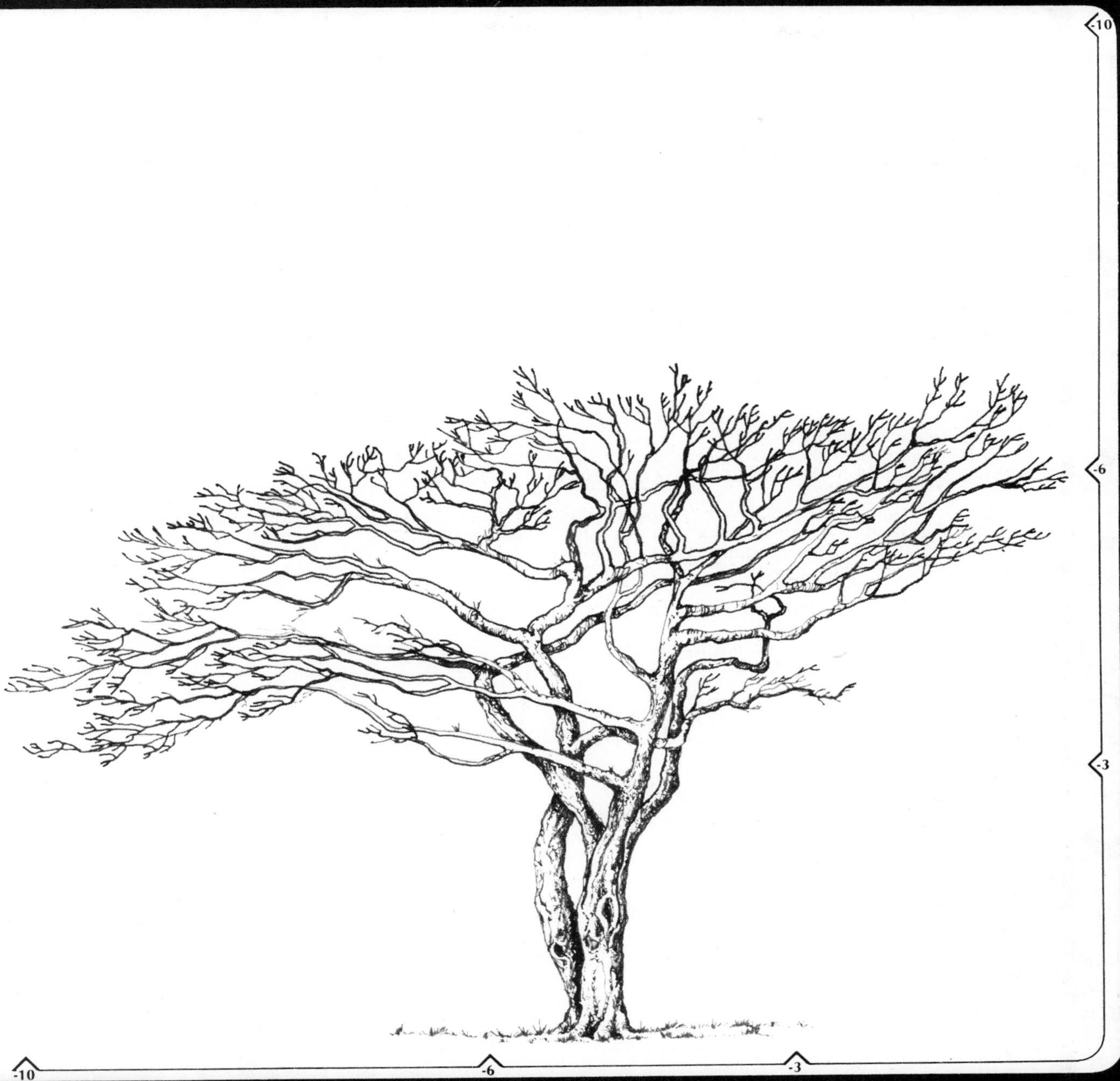
-10
-6
-3
-10
-6
-3

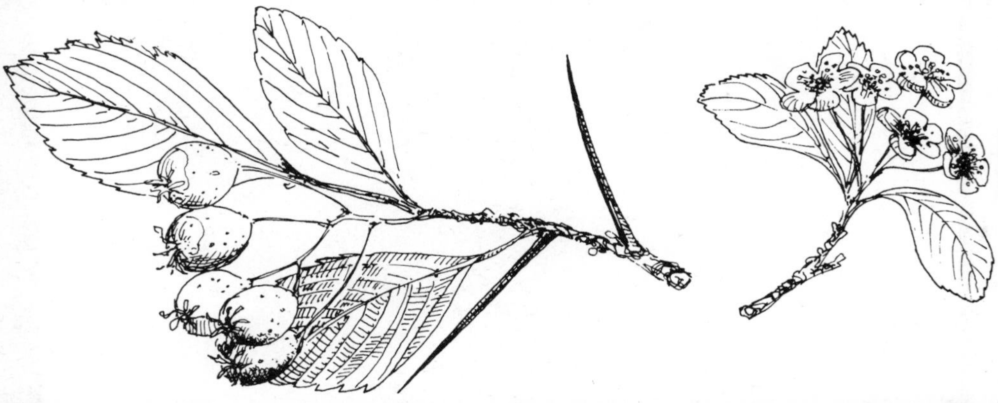

Diospyros virginiana

FORM: ovoid
Size: **small canopy** - 15 to 22.5 m (50 to 75 ft)
Spread: **intermediate** - 10 to 15 m (35 to 50 ft), 2/3 the height
Mass: **open**

BRANCHING: **leggy, picturesque** contorted, short crooked rigid angular branchlets, **medium** texture
Twig: flexible, slightly **zig zag, gray brown**
Bud: **two scales,** small red brown
Bark: squarish thick **blocky** grid-like pattern; **black** with orange fissures visible between the blocks

FOLIAGE: alternate, **simple, elliptic-oval,** entire margin, petiole fuzzy, **medium** texture
Surface: **glossy,** pale woolly beneath
Color: spring - **light green;** summer - **dark green;** autumn - remaining **green or yellowish orange,** late
Season: **deciduous;** emergence - late **May,** drop - early **October**

FLOWER: **bell shaped,** 13 mm (1/2 in) long, female solitary, 4 petals curling outwards
Color: **yellow**
Season: early through mid **June,** after leaves are half grown, hidden
Sex: **dioecious**

FRUIT: large fleshy globular **berry,** 2.5 to 4 cm (1 to 1 1/2 in) diameter, wrinkled when ripe
Color: **yellow orange**
Season: **September through** late **November**
Wildlife Value: **high;** man, birds, small mammals, sweet edible

HABITAT: formation - **forest, savanna;** region - **central;** gradient - **lowland wet-mesic, upland dry;** rocky fields, pastures,
waste ground, rich alluvial bottomlands or open hillside woods
Shade Tolerance: **intolerant;** index range 2.0-3.9
Flood Tolerance: **intermediate**

SOIL; Texture: **medium to moderately fine;** best on alluvial soils such as clay and heavy loams, sandy loam
Drainage: **well to moderately well**
Moisture: **average,** tolerates **droughty** conditions
Reaction: **slightly acid,** pH 6.1-6.5

HARDINESS: **zone 5a**
Rate: **slow** - 4.5 m (15 ft) over 20 year period
Longevity: **short** - generally mature at 50 to 75 years, commonly survives 100 years

SUSCEPTIBILITY; Physiological: **infrequent**
Disease: **frequent** - persimmon wilt, heartwood rot
Insect: **infrequent** - hickory horned devil and webworms cause local damage
Wind-Ice: **infrequent**

URBAN TOLERANCE; Pollution:
Lighting: Drought-Heat: **resistant**   Mine Spoils: **resistant**
Salt: Soil Compaction: **intermediate**
Root Pattern: strong deep **taproot;** difficult to transplant, move as small tree B&B in early spring

SPECIES; Associate: dry - Sassafras, American Elm, Green Ash, Eastern Redcedar, Flameleaf and Smooth Sumacs,
Sourwood, Black Tupelo, Eastern Redbud, Flowering Dogwood, hickories, oaks, hawthorn species
Similar: Sourwood and Black Tupelo, Diospyros kakai (Asia) is related
Cultivars: none available commercially at this time

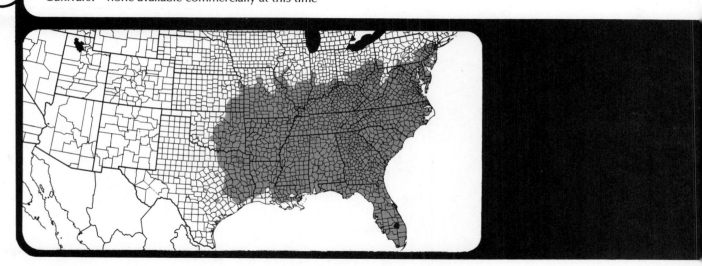

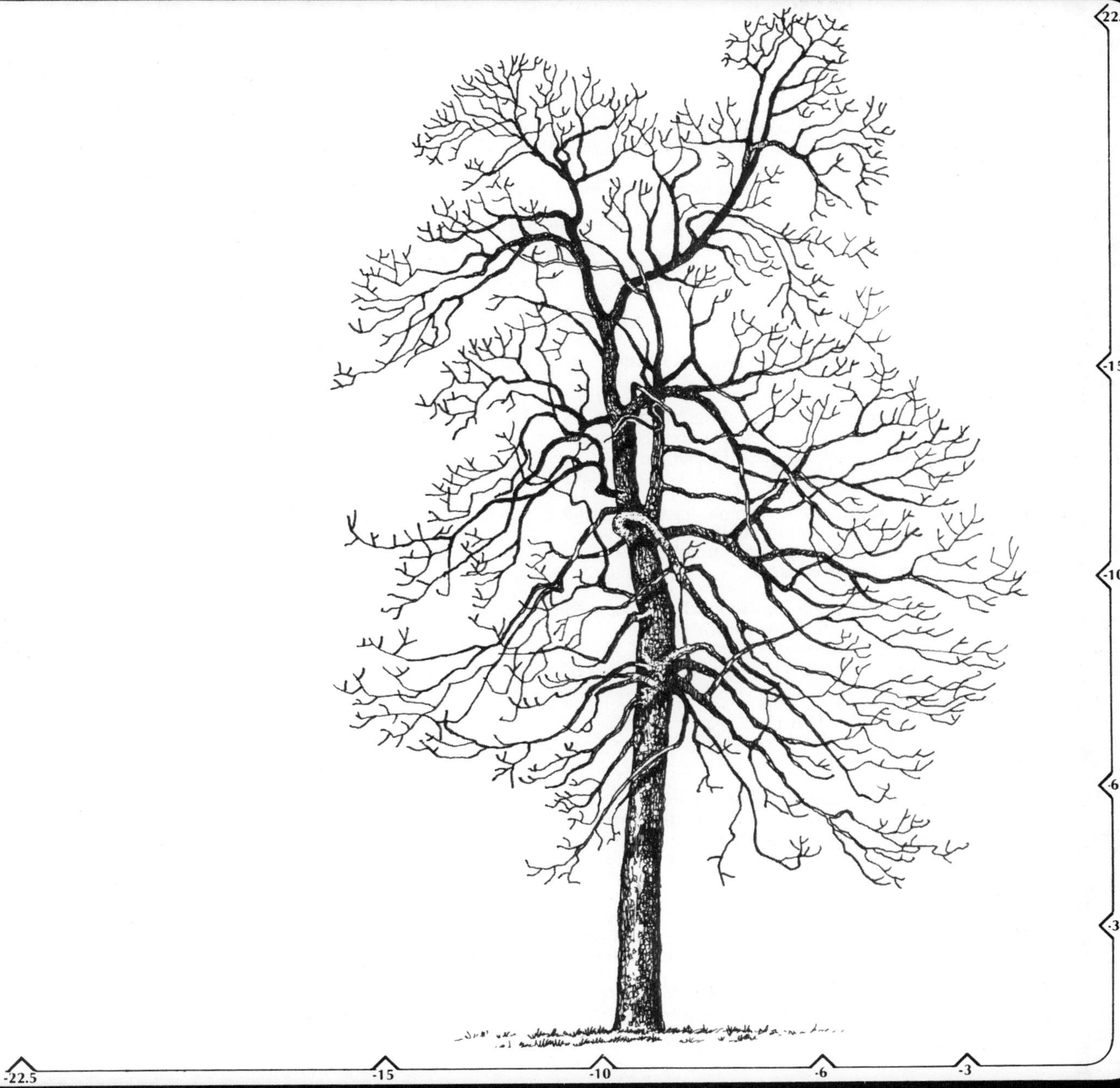
22.5
15
10
6
3
22.5
15
10
6
3

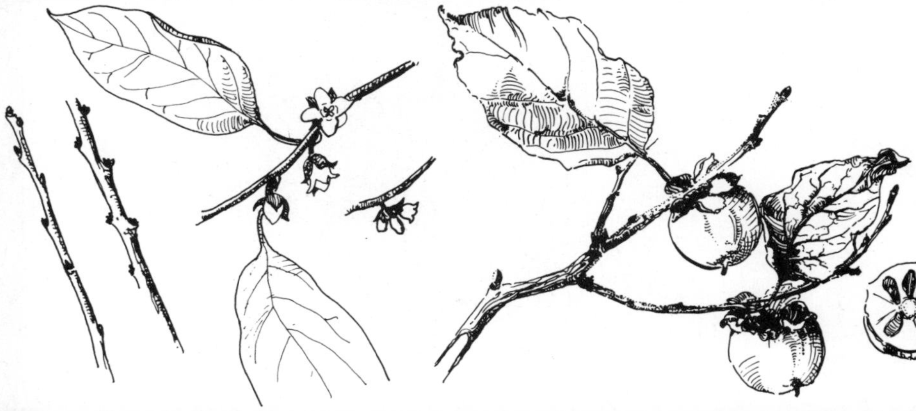

Euonymus atropurpureus

FORM: **globular**
Size: **small understory -** 6 to 10 m (20 to 35 ft), commonly 3 to 6 m
Spread: **narrow** 6 to 10 m (20 to 35 ft), as wide as tall
Mass: **moderate**

BRANCHING: commonly multiple trunks, stiff **upright** becoming arching, **medium** texture
Twig: squarish, 4 **longitudinal** striped **lines**, occasionally **winged**, lime **green**, rigid
Bud: small, conical, purplish **green**
Bark: thin minute flaky scales, younger trunks **smooth**, green purple becoming ashy **gray**

FOLIAGE: opposite, **simple, ovate-oblong ovate,** finely toothed margin, prominent veins, **medium** texture
Surface: **dull**
Color: spring - **light green;** summer - grass **green;** autumn - unusual carmen pink to bright **red**
Season: **deciduous;** emergence - early **May,** drop - early **October**

FLOWER: **small** loose **clusters** along undersides of twigs, 6 to 13 mm (1/4 to 1/2 in) diameter, individual 4 petaled
Color: bright red and **purplish red**
Season: late **June through** early **July,** after leaves are fully grown
Sex: monoecious

FRUIT: three and four chambered fleshy **capsule,** 19 mm (3/4 in) diameter, in loose drooping clusters
Color: capsule - fuchsia pink; seeds - bright glossy **red**
Season: **September through** early **December**
Wildlife Value: **very low**

HABITAT: formation - **forest;** region - **central;** gradient - **lowland wet-mesic;** alluvial floodplain, border of small streams, base of mesic slope, rocky sheltered ravines
Shade Tolerance: **tolerant;** index range 6.0-7.9
Flood Tolerance: **intermediate**

SOIL; Texture: **moderately coarse** sandy loams, medium loams, **to moderately fine** silt loams
Drainage: **moderately well to moderately poor**
Moisture: **moist to average** conditions
Reaction: **neutral,** pH 6.6-7.5

HARDINESS: **zone 4b**
Rate: **medium -** 46 cm (18 in) in a year
Longevity: **medium**

SUSCEPTIBILITY; Physiological: **infrequent**
Disease: **frequent -** severe powdery mildew on leaves and twigs in wet seasons
Insect: **infrequent -** occasional scale
Wind-Ice: **infrequent**

URBAN TOLERANCE; Pollution:
Lighting: Drought-Heat: **intermediate**   Mine Spoils: **intermediate**
Salt: Soil Compaction: **intermediate**
Root Pattern: **shallow** spreading; transplants easily B&B in early spring

SPECIES; Associate: Red Mulberry, American Elm, Eastern Redbud, Black Walnut, Common Hackberry, Silver Maple, American Hornbeam, Pagoda Dogwood, Green Ash, American Sweetgum, Black Tupelo
Similar: Mountain Maple exhibits similar form, branching, bark, autumn color, European Spindletree is related
Cultivars: none commercially obtainable

Fagus grandifolia

FORM: conical or ovoid
Size: **large canopy** - 22.5 to 30 m (75 to 100 ft)
Spread: **wide -** 15 to 22.5 m (50 to 75 ft), 2/3 the height
Mass: very **dense**

BRANCHING: **horizontal** branches often sweeping ground, picturesque undulating drooping branchlets, **fine** texture
Twig: **zig zag,** slender, silvery **gray**
Bud: **narrow, long pointed,** 2.5 cm (1 in) cigar shaped, laterals at right angles to twig, glossy chestnut brown
Bark: **smooth** with sagging parallel folds or wrinkles; light silvery gray, old trunks slate **gray**

FOLIAGE: alternate, **simple, oblong-lanceolate** to **elliptic-oval,** margin coarsely toothed, **medium coarse** texture
Surface: leathery, smooth **dull** above, glossy yellow green beneath
Color: spring - **light green;** summer - **blue green;** autumn - clear **yellow becoming brown** first along margin
Season: deciduous - **persistent;** emergence - mid **April,** drop - dried leaves remaining **through** winter until late **January**

FLOWER: **small** drooping globe shaped **clusters**
Color: **yellow green**
Season: late **April through** early May, after new leaves unfold
Sex: monoecious

FRUIT: pyramidal **nut,** 4 parted bur-like husk, 2.5 cm (1 in) long
Color: **tan brown**
Season: mid **September through** mid **November**
Wildlife Value: **high;** man, songbirds, upland ground birds, small mammals, hoofed browsers

HABITAT: formation - **forest;** region - **northern, central;** gradient - **upland mesic;** floodplain knolls, elevated terrace, mesic
  ravines, coves, north and east slope aspects, areas of cool air drainage
Shade Tolerance: **very tolerant;** index 9.3
Flood Tolerance: **very intolerant;** more tolerant of poorly drained sites than Sugar Maple

SOIL; Texture: **moderately coarse to moderately fine,** loamy sands, sandy loams, loams and silt loams
Drainage: **well to moderately well**
Moisture: **moist to average,** more sensitive to reduced soil moisture than Sugar Maple
Reaction: **moderately acid to slightly acid,** pH 5.5-6.5

HARDINESS: zone 3b
Rate: **slow to medium -** 2.7 to 3.6 m (9 to 12 ft) over 10 year period, decidedly slow after first 5 years
Longevity: **long -** 200 to 300 years

SUSCEPTIBILITY; Physiological: **frequent -** sunscald injures open grown trees and new plantings
Disease: **infrequent -** none particularly severe
Insect: **infrequent -** occasional severe infestations of beech scale
Wind-Ice: **infrequent**

URBAN TOLERANCE; Pollution: **resistant -** SO_2, O_3
Lighting: **sensitive**   Drought-Heat: **sensitive**   Mine Spoils: **sensitive**
Salt: **sensitive**   Soil Compaction: **sensitive**
Root Pattern: widespreading, **shallow,** commonly producing sprouts; transplants readily B&B in early spring

SPECIES; Associate: Sugar, Striped, Mountain and Red Maple, Red Spruce, Eastern White Pine, Yellow Birch, Northern
  Red Oak, American Linden, Cucumbertree Magnolia, Canada Hemlock, White Ash
Similar: American Yellowwood has similar bark; European Beech is related - more adaptable in hot, dry climate
Cultivars: none commercially available

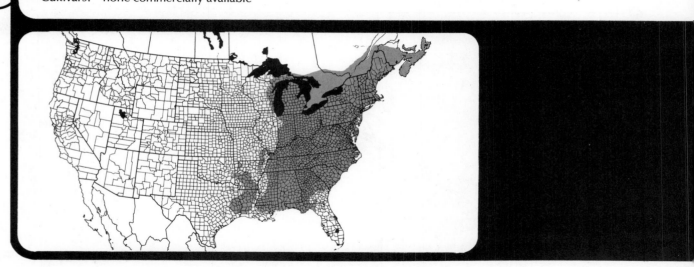

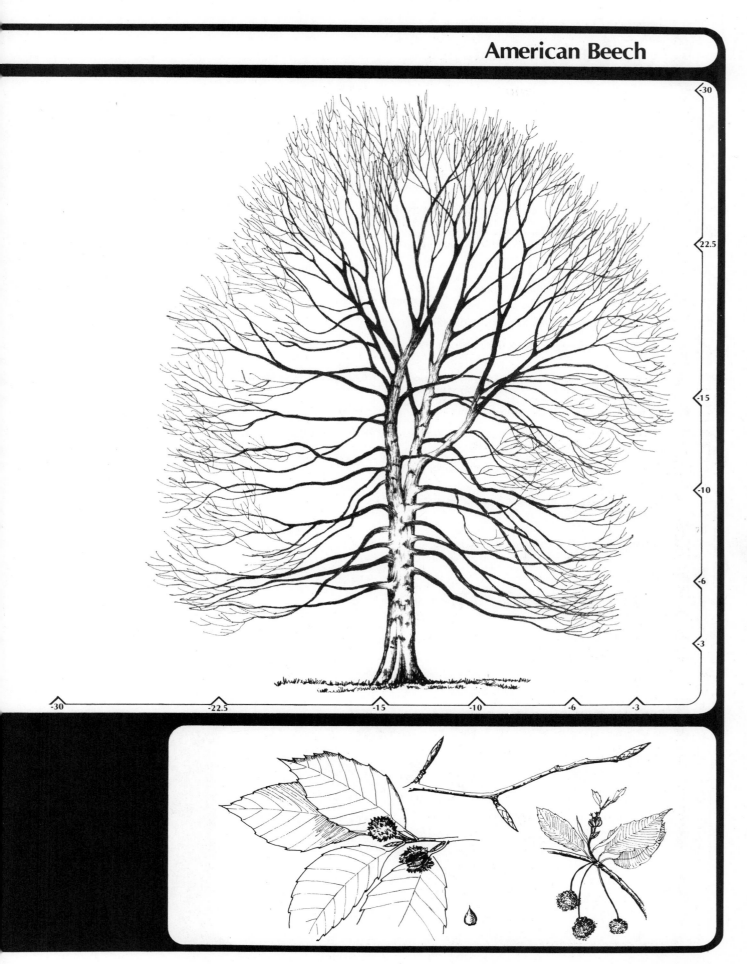

Franklinia alatamaha

FORM: conical
Size: **small understory -** 6 to 10 m (20 to 35 ft)
Spread: **narrow -** 6 to 10 m (20 to 35 ft), usually 3 to 6 m (10 to 20 ft), 1/2 the height
Mass: **open**

BRANCHING: multiple trunks, stiff **upright, coarse** texture
Twig: angular, squarish, **large** prominent **leaf scars, red brown**
Bud: small 6 mm (1/4 in) long, red brown
Bark: **smooth** becoming slightly scaly; dark **gray brown**

FOLIAGE: alternate, **simple, oblong-obovate,** toothed above the middle, winged petiole, **coarse** texture
Surface: **glossy**
Color: spring - **light green;** summer - **bright green;** autumn - **orange to** scarlet **red**
Season: **deciduous;** emergence - late **May,** drop - early **November**

FLOWER: large singular, 7.5 to 9 cm (3 to 3 1/2 in) diameter, 5 petals
Color: **white,** bright yellow stamens in center
Season: early through mid **September**
Sex: monoecious   **Fragrant:** sweet, spicy

FRUIT: woody **capsule,** 19 mm (3/4 in) diameter
Color: **tan brown**
Season: **October** persisting through winter season **until** late **January**
Wildlife Value: **low**

HABITAT: found by George Bartrum in Georgia in 1770, no plants have been found in wild since 1790, along banks of
    the Alatamaha River; gradient - **lowland wet and wet-mesic**
Shade Tolerance: **intermediate;** index range 4.0-5.9
Flood Tolerance: **intermediate**

SOIL; Texture: moderately coarse sandy loams, medium loams **to fine** sandy and silty clays
Drainage: **well to moderately well**
Moisture: **moist to average**
Reaction: **strongly acid to moderately acid,** pH 4.6-6.0

HARDINESS: zone 6
Rate: **slow -** 15 to 20 cm (6 to 8 in) in one year period
Longevity: **medium**

SUSCEPTIBILITY; Physiological: infrequent
Disease: **frequent -** Fusarium wilt causes lethal damage
Insect: **infrequent**
Wind-Ice: **infrequent**

URBAN TOLERANCE; Pollution:
Lighting: Drought-Heat: **sensitive**   Mine Spoils: **sensitive**
Salt: Soil Compaction: **intermediate**
Root Pattern: **deep** sparsely fibrous; somewhat difficult to transplant, move small B&B or container in early spring

SPECIES; Associate: Black Tupelo, Baldcypress, Red Maple, Water Hickory, Pecan, Eastern Cottonwood, American
    Planetree, American Sweetgum, River Birch, lowland oaks
Similar: Star and Virginia Magnolia
Cultivars: none commercially obtainable

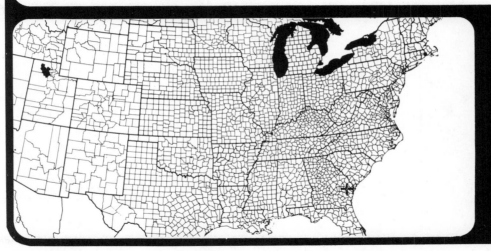

Franklinia

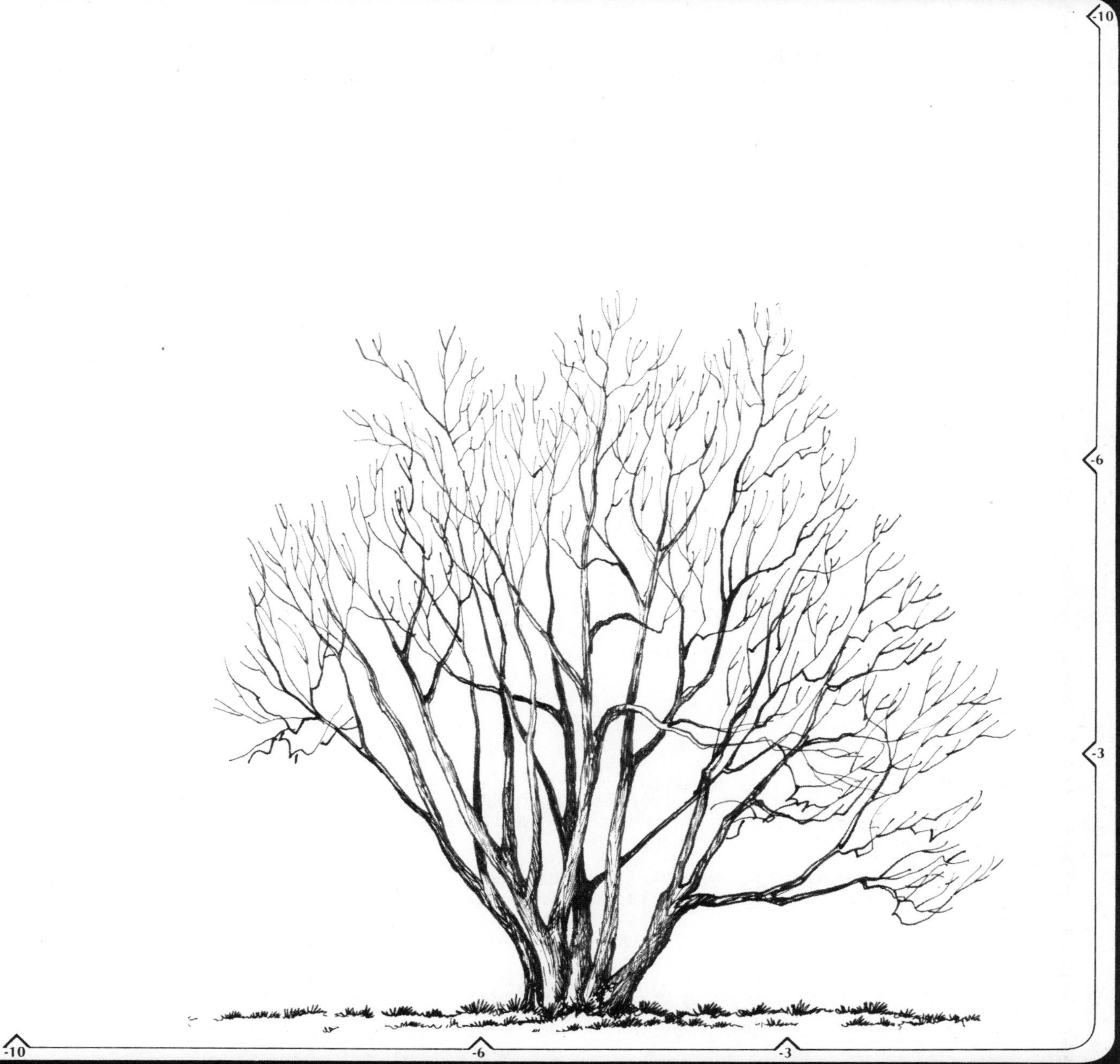

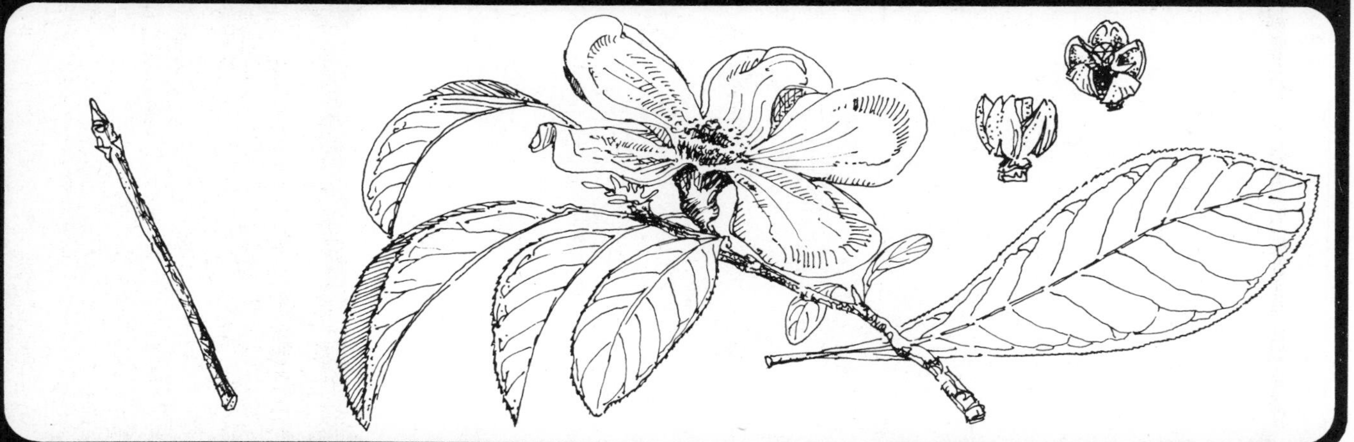

Fraxinus americana

FORM: irregular-ovoid
Size: **large canopy** - 22.5 to 30 m (75 to 100 ft)
Spread: **wide** - 15 to 22.5 m (50 to 75 ft), 2/3 of height
Mass: **moderate**

BRANCHING: **recurving,** very **coarse** texture
Twig: **large leaf scars,** conspicuous lenticels, coarse rigid, brittle, smooth, gray or **yellow brown**
Bud: **naked,** triangular end buds, **chocolate brown**
Bark: **shallow furrowed,** tight **narrow** fissures cross-checking in diamond-like pattern; silvery to ashy **gray**

FOLIAGE: opposite, **pinnately compound,** 5 to 9 mostly 7 leaflets, **lanceolate-oblong lanceolate, medium fine** texture
Surface: **dull** above, pale and smooth beneath
Color: spring - **light green;** summer - **bright green;** autumn - golden **yellow with purple** mottling
Season: **deciduous;** emergence - early **May,** drop - late **September**

FLOWER: **compact** many flowered **clusters**
Color: deep **purple**
Season: late **April through** early **May,** appearing just before leaves
Sex: **dioecious**

FRUIT: winged **samara,** 2.5 cm (1 in) long, borne in dense drooping terminal clusters
Color: **tan brown**
Season: early **August** persisting through winter months **through** late **February**
Wildlife Value: **low;** songbirds, small mammals

HABITAT: formation - **forest;** region - **northern, central;** gradient - **upland mesic, mesic-dry;** upland slopes and ravines, frequent on higher floodplain elevations
Shade Tolerance: **tolerant;** index range 6.0-7.9
Flood Tolerance: **intermediate**

SOIL; Texture: **moderately coarse to moderately fine;** loamy sands, sandy loams, loams and silt loams
Drainage: **well to moderately poor**
Moisture: **moist to average**
Reaction: **slightly acid to neutral,** pH 6.1-7.5

HARDINESS: zone 3b
Rate: **medium** - 46 cm (18 in) a year generally
Longevity: **medium** to long- 150 to 200 years common, longer lived than other ashes

SUSCEPTIBILITY; Physiological: **infrequent**
Disease: **frequent** - leaf rusts, leafspots, dieback, many cankers
Insect: **frequent** - ash borer, ash flower gall, brown headed ash sawfly
Wind-Ice: **frequent** - brittle twigs frequently broken

URBAN TOLERANCE; Pollution: **sensitive** - O$_3$; **resistant** - 2,4-D
Lighting: **resistant**　　　　　　　Drought-Heat: **intermediate**　　　　　Mine Spoils: **intermediate**
Salt: **intermediate**　　　　　　Soil Compaction: **intermediate**
Root Pattern: **shallow** fibrous widespreading; readily transplanted B&B in early spring or late autumn

SPECIES; Associate: Pin Cherry, Eastern White Pine, Yellow Birch, Sugar and Black Maples, Black Cherry, American Linden, American Beech, Northern Red and White Oaks, Tuliptree, Cucumbertree Magnolia
Similar: Green Ash has dissimilar autumn coloration, Yellow Buckeye
Cultivars: 'Autumn purple' - dark purple autumn color, 'Rosehill' - seedless and tolerates alkaline soils

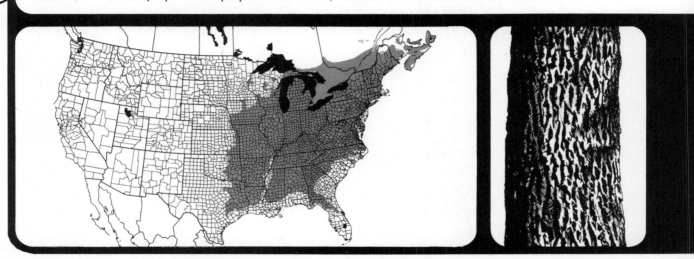

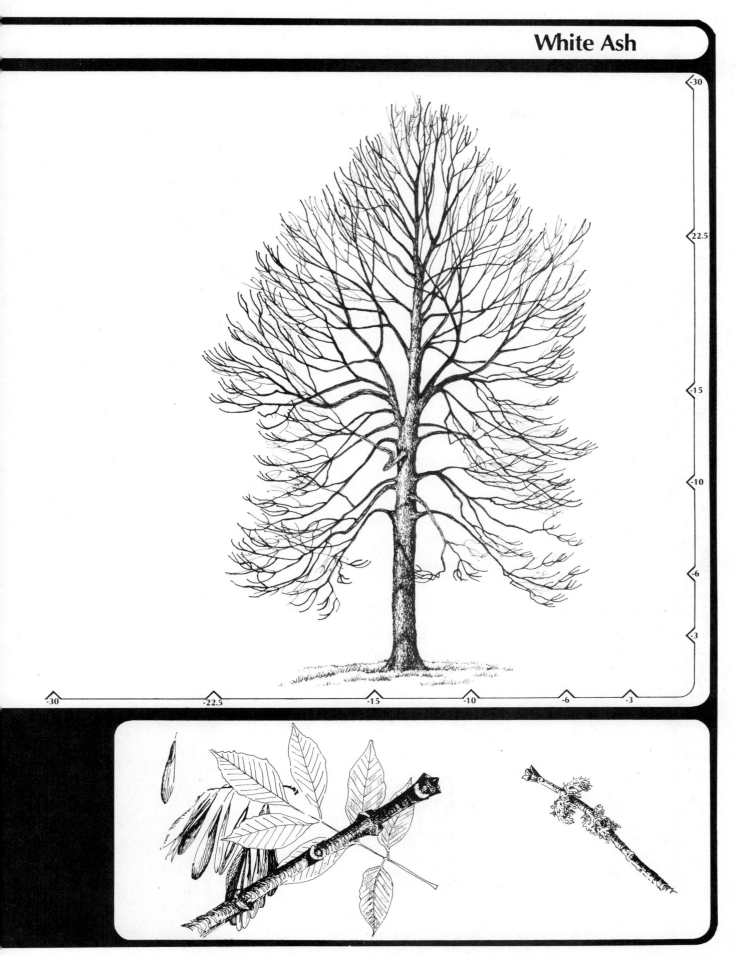

-30
-22.5
-15
-10
-6
-3

-30   -22.5   -15   -10   -6   -3

Fraxinus nigra

FORM: **irregular**
Size: **small canopy** - 15 to 22.5 cm (50 to 75 ft)
Spread: **intermediate** - 10 to 15 m (35 to 50 ft), 1/4 to 1/3 the height
Mass: **moderate**

BRANCHING: **recurving** branches, very **coarse** texture
Twig: dull with conspicuous lenticels and **large leaf scars**, coarse, brittle, rigid, smooth, **yellow brown**
Bud: **naked,** triangular end buds, very dark **brown to black**
Bark: thin loose **scaly** developing soft corky ridges which rub off easily by hand; light **gray**

FOLIAGE: opposite, **pinnately compound,** 7 to 13 leaflets, **lanceolate-oblong lanceolate, medium** texture
Surface: **dull,** smooth above, paler below
Color: spring - **light green;** summer - **dark green;** autumn - burgundy **purple to brown**
Season: **deciduous;** emergence - early **May,** drop - late **September**

FLOWER: **compact** many flowered **clusters**
Color: deep **purple**
Season: mid through late **April,** definitely before leaf emergence
Sex: **dioecious**

FRUIT: winged singular **samara,** 2.5 cm (1 in) long, borne in dense drooping clusters
Color: **tan brown**
Season: mid **July** persisting through winter months, **through** mid **February**
Wildlife Value: **low;** songbirds, small mammals

HABITAT: formation - **forest;** region - **northern;** gradient - **lowland wet;** edge of bogs, along streams, low lake margin,
alluvial flats
Shade Tolerance: **intolerant;** index range 2.0-3.9
Flood Tolerance: **very tolerant**

SOIL; Texture: **moderately coarse to fine;** peat soils, also fine sand and sandy loams underlain with clayey till
Drainage: **moderately poor to very poor,** high water table
Moisture: **demands wet to moist** conditions
Reaction: **strongly acid to slightly acid,** pH 4.6-6.5

HARDINESS: **zone 2**
Rate: **fast -** 60 to 90 cm (2 to 3 ft) per year generally, up to 1.2 m (4 ft) common
Longevity: **short -** rarely survives 100 years

SUSCEPTIBILITY; Physiological: **infrequent**
Disease: **frequent -** leaf spot, Anthracnose, rust, canker
Insect: **frequent -** oystershell scale, ash borer
Wind-Ice: **frequent -** brittle twigs

URBAN TOLERANCE; Pollution: **resistant -** 2,4-D
Lighting: **resistant**   Drought - Heat: **resistant**   Mine Spoils: **resistant**
Salt: **intermediate**   Soil Compaction: **resistant**
Root Pattern: very **shallow** and wide spreading; readily transplanted BR or B&B in spring or autumn with care

SPECIES; Associate: American Elm, Red Maple, Eastern Arborvitae, Balsam Fir, Black Spruce, Paper Birch, American Larch,
Hazel Alder
Similar: Green Ash, Blue Ash
Cultivars: none available commerically

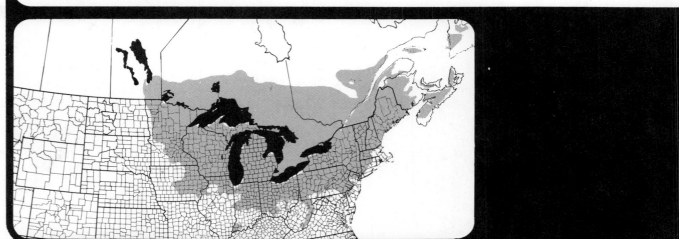

Black Ash

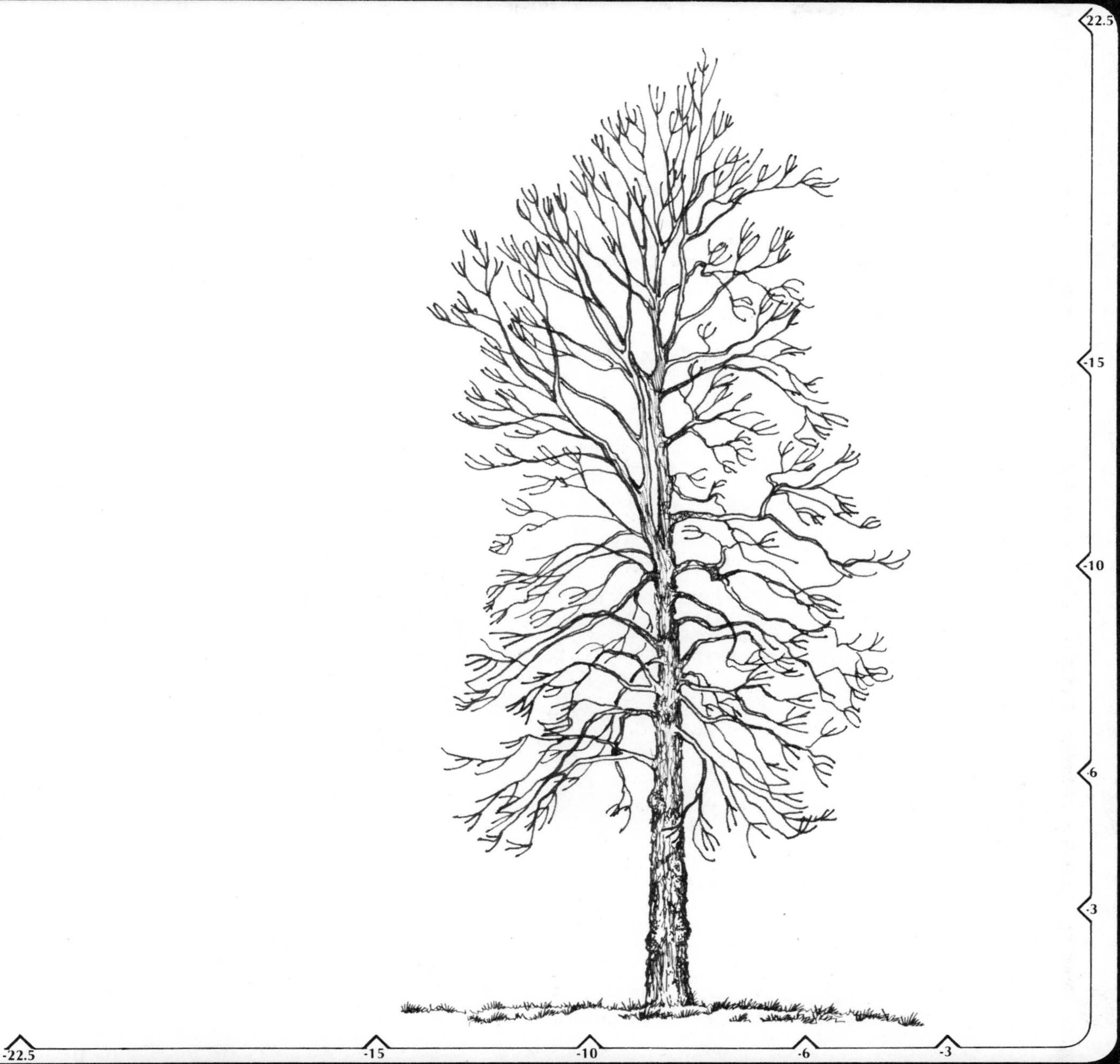

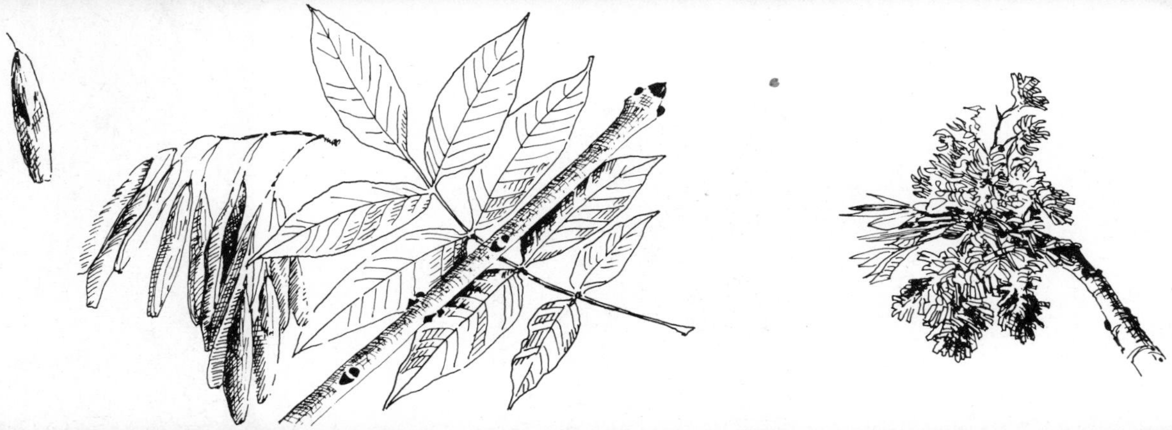

Fraxinus pennsylvanica lanceolata

FORM: irregular-ovoid
Size: **small canopy** - 15 to 22.5 m (50 to 75 ft)
Spread: **intermediate** - 10 to 15 m (35 to 50 ft), 2/3 of height
Mass: **moderate**

BRANCHING: recurving, very **coarse** texture
Twig: **large leaf scars** with conspicuous lenticels, mostly shiny, rigid, smooth **yellowish brown**
Bud: **naked,** triangular, **chocolate brown** end buds
Bark: **shallow furrowed,** close **narrow** ridges cross-checking into diamond-like pattern; silvery to ashy **gray**

FOLIAGE: opposite, **pinnately compound,** 7-9 short-stalked leaflets, **lanceolate-oblong lanceolate, medium** texture
Surface: **glossy** upper, pale smooth lower
Color: spring - **light green;** summer - **dark green;** autumn - golden **yellow to orangish**
Season: **deciduous;** emergence - early **May,** drop - early **October**

FLOWER: compact many flowered **clusters**
Color: deep **purple**
Season: late **April through** early **May,** before the leaves
Sex: **dioecious**

FRUIT: winged singular **samara, 2.5 cm (1 in) long, borne in dense drooping clusters**
Color: **tan brown**
Season: early **August** persisting through winter months **to late February**
Wildlife Value: **low;** songbirds, small mammals

HABITAT: formation - **forest, savanna;** region - **northern, central;** gradient - **lowland wet-mesic and upland mesic-dry;**
   along streams and lakes, floodplain, midwest windbreak and farmstead plantings
Shade Tolerance: **intolerant;** index range 2.0-3.9
Flood Tolerance: **tolerant**

SOIL; Texture: **coarse to medium** sands, sandy loams and loamy sands
Drainage: **moderately poor to well**
Moisture: **wet to** porous **droughty** granular soils
Reaction: **slightly acid to neutral,** pH 6.1-7.5

HARDINESS: zone 2
Rate: **fast** - 76 cm (2 1/2 ft) a year is average, commonly 91 cm (36 in) and more in some years
Longevity: **medium** - 100 to 150 years

SUSCEPTIBILITY; Physiological: **infrequent**
Disease: **infrequent** - heartwood rot, leafspots, many cankers
Insect: **frequent** - ash borer, oystershell scale, brown headed ash sawfly, lilac leaf minor, lilac borer
Wind-Ice: **frequent** - brittle twigs commonly broken

URBAN TOLERANCE; Pollution: **sensitive** - SO$_2$, O$_3$; **intermediate** - HFl; **resistant** - 2,4-D
Lighting: **resistant**   Drought - Heat: **resistant** - most tolerant ash
Salt: **intermediate**   Soil Compaction: **resistant**   Mine Spoils: **resistant**
Root Pattern: **shallow** fibrous pattern; transplants readily BR or B&B in spring or autumn with care

SPECIES; Associate: Bur Oak, Silver Maple, American Elm, Common Hackberry, Eastern Poplar, Pin Oak, American
   Sweetgum, Pecan, American Planetree, Black Willow, Eastern Wahoo, Eastern Redbud, hawthorn species
Similar: Black Ash, White Ash is less tolerant of flooding, not as drought tolerant, Boxelder
Cultivars: 'Honeyshade' - glossy green leaves, selected form; Marshall's Seedless; 'Summit' - pyramidal form

22.5

-15

-10

-6

-3

-22.5   -15   -10   -6   -3

Fraxinus quadrangulata

FORM: irregular
Size: **small canopy -** 15 to 22.5 m (50 to 75 ft)
Spread: **intermediate -** 10 to 15 m (35 to 50 ft), 2/3 of height
Mass: **moderate**

BRANCHING: recurving, coarse texture
Twig: squarish, 4 low corky **winged lines,** conspicuous lenticels, **large leaf scars,** light **yellow brown,** rigid
Bud: **naked,** triangular tan **brown** end buds
Bark: broken into loose fitting **scales,** old trees with loose hanging shaggy exfoliating plates; tan **gray**

FOLIAGE: opposite, pinnately compound, 5 to 11 leaflets, **lanceolate-oblong lanceolate, medium** texture
Surface: **dull** above, paler beneath
Color: spring - light **yellow green;** summer - **yellow green;** autumn - golden **yellow**
Season: **deciduous;** emergence - **May,** drop-late **September**

FLOWER: compact open **clusters**
Color: deep **purple**
Season: early to mid **May,** appearing with new leaves
Sex: monoecious

FRUIT: singular linear samaras, 2.5 cm (1 in) long, borne in dense drooping clusters
Color: **tan brown**
Season: mid **July through** winter months to mid **February**
Wildlife Value: **low;** songbirds, small mammals

HABITAT: formation - forest, savanna; region - **central;** gradient - **lowland wet mesic, upland dry;** dry rocky hillsides,
ravines, ridgetops, calcareous cliffs, along creek banks, floodplain
Shade Tolerance: **intermediate;** index range 4.0-5.9
Flood Tolerance: **very intolerant**

SOIL; Texture: **coarse** sandy or gravelly loams, **to moderately fine** silt loams, shallow soils over limestone, sandstone
Drainage: **moderately poor to excessive**
Moisture: **wet to** porous **droughty** granular soils
Reaction: **neutral to alkaline,** pH 6.6-8.0

HARDINESS: zone 5a
Rate: **fast -** 6 cm (24 in) a year on lowland sites, slow to medium on upland sites
Longevity: **medium -** 100 to 150 years

SUSCEPTIBILITY; Physiological: **infrequent**
Disease: **infrequent -** none serious
Insect: **frequent -** lilac leaf miner, lilac borer, fall webworm, ash borer
Wind-Ice: **infrequent**

URBAN TOLERANCE; Pollution: **resistant -** 2,4-D
Lighting: **resistant**   Drought - Heat: **resistant**   Mine Spoils: **resistant**
Salt: **intermediate**   Soil Compaction: **intermediate**
Root Pattern: **shallow** fibrous; readily transplanted B&B or BR in spring or autumn with care

SPECIES; Associate: wet mesic - Black Walnut, American Elm, Green Ash, Common Honeylocust; upland dry - Chinkapin
Oak, Post Oak, Blackjack Oak, Common Hoptree, Eastern Redcedar, sumac, Gray Dogwood, cherry, hawthorns
Similar: Green Ash, Black Ash
Cultivars: 'Urbana" - colorful bark, not yet generally available

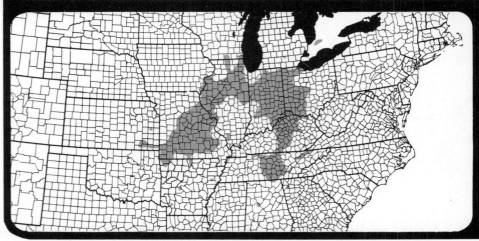

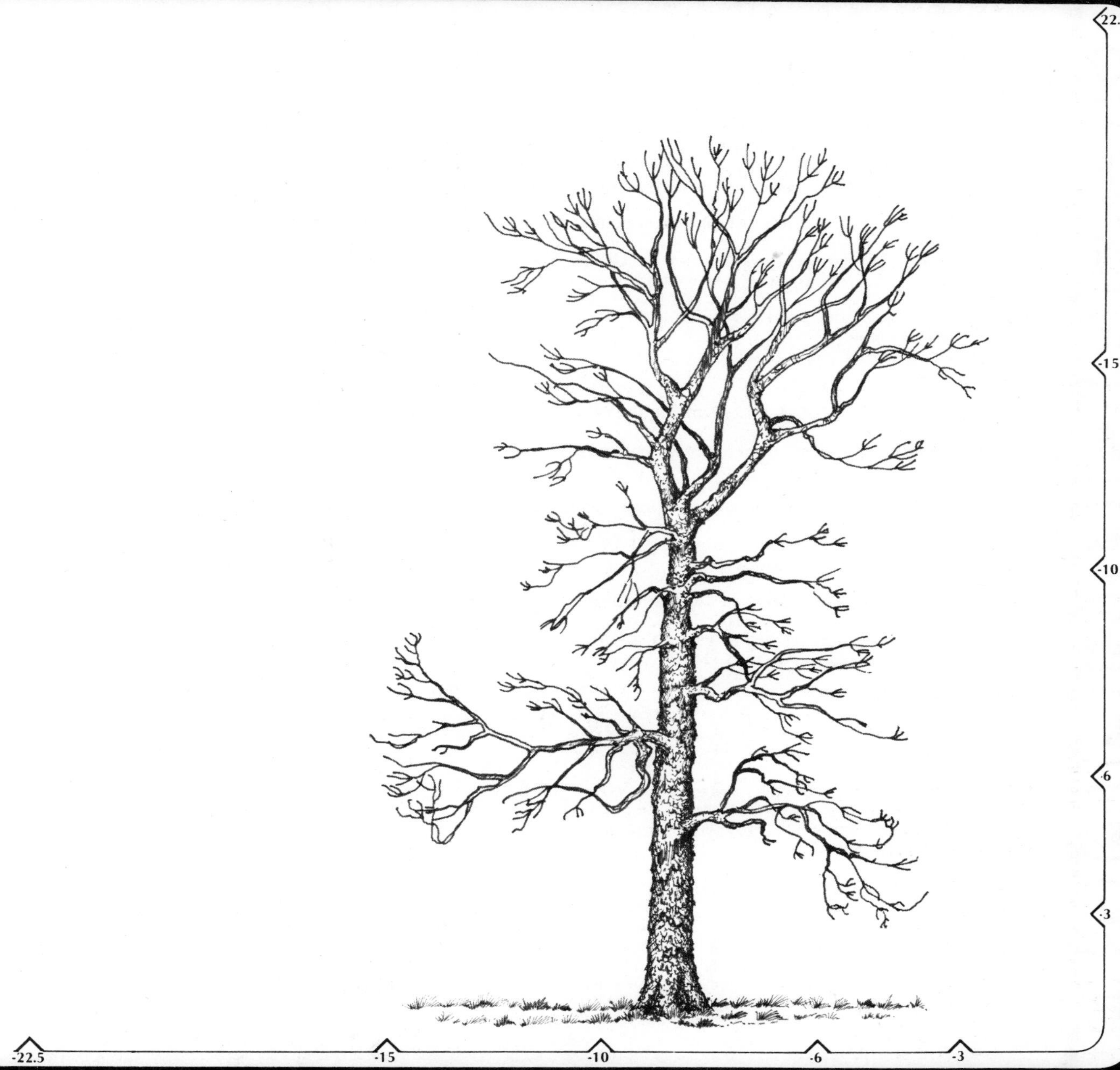
22.5
15
10
6
3
22.5
15
10
6
3

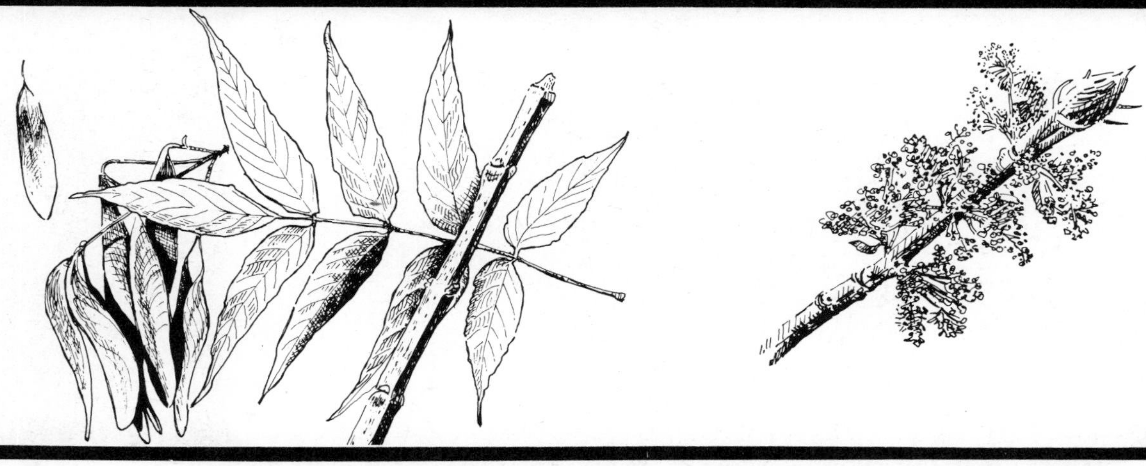

Gleditsia triacanthos

FORM: irregular - globular
Size: **small canopy -** 15 to 22.5 m (50 to 75 ft)
Spread: **wide -** 15 to 22.5 m (50 to 75 ft), as wide as tall
Mass: **open**

BRANCHING: **horizontal, picturesque,** irregular, **coarse** texture
Twig: **zig zag,** swollen at the nodes, **red brown; armed** with 3 branched thorns, trunks with massive clusters
Bud: small, mostly hidden
Bark: **shallow furrowed, wide** long flat irregular plate-like ridges curling along vertical margin; **brown black**

FOLIAGE: alternate, **pinnately or bipinnately compound,** 26-32 leaflets, **elliptic-oval,** entire, very **fine** texture
Surface: **dull**
Color: spring - **light green;** summer - bright **yellow green;** autumn - pale **yellow**
Season: **deciduous;** emergence - late **May,** drop - late **September**

FLOWER: small slender **pyramidal spike**-like clusters up to 10 cm (4 in) in length
Color: **yellow green**
Season: early through mid **June**
Sex: **dioecious**

FRUIT: **legume,** 30 cm (12 in) long, twisting flat bean-like pod, pendant
Color: **purplish brown**
Season: late **July** persisting until mid winter, **through January**
Wildlife Value: **very low**

HABITAT: formation - **forest, savanna;** region - **central;** gradient - **lowland wet-mesic and upland mesic-dry;** alluvial bottom-
lands, rocky hillsides, open or wooded pastures, fence rows, abandoned fields (especially in midwest), windbreaks
Shade Tolerance: **intolerant;** index range 2.0-3.9
Flood Tolerance: **intermediate**

SOIL; Texture: prefers **fine** clay, heavy loams, fine sandy and silty clay; tolerant of **moderately coarse** sandy loams
Drainage: **moderately poor to well**
Moisture: **wet to porous droughty** granular soils
Reaction: **slightly acid to neutral,** pH 6.1-7.5

HARDINESS: zone 4b
Rate: **fast -** 61 to 76 cm (2 to 2 1/2 ft a year) over a 20 year period
Longevity: **medium -** mature around 100 to 125 years, rarely survives 200 years

SUSCEPTIBILITY; Physiological: **infrequent**
Disease: **infrequent -** occasional canker, witches broom, leaf spot
Insect: **frequent -** honeylocust borer, Mimosa webworm is most serious in the midwest
Wind-Ice: **infrequent**

URBAN TOLERANCE; Pollution: **sensitive -** O_3
Lighting: Drought - Heat: **resistant**   Mine Spoils: **resistant**
Salt: **resistant**   Soil Compaction: **resistant**
Root Pattern: variable **taproot, deep laterals** to **shallow** fibrous spreading; easily transplanted B&B in spring, autumn

SPECIES; Associate: American Sweetgum, American Elm, Green Ash, Red Maple, Silver Maple, Boxelder, Pecan, Kentucky
Coffeetree, Black Walnut, Pin and Swamp White Oaks, Common Hackberry
Similar: Kentucky Coffeetree is less regular, coarser; Black Locust is narrower, less tolerant of flooding
Cultivars: 'Moraine' - seedless, 'Shademaster' - ascending habit, 'Skyline' - pyramidal, 'Sunburst' - yellow foliage

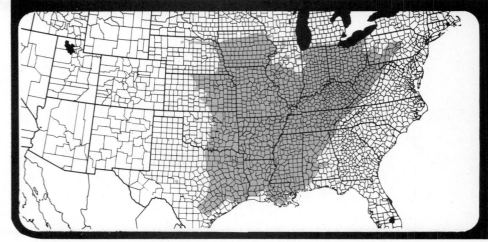

Gymnocladus dioicus

FORM: **irregular** - ovoid
Size: **large canopy** - 22.5 to 30 m (75 to 100 ft)
Spread: **wide** - 15 to 22.5 m (50 to 75 ft), 2/3 the height
Mass: **open**

BRANCHING: 3 or 4 sharply ascending limbs, **picturesque** contorted sparse lateral branching, **very coarse** texture
Twig: **large leaf scar**, blunt ended, **brown**
Bud: minute, blackish
Bark: **shallow furrowed** with **narrow** ridges curling outwards along vertical margin; **gray brown,** fissures bright orange

FOLIAGE: alternate, **bipinnately compound, ovate-oblong ovate** leaflets, entire margin, **medium fine** texture
Surface: **dull**
Color: spring - glossy **maroon green;** summer - dark **blue-green;** autumn - lemon **yellow,** early
Season: **deciduous;** emergence - early **June,** drop - mid to late **September**

FLOWER: open loose **pyramidal spike**-like cluster, 7.5 to 10 cm (3 to 4 in) long, terminal
Color: **yellow green**
Season: mid through late **June,** after leaf emergence
Sex: monoecious

FRUIT: **legume,** 12.5 cm (5 in) long, blunt leathery bean-like pod, hard shelled
Color: **purplish brown,** with bluish film, seeds imbedded in bright green sticky pulp
Season: **August** persisting **until** mid **February**
Wildlife Value: **very low**

HABITAT: formation - **forest;** region - **central;** gradient - **lowland wet-mesic;** floodplain, lower slope, farmstead
plantation, shelterbelts
Shade Tolerance: **intolerant;** index range 2.0-3.9
Flood Tolerance: **intermediate**

SOIL; Texture: grows poorly on gravelly or heavy clays, prefers **moderately coarse** sandy loams **to fine** sandy or silty clays
Drainage: **moderately poor to moderately well**
Moisture: prefers **wet to average** soils
Reaction: **neutral,** pH 6.6-7.5

HARDINESS: zone 5a
Rate: **slow to medium** - forestry plots (Morton Arboretum) average just over 30 cm (1 ft) per year for 10 year period
Longevity: **medium** - generally mature at 100 to 125 years

SUSCEPTIBILITY; Physiological: infrequent
Disease: **infrequent** - noticeably free from biological disorders
Insect: **infrequent**
Wind-Ice: **infrequent**

URBAN TOLERANCE; Pollution:
Lighting: Drought-Heat: **resistant**   Mine Spoils: **resistant**
Salt: **resistant**   Soil Compaction: **intermediate**
Root Pattern: **deep** coarse **laterals;** more difficult to transplant than honeylocust or ash, B&B in early spring

SPECIES; Associate: Green Ash, Common Honeylocust, Silver Maple, Black Walnut, Common Hackberry, Bitternut
Hickory, American Elm, Red Mulberry, Cockspur Hawthorn, Eastern Wahoo, Butternut
Similar: Northern Catalpa has dissimilar leaves, Common Honeylocust exhibits finer foliage texture
Cultivars: none available commercially

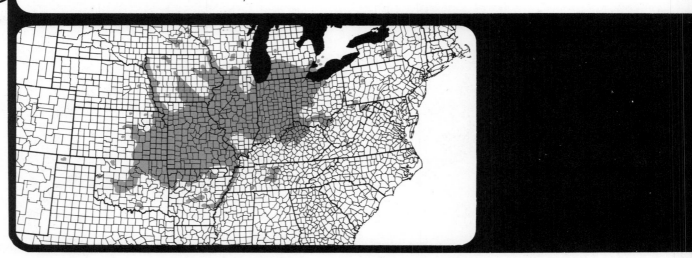

216

Halesia carolina

FORM: obovoid to globular
Size: **small understory** - 6 to 10 m (20 to 35 ft)
Spread: **narrow** - 6 to 10 m (20 to 35 ft) wide as tall
Mass: **dense**

BRANCHING: multiple upright trunks, branches **ascending** and widespreading, **medium** texture
Twig: slender, **brown**
Bud: elliptic, 3 mm (1/8 in) long, scaly
Bark: **smooth,** slightly ridged, narrow longitudinal stripes, old trunks scaly; **gray** with pale white stripes

FOLIAGE: alternate, **simple, elliptic-oval,** finely toothed margin, **medium** texture
Surface: **dull**
Color: spring - **light green;** summer - **bright green;** autumn - clear lemon **yellow**
Season: **deciduous;** emergence - mid **May,** drop - early **October**

FLOWER: bell-shaped, 13 mm (1/2 in) long, drooping delicately along undersides of twigs
Color: **white**
Season: early through mid **May,** before the new leaves
Sex: monoecious

FRUIT: elliptic 4 winged **samara,** 2.5 cm (1 in) long, in clusters along undersides of twigs
Color: **tan brown**
Season: **September through** mid winter until mid **January**
Wildlife Value: **very low**

HABITAT: formation - **forest;** region - **central;** gradient - **upland mesic;** sheltered coves, mesic ravines, north and east facing slopes
Shade Tolerance: **tolerant;** index range 6.0-7.9
Flood Tolerance: **intolerant**

SOIL; Texture: moderately coarse to moderately fine; sandy loams, loamy sands, medium loams
Drainage: **well to moderately well**
Moisture: **moist to average**
Reaction: **strongly acid to moderately acid,** pH 4.6-6.0

HARDINESS: zone 5b
Rate: **medium** - 2.7 to 3.6 m (9 to 12 ft) in 6 to 8 year period
Longevity: **medium**

SUSCEPTIBILITY; Physiological: infrequent
Disease: **infrequent**
Insect: **infrequent** - rarely attacked by pests
Wind-Ice: **infrequent**

URBAN TOLERANCE; Pollution:
Lighting: Drought-Heat: **sensitive**   Mine Spoils: **sensitive**
Salt: **sensitive**   Soil Compaction: **sensitive**
Root Pattern: **deep** coarse widespreading **laterals;** transplants readily B&B in early spring

SPECIES; Associate: Cucumbertree Magnolia, Bitternut Hickory, Yellow Buckeye, Tuliptree, Sourwood, Eastern White Pine, American Beech, Common Witchhazel, maple, oaks
Similar: Mountain Silverbell is related, larger fruits, flowers and size
Cultivars: none available

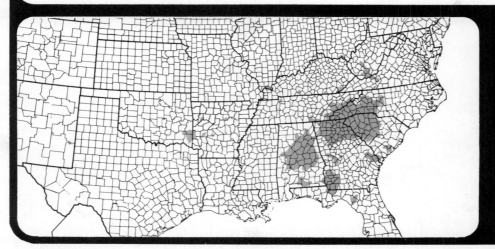

Carolina Silverbell

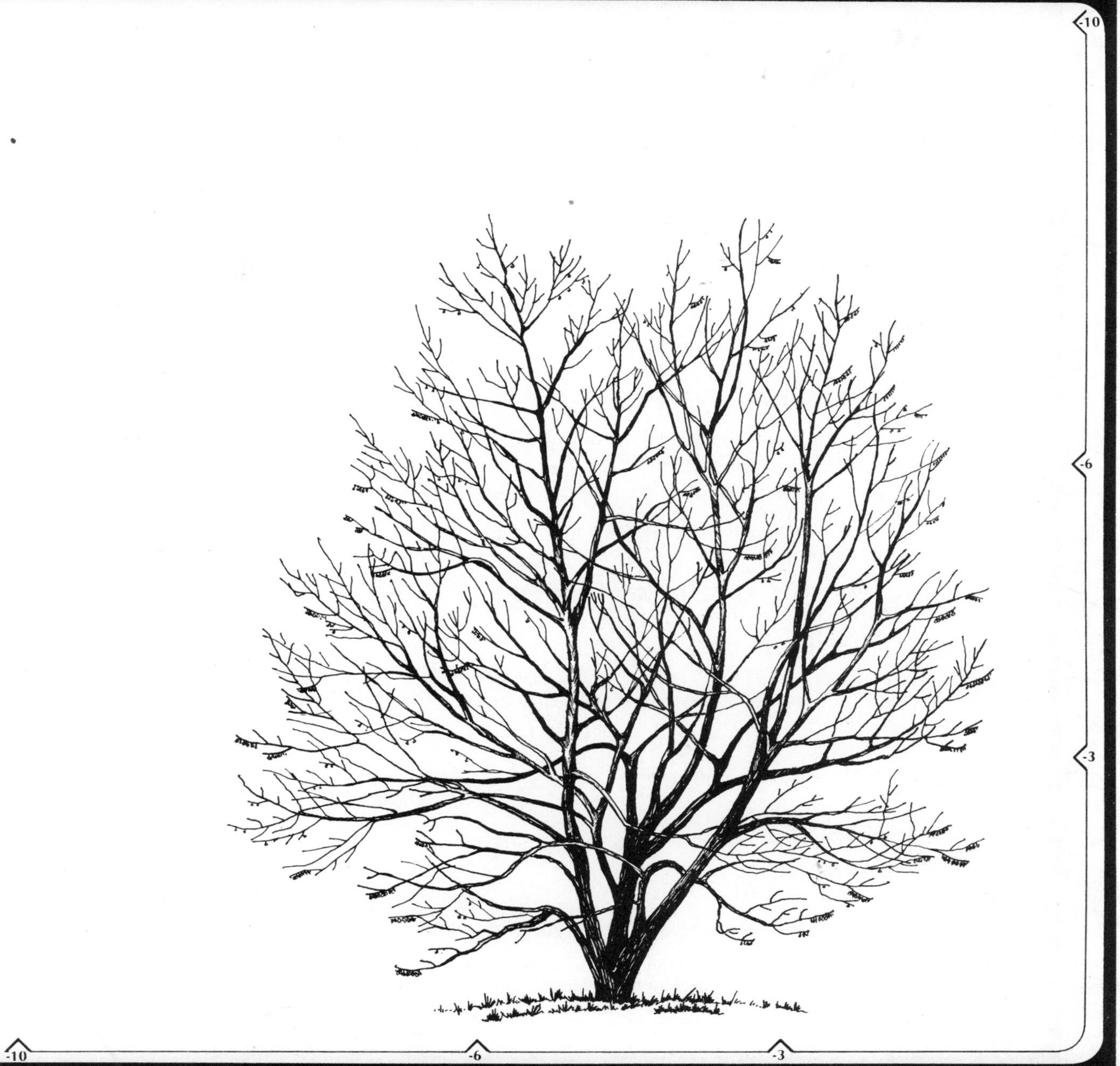

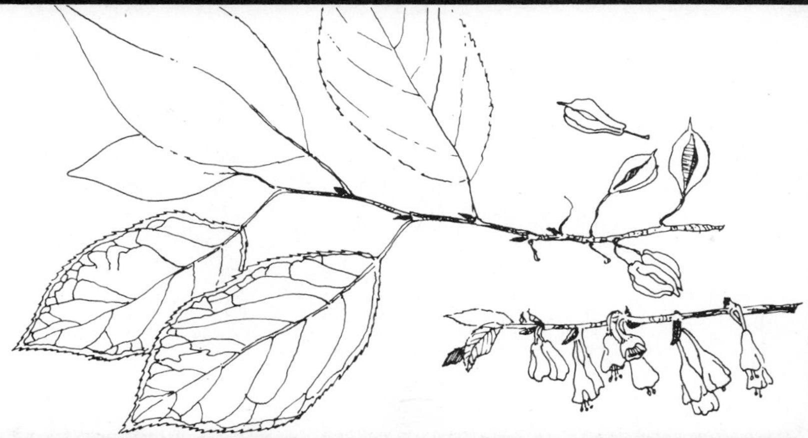

Hamamelis virginiana

FORM: globular or obovoid
Size: **small understory** - 6 to 10 m (20 to 35 ft)
Spread: **narrow** - 6 to 10 m (20 to 35 ft), commonly to 12 m, wider than tall
Mass: **dense**

BRANCHING: crooked leaning trunks, **horizontal picturesque,** twigs crowded above lateral branches, **medium** texture
Twig: velvety, slender, **yellowish brown**
Bud: **naked, stalked,** several clustered buds at a leaf scar, mustard **yellow**
Bark: **smooth** or slightly scaly, often mottled, conspicuous short horizontal lenticels; light **gray brown**

FOLIAGE: alternate, **simple, obovate-oblong obovate,** uneven base, margin wavy above middle, **medium coarse** texture
Surface: **dull,** slightly **tomentose**
Color: spring - **light green;** summer - **bright green;** autumn - clear lemon **yellow**
Season: **deciduous;** emergence - mid **May,** drop - early **October**

FLOWER: small clusters, 13 to 25 mm (1/2 to 1 in) across, spider-like linear kinky petals, clusters of 3
Color: bright **yellow**
Season: late **September** as leaves drop persisting **until** early **November,** commonly to December
Sex: monoecious

FRUIT: fuzzy two beaked woody **capsules,** 19 mm (3/4 in) long, splitting mechanically ejecting seeds
Color: **tan brown**
Season: **year round,** maturing in summer, opening when tree is in bloom, persisting another year
Wildlife Value: **low;** songbirds, small mammals

HABITAT: formation - **forest;** region - **central;** gradient - **upland mesic;** most abundant in mesic woods of ravine slopes
    and bottoms, often in drier sites
Shade Tolerance: **very tolerant;** index range 8.0-10.0
Flood Tolerance: **intolerant**

SOIL; Texture: **moderately coarse to moderately fine;** sandy loams, loamy sands, medium loams
Drainage: **well to moderately poor**
Moisture: **moist to average**
Reaction: **slightly acid,** pH 6.1-6.5

HARDINESS: zone 5a
Rate: **medium** - 23 to 38 cm (9 to 15 in) per year on favorable sites
Longevity: **medium**

SUSCEPTIBILITY; Physiological: **infrequent**
Disease: **infrequent**
Insect: **infrequent** - exceptionally pest resistant
Wind-Ice: **infrequent**

URBAN TOLERANCE; Pollution:
Lighting: Drought-Heat: **sensitive**   Mine Spoils: **sensitive**
Salt: **sensitive**   Soil Compaction: **sensitive**
Root Pattern: **deep** coarse **laterals;** somewhat difficult to transplant, move B&B or container in early spring

SPECIES; Associate: Tuliptree, American Hophornbeam, Common Chokecherry, American Linden, Black and
    Sugar Maple, Carolina Silverbell, American Beech, White and Northern Red Oaks, rhododendron, serviceberry,
    dogwood, hickory
Similar: Large Fothergilla is rarely larger than 3 m (10 ft), Vernal Witchhazel is upright shrub
Cultivars: none available commercially

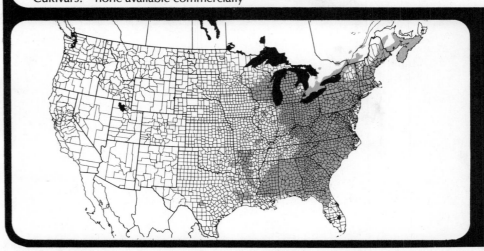

Common Witchhazel

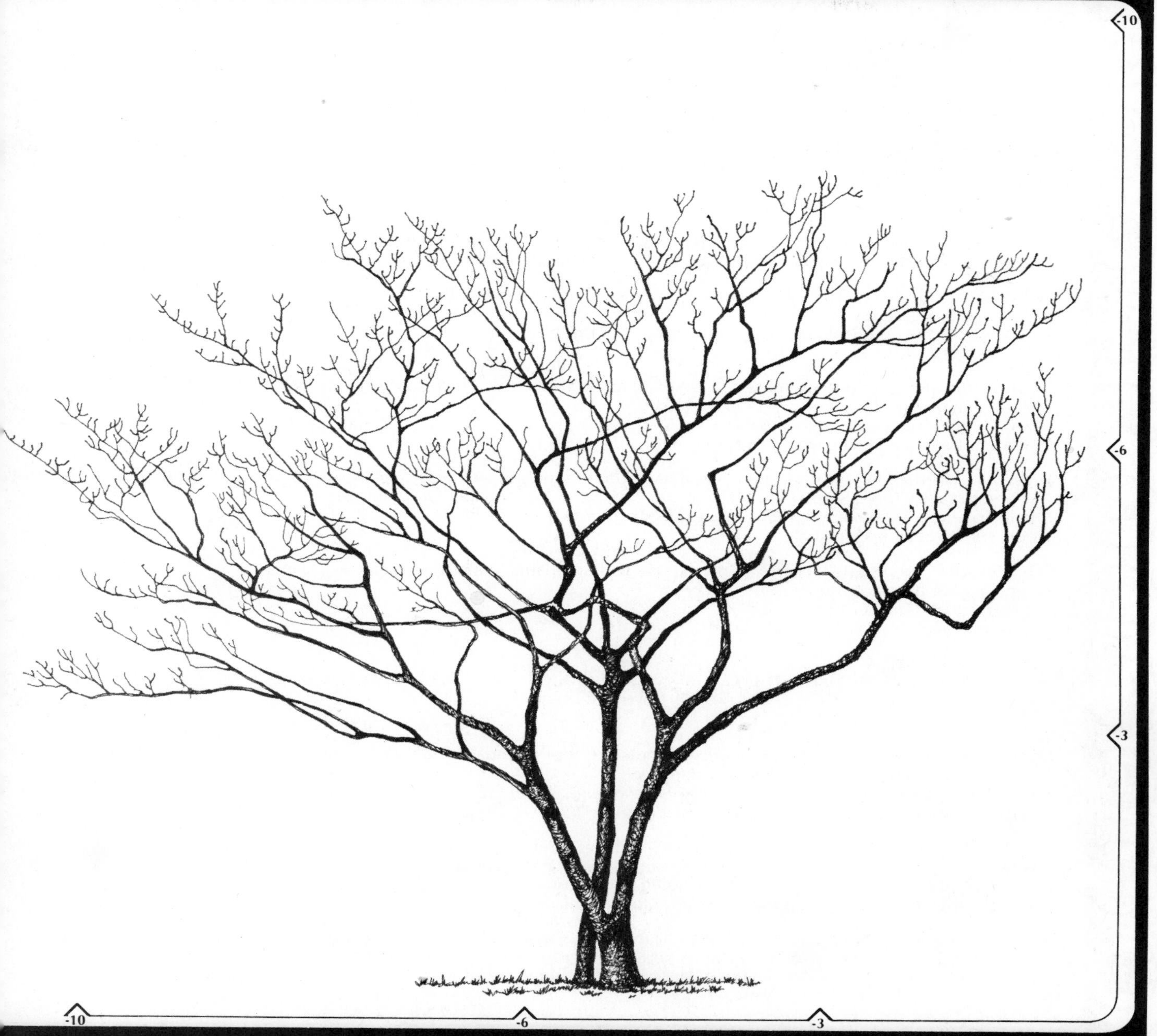

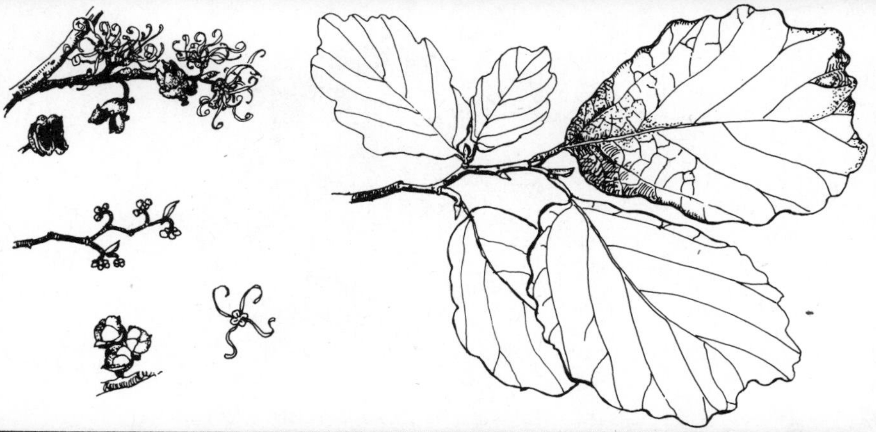

FORM: irregular
Size: **small canopy** - 15 to 22.5 cm (50 to 75 ft)
Spread: **wide** - 15 to 22.5 m (50 to 75 ft), commonly wider than tall
Mass: **open**

BRANCHING: trunk short, low number of large **ascending** branches with relatively few stout twigs, very **coarse** texture
Twigs: **large conspicuous leaf scars, velvety, tan brown,** diaphragmed pith
Bud: **naked, woolly,** tan brown
Bark: smooth becoming **shallow furrowed** with **wide** flat platy ridges; silvery white, young trees ashy **gray**

FOLIAGE: alternate, **pinnately compound,** 11 - 17 stalkless leaflets, **lanceolate-oblong lanceolate, medium** texture
Surface: **dull,** smooth above, **tomentose** beneath, terminal leaflet commonly absent
Color: spring - **yellow green;** summer - **yellow green;** autumn - golden **yellow**
Season: **deciduous;** emergence - late **May,** drop - early to mid **September**

FLOWER: male clustered in slender drooping **catkins,** 7.5 to 10 cm (3 to 4 in) long
Color: **yellow green**
Season: late **May through** early **June,** appearing with the leaves
Sex: monoecious

FRUIT: **nut,** elliptical football shaped, 5 cm (2 in) long, fuzzy husk which rots away exposing corrugated nut
Color: **tan brown**
Season: mid August through late October
Wildlife value: **low;** man, small mammals

HABITAT: formation - **forest;** region - **central;** gradient - **lowland wet-mesic, upland mesic;** mesic coves on stream benches
and terraces, lower slope in the talus of rock ledges, sites with cool air drainage
Shade Tolerance: **intolerant;** index range 2.0-3.9, intermediate on mesic sites
Flood Tolerance: **intermediate**

SOIL; Texture: **moderately coarse** loamy sands, medium loams **to moderately fine** silt loams
Drainage: **well to moderately well**
Moisture: prefers **moist to average**
Reaction: **neutral to alkaline,** pH 6.6-8.0

HARDINESS: **zone 3a**
Rate: **fast** - 60 to 90 cm (2 to 3 ft) a year on favorable sites, 9 to 12 m (30 to 40 ft) in 20 years
Longevity: very **short** - usually does not live beyond 75 years

SUSCEPTIBILITY; Physiological: **infrequent** - roots produce material toxic to many plants
Disease: **infrequent** - occasional canker dieback
Insect: **infrequent** - wood borers, nut weevils, lace bugs, bark beetles
Wind-Ice: **frequent** - extremely weak wooded, brittle

URBAN TOLERANCE; Pollution: **intermediate** - HFl; **resistant** - O$_3$
Lighting: Drought-Heat: **intermediate** Mine Spoils: **intermediate**
Salt: **sensitive** Soil Compaction: **intermediate**
Root Pattern: **taproot;** difficult to transplant, move small tree B&B in early spring

SPECIES; Associate: American Linden, American Beech, Sugar and Black Maples, Black Walnut, American Elm, Black
Cherry, Tuliptree, White Ash, Northern Red Oak, Kentucky Coffeetree, Common Hackberry
Similar: Amur Corktree (Asiatic) has similar form, branching character, foliage texture and autumn color
Cultivars: none commercially available

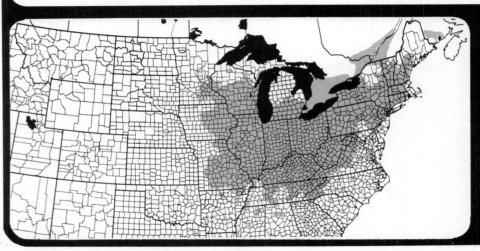

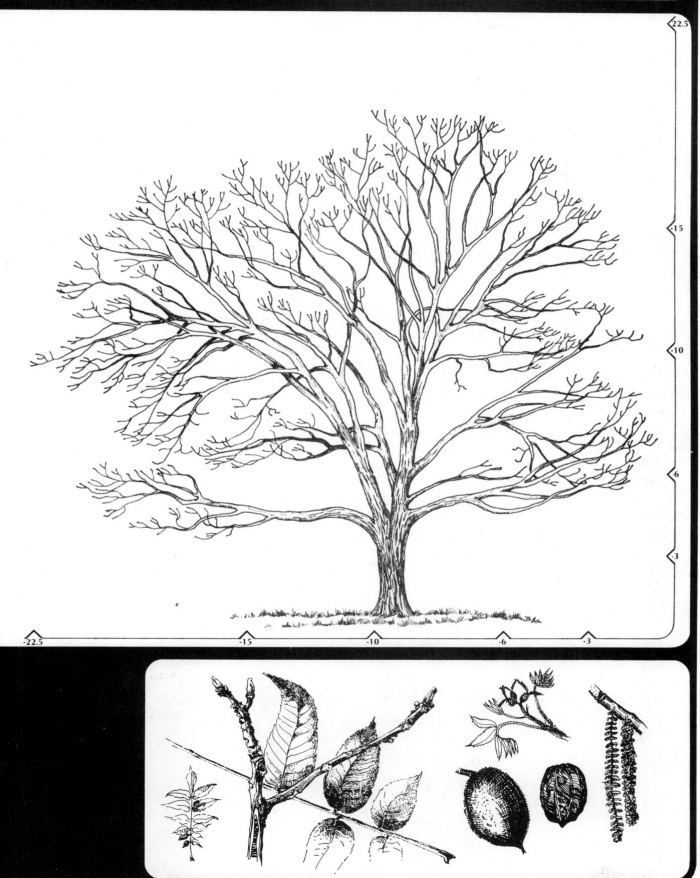

22.5
-15
-10
-6
-3

-22.5
-15
-10
-6
-3

Juglans nigra

FORM: irregular
Size: **large canopy** - 22.5 to 30 m (75 to 100 ft)
Spread: **very wide** - 22.5 to 30 m (75 to 100 ft), wide as tall
Mass: **open**

BRANCHING: high straight clear trunk, broadly **ascending** branches with relatively few stout twigs, **coarse** texture
Twig: **large** conspicuous **leaf scars,** dense **velvety,** very stout, **tan brown** with diaphragmed pith
Bud: **naked, woolly,** tan brown
Bark: **deeply furrowed** with fine lateral crack-like fissures divide ridges into rectilinear blocks; **brown black**

FOLIAGE: alternate, **pinnately compound,** 15-23 leaflets, **lanceolate-oblong lanceolate, medium fine** texture
Surface: **dull,** smooth, faintly hairy beneath
Color: spring - **yellow green;** summer - **yellow green;** autumn - golden **yellow**
Season: **deciduous;** emergence - late **May,** drop - early to mid **September**

FLOWER: male clustered in short pencil-like drooping **catkins,** 10 cm (4 in) long
Color: **yellow green**
Season: late **May through** early **June,** with the leaves
Sex: monoecious

FRUIT: **nut,** basketball shaped, 5 cm (2 in) diameter, smooth husk which rots on ground exposing corrugated nut
Color: **yellow green** becoming black
Season: late **August to** late **September**
Wildlife Value: **low;** man, small mammals

HABITAT: formation - **forest, savanna;** region - **central;** gradient - **lowland wet-mesic, upland mesic dry;** alluvial floodplain, stream banks, upland in open or abandoned fields, midwest windbreak and farmstead
Shade Tolerance: **intolerant;** index 3.9
Flood Tolerance: **intermediate**

SOIL; Texture: **moderately coarse** loamy sands, sandy loams, prefers deep loams **to moderately fine** silt loams
Drainage: **well to moderately well**
Moisture: prefers **moist,** tolerates **droughty** conditions
Reaction: **neutral to alkaline,** pH 6.6-8.0

HARDINESS: zone 4b
Rate: **fast** - 60 to 90 cm (2 to 3 ft) a year on favorable sites when young, 9 to 12 m (30 to 40 ft) in 20 years
Longevity: **long** - matures at about 150 years, may live to 250

SUSCEPTIBILITY; Physiological: **infrequent** - roots are toxic to many plants
Disease: **infrequent** - European canker can be destructive in weakened trees
Insect: **infrequent** - locally severe attacks by caterpillars can defoliate trees
Wind-Ice: **infrequent**

URBAN TOLERANCE; Pollution: **intermediate** - HFl; **resistant** - O$_3$
Lighting: Drought-Heat: **resistant**   Mine Spoils: **resistant**
Salt: **sensitive**   Soil Compaction: **intermediate**
Root Pattern: **taproot;** difficult to transplant, move B&B in early spring

SPECIES; Associate: lowland - American Elm, Kentucky Coffeetree, Common Hackberry, Green Ash, Boxelder, Silver Maple, Butternut, American Linden, Bitternut Hickory, Eastern Redbud, Red Mulberry, hawthorn species
Similar: Green Ash, Eastern Poplar, Silver Maple, all exhibit similar form, branching habit, mass, texture
Cultivars: 'Laciniata' - finely dissected foliage, not yet available commercially

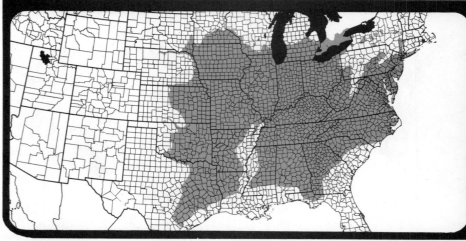

Eastern Black Walnut

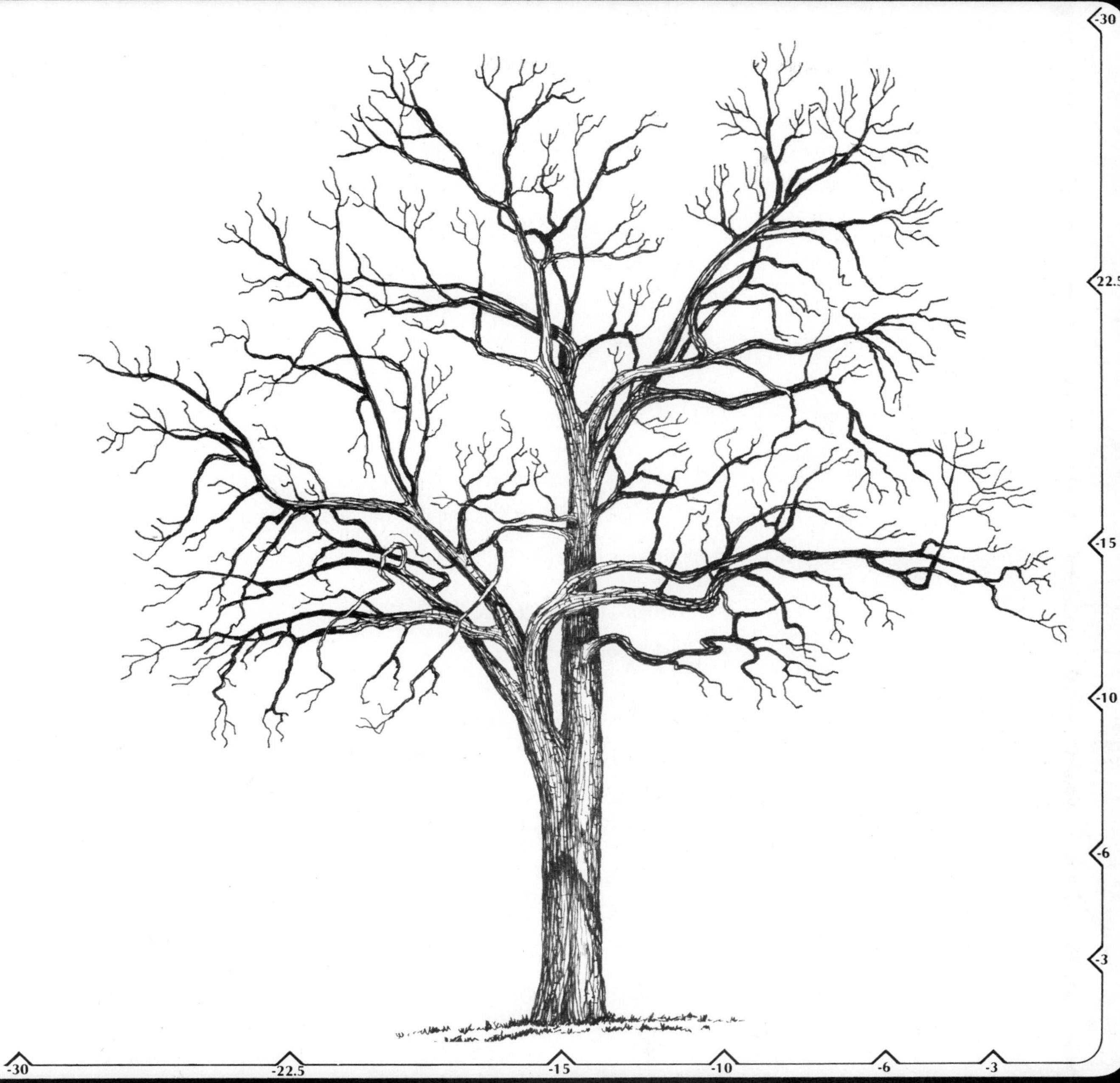

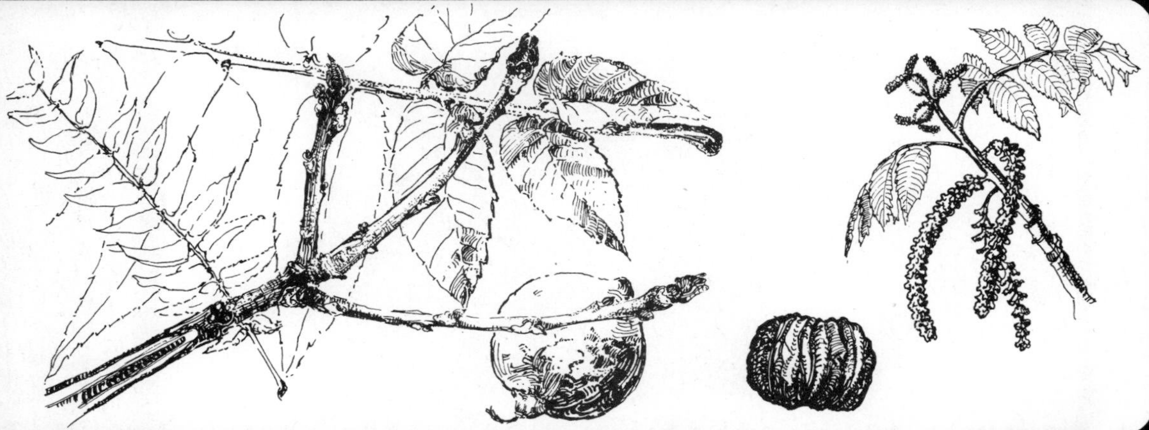

Juniperus virginiana

FORM: broadly **conical,** commonly columnar
Size: **small canopy** - 15 to 22.5 m (50 to 75 ft)
Spread: **intermediate** - 10 to 15 m (35 to 50 ft), 1/2 to 2/3 the height
Mass: very **dense**

BRANCHING: **horizontal** becoming ascending at ends; branchlets frequently drooping on mature trees, **medium** texture
Twig: slender, **green** becoming coppery or yellow brown in winter
Bud: minute
Bark: thin fibrous **exfoliating,** narrow shreddy long strips peeling **vertically; red brown** to silvery gray

FOLIAGE: mature **scale-like,** juvenile short prickly **acicular,** very **fine** texture
Surface: **dull,** aromatic
Color: spring - dark **blue green;** summer and autumn - **dark** olive **green;** late autumn through winter - **maroon green to**
Season: coniferous **evergreen**
                                                                                                            brown green

FLOWER: small **cone**
Color: female - **red purple;** male - yellowish
Season: mid through late **May**
Sex: **dioecious**

FRUIT: **berry**-like cone, 3 to 6 mm (1/8 to 1/4 in), cone scales are fused
Color: gray or **blue** green
Season: **July** persisting **until** late **March**
Wildlife Value: **very high;** man (distilled in gin), songbirds, upland ground birds, small mammals, hoofed browsers

HABITAT: formation - **savanna;** region - **central;** gradient - **upland dry;** dry hillsides or semi-barren lands, calcareous
    cliffs, steep rocky land, occasional in open alluvial woods, abandoned farmlands, midwest shelterbelt plantings
Shade Tolerance: intermediate in youth, **very intolerant** with maturity; index range 0-1.9
Flood Tolerance: **intolerant**

SOIL; Texture: **coarse** sands and sandy loams **to fine** silty clays
Drainage: **moderately poor to excessive**
Moisture: prefers **moist,** tolerates **droughty** conditions
Reaction: **slightly acid to alkaline,** pH 6.1-8.0

HARDINESS: zone 3a
Rate: **slow** - 20 to 30 year old trees generally 5.4 to 7.2 m (18 to 24 ft) tall
Longevity: **long** - maximum age about 300 years

SUSCEPTIBILITY; Physiological: **infrequent**
Disease: **frequent** - cedar apple rust, many other rusts, twig blight
Insect: **infrequent** - few cause damage, bagworms can defoliate entire crown
Wind-Ice: **infrequent** - decidedly windfirm

URBAN TOLERANCE; Pollution: **resistant** - SO_2, O_3, HFl
Lighting: Drought-Heat: **resistant**   Mine Spoils: **resistant**
Salt: **resistant**   Soil Compaction: **sensitive**
Root Pattern: **taproot;** more easily transplanted if root pruned, move B&B in early spring, late autumn

SPECIES; Associate: pure stands - cedar glades, Common Persimmon, Sassafras, Common Honeylocust, Post, Black, and
    Blackjack Oaks, Devils-Walkingstick, hickories, hawthorns, sumac, cherry
Similar: Eastern Arborvitae, Chinese Juniper (Asiatic), Western Redcedar
Cultivars: 'Burkii' - narrow pyramidal, steel blue cast in winter, 'Skyrocket' - extremely narrow, many others

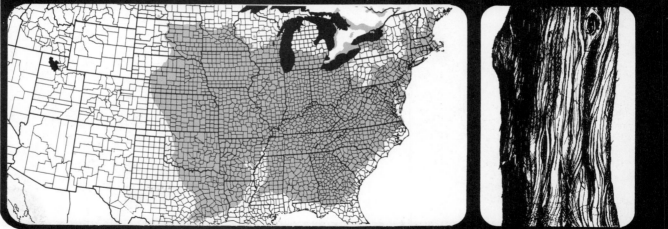

Larix laricina

FORM: conical
Size: **small canopy** - 15 to 22.5 m (50 to 75 ft)
Spread: **intermediate** - 10 to 15 m (35 to 50 ft), 1/2 to 2/3 the height
Mass: **open**

BRANCHING: strongly **horizontal,** slender tertiary branchlets **pendulous, fine** texture
Twig: short compressed, dwarf spur-like, **green yellow**
Bud: **stalked,** minute, bright red
Bark: **scaly,** very fine tight flaky appearance; **red brown,** exposed inner bark dark reddish purple

FOLIAGE: acicular, 2.5 cm (1 in) long, spirally arranged in clusters of 10 to 20, **very fine** texture
Surface: **glossy,** soft, flexible
Color: spring - **light green;** summer - **bright green;** autumn - golden **yellow,** late
Season: **deciduous** conifer; emergence - early **May,** drop - mid **November**

FLOWER: cone, 13 to 19 mm (1/2 to 3/4 in) long, borne upright along twigs
Color: female - bright **purplish red**
Season: early through mid **May,** with new leaves
Sex: monoecious

FRUIT: small oval **cone,** 13 mm (1/2 in) long, 8 to 14 scales, erect
Color: light **tan brown**
Season: **year around;** opening in autumn, persisting for an additional year
Wildlife Value: **intermediate;** small mammals, songbirds

HABITAT: formation - **forest;** region - **northern;** gradient - **lowland wet;** swamp, muck, lake margin, stream borders, seep areas
Shade Tolerance: **very intolerant;** index 0.8
Flood Tolerance: **very tolerant**

SOIL; Texture: not limiting - ranges from **fine** heavy clay **to coarse** wet sand
Drainage: **moderately poor to very poor**
Moisture: **wet,** will grow fairly well on **dry** soils due to shallow bedrock or low water table
Reaction: **strongly acid to neutral,** pH 4.8-7.5

HARDINESS: zone 2
Rate: **fast** - 46 to 61 cm (1 1/2 to 2 ft) annually in youth, slowing after 50 years
Longevity: **medium** - maximum age generally 150 to 180 years

SUSCEPTIBILITY; Physiological: **infrequent**
Disease: **infrequent** - occasional wood rot, several rust fungi
Insect: **frequent** - larch casebearer, larch sawfly
Wind-Ice: **frequent** - wind throw

URBAN TOLERANCE; Pollution: **sensitive** - SO_2, O_3, HFl, HCl, Cl
Lighting: Drought-Heat: **sensitive**   Mine Spoils: **sensitive;**
Salt: **resistant**   Soil Compaction: **resistant**   vigorous on wet sites
Root Pattern: **shallow** fibrous; readily transplanted BB when dormant

SPECIES; Associate: Black Ash, Black Spruce, Red Maple, Black Willow, Balsam Fir, Jack Pine, Gray Birch, Hazel Alder, Eastern Arborvitae, Boxelder
Similar: European Larch is related, Baldcypress
Cultivars: none available commercially

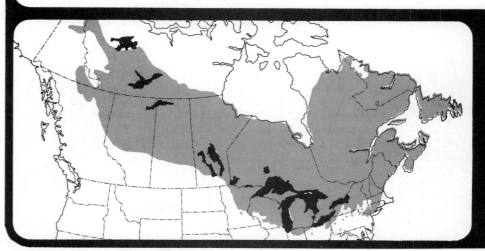

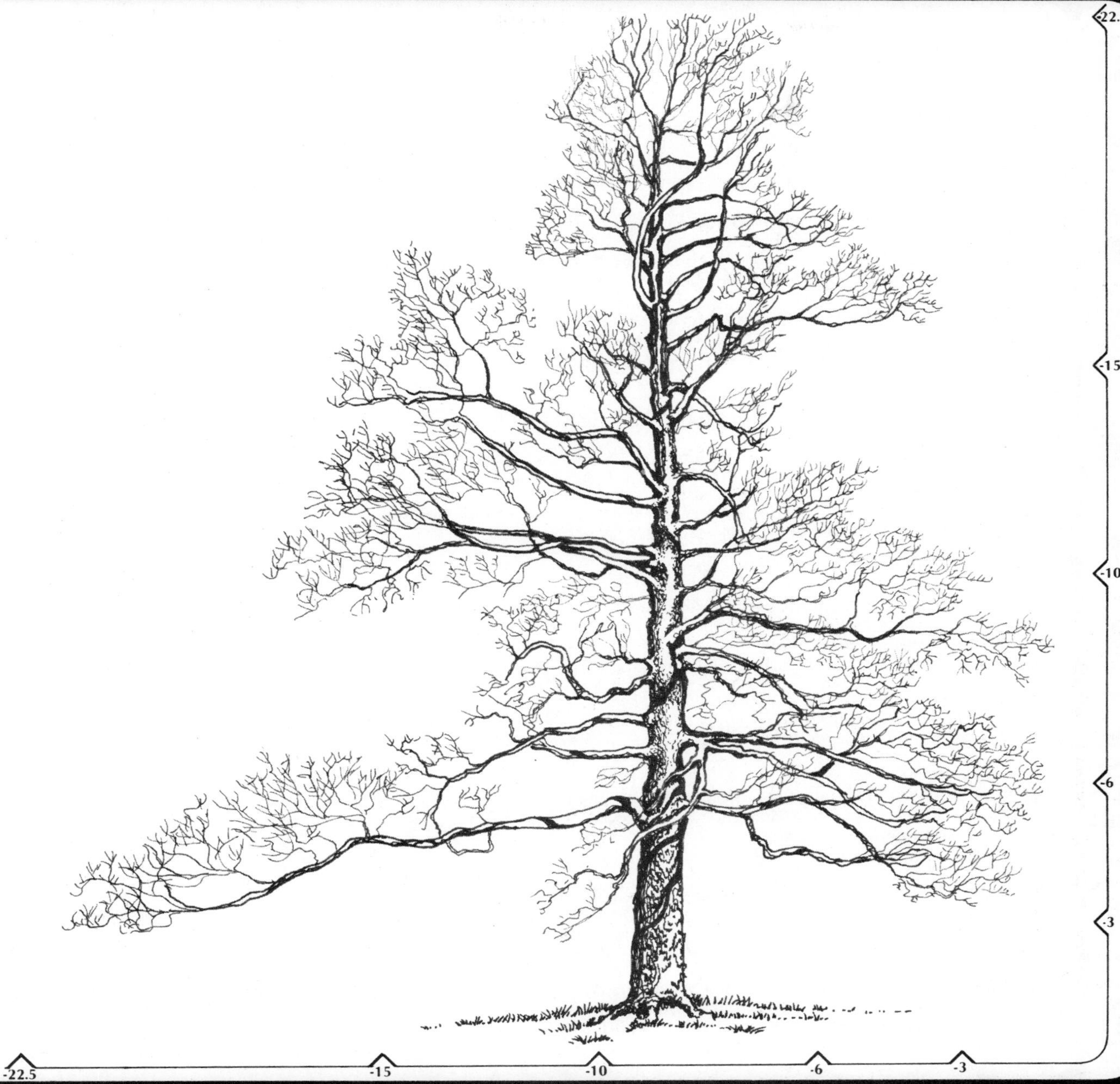
-22.5
-15
-10
-6
-3
-22.5
-15
-10
-6
-3

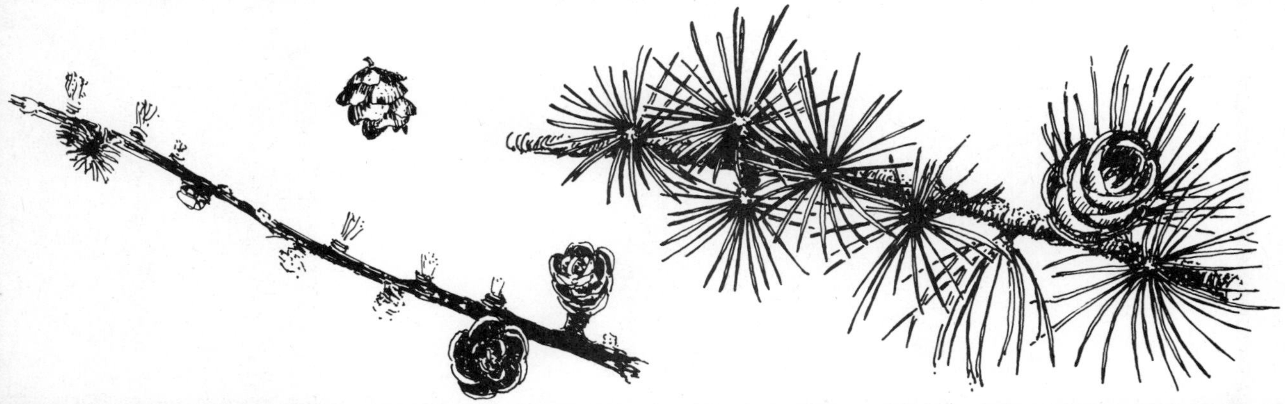

Liquidambar styraciflua

FORM: **conical** in youth becoming **ovoid**
Size: **large canopy** - 22.5 to 30 m (75 to 100 ft)
Spread: **wide** - 15 to 22.5 m (50 to 75 ft), 2/3 the crown height
Mass: **dense**

BRANCHING: long clear trunk, occasionally buttressed, **ascending,** strong candelabra appearance, **medium** texture
Twig: stout corky **wings,** silvery **gray**
Bud: scaly, 6 mm (1/4 in) long, orange-brown
Bark: **deep furrowed,** ridges with coarse irregular scales; silvery **gray**

FOLIAGE: alternate, **simple, palmately lobed,** 5 sharp pointed star-shaped lobes, toothed, **medium** texture
Surface: **glossy,** dull beneath, leathery
Color: spring - **light** glossy **green;** summer - **bright green;** autumn - scarlet **red to purple**
Season: **deciduous;** emergence - late **April,** drop - late **October**

FLOWER: **small** globular **clusters** on long stem
Color: **yellow green**
Season: late **April through** early **May,** appearing with new foliage
Sex: monoecious

FRUIT: **multiple,** globular horny woody ball, 2.5 to 4 cm (1 to 1 1/2 in) diameter, pendant on long stem
Color: **tan brown**
Season: late **July** persisting **through January**
Wildlife Value: **low**

HABITAT: formation - **forest;** region - **central;** gradient - **lowland wet mesic;** alluvial floodplain, stream borders
Shade Tolerance: **intolerant;** index range 2.0-3.9
Flood Tolerance: **tolerant**

SOIL: Texture: **moderately coarse to fine;** prefers alluvial clays and loams, silty clay loams, silt loams
Drainage: **well to poor**
Moisture: prefers **moist to average**
Reaction: **slightly acid,** pH 6.1-6.5

HARDINESS: zone 6
Rate: **slow to medium** - 30 to 61 cm (1 to 2 ft) a year, somewhat faster on alluvial sites
Longevity: **long** - mature at 150 to 300 years

SUSCEPTIBILITY; Physiological: **frequent** - iron chlorosis on high pH soils, frost damages late summer shoot growth
Disease: **infrequent** - occasional bleeding necrosis, leader dieback, sweetgum blight
Insect: **infrequent** - very resistant
Wind-Ice: **infrequent** - decidedly windfirm

URBAN TOLERANCE; Pollution: **sensitive** - HCl, Cl; **intermediate** - O$_3$, 2,4-D
Lighting: Drought-Heat: **intermediate** Mine Spoils: **intermediate**
Salt: Soil Compaction: **resistant**
Root Pattern: deep **taproot;** somewhat difficult to transplant, move B&B in early spring, re-establishes slowly

SPECIES; Associate: Pin Oak, Eastern Poplar, Baldcypress, American Planetree, Pecan, American Elm, Northern Catalpa, Tuliptree, River Birch, Black Willow, Black Tupelo
Similar: Sugar Maple exhibits similar shape and texture, not flood tolerant
Cultivars: 'Burgundy' - wine colored leaves in autumn, 'Festival' - slender columnar form, others

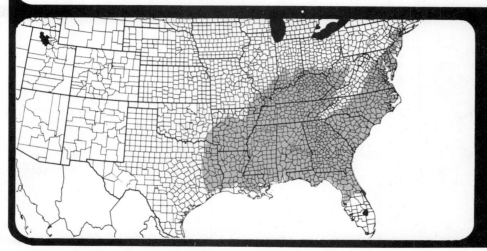

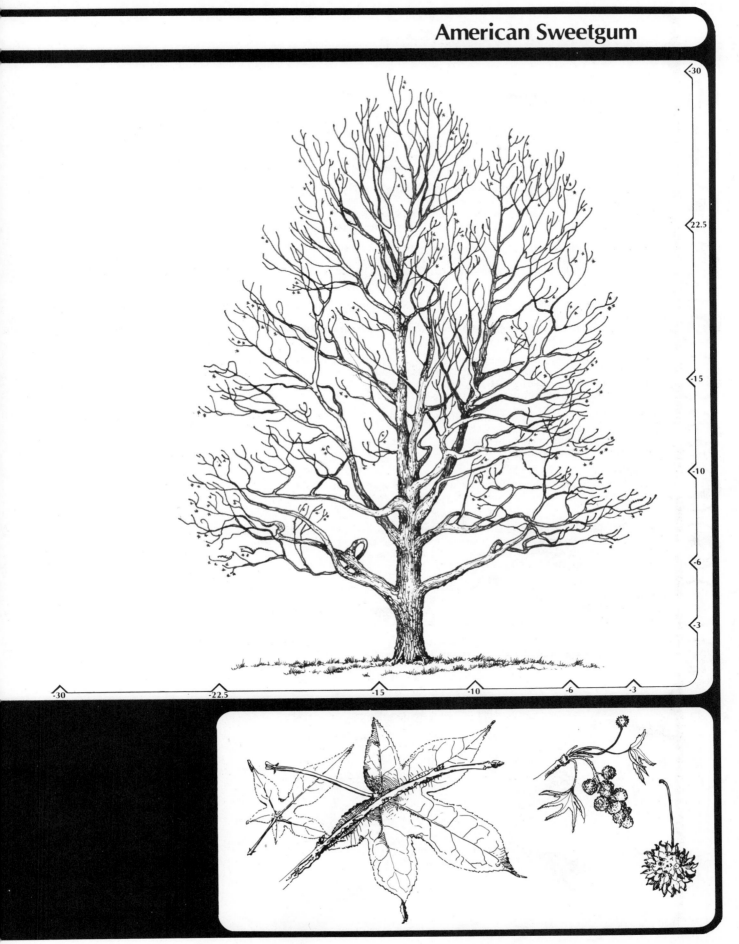

Liriodendron tulipifera

FORM: **columnar** to conical
Size: **large canopy** - 22.5 to 30 m (75 to 100 ft)
Spread: **intermediate** - 10 to 15 m (35 to 50 ft), 1/2 the height
Mass: **moderate**

BRANCHING: irregular **ascending,** high crowned, **medium** texture
Twig: encircled at each leaf scar by a line-like mark, slender, glossy, **red brown**
Bud: **two scales,** flattened duckbill-like terminal bud, dark **red** flower bud tulip-like 2.5 to 5 cm (1 to 2 in)
Bark: **shallow furrowed, narrow** elongated longitudinal flat topped or rounded ridges; **gray,** orange fissures

FOLIAGE: alternate, **simple, palmately lobed,** long petiole, leaf appears cut off at top, **medium coarse** texture
Surface: somewhat **glossy,** paler beneath
Color: spring - **light green;** summer - **bright green;** autumn - clear lemon **yellow**
Season: **deciduous;** emergence - mid May, drop - mid **October**

FLOWER: **large single,** cup shaped, 5 to 7.5 cm (2 to 3 in) diameter, at ends of twigs, borne upright along branches
Color: **yellow green** with orange splotches toward base of petals
Season: early through mid **June,** after leaves are half grown
Sex: **dioecious**   Fragrant: slightly

FRUIT: winged woody **samara,** 5 cm (2 in), erect pyramidal cluster, central stalk remaining after seed dispersal
Color: **tan brown**
Season: **August through** late **November,** frequently persisting into late winter
Wildlife Value: **low;** songbirds, small mammals

HABITAT: formation - **forest;** region - **central;** gradient - **upland mesic-dry;** sheltered coves, lower slopes and hills, stream
valleys near northern and southern limits of range
Shade Tolerance: **intermediate;** index range 4.0-5.9
Flood Tolerance: **very intolerant**

SOIL; Texture: prefers loose **moderately fine** sandy soils, sandy loams, loamy sands, **to medium** loams
Drainage: **well to moderately well**
Moisture: prefers **moist to average**
Reaction: **slightly acid,** pH 6.1-6.5

HARDINESS: zone 5a
Rate: **medium to fast** - 9 to 12 m (30 to 40 ft) in 15 year period
Longevity: **medium** - 125 to 175 years at maturity; maximum age known to be over 200 years

SUSCEPTIBILITY; Physiological: **frequent** - leaf yellowing and premature leaf drop in dry seasons
Disease: **infrequent** - cankers, powdery mildew, Verticillium wilt
Insect: **infrequent** - scale, Tuliptree spot gall, aphids
Wind-Ice: **frequent** - weak wooded

URBAN TOLERANCE; Pollution: **sensitive** - O_3, PAN; **resistant** - SO_2
Lighting: **sensitive**   Drought-Heat: **sensitive**   Mine Spoils: **sensitive**
Salt: Soil Compaction: **sensitive**
Root Pattern: **shallow to deep** fibrous, fleshy and poorly branched; transplants best B&B in early spring

SPECIES; Associate: Sugar Maple, American Beech, Yellow Birch, Cucumbertree Magnolia, White Ash, Northern Red Oak,
Carolina Silverbell, American Linden, Flowering Dogwood, Canada Hemlock
Similar: none, distinctive in most seasons
Cultivars: 'Crispum' - leaves broader with wavy margin, 'Compactum' - dwarf form, 'Tortuosum' - contorted branching

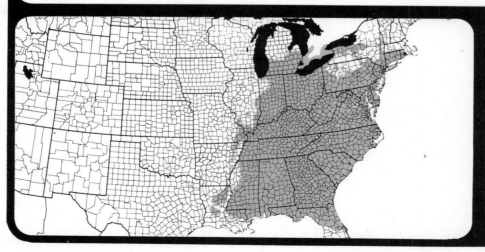

232

Maclura pomifera

FORM: globular
Size: **large understory** - 10 to 15 m (35 to 50 ft)
Spread: **intermediate** - 10 to 15 m (35 to 50 ft), wide as tall
Mass: **dense**

BRANCHING: **recurving**, abrupt scythe-like arching habit repeating at regular interval along limbs, **coarse** texture
Twig: stout, **zig zag, orange brown; armed** with 13 mm (1/2 in) long straight spine at each node
Bud: small depressed and partially imbedded in bark
Bark: **deeply furrowed**, fibrous, flattened ridges cross-checking in irregular pattern; dark **yellow-orange brown**

FOLIAGE: alternate, **simple, ovate-oblong ovate**, entire margin, **medium** texture
Surface: thick, firm, **glossy**, paler and smooth beneath
Color: spring - **light green**; summer - **bright green**; autumn - **yellow**
Season: **deciduous**; emergence - late **May**, drop - early **November**

FLOWER: dense **small** globular **clusters**
Color: **yellow green**
Season: mid through late **June**, appearing after the leaves
Sex: **dioecious**

FRUIT: large **multiple**, 10 to 12.5 cm (4 to 5 in) diameter, resembling woody orange, covered with fibrous hairs
Color: pale **green yellow**
Season: **September through** early **November**
Wildlife Value: **very low**

HABITAT: formation - **savanna**; region - **central**; gradient - **lowland wet-mesic, upland dry;** open alluvial floodplain, hillsides in open rocky pasture, midwest windbreak plantings and fencerows
Shade Tolerance: **intolerant;** index range 2.0-3.9
Flood Tolerance: **intermediate**

SOIL; Texture: **moderately fine** silt loams, sandy loams, loamy sands **to moderately coarse** sandy plains
Drainage: **moderately poor to excessive**
Moisture: prefers **moist**, tolerates **droughty** condition
Reaction: **slightly acid to alkaline**, pH 6.1-8.0

HARDINESS: zone 5a
Rate: **fast** - approximately 76 cm (30 in) per year
Longevity: **long**

SUSCEPTIBILITY; Physiological: **infrequent**
Disease: **infrequent** - occasional leaf spot
Insect: **infrequent** - very resistant
Wind-Ice: **infrequent**

URBAN TOLERANCE; Pollution:
Lighting: Drought-Heat: **resistant**   Mine Spoils: **resistant**
Salt: **resistant**   Soil Compaction: **sensitive**
Root Pattern: **shallow** fibrous; transplants readily as BR or B&B in any season with care

SPECIES; Associate: Red Mulberry, Eastern Redcedar, Black Cherry, Common Chokecherry American Plum, Common Prickly Ash, Sassafras, Eastern Redbud, hawthorns, crabapples, viburnums, sumacs
Similar: Red Mulberry
Cultivars: 'Inermis' - thornless, 'Pawhuska' and 'Chetapa' - thornless, male - produces no fruit

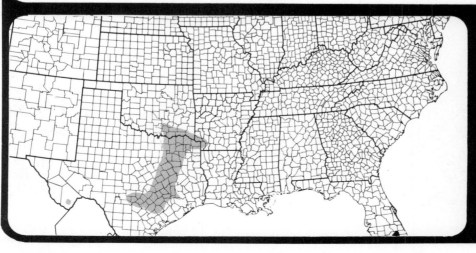

234

Magnolia acuminata

FORM: ovoid
Size: **large canopy** - 22.5 to 30 m (75 to 100 ft)
Spread: **intermediate** - 10 to 15 m (35 to 50 ft), 1/2 to 3/4 the height
Mass: **moderate**

BRANCHING: **recurving,** frequently sweeping the ground, **coarse** texture
Twig: stout, ringed at leaf scar, **red brown**
Bud: **naked, woolly, green** with **silvery hairs,** 13 to 25 mm (1/2 to 1 in) long
Bark: **shallow furrowed, narrow** flat-topped plate-like longitudinal ridges; **gray brown**

FOLIAGE: alternate, **simple, elliptic-oval,** entire slightly wavy margin, **coarse** texture
Surface: **dull,** leathery
Color: spring - **yellow green;** summer - **yellow green;** autumn - remains **yellow green** until drop
Season: **deciduous;** emergence - mid **May,** drop - mid **October**

FLOWER: **large singular** tulip-like at ends of twigs, 5 cm (2 in) across, fleshy petals
Color: **yellow green**
Season: late **May through** early **June,** after leaves are full grown
Sex: monoecious   **Fragrant:** slightly

FRUIT; **follicle,** aggregate of small fleshy pods on stout short stem resembling a cucumber
Color: green turning bright **red**
Season: **September through** early **November**
Wildlife Value: **very low**

HABITAT: formation - **forest;** region - **central;** gradient - **upland mesic;** sheltered coves, mesic ravines, lower slopes
          protected valleys
Shade Tolerance: **intermediate;** index range 4.0-5.9
Flood Tolerance: **intolerant**

SOIL; Texture: **moderately coarse** loamy sands, medium loams **to moderately fine** silt loams, better aeration
Drainage: **well to moderately well**
Moisture: prefers **moist to average**
Reaction: **strongly acid to neutral;** pH 4.6-7.0

HARDINESS: **zone 5a**
Rate: **medium** - 3 to 4.5 m (10 to 15 ft) over 4 to 5 year period
Longevity: **medium** - generally matures at 125 years

SUSCEPTIBILITY; Physiological: **infrequent**
Disease: **infrequent** - noticeably free of biological disorders
Insect: **infrequent** - occasional scale
Wind-Ice: **infrequent**

URBAN TOLERANCE; Pollution:
Lighting: Drought-Heat: **sensitive**   Mine Spoils: **sensitive**
Salt: **sensitive**   Soil Compaction: **sensitive**
Root Pattern: **deep** coarse **laterals,** fleshy; difficult to transplant, move as small tree B&B in early spring

SPECIES; Associate: Tuliptree, Sugar Maple, Yellow Buckeye, White and American Lindens, American Beech, Carolina
          Silverbell, Northern Red Oak, Umbrella Magnolia, Sourwood, Eastern Redbud, dogwood
Similar: Common Pawpaw has similar foliage but is small tree, other magnolias not hardy in north, Tuliptree
Cultivars: 'Subcordata' - smaller tree, pale yellow flowers in early May

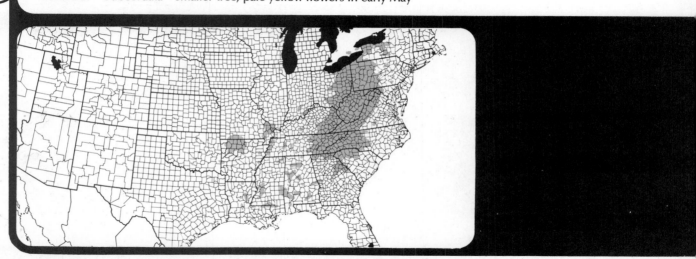

Malus ioensis

FORM: globular
Size: **small understory** - 6 to 10 m (20 to 35 ft)
Spread: **narrow** - 6 to 10 m (20 to 35 ft), wide as tall
Mass: **dense**

BRANCHING: crooked trunk, irregular **horizontal, medium** texture
Twig: slender **reddish brown** with thin grayish **flaky** skin; **armed** with short thorn-like right angle spur branches
Bud: blunt, bright **red**
Bark: **scaly** exfoliating in irregular papery sheets revealing smooth inner bark; silvery **gray**

FOLIAGE: alternate, **simple, wedge,** doubly serrate, somewhat 3 lobed-terminal elongated, **medium fine** texture
Surface: **tomentose,** dull
Color: spring - **red to maroon green;** summer - **bright green;** autumn - **yellowish to orange**
Season: **deciduous;** emergence - early **May,** drop - mid **September,** early

FLOWER: large single, 4 cm (1 1/2 in) across, in 3-6 flowered clusters
Color: **pink** to whitish with pink flush
Season: mid through late **May,** just following leaf emergence
Sex: monoecious   **Fragrant:** sweet spicy

FRUIT: large single apple-like **berry,** 2.5 cm (1 in) diameter, pendant on long stems
Color: **yellow green**
Season: **September through** mid **October**
Wildlife Value: **intermediate;** man, songbirds, upland ground birds, large and small mammals

HABITAT: formation - **savanna;** region - **central;** gradient - **upland dry;** open woods, rocky hillsides, open pastures,
      margin of woods, creek banks, waste ground, common on limestone areas, windbreak and shelterbelt
Shade Tolerance: **intolerant;** index range 2.0-3.9
Flood Tolerance: **intermediate**

SOIL; Texture: **moderately coarse** sandy and gravelly loams, **to fine** silty clay loams and heavy clays
Drainage: **well to poor**
Moisture: prefers **moist,** tolerates **dry** soils
Reaction: **strongly acid to neutral,** pH 4.8-7.5

HARDINESS: zone 2
Rate: **medium** - 3 to 4.5 m (10 to 15 ft) over 6 to 10 years
Longevity: **short** - 50 to 75 years, rarely survives 100 years

SUSCEPTIBILITY; Physiological: **infrequent**
Disease: **frequent** - cedar apple rust is severe, fire blight, scab, canker
Insect: **frequent** - scale, borers, aphids
Wind-Ice: **infrequent**

URBAN TOLERANCE; Pollution: **sensitive** - SO$_2$, HCl, Cl, 2,4-D
Lighting: Drought-Heat: **resistant**   Mine Spoils: **resistant**
Salt: **intermediate**   Soil Compaction: **intermediate**
Root Pattern: **shallow** fibrous; transplants easily B&B in early spring or autumn

SPECIES; Associate: Eastern Redcedar, Bur Oak, American Plum, American Filbert, Blackhaw Viburnum,
      Red Mulberry, Eastern Redbud, Flowering Dogwood, sumac and hawthorn species
Similar: other native (specifically M. coronaria) and exotic crabs, American Plum, hawthorn species
Cultivars: 'Plena' - double flowering form, 'Prairie Rose' - rarely fruits, symmetrical and very dense, others

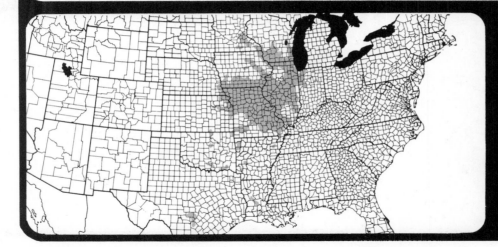

Morus rubra

FORM: globular
Size: **large understory** - 10 to 15 m (35 to 50 ft)
Spread: **intermediate** - 10 to 15 m (35 to 50 ft), wide as tall
Mass: very **dense**

BRANCHING: short trunk, stout **ascending,** short crowded aggregated entangled branchlets, **coarse** texture
Twig: slender, exudes a milky juice, **orangish brown**
Bud: on raised projection above leaf scar, glossy
Bark: young trees smooth with raised lenticels, adult **deeply furrowed** with fibrous ridges; **orange brown**

FOLIAGE: alternate, **simple, cordate or** occasionally **pinnately lobed,** coarsely toothed, **medium coarse** texture
Surface: **tomentose, dull,** thick
Color: spring - **yellow green;** summer - **yellow green;** autumn - golden **yellow**
Season: **deciduous;** emergence - mid **May,** drop - late **September**

FLOWER: small dense elliptic **catkin,** 19 to 25 mm (3/4 to 1 in) long
Color: **yellow green**
Season: late **May through** early **June,** after the new leaves
Sex: **dioecious**

FRUIT: cylindric **berry,** multiple aggregate resembling a blackberry, 2.5 cm (1 in) long
Color: dark **reddish purple** becoming almost black
Season: mid **June through** mid **July**
Wildlife Value: **high;** man, large and small mammals, songbirds, upland birds

HABITAT: formation - **forest, savanna;** region - **central;** gradient - **lowland wet-mesic, upland dry;** alluvial floodplain, creek
banks, open prairie hills and pastures, planted in windbreaks
Shade Tolerance: **intermediate;** index range 4.0-5.9
Flood Tolerance: **intermediate**

SOIL; Texture: **moderately coarse** sandy loams, loamy sands, **to moderately fine** silt loams
Drainage: **well to poor**
Moisture: prefers **moist,** tolerates **dry** soils
Reaction: **slightly acid to alkaline,** pH 6.3-8.0

HARDINESS: zone 5b
Rate: **fast** - 3 to 4 m (10 to 12 ft) in 5 year period
Longevity: **short** - mature at 75 years

SUSCEPTIBILITY; Physiological: **infrequent**
Disease: **frequent** - bacterial blight on leaves, leaf spot, witches broom, canker, powdery mildew
Insect: **frequent** - two-spotted mites, scale
Wind-Ice: **frequent**

URBAN TOLERANCE; Pollution: **sensitive** - SO_2, O_3; **intermediate** - HFl, 2,4-D
Lighting: Drought-Heat: **resistant**   Mine Spoils: **resistant**
Salt: **resistant**   Soil Compaction: **intermediate**
Root Pattern: **taproot, or deep laterals;** transplants easily B&B or BR at any season with care

SPECIES; Associate: Eastern Wahoo, Common Hackberry, Black Walnut, American Elm, Common Honeylocust, Silver
Maple, Kentucky Coffeetree, Eastern Redbud, Cockspur Hawthorn
Similar: White Mulberry (European) is related, Osageorange, Eastern Redbud exhibits similar form and texture
Cultivars: none available commercially

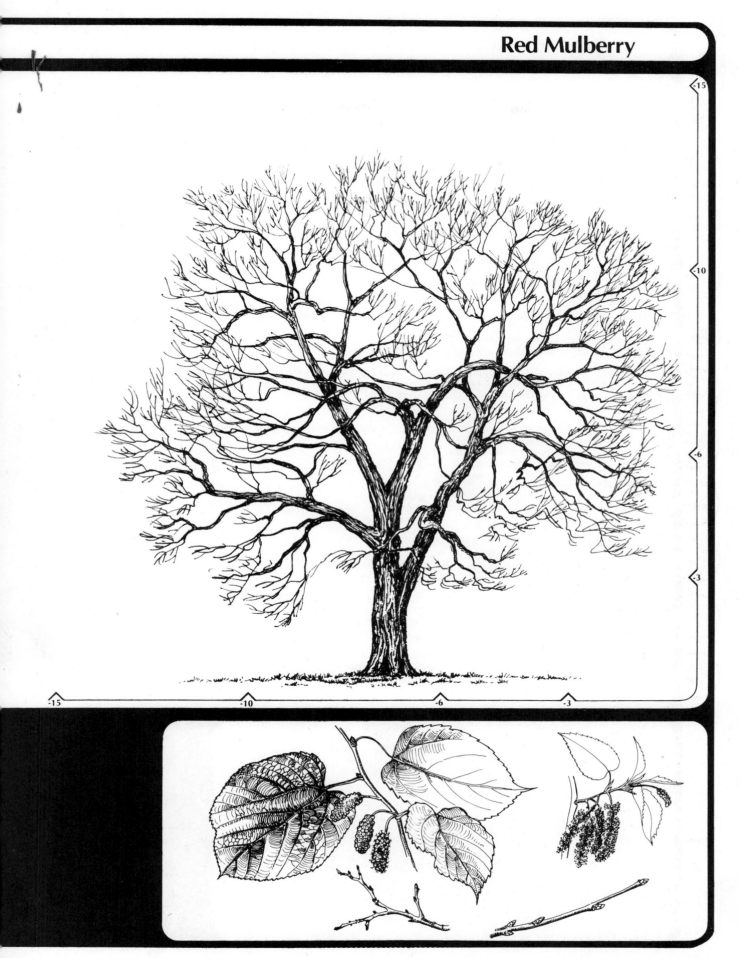

Nyssa sylvatica

FORM: broadly **conical**
Size: **small canopy** - 15 to 22.5 cm (50 to 75 ft)
Spread: **intermediate** - 10 to 15 m (35 to 50 ft), 2/3 the height
Mass: **dense**

BRANCHING: **horizontal,** crooked **picturesque,** entangled, aggregated spur-like rigid branchlets, **medium** texture
Twig: slender, with **grayish flaky skin; armed** with short thorn-like right angle stiff spur branches
Bud: pointed, tip curved, often hairy, spread widely from twig
Bark: fine horizontal crack-like fissures separate ridges into rectilinear **blocky** segments; coal **black**

FOLIAGE: alternate, **simple,** variable, **obovate-oblong obovate,** entire, **medium** texture
Surface: very **glossy,** leathery
Color: spring - **light green;** summer - **dark green;** autumn - scarlet **red**
Season: **deciduous;** emergence - late **May,** drop - late **October**

FLOWER: **small clusters** on long stems
Color: greenish **white**
Season: late **May through** early **June,** with the new leaves
Sex: **dioecious**

FRUIT: fleshy **berry,** 8 mm (3/8 in) long, in clusters of 1 to 3, on long stems
Color: **blue**
Season: mid **September through** mid **October**
Wildlife Value: **intermediate;** songbirds, small mammals

HABITAT: formation - **forest;** region - **central;** gradient - **lowland wet, wet-mesic, upland dry;** low ridges or second bottoms, alluvial flats, dry upper and middle slopes
Shade Tolerance: **intolerant;** index range 2.0-3.9
Flood Tolerance: **intermediate**

SOIL; Texture: **coarse to moderately fine;** upland loams, clay loams on lower slope, silt loams on alluvial benches
Drainage: **well to poor**
Moisture: demands **wet,** tolerates **dry**
Reaction: **moderately acid,** pH 6.1-6.5

HARDINESS: **zone 5a**
Rate: **slow** - 10 to 12.5 cm (4 to 5 in) a year generally
Longevity: **medium** - generally mature between 120 to 150 years of age

SUSCEPTIBILITY; Physiological: **infrequent**
Disease: **infrequent** - canker, leafspot
Insect: **infrequent** - occasional tupelo leaf miner, scale
Wind-Ice: **infrequent**

URBAN TOLERANCE; Pollution: **resistant** - SO_2, O_3; **intermediate** - HCl, Cl
Lighting: Drought-Heat: **resistant**   Mine Spoils: **resistant**
Salt: **resistant**   Soil Compaction: **intermediate**
Root Pattern: **taproot;** difficult to transplant, move B & B in early spring

SPECIES; Associate: Sourwood, Post, Scarlet, Chestnut, and Black Oaks, Eastern Redcedar, Mockernut Hickory, Eastern Redbud, American Hornbeam, American Hophornbeam, Common Pawpaw, Flowering Dogwood, hawthorns
Similar: Water Tupelo is related - less hardy, Sourwood and Common Persimmon exhibit same form and branching
Cultivars: none commercially obtainable

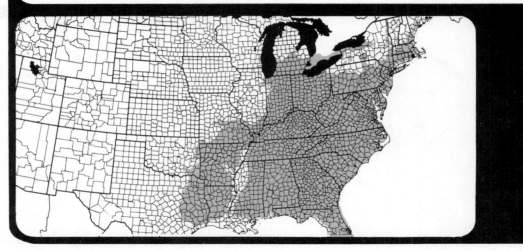

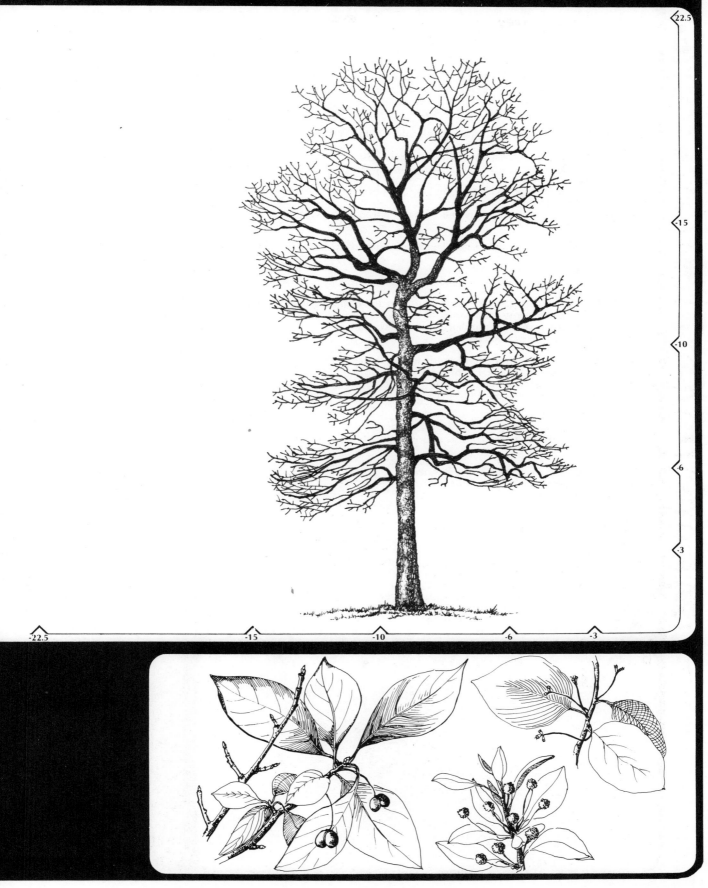

Ostrya virginiana

FORM: **conical** especially in youth
Size: **large understory - 10 to 15 m (35 to 50 ft)**
Spread: **narrow - 6 to 10 m (20 to 35 ft)**, 2/3 the height
Mass: very **dense**

BRANCHING: twisting trunks with large burls, **horizontal,** irregular, branchlets slightly **pendant, fine** texture
Twig: long slender, often **zig zag,** dark **red brown** to bronze, smooth, glossy
Bud: at right angle from twigs
Bark: **scaly** loose narrow rectilinear strips, rubbing off under light hand pressure; **gray brown**

FOLIAGE: alternate, **simple, elliptic-oval,** toothed, uneven base, **medium** texture
Surface: **dull,** fuzzy beneath
Color: spring - **maroon green;** summer - **yellow green;** autumn - pale golden **yellow**
Season: **deciduous - persistent;** emergence - early **May,** drop - dried leaves **persist** until late **February**

FLOWER: short slender **catkins,** male in groups of three at end of twig, forming previous fall, conspicuous in winter
Color: **red brown**
Season: early through mid **May,** before or with the leaves
Sex: monoecious

FRUIT: flattened oval inflated sac-like **samara,** 13 mm (1/2 in), male clusters in 3's at ends of drooping twigs
Color: **tan brown**
Season: late **June through** late **October**
Wildlife Value: **low;** songbirds, small mammals

HABITAT: formation - **forest;** region - **northern and central;** gradient - **upland mesic, mesic-dry;** variable - moist to dry
upland slopes, coves and ravines, along rocky streams
Shade Tolerance: **very tolerant;** index range 8.0-10.0
Flood Tolerance: **very intolerant**

SOIL; Texture: **moderately coarse** sandy loams, loams **to fine** sandy clays, silty clays, heavy clays
Drainage: **excessive to moderately well**
Moisture: prefers **moist,** tolerates **dry**
Reaction: **slightly acid to alkaline,** pH 6.1-8.0

HARDINESS: **zone 5a**
Rate: **slow - 20 to 25 cm (8 to 10 in)** a year generally 3m (10 ft) in 15 year period
Longevity: **medium - around 150 years**

SUSCEPTIBILITY; Physiological: **infrequent**
Disease: **infrequent - none serious**
Insect: **infrequent - very resistant**
Wind-Ice: **infrequent - extremely strong and durable**

URBAN TOLERANCE; Pollution:
Lighting: Drought-Heat: **intermediate**   Mine Spoils: **intermediate**
Salt: Soil Compaction: **sensitive**
Root Pattern: deep **taproot;** difficult to transplant, recovers slowly, move B&B in early spring as small tree

SPECIES; Associate: White, Bur, and Northern Red Oaks, Shagbark Hickory, Black and Sugar Maple, American Beech,
Carolina Silverbell, Allegany Serviceberry, Flowering Dogwood, American Hornbeam
Similar: American Hornbeam exhibits red fall color and smooth bark, demands moist sites
Cultivars: none available commercially

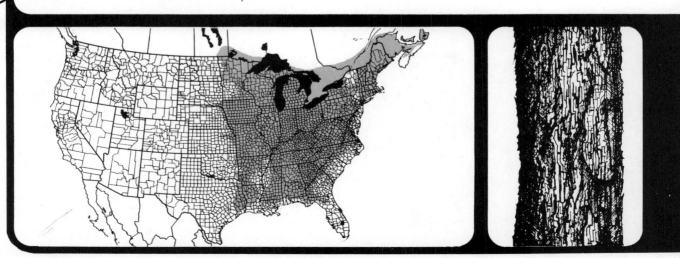

American Hophornbeam

Ironwood

245

Oxydendrum arboreum

FORM: **conical to** columnar becoming **ovoid**
Size: **large understory** - 10 to 15 m (35 to 50 ft)
Spread: **narrow** - 6 to 10 m (20 to 35 ft), 1/2 the height
Mass: **moderate**

BRANCHING: tall straight trunk, **ascending,** branchlets commonly **pendulous, medium** texture
Twig: slender, olive **green** or bright red
Bud: small, scaly, red brown
Bark: **deeply furrowed** with broad scaly rounded ridges; **gray** tinged with red

FOLIAGE: alternate, **simple, lanceolate-oblong lanceolate,** finely toothed margin, **medium coarse** texture
Surface: **glossy,** thick leathery
Color: spring - **light green;** summer - **dark green;** autumn - scarlet **red**
Season: **deciduous;** emergence - early **June,** drop - mid **October**

FLOWER: small **bell shaped,** in slightly pendulous spikelets, 15 to 20 cm (6 to 8 in) long, crowded to upper side
Color: **white**
Season: mid through late **July,** appearing after leaves are fully grown
Sex: monoecious   **Fragrant:** slightly

FRUIT: dried **capsules,** 8 to 13 mm (1/3 to 1/2 in) long, in drooping linear spikelets up to 30 cm (1 ft) long
Color: **tan brown**
Season: **September through November**
Wildlife Value: **low;** songbirds, upland ground birds, small mammals

HABITAT: formation - **forest;** region - **central;** gradients - **upland mesic-dry and dry;** gravelly upland slopes, ridges rising
above banks of streams, warm south and west slope aspects
Shade Tolerance: **tolerant;** index range 6.0-7.9
Flood Tolerance: **intolerant**

SOIL; Texture: **coarse** granular sands and gravels, **to moderately fine** clay loams
Drainage: **well to moderately well**
Moisture: prefers **moist to average**
Reaction: **strongly acid to moderately acid,** pH 4.5-6.0

HARDINESS: zone 6
Rate: **slow** - 20 to 25 cm (8 to 10 in) a year generally, 4.5 m (15 ft) in 15 year period
Longevity: **medium** - maturity between 125 and 175 years

SUSCEPTIBILITY; Physiological: **infrequent**
Disease: **infrequent** - none serious, occasional leaf spot, twig blight
Insect: **infrequent** - very resistant
Wind-Ice: **infrequent**

URBAN TOLERANCE; Pollution: **resistant** - SO_2
Lighting: Drought-Heat: **intermediate**   Mine Spoils: **intermediate**
Salt: Soil Compaction: **sensitive**
Root Pattern: **deep** coarse **laterals;** somewhat difficult to transplant, move as small tree B&B in early spring

SPECIES; Associate: Black Tupelo, Mockernut Hickory, Post, Chestnut, Black and Scarlet Oaks, Eastern Redbud,
Flowering Dogwood, Common Pawpaw, American Chestnut, Sassafras
Similar: Common Persimmon and Black Tupelo
Cultivars: none available

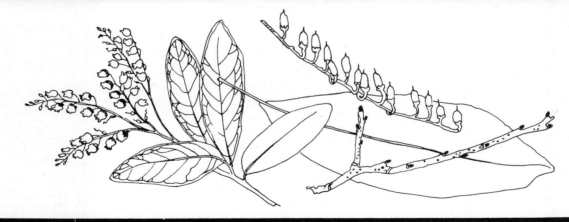

Picea engelmanni

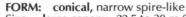

FORM: **conical,** narrow spire-like
Size: **large canopy -** 22.5 to 30 m (75 to 100 ft)
Spread: **narrow -** 6 to 10 m (20 to 35 ft), commonly 1/6 to 1/4 the height
Mass: **dense**

BRANCHING: central trunk, **descending** sweeping to ground concealing trunk, upper limbs horizontal, **medium** texture
Twig: with short woody pegs supporting foliage, **yellow brown**
Bud: ovoid, yellow brown
Bark: broken into large, loose coarse **scales,** thin; silvery gray to **red brown**

FOLIAGE: spirally arranged, broad **acicular,** stiff, sharp pointed, curved, 4 sided, **fine** texture
Surface: **dull;** aromatic
Color: all seasons - **blue green,** new growth **silvery gray** with whitish bloom
Season: **evergreen**

FLOWER: **cone,** concentrated in upper crown
Color: green tinged with **red purple** (female)
Season: **June**
Sex: monoecious

FRUIT: cylindrical **cones,** 2.5 to 7.5 cm (1 to 3 in) long, notched papery scales, wavy margin
Color: **tan brown**
Season: early **August through** late **winter**
Wildlife Value: **high;** songbirds, small mammals, hoofed browsers

HABITAT: formation - **forest** (mountain); region - **western;** gradient - **lowland wet-mesic, and upland mesic;** moist valley
slopes and cold bottoms along streams
Shade Tolerance: **tolerant;** index range 6.0-7.9
Flood Tolerance: **intolerant**

SOIL; Texture: medium to moderately fine; best on silt and clay loams, poor on sands, gravels or heavy clay
Drainage: **well to moderately well**
Moisture: prefers **moist to average**
Reaction: **strongly acid to slightly acid,** pH 4.6-6.5

HARDINESS: zone 2
Rate: **slow -** 7.5 m (25 ft) in 40 year period
Longevity: **long -** mature in about 300 years, trees over 500 years of age are not uncommon

SUSCEPTIBILITY; Physiological: infrequent
Disease: **frequent -** wood rot, brown rot, spruce broom rust
Insect: **frequent -** spruce bark beetle, spruce budworm
Wind-Ice: **frequent -** susceptible to wind throw

URBAN TOLERANCE; Pollution: sensitive - SO_2
Lighting: **resistant**   Drought-Heat: **sensitive**   Mine Spoils: **sensitive**
Salt: Soil Compaction: **sensitive**
Root Pattern: **shallow** fibrous widespreading **laterals;** transplants readily, move small trees B&B in early spring

SPECIES; Associate: White Spruce, Paper Birch, Quaking Aspen, Colorado Spruce, Douglasfir, western species of
larch, hemlock and fir
Similar: Colorado and White Spruces, White and Alpine Firs, Douglasfir
Cultivars: 'Argentea' - silvery gray needles, 'Glauca' - steel blue needles

Picea glauca

FORM: conical
Size: **small canopy** - 15 to 22.5 m (50 to 75 ft)
Spread: **narrow** - 6 to 10 m (20 to 35 ft), 1/4 to 1/3 the height
Mass: **dense**

BRANCHING: single central trunk, **descending** to horizontal sweeping ground, concealing trunk, **medium** texture
Twig: conspicuous woody peg-like projections supporting foliage, **yellow brown**
Bud: 3 to 6 mm (1/8 to 1/4 in) long, chestnut brown
Bark: separated into irregular thin **scales**; silvery **gray**

FOLIAGE: spirally arranged, broad **acicular**, stiff, straight, 4 sided in cross section, single, **fine** texture
Surface: **dull**; aromatic
Color: all seasons - **bluish green;** new growth - **silvery gray** with whitish bloom
Season: **evergreen**

FLOWER: **cone,** concentrated in upper crown
Color: **red purple** (female)
Season: late **May through** mid **June**
Sex: monoecious

FRUIT: small cylindrical **cone,** 2.5 to 5 cm (1 to 2 in) long, smooth continuous rounded scale margin
Color: **tan brown** weathering to silvery gray
Season: late **July** with many persisting **through** late **January**
Wildlife Value: **high;** songbirds, small mammals, hoofed browsers

HABITAT: formation - **forest;** region - **northern;** gradient - **lowland wet mesic, upland mesic;** along streams and lakes, moist
slopes, pioneer species in abandoned fields, midwest windbreak and shelterbelt
Shade Tolerance: **tolerant;** index range 6.0-7.9
Flood Tolerance: **tolerant**

SOIL; Texture: **medium** loams **to fine** clays
Drainage: **moderately poor to well**
Moisture: prefers **moist to average**
Reaction: **strongly acid to alkaline,** pH 4.6-8.0

HARDINESS: **zone 2**
Rate: **slow, medium** - 4.5 m (15 ft) in 10 year period
Longevity: **long** - attains age of 250 to 300 years generally

SUSCEPTIBILITY; Physiological: **infrequent** - potassium deficiency results in yellowing and needle loss
Disease: **frequent** - needle rusts, cankers, trunk and root rots
Insect: **frequent** - spruce needle minor, spruce budworm, European spruce sawfly, eastern spruce beetle
Wind-Ice: **frequent** - more wind firm than Black Spruce or Balsam Fir, more resistant to winter drying than other spruces

URBAN TOLERANCE; Pollution: **sensitive** - NOx; **intermediate** - SO$_2$, HFl; **resistant** - O$_3$, PAN
Lighting: **resistant**   Drought-Heat: **intermediate**   Mine Spoils: **intermediate**
Salt: **sensitive**   Soil Compaction: **intermediate**
Root Pattern: **shallow** fibrous, many widespreading **laterals;** transplants readily, move young trees B&B in early spring

SPECIES; Associate: Black and Red Spruces, Balsam Fir, Quaking Aspen, Paper Birch, Jack Pine, Sugar Maple, American
Beech, Yellow Birch, Mountain and Striped Maple
Similar: Engelmann, Colorado and BlackHills White Spruces are related, Douglasfir, other firs
Cultivars: 'Albertiana'- slow growing, narrow pyramidal form, 'Conica' - dwarf, broadly conical at maturity

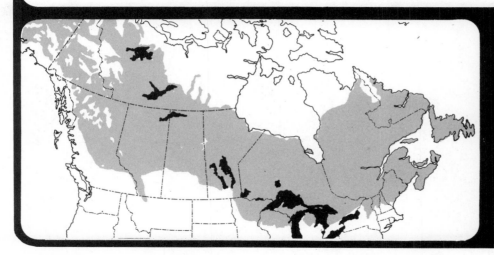

White Spruce

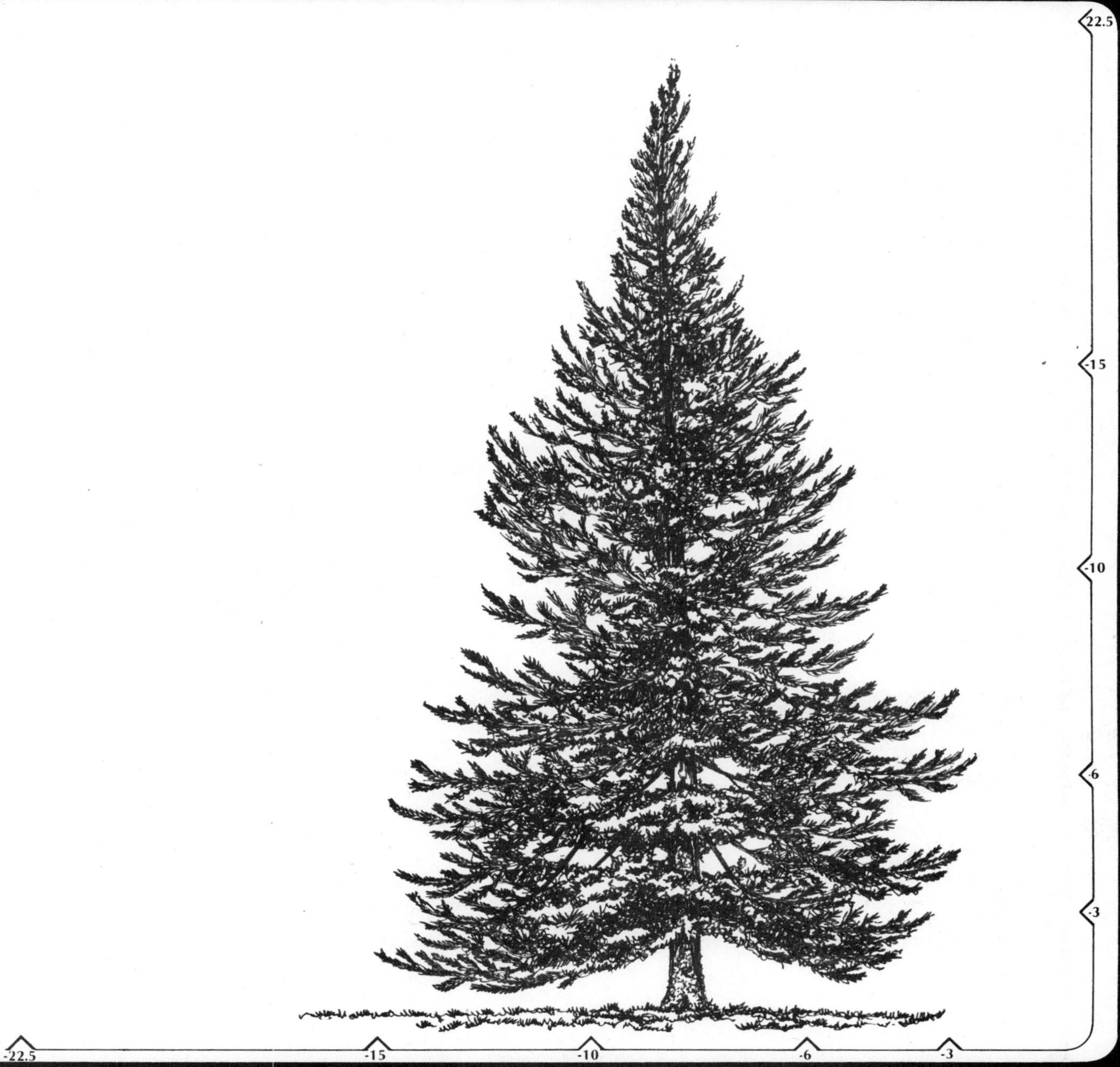

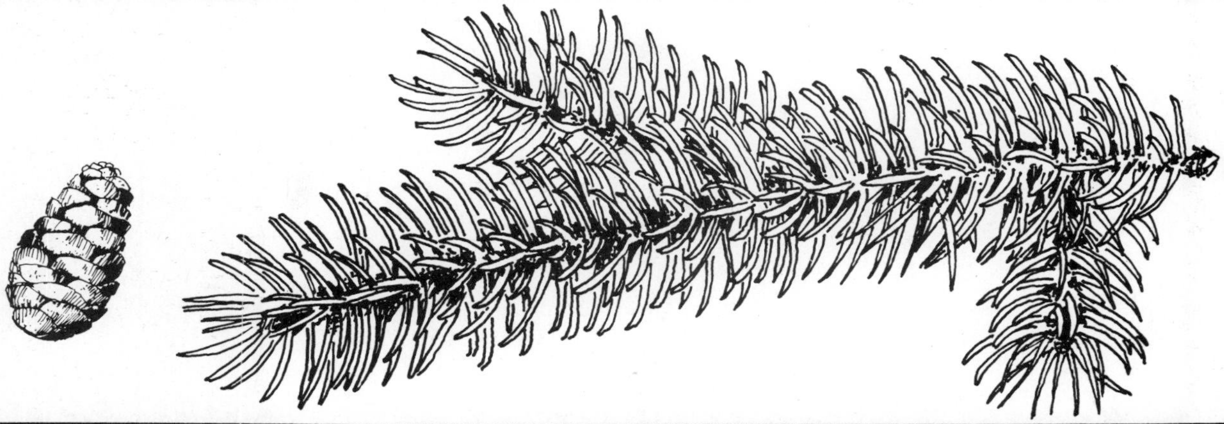

Picea glauca densata

FORM: conical
Size: **small canopy** - 15 to 22.5 m (50 to 75 ft)
Spread: **narrow** - 6 to 10 m (20 to 35 ft), 1/4 to 1/3 the height
Mass: **dense**

BRANCHING: single central trunk, **descending** lower limbs sweeping the ground, **medium** texture
Twig: with slender woody pegs supporting singular leaf, **yellow brown**
Bud: blunt 6 mm (1/4 in) long, chestnut brown, splotched with whitish resin spots
Bark: separated into thin flaky **scales**; ashy **gray**, exposed inner bark layers somewhat silvery

FOLIAGE: spirally arranged, **acicular,** crowded to upperside of twig by twisting of those on lower, **fine** texture
Surface: **dull;** aromatic
Color: all seasons - **yellow green** to **blue green**
Season: **evergreen**

FLOWER: elliptic **cone**, erect, mostly near top of crown
Color: male - tan to pale **red purple**, female - red brown
Season: late **May through** early **June**
Sex: monoecious

FRUIT: small cylindrical **cone**, 2.5 to 5 cm (1 to 2 in) long, smooth continuous rounded scale margin
Color: **tan brown**
Season: late **July**, with many persisting **through** mid **January**
Wildlife Value: **high;** songbirds, upland ground birds, small mammals, hoofed browsers

HABITAT: formation - **forest** (mountain); region - **western;** gradient - **upland dry;** dry valley slopes, steep rocky land, midwest windbreak and shelterbelt
Shade Tolerance: **tolerant;** index range 6.0-7.9
Flood Tolerance: **intolerant**

SOIL; Texture: **moderately coarse** gravelly or sandy loams, medium loams **to fine** clays
Drainage: **moderately poor to well**
Moisture: prefers **moist to average** soils
Reaction: **strongly acid to slightly acid,** pH 4.6-6.5

HARDINESS: zone 2
Rate: **slow** - 6 m (20 ft) in 30 year period
Longevity: **long** - attains age of 200 to 300 years

SUSCEPTIBILITY; Physiological: **infrequent**
Disease: **frequent** - needle rusts, needle cast, canker (Cytospora), pine needle scale
Insect: **frequent** - spruce spider mite, spruce gall aphid, bagworms
Wind-Ice: **infrequent**

URBAN TOLERANCE; Pollution: **resistant** - O$_3$
Lighting: **resistant**   Drought-Heat: **resistant**   Mine Spoils: **resistant**
Salt: **resistant**   Soil Compaction: **sensitive**
Root Pattern: **shallow** fibrous, widespreading; transplants readily B&B in early spring

SPECIES; Associate: Ponderosa Pine, Quaking Aspen, Common Chokecherry, American Elm, Bur Oak, Common Hackberry
Similar: White and Colorado Spruce, White Fir, Douglasfir
Cultivars: none available commercially

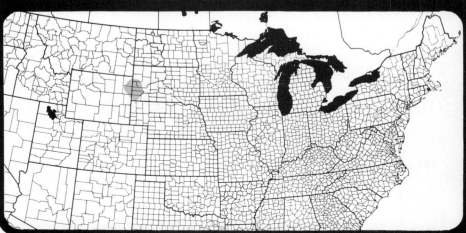

22.5

-15

-10

-6

-3

-22.5   -15   -10   -6   -3

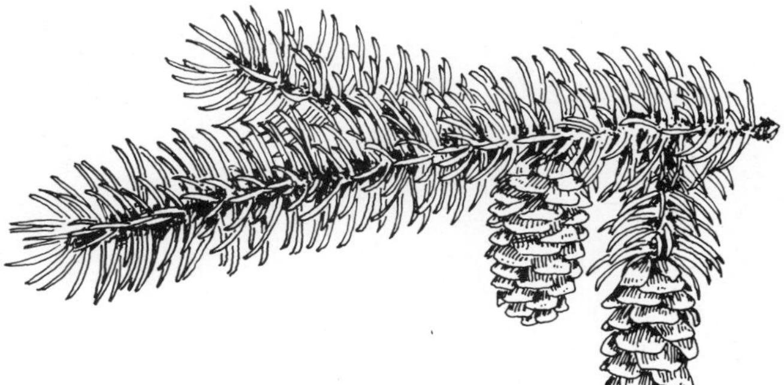

Picea mariana

FORM: narrow **conical**, spire-like
Size: **small canopy -** 15 to 22.5 m (50 to 75 ft)
Spread: **narrow -** 6 to 10 m (20 to 35 ft), commonly 3 to 6 m, 1/6 to 1/4 the height
Mass: very **dense**

BRANCHING: single central trunk, **descending** with upturned ends, lower limbs sweeping ground, **medium** texture
Twig: dense hairy with peg-like projections supporting foliage, **yellow brown**
Bud: broadly conical, blunt, yellowish brown
Bark: mature bark is thin and **scaly;** dark **gray**

FOLIAGE: spirally arranged, **acicular,** stiff, straight, blunt, 4 sided in cross-section, singular, very **fine** texture
Surface: **dull**
Color: all seasons - **bluish green**
Season: **evergreen**

FLOWER: cone, concentrated in upper crown
Color: **red to purplish**
Season: late **June**
Sex: monoecious

FRUIT: spherical **cones,** 2.5 cm (1 in) scales spreading only slightly on open cone, scale margin roughly toothed
Color: purplish to dark **tan brown**
Season: cones **persist** for many years
Wildlife Value: **high;** songbirds, small mammals, hoofed browsers

HABITAT: formation - **forest;** region - **northern;** gradient - **lowland wet;** confined to peat bogs, seepages, streams, slow
draining flats, swamps, gently sloping glacial lake beds, river floodplains
Shade Tolerance: **tolerant;** index range 6.0-7.9
Flood Tolerance: **very tolerant**

SOIL; Texture: **coarse to fine;** organic soils, clay, loams, sandy loams, even on sands, gravels or rocky soils
Drainage: **very poor to moderately poor**
Moisture: demands **wet** conditions
Reaction: **strongly acid to slightly acid,** pH 4.6-6.5

HARDINESS: zone 2
Rate: **slow -** 6 m (20 ft) in 30 year period
Longevity: **medium -** commonly mature at 125 to 200 years

SUSCEPTIBILITY; Physiological: **infrequent**
Disease: **frequent -** butt rots, black spruce dwarf mistletoe, needle rusts
Insect: **frequent -** spruce budworm, eastern spruce beetle, spruce sawfly
Wind-Ice: **frequent -** shallow root system makes it notably susceptible to uprooting by wind

URBAN TOLERANCE; Pollution:
Lighting: **resistant**   Drought-Heat: **resistant**   Mine Spoils: **resistant**
Salt: Soil Compaction: **resistant**
Root Pattern: **shallow** fibrous, reproduces by layering; transplants easily B&B in early spring, late autumn

SPECIES; Associate: White Spruce, Jack Pine, Balsam Fir, Quaking Aspen, American Larch, Black Ash, Red Maple,
Eastern Arborvitae, Hazel Alder, Gray Birch
Similar: Engelmann Spruce or Balsam Fir
Cultivars: 'Donumentii' - slow growing broadly conical form

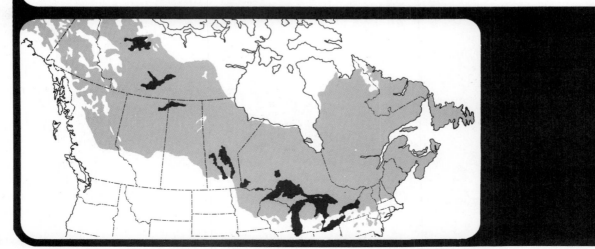

Picea pungens

FORM: conical
Size: **large canopy** - 22.5 to 30m (75 to 100 ft)
Spread: **narrow** - 6 to 10 m (20 to 35 ft), 1/4 the height
Mass: **dense**

BRANCHING: central trunk, **descending,** lower limbs sweeping ground, **medium** texture
Twig: divergent slender woody pegs support single leaf, **orange brown**
Bud: broadly conical, blunt, yellowish brown
Bark: broken into large loose coarse **scales,** with thin papery concave flaky appearance; silvery **gray**

FOLIAGE: spirally arranged, **acicular,** extremely stiff, radiate at right angles from twig, **medium fine** texture
Surface: **dull;** aromatic
Color: all seasons - **blue green** often silvery, new growth **silvery gray** with whitish bloom
Season: **evergreen**

FLOWER: **cone,** concentrated in upper crown
Color: male - orange, female - greenish to **red purple**
Season: late **May through** mid **June**
Sex: monoecious

FRUIT: broad cylindrical **cone,** 6 to 10 cm (2 1/2 to 4 in), papery scales exhibit wavy irregularly toothed margins
Color: light **tan brown**
Season: early **July through January**
Wildlife Value: **high;** songbirds, upland ground birds, small mammals, hoofed browsers

HABITAT: formation - **forest** (mountain); region - **western;** gradient - **upland mesic and mesic dry;** moist valley slopes and
cool bottoms along streams, midwest windbreaks
Shade Tolerance: **intermediate;** index range 4.0-5.9
Flood Tolerance: **intolerant**

SOIL; Texture: **moderately coarse to moderately fine;** best on silt and clay loams, tolerates sandy loams, heavy clay
Drainage: **moderately poor to well**
Moisture: prefers **moist to average** soils, most tolerant spruce for **dry** sites
Reaction: **strongly acid to slightly acid,** pH 4.6-6.5

HARDINESS: **zone 2**
Rate: **slow** - 1.5 to 1.8 m (5 to 6 ft) in 10 year period
Longevity: **long** - mature at 225 to 350 years, commonly beyond 400 years

SUSCEPTIBILITY; Physiological: **frequent** - lower limbs commonly defoliated
Disease: **frequent** - canker, needle casts, needle rust, wood decay
Insect: **frequent** - spruce gall aphid, Cooley spruce gall aphid, bagworms, spider mites, spruce budworm
Wind-Ice: **infrequent** - wind firm

URBAN TOLERANCE; Pollution: **sensitive** - NOx, HFl; **intermediate** - 2,4-D; **resistant** - SO_2, O_3, PAN
Lighting: **resistant**   Drought-Heat: **sensitive**   Mine Spoils: **sensitive**
Salt: **resistant**   Soil Compaction: **sensitive**
Root Pattern: **deep** coarse **laterals;** more difficult than other spruces to transplant, move B&B in early spring

SPECIES; Associate: Engelmann Spruce, Douglasfir, White Spruce, Paper Birch, Quaking Aspen, western species of
hemlock, Limber Pine, Subalpine Fir, Lodgepole Pine
Similar: Engelmann and White Spruces are related, Subalpine and White Fir, Douglasfir
Cultivars: 'Hoopsii' - extremely glaucous foliage, 'Moerheimii' - irregular form, very blue foliage, other hybrids

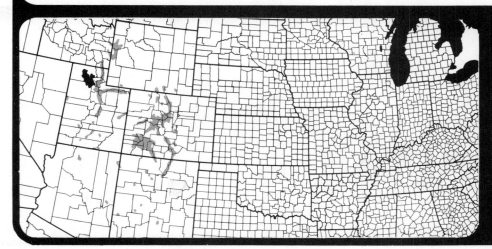

Pinus banksiana

FORM: **conical-irregular**
Size: **small canopy -** 15 to 22.5 m (50 to 75 ft)
Spread: **narrow -** 6 to 10 m (20 to 35 ft), 1/3 the height
Mass: **open**

BRANCHING: **recurving** irregular, lower limbs commonly mostly defoliated, **coarse** texture
Twig: smooth, **red brown**
Bud: **resinous,** rounded pale red brown, 6 mm (1/4 in) long, cylindrical
Bark: **scaly,** irregular flaky plates; brown black with patches of exposed **yellow orange**

FOLIAGE: **acicular,** bundles of 2, straight, widely divergent, sharp pointed, often twisted, **medium fine** texture
Surface: **dull;** aromatic
Color: all seasons - **yellow green**
Season: **evergreen**

FLOWER: **cone,** clustered, borne throughout crown
Color: male - yellowish, female - **purple**
Season: **June**
Sex: monoecious

FRUIT: **cone,** 2.5 to 7.5 cm (1 to 3 in) long, variable in shape, assymetric, curved inwards, usually remaining closed
Color: **tan brown** becoming black
Season: **persisting** for many years usually opening only when exposed to fire
Wildlife Value: **very high;** songbirds, upland ground birds, small mammals, browsers; cones produced at early age

HABITAT: formation - **forest;** region - **northern;** gradient - **upland dry;** rolling sand plains, sand dunes, rock outcrops, bald rock ridges, steep rocky land, midwest windbreak, shelterbelt and forestry plantings
Shade Tolerance: **very intolerant;** index 1.8
Flood Tolerance: **very intolerant**

SOIL; Texture: **coarse** sands and gravels, **to moderately coarse** loamy sands, intolerant of clay soils
Drainage: **well to excessive**
Moisture: **average,** tolerates **droughty** conditions
Reaction: **strongly acid to slightly acid,** pH 4.6-6.5, intolerant of alkaline soils

HARDINESS: zone 2
Rate: **fast -** 61 to 91 cm (2 to 3 ft) per year generally
Longevity: **short -** matures in about 60 years and subsequently deteriorates rapidly thereafter

SUSCEPTIBILITY; Physiological: **infrequent**
Disease: **frequent -** several needle rusts, other rusts, shoestring fungus
Insect: **frequent -** Jack Pine budworm, sawflies, pine sawfly, pine tussock moth, pine needle miner
Wind-Ice: **frequent -** windthrow

URBAN TOLERANCE; Pollution: **sensitive -** SO_2, O_3, **intermediate -** HCl, Cl; **resistant -** PAN
Lighting: **resistant** Drought-Heat: **resistant** Mine Spoils: **resistant**
Salt: **resistant** Soil Compaction: **sensitive**
Root Pattern: moderately **deep,** without a taproot; transplants well B&B if root pruned, move in early spring

Species; Associate: pure stands, Paper Birch, Black Spruce, Quaking Aspen, Northern Pin Oak, Red Pine, White Spruce, Bigtooth Aspen, Eastern White Pine, Pin Cherry, Common Chokecherry
Similar: Pitch Pine, Virginia Pine
Cultivars: 'Uncle Fogy' - weeping form

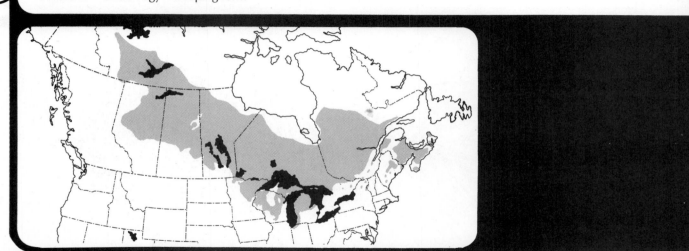

Pinus flexilis

FORM: **conical** in youth, **ovoid** at maturity
Size: **small canopy** - 15 to 22.5 m (20 to 35 ft)
Spread: **intermediate** - 10 to 15 m (35 to 50 ft), 1/2 to 3/4 the height
Mass: **open**

BRANCHING: short trunk, abruptly tapering, crooked, irregularly limbed, lower branches **horizontal, coarse** texture
Twig: young twigs flexible, **gray**
Bud: oval pointed, 9 mm (3/8 in) long with overlapping loose scales
Bark: immature trees smooth, mature bark broken into fine **scaly** plates; silvery **gray** to nearly black

FOLIAGE: **acicular,** bundles of 5, stiff, slightly curved, clustered toward ends of branches, **medium fine** texture
Surface: **dull;** aromatic
Color: all seasons - dark **blue green**
Season: **evergreen**

FLOWER: **cone,** clustered, borne throughout crown
Color: male - **rose** becoming **purple**
Season: late **June through** mid **July**
Sex: monoecious

FRUIT: oval **cone,** 7.5 to 15 cm (3 to 6 in) long, scales bearing rigid sharp curved prickles
Color: **tan brown**
Season: mid **August through** late **October**
Wildlife Value: **very high;** songbirds, upland ground birds, small mammals, hoofed browsers

HABITAT: formation - **forest** (mountain); region - **western;** gradient - **upland dry;** dry eroded slopes,
steep rocky land
Shade Tolerance: **very intolerant;** index range 0-1.9
Flood Tolerance: **very intolerant**

SOIL; Texture: **coarse to moderately fine;** sandy loams, gravelly loam, silt loams, clay loam, loamy sand and gravel
Drainage: **well to excessive**
Moisture: **average,** tolerates **droughty** conditions
Reaction: **strongly acid to slightly acid,** pH 4.6-6.5

HARDINESS: zone 2
Rate: **slow** - 15 cm (6 in) a year average 1.8 to 3.6 m (6 to 12 ft) in 10 year period
Longevity: **long** - maturity reached in 200 to 300 years

SUSCEPTIBILITY; Physiological: **infrequent**
Disease: **frequent** - root rot, dieback, tip blight, stem blister rust, leaf cast, rust
Insect: **frequent** - sawflies, weevils, pine webworm, pine needle scale, spittle needle
Wind-Ice: **infrequent**

URBAN TOLERANCE; Pollution: **resistant** - SO_2
Lighting: **resistant**   Drought-Heat: **resistant**   Mine Spoils: **resistant**
Salt: **resistant**   Soil Compaction: **sensitive**
Root Pattern: long **taproot** with several coarse deep laterals; somewhat difficult, transplant B&B in early spring

SPECIES; Associate: pure stands - Ponderosa Pine, Douglasfir, Quaking Aspen, Subalpine Fir, Engelmann
Spruce, Bristlecone Pine
Similar: Chinese White Pine is related
Cultivars: 'Columnaris' - fastigiate upright form, 'Glauca' - foliage deep blue green, 'Nana' - dwarf, slow growing

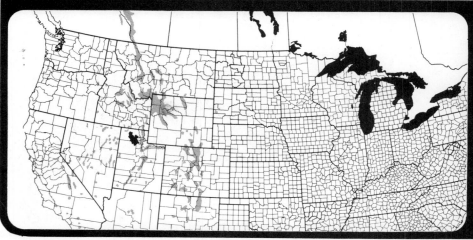

Pinus ponderosa

FORM: conical to ovoid
Size: **large canopy** - 22.5 to 30 m (75 to 100 ft)
Spread: **wide** - 15 to 22.5 m (50 to 75 ft) 1/2 to 3/4 the height
Mass: **open**

BRANCHING: straight trunks, little taper, **horizontal,** old trees with high clear flat topped crowns, **coarse** texture
Twig: stout, orange to **orange brown**
Bud: sharp pointed, **resinous,** 13 to 25 mm (1/2 to 1 in) long
Bark: young trees rough scaly, mature **shallow furrowed** with **wide** flaky plates; nearly black, becoming **yellow orange**

FOLIAGE: **acicular,** in 2's, 3's and rarely 4's, stout flexible, **coarse** texture
Surface: **dull,** aromatic
Color: all seasons - **dark** olive **green**
Season: **evergreen**

FLOWER: **cone,** female in pairs, borne throughout crown
Color: male - yellow, female - **red purple**
Season: **June**
Sex: monoecious

FRUIT: terminal oval **cone,** 7.5 to 15 cm (3 to 6 in) long, scales bearing rigid sharp prickles
Color: **tan brown** weathering to silver gray
Season: early **August through** late **October**
Wildlife Value: **very high;** songbirds, upland ground birds, hoofed browsers, small mammals

HABITAT: formation - **forest** (mountain); region - **western;** gradients - **upland mesic-dry and dry;** benches, plateaus,
west and south facing slope aspects, midwest windbreaks and shelterbelts
Shade Tolerance: **intolerant;** index range 2.0-3.9
Flood Tolerance: **intolerant**

SOIL; Texture: **coarse to moderately fine;** gravel, loamy sand, best on deep sandy, gravelly, silt and clay loams
Drainage: **moderately poor to excessive**
Moisture: **average to droughty**
Reaction: **strongly acid to acid,** pH 4.5-6.5

HARDINESS: zone 4b
Rate: **medium** - 22.5 m (75 ft) in 50 years
Longevity: **long** - maturity reached at 350 years, trees rarely survive 500 years

SUSCEPTIBILITY; Physiological: **infrequent** - hurt by late frosts
Disease: **frequent** - root and butt rots, dwarf mistletoe, needle blight is severe, several blister rusts
Insect: **frequent** - at least 50 species reportedly attack, consult local county extension service expertise
Wind-Ice: **infrequent**

URBAN TOLERANCE; Pollution: **sensitive** - SO_2, NOx, HFl
Lighting: **resistant**   Drought-Heat: **resistant**   Mine Spoils: **resistant**
Salt: **intermediate**   Soil Compaction: **sensitive**
Root Pattern: **taproot** with moderately deep laterals; transplants well B&B if root pruned, move in early spring

SPECIES; Associate: pure stands - Douglasfir, Quaking Aspen, Colorado and White Spruce, Limber Pine, western species
of oak and fir
Similar: Austrian Pine (European) silvery bark, Red Pine, Scotch Pine (European), Pitch Pine
Cultivars: 'Scopulorum' - smaller size, shorter needle length

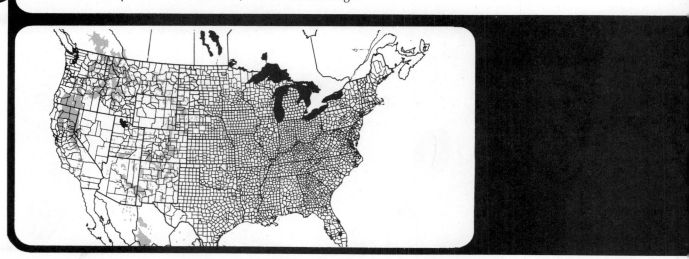

Pinus resinosa

FORM: **conical to ovoid**
Size: **large canopy** - 22.5 to 30 m (75 to 100 ft)
Spread: **wide** - 15 to 22.5 m (50 to 75 ft), 1/2 to 3/4 the height
Mass: **moderate**

BRANCHING: often irregular, **horizontal** to ascending, **medium** texture, coarser than Eastern White Pine
Twig: shiny **green yellow**
Bud: sharp pointed, **resinous,** 13 mm (1/2 in) long, loose overlapping hairy red brown scales
Bark: **shallow furrowed wide** longitudinal flat flaky ridges; **gray** with **reddish** to pinkish tinge

FOLIAGE: **acicular,** clusters of 2, straight, slender, brittle, clustered near branch ends, **medium** texture
Surface: **glossy; aromatic**
Color: **bright green becoming dark green** by midsummer
Season: **evergreen**

FLOWER: **cone,** clustered, born throughout crown
Color: male - red, female - **reddish purple**
Season: mid **May through** early **June**
Sex: monoecious

FRUIT: broadly oval **cone,** 4 to 6 cm (1 1/2 to 2 1/2 in) long, solitary or in pairs
Color: **tan brown** weathering to silvery gray
Season: mid **August through** late **October**
Wildlife Value: **very high;** songbirds, upland ground birds, small mammals, hoofed browsers

HABITAT: formation - **forest;** region - **northern;** gradient - **upland mesic-dry;** sand plains, low ridges adjacent lakes, steep rocky land, ridgetops, outwash plains, windbreak and shelterbelt plantings
Shade Tolerance: **intermediate;** index 2.4
Flood Tolerance: **intolerant**

SOIL; Texture: **coarse** sands and gravels, sandy loams **to fine** sands, medium loams, very poor growth on clay soils
Drainage: **moderately poor to excessive**
Moisture: **moist,** tolerates **dry** condition; intermediate between White Pine and Jack Pine
Reaction: **strongly acid to slightly acid,** pH 4.6-6.5

HARDINESS: **zone 2**
Rate: **medium** - 11 m (36 ft) in 25 years, generally exceeds growth of Eastern White Pine over same period of time
Longevity: **long** - maximum age 350 years

SUSCEPTIBILITY; Physiological: **frequent** - stunt (possibly due to poor drainage), potassium chlorosis
Disease: **frequent** - bark canker, shoestring fungus, needle blight, root rots
Insect: **frequent** - pine beetles, pine gall weevil, pine chafer, Zimmerman pine moth, and so forth
Wind-Ice: **infrequent**

URBAN TOLERANCE; Pollution: **resistant** - O_3
Lighting: **resistant**   Drought-Heat: **intermediate**   Mine Spoils: **intermediate**
Salt: **sensitive**   Soil Compaction: **sensitive**
Root Pattern: **deep** spreading **laterals;** transplants well B&B if root pruned, move in early spring

SPECIES; Associate: dry sites - Jack Pine, Bigtooth and Quaking Aspen, Northern Pin Oak, Black Cherry, Chestnut Oak, White Oak; moist sites - Sugar Maple, Eastern White Pine, American Linden, Yellow Birch, American Beech
Similar: Scotch Pine (European), Ponderosa Pine is coarser
Cultivars: none available commercially

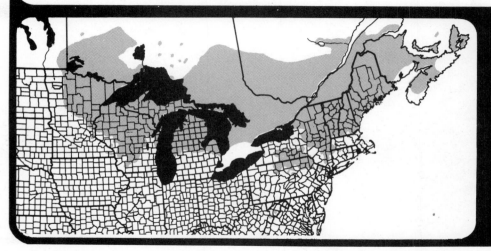

-30

-22.5

-15

-10

-6

-3

-30   -22.5   -15   -10   -6   -3

Pinus rigida

FORM: irregular - globular
Size: **small canopy** - 15 to 22.5 m (50 to 75 ft)
Spread: **wide** - 15 to 22.5 m (50 to 75 ft), 3/4 to equal to height
Mass: **open**

BRANCHING: **recurving,** twisted gnarled drooping, **coarse** texture
Twig: often in clusters on tree trunk, prominently ridged, **orange brown**
Bud: sharp pointed, **resinous,** 13 mm (1/2 in) long, loose chestnut brown scales
Bark: **shallow furrowed** with **wide** flat-topped scaly plates; **reddish brown** becoming nearly black

FOLIAGE: **acicular,** in 3's, twisted, at right angle to twig, often in tufts along trunk, **medium coarse** texture
Surface: **dull,** aromatic
Color: all seasons - dark **yellow green**
Season: **evergreen**

FLOWER: **cone,** clustered, borne throughout crown
Color: male - yellow, female - **red purple**
Season: **May**
Sex: monoecious

FRUIT: broadly oval **cone,** 5 to 9 mm (2 to 3 1/2 in), clusters of 3 to 5, scales bearing rigid sharp prickles
Color: **tan brown** weathering to silvery gray and black
Season: **persist** on trees for many seasons
Wildlife Value: **very high;** songbirds, upland birds, small mammals, hoofed browsers; cones produced at early age

HABITAT: formation - **forest;** region - **central;** gradient - **upland dry;** shallow soils on steep rocky land, ridges, south or west facing slopes, windbreak
Shade Tolerance: **very intolerant;** index range 0-1.9
Flood Tolerance: **very intolerant**

SOIL; Texture: **coarse** sands and gravels **to moderately coarse** sandy loams
Drainage: **well to excessive**
Moisture: **average,** tolerates **droughty** conditions
Reaction: **strongly acid to slightly acid,** pH 4.6-6.5

HARDINESS: **zone 5a**
Rate: **fast** - 61 to 91 cm (2 to 3 ft) in a year
Longevity: **short** - reaching maturity at 60 to 90 years, maximum age 150 years

SUSCEPTIBILITY; Physiological: **infrequent**
Disease: **frequent** - gall rusts, needle cast, needle blight, heart rot
Insect: **frequent** - tip moth, pitch pine looper, sawflies, pine webworm, pine needle miner
Wind-Ice: **frequent** - wet snow and ice glaze break leaders and limbs

URBAN TOLERANCE; Pollution: **sensitive** - O_3; **resistant** - PAN
Lighting: **resistant**   Drought-Heat: **resistant**   Mine Spoils: **resistant**
Salt: **resistant**   Soil Compaction: **sensitive**
Root Pattern: short **taproot;** transplants easily B&B if root pruned, move in early spring

SPECIES; Associate: Scarlet Oak, Chestnut Oak, White Oak, Black Oak, Post Oak, Blackjack Oak, Shortleaf Pine, Virginia Pine, Red Pine, Mountain Laurel
Similar: Jack Pine, Virginia Pine
Cultivars: none available commercially

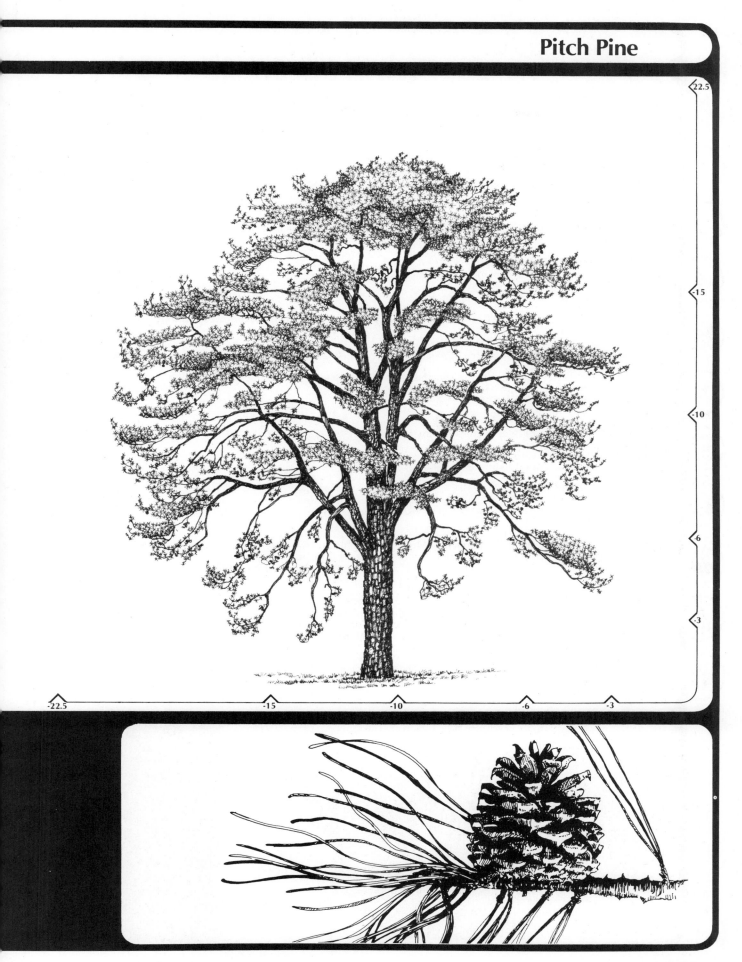

Pinus strobus

FORM: conical to ovoid, old trees irregular
Size: **large canopy -** 22.5 to 30 m (75 to 100 ft)
Spread: **wide -** 15 to 22.5 m (50 to 75 ft), 3/4 the height
Mass: **moderate**

BRANCHING: horizontal, tiered, windswept appearance, **medium** texture
Twig: slender, **green** becoming **gray**
Bud: ovoid, 6 mm (1/4 in) long, sharp pointed, **resinous**
Bark: **deeply furrowed,** longitudinal broad scaly ridges; dark **brown** to nearly **black**

FOLIAGE: acicular, in bundles of 5, slender, straight, soft, **medium** texture
Surface: **glossy,** aromatic
Color: spring - **light green;** summer - **bright green;** autumn - **bright green;** winter - **bright green** with some yellowing
Season: **evergreen**

FLOWER: cone, clustered, borne throughout crown
Color: female - **red to purplish,** male - yellowish
Season: late **May through** mid **July**
Sex: monoecious

FRUIT: cylindrical cone, 15 to 20 cm (6 to 8 in) long, pendulous, slightly curved, scales resinous
Color: **tan brown**
Season: early **August through** mid October
Wildlife Value: **very high;** songbirds, upland ground birds, small mammals, hoofed browsers, produces cones at early age

HABITAT: formation - forest; regions - **northern, central;** gradients - **upland mesic;** northerly slope aspects, sheltered
    coves, along rocky streams, steep rocky land
Shade Tolerance: **intermediate;** index 4.4
Flood Tolerance: **intolerant**

SOIL; Texture: coarse to fine; loam, silt loam, loamy sand, less common in clay
Drainage: **moderately poor to well**
Moisture: prefers **moist to average**
Reaction: **strongly acid to slightly acid,** pH 4.5-6.5

HARDINESS: zone 3b
Rate: **medium -** 46 to 61 cm (1 1/2 to 2 ft) per year on the average for first 50 years
Longevity: **long -** maturity reached in 200 to 350 years, extreme age potential 400-500 years

SUSCEPTIBILITY; Physiological: frequent - White Pine blight causes browning of needles
Disease: **frequent -** tip blight, Cenangium twig blight, stem blister rust, needle rust
Insect: **frequent -** White Pine shoot borer, White Pine tube moth, Zimmerman moth, White Pine weevil and so forth
Wind-Ice: **infrequent**

URBAN TOLERANCE; Pollution: sensitive - SO_2, O_3, NOx, HFl, Cl; **resistant -** PAN
Lighting: **resistant**   Drought-Heat: **sensitive**   Mine Spoils: **sensitive**
Salt: **sensitive**   Soil Compaction: **sensitive**
Root Pattern: weak taproot, several large coarse **deep laterals;** transplants readily B&B in early spring

SPECIES; Associate: pure stands - White Ash, Canada Hemlock, Northern Red Oak, Chestnut Oak, Balsam Fir, Paper
    Birch, Red Pine, Sugar Maple, American Beech, American Linden
Similar: Red Pine exhibits a more tufted foliage appearance, reddish bark
Cultivars: 'Compacta' - dwarf globular form, 'Fastigiata' - narrowly upright, 'Pendula' - weeping form, others

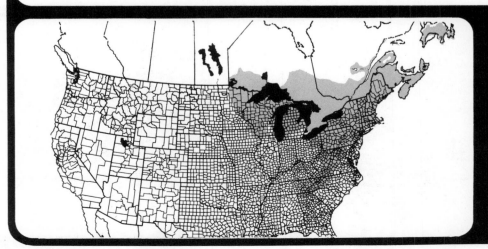

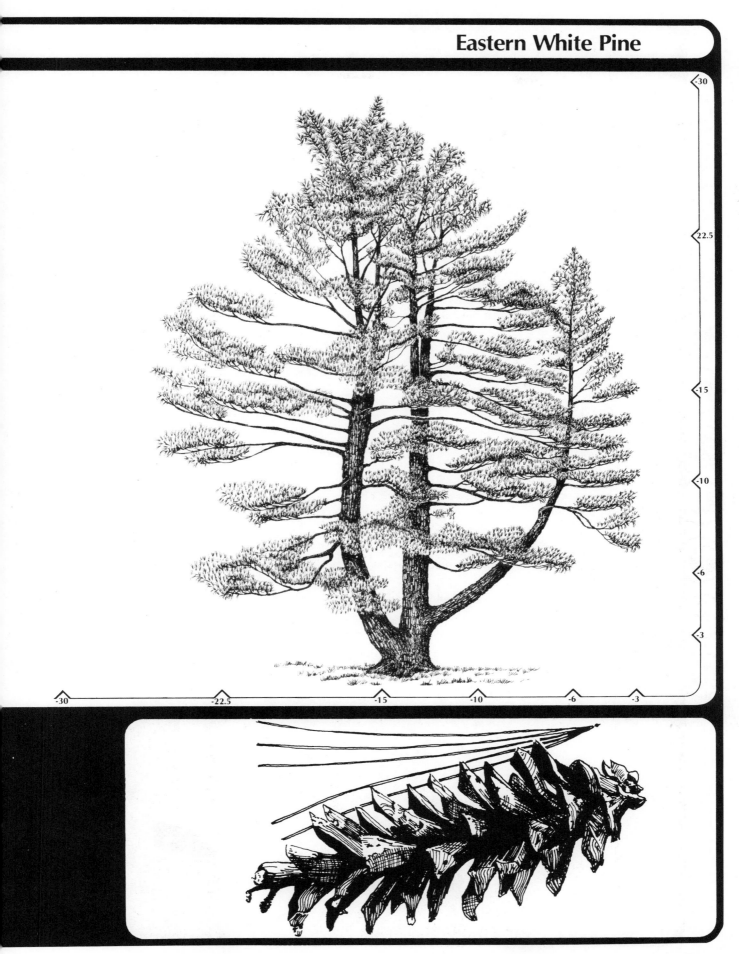

Platanus occidentalis

FORM: **globular**
Size: **large canopy -** 22.5 to 30 m (75 to 100 ft)
Spread: **very wide -** 22.5 to 30 m, (75 to 100 ft), up to 40 m, wider than tall
Mass: **open**

BRANCHING: massive **horizontal picturesque** gnarled branches, **coarse** texture
Twig: stout **zig zag** pattern, **orange brown**
Bud: small **dome shaped, encircled by leaf scar**, reddish brown
Bark: mottled **patchy exfoliating** sheets; creamy **white**, greens, tans, lower trunk with tan brown squarish flakes

FOLIAGE: alternate, **simple, palmately** 3-5 **lobed,** coarsely toothed, **coarse** texture
Surface: **dull**, smooth above, paler and hairy along veins beneath
Color: spring - **light green;** summer - **bright green;** autumn - **tan brown**
Season: deciduous often **persisting** through winter; emergence - late **May or** early **June,** drop - late **December**

FLOWER: **small clusters,** both sexes together in 2.5 cm (1 in) diameter ball-like clusters
Color: **yellow green**
Season: late **May through** early **June** with new leaves
Sex: monoecious

FRUIT: globular **multiple,** 2.5 cm (1 in) diameter, disintegrating when ripe, wind disseminated
Color: **tan brown**
Season: early **August** persisting **through** winter to late **December**
Wildlife Value: **very low**

HABITAT: formation - **forest;** region - **central;** gradient - **lowland wet and wet-mesic;** rich bottomlands, alluvial
floodplains, creek banks, lake margin
Shade Tolerance: **intermediate;** index 4.0
Flood Tolerance: **intermediate**

SOIL; Texture: **coarse** sandy and gravelly loams **to moderately fine** sandy and silty clays
Drainage: **well to poor**
Moisture: demands **wet to average** soils, best growth where there is good ground water supply
Reaction: **neutral to alkaline,** pH 6.6-8.0

HARDINESS: zone 4a
Rate: **very fast -** 21 m (70 ft) in 20 year period not uncommon
Longevity: **long -** many trees survive 350 years

SUSCEPTIBILITY; Physiological: **infrequent**
Disease: **frequent -** Anthracnose is severe, leaf spots
Insect: **infrequent -** sycamore tussock moth, scales, borers, bagworms
Wind-Ice: **infrequent**

URBAN TOLERANCE; Pollution: **resistant -** SO_2, HFl; **sensitive -** O_3, 2,4-D
Lighting: **sensitive**   Drought-Heat: **resistant**   Mine Spoils: **resistant**
Salt: Soil Compaction: **resistant**
Root Pattern: **shallow** fibrous; easily transplanted, move BR or B&B in spring or autumn with care

SPECIES; Associate: American Sweetgum, Northern Catalpa, Eastern Poplar, Black Willow, River Birch, Silver Maple,
American Elm, Green Ash, Pecan, Pin Oak, Boxelder, Swamp White Oak
Similar: Oriental and London Planetrees are related, White Poplar has massive crown, white bark, streamside habitat
Cultivars: none available commercially

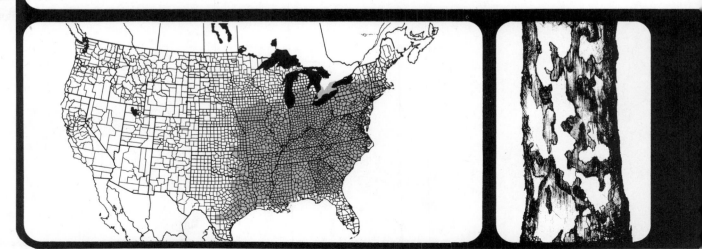

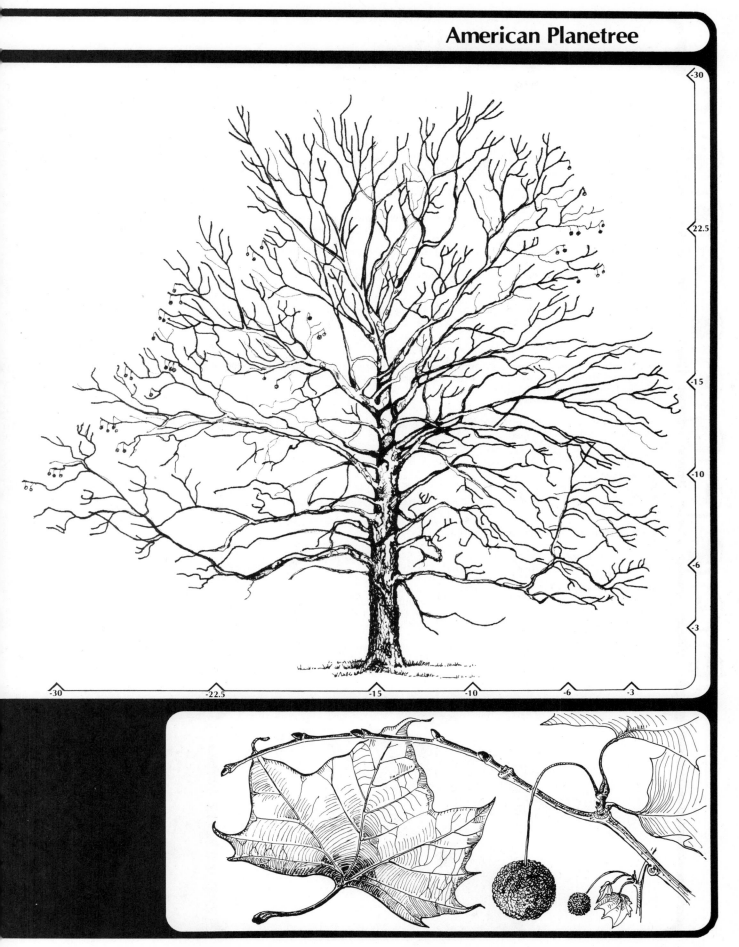

Populus deltoides

FORM: **obovoid-globular,** young trees **columnar**
Size: **large canopy** - 22.5 to 30 m (75 to 100 ft)
Spread: **very wide** - 22.5 to 30 m (75 to 100 ft), as wide as tall
Mass: **open**

BRANCHING: massive **upright** limbs, becoming arching to descending at tips, high crown, very **coarse** texture
Twig: stout, creamy **yellow brown**
Bud: **resinous,** large **clustered sharp pointed** end buds, **red to yellow brown**
Bark: **deeply furrowed,** irregular cross checked pattern, branches smooth, creamy tan; trunk **gray brown**

FOLIAGE: alternate, **simple, deltoid,** coarse incurved teeth, long flat petiole, **medium fine** texture
Surface: **glossy**
Solor: spring - **light green;** summer - **bright green;** autumn - pale **yellow**
Season: **deciduous;** emergence - early **May,** drop - mid **September,** early

FLOWER: linear drooping **catkins,** 7.5 cm (3 in) long, resemble miniature corncobs
Color: bright **red**
Season: mid through late **April,** before leaf emergence
Sex: **dioecious**

FRUIT: small conical **capsules,** in loose drooping catkin-like clusters, splitting - releasing cottony seeds
Color: **yellow green;** silvery white seed tufts
Season: late **May through** mid **June**
Wildlife Value: **high;** songbirds, small mammals, waterfowl, hoofed browsers

HABITAT: formation - **forest, savanna;** region - **central;** gradient - **lowland wet, wet-mesic;** almost any moist situation,
along streams, wet ravines, floodplain, windbreak and shelterbelt plantings
Shade Tolerance: **intolerant;** index 2.2
Flood Tolerance: **tolerant**

SOIL; Texture: **coarse** infertile sands, sandy loams, stiff clays, prefers **fine** sandy loams or silts
Drainage: **poor to excessive**
Moisture: **wet to** porous **droughty** granular soils
Reaction: **neutral,** pH 6.6-7.5

HARDINESS: zone 3b
Rate: very **fast** - 1.2 to 1.5 m (4 to 5 ft) a year, 36 m (120 ft) in 35 year period common on wet sites
Longevity: **short** - mature at 60 to 75 years, decadence is rapid thereafter, rarely survives 125 years

SUSCEPTIBILITY; Physiological: **infrequent**
Disease: **frequent** - poplar canker, Cytospora canker, Fusarium canker, leaf blister, branch gall, dieback
Insect: **frequent** - bronze birch borer, poplar borer, poplar tent maker
Wind-Ice: **frequent** - very weak wooded, brittle limbs

URBAN TOLERANCE; Pollution: **resistant** - SO$_2$
Lighting: **sensitive**   Drought-Heat: **resistant**   Mine Spoils: **resistant**
Salt: **resistant**   Soil Compaction: **resistant**
Root Pattern: **shallow** fibrous; easily transplanted, move BR or B&B in spring or autumn with care

SPECIES; Associate: Black Willow, Red Maple, American Planetree, American Sweetgum, Northern Catalpa,
Osageorange, Red Mulberry, Silver Maple, Boxelder, Bur Oak, River Birch, Green Ash, Black Tupelo
Similar: American Elm, Common Hackberry, Silver Maple, White Poplar (European)
Cultivars: 'Siouxland' - male tree, somewhat more resistant to biological disorders

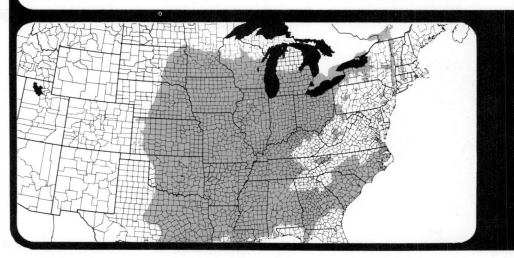

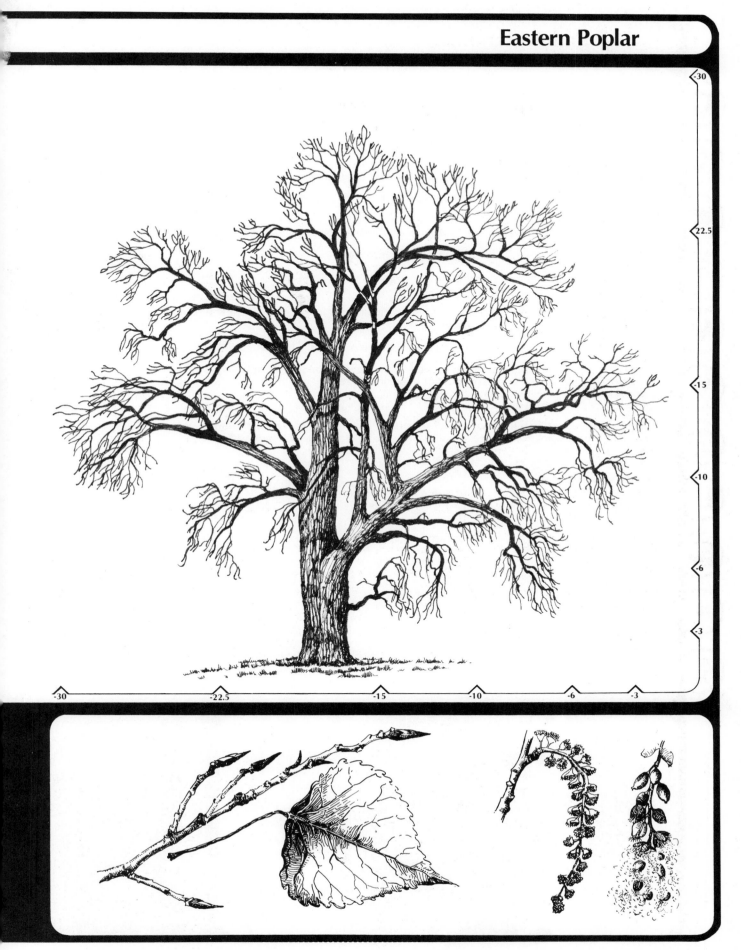

Populus grandidentata

FORM: **columnar**
Size: **small canopy** - 15 to 22.5 m (50 to 75 ft)
Spread: **narrow** - 6 to 10 m (20 to 35 ft), 1/3 to 1/2 the height
Mass: **open**

BRANCHING: high slender clear trunk, **leggy, picturesque,** spreading into large colonies, **coarse** texture
Twig: **gray brown**
Bud: **clustered sharp pointed** end buds, **woolly**
Bark: **smooth,** very old trunks deeply fissured at base; **yellowish to orange,** dark gray at base

FOLIAGE: alternate, **simple, ovate-oblong ovate,** coarse right angle teeth, flattened petiole, **medium fine** texture
Surface: **dull**
Color: spring - **light green;** summer - **bright green;** autumn - golden **yellow**
Season: **deciduous;** emergence - early **May,** drop - early **October,** variable - commonly as early as mid September

FLOWER: slender drooping **catkin,** up to 10 cm (4 in) long
Color: **silvery gray**
Season: mid through late **April,** before leaf emergence
Sex: **dioecious**

FRUIT: small **capsules,** 3 mm (1/8 in), splitting in drooping catkin-like clusters releasing cottony seeds
Color: **yellow green;** seeds silvery white
Season: late **May through** mid **June**
Wildlife Value: **high;** songbirds, upland ground birds, small mammals

HABITAT: formation - **savanna;** region - **northern;** gradient - **upland mesic and mesic dry;** lower slopes with northeast aspects or high terraces, mesic shoulder of upland ridges
Shade Tolerance: **very intolerant;** index 1.0
Flood Tolerance: **intolerant**

SOIL; Texture: **coarse** sand, loamy sand, sandy loam, gravel, rock covered with humus, **to medium** loams
Drainage: **moderately well to excessively** drained, high water tables interfere with aeration
Moisture: demands **wet to moist soils**
Reaction: **moderately acid to slightly acid,** pH 5.1-6.3

HARDINESS: **zone 3a**
Rate: **fast** - .76 to 1 m (2 1/2 to 3 1/2 ft) over a 20 year period
Longevity: **short** - deteriorates rapidly after 60 to 70 years

SUSCEPTIBILITY; Physiological: **infrequent**
Disease: **frequent** - Hypoxylon canker, Valsa canker, Nectria canker, twig blight
Insect: **frequent** - forest tent caterpillar, aspen tortrix, gypsy moth, poplar borer, poplar gall
Wind-Ice: **frequent** - windthrow is common, very weak wooded

URBAN TOLERANCE; Pollution: **intermediate** - SO$_2$
Lighting: Drought-Heat: **intermediate**   Mine Spoils: **intermediate**
Salt: **intermediate**   Soil Compaction: **sensitive**
Root Pattern: **shallow** fibrous, prolific sprouts form broad colonies; transplanted B&B or BR in early spring, autumn

SPECIES; Associate: Jack Pine, Balsam fir, Quaking Aspen, Paper and Gray Birch, Pin Cherry, White Spruce, Red Maple, Eastern White and Red Pines, Northern Pin Oak, Common Chokecherry
Similar: Quaking Aspen, Paper and Gray Birches
Cultivars: none available commercially

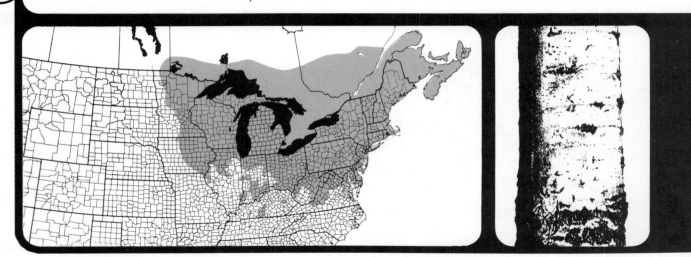

Bigtooth Aspen

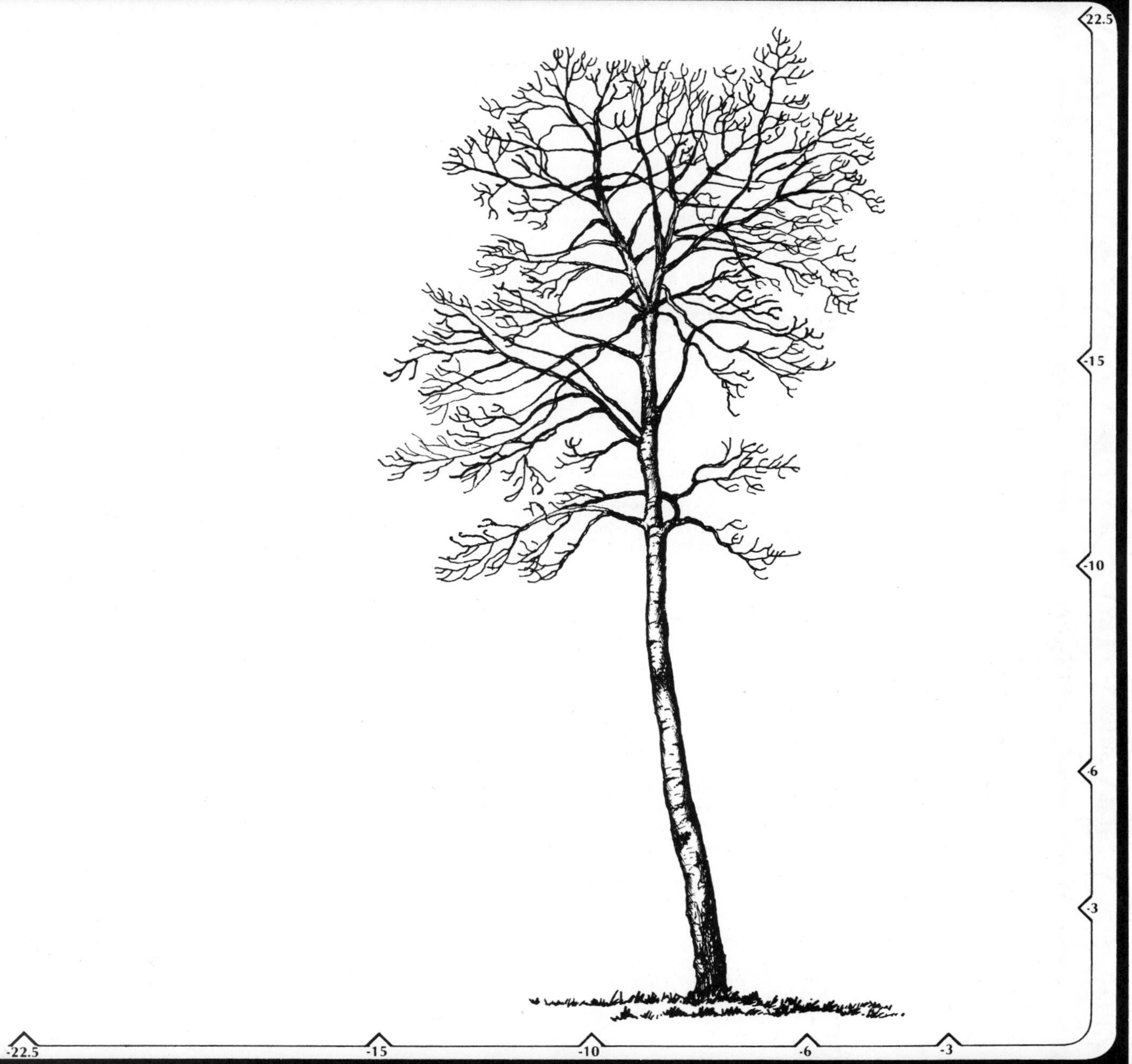

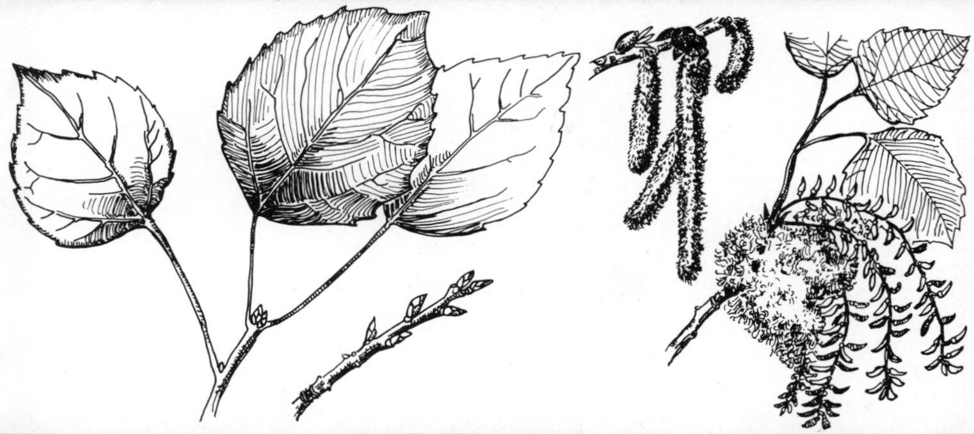

Populus tremuloides

FORM: columnar
Size: **large understory -** 10 to 15 m (35 to 50 ft)
Spread: **narrow -** 6 to 10 m (20 to 35 ft), 1/3 to 1/2 the height
Mass: **open**

BRANCHING: slender, long clear trunk, **leggy, picturesque,** forming extensive colonies, **coarse** texture
Twig: slender, glossy, **gray brown**
Bud: **clustered sharp pointed** buds, **reddish,** glossy
Bark: **smooth** with waxy appearance, old trunks deeply furrowed at base; **white** to greenish, old trunks brown-black

FOLIAGE: alternate, **simple, cordate,** long flattened petiole, rustling in slightest breeze, **medium fine** texture
Surface: **glossy**
Color: spring - **light green;** summer - **bright green;** autumn - bright **yellow**
Season: **deciduous;** emergence - mid **April,** drop - late **October,** variable commonly as early as mid September

FLOWER: both sexes in slender drooping hairy appearing **catkins,** 10 cm (4 in) long
Color: **silvery gray**
Season: mid **March through** early **April,** before leaf emergence
Sex: **dioecious**

FRUIT: small conical **capsule,** in linear catkin-like clusters, releasing cottony tufted seeds
Color: **yellow green,** silvery white cottony seeds
Season: wind dispersal throughout **May**
Wildlife Value: **high;** songbirds, upland ground birds, small mammals, hoofed browsers

HABITAT: formation - **savanna;** region - **northern;** gradient - **upland mesic and mesic-dry;** seeps, slopes with cool air
   drainage, rocky streams, north and east slope aspects, disturbed sites
Shade Tolerance: **very intolerant;** index 0.7
Flood Tolerance: **intolerant**

SOIL; Texture: prefers shallow **coarse** rocky soils, loamy sands, also common **to heavy fine** clays, silt loams
Drainage: **moderately well to excessive**
Moisture: demands **wet to moist**
Reaction: **strongly acid to slightly acid,** pH 4.8-6.5

HARDINESS: zone 2
Rate: **fast -** .90 to 1.2 m (3 to 4 ft) per year is common
Longevity: **short -** deteriorates rapidly after 50 to 60 years in midwest, seldom survives 100 years

SUSCEPTIBILITY; Physiological: **infrequent**
Disease: **frequent -** Cytospora canker, Hypoxylon canker, leaf spot, shoot blight, other cankers
Insect: **frequent -** poplar borer, poplar gall, scale, red humped caterpillar
Wind-Ice: **frequent -** windthrow, brittle limbs damage easily

URBAN TOLERANCE; Pollution: **sensitive -** SO_2, O_3; **intermediate -** HFl
Lighting: **sensitive**   Drought-Heat: **intermediate**   Mine Spoils: **intermediate**
Salt: **intermediate**   Soil Compaction: **sensitive**
Root Pattern: **shallow** fibrous, prolific sprouts form broad colonies; transplanted BR or B&B in early spring, autumn

SPECIES: Associate: Jack, Red and Eastern White Pines, Gray and Paper Birches, Mountain and Red Maples, Bigtooth
   Aspen, Pin and Chokecherry, Engelmann and Colorado Spruce, Subalpine Fir
Similar: Bigtooth Aspen, Paper Birch, Gray Birch
Cultivars: none available commercially

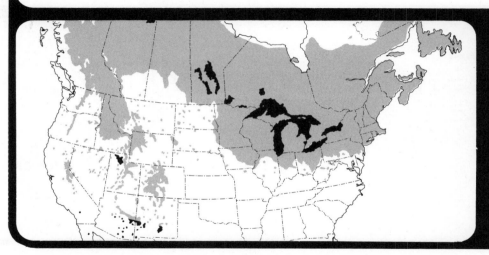

Prunus americana

FORM: globular
Size: **small understory** - 6 to 10 m (20 to 35 ft)
Spread: **narrow** - 6 to 10 m (20 to 35 ft), wider than tall
Mass: **dense**

BRANCHING: short crooked trunk, stiff **horizontal** laterals, irregular flat-topped crown, **medium** texture
Twig: slender, **red brown, flaky** blue gray skin; **armed** with short thorn-like right angle stiff spur branches
Bud: commonly **clustered, sharp pointed**
Bark: **scaly,** splitting vertically and curling along margin, horizontal lenticels; reddish **brown to** nearly **black**

FOLIAGE: alternate, **simple, elliptic-oval,** toothed margin, glands on petiole, deep seated veination, **medium** texture
Surface: **dull,** paler beneath
Color: spring - **light green;** summer - **dark green;** autumn - pale golden **yellow**
Season: **deciduous;** emergence - late **May,** drop - late **September**

FLOWER: flowers in rounded to **flat-topped clusters,** small 13 mm (1/2 in), profuse
Color: **white**
Season: early through mid **May,** before leaf emergence
Sex: monoecious   **Fragrant:** strong sweet spicy

FRUIT: large fleshy plum-like **berry,** 2.5 to 3 cm (1 to 1 1/4 in) diameter
Color: dull **red to purplish**
Season: mid **August through** early **September**
Wildlife Value: **very low;** man, songbirds, upland ground birds, small mammals; very sweet

HABITAT: formation - **savanna;** region - **central;** gradient - **upland dry;** upland pastures, margin of woods, thickets, fencerows, steep rocky hillsides, streambanks, open oak woods, midwest windbreaks
Shade Tolerance: **intolerant;** index range 2.0-3.9
Flood Tolerance: **very intolerant**

SOIL; Texture: deep black prairie loams, **moderately coarse** loamy sands, sandy loams, **to moderately fine** clay loam
Drainage: **moderately well to excessive**
Moisture: prefers **average,** tolerates **droughty** conditions
Reaction: **neutral,** pH 6.6-7.5

HARDINESS: zone 3a
Rate: **fast** - 32 to 46 cm (18 to 30 in) per year
Longevity: **short** - 35 to 65 years commonly

SUSCEPTIBILITY; Physiological: **infrequent**
Disease: **infrequent** - not as susceptible as many other cherries
Insect: **infrequent**
Wind-Ice: **infrequent**

URBAN TOLERANCE; Pollution: **sensitive** - HCl, Cl
Lighting: Drought-Heat: **resistant**   Mine Spoils: **resistant**
Salt: Soil Compaction: **sensitive**
Root Pattern: **shallow** fibrous; transplants readily B&B in early spring or late autumn

SPECIES; Associate: Nannyberry and Blackhaw Viburnums, Bur Oak, Prairie Crabapple, Common Chokecherry, Pin Cherry, Eastern Redcedar, Common Prickly Ash, Northern Pin Oak, hawthorn and sumac species
Similar: many crabapples, hawthorns, and plums would substitute, especially Beach Plum
Cultivars: none available commercially

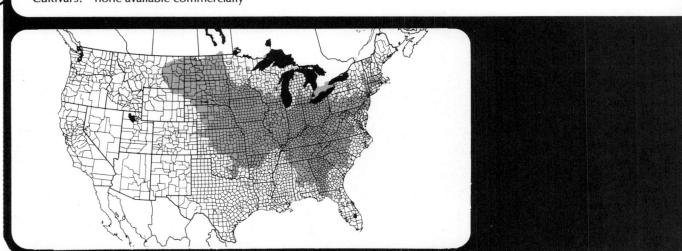

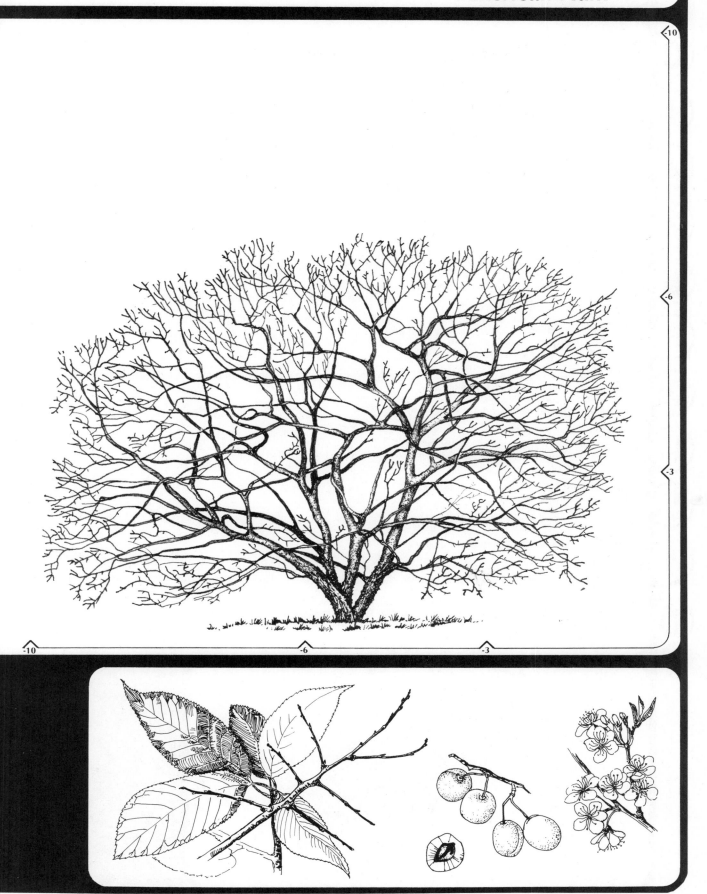

-10

-6

-3

-10

-6

-3

Prunus pensylvanica

FORM: ovoid to columnar
Size: **small understory -** 6 to 10 m (20 to 35 ft)
Spread: **narrow -** 6 to 10 m (20 to 35 ft), about 1/3 to 2/3 the mature height
Mass: **open**

BRANCHING: short trunk, **ascending** in youth becoming more or less horizontal spreading at maturity, **fine** texture
Twig: very slender, thin **flaky** exfoliation, bright **red;** sharp spur branches are common
Bud: small, 15 mm (1/16 in) long, rounded, **clustered sharp pointed** end buds, bright **red**
Bark: **smooth,** conspicuous bright orange widely spaced horizontal lenticels; dark **reddish brown to yellow orange**

FOLIAGE: alternate, **simple, lanceolate-oblong lanceolate,** finely toothed margin, **medium** texture
Surface: **glossy,** thin and fragile, petiole with 2 glands near the blade
Color: spring - **orange green;** summer - **bright green;** autumn - bright **red or orangish**
Season: **deciduous;** emergence - late **April,** drop - late **September**

FLOWER: **flat-topped clusters,** 5 to 7 per cluster, individuals 10 to 15 mm (2/5 to 3/5 in) wide
Color: **white**
Season: early to mid **May,** after leaf emergence
Sex: monoecious   **Fragrant:**   sweet, spicy

FRUIT: globular **berry,** 13 mm (1/2 in) diameter, on long stalk
Color: **bright red**
Season: late **July through** mid **September**
Wildlife Value: **very high;** man, songbirds, small and large mammals, hoofed browsers

HABITAT: formation - **savanna;** region - **northern;** gradient - **upland mesic dry and dry;** clearings, open woods, margin of
woods, fencerow, abandoned pastureland
Shade Tolerance: **very intolerant;** index 0.7, demands full sun
Flood Tolerance: **very intolerant**

SOIL; Texture: **coarse** sands and gravels, sandy and gravelly loams, medium loams **to moderately fine** sandy loams
Drainage: **moderately well to excessive**
Moisture: **moist to droughty**
Reaction: **slightly acid or neutral,** pH range 6.1-7.5

HARDINESS: zone 2
Rate: **fast -** 60 to 90 cm (24 to 36 in) per year
Longevity: **short -** 40 to 60 years commonly, rarely survives 75 years

SUSCEPTIBILITY; Physiological: **infrequent**
Disease: **infrequent**
Insect: **infrequent**
Wind-Ice: **frequent -** low in strength, breakage is common

URBAN TOLERANCE; Pollution: **sensitive -** HCl, Cl
Lighting: Drought-Heat: **resistant**   Mine Spoils: **resistant**
Salt: **resistant**   Soil Compaction: **sensitive**
Root Pattern: **deep** widespreading **laterals;** transplants with difficulty, move small trees B&B in early spring, autumn

SPECIES; Associate: Black Cherry, Common Chokecherry, Gray Dogwood, Beaked Filbert, Quaking
and Bigtooth Aspen, Bur Oak, Northern Pin Oak, American Plum, hawthorns
Similar: Common Chokecherry; Black Cherry has narrow leaves, orange red fall color
Cultivars: none commercially obtainable

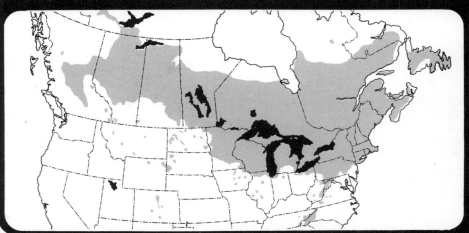

Pin Cherry

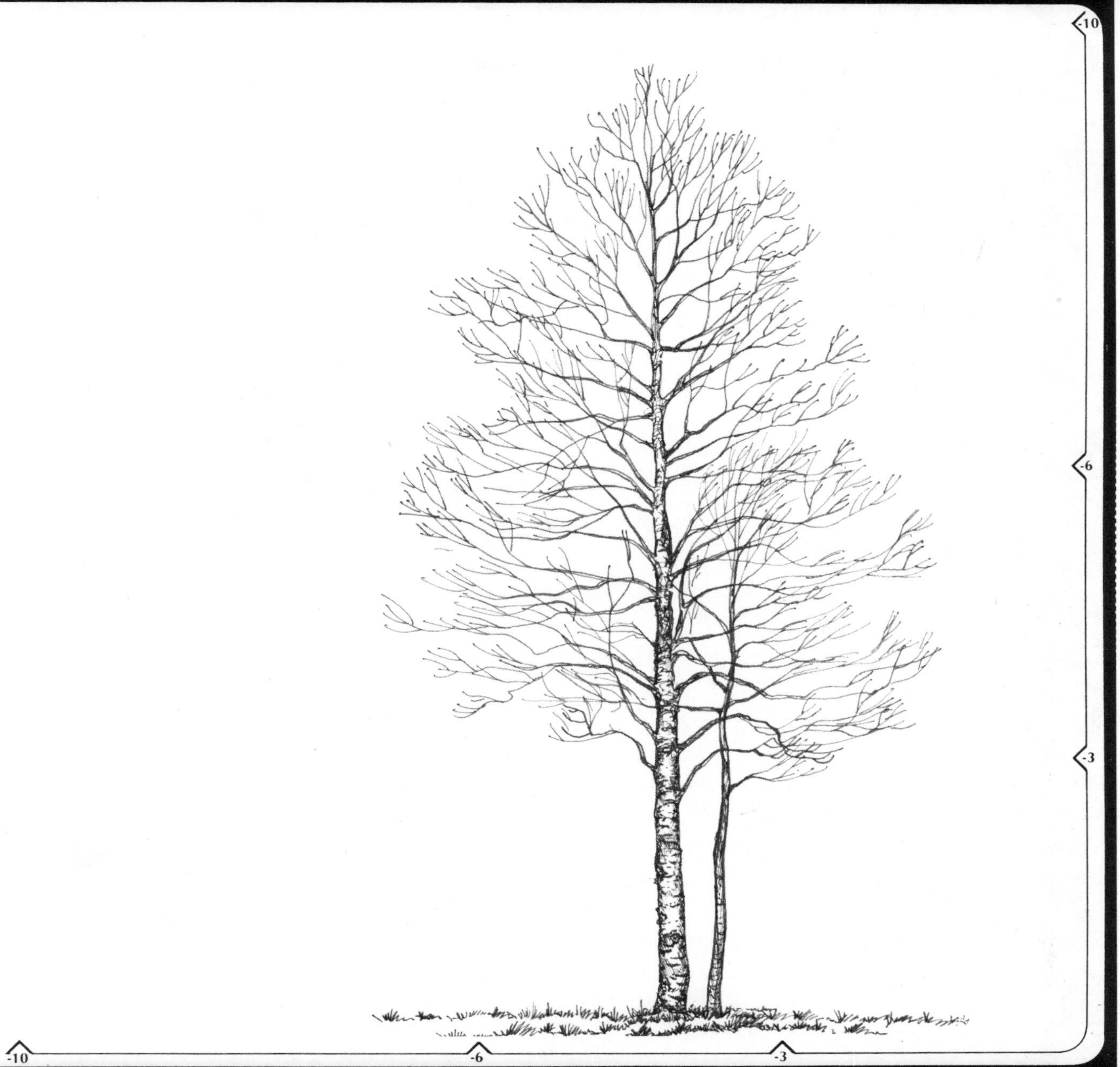

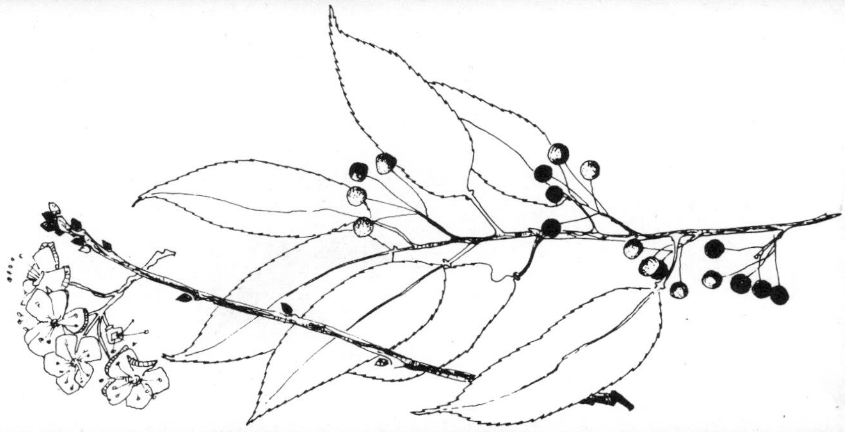

Prunus serotina

FORM: columnar to ovoid
Size: **small canopy** - 15 to 22.5 m
Spread: **intermediate** - 10 to 15 m (35 to 50 ft), 1/2 the height
Mass: **open**

BRANCHING: **ascending** branches with slender **pendulous** branchlets, **fine** texture
Twig: conspicuous lenticels, slender **reddish brown** glossy branchlets
Bud: 3 mm (1/8 in), red brown
Bark: squarish **scales** curving outward along their vertical edges, horizontal lenticels; red **brown** becoming **black**

FOLIAGE: alternate, **simple, lanceolate-oblong lanceolate,** margin with incurved teeth, **medium** texture
Surface: **glossy**, thick leathery, reddish petiole with 2 glands near the blade
Color: spring - **maroon green;** summer - **dark green;** autumn - **yellow to orange**
Season: **deciduous;** emergence - mid **May,** drop - mid **October**

FLOWER: loose pendulous **pyramidal spikes,** 10 to 15 mm (4 to 6 in) long, individual bloom 10 mm (2/5 in) across
Color: **white**
Season: late **May through** early **June,** after the leaves
Sex: monoecious   **Fragrant:**   strong sweet spicy

FRUIT: **berry,** 9 mm (3/8 in) across, in drooping 10 to 15 cm (4 to 6 in) spikes
Color: dark glossy red changing to **black**
Season: mid **August through** late **September**
Wildlife Value: **very high;** songbirds, small mammals

HABITAT: formation - **forest, savanna;** region - **central;** gradient - **upland mesic, mesic dry;** rocky hillsides, fence rows,
        borders of wooded areas, abandoned fields, also common to alluvial bottomlands, midwest windbreaks
Shade Tolerance: **intolerant;** index 2.4
Flood Tolerance: **very intolerant**

SOIL; Texture: **moderately coarse to moderately fine;** stony and sandy loams, silt loam
Drainage: **well to moderately well**
Moisture: prefers **moist,** tolerates **dry**
Reaction: **slightly acid to neutral,** pH 6.1-7.5

HARDINESS: zone 3b
Rate: **fast -** 46 to 76 cm (1 1/2 to 2 1/2 ft) a year is average
Longevity: **medium -** mature at 125 to 175 years

SUSCEPTIBILITY; Physiological: **infrequent**
Disease: **infrequent -** gum spot, leaf spots, black knot, wood rots
Insect: **infrequent -** eastern tent and ugly nest caterpillars, borers
Wind-Ice: **infrequent**

URBAN TOLERANCE; Pollution: **intermediate -** HCl, Cl
Lighting: Drought-Heat: **resistant**   Mine Spoils: **resistant**
Salt: **resistant**   Soil Compaction: **sensitive**
Root Pattern: deep coarse **taproot;** somewhat difficult to transplant, move B&B in early spring, late fall

SPECIES; Associate: moist - Eastern White Pine, Northern Red Oak, White Oak, White Ash, Canada Hemlock, Sugar
        Maple, American Beech, Shagbark Hickory
Similar: European Alder, River Birch, other cherries
Cultivars: none available commercially

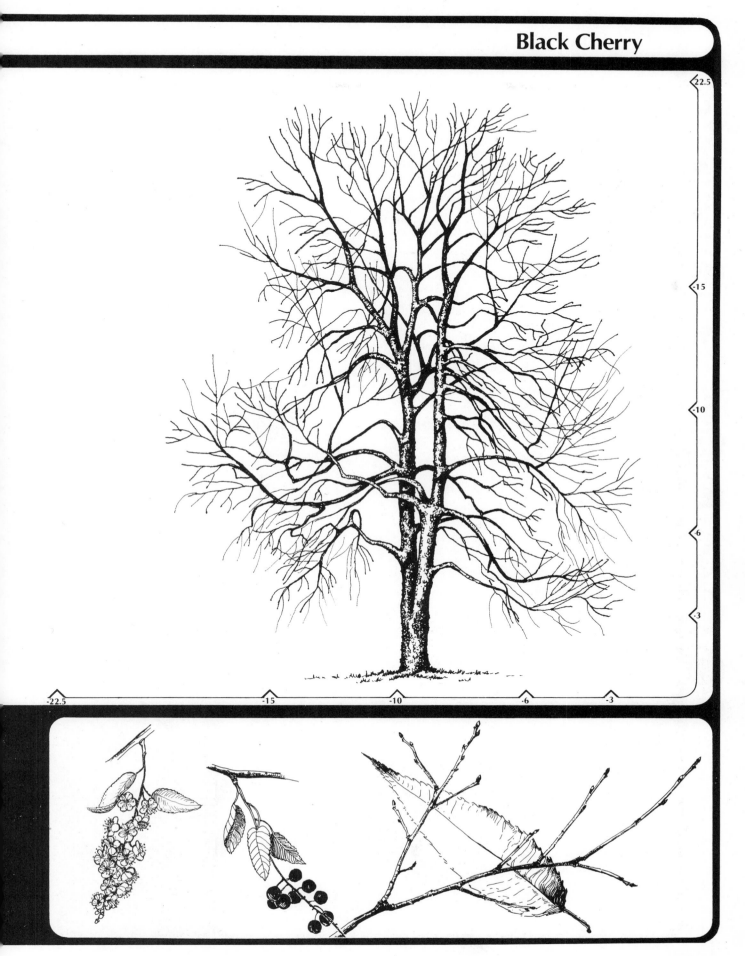

Prunus virginiana

FORM: obovoid
Size: **large understory** - 10 to 15 m (35 to 50 ft)
Spread: **narrow** - 6 to 10 m (20 to 35 ft), 2/3 the height
Mass: **moderate**

BRANCHING: multiple trunks, **leggy**, lateral branches **ascending**, forming thicket-like colonies, **medium** texture
Twig: conspicuous lenticels, crushed twig with cyanide taste and fragrance, **red brown**
Bud: **clustered, sharp pointed**, brown scales with whitish margin
Bark: **smooth**, pocked with conspicuous raised circular lenticels; ashy to slate **gray**

FOLIAGE: alternate, **simple, obovate-oblong obovate**, serrate margin, 2 small glands on petiole, **medium** texture
Surface: **dull**
Color: spring - copper to **red green;** summer - **bright green;** autumn - golden **yellow to orange**
Season: **deciduous;** emergence - early **May**, drop - mid **October**

FLOWER: **pyramidal spike**, 7.5 to 15 cm (3 to 6 in) long, somewhat pendant
Color: **white**
Season: mid through late **May**, after leaf emergence
Sex: monoecious   **Fragrant:**   strong

FRUIT: **berry,** 8 mm (1/3 in) across, clustered in loose open pendant clusters
Color: dark purple to **black**
Season: **August** until mid **September**
Wildlife Value: **very high;** popular with songbirds, also small mammals, large mammals, man

HABITAT: formation - **forest, savanna;** region - **northern, central;** gradient - **upland mesic-dry;** open wooded slopes,
     margin of woods, open field, fencerows
Shade Tolerance: **intermediate;** index range 4.0-5.9
Flood Tolerance: **intolerant**

SOIL; Texture: **moderately coarse to moderately fine;** sandy loams, loamy sands, loams, silt loams, clay loams
Drainage: **moderately well to well**
Moisture: **moist to dry**
Reaction: prefers **neutral** soils, pH 6.5-7.5

HARDINESS: **zone 2**
Rate: **fast** - 60 to 90 cm (24 to 36 in) annually
Longevity: **medium**

SUSCEPTIBILITY; Physiological: **infrequent**
Disease: **frequent** - black knot is locally severe
Insect: **infrequent** - occasional borers
Wind-Ice: **frequent** - weak wooded, ice glaze contributes to broken branchlets

URBAN TOLERANCE; Pollution: **sensitive** - HCl, Cl; **intermediate** - SO_2, HFl
Lighting: Drought-Heat: **resistant**   Mine Spoils: **resistant**
Salt: **resistant**   Soil Compaction: **sensitive**
Root Pattern: **shallow** fibrous; transplants readily B&B in spring or autumn

SPECIES; Associate: oaks, hickories, Black Maple, Flowering Dogwood, Tuliptree, American Hophornbeam,
     Black Cherry, Sassafras, viburnum, American Linden, Bur Oak
Similar: American Hornbeam, Shadblow or Allegany Serviceberry, Red and Purple Chokeberry are shrubs
Cultivars: 'Shubert' - pyramidal habit, dense, reddish purple summer foliage

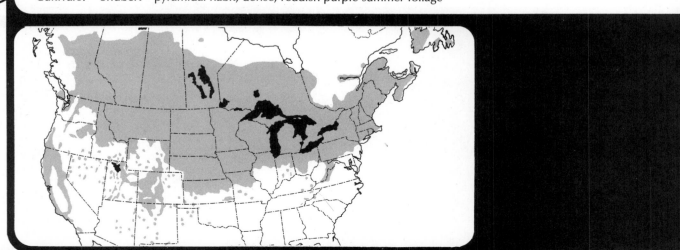

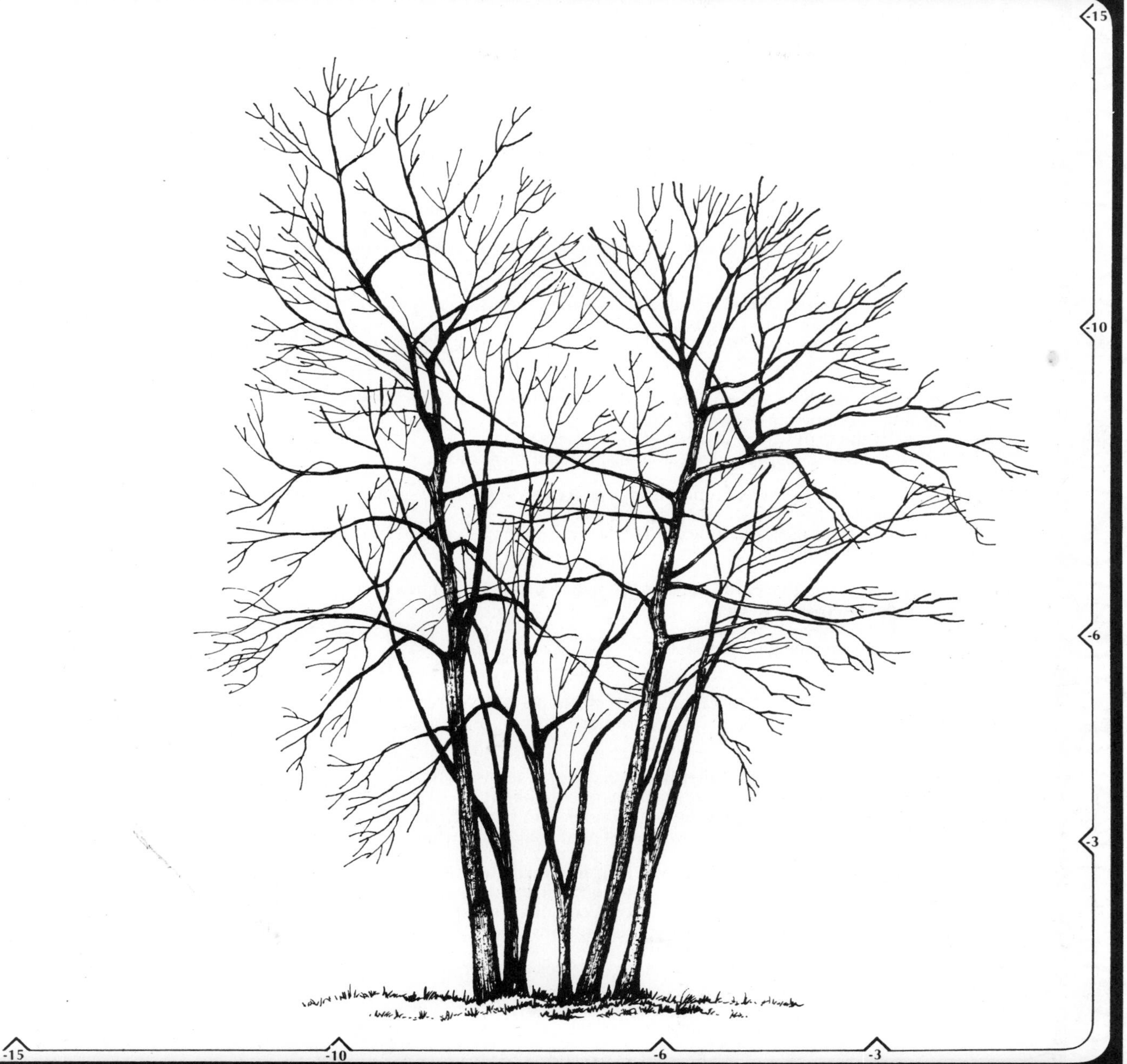
-15
-10
-6
-3
-15
-10
-6
-3

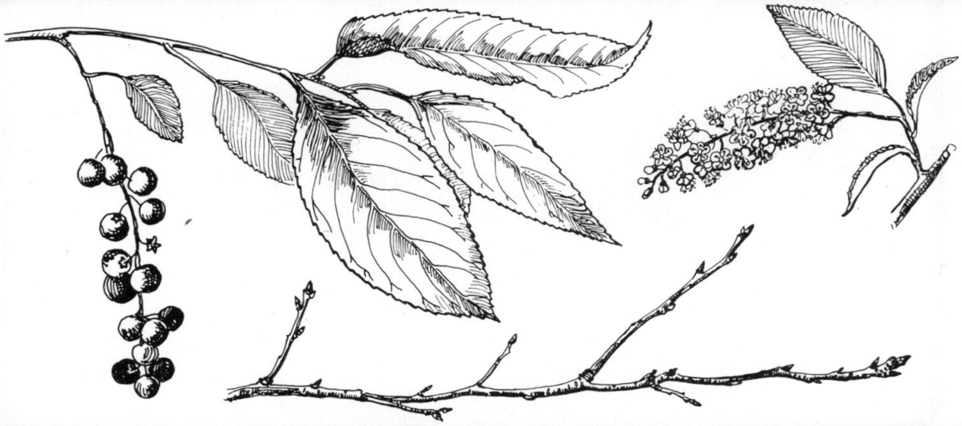

Pseudotsuga taxifolia

FORM: conical
Size: **large canopy -** 22.5 to 30 m (75 to 100 ft)
Spread: **narrow -** 6 to 10 m (20 to 35 ft), 1/3 the height
Mass: **dense,** commonly moderate at maturity

BRANCHING: central trunk, **horizontal** straight stiff, lower somewhat drooping, **medium** texture
Twig: **gray brown**
Bud: conical sharp pointed, 10 mm (2/5 in) long, papery flared scales, **red** to red-brown
Bark: **deep furrowed** into scaly ridges, young trees smooth, with resin blisters; **red brown**

FOLIAGE: spirally arranged, broad **acicular,** straight, blunt rounded at tip, flat, **fine** texture
Surface: **dull; aromatic**
Color: all seasons - **dark green to blue green;** new spring growth **light green to blue green**
Season: **evergreen**

FLOWER: cylindric **cone,** borne throughout crown, pendulous
Color: male and female - bright **red**
Season: late **April or** early **May**
Sex: monoecious

FRUIT: cylindric **cone,** 5 to 7.5 cm (2 to 3 in) long, pendant, seed bracts extend beyond scales
Color: green becoming **tan brown** at maturity
Season: persist through winter, **August until February**
Wildlife Value: **high;** songbirds, small animals, hoofed browsers

HABITAT: formation - **forest** (mountain); region - **western;** gradient - **upland mesic;** northerly slopes, canyon bottoms,
      midwest windbreaks and farmstead plantations
Shade Tolerance: **intermediate;** index range 4.0-5.9
Flood Tolerance: **intolerant**

SOIL; Texture: **medium** loams **to coarse** gravelly or sandy loams, grows poorly in clay soils
Drainage: **moderately well to well**
Moisture: **moist to average,** tolerates dry
Reaction: prefers **slightly acid,** pH 6.0-6.5

HARDINESS: zone 5b
Rate: **medium -** 30 to 60 cm (1 to 2 ft) in youth, 4.5 m (15 ft) in 10 year period
Longevity: **long -** 200 to 300 years not uncommon

SUSCEPTIBILITY; Physiological: **infrequent -** occasional leaf scorch
Disease: **infrequent -** cankers, witches broom, needle blight
Insect: **infrequent -** Douglasfir bark beetle, Zimmerman moth, gypsy moth, scales
Wind-Ice: **frequent -** high winds following heavy rainfall cause wind throw

URBAN TOLERANCE; Pollution: **sensitive -** HFl; **intermediate -** SO$_2$; **resistant -** O$_3$, PAN
Lighting: Drought-Heat: **intermediate**   Mine Spoils: **intermediate**
Salt: **intermediate**   Soil Compaction: **sensitive**
Root Pattern: **deep** to shallow spreading **laterals;** transplants with ease B&B in early spring

SPECIES; Associate: pure stands with western species of alder, hemlock, redcedar, fir, oak, maple, rhododendron and
      spruce
Similar: White or Alpine Fir are first choice followed by Limber Pine or several spruces
Cultivars: 'Compacta' - compact dense, 'Fastigiata' - very narrow, 'Glauca' - leaves bluish green, others available

Ptelea trifoliata

FORM: irregular
Size: **small understory** - 6 to 10 m (20 to 35 ft), commonly 6 m
Spread: **narrow** - 6 to 10 m (20 to 35 ft), commonly 4 to 6 m (15 to 20 ft), 2/5 or equal to height
Mass: **open**

BRANCHING: slender crooked trunk, many short twisting interwoven **ascending** branches, **medium** texture
Twig: conspicuous warty raised dot-like lenticels, leaf scars somewhat raised, **red brown**
Bud: small **woolly, dome shaped, surrounded by leaf scar,** yellowish
Bark: **smooth** or with a slight warty roughness; **red brown** to dark gray

FOLIAGE: alternate, **palmately compound,** tri-foliate, **ovate-oblong ovate,** margin entire, **medium fine** texture
Surface: **glossy,** pale beneath, aromatic orange peel odor when crushed
Color: spring - **pale** lime **green;** summer - **dark green;** autumn - pale **yellow**
Season: **deciduous;** emergence - late **May,** drop - late **September**

FLOWER: flat-topped terminal **cluster** borne on short lateral branches
Color: **yellow-green**
Season: early and mid **June**
Sex: monoecious

FRUIT: circular **samara,** 15 mm (3/5 in) wide, dense clusters, flat papery disc with seed positioned in middle
Color: green becoming **tan brown**
Season: mid **August through** late **November**
Wildlife Value: **intermediate;** songbirds, upland ground birds, small mammals, hoofed browsers

HABITAT: formation - **forest, savanna;** region - **central;** gradient - **upland mesic dry and dry;**
    sandy beaches, dry rocky soils bordering wooded areas
Shade Tolerance: **tolerant;** index range 6.0-7.9
Flood Tolerance: **very intolerant**

SOIL; Texture: **moderately coarse** sandy and gravelly loams, medium loams, **to moderately fine** sandy loams
Drainage: **moderately well to excessive**
Moisture: **moist to dry**
Reaction: **neutral,** pH 6.6-7.5

HARDINESS: zone 5a
Rate: **medium to slow** - 23 to 46 cm (9 to 18 in) annually
Longevity: **medium**

SUSCEPTIBILITY; Physiological: **infrequent**
Disease: **infrequent** - leaf spot, rust-not serious
Insect: **infrequent**
Wind-Ice: **infrequent** - strong wooded

URBAN TOLERANCE; Pollution:
Lighting: Drought-Heat: **resistant**   Mine Spoils: **resistant**
Salt: **resistant**   Soil Compaction: **senstive**
Root Pattern: shallow spreading or **deep laterals;** transplants readily B&B in early spring

SPECIES; Associate: Common Chokecherry, Flameleaf and Smooth Sumacs, Nannyberry
    and Blackhaw Viburnums, hawthorn, upland oak and hickory
Similar: American Bladdernut is a large shrub
Cultivars: none available commercially

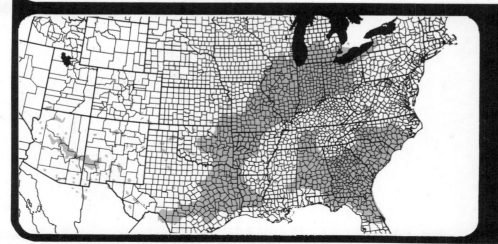

Common Hoptree

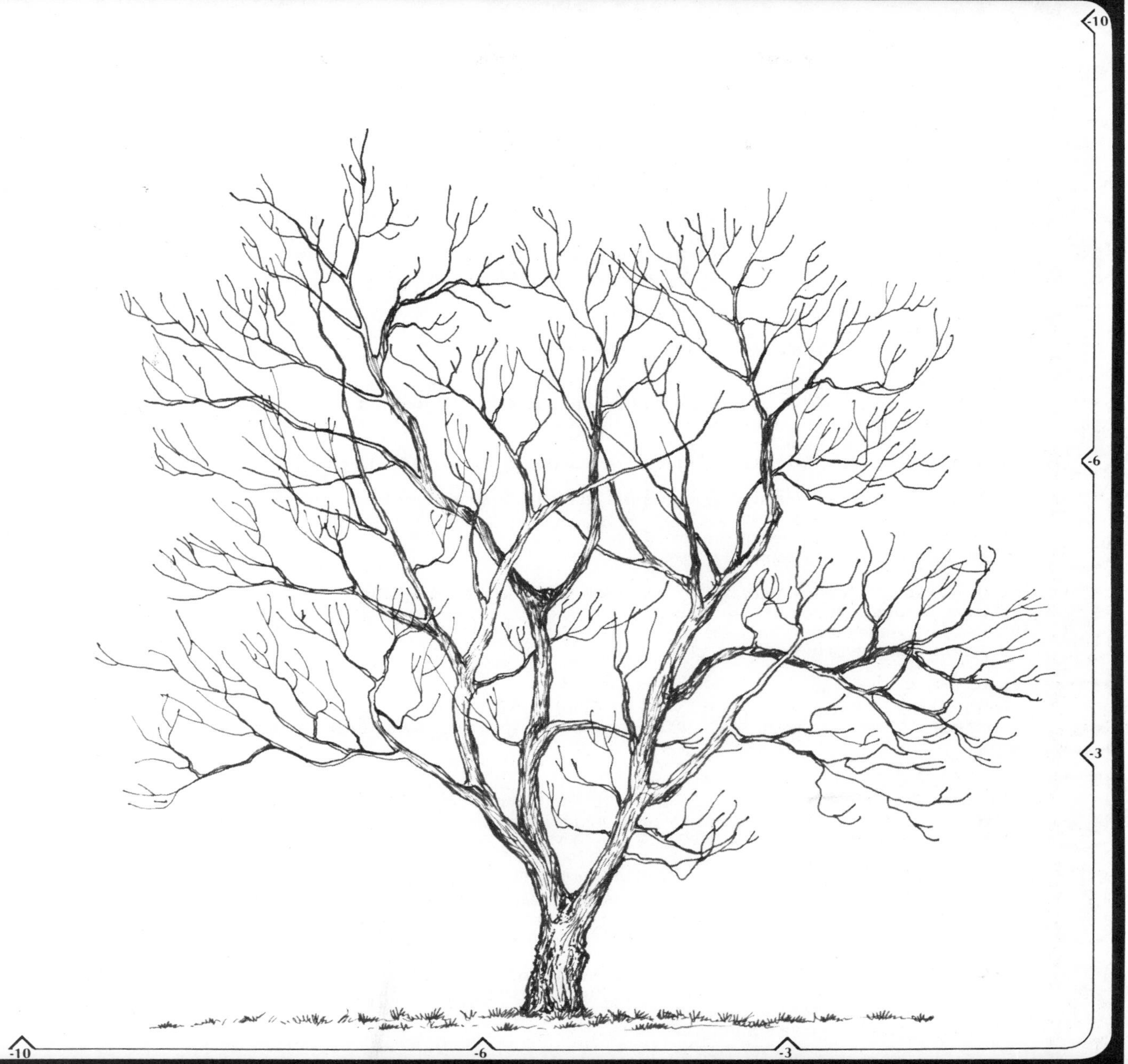

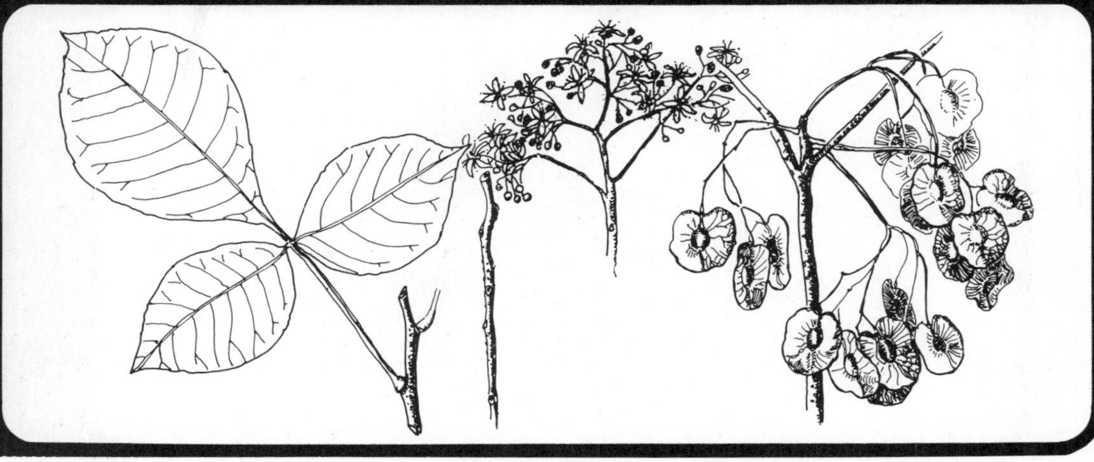

Quercus alba

FORM: globular
Size: **large canopy** - 22.5 to 30 m (75 to 100 ft)
Spread: **very wide** - 22.5 to 30 m (75 to 100 ft), up to 40 m, commonly wider than tall
Mass: **moderate**

BRANCHING: short stocky trunk, massive **horizontal picturesque** limbs, strong bold appearance, **coarse** texture
Twig: moderately stout, **red** often with a purplish tinge
Bud: **clustered, blunt oval** end buds, 3 mm (1/8 in), reddish brown to brown
Bark: **scaly** or **shallow furrowed** with small **narrow** rectangular blocks; light ashy **gray**

FOLIAGE: alternate, **simple, pinnately lobed,** sinuses reaching nearly to midrib, lobes entire, **medium** texture
Surface:: **dull**, leathery, pale and whitish below
Color: spring - bright **red** to pink becoming **silvery gray**; summer - **medium green** to blue green; autumn - **burgundy**
Season: deciduous - **persistent**; emergence - mid **May,** drop - many interior leaves persisting **through January**

FLOWER: male in drooping clustered **catkins**, 2.5 to 5 cm (1 to 2 in) long
Color: **yellow green**
Season: mid through late **May,** shortly after leaves unfold
Sex: monoecious

FRUIT: acorn, 19 mm (3/4 in) long, cup with warty scales, enclosing about 1/4 of nut, solitary or paired
Color: light green becoming **tan brown** at maturity
Season: **September through early October**
Wildlife Value: **very high;** man, songbirds, upland ground birds, small mammals, hoofed browsers

HABITAT: formation - **forest;** region - **central;** gradient - **upland mesic-dry;** moist warm south and west facing slopes, upland flats, rocky hillsides
Shade Tolerance: **intermediate;** index 5.7
Flood Tolerance: **intolerant**

SOIL; Texture: **coarse to fine;** heavy clay, sandy plains, sandy loams, loams
Drainage: **moderately well to excessive**
Moisture: prefers **moist,** tolerates **dry**
Reaction: **slightly acid to neutral,** pH 6.1-7.5

HARDINESS: zone 4a
Rate: **slow** - 3.6 m (12 ft) in 12 years, very slow after first 30 years
Longevity: **long** - commonly 350 to 400 years, old trees to 500 years not uncommon

SUSCEPTIBILITY; Physiological: **infrequent**
Disease: **frequent -** oak wilt, shoestring root rot, Anthracnose, oak leaf blister
Insect: **frequent -** orange striped oak worm, golden oak scale, oak skeletonizer
Wind-Ice: **infrequent**

URBAN TOLERANCE; Pollution: **intermediate** - SO_2, HFl, **sensitive** - O_3
Lighting: **intermediate**   Drought-Heat: **intermediate**   Mine Spoils: **intermediate**
Salt: **resistant**   Soil Compaction: extremely **sensitive** to compaction and grade change
Root Pattern: deep **taproot,** and deep laterals; difficult to transplant, move as small tree B&B in early spring

SPECIES; Associate: Tuliptree, American Linden, White Ash, Black Cherry, American Beech, Sugar Maple, Eastern White Pine and Canada Hemlock, Cucumbertree Magnolia, buckeye, oak and hickory
Similar: Bur Oak, Post Oak, English Oak (European)
Cultivars: none available commercially

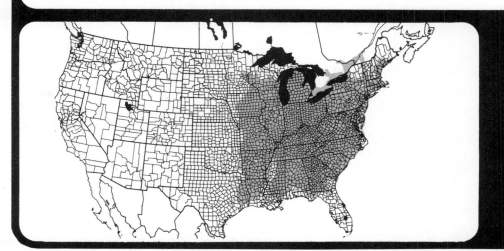

Quercus bicolor

FORM: ovoid
Size: **large canopy - 22.5 to 30 m (75 to 100 ft)**
Spread: **wide -** 15 to 22.5 m (50 to 75 ft), 2/3 that of height
Mass: **moderate**

BRANCHING: short trunk, lower limbs **descending,** upper crown ascending, **medium** texture
Twig: moderately stout, pale raised lenticels, **red brown**
Bud: **clustered blunt globular** end buds, light chestnut brown
Bark: young trees shedding in ragged papery flakes, adult **deeply furrowed;** dark **gray-brown**

FOLIAGE: alternate, **simple, obovate-oblong obovate,** shallow lobed to wavy margin, **medium coarse** texture
Surface: **dull,** leathery appearance, pale grayish green beneath and tomentose
Color: spring - **purplish green;** summer - **dark green;** autumn - golden **yellow brown**
Season: **deciduous;** emergence - early **May,** drop - early **November**

FLOWER: male in pendulous **catkins,** 5 to 7.5 cm (2 to 3 in) long
Color: **yellow green**
Season: early through mid **May,** with or soon after leaf emergence
Sex: monoecious

FRUIT: **acorn,** 19 to 38 mm (3/4 to 1 1/2 in) long, cap enclosing 1/3 to 1/2 length, long stem, usually in pairs
Color: **tan brown**
Season: **September through** early **October**
Wildlife Value: **very high;** man, water birds, upland ground birds, songbirds, small mammals, hoofed browsers

HABITAT: formation - **forest;** region - **central;** gradient - **lowland wet and wet-mesic;** second bottoms, alluvial flats, border of small streams, lake margin
Shade Tolerance: **intermediate;** index range 4.0-5.9
Flood Tolerance: **tolerant**

SOIL; Texture: **medium to fine;** stiff hard pan clay, silty clay, fine sandy clays, fine sandy loams
Drainage: **moderately poor to very poor**
Moisture: demands **wet to moist**
Reaction: **neutral,** pH 6.0-6.5

HARDINESS: **zone 4a**
Rate: **medium to fast -** one of faster growing oaks, 46 to 60 cm (1 1/2 to 2 ft) per year, slowing with maturity
Longevity: **medium -** generally mature in 125 to 175 years

SUSCEPTIBILITY; Physiological: **frequent -** severe iron chlorosis, requires acid soils
Disease: **infrequent -** oak wilt, Anthracnose, canker, Phomopsis canker, Coniothyrium dieback
Insect: **infrequent**
Wind-Ice: **infrequent**

URBAN TOLERANCE; Pollution:
Lighting: Drought-Heat: **resistant**   Mine Spoils: **resistant**
Salt: **resistant**   Soil Compaction: **resistant**
Root Pattern: **shallow** fibrous; transplant readily B&B in early spring or late autumn

SPECIES; Associate: Black Ash, Red Maple, Silver Maple, Tuliptree, American Sweetgum, River Birch, Pecan, Boxelder, American Planetree, Green Ash, Shingle Oak, Bur Oak, Pin Oak
Similar: Pin Oak exhibits comparable cultural requirements, shape and branching form
Cultivars: none available commercially

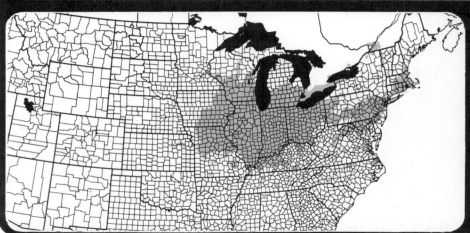

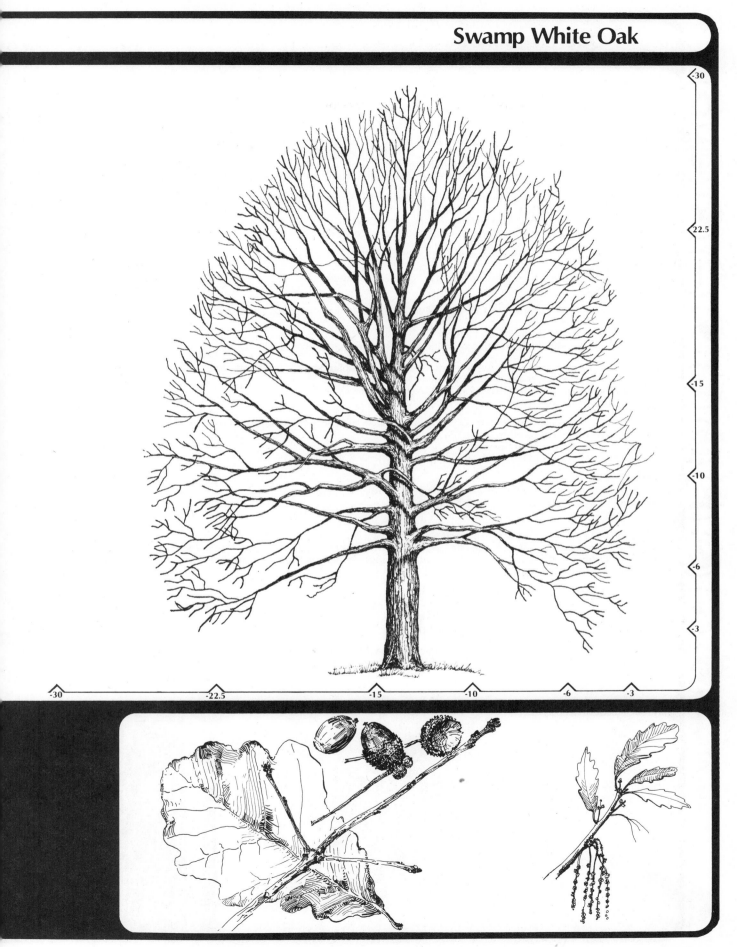

Quercus borealis

FORM: ovoid, commonly **globular**
Size: **large canopy -** 22.5 to 30 m (75 to 100 ft)
Spread: **very wide -** 22.5 to 30 m (75 to 100 ft), commonly 3/4 that of height
Mass: **dense**

BRANCHING: moderately stout **ascending** symmetrical limbs, **medium** texture
Twig: slender, glossy, **reddish brown**
Bud: **clustered** end buds, **sharp pointed,** 6 mm (1/4 in) long, smooth
Bark: **shallow furrowed** with **wide** flat ridges, deeply fissured base; trunk commonly **black,** plates ashy gray

FOLIAGE: alternate, **simple, pinnately lobed,** shallow to moderately deep bristle tipped sinuses, **medium coarse** texture
Surface: **dull,** pale yellow green beneath
Color: spring - juvenile leaves woolly **pink** becoming **light green;** summer - **dark green;** autumn - golden **yellow brown**
Season: **deciduous;** emergence - mid **May,** drop - mid **November**

FLOWER: slender drooping staminate **catkins,** 7.5 to 10 cm (3 to 4 in) long
Color: **yellow green**
Season: mid through late **May,** with or soon following leaf emergence
Sex: monoecious

FRUIT: large broad **acorn,** 19 to 32 mm (3/4 to 1 1/4 in), shallow cap covers 1/10 of nut, acorn frequently woolly
Color: **chocolate brown**
Season: **September through** mid October
Wildlife Value: **very high;** songbirds, upland ground birds, small mammals, hoofed browsers

HABITAT: formation - **forest;** region - **central;** gradient - **upland mesic and mesic-dry;** most frequent on north and east
slope aspects, lower and middle slopes, coves and ravines
Shade Tolerance: **tolerant;** index 7.8, most tolerant oak
Flood Tolerance: **intolerant**

SOIL; Texture: **moderately coarse to fine;** prefers clay loams and loamy sands, tolerates heavy clay loams and clays
Drainage: **moderately well to well**
Moisture: prefers **moist to average**
Reaction: **strongly acid to slightly acid,** pH 4.8-6.5

HARDINESS: **zone 3a**
Rate: **medium -** generally around 46 to 60 cm (1 1/2 to 2 ft) per year
Longevity: **long -** maturity at 200 to 300 years

SUSCEPTIBILITY; physiological: **infrequent**
Disease: **frequent -** oak wilt, Strumella canker, Nectria canker, leaf blister, powdery mildew
Insect: **frequent -** gypsy moth, brown tail moth, orange striped oakworm, trunk borers
Wind-Ice: **infrequent**

URBAN TOLERANCE; Pollution: **resistant -** SO_2, O_3, Cl; **intermediate -** HFl, 2,4-D
Lighting: **intermediate**   Drought-Heat: **intermediate**   Mine Spoils: **intermediate**
Salt: **resistant**   Soil Compaction: **sensitive**
Root Pattern: **deep lateral** spreading; transplants readily due to negligible taproot, move B&B in early spring

SPECIES; Associate: Eastern White Pine, Red Pine, White Ash, Pin and Black Cherries, Canada Hemlock, Sugar, Black,
Striped and Mountain Maples, White Oak, American Linden, Shadblow Serviceberry, American Hophornbeam
Similar: Black Oak (difficult to tell these species apart)
Cultivars: none available commercially

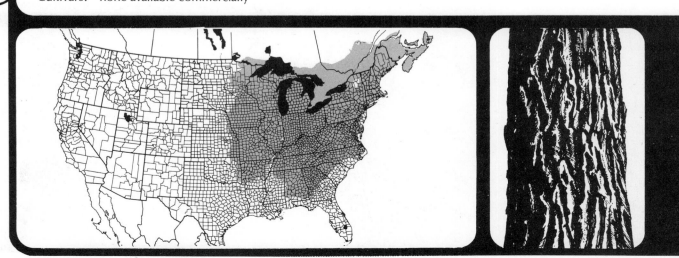

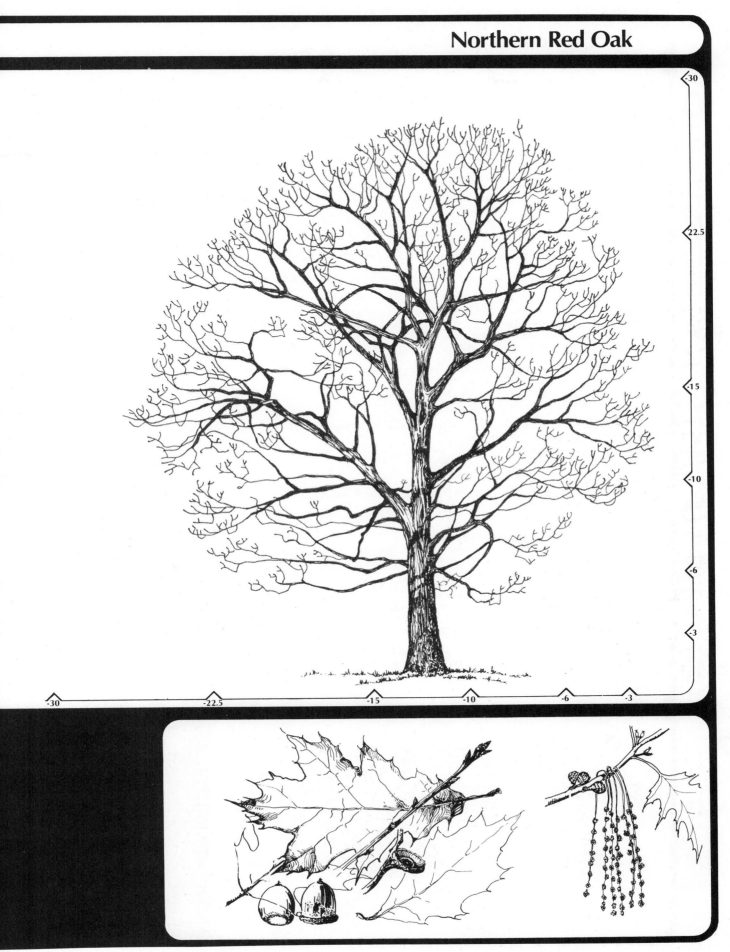

Quercus coccinea

FORM: globular
Size: **small canopy** - 15 to 22.5 m (50 to 75 ft)
Spread: **wide** - 15 to 22.5 m plus (50 to 75 ft), commonly as wide as tall
Mass: **moderate**

BRANCHING: rapidly tapering trunk, stout **ascending** branches drooping slightly at ends, **medium** texture
Twig: moderately stout, smooth, **red brown**
Bud: **clustered** conical end buds, **blunt rounded**
Bark: **smooth** becoming divided by shallow fissures with rounded knobby irregular ridges; **black**

FOLIAGE: alternate, **simple, pinnately lobed,** deep "C" shaped sinuses, bristle tipped, **medium** texture
Surface: very **glossy,** under surface silvery white tomentose
Color: spring - new leaf **green;** summer - **bright green;** autumn - scarlet **red**
Season: **deciduous;** emergence - mid **May,** drop - late **November**

FLOWER: male in slender drooping **catkins** 7.5 to 10 cm (3 to 4 in) long
Color: bright red before opening becoming **yellow green**
Season: mid **May through** early **June,** appearing with or a few days after leaves
Sex: monoecious

FRUIT: oval, **acorn,** 13 to 25 mm (1/2 to 1 in) long, enclosed 1/3 to 1/2 of length by cap
Color: light **tan brown**
Season: early **September through** early **October**
Wildlife Value: **very high;** songbirds, upland ground birds, small mammals, hoofed browsers

HABITAT: formation - **forest;** region - **central;** gradient - **upland dry;** steep rocky land, ridgetops, warm upper and middle slopes, south and west slope aspects
Shade Tolerance: **intolerant;** index 2.0-3.9
Flood Tolerance: **very intolerant**

SOIL; Texture: shallow infertile soils over sandstone or limestone, **coarse** sandy loams **to fine** heavy clay
Drainage: **moderately well to excessive**
Moisture: prefers **average to dry**
Reaction: **slightly acid,** pH 6.1-6.5

HARDINESS: zone 5a
Rate: **medium to fast** - 46 to 60 cm (1 1/2 to 2 ft) a year is average in youth
Longevity: **long** - 200 to 300 years

SUSCEPTIBILITY; Physiological: **infrequent**
Disease: **frequent** - oak wilt, Nectria and Strumella cankers
Insect: **frequent** - cankerworm, forest tent caterpillar, carpenterworms
Wind-Ice: **infrequent**

URBAN TOLERANCE; Pollution: **intermediate** - O_3, HFl
Lighting: Drought-Heat: **resistant** Mine Spoils: **resistant**
Salt: **resistant** Soil Compaction: **sensitive**
Root Pattern: deep **taproot** with shallow coarse laterals; difficult to transplant, move B&B in early spring

SPECIES; Associate: Sourwood, Flowering Dogwood, Chestnut, Post, Black and Blackjack Oaks, Northern Pin Oak, Pitch and Virginia Pines, Shagbark and Pignut Hickories
Similar: Northern Pin Oak, Pin Oak will grow reasonably well on dry upland sites
Cultivars: none available commercially

Quercus ellipsoidalis

FORM: ovoid
Size: **small canopy -** 15 to 22.5 m (50 to 75 ft)
Spread: **wide -** 15 to 22.5 m (50 to 75 ft), 3/4 the height
Mass: **moderate**

BRANCHING: short **descending** or deflected lower branchlets, upper crown ascending, **medium** texture
Twig: slender, **red brown**
Bud: **clustered sharp pointed** angular end buds, red brown
Bark: rather **smooth,** divided by shallow connected fissures into narrow knobby plates; dark **brown black**

FOLIAGE: alternate, **simple, pinnately lobed,** deep wide open sinuses with bristle tips, **medium** texture
Surface: very **glossy,** pale beneath
Color: spring - fuzzy **pink turning light green;** summer - **bright green;** autumn - late, scarlet **red**
Season: deciduous - **persistent;** emergence - mid **May,** drop - dried leaves remaining **through February**

FLOWER: staminate **catkins,** 36 to 50 mm (1 1/2 to 2 in) long, pendant
Color: **yellow green** occasionally tinged with red
Season: mid through late **May,** with or shortly after leaves unfold
Sex: monoecious

FRUIT: elliptic **acorn,** 8 to 17 mm (1/3 to 2/3 in) long, cup enclosing 1/3 to 1/2 of length
Color: chestnut **brown**
Season: early **September through** early **October**
Wildlife Value: **very high;** songbirds, upland ground birds, small mammals, hoofed browsers

HABITAT: formation - **savanna;** region - **northern;** gradient - **upland dry;** gravelly morainal hills, dry sandy and clayey uplands
Shade Tolerance: **very intolerant;** index range 0-1.9, least tolerant of the oaks
Flood Tolerance: **very intolerant**

SOIL; Texture: **coarse to fine;** heavy clay, coarse gravelly and sandy loams, sandy plains
Drainage: **moderately well to excessive**
Moisture: prefers **average,** tolerates **dry** soils
Reaction: **slightly acid to neutral,** pH 6.1-7.5

HARDINESS: zone 3b
Rate: **slow -** about 6 m (20 ft) in 20 years
Longevity: **long -** mature at 150 to 250 years

SUSCEPTIBILITY; Physiological: **infrequent**
Disease: **infrequent -** oak wilt, Anthracnose are occasional problems
Insect: **infrequent -** not particularly serious
Wind-Ice: **infrequent**

URBAN TOLERANCE; Pollution:
Lighting: Drought-Heat: **resistant**   Mine Spoils: **resistant**
Salt: **resistant**   Soil Compaction: **sensitive**
Root Pattern: **taproot;** difficult to transplant, move in early spring B&B

SPECIES; Associate: Bur Oak, Scarlet Oak, Bigtooth and Quaking Aspens, Jack Pine, Common Chokecherry, Prairie Crabapple, Black Cherry, Nannyberry and Blackhaw Viburnums
Similar: Pin Oak, Scarlet Oak
Cultivars: none available commercially

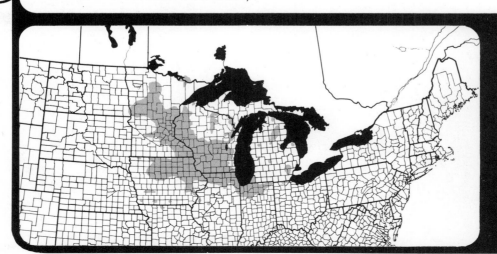

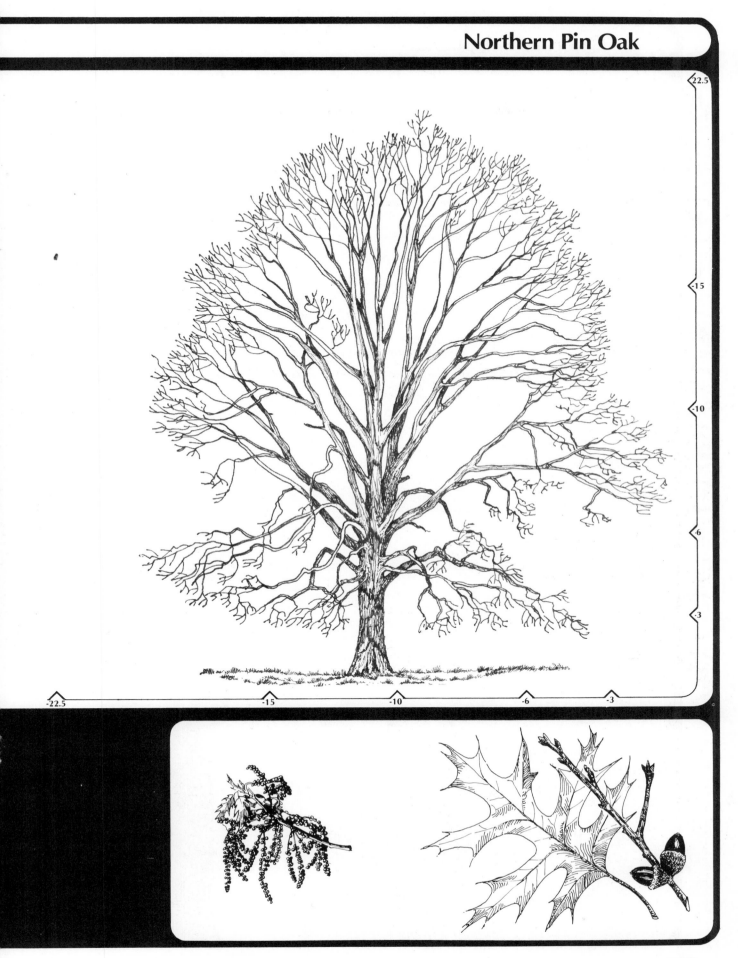

Quercus imbricaria

FORM: conical
Size: **large understory -** 10 to 15 m (30 to 45 ft)
Spread: **intermediate -** 10 to 15 m (30 to 45 ft), 2/3 that of height
Mass: **open**

BRANCHING: limbs **descending** or strongly **horizontal, medium** texture
Twig: moderately stout to slender, glossy, smooth, **green brown**
Bud: **clustered blunt globular** end buds
Bark: thin loose **scaly** or slightly fissured into broad scaly ridges; light **gray brown**

FOLIAGE: alternate, **simple, elliptic-oval,** entire undulate margin, one bristle at apex, **medium** texture
Surface: very **glossy,** thick leathery, pale green beneath
Color: spring - light green to **yellow green;** summer - **dark green;** autumn - turns late, golden **yellow brown** to russet-red
Season: deciduous - **persistent;** emergence - mid **May,** drop - dried leaves persisting through winter **to late March**

FLOWER: drooping male **catkins,** 5 to 7.5 cm (2 to 3 in) long
Color: light yellow or **yellow green**
Season: mid through late **May,** shortly after leaves unfold
Sex: monoecious

FRUIT: broad dome shaped **acorns,** 13 to 17 mm (1/2 to 2/3 in) long, cup enclosing 1/3 to 1/2 of nut
Color: dark **brown**
Season: early **September through** early **October**
Wildlife Value: **very high;** waterbirds, upland ground birds, songbirds, small mammals, hoofed browsers

HABITAT: formation - **forest;** region - **central;** gradient - **lowland wet mesic and upland mesic-dry;** rocky uplands, alluvial
floodplain and stream bank, elevated sandy knobs
Shade Tolerance: **intermediate;** index range 4.0-5.9
Flood Tolerance: **intermediate**

SOIL; Texture: **moderately coarse to moderately fine;** silt loams, sandy loams, clay loams
Drainage: **moderately well to well**
Moisture: prefers **moist,** tolerates **dry**
Reaction: **strongly acid,** pH 4.5-6.0

HARDINESS: **zone 5a**
Rate: **slow -** about 15 to 30 cm (6 to 12 in) per year during first 30 year period
Longevity: **long -** maximum age around 250 years

SUSCEPTIBILITY; Physiological: **infrequent**
Disease: **infrequent -** oak wilt, Anthracnose, canker, leaf blister, twig blight, wood decay
Insect: **infrequent -** yellow necked caterpillar, oak skeletonizer, oak lacebug, oak mite
Wind-Ice: **infrequent**

URBAN TOLERANCE; Pollution: **resistant -** O_3, HCl, Cl; **intermediate -** HFl
Lighting: Drought-Heat: **resistant**   Mine Spoils: **resistant**
Salt: **resistant**   Soil Compaction: **intermediate**
Root Pattern: **taproot;** transplants with less difficulty than many other oaks, move B&B in early spring

SPECIES; Associate: lowlands - Pin and Swamp White Oaks, Bur Oak; uplands - White Oak, Shagbark Hickory,
Ohio Buckeye
Similar: Willow Oak is less hardy
Cultivars: none available commercially

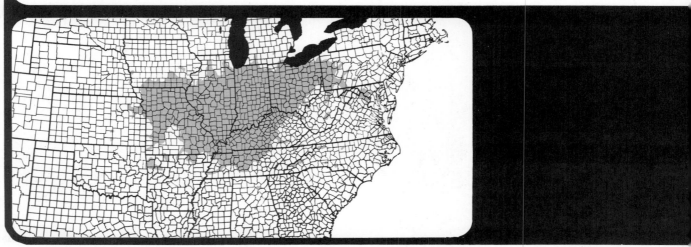

Shingle Oak

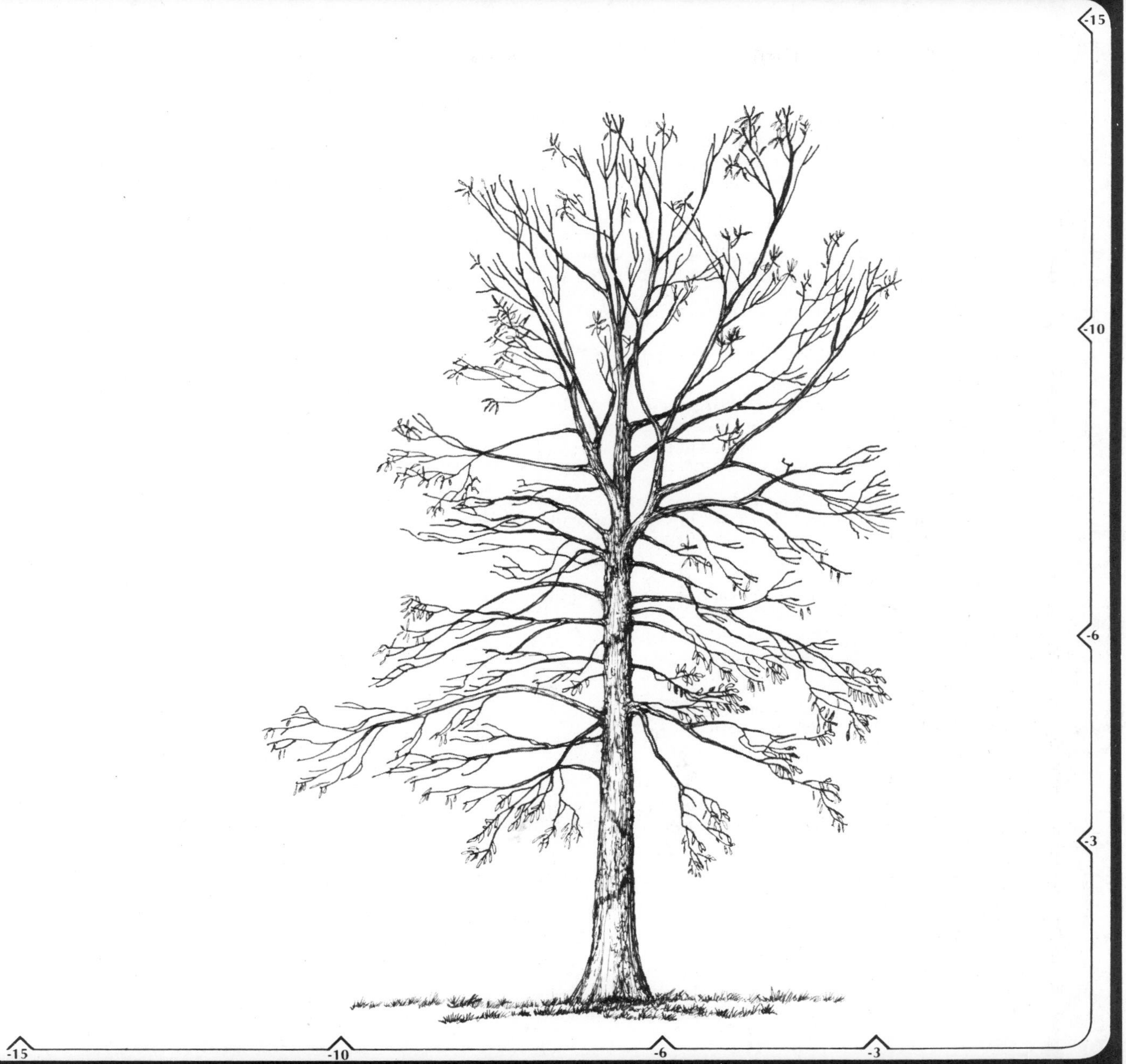

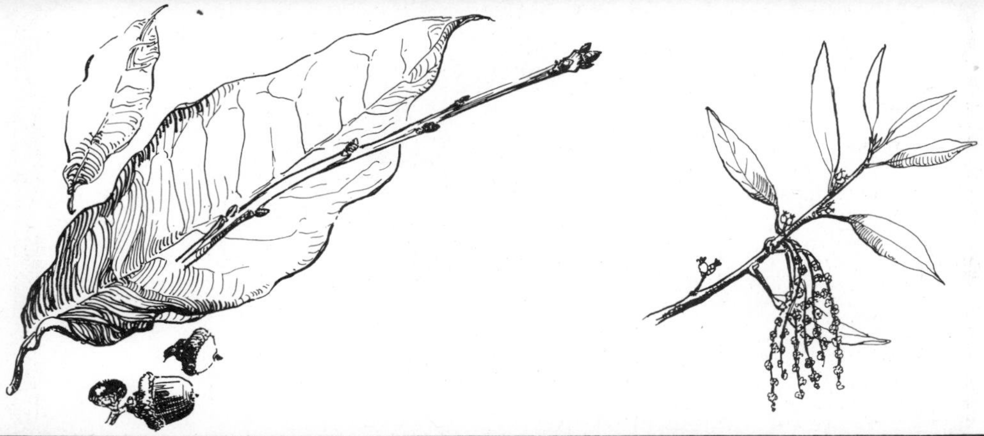

Quercus macrocarpa

FORM: globular
Size: **large canopy** - 22.5 to 30 m (75 to 100 ft)
Spread: **very wide** - 22.5 to 30 m or more (75 to 100 ft), open crown usually wider than tall
Mass: **open**

BRANCHING: short massive trunk, **horizontal** widespreading **picturesque** limbs, majestic appearance, **coarse** texture
Twig: stout, with **corky ridges** or **wings** on some trees, **yellowish brown**
Bud: **clustered** 3 to 6 mm (1/8 to 1/4 in) **blunt** end buds, tan-brown coloration
Bark: **deeply furrowed** into coarse scaly or rectangular plates; dark **gray brown**

FOLIAGE: alternate, **simple, pinnately lobed,** central pair of sinuses reach nearly to midrib, **coarse** texture
Surface: **glossy** above, paler and silvery white tomentose beneath
Color: spring - light green to **yellow green;** summer - **dark green;** autumn - golden **yellow brown**
Season: **deciduous;** emergence - early **May**, drop - early **November**

FLOWER: male in drooping **catkins,** 2.5 to 5 cm (1 to 2 in) long
Color: **yellowish green**
Season: early through mid **May**, appearing shortly after leaf emergence
Sex: monoecious

FRUIT: **acorn,** 19 to 32 mm (3/4 to 1 1/4 in) long, burly fringed cup covers 1/2 or more of nut, solitary
Color: light green becoming **tan-brown** at maturity
Season: **September through** early **October**
Wildlife Value: **very high;** songbirds, upland ground birds, waterbirds, small mammals

HABITAT: formation - **forest, savanna;** region - **northern, central;** gradients - **lowland wet-mesic, upland mesic-dry and dry;**
    floodplain, south and west facing slopes, forest - prairie margin, open field
Shade Tolerance: **intolerant;** index 3.0
Flood Tolerance: **intermediate**

SOIL; Texture: **coarse to fine;** sandy plain, loamy slopes, heavy clay pan, prairie loam, silt loams
Drainage: **moderately poor to well**
Moisture: **wet soils** to porous **droughty** granular
Reaction: **strongly acid to alkaline,** pH 4.6-8.0

HARDINESS: zone 2
Rate: **slow** - 4.5 m (15 ft) in 20 year period is average
Longevity: **long** - 200 to 300 years

SUSCEPTIBILITY; Physiological: **infrequent**
Disease: **frequent** - oak wilt, cottonroot rot, Strumella canker, Conothyrium dieback
Insect: **infrequent** - oak leaf caterpillar, Bur Oak kermes
Wind-Ice: **infrequent**

URBAN TOLERANCE; Pollution: **resistant** - O$_3$; **intermediate** - HFl
Lighting: Drought-Heat: **resistant**   Mine Spoils: **resistant**
Salt: **resistant**   Soil Compaction: **sensitive**
Root Pattern: **taproot;** difficult to transplant, move B&B in early spring

SPECIES; Associate: upland - pure stands, Prairie Crabapple, Northern Pin, White, and Black Oaks, Shagbark and
    Bitternut Hickories, hawthorns; lowland - American Elm, Common Hackberry, Swamp White Oak, Eastern Poplar
Similar: White and Post Oaks, English Oak (European)
Cultivars: none available commercially

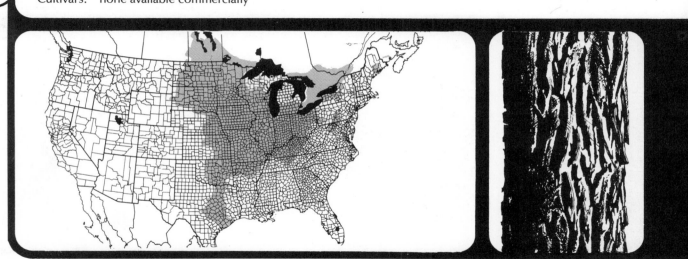

302

Bur Oak

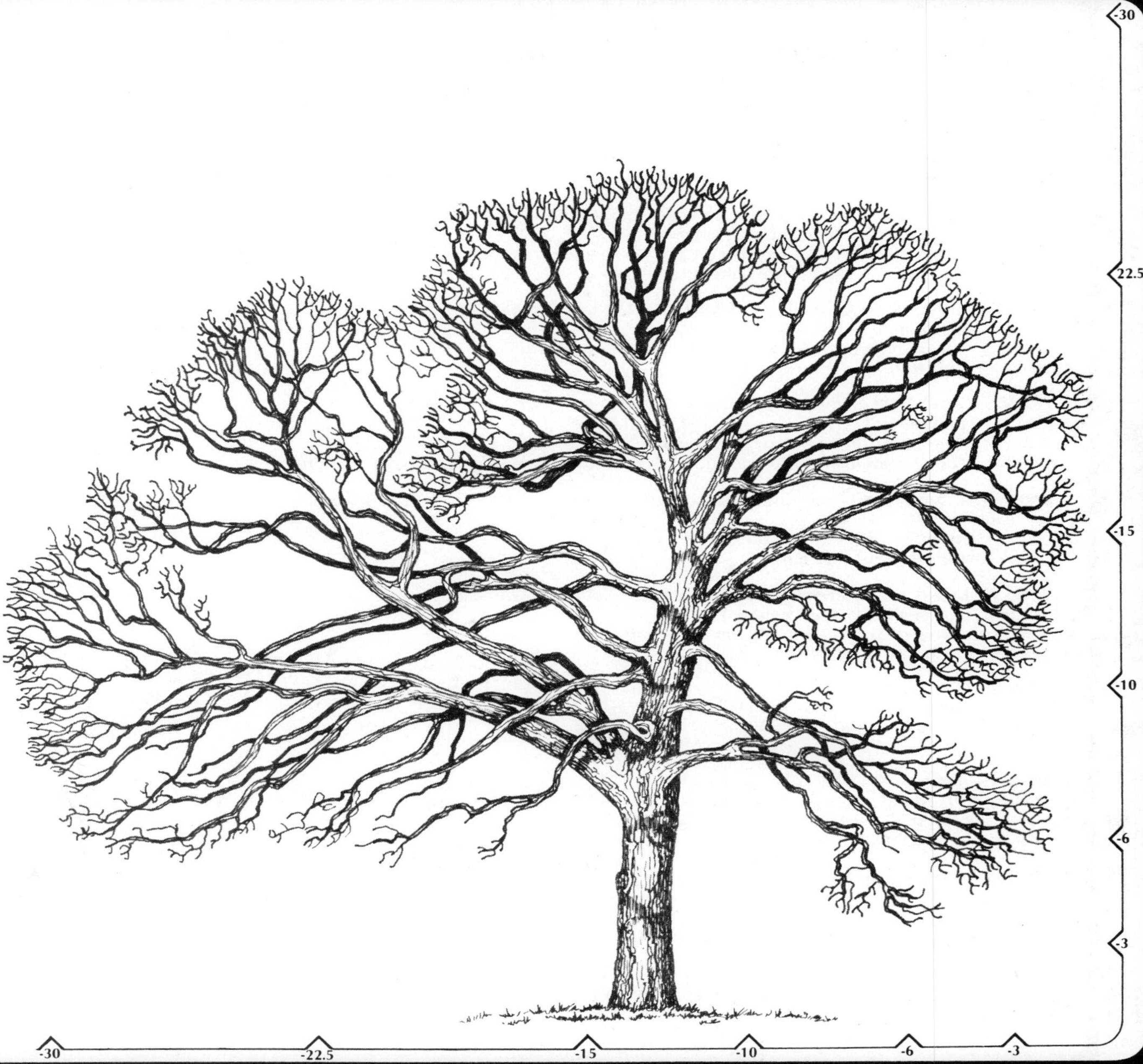

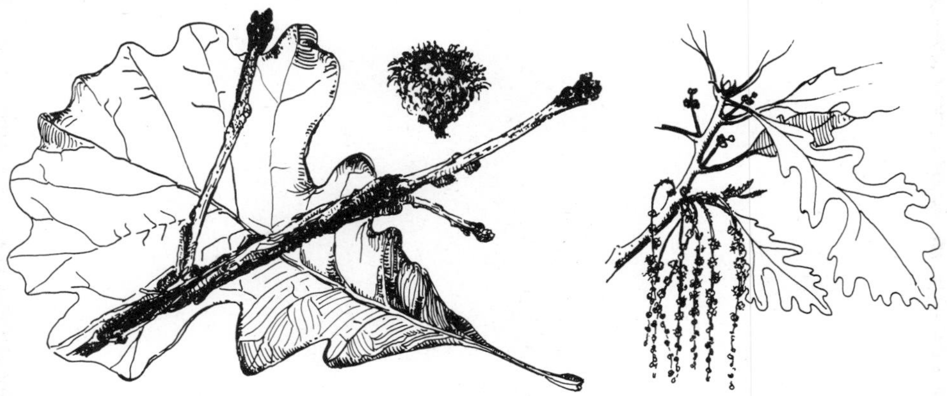

Quercus marilandica

FORM: ovoid
Size: **large understory -** 10 to 15 m (35 to 50 ft)
Spread: **intermediate -** 10 to 15 m (35 to 50 ft), 2/3 the height
Mass: dense through upper crown, **moderate** overall

BRANCHING: short trunk dividing into many dense **picturesque** contorted **horizontal** limbs, **coarse** texture
Twig: stout, **red brown**
Bud: **clustered** angular end buds, **sharp pointed**
Bark: thick squarish **blocky** flat-topped ridges; coal **black**

FOLIAGE: alternate, **simple,** broadly **obovate-oblong obovate,** 3 broad bristle tipped lobes, **coarse** texture
Surface: **glossy,** lower surface pale orangish
Color: spring - bright **red** to pink **becoming yellow green;** summer - **yellow green;** autumn - **red**
Season: **deciduous** commonly **persistent;** emergence - mid **May,** drop - late November or early **December**

FLOWER: slender drooping male **catkins,** 7.5 to 10 cm (3 to 4 in) long
Color: pale orange red or **yellowish green**
Season: mid **May through** early **June,** soon after leaves unfold
Sex: monoecious

FRUIT: egg shaped **acorn,** 19 mm (3/4 in) long, cup encloses 1/3 to 1/2 of nut
Color: **tan brown**
Season: **September through** early **October**
Wildlife Value: **very high;** upland ground birds, songbirds, hoofed browsers, small mammals

HABITAT: formation - **forest and savanna;** region - **central;** gradient - **upland dry;** rocky sandy ridgetops, edge of woods, sand terrace
Shade Tolerance: **intolerant;** index range 2.0-3.9
Flood Tolerance: **very intolerant**

SOIL; Texture: **coarse to medium;** pure sand, shallow soils over sandstone or limestone, sandy loams
Drainage: **moderately well to excessive**
Moisture: tolerates **dry,** tolerates droughty soils
Reaction: **strongly acid,** pH 4.6-5.0

HARDINESS: zone 5b
Rate: **slow -** generally 15 cm (6 in) annually
Longevity: **long -** mature at 200 to 300 years

SUSCEPTIBILITY; Physiological: **infrequent**
Disease: **frequent -** oak wilt, cottonroot rot, Strumella canker, Conothyrium dieback, Anthracnose
Insect: **infrequent -** oak leaf caterpillar, oak skeletonizer
Wind-Ice: **infrequent -** very strong, decidedly windfirm

URBAN TOLERANCE; Pollution:
Lighting: Drought-Heat: **resistant**   Mine Spoils: **resistant**
Salt: **resistant**   Soil Compaction: **sensitive**
Root Pattern: **taproot;** difficult to transplant, move B&B in early spring

SPECIES; Associate: Post, Black, Scarlet and Chestnut Oaks, Mockernut Hickory, Pignut Hickory, Black Locust, Flowering Dogwood, Shortleaf and Pitch Pines, Eastern Redbud, sumac, hawthorns
Similar: Northern Pin Oak
Cultivars: none available commercially

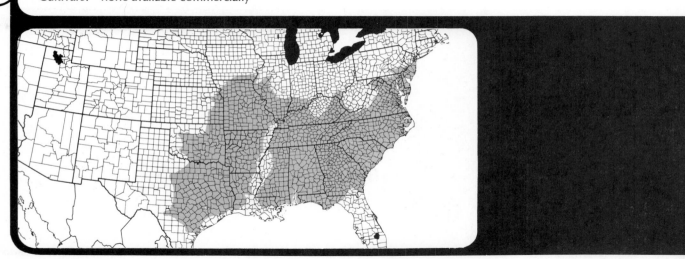

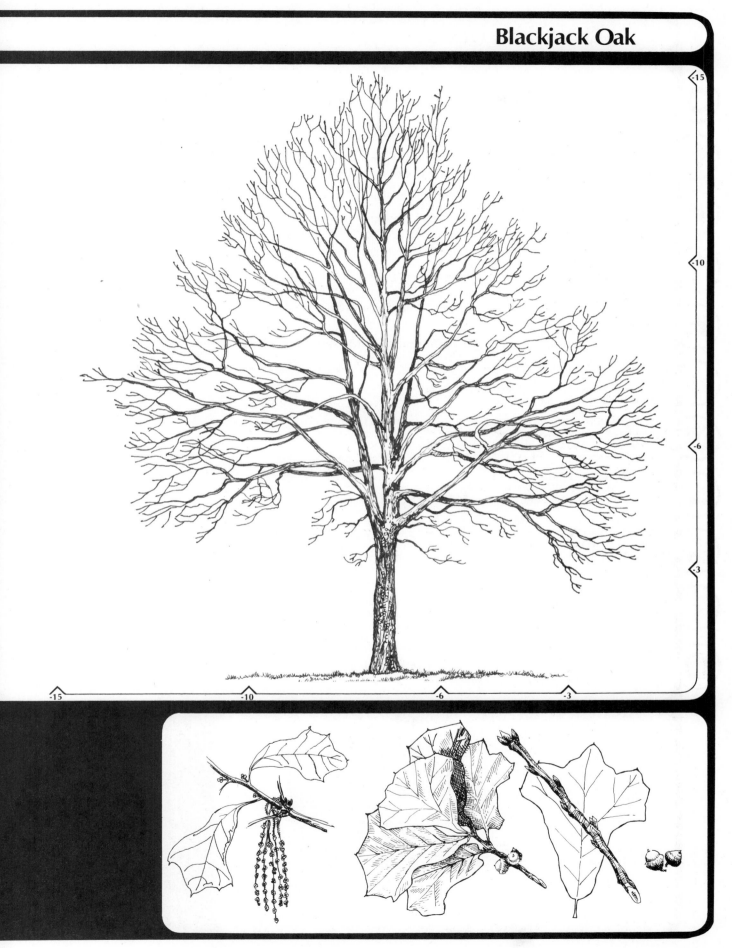

Quercus montana

FORM: globular
Size: **small canopy -** 15 to 22.5 m (50 to 75 ft)
Spread: **very wide -** 22.5 to 30 m (75 to 100 ft), usually much wider than tall
Mass: **moderate** to open

BRANCHING: trunk forking shortly above ground, large **ascending** limbs, high arching crown, **coarse** texture
Twig: stout, **red brown**
Bud: **clustered, sharp pointed** end buds, slightly hairy, chestnut brown
Bark: **deeply furrowed** with broad rounded ridges; dark reddish **brown** becoming **black**

FOLIAGE: alternate, **simple, obovate-oblong obovate**, shallow undulate margin, **medium coarse** texture
Surface: **glossy**, thick, leathery, pale green or silvery white beneath
Color: spring - bright **yellow green;** summer - **dark green;** autumn - dark crimson **red**
Season: **deciduous;** emergence - mid **May**, drop - mid **November**

FLOWER: slender, drooping male **catkins,** 7.5 to 10 cm (3 to 4 in) long
Color: light **yellow green**
Season: mid through late **May,** usually appearing after the leaves unfold
Sex: monoecious

FRUIT: elliptic **acorn,** 25 to 38 mm (1 to 1 1/2 in), cap enclosing one half of length
Color: **tan brown** and glossy
Season: **September through** early **October**
Wildlife Value: **very high;** songbirds, upland ground birds, small mammals, hoofed browsers

HABITAT: formation - **forest**, region - **central;** gradient - **upland dry;** sandy or gravelly upland ridges, steep rocky land
Shade Tolerance: **intermediate;** index range 4.0-5.9
Flood Tolerance: **intolerant**

SOIL; Texture: **coarse** dry sandy or gravelly loams, **to fine** heavy loams, clays, silt loams
Drainage: **moderately poor to well**
Moisture: tolerates **average to dry**
Reaction: **slightly acid,** pH 6.1-6.5

HARDINESS: zone 5a
Rate: **slow -** 6 m (20 ft) in 20 year period
Longevity: **long -** maturity reached between 200 and 300 years

SUSCEPTIBILITY; Physiological: **infrequent**
Disease: **frequent -** oak wilt, twig blight, canker fungi, shoestring root rot
Insect: **frequent -** Ambrosia beetle, resistant to borers, carpenterworms, cankerworms
Wind-Ice: **infrequent**

URBAN TOLERANCE; Pollution:
Lighting: **intermediate**   Drought-Heat: **resistant**   Mine Spoils: **resistant**
Salt: **resistant**   Soil Compaction: **sensitive**
Root Pattern: deep **taproot;** difficult to transplant, move B&B in early spring

SPECIES; Associate: Red Pine, Scarlet, Post, Bear and Southern Red Oaks, Pitch and Virginia Pines, Eastern Redcedar, Mountain-Laurel, Tuliptree, Black Tupelo
Similar: Sawtooth Oak (Asiatic), Chinkapin Oak is smaller
Cultivars: none available commercially

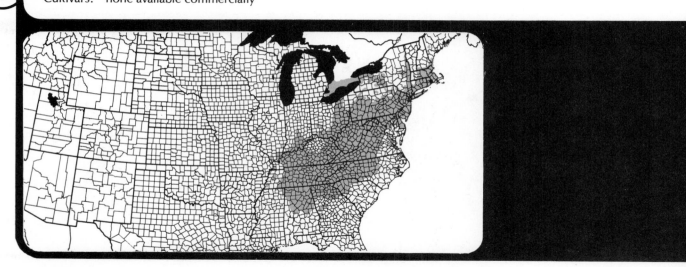

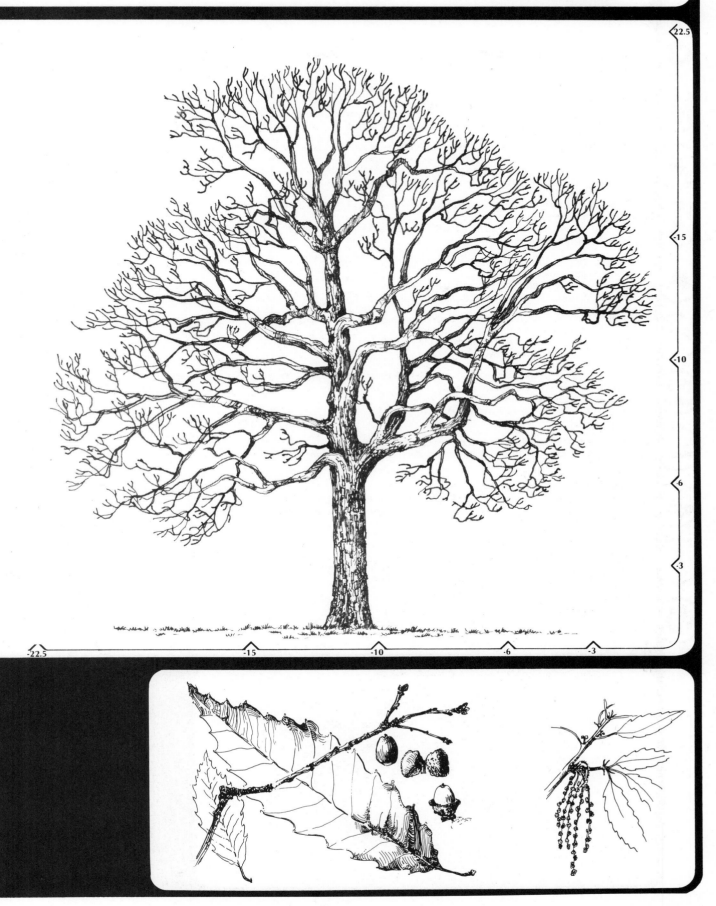

Quercus muhlenbergi

FORM: irregular-globular
Size: **large understory -** 10 to 15 m (35 to 50 ft)
Spread: **intermediate -** 10 to 15 m (35 to 50 ft), as wide as tall
Mass: **open**

BRANCHING: short irregularly **ascending** branches, **medium** texture
Twig: slender, **gray brown**
Bud: **clustered sharp pointed** conical end buds, chestnut brown
Bark: thin loose **scaly** or shallow furrowed with short flaky ridges; ashy gray tinged with brown

FOLIAGE: alternate, **simple, obovate-oblong obovate,** sharp coarse teeth, **medium** texture
Surface: **dull,** lower surface pale silvery white and short hairy
Color: spring - embrionic leaf fuzzy **pink;** summer - **yeilow green;** autumn - golden **yellow brown**
Season: **deciduous;** emergence - early **May,** drop - mid **October**

FLOWER: male in singular pendulous **catkins,** 7.5 to 10 cm (3 to 4 in) long
Color: **yellow green**
Season: early through mid **May,** with or soon after leaves unfold
Sex: monoecious

FRUIT: **acorn,** 13 to 19 mm (1/2 to 3/4 in) long, approximately half enclosed by cap
Color: **tan brown**
Season: early **September through** early **October**
Wildlife Value: **very high;** upland ground birds, songbirds, hoofed browsers, small mammals

HABITAT: formation - **savanna;** region - **central;** gradient - **upland dry;** dry banks of streams, rocky limestone bluffs
      above streams, clay or rocky ridgetops
Shade Tolerance: **intolerant;** index range 2.0-3.9
Flood Tolerance: **very intolerant**

SOIL; Texture: shallow soils over sandstone or limestone, **moderately coarse to moderately fine** sandy loams
Drainage: **well to excessive**
Moisture: tolerates **dry to droughty**
Reaction: **neutral to alkaline,** pH 6.6-8.0

HARDINESS: zone 4b
Rate: **slow -** 6 m (20 ft) in 18 to 25 year period
Longevity: **long -** maturity reached between 150 and 200 years, shorter lived than other upland oaks

SUSCEPTIBILITY; Physiological: **infrequent**
Disease: **infrequent -** oak wilt, Anthracnose, not particularly serious
Insect: **frequent -** leaf miners, twig pruner, acorn weevils, gypsy moth, orange striped oak worm
Wind-Ice: **infrequent**

URBAN TOLERANCE; Pollution:
Lighting: Drought-Heat: **resistant**   Mine Spoils: **resistant**
Salt: **resistant**   Soil Compaction: **sensitive**
Root Pattern: **deep** coarse **laterals;** difficult to transplant, move B&B in early spring

SPECIES; Associate: Post, Black, Blackjack Oaks, Pignut, Mockernut Hickories, Black Cherry, Black Walnut,
      American Linden, American Elm, White Ash, Common Hoptree, Hawthorns
Similar: Sawtooth Oak and Chestnut Oak become large canopy trees
Cultivars: none available commercially

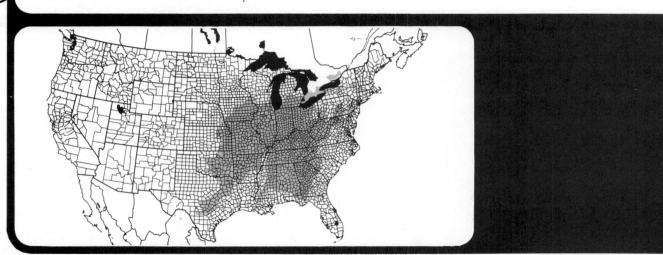

Chinkapin Oak

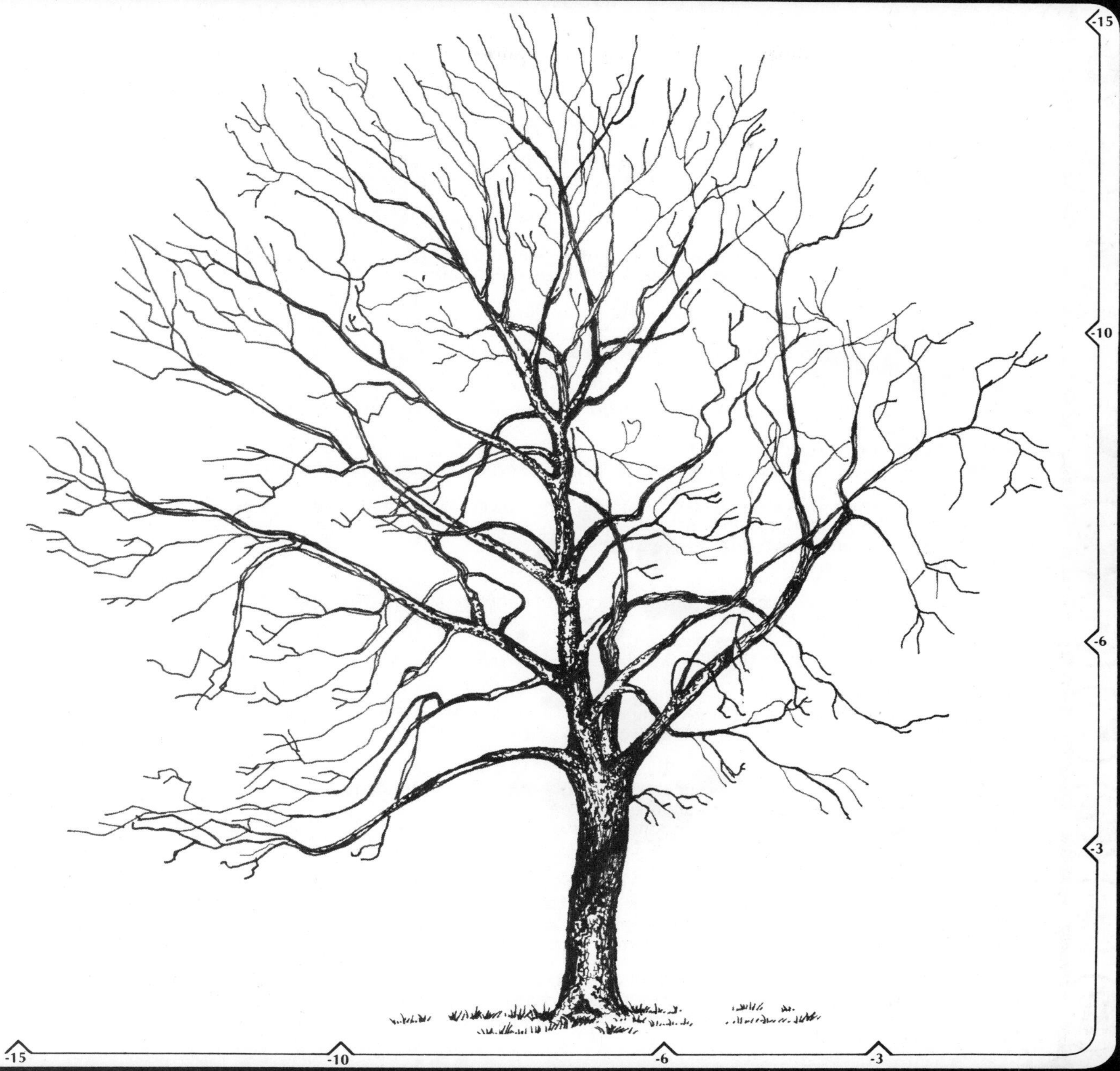

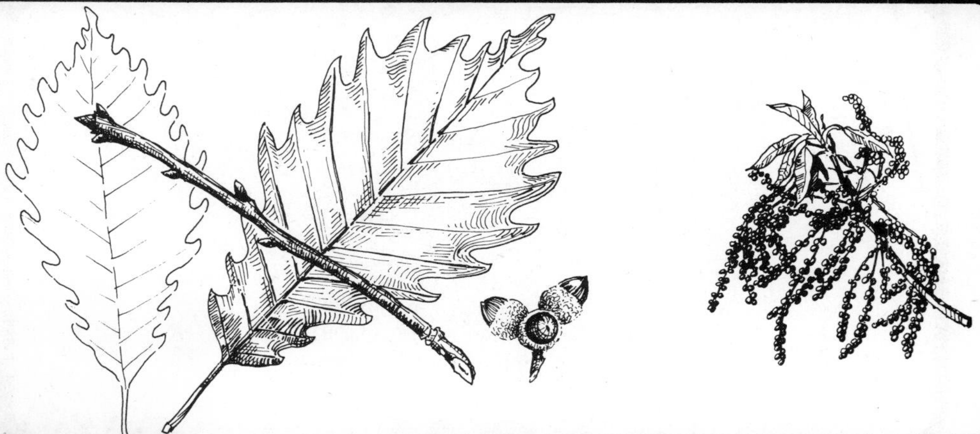

Quercus palustris

FORM: **conical**, old trees high crowned shedding lower limbs
Size: **small canopy** - 15 to 22.5 m (50 to 75 ft)
Spread: **wide** - 15 to 22.5 m (50 to 75 ft), 2/3 that of height
Mass: **moderate**

BRANCHING: single trunk, small side branches, lower limbs **descending** frequently sweeping ground, **medium** texture
Twig: slender (for oak), smooth, **green becoming red brown**
Bud: **clustered sharp pointed** end buds, side buds at right angle, red brown
Bark: **smooth** or with shallow fissures and low knobby tight fitted ridges; **black** with reflective ashy gray ridges

FOLIAGE: alternate, **simple, pinnately lobed**, deep open sinuses, bristle tipped, **medium fine** texture
Surface: very **glossy**, pale beneath
Color: spring - light **maroon green**; summer - **dark green**; autumn - late, deep scarlet **red**
Season: deciduous - **persistent**; emergence - early **May**, drop - dried leaves persist **through February**

FLOWER: male in drooping **catkins,** 5 to 7.5 (2 to 3 in) long
Color: **yellow green**
Season: early through mid **May,** with or shortly after leaves unfold
Sex: monoecious

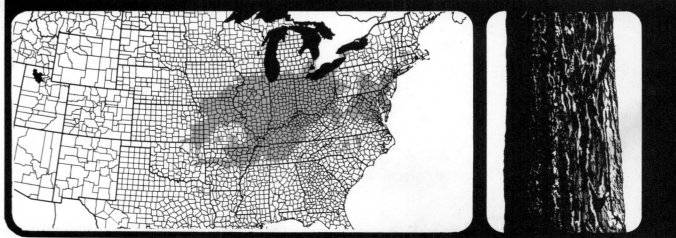

FRUIT: short squat flattened dome shaped **acorn,** 13 mm (1/2 in) long, cap covering base only
Color: red brown
Season: **September through** early **October**
Wildlife Value: **very high;** waterbirds, songbirds, upland ground birds, small mammals, hoofed browsers

HABITAT: formation - **forest;** region - **central;** gradient - **lowland wet and wet-mesic;** second bottoms, alluvial flats, occasional to upland open sites
Shade Tolerance: **intolerant;** index range 2.0-3.9
Flood Tolerance: **tolerant**

SOIL; Texture: **moderately coarse to fine;** prefers hard compact clay soils, silty clay loams
Drainage: **poor to well**
Moisture: **demands wet,** tolerates **average**
Reaction: **moderately acid to slightly acid,** pH 5.5-6.5, intolerant of high neutral and alkaline soils

HARDINESS: **zone 5a**
Rate: **medium to fast;** one of faster growing oaks, 9 m (30 ft) in 12 to 15 year period
Longevity: **medium -** maturity reached between 125 and 175 years

SUSCEPTIBILITY; Physiological: **frequent -** iron chlorosis causes severe damage
Disease: **infrequent -** oak wilt, Dothiorella canker, oak blister, oak rust
Insect: **infrequent -** relatively free, galls, pin oak sawfly
Wind-Ice: **infrequent**

URBAN TOLERANCE; Pollution: **resistant -** SO_2; intermediate - O_3, HFl, 2,4-D; sensitive - HCl,
Lighting: Drought-Heat: **resistant**   Mine Spoils: **resistant**
Salt: **resistant**   Soil Compaction: **resistant**
Root Pattern: **shallow** fibrous without a distinct taproot; easily transplanted, move B&B in early spring or autumn

SPECIES; Associate: pure stands, Swamp White Oak, Shingle and Bur Oaks, Pecan, River Birch, Eastern Poplar, American Sweetgum, Black Willow, Common Honeylocust, elms
Similar: Scarlet Oak, Northern Pin Oak; Swamp White Oak exhibits most similar cultural requirements
Cultivars: none available commercially

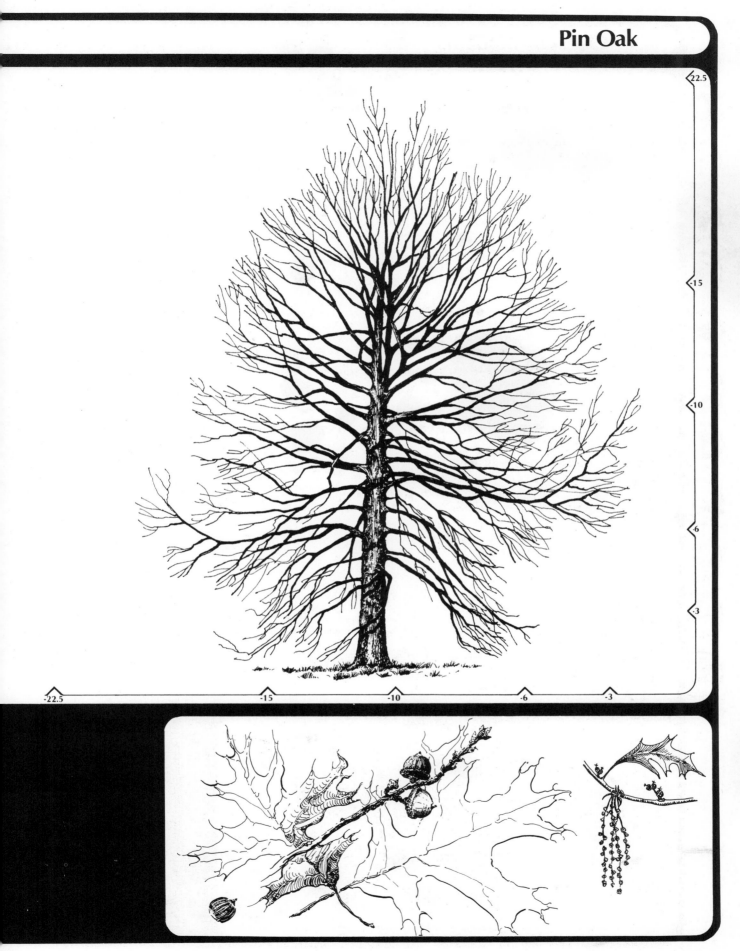

22.5

-15

-10

-6

-3

-22.5   -15   -10   -6   -3

Quercus stellata

FORM: **globular**
Size: **large understory -** commonly larger - 10 to 15 m (35 to 50 ft)
Spread: **intermediate -** 10 to 15 m (35 to 50 ft) plus, as wide or wider than tall
Mass: **open**

BRANCHING: widespread **horizontal** massive **picturesque** twisted limbs, **coarse** texture
Twig: more or less **velvety,** stout, **reddish to orange**
Bud: **clustered blunt** 13 mm (1/2 in) long buds, lightly hairy
Bark: **deeply furrowed** into broad rectilinear ridges with narrow tight scales; **gray** to **reddish brown**

FOLIAGE: alternate, **simple, pinnately lobed,** prominently 3 lobed resembling a "cross", **medium coarse** texture
Surface: **glossy,** thick leathery, paler gray or silvery **tomentose** beneath
Color: spring - dark **red;** summer - deep **dark green;** autumn - golden **yellow brown**
Season: **deciduous;** emergence - early **May,** drop - early **November**

FLOWER: staminate in drooping **catkins,** 7.5 to 10 cm (3 to 4 in) long
Color: **yellow green**
Season: mid **May through** early **June,** shortly following leaf emergence
Sex: monoecious

FRUIT: dome shaped **acorn,** 13 to 19 mm (1/2 to 3/4 in), cup encloses 1/3 to 1/2 of nut
Color: light **brown** to nearly black
Season: **September through** early **October**
Wildlife Value: **very high;** songbirds, upland ground birds, small mammals, hoofed browsers

HABITAT: formations - **forest, savanna;** region - **central;** gradient - **upland dry;** sandy ridges, dry rocky hillsides,
    southern slope exposure
Shade Tolerance: **intolerant;** index range 2.0-3.9
Flood Tolerance: **very intolerant**

SOIL; Texture: **coarse** gravelly-sandy loams of low organic content, sandy plains, **to moderately fine** clay loams
Drainage: **moderately poor to well**
Moisture: tolerates **dry to droughty**
Reaction: **strongly acid to slight acid,** pH 4.6-6.5

HARDINESS: zone 5b
Rate: **slow -** generally between 15 to 22.5 cm (6 to 9 in) annually
Longevity: **long -** maturity at 200 to 300 years, commonly surviving 400 years

SUSCEPTIBILITY; Physiological: **infrequent**
Disease: **frequent -** oak wilt, chestnut blight, smooth patch
Insect: **frequent -** flag worms, gall wasp, nut weevils
Wind-Ice: **infrequent**

URBAN TOLERANCE; Pollution:
Lighting: **intermediate**   Drought-Heat: **resistant**   Mine Spoils: **resistant**
Salt: **resistant**   Soil Compaction: **sensitive**
Root Pattern: **taproot** with several **deep** spreading **laterals;** transplant small trees B&B in early spring

SPECIES; Associate: Black Oak, Scarlet Oak, Chestnut Oak, Blackjack Oak, Shingle Oak and Chinkapin
    Oak, Rusty Blackhaw Viburnum, Eastern Redbud, Eastern Redcedar, Shagbark Hickory, hawthorn species, sumac
Similar: Bur and White Oaks, English Oak (European)
Cultivars: none available commercially

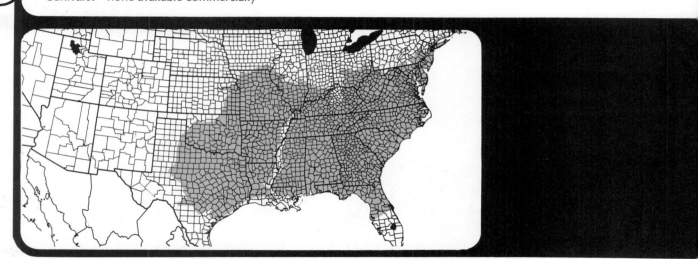

Quercus velutina

FORM: ovoid, commonly **globular**
Size: **large canopy -** 22.5 to 30 m (75 to 100 ft)
Spread: **very wide -** 22.5 to 30 m (75 to 100 ft), commonly 3/4 that of height
Mass: **moderate**

BRANCHING: symmetrical **ascending** limbs, **medium** texture
Twig: lenticels conspicuous, moderately stout, **red brown**
Bud: **clustered sharp pointed** end buds, pale **woolly**, strongly 5 sided
Bark: mature trunks **shallow** to deeply **furrowed, black ,** upper trunk developing **wide** flat ridges, ashy gray

FOLIAGE: alternate, **simple, pinnately lobed,** shallow to moderately deep sinuses, bristle tips, **medium coarse** texture
Surface: **glossy**, pale yellow green beneath
Color: spring - bright crimson **red;** summer - **dark green;** autumn - **yellow to** golden **yellow brown**
Season: deciduous - **persistent;** emergence - early to mid **May,** drop - mid **October**

FLOWER: staminate in drooping **catkins,** 7.5 to 10 cm (3 to 4 in) long
Color: **yellow green**
Season: mid through late **May,** shortly after leaf emergence
Sex: monoecious

FRUIT: elliptic **acorn,** 19 mm (3/4 in), cap encloses 1/2 to 3/4 of nut, scales slightly fringed and hairy
Color: light red **brown**
Season: **September through** early October
Wildlife Value: **very high;** upland ground birds, songbirds, small mammals, hoofed browsers

HABITAT: formation - **forest, savanna;** region - **central;** gradients - **upland mesic-dry and dry;** clay and gravelly ridges, sand
dunes, sand ridges, barren lands, also common on middle and upper slopes
Shade Tolerance: **intermediate;** index range 6.0-7.9
Flood Tolerance: **very intolerant**

SOIL; Texture: **coarse** sands and gravels, sandy loams **to fine** clay, heavy loams
Drainage: **moderately well to excessively** drained soils
Moisture: prefers **moist,** tolerates **droughty** conditions
Reaction: **slightly acid,** pH 6.1-6.5

HARDINESS: zone 4b
Rate: **medium -** 60 cm (2 ft) per year slowing with maturity
Longevity: **medium -** maturity at 150 to 200 years, shorter lived than Northern Red Oak

SUSCEPTIBILITY; Physiological: **infrequent**
Disease: **frequent -** oak wilt, canker, leaf blister, rust, twig blights
Insect: **frequent -** various galls, scales, two lined chestnut borer, leaf miner
Wind-Ice: **infrequent**

URBAN TOLERANCE; Pollution: **sensitive -** 2,4-D; **intermediate -** O_3, HFl
Lighting: Drought-Heat: **resistant** Mine Spoils: **resistant**
Salt: **resistant** Soil Compaction: **sensitive**
Root Pattern: deep **taproot,** some widespreading and **deep lateral** roots; difficult to transplant, move B&B in early spring

SPECIES; Associate: Northern Pin, Bur, Post, Blackjack, Scarlet and Chestnut Oaks; Pitch, Virginia and Shortleaf
Pines; Eastern Redcedar, Tuliptree, White Ash, Black Locust, hickories
Similar: Northern Red Oak demands moist soils
Cultivars: none available commercially

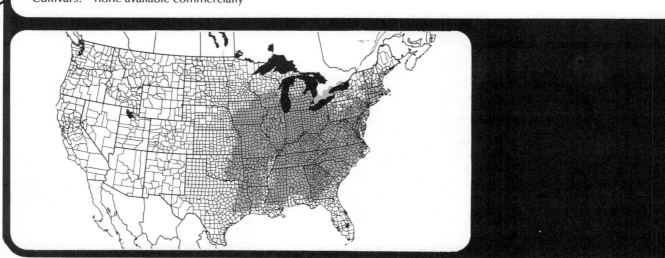

Black Oak

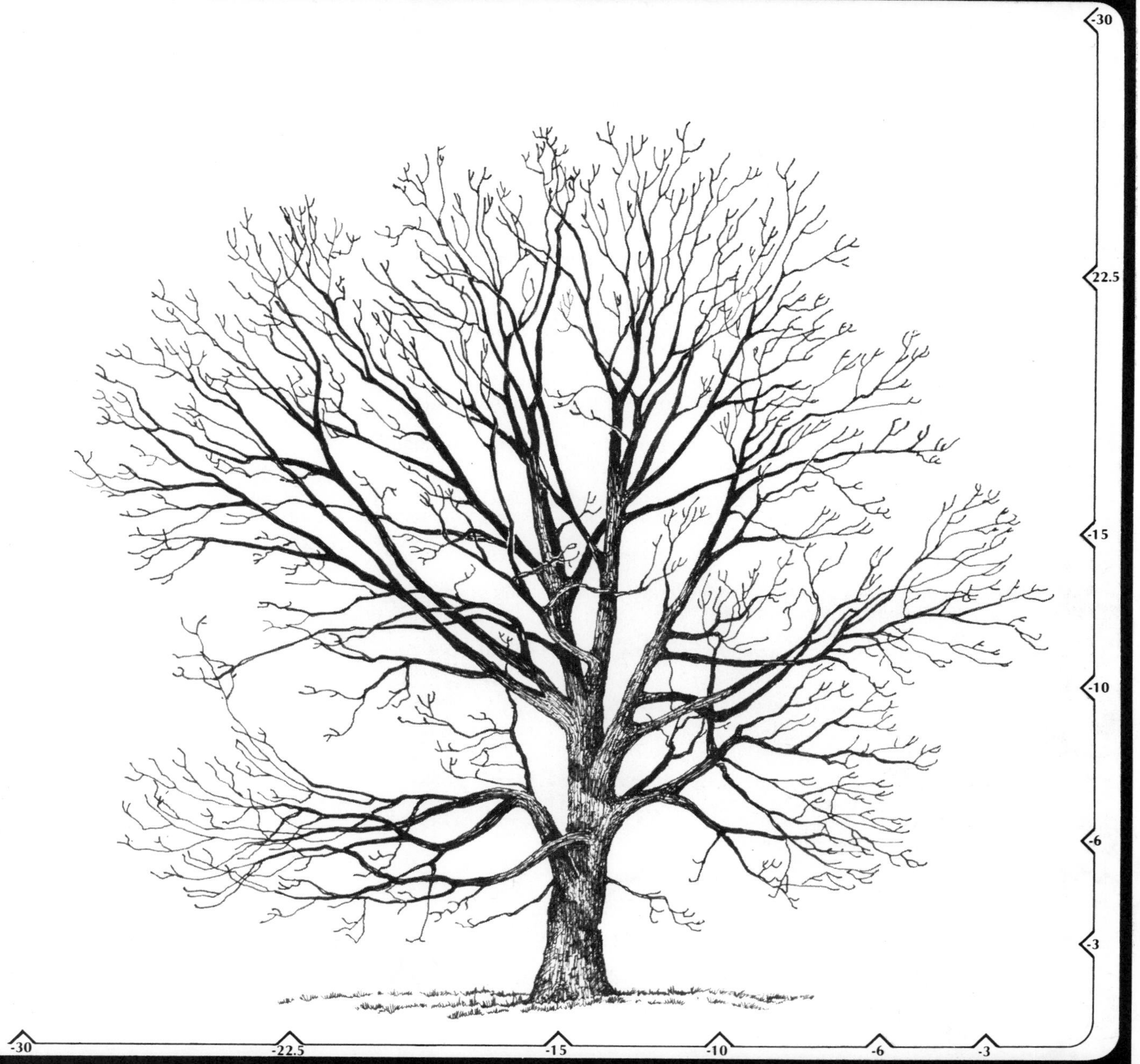

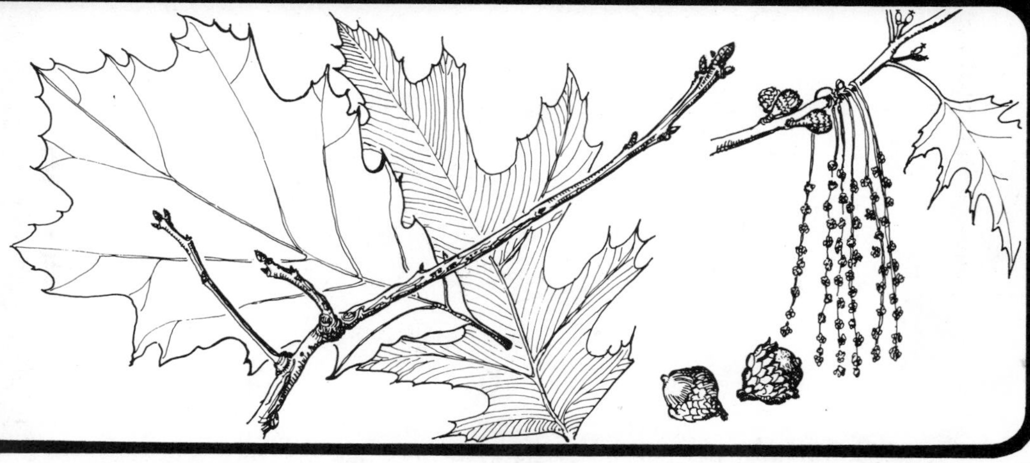

Rhododendron maximum

FORM: obovoid-irregular
Size: **small understory -** 6 to 10 m (20 to 35 ft)
Spread: **narrow -** 6 to 10 m (20 to 35 ft), commonly 3 to 6 m, 1/3 to 1/2 the height
Mass: **open**

BRANCHING: short multiple inclined trunks, **picturesque upright,** forms thickets, **coarse** texture
Twig: stout, velvety, dark green becoming **red brown**
Bud: **large papery** flower buds, 25 to 38 mm (1 to 1 1/2 in) long
Bark: **scaly,** broken into thin flakes; **red brown**

FOLIAGE: alternate, **simple, oblong-obovate,** entire, edges rolled, **coarse** texture
Surface: **glossy,** leathery, stiff, somewhat tomentose, and whitish beneath
Color: all seasons - dark **blue green;** spring growth - **light green**
Season: broadleaf **evergreen**

FLOWER: large **bell shaped** bloom, 25 mm (1 in) across, terminal clusters of 16-24
Color: rose **pink to lavender** or white, upper lobe with yellow spots on inside
Season: mid through late **June,** after the leaves
Sex: monoecious

FRUIT: elongate **capsules,** 13 mm (1/2 in) long, occasionally resinous
Color: **tan brown** to red brown
Season: **September through** mid **November,** often persisting throughout winter
Wildlife Value: **very low;** songbirds, small mammals

HABITAT: formation - **forest;** region - **central;** gradient - **lowland wet, wet mesic, upland mesic;** cool mountain slopes,
moist woods, sheltered coves, steep banks along streams, cold swamps in north
Shade Tolerance: **tolerant;** index range 6.0-7.9
Flood Tolerance: **tolerant**

SOIL; Texture: moderately fine to moderately coarse; sandy or gravelly loams, silt loams
Drainage: **moderately poor to well**
Moisture: **moist to average**
Reaction: prefers **strongly acid to moderately acid,** pH 4.5-6.0, does not like lime soils

HARDINESS: zone 3b
Rate: **medium -** generally 30 to 46 cm (12 to 18 in) annually
Longevity: **medium**

SUSCEPTIBILITY; Physiological: frequent - chlorosis in high pH soils, winter injury
Disease: **frequent -** Botryosphaeria canker, bud and twig blights, crown rot, dieback, root rot, many others
Insect: **frequent -** azalea stem borer, azalea leaf miner, a host of others
Wind-Ice: **infrequent -** strong and resistant

URBAN TOLERANCE; Pollution: intermediate - HFl
Lighting: Drought-Heat: **sensitive**   Mine Spoils: **sensitive**
Salt: extremely **sensitive**   Soil Compaction: **sensitive**
Root Pattern: **shallow** fibrous **laterals;** transplants readily B&B as small plant in early spring

SPECIES; Associate: pure stands, Striped, Sugar, and Mountain Maples, Flowering Dogwood, Butternut,
Tuliptree, Eastern Arborvitae, Canada Hemlock, Mountain Laurel, Common Witch-hazel
Similar: Catawba Rhododendron is related but smaller, Mountain Laurel
Cultivars: 'Album' - white flowers, 'Purpureum' - deep purple flowers

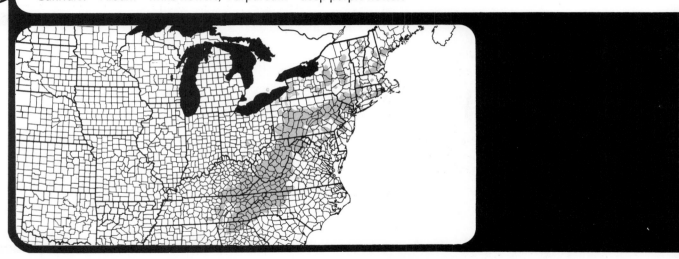

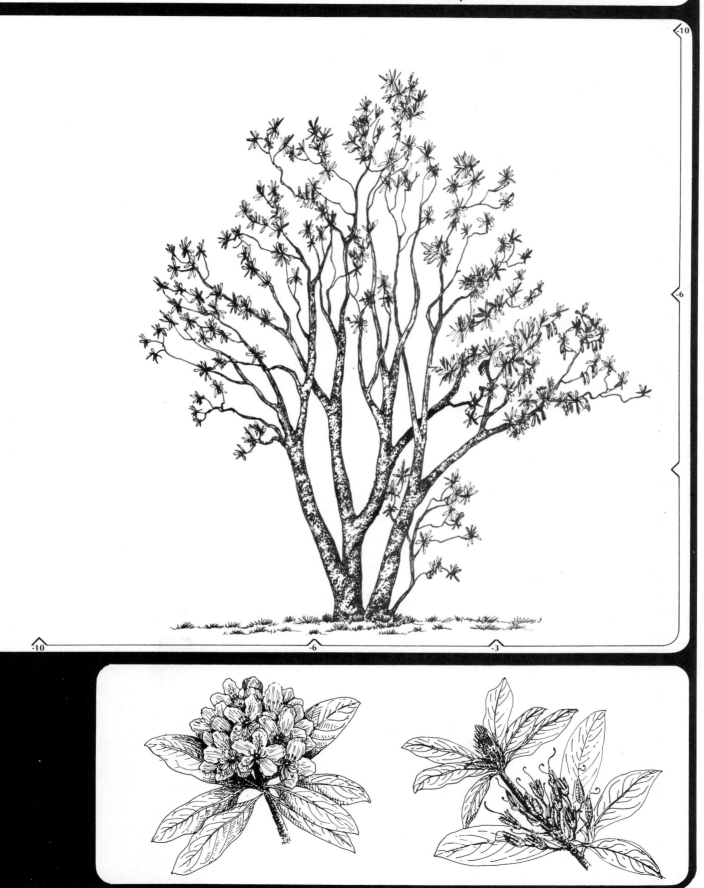

Rhus copallina

FORM: **irregular-obovoid**
Size: **small understory -** 6 to 10 m (20 to 35 ft)
Spread: **narrow -** 6 to 10 m (20 to 35 ft), as wide or wider than tall
Mass: **open,** dense in youth

BRANCHING: short crooked leaning trunks with few **leggy** branches, forming large colonies, **coarse** texture
Twig: stout, **large leaf scars** often hairy to smooth, **red**
Bud: small, leaf scar encircling bud, **woolly**
Bark: **smooth** with conspicuous raised dot-like lenticels, becoming scaly at maturity; silvery **gray**

FOLIAGE: alternate, **pinnately compound,** 9 to 21 leaflets, **lanceolate,** winged leaf stalk, **medium fine** texture
Surface: **glossy,** fuzzy beneath
Color: spring - **dark green;** summer - **dark green;** autumn - scarlet to crimson **red**
Season: **deciduous;** emergence - late **May,** drop - early **October**

FLOWER: erect **pyramidal spike,** 10 to 20 cm (4 to 8 in) tall, dense
Color: **yellowish green**
Season: mid through late **July**
Sex: **dioecious**

FRUIT: small globular woolly **berry** in dense erect pyramidal spikes, 10 to 20 cm (4 to 8 in) tall, terminal
Color: bright **red**
Season: persisting through winter, **August through March**
Wildlife Value: **high;** songbirds, upland ground birds, small and large mammals

HABITAT: formation - **savanna;** region - **central;** gradient - **upland dry;** old fields, prairies, warm dry ridges, dry rocky open
hillsides, fencerows, dry open woods, margin of woods
Shade tolerance: **very intolerant;** index range 0-1.9, demands full sun
Flood Tolerance: **intolerant**

SOIL; Texture: almost any soil, **coarse to fine**
Drainage; **moderately well to excessive**
Moisture: **average to droughty**
Reaction: **slightly acid to neutral;** pH 6.1-7.0

HARDINESS: **zone 5a**
Rate: **fast -** 1 to 1.2 m (3 to 4 ft) annually
Longevity: **short -** 15 to 25 years, rarely survives 50 years; long lived root system perpetuates colony

SUSCEPTIBILITY; Physiological: **infrequent**
Disease: **infrequent**
Insect: **infrequent**
Wind-Ice: **frequent -** windthrow, brittle twigs

URBAN TOLERANCE; Pollution:
Lighting: **sensitive**   Drought-Heat: **resistant**   Mine Spoils: **resistant**
Salt: **resistant**   Soil Compaction: **sensitive**
Root Pattern: **shallow** widespreading, coarse; transplants readily B&B or BR in any season with care

SPECIES; Associate: pure stands, Prairie Crabapple, Smooth Sumac, Black Cherry, Common Chokecherry, Blackhaw and
Rusty Blackhaw Viburnum, Bur, Post, and Blackjack Oaks, Eastern Redcedar, hawthorns
Similar: Smooth Sumac is related, smaller
Cultivars: none available commercially

Rhus glabra

FORM: irregular-obovoid
Size: **small understory** - 6m (20 ft) maximum, commonly 3 to 6 m (10 to 20 ft)
Spread: **narrow** - 6 to 10 m (20 to 35 ft), as wide or wider than tall
Mass: **open**

BRANCHING: short crooked leaning trunks, **leggy** branches, forms broad colonies, **coarse** texture
Twig: **large leaf scars**, smooth, **red** to purplish with bluish **bloom**
Bud: small ovoid, **dome shaped, leaf scar encircling bud**
Bark: **smooth** with conspicuous raised dot-like lenticels, thin becoming scaly with age; **gray**

FOLIAGE: alternate, **pinnately compound**, 9-27 leaflets, **oblong lanceolate**, coarsely toothed, **medium fine** texture
Surface: **glossy**, whitish beneath
Color: spring - **bright green;** summer - **dark green;** autumn - flame or scarlet **red**
Season: **deciduous;** emergence - late **May,** drop - early **October**

FLOWER: erect **pyramidal spikes,** 7.5 to 12.5 (3 to 5 in) tall, dense
Color: **yellow green**
Season: early through mid **July**
Sex: **dioecious**

FRUIT: small globe-shaped hairy **berry** in dense erect pyramidal spikes, at ends of branches
Color: **red** with bright crimson hairs
Season: persist throughout winter, early **September through March**
Wildlife Value: **high;** songbirds, upland ground birds, small and large mammals, hoofed browsers

HABITAT: formation - **savanna;** region - **northern, central;** gradient - **upland dry;** vigorous invader of upland prairie, abandoned fields, woods edge, waste areas, sandy plains, open rocky hillsides, bluffs
Shade Tolerance: **very intolerant;** index range 0-1.9, demands full sun
Flood Tolerance: **intolerant**

SOIL; Texture: vigorous growth in most soils from **coarse** sandy and gravelly loam **to fine** heavy clays
Drainage: **moderately well to excessive**
Moisture: **average to droughty**
Reaction: **slightly acid to neutral,** pH 6.1-7.0

HARDINESS: **zone 2**
Rate: **fast** - 60 to 90 cm (24 to 36 in) per year plus
Longevity: **short** - 10 to 15 years, rarely survives 30 years; long lived root system perpetuates colony

SUSCEPTIBILITY; Physiological: **infrequent**
Disease: **infrequent** - none serious
Insect: **infrequent** - aphids, scale have been noted
Wind-Ice: **frequent** - heavy snows and high winds cause blow down

URBAN TOLERANCE; Pollution: **intermediate** - HFl; **resistant** - SO$_2$
Lighting: **sensitive**   Drought-Heat: **resistant**   Mine Spoils: **resistant**
Salt: **resistant**   Soil Compaction: **sensitive**
Root Pattern: **shallow** widespreading, new stems from root suckers; easily transplanted B&B or BR in any season

SPECIES; Associate: pure stands, Eastern Redcedar, Sassafras, Common Persimmon, Black Cherry, Post, Black and Bur Oaks, American Plum, Prairie Crabapple, hawthorns, viburnums, filbert
Similar: Flameleaf Sumac is related
Cultivars: none commerically obtainable

320

Rhus typhina

FORM: **irregular-obovoid**
Size: **large understory** - 10 to 15 cm (35 to 50 ft)
Spread: **intermediate** - 10 to 15 m (35 to 50 ft), equal to height
Mass: **open**

BRANCHING: multiple trunks, spreading into extensive colonies, **leggy,** high umbrella crown, **coarse** texture
Twig: very stout, densely covered with dark **velvety** hairs, **large leaf scars, red brown**
Bud: small roundish, **woolly,** surrounded by leafscar
Bark: **smooth** with conspicuous raised dot-like lenticels, becoming scaly with age; gray

FOLIAGE: alternate, **pinnately compound,** 11 to 31 leaflets, **oblong lanceolate,** sharply toothed **medium** texture
Surface: **dull,** velvety **tomentose** beneath
Color: spring - **yellow green;** summer - **medium green;** autumn - golden **yellows, orange** to bright **red**
Season: **deciduous;** emergence - late **May,** drop - early **October**

FLOWER: upright **pyramidal spike,** 5 to 30 cm (6 to 12 in) tall, dense
Color: **yellowish green**
Season: late **June through** early **July**
Sex: **dioecious**

FRUIT: small globe shaped velvety **berries** in dense erect pyramidal spikes, terminal
Color: bright **red**
Season: persisting through winter, mid **August through** late **March**
Wildlife Value: **high;** songbirds, upland ground birds, small and large mammals, hoofed browsers

HABITAT: formation - **savanna;** region - **northern;** gradient - **upland dry;** open woods, rocky hillsides, open pastures, margin
of woods, creek banks, waste ground, common in limestone areas
Shade Tolerance: **very intolerant;** index range 0-1.9, demands full sun
Flood Tolerance: **intolerant**

SOIL; Texture: almost any soil, **coarse** sandy and gravelly loams **to fine** heavy clays
Drainage: **moderately well to excessive**
Moisture: **average to droughty**
Reaction: **slightly acid or neutral;** pH 6.1-7.0

HARDINESS: **zone 3a**
Rate: **fast** - 1 to 2 m (3 to 7 ft.) annually
Longevity: **short** - rarely survives 50 years; long lived root system perpetuates colony

SUSCEPTIBILITY; Physiological: **infrequent**
Disease: **infrequent** - Verticillium wilt is most serious
Insect: **infrequent**
Wind-Ice: **frequent** - heavy snow, ice and wind cause wind throw, also brittle stems

URBAN TOLERANCE; Pollution: **sensitive** - SO_2; **intermediate** - HFl
Lighting: **sensitive**   Drought-Heat: **resistant**   Mine Spoils: **resistant**
Salt: **resistant**   Soil Compaction: **sensitive**
Root Pattern: **shallow** widespreading, produces new stems from root suckers; transplants readily B&B in any season

SPECIES; Associate: pure stands, Prairie Crabapple, Common Chokecherry, Black Cherry, American Plum, Eastern
Redcedar, Pin Cherry, Bur, Black and Northern Pin Oaks, Quaking Aspen, viburnums, hawthorns
Similar: other sumacs, Tree of Heaven Ailanthus (Asiatic)
Cultivars: 'Laciniata' and 'Disecta' - fine lacy dissected foliage

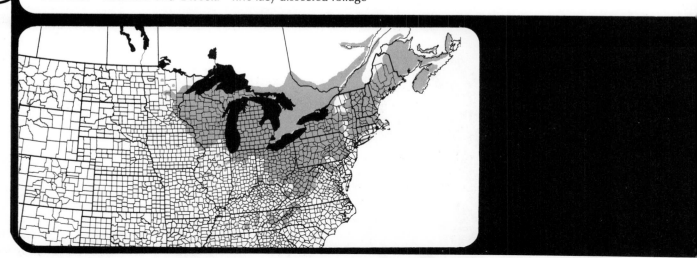

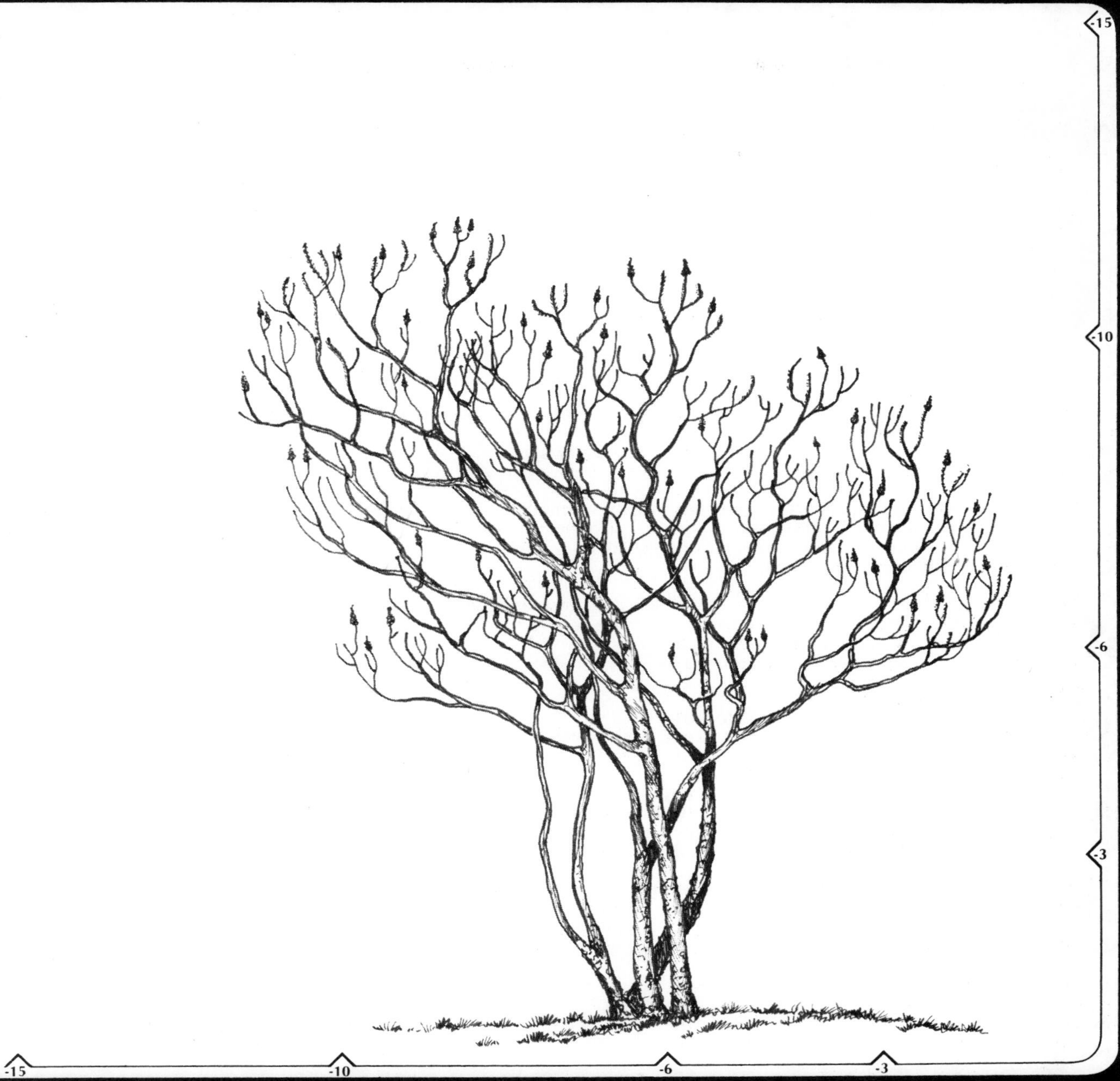
-15
-10
-6
-3
-15
-10
-6
-3

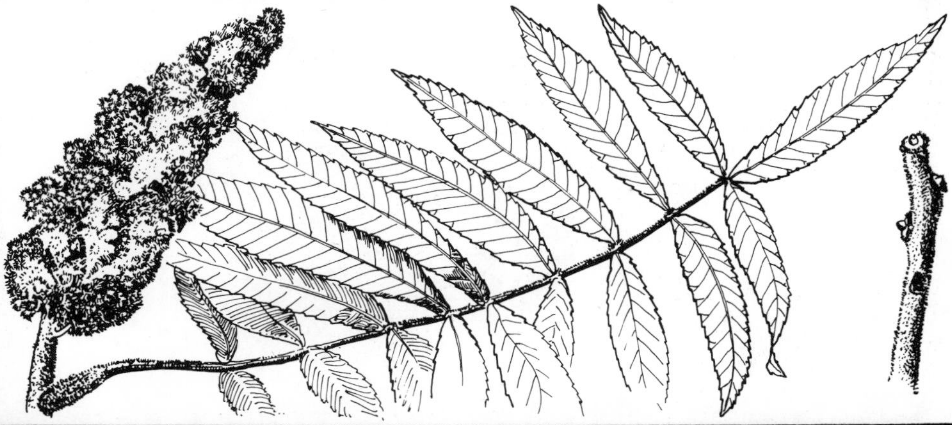

Robinia pseudoacacia

FORM: **irregular, columnar**
Size: **small canopy -** 15 to 22.5 m (50 to 75 ft)
Spread: **intermediate -** 10 to 15 m (35 to 50 ft), commonly narrower, 1/4 to 1/3 the height
Mass: **open**

BRANCHING: **ascending,** tendency to fork and be crooked and limby, **coarse** texture
Twig: **zig zag,** somewhat angular, **longitudinal lines, red brown; armed** with straight, spiny paired prickles
Bud: minute, rusty brown
Bark: **deeply furrowed** with convex rounded ridges, fibrous; **red brown** to black

FOLIAGE: alternate, **pinnately compound,** 7-19 leaflets, **elliptic-oval,** entire margin, **fine** texture
Surface: **dull**
Color: spring - light **blue green;** summer - **dark blue green;** autumn - **yellow green to yellow**
Season: **deciduous;** emergence - late **May;** drop - late **September**

FLOWER: dense **pyramidal spikes,** 20 to 30 cm (8 to 12 in) long, pea-like blossom, 2.5 cm (1 in) across
Color: creamy **white**
Season: early through mid **June,** after leaf emergence
Sex: **dioecious**   **Fragrant:** extremely sweet

FRUIT: **legume,** 5 to 10 cm (2 to 4 in) long, flat paper thin pod, blunt rounded at tip
Color: **tan brown**
Season: persists through winter, **September until March**
Wildlife Value: **very low**

HABITAT: formation - **forest, savanna;** region - **central;** gradient - **upland dry;** borders of forest, south and west slope
aspects, open pasture, erosion control plantings
Shade Tolerance: **intolerant;** index range 2.0-3.9
Flood Tolerance: **intolerant**

SOIL; Texture: **coarse to moderately fine;** silt loams, sandy loams, limestone soils, poor growth on clay
Drainage: **moderately well to well,** tolerates **excessive**
Moisture: **average to dry,** tolerates **droughty**
Reaction: **moderately acid through alkaline,** pH range 5.1-7.7

HARDINESS: **zone 3b**
Rate: very **fast -** 60 to 90 cm (2 to 3 ft) annually
Longevity: **short -** 50 to 75 years, rarely survives 100 years

SUSCEPTIBILITY; Physiological: **infrequent**
Disease: **infrequent -** canker, powdery mildew, wood decay, witches' broom, dampening off
Insect: **frequent -** locust borer, carpenterworm, locust twig borer, locust leaf miner
Wind-Ice: **frequent -** weak wooded, brittle, breakage to major limbs, windfall

URBAN TOLERANCE; Pollution: **sensitive -** O_3, NOx; **intermediate -** HFl; **resistant -** SO_2
Lighting: **sensitive**   Drought-Heat: **resistant**   Mine Spoils: **resistant**
Salt: **resistant**   Soil Compaction: **sensitive**
Root Pattern: **shallow** fibrous, prolific root suckering forms colony, easily transplanted B&B in early spring

SPECIES; Associate: Eastern Redcedar, Scarlet, Bear, Black and Chestnut Oaks, Pignut Hickory, and in mesic dry coves
with Tuliptree
Similar: Commom Honeylocust
Cultivars: 'Aurea' - new leaves yellow, 'Decaisneana' - pinkish flowers, 'Semperflorens' - flowers throughout summer

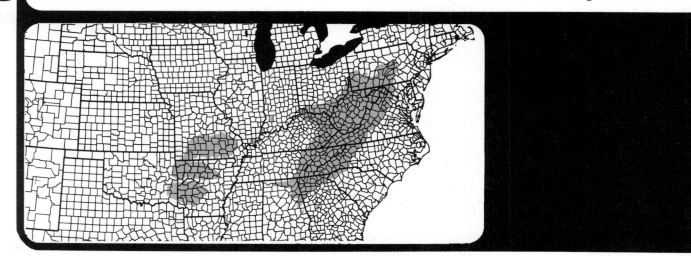

Black Locust

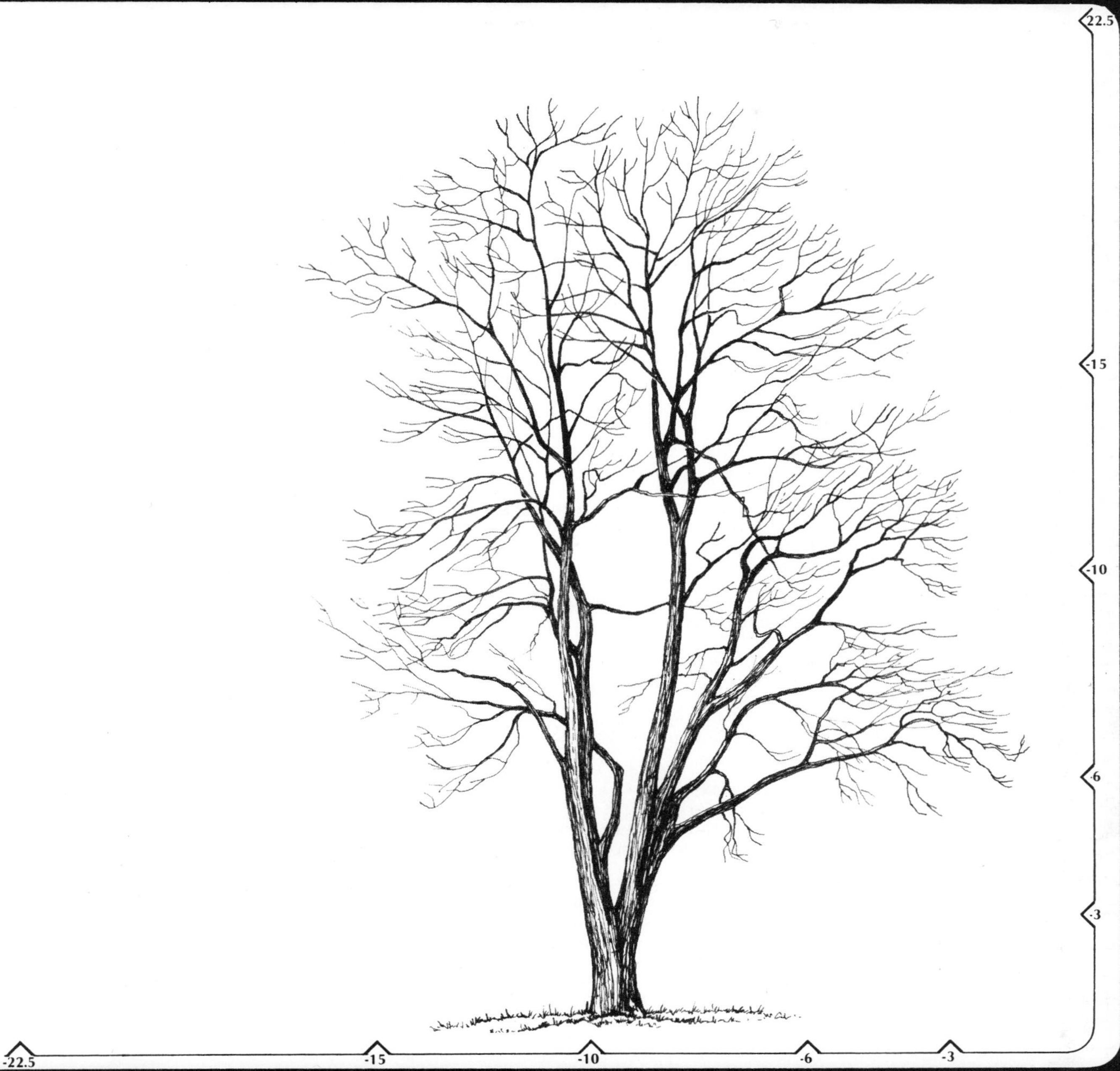

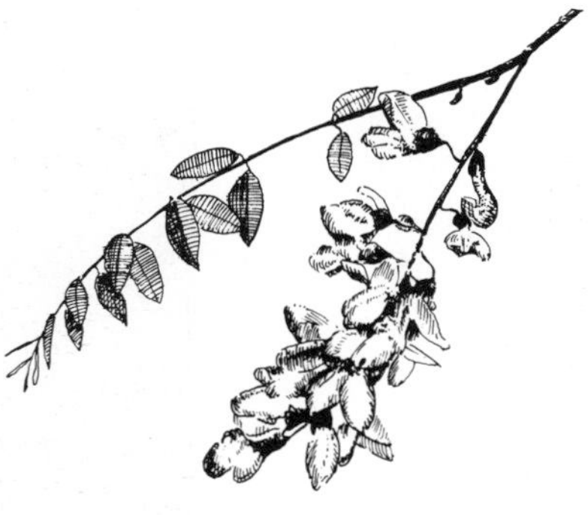

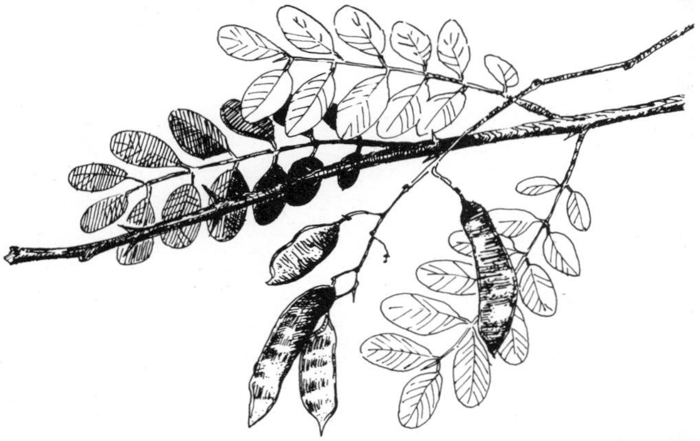

Salix amygdaloides

FORM: columnar
Size: **large understory -** 10 to 15 m (35 to 50 ft)
Spread: **intermediate -** 10 to 15 m (35 to 50 ft)
Mass: **open**

BRANCHING: multiple leaning trunks, **upright or ascending,** branchlets drooping, **fine** texture
Twig: slender, glossy, flexible, bright **orange** or **yellow** colored
Bud: **one scale,** crescent shaped, hugs twig, glossy, brown
Bark: **shallow** to **deeply furrowed,** irregular, **wide flat ridges,** shaggy appearance; **red brown**

FOLIAGE: alternate, **simple, lanceolate-oblong lanceolate,** fine toothed, twisted petiole, **medium** texture
Surface: **glossy,** whitened beneath, somewhat leathery
Color: spring - **light green;** summer - **light green;** autumn - pale **yellow green**
Season: **deciduous;** emergence - late **March,** drop - late **October**

FLOWER: **catkin,** 2.5 cm (1 in) long
Color: **yellow green**
Season: **March,** before leaf emergence
Sex: **dioecious**

FRUIT: **strobile,** 2.5 cm (1 in)
Color: **green to yellow**
Season: mid **April through** early **May**
Wildlife Value: **high;** early season harvest for songbirds, waterfowl, small mammals

HABITAT: formation - **savanna;** region - **northern, central;** gradient - **lowland wet and wet-mesic;** along streams, lake
margin, farm ponds, sloughs, oxbows
Shade Tolerance: **very intolerant;** index range 0-1.9
Flood Tolerance: **very tolerant**

SOIL; Texture: coarse to fine; sand, gravel, loamy sands, silt loams, silty clay loam
Drainage: **very poor to moderately poor**
Moisture: **wet to moist**
Reaction: **neutral,** pH 6.6-7.5

HARDINESS: zone 3a
Rate: **fast -** generally 1 to 1.5 m (3 to 5 ft) per year
Longevity: **short -** rarely survives 75 years

SUSCEPTIBILITY; Physiological: infrequent
Disease: **frequent -** fungus scab, black canker, Cytospora canker, twig and leaf blight, leaf spot, crown gall, others
Insect: **frequent -** willow sawfly, willow lacebug, poplar borer, willow scurfy scale; many others
Wind-Ice: **frequent -** weak wooded, brittle, most adult trees exhibit some damage

URBAN TOLERANCE; Pollution: sensitive - SO_2, O_3; **resistant -** HFl
Lighting: Drought-Heat: **resistant** Mine Spoils: **resistant**
Salt: **resistant** Soil Compaction: **resistant**
Root Pattern: **shallow** fibrous, extensive; readily transplanted B&B or BR in spring

SPECIES; Associate: pure stands, Boxelder, Silver Maple, Green Ash, Eastern Poplar, American Elm,
Common Hackberry, Black Willow, other willows
Similar: Missouri or Black Willow, White Willow (European)
Cultivars: none available commercially

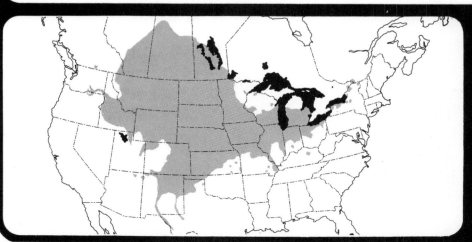

326

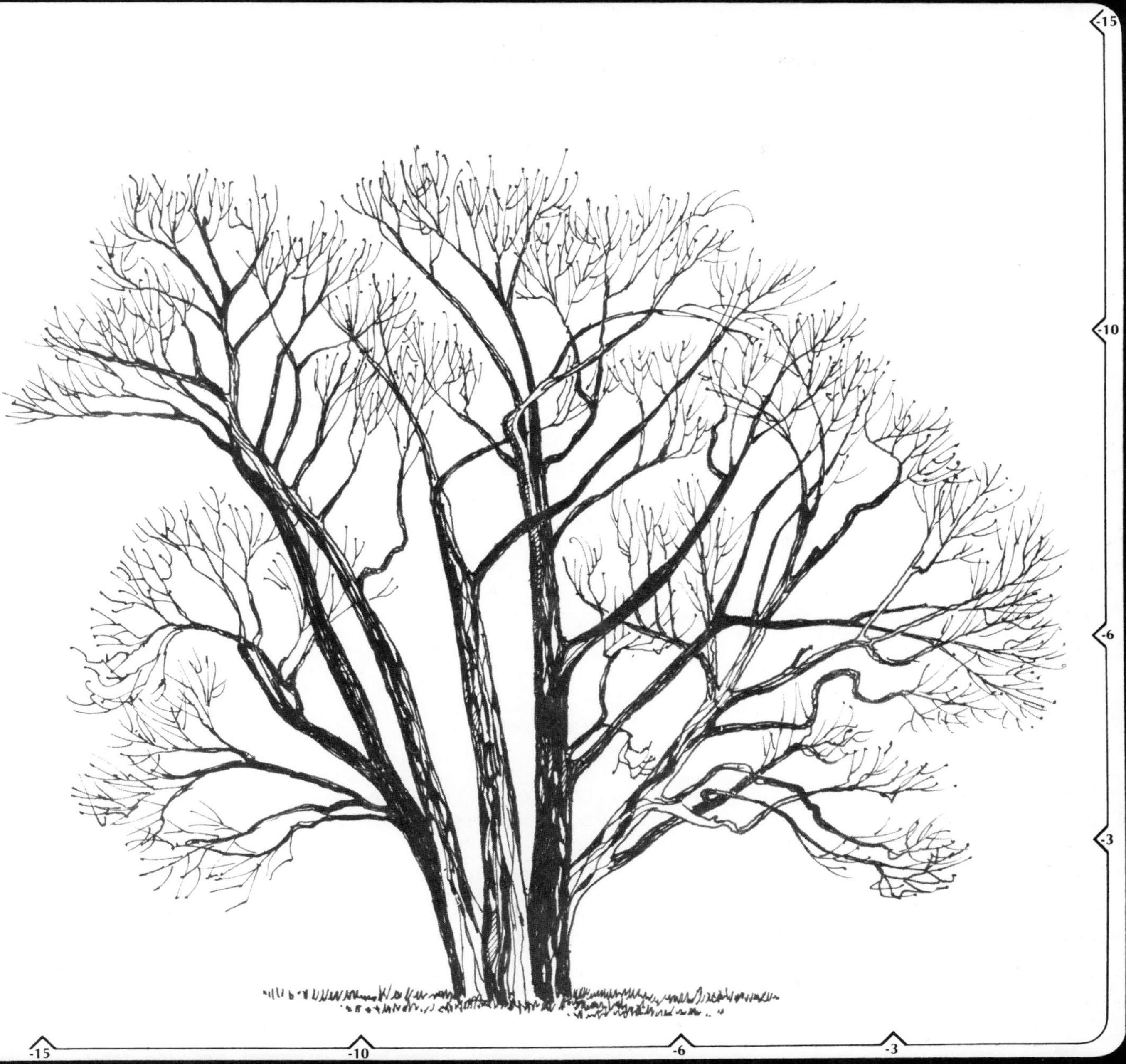
-15
-10
-6
-3
-15
-10
-6
-3

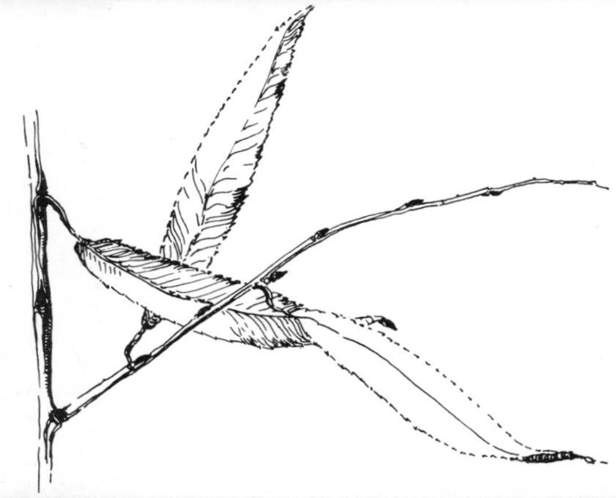

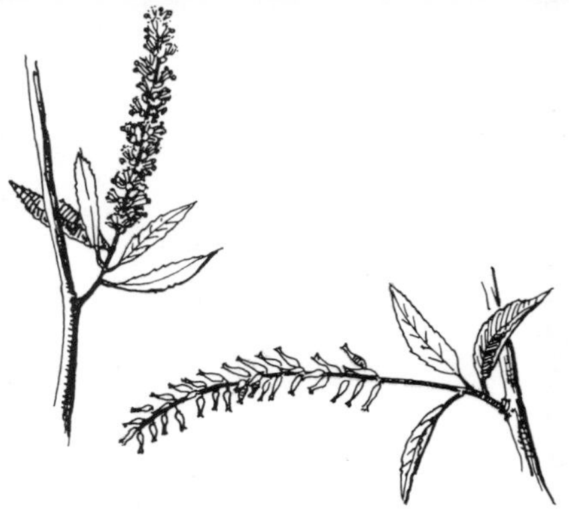

Salix bebbiana

FORM: columnar
Size: **small understory -** 6 to 10 m (20 to 35 ft)
Spread: **narrow -** 6 to 10 m (20 to 35 ft), commonly 3 to 6 m, 1/3 the height
Mass: **moderate**

BRANCHING: one to multiple trunks, **upright leggy, fine** texture
Twig: velvety to smooth, **green** with **gray** hairs
Bud: **one scale,** incurved buds hug twigs
Bark: **smooth,** irregularly scaly with age; **green, maroon purple** to red brown

FOLIAGE: alternate, **simple, obovate-oblong obovate,** coarsely toothed, commonly entire, **medium fine** texture
Surface: **dull,** grayish **tomentose** and veiny beneath
Color: spring - **silvery gray;** summer - **medium green;** autumn - pale **yellow green**
Season: **deciduous;** emergence - early **April,** drop - early **October**

FLOWER: stiff **catkin,** 25 mm (1 in) long
Color: **yellow green**
Season: mid **March through** early **April,** before leaf emergence
Sex: **dioecious**

FRUIT: **strobile,** 25 cm (1 in) long, releasing minute seeds with long tufted silky white hairs
Color: **green to yellow**
Season: **May through** early **June**
Wildlife Value: **high;** songbirds, waterfowl, small mammals

HABITAT: formation - **savanna;** region - **northern;** gradient - **lowland wet, wet mesic;** river margins, lake margin, swamp, bog, common to dryer upland sites and gullies
Shade Tolerance: **very intolerant;** index range 0-1.9
Flood Tolerance: **very tolerant**

SOIL; Texture: **coarse to fine;** virtually any soil
Drainage: **very poor to moderately poor**
Moisture: **wet to moist**
Reaction: **neutral,** pH 6.6-7.5

HARDINESS: zone 2
Rate: **fast -** between 1 to 1.8 m (3 to 6 ft) per year
Longevity: **short -** mature in 25 years; rarely survives 50 years

SUSCEPTIBILITY; Physiological: **infrequent**
Disease: **frequent -** bacterial twig blight, leaf blight, black canker, many other cankers, leaf spot, powdery mildew, others
Insect: **frequent -** pine cone gall, mottled willow borer, poplar borer, willow shoot sawfly, others
Wind-Ice: **frequent -** weak wooded, brittle

URBAN TOLERANCE; Pollution: **sensitive -** SO$_2$, O$_3$; **resistant -** HFl
Lighting: Drought-Heat: **resistant**   Mine Spoils: **resistant**
Salt: **resistant**   Soil Compaction: **resistant**
Root Pattern: **shallow** fibrous, extensive; easily transplanted B&B or BR in any season with care

SPECIES: Associate: pure stands, other willows, Eastern Poplar, Hazel Alder, American Mountain Ash, Boxelder, Quaking and Bigtooth Aspen, Balsam Poplar
Similar:
Cultivars: none available commercially

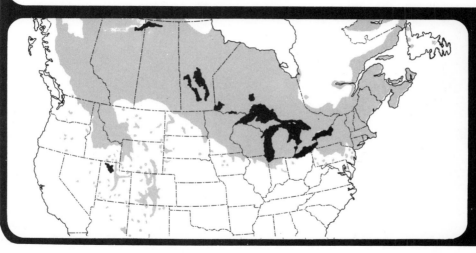

-10

-6

-3

-10   -6   -3

Salix discolor

FORM: columnar
Size: **small understory** - 6 to 10 m (20 to 35 ft)
Spread: narrow - 6 to 10 m (20 to 35 ft), commonly 3 to 6 m, 1/4 to 1/3 the height
Mass: **moderate**

BRANCHING: multiple trunks, **upright leggy, fine** texture
Twig: stout, smooth, glossy, bright **green or red** becoming dark brown
Bud: **one scale,** incurved buds hug twig, bright **green to red** or purplish
Bark: **smooth,** old trunks, irregularly scaly; **red brown** to gray brown

FOLIAGE: alternate, **simple, elliptic-oval,** toothed mostly above middle, **medium** texture
Surface: **dull,** whitened beneath
Color: spring - **light lime green;** summer - **medium green;** autumn - pale **yellow green**
Season: **deciduous;** emergence - early **April,** drop - early **October**

FLOWER: **catkin,** 25 mm (1 in) long, furry appearance
Color: **silvery gray**
Season: late **February through March** before leaf emergence, harbinger of spring
Sex: **dioecious**

FRUIT: **strobile,** 25 mm (1 in) long, releasing minute seeds with long tufted white hairs
Color: **green to yellow**
Season: mid **April through** early **May**
Wildlife Value: **high;** early season harvest for songbirds, waterfowl, small mammals

HABITAT: formation - **savanna;** region - **northern;** gradient - **lowland wet, wet-mesic;** river margins, low lying lakeshore, swamp and bog, swales
Shade Tolerance: **very intolerant;** index range 0-1.9
Flood Tolerance: **very tolerant**

SOIL; Texture: **coarse to fine;** sand, gravel, sandy loams, fine silt loams, silty clay loams
Drainage: **very poor to moderately poor**
Moisture: **wet to moist**
Reaction: **neutral,** pH 6.6-7.5

HARDINESS: **zone 2**
Rate: **fast** - generally 1.2 to 1.8 m (4 to 6 ft) annually
Longevity: **short** - maturity in 20 years, few survive 50 years

SUSCEPTIBILITY; Physiological: **infrequent**
Disease: **frequent** - twig and leaf blight, several cankers, gray scab, powdery mildew, rust; many others
Insect: **frequent** - aphids, several galls, willow lacebug, willow borer, scale and other insects
Wind-Ice: **frequent** - weak wooded, very brittle, stems commonly break to ground

URBAN TOLERANCE; Pollution: **sensitive** - SO_2, O_3; **resistant** - HFl
Lighting: Drought-Heat: **resistant** Mine Spoils: **resistant**
Salt: **resistant** Soil Compaction: **resistant**
Root Pattern: **shallow** fibrous, extensive; easily transplanted B&B or BR in any season with care

SPECIES; Associate: Bebb Willow, Boxelder, Hazel Alder, American Mountain Ash, Balsam Poplar, Quaking Aspen, Paper Birch, Black Ash
Similar: Goat Willow which is European
Cultivars: none available commercially

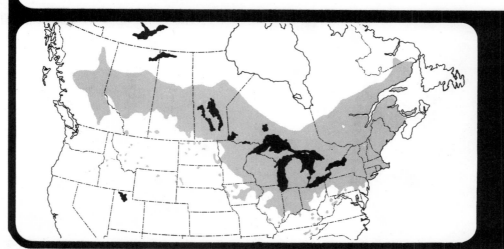

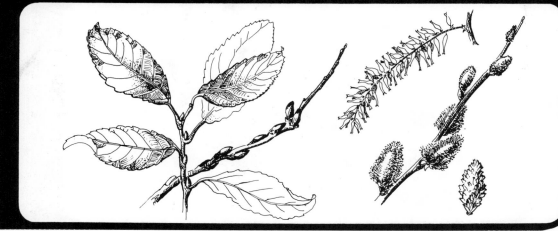

Salix nigra

FORM: **columnar**
Size: **large understory -** 10 to 15 m (35 to 50 ft)
Spread: **narrow -** 6 to 10 m (20 to 35 ft), 1/3 the height commonly
Mass: **open**

BRANCHING: straight, singular or multiple trunks, high crowned, **ascending** limbs, **fine** texture
Twig: slender, glossy, smooth, flexible, bright **green yellow**
Bud: buds hug twig, incurved, **single** bud **scale,** bright **yellow brown** to orange
Bark: **deep furrowed,** fibrous; **gray brown to brown black**

FOLIAGE: alternate, **simple, lanceolate-oblong lanceolate,** finely serrate margin, **medium fine** texture
Surface: **glossy**
Color: spring - **light green;** summer - **bright green;** autumn - **yellow green**
Season: **deciduous;** emergence - mid **April,** drop - late **October**

FLOWER: stiff **catkins,** 25 mm (1 in) long
Color: **yellow green**
Season: mid **March through** early **April,** before leaf emergence
Sex: **dioecious**

FRUIT: strobile, 25 mm (1 in) long, releasing minute seeds with long tufted silky white hairs
Color: **green yellow**
Season: late **April until** mid **May**
Wildlife Value: **high;** early season harvest for songbirds, waterfowl, small mammals

HABITAT: formation - **savanna;** region - **central;** gradient - **lowland wet, wet-mesic;** river margins, low lying lakeshore,
swamps, sloughs, swales, gullies
Shade Tolerance: **very intolerant;** more intolerant than any of its associates, index 1.4
Flood Tolerance: **very tolerant;** flourishing at or slightly below water level

SOIL; Texture: almost any soil, **coarse** sands and gravels, loamy sands **to fine** silt loams, silty clay loams
Drainage: **very poor to moderately poor**
Moisture: **wet to moist**
Reaction: **neutral,** pH 6.5-7.5, tolerates alkaline, pH 7.6-8.0

HARDINESS: zone 3a
Rate: very **fast -** 1 to 2 m (3 to 6 ft) annually, 10 year old trees average 15 m (50 ft) in height
Longevity: **short -** average trees mature in 55 years, few survive 85 years

SUSCEPTIBILITY; Physiological: **infrequent**
Disease: **frequent -** fungus scab and black canker cause leaf and shoot destruction
Insect: **infrequent -** willow sawfly occasionally defoliates trees
Wind-Ice: **frequent -** weak, especially subject to breakage, almost all large trees have large limbs broken off

URBAN TOLERANCE; Pollution: **sensitive -** SO_2, O_3; **resistant -** HFl
Lighting: Drought-Heat: **resistant**   Mine Spoils: **resistant**
Salt: **intermediate**   Soil Compaction: **resistant**
Root Pattern: **shallow** roots divide into a multitude of rootlets; transplants readily B&B in any season

SPECIES; Associate: pure stands - central - River Birch, American Planetree, Eastern Poplar, Boxelder, Red Mulberry,
Sandbar Willow; north - Black Spruce, Red Maple, Black Ash; south - Baldcypress, Water Tupelo, Water Locust
Similar: Peachleaf Willow, White Willow (European), other native or exotic willows
Cultivars: none available commercially

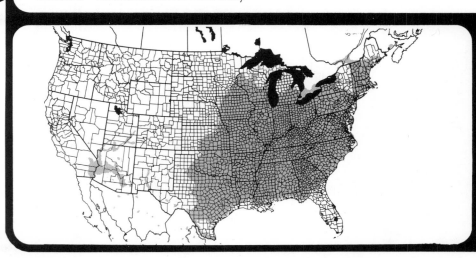

Sassafras albidum

FORM: broadly **conical, irregular**
Size: **large understory** - 10 to 15 m (35 to 50 ft)
Spread: **intermediate** - 10 to 15 m (35 to 50 ft), 2/3 the height
Mass: **open**

BRANCHING: **horizontal** cloud-like tiers, **picturesque,** broad flat topped crown, forms colonies, **medium** texture
Twig: crowded to upperside of branch, leaf scar encircling twig, bright **yellow to green;** aromatic
Bud: ovoid, **green** tinged with red
Bark: **deep furrowed,** thick corky ridges; **gray brown**

FOLIAGE: alternate, **simple, ovate-oblong ovate, palmately lobed** or unlobed, **medium fine** texture
Surface: **dull**
Color: spring and summer - **yellow green;** autumn - various **yellows, oranges, reds and purples,** dull
Season: **deciduous;** emergence - early **May,** drop - late **September**

FLOWER: **small clusters,** borne in loose drooping open spikes
Color: bright **yellow**
Season: late **April through** early **May,** before leaf emergence
Sex: **dioecious**   **Fragrant:** sweet smell

FRUIT: **berry,** 5 mm (1/5 in) across
Color: dark **blue,** fruit stem is brilliant red
Season: **August through September**
Wildlife Value: **low;** songbirds

HABITAT: formation - **forest, savanna;** region - **central;** gradient - **upland dry;** open woods, abandoned fields,
    on dry ridges and upper slopes
Shade Tolerance: **intolerant;** index range 2.0-3.9
Flood Tolerance: **very intolerant**

SOIL; Texture: **moderately coarse** sandy loams, loamy sands **to medium** loams, tolerates **fine** loamy clays and heavy clays
Drainage: **well to excessive**
Moisture: **moist to droughty**
Reaction: **acid,** pH 6.0-6.5

HARDINESS: **zone 5b**
Rate: **medium** - 45 to 60 (1 1/2 to 2 ft) long
Longevity: **short** - 50 to 75 years, rarely survives 100 years

SUSCEPTIBILITY; Physiological: **frequent** - iron chlorosis
Disease: **infrequent** - leaf spots, mildew
Insect: **infrequent** - sassafras weevil, Japanese Beetle, scale
Wind-Ice: **frequent** - weak wooded

URBAN TOLERANCE; Pollution: **sensitive** - HCl, Cl
Lighting: Drought-Heat: **resistant**   Mine Spoils: **resistant**
Salt: Soil Compaction: **sensitive**
Root Pattern: **taproot** with coarse laterals, sprouting from roots; difficult to transplant, move B&B in early spring

SPECIES; Associate: pure stands, Common Persimmon, American Sweetgum, Flowering Dogwood, American Elm,
    Eastern Redcedar, White Ash, Common Pawpaw, American Hophornbeam, American Hornbeam,
    Black Locust, Sourwood, hickories, oaks
Similar: Pagoda Dogwood, foliage texture, autumn color, fruit color, size and branching habit
Cultivars: none available commercially

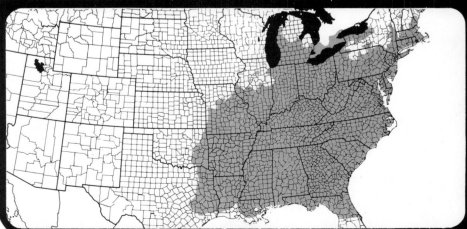

334

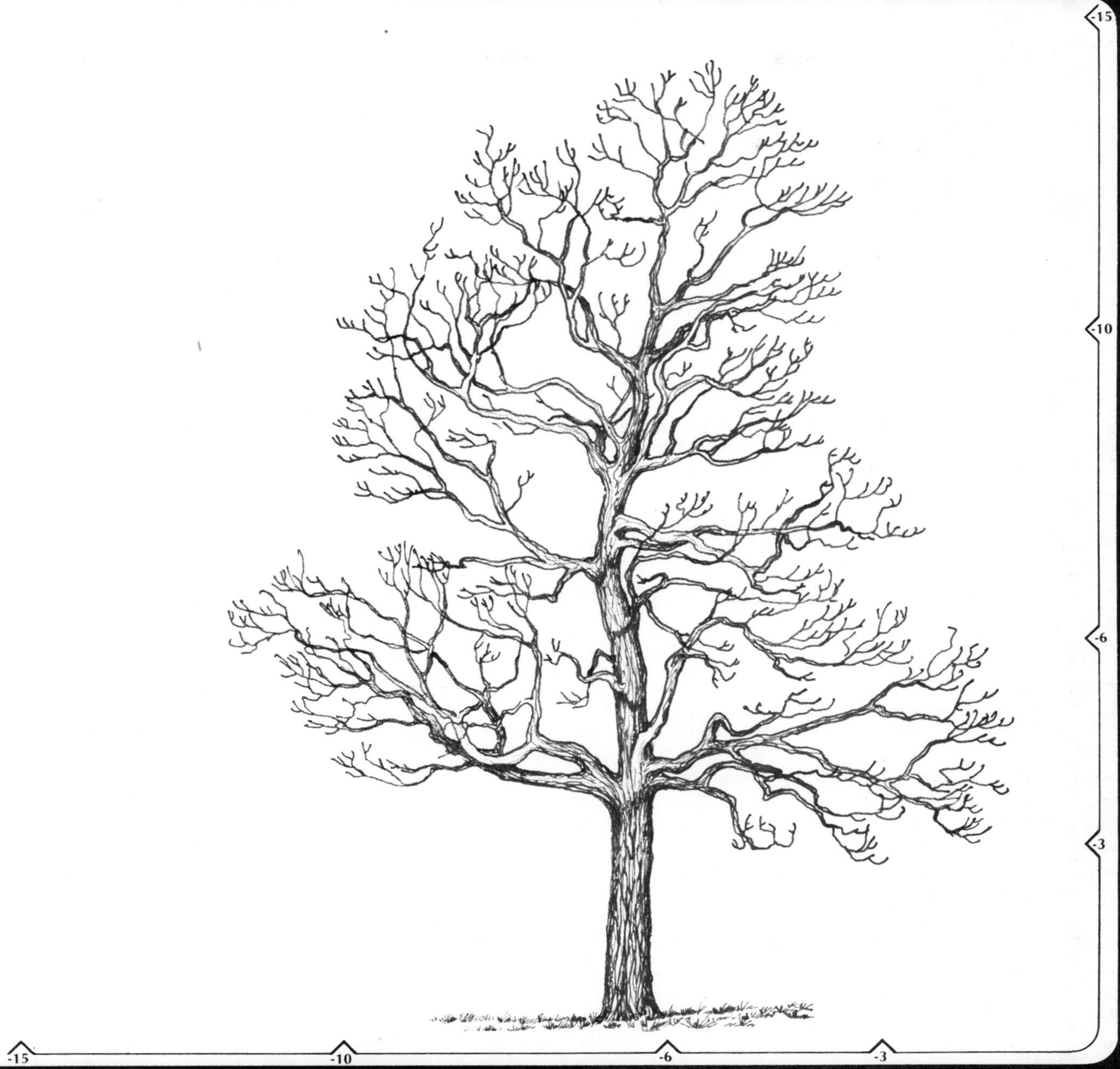

15
10
6
3
15
10
6
3

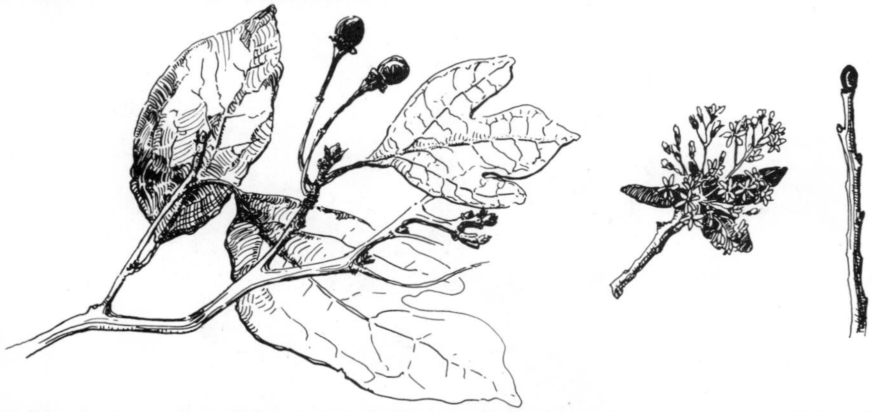

Sorbus decora

FORM: ovoid
Size: **small understory** - 6 to 10 m (20 to 35 ft), commonly larger
Spread: **narrow** - 6 to 10 m (20 to 35 ft), often less than 6 m, 2/3 to 3/4 the height
Mass: **open**

BRANCHING: branching low to ground, **ascending to upright, medium** texture
Twig: **flaky** skin weathers off, **red brown** or **yellow bronze**
Bud: narrow conical, 8 mm (1/3 in) shiny, **stalked, resinous,** hooked at tip, bright **red** to red brown
Bark: **smooth** with conspicuous horizontal lenticels, slightly scaly with age; **yellowish orange** to bronze

FOLIAGE: alternate, **pinnately compound,** 11-15 leaflets, **lanceolate-oblong lanceolate,** finely toothed, **fine** texture
Surface: **dull,** grayish beneath
Color: spring - **light green;** summer - **blue green;** autumn - golden **yellow orange, red to purple**
Season: **deciduous;** emergence - mid **May,** drop - mid **October**

FLOWER: broad **flat-topped** head up to 10 cm (4 in) across, upright terminal **clusters**
Color: **white**
Season: late **May** or early **June,** after leaves are fully grown
Sex: monoecious   **Fragrant:** sweet scented

FRUIT: globular **berry,** 1 cm (2/5 in) across, heavy drooping terminal clusters, glossy
Color: bright scarlet **red or** vermillion **orange**
Season: mid **August through** late **October**
Wildlife Value: **intermediate;** waterfowl, songbirds, small and large mammals, man

HABITAT: formation - **forest;** region - **northern;** gradient - **lowland wet and wet mesic, upland mesic;** swamps, bogs and
sites with cool air drainage, lake shore, open mesic coves, moist open rocky hillside
Shade Tolerance: **intolerant;** index range 2.0-3.9
Flood Tolerance: **tolerant**

SOIL; Texture: virtually any soil, **coarse** granular soils **to fine** clays
Drainage: **very poor to well**
Moisture: **wet to average**
Reaction: **acid to neutral,** pH range from 5.1-7.0

HARDINESS: **zone 2**
Rate: **medium** - 30 to 46 cm (12 to 18 in) annually
Longevity: **short** - 25 to 50 years, often less due to borers, protect in cool moist light shaded areas

SUSCEPTIBILITY; Physiological: **infrequent**
Disease: **frequent** - fire blight is serious, scab, cankers
Insect: **frequent** - borers are serious, crown gall, pear leaf blister mite, mountain ash sawfly, scales
Wind-Ice: **frequent** - very weak wooded

URBAN TOLERANCE; Pollution: **sensitive** - SO_2, O_3; **resistant** - HFl
Lighting: Drought-Heat: **sensitive,**   Mine Spoils: **sensitive**
Salt: **intermediate**   Soil Compaction: **intermediate**
Root Pattern: **shallow** fibrous; transplants readily B&B in early spring

SPECIES; Associate: Gray and Paper Birch, Eastern White Pine, Black Spruce, Balsam Fir, Quaking Aspen, Black Ash,
American Elm, Red Maple
Similar: American and European Mountain Ashes are related
Cultivars: many hybrids of European Mountain Ash available; 'Wilson' - columnar habit, 'Pendula' - weeping habit

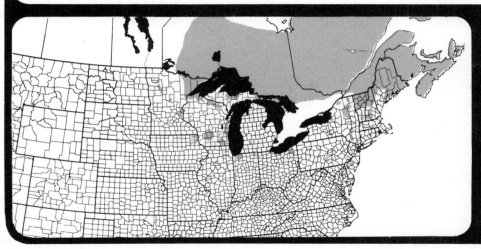

Showy Mountainash

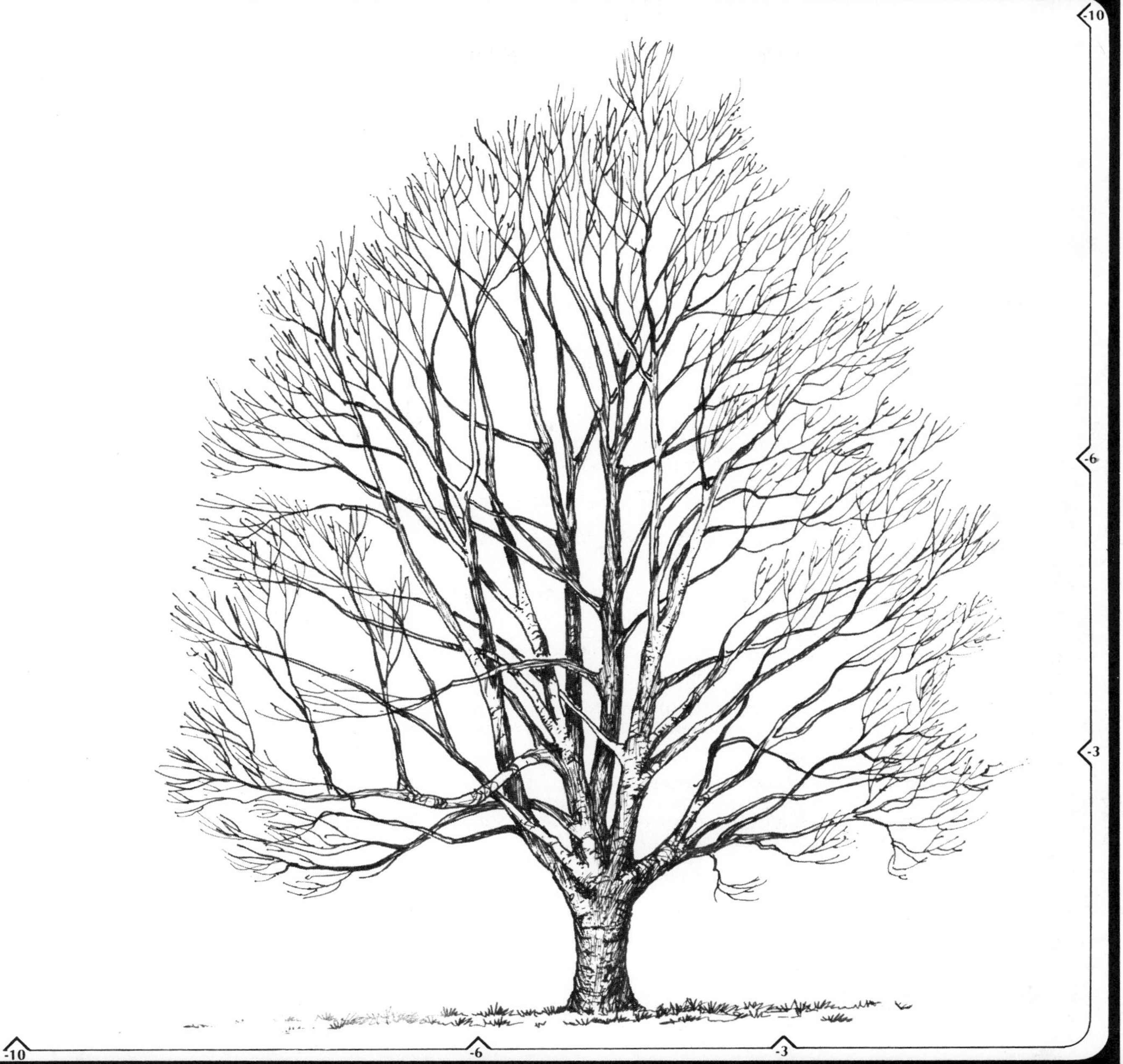

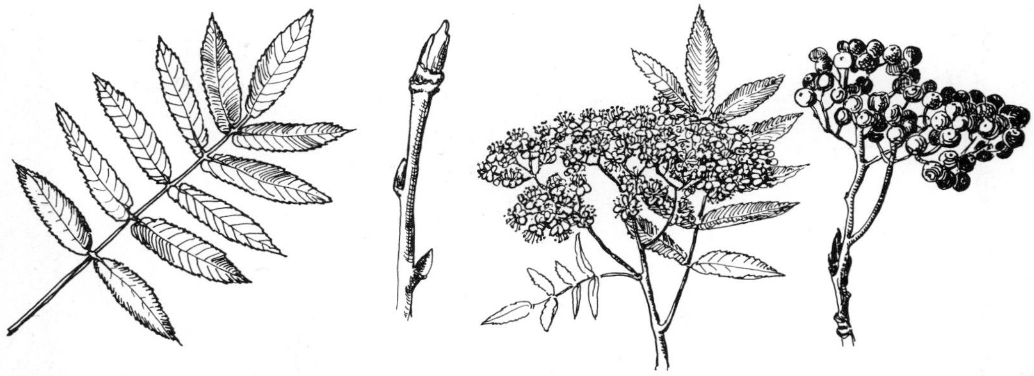

Taxodium distichum

FORM: **conical,** commonly **columnar** in youth, irregular, with extreme age, flat-topped
Size: **large canopy** - 22.5 to 30 m (75 to 100 ft)
Spread: **narrow** - 6 to 10 m (20 to 35 ft), 1/6 to 1/3 the height
Mass: **open**

BRANCHING: central trunk, buttressed at base, **horizontal,** branchlets **pendulous,** picturesque in old age, **fine** texture
Twig: short stout, **green** to green brown
Bud: inconspicuous
Bark: fibrous **exfoliating,** narrow shreddy long strips peeling **vertically; red brown** to silvery gray

FOLIAGE: spiral, pinnately and **bipinnately compound, linear,** 2 ranked in flat plane, **fine** texture
Surface: **dull**
Color: spring - **light green;** summer - **blue green;** autumn - **maroon purple to chocolate brown**
Season: **deciduous** conifer; emergence - late **May,** drop - early **October**

FLOWER: drooping **cones,** born throughout crown
Color: female - **deep purple**
Season: mid **March through** early **April,** before leaf emergence
Sex: monoecious

FRUIT: globular or elliptic **cone,** 25 mm (1 in) long, peltate scales
Color: **purple brown**
Season: early **October through December**
Wildlife Value: **very low**

HABITAT: formation - **forest;** region - **southern, adaptable in central;** gradient - **lowland wet, wet - mesic;** swamp, along
rivers, oxbows, flat alluvial bottoms
Shade Tolerance: **intermediate to intolerant;** index range 2.0-5.0
Flood Tolerance: **very tolerant** - grows in shallow standing water

SOIL; Texture: prefers mucks, clays, **fine** sands, fine sandy loams, **to medium** loams
Drainage: **very poor to moderately well,** grows in shallow water in south
Moisture: **wet to moist**
Reaction: **prefers acid,** pH 6.1-6.5

HARDINESS: **zone 5a**
Rate: **medium** - 30 to 60 cm (12 to 24 in) per year during first 50 years
Longevity: **long** - trees 400 to 600 years old are common, extreme age 1200 years

SUSCEPTIBILITY; Physiological: **frequent** - iron chlorosis on neutral or alkaline soils
Disease: **infrequent** - twig blight, wood decay
Insect: **infrequent** - cypress moth, spider mites
Wind-Ice: **infrequent** - decidedly wind firm

URBAN TOLERANCE; Pollution:
Lighting: Drought-Heat: **sensitive**   Mine Spoils: **sensitive**
Salt: Soil Compaction: **very resistant**
Root Pattern: **shallow** fibrous, submerged roots develop knees; transplants readily B&B in early spring

SPECIES; Associate: central - pure stands, American Sweetgum, Black Willow, Red Maple, American Elm, Green Ash;
south - Pumpkin Ash, Loblolly Pine, Pond Pine and Slash Pine
Similar: larch species share form and habitat requirements, also deciduous conifers
Cultivars: 'Monarch of Illinois' - widespreading to 15 m (50 ft), 'Shawnee Brave' - narrow pyramidal form

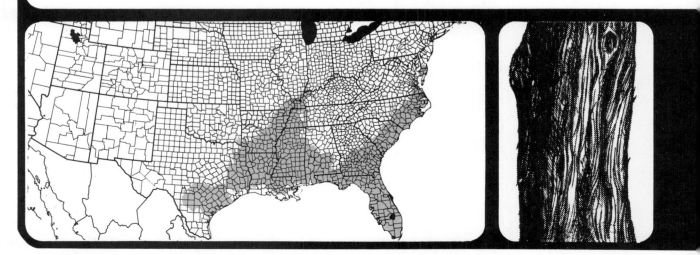

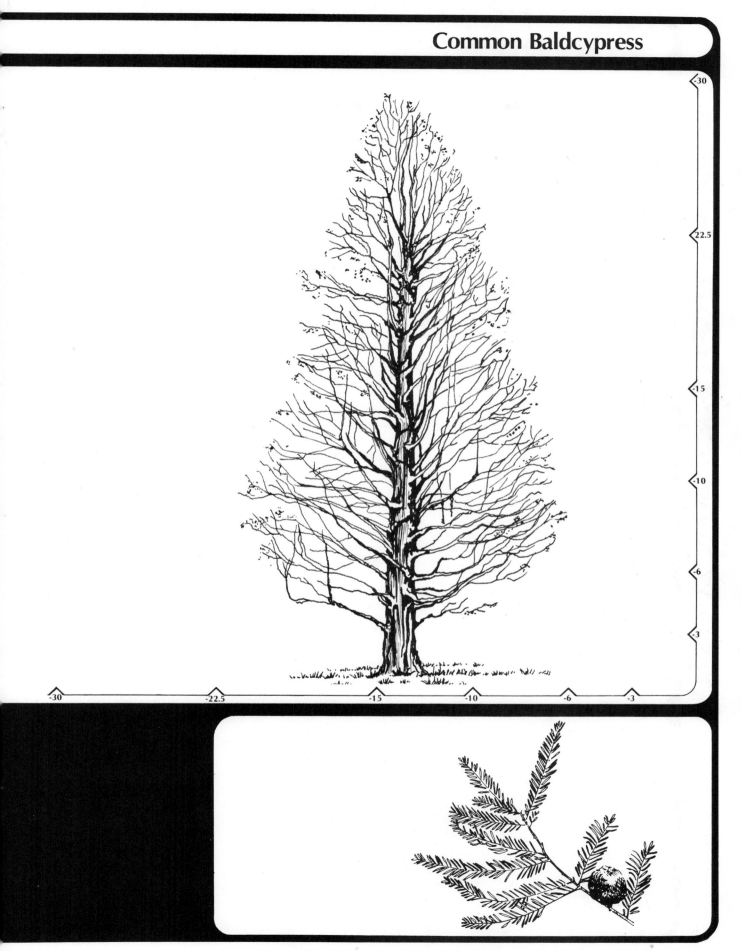

Thuja occidentalis

FORM: broad **conical,** young trees commonly columnar
Size: **small canopy -** 15 to 22.5 m (50 to 75 ft)
Spread: **intermediate -** 10 to 15 m (35 to 50 ft), commonly less
Mass: very **dense**

BRANCHING: singular or multiple trunks, generally **horizontal** bending downwards ascending at tips, **medium** texture
Twig: minute, **yellow green** becoming **green gray**
Bud: inconspicuous
Bark: fibrous **exfoliating,** narrow shreddy long strips peeling **vertically; red brown** to silvery gray

FOLIAGE: **scale-like** in broad flat horizontal fan shaped sprays, conspicuous glandular spots, very **fine** texture
Surface: **dull**
Color: all seasons - **yellow green;** winter - commonly **brownish green**
Season: **evergreen**

FLOWER: small **cone,** 3 mm (1/8 in) long, at foliage tips
Color: both sexes **red brown**
Season: early through late **May**
Sex: monoecious

FRUIT: erect egg shaped **cone,** 10 mm (2/5 in) long, 8 to 12 scales
Color: **tan brown** weathering to silvery gray
Season: persist into winter, early **August through February**
Wildlife Value: **low;** songbirds, waterfowl, small mammals

HABITAT: formation - **forest;** region - **northern;** gradient - **lowland wet, wet mesic, upland mesic, mesic dry;** swampy areas,
bogs, lake margin, mesic coves, open rocky hillside, invades open rocky pastureland, prefers humid atmosphere
Shade Tolerance: **intermediate;** index range 4.0-5.9, more tolerant than Eastern Redcedar
Flood Tolerance: **tolerant**

SOIL; Texture: common on soils over limestone, calcareous **fine** clay, medium loams **to moderately coarse** sandy loams
Drainage: **poor to well**
Moisture: **wet to dry**
Reaction: **slightly acid to alkaline,** pH range 6.0-8.0

HARDINESS: zone 2
Rate: **fast to medium -** more rapid on upland sites, generally 60 cm (2 ft) per year
Longevity: **long -** 400 year old trees are common

SUSCEPTIBILITY; Physiological: **infrequent -** leaf browning, winter browning caused by rapid temperature change
Disease: **infrequent -** leaf blight, juniper blight, cedar tree canker
Insect: **infrequent -** mealybugs, scale, arborvitae leaf miner
Wind-Ice: **frequent -** strong winds cause windthrow

URBAN TOLERANCE; Pollution: **intermediate -** HFl; **resistant -** SO$_2$, O$_3$, HCl, Cl
Lighting: **resistant**   Drought-Heat: **resistant**   Mine Spoils: **resistant**
Salt: **intermediate**   Soil Compaction: **resistant**
Root Pattern: **shallow** widespread; transplants readily if root pruned, any time of year

SPECIES; Associate: pure stands; lowland - Black Spruce, American Larch, Black Ash, Red Maple; upland - Eastern White
Pine, Yellow Birch, Canada Hemlock, Sugar, Striped and Mountain Maple
Similar: Eastern Redcedar
Cultivars: many including 'Globose' - dwarf 1.8 m (6 ft) tall, 'Nigra' - pyramidal form, dark green in winter

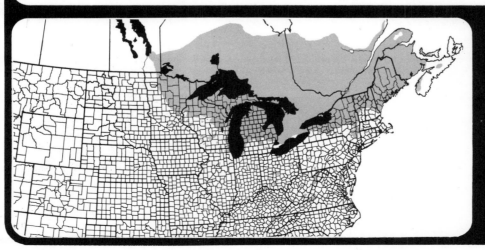

Tilia americana

FORM: **ovoid**, conical in youth
Size: **large canopy** - 22.5 to 30 m (75 to 100 ft)
Spread: **wide** - 15 to 22.5 m (50 to 75 ft), usually 2/3 that of mature height
Mass: **dense**

BRANCHING: dividing near the ground or with multiple trunks (10 or more common), **recurving, medium** texture
Twig: **flaky**, bright **red** in winter
Bud: **two scaled**, ovoid, 3 mm (1/8 in) long, glossy, bright **red**
Bark: smooth becoming **shallow furrowed** with long **narrow** uninterrupted longitudinal ridges; **gray brown**

FOLIAGE: alternate, **simple, cordate to ovate**, uneven base, coarsely toothed, **medium coarse** texture
Surface: **dull**, light green beneath
Color: spring - **light** lime **green;** summer - **medium green;** autumn - golden **yellow**
Season: **deciduous;** emergence - late **April or** early **May,** drop - early **October**

FLOWER: **flat topped** terminal **clusters**, 5 to 7.5 cm (2 to 3 in) across, pendulous, 5 to 10 blossoms per cluster
Color: pale **yellowish**
Season: late **June until** early **July,** after the leaves are fully grown
Sex: monoecious   **Fragrant:** sweet arresting scent

FRUIT: **samara,** small woody pendulous balls in open clusters attached to bract-like wing
Color: **tan brown**
Season: early **September through** late **October**
Wildlife Value: **very low**

HABITAT: formation - **forest;** region - **northern, central;** gradient - **upland mesic;** mesic ravines, coves, north and east
    slope aspects, lower slopes, floodplain knobs, areas of cool air drainage
Shade Tolerance: **very tolerant;** index 8.0
Flood Tolerance: **intolerant**

SOIL; Texture: **moderately coarse** sandy loams **to medium** loams, silt loams
Drainage: **moderately well to well**
Moisture: **moist to average**
Reaction: **neutral,** pH 6.5-7.5

HARDINESS: **zone 3a**
Rate: **medium** - 9 m (30 ft) in 20 years
Longevity: **medium** - commonly to 150 to 200 years, long lived root systems perpetuate crown

SUSCEPTIBILITY; Physiological: **infrequent**
Disease: **frequent** - Verticillium wilt, powdery mildew, leaf blight, canker
Insect: **frequent** - linden aphid, linden borer, basswood lace miner, linden mite, many others
Wind-Ice: **infrequent** - windfirm

URBAN TOLERANCE; Pollution: **sensitive** - 2,4-D, NOx; **intermediate** - SO 2; **resistant** - O_3, HFl
Lighting: Drought-Heat: **sensitive**   Mine Spoils: **sensitive**
Salt: **sensitive**   Soil Compaction: **sensitive**
Root Pattern: **deep** coarse **laterals;** transplants easily B&B in early spring

SPECIES; Associate: northern - American Beech, American Hophornbeam, Sugar Maple, Northern Red Oak, Yellow Birch,
    Canada Hemlock; central - American Beech, Sugar Maple, Black Maple, Yellow Buckeye, White Oak,
    Cucumbertree Magnolia
Similar: Black and Sugar Maple, Norway Maple (European), Littleleaf Linden (European), other lindens
Cultivars: 'Fastigiata'- pyramidal form

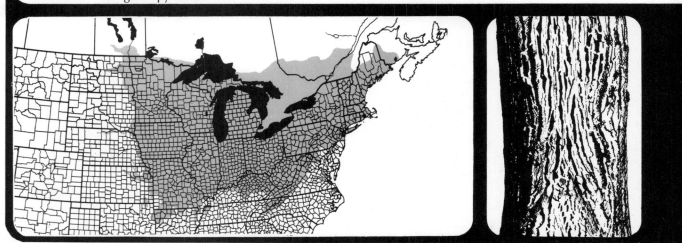

342

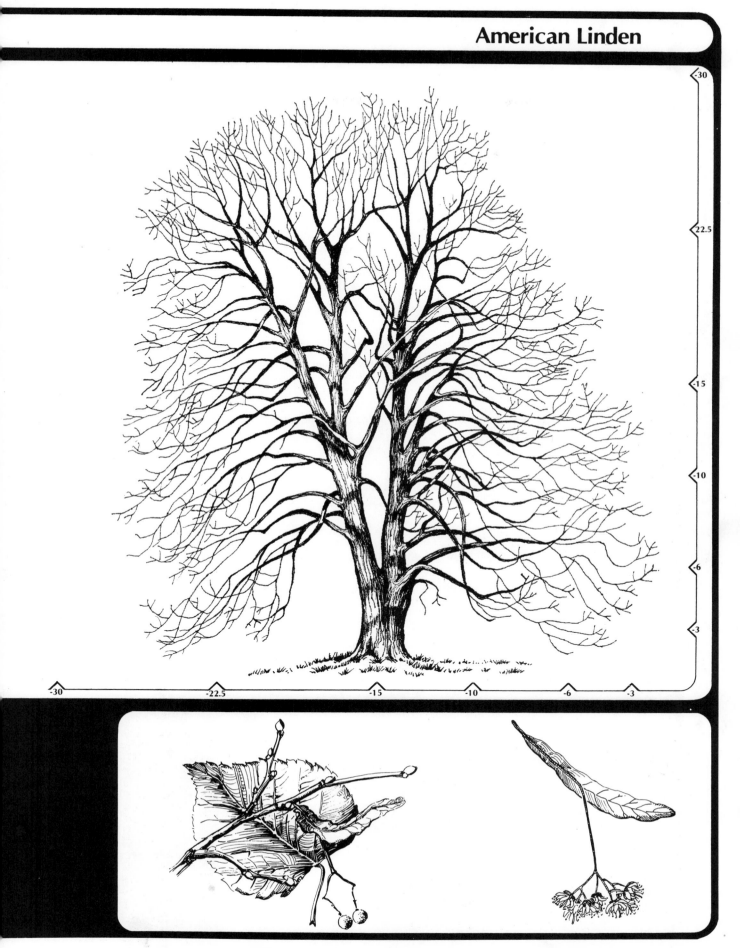

Tsuga canadensis

FORM: broadly **conical**
Size: **large canopy -** 22.5 to 30 m (75 to 100 ft)
Spread: **intermediate -** 10 to 15 m (35 to 50 ft), usually 1/2 to 3/4 the height
Mass: very **dense**

BRANCHING: slender **horizontal** spreading, **pendulous** at ends, terminal leader droops slightly, **medium** texture
Twig: slender, **yellowish brown**
Bud: very small, 1.6 mm (1/16 in) long, blunt brownish
Bark: scaly, when young becoming **deeply furrowed** into wide flat topped ridges; **red brown**

FOLIAGE: **linear,** flat, rounded or indented at tip, ranked in flat plane along twig, very **fine** texture
Surface: **glossy**
Color: **dark green** year around, 2 whitish bands on leaf undersides
Season: coniferous **evergreen**

FLOWER: **cone,** born throughout the crown, terminal, singular
Color: male - light **yellow,** female - pale green
Season: late **May through** early **June**
Sex: monoecious

FRUIT: small elliptical **cone,** 19 mm (3/4 in) long, smooth rounded scale margin, pendulous
Color: **tan brown**
Season: **September through January**
Wildlife Value: **intermediate;** songbirds, small mammals, hoofed browsers

HABITAT: formation - **forest;** region - **northern;** gradient - **upland mesic;** protected coves, mesic ravines, moist cool valleys, north and east slope aspects, benches, hollows under cliffs
Shade Tolerance: **very tolerant;** index 10.0
Flood Tolerance: **very intolerant**

SOIL; Texture: **moderately coarse** sandy and gravelly loams, medium loams **to moderately fine** silt loams, clay
Drainage: **well to poor**
Moisture: demands **wet to average**
Reaction: **strongly acid to slightly acid,** pH 4.6-6.5

HARDINESS: zone 3b
Rate: **medium to slow -** 15 to 46 cm (1/2 to 1 1/2 ft) a year
Longevity: **long -** commonly 300 to 400 years

SUSCEPTIBILITY; Physiological: **frequent -** sunscorch with temperatures above 95 degrees, drought injury
Disease: **infrequent**
Insect: **frequent -** hemlock borer, bagworm, gypsy moth, hemlock sawfly, many scales and mites
Wind - Ice: **infrequent**

URBAN TOLERANCE; Pollution: **sensitive -** O_3; **intermediate -** 2,4-D; **resistant -** HCl, Cl, PAN
Lighting: **sensitive**   Drought-Heat: **very sensitive**   Mine Spoils: **sensitive**
Salt: **sensitive**   Soil Compaction: **sensitive**
Root Pattern: **shallow** fibrous, wide spreading; somewhat difficult, move root pruned trees B&B in early spring

SPECIES; Associate: Sugar Maple, American Beech, Yellow and Sweet Birches, Tuliptree, Red and Eastern White Pines, Eastern Arborvitae, Red Spruce, Fraser Fir, Striped and Mountain Maples, Rosebay Rhododendron
Similar: Balsam Fir, Upright Japanese Yew is small understory tree, Carolina Hemlock is related
Cultivars: 'Sargentii' - mound-like habit two or three times broader than tall, also listed as 'Pendula'

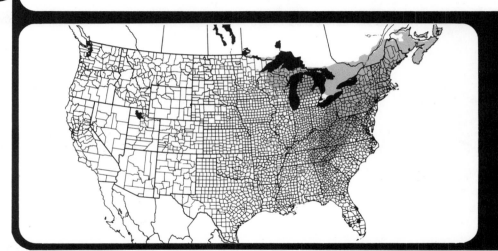

344

Ulmus americana

FORM: globular
Size: **large canopy -** 22.5 to 30 m (75 to 100 ft)
Spread: **very wide -** 22.5 to 30 m (75 to 100 ft), as wide or wider than height
Mass: **moderate**

BRANCHING: upright with high arching crown, branchlets drooping (umbrella-like appearance), **medium** texture
Twig: **zig zag,** slender, **red brown,** conspicuous lenticels
Bud: conical pointed, 10 mm (2/5 in) long, red with dark margin, hugs twig
Bark: **shallow to deeply furrowed** with **narrow** ridges; **gray brown** frequently with bleached streaky appearance

FOLIAGE: alternate, **simple, ovobate-oblong obovate,** uneven base, doubly serrate margin, **medium** texture
Surface: **glossy to dull,** smooth
Color: spring - **light green;** summer - **bright green;** autumn - golden **yellow**
Season: **deciduous;** emergence - late **April,** drop - mid **October**

FLOWER: small clusters, 5 mm (1/5 in) bell shaped blooms, borne on slender pendulous stringy filaments
Color: **red brown**
Season: early through mid **April,** before leaf emergence
Sex: monoecious

FRUIT: circular wafer-like **samara,** 15 mm (3/5 in) across, clustered, seed positioned in middle, notched at apex
Color: **tan brown**
Season: throughout **May**
Wildlife Value: **intermediate;** waterfowl, songbirds, upland ground birds, small mammals

HABITAT: formation - **forest, savanna;** region - **northern, central;** gradient - **lowland wet mesic, upland mesic, mesic-dry;**
  alluvial flats, mesic ravines, moist slopes, invades abandoned field
Shade Tolerance: **intermediate;** index 6.4
Flood Tolerance: **intermedaite**

SOIL; Texture: **moderately coarse** sandy and gravelly loams **to moderately fine** silt loams, silty clay loams
Drainage: **moderately poor to well**
Moisture: **moist to dry**
Reaction: **neutral and alkaline,** pH range 6.6-8.0

HARDINESS: zone 2
Rate: **medium -** 6 m (20 ft) in 10 years
Longevity: **medium -** matures at about 150 years, often lives for 175 to 200 years

SUSCEPTIBILITY; Physiological: **infrequent**
Disease: **frequent -** wet wood, Dutch Elm disease, many cankers, Verticillium wilt, many others
Insect: **frequent -** gypsy moth, bark beetles, elm borer, cankerworms, elm cockscomb gall, many others
Wind-Ice: **infrequent**

URBAN TOLERANCE; Pollution: **sensitive -** SO_2; **resistant -** HFl
Lighting: **sensitive**   Drought-Heat: **resistant**   Mine Spoils: **resistant**
Salt: **intermediate**   Soil Compaction: **intermediate**
Root Pattern: varies with site, usually **shallow to deep laterals;** transplants reaily B&B in spring or autumn

SPECIES; Associate: lowland - Green Ash, Eastern Poplar, Boxelder, Silver Maple, Red Mulberry, Black Walnut, Common
  Hackberry; upland - White Ash, Common Hackberry, Butternut, Bitternut Hickory, American Linden, maple and beech
Similar: Common Hackberry is best, Siberian Elm, Chinese Elm is smaller with red autumn color, Silver Maple
Cultivars: consideration no longer practical due to Dutch Elm disease

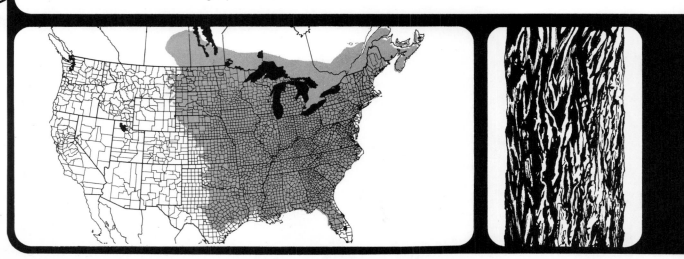

American Elm

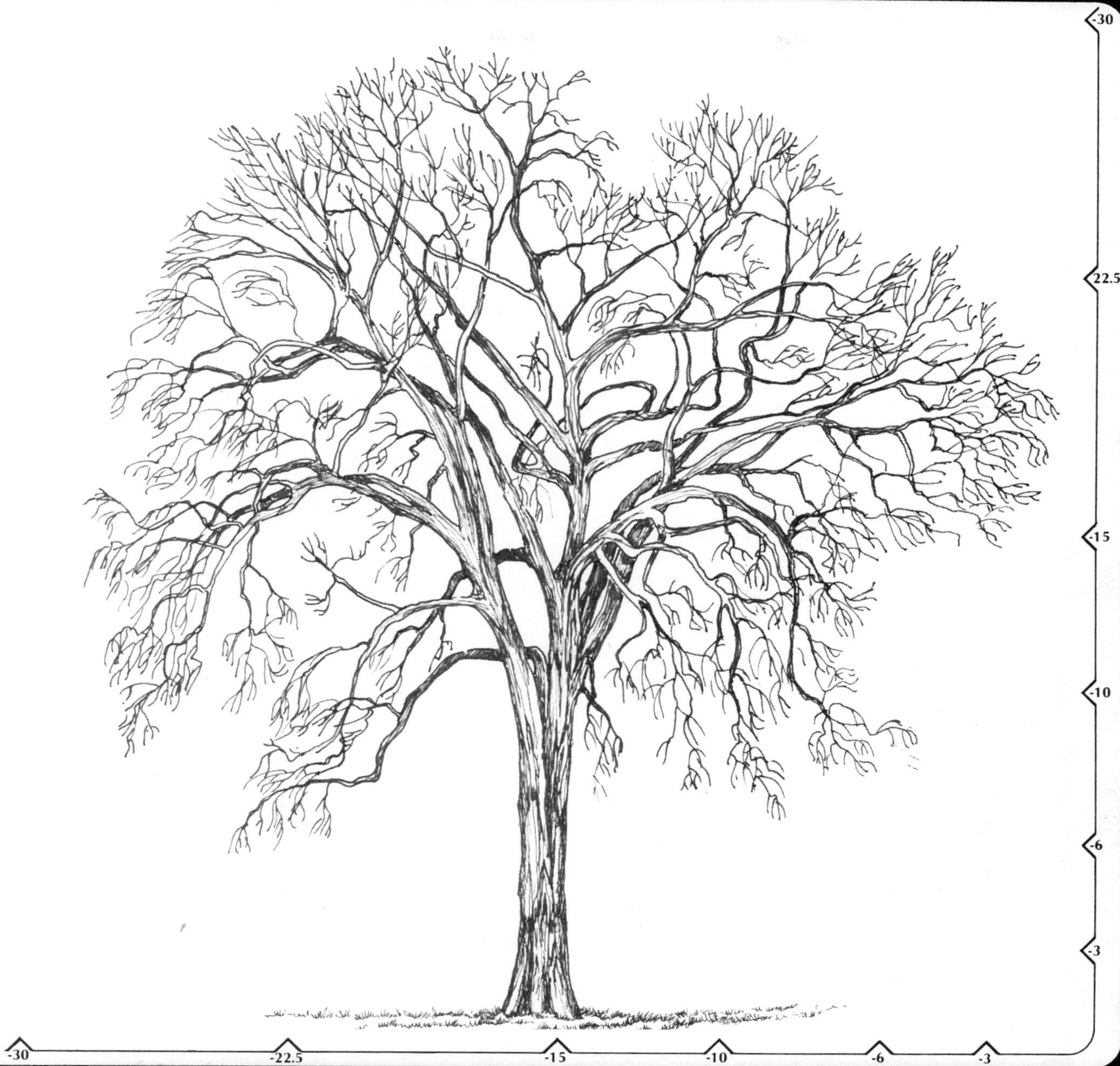

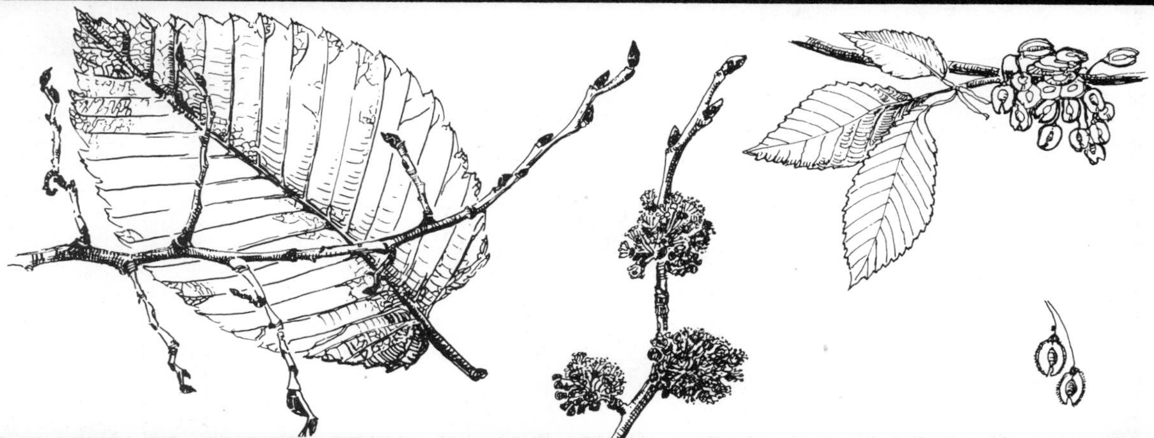

Viburnum lentago

FORM: obovoid
Size: **small understory** - 6 to 10 m (20 to 35 ft)
Spread: **narrow** - 6 to 10 m (20 to 35 ft), commonly 3 to 6 m (10 to 20 ft), 3/4 the height
Mass: **dense**

BRANCHING: multiple trunks, **upright** spreading becoming arching, **medium** texture
Twig: slender, **gray brown**
Bud: **naked, long pointed**, 25 mm (1 in) long, flower bud swollen at base, flesh **pink** coloration
Bark: blocky, squarish grid-like pattern; **brown black**

FOLIAGE: opposite, **simple, ovate-oblong ovate**, finely toothed, petiole with winged margin, **medium coarse** texture
Surface: **glossy**
Color: spring - **light green;** summer - bright **medium green;** autumn - mottled with **yellow, orange red** becoming **purple**
Season: **deciduous;** emergence - early **May**, drop - mid **October**

FLOWER: broad **flat-topped** terminal **clusters**, 7.5 to 10 cm (3 to 4 in) across
Color: creamy **white**
Season: mid through late **May**, after leaf emergence
Sex: monoecious   **Fragrant:** strong scented

FRUIT: **berry**, 10 to 15 mm (2/5 to 3/5 in) long, football shaped, in open loose drooping terminal clusters
Color: yellows and reds ripening to **black** with powder **blue** bloom, on bright red stems
Season: early **September through** early **December**
Wildlife Value: **high;** songbirds, upland ground birds, small mammals, man

HABITAT: formation - **forest, savanna;** region - **northern, central;** gradient - **upland mesic dry and dry;** along banks of
streams, lakeshores, sheltered coves, wooded slopes, margin of woods, open rocky pastureland, fencerows
Shade Tolerance: **intermediate;** index range 4.0-5.9
Flood Tolerance: **intolerant**

SOIL; Texture: **moderately coarse** sandy of gravelly loam, medium loam **to moderately fine** light loamy clay
Drainage: **moderately poor to well**
Moisture: **moist to dry**
Reaction: **slightly acid to neutral,** pH 6.1-7.5, tolerates **alkaline**

HARDINESS: zone 2
Rate: **fast -** 60 to 90 cm (24 to 36 in) annually
Longevity: **short**

SUSCEPTIBILITY; Physiological: **infrequent**
Disease: **infrequent -** mildew is common and locally severe on plants in shaded area
Insect: **infrequent**
Wind-Ice: **infrequent**

URBAN TOLERANCE; Pollution:
Lighting: Drought-Heat: **resistant**   Mine Spoils: **resistant**
Salt: **sensitive**   Soil Compaction: **sensitive**
Root Pattern: **shallow fibrous rooted; transplants easily B&B in early spring**

SPECIES; Associate: mesic dry - Black and Sugar Maples, American Linden, Northern Red Oak, White Oak, Leatherwood;
dry - Blackhaw Viburnum, Black Cherry, American Plum, sumacs, filbert, chokecherry, hawthorn species
Similar: Witherod Viburnum is smaller
Cultivars: none commercially obtainable

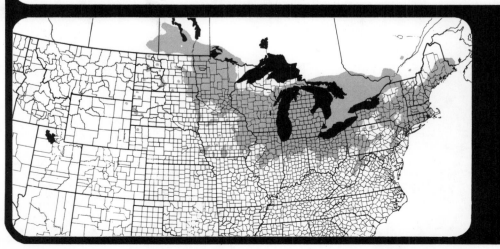

Nannyberry Viburnum

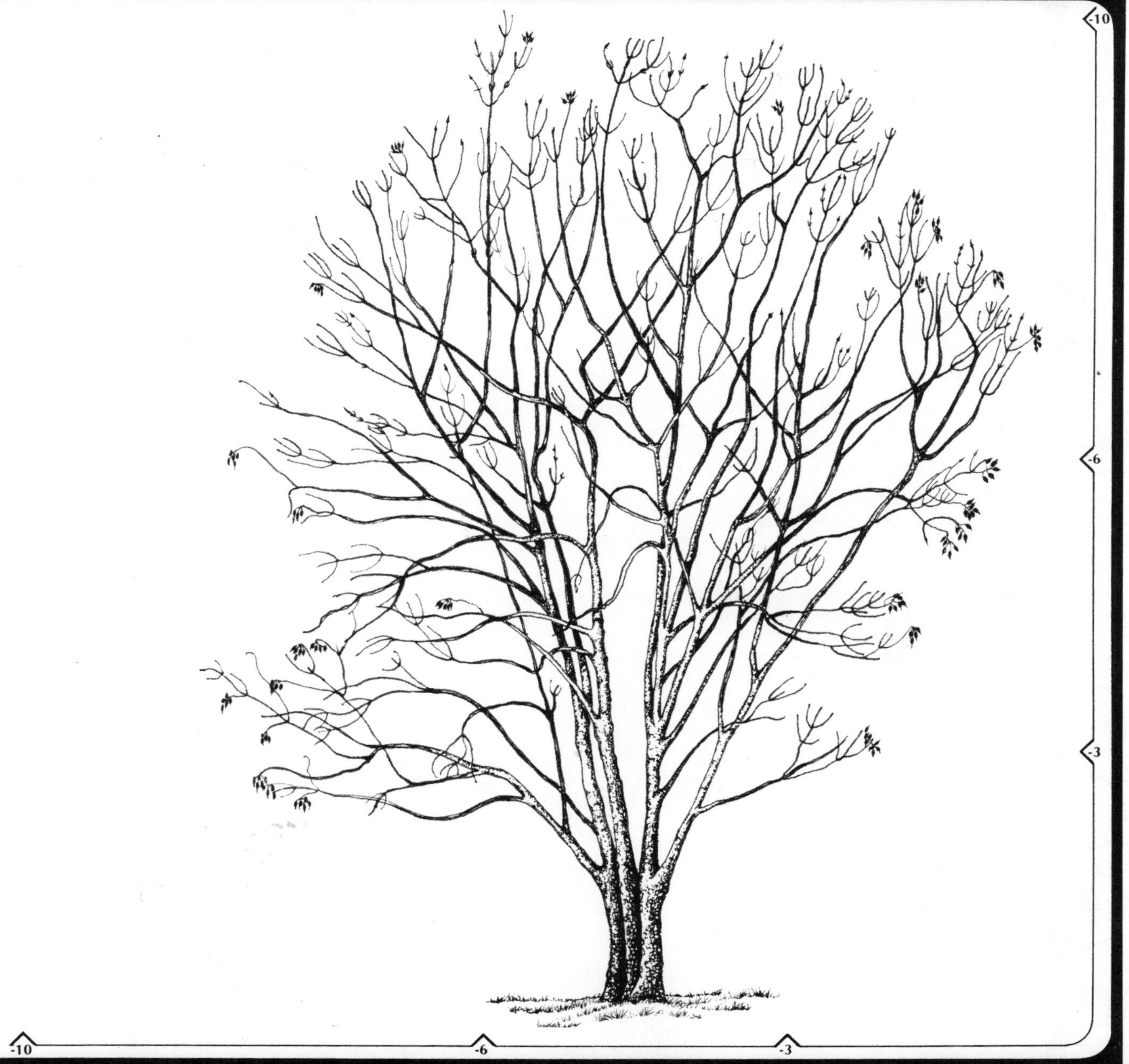

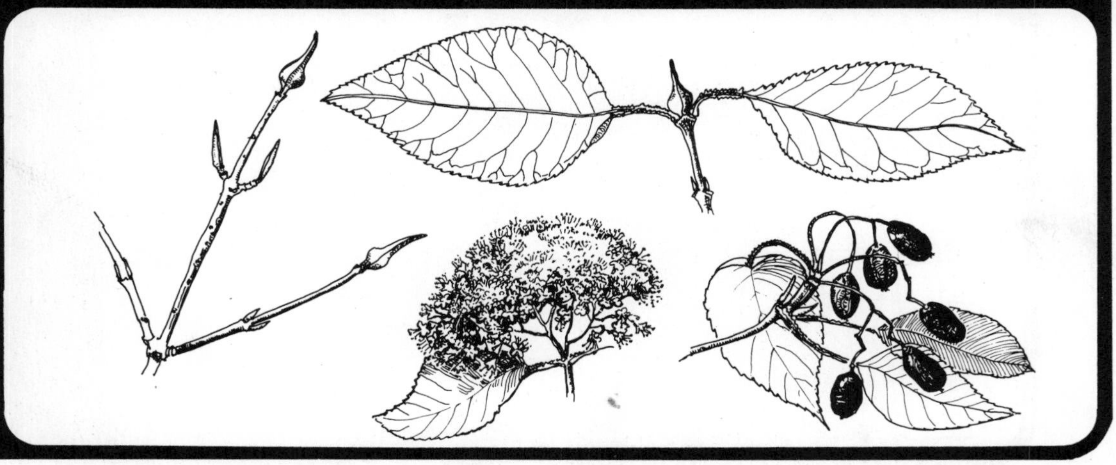

Viburnum prunifolium

FORM: obovoid
Size: **small understory** - 6 to 10 m (20 to 35 ft)
Spread: **narrow** - 6 to 10 m (20 to 35 ft), commonly 3/4 the adult height
Mass: **dense**

BRANCHING: multiple trunks, stiffly **horizontal** fishbone habit, **medium** texture
Twig: slender, smooth, **gray brown; armed** with short thorn-like right angle spur branches
Bud: **naked,** flower bud swollen at base, short pointed, flesh **pink**
Bark: squarish thick **blocks,** narrow fissures checked into grid-like pattern; **brown black**

FOLIAGE: opposite, **simple, elliptic-oval,** finely toothed, **medium fine** texture
Surface: **dull,** smooth
Color: spring - light **yellow green;** summer - bright **medium green;** autumn - scarlet **red** to crimson
Season: **deciduous;** emergence - early **May,** drop - mid **October**

FLOWER: large **flat-topped clusters,** 7.5 to 10 m (3 to 4 in) wide, on the ends of the branches, prolific
Color: creamy **white**
Season: late **May through** early **June**
Sex: monoecious   **Fragrant:** slightly

FRUIT: **berry,** 10 to 15 mm (2/5 to 3/5 in) long, football shaped, in open loose drooping terminal clusters
Color: dark **blue** almost **black** covered with a white frost-like bloom, on bright red stems
Season: early **September through December**
Wildlife Value: **high;** songbirds, upland ground birds, small mammals, hoofed browsers

HABITAT: formation - **savanna;** region - **central;** gradient - **upland dry;** dry rocky woods, upland pastures, margin of woods, thickets, fencerows, steep rocky hillsides, rocky creek banks
Shade Tolerance: **intolerant;** index range 2.0-3.9
Flood Tolerance: **very intolerant**

SOIL; Texture: **moderately coarse** sandy or gravelly loams, loamy sands, medium loams, **to moderately fine** loamy clay
Drainage: **moderately well to well**
Moisture: **average to droughty**
Reaction: **neutral to alkaline,** pH 6.6-8.0

HARDINESS: zone 3b
Rate: **slow to medium** - 32 to 46 cm (18 to 30 in) per year
Longevity: **short**

SUSCEPTIBILITY; Physiological: **infrequent**
Disease: **infrequent** - remarkably free from biological disorders
Insect: **infrequent**
Wind-Ice: **infrequent**

URBAN TOLERANCE; Pollution:
Lighting: **resistant**   Drought-Heat: **resistant**   Mine Spoils: **resistant**
Salt: **sensitive**   Soil Compaction: **sensitive**
Root Pattern: **shallow** widespreading; transplants readily B&B in early spring

SPECIES; Associate: Black Cherry, Common Chokecherry, American Plum, Prairie Crabapple, Red Mulberry, Sassafras, Nannyberry Viburnum, Common Persimmon, hawthorns, sumacs
Similar: Rusty Blackhaw Viburnum, buckthorn species
Cultivars: 'Mrs. George Large' - compact habit, leathery foliage, not readily available

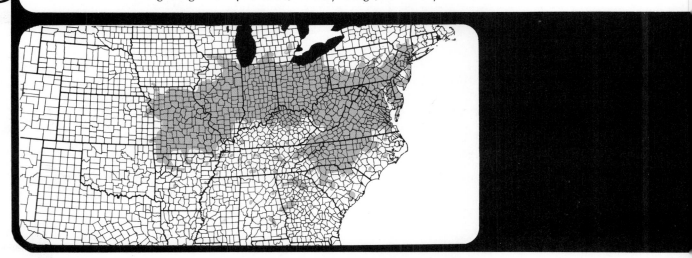

Viburnum rufidulum

FORM: obovoid to globular
Size: **small understory -** 6 to 10 m (20 to 35 ft)
Spread: **narrow -** 6 to 10 m (20 to 35 ft), 3 to 6 m commonly, 3/4 to equal height
Mass: **dense**

BRANCHING: multiple or single trunk, **horizontal** to arching, low umbrella-like crown, **medium** texture
Twig: slender, **velvety**, dark **red brown; armed** with sharp spur-like modified twigs, fishbone angular appearance
Bud: short, **naked, woolly,** dark **chocolate brown**
Bark: fine horizontal crack-like fissures separate ridges into short squarish **blocky** segments; **brown black**

FOLIAGE: opposite, **simple, elliptic-oval,** finely toothed, leaf petiole woolly, **medium fine** texture
Surface: very **glossy,** smooth upper, lighter with rust colored **tomentum** beneath
Color: spring - **bright** lime **green;** summer - **dark green;** autumn - scarlet **red to purple**
Season: **deciduous:** emergence - early **May,** drop - mid **October**

FLOWER: broad **flat-topped** terminal **clusters,** 7.5 to 10 m (3 to 4 in) across
Color: creamy **white**
Season: mid **May through** early **June**
Sex: monoecious   **Fragrant:** slightly

FRUIT: berry, 10 to 15 mm (2/5 to 3/5 in) long, football shaped, in open loose drooping terminal clusters
Color: dark **blue to black,** covered with a white frost-like bloom, borne on bright red stems
Season: mid **August through** mid **November**
Wildlife Value: **high;** songbirds, upland ground birds, small and large animals

HABITAT: formation - **savanna;** region - **central, southern;** gradient - **upland dry;** dry rocky woods, glades along rocky
     streams, steep rocky hillsides, margin of woods, fencerow, abandoned fields
Shade Tolerance: **intolerant;** index range 2.0-3.9
Flood Tolerance: **very intolerant**

SOIL; Texture: moderately coarse gravelly or sandy loams, medium loams **to moderately fine** loamy clays
Drainage: **moderately well to well**
Moisture: **average to droughty**
Reaction: **neutral,** pH 6.6-7.5, tolerates alkaline pH 7.6-8.0

HARDINESS: zone 5a
Rate: **medium -** 30 to 60 cm (12 to 24 in) annually
Longevity: **short**

SUSCEPTIBILITY; Physiological: infrequent
Disease: **infrequent -** basically free from biological disorders
Insect: **infrequent**
Wind-Ice: **infrequent**

URBAN TOLERANCE; Pollution:
Lighting: Drought-Heat: **resistant**   Mine Spoils: **resistant**
Salt: **sensitive**   Soil Compaction: **sensitive**
Root Pattern: **shallow** widespreading; transplants readily B&B in early spring

SPECIES; Associate: Blackhaw Viburnum, Blackjack and Post Oaks, Osageorange,
     Common Persimmon, Flowering Dogwood, hawthorns, sumacs cherries, mulberry, crabapples
Similar: Blackhaw Viburnum
Cultivars: none available commercially

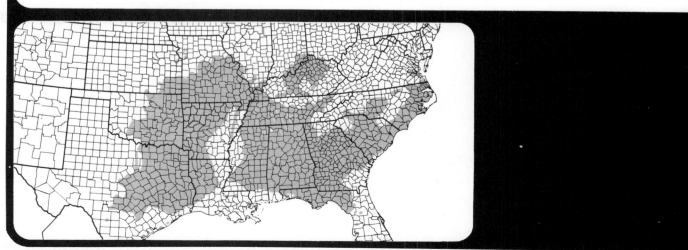

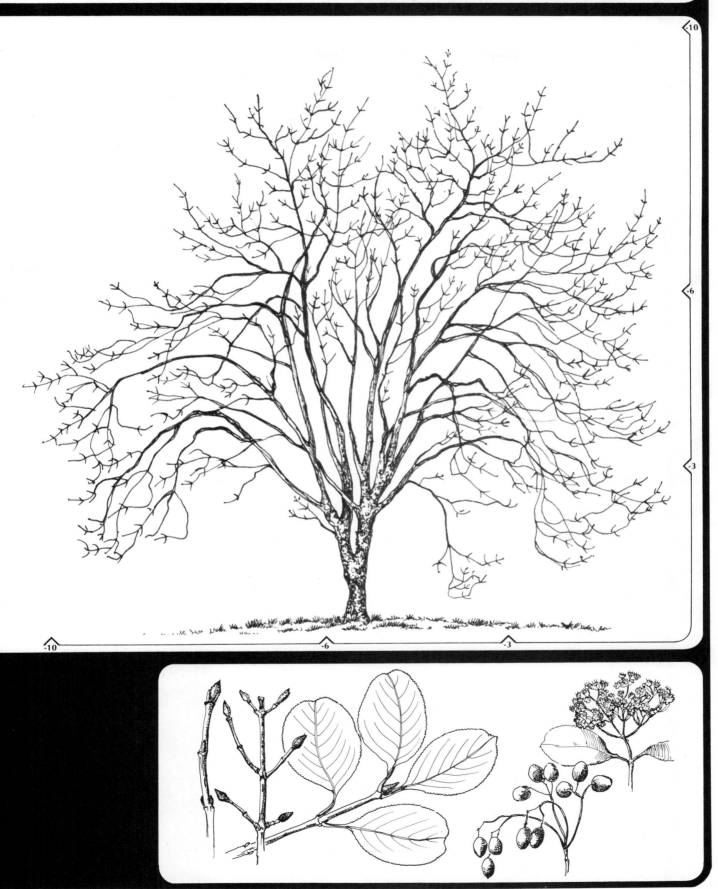

Zanthoxylum americanum

FORM: obovoid, irregular
Size: **small understory** - 6 to 10 m (20 to 35 ft)
Spread: **narrow** - 6 to 10 m (20 to 35 ft), commonly 3 to 6 m
Mass: **open**

BRANCHING: slender inclined trunk, short club-like branches, forms extensive colonies, **coarse** texture
Twig: smooth, stout, **red; armed** with stout prickles, paired at each node
Bud: **woolly**, globular, bright **red** or red brown
Bark: **smooth** becoming broken into fine scales with age; gray to **red brown**

FOLIAGE: alternate, **pinnately compound, ovate lanceolate,** 7-11 leaflets, prickly rachis, **medium fine** texture
Surface: **glossy**, aromatic when crushed
Color: spring - **light** lime **green;** summer - **bright green;** autumn - golden **yellow**
Season: **deciduous;** emergence - mid **May,** drop - late **September**

FLOWER: small clusters
Color: **yellow green**
Season: early through mid **May,** before or with new leaves
Sex: **dioecious**

FRUIT: **berry,** 3 mm (1/8 in) long, in loose drooping clusters, aromatic
Color: bright crimson **red,** seeds glossy jet black
Season: mid **August through** mid **September**
Wildlife Value: **high;** popular with songbirds, upland ground birds, small mammals

HABITAT: formation - **forest, savanna;** region - **northern, central;** gradient - **upland mesic dry, dry;** margin of woods, open
field, open woods, open rocky slopes, ridgetops
Shade Tolerance: **intolerant;** index range 2.0-3.9
Flood Tolerance: **intermediate**

SOIL; Texture: **moderately coarse** sandy or gravelly loams **to moderately fine** clay loams
Drainage: **moderately well to well**
Moisture: **average to dry,** tolerates **droughty**
Reaction: **slightly acid to alkaline,** pH 6.6-8.0

HARDINESS: zone 3a
Rate: **fast** - 60 to 90 cm (24 to 36 in) annually
Longevity: **short** - rarely survives 40 years; long lived root system perpetuates colony

SUSCEPTIBILITY; Physiological: **infrequent**
Disease: **infrequent**
Insect: **frequent** - many leaf eating insects commonly defoliate crown in late summer
Wind-Ice: **infrequent** - strong, windfirm

URBAN TOLERANCE; Pollution:
Lighting: Drought-Heat: **resistant**   Mine Spoils: **resistant**
Salt: Soil Compaction: **sensitive**
Root Pattern: **shallow** fibrous, prolific suckers; transplants readily B&B or BR in any season with care

SPECIES; Associate: Shagbark and Pignut Hickories, Common Hoptree, Common Chokecherry, Black Cherry,
oaks, sumac, hawthorn, crabapple, viburnum
Similar: Bristly Locust, Bristly Sarsaparilla, Devils Club, Devils Walking-stick
Cultivars: none available commercially

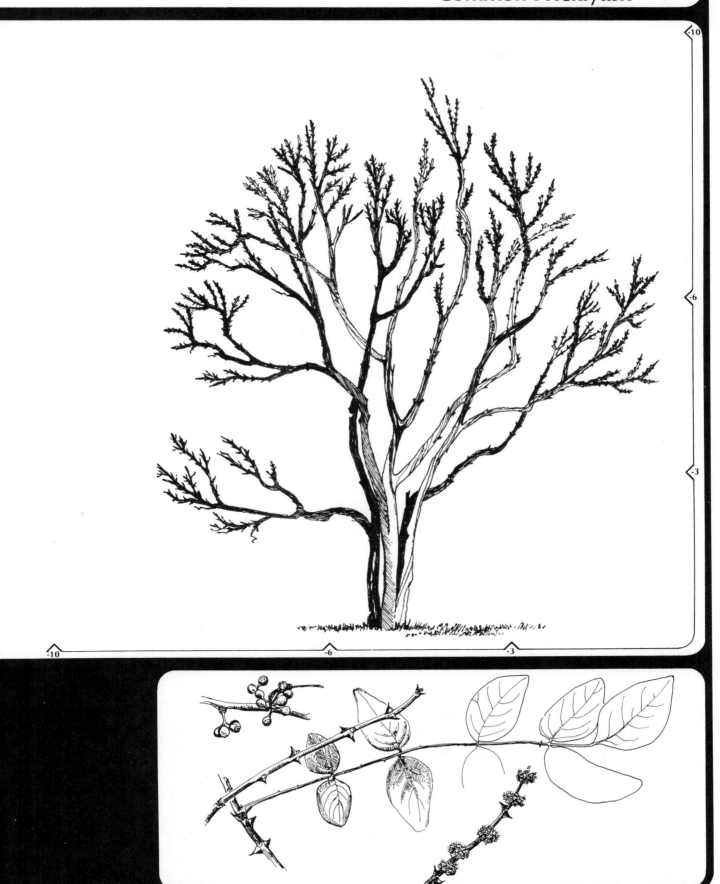

PART II

NATIVE SHRUBS AND VINES

CONTENTS

LIST OF TABLES AND FIGURES

INTRODUCTION

Land of Milk and Honey

Three hundred and fifty years ago, the North American continent was essentially virgin land — wild and undisturbed. When the first settlers colonized the Atlantic Seaboard and a few explorers had penetrated our land westward over the mountains and along the rivers, they found an endless expanse of forest, broken only by swamps and bogs, by cliffs and bluffs too steep for forest, and by openings in the forest where meadow and prairie grasses flourished. The land was still occupied by Indian tribes of many nations and European Settlement had not begun in earnest.

What was the landscape like then? What did the Indians and earliest European settlers see? Something of the primeval beauty and bounty of this new land is suggested in the diaries and writings of the early explorers, surveyors, naturalists, and poets of that time.

> There were then still miles upon miles of almost undisturbed timber, fine white oaks predominating on the uplands, the hard maple occasionally dominating the river-bluffs, and the red cedar finding an anchorage on the limestone ledges, while the black walnut and various softwood trees occupied the narrow bottom lands. The upland woods were carpeted in early spring with hepaticas (chiefly on the steeper slopes) and the rue anemone, while the ravines were decked with beautiful ferns, interspersed with pink and yellow ladies'-slippers and many other wild flowers, all in great profusion, while the lowland woods displayed their gorgeous raiment of spring-beauties, *Mertensia*, buttercup, *Phlox* and *Isopyrum*, the whole making a wonderful flower garden.
>
> Nor did plant-life furnish the only interest. The wild turkey persisted, the drumming of the ruffed grouse, now almost extinct, was one of the most familiar sounds in our woods, and the passenger pigeon still came in great clouds to seek shelter amid the oaks of our uplands.
>
> Bohumil Shimek, as quoted in
> *Iowa's Natural Heritage*
> by Tom C. Cooper

Times of Change

In the next three and one-half centuries the lure of furs, mineral deposits and land attracted settlers farther and farther west in ever growing numbers. When the people began to come, they found a rich land which had been waiting for them for thousands of years. "They marveled at the sight of seemingly unlimited quantities of land — enough, it seemed, to fully satisfy one of man's oldest hungers — cheap, rich land which he could call his own" (McFarland, 1969). The forests were cut for building and fencing materials and for fuel. Native birds and animals provided the settler with some food, but mainly with irritation. In an effective and systematic way these creatures were eliminated, like the American Indian — killed or pushed out. Forests, prairie and meadow fared no better. Most of the forest was cut for the construction of rail lines to the west and the farmer plowed up the meadow and prairie. Settlement changed and adapted some natural landscape features, but most were simply eliminated.

> Looking back, we find we owe much to the pioneers. Those hardy men and women were imbued with the New World spirit of getting ahead, of seeking new opportunities, of competition, free enterprise, of using their hands and their minds and their ingenuity to open up the land and "conquer the wilderness." But in their zeal they viewed the land as a limitless resource. It was there to be claimed, farmed, mined, or cut over for timber until the resource was expended. Then they "pulled up stakes" and moved on. Always there seemed to be more and better land ahead . . . to be used, and again exploited.
>
> John O. Simonds, *Earthscape*

Heritage Lost

The Jefferson agrarian plan was realized throughout the east and midwest by the end of the 19th century. Yeoman farmers of this period each owned a small plot of land and were able to profit personally by the fruits of their labor. Today regional farm land is becoming increasingly centralized in the hands of fewer people who are often removed from the land. Yesterday's subsistance agriculture has become today's agribusiness where any part of the land that is not contributing a marketable product to its owner is of no value. Meta-economic values of the landscape are commonly overlooked in the rush to make every acre pay for itself. With modern agriculture and forestry has come the homogenization of the landscape throughout the east and midwest. As natural areas are eliminated by development pressures, the continued decline in biological diversity, productivity and stability of remaining areas can be anticipated.

In the early twentieth century Dr. Robert I. Cratty (Pammel et al. 1919), respected Iowa naturalist and botanist, wrote:

> So large a proportion of our state is suitable for cultivation that our native flora is being rapidly swept away, and while many of the species may survive along the roadsides, in hilly and stony locations and along the streamside, others which are local or rare must eventually disappear altogether.

Today almost all of the midwest and eastern forest resource is second and third generation growth with present forest community structures which hardly measure up to the forest descriptions of the early explorers, surveyors, and naturalists. A few relict Prairie Preserves are the only reminders of the past expanse of grassland that stretched across the midwest landscape like an inland sea.

A publication by the Smithsonian Institution Press (1978) lists *Endangered and Threatened Plants of the United States*. According to this report 90 species of taxa (or 0.4 percent of the native flora) have become extinct since the early settlement period. At the present time 839 kinds, or 4.2 percent of the native plants, are endangered species and 1211 kinds representing 6.1 percent are considered threatened in the continental United States. In little over three hundred years an inconceivable 10.7 percent of our native flora has been or is in the process of being extirpated from the face of the continent.

Endangered and Threatened Wildlife (U.S. Fish and Wildlife Service, 1982) includes over 90 species of mammals, birds, reptiles, amphibians, and fishes that have become rare in the continental United States over the same short time period.

The causes of the rarity are legion. Some of the primary causes include; forestry practices, surface mining, biocide (insecticide and herbicide) spraying, real estate development and construction, overgrazing, off road vehicles, agriculture, commercial exploitation, illegal poaching, and collecting by private individuals.

Landscape for Living

With the advance of American civilizaton came civilized landscapes. These highly structured, totally designed landscapes were of two basic types, either formal - where the plants were pruned and carved into shapes and forms, or naturalistic - with great flowing romantic lines and irregular shapes and forms. Both were born from man's imagination and not from the observation and appreciation of natural landscape as a biological system.

> Here the ornamental qualities of plants are paramount - no ecological concepts of community or association becloud the objective. Plants are analogous to domestic pets, dogs, cats, ponies, canaries and goldfish, tolerant to man and dependent upon him; lawn grasses, hedges, flowering shrubs and trees, tractable and benign, are thus man's companions, sharing his domestication.
>
> Ian McHarg, *Design with Nature*

Ecologists consider many of today's urban and rural landscapes to be biologically sterile, while landscape architects consider them to be esthetically impoverished. The heavy use of exotic species for ornament has resulted in a sameness in traditional American landscapes across broad regions.

> Once non-natives were considered rare; now they are common in landscapes. The opposite is true of native plants in the landscape, which now seem exotic because of their lack of use in recent years.
>
> C. Ann Norris, *American Nurseryman*

The result has been home and work landscapes of low human interest and use, landscapes often pretty to look at but not for living.

> It is wrong to think that landscaping is a collection of specimens from all parts of the world. Museums are not made to live with. The finding of plant varieties is a scientific venture, fine and noble in itself, but it must not be confused with art, as is so often done. To be inspired by and to create parks and gardens out of the beauty and composition of our native landscape is a much higher accomplishment than to form a garden with varieties of plants that have no intimate association with each other or with us and which at best become mere patch work influenced by the curious and scientific mind.
>
> Jens Jensen, *Siftings, A Major Portion of the Clearing and Collected Writings*

As a result we find ourselves making more frequent and longer pilgrimages and retreats to rapidly disappearing wild land and countryside landscapes for recreation, relaxation, education, and inspiration.

> Thus speaks the soul of our native landscape. Nothing can take its place. It is given to us when we are born, and with it we live. It speaks of freedom and friendliness. It speaks of a hope that gives joy and peace to the mind.
>
> Jens Jensen, *Siftings, A Major Portion of the Clearing and Collected Writings*

Yet it is a measure of our progress today that we are in the midst of a dynamic new movement to protect, to restore, and to reconstruct natural environments. In today's world, principles of ecology and environmental processes are becoming increasingly important concerns reflected in architectural design. More residential homes, office buildings, and businesses are being heated by solar energy than ever before. Design and construction methods also reflect the concern for nature and for increased oil, gas, and electric costs.

> . . . Buildings perform their highest function in relation to human life within and the natural efflorescence without; and to develop and maintain the harmony of a true chord between them, making of the building in this sense a sure foil for life . . .
>
> You must read the book of nature. What we must know in organic architecture is not found in books. It is necessary to have recourse to Nature with a capital N in order to get an education. Necessary to learn from trees, flowers, shells — objects which contain truths of form following function. If we stopped there, then it would be merely imitation. But if we dig deep enough to read the priniciples upon which these are activated, we arrive at secrets of form related to purpose that would make of the tree a building and of the building a tree.
>
> Frank Lloyd Wright, as quoted in *An American Architecture*   by Edgar Kaufman

Landscape design has also become maintenance conscious and attuned to nature. An increasing number of people are applynig the lessons of ecology to their own lives and enjoying once again a natural landscape for living similar to the one enjoyed by their grandparents and great grandparents who settled the land centuries before. They are accomplishing this by planting native trees, shrubs, and wildflowers; by stocking ponds with native fish species; and by providing preferred food, shelter and nesting habitat for native wildlife species.

A Natural Alternative

Natural landscaping is a design term that has become increasingly popular within the last decade. A natural landscape requires that the designer have an understanding of the unique environmental conditions of a site and region and of the environmental requirements of the plant materials that are indigenous to it. Each site and region is treated as a living, growing, evolving ecosystem with its own unique geology, physiography, hydrology, soils, climate, vegetation, and wildlife. The use of native plants best suited to this site environment is what natural landscaping is all about.

Natural landscaping is used basically to describe two similar, yet quite different, contemporary approaches in landscape design. The *floristic* approach promotes the use of indigenous species for their singular beauty, texture, color, and shape. The design emphasis is placed on the beauty or function of one individual species or mosaic of separate species indigenous to the site environment, but with no attempt to group species commonly found growing together in nature.

A second approach focuses on the mutual dependencies and interrelationships between a community of plants indigenous to the site environment. A different image of beauty and function is characteristic of this *community* approach to natural landscaping. The subtle textures, colors and shapes of the whole (community) rather than the sum of parts (flora) is the emphasis here. The woodland, marsh or prairie landscapes created by the designer in this approach most closely approximates the assemblages found in nature.

> There are but few plants that do not love company. On the other hand, most of them are particular about their associates. The spiritual message or character of the individual plant is often enhanced by its association with other plants which are attune with it. Together they form a tonal quality expressed by an orchestra when certain instruments in chorus bring out a much higher and a much finer feeling than a combination of others. The different plants are then given a chance to speak their best.
>
> Jens Jensen, *Siftings, A Major Portion of the Clearing and Collected Writings*

Both approaches emphasize the ability of native species/communities to exploit the resources available to them in a suitable environment and to survive the competition of other plants also adapted to it. Selecting plants first for their environmental fitness is critical and must precede selection based on texture, color, and shape.

> To me no plant is more refined than that which belongs. There is no comparison between native plants and those imported from foreign shores which are, and shall always remain so, novelties.
>
> Jens Jensen, *Siftings, A Major Portion of the Clearing and Collected Writings*

Advantages of Going Native

Landscaping with native plants has both aesthetic and practical advantages. The native species are best suited to the soil and climate in which they grow and are less demanding in cost and care, if planted in a situation similar to their natural habitat.

Low Maintenance: Most contemporary landscapes are expensive to maintain. The lawn, for example, must be mowed regularly. Small mowers use 5 gallons of gasoline a year and a large riding mower 25 gallons (Gottehrer, 1978), with over 40 million lawnmowers consuming 200 million gallons of gasoline annually (Diekelmann and Schuster, 1982).

The same lawn, in order to be the envy of friends and neighbors for blocks around, requires fertilization to keep it growing in a healthy and vigorous way. We use more fertilizer in the United States on our lawns in one year than is used in India each year for food production (Gottehrer, p. 15). While millions of persons are affected by food shortages, as much as one-sixth of all commercial fertilizers (Diekelmann and Schuster, p. 3) are used to produce verdant green lawns instead of food. Forty percent (Norris, 1982) of all pesticides are used on lawns and gardens, with often harmful effects to surrounding plants and animals. The tremendous waste of water resources to sprinkle lawns each summer when semi-arid regions spend billions of dollars to pipe life-giving water hundreds of miles is a travesty. The result of this sad waste is that more and more consumers are expressing preference for low maintenance landscapes.

The use of native plants in landscape design requires less maintenance because they have evolved so that they maintain the competitive advantage in their niche in the environment. In stressful situations native plants growing in their natural environment are more resistant to disease, insects, physiological disorders, heat, drought, or flooding and are better suited to the conditions of these environments than are most exotics.

Unique Individuality: A second advantage of using native plants is the unique individuality and beauty of any particular place. We plan weekend and extended trips across the country to visit diminishing wild lands whose unique expression of regional and local environment are, for many, the most inspirational and memorable part.

> Vegetation that is native to Iowa is different from vegetation that is native to Florida, and both of those kinds of vegetation are different from Utah's. Sadly, landscaping in any of those places looks pretty much the same. And it is more than the designs that make it so, it's the plants that are used. Think how much more interesting a trip across the country would be if you could see the uniqueness of each environment expressed in its (urban and rural) residential areas.
>
> Carol A. Smyser, *Nature's Design*

Bilogical Diversity: It is one of the primary goals of natural landscaping to improve biological diversity and to contribute to ecological stability. An important advantage of natural landscaping is that biological health and sound ecologic function can be restored to badly damaged landscapes.

Preferred Wildlife Habitat: Planting native species/communities also provides native wildlife with their preferred food, protective cover, and nesting habitat. Since the settlement period, the unabated destruction and degradation of prime wildlife habitats has resulted in the local extirpation of many species. Expanding development pressures into remaining habitat areas threatens the survival of a growing number of others. Remaining wild land areas must be protected and managed effectively. The reintroduction of native species and communites may once again provide islands of refuge for native wildlife in urban areas and help reconnect fragmented habitat and wildlife corridors in rural areas.

Heritage Reclaimed: Plants that are native have evolved through millions of years of competition. They are the most fit to survive each kind of environment. When we plant native species or communities we are endeavoring to reclaim all of the evolutionary history of the site. To restore some of this history for our personal enjoyment and the enjoyment of future generations and to gain knowledge in the process itself is perhaps the most noble and satisfying reason for using native plants.

Planning Natural Landscapes

Recognizing the many advantages of "going native" the question then is how do we go about it? Personal field observation of the relationship of native plants to their natural environment provides a point of beginning. Correlation and support for these observations can be substantiated by review of the local records and writings of amateurs and professionals with expertise and interest in this subject area. Recent university Master's and Ph.D. theses offer detailed community dynamics information.

The most important environmental factor influencing plant distribution at continental scale is climate. Differences in measures of precipitation, light, temperature, radiation, humidity and air movement variously combine to divide the land into many regions of distinctly different habitat and adapted vegetation. The coniferous forests of Canada, deciduous forests of the Eastern United States, and tallgrass prairie landscape of the Midwest are representative.

Throughout each region, plant available moisture is a major limiting environmental factor determining the local distribution of plants. The moisture regimen is associated with differences in topography and soil structure and varies sufficiently to provide a multitude of distinctive habitats and adapted vegetation. Within any given region where similar habitat occurs, then communities of fairly homogenous species consistently recur. This integral relationship between plant community and habitat is predictive and represents the best fit and utilization of available environmental resources.

These collective observations and written documentation become the biological models which influence natural landscaping decisions. By using our knowledge of the different kinds of flora/communities and their most suitable habitat it is possible to develop scenarios that match the most appropriate vegetation expression with the physical resource potential of any restoration site. The potential natural vegetation concept is a particularly important object of natural landscape education, planning, and management because it reveals the biological potential of all urban and rural landscape.

> The little world about us has within it all the joy and happiness that we need. It has all the creative sources essential to making the man-made world beautiful for us to live with and enjoy. Each little world is somewhat different from the next one. Sometimes the difference is great, as between hills and valleys or between mountains and plains, but each speaks its own language. It is by listening to these messages and being inspired by these masterly creations that the world may become in its art expression as rich and as different as the expression of its local color. It is out of this, and out of this alone, that great arts can grow.
>
> Jens Jensen, *Siftings, A Major Portion of the Clearing and Collected Writings*

Natural Succession

The biological models presented above are used by environmental designers as guides in the restoration of natural landscapes. These models, as presented, are incomplete because they consider only relatively stable, self-perpetuating (climax) plant communities. If a major natural or man-made disturbance should occur, the existing environment is dramatically altered. Fire, flooding, logging and surface mining of valuable mineral resources are representative examples of such common disturbance.

A series of dynamic long-term plant recovery changes known as "plant succession" follows. The composition changes with time and varies from habitat to habitat. First weedy herbaceous and grass species colonize the disturbed area, then woody shrubs and vines, followed by tree saplings. With increased competition and shade the grassy colonizers are eliminated. As species/communities with increased shade tolerance assume dominance, others, less tolerant, will decline and disappear. Finally, over the course of several hundred years, a stable climax plant community similar to the original will be achieved — assuming the regional climate has changed little. The vegetation sequence in a particular disturbed habitat is predictable. Similar habitats support similar species/communities that succeed each other in the same order. Contrasting habitats do not support the same sequence.

In disturbed landscapes the environmental designer now has even a broader palette of potential plant to habitat expression. Early or intermediate successional communities may be passed by, for example, by planting a more advanced successional stage. Biologists might plant an intermediate successional community whose cover, nesting habitat, and food opportunities are known to be preferred by an endangered species of wildlife. Other design criteria may favor the selection of a particular successional community over a climax one. For example, on harsh exposed sites, the selection of a vigorous successional community can provide a nursery canopy that will ameliorate the climate beneath for the planting of a more sensitive community.

Ecologist Rexford Daubenmire (Daubenmire and Daubenmire, 1968) has determined the basic ecologic subdivisions of landscapes and describes their distinctive potential to support a specific type of successional or climax vegetation:

> Most of the land has been disturbed by lightning-induced fires or by man's activities in the past century. Therefore, the majority of communities represent varying stages of secondary succession progressing toward one of the climax types, and attention is inevitably directed toward the potentialities of the land. Habitat types are considered the basic ecologic subdivisions of landscapes. Each has a distinctive potential as to sere (successional stage) and climax.

Reading the Landscape

The first step in the planning process is to inventory the potential habitat conditions of the restoration site. Analysis of geologic, physiographic, hydrologic, soils, regional and local climate, vegetation, and wildlife features will reveal the kinds of site habitat present. The potential of each inventoried unit of land must come under scrutiny, for the natural landscape approach requires that each unit be planned on site and mapped for the purpose it serves best. The on/adjacent site presence of native plants in natural groupings has proven to be of high value for indicating habitat potentialities (Küchler, 1964).

Plant Sources

Native plants or seeds are available from several sources. A local source within 100 miles of the site is preferred because these plants have been acclimated and genetically adapted to the area and will have a much better chance of survival. They are also more representative of the local native flora. Plant sales at regional arboretums and at forest and wild-flower preserves can fill some gaps. These same preserves often organize seed collection opportunities at local prairies and woodlands. Sexual and vegetative propagation of native plants is another way of acquiring the materials you need to implement the planting plan.

Plants should never be dug from wild land or rural landscapes. The willingness of some commercial interests, private individuals, and poachers to forage for native plants will be deplored by responsible amateurs and by professional landscape architects, wildlife biologists, ecologists, and nursery people. Foraging on public and private lands does much to offset the value of natural landscape design and is philosophically inconsistent. Digging plants in these areas can lead to prosecution.

> To me it is stupid to transplant trees into an environment they dislike and in which their length of life will be shortened and their real beauty never revealed. Of course the reason for this stupidity is ignorance and commercialism. It is a crime to deface a beautiful countryside, to mutilate what has been

given us, by greed and ignorance. Landscaping will never flourish under those banners.

Jens Jensen, *Siftings, A Major Portion of the Clearing and Collected Writings*

The one obvious exception is the salvage of native plants from permanent destruction by highway, utility, reservoir or other development.

The best source of native plants and seeds is a nursery where they have been propagated. Nursery grown plants are hardier than those collected in the wild because they have been cultivated with more compact root systems, they are less susceptible to disease, they establish more quickly, and are less susceptible to injury or death caused by transplant shock.

A listing of 272 commercial suppliers of wildflower seed and native plants, nursery stock of native trees and shrubs, native grass seed, and tree and shrub seed can be obtained for $3 by writing The Soil Conservation Society of America, 7515 NE Ankeny Road, Ankeny, Iowa 50021.

There has been a swing toward natural landscapes that has, in turn, greatly increased the demand for native plants. Landscape Architects, Urban Foresters, and Wildlife Biologists are specifying native plants for an increasing number of projects. There is a rapidly growing series of articles, books, and journals that have come out recently in response to the rising interest in natural landscaping. Some nurserymen are realizing the value of native plants in landscapes and have begun stocking them. An increasing number of nurseries specialize in native plants.

Management and Maintenance

It is a common misconception that the management of natural landscapes established by man is maintenance free. However, it is true that these landscapes are much less maintenance intensive than exotic or agricultural landscapes.

The primary distinction between management and maintenance is that the first focuses on developing a strategy or plan that will insure the desired landscape effect over time while the latter is the physical act of mowing, weeding or spraying required to implement the management plan.

Maintenance is generally divided into two time periods. Short-term envelops the first 3 years and long-term, after the third year. The short-term program is the more labor intensive of the two because it involves the establishment and monitoring of initial growth in the direction of the intended landscape expression. Examples of short-term maintenance routine include the removal of weed competition by pulling, mowing, or burning, the judicious application of organic fertilizers, and watering in drought periods. Long-term maintenance is minor and may require the organic control of diseases and plant or animal pests.

The management and maintenance of glades, forest openings, barrens, savannas, edges, and old field landscapes is different than that required in forested landscapes. These landscapes are transitional in character with a mosaic pattern of both prairie and forest elements. These landscapes would eventually become forest in environments with enough yearly precipitation to support forest. In order to keep the woody portion from quickly spreading and eventually replacing the shade intolerant prairie grasses, it is necessary to burn or mow the grassland portion. Burning is ideal because it was one of the forces in primeval savanna landscape that kept the advance of woody plants in check. Burning or mowing (in urban or suburban areas where burning is prohibited by closeness of neighbors and laws) at regular intervals weakens competition by early-season weeds, eliminates thatch build-up that hinders seedling development, and eliminates fire sensitive woody plants. Weeds are the primary target of short-term maintenance and woody plant control beyond designated areas is a long-term target. Many of the woody trees and shrubs characteristic of savanna landscapes are fire sensitive and tolerant of open or moderate shade only. In the long-term these open groves will increase their density becoming thickets and will be succeeded by more shade tolerant species typical of forest environments. It will be necessary to prune some stems annually to retain the open character of the grove. Mowing may also prove effective. Fire can be used only if the desired woody species are known to be fire resistant.

The greater stability of climax woodland communities, when married with appropriate habitat, requires much less maintenance than successional or transitional ones. Weeds are a maintenance problem during establishment only. Most are intolerant of shade and will be eliminated with increased closure of the canopy. It may also be necessary to remove volunteer native species over the long-term that are inappropriate to the community planting desired. Young woodland plantings often require protection from wind and sun. Many woods shrub and groundcover species demand shade and stable temperature near the ground. They are sensitive to drought and burn or dehydrate easily when exposed to intense sun or wind. Nursery canopies of quick growing successional species planted with the desired but slower growing trees will provide overhead protection. Heavy edge plantings of quick growing drought resistant shrub species will provide side protection. Both will encourage the health and survival of sensitive woodland species/communities and bring about optimum results.

The New Landscape Ethic

It is only within the past few centuries that the people of the Western world, in their arrogance, have set out to conquer nature, to wrest from her meadows, forests, and waters far more than required to meet human needs — to deplete, lay waste, and to squander. It is this new contemptuous attitude toward nature to which we, haplessly, have fallen heir. It is this recently acquired habit of wanton destruction, this acceptance of mass slaughter of wildlife to the point of extinction, this compulsion to reshape and reorder the landforms and waterways, that has led us in the United States to ravish and befoul to a shameful degree this "Land that we love."
John O. Simonds, *Earthscape*

Within the present decade the citizenry of this country have been stirred by a sense of revulsion of technological advances made at great environmental expense. There is an urgent demand for reform and a new yearning for a way of life attuned to nature's way. What is emerging is a whole new ethic of environmental protection and design.

In 1949 the book *A Sand County Almanac* was published and was modestly received. Two decades later the present environmental movement discovered in its author, Aldo Leopold, the father of the American conservation ethic. Leopold, an extraordinary naturalist, elevated ecology to philosophy and literature. "He tied the future of the natural world — what he called land, what we now call environment — to man's conscience. His message — the keel of his thinking — was a gentle plea for self-inquiry" (Gibbons, 1981).

There is as yet no ethic dealing with man's relation to land and to the animals and plants which grow upon it... The land-relation is still strictly economic, entailing privileges but not obligations... Obligations have no meaning without conscience, and the problem we face is the extension of the social conscience from people to land.

No important change in ethics was ever accomplished without an internal change in our intellectual emphasis, loyalties, affections, and convictions. The proof that conservation has not yet touched these foundations of conduct lies in the fact that philosophy and religion have not yet heard of it.

We shall never achieve harmony with land, any more than we shall achieve justice or liberty for people. In these higher aspirations the important thing is not to achieve, but to strive...

That land is a community is the basic concept of ecology, but that land is
to be loved and respected is an extension of ethics.
Aldo Leopold, as quoted in
National Geographic
by Boyd Gibbons

To preserve our superlative remaining natural landscape and wilderness, to conserve rural landscape character, and to design and restore appropriate developed landscapes to natural condition, especially in urban and rural areas, and to manage all for the enjoyment and use of present and future generations: these are the goals of this dynamic new landscape ethic.

Only two kinds of landscape are fully satisfying. One is primeval nature undisturbed by man; we shall have less and less of it as the world population increases. The other is one in which man has toiled and created through trial and error a kind of harmony between himself and the physical environment. What we long for is rarely nature in the raw; more often it is an atmosphere suited to human limitations, and determined by emotional aspirations engendered during centuries of civilized life. The charm of the New England or Pennsylvania Dutch countryside should not be taken for granted, as a product of chance. It did not result from man's conquest of nature. Rather it is the expression of a subtle process through which the natural environment was humanized, yet retained its own individual genius.
Rene Dubos, as quoted in
Earthscape
by John O. Simonds

Viewpoint

At first glance the concept of natural landscaping appears to promote the design and restoration of wilderness-type landscapes only. Although wild land restoration is appropriate to many large scale quasi-wild and rural areas; to public parks, gardens, and arboretums; to corporate or commercial sites; and to large private estates: it is not generally appropriate to small scale residential landscape situations in urban and suburban areas. The apparent chaos and primeval character of "wilderness" in this setting is as uncomfortable and as unlivable as the "civilized" structure of formal garden and bluegrass lawn. In the small-lot residential situation a different expression of natural landscape is required. This "cultured" type of landscape is intermediate between the other two and is most appropriate and acceptable. Border plantings of native species or communities surrounding grass lawn areas with flowing irregular defined edges are characteristic of this second natural landscape type. Use of the cultured-type in residential settings often avoids the controversy associated with the wilderness expression.

Still, there will continue to be those skeptics with the opposing view that even cultured natural landscape designs are eyesores of maintenance neglect and homeowner laziness. This view also embraces the belief that native plants are "weeds" and landscapes that exhibit them — weedy! Sadly, these are the perceptions of the arrogant and the uneducated.

There is probably no word used to describe plants which is so misapplied and misunderstood as the term — weed. To many persons weeds are those plants which are unfamiliar, undesirable, useless, or harmful. Such definitions are based on physiological and psychological human responses and could apply to any plant, anywhere!

Botanists have defined weeds as plants that grow spontaneously in a habitat that has been greatly modified by man, and especially a species confined chiefly or exclusively to such habitats. Rarely then, does a member of a native plant community become a weed if we apply this definition. In fact, many of the worst weed offenders are exotic species, originating from another continent. These cannot compete successfully with the native species in stable natural environments. The majority of exotic trees, shrubs, and vines planted for ornament are also weeds since they cannot reproduce and survive without manmade and maintained environment. Most agricultural crops then are also weeds.

All of this discussion is leading up to one fundamental conclusion: that any plant can be considered a weed if the appropriate definition, as determined by the individual, is applied. Of course, exotics planted for ornament and agrinomic crops planted to help feed the world's hungry are not considered by most persons to be weeds by any stretch of the imagination.

To consider native plants as weeds is also unfair. It is a fundamental educational objective of natural landscaping enthusiasts, professionals, and industry to correct this misconception that equates weeds with native plants and natural landscape design with eyesores and laziness. The lack of public awareness and education regarding the beauty and practicality of using natives in landscape design is a major contemporary concern and challenge.

It is often remarked, "native plants are coarse." How humiliating to hear an American speak so of plants with which the Great Master has decorated his land! To me no plant is more refined than that which belongs. There is no comparison between native plants and those imported from foreign shores which are, and shall always remain so, novelties. If, however, as is said, our native landscape is coarse, then as times goes by we, the American people, shall also become coarse because we shall be molded into our environment.
Jens Jensen, *Siftings, A Major Portion of the Clearing and Collected Writings*

Part II of this volume offers a classification format and text that identifies, categorizes, and theorizes about the benefits and uses of native shrubs and vines.

How to Use Part II
Part II is divided into two principal parts: an **ELIMINATION KEY** section followed by a **MASTER PLATES** section.

ELIMINATION KEY
Shrub and vine selection is based on definite classifiable characteristics. No two shrubs/vines exhibit all the same characteristics. If the list of plant performance criteria is expanded it becomes possible to narrow the selection field to a few suitable species by eliminating the unsuitable from consideration. This is done simply and quickly in this book by employing the elimination key format.

Plants that exhibit similar design characteristics are grouped together in plant lists. These plant lists are organized and classified according to various design attributes under three primary categories which include visual characteristics, cultural requirements, and ecological relationships. When choosing a suitable shrub or vine for a specific design criteria (for example, shrubs with colorful white flowers), the process would be to 1) consult the general category (flower coloration), 2) identify the specific color feature (white) and 3) review the corresponding plant list. Such plant lists facilitate efficient comparison between plants exhibiting similar design characteristics. Shrubs and vines within each category are listed in alphabetical order according to their botanic or scientific names, genus first, followed by the species name. Preferred common names are included in parenthesis. Important botanic nomenclature is quickly learned through repeated association with the more famliar preferred common name.

The **ELIMINATION KEY** section presents basic classification terminology and descriptions used in this book. The principle advantage of the **ELIMINATION KEY** is that the designer need be familiar only with the plant performance criteria. Prior knowledge regarding specific plant species, although helpful, is not necessary. The plants under consideration can be explored in greater written and illustrated detail by consulting the **MASTER PLATE** section.

MASTER PLATES

This section brings together all the design information for any given shrub or vine. If the designer is familiar with the specific plant under consideration, consulting directly the **MASTER PLATE** text and illustrations would be the next step in determining the plant's suitability in the design program. If the botanic or preferred common name is known, it is not necessary to consult the key, and the **MASTER PLATE** can be consulted directly by using the index in the back of the book. At the heading of each **MASTER PLATE** the botanical name (left page) and the preferred common name (right page) are given.

Text: The format of the **MASTER PLATE** text offers the designer a classification system which facilitates efficient plant comparison and the analysis and synthesis of important design criteria. The classification system employed in this manual establishes a rational hierarchy showing relationships among and between categories. This hierarchy is organized as follows:

GENERAL CHARACTERISTIC GROUP, all plant information is organized into three areas of designer concern, e.g. *VISUAL CHARACTERISTICS, ECOLOGICAL RELATIONSHIPS,* and *CULTURAL REQUIREMENTS.*

PRIMARY CHARACTERISTIC CLASS e.g. **FORM, BRANCHING, FOLIAGE, FLOWER, FRUIT** (Identified by bold face caps).

Seconday Characteristic Class, e.g. Size, Spread, Mass, Twig, Bud, Bark (Identified by medium face, first letter caps).

Specific design data, e.g. **small shrub, wide, dense** (Identified by bold face, lower case. These are key words which are cross-referenced to the plant lists presented in the **ELIMINATION KEY** section).

Specific design data, e.g. from 1 to 2 m (3 to 6 ft) (Identified by medium face, lower case. This is additional text presented for clarity and designer review. This information is not of key word importance and is not reflected in the **ELIMINATION KEY** section).

The classification system as it appears in the **MASTER PLATE** text is summarized below and the major categories are identified.

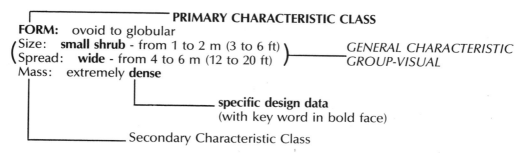

PRIMARY CHARACTERISTIC CLASS

FORM: ovoid to globular

Size: **small shrub** - from 1 to 2 m (3 to 6 ft)

Spread: **wide** - from 4 to 6 m (12 to 20 ft)

Mass: extremely **dense**

GENERAL CHARACTERISTIC GROUP-VISUAL

specific design data
(with key word in bold face)

Secondary Characteristic Class

Metric and Standard Measure: The metric system has been used throughout. The following table of approximate equivalents will clarify the measurements for the reader who is not familiar with metric measure. In the text all metric measurements are followed by the American Standard Equivalent in parentheses. It was felt that by repeatedly seeing both systems of measure side by side the reader would quickly become familiar with the metric equivalent through association.

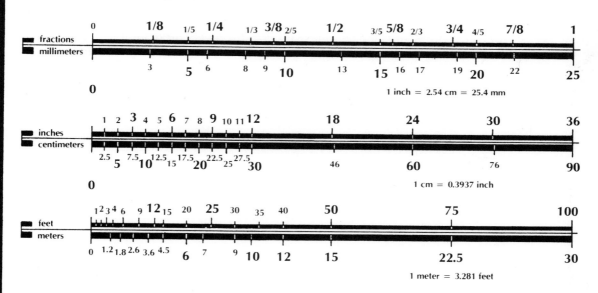

Common metric conversion factors
   1 cm = 0.3937 inch
   1 inch = 2.54 cm = 25.4 mm
   1 meter = 3.281 feet
   1 foot = 0.3048 meter

Symbols: For convenience and quick cross-reference between sections, a system of abstract pictorial symbols is used in the margins of both the **ELIMINATION KEY** section and the **MASTER PLATE** section opposite the corresponding written characteristics description.

Range Map: The natural range of each native shrub/vine is mapped showing geographic distribution by county. The use of geographic distribution maps as general guides to the preservation, conservation, and restoration of natural landscapes is encouraged. Even though a species is not recorded for a certain county, its proved occurrence in an adjacent county or within the same floristic region may be taken to mean that its adaptability is possible (providing suitable habitat exists).

Photography: We have elected in this part to use black-and-white photography to show important bark and shrub crown characteristics. Freehand illustration could not adequately capture the finer texture of bark and greater density of shrub crown stems and branches. Several adjustments were made to alleviate the objections to the use of photographic images cited in part I.

All of the bark details and shrub crowns were photographed by the author in the field at various arboretums and botanic gardens throughout the east and midwest. Care was taken to select representative plants with typical bark and adult crown form for each species. Separation of the photographic subject from competing background images was accomplished by the use of styrofoam screens placed immediately behind the subject. Light direction (side light) was selected to enhance perception of detailed bark/crown differences and to eliminate screen shadow (back light) or plant shadow (front light).

Drawings: Freehand illustrations of important plant details (for example; twig, bud, foliage, flower, fruit, and armament) are also included for reference and clarification. The majority of the illustrations of twig and leaf were drawn from photographic records with a few from fresh or herbarium specimens. The artwork in combination with the photography is intended to assist the amateur, student, and professional in the selection of native shrub and vine species that fulfill the design program. Over 430 photographs and freehand drawings capture the visual spirit of 145 native shrubs and vines.

Region of Use: The region of application and use of this manual includes southeastern and south central Canada; north central, northeastern, central, east central, south central and southeastern United States.

ACKNOWLEDGMENTS

The author wishes to express his thanks to the many students, colleagues, professionals, and laypersons who have kindly given criticism, advice, and encouragement, particularly Daniel L. Griffen, Jr., Executive Director of the Iowa State University Research Foundation. His cooperation, interest in native plant materials, patience, and enthusiasm for this project are greatly appreciated.

Part II could not have been successfully written without the invaluable artistic, photographic, research, and secretarial skills and assistance of the following persons, who carried a major share of the responsibility:

Harlen D. Groe, Landscape Architect, Ames, Iowa; for his ingenious and painstaking labor in creating and producing the design format, graphic and copy layout, drafting the range maps, symbol design, and providing the author with technical advice and field assistance in the photographing of crown and bark details.

Craig D. Ritland, Landscape Architect, Waterloo, Iowa; for over 165 original illustrations. His artistic skills capture so well the detailed spirit of the native shrubs and trees.

Nancy M. Santen; for her secretarial skills and dedication in typing the many drafts of the text and plant lists.

Laura Knowles Verden, Landscape Architect, Wilton, Iowa; for her research assistance and painstaking review of the published plant literature.

I am especially indebted to the many arboreta, public gardens, and university campuses whose nationally recognized libraries, plant collections, and staff were critical resources consulted.

Arnold Arboretum, Jamaica Plain (Boston), MA
Bernheim Forest, Clermont, KY
Bickelhaupt Arboretum, Clinton, IA
Brookgreen Gardens, Murrels Inlet, SC
Brooklyn Botanic Garden, New York, NY
Calloway Gardens, Pine Mountain, GA
Core Arboretum, Morgantown, WV
Dawes Arboretum, Newark, OH
Gardens de Pajarito, Canton, GA
Harvard University, Cambridge, MA
Holden Arboretum, Mentor, OH
Iowa State University, Ames, IA
Longwood Gardens, Kennet Square, PA
Middleton Place, Charleston, SC
Missouri Botanical Gardens, St. Louis, MO
Morton Arboretum, Lisle, IL
North Carolina Botanical Gardens, Chapel Hill, NC
Secrest Arboretum, Wooster, OH
University of Minnesota Landscape Arboretum, Chaska, MN
University of Wisconsin Arboretum, Madison, WI
U.S. National Arboretum, Washington, D.C.

A special thank you to Bob and Frances Bicklehaupt for the warm hospitality shown the author in the initial stages of the project and for their help in identifying important resource persons and places to visit.

Several State Herbaria maintain unpublished card files of maps showing where herbarium specimens were collected. In 9 states species maps with county locality records of specimens kindly were made available or were compiled by the curators as follows:

William A. Anderson, University of Michigan, Ann Arbor
Lois Arnow, University of Utah, Salt Lake City
Dennis E. Breedlove, California Academy of Sciences, San Francisco
R. Brook, Simon Fraser University, Burnaby, British Columbia
C. C. Chinnappa, University of Calgary, Calgary, Alberta
Nancy C. Coile, University of Georgia, Athens
Bernard De Vries, Fort Qu'Appelle, Saskachewan
Ronald L. Harman, University of Wyoming, Laramie
Vernon L. Harms, University of Saskachewan, Saskatoon
Douglass M. Henderson, University of Idaho, Moscow
Harold R. Hinds, University of New Brunswick, Fredericton
Karl E. Holte, Idaho State University, Pocatello
Hugh H. Iltis, University of Wisconsin, Madison
Frederick D. Johnson, University of Idaho, Moscow
Walter S. Judd, University of Florida, Gainesville
Helen Kennedy, University of Manitoba, Winnipeg
Jan Looman, Agriculture Canada, Swift Current, Saskatchewan
Sidney McDaniel, Mississippi State University, Mississippi State
William C. Martin, University of New Mexico, Albuquerque
Charles T. Mason, Jr., University of Arizona, Tucson
Joy Mastrogiuseppe, Washington State University, Pullman
J. R. Maze, University of British Columbia, Vancouver
Willem Meijer, University of Kentucky, Lexington
Hugh N. Mozingo, University of Nevada, Reno
Wesley E. Niles, University of Nevada, Las Vegas
R. T. Ogilvie, British Columbia Provincial Museum, Victoria
Gerald B. Ownbey, University of Minnesota, Saint Paul
John G. Packer, University of Alberta, Edmonton
Ann Pinzl, Nevada State Museum, Carson City
Richard W. Pohl, Iowa State University, Ames
Jackie M. Poole, University of Texas, Austin
Sherman J. Preece, University of Montana, Missoula
Thomas M. Pullen, University of Mississippi, University
John H. Rumely, Montana State University, Bozeman
Charles J. Sheviek, New York State Museum, Albany
Leila M. Shultz, Utah State University, Logan
Peter F. Stickney, USDA Forestry Sciences Laboratory, Missoula
R. Dale Thomas, Northeast Louisiana University, Monroe
Kaye H. Thorne, Brigham Young University, Provo
David H. Wagner, University of Oregon, Eugene
William A. Webber, University of Colorado Museum, Boulder
Dieter H. Wilken, Colorado State University, Fort Collins
B. Eugene Wofford, University of Tennessee, Knoxville

We acknowledge our fundamental debt to the many botanists, horticulturists, foresters, landscape architects, and landscape gardeners past and present, whose popular writings and teachings form the background upon which we have relied. The author, of course, accepts full responsibility for any inaccuracies or misrepresentation of the information herein.

I am forever grateful to my wife Joan, daughters Kate and Jessica, and son Tobin, for their unwavering support of my professional interests and writing.

SHRUB AND VINE ELIMINATION KEY

NOMENCLATURE:

The scientific and common names used in this book are given in Kelsey and Dayton (1942). Shrubs and vines are listed alphabetically according to their scientific or botanical name. *Standardized Plant Names,* second edition, is approved by the American Committee on Horticultural Nomenclature and the American Society of Landscape Architects. Botanical nomenclature has several principal advantages: it is understood in all countries, is based on natural relationships of plants and is consistent in form. Common names, however, were not originated with these features in mind. Many common names for the same plant are encountered and reflect local usage. Many plants also share the same common names. The plants used in landscape design can be designated by using the generic and specific name. Generic names (genus) distinguish groups of plants such as azaleas and viburnums. Specific names (species) are used to distinguish variables within a genus and are generally descriptive of some visual or physiological aspect such as (leaf) size, shape, color, texture and surface, or geographical aspect (virginiana, canadensis, americana).

FORM:

Each species of shrub or vine has a characteristic shape when grown in an open field under favorable environmental conditions. The shape of a particular shrub or vine refers to the outline of the crown as perceived in silhouette. Volumetric description (shrubs) and life form (vines) best expresses the adult crown form for each species. Nine basic crown forms for natural, open grown shrubs and vines are classified.

GLOBULAR:
rounded circular form, vertical and horizontal axis about equal,
indicator — *Potentilla fruticosa* (Bush Cinquefoil)

Aesculus parviflora (Bottlebrush Buckeye)
Aesculus pavia (Red Buckeye)
Alnus serrulata (Common Alder)
Amorpha canescens (Leadplant Amorpha)
Amorpha fruticosa (Indigobush Amorpha)
Aronia melanocarpa (Black Chokeberry)
Aronia prunifolia (Purplefruit Chokeberry)
Baccharis halimifolia (Eastern Baccharis)
Betula pumila (Low Birch)
Calycanthus floridus (Common Sweetshrub)
Castanea pumila (Allegany Chinkapin)
Cephalanthus occidentalis (Common Buttonbush)
Comptonia peregrina (Sweetfern)
Cornus amomum (Silky Dogwood)
Cornus stolonifera (Redosier Dogwood)
Corylus americana (American Filbert)
Corylus cornuta (Beaked Filbert)
Cyrilla racemiflora (American Cyrilla)
Dirca palustris (Atlantic Leatherwood)
Elaeagnus commutata (Silverberry)
Fothergilla gardeni (Dwarf Fothergilla)
Hamamelis vernalis (Vernal Witchhazel)
Hydrangea arborescens (Smooth Hydrangea)
Hydrangea quercifolia (Oakleaf Hydrangea)

Hypericum frondosum (Golden St.Johnswort)
Ilex glabra (Inkberry)
Itea virginica (Virginia Sweetspire)
Ledum groenlandicum (Labradortea Ledum)
Lindera benzoin (Common Spicebush)
Neviusia alabamensis (Snowwreath)
Pinus aristata (Bristlecone Pine)
Potentilla fruticosa (Bush Cinquefoil)
Prunus hortulana (Hortulan Plum)
Quercus ilicifolia (Scrub Oak)
Quercus prinoides (Dwarf Chinkapin Oak)
Rhododendron arborescens (Sweet Azalea)
Rhododendron calendulaceum (Flame Azalea)
Rhododendron carolinianum (Carolina Rhododendron)
Rhododendron catawbiense (Catawba Rhododendron)
Rhododendron nudiflorum (Pinxterbloom Azalea)
Rhododendron roseum (Roseshell Azalea)
Rhododendron vaseyi (Pinkshell Azalea)
Rhododendron viscosum (Swamp Azalea)
Ribes americanum (American Black Currant)
Ribes cynosbati (Pasture Gooseberry)
Ribes missouriense (Missouri Gooseberry)
Ribes odoratum (Clove Currant)
Salix humilis (Prairie Willow)

Form (cont.)

Salix lucida (Shining Willow)
Sambucus canadensis (American Elder)
Sambucus pubens (Scarlet Elder)
Shepherdia argentea (Silver Buffaloberry)
Shepherdia canadensis (Russet Buffaloberry)
Symphoricarpos albus (Common Snowberry)
Vaccinium angustifolium (Lowbush Blueberry)
Vaccinium corymbosum (Highbush Blueberry)
Vaccinium stamineum (Common Deerberry)

Viburnum acerifolium (Mapleleaf Viburnum)
Viburnum alnifolium (Hobblebush Viburnum)
Viburnum cassinoides (Witherod Viburnum)
Viburnum dentatum (Arrowwood Viburnum)
Viburnum nudum (Possumhaw Viburnum)
Viburnum rafinesquianum (Rafinesque Viburnum)
Viburnum trilobum (American Cranberrybush Viburnum)
Yucca filamentosa (Adamsneedle Yucca)
Zenobia pulverulenta (Dusty Zenobia)

OVOID:
elliptic to egg-shaped, broadest at base, vertical axis exceeding horizontal by 2 to 1 ratio,
indicator — Stewartia ovata (Mountain Stewartia)

Clethra alnifolia (Summersweet Clethra)
Hypericum densiflorum (Dense Hypericum)

Rhododendron vaseyi (Pinkshell Azalea)
Stewartia ovata (Mountain Stewartia)

OBOVOID:
elliptic to egg-shaped, broadest at crown apex, vertical axis exceeding horizontal by 2 to 1 ratio,
indicator — Viburnum dentatum (Arrowwood Viburnum)

Aesculus pavia (Red Buckeye)
Alnus serrulata (Common Alder)
Aronia arbutifolia (Red Chokeberry)
Aronia prunifolia (Purplefruit Chokeberry)
Baccharis halimifolia (Eastern Baccharis)
Clethra alnifolia (Summersweet Clethra)
Cornus racemosa (Gray Dogwood)
Cornus rugosa (Roundleaf Dogwood)
Elaeagnus commutata (Silverberry)
Euonymus americanus (Brook Euonymus)
Fothergilla major (Large Fothergilla)
Hamamelis vernalis (Vernal Witchhazel)
Hypericum densiflorum (Dense Hypericum)
Ilex decidua (Possumhaw)
Ilex verticillata (Common Winterberry)
Lyonia ligustrina (He-huckleberry)
Magnolia virginiana (Sweetbay Magnolia)

Philadelphus grandiflorus (Big Scentless Mockorange)
Rhododendron vaseyi (Pinkshell Azalea)
Robinia hispida (Roseacacia Locust)
Robinia viscosa (Clammy Locust)
Sambucus canadensis (American Elder)
Sambucus pubens (Scarlet Elder)
Shepherdia argentea (Silver Buffaloberry)
Shepherdia canadensis (Russet Buffaloberry)
Staphylea trifolia (American Bladdernut)
Viburnum acerifolium (Mapleleaf Viburnum)
Viburnum alnifolium (Hobblebush Viburnum)
Viburnum cassinoides (Witherod Viburnum)
Viburnum dentatum (Arrowwood Viburnum)
Viburnum nudum (Possumhaw Viburnum)
Viburnum rafinesquianum (Rafinesque Viburnum)
Viburnum trilobum (American Cranberrybush Viburnum)

IRREGULAR:
asymmetrical, uneven outline,
indicator — Robinia hispida (Roseacacia Locust)

Pinus aristata (Bristlecone Pine)
Robinia hispida (Roseacacia Locust)

Robinia viscosa (Clammy Locust)

MOUND:
broad elliptic shape; horizontal axis exceeding vertical by 2 to 1 or 3 to 1 ratio,
indicator — Myrica pensylvanica (Northern Bayberry)

Aesculus parviflora (Bottlebrush Buckeye)
Amelanchier sanguinea (Roundleaf Serviceberry)
Amorpha canescens (Leadplant Amorpha)
Amorpha fruticosa (Indigobush Amorpha)
Andromeda polifolia (Bogrosemary Andromeda)
Aronia melanocarpa (Black Chokeberry)
Betula pumila (Low Birch)

Calycanthus floridus (Common Sweetshrub)
Ceanothus americanus (Jerseytea Ceanothus)
Ceanothus ovatus (Inland Ceanothus)
Cephalanthus occidentalis (Common Buttonbush)
Chamaedaphne calyculata (Leatherleaf)
Clethra acuminata (Cinnamon Clethra)
Comptonia peregrina (Sweetfern)

Cornus amomum   (Silky Dogwood)
Cornus stolonifera   (Redosier Dogwood)
Corylus americana   (American Filbert)
Corylus cornuta   (Beaked Filbert)
Diervilla lonicera   (Dwarf Bushhoneysuckle)
Fothergilla gardeni   (Dwarf Fothergilla)
Hydrangea arborescens   (Smooth Hydrangea)
Hydrangea quercifolia   (Oakleaf Hydrangea)
Hypericum kalmianum   (Kalm St.Johnswort)
Hypericum prolificum   (Shrubby St.Johnswort)
Ilex glabra   (Inkberry)
Itea virginica   (Virginia Sweetspire)
Kalmia latifolia   (Mountainlaurel Kalmia)
Leiophyllum buxifolium   (Box Sandmyrtle)
Leucothoe catesbaei   (Drooping Leucothoe)
Lonicera canadensis   (American Fly Honeysuckle)
Mahonia aquifolium   (Oregongrape)
Myrica pensylvanica   (Northern Bayberry)
Physocarpus opulifolius   (Common Ninebark)
Pieris floribunda   (Mountain Pieris)

Potentilla fruticosa   (Bush Cinquefoil)
Rhododendron arborescens   (Sweet Azalea)
Rhododendron catawbiense   (Catawba Rhododendron)
Rhus aromatica   (Fragrant Sumac)
Rosa carolina   (Carolina Rose)
Rosa setigera   (Prairie Rose)
Rubus allegheniensis   (Allegany Blackberry)
Rubus occidentalis   (Blackcap Raspberry)
Rubus odoratus   (Fragrant Thimbleberry)
Rubus strigosus   (American Red Raspberry)
Salix humilis   (Prairie Willow)
Salix lucida   (Shining Willow)
Shepherdia argentea   (Silver Buffaloberry)
Spiraea alba   (Narrowleaf Meadowsweet Spirea)
Spiraea corymbosa   (Corymed Spirea)
Spiraea tomentosa   (Hardhack Spirea)
Symphoricarpos albus   (Common Snowberry)
Symphoricarpos occidentalis   (Western Snowberry)
Symphoricarpos orbiculatus   (Indiancurrant Coralberry)
Zenobia pulverulenta   (Dusty Zenobia)

MAT:
      prostrate, low, widespreading form; horizontal axis greatly exceeds vertical, from 3 to 1 up to 10 to 1
      ratio or more,
      indicator — Juniperus horizontalis (Creeping Juniper)

Arctostaphylos uva-ursi   (Bearberry)
Cornus canadensis   (Bunchberry Dogwood)
Epigaea repens   (Trailing-arbutus)
Euonymus obovatus   (Running Euonymus)
Gaultheria procumbens   (Checkerberry Wintergreen)
Juniperus communis   (Common Juniper)
Juniperus horizontalis   (Creeping Juniper)

Kalmia angustifolia   (Lambkill Kalmia)
Kalmia polifolia   (Bog Kalmia)
Pachistima canbyi   (Canby Pachistima)
Taxus canadensis   (Canada Yew)
Vaccinium macrocarpum   (Cranberry)
Xanthorhiza simplicissima   (Yellowroot)

CLIMBING:
      tall growing vines which use other plants or objects for vertical support,
      indicator — Campsis radicans (Common Trumpetcreeper)

Ampelopsis arborea   (Peppervine)
Ampelopsis cordata   (Heartleaf Ampelopsis)
Aristolochia durior   (Common Dutchmanspipe)
Berchemia scandens   (Alabama Supplejack)
Bignonia capreolata   (Crossvine)
Campsis radicans   (Common Trumpetcreeper)
Celastrus scandens   (American Bittersweet)
Clematis verticillaris   (Rock Clematis)
Clematis virginiana   (Virginsbower)
Cocculus carolinus   (Carolina Snailseed)
Lonicera dioica   (Limber Honeysuckle)

Lonicera sempervirens   (Trumpet Honeysuckle)
Menispermum canadense   (Common Moonseed)
Parthenocissus quinquefolia   (Virginia Creeper)
Smilax glauca   (Cat Greenbrier)
Smilax rotundifolia   (Common Greenbrier)
Smilax tamnoides   (Bamboo Greenbrier)
Toxicodendron radicans   (Common Poisonivy)
Vitis labrusca   (Fox Grape)
Vitis riparia   (Riverbank Grape)
Wistaria macrostachya   (Kentucky Wistaria)

SHRUB-LIKE:
      multi-branched vines which resemble a woody shrub in appearance and structure,
      indicator — Lonicera dioica (Limber Honeysuckle)

Ampelopsis arborea   (Peppervine)
Ampelopsis cordata   (Heartleaf Ampelopsis)

Lonicera dioica   (Limber Honeysuckle)
Toxicodendron radicans   (Common Poisonivy)

Form (cont.)

GROUNDCOVER-LIKE:
   low growing vines which trail on the ground resembling herbaceous groundcover,
   indicator — *Parthenocissus quinquefolia* (Virginia Creeper)

Ampelopsis arborea (Peppervine)
Menispermum canadense (Common Moonseed)

Parthenocissus quinquefolia (Virginia Creeper)
Toxicodendron radicans (Common Poisonivy)

SIZE:

The compatibility of the dimensional measure of a selected plant crown with the designed program function is essential. Designer knowledge of the relative mature height and spread is especially critical where spatial limitations exist. Failure to recognize the potential adult size of a plant results in spatial overcrowding and often necessitates severe and unsightly maintenance, which alters the natural form of the plant and consequently the designer's intent. Knowledge of mature crown size is demanded if proper scale and proportion are to be achieved in the designed landscape expression.

SHRUB HEIGHT: Four strata of relative mature height are classified

LARGE SHRUB:
   from 4 to 6 meters (12 to 20 feet) or more,
   indicator — *Magnolia virginiana* (Sweetbay Magnolia)

Aesculus pavia (Red Buckeye)
Alnus serrulata (Common Alder)
Betula pumila (Low Birch)
Castanea pumila (Allegany Chinkapin)
Clethra acuminata (Cinnamon Clethra)
Cyrilla racemiflora (American Cyrilla)
Ilex decidua (Possumhaw)
Kalmia latifolia (Mountainlaurel Kalmia)

Magnolia virginiana (Sweetbay Magnolia)
Pinus aristata (Bristlecone Pine)
Prunus hortulana (Hortulan Plum)
Quercus prinoides (Dwarf Chinkapin Oak)
Rhododendron arborescens (Sweet Azalea)
Salix lucida (Shining Willow)
Stewartia ovata (Mountain Stewartia)
Viburnum nudum (Possumhaw Viburnum)

MID-HEIGHT SHRUB:
   from 2 to 4 meters (6 to 12 feet),
   indicator — *Cornus stolonifera* (Redosier Dogwood)

Aesculus parviflora (Bottlebrush Buckeye)
Amorpha fruticosa (Indigobush Amorpha)
Aronia arbutifolia (Red Chokeberry)
Aronia prunifolia (Purplefruit Chokeberry)
Baccharis halimifolia (Eastern Baccharis)
Calycanthus floridus (Common Sweetshrub)
Cephalanthus occidentalis (Common Buttonbush)
Clethra alnifolia (Summersweet Clethra)
Cornus amomum (Silky Dogwood)
Cornus racemosa (Gray Dogwood)
Cornus rugosa (Roundleaf Dogwood)
Cornus stolonifera (Redosier Dogwood)
Corylus americana (American Filbert))
Corylus cornuta (Beaked Filbert)
Elaeagnus commutata (Silverberry)
Euonymus americanus (Brook Euonymus)
Fothergilla major (Large Fothergilla)
Hamamelis vernalis (Vernal Witchhazel)

Ilex glabra (Inkberry)
Ilex verticillata (Common Winterberry)
Itea virginica (Virginia Sweetspire)
Lindera benzoin (Common Spicebush)
Lyonia ligustrina (He-huckleberry)
Myrica pensylvanica (Northern Bayberry)
Philadelphus grandiflorus (Big Scentless Mockorange)
Physocarpus opulifolius (Common Ninebark)
Quercus ilicifolia (Scrub Oak)
Rhododendron calendulaceum (Flame Azalea)
Rhododendron catawbiense (Catwaba Rhododendron)
Rhododendron nudiflorum (Pinxterbloom Azalea)
Rhododendron roseum (Roseshell Azalea)
Rhododendron vaseyi (Pinkshell Azalea)
Rhododendron viscosum (Swamp Azalea)
Rhus aromatica (Fragrant Sumac)
Ribes odoratum (Clove Currant)
Robinia hispida (Roseacacia Locust)

Robinia viscosa (Clammy Locust)
Rosa setigera (Prairie Rose)
Salix humilis (Prairie Willow)
Sambucus canadensis (American Elder)
Sambucus pubens (Scarlet Elder)
Shepherdia argentea (Silver Buffaloberry)
Shepherdia canadensis (Russet Buffaloberry)

Staphylea trifolia (American Bladdernut)
Vaccinium corymbosum (Highbush Blueberry)
Vaccinium stamineum (Common Deerberry)
Viburnum alnifolium (Hobblebush Viburnum)
Viburnum cassinoides (Witherod Viburnum)
Viburnum dentatum (Arrowwood Viburnum)
Viburnum trilobum (American Cranberrybush Viburnum)

SMALL SHRUB:
from 1 to 2 meters (3 to 6 feet),
indicator — Ribes cynosbati (Pasture Gooseberry)

Amelanchier sanguinea (Roundleaf Serviceberry)
Aronia melanocarpa (Black Chokeberry)
Dirca palustris (Atlantic Leatherwood)
Hydrangea arborescens (Smooth Hydrangea)
Hydrangea quercifolia (Oakleaf Hydrangea)
Hypericum densiflorum (Dense Hypericum)
Juniperus communis (Common Juniper)
Leucothoe catesbaei (Drooping Leucothoe)
Lonicera canadensis (American Fly Honeysuckle)
Mahonia aquifolium (Oregongrape)
Neviusia alabamensis (Snowwreath)
Pieris floribunda (Mountain Pieris)
Rhododendron carolinianum (Carolina Rhododendron)
Ribes americanum (American Black Currant)
Ribes cynosbati (Pasture Gooseberry)

Ribes missouriense (Missouri Gooseberry)
Rubus allegheniensis (Allegany Blackberry)
Rubus occidentalis (Blackcap Raspberry)
Rubus odoratus (Fragrant Thimbleberry)
Rubus strigosus (American Red Raspberry)
Spiraea alba (Narrowleaf Meadowsweet Spirea)
Spiraea corymbosa (Corymed Spirea)
Spiraea tomentosa (Hardhack Spirea)
Symphoricarpos albus (Common Snowberry)
Symphoricarpos occidentalis (Western Snowberry)
Symphoricarpos orbiculatus (Indiancurrant Coralberry)
Taxus canadensis (Canada Yew)
Viburnum acerifolium (Mapleleaf Viburnum)
Viburnum rafinesquianum (Rafinesque Viburnum)
Zenobia pulverulenta (Dusty Zenobia)

VERY SMALL SHRUB:
generally less than 1 meter (3 feet),
indicator — Ceanothus americanus (Jerseytea Ceanothus)

Amorpha canescens (Leadplant Amorpha)
Andromeda polifolia (Bogrosemary Andromeda) *
Arctostaphylos uva-ursi (Bearberry) *
Ceanothus americanus (Jerseytea Ceanothus)
Ceanothus ovatus (Inland Ceanothus)
Chamaedaphne calyculata (Leatherleaf)
Comptonia peregrina (Sweetfern)
Cornus canadensis (Bunchberry Dogwood) *
Diervilla lonicera (Dwarf Bushhoneysuckle)
Epigaea repens (Trailing-arbutus) *
Euonymus obovatus (Running Euonymus) *
Fothergilla gardeni (Dwarf Fothergilla)
Gaultheria procumbens (Checkerberry Wintergreen) *
Hypericum frondosum (Golden St.Johnswort)

Hypericum kalmianum (Kalm St.Johnswort)
Hypericum prolificum (Shrubby St.Johnswort)
Juniperus horizontalis (Creeping Juniper)
Kalmia angustifolia (Lambkill Kalmia)
Kalmia polifolia (Bog Kalmia)
Ledum groenlandicum (Labradortea Ledum)
Leiophyllum buxifolium (Box Sandmyrtle)
Pachistima canbyi (Canby Pachistima) *
Potentilla fruticosa (Bush Cinquefoil)
Rosa carolina (Carolina Rose)
Vaccinium angustifolium (Lowbush Blueberry)
Vaccinium macrocarpum (Cranberry) *
Xanthorhiza simplicissima (Yellowroot)
Yucca filamentosa (Adamsneedle Yucca)

*Commonly less than 15 centimeters (6 inches) in height

VINE HEIGHT: Four strata of relative mature height are classified

TALL VINE:
climbing vine with adult height 10 meters (35 feet) or more,
indicator — Ampelopsis arborea (Peppervine)

Ampelopsis arborea (Peppervine)
Ampelopsis cordata (Heartleaf Ampelopsis)
Bignonia capreolata (Crossvine)
Campsis radicans (Common Trumpetcreeper)

Parthenocissus quinquefolia (Virginia Creeper)
Toxicodendron radicans (Common Poisonivy)
Vitis labrusca (Fox Grape)
Vitis riparia (Riverbank Grape)

Height (cont.)

MID-HEIGHT VINE:
   climbing vine with adult height from 6 to 10 meters (20 to 35 feet),
   indicator — *Celastrus scandens* (American Bittersweet)

Aristolochia durior (Common Dutchmanspipe)
Celastrus scandens (American Bittersweet)
Smilax rotundifolia (Common Greenbrier)

Smilax tamnoides (Bamboo Greenbrier)
Wistaria macrostachya (Kentucky Wistaria)

LOW VINE:
   climbing vine with adult height from 1 to 6 meters (3 to 20 feet),
   indicator — *Menispermum canadense* (Common Moonseed)

Berchemia scandens (Alabama Supplejack)
Celastrus scandens (American Bittersweet)
Clematis verticillaris (Rock Clematis)
Clematis virginiana (Virginsbower)
Cocculus carolinus (Carolina Snailseed)

Lonicera sempervirens (Trumpet Honeysuckle)
Menispermum canadense (Common Moonseed)
Rosa setigera (Prairie Rose)
Smilax glauca (Cat Greenbrier)

VERY LOW VINE:
   primarily groundcover/shrub-like vines with adult height generally less than 1 meter (3 feet),
   indicator — *Lonicera dioica* (Limber Honeysuckle)

Lonicera dioica (Limber Honeysuckle)

SHRUB SPREAD: Four categories of mature crown width are classified

WIDE:
   from 4 to 6 meters (12 to 20 feet) or more,
   indicator — *Rhus aromatica* (Fragrant Sumac)

Aesculus parviflora (Bottlebrush Buckeye)
Aesculus pavia (Red Buckeye)
Alnus serrulata (Common Alder)
Amorpha fruticosa (Indigobush Amorpha)
Betula pumila (Low Birch)
Castanea pumila (Allegany Chinkapin)
Cephalanthus occidentalis (Common Buttonbush)
Clethra acuminata (Cinnamon Clethra)
Cyrilla racemiflora (American Cyrilla)
Ilex decidua (Possumhaw)
Juniperus communis (Common Juniper)
Kalmia latifolia (Mountainlaurel Kalmia)

Lyonia ligustrina (He-huckleberry)
Magnolia virginiana (Sweetbay Magnolia)
Pinus aristata (Bristlecone Pine)
Quercus ilicifolia (Scrub Oak)
Quercus prinoides (Dwarf Chinkapin Oak)
Rhododendron arborescens (Sweet Azalea)
Rhus aromatica (Fragrant Sumac)
Rosa setigera (Prairie Rose)
Salix lucida (Shining Willow)
Stewartia ovata (Mountain Stewartia)
Viburnum nudum (Possumhaw Viburnum)

INTERMEDIATE:
   from 2 to 4 meters (6 to 12 feet),
   indicator — *Fothergilla major* (Large Fothergilla)

Baccharis halimifolia (Eastern Baccharis)
Calycanthus floridus (Common Sweetshrub)
Cornus amomum (Silky Dogwood)
Cornus racemosa (Gray Dogwood)
Cornus rugosa (Roundleaf Dogwood)
Cornus stolonifera (Redosier Dogwood)
Corylus americana (American Filbert)
Corylus cornuta (Beaked Filbert)

Elaeagnus commutata (Silverberry)
Euonymus americanus (Brook Euonymus)
Fothergilla major (Large Fothergilla)
Hamamelis vernalis (Vernal Witchhazel)
Ilex glabra (Inkberry)
Ilex verticillata (Common Winterberry)
Itea virginica (Virginia Sweetspire)
Juniperus horizontalis (Creeping Juniper)

Lindera benzoin   (Common Spicebush)
Myrica pensylvanica   (Northern Bayberry)
Philadelphus grandiflorus   (Big Scentless Mockorange)
Physocarpus opulifolius   (Common Ninebark)
Rhododendron calendulaceum   (Flame Azalea)
Rhododendron catawbiense   (Catawba Rhododendron)
Rhododendron nudiflorum   (Pinxterbloom Azalea)
Rhododendron roseum   (Roseshell Azalea)
Rhododendron vaseyi   (Pinkshell Azalea)
Rhododendron viscosum   (Swamp Azalea)
Ribes odoratum   (Clove Currant)
Rosa carolina   (Carolina Rose)
Rubus allegheniensis   (Allegany Blackberry)
Rubus occidentalis   (Blackcap Raspberry)
Rubus odoratus   (Fragrant Thimbleberry)

Rubus strigosus   (American Red Raspberry)
Salix humilis   (Prairie Willow)
Sambucus canadensis   (American Elder)
Sambucus pubens   (Scarlet Elder)
Shepherdia argentea   (Silver Buffaloberry)
Shepherdia canadensis   (Russet Buffaloberry)
Staphylea trifolia   (American Bladdernut)
Taxus canadensis   (Canada Yew)
Vaccinium corymbosum   (Highbush Blueberry)
Vaccinium stamineum   (Common Deerberry)
Viburnum alnifolium   (Hobblebush Viburnum)
Viburnum cassinoides   (Witherod Viburnum)
Viburnum dentatum   (Arrowwood Viburnum)
Viburnum trilobum   (American Cranberrybush Viburnum)
Xanthorhiza simplicissima   (Yellowroot)

NARROW:
from 1 to 2 meters (3 to 6 feet),
indicator — *Hypericum prolificum* (Shrubby St.Johnswort)

Amelanchier sanguinea   (Roundleaf Serviceberry)
Aronia arbutifolia   (Red Chokeberry)
Aronia melanocarpa   (Black Chokeberry)
Aronia prunifolia   (Purplefruit Chokeberry)
Clethra alnifolia   (Summersweet Clethra)
Dirca palustris   (Atlantic Leatherwood)
Hydrangea arborescens   (Smooth Hydrangea)
Hydrangea quercifolia   (Oakleaf Hydrangea)
Hypericum densiflorum   (Dense Hypericum)
Hypericum prolificum   (Shrubby St.Johnswort)
Kalmia angustifolia   (Lambkill Kalmia)
Leiophyllum buxifolium   (Box Sandmyrtle)
Leucothoe catesbaei   (Drooping Leucothoe)
Lonicera canadensis   (American Fly Honeysuckle)
Neviusia alabamensis   (Snowwreath)
Pieris floribunda   (Mountain Pieris)

Rhododendron carolinianum   (Carolina Rhododendron)
Ribes americanum   (American Black Currant)
Ribes cynosbati   (Pasture Gooseberry)
Ribes missouriense   (Missouri Gooseberry)
Robinia hispida   (Roseacacia Locust)
Robinia viscosa   (Clammy Locust)
Spiraea alba   (Narrowleaf Meadowsweet Spirea)
Spiraea corymbosa   (Corymed Spirea)
Spiraea tomentosa   (Hardhack Spirea)
Symphoricarpos albus   (Common Snowberry)
Symphoricarpos occidentalis   (Western Snowberry)
Symphoricarpos orbiculatus   (Indiancurrant Coralberry)
Viburnum acerifolium   (Mapleleaf Viburnum)
Viburnum rafinesquianum   (Rafinesque Viburnum)
Zenobia pulverulenta   (Dusty Zenobia)

VERY NARROW:
less than 1 meter (3 feet),
indicator — *Yucca filamentosa* (Adamsneedle Yucca)

Amorpha canescens   (Leadplant Amorpha)
Andromeda polifolia   (Bogrosemary Andromeda)
Arctostaphylos uva-ursi   (Bearberry)
Ceanothus americanus   (Jerseytea Ceanothus)
Ceanothus ovatus   (Inland Ceanothus)
Chamaedaphne calyculata   (Leatherleaf)
Comptonia peregrina   (Sweetfern)
Cornus canadensis   (Bunchberry Dogwood)
Diervilla lonicera   (Dwarf Bushhoneysuckle)
Epigaea repens   (Trailing-arbutus)
Euonymus obovatus   (Running Euonymus)
Fothergilla gardeni   (Dwarf Fothergilla)

Gaultheria procumbens   (Checkerberry Wintergreen)
Hypericum frondosum   (Golden St.Johnswort)
Hypericum kalmianum   (Kalm St.Johnswort)
Kalmia polifolia   (Bog Kalmia)
Ledum groenlandicum   (Labradortea Ledum)
Mahonia aquifolium   (Oregongrape)
Pachistima canbyi   (Canby Pachistima)
Potentilla fruticosa   (Bush Cinquefoil)
Vaccinium angustifolium   (Lowbush Blueberry)
Vaccinium macrocarpum   (Cranberry)
Yucca filamentosa   (Adamsneedle Yucca)

VINE SPREAD: Four categories of mature crown width are classified

WIDE:
10 meters (35 feet) or more,
indicator — *Bignonia capreolata* (Crossvine)

Ampelopsis arborea   (Peppervine)   Ampelopsis cordata   (Heartleaf Ampelopsis)

Spread (cont.)

Bignonia capreolata (Crossvine)
Campsis radicans (Common Trumpetcreeper)
Parthenocissus quinquefolia (Virginia Creeper)

Toxicodendron radicans (Common Poisonivy)
Vitis labrusca (Fox Grape)
Vitis riparia (Riverbank Grape)

INTERMEDIATE:
from 6 to 10 meters (20 to 35 feet),
indicator — *Wistaria macrostachya* (Kentucky Wistaria)

Aristolochia durior (Common Dutchmanspipe)
Celastrus scandens (American Bittersweet)
Smilax rotundifolia (Common Greenbrier)

Smilax tamnoides (Bamboo Greenbrier)
Wistaria macrostachya (Kentucky Wistaria)

NARROW:
from 1 to 6 meters (3 to 20 feet),
indicator — *Menispermum canadense* (Common Moonseed)

Berchemia scandens (Alabama Supplejack)
Celastrus scandens (American Bittersweet)
Clematis verticillaris (Rock Clematis)
Clematis virginiana (Virginsbower)

Cocculus carolinus (Carolina Snailseed)
Lonicera sempervirens (Trumpet Honeysuckle)
Menispermum canadense (Common Moonseed)
Smilax glauca (Cat Greenbrier)

VERY NARROW
less than 1 meter (3 feet),
indicator — *Lonicera dioica* (Limber Honeysuckle)

Lonicera dioica (Limber Honeysuckle)

MASS:

The complexity of foliage and branching which is controlled by the genetic code of each species produces a predictable density which can be measured and quantified. Density can be measured as a ratio of positive to negative space within the plant crown. Positive space includes branching, foliage, and other plant parts perceived as line or mass in two-dimensional silhouette.

Negative space is the illusory space between the branching and foliage perceived as sky or background. This space determines the degree of opacity, translucency, or transparency for each species. Three categories of crown mass are classified.

DENSE:
extremely well developed branching system, heavily clothed with foliage, negative space minimal or absent,
indicator — *Hypericum kalmianum* (Kalm St.Johnswort)

Aesculus parviflora (Bottlebrush Buckeye)
Arctostaphylos uva-ursi (Bearberry)
Calycanthus floridus (Common Sweetshrub)
Castanea pumila (Allegany Chinkapin)
Ceanothus americanus (Jerseytea Ceanothus)
Ceanothus ovatus (Inland Ceanothus)

Chamaedaphne calyculata (Leatherleaf)
Cornus racemosa (Gray Dogwood)
Corylus americana (American Filbert)
Corylus cornuta (Beaked Filbert)
Epigaea repens (Trailing-arbutus)
Euonymus obovatus (Running Euonymus)

Fothergilla gardeni (Dwarf Fothergilla)
Fothergilla major (Large Fothergilla)
Gaultheria procumbens (Checkerberry Wintergreen)
Hamamelis vernalis ((Vernal Witchhazel)
Hydrangea arborescens (Smooth Hydrangea)
Hypericum densiflorum (Dense Hypericum)
Hypericum frondosum (Golden St.Johnswort)
Hypericum kalmianum (Kalm St.Johnswort)
Hypericum prolificum (Shrubby St.Johnswort)
Ilex decidua (Possumhaw)
Ilex verticillata (Common Winterberry)
Juniperus communis (Common Juniper)
Juniperus horizontalis (Creeping Juniper)
Kalmia angustifolia (Lambkill Kalmia)
Kalmia latifolia (Mountainlaurel Kalmia)
Leucothoe catesbaei (Drooping leucothoe)
Mahonia aquifolium (Oregongrape)
Pachistima canbyi (Canby Pachistima)
Philadelphus grandiflorus (Big Scentless Mockorange)
Physocarpus opulifolius (Common Ninebark)

Pieris floribunda (Mountain Pieris)
Potentilla fruticosa (Bush Cinquefoil)
Prunus hortulana (Hortulan Plum)
Quercus ilicifolia (Scrub Oak)
Rhus aromatica (Fragrant Sumac)
Ribes cynosbati (Pasture Gooseberry)
Ribes missouriense (Missouri Gooseberry)
Rosa carolina (Carolina Rose)
Rosa setigera (Prairie Rose)
Spiraea alba (Narrowleaf Meadowsweet Spirea)
Symphoricarpos albus (Common Snowberry)
Symphoricarpos occidentalis (Western Snowberry)
Symphoricarpos orbiculatus (Indiancurrant Coralberry)
Vaccinium corymbosum (Highbush Blueberry)
Viburnum acerifolium (Mapleleaf Viburnum)
Viburnum cassinoides (Witherod Viburnum)
Viburnum trilobum (American Cranberrybush Viburnum)
Yucca filamentosa (Adamsneedle Yucca)
Zenobia pulverulenta (Dusty Zenobia)

Aristolochia durior (Common Dutchmanspipe)
Bignonia capreolata (Crossvine)
Celastrus scandens (American Bittersweet)
Cocculus carolinus (Carolina Snailseed)
Menispermum canadense (Common Moonseed)
Smilax glauca (Cat Greenbrier)

Smilax rotundifolia (Common Greenbrier)
Smilax tamnoides (Bamboo Greenbrier)
Vitis labrusca (Fox Grape)
Vitis riparia (Riverbank Grape)
Wistaria macrostachya (Kentucky Wistaria)

MODERATE:
branching and foliage of intermediate density, positive to negative space ratio ranging between 2 to 1 and 1 to 1,
indicator — *Aronia arbutifolia* (Red Chokeberry)

Aesculus pavia (Red Buckeye)
Aronia arbutifolia (Red Chokeberry)
Aronia melanocarpa (Black Chokeberry)
Aronia prunifolia (Purplefruit Chokeberry)
Cornus amomum (Silky Dogwood)
Cornus stolonifera (Redosier Dogwood)
Cyrilla racemiflora (American Cyrilla)
Euonymus americanus (Brook Euonymus)
Kalmia polifolia (Bog Kalmia)
Ledum groenlandicum (Labradortea Ledum)
Lindera benzoin (Common Spicebush)
Myrica pensylvanica (Northern Bayberry)
Quercus prinoides (Dwarf Chinkapin Oak)

Rhododendron arborescens (Sweet Azalea)
Rhododendron calendulaceum (Flame Azalea)
Rhododendron carolinianum (Carolina Rhododendron)
Rhododendron catawbiense (Catawba Rhododendron)
Rhododendron nudiflorum (Pinxterbloom Azalea)
Rhododendron roseum (Roseshell Azalea)
Rhododendron vaseyi (Pinkshell Azalea)
Rhododendron viscosum (Swamp Azalea)
Ribes americanum (American Black Currant)
Ribes odoratum (Clove Currant)
Vaccinium stamineum (Common Deerberry)
Viburnum dentatum (Arrowwood Viburnum)
Viburnum nudum (Possumhaw Viburnum)

Parthenocissus quinquefolia (Virginia Creeper)
Toxicodendron radicans (Common Poisonivy)

OPEN:
sparse branching, clothed with relatively small quantity of foliage, high percentage of negative space visible,
indicator — *Diervilla lonicera* (Dwarf Bushhoneysuckle)

Alnus serrulata (Common Alder)
Amelanchier sanguinea (Roundleaf Serviceberry)
Amorpha canescens (Leadplant Amorpha)
Amorpha fruticosa (Indigobush Amorpha)
Andromeda polifolia (Bogrosemary Andromeda)
Baccharis halimifolia (Eastern Baccharis)
Betula pumila (Low Birch)

Cephalanthus occidentalis (Common Buttonbush)
Clethra acuminata (Cinnamon Clethra)
Clethra alnifolia (Summersweet Clethra)
Comptonia peregrina (Sweetfern)
Cornus canadensis (Bunchberry Dogwood)
Cornus rugosa (Roundleaf Dogwood)
Diervilla lonicera (Dwarf Bushhoneysuckle)

Mass (cont.)

Dirca palustris (Atlantic Leatherwood)
Elaeagnus commutata (Silverberry)
Hydrangea quercifolia (Oakleaf Hydrangea)
Ilex glabra (Inkberry)
Itea virginica (Virginia Sweetspire)
Leiophyllum buxifolium (Box Sandmyrtle)
Lonicera canadensis (American Fly Honeysuckle)
Lyonia ligustrina (He-huckleberry)
Magnolia virginiana (Sweetbay Magnolia)
Neviusia alabamensis (Snowwreath)
Pinus aristata (Bristlecone Pine)
Robinia hispida (Roseacacia Locust)
Robinia viscosa (Clammy Locust)
Rubus allegheniensis (Allegany Blackberry)
Rubus occidentalis (Blackcap Raspberry)
Rubus odoratus (Fragrant Thimbleberry)
Rubus strigosus (American Red Raspberry)

Salix humilis (Prairie Willow)
Salix lucida (Shining Willow)
Sambucus canadensis (American Elder)
Sambucus pubens (Scarlet Elder)
Shepherdia argentea (Silver Buffaloberry)
Shepherdia canadensis (Russet Buffaloberry)
Spiraea corymbosa (Corymed Spirea)
Spiraea tomentosa (Hardhack Spirea)
Staphylea trifolia (American Bladdernut)
Stewartia ovata (Mountain Stewartia)
Taxus canadensis (Canada Yew)
Vaccinium angustifolium (Lowbush Blueberry)
Vaccinium macrocarpum (Cranberry)
Viburnum alnifolium (Hobblebush Viburnum)
Viburnum rafinesquianum (Rafinesque Viburnum)
Xanthorhiza simplicissima (Yellowroot)

Ampelopsis arborea (Peppervine)
Ampelopsis cordata (Heartleaf Ampelopsis)
Berchemia scandens (Alabama Supplejack)
Campsis radicans (Common Trumpetcreeper)

Clematis verticillaris (Rock Clematis)
Clematis virginiana (Virginsbower)
Lonicera dioica (Limber Honeysuckle)
Lonicera sempervirens (Trumpet Honeysuckle)

BRANCHING CHARACTER:

The shape or form of a plant is greatly affected by the structure of the main stems and primary branches. The following structural arrangements may occur within almost any plant form.

ERECT:

stems and main branches stiffly vertical or diverging at a very slight angle from the vertical, indicator — Spiraea alba (Narrowleaf Meadowsweet Spirea)

Alnus serrulata (Common Alder)
Amelanchier sanguinea (Roundleaf Serviceberry)
Andromeda polifolia (Bogrosemary Andromeda)
Aronia arbutifolia (Red Chokeberry)
Aronia melanocarpa (Black Chokeberry)
Aronia prunifolia (Purplefruit Chokeberry)
Ceanothus americanus (Jerseytea Ceanothus)
Ceanothus ovatus (Inland Ceanothus)
Chamaedaphne calyculata (Leatherleaf)
Clethra acuminata (Cinnamon Clethra)
Clethra alnifolia (Summersweet Clethra)
Comptonia peregrina (Sweetfern)
Cornus canadensis (Bunchberry Dogwood)
Corylus americana (American Filbert)
Corylus cornuta (Beaked Filbert)
Diervilla lonicera (Dwarf Bushhoneysuckle)
Euonymus americanus (Brook Euonymus)
Fothergilla gardeni (Dwarf Fothergilla)
Fothergilla major (Large Fothergilla)
Hydrangea arborescens (Smooth Hydrangea)
Hypericum densiflorum (Dense Hypericum)
Hypericum frondosum (Golden St.Johnsort)
Hypericum kalmianum (Kalm St.Johnsowrt)

Itea virginica (Virginia Sweetspire)
Juniperus communis (Common Juniper)
Kalmia angustifolia (Lambkill Kalmia)
Ledum groenlandicum (Labradortea Ledum)
Leiophyllum buxifolium (Box Sandmyrtle)
Lyonia ligustrina (He-huckleberry)
Mahonia aquifolium (Oregongrape)
Philadelphus grandiflorus (Big Scentless Mockorange)
Ribes americanum (American Black Currant)
Ribes odoratum (Clove Currant)
Robinia hispida (Roseacacia Locust)
Robinia viscosa (Clammy Locust)
Rosa carolina (Carolina Rose)
Rubus allegheniensis (Allegany Blackberry)
Rubus occidentalis (Blackcap Raspberry)
Rubus odoratus (Fragrant Thimbleberry)
Rubus strigosus (American Red Raspberry)
Spiraea alba (Narrowleaf Meadowsweet Spirea)
Spiraea corymbosa (Corymed Spirea)
Spiraea tomentosa (Hardhack Spirea)
Symphoricarpos albus (Common Snowberry)
Symphoricarpos occidentalis (Western Snowberry)
Symphoricarpos orbiculatus (Indiancurrant Coralberry)

Vaccinium macrocarpum (Cranberry)   Xanthorhiza simplicissima (Yellowroot)
Viburnum alnifolium (Hobblebush Viburnum) Yucca filamentosa (Adamsneedle Yucca)

UPRIGHT:
  stems and main branches diverging at near 25 degrees from the vertical,
  indicator — Cornus racemosa (Gray Dogwood)

Alnus serrulata (Common Alder)   Ilex verticillata (Common Winterberry)
Amelanchier sanguinea (Roundleaf Serviceberry)   Itea virginica (Virginia Sweetspire)
Andromeda polifolia (Bogrosemary Andromeda)   Ledum groenlandicum (Labradortea Ledum)
Aronia arbutifolia (Red Chokeberry)   Leiophyllum buxifolium (Box Sandmyrtle)
Aronia melanocarpa (Black Chokeberry)   Neviusia alabamensis (Snowwreath)
Aronia prunifolia (Purplefruit Chokeberry)   Philadelphus grandiflorus (Big Scentless Mockorange)
Baccharis halimifolia (Eastern Baccharis)   Physocarpus opulifolius (Common Ninebark)
Betula pumila (Low Birch)   Potentilla fruticosa (Bush Cinquefoil)
Calycanthus floridus (Common Sweetshrub)   Rhododendron vaseyi (Pinkshell Azalea)
Ceanothus americanus (Jerseytea Ceanothus)   Rhododendron viscosum (Swamp Azalea)
Ceanothus ovatus (Inland Ceanothus)   Ribes americanum (American Black Currant)
Cephalanthus occidentalis (Common Buttonbush)   Ribes cynosbati (Pasture Gooseberry)
Chamaedaphne calyculata (Leatherleaf)   Ribes missouriense (Missouri Gooseberry)
Clethra acuminata (Cinnamon Clethra)   Ribes odoratum (Clove Currant)
Comptonia peregrina (Sweetfern)   Salix humilis (Prairie Willow)
Cornus amomum (Silky Dogwood)   Salix lucida (Shining Willow)
Cornus racemosa (Gray Dogwood))   Sambucus canadensis (American Elder)
Cornus rugosa (Roundleaf Dogwood)   Sambucus pubens (Scarlet Elder)
Cornus stolonifera (Redosier Dogwood)   Staphylea trifolia (American Bladdernut)
Corylus americana (American Filbert)   Symphoricarpos albus (Common Snowberry)
Corylus cornuta (Beaked Filbert)   Symphoricarpos occidentalis (Western Snowberry)
Diervilla lonicera (Dwarf Bushhoneysuckle)   Symphoricarpos orbiculatus (Indiancurrant Coralberry)
Euonymus americanus (Brook Euonymus)   Vaccinium angustifolium) (Lowbush Blueberry)
Fothergilla gardeni (Dwarf Fothergilla)   Vaccinium corymbosum (Highbush Blueberry)
Fothergilla major (Large Fothergilla)   Vaccinium stamineum (Common Deerberry)
Hamamelis vernalis (Vernal Witchhazel)   Viburnum acerifolium (Mapleleaf Viburnum)
Hydrangea arborescens (Smooth Hydrangea)   Viburnum alnifolium (Hobblebush Viburnum)
Hydrangea quercifolia (Oakleaf Hydrangea)   Viburnum cassinoides (Witherod Viburnum)
Hypericum densiflorum (Dense Hypericum)   Viburnum dentatum (Arrowwood Viburnum)
Hypericum frondosum (Golden St.Johnswort)   Viburnum nudum (Possumhaw Viburnum)
Hypericum kalmianum (Kalm St.Johnswort)   Viburnum rafinesquianum (Rafinesque Viburnum)
Hypericum prolificum (Shrubby St.Johnswort)   Viburnum trilobum (American Cranberrybush Viburnum)
Ilex glabra (Inkberry)   Zenobia pulverulenta (Dusty Zenobia)

ASCENDING:
  stems and main branches diverging at near 45 degree angle from the vertical,
  indicator — Rhododendron nudiflorum (Pinxterbloom Azalea)

Aesculus parviflora (Bottlebrush Buckeye)   Myrica pensylvanica (Northern Bayberry)
Aesculus pavia (Red Buckeye)   Pieris floribunda (Mountain Pieris)
Amorpha canescens (Leadplant Amorpha)   Pinus aristata (Bristlecone Pine)
Amorpha fruticosa (Indigobush Amorpha)   Prunus hortulana (Hortulan Plum)
Calycanthus floridus (Common Sweetshrub)   Rhododendron arborescens (Sweet Azalea)
Cephalanthus occidentalis (Common Buttonbush)   Rhododendron calendulaceum (Flame Azalea)
Cyrilla racemiflora (American Cyrilla)   Rhododendron carolinianum (Carolina Rhododendron)
Dirca palustris (Atlantic Leatherwood)   Rhododendron catawbiense (Catawba Rhododendron)
Elaeagnus commutata (Silverberry)   Rhododendron nudiflorum (Pinxterbloom Azalea)
Hamamelis vernalis (Vernal Witchhazel)   Rhododendron roseum (Roseshell Azalea)
Hypericum kalmianum (Kalm St.Johnswort)   Rhus aromatica (Fragrant Sumac)
Hypericum prolificum (Shrubby St.Johnswort)   Salix humilis (Prairie Willow)
Ilex decidua (Possumhaw)   Shepherdia argentea (Silver Buffaloberry)
Ilex glabra (Inkberry)   Shepherdia canadensis (Russet Buffaloberry)
Kalmia latifolia (Mountainlaurel Kalmia)   Stewartia ovata (Mountain Stewartia)
Leiophyllum buxifolium (Box Sandmyrtle)   Taxus canadensis (Canada Yew)
Lindera benzoin (Common Spicebush)   Vaccinium corymbosum (Highbrush Blueberry)

Branching character (cont.)

HORIZONTAL:
>   stems and main branches predominantly oriented at near 90 degree angle from the vertical,
>   indicator — *Aesculus parviflora* (Bottlebrush Buckeye)

Aesculus parviflora   (Bottlebrush Buckeye)
Amorpha fruticosa   (Indigobush Amorpha)
Castanea pumila   (Allegany Chinkapin)
Ilex decidua   (Possumhaw)
Juniperus horizontalis   (Creeping Juniper)
Kalmia latifolia   (Mountainlaurel Kalmia)
Lindera benzoin   (Common Spicebush)
Magnolia virginiana   (Sweetbay Magnolia)

Myrica pensylvanica   (Northern Bayberry)
Pachistima canbyi   (Canby Pachistima)
Pieris floribunda   (Mountain Pieris)
Pinus aristata   (Bristlecone Pine)
Quercus ilicifolia   (Scrub Oak)
Quercus prinoides   (Dwarf Chinkapin Oak)
Rhododendron nudiflorum   (Pinxterbloom Azalea)
Rhus aromatica   (Fragrant Sumac)

ARCHING:
>   stems or main branches changing from erect near plant base, curving horizontal near the middle, and
>   becoming descending at tips, umbrella-like,
>   indicator — *Rosa setigera* (Prairie Rose)

Amelanchier sanguinea   (Roundleaf Serviceberry)
Cephalanthus occidentalis   (Common Buttonbush)
Cornus amomum   (Silky Dogwood)
Cornus stolonifera   (Redosier Dogwood)
Diervilla lonicera   (Dwarf Bushhoneysuckle)
Leucothoe catesbaei   (Drooping Leucothoe)
Lonicera canadensis   (American Fly Honeysuckle)
Philadelphus grandiflorus   (Big Scentless Mockorange)
Physocarpus opulifolius   (Common Ninebark)
Potentilla fruticosa   (Bush Cinquefoil)
Ribes cynosbati   (Pasture Gooseberry)
Ribes missouriense   (Missouri Gooseberry)
Ribes odoratum   (Clove Currant)

Robinia hispida   (Roseacacia Locust)
Rosa setigera   (Prairie Rose)
Rubus allegheniensis   (Allegany Blackberry)
Rubus occidentalis   (Blackcap Raspberry)
Rubus odoratus   (Fragrant Thimbleberry)
Rubus strigosus   (American Red Raspberry)
Sambucus canadensis   (American Elder)
Symphoricarpos occidentalis   (Western Snowberry)
Symphoricarpos orbiculatus   (Indiancurrant Coralberry)
Viburnum cassinoides   (Witherod Viburnum)
Viburnum dentatum   (Arrowwood Viburnum)
Viburnum trilobum   (American Cranberrybush Viburnum)

TRAILING:
>   horizontal orientation but with most stems hugging the ground,
>   indicator — *Arctostaphylos uva-ursi* (Bearberry)

Arctostaphylos uva-ursi   (Bearberry)
Cornus canadensis   (Bunchberry Dogwod)
Epigaea repens   (Trailing-arbutus)
Euonymus obovatus   (Running Euonymus)
Gaultheria procumbens   (Checkerberry Wintergreen)
Juniperus communis   (Common Juniper)
Juniperus horizontalis   (Creeping Juniper)

Kalmia angustifolia   (Lambkill Kalmia)
Kalmia polifolia   (Bog Kalmia)
Lonicera canadensis   (American Fly Honeysuckle)
Pachistima canbyi   (Canby Pachistima)
Taxus canadensis   (Canada Yew)
Vaccinium macrocarpum   (Cranberry)

TENDRILS:
>   a coiling thread-like organ by which certain vines grasp an object for support,
>   indicator — *Bignonia capreolata* (Crossvine)

Ampelopsis arborea   (Peppervine)
Ampelopsis cordata   (Heartleaf Ampelopsis)
Bignonia capreolata   (Crossvine)
Smilax glauca   (Cat Greenbrier)

Smilax rotundifolia   (Common Greenbrier)
Smilax tamnoides   (Bamboo Greenbrier)
Vitis labrusca   (Fox Grape)
Vitis riparia   (Riverbank Grape)

SUCTION DISCS:
>   a suction cup-like organ by which some climbing vines fasten to an object for support,
>   indicator — *Parthenocissus quinquefolia* (Virginia Creeper)

Bignonia capreolata   (Crossvine)

Parthenocissus quinquefolia   (Virginia Creeper)

AERIAL ROOTLETS:
small root-like organs along stems of some climbing vines, used for support,
indicator — *Campsis radicans* (Common Trumpetcreeper)

Campsis radicans   (Common Trumpetcreeper)
Toxicodendron radicans   (Common Poisonivy)

TWINING:
clasping method by which certain climbing vines wind stems around an object for support,
indicator — *Aristolochia durior* (Common Dutchmanspipe)

Aristrolochia durior   (Common Dutchmanspipe)
Berchemia scandens   (Alabama Supplejack)
Celastrus scandens   (American Bittersweet)
Cocculus carolinus   (Carolina Snailseed)

Lonicera dioica   (Limber Honeysuckle)
Lonicera sempervirens   (Trumpet Honeysuckle)
Menispermum canadense   (Common Moonseed)
Wistaria macrostachya   (Kentucky Wistaria)

TWISTING LEAFSTALK:
clasping method by which certain climbing vines wind leafstalks around an object for support,
indicator — *Clematis verticillaris* (Rock Clematis)

Clematis verticillaris   (Rock Clematis)
Clematis virginiana   (Virginsbower)

BRANCHING APPEARANCE IS FURTHER MODIFIED IN SEVERAL WAYS:

LEGGY:
multiple stemmed plant devoid of foliage below, frequently observed in shade intolerant pioneer
species that spread into large colonies by vegetative root propagation,
indicator — *Robinia viscosa* (Clammy Locust)

Amorpha fruticosa   (Indigobush Amorpha)
Aronia arbutifolia   (Red Chokeberry)
Corylus americana   (American Filbert)
Corylus cornuta   (Beaked Filbert)
Diervilla lonicera   (Dwarf Bushhoneysuckle)
Lonicera canadensis   (American Fly Honeysuckle)
Robinia hispida   (Roseacacia Locust)
Robinia viscosa   (Clammy Locust)

Rosa carolina   (Carolina Rose)
Rubus allegheniensis   (Allegany Blackberry)
Rubus occidentalis   (Blackcap Raspberry)
Rubus odoratus   (Fragrant Thimbleberry)
Rubus strigosus   (American Red Raspberry)
Sambucus canadensis   (American Elder)
Sambucus pubens   (Scarlet Elder)
Xanthorhiza simplicissima   (Yellowroot)

Ampelopsis arborea   (Peppervine)
Ampelopsis cordata   (Heartleaf Ampelopsis)

Vitis labrusca   (Fox Grape)
Vitis riparia   (Riverbank Grape)

PICTURESQUE:
naturally irregular or contorted branching occurring commonly in some species,
indicator — *Quercus ilicifolia* (Scrub Oak)

Aesculus parviflora   (Bottlebrush Buckeye)
Alnus serrulata   (Common Alder)
Dirca palustris   (Atlantic Leatherwood)
Fothergilla gardeni   (Dwarf Fothergilla)
Hydrangea quercifolia   (Oakleaf Hydrangea)
Hypericum prolificum   (Shrubby St.Johnswort)
Ilex glabra   (Inkberry)
Kalmia latifolia   (Mountainlaurel Kalmia)
Magnolia virginiana   (Sweetbay Magnolia)
Myrica pensylvanica   (Northern Bayberry)
Pinus aristata   (Bristlecone Pine)

Quercus ilicifolia   (Scrub Oak)
Quercus prinoides   (Dwarf Chinkapin Oak)
Rhododendron arborescens   (Sweet Azalea)
Rhododendron calendulaceum   (Flame Azalea)
Rhododendron carolinianum   (Carolina Rhododendron)
Rhododendron catawbiense   (Catawba Rhododendron)
Rhododendron nudiflorum   (Pinxterbloom Azalea)
Rhododendron roseum   (Roseshell Azalea)
Rhododendron vaseyi   (Pinkshell Azalea)
Robinia hispida   (Roseacacia Locust)

Branching character (cont.)

Aristolochia durior (Common Dutchmanspipe)
Berchemia scandens (Alabama Supplejack)
Celastrus scandens (American Bittersweet)
Cocculus carolinus (Carolina Snailseed)

Lonicera dioica (Limber Honeysuckle)
Lonicera sempervirens (Trumpet Honeysuckle)
Menispermum canadense (Common Moonseed)
Wistaria macrostachya (Kentucky Wistaria)

PENDULOUS:
> secondary branchlets or tertiary branch tips and twigs pendant,
> indicator — *Betula pumila* (Low Birch)

Betula pumila (Low Birch)
Calycanthus floridus (Common Sweetshrub)
Ilex decidua (Possumhaw)
Symphoricarpos albus (Common Snowberry)

Symphoricarpos occidentalis (Western Snowberry)
Symphoricarpos orbiculatus (Indiancurrant Coralberry)
Viburnum trilobum (American Cranberrybush Viburnum)

SPREADING:
> stems commonly erect or upright through the lower and middle crown with secondary branchlets or
> tertiary branch tips and twigs diverging to a 45° angle in the upper crown,
> indicator — *Philadelphus grandiflorus* (Big Scentless Mockorange)

Alnus serrulata (Common Alder)
Amelanchier sanguinea (Roundleaf Serviceberry)
Aronia arbutifolia (Red Chokeberry)
Aronia melanocarpa (Black Chokeberry)
Aronia prunifolia (Purplefruit Chokeberry)
Baccharis halimifolia (Eastern Baccharis)
Betula pumila (Low Birch)
Calycanthus floridus (Common Sweetshrub)
Cephalanthus occidentalis (Common Buttonbush)
Clethra acuminata (Cinnamon Clethra)
Comptonia peregrina (Sweetfern)
Cornus racemosa (Gray Dogwood)
Cornus rugosa (Roundleaf Dogwood)
Cornus stolonifera (Redosier Dogwood)
Corylus americana (American Filbert)
Corylus cornuta (Beaked Filbert)
Diervilla lonicera (Dwarf Bushhoneysuckle)
Fothergilla gardeni (Dwarf Fothergilla)
Fothergilla major (Large Fothergilla)
Hamamelis vernalis (Vernal Witchhazel)
Hydrangea arborescens (Smooth Hydrangea)
Hypericum densiflorum (Dense Hypericum)
Hypericum frondosum (Golden St.Johnswort)
Hypericum kalmianum (Kalm St.Johnswort)
Hypericum prolificum (Shrubby St.Johnswort)
Ilex verticillata (Common Winterberry)
Itea virginica (Virginia Sweetspire)
Ledum groenlandicum (Labradortea Ledum)

Leiophyllum buxifolium (Box Sandmyrtle)
Neviusia alabamensis (Snowwreath)
Philadelphus grandiflorus (Big Scentless Mockorange)
Physocarpus opulifolius (Common Ninebark)
Potentilla fruticosa (Bush Cinquefoil)
Rhododendron viscosum (Swamp Azalea)
Ribes americanum (American Black Currant)
Ribes cynosbati (Pasture Gooseberry)
Ribes missouriense (Missouri Gooseberry)
Ribes odoratum (Clove Currant)
Salix humilis (Prairie Willow)
Salix lucida (Shining Willow)
Sambucus canadensis (American Elder)
Sambucus pubens (Scarlet Elder)
Staphylea trifolia (American Bladdernut)
Symphoricarpos albus (Common Snowberry)
Symphoricarpos occidentalis (Western Snowberry)
Symphoricarpos orbiculatus (Indiancurrant Coralberry)
Vaccinium angustifolium (Lowbush Blueberry)
Vaccinium corymbosum (Highbush Blueberry)
Vaccinium stamineum (Common Deerberry)
Viburnum acerifolium (Mapleleaf Viburnum)
Viburnum alnifolium (Hobblebush Viburnum)
Viburnum cassinoides (Witherod Viburnum)
Viburnum dentatum (Arrowwood Viburnum)
Viburnum nudum (Possumhaw Viburnum)
Viburnum rafinesquianum (Rafinesque Viburnum)
Zenobia pulverulenta (Dusty Zenobia)

BRANCHING TEXTURE:

Texture in the landscape is the result of the detailed structure of plant growth or of the total plant mass, influenced by the distance from which the scene is viewed. In the winter landscape, texture in deciduous plants is a product of the size, surface, spacing, disposition, grouping and attitude of twigs and branches, persisting seeds and dried leaves. Every species exhibits its own characteristic branching personality which produces a consistent texture within a limited range. Some plants are coarse, medium or fine the year around. Others are fine or medium in summer and coarser in winter. The following textural categories (winter) are considered.

COARSE:
    large prominent branches and twigs, spacing open,
    indicator — *Hydrangea quercifolia* (Oakleaf Hydrangea)

Aesculus parviflora (Bottlebrush Buckeye)
Aesculus pavia (Red Buckeye)
Amorpha canescens (Leadplant Amorpha)
Cephalanthus occidentalis (Common Buttonbush)
Cornus rugosa (Roundleaf Dogwood)
Diervilla lonicera (Dwarf Bushhoneysuckle)
Hamamelis vernalis (Vernal Witchhazel)
Hydrangea arborescens (Smooth Hydrangea)
Hydrangea quercifolia (Oakleaf Hydrangea)
Philadelphus grandiflorus (Big Scentless Mockorange)
Physocarpus opulifolius (Common Ninebark)
Rhododendron catawbiense (Catawba Rhododendron)
Rhus aromatica (Fragrant Sumac)
Robinia hispida (Roseacacia Locust)

Robinia viscosa (Clammy Locust)
Rosa setigera (Prairie Rose)
Rubus allegheniensis (Allegany Blackberry)
Rubus occidentalis (Blackcap Raspberry)
Rubus odoratus (Fragrant Timbleberry)
Rubus strigosus (American Red Raspberry)
Sambucus canadensis (American Elder)
Sambucus pubens (Scarlet Elder)
Viburnum alnifolium (Hobblebush Viburnum)
Viburnum nudum (Possumhaw Viburnum)
Viburnum trilobum (American Cranberrybush Viburnum)
Xanthorhiza simplicissima (Yellowroot)
Yucca filamentosa (Adamsneedle Yucca)

Aristolochia durior (Common Dutchmanspipe)
Bignonia capreolata (Crossvine)
Campsis radicans (Common Trumpetcreeper)
Lonicera sempervirens (Trumpet Honeysuckle)
Smilax glauca (Cat Greenbrier)

Smilax tamnoides (Bamboo Greenbrier)
Toxicodendron radicans (Common Poisonivy)
Vitis labrusca (Fox Grape)
Vitis riparia (Riverbank Grape)

MEDIUM:
    branches and twigs of intermediate diameter and spacing,
    indicator — *Viburnum cassinoides* (Witherod Viburnum)

Alnus serrulata (Common Alder)
Amorpha fruticosa (Indigobush Amorpha)
Aronia arbutifolia (Red Chokeberry)
Aronia melanocarpa (Black Chokeberry)
Aronia prunifolia (Purplefruit Chokeberry)
Calycanthus floridus (Common Sweetshrub)
Castanea pumila (Allegany Chinkapin)
Ceanothus americanus (Jerseytea Ceanothus)
Ceanothus ovatus (Inland Ceanothus)
Clethra acuminata (Cinnamon Clethra)
Clethra alnifolia (Summersweet Clethra)
Cornus amomum (Silky Dogwood)
Cornus canadensis (Bunchberry Dogwood)
Cornus racemosa (Gray Dogwood)
Cornus stolonifera (Redosier Dogwood)
Corylus americana (American Filbert)
Corylus cornuta (Beaked Filbert)
Dirca palustris (Atlantic Leatherwood)
Elaeagnus commutata (Silverberry)
Epigaea repens (Trailing-arbutus)
Euonymus obovatus (Running Euonymus)
Fothergilla gardeni (Dwarf Fothergilla)
Fothergilla major (Large Fothergilla)
Ilex decidua (Possumhaw)
Ilex glabra (Inkberry)
Ilex verticillata (Common Winterberry)
Itea virginica (Virginia Sweetspire)
Juniperus communis (Common Juniper)
Kalmia angustifolia (Lambkill Kalmia)
Kalmia latifolia (Mountainlaurel Kalmia)
Ledum groenlandicum (Labradortea Ledum)
Leucothoe catesbaei (Drooping Leucothoe)
Lonicera canadensis (American Fly Honeysuckle)

Magnolia virginiana (Sweetbay Magnolia)
Mahonia aquifolium (Oregongrape)
Myrica pensylvanica (Northern Bayberry)
Neviusia alabamensis (Snowwreath)
Pieris floribunda (Mountain Pieris)
Pinus aristata (Bristlecone Pine)
Prunus hortulana (Hortulan Plum)
Quercus ilicifolia (Scrub Oak)
Quercus prinoides (Dwarf Chinkapin Oak)
Rhododendron arborescens (Sweet Azalea)
Rhododendron calendulaceum (Flame Azalea)
Rhododendron carolinianum (Carolina Rhododendron)
Rhododendron nudiflorum (Pinxterbloom Azalea)
Rhododendron roseum (Roseshell Azalea)
Rhododendron vaseyi (Pinkshell Azalea)
Rhododendron viscosum (Swamp Azalea)
Ribes americanum (American Black Currant)
Ribes odoratum (Clove Currant)
Rosa carolina (Carolina Rose)
Salix humilis (Prairie Willow)
Shepherdia argentea (Silver Buffaloberry)
Shepherdia canadensis (Russet Buffaloberry)
Staphylea trifolia (American Bladdernut)
Stewartia ovata (Mountain Stewartia)
Vaccinium angustifolium (Lowbush Blueberry)
Vaccinium corymbosum (Highbush Blueberry)
Vaccinium stamineum (Common Deerberry)
Viburnum acerifolium (Mapleleaf Viburnum)
Viburnum cassinoides (Witherod Viburnum)
Viburnum dentatum (Arrowwood Viburnum)
Viburnum rafinesquianum (Rafinesque Viburnum)
Zenobia pulverulenta (Dusty Zenobia)

Branching texture (cont.)

Ampelopsis arborea (Peppervine)
Ampelopsis cordata (Heartleaf Ampelopsis)
Berchemia scandens (Alabama Supplejack)
Celastrus scandens (American Bittersweet)
Cocculus carolinus (Carolina Snailseed)

Lonicera dioica (Limber Honeysuckle)
Menispermum canadense (Common Moonseed)
Parthenocissus quinquefolia (Virginia Creeper)
Smilax rotundifolia (Common Greenbrier)
Wistaria macrostachya (Kentucky Wistaria)

FINE:
  branches and twigs conspicuously slender, spacing closed,
  indicator — *Spiraea alba* (Narrowleaf Meadowsweet Spirea)

Amelanchier sanguinea (Roundleaf Serviceberry)
Andromeda polifolia (Bogrosemary Andromeda)
Arctostaphylos uva-ursi (Bearberry)
Baccharis halimifolia (Eastern Baccharis)
Betula pumila (Low Birch)
Chamaedaphne calyculata (Leatherleaf)
Comptonia peregrina (Sweetfern)
Euonymus americanus (Brook Euonymus)
Gaultheria procumbens (Checkerberry Wintergreen)
Hypericum densiflorum (Dense Hypericum)
Hypericum frondosum (Golden St.Johnswort)
Hypericum kalmianum (Kalm St.Johnswort)
Hypericum prolificum (Shrubby St.Johnswort)
Juniperus horizontalis (Creeping Juniper)
Kalmia polifolia (Bog Kalmia)
Leiophyllum buxifolium (Box Sandmyrtle)

Lindera benzoin (Common Spicebush)
Lyonia ligustrina (He-huckleberry)
Pachistima canbyi (Canby Pachistima)
Potentilla fruticosa (Bush Cinquefoil)
Ribes cynosbati (Pasture Gooseberry)
Ribes missouriense (Missouri Gooseberry)
Salix lucida (Shining Willow)
Spiraea alba (Narrowleaf Meadowsweet Spirea)
Spiraea corymbosa (Corymed Spirea)
Spiraea tomentosa (Hardhack Spirea)
Symphoricarpos albus (Common Snowberry)
Symphoricarpos occidentalis (Western Snowberry)
Symphoricarpos orbiculatus (Indiancurrant Coralberry)
Taxus canadensis (Canada Yew)
Vaccinium macrocarpum (Cranberry)

Clematis verticillaris (Rock Clematis)
Clematis virginiana (Virginsbower)

TWIG AND BUD:

Twigs and buds may be distinctive in color, size and shape. Buds of many plants are naked, scaly, gummy, hairy or smooth. Some twigs frequently are marked with large leaf scars while others are smooth or covered with hair. Although unusual twig and bud characteristics exhibit greatest visual impact in the winter landscape, it is the subtle discovery of this detail in other seasons which produces a richer environmental perception of the design.

TWIG CHARACTER:

LARGE LEAF SCARS:
  indicator — *Sambucus canadensis* (American Elder)

Sambucus canadensis (American Elder)
Sambucus pubens (Scarlet Elder)

Symphoricarpos occidentalis (Western Snowberry)

Aristolochia durior (Common Dutchmanspipe)
Campsis radicans (Common Trumpetcreeper)

Menispermum canadense (Common Moonseed)
Toxicodendron radicans (Common Poisonivy)

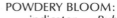

POWDERY BLOOM:
  indicator — *Rubus occidentalis* (Blackcap Raspberry)

Rhododendron arborescens (Sweet Azalea)
Rosa setigera (Prairie Rose)
Rubus occidentalis (Blackcap Raspberry)

Rubus strigosus (American Red Raspberry)
Zenobia pulverulenta (Dusty Zenobia)

Smilax glauca (Cat Greenbrier)

VELVETY:
indicator — *Aronia arbutifolia* (Red Chokeberry)

Amorpha canescens (Leadplant Amorpha)
Arctostaphylos uva-ursi (Bearberry)
Aronia arbutifolia (Red Chokeberry)
Betula pumila (Low Birch)
Ceanothus ovatus (Inland Ceanothus)
Cephalanthus occidentalis (Common Buttonbush)
Clethra acuminata (Cinnamon Clethra)
Clethra alnifolia (Summersweet Clethra)
Comptonia peregrina (Sweetfern)
Cornus amomum (Silky Dogwood)
Corylus americana (American Filbert))
Cyrilla racemiflora (American Cyrilla)
Epigaea repens (Trailing-arbutus)
Hamamelis vernalis (Vernal Witchhazel)
Hydrangea quercifolia (Oakleaf Hydrangea)
Itea virginica (Virginia Sweetspire)
Ledum groenlandicum (Labradortea Ledum)
Myrica pensylvanica (Northern Bayberry)
Pieris floribunda (Mountain Pieris)
Quercus ilicifolia (Scrub Oak)

Rhododendron calendulaceum (Flame Azalea)
Rhododendron nudiflorum (Pinxterbloom Azalea)
Rhododendron roseum (Roseshell Azalea)
Rhododendron viscosum (Swamp Azalea)
Rhus aromatica (Fragrant Sumac)
Ribes odoratum (Clove Currant)
Robinia hispida (Roseacacia Locust)
Robinia viscosa (Clammy Locust)
Rubus odoratus (Fragrant Thimbleberry)
Salix humilis (Prairie Willow)
Spiraea tomentosa (Hardhack Spirea)
Symphoricarpos occidentalis (Western Snowberry)
Symphoricarpos orbiculatus (Indiancurrant Coralberry)
Vaccinium angustifolium (Lowbush Blueberry)
Vaccinium corymbosum (Highbush Blueberry)
Vaccinium stamineum (Common Deerberry)
Viburnum acerifolium (Mapleleaf Viburnum)
Viburnum alnifolium (Hobblebush Viburnum)
Viburnum cassinoides (Witherod Viburnum)
Viburnum dentatum (Arrowwood Viburnum)

Cocculus carolinus (Carolina Snailseed)
Vitis labrusca (Fox Grape)

ANGULAR/RIDGED:
indicator — *Euonymus americanus* (Brook Euonymus)

Amorpha canescens (Leadplant Amorpha)
Calycanthus floridus (Common Sweetshrub)
Cornus rugosa (Roundleaf Dogwood)
Diervilla lonicera (Dwarf Bushhoneysuckle)
Euonymus americanus (Brook Euonymus)
Euonymus obovatus (Running Euonymus)
Fothergilla gardeni (Dwarf Fothergilla)
Hypericum densiflorum (Dense Hypericum)
Hypericum frondosum (Golden St.Johnswort)
Hypericum kalmianum (Kalm St.Johnswort)
Hypericum prolificum (Shrubby St.Johnswort)
Juniperus communis (Common Juniper)

Kalmia polifolia (Bog Kalmia)
Lonicera canadensis (American Fly Honeysuckle)
Pachistima canbyi (Canby Pachistima)
Philadelphus grandiflorus (Big Scentless Mockorange)
Physocarpus opulifolius (Common Ninebark)
Ribes americanum (American Black Currant)
Rubus allegheniensis (Allegany Blackberry)
Sambucus canadensis (American Elder)
Sambucus pubens (Scarlet Elder)
Vaccinium angustifolium (Lowbush Blueberry)
Viburnum dentatum (Arrowwood Viburnum)

Clematis verticillaris (Rock Clematis)
Menispermum canadense (Common Moonseed)

Smilax rotundifolia (Common Greenbrier)
Vitis riparia (Riverbank Grape)

FLAKY/SCALY:
indicator — *Shepherdia argentea* (Silver Buffaloberry)

Amelanchier sanguinea (Roundleaf Serviceberry)
Aronia melanocarpa (Black Chokeberry)
Aronia prunifolia (Purplefruit Chokeberry)
Elaeagnus commutata (Silverberry)

Prunus hortulana (Hortulan Plum)
Shepherdia argentea (Silver Buffaloberry)
Shepherdia canadensis (Russet Buffaloberry)
Viburnum cassinoides (Witherod Viburnum

ZIGZAG:

indicator — *Vaccinium corymbosum* (Highbush Blueberry)

Alnus serrulata (Common Alder)
Corylus americana (American Filbert)
Corylus cornuta (Beaked Filbert)
Fothergilla gardeni (Dwarf Fothergilla)
Fothergilla major (Large Fothergilla)
Hamamelis vernalis (Vernal Witchhazel)
Ilex decidua (Possumhaw)
Ilex glabra (Inkberry)
Ilex verticillata (Common Winterberry)

Lindera benzoin (Common Spicebush)
Rosa carolina (Carolina Rose)
Rosa setigera (Prairie Rose)
Rubus allegheniensis (Allegany Blackberry)
Rubus occidentalis (Blackcap Raspberry)
Rubus odoratus (Fragrant Thimbleberry)
Rubus strigosus (American Red Raspberry)
Vaccinium angustifolium (Lowbush Blueberry)
Vaccinium corymbosum (Highbush Blueberry)

RESINOUS:

indicator — *Juniperus horizontalis* (Creeping Juniper)

Comptonia peregrina (Sweetfern)
Juniperus communis (Common Juniper)

Myrica pensylvanica (Northern Bayberry)
Ribes americanum (American Black Currant)

TWIG COLORATION:

WHITE:

Arctostaphylos uva-ursi (Bearberry)
Rubus occidentalis (Blackcap Raspberry)
Rubus strigosus (American Red Raspberry)

Shepherdia argentea (Silver Buffaloberry)
Staphylea trifolia (American Bladdernut)
Zenobia pulverulenta (Dusty Zenobia)

Smilax glauca (Cat Greenbrier)

SILVER-GRAY:

Elaeagnus commutata (Silverberry)

Shepherdia argentea (Silver Buffaloberry)

GRAY:

Aronia arbutifolia (Red Chokeberry)
Elaeagnus commutata (Silverberry)
Hamamelis vernalis (Vernal Witchhazel)
Ilex decidua (Possumhaw)
Ilex verticillata (Common Winterberry)
Lonicera canadensis (American Fly Honeysuckle)

Myrica pensylvanica (Northern Bayberry)
Quercus prinoides (Dwarf Chinkapin Oak)
Ribes americanum (American Black Currant)
Shepherdia argentea (Silver Buffaloberry)
Viburnum trilobum (American Cranberrybush Viburnum)

Lonicera dioica (Limber Honeysuckle)

GREEN:

Baccharis halimifolia (Eastern Baccharis)
Cornus amomum (Silky Dogwood)
Cornus rugosa (Roundleaf Dogwood)
Dirca palustris (Atlantic Leatherwood)
Euonymus americanus (Brook Euonymus)
Euonymus obovatus (Running Euonymus)
Ilex glabra (Inkberry)
Itea virginica (Virginia Sweetspire)
Kalmia latifolia (Mountainlaurel Kalmia)

Leucothoe catesbaei (Drooping Leucothoe)
Lindera benzoin (Common Spicebush)
Lonicera canadensis (American Fly Honeysuckle)
Lyonia ligustrina (He-huckleberry)
Magnolia virginiana (Sweetbay Magnolia)
Quercus ilicifolia (Scrub Oak)
Rosa carolina (Carolina Rose)
Rosa setigera (Prairie Rose)
Rubus allegheniensis (Allegany Blackberry)

Rubus occidentalis (Blackcap Raspberry)
Staphylea trifolia (American Bladdernut)
Taxus canadensis (Canada Yew)

Vaccinium angustifolium (Lowbush Blueberry)
Vaccinium corymbosum (Highbush Blueberry)
Xanthorhiza simplicissima (Yellowroot)

Aristolochia durior (Common Dutchmanspipe)
Menispermum canadense (Common Moonseed)
Smilax glauca (Cat Greenbrier)

Smilax rotundifolia (Common Greenbrier)
Smilax tamnoides (Bamboo Greenbrier)
Vitis riparia (Riverbank Grape)

YELLOW-BROWN:

Aronia melanocarpa (Black Chokeberry)
Hypericum densiflorum (Dense Hypericum)
Kalmia polifolia (Bog Kalmia)
Lyonia ligustrina (He-huckleberry)
Neviusia alabamensis (Snowwreath)
Philadelphus grandiflorus (Big Scentless Mockorange)
Rhododendron arborescens (Sweet Azalea)

Rubus odoratus (Fragrant Thimbleberry)
Salix humilis (Prairie Willow)
Sambucus canadensis (American Elder)
Spiraea alba (Narrowleaf Meadowsweet Spirea)
Taxus canadensis (Canada Yew)
Viburnum trilobum (American Cranberrybush Viburnum)

Ampelopsis cordata (Heartleaf Ampelopsis)
Campsis radicans (Common Trumpetcreeper)

ORANGE-BROWN:

Aesculus parviflora (Bottlebrush Buckeye)
Aesculus pavia (Red Buckeye)
Betula pumila (Low Birch)
Diervilla lonicera (Dwarf Bushhoneysuckle)
Elaeagnus commutata (Silverberry)

Potentilla fruticosa (Bush Cinquefoil)
Quercus prinoides (Dwarf Chinkapin Oak)
Rhododendron calendulaceum (Flame Azalea)
Ribes americanum (American Black Currant)

Campsis radicans (Common Trumpetcreeper)

GRAY-BROWN:

Amorpha canescens (Leadplant Amorpha)
Cephalanthus occidentalis (Common Buttonbush)
Chamaedaphne calyculata (Leatherleaf)
Clethra acuminata (Cinnamon Clethra)
Clethra alnifolia (Summersweet Clethra)
Hydrangea arborescens (Smooth Hydrangea)
Ilex decidua (Possumhaw)
Ilex verticillata (Common Winterberry)
Kalmia angustifolia (Lambkill Kalmia)
Lonicera canadensis (American Fly Honeysuckle)
Pinus aristata (Bristlecone Pine)
Rhododendron calendulaceum (Flame Azalea)

Rhododendron carolinianum (Carolina Rhododendron)
Rhododendron catawbiense (Catawba Rhododendron)
Rhododendron nudiflorum (Pinxterbloom Azalea)
Rhododendron roseum (Roseshell Azalea)
Sambucus pubens (Scarlet Elder)
Symphoricarpos albus (Common Snowberry)
Symphoricarpos orbiculatus (Indiancurrant Coralberry)
Viburnum acerifolium (Mapleleaf Viburnum)
Viburnum cassinoides (Witherod Viburnum)
Viburnum dentatum (Arrowwood Viburnum)
Viburnum rafinesquianum (Rafinesque Viburnum)
Xanthorhiza simplicissima (Yellowroot)

Clematis virginiana (Virginsbower)
Cocculus carolinus (Carolina Snailseed)

Lonicera sempervirens (Trumpet Honeysuckle)

GREEN-BROWN:

Aesculus pavia (Red Buckeye)
Alnus serrulata (Common Alder)
Comptonia peregrina (Sweetfern)
Dirca palustris (Atlantic Leatherwood)
Fothergilla gardeni (Dwarf Fothergilla)
Fothergilla major (Large Fothergilla)

Lindera benzoin (Common Spicebush)
Myrica pensylvanica (Northern Bayberry)
Quercus ilicifolia (Scrub Oak)
Staphylea trifolia (American Bladdernut)
Viburnum alnifolium (Hobblebush Viburnum)

Toxicodendron radicans (Common Poisonivy)
Wistaria macrostachya (Kentucky Wistaria)

Twig coloration (cont.)

BROWN:

Andromeda polifolia (Bogrosemary Andromeda)
Calycanthus floridus (Common Sweetshrub)
Castanea pumila (Allegany Chinkapin)
Comptonia peregrina (Sweetfern)
Epigaea repens (Trailing-arbutus)
Hydrangea quercifolia (Oakleaf Hydrangea)
Juniperus communis (Common Juniper)
Juniperus horizontalis (Creeping Juniper)
Kalmia angustifolia (Lambkill Kalmia)
Kalmia polifolia (Bog Kalmia)

Lyonia ligustrina (He-huckleberry)
Philadelphus grandiflorus (Big Scentless Mockorange)
Quercus prinoides (Dwarf Chinkapin Oak)
Rhododendron viscosum (Swamp Azalea)
Ribes cynosbati (Pasture Gooseberry)
Ribes missouriense (Missouri Gooseberry)
Salix lucida (Shining Willow)
Shepherdia canadensis (Russet Buffaloberry)
Symphoricarpos orbiculatus (Indiancurrant Coralberry)
Vaccinium macrocarpum (Cranberry)

Ampelopsis arborea (Peppervine)
Ampelopsis cordata (Heartleaf Ampelopsis)
Celastrus scandens (American Bittersweet)
Clematis verticillaris (Rock Clematis)
Menispermum canadense (Common Moonseed)

Pathenocissus quinquefolia (Virginia Creeper)
Toxicodendron radicans (Common Poisonivy)
Vitis labrusca (Fox Grape)
Vitis riparia (Riverbank Grape)

RED-BROWN:

Alnus serrulata (Common Alder)
Amelanchier sanguinea (Roundleaf Serviceberry)
Amorpha fruticosa (Indigobush Amorpha)
Andromeda polifolia (Bogrosemary Andromeda)
Arctostaphylos uva-ursi (Bearberry)
Aronia arbutifolia (Red Chokeberry)
Aronia prunifolia (Purplefruit Chokeberry)
Castanea pumila (Allegany Chinkapin)
Ceanothus americanus (Jerseytea Ceanothus)
Ceanothus ovatus (Inland Ceanothus)
Cephalanthus occidentalis (Common Buttonbush)
Chamaedaphne calyculata (Leatherleaf)
Cornus racemosa (Gray Dogwood)
Corylus americana (American Filbert)
Corylus cornuta (Beaked Filbert)
Cyrilla racemiflora (American Cyrilla)
Dirca palustris (Atlantic Leatherwood)
Hydrangea arborescens (Smooth Hydrangea)
Hypericum densiflorum (Dense Hypericum)

Hypericum frondosum (Golden St.Johnswort)
Hypericum kalmianum (Kalm St.Johnswort)
Hypericum prolificum (Shrubby St.Johnswort)
Kalmia latifolia (Mountainlaurel Kalmia)
Ledum groenlandicum (Labradortea Ledum)
Pachistima canbyi (Canby Pachistima)
Physocarpus opulifolius (Common Ninebark)
Quercus ilicifolia (Scrub Oak)
Rhododendron vaseyi (Pinkshell Azalea)
Rhus aromatica (Fragrant Sumac)
Ribes odoratum (Clove Currant)
Robinia hispida (Roseacacia Locust)
Robinia viscosa (Clammy Locust)
Shepherdia canadensis (Russet Buffaloberry)
Spiraea alba (Narrowleaf Meadowsweet Spirea)
Spiraea corymbosa (Corymed Spirea)
Stewartia ovata (Mountain Stewartia)
Viburnum nudum (Possumhaw Viburnum)
Zenobia pulverulenta (Dusty Zenobia)

RED:

Amelanchier sanguinea (Roundleaf Serviceberry)
Chamaedaphne calyculata (Leatherleaf)
Cornus amomum (Silky Dogwood)
Cornus stolonifera (Redosier Dogwood)
Itea virginica (Virginia Sweetspire)
Ledum groenlandicum (Labradortea Ledum)
Leucothoe catesbaei (Drooping Leucothoe)
Myrica pensylvanica (Northern Bayberry)
Rhododendron arborescens (Sweet Azalea)
Robinia hispida (Roseacacia Locust)
Robinia viscosa (Clammy Locust)
Rosa carolina (Carolina Rose)

Rosa setigera (Prairie Rose)
Rubus allegheniensis (Allegany Blackberry)
Rubus occidentalis (Blackcap Raspberry)
Rubus strigosus (American Red Raspberry)
Salix humilis (Prairie Willow)
Spiraea corymbosa (Corymed Spirea)
Vaccinium angustifolium (Lowbush Blueberry)
Vaccinium corymbosum (Highbush Blueberry)
Vaccinium stamineum (Common Deerberry)
Viburnum alnifolium (Hobblebush Viburnum)
Zenobia pulverulenta (Dusty Zenobia)

Clematis virginiana (Virginsbower)
Vitis riparia (Riverbank Grape)

PURPLE:

Cornus amomum (Silky Dogwood)
Cornus rugosa (Roundleaf Dogwood)

Cornus stolonifera (Redosier Dogwood)
Euonymus americanus (Brook Euonymus)

Euonymus obovatus   (Running Euonymus)
Mahonia aquifolium   (Oregongrape)
Rubus allegheniensis   (Allegany Blackberry)
Rubus occidentalis   (Blackcap Raspberry)
Rubus strigosus   (American Red Raspberry)

Sambucus pubens   (Scarlet Elder)
Spiraea corymbosa   (Corymed Spirea)
Vaccinium stamineum   (Common Deerberry)
Viburnum alnifolium   (Hobblebush Viburnum)

Aristolochia durior   (Common Dutchmanspipe)
Clematis virginiana   (Virginsbower)

BLACK:

Lyonia ligustrina   (He-huckleberry)
Rubus occidentalis   (Blackcap Raspberry)

Rubus strigosus   (American Red Raspberry)

BUD CHARACTER:

NAKED:
indicator — *Viburnum alnifolium* (Hobblebush Viburnum)

Calycanthus floridus   (Common Sweetshrub)
Fothergilla gardeni   (Dwarf Fothergilla)
Fothergilla major   (Large Fothergilla)
Hamamelis vernalis   (Vernal Witchhazel)
Juniperus communis   (Common Juniper)
Juniperus horizontalis   (Creeping Juniper)

Kalmia angustifolia   (Lambkill Kalmia)
Kalmia latifolia   (Mountainlaurel Kalmia)
Kalmia polifolia   (Bog Kalmia)
Shepherdia argentea   (Silver Buffaloberry)
Shepherdia canadensis   (Russet Buffaloberry)
Viburnum alnifolium   (Hobblebush Viburnum)

Toxicodendron radicans   (Common Poisonivy)

RESINOUS:
indicator — *Ribes americanum* (American Black Currant)

Alnus serrulata   (Common Alder)
Baccharis halimifolia   (Eastern Baccharis)
Comptonia peregrina   (Sweetfern)
Myrica pensylvanica   (Northern Bayberry)

Pinus aristata   (Bristlecone Pine)
Ribes americanum   (American Black Currant)
Viburnum trilobum   (American Cranberrybush Viburnum)

WOOLLY:
indicator — *Magnolia virginiana* (Sweetbay Magnolia)

Amorpha canescens   (Leadplant Amorpha)
Amorpha fruticosa   (Indigobush Amorpha)
Calycanthus floridus   (Common Sweetshrub)
Castanea pumila   (Allegany Chinkapin)
Ceanothus ovatus   (Inland Ceanothus)
Clethra acuminata   (Cinnamon Clethra)
Comptonia peregrina   (Sweetfern)
Cornus amomum   (Silky Dogwood)
Corylus americana   (American Filbert)
Dirca palustris   (Atlantic Leatherwood)
Fothergilla gardeni   (Dwarf Fothergilla)
Fothergilla major   (Large Fothergilla)
Hamamelis vernalis   (Vernal Witchhazel)

Magnolia virginiana   (Sweetbay Magnolia)
Potentilla fruticosa   (Bush Cinquefoil)
Rhododendron roseum   (Roseshell Azalea)
Rhododendron viscosum   (Swamp Azalea)
Rhus aromatica   (Fragrant Sumac)
Ribes odoratum   (Clove Currant)
Robinia viscosa   (Clammy Locust)
Salix humilis   (Prairie Willow)
Spiraea alba   (Narrowleaf Meadowsweet Spirea)
Spiraea tomentosa   (Hardhack Spirea)
Stewartia ovata   (Mountain Stewartia)
Viburnum alnifolium   (Hobblebush Viburnum)

Aristolochia durior   (Common Dutchmanspipe)
Toxicodendron radicans   (Common Poisonivy)

Wistaria macrostachya   (Kentucky Wistaria)

Bud character (cont.)

STALKED:
    indicator — *Alnus serrulata* (Common Alder)

Alnus serrulata   (Common Alder)
Betula pumila   (Low Birch)
Fothergilla gardeni   (Dwarf Fothergilla)
Fothergilla major   (Large Fothergilla)
Hamamelis vernalis   (Vernal Witchhazel)

Ilex decidua   (Possumhaw)
Lindera benzoin   (Common Spicebush)
Ribes americanum   (American Black Currant)
Ribes odoratum   (Clove Currant)
Sambucus pubens   (Scarlet Elder)

Toxicodendron radicans   (Common Poisonivy)

ONE/TWO SCALES:
    indicator — *Salix humilis* (Prairie Willow)

Alnus serrulata   (Common Alder)
Betula pumila   (Low Birch)
Clethra acuminata   (Cinnamon Clethra)
Clethra alnifolia   (Summersweet Clethra)
Cornus amomum   (Silky Dogwood)
Cornus canadensis   (Bunchberry Dogwood)
Cornus racemosa   (Gray Dogwood)
Cornus rugosa   (Roundleaf Dogwood)
Cornus stolonifera   (Redosier Dogwood)
Hypericum densiflorum   (Dense Hypericum)
Hypericum frondosum   (Golden St.Johnswort)
Hypericum kalmianum   (Kalm St.Johnswort)
Hypericum prolificum   (Shrubby St.Johnswort)

Leiophyllum buxifolium   (Box Sandmyrtle)
Lyonia ligustrina   (He-huckleberry)
Magnolia virginiana   (Sweetbay Magnolia)
Pachistima canbyi   (Canby Pachistima)
Philadelphus grandiflorus   (Big Scentless Mockorange)
Salix humilis   (Prairie Willow)
Salix lucida   (Shining Willow)
Staphylea trifolia   (American Bladdernut)
Stewartia ovata   (Mountain Stewartia)
Viburnum alnifolium   (Hobblebush Viburnum)
Viburnum cassinoides   (Witherod Viburnum)
Viburnum nudum   (Possumhaw Viburnum)
Viburnum trilobum   (American Cranberrybush Viburnum)

Vitis labrusca   (Fox Grape)
Vitis riparia   (Riverbank Grape)

Wistaria macrostachya   (Kentucky Wistaria)

LARGE:
    indicator — *Aesculus pavia* (Red Buckeye)

Aesculus parviflora   (Bottlebrush Buckeye)
Aesculus pavia   (Red Buckeye)
Clethra acuminata   (Cinnamon Clethra)
Clethra alnifolia   (Summersweet Clethra)
Leucothoe catesbaei   (Drooping Leucothoe)
Magnolia virginiana   (Sweetbay Magnolia)
Rhododendron arborescens   (Sweet Azalea)
Rhododendron calendulaceum   (Flame Azalea)
Rhododendron carolinianum   (Carolina Rhododendron)
Rhododendron catawbiense   (Catawba Rhododendron)

Rhododendron nudiflorum   (Pinxterbloom Azalea)
Rhododendron roseum   (Roseshell Azalea)
Rhododendron vaseyi   (Pinkshell Azalea)
Rhododendron viscosum   (Swamp Azalea)
Sambucus pubens   (Scarlet Elder)
Viburnum alnifolium   (Hobblebush Viburnum)
Viburnum cassinoides   (Witherod Viburnum)
Viburnum nudum   (Possumhaw Viburnum)
Xanthorhiza simplicissima   (Yellowroot)

NARROW, LONG POINTED:
    indicator — *Amelanchier sanguinea* (Roundleaf Serviceberry)

Amelanchier sanguinea   (Roundleaf Serviceberry)
Aronia arbutifolia   (Red Chokeberry)
Aronia melanocarpa   (Black Chokeberry)
Aronia prunifolia   (Purplefruit Chokeberry)
Diervilla lonicera   (Dwarf Bushhoneysuckle)

Leucothoe catesbaei   (Drooping Leucothoe)
Stewartia ovata   (Mountain Stewartia)
Viburnum cassinoides   (Witherod Viburnum)
Viburnum nudum   (Possumhaw Viburnum)

Berchemia scandens   (Alabama Supplejack)
Wistaria macrostachya   (Kentucky Wistaria)

CLUSTERED:
    indicator — *Rhododendron calendulaceum* (Flame Azalea)

400

Betula pumila (Low Birch)
Castanea pumila (Allegany Chinkapin)
Lindera benzoin (Common Spicebush)
Myrica pensylvanica (Northern Bayberry)
Prunus hortulana (Hortulan Plum)
Quercus ilicifolia (Scrub Oak)
Quercus prinoides (Dwarf Chinkapin Oak)
Rhododendron arborescens (Sweet Azalea)
Rhododendron calendulaceum (Flame Azalea)

Rhododendron carolinianum (Carolina Rhododendron)
Rhododendron catawbiense (Catawba Rhododendron)
Rhododendron nudiflorum (Pinxterbloom Azalea)
Rhododendron roseum (Roseshell Azalea)
Rhododendron vaseyi (Pinkshell Azalea)
Rhododendron viscosum (Swamp Azalea)
Ribes americanum (American Black Currant)
Ribes odoratum (Clove Currant)
Sambucus canadensis (American Elder)

Aristolochia durior (Common Dutchmanspipe)

DOME-SHAPED, SURROUNDED BY LEAF SCAR:
    indicator — Dirca palustris (Atlantic Leatherwood)

Dirca palustris (Atlantic Leatherwood)
Rhus aromatica (Fragrant Sumac)

BUD COLORATION:

WHITE/SILVER-GRAY:

Cornus amomum (Silky Dogwood)
Elaeagnus commutata (Silverberry)

Myrica pensylvanica (Northern Bayberry)
Shepherdia argentea (Silver Buffaloberry)

GRAY:

Clethra acuminata (Cinnamon Clethra)
Clethra alnifolia (Summersweet Clethra)
Dirca palustris (Atlantic Leatherwood)

Magnolia virginiana (Sweetbay Magnolia)
Rhododendron roseum (Roseshell Azalea)
Shepherdia argentea (Silver Buffaloberry)

Aristolochia durior (Common Dutchmanspipe)

GREEN:

Baccharis halimifolia (Eastern Baccharis)
Hypericum prolificum (Shrubby St.Johnswort)
Lindera benzoin (Common Spicebush)
Magnolia virginiana (Sweetbay Magnolia)
Rhododendron calendulaceum (Flame Azalea)

Rhododendron catawbiense (Catawba Rhododendron)
Rhododendron nudiflorum (Pinxterbloom Azalea)
Vaccinium corymbosum (Highbush Blueberry)
Viburnum acerifolium (Mapleleaf Viburnum)
Viburnum trilobum (American Cranberrybush Viburnum)

Smilax glauca (Cat Greenbrier)
Smilax rotundifolia (Common Greenbrier)

Smilax tamnoides (Bamboo Greenbrier)

YELLOW-BROWN:

Rhododendron arborescens (Sweet Azalea)
Rhododendron calendulaceum (Flame Azalea)
Rhus aromatica (Fragrant Sumac)
Rubus occidentalis (Blackcap Raspberry)

Salix humilis (Prairie Willow)
Viburnum alnifolium (Hobblebush Viburnum)
Viburnum cassinoides (Witherod Viburnum)

ORANGE-BROWN:

Salix lucida (Shining Willow)

Bud coloration (cont.)

GREEN-BROWN:

Hypericum densiflorum   (Dense Hypericum)
Hypericum frondosum   (Golden St.Johnswort)
Hypericum kalmianum   (Kalm St.Johnswort)
Hypericum prolificum   (Shrubby St.Johnswort)

GRAY-BROWN:

Aesculus parviflora   (Bottlebrush Buckeye)
Cornus amomum   (Silky Dogwood)
Hamamelis vernalis   (Vernal Witchhazel)
Ilex decidua   (Possumhaw)
Ilex glabra   (Inkberry)
Ilex verticillata   (Common Winterberry)
Viburnum rafinesquianum   (Rafinesque Viburnum)

BROWN:

Aesculus pavia   (Red Buckeye)
Amelanchier sanguinea   (Roundleaf Serviceberry)
Aronia prunifolia   (Purplefruit Chokeberry)
Betula pumila   (Low Birch)
Calycanthus floridus   (Common Sweetshrub)
Castanea pumila   (Allegany Chinkapin)
Cephalanthus occidentalis   (Common Buttonbush)
Chamaedaphne calyculata   (Leatherleaf)
Cornus racemosa   (Gray Dogwood)
Cornus rugosa   (Roundleaf Dogwood)
Cornus stolonifera   (Redosier Dogwood)
Corylus cornuta   (Beaked Filbert)
Diervilla lonicera   (Dwarf Bushhoneysuckle)
Dirca palustris   (Atlantic Leatherwood)
Euonymus americanus   (Brook Euonymus)
Euonymus obovatus   (Running Euonymus)
Hydrangea quercifolia   (Oakleaf Hydrangea)
Physocarpus opulifolius   (Common Ninebark)
Potentilla fruticosa   (Bush Cinquefoil)
Quercus ilicifolia   (Scrub Oak)
Quercus prinoides   (Dwarf Chinkapin Oak)
Ribes americanum   (American Black Currant)
Robinia hispida   (Roseacacia Locust)
Robinia viscosa   (Clammy Locust)
Rubus strigosus   (American Red Raspberry)
Salix humilis   (Prairie Willow)
Salix lucida   (Shining Willow)
Sambucus canadensis   (American Elder)
Spiraea alba   (Narrowleaf Meadowsweet Spirea)
Spiraea corymbosa   (Corymed Spirea)
Spiraea tomentosa   (Hardhack Spirea)
Symphoricarpos albus   (Common Snowberry)
Symphoricarpos occidentalis   (Western Snowberry)
Symphoricarpos orbiculatus   (Indiancurrant Coralberry)

Clematis virginiana   (Virginsbower)
Lonicera dioica   (Limber Honeysuckle)
Lonicera sempervirens   (Trumpet Honeysuckle)
Parthenocissus quinquefolia   (Virginia Creeper)
Vitis labrusca   (Fox Grape)
Wistaria macrostachya   (Kentucky Wistaria)

RED-BROWN:

Alnus serrulata   (Common Alder)
Amorpha canescens   (Leadplant Amorpha)
Amorpha fruticosa   (Indigobush Amorpha)
Ceanothus americanus   (Jerseytea Ceanothus)
Ceanothus ovatus   (Inland Ceanothus)
Comptonia peregrina   (Sweetfern)
Corylus americana   (American Filbert)
Rhododendron arborescens   (Sweet Azalea)
Rhododendron viscosum   (Swamp Azalea)
Ribes cynosbati   (Pasture Gooseberry)
Ribes missouriense   (Missouri Gooseberry)
Ribes odoratum   (Clove Currant)
Rubus occidentalis   (Blackcap Raspberry)
Sambucus canadensis   (American Elder)
Shepherdia canadensis   (Russet Buffaloberry)
Staphylea trifolia   (American Bladdernut)
Vaccinium angustifolium   (Lowbush Blueberry)
Vaccinium stamineum   (Common Deerberry)
Viburnum alnifolium   (Hobblebush Viburnum)
Viburnum dentatum   (Arrowwood Viburnum)
Viburnum nudum   (Possumhaw Viburnum)
Xanthorhiza simplicissima   (Yellowroot)

Ampelopsis arborea   (Peppervine)
Celastrus scandens   (American Bittersweet)
Vitis riparia   (Riverbank Grape)

RED:

Alnus serrulata   (Common Alder)
Amelanchier sanguinea   (Roundleaf Serviceberry)
Aronia arbutifolia   (Red Chokeberry)
Aronia melanocarpa   (Black Chokeberry)
Aronia prunifolia   (Purplefruit Chokeberry)
Baccharis halimifolia   (Eastern Baccharis)
Castanea pumila   (Allegany Chinkapin)
Clethra acuminata   (Cinnamon Clethra)
Clethra alnifolia   (Summersweet Clethra)
Cornus racemosa   (Gray Dogwood)
Euonymus americanus   (Brook Euonymus)
Euonymus obovatus   (Running Euonymus)
Lyonia ligustrina   (He-huckleberry)
Rhododendron nudiflorum   (Pinxterbloom Azalea)
Rosa carolina   (Carolina Rose)
Rosa setigera   (Prairie Rose)

Rubus allegheniensis   (Allegany Blackberry)
Salix humilis   (Prairie Willow)
Vaccinium angustifolium   (Lowbush Blueberry)
Vaccinium corymbosum   (Highbush Blueberry)

Vaccinium stamineum   (Common Deerberry)
Viburnum acerifolium   (Mapleleaf Viburnum)
Viburnum trilobum   (American Cranberrybush Viburnum)

Parthenocissus quinquefolia   (Virginia Creeper)
Toxicodendron radicans   (Common Poisonivy)

PURPLE:

Alnus serrulata   (Common Alder)
Amelanchier sanguinea   (Roundleaf Serviceberry)
Aronia arbutifolia   (Red Chokeberry)
Aronia melanocarpa   (Black Chokeberry)

Corylus americana   (American Filbert)
Ribes americanum   (American Black Currant)
Sambucus canadensis   (American Elder)
Sambucus pubens   (Scarlet Elder)

BLACK:

Staphylea trifolia   (American Bladdernut)

BARK CHARACTER:

The distinctive textural characteristics of shrub and vine bark is most interesting, especially on deciduous plants during the winter season. The surface on stems and main branches for many species change with the advance of maturity. The bark of most young shrubs and vines is smooth while that of a many season veteran may become scaly, exfoliated, or divided into longitudinal ridges and fissures. Many species are valued primarily for their ornamental bark. The knowledgeable designer appreciates the palette of bark variation and shows this to best advantage. Six categories of bark character are recognized.

SMOOTH:
>   having a continuous even surface with a minimum of fissures,
>   indicator — *Wistaria macrostachya* (Kentucky Wistaria)

Aesculus parviflora   (Bottlebrush Buckeye)
Aesculus pavia   (Red Buckeye)
Alnus serrulata   (Common Alder)
Amelanchier sanguinea   (Roundleaf Serviceberry)
Amorpha canescens   (Leadplant Amorpha)
Amorpha fruticosa   (Indigobush Amorpha)
Andromeda polifolia   (Bogrosemary Andromeda)
Arctostaphylos uva-ursi   (Bearberry)
Aronia arbutifolia   (Red Chokeberry)
Aronia melanocarpa   (Black Chokeberry)
Aronia prunifolia   (Purplefruit Chokeberry)
Betula pumila   (Low Birch)
Calycanthus floridus   (Common Sweetshrub)
Ceanothus americanus   (Jerseytea Ceanothus)
Ceanothus ovatus   (Inland Ceanothus)
Comptonia peregrina   (Sweetfern)
Cornus amomum   (Silky Dogwood)
Cornus canadensis   (Bunchberry Dogwood)
Cornus rugosa   (Roundleaf Dogwood)
Cornus stolonifera   (Redosier Dogwood)
Corylus americana   (American Filbert)
Corylus cornuta   (Beaked Filbert)

Dirca palustris   (Atlantic Leatherwood)
Epigaea repens   (Trailing-arbutus)
Euonymus americanus   (Brook Euonymus)
Euonymus obovatus   (Running Euonymus)
Fothergilla gardeni   (Dwarf Fothergilla)
Fothergilla major   (Large Fothergilla)
Gaultheria procumbens   (Checkerberry Wintergreen)
Hamamelis vernalis   (Vernal Witchhazel)
Hydrangea arborescens   (Smooth Hydrangea)
Ilex decidua   (Possumhaw)
Ilex glabra   (Inkberry)
Ilex verticillata   (Common Winterberry)
Kalmia angustifolia   (Lambkill Kalmia)
Kalmia latifolia   (Mountainlaurel Kalmia)
Kalmia polifolia   (Bog Kalmia)
Ledum groenlandicum   (Labradortea Ledum)
Lindera benzoin   (Common Spicebush)
Magnolia virginiana   (Sweetbay Magnolia)
Myrica pensylvanica   (Northern Bayberry)
Pachistima canbyi   (Canby Pachistima)
Pieris floribunda   (Mountain Pieris)
Rhododendron arborescens   (Sweet Azalea)

Bark character (cont.)

Rhododendron calendulaceum (Flame Azalea)
Rhododendron carolinianum (Carolina Rhododendron)
Rhododendron catawbiense (Catawba Rhododendron)
Rhododendron nudiflorum (Pinxterbloom Azalea)
Rhododendron roseum (Roseshell Azalea)
Rhododendron vaseyi (Pinkshell Azalea)
Rhododendron viscosum (Swamp Azalea)
Rhus aromatica (Fragrant Sumac)
Ribes americanum (American Black Currant)
Ribes odoratum (Clove Currant)
Robinia viscosa (Clammy Locust)
Rosa carolina (Carolina Rose)
Rosa setigera (Prairie Rose)
Rubus allegheniensis (Allegany Blackberry)
Rubus occidentalis (Blackcap Raspberry)

Rubus odoratus (Fragrant Thimbleberry)
Rubus strigosus (American Red Raspberry)
Salix lucida (Shining Willow)
Sambucus canadensis (American Elder)
Sambucus pubens (Scarlet Elder)
Staphylea trifolia (American Bladdernut)
Stewartia ovata (Mountain Stewartia)
Viburnum acerifolium (Mapleleaf Viburnum)
Viburnum cassinoides (Witherod Viburnum)
Viburnum dentatum (Arrowwood Viburnum)
Viburnum rafinesquianum (Rafinesque Viburnum)
Viburnum trilobum (American Cranberrybush Viburnum)
Xanthorhiza simplicissima (Yellowroot)
Yucca filamentosa (Adamsneedle Yucca)

Ampelopsis arborea (Peppervine)
Aristolochia durior (Common Dutchmanspipe)
Celastrus scandens (American Bittersweet)
Menispermum canadense (Common Moonseed)
Smilax glauca (Cat Greenbrier)

Smilax rotundifolia (Common Greenbrier)
Smilax tamnoides (Bamboo Greenbrier)
Toxicodendron radicans (Common Poisonivy)
Wistaria macrostachya (Kentucky Wistaria)

SCALY:

regular thin papery flakes separated by a mesh pattern of fine shallow vertical and horizontal fissures, indicator — *Clethra alnifolia* (Summersweet Clethra)

Amorpha canescens (Leadplant Amorpha)
Baccharis halimifolia (Eastern Baccharis)
Chamaedaphne calyculata (Leatherleaf)
Clethra acuminata (Cinnamon Clethra)
Clethra alnifolia (Summersweet Clethra)
Cornus racemosa (Gray Dogwood)
Elaeagnus commutata (Silverberry)
Hamamelis vernalis (Vernal Witchhazel)
Kalmia latifolia (Mountainlaurel Kalmia)
Leucothoe catesbaei (Drooping Leucothoe)
Lyonia ligustrina (He-huckleberry)
Prunus hortulana (Hortulan Plum)
Quercus ilicifolia (Scrub Oak)
Quercus prinoides (Dwarf Chinkapin Oak)
Rhododendron arborecens (Sweet Azalea)
Rhododendron calendulaceum (Flame Azalea)
Rhododendron carolinianum (Carolina Rhododendron)
Rhododendron catawbiense (Catawba Rhododendron)
Rhododendron nudiflorum (Pinxterbloom Azalea)

Rhododendron roseum (Roseshell Azalea)
Rhododendron vaseyi (Pinkshell Azalea)
Rhododendron viscosum (Swamp Azalea)
Rhus aromatica (Fragrant Sumac)
Robinia hispida (Roseacacia Locust)
Shepherdia argentea (Silver Buffaloberry)
Shepherdia canadensis (Russet Buffaloberry)
Staphylea trifolia (American Bladdernut)
Taxus canadensis (Canada Yew)
Vaccinium angustifolium (Lowbush Blueberry)
Vaccinium corymbosum (Highbush Blueberry)
Vaccinium macrocarpum (Cranberry)
Vaccinium stamineum (Common Deerberry)
Viburnum acerifolium (Mapleleaf Viburnum)
Viburnum alnifolium (Hobblebush Viburnum)
Viburnum cassinoides (Witherod Viburnum)
Viburnum dentatum (Arrowwood Viburnum)
Viburnum nudum (Possumhaw Viburnum)
Xanthorhiza simplicissima (Yellowroot)

Aristolochia durior (Common Dutchmanspipe)
Celastrus scandens (American Bittersweet)

Parthenocissus quinquefolia (Virginia Creeper)

EXFOLIATING:

thin or coarse strips or sheets peeling either vertically, horizontally or into irregular mottled patches, indicator — *Hydrangea quercifolia* (Oakleaf Hydrangea)

Archtostaphylus uva-ursi (Bearberry)
Cephalanthus occidentalis (Common Buttonbush)
Clethra acuminata (Cinnamon Clethra)
Clethra alnifolia (Summersweet Clethra)
Diervilla lonicera (Dwarf Bushhoneysuckle)
Hydrangea arborescens (Smooth Hydrangea)
Hydrangea quercifolia (Oakleaf Hydrangea)
Hypericum densiflorum (Dense Hypericum)
Hypericum frondosum (Golden St.Johnswort)
Hypericum kalmianum (Kalm St.Johnswort)

Hypericum prolificum (Shrubby St.Johnswort)
Juniperis communis (Common Juniper)
Juniperus horizontalis (Creeping Juniper)
Leiophyllum buxifolium (Box Sandmyrtle)
Lonicera canadensis (American Fly Honeysuckle)
Neviusia alabamensis (Snowwreath)
Philadelphus grandiflorus (Big Scentless Mockorange)
Physocarpus opulifolius (Common Ninebark)
Potentilla fruticosa (Bush Cinquefoil)
Ribes cynosbati (Pasture Gooseberry)

Ribes missouriense (Missouri Gooseberry)
Ribes odoratum (Clove Currant)
Rubus odoratus (Fragrant Thimbleberry)
Spiraea alba (Narrowleaf Meadowsweet Spirea)
Spiraea corymbosa (Corymed Spirea)
Spiraea tomentosa (Hardhack Spirea)

Stewartia ovata (Mountain Stewartia)
Symphoricarpos albus (Common Snowberry)
Symphoricarpos occidentalis (Western Snowberry)
Symphoricarpos orbiculatus (Indiancurrant Coralberry)
Taxus canadensis (Canada Yew)
Zenobia pulverulenta (Dusty Zenobia)

Bignonia capreolata (Crossvine)
Campsis radicans (Common Trumpetcreeper)
Clematis verticillaris (Rock Clematis)
Clematis virginiana (Virginsbower)
Lonicera dioica (Limber Honeysuckle)

Lonicera sempervirens (Trumpet Honeysuckle)
Toxicodendron radicans (Common Poisonivy)
Vitis labrusca (Fox Grape)
Vitis riparia (Riverbank Grape)

BLOCKY:
> short knobby, warty, flat-topped squarish plates or ridges,
> indicator — *Ilex decidua* (Possumhaw)

Ilex decidua (Possumhaw)
Ilex glabra (Inkberry)

Itea virginica (Virginia Sweetspire)
Sambucus pubens (Scarlet Elder)

Cocculus carolinus (Carolina Snailseed)
Menispermum canadense (Common Moonseed)

SHALLOW-FURROWED:
> grooved by shallow longitudinal cracks becoming checked across into elongated rectangular platy
> segments,
> indicator — *Castanea pumila* (Allegany Chinkapin)

Amorpha fruticosa (Indigobush Amorpha)
Baccharis halimifolia (Eastern Baccharis)
Castanea pumila (Allegany Chinkapin)
Ceanothus americanus (Jerseytea Ceanothus)
Ceanothus ovatus (Inland Ceanothus)
Cephalanthus occidentalis (Common Buttonbush)
Cornus amomum (Silky Dogwood)
Corylus americana (American Filbert)
Corylus cornuta (Beaked Filbert)
Kalmia latifolia (Mountainlaurel Kalmia)
Lindera benzoin (Common Spicebush)
Lyonia ligustrina (He-huckleberry)

Mahonia aquifolium (Oregongrape)
Pinus aristata (Bristlecone Pine)
Rhus aromatica (Fragrant Sumac)
Ribes cynosbati (Pasture Gooseberry)
Ribes missouriense (Missouri Gooseberry)
Salix humilis (Prairie Willow)
Shepherdia argentea (Silver Buffaloberry)
Shepherdia canadensis (Russet Buffaloberry)
Staphylea trifolia (American Bladdernut)
Viburnum dentatum (Arrowwood Viburnum)
Viburnum rafinesquianum (Rafinesque Viburnum)

Clematis verticillaris (Rock Clematis)
Clematis virginiana (Virginsbower)

Cocculus carolinus (Carolina Snailseed)
Parthenocissus quinquefolia (Virginia Creeper)

DEEP-FURROWED:
> grooved by coarse, deep longitudinal cracks becoming checked across into rectangular segments,
> indicator — *Ampelopsis cordata* (Heartleaf Ampelopsis)

Ampelopsis cordata (Heartleaf Ampelopsis)
Parthenocissus quinquefolia (Virginia Creeper)

BARK COLORATION:

The vast palette of color in plants is a basic aesthetic consideration in their use. The use of dynamic bark coloration achieves emphasis, accent, decoration, attraction, and organization in the landscape. Bark character and color form one of the most interesting visual features of the winter landscape when

contrasted with the white background of snow or the green background of evergreens. Seven classes represent the basic bark color possibilities.

GRAY:

Alnus serrulata (Common Alder)
Amelanchier sanguinea (Roundleaf Serviceberry)
Amorpha canescens (Leadplant Amorpha)
Andromeda polifolia (Bogrosemary Andromeda)
Baccharis halimifolia (Eastern Baccharis)
Cornus amomum (Silky Dogwood)
Cornus racemosa (Gray Dogwood)
Cornus rugosa (Roundleaf Dogwood)
Elaeagnus commutata (Silverberry)
Fothergilla gardeni (Dwarf Fothergilla)
Fothergilla major (Large Fothergilla)
Hamamelis vernalis (Vernal Witchhazel)
Ilex decidua (Possumhaw)
Ilex verticillata (Common Winterberry)
Kalmia latifolia (Mountainlaurel Kalmia)
Lyonia ligustrina (He-huckleberry)
Magnolia virginiana (Sweetbay Magnolia)
Mahonia aquifolium (Oregongrape)

Myrica pensylvanica (Northern Bayberry)
Rhododendron arborescens (Sweet Azalea)
Rhododendron calendulaceum (Flame Azalea)
Rhododendron carolinianum (Carolina Rhododendron)
Rhododendron catawbiense (Catawba Rhododendron)
Rhododendron nudiflorum (Pinxterbloom Azalea)
Rhododendron roseum (Roseshell Azalea)
Rhododendron vaseyi (Pinkshell Azalea)
Rhododendron viscosum (Swamp Azalea)
Ribes cynosbati (Pasture Gooseberry)
Ribes missouriense (Missouri Gooseberry)
Ribes odoratum (Clove Currant)
Rubus odoratus (Fragrant Thimbleberry)
Sambucus pubens (Scarlet Elder)
Shepherdia argentea (Silver Buffaloberry)
Shepherdia canadensis (Russet Buffaloberry)
Vaccinium angustifolium (Lowbush Blueberry)
Vaccinium stamineum (Common Deerberry)

Aristolochia durior (Common Dutchmanspipe)
Celastrus scandens (American Bittersweet)
Clematis virginiana (Virginsbower)

Toxicodendron radicans (Common Poisonivy)
Wistaria macrostachya (Kentucky Wistaria)

GREEN:

Comptonia peregrina (Sweetfern)
Cornus amomum (Silky Dogwood)
Cornus rugosa (Roundleaf Dogwood)
Euonymus americanus (Brook Euonymus)

Euonymus obovatus (Running Euonymus)
Leucothoe catesbaei (Drooping Leucothoe)
Rosa carolina (Carolina Rose)
Rosa setigera (Prairie Rose)

Smilax glauca (Cat Greenbrier)
Smilax rotundifolia (Common Greenbrier)

Smilax tamnoides (Bamboo Greenbrier)

YELLOW-BROWN:

Comptonia peregrina (Sweetfern)
Mahonia aquifolium (Oregongrape)

Rubus odoratus (Fragrant Thimbleberry)
Sambucus canadensis (American Elder)

ORANGE-BROWN:

Betula pumila (Low Birch)
Hydrangea arborescens (Smooth Hydrangea)
Hydrangea quercifolia (Oakleaf Hydrangea)
Ledum groenlandicum (Labradortea Ledum)
Neviusia alabamensis (Snowwreath)
Philadelphus grandiflorus (Big Scentless Mockorange)
Physocarpus opulifolius (Common Ninebark)

Potentilla fruticosa (Bush Cinquefoil)
Rubus odoratus (Fragrant Thimbleberry)
Salix humilis (Prairie Willow)
Spiraea alba (Narrowleaf Meadowsweet Spirea)
Spiraea corymbosa (Corymed Spirea)
Spiraea tomentosa (Hardhack Spirea)
Stewartia ovata (Mountain Stewartia)

Campsis radicans (Common Trumpetcreeper)
Lonicera sempervirens (Trumpet Honeysuckle)

GRAY-BROWN:

Alnus serrulata (Common Alder)
Amorpha fruticosa (Indigobush Amorpha)
Calycanthus floridus (Common Sweetshrub)
Cephalanthus occidentalis (Common Buttonbush)
Chamaedaphne calyculata (Leatherleaf)
Clethra alnifolia (Summersweet Clethra)
Cornus racemosa (Gray Dogwood)
Corylus americana (American Filbert)
Corylus cornuta (Beaked Filbert)
Diervilla lonicera (Dwarf Bushhoneysuckle)
Dirca palustris (Atlantic Leatherwood)
Ilex decidua (Possumhaw)
Ilex glabra (Inkberry)
Juniperus communis (Common Juniper)
Juniperus horizontalis (Creeping Juniper)
Kalmia angustifolia (Lambkill Kalmia)
Lindera benzoin (Common Spicebush)
Magnolia virginiana (Sweetbay Magnolia)
Myrica pensylvanica (Northern Bayberry)
Philadelphus grandiflorus (Big Scentless Mockorange)
Pieris floribunda (Mountain Pieris)
Potentilla fruticosa (Bush Cinquefoil)

Quercus ilicifolia (Scrub Oak)
Quercus prinoides (Dwarf Chinkapin Oak)
Robinia hispida (Roseacacia Locust)
Robinia viscosa (Clammy Locust)
Sambucus canadensis (American Elder)
Shepherdia argentea (Silver Buffaloberry)
Shepherdia canadensis (Russet Buffaloberry)
Staphylea trifolia (American Bladdernut)
Symphoricarpos albus (Common Snowberry)
Symphoricarpos occidentalis (Western Snowberry)
Symphoricarpos orbiculatus (Indiancurrant Coralberry)
Vaccinium angustifolium (Lowbush Blueberry)
Vaccinium corymbosum (Highbush Blueberry)
Vaccinium stamineum (Common Deerberry)
Viburnum acerifolium (Mapleleaf Viburnum)
Viburnum cassinoides (Witherod Viburnum)
Viburnum dentatum (Arrowwood Viburnum)
Viburnum nudum (Possumhaw Viburnum)
Viburnum rafinesquianum (Rafinesque Viburnum)
Viburnum trilobum (American Cranberrybush Viburnum)
Xanthorhiza simplicissima (Yellowroot)

Campsis radicans (Common Trumpetcreeper)
Cocculus carolinus (Carolina Snailseed)

Lonicera dioica (Limber Honeysuckle)

BROWN:

Aesculus parviflora (Bottlebrush Buckeye)
Aesculus pavia (Red Buckeye)
Betula pumila (Low Birch)
Castanea pumila (Allegany Chinkapin)
Epigaea repens (Trailing-arbutus)
Lonicera canadensis (American Fly Honeysuckle)
Pachistima canbyi (Canby Pachistima)
Physocarpus opulifolius (Common Ninebark)

Prunus hortulana (Hortulan Plum)
Ribes cynosbati (Pasture Gooseberry)
Spiraea alba (Narrowleaf Meadowsweet Spirea)
Stewartia ovata (Mountain Stewartia)
Symphoricarpos orbiculatus (Indiancurrant Coralberry)
Vaccinium macrocarpum (Cranberry)
Viburnum alnifolium (Hobblebush Viburnum)
Zenobia pulverulenta (Dusty Zenobia)

Ampelopsis arborea (Peppervine)
Ampelopsis cordata (Heartleaf Ampelopsis)
Celastrus scandens (American Bittersweet)

Clematis verticillaris (Rock Clematis)
Cocculus carolinus (Carolina Snailseed)
Parthenocissus quinquefolia (Virginia Creeper)

RED-BROWN:

Aesculus parviflora (Bottlebrush Buckeye)
Aesculus pavia (Red Buckeye)
Arctostaphylos uva-ursi (Bearberry)
Aronia arbutifolia (Red Chokeberry)
Aronia melanocarpa (Black Chokeberry)
Aronia prunifolia (Purplefruit Chokeberry)
Ceanothus americanus (Jerseytea Ceanothus)
Ceanothus ovatus (Inland Ceanothus)
Chamaedaphne calyculata (Leatherleaf)
Clethra acuminata (Cinnamon Clethra)
Cyrilla racemiflora (American Cyrilla)
Hydrangea arborescens (Smooth Hydrangea)
Hydrangea quercifolia (Oakleaf Hydrangea)
Hypericum densiflorum (Dense Hypericum)
Hypericum frondosum (Golden St. Johnswort)
Hypericum kalmianum (Kalm St. Johnswort)
Hypericum prolificum (Shrubby St. Johnswort)

Itea virginica (Virginia Sweetspire)
Juniperus communis (Common Juniper)
Juniperus horizontalis (Creeping Juniper)
Kalmia latifolia (Mountainlaurel Kalmia)
Ledum groenlandicum (Labradortea Ledum)
Rhus aromatica (Fragrant Sumac)
Ribes cynosbati (Pasture Gooseberry)
Ribes missouriense (Missouri Gooseberry)
Ribes odoratum (Clove Currant)
Rosa setigera (Prairie Rose)
Rubus occidentalis (Blackcap Raspberry)
Rubus strigosus (American Red Raspberry)
Salix lucida (Shining Willow)
Spiraea tomentosa (Hardhack Spirea)
Staphylea trifolia (American Bladdernut)
Taxus canadensis (Canada Yew)
Zenobia pulverulenta (Dusty Zenobia)

Clematis verticillaris (Rock Clematis)

Menispermum canadense (Common Moonseed)

Bark coloration - red brown (cont.)

Toxicodendron radicans   (Common Poisonivy)
Vitis labrusca   (Fox Grape)

Vitis riparia   (Riverbank Grape)

RED:

Comptonia peregrina   (Sweetfern)
Cornus stolonifera   (Redosier Dogwood)
Leucothoe catesbaei   (Drooping Leucothoe)
Rosa carolina   (Carolina Rose)
Rosa setigera   (Prairie Rose)

Rubus allegheniensis   (Allegany Blackberry)
Rubus occidentalis   (Blackcap Raspberry)
Rubus strigosus   (American Red Raspberry)
Taxus canadensis   (Canada Yew)

PURPLE:

Comptonia peregrina   (Sweetfern)
Cornus amomum   (Silky Dogwood)
Cornus rugosa   (Roundleaf Dogwood)
Cornus stolonifera   (Redosier Dogwood)
Hypericum densiflorum   (Dense Hypericum)
Hypericum frondosum   (Golden St.Johnswort)
Hypericum kalmianum   (Kalm St.Johnswort)
Hypericum prolificum   (Shrubby St.Johnswort)

Leucothoe catesbaei   (Drooping Leucothoe)
Ribes americanum   (American Black Currant)
Rubus allegheniensis   (Allegany Blackberry)
Rubus occidentalis   (Blackcap Raspberry)
Rubus strigosus   (American Red Raspberry)
Sambucus pubens   (Scarlet Elder)
Viburnum acerifolium   (Mapleleaf Viburnum)

BROWN-BLACK:

Andromeda polifolia   (Bogrosemary Andromeda)
Clethra alnifolia   (Summersweet Clethra)
Dirca palustris   (Atlantic Leatherwood)

Pinus aristata   (Bristlecone Pine)
Ribes americanum   (American Black Currant)
Vaccinium stamineum   (Common Deerberry)

ARMAMENT:

Many plant species have ornamental prickles, spines, true thorns or sharp modified twigs which contribute special color and textural beauty in the landscape. Where personal injury liability is a real concern, use of these species should be limited. However, in many design situations, species with ornamental armament add interest and dimension not afforded by other plants.

indicator — *Smilax rotundifolia* (Common Greenbrier)

Elaeagnus commutata   (Silverberry)
Ilex decidua   (Possumhaw)
Juniperus communis   (Common Juniper)
Mahonia aquifolium   (Oregongrape)
Myrica pensylvanica   (Northern Bayberry)
Pinus artistata   (Bristlecone Pine)
Prunus hortulana   (Hortulan Plum)
Ribes cynosbati   (Pasture Gooseberry)
Ribes missouriense   (Missouri Gooseberry)
Robinia hispida   (Roseacacia Locust)

Robinia viscosa   (Clammy Locust)
Rosa carolina   (Carolina Rose)
Rosa setigera   (Prairie Rose)
Rubus allegheniensis   (Allegany Blackberry)
Rubus occidentalis   (Blackcap Raspberry)
Rubus strigosus   (American Red Raspberry)
Shepherdia argentea   (Silver Buffaloberry)
Shepherdia canadensis   (Russet Buffaloberry)
Yucca filamentosa   (Adamsneedle Yucca)

Parthenocissus quinquefolia   (Virginia Creeper)
Smilax glauca   (Cat Greenbrier)

Smilax rotundifolia   (Common Greenbrier)
Smilax tamnoides   (Bamboo Greenbrier)

FOLIAGE DURATION:

As we travel through the forest or savanna landscape and look about us, it soon becomes apparent that there are two predominant races of plants visually quite different from each other. The first includes species of dogwood, viburnum, raspberry, and others with large spreading leaves that fall each autumn (deciduous). Species of juniper, yew, rhododendron and holly represent the second great group. The leaves of these remain for many years (evergreen). The evergreen species are considered masculine in gender and are symbols of constancy and endurance while the feminine moods of the deciduous shrubs and vines change in patterned response to the influence of season, day and hour. This dynamic contrast must be considered one of the most enriching landscape experiences perceived by man.

DECIDUOUS:
> leaves shed annually in autumn,
> indicator — *Itea virginica* (Virginia Sweetspire)

Aesculus parviflora   (Bottlebrush Buckeye)
Aesculus pavia   (Red Buckeye)
Alnus serrulata   (Common Alder)
Amelanchier sanguinea   (Roundleaf Serviceberry)
Amorpha canescens   (Leadplant Amorpha)
Amorpha fruticosa   (Indigobush Amorpha)
Aronia arbutifolia   (Red Chokeberry)
Aronia melanocarpa   (Black Chokeberry)
Aronia prunifolia   (Purplefruit Chokeberry)
Betula pumila   (Low Birch)
Calycanthus floridus   (Common Sweetshrub)
Castanea pumila   (Allegany Chinkapin)
Ceanothus americanus   (Jerseytea Ceanothus)
Ceanothus ovatus   (Inland Ceanothus)
Clethra acuminata   (Cinnamon Clethra)
Clethra alnifolia   (Summersweet Clethra)
Cornus amomum   (Silky Dogwood)
Cornus racemosa   (Gray Dogwood)
Cornus rugosa   (Roundleaf Dogwood)
Cornus stolonifera   (Redosier Dogwood)
Corylus americana   (American Filbert))
Corylus cornuta   (Beaked Filbert)
Diervilla lonicera   (Dwarf Bushhoneysuckle)
Dirca palustris   (Atlantic Leatherwood)
Elaeagnus commutata   (Silverberry)
Euonymus americanus   (Brook Euonymus)
Euonymus obovatus   (Running Euonymus)
Fothergilla gardeni   (Dwarf Fothergilla)
Fothergilla major   (Large Fothergilla)
Hydrangea aborescens   (Smooth Hydrangea)
Hydrangea quercifolia   (Oakleaf Hydrangea)
Hypericum densiflorum   (Dense Hypericum)
Hypericum frondosum   (Golden St.Johnswort)
Hypericum kalmianum   (Kalm St.Johnswort)
Hypericum prolificum   (Shrubby St.Johnswort)
Ilex decidua   (Possumhaw)
Ilex verticillata   (Common Winterberry)
Itea virginica   (Virginia Sweetspire)
Lindera benzoin   (Common Spicebush)
Lonicera canadensis   (American Fly Honeysuckle)
Neviusia alabamensis   (Snowwreath)
Philadelphus grandiflorus   (Big Scentless Mockorange)
Physocarpus opulifolius   (Common Ninebark)
Potentilla fruticosa   (Bush Cinquefoil)

Prunus hortulana   (Hortulan Plum)
Rhododendron arborescens   (Sweet Azalea)
Rhododendron calendulaceum   (Flame Azalea)
Rhododendron nudiflorum   (Pinxterbloom Azalea)
Rhododendron roseum   (Roseshell Azalea)
Rhododendron vaseyi   (Pinkshell Azalea)
Rhododendron viscosum   (Swamp Azalea)
Rhus aromatica   (Fragrant Sumac)
Ribes cynosbati   (Pasture Gooseberry)
Ribes missouriense   (Missouri Gooseberry)
Ribes odoratum   (Clove Currant)
Robinia hispida   (Roseacacia Locust)
Robinia viscosa   (Clammy Locust)
Rosa carolina   (Carolina Rose)
Rosa setigera   (Prairie Rose)
Rubus allegheniensis   (Allegany Blackberry)
Rubus occidentalis   (Blackcap Raspberry)
Rubus odoratus   (Fragrant Thimbleberry)
Rubus strigosus   (American Red Raspberry)
Salix humilis   (Prairie Willow)
Salix lucida   (Shining Willow)
Sambucus canadensis   (American Elder)
Sambucus pubens   (Scarlet Elder)
Shepherdia argentea   (Silver Buffaloberry)
Shepherdia canadensis   (Russet Buffaloberry)
Spiraea alba   (Narrowleaf Meadowsweet Spirea)
Spiraea corymbosa   (Corymed Spirea)
Spiraea tomentosa   (Hardhack Spirea)
Staphylea trifolia   (American Bladdernut)
Stewartia ovata   (Mountain Stewartia)
Symphoricarpos albus   (Common Snowberry)
Symphoricarpos orbiculatus   (Indiancurrant Coralberry)
Vaccinium angustifolium   (Lowbush Blueberry)
Vaccinium corymbosum   (Highbush Blueberry)
Vaccinium stamineum   (Common Deerberry)
Viburnum acerifolium   (Mapleleaf Viburnum)
Viburnum alnifolium   (Hobblebush Viburnum)
Viburnum cassinoides   (Witherod Viburnum)
Viburnum dentatum   (Arrowwood Viburnum)
Viburnum nudum   (Possumhaw Viburnum)
Viburnum rafinesquianum   (Rafinesque Viburnum)
Viburnum trilobum   (American Cranberrybush Viburnum)
Xanthorhiza simplicissima   (Yellowroot)

Ampelopsis cordata   (Heartleaf Ampelopsis)

Aristolochia durior   (Common Dutchmanspipe)

Foliage duration - deciduous (cont.)

Berchemia scandens (Alabama Supplejack)
Campsis radicans (Common Trumpetcreeper)
Celastrus scandens (American Bittersweet)
Clematis verticillaris (Rock Clematis)
Clematis virginiana (Virginsbower)
Lonicera dioica (Limber Honeysuckle)

Menispermum canadense (Common Moonseed)
Parthenocissus quinquefolia (Virginia Creeper)
Toxicodendron radicans (Common Poisonivy)
Vitis labrusca (Fox Grape)
Vitis riparia (Riverbank Grape)
Wistaria macrostachya (Kentucky Wistaria)

EVERGREEN:
coniferous or broadleaved plants whose leaves remain throughout the year and are continually dropping and being replaced by new springtime growth,
indicator — *Leiophyllum buxifolium* (Box Sandmyrtle)

Andromeda polifolia (Bogrosemary Andromeda)
Arctostaphylos uva-ursi (Bearberry)
Chamaedaphne calyculata (Leatherleaf)
Cornus canadensis (Bunchberry Dogwood)
Cyrilla racemiflora (American Cyrilla)
Epigaea repens (Trailing-arbutus)
Gaultheria procumbens (Checkerberry Wintergreen)
Ilex glabra (Inkberry)
Juniperus communis (Common Juniper)
Juniperus horizontalis (Creeping Juniper)
Kalmia angustifolia (Lambkill Kalmia)
Kalmia latifolia (Mountainlaurel Kalmia)
Kalmia polifolia (Bog Kalmia)

Ledum groenlandicum (Labradortea Ledum)
Leiophyllum buxifolium (Box Sandmyrtle)
Leucothoe catesbaei (Drooping Leucothoe)
Mahonia aquifolium (Oregongrape)
Pachistima canbyi (Canby Pachistima)
Pieris floribunda (Mountain Pieris)
Pinus aristata (Bristlecone Pine)
Rhododendron carolinianum (Carolina Rhododendron)
Rhododendron catawbiense (Catawba Rhododendron)
Taxus canadensis (Canada Yew)
Vaccinium macrocarpum (Cranberry)
Yucca filamentosa (Adamsneedle Yucca)

Bignonia capreolata (Crossvine)
Lonicera sempervirens (Trumpet Honeysuckle)

SEMI-EVERGREEN:
many leaves remain green throughout autumn and occasionally early winter before turning brown,
indicator — *Lonicera sempervirens* (Trumpet Honeysuckle)

Baccharis halimifolia (Eastern Baccharis)
Cornus canadensis (Bunchberry Dogwood)

Magnolia virginiana (Sweetbay Magnolia)
Zenobia pulverulenta (Dusty Zenobia)

Ampelopsis arborea (Peppervine)
Bignonia capreolata (Crossvine)

Lonicera sempervirens (Trumpet Honeysuckle)
Smilax glauca (Cat Greenbrier)

PERSISTANT:
leaves losing summer color in autumn, but with a significant percentage persisting into winter or early spring,
indicator — *Myrica pensylvanica* (Northern Bayberry)

Cephalanthus occidentalis (Common Buttonbush)
Comptonia peregrina (Sweetfern)
Hamamelis vernalis (Vernal Witchhazel)
Ilex decidua (Possumhaw)
Myrica pensylvanica (Northern Bayberry)

Quercus ilicifolia (Scrub Oak)
Quercus prinoides (Dwarf Chinkapin Oak)
Ribes americanum (American Black Currant)
Symphoricarpos occidentalis (Western Snowberry)
Xanthorhiza simplicissima (Yellowroot)

Cocculus carolina (Carolina Snailseed)
Smilax rotundifolia (Common Greenbrier)

Smilax tamnoides (Bamboo Greenbrier)

FOLIAGE STRUCTURE:

Relatively few woody plants in this region exhibit ornamentally colorful flowers, fruit, or foliage during

the summer season. Leaves, with their variety of structure and shape are the most important visual interest in the summer landscape. Four basic leaf structures are recognized.

SIMPLE:
> leaf having only one blade in which the midrib is unbranched and is united continuously along the blade margin,
> indicator — *Neviusia alabamensis* (Snowwreath)

Alnus serrulata (Common Alder)
Amelanchier sanguinea (Roundleaf Serviceberry)
Andromeda polifolia (Bogrosemary Andromeda)
Arctostaphylos uva-ursi (Bearberry)
Aronia arbutifolia (Red Chokeberry)
Aronia melanocarpa (Black Chokeberry)
Aronia prunifolia (Purplefruit Chokeberry)
Baccharis halimifolia (Eastern Baccharis)
Betula pumila (Low Birch)
Calycanthus floridus (Common Sweetshrub)
Castanea pumila (Allegany Chinkapin)
Ceanothus americanus (Jerseytea Ceanothus)
Ceanothus ovatus (Inland Ceanothus)
Cephalanthus occidentalis (Common Buttonbush)
Clethra acuminata (Cinnamon Clethra)
Clethra alnifolia (Summersweet Clethra)
Comptonia peregrina (Sweetfern)
Cornus amomum (Silky Dogwood)
Cornus canadensis (Bunchberry Dogwood)
Cornus racemosa (Gray Dogwood)
Cornus rugosa (Roundleaf Dogwood)
Cornus stolonifera (Redosier Dogwood)
Corylus americana (American Filbert))
Corylus cornuta (Beaked Filbert)
Cyrilla racemiflora (American Cyrilla)
Diervilla lonicera (Dwarf Bushhoneysuckle)
Dirca palustris (Atlantic Leatherwood)
Elaeagnus commutata (Silverberry)
Epigaea repens (Trailing-arbutus)
Euonymus americanus (Brook Euonymus)
Euonymus obovatus (Running Euonymus)
Fothergilla gardeni (Dwarf Fothergilla)
Fothergilla major (Large Fothergilla)
Gaultheria procumbens (Checkerberry Wintergreen)
Hamamelis vernalis (Vernal Witchhazel)
Hydrangea aborescens (Smooth Hydrangea)
Hydrangea quercifolia (Oakleaf Hydrangea)
Hypericum densiflorum (Dense Hypericum)
Hypericum frondosum (Golden St.Johnswort)
Hypericum kalmianum (Kalm St.Johnswort)
Hypericum prolificum (Shrubby St.Johnswort)
Ilex decidua (Possumhaw)
Ilex glabra (Inkberry)
Ilex verticillata (Common Winterberry)
Itea virginica (Virginia Sweetspire)
Juniperus communis (Common Juniper)
Juniperus horizontalis (Creeping Juniper)
Kalmia angustifolia (Lambkill Kalmia)
Kalmia latifolia (Mountainlaurel Kalmia)
Ledum groenlandicum (Labradortea Ledum)
Leiophyllum buxifolium (Box Sandmyrtle)
Leucothoe catesbaei (Drooping Leucothoe)

Lindera benzoin (Common Spicebush)
Lonicera canadensis (American Fly Honeysuckle)
Lyonia ligustrina (He-huckleberry)
Magnolia virginiana (Sweetbay Magnolia)
Myrica pensylvanica (Northern Bayberry)
Neviusia alabamensis (Snowwreath)
Pachistima canbyi (Canby Pachistima)
Philadelphus grandiflorus (Big Scentless Mockorange)
Physocarpus opulifolius (Common Ninebark)
Pieris floribunda (Mountain Pieris)
Pinus aristata (Bristlecone Pine)
Prunus hortulana (Hortulan Plum)
Quercus ilicifolia (Scrub Oak)
Quercus prinoides (Dwarf Chinkapin Oak)
Rhododendron arborescens (Sweet Azalea)
Rhododendron calendulaceum (Flame Azalea)
Rhododendron carolinianum (Carolina Rhododendron)
Rhododendron catawbiense (Catawba Rhododendron)
Rhododendron nudiflorum (Pinxterbloom Azalea)
Rhododendron roseum (Roseshell Azalea)
Rhododendron vaseyi (Pinkshell Azalea)
Rhododendron viscosum (Swamp Azalea)
Ribes americanum (American Black Currant)
Ribes cynosbati (Pasture Gooseberry)
Ribes missouriense (Missouri Gooseberry)
Ribes odoratum (Clove Currant)
Rubus odoratus (Fragrant Thimbleberry)
Salix humilis (Prairie Willow)
Salix lucida (Shining Willow)
Shepherdia argentea (Silver Buffaloberry)
Shepherdia canadensis (Russet Buffaloberry)
Spiraea alba (Narrowleaf Meadowsweet Spirea)
Spiraea corymbosa (Corymed Spirea)
Spiraea tomentosa (Hardhack Spirea)
Stewartia ovata (Mountain Stewartia)
Symphoricarpos albus (Common Snowberry)
Symphoricarpos occidentalis (Western Snowberry)
Symphoricarpos orbiculatus (Indiancurrant Coralberry)
Taxus canadensis (Canada Yew)
Vaccinium angustifolium (Lowbush Blueberry)
Vaccinium corymbosum (Highbush Blueberry)
Vaccinium macrocarpum (Cranberry)
Vaccinium stamineum (Common Deerberry)
Viburnum acerifolium (Mapleleaf Viburnum)
Viburnum alnifolium (Hobblebush Viburnum)
Viburnum cassinoides (Witherod Viburnum)
Viburnum dentatum (Arrowwood Viburnum)
Viburnum nudum (Possumhaw Viburnum)
Viburnum rafinesquianum (Rafinesque Viburnum)
Viburnum trilobum (American Cranberrybush Viburnum)
Yucca filamentosa (Adamsneedle Yucca)
Zenobia pulverulenta (Dusty Zenobia)

Foliage structure - simple (cont.)

Ampelopsis cordata (Heartleaf Ampelopsis)
Aristolochia durior (Common Dutchmanspipe)
Berchemia scandens (Alabama Supplejack)
Bignonia capreolata (Crossvine)
Celastrus scandens (American Bittersweet)
Cocculus carolinus (Carolina Snailseed)
Lonicera dioica (Limber Honeysuckle)

Lonicera sempervirens (Trumpet Honeysuckle)
Menispermum canadense (Common Moonseed)
Smilax glauca (Cat Greenbrier)
Smilax rotundifolia (Common Greenbrier)
Smilax tamnoides (Bamboo Greenbrier)
Vitis labrusca (Fox Grape)
Vitis riparia (Riverbank Grape)

PINNATELY COMPOUND:
    several individual leaflets arranged along each side of a common unbranched axis (rachis), resembling the pattern of a feather,
    indicator — *Rosa carolina* (Carolina Rose)

Amorpha canescens (Leadplant Amorpha)
Amorpha fruticosa (Indigobush Amorpha)
Mahonia aquifolium (Oregongrape)
Potentilla fruticosa (Bush Cinquefoil)
Rhus aromatica (Fragrant Sumac)
Robinia hispida (Roseacacia Locust)
Robinia viscosa (Clammy Locust)
Rosa carolina (Carolina Rose)

Rosa setigera (Prairie Rose)
Rubus allegheniensis (Allegany Blackberry)
Rubus occidentalis (Blackcap Raspberry)
Rubus strigosus (American Red Raspberry)
Sambucus canadensis (American Elder)
Sambucus pubens (Scarlet Elder)
Staphylea trifolia (American Bladdernut)
Xanthorhiza simplicissima (Yellowroot)

———

Campsis radicans (Common Trumpetcreeper)
Clematis verticillaris (Rock Clematis)
Clematis virginiana (Virginsbower)

Toxicodendron radicans (Common Poisonivy)
Wistaria macrostachya (Kentucky Wistaria)

PALMATELY COMPOUND:
    several individual leaflets radiating from a single point at the apex of the petiole,
    indicator — *Parthenocissus quinquefolia* (Virginia Creeper)

Aesculus parviflora (Bottlebrush Buckeye)
Aesculus pavia (Red Buckeye)

Rubus allegheniensis (Allegany Blackberry)
Rubus occidentalis (Blackcap Raspberry)

———

Parthenocissus quinquefolia   (Virginia Creeper)

BIPINNATELY COMPOUND:
    several individual leaflets arranged along each side of a branched axis,
    indicator — *Ampelopsis arborea* (Peppervine)

Xanthorhiza simplicissima (Yellowroot)

———

Ampelopsis arborea (Peppervine)

LEAF SHAPE:

The most conspicuous feature of foliage is leaf shape. The shape of a leaf or leaflet is usually characteristic of a species. The following shape terminology has the authority of precedence and of wide usage (Bailey 1978, Gleason 1974, Radford 1968, Rehder 1940).

SCALE:
small, short leaves resembling scales and overlapping one another like the shingles on a roof,
indicator — *Juniperus horizontalis* (Creeping Juniper)

Juniperus horizontalis   (Creeping Juniper)

ACICULAR:
needle-like, very slender, long and pointed,
indicator — *Pinus aristata* (Bristlecone Pine)

Pinus aristata   (Bristlecone Pine)

LINEAR:
much longer than wide, with nearly parallel margins,
indicator — *Taxus canadensis* (Canada Yew)

Andromeda polifolia   (Bogrosemary Andromeda)
Comptonia peregrina   (Sweetfern)
Hypericum densiflorum   (Dense Hypericum)
Hypericum frondosum   (Golden St.Johnswort)
Hypericum kalmianum   (Kalm St.Johnswort)
Hypericum prolificum   (Shrubby St.Johnswort)
Kalmia polifolia   (Bog Kalmia)
Pachistima canbyi   (Canby Pachistima)
Taxus canadensis   (Canada Yew)
Yucca filamentosa   (Adamsneedle Yucca)

LANCEOLATE-OBLONG LANCEOLATE:
about 4 times as long as wide, widest near petiole end, lance-shaped,
indicator — *Leucothoe catesbaei* (Drooping Leucothoe)

Castanea pumila   (Allegany Chinkapin)
Cephalanthus occidentalis   (Common Buttonbush)
Elaeagnus commutata   (Silverberry)
Leucothoe catesbaei   (Drooping Leucothoe)
Magnolia virginiana   (Sweetbay Magnolia)
Prunus hortulana   (Hortulan Plum)
Quercus prinoides   (Dwarf Chinkapin Oak)
Sambucus canadensis   (American Elder)
Sambucus pubens   (Scarlet Elder)
Vaccinium corymbosum   (Highbush Blueberry)
Viburnum nudum   (Possumhaw Viburnum)

Bignonia capreolata   (Crossvine)
Wistaria macrostachya   (Kentucky Wistaria)

OVATE LANCEOLATE:
about 3 times as long as wide, widest near tip base,
indicator — *Kalmia latifolia* (Mountainlaurel Kalmia)

Cornus racemosa   (Gray Dogwood)
Kalmia latifolia   (Mountainlaurel Kalmia)
Leucothoe catesbaei   (Drooping Leucothoe)
Salix lucida   (Shining Willow)

Toxicodendron radicans   (Common Poisonivy)

OBLANCEOLATE:
about 4 times as long as wide, widest near tip end,
indicator — *Hypericum kalmianum* (Kalm St.Johnswort)

Aesculus parviflora   (Bottlebrush Buckeye)
Aesculus pavia   (Red Buckeye)
Cyrilla racemiflora   (American Cyrilla)
Hypericum densiflorum   (Dense Hypericum)
Hypericum frondosum   (Golden St.Johnswort)
Hypericum kalmianum   (Kalm St.Johnswort)
Hypericum prolificum   (Shrubby St.Johnswort)
Ilex glabra   (Inkberry)
Myrica pensylvanica   (Northern Bayberry)
Pieris floribunda   (Mountain Pieris)
Potentilla fruticosa   (Bush Cinquefoil)
Rhododendron nudiflorum   (Pinxterbloom Azalea)
Rhododendron roseum   (Roseshell Azalea)
Salix humilis   (Prairie Willow)

ELLIPTIC-OVAL:
twice as long as broad, widest at middle, both ends rounded or blunt pointed,
indicator — *Epigaea repens* (Trailing-arbutus)

Leaf shape - elliptic oval (cont.)

Amelanchier sanguinea (Roundleaf Serviceberry)
Amorpha canescens (Leadplant Amorpha)
Amorpha fruticosa (Indigobush Amorpha)
Calycanthus floridus (Common Sweetshrub)
Chamaedaphne calyculata (Leatherleaf)
Clethra acuminata (Cinnamon Clethra)
Cornus amomum (Silky Dogwood)
Cornus canadensis (Bunchberry Dogwood)
Dirca palustris (Atlantic Leatherwood)
Epigaea repens (Trailing-arbutus)
Hydrangea aborescens (Smooth Hydrangea)
Kalmia angustifolia (Lambkill Kalmia)
Ledum groenlandicum (Labradortea Ledum)
Leiophyllum buxifolium (Box Sandmyrtle)

Rhododendron calendulaceum (Flame Azalea)
Rhododendron carolinianum (Carolina Rhododendron)
Rhododendron catawbiense (Catawba Rhododendron)
Rhododendron vaseyi (Pinkshell Azalea)
Robinia hispida (Roseacacia Locust)
Robinia viscosa (Clammy Locust)
Rosa carolina (Carolina Rose)
Shepherdia argentea (Silver Buffaloberry)
Shepherdia canadensis (Russet Buffaloberry)
Staphylea trifolia (American Bladdernut)
Stewartia ovata (Mountain Stewartia)
Vaccinium angustifolium (Lowbush Blueberry)
Vaccinium macrocarpum (Cranberry)
Zenobia pulverulenta (Dusty Zenobia)

Berchemia scandens (Alabama Supplejack)
Lonicera dioica (Limber Honeysuckle)

Lonicera sempervirens (Trumpet Honeysuckle)
Smilax glauca (Cat Greenbrier)

OVATE-OBLONG OVATE:
egg-shaped, widest near petiole end,
indicator — *Corylus cornuta* (Beaked Filbert)

Ceanothus americanus (Jerseytea Ceanothus)
Ceanothus ovatus (Inland Ceanothus)
Cornus stolonifera (Redosier Dogwood)
Corylus americana (American Filbert))
Corylus cornuta (Beaked Filbert)
Diervilla lonicera (Dwarf Bushhoneysuckle)
Euonymus americanus (Brook Euonymus)
Lonicera canadensis (American Fly Honeysuckle)
Mahonia aquifolium (Oregongrape)
Neviusia alabamensis (Snowwreath)
Philadelphus grandiflorus (Big Scentless Mockorange)
Quercus prinoides (Dwarf Chinkapin Oak)

Rhus aromatica (Fragrant Sumac)
Rosa setigera (Prairie Rose)
Rubus allegheniensis (Allegany Blackberry)
Rubus occidentalis (Blackcap Raspberry)
Rubus strigosus (American Red Raspberry)
Spiraea tomentosa (Hardhack Spirea)
Viburnum alnifolium (Hobblebush Viburnum)
Viburnum cassinoides (Witherod Viburnum)
Viburnum dentatum (Arrowwood Viburnum)
Viburnum rafinesquianum (Rafinesque Viburnum)
Xanthorhiza simplicissima (Yellowroot)

Ampelopsis arborea (Peppervine)
Campsis radicans (Common Trumpetcreeper)
Celastrus scandens (American Bittersweet)
Clematis verticillaris (Rock Clematis)

Clematis virginiana (Virginsbower)
Cocculus carolinus (Carolina Snailseed)
Smilax walteri (Redbead Greenbrier)

OBOVATE-OBLONG OBOVATE:
egg-shaped, widest near tip end,
indicator — *Fothergilla gardeni* (Dwarf Fothergilla)

Aesculus parviflora (Bottlebrush Buckeye)
Alnus serrulata (Common Alder)
Arctostaphylos uva-ursi (Bearberry)
Aronia arbutifolia (Red Chokeberry)
Aronia melanocarpa (Black Chokeberry)
Aronia prunifolia (Purplefruit Chokeberry)
Baccharis halimifolia (Eastern Baccharis)
Clethra alnifolia (Summersweet Clethra)
Euonymus obovatus (Running Euonymus)
Fothergilla gardeni (Dwarf Fothergilla)
Fothergilla major (Large Fothergilla)
Gaultheria procumbens (Checkerberry Wintergreen)

Hamamelis vernalis (Vernal Witchhazel)
Ilex decidua (Possumhaw)
Ilex verticillata (Common Winterberry)
Itea virginica (Virginia Sweetspire)
Lindera benzoin (Common Spicebush)
Lyonia ligustrina (He-huckleberry)
Rhododendron arborescens (Sweet Azalea)
Rhododendron viscosum (Swamp Azalea)
Spiraea alba (Narrowleaf Meadowsweet Spirea)
Spiraea corymbosa (Corymed Spirea)
Vaccinium stamineum (Common Deerberry)

CORDATE:
heart-shaped,
indicator — *Ampelopsis cordata* (Heartleaf Ampelopsis)

Ampelopsis cordata (Heartleaf Ampelopsis)

Aristolochia durior (Common Dutchmanspipe)

Menispermum canadense (Common Moonseed)   *Smilax rotundifolia* (Common Greenbrier)

ORBICULAR-SUBORBICULAR:
    circular, width and length about equal,
    indicator — *Smilax rotundifolia* (Common Greenbrier)

Amelanchier sanguinea (Roundleaf Serviceberry)   *Symphoricarpos albus* (Common Snowberry)
Betula pumila (Low Birch)   *Symphoricarpos occidentalis* (Western Snowberry)
Cornus rugosa (Roundleaf Dogwood)   *Symphoricarpos orbiculatus* (Indiancurrant Coralberry)
Hydrangea arborescens (Smooth Hydrangea)   *Viburnum alnifolium* (Hobbebush Viburnum)

Cocculus carolinus (Carolina Snailseed)   *Smilax rotundifolia* (Common Greenbrier)
Menispermum canadense (Common Moonseed)

PALMATELY-LOBED:
    major lobes (sinuses) radiating from central point at leaf base, fan-lobed,
    indicator — *Rubus odoratus* (Fragrant Thimbleberry)

Physocarpus opulifolius (Common Ninebark)   *Ribes odoratum* (Clove Currant)
Ribes americanum (American Black Currant)   *Rubus odoratus* (Fragrant Thimbleberry)
Ribes cynosbati (Pasture Gooseberry)   *Viburnum acerifolium* (Mapleleaf Viburnum)
Ribes missouriense (Missouri Gooseberry)   *Viburnum trilobum* (American Cranberrybush Viburnum)

Cocculus carolinus (Carolina Snailseed)   *Vitis labrusca* (Fox Grape)
Menispermum canadense (Common Moonseed)   *Vitis riparia* (Riverbank Grape)

PINNATELY-LOBED:
    lobes at more or less right angles along parallel leaf margins,
    indicator — *Quercus ilicifolia* (Scrub Oak)

Comptonia peregrina (Sweetfern)   *Quercus ilicifolia* (Scrub Oak)
Hydrangea quercifolia (Oakleaf Hydrangea)

AWL:
    leaf tapering from the base to a slender and stiff point,
    indicator — *Juniperus communis* (Common Juniper)

Juniperus communis (Common Juniper)
Juniperus horizontalis (Creeping Juniper)

FOLIAGE TEXTURE:

Texture in the summer landscape is due essentially to different foliage patterns. Texture appears coarse or medium or fine because of leaf size which is a function primarily of leaf length and width. Texture is more subtly influenced by spacing of leaves, shape and division of leaves, surface quality of leaves or by length and stiffness of petioles. Coarse textures, for example, are found in Smooth Hydrangea and Hobblebush Viburnum. Since hydrangea leaves are spaced closer together and denser, the effect is somewhat less coarse than viburnum. Fineness, like coarseness, may be more apparent when leaves are more widely spaced or sparser. Fine textures are represented by Roseacia Locust and Canby Pachistima, yet Roseacia Locust appears finer because of its more open character. Five foliage texture categories are classified.

Foliage texture (cont.)

COARSE:
- ☐ deciduous — leaf blades expansive, greater than 100 square centimeters (15 square inches) in total leaf surface area,
  indicator — *Viburnum alnifolium* (Hobblebush Viburnum)
- ☐ conifers — leaf blades greater than 16 centimeters (6 inches) long,
  indicator — *Yucca filamentosa* (Adamsneedle Yucca)*

Hydrangea arborescens (Smooth Hydrangea)
Hydrangea quercifolia (Oaklef Hydrangea)
Rubus odoratus (Fragrant Thimbleberry)

Viburnum alnifolium (Hobblebush Viburnum)
Yucca filamentosa (Adamsneedle Yucca)

Ampelopsis cordata (Heartleaf Ampelopsis)
Aristolochia durior (Common Dutchmanspipe)
Cocculus carolinus (Carolina Snailseed)
Menispermum canadense (Common Moonseed)
Smilax glauca (Cat Greenbrier)

Smilax rotundifolia (Common Greenbrier)
Smilax tamnoides (Bamboo Greenbrier)
Vitis labrusca (Fox Grape)
Vitis riparia (Riverbank Grape)

MEDIUM COARSE:
- ☐ deciduous — leaf blades between 60 and 100 square centimeters (9 and 15 square inches) in total leaf surface area,
  indicator — *Rhododendron catawbiense* (Catawba Rhododendron)
- ☐ conifers — leaf blades between 10 and 16 centimeters (4 and 6 inches) long,
  indicator—*Pinus attenuata* (Knob-Cone Pine)

Aesculus parviflora (Bottlebrush Buckeye)
Aesculus pavia (Red Buckeye)
Calycanthus floridus (Common Sweetshrub)
Cephalanthus occidentalis (Common Buttonbush)
Cornus rugosa (Roundleaf Dogwood)
Corylus americana (American Filbert))
Corylus cornuta (Beaked Filbert)

Fothergilla gardeni (Dwarf Fothergilla)
Fothergilla major (Large Fothergilla)
Hamamelis vernalis (Vernal Witchhazel)
Kalmia latifolia (Mountainlaurel Kalmia)
Quercus prinoides (Dwarf Chinkapin Oak)
Rhododendron catawbiense (Catawba Rhododendron)

Celastrus scandens (American Bittersweet)
Toxicodendron radicans (Common Poisonivy)

MEDIUM:
- ☐ deciduous — leaf blades between 20 and 60 square centimeters (3 and 9 square inches) in total leaf surface area,
  indicator — *Lindera benzoin* (Common Spicebush)
- ☐ conifers — leaf blades between 5 and 10 centimeters (2 and 4 inches) long,
  indicator—*Pinus pungens* (Table-Mountain Pine)

Alnus serrulata (Common Alder)
Castanea pumila (Allegany Chinkapin)
Clethra acuminata (Cinnamon Clethra)
Cyrilla racemiflora (American Cyrilla)
Dirca palustris (Atlantic Leatherwood)
Euonymus americanus (Brook Euonymus)
Leucothoe catesbaei (Drooping Leucothoe)
Lindera benzoin (Common Spicebush)
Magnolia virginiana (Sweetbay Magnolia)
Prunus hortulana (Hortulan Plum)
Quercus ilicifolia (Scrub Oak)

Rhododendron calendulaceum (Flame Azalea)
Rhododendron roseum (Roseshell Azalea)
Rhododendron vaseyi (Pinkshell Azalea)
Sambucus canadensis (American Elder)
Sambucus pubens (Scarlet Elder)
Stewartia ovata (Mountain Stewartia)
Viburnum acerifolium (Mapleleaf Viburnum)
Viburnum cassinoides (Witherod Viburnum)
Viburnum nudum (Possumhaw Viburnum)
Viburnum trilobum (American Cranberrybush Viburnum)

Berchemia scandens (Alabama Supplejack)
Bignonia capreolata (Crossvine)

Campsis radicans (Common Trumpetcreeper)
Parthenocissus quinquefolia (Virginia Creeper)

MEDIUM FINE:
- ☐ deciduous — leaf blades between 6 and 20 square centimeters (1 and 3 square inches) in total leaf surface area,
  indicator — *Amelanchier sanguinea* (Roundleaf Serviceberry)

☐ conifers — leaf blades between 2.5 and 5 centimeters (1 and 2 inches) long,
    indicator — *Pinus aristata* (Bristlecone Pine)

Amelanchier sanguinea   (Roundleaf Serviceberry)
Aronia arbutifolia   (Red Chokeberry)
Aronia melanocarpa   (Black Chokeberry)
Aronia prunifolia   (Purplefruit Chokeberry)
Baccharis halimifolia   (Eastern Baccharis)
Betula pumila   (Low Birch)
Ceanothus americanus   (Jerseytea Ceanothus)
Ceanothus ovatus   (Inland Ceanothus)
Clethra alnifolia   (Summersweet Clethra)
Comptonia peregrina   (Sweetfern)
Cornus amomum   (Silky Dogwood)
Cornus canadensis   (Bunchberry Dogwood)
Cornus racemosa   (Gray Dogwood)
Cornus stolonifera   (Redosier Dogwood)
Diervilla lonicera   (Dwarf Bushhoneysuckle)
Elaeagnus commutata   (Silverberry)
Epigaea repens   (Trailing-arbutus)
Euonymus obovatus   (Running Euonymus)
Ilex decidua   (Possumhaw)
Ilex verticillata   (Common Winterberry)
Itea virginica   (Virginia Sweetspire)
Kalmia angustifolia   (Lambkill Kalmia)
Lonicera canadensis   (American Fly Honeysuckle)
Lyonia ligustrina   (He-huckleberry)
Mahonia aquifolium   (Oregongrape)
Myrica pensylvanica   (Northern Bayberry)
Neviusia alabamensis   (Snowwreath)
Philadelphus grandiflorus   (Big Scentless Mockorange)
Physocarpus opulifolius   (Common Ninebark)

Pieris floribunda   (Mountain Pieris)
Pinus aristata   (Bristlecone Pine)
Rhododendron arborescens   (Sweet Azalea)
Rhododendron carolinianum   (Carolina Rhododendron)
Rhododendron nudiflorum   (Pinxterbloom Azalea)
Rhododendron viscosum   (Swamp Azalea)
Rhus aromatica   (Fragrant Sumac)
Ribes americanum   (American Black Currant)
Ribes cynosbati   (Pasture Gooseberry)
Ribes missouriense   (Missouri Gooseberry)
Ribes odoratum   (Clove Currant)
Rosa setigera   (Prairie Rose)
Rubus allegheniensis   (Allegany Blackberry)
Rubus occidentalis   (Blackcap Raspberry)
Rubus strigosus   (American Red Raspberry)
Salix humilis   (Prairie Willow)
Spiraea alba   (Narrowleaf Meadowsweet Spirea)
Spiraea corymbosa   (Corymed Spirea)
Spiraea tomentosa   (Hardhack Spirea)
Staphylea trifolia   (American Bladdernut)
Symphoricarpos albus   (Common Snowberry)
Symphoricarpos occidentalis   (Western Snowberry)
Vaccinium corymbosum   (Highbush Blueberry)
Vaccinium macrocarpum   (Cranberry)
Vaccinium stamineum   (Common Deerberry)
Viburnum dentatum   (Arrowwood Viburnum)
Viburnum rafinesquianum   (Rafinesque Viburnum)
Xanthorhiza simplicissima   (Yellowroot)
Zenobia pulverulenta   (Dusty Zenobia)

Ampelopsis arborea   (Peppervine)
Campsis radicans   (Common Trumpetcreeper)
Clematis verticillaris   (Rock Clematis)
Clematis virginiana   (Virginsbower)

Lonicera dioica   (Limber Honeysuckle)
Lonicera sempervirens   (Trumpet Honeysuckle)
Wistaria macrostachya   (Kentucky Wistaria)

FINE:
☐ deciduous — leaf blades compact or divided, less than 6 square centimeters (one square inch) in total
    leaf surface area,
    indicator — *Amorpha fruticosa* (Indigobush Amorpha)
☐ conifers — leaf blades less than 2.5 centimeters (1 inch) long,
    indicator — *Taxus canadensis* (Canada Yew)

Amorpha canescens   (Leadplant Amorpha)
Amorpha fruticosa   (Indigobush Amorpha)
Andromeda polifolia   (Bogrosemary Andromeda)
Arctostaphylos uva-ursi   (Bearberry)
Chamaedaphne calyculata   (Leatherleaf)
Elaeagnus commutata   (Silverberry)
Gaultheria procumbens   (Checkerberry Wintergreen)
Hypericum densiflorum   (Dense Hypericum)
Hypericum frondosum   (Golden St.Johnswort)
Hypericum kalmianum   (Kalm St.Johnswort)
Hypericum prolificum   (Shrubby St.Johnswort)
Ilex glabra   (Inkberry)
Juniperus communis   (Common Juniper)
Juniperus horizontalis   (Creeping Juniper)
Kalmia polifolia   (Bog Kalmia)

Ledum groenlandicum   (Labradortea Ledum)
Leiophyllum buxifolium   (Box Sandmyrtle)
Pachistima canbyi   (Canby Pachistima)
Potentilla fruticosa   (Bush Cinquefoil)
Robinia hispida   (Roseacacia Locust)
Robinia viscosa   (Clammy Locust)
Rosa carolina   (Carolina Rose)
Salix lucida   (Shining Willow)
Shepherdia argentea   (Silver Buffaloberry)
Shepherdia canadensis   (Russet Buffaloberry)
Symphoricarpos orbiculatus   (Indiancurrant Coralberry)
Taxus canadensis   (Canada Yew)
Vaccinium angustifolium   (Lowbush Blueberry)
Vaccinium macrocarpum   (Cranberry)

FOLIAGE COLORATION:

The tremendous palette of foliage colors with a wide selection of hues, intensities and values provides the designer with a color spectrum which changes with the season. Through the judicious selection of vegetation species, designers can provide spots or splashes of color in either the natural or the cultural landscape in much the same manner that an artist uses paints on canvas. Although the leaves of most deciduous woody plants are of little tonal contrast during the summer growing season, most species have leaves which are differently colored at other seasons. Leaves are green because they contain chlorophyll which is continually manufactured during the growing season by the plant under the heat and light of day.

Seasonal coloration is determined by the amount of two general groups of coloring pigments in the leaf which mask the chlorophyll. These pigments are the carotins (yellow-producing pigments) and the anthocyanins (red-producing pigments). These pigments become most pronounced during the autumn season when most of the cholorphyll is destroyed in many deciduous plants. The coloration of new spring foliage can be as beautiful as that in autumn but is usually more subtle and does not last as long. As the spring season progresses and more and more chlorophyll is manufactured, most deciduous plants produce sufficient chlorophyll to completely mask any coloration exhibited at leaf emergence.

Coniferous and broadleaf evergreens along with a few deciduous plants with persisting leaves offer foliage coloration throughout the winter landscape that are strongly contrasted with the defoliated crowns of other species. Table I correlates foliage color variation of plants for quick cross reference, comparison, and evaluation. This table can be used to assist designers in making decisions concerning intraseasonal landscape color composition.

AROMATIC FOLIAGE:

Who could ever forget a camping trip spent beneath towering, noble pines and on a carpet thick and spongy with needles. The arresting aroma exuded by the pine foliage permeates the atmosphere and human mind in a way that relaxes and refreshes the soul. The consideration of plants in landscape design with aromatic leaves, twigs, and bark enriches their sensual dimension and appeal.

indicator — *Comptonia peregrina* (Sweetfern)

Calycanthus floridus (Common Sweetshrub)
Comptonia peregrina (Sweetfern)
Epigaea repens (Trailing-arbutus)
Fothergilla gardeni (Dwarf Fothergilla)
Gaultheria procumbens (Checkerberry Wintergreen)
Hamamelis vernalis (Vernal Witchhazel)
Itea virginica (Virginia Sweetspire)
Juniperus communis (Common Juniper)

Juniperus horizontalis (Creeping Juniper)
Ledum groenlandicum (Labradortea Ledum)
Lindera benzoin (Common Spicebush)
Myrica pensylvanica (Northern Bayberry)
Pinus aristata (Bristlecone Pine)
Rhus aromatica (Fragrant Sumac)
Ribes americanum (American Black Currant)
Taxus canadensis (Canada Yew)

Aristolochia durior (Common Dutchmanspipe)

	Winter									Spring									Summer									Autumn								
	silver-gray green	light green	med. green	dark green	blue green	yellow green	or-red green	maroon green	tan brown	silver-gray green	light green	med. green	dark green	blue green	yellow green	or-red green	maroon-purple	tan brown	silver-gray green	light green	med. green	dark green	blue green	yellow green	or-red green	maroon green	tan brown	silver-gray green	med. green	dark green	blue green	yellow green	yellow	orange-red	maroon-purple	tan brown
Aesculus parviflora											▓										■												▓			
Aesculus pavia											▓											■														
Alnus serrulata											▓											■											▓	■		
Amelanchier sanguinea															▓							■												■		
Amorpha canescens											▓										▓								▓				▓			
Amorpha fruticosa												▓										■														
Andromeda polifolia				■							▓											■								■						
Arctostaphylos uva-ursi							■						■										■											■		
Aronia arbutifolia													■									■								■						
Aronia melanocarpa													■									■								■						
Aronia prunifolia													■									■								■						
Baccharis halimifolia						▓					▓								▓										▓							■
Betula pumila												▓									■											▓				
Calycanthus floridus														▓								▓														
Castanea pumila													■									■														■
Ceanothus americanus											▓										■													▓		
Ceanothus ovatus												■										■														
Cephalanthus occidentalis															▓							■										▓				
Chamaedaphne calyculata								■				■																	■					■		
Clethra acuminata											▓										■															
Clethra alnifolia																																▓				
Comptonia peregrina											▓										■											■				
Cornus amomum												▓									■														■	
Cornus canadensis							■						■								■														■	
Cornus racemosa													■							▓															■	
Cornus rugosa														■							■														■	

Foliage Coloration: Shrubs   Table I

	Winter									Spring									Summer									Autumn								
	silver-gray green	light green	med. green	dark green	blue green	yellow green	or-red green	maroon green	tan brown	silver-gray green	light green	med. green	dark green	blue green	yellow green	or-red green	maroon-purple	tan brown	silver-gray green	light green	med. green	dark green	blue green	yellow green	or-red green	maroon green	tan brown	silver-gray green	med. green	dark green	blue green	yellow green	yellow	orange-red	maroon-purple	tan brown
Cornus stolonifera																■				■															■	■
Corylus americana															■						■												■			
Corylus cornuta															■						■												■			
Cyrilla racemiflora				■										■								■												■		
Diervilla lonicera												■										■												■		
Dirca palustris												■										■											■			
Elaeagnus commutata										■									■									■								
Epigaea repens		■											■									■								■						
Euonymus americanus													■								■									■						
Euonymus obovatus										■											■									■						
Fothergilla gardeni																					■													■		
Fothergilla major																					■													■		
Gaultheria procumbens			■		■								■	■																					■	■
Hamamelis vernalis							■			■											■													■		
Hydrangea arborescens														■						■												■			■
Hydrangea quercifolia										■												■												■	■	
Hypericum densiflorum												■									■											■				
Hypericum frondosum												■										■									■					
Hypericum kalmianum												■										■	■							■						
Hypericum prolificum												■										■									■					
Ilex decidua							■			■											■									■						
Ilex glabra			■									■										■								■						
Ilex verticillata														■							■									■						
Itea virginica										■											■													■		
Juniperus communis					■					■			■									■								■						
Juniperus horizontalis					■									■									■								■					

Foliage Coloration: Shrubs — Table I

	Winter									Spring									Summer									Autumn								
	silver-gray green	light green	med. green	dark green	blue green	yellow green	or-red green	maroon green	tan brown	silver-gray green	light green	med. green	dark green	blue green	yellow green	or-red green	maroon-purple	tan brown	silver-gray green	light green	med. green	dark green	blue green	yellow green	or-red green	maroon green	tan brown	silver-gray green	med. green	dark green	blue green	yellow green	yellow	orange-red	maroon-purple	tan brown
Kalmia angustifolia				■			■					■										■								■						
Kalmia latifolia			■					■				■				■						■								■						
Kalmia polifolia				■																			■								■					
Ledum groenlandicum			■																			■								■						
Leiophyllum buxifolium				■				■					■									■								■						
Leucothoe catesbaei				■			■	■				■										■								■						
Lindera benzoin															■					■													■			
Lonicera canadensis																					■											■				
Lyonia ligustrina										■																							■			
Magnolia virginiana			■				■					■				■						■								■			■			
Mahonia aquifolium			■												■	■					■									■			■			
Myrica pensylvanica			■									■										■								■						
Neviusia alabamensis											■										■									■						
Pachistima canbyi			■										■									■								■			■			
Philadelphus grandiflorus											■										■								■							
Physocarpus opulifolius																					■											■				
Pieris floribunda				■				■					■									■								■						
Pinus aristata	■			■									■						■			■						■		■						
Potentilla fruticosa																													■							
Prunus hortulana											■										■									■						
Quercus ilicifolia								■					■									■								■			■		■	
Quercus prinoides								■					■									■								■			■			
Rhododendron arborescens											■											■								■						
Rhododendron calendulaceum																																				
Rhododendron carolinianum			■				■																													
Rhododendron catawbiense			■																			■								■						

421

	Winter									Spring									Summer									Autumn								
	silver-gray green	light green	med. green	dark green	blue green	yellow green	or-red green	maroon green	tan brown	silver-gray green	light green	med. green	dark green	blue green	yellow green	or-red green	maroon-purple	tan brown	silver-gray green	light green	med. green	dark green	blue green	yellow green	or-red green	maroon green	tan brown	silver-gray green	med. green	dark green	blue green	yellow green	yellow	orange-red	maroon-purple	tan brown
Rhododendron nudiflorum											░					■					▓												░			
Rhododendron roseum											░					■						▓							▓						■	
Rhododendron vaseyi																■						▓	▓									░		■		
Rhododendron viscosum																■						▓										░		■		
Rhus aromatica														░		■									■									■		
Ribes americanum								■																												
Ribes cynosbati																																				
Ribes missouriense											░																									
Ribes odoratum											▓																									
Robinia hispida															■						■											■				
Robinia viscosa															■						■											■	░			
Rosa carolina											░				■					░			■													
Rosa setigera																														■						
Rubus allegheniensis															■															■						
Rubus occidentalis															░						■									■	░					
Rubus odoratus															■						▓															
Rubus strigosus															■																			■		
Salix humilis											░									░			■									░				
Salix lucida													░								▓											░				
Sambucus canadensis												▓																								
Sambucus pubens																																				
Shepherdia argentea											░									░												░				
Shepherdia canadensis											░																								■	
Spiraea alba															▓	■					▓											░				
Spiraea corymbosa															▓																					
Spiraea tomentosa											░										░													■		

	Winter									Spring									Summer									Autumn								
	silver-gray green	light green	med. green	dark green	blue green	yellow green	or-red green	maroon green	tan brown	silver-gray green	light green	med. green	dark green	blue green	yellow green	or-red green	maroon-purple	tan brown	silver-gray green	light green	med. green	dark green	blue green	yellow green	or-red green	maroon green	tan brown	silver-gray green	med. green	dark green	blue green	yellow green	yellow	orange-red	maroon-purple	tan brown
Staphylea trifolia											▓									▓												▓				
Stewartia ovata													▓									▓													▓	
Symphoricarpos albus														▓									▓								▓					
Symphoricarpos occidentalis									▓					▓									▓								▓					
Symphoricarpos orbiculatus																▓							▓							▓						
Taxus canadensis			▓								▓											▓								▓						
Vaccinium angustifolium																▓							▓											▓		
Vaccinium corymbosum																▓							▓									▓		▓		
Vaccinium macrocarpum					▓	▓					▓											▓								▓				▓		
Vaccinium stamineum												▓	▓									▓								▓						
Viburnum acerifolium															▓							▓										▓				
Viburnum alnifolium														▓									▓							▓						
Viburnum cassinoides														▓									▓								▓					
Viburnum dentatum														▓									▓								▓					
Viburnum nudum															▓							▓	▓								▓					
Viburnum rafinesquianum														▓									▓								▓					
Viburnum trilobum														▓								▓								▓						
Xanthorhiza simplicissima									▓		▓											▓										▓		▓		
Yucca filamentosa			▓									▓											▓							▓						
Zenobia pulverulenta											▓									▓									▓							

Foliage Coloration: Vines   Table I

	Winter									Spring									Summer									Autumn								
	silver-gray green	light green	med. green	dark green	blue green	yellow green	or-red green	maroon green	tan brown	silver-gray green	light green	med. green	dark green	blue green	yellow green	or-red green	maroon-purple	tan brown	silver-gray green	light green	med. green	dark green	blue green	yellow green	or-red green	maroon green	tan brown	silver-gray green	med. green	dark green	blue green	yellow green	yellow	orange-red	maroon-purple	tan brown
Ampelopsis arborea																	■				■															
Ampelopsis cordata																■					■			▦												
Aristolochia durior											▦										■								■			▦				
Berchemia scandens											▦										■															
Bignonia capreolata								■			▦																									■
Campsis radicans																■	■							▦								▦				
Celastrus scandens																				▦																
Clematis verticillaris																																				
Clematis virginiana																															■					
Cocculus carolinus																					■															
Lonicera dioica											■																					▦				
Lonicera sempervirens										▦													■							■						
Menispermum canadense											▦										■			·												
Parthenocissus quinquefolia													■								■									▦						
Smilax glauca											■										■								■							
Smilax rotundifolia			▦								■										■								■							
Smilax tamnoides											▦										■								■							
Toxicodendron radicans																■	■				■									■						
Vitis labrusca																■	■			▦									■			▦				
Vitis riparia																					■								■							
Wistaria macrostachya													■																							

FOLIAGE SURFACE:

Glossy leaves or leaves that are very light on either upper or lower surface (such as Shining Willow) tend to appear fine textured because there is more sparkle and reflected light. The resulting appearance is that there are many small leaves. Foliage which is noticeably light or silvery on the underside (such as Sweetbay Magnolia) assumes a lightened dancing ornamental quality when whipped by summer breezes. Such ephemeral qualities strongly contrast the normal reflective foliage values on breezeless days. Three leaf surface categories indicate the amount of light reflected or absorbed.

GLOSSY:
>   one or both blade surfaces lustrous, often thick leathery appearance,
>   indicator — *Salix lucida* (Shining Willow)

Alnus serrulata   (Common Alder)
Andromeda polifolia   (Bogrosemary Andromeda)
Arctostaphylos uva-ursi   (Bearberry)
Aronia arbutifolia   (Red Chokeberry)
Aronia melanocarpa   (Black Chokeberry)
Aronia prunifolia   (Purplefruit Chokeberry)
Calycanthus floridus   (Common Sweetshrub)
Ceanothus americanus   (Jerseytea Ceanothus)
Ceanothus ovatus   (Inland Ceanothus)
Cephalanthus occidentalis   (Common Buttonbush)
Clethra alnifolia   (Summersweet Clethra)
Comptonia peregrina   (Sweetfern)
Cyrilla racemiflora   (American Cyrilla)
Gaultheria procumbens   (Checkerberry Wintergreen)
Ilex decidua   (Possumhaw)
Kalmia angustifolia   (Lambkill Kalmia)
Kalmia latifolia   (Mountainlaurel Kalmia)
Kalmia polifolia   (Bog Kalmia)
Ledum groenlandicum   (Labradortea Ledum)
Leiophyllum buxifolium   (Box Sandmyrtle)
Leucothoe catesbaei   (Drooping Leucothoe)
Lindera benzoin   (Common Spicebush)
Lyonia ligustrina   (He-huckleberry)

Magnolia virginiana   (Sweetbay Magnolia)
Mahonia aquifolium   (Oregongrape)
Myrica pensylvanica   (Northern Bayberry)
Pachistima canbyi   (Canby Pachistima)
Pieris floribunda   (Mountain Pieris)
Pinus aristata   (Bristlecone Pine)
Quercus ilicifolia   (Scrub Oak)
Quercus prinoides   (Dwarf Chinkapin Oak)
Rhododendron arborescens   (Sweet Azalea)
Rhododendron catawbiense   (Catawba Rhododendron)
Rhododendron vaseyi   (Pinkshell Azalea)
Rhododendron viscosum   (Swamp Azalea)
Rosa setigera   (Prairie Rose)
Rubus allegheniensis   (Allegany Blackberry)
Salix lucida   (Shining Willow)
Taxus canadensis   (Canada Yew)
Vaccinium angustifolium   (Lowbush Blueberry)
Vaccinium macrocarpum   (Cranberry)
Viburnum cassinoides   (Witherod Viburnum)
Viburnum dentatum   (Arrowwood Viburnum)
Viburnum nudum   (Possumhaw Viburnum)
Xanthorhiza simplicissima   (Yellowroot)

Ampelopsis arborea   (Peppervine)
Berchemia scandens   (Alabama Supplejack)
Campsis radicans   (Common Trumpetcreeper)
Celastrus scandens   (American Bittersweet)

Menispermum canadense   (Common Moonseed)
Smilax rotundifolia   (Common Greenbrier)
Smilax tamnoides   (Bamboo Greenbrier)

DULL:
>   both blade surfaces lacking luster,
>   indicator — *Symphoricarpos albus* (Common Snowberry)

Aesculus parviflora   (Bottlebrush Buckeye)
Aesculus pavia   (Red Buckeye)
Amelanchier sanguinea   (Roundleaf Serviceberry)
Baccharis halimifolia   (Eastern Baccharis)
Betula pumila   (Low Birch)
Castanea pumila   (Allegany Chinkapin)
Ceanothus americanus   (Jerseytea Ceanothus)
Chamaedaphne calyculata   (Leatherleaf)
Clethra acuminata   (Cinnamon Clethra)
Cornus amomum   (Silky Dogwood)
Cornus canadensis   (Bunchberry Dogwood)
Cornus racemosa   (Gray Dogwood)
Cornus rugosa   (Roundleaf Dogwood)
Cornus stolonifera   (Redosier Dogwood)

Diervilla lonicera   (Dwarf Bushhoneysuckle)
Dirca palustris   (Atlantic Leatherwood)
Epigaea repens   (Trailing-arbutus)
Euonymus americanus   (Brook Euonymus)
Euonymus obovatus   (Running Euonymus)
Fothergilla gardeni   (Dwarf Fothergilla)
Fothergilla major   (Large Fothergilla)
Hamamelis vernalis   (Vernal Witchhazel)
Hydrangea aborescens   (Smooth Hydrangea)
Hydrangea quercifolia   (Oakleaf Hydrangea)
Hypericum densiflorum   (Dense Hypericum)
Hypericum frondosum   (Golden St.Johnswort)
Hypericum kalmianum   (Kalm St.Johnswort)
Hypericum prolificum   (Shrubby St.Johnswort)

Foliage surface - dull (cont.)

Ilex verticillata (Common Winterberry)
Itea virginica (Virginia Sweetspire)
Juniperus communis (Common Juniper)
Juniperus horizontalis (Creeping Juniper)
Lonicera canadensis (American Fly Honeysuckle)
Neviusia alabamensis (Snowwreath)
Philadelphus grandiflorus (Big Scentless Mockorange)
Physocarpus opulifolius (Common Ninebark)
Prunus hortulana (Hortulan Plum)
Rhododendron calendulaceum (Flame Azalea)
Rhododendron carolinianum (Carolina Rhododendron)
Rhododendron nudiflorum (Pinxterbloom Azalea)
Rhododendron roseum (Roseshell Azalea)
Ribes americanum (American Black Currant)
Ribes missouriense (Missouri Gooseberry)
Ribes odoratum (Clove Currant)
Robinia hispida (Roseacacia Locust)
Robinia viscosa (Clammy Locust)
Rosa carolina (Carolina Rose)
Rubus occidentalis (Blackcap Raspberry)

Rubus strigosus (American Red Raspberry)
Salix humilis (Prairie Willow)
Sambucus canadensis (American Elder)
Sambucus pubens (Scarlet Elder)
Shepherdia argentea (Silver Buffaloberry)
Shepherdia canadensis (Russet Buffaloberry)
Spiraea alba (Narrowleaf Meadowsweet Spirea)
Spiraea corymbosa (Corymed Spirea)
Staphylea trifolia (American Bladdernut)
Stewartia ovata (Mountain Stewartia)
Symphoricarpos albus (Common Snowberry)
Symphoricarpos occidentalis (Western Snowberry)
Symphoricarpos orbiculatus (Indiancurrant Coralberry)
Vaccinium corymbosum (Highbush Blueberry)
Vaccinium stamineum (Common Deerberry)
Viburnum rafinesquianum (Rafinesque Viburnum)
Viburnum trilobum (American Cranberrybush Viburnum)
Yucca filamentosa (Adamsneedle Yucca)
Zenobia pulverulenta (Dusty Zenobia)

Ampelopsis arborea (Peppervine)
Ampelopsis cordata (Heartleaf Ampelopsis)
Aristolochia durior (Common Dutchmanspipe)
Campsis radicans (Common Trumpetcreeper)
Clematis verticillaris (Rock Clematis)
Clematis virginiana (Virginsbower)
Lonicera dioica (Limber Honeysuckle)
Lonicera sempervirens (Trumpet Honeysuckle)

Menispermum canadense (Common Moonseed)
Parthenocissus quinquefolia (Virginia Creeper)
Smilax glauca (Cat Greenbrier)
Toxicodendron radicans (Common Poisonivy)
Vitis labrusca (Fox Grape)
Vitis riparia (Riverbank Grape)
Wistaria macrostachya (Kentucky Wistaria)

TOMENTOSE:
> blade covered on one or both surfaces by woolly hairlike fibers,
> indicator — *Amorpha canescens* (Leadplant Amorpha)

Amorpha canescens (Leadplant Amorpha)
Amorpha fruticosa (Indigobush Amorpha)
Corylus americana (American Filbert)
Corylus cornuta (Beaked Filbert)
Elaeagnus commutata (Silverberry)
Hamamelis vernalis (Vernal Witchhazel)
Potentilla fruticosa (Bush Cinquefoil)

Rhus aromatica (Fragrant Sumac)
Ribes cynosbati (Pasture Gooseberry)
Rubus odoratus (Fragrant Thimbleberry)
Spiraea tomentosa (Hardhack Spirea)
Viburnum acerifolium (Mapleleaf Viburnum)
Viburnum alnifolium (Hobblebush Viburnum)

Cocculus carolinus (Carolina Snailseed)

FLOWER STRUCTURE:

One of a child's first consciousness of plant characteristics is the bright colors and fragile form of flowers. The diversity of shape and arrangement of parts is captivating. Flower qualities are one of the most popular design criteria influencing plant selection. Eight structural arrangements are considered:

CONE:
> small staminate and pistillate flowers clustered into tight cylindrical cones (conifers),
> Note: The reproductive organs of conifers are not considered true flowers. They are not accompanied

by the greenish sepals and colorful petals of a normal flower, but by minute bodies borne on scales and placed very close to one another to form a structure called a cone.
indicator — *Juniperus communis* (Common Juniper)

Juniperus communis (Common Juniper)
Juniperus horizontalis (Creeping Juniper)

Pinus aristata (Bristlecone Pine)
Taxus canadensis (Canada Yew)

CLUSTERED, SMALL:
    flowers mostly in small clusters along the stems,
        indicator — *Hamamelis vernalis* (Vernal Witchhazel)

Baccharis halimifolia (Eastern Baccharis)
Cephalanthus occidentalis (Common Buttonbush)
Elaeagnus commutata (Silverberry)
Euonymus americanus (Brook Euonymus)
Euonymus obovatus (Running Euonymus)
Hamamelis vernalis (Vernal Witchhazel)
Ilex decidua (Possumhaw)
Ilex glabra (Inkberry)
Ilex verticillata (Common Winterberry)
Lindera benzoin (Common Spicebush)
Pachistima canbyi (Canby Pachistima)
Prunus hortulana (Hortulan Plum)
Rhododendron arborescens (Sweet Azalea)
Rhododendron carolinianum (Carolina Rhododendron)
Rhododendron catawbiense (Catawba Rhododendron)

Rhododendron nudiflorum (Pinxterbloom Azalea)
Rhododendron roseum (Roseshell Azalea)
Rhododendron vaseyi (Pinkshell Azalea)
Rhododendron viscosum (Swamp Azalea)
Rhus aromatica (Fragrant Sumac)
Salix humilis (Prairie Willow)
Salix lucida (Shining Willow)
Shepherdia argentea (Silver Buffaloberry)
Shepherdia canadensis (Russet Buffaloberry)
Symphoricarpos albus (Common Snowberry)
Symphoricarpos occidentalis (Western Snowberry)
Symphoricarpos orbiculatus (Indiancurrant Coralberry)
Xanthorhiza simplicissima (Yellowroot)
Zenobia pulverulenta (Dusty Zenobia)

Celastrus scandens (American Bittersweet)
Menispermum canadense (Common Moonseed)
Smilax glauca (Cat Greenbrier)

Smilax rotundifolia (Common Greenbrier)
Smilax tamnoides (Bamboo Greenbrier)

CLUSTERED, LARGE:
    flowers large, mostly in clusters along the stems,
        indicator — *Rhododendron roseum* (Roseshell Azalea)

Rhododendron arborescens (Sweet Azalea)
Rhododendron carolinianum (Carolina Rhododendron)
Rhododendron catawbiense (Catawba Rhododendron)
Rhododendron nudiflorum (Pinxterbloom Azalea)

Rhododendron roseum (Roseshell Azalea)
Rhododendron vaseyi (Pinkshell Azalea)
Rhododendron viscosum (Swamp Azalea)
Yucca filamentosa (Adamsneedle Yucca)

SOLITARY, LARGE:
    flowers widely open with conspicuous distinct petals,
        indicator — *Rosa carolina* (Carolina Rose)

Calycanthus floridus (Common Sweetshrub)
Cornus canadensis (Bunchberry Dogwood)
Hypericum frondosum (Golden St.Johnswort)
Hypericum kalmianum (Kalm St.Johnswort)
Hypericum prolificum (Shrubby St.Johnswort)
Magnolia virginiana (Sweetbay Magnolia)

Philadelphus grandiflorus (Big Scentless Mockorange)
Potentilla fruticosa (Bush Cinquefoil)
Rosa carolina (Carolina Rose)
Rosa setigera (Prairie Rose)
Rubus odoratus (Fragrant Thimbleberry)
Stewartia ovata (Mountain Stewartia)

Clematis verticillaris (Rock Clematis)

CATKIN:
    flowers in the form of slender elongated catkins,
        indicator — *Corylus americana* (American Filbert)

Alnus serrulata (Common Alder)
Betula pumila (Low Birch)
Comptonia peregrina (Sweetfern)
Corylus americana (American Filbert)
Corylus cornuta (Beaked Filbert)
Leucothoe catesbaei (Drooping Leucothoe)

Myrica pensylvanica (Northern Bayberry)
Quercus ilicifolia (Scrub Oak)
Quercus prinoides (Dwarf Chinkapin Oak)
Rhus aromatica (Fragrant Sumac)
Salix humilis (Prairie Willow)
Salix lucida (Shining Willow)

Flower structure (cont.)

PYRAMIDAL SPIKE:
> flowers in elongated pyramidal or cylindrical clusters mostly at the ends of twigs,
> indicator — *Clethra acuminata* (Cinnamon Clethra)

Aesculus parviflora   (Bottlebrush Buckeye)
Aesculus pavia   (Red Buckeye)
Amelanchier sanguinea   (Roundleaf Serviceberry)
Amorpha canescens   (Leadplant Amorpha)
Amorpha fruticosa   (Indigobush Amorpha)
Castanea pumila   (Allegany Chinkapin)
Ceanothus americanus   (Jerseytea Ceanothus)
Clethra acuminata   (Cinnamon Clethra)
Clethra alnifolia   (Summersweet Clethra)
Cornus racemosa   (Gray Dogwood)
Cyrilla racemiflora   (American Cyrilla)

Fothergilla gardeni   (Dwarf Fothergilla)
Fothergilla major   (Large Fothergilla)
Hydrangea quercifolia   (Oakleaf Hydrangea)
Itea virginica   (Virginia Sweetspire)
Neviusia alabamensis   (Snowwreath)
Robinia hispida   (Roseacacia Locust)
Robinia viscosa   (Clammy Locust)
Rubus allegheniensis   (Allegany Blackberry)
Sambucus pubens   (Scarlet Elder)
Spiraea alba   (Narrowleaf Meadowsweet Spirea)
Spiraea tomentosa   (Hardhack Spirea)

Aristolochia durior   (Common Dutchmanspipe)
Berchemia scandens   (Alabama Supplejack)
Cocculus carolinus   (Carolina Snailseed)
Toxicodendron radicans   (Common Poisonivy)

Vitis labrusca   (Fox Grape)
Vitis riparia   (Riverbank Grape)
Wistaria macrostachya   (Kentucky Wistaria)

FLAT TOP:
> small flowers in rounded or flat-topped clusters mostly at the ends of twigs,
> indicator — *Sambucus canadensis* (American Elder)

Aronia arbutifolia   (Red Chokeberry)
Aronia melanocarpa   (Black Chokeberry)
Aronia prunifolia   (Purplefruit Chokeberry)
Ceanothus ovatus   (Inland Ceanothus)
Cornus amomum   (Silky Dogwood)
Cornus rugosa   (Roundleaf Dogwood)
Cornus stolonifera   (Redosier Dogwood)
Hydrangea arborescens   (Smooth Hydrangea)
Hypericum densiflorum   (Dense Hypericum)
Kalmia angustifolia   (Lambkill Kalmia)
Kalmia latifolia   (Mountainlaurel Kalmia)
Leiophyllum buxifolium   (Box Sandmyrtle)

Physocarpus opulifolius   (Common Ninebark)
Rubus strigosus   (American Red Raspberry)
Sambucus canadensis   (American Elder)
Spiraea corymbosa   (Corymed Spirea)
Viburnum acerifolium   (Mapleleaf Viburnum)
Viburnum alnifolium   (Hobblebush Viburnum)
Viburnum cassinoides   (Witherod Viburnum)
Viburnum dentatum   (Arrowwood Viburnum)
Viburnum nudum   (Possumhaw Viburnum)
Viburnum rafinesquianum   (Rafinesque Viburnum)
Viburnum trilobum   (American Cranberrybush Viburnum)

Ampelopsis arborea   (Peppervine)
Ampelopsis cordata   (Heartleaf Ampelopsis)

Parthenocissus quinquefolia   (Virginia Creeper)

BELL/TRUMPET:
> bell-shaped and cup-like, or tubular trumpet shaped,
> indicator — *Rhododendron calendulaceum* (Flame Azalea)

Andromeda polifolia   (Bogrosemary Andromeda)
Arctostaphylos uva-ursi   (Bearberry)
Chamaedaphne calyculata   (Leatherleaf)
Diervilla lonicera   (Dwarf Bushhoneysuckle)
Dirca palustris   (Atlantic Leatherwood)
Epigaea repens   (Trailing-arbutus)
Gaultheria procumbens   (Checkerberry Wintergreen)
Kalmia angustifolia   (Lambkill Kalmia)
Kalmia latifolia   (Mountainlaurel Kalmia)
Kalmia polifolia   (Bog Kalmia)
Ledum groenlandicum   (Labradortea Ledum)
Leucothoe catesbaei   (Drooping Leucothoe)
Lonicera canadensis   (American Fly Honeysuckle)
Lyonia ligustrina   (He-huckleberry)
Mahonia aquifolium   (Oregongrape)
Pieris floribunda   (Mountain Pieris)
Rhododendron arborescens   (Sweet Azalea)

Rhododendron calendulaceum   (Flame Azalea)
Rhododendron carolinianum   (Carolina Rhododendron)
Rhododendron catawbiense   (Catawba Rhododendron)
Rhododendron nudiflorum   (Pinxterbloom Azalea)
Rhododendron roseum   (Roseshell Azalea)
Rhododendron vaseyi   (Pinkshell Azalea)
Rhododendron viscosum   (Swamp Azalea)
Shepherdia argentea   (Silver Buffaloberry)
Shepherdia canadensis   (Russet Buffaloberry)
Ribes americanum   (American Black Currant)
Ribes cynosbati   (Pasture Gooseberry)
Ribes missouriense   (Missouri Gooseberry)
Ribes odoratum   (Clove Currant)
Staphylea trifolia   (American Bladdernut)
Symphoricarpos albus   (Common Snowberry)
Symphoricarpos occidentalis   (Western Snowberry)
Symphoricarpos orbiculatus   (Indiancurrant Coralberry)

Vaccinium angustifolium (Lowbush Blueberry)
Vaccinium corymbosum (Highbush Blueberry)
Vaccinium macrocarpum (Cranberry)

Vaccinium stamineum (Common Deerberry)
Yucca filamentosa (Adamsneedle Yucca)

Aristolochia durior (Common Dutchmanspipe)
Bignonia capreolata (Crossvine)
Campsis radicans (Common Trumpetcreeper)

Lonicera dioica (Limber Honeysuckle)
Lonicera sempervirens (Trumpet Honeysuckle)

FLOWER COLOR:

The flowers of many shrubs and vines contribute a pageant of color which brightens the landscape. After the long winter season, the yellow orange blossoms of Vernal Witchhazel and the bright red and brown blooms of American Filbert become the harbingers of spring. Although the majority of species flower during the spring season, a few bloom in late summer and autumn. The great spectrum of brilliant flower hues and the dramatic visual impact achieved by mass plantings has an arresting power that has long been appealing to the designer. A range of ten color classes is used. Where appropriate, symbols distinguish between pistillate (*) and staminate (+) flowers.

WHITE:

Aesculus parviflora (Bottlebrush Buckeye)
Amelanchier sanguinea (Roundleaf Serviceberry)
Andromeda polifolia (Bogrosemary Andromeda)
Arctostaphylos uva-ursi (Bearberry)
Aronia arbutifolia (Red Chokeberry)
Aronia melanocarpa (Black Chokeberry)
Aronia prunifolia (Purplefruit Chokeberry)
Baccharis halimifolia (Eastern Baccharis)
Ceanothus americanus (Jerseytea Ceanothus)
Ceanothus ovatus (Inland Ceanothus)
Cephalanthus occidentalis (Common Buttonbush)
Chamaedaphne calyculata (Leatherleaf)
Clethra acuminata (Cinnamon Clethra)
Clethra alnifolia (Summersweet Clethra)
Cornus amomum (Silky Dogwood)
Cornus canadensis (Bunchberry Dogwood)
Cornus racemosa (Gray Dogwood)
Cornus rugosa (Roundleaf Dogwood)
Cornus stolonifera (Redosier Dogwood)
Cyrilla racemiflora (American Cyrilla)
Epigaea repens (Trailing-arbutus)
Fothergilla gardeni (Dwarf Fothergilla)
Fothergilla major (Large Fothergilla)
Gaultheria procumbens (Checkerberry Wintergreen)
Hydrangea arborescens (Smooth Hydrangea)
Hydrangea quercifolia (Oakleaf Hydrangea)
Ilex decidua (Possumhaw)
Ilex glabra (Inkberry)
Ilex verticillata (Common Winterberry)
Itea virginica (Virginia Sweetspire)
Kalmia latifolia (Mountainlaurel Kalmia)
Ledum groenlandicum (Labradortea Ledum)
Leiophyllum buxifolium (Box Sandmyrtle)
Leucothoe catesbaei (Drooping Leucothoe)

Lyonia ligustrina (He-huckleberry)
Magnolia virginiana (Sweetbay Magnolia)
Neviusia alabamensis (Snowwreath)
Philadelphus grandiflorus (Big Scentless Mockorange)
Physocarpus opulifolius (Common Ninebark)
Pieris floribunda (Mountain Pieris)
Prunus hortulana (Hortulan Plum)
Rhododendron arborescens (Sweet Azalea)
Rhododendron viscosum (Swamp Azalea)
Ribes americanum (American Black Currant)
Ribes cynosbati (Pasture Gooseberry)
Ribes missouriense (Missouri Gooseberry)
Rubus allegheniensis (Allegany Blackberry)
Rubus occidentalis (Blackcap Raspberry)
Rubus strigosus (American Red Raspberry)
Sambucus canadensis (American Elder)
Sambucus pubens (Scarlet Elder)
Spiraea alba (Narrowleaf Meadowsweet Spirea)
Spiraea corymbosa (Corymed Spirea)
Staphylea trifolia (American Bladdernut)
Stewartia ovata (Mountain Stewartia)
Vaccinium angustifolium (Lowbush Blueberry)
Vaccinium corymbosum (Highbush Blueberry)
Vaccinium macrocarpum (Cranberry)
Vaccinium stamineum (Common Deerberry)
Viburnum acerifolium (Mapleleaf Viburnum)
Viburnum alnifolium (Hobblebush Viburnum)
Viburnum cassinoides (Witherod Viburnum)
Viburnum dentatum (Arrowwood Viburnum)
Viburnum nudum (Possumhaw Viburnum)
Viburnum rafinesquianum (Rafinesque Viburnum)
Viburnum trilobum (American Cranberrybush Viburnum)
Yucca filamentosa (Adamsneedle Yucca)
Zenobia pulverulenta (Dusty Zenobia)

Flower color - white (cont.)

Berchemia scandens (Alabama Supplejack)
Clematis virginiana (Virginsbower)

Cocculus carolinus (Carolina Snailseed)
Toxicodendron radicans (Common Poisonivy)

GREEN:

Baccharis halimifolia (Eastern Baccharis)
Elaeagnus commutata (Silverberry)
Euonymus americanus (Brook Euonymus)
Euonymus obovatus (Running Euonymus)
Ilex decidua (Possumhaw)
Ilex glabra (Inkberry)
Ilex verticillata (Common Winterberry)

Myrica pensylvanica (Northern Bayberry)
Pachistima canbyi (Canby Pachistima)
Ribes cynosbati (Pasture Gooseberry)
Ribes missouriense (Missouri Gooseberry)
Salix humilis (Prairie Willow)
Salix lucida (Shining Willow)
Symphoricarpos orbiculatus (Indiancurrant Coralberry)

Ampelopsis arborea (Peppervine)
Ampelopsis cordata (Heartleaf Ampelopsis)
Berchemia scandens (Alabama Supplejack)
Celastrus scandens (American Bittersweet)
Parthenocissus quinquefolia (Virginia Creeper)

Smilax glauca (Cat Greenbrier)
Smilax rotundifolia (Common Greenbrier)
Smilax tamnoides (Bamboo Greenbrier)
Vitis labrusca (Fox Grape)
Vitis riparia (Riverbank Grape)

YELLOW-GREEN:

Betula pumila (Low Birch)
Juniperus communis (Common Juniper) [+]
Juniperus horizontalis (Creeping Juniper) [+]
Quercus ilicifolia (Scrub Oak)

Quercus prinoides (Dwarf Chinkapin Oak)
Salix humilis (Prairie Willow)
Salix lucida (Shining Willow)
Taxus canadensis (Canada Yew) [+]

Menispermum canadense (Common Moonseed)

YELLOW:

Castanea pumila (Allegany Chinkapin)
Diervilla lonicera (Dwarf Bushhoneysuckle)
Dirca palustris (Atlantic Leatherwood)
Hamamelis vernalis (Vernal Witchhazel)
Hypericum densiflorum (Dense Hypericum)
Hypericum frondosum (Golden St.Johnswort)
Hypericum kalmianum (Kalm St.Johnswort)
Hypericum prolificum (Shrubby St.Johnswort)
Lindera benzoin (Common Spicebush)

Lonicera canadensis (American Fly Honeysuckle)
Mahonia aquifolium (Oregongrape)
Pinus aristata (Bristlecone Pipe) [+]
Potentilla fruticosa (Bush Cinquefoil)
Rhododendron calendulaceum (Flame Azalea)
Rhus aromatica (Fragrant Sumac)
Ribes odoratum (Clove Currant)
Shepherdia argentea (Silver Buffaloberry)
Shepherdia canadensis (Russet Buffaloberry)

Lonicera dioica (Limber Honeysuckle)

ORANGE:

Diervilla lonicera (Dwarf Bushhoneysuckle)
Hamamelis vernalis (Vernal Witchhazel)

Lonicera canadensis (American Fly Honeysuckle)
Rhododendron calendulaceum (Flame Azalea)

Bignonia capreolata (Crossvine)
Campsis radicans (Common Trumpetcreeper)

Lonicera dioica (Limber Honeysuckle)
Lonicera sempervirens (Trumpet Honeysuckle)

PINK:

Arctostaphylos uva-ursi (Bearberry)
Epigaea repens (Trailing-arbutus)
Gaultheria procumbens (Checkerberry Wintergreen)
Kalmia latifolia (Mountainlaurel Kalmia)
Rhododendron carolinianum (Carolina Rhododendron)
Rhododendron nudiflorum (Pinxterbloom Azalea)
Rhododendron roseum (Roseshell Azalea)
Robinia hispida (Roseacacia Locust)
Robinia viscosa (Clammy Locust)

Rosa carolina (Carolina Rose)
Rosa setigera (Prairie Rose)
Spiraea tomentosa (Hardhack Spirea)
Symphoricarpos albus (Common Snowberry)
Symphoricarpos occidentalis (Western Snowberry)
Vaccinium corymbosum (Highbush Blueberry)
Vaccinium macrocarpum (Cranberry)
Vaccinium stamineum (Common Deerberry)

RED:

Aesculus pavia   (Red Buckeye)
Calycanthus floridus   (Common Sweetshrub)
Corylus americana   (American Filbert)
Corylus cornuta   (Beaked Filbert)
Diervilla lonicera   (Dwarf Bushhoneysuckle)

Hamamelis vernalis   (Vernal Witchhazel)
Kalmia angustifolia   (Lambkill Kalmia)
Rhododendron vaseyi   (Pinkshell Azalea)
Robinia hispida   (Roseacacia Locust)

————

Bignonia capreolata   (Crossvine)
Campsis radicans   (Common Trumpetcreeper)

Lonicera sempervirens   (Trumpet Honeysuckle)

BLUE:

Amorpha canescens   (Leadplant Amorpha)
Amorpha fruticosa   (Indigobush Amorpha)

PURPLE:

Alnus serrulata   (Common Alder)
Amorpha canescens   (Leadplant Amorpha)
Amorpha fruticosa   (Indigobush Amorpha)
Euonymus americanus   (Brook Euonymus)
Euonymus obovatus   (Running Euonymus)
Kalmia angustifolia   (Lambkill Kalmia)
Rhododendron carolinianum   (Carolina Rhododendron)
Rhododendron catawbiense   (Catawba Rhododendron)

Rhododendron nudiflorum   (Pinxterbloom Azalea)
Rhododendron roseum   (Roseshell Azalea)
Robinia hispida   (Roseacacia Locust)
Robinia viscosa   (Clammy Locust)
Rubus odoratus   (Fragrant Thimbleberry)
Spiraea tomentosa   (Hardhack Spirea)
Xanthorhiza simplicissima   (Yellowroot)

————

Clematis verticillaris   (Rock Clematis)
Wistaria macrostachya   (Kentucky Wistaria)

BROWN:

Calycanthus floridus   (Common Sweetshrub)
Comptonia peregrina   (Sweetfern)
Corylus americana   (American Filbert)

Corylus cornuta   (Beaked Filbert)
Xanthorhiza simplicissima   (Yellowroot)

————

Aristolochia durior   (Common Dutchmanspipe)

FLOWER FRAGRANCE:

The flowers and foliage of certain plants create pleasant scents. The spicy blossoms of viburnums and buttonbush are plants which exude pleasant scents. Plants with olfactory values should be studied and used by environmental designers to enrich the sensual dimension of the rural and urbanized landscape. Plants with fragrant flowers include:

indicator — Ribes odoratum (Clove Currant)

Aesculus parviflora   (Bottlebrush Buckeye)
Calycanthus floridus   (Common Sweetshrub)
Ceanothus americanus   (Jerseytea Ceanothus)
Cephalanthus occidentalis   (Common Buttonbush)
Clethra acuminata   (Cinnamon Clethra)
Clethra alnifolia   (Summersweet Clethra)

Elaeagnus commutata   (Silverberry)
Epigaea repens   (Trailing-arbutus)
Fothergilla gardeni   (Dwarf Fothergilla)
Fothergilla major   (Large Fothergilla)
Hamamelis vernalis   (Vernal Witchhazel)
Hydrangea arborescens   (Smooth Hydrangea)

Flower fragrance (cont.)

Hydrangea quercifolia (Oakleaf Hydrangea)
Itea virginica (Virginia Sweetspire)
Kalmia latifolia (Mountainlaurel Kalmia)
Leucothoe catesbaei (Drooping Leucothoe)
Lindera benzoin (Common Spicebush)
Lonicera canadensis (American Fly Honeysuckle)
Magnolia virginiana (Sweetbay Magnolia)
Mahonia aquifolium (Oregongrape)
Physocarpus opulifolius (Common Ninebark)
Pieris floribunda (Mountain Pieris)
Prunus hortulana (Hortulan Plum)
Rhododendron arborescens (Sweet Azalea)
Rhododendron nudiflorum (Pinxterbloom Azalea)

Rhododendron roseum (Roseshell Azalea)
Rhododendron viscosum (Swamp Azalea)
Ribes cynosbati (Pasture Gooseberry)
Ribes missouriense (Missouri Gooseberry)
Ribes odoratum (Clove Currant)
Rosa carolina (Carolina Rose)
Rosa setigera (Prairie Rose)
Rubus odoratus (Fragrant Thimbleberry)
Sambucus canadensis (American Elder)
Sambucus pubens (Scarlet Elder)
Viburnum cassinoides (Witherod Viburnum)
Yucca filamentosa (Adamsneedle Yucca)

Lonicera dioica (Limber Honeysuckle)
Vitis labrusca (Fox Grape)

Vitis riparia (Riverbank Grape)
Wistaria macrostachya (Kentucky Wistaria)

PLANT SEX:

Most shrubs and vines have both staminate (male) and pistillate (female) flowers on the same plant allowing self-fertilization. Some groups of plants are dioecious and bear staminate flowers on one plant and pistillate flowers on another. The selection of a staminate plant might be desirable where seed becomes a nuisance maintenance problem. Of course the pistillate plant will not bear heavy fruit crops unless the pollen-bearing staminate plant is located in close proximity. The following species are frequently dioecious.

indicator — *Ilex glabra* (Inkberry)

Baccharis halimifolia (Eastern Baccharis)
Comptonia peregrina (Sweetfern)
Epigaea repens (Trailing-arbutus)
Ilex decidua (Possumhaw)
Ilex glabra (Inkberry)
Ilex verticillata (Common Winterberry)
Juniperus communis (Common Juniper)
Juniperus horizontalis (Creeping Juniper)
Lindera benzoin (Common Spicebush)
Myrica pensylvanica (Northern Bayberry)

Rhus aromatica (Fragrant Sumac)
Ribes americanum (American Black Currant)
Ribes cynosbati (Pasture Gooseberry)
Ribes missouriense (Missouri Gooseberry)
Ribes odoratum (Clove Currant)
Salix humilis (Prairie Willow)
Salix lucida (Shining Willow)
Shepherdia argentea (Silver Buffaloberry)
Shepherdia canadensis (Russet Buffaloberry)
Taxus canadensis (Canada Yew)

Ampelopsis arborea (Peppervine)
Ampelopsis cordata (Heartleaf Ampelopsis)
Celastrus scandens (American Bittersweet)
Clematis verticillaris (Rock Clematis)
Clematis virginiana (Virginsbower)
Cocculus carolinus (Carolina Snailseed)
Menispermum canadense (Common Moonseed)

Smilax glauca (Cat Greenbrier)
Smilax rotundfolia (Common Greenbrier)
Smilax tamnoides (Bamboo Greenbrier)
Toxicodendron radicans (Common Poisonivy)
Vitis labrusca (Fox Grape)
Vitis riparia (Riverbank Grape)

FRUIT STRUCTURE:

Ornamental fruits are often as interesting as the flowers they follow. Some, like the white berries of Gray Dogwood cling to the branches until late autumn. The brilliant fruits of American Cranberrybush Viburnum and American Bittersweet hang like Christmas ornaments throughout much of the winter season. The fruits of a few plants, such as the fuzzy woody capsules of Verna Witchhazel, persist throughout the year and exhibit ornamental characteristics during each season. Nine categories of fruit structure are distinguished for designer consideration.

BERRY:
>   fruits with soft flesh covering over the seed,
>   indicator — *Vitis labrusca* (Fox Grape)

Amelanchier sanguinea (Roundleaf Serviceberry)
Arctostaphylos uva-ursi (Bearberry)
Aronia arbutifolia (Red Chokeberry)
Aronia melanocarpa (Black Chokeberry)
Aronia prunifolia (Purplefruit Chokeberry)
Cornus amomum (Silky Dogwood)
Cornus canadensis (Bunchberry Dogwood)
Cornus racemosa (Gray Dogwood)
Cornus rugosa (Roundleaf Dogwood)
Cornus stolonifera (Redosier Dogwood)
Dirca palustris (Atlantic Leatherwood)
Elaeagnus commutata (Silverberry)
Epigaea repens (Trailing-arbutus)
Gaultheria procumbens (Checkerberry Wintergreen)
Ilex decidua (Possumhaw)
Ilex glabra (Inkberry)
Ilex verticillata (Common Winterberry)
Juniperus communis (Common Juniper)
Juniperus horizontalis (Creeping Juniper)
Lindera benzoin (Common Spicebush)
Lonicera canadensis (American Fly Honeysuckle)
Mahonia aquifolium (Oregongrape)
Myrica pensylvanica (Northern Bayberry)
Prunus hortulana (Hortulan Plum)
Rhus aromatica (Fragrant Sumac)
Ribes americanum (American Black Currant)
Ribes cynosbati (Pasture Gooseberry)

Ribes missouriense (Missouri Gooseberry)
Ribes odoratum (Clove Currant)
Rosa carolina (Carolina Rose)
Rosa setigera (Prairie Rose)
Rubus allegheniensis (Allegany Blackberry)
Rubus occidentalis (Blackcap Raspberry)
Rubus odoratus (Fragrant Thimbleberry)
Rubus strigosus (American Red Raspberry)
Sambucus canadensis (American Elder)
Sambucus pubens (Scarlet Elder)
Shepherdia argentea (Silver Buffaloberry)
Shepherdia canadensis (Russet Buffaloberry)
Symphoricarpos albus (Common Snowberry)
Symphoricarpos occidentalis (Western Snowberry)
Symphoricarpos orbiculatus (Indiancurrant Coralberry)
Taxus canadensis (Canada Yew)
Vaccinium angustifolium (Lowbush Blueberry)
Vaccinium corymbosum (Highbush Blueberry)
Vaccinium macrocarpum (Cranberry)
Vaccinium stamineum (Common Deerberry)
Viburnum acerifolium (Mapleleaf Viburnum)
Viburnum alnifolium (Hobblebush Viburnum)
Viburnum cassinoides (Witherod Viburnum)
Viburnum dentatum (Arrowwood Viburnum)
Viburnum nudum (Possumhaw Viburnum)
Viburnum rafinesquianum (Rafinesque Viburnum)
Viburnum trilobum (American Cranberrybush Viburnum)

Ampelopsis arborea (Peppervine)
Ampelopsis cordata (Heartleaf Ampelopsis)
Berchemia scandens (Alabama Supplejack)
Cocculus carolinus (Carolina Snailseed)
Lonicera dioica (Limber Honeysuckle)
Lonicera sempervirens (Trumpet Honeysuckle)
Menispermum canadense (Common Moonseed)

Parthenocissus quinquefolia (Virginia Creeper)
Smilax glauca (Cat Greenbrier)
Smilax rotundifolia (Common Greenbrier)
Smilax tamnoides (Bamboo Greenbrier)
Toxicodendron radicans (Common Poisonivy)
Vitis labrusca (Fox Grape)
Vitis riparia (Riverbank Grape)

NUT OR ACORN:
>   nut partially or wholly enclosed in a husk which may be papery, woody, leafy, or spiny in character,
>   indicator — *Castanea pumila* (Allegany Chinkapin)

Aesculus parviflora (Bottlebrush Buckeye)
Aesculus pavia (Red Buckeye)
Castanea pumila (Allegany Chinkapin)
Corylus americana (American Filbert)

Corylus cornuta (Beaked Filbert)
Quercus ilicifolia (Scrub Oak)
Quercus prinoides (Dwarf Chinkapin Oak)

433

Fruit structure (cont.)

LEGUME:
elongated bean-like pod splitting open at maturity along two seams,
indicator — *Wistaria macrostachya* (Kentucky Wistaria)

Amorpha canescens (Leadplant Amorpha)
Amorpha fruticosa (Indigobush Amorpha)

Robinia hispida (Roseacacia Locust)
Robinia viscosa (Clammy Locust)

Aristolochia durior (Common Dutchmanspipe)
Bignonia capreolata (Crossvine)

Campsis radicans (Common Trumpetcreeper)
Wistaria macrostachya (Kentucky Wistaria)

CONE:
woody fruit, primarily of coniferous plants, having stiff overlapping scales which support naked seeds,
indicator — *Pinus aristata* (Bristlecone Pine)

Pinus aristata (Bristlecone Pine)

MULTIPLE:
small unwinged but sometimes plumed, one-celled, one-seeded fruit compounded to form a globose or ball-like head,
indicator — *Cephalanthus occidentalis* (Common Buttonbush)

Cephalanthus occidentalis (Common Buttonbush)

CAPSULE:
fruit of more than one chamber usually splitting lengthwise from one end along multiple seams,
indicator — *Celastrus scandens* (American Bittersweet)

Andromeda polifolia (Bogrosemary Andromeda)
Calycanthus floridus (Common Sweetshrub)
Ceanothus americanus (Jerseytea Ceanothus)
Ceanothus ovatus (Inland Ceanothus)
Clethra acuminata (Cinnamon Clethra)
Clethra alnifolia (Summersweet Clethra)
Cyrilla racemiflora (American Cyrilla)
Diervilla lonicera (Dwarf Bushhoneysuckle)
Epigaea repens (Trailing-arbutus)
Euonymus americanus (Brook Euonymus)
Euonymus obovatus (Running Euonymus)
Fothergilla gardeni (Dwarf Fothergilla)
Fothergilla major (Large Fothergilla)
Hamamelis vernalis (Vernal Witchhazel)
Hydrangea arborescens (Smooth Hydrangea)
Hydrangea quercifolia (Oakleaf Hydrangea)
Hypericum densiflorum (Dense Hypericum)
Hypericum frondosum (Golden St.Johnswort)
Hypericum kalmianum (Kalm St.Johnswort)
Hypericum prolificum (Shrubby St.Johnswort)
Itea virginica (Virginia Sweetspire)
Kalmia angustifolia (Lambkill Kalmia)
Kalmia latifolia (Mountainlaurel Kalmia)
Kalmia polifolia (Bog Kalmia)
Ledum groenlandicum (Labradortea Ledum)

Leiophyllum buxifolium (Box Sandmyrtle)
Leucothoe catesbaei (Drooping Leucothoe)
Lyonia ligustrina (He-huckleberry)
Pachistima canbyi (Canby Pachistima)
Philadelphus grandiflorus (Big Scentless Mockorange)
Physocarpus opulifolius (Common Ninebark)
Pieris floribunda (Mountain Pieris)
Potentilla fruticosa (Bush Cinquefoil)
Rhododendron arborescens (Sweet Azalea)
Rhododendron calendulaceum (Flame Azalea)
Rhododendron carolinianum (Carolina Rhododendron)
Rhododendron catawbiense (Catawba Rhododendron)
Rhododendron nudiflorum (Pinxterbloom Azalea)
Rhododendron roseum (Roseshell Azalea)
Rhododendron vaseyi (Pinkshell Azalea)
Rhododendron viscosum (Swamp Azalea)
Salix humilis (Prairie Willow)
Salix lucida (Shining Willow)
Spiraea alba (Narrowleaf Meadowsweet Spirea)
Spiraea corymbosa (Corymed Spirea)
Spiraea tomentosa (Hardhack Spirea)
Staphylea trifolia (American Bladdernut)
Stewartia ovata (Mountain Stewartia)
Yucca filamentosa (Adamsneedle Yucca)
Zenobia pulverulenta (Dusty Zenobia)

Celastrus scandens (American Bittersweet)

STROBILE:
slender pendant or erect catkin-like or cone-like fruits with papery, overlapping seeds,
indicator — *Betula pumila* (Low Birch)

Alnus serrulata (Common Alder)
Betula pumila (Low Birch)

Comptonia peregrina (Sweetfern)

FOLLICLE:
    aggregate of small fleshy pods on stout short erect stems resembling a cucumber,
    indicator — *Magnolia virginiana* (Sweetbay Magnolia)

Magnolia virginiana   (Sweetbay Magnolia)
Xanthorhiza simplicissima   (Yellowroot)

ACHENE:
    a small, dry, hard, nonsplitting fruit with one seed,
    indicator — *Baccharis halimifolia* (Eastern Baccharis)

Baccharis halimifolia   (Eastern Baccharis)
Neviusia alabamensis   (Snowwreath)

———

Clematis verticillaris   (Rock Clematis)
Clematis virginiana   (Virginsbower)

FRUIT COLORATION:

Fruit colors frequently afford beauty in the landscape in much the same manner as flowers, foliage, and bark. Species with conspicuous early fruit production are a welcome contrast against the summer background of green leaves. Others hold significant quantities of fruit which brightly decorate the winter landscape. Fruit coloration is considered for the period during which the ripe fruits remain ornamentally effective. Ten color classes are presented for designer consideration:

WHITE:

Cornus racemosa   (Gray Dogwood)
Cornus stolonifera   (Redosier Dogwood)
Elaeagnus commutata   (Silverberry)
Myrica pensylvanica   (Northern Bayberry)
Symphoricarpos albus   (Common Snowberry)
Symphoricarpos occidentalis   (Western Snowberry)

GRAY:

Elaeagnus commutata   (Silverberry)
Juniperus communis   (Common Juniper)
Juniperus horizontalis   (Creeping Juniper)
Myrica pensylvanica   (Northern Bayberry)

———

Clematis verticillaris   (Rock Clematis)
Clematis virginiana   (Virginsbower)

GREEN:

Dirca palustris   (Atlantic Leatherwood)
Symphoricarpos occidentalis   (Western Snowberry)

———

Aristolochia durior   (Common Dutchmanspipe)

YELLOW:

Prunus hortulana   (Hortulan Plum)
Shepherdia argentea   (Silver Buffaloberry)
Shepherdia canadensis   (Russet Buffaloberry)
Viburnum cassinoides   (Witherod Viburnum)
Xanthorhiza simplicissima   (Yellowroot)

Fruit coloration (cont.)

YELLOW-GREEN:

Hamamelis vernalis   (Vernal Witchhazel)

ORANGE:

Euonymus americanus   (Brook Euonymus)
Euonymus obovatus   (Running Euonymus)
Ilex decidua   (Possumhaw)

Shepherdia argentea   (Silver Buffaloberry)
Taxus canadensis   (Canada Yew)

——

Celastrus scandens   (American Bittersweet)

RED:

Amelanchier sanguinea   (Roundleaf Serviceberry)
Arctostaphylos uva-ursi   (Bearberry)
Aronia arbutifolia   (Red Chokeberry)
Ceanothus ovatus   (Inland Ceanothus)
Cephalanthus occidentalis   (Common Buttonbush)
Cornus canadensis   (Bunchberry Dogwood)
Dirca palustris   (Atlantic Leatherwood)
Euonymus americanus   (Brook Euonymus)
Euonymus obovatus   (Running Euonymus)
Gaultheria procumbens   (Checkerberry Wintergreen)
Ilex decidua   (Possumhaw)
Ilex verticillata   (Common Winterberry)
Lindera benzoin   (Common Spicebush)
Lonicera canadensis   (American Fly Honeysuckle)
Magnolia virginiana   (Sweetbay Magnolia)

Physocarpus opulifolius   (Common Ninebark)
Prunus hortulana   (Hortulan Plum)
Rhus aromatica   (Fragrant Sumac)
Rosa carolina   (Carolina Rose)
Rosa setigera   (Prairie Rose)
Rubus odoratus   (Fragrant Thimbleberry)
Rubus strigosus   (American Red Raspberry)
Sambucus pubens   (Scarlet Elder)
Shepherdia argentea   (Silver Buffaloberry)
Shepherdia canadensis   (Russet Buffaloberry)
Symphoricarpos orbiculatus   (Indiancurrant Coralberry)
Taxus canadensis   (Canada Yew)
Vaccinium macrocarpum   (Cranberry)
Viburnum cassinoides   (Witherod Viburnum)
Viburnum trilobum   (American Cranberrybush Viburnum)

Celastrus scandens   (American Bittersweet)
Cocculus carolinus   (Carolina Snailseed)

Lonicera dioica   (Limber Honeysuckle)
Lonicera sempervirens   (Trumpet Honeysuckle)

RED-BROWN:

Hypericum densiflorum   (Dense Hypericum)
Hypericum frondosum   (Golden St.Johnswort)
Hypericum kalmianum   (Kalm St.Johnswort)
Hypericum prolificum   (Shrubby St.Johnswort)
Pinus aristata   (Bristlecone Pine)
Robinia hispida   (Roseacacia Locust)

Robinia viscosa   (Clammy Locust)
Spiraea alba   (Narrowleaf Meadowsweet Spirea)
Spiraea corymbosa   (Corymed Spirea)
Spiraea tomentosa   (Hardhack Spirea)
Staphylea trifolia   (American Bladdernut)

BROWN:

Aesculus parviflora   (Bottlebrush Buckeye)
Aesculus pavia   (Red Buckeye)
Alnus serrulata   (Common Alder)
Amorpha canescens   (Leadplant Amorpha)
Amorpha fruticosa   (Indigobush Amorpha)
Andromeda polifolia   (Bogrosemary Andromeda)
Betula pumila   (Low Birch)
Calycanthus floridus   (Common Sweetshrub)
Castanea pumila   (Allegany Chinkapin)
Ceanothus americanus   (Jerseytea Ceanothus)
Ceanothus ovatus   (Inland Ceanothus)
Cephalanthus occidentalis   (Common Buttonbush)
Clethra acuminata   (Cinnamon Clethra)
Clethra alnifolia   (Summersweet Clethra)
Comptonia peregrina   (Sweetfern)
Corylus americana   (American Filbert)
Corylus cornuta   (Beaked Filbert)
Cyrilla racemiflora   (American Cyrilla)
Diervilla lonicera   (Dwarf Bushhoneysuckle)

Fothergilla gardeni   (Dwarf Fothergilla)
Fothergilla major   (Large Fothergilla)
Hamamelis vernalis   (Vernal Witchhazel)
Hydrangea arborescens   (Smooth Hydrangea)
Hydrangea quercifolia   (Oakleaf Hydrangea)
Itea virginica   (Virginia Sweetspire)
Kalmia angustifolia   (Lambkill Kalmia)
Kalmia latifolia   (Mountainlaurel Kalmia)
Ledum groenlandicum   (Labradortea Ledum)
Leiophyllum buxifolium   (Box Sandmyrtle)
Leucothoe catesbaei   (Drooping Leucothoe)
Lyonia ligustrina   (He-huckleberry)
Neviusia alabamensis   (Snowwreath)
Pachistima canbyi   (Canby Pachistima)
Philadelphus grandiflorus   (Big Scentless Mockorange)
Physocarpus opulifolius   (Common Ninebark)
Pieris floribunda   (Mountain Pieris)
Pinus aristata   (Bristlecone Pine)
Potentilla fruticosa   (Bush Cinquefoil)

436

Quercus ilicifolia (Scrub Oak)
Quercus prinoides (Dwarf Chinkapin Oak)
Rhododendron arborescens (Sweet Azalea)
Rhododendron calendulaceum (Flame Azalea)
Rhododendron carolinianum (Carolina Rhododendron)
Rhododendron catawbiense (Catawba Rhododendron)
Rhododendron nudiflorum (Pinxterbloom Azalea)
Rhododendron roseum (Roseshell Azalea)
Rhododendron vaseyi (Pinkshell Azalea)
Rhododendron viscosum (Swamp Azalea)
Robinia hispida (Roseacacia Locust)

Robinia viscosa (Clammy Locust)
Salix humilis (Prairie Willow)
Salix lucida (Shining Willow)
Spiraea alba (Narrowleaf Meadowsweet Spirea)
Spiraea corymbosa (Corymed Spirea)
Spiraea tomentosa (Hardhack Spirea)
Staphylea trifolia (American Bladdernut)
Stewartia ovata (Mountain Stewartia)
Yucca filamentosa (Adamsneedle Yucca)
Zenobia pulverulenta (Dusty Zenobia)

Aristolochia durior (Common Dutchmanspipe)
Bignonia capreolata (Crossvine)

Campsis radicans (Common Trumpetcreeper)
Wistaria macrostachya (Kentucky Wistaria)

BLUE:

Amelanchier sanguinea (Roundleaf Serviceberry)
Cornus amomum (Silky Dogwood)
Cornus rugosa (Roundleaf Dogwood)
Juniperus communis (Common Juniper)
Juniperus horizontalis (Creeping Juniper)
Mahonia aquifolium (Oregongrape)
Vaccinium angustifolium (Lowbush Blueberry)
Vaccinium corymbosum (Highbush Blueberry)

Vaccinium stamineum (Common Deerberry)
Viburnum acerifolium (Mapleleaf Viburnum)
Viburnum alnifolium (Hobblebush Viburnum)
Viburnum cassinoides (Witherod Viburnum)
Viburnum dentatum (Arrowwood Viburnum)
Viburnum nudum (Possumhaw Viburnum)
Viburnum rafinesquianum (Rafinesque Viburnum)

Ampelopsis arborea (Peppervine)
Ampelopsis cordata (Heartleaf Ampelopsis)
Berchemia scandens (Alabama Supplejack)
Menispermum canadense (Common Moonseed)
Parthenocissus quinquefolia (Virginia Creeper)

Smilax glauca (Cat Greenbrier)
Smilax rotundifolia (Common Greenbrier)
Smilax tamnoides (Bamboo Greenbrier)
Vitis labrusca (Fox Grape)
Vitis riparia (Riverbank Grape)

PURPLE:

Amelanchier sanguinea (Roundleaf Serviceberry)
Aronia prunifolia (Purplefruit Chokeberry)
Hypericum densiflorum (Dense Hypericum)
Hypericum frondosum (Golden St.Johnswort)
Hypericum kalmianum (Kalm St.Johnswort)
Hypericum prolificum (Shrubby St.Johnswort)
Prunus hortulana (Hortulan Plum)

Ribes americanum (American Black Currant)
Ribes cynosbati (Pasture Gooseberry)
Ribes missouriense (Missouri Gooseberry)
Rubus odoratus (Fragrant Thimbleberry)
Sambucus canadensis (American Elder)
Symphoricarpos orbiculatus (Indiancurrant Coralberry)

Ampelopsis arborea (Peppervine)
Ampelopsis cordata (Heartleaf Ampelopsis)

BLACK:

Aronia melanocarpa (Black Chokeberry)
Ceanothus americanus (Jerseytea Ceanothus)
Ilex glabra (Inkberry)
Mahonia aquifolium (Oregongrape)
Ribes americanum (American Black Currant)
Ribes cynosbati (Pasture Gooseberry)
Ribes missouriense (Missouri Gooseberry)
Ribes odoratum (Clove Currant)
Rubus allegheniensis (Allegany Blackberry)
Rubus occidentalis (Blackcap Raspberry)

Sambucus canadensis (American Elder)
Vaccinium angustifolium (Lowbush Blueberry)
Vaccinium corymbosum (Highbush Blueberry)
Vaccinium stamineum (Common Deerberry)
Viburnum acerifolium (Mapleleaf Viburnum)
Viburnum alnifolium (Hobblebush Viburnum)
Viburnum cassinoides (Witherod Viburnum)
Viburnum dentatum (Arrowwood Viburnum)
Viburnum nudum (Possumhaw Viburnum)
Viburnum rafinesquianum (Rafinesque Viburnum)

Berchemia scandens (Alabama Supplejack)
Menisperum canadense (Common Moonseed)
Parthenocissus quinquefolia (Virginia Creeper)
Smilax glauca (Cat Greenbrier)

Smilax rotundifolia (Common Greenbrier)
Smilax tamnoides (Bamboo Greenbrier)
Vitis labrusca (Fox Grape)
Vitis riparia (Riverbank Grape)

WILDLIFE VALUE:

Food is one of the primary necessities of all life forms, and cover for wild animals is also a vital requirement. Survival in critical periods — during inclement weather, during spring and summer rearing of young, or when subjected to attack by enemies — depends largely on these fundamental factors of food and cover (Martin, Zim, Nelson 1961). These factors dominate the welfare of all kinds of wildlife and determine to a large degree the increase or decrease of animal populations.

Grass and shrub species constitute the bulk of plants used for food and cover. Many vine species also provide fruits, seeds, leaves, twigs, bark, stems and roots for many kinds of wildlife.

Wildlife biologists have been alarmed of the rapid decrease in wildlife habitat within the last decade to expanded agriculture, forestry, and urbanization. For example, methods of seeding, harvesting and the size of machinery have necessitated the farming of large acreages. Fence rows and shelterbelts are destroyed because woody pioneer plants compete with agronomic crops for available soil moisture at distances up to 12.5 meters (40 feet) from the row, reducing crop yield.

Animal food use information can aid the environmental designer in planning wildlife habitat developments for forests, marshlands, grazing ranges, wildlife refuges, farms, and residential areas. The following classification reflects the relative attractiveness values for different plant genera as wildlife food sources in the east and midwest regions. Five categories are considered.

VERY HIGH:
50 wildlife users or more,
indicator — *Cornus amomum* (Silky Dogwood)

Amelanchier sanguinea (Roundleaf Serviceberry)
Betula pumila (Low Birch)
Cornus amomum (Silky Dogwood)
Cornus racemosa (Gray Dogwood)
Cornus rugosa (Roundleaf Dogwood)
Cornus stolonifera (Redosier Dogwood)
Juniperus communis (Common Juniper)
Juniperus horizontalis (Creeping Juniper)
Lindera benzoin (Common Spicebush)
Pinus aristata (Bristlecone Pine)
Quercus ilicifolia (Scrub Oak)

Quercus prinoides (Dwarf Chinkapin Oak)
Rhus aromatica (Fragrant Sumac)
Rubus allegheniensis (Allegany Blackberry)
Rubus occidentalis (Blackcap Raspberry)
Rubus odoratus (Fragrant Thimbleberry)
Rubus strigosus (American Red Raspberry)
Sambucus canadensis (American Elder)
Sambucus pubens (Scarlet Elder)
Vaccinium angustfolium (Lowbush Blueberry)
Vaccinium corymbosum (Highbush Blueberry)
Vaccinium stamineum (Common Deerberry)

Vitis labrusca (Fox Grape)
Vitis riparia (Riverbank Grape)

HIGH:
25 to 49 wildlife users,
indicator — *Viburnum acerifolium* (Mapleleaf Viburnum)

Ilex decidua (Possumhaw)
Ilex glabra (Inkberry)
Ilex verticillata (Common Winterberry)
Mahonia aquifolium (Oregongrape)
Myrica pensylvanica (Northern Bayberry)
Ribes americanum (American Black Currant
Ribes cynosbati (Pasture Gooseberry)
Ribes missouriense (Missouri Gooseberry)
Ribes odoratum (Clove Currant)
Salix humilis (Prairie Willow)
Salix lucida (Shining Willow)

Symphoricarpos albus (Common Snowberry)
Symphoricarpos occidentalis (Western Snowberry)
Symphoricarpos orbiculatus (Indiancurrant Coralberry)
Viburnum acerifolium (Mapleleaf Viburnum)
Viburnum alnifolium (Hobblebush Viburnum)
Viburnum cassinoides (Witherod Viburnum)
Viburnum dentatum (Arrowwood Viburnum)
Viburnum nudum (Possumhaw Viburnum)
Viburnum rafinesquianum (Rafinesque Viburnum)
Viburnum trilobum (American Cranberrybush Viburnum)
Xanthorhiza simplicissima (Yellowroot)

Menispermum canadense (Common Moonseed)
Parthenocissus quinquefolia (Virginia Creeper)

Toxicodendron radicans (Common Poisonivy)

INTERMEDIATE:
    15 to 24 wildlife users.
    indicator — *Spiraea tomentosa* (Hardhack Spirea)

Alnus serrulata (Common Alder)
Amorpha canescens (Leadplant Amorpha)
Amorpha fruticosa (Indigobush Amorpha)
Aronia arbutifolia (Red Chokeberry)
Aronia melanocarpa (Black Chokeberry)
Aronia prunifolia (Purplefruit Chokeberry)
Ceanothus americanus (Jerseytea Ceanothus)
Ceanothus ovatus (Inland Ceanothus)
Clethra acuminata (Cinnamon Clethra)
Clethra alnifolia (Summersweet Clethra)
Corylus americana (American Filbert)
Corylus cornuta (Beaked Filbert)

Hypericum densiflorum (Dense Hypericum)
Hypericum frondosum (Golden St.Johnswort)
Hypericum kalmianum (Kalm St.Johnswort)
Hypericum prolificum (Shrubby St.Johnswort)
Physocarpus opulifolius (Common Ninebark)
Prunus hortulana (Hortulan Plum)
Rosa carolina (Carolina Rose)
Rosa setigera (Prairie Rose)
Spiraea alba (Narrowleaf Meadowsweet Spirea)
Spiraea corymbosa (Corymed Spirea)
Spiraea tomentosa (Hardhack Spirea)

Ampelopsis arborea (Peppervine)
Ampelopsis cordata (Heartleaf Ampelopsis)
Berchemia scandens (Alabama Supplejack)
Cocculus carolinus (Carolina Snailseed)
Lonicera dioica (Limber Honeysuckle)

Lonicera sempervirens (Trumpet Honeysuckle)
Smilax glauca (Cat Greenbrier)
Smilax rotundifolia (Common Greenbrier)
Smilax tamnoides (Bamboo Greenbrier)

LOW:
    5 to 14 wildlife users,
    indicator — *Staphylea trifolia* (American Bladdernut)

Arctostaphylos uva-ursi (Bearberry)
Castanea pumila (Allegany Chinkapin)
Cephalanthus occidentalis (Common Buttonbush)
Comptonia peregrina (Sweetfern)
Cornus canadensis (Bunchberry Dogwood)
Cyrilla racemiflora (American Cyrilla)
Diervilla lonicera (Dwarf Bushhoneysuckle)
Dirca palustris (Atlantic Leatherwood)
Elaeagnus commutata (Silverberry)
Epigaea repens (Trailing-arbutus)
Euonymus americanus (Brook Euonymus)
Euonymus obovatus (Running Euonymus)
Fothergilla gardeni (Dwarf Fothergilla)
Fothergilla major (Large Fothergilla)
Gaultheria procumbens (Checkerberry Wintergreen)
Hamamelis vernalis (Vernal Witchhazel)
Hydrangea arborescens (Smooth Hydrangea)
Hydrangea quercifolia (Oakleaf Hydrangea)
Itea virginica (Virginia Sweetspire)
Ledum groenlandicum (Labradortea Ledum)
Leiophyllum buxifolium (Box Sandmyrtle)
Leucothoe catesbaei (Drooping Leucothoe)
Lonicera canadensis (American Fly Honeysuckle)

Lyonia ligustrina (He-huckleberry)
Neviusia alabamensis (Snowwreath)
Pachistima canbyi (Canby Pachistima)
Philadelphus grandiflorus (Big Scentless Mockorange)
Pieris floribunda (Mountain Pieris)
Potentilla fruticosa (Bush Cinquefoil)
Rhododendron arborescens (Sweet Azalea)
Rhododendron calendulaceum (Flame Azalea)
Rhododendron carolinianum (Carolina Rhododendron)
Rhododendron catawbiense (Catawba Rhododendron)
Rhododendron nudiflorum (Pinxterbloom Azalea)
Rhododendron roseum (Roseshell Azalea)
Rhododendron vaseyi (Pinkshell Azalea)
Rhododendron viscosum (Swamp Azalea)
Robinia hispida (Roseacacia Locust)
Robinia viscosa (Clammy Locust)
Shepherdia argentea (Silver Buffaloberry)
Shepherdia canadensis (Russet Buffaloberry)
Staphylea trifolia (American Bladdernut)
Stewartia ovata (Mountain Stewartia)
Taxus canadensis (Canada Yew)
Zenobia pulverulenta (Dusty Zenobia)

Bignonia capreolata (Crossvine)
Celastrus scandens (American Bittersweet)

VERY LOW:
    fewer than 5 wildlife users,
    indicator — *Calycanthus floridus* (Common Sweetshrub)

Aesculus parviflora (Bottlebrush Buckeye)
Aesculus pavia (Red Buckeye)
Andromeda polifolia (Bogrosemary Andromeda)
Baccharis halimifolia (Eastern Baccharis)
Calycanthus floridus (Common Sweetshrub)

Kalmia angustifolia (Lambkill Kalmia)
Kalmia latifolia (Mountainlaurel Kalmia)
Kalmia polifolia (Bog Kalmia)
Magnolia virginiana (Sweetbay Magnolia)
Vaccinium macrocarpum (Cranberry)

Wildlife value - very low (cont.)

Yucca filamentosa (Adamsneedle Yucca)

Aristolochia durior (Common Dutchmanspipe)
Campsis radicans (Common Trumpetcreeper)
Clematis verticillaris (Rock Clematis)

Clematis virginiana (Virginsbower)
Wistaria macrostachya (Kentucky Wistaria)

HUMAN VALUE:

To many people, the joy of collecting and cooking with edible wild plants brings tremendous satisfaction while stretching grocery dollars. The ability to successfully identify and harvest edible native plants has become popular with self-sufficient individuals and families. Eight categories of edible and poisonous plants are recognized:

EDIBLE, ALL PARTS:
   entire plant edible and nutritious,
   indicator — *Lindera benzoin* (Common Spicebush)

Lindera benzoin (Common Spicebush)

POISONOUS, ALL PARTS:
   entire plant poisonous if eaten and/or contacted with skin,
   indicator — *Toxicodendron radicans* (Common Poisonivy)

Aesculus parviflora (Bottlebrush Buckeye)
Aesculus pavia (Red Buckeye)
Kalmia angustifolia (Lambkill Kalmia)
Kalmia latifolia (Mountainlaurel Kalmia)
Kalmia polifolia (Bog Kalmia)
Rhododendron arborescens (Sweet Azalea)
Rhododendron calendulaceum (Flame Azalea)
Rhododendron carolinianum (Carolina Rhododendron)
Rhododendron catawbiense (Catawba Rhododendron)

Rhododendron nudiflorum (Pinxterbloom Azalea)
Rhododendron roseum (Roseshell Azalea)
Rhododendron vaseyi (Pinkshell Azalea)
Rhododendron viscosum (Swamp Azalea)
Robinia hispida (Roseacacia Locust)
Robinia viscosa (Clammy Locust)
Sambucus pubens (Scarlet Elder)
Taxus canadensis (Canada Yew)

Celastrus scandens (American Bittersweet)
Toxicodendron radicans (Common Poisonivy)

EDIBLE FRUIT:
   fruits edible and nutritious,
   indicator — *Vitis labrusca* (Fox Grape)

Amelanchier sanguinea (Roundleaf Serviceberry)
Arctostaphylos uva-ursi (Bearberry)
Aronia arbutifolia (Red Chokeberry)
Aronia melanocarpa (Black Chokeberry)
Aronia prunifolia (Purplefruit Chokeberry)
Castanea pumila (Allegany Chinkapin)
Cornus canadensis (Bunchberry Dogwood)
Corylus americana (American Filbert)
Corylus cornuta (Beaked Filbert)
Elaeagnus commutata (Silverberry)
Gaultheria procumbens (Checkerberry Wintergreen)
Juniperus communis (Common Juniper)

Juniperus horizontalis (Creeping Juniper)
Lonicera canadensis (American Fly Honeysuckle)
Myrica pensylvanica (Northern Bayberry)
Prunus hortulana (Hortulan Plum)
Quercus ilicifolia (Scrub Oak)
Quercus prinoides (Dwarf Chinkapin Oak)
Rhus aromatica (Fragrant Sumac)
Ribes americanum (American Black Currant
Ribes cynosbati (Pasture Gooseberry)
Ribes missouriense (Missouri Gooseberry)
Ribes odoratum (Clove Currant)
Rosa carolina (Carolina Rose)

Rosa setigera (Prairie Rose)
Rubus allegheniensis (Allegany Blackberry)
Rubus occidentalis (Blackcap Raspberry)
Rubus odoratus (Fragrant Thimbleberry)
Rubus strigosus (American Red Raspberry)
Sambucus canadensis (American Elder)
Shepherdia argentea (Silver Buffaloberry)
Shepherdia canadensis (Russet Buffaloberry)
Vaccinium angustifolium (Lowbush Blueberry)

Vaccinium corymbosum (Highbush Blueberry)
Vaccinium macrocarpum (Cranberry)
Vaccinium stamineum (Common Deerberry)
Viburnum acerifolium (Mapleleaf Viburnum)
Viburnum alnifolium (Hobblebush Viburnum)
Viburnum cassinoides (Witherod Viburnum)
Viburnum nudum (Possumhaw Viburnum)
Viburnum trilobum (American Cranberrybush Viburnum)

Vitis labrusca (Fox Grape)
Vitis riparia (Riverbank Grape)

POISONOUS FRUIT:
fruit poisonous if eaten,
indicator — *Ilex verticillata* (Common Winterberry)

Euonymus americanus (Brook Euonymus)
Euonymus obovatus (Running Euonymus)
Ilex decidua (Possumhaw)

Ilex glabra (Inkberry)
Ilex verticillata (Common Winterberry)

Cocculus carolinus (Carolina Snailseed)
Menispermum canadense (Common Moonseed)

Parthenocissus quinquefolia (Virginia Creeper)
Wistaria macrostachya (Kentucky Wistaria)

EDIBLE LEAVES:
foliage edible and nutritious,
indicator — *Comptonia peregrina* (Sweetfern)

Arctostaphylos uva-ursi (Bearberry)
Ceanothus americanus (Jerseytea Ceanothus)
Comptonia peregrina (Sweetfern)
Gaultheria procumbens (Checkerberry Wintergreen)
Ledum groenlandicum (Labradortea Ledum)

Myrica pensylvanica (Northern Bayberry)
Pinus aristata (Bristlecone Pine)
Potentilla fruticosa (Bush Cinquefoil)
Salix humilis (Prairie Willow)
Salix lucida (Shining Willow)

Smilax glauca (Cat Greenbrier)
Smilax rotundifolia (Common Greenbrier)

Smilax tamnoides (Bamboo Greenbrier)

POISONOUS LEAVES:
foliage poisonous if eaten and/or contacted with skin,
indicator — *Hydrangea arborescens* (Smooth Hydrangea)

Cephalanthus occidentalis (Common Buttonbush)
Hydrangea arborescens (Smooth Hydrangea)
Hydrangea quercifolia (Oakleaf Hydrangea)

Leucothoe catesbaei (Drooping Leucothoe)
Lyonia ligustrina (He-hucklberry)

Campsis radicans (Common Trumpetcreeper)
Clematis verticillaris (Rock Clematis)

Clematis virginiana (Virginsbower)

EDIBLE ROOTS:
tubers, rhizomes, corms, bulbs, or roots edible and nutritious,
indicator — *Smilax glauca* (Cat Greenbrier)

Smilax glauca (Cat Greenbrier)
Smilax rotundifolia (Common Greenbrier)

Smilax tamnoides (Bamboo Greenbrier)

EDIBLE FLOWERS:
flower petals and parts edible and nutritious,
indicator — *Rosa carolina* (Carolina Rose)

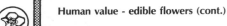

Epigaea repens (Trailing-arbutus)
Rosa carolina (Carolina Rose)
Rosa setigera (Prairie Rose)

Sambucus canadensis (American Elder)
Yucca filamentosa (Adamsneedle Yucca)

PHENOLOGICAL CALENDAR:

Rain, snow, fog, and seasonal change alter human perception of plant qualities. The plant is viewed as a dynamic changeable element. Plants are the most dynamic materials used by the designer. Different plants have different timing in the emergence, development, maturity, senescence, and drop periods of their leaves. Flowering and fruiting periods also vary from species to species. The life cycle stages correlate with seasonal variation in temperature in temperate regions. Phenological phases delineated in Table II include calendar dates for leaf emergence, flowering, fruit ripeness, fruit dissemination, and leaf drop.

The periods of leaf emergence presented in this book represent the average date for the first fully formed leaf for each species. Leaf drop refers to the autumn calendar period when the leaves of deciduous plants are falling to the ground in large numbers. Drop periods distinguished in this book represent the average date when each species is divested of 50% of its leaves. Flower season refers to the period of time the blossoms remain ornamentally effective. Similarly, fruit season refers to the period of time during which the ripe fruits remain ornamentally effective.

Phenophase periods have been coded on two levels of detail giving the designer the opportunity to select plants which generally flower, for example, during a particular month or specifically flower for a designated part of that month. Three partial month categories are distinguished for designer consideration.

EARLY:
   Month days 1-10

MID:
   Month days 11-20

LATE:
   Month days 21-31

The actual calendar day which a certain plant initiates a particular phenophase varies from year to year in response to the unpredictability of optimum temperature and moisture conditions. Similarly the length of phenophase duration or the amount of time that particular plant characteristics remains ornamentally effective varies with annual weather fluctuations. However, observations suggest that certain species always coincide in phenophase periods and that the progressive sequencing between other species can be forecast.

For example, American Filbert (*Corylus americana*) and Common Alder (*Alnus serrulata*) consistently bloom at the same time. These species are followed several weeks later by Atlantic Leatherwood (*Dirca palustris*). The actual dates vary annually, but the sequence is the same.

Another important factor causing a variance in the specific phenophase dates is the geographic distribution of the species. Common Buttonbush (*Cephalanthus occidentalis*) blooms up to six weeks earlier in the southern latitude of its natural range than along the northern limits. Differences in phenophase dates at higher altitudes is also apparent. Common Deerberry (*Vaccinium stamineum*) leafs out many days later in the higher elevations of the North Carolina mountains than it does in the surrounding valleys and the coastal plain.

Plant phenophases have been annually monitored by professional groups and respected individuals for most areas of the United States and Southern Canada. The phenological calendar presented in Table II, plots the normal phenophase periods for shrubs and vines in our area (latitude 45° north). These can easily

Phenological Calendar: Shrubs — Table II

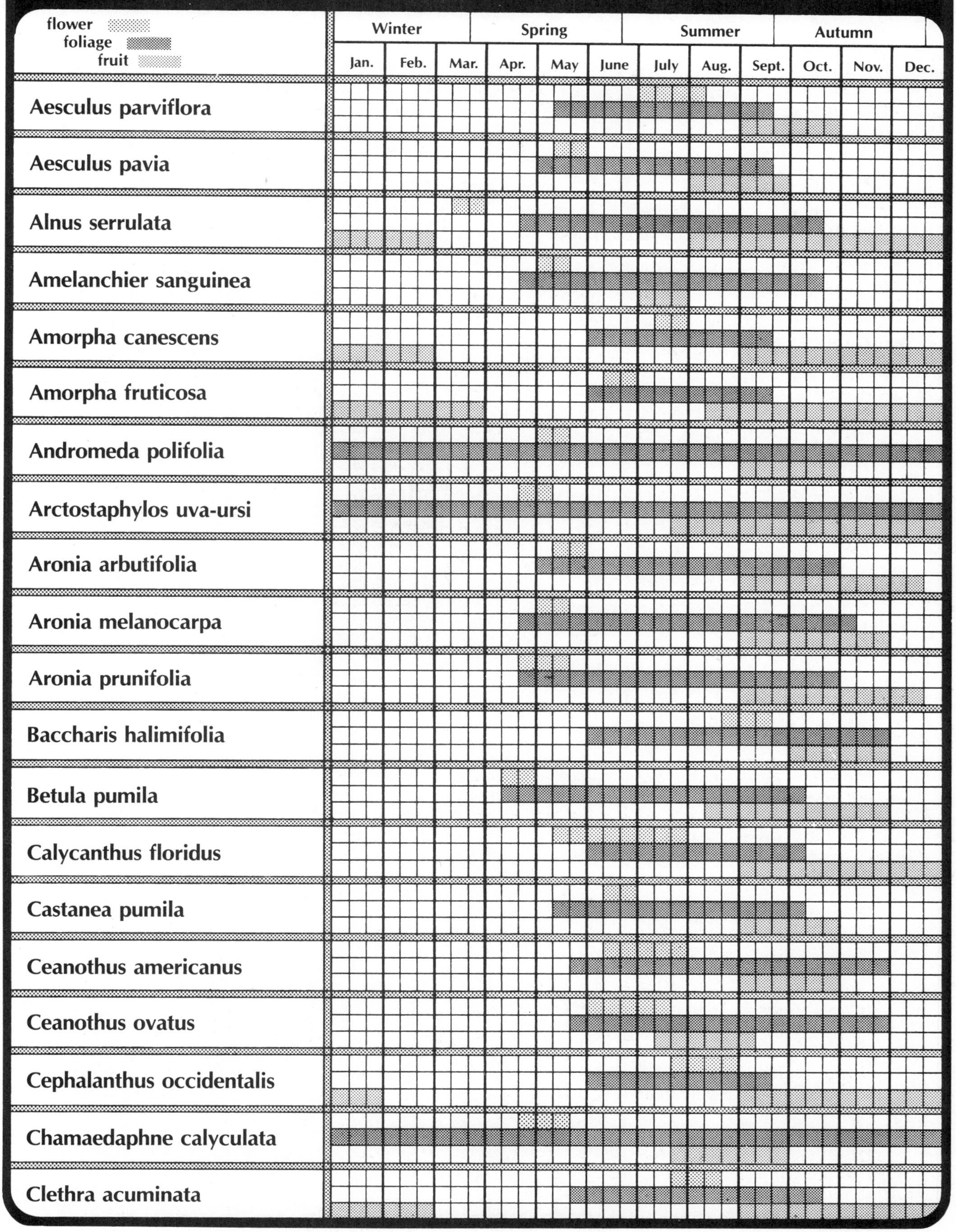

Legend:
- flower
- foliage
- fruit

	Winter			Spring			Summer			Autumn		
	Jan.	Feb.	Mar.	Apr.	May	June	July	Aug.	Sept.	Oct.	Nov.	Dec.
Aesculus parviflora												
Aesculus pavia												
Alnus serrulata												
Amelanchier sanguinea												
Amorpha canescens												
Amorpha fruticosa												
Andromeda polifolia												
Arctostaphylos uva-ursi												
Aronia arbutifolia												
Aronia melanocarpa												
Aronia prunifolia												
Baccharis halimifolia												
Betula pumila												
Calycanthus floridus												
Castanea pumila												
Ceanothus americanus												
Ceanothus ovatus												
Cephalanthus occidentalis												
Chamaedaphne calyculata												
Clethra acuminata												

443

		Winter			Spring			Summer			Autumn		
flower ▒		Jan.	Feb.	Mar.	Apr.	May	June	July	Aug.	Sept.	Oct.	Nov.	Dec.
foliage ▓													
fruit ▒													
Clethra alnifolia													
Comptonia peregrina													
Cornus amomum													
Cornus canadensis													
Cornus racemosa													
Cornus rugosa													
Cornus stolonifera													
Corylus americana													
Corylus cornuta													
Cyrilla racemiflora													
Diervilla lonicera													
Dirca palustris													
Elaeagnus commutata													
Epigaea repens													
Euonymus americanus													
Euonymus obovatus													
Fothergilla gardeni													
Fothergilla major													
Gaultheria procumbens													
Hamamelis vernalis													

Phenological Calendar: Shrubs — Table II

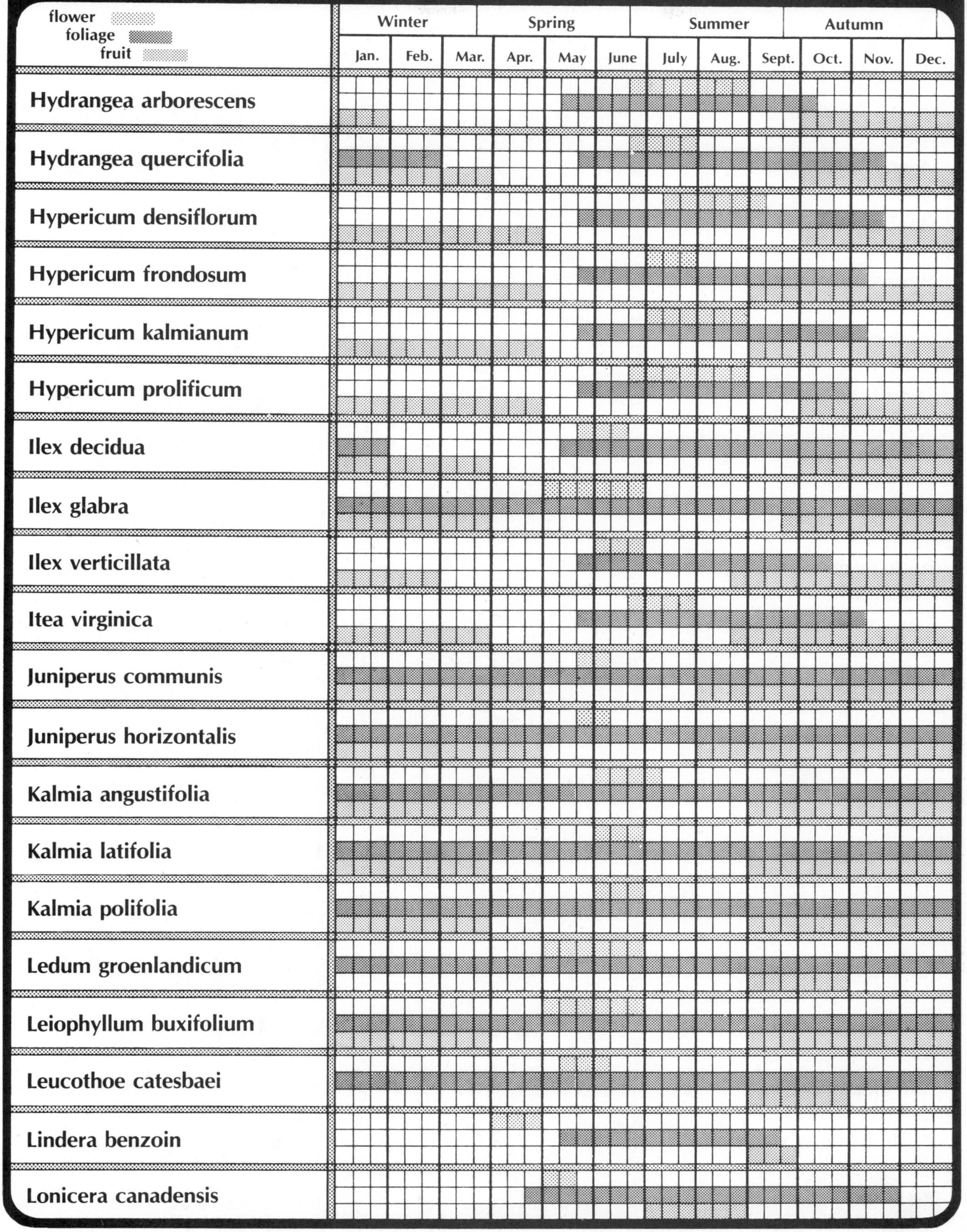

Legend:
- flower
- foliage
- fruit

Species	Winter			Spring			Summer			Autumn		
	Jan.	Feb.	Mar.	Apr.	May	June	July	Aug.	Sept.	Oct.	Nov.	Dec.
Hydrangea arborescens												
Hydrangea quercifolia												
Hypericum densiflorum												
Hypericum frondosum												
Hypericum kalmianum												
Hypericum prolificum												
Ilex decidua												
Ilex glabra												
Ilex verticillata												
Itea virginica												
Juniperus communis												
Juniperus horizontalis												
Kalmia angustifolia												
Kalmia latifolia												
Kalmia polifolia												
Ledum groenlandicum												
Leiophyllum buxifolium												
Leucothoe catesbaei												
Lindera benzoin												
Lonicera canadensis												

flower ▒ foliage ▓ fruit ▒	Winter			Spring			Summer			Autumn		
	Jan.	Feb.	Mar.	Apr.	May	June	July	Aug.	Sept.	Oct.	Nov.	Dec.
Lyonia ligustrina												
Magnolia virginiana												
Mahonia aquifolium												
Myrica pensylvanica												
Neviusia alabamensis												
Pachistima canbyi												
Philadelphus grandiflorus												
Physocarpus opulifolius												
Pieris floribunda												
Pinus aristata												
Potentilla fruticosa												
Prunus hortulana												
Quercus ilicifolia												
Quercus prinoides												
Rhododendron arborescens												
Rhododendron calendulaceum												
Rhododendron carolinianum												
Rhododendron catawbiense												
Rhododendron nudiflorum												
Rhododendron roseum												

Phenological Calendar: Shrubs

Table II

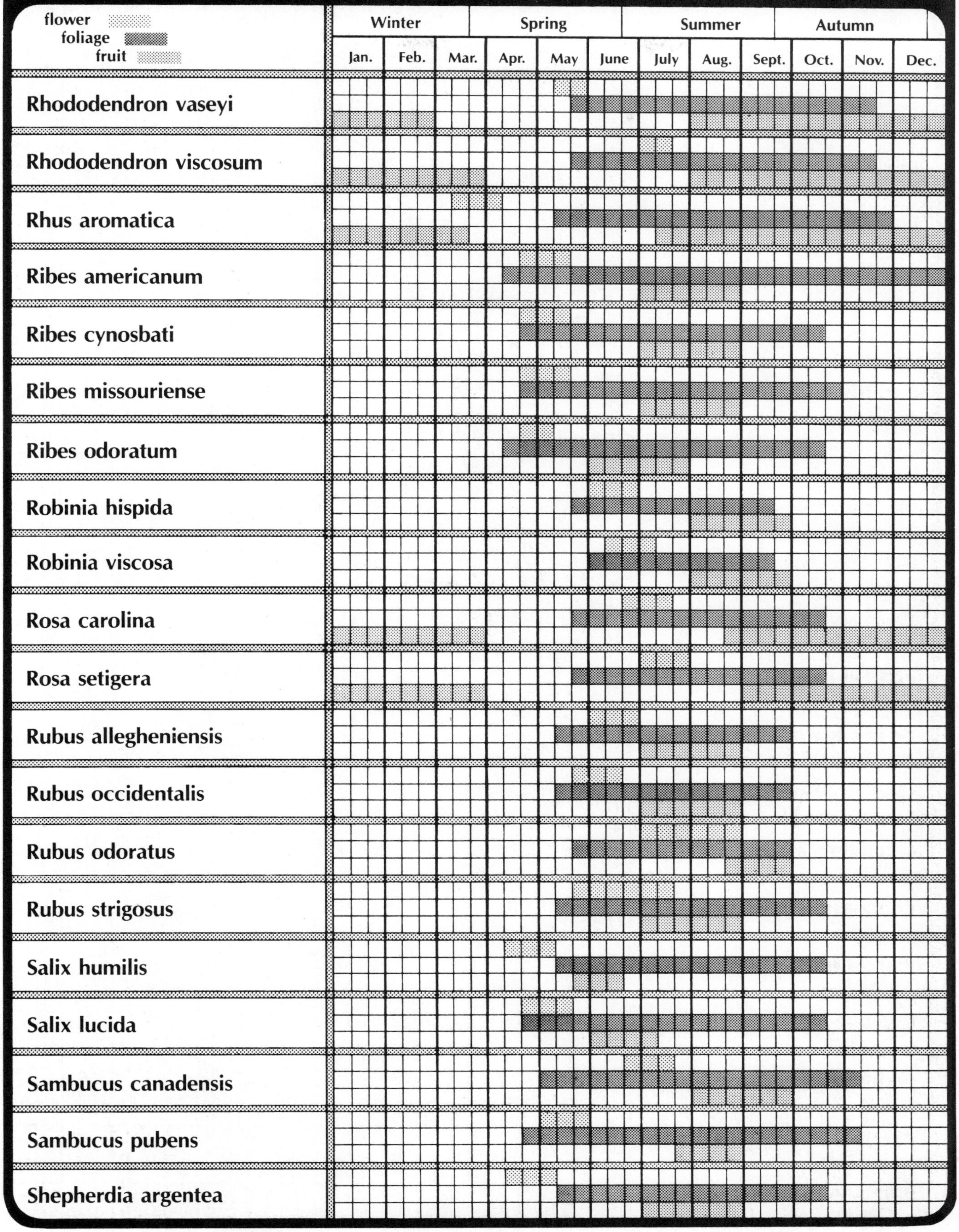

		Winter			Spring			Summer			Autumn		
flower / foliage / fruit		Jan.	Feb.	Mar.	Apr.	May	June	July	Aug.	Sept.	Oct.	Nov.	Dec.
Rhododendron vaseyi													
Rhododendron viscosum													
Rhus aromatica													
Ribes americanum													
Ribes cynosbati													
Ribes missouriense													
Ribes odoratum													
Robinia hispida													
Robinia viscosa													
Rosa carolina													
Rosa setigera													
Rubus allegheniensis													
Rubus occidentalis													
Rubus odoratus													
Rubus strigosus													
Salix humilis													
Salix lucida													
Sambucus canadensis													
Sambucus pubens													
Shepherdia argentea													

447

Phenological Calendar: Shrubs

Table II

	Winter			Spring			Summer			Autumn		
flower / foliage / fruit	Jan.	Feb.	Mar.	Apr.	May	June	July	Aug.	Sept.	Oct.	Nov.	Dec.
Shepherdia canadensis												
Spiraea alba												
Spiraea corymbosa												
Spiraea tomentosa												
Staphylea trifolia												
Stewartia ovata												
Symphoricarpos albus												
Symphoricarpos occidentalis												
Symphoricarpos orbiculatus												
Taxus canadensis												
Vaccinium angustifolium												
Vaccinium corymbosum												
Vaccinium macrocarpum												
Vaccinium stamineum												
Viburnum acerifolium												
Viburnum alnifolium												
Viburnum cassinoides												
Viburnum dentatum												
Viburnum nudum												
Viburnum rafinesquianum												

Phenological Calendar: Shrubs

Table II

		Winter			Spring			Summer			Autumn		
flower ▓ foliage ▓ fruit ▓		Jan.	Feb.	Mar.	Apr.	May	June	July	Aug.	Sept.	Oct.	Nov.	Dec.
Viburnum trilobum													
Xanthorhiza simplicissima													
Yucca filamentosa													
Zenobia pulverulenta													

Phenological Calendar: Vines

Table II

	flower	foliage	fruit	Winter			Spring			Summer			Autumn		
				Jan.	Feb.	Mar.	Apr.	May	June	July	Aug.	Sept.	Oct.	Nov.	Dec.
Ampelopsis arborea															
Ampelopsis cordata															
Aristolochia durior															
Berchemia scandens															
Bignonia capreolata															
Campsis radicans															
Celastrus scandens															
Clematis verticillaris															
Clematis virginiana															
Cocculus carolinus															
Lonicera dioica															
Lonicera sempervirens															
Menispermum canadense															
Parthenocissus quinquefolia															
Smilax glauca															
Smilax rotundifolia															
Smilax tamnoides															
Toxicodendron radicans															
Vitis labrusca															
Vitis riparia															

450

Phenological Calendar: Vines

Table II

	flower ▨			Winter			Spring			Summer			Autumn		
	foliage ▨			Jan.	Feb.	Mar.	Apr.	May	June	July	Aug.	Sept.	Oct.	Nov.	Dec.
Wistaria macrostachya															

be adjusted for other regions where the same species is hardy. Once the normal phenophase periods for several key indicator shrubs or vines can be established in other areas and correlated with the calendar herein, the corresponding periods for all other species can be projected.

Phenological calendars of this type are tools which enable the designer to compare, organize, explore, and evaluate the complex of possible plant to plant and plant to man relationships. It remains the challenge of the designer to develop a viable program which demonstrates this understanding.

MOST SUITABLE HABITAT:

A community is an assemblage of living organisms having a mutual relationship among themselves and to their environment (habitat). Each vegetation assemblage then is a kind of plant community of definite composition presenting a uniform appearance and growing in a uniform suitable habitat. The community concept is a useful guide to the environmental planner. Knowing the correlation between specific communities and their specific habitat tolerances is essential because growth and survival for a particular community/species varies significantly from one habitat to another.

Environmental factors that influence plant distribution include those of climate, such as various measures of light, radiation, humidity, precipitation and air movement. Distribution is also influenced by soil characteristics such as texture, structure and depth, moisture capacity and drainage, nutrient content, and topographic position. Species vary in their ability to survive and reproduce in different habitats. Some survive extreme heat, others extreme cold. Many require much continuous moisture, others small amounts periodically. Some species such as Pasture Gooseberry (*Ribes cynosbati*) have a broad ecologic amplitude and are found over wide ranges of climate and site. Other species, like Snowwreath (*Neviusia alabamensis*), have a narrow amplitude with limited geographic distribution and specific habitat preference. Within any given region where habitat is held in dynamic equilibrium, plant communities of fairly homogeneous composition consistently recur. This integral relationship of plant and habitat represents the maximum utilization of available environmental resources.

The first step in the recognition of the major or minor habitat types for general landscape use is to identify the broad vegetational cover differences present in southern Canada and eastern and central United States (Fig. 1). The major portion of the vegetation can be divided into ten formation types based upon differences as expressed by their growth form characteristics:

 FOREST, WOODLAND:
    trees forming closed stands, greater than 50 percent crown cover.

 SAVANNA, GLADE, BARRENS:
    grasslands with scattered trees only, 5 to 50 percent tree crown cover.

 PRAIRIE:
    communities with over half of the dominance contributed by grasses, less than 5 percent tree crown cover.

 MEADOW:
    communities dominated by herbaceous plants, less than 5 percent tree crown cover.

 BOG, SWAMP:
    communities dominated by shrubs, water table at or just below soil surface during most of growing season; low, evergreen, ericaceous shrubs, sphagnum understory (Bog) or tall deciduous shrubs, no sphagnum (Swamp).

 SPRING, FEN:
    communities of spring-fed, internally flowing calcareous waters, over half of the dominance contributed by grass and sedge-like species.

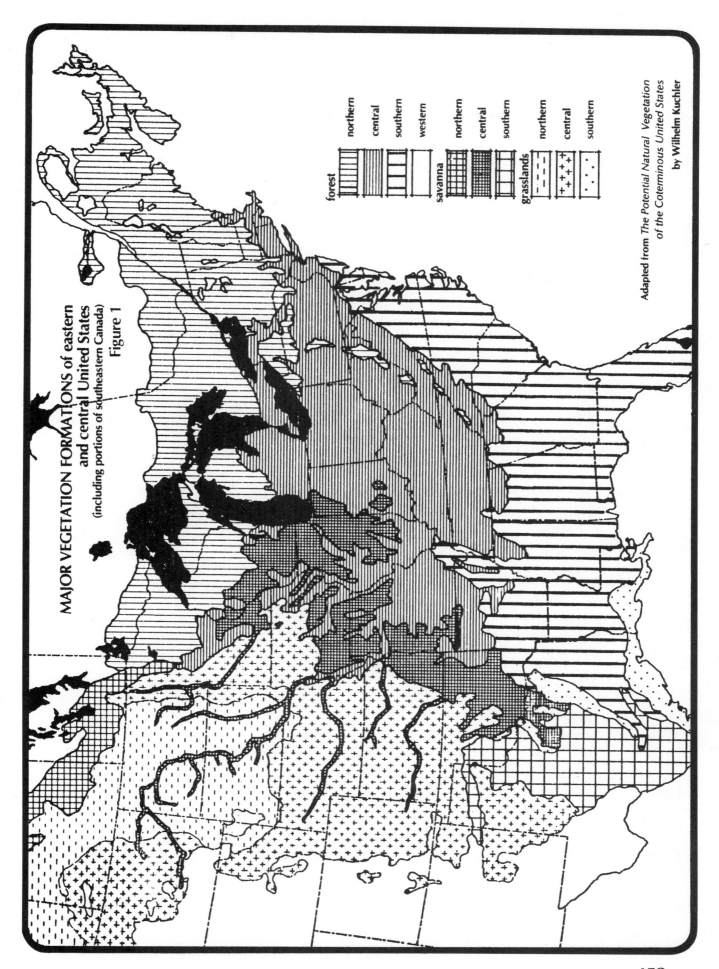

MAJOR VEGETATION FORMATIONS of eastern
and central United States
(including portions of southeastern Canada)
Figure 1

forest
northern
central
southern
western

savanna
northern
central
southern

grasslands
northern
central
southern

Adapted from *The Potential Natural Vegetation
of the Coterminous United States*
by Wilhelm Kuchler

DUNE:
relatively open communities of essentially level topographies with rocky or sandy soils, often less than 50 percent coverage in the ground layer; communities of lake/marine dunes.

CLIFF; OPEN:
relatively open communities of rock outcrops and cliffs, often less than 50 percent coverage in ground layer, exposed to full sun.

CLIFF; SHADED:
similar to above but shaded by trees or other cliffs.

OLD FIELD:
pioneer species colonizing open disturbed areas, including abandoned fields and pasture lands, roadsides, fence rows, waste areas and edge zones between forest and field.

The various flora are not distributed uniformly within each vegetation formation, rather there are several distinct floristic regions (Fig. 1). The significance of floristic regions lies in the influences that these regional climates have on the floristic composition of the individual communities adapted to each. Four floristic regions are classified below.

NORTHERN:
cold climate region of southern Canada and the northern United States dominated by both coniferous and deciduous forest flora or cool season grassland flora.

CENTRAL:
primarily temperate cimate region of the central United States dominated by deciduous forest flora or by temperate season grassland flora.

SOUTHERN:
warm climate region of the southern United States dominated by mixed forest including broadleaf deciduous, broadleaf evergreen, and coniferous evergreen species or by warm season grassland flora.

WESTERN:
primarily cold climate region of the western United States dominated by mountain coniferous forest.

The over-riding environmental factor determining the disposition of plant communities is plant available soil moisture. The assembled plant species are placed under selective stress along the moisture gradients of the landscape. Five soil moisture gradient segments are delineated:

DRY:
high banks, calcareous waterworn cliffs, steep rocky land, droughty excessively drained sandy soils or shallow stony soils over rock.

MESIC-DRY:
dryer slopes and upland flats, generally warmer south- and west-facing slope aspects, upland ridges and ravines; direct sun exposure accelerates evaporation stress, reduces available soil moisture and greatly increases temperature near the ground.

MESIC:
moist ravines and sheltered coves, moist but well drained slopes and uplands, generally north- and east-facing slope aspects; protection from direct sun exposure and to prevailing dry winds together with cool air drainage into these areas maintains a regimen of greater available soil moisture, reduced evaporation stress and stable temperature near the ground.

WET-MESIC:
alluvial bottomlands and elevated terraces of major streams, where soil moisture supply is in excess of that falling as rain, areas of intermittent yearly flooding of short duration, characterized by excess surface wetness in winter and spring to nearly droughty conditions during mid-summer low water stages.

WET:
river and streamside margins, floodplain depressions (areas subject to frequent and violent inundation due to cyclic flooding in late winter and spring), lake margin and swamp, potholes, slow draining flats

	Floristic Region				Vegetation Formation										Moisture Gradient				
	northern	central	southern	western	bog-swamp	spring-fen	meadow	prairie	savanna-glade-barrens	forest-woodland	cliff-moist/dry	summits-balds	dune	old field-woods edge	wet	wet-mesic	mesic	mesic-dry	dry
Aesculus parviflora			■							■							■		
Aesculus pavia			■							■				■			■		
Alnus serrulata		■	■		■										■	■			
Amelanchier sanguinea	■	■							■									■	■
Amorpha canescens		■						■											■
Amorpha fruticosa		■	■				■									■	■		
Andromeda polifolia	■				■										■				
Arctostaphylos uva-ursi	■											■	■						■
Aronia arbutifolia		■			■										■	■			
Aronia melanocarpa	■				■										■	■			
Aronia prunifolia	■				■										■	■			
Baccharis halimifolia			■										■		■	■			
Betula pumila	■				■	■									■				
Calycanthus floridus			■							■							■	■	
Castanea pumila			■						■					■				■	■
Ceanothus americanus		■						■	■									■	■
Ceanothus ovatus		■						■										■	■
Cephalanthus occidentalis		■	■		■										■	■			
Chamaedaphne calyculata	■				■										■				
Clethra acuminata			■							■	■						■	■	
Clethra alnifolia			■		■										■	■			
Comptonia peregrina	■												■					■	■
Cornus amomum		■	■				■								■	■			
Cornus canadensis	■									■						■	■		
Cornus racemosa	■	■					■							■		■	■		

	Floristic Region				Vegetation Formation										Moisture Gradient				
	northern	central	southern	western	bog-swamp	spring-fen	meadow	prairie	savanna-glade-barrens	forest-woodland	cliff-moist/dry	summits-balds	dune	old field-woods edge	wet	wet-mesic	mesic	mesic-dry	dry
Cornus rugosa	■									■								■	
Cornus stolonifera	■				■	■								■	■				
Corylus americana	■	■	■						■	■				■			■	■	
Corylus cornuta	■								■	■				■			■	■	
Cyrilla racemiflora			■		■								■		■				
Diervilla lonicera	■									■	■						■	■	
Dirca palustris	■	■								■							■		
Elaeagnus commutata	■												■				■	■	
Epigaea repens	■									■			■				■	■	
Euonymus americanus		■	■							■				■		■	■		
Euonymus obovatus		■	■							■							■		
Fothergilla gardeni			■		■										■				
Fothergilla major			■							■							■		
Gaultheria procumbens	■				■					■			■		■		■		
Hamamelis vernalis			■							■					■		■		
Hydrangea arborescens			■							■	■						■		
Hydrangea quercifolia			■							■							■		
Hypericum densiflorum		■	■			■					■				■		■		
Hypericum frondosum			■					■	■		■						■	■	
Hypericum kalmianum	■					■							■		■		■		
Hypericum prolificum		■	■						■	■	■						■	■	
Ilex decidua			■		■					■					■				
Ilex glabra			■		■								■		■				
Ilex verticillata	■	■	■		■					■					■				
Itea virginica			■		■										■				

	Floristic Region				Vegetation Formation										Moisture Gradient				
	northern	central	southern	western	bog-swamp	spring-fen	meadow	prairie	savanna-glade-barrens	forest-woodland	cliff-moist/dry	summits-balds	dune	old field-woods edge	wet	wet-mesic	mesic	mesic-dry	dry
Juniperus communis	•			•					•		•	•						•	
Juniperus horizontalis	•			•														•	•
Kalmia angustifolia	•						•				•						•		
Kalmia latifolia		•	•						•	•							•	•	
Kalmia polifolia	•				•										•	•			
Ledum groenlandicum	•				•										•				
Leiophyllum buxifolium		•	•						•		•	•						•	•
Leucothoe catesbaei		•	•		•					•						•	•		
Lindera benzoin		•	•							•						•	•		
Lonicera canadensis	•									•	•						•		
Lyonia ligustrina		•	•		•					•						•	•		
Magnolia virginiana		•	•		•					•						•	•		
Mahonia aquifolium			•	•						•	•						•	•	
Myrica pensylvanica		•	•						•				•	•			•	•	
Neviusia alabamensis		•	•							•	•						•	•	
Pachistima canbyi		•	•							•	•						•	•	
Philadelphus grandiflorus		•	•							•	•					•	•		
Physocarpus opulifolius		•	•							•	•					•	•	•	
Pieris floribunda		•	•		•					•		•				•	•		
Pinus aristata				•						•		•						•	•
Potentilla fruticosa	•			•		•	•				•					•	•		
Prunus hortulana		•	•					•	•					•				•	
Quercus ilicifolia	•	•							•	•	•			•					•
Quercus prinoides	•	•							•	•	•							•	•
Rhododendron arborescens		•	•		•					•						•	•		

	Floristic Region				Vegetation Formation										Moisture Gradient				
	northern	central	southern	western	bog-swamp	spring-fen	meadow	prairie	savanna-glade-barrens	forest-woodland	cliff-moist/dry	summits-balds	dune	old field-woods edge	wet	wet-mesic	mesic	mesic-dry	dry
Rhododendron calendulaceum		X								X		X						X	
Rhododendron carolinianum			X							X		X					X		
Rhododendron catawbiense			X							X		X					X		
Rhododendron nudiflorum		X								X		X					X		
Rhododendron roseum	X									X		X					X		
Rhododendron vaseyi			X							X		X					X		
Rhododendron viscosum		X			X	X									X				
Rhus aromatica	X								X	X	X		X					X	X
Ribes americanum	X				X	X				X					X	X			
Ribes cynosbati	X	X								X	X			X			X		
Ribes missouriense		X								X	X			X			X		
Ribes odoratum				X						X	X			X				X	X
Robinia hispida			X							X		X					X		
Robinia viscosa			X							X		X					X		
Rosa carolina	X	X					X	X	X				X	X				X	X
Rosa setigera		X					X	X		X				X		X	X		
Rubus allegheniensis	X						X			X				X			X		
Rubus occidentalis	X						X			X				X			X	X	
Rubus odoratus	X									X	X			X		X	X		
Rubus strigosus	X				X	X				X				X	X	X			
Salix humilis	X					X	X		X				X	X	X	X			
Salix lucida	X				X	X									X				
Sambucus canadensis	X	X					X			X				X	X	X			
Sambucus pubens	X									X	X			X		X	X		
Shepherdia argentea				X									X					X	X

	Floristic Region				Vegetation Formation										Moisture Gradient				
	northern	central	southern	western	bog-swamp	spring-fen	meadow	prairie	savanna-glade-barrens	forest-woodland	cliff-moist/dry	summits-balds	dune	old field-woods edge	wet	wet-mesic	mesic	mesic-dry	dry
Shepherdia canadensis	■			■						■								■	
Spiraea alba	■	■	■	■	■	■	■						■	■		■			
Spiraea corymbosa	■	■	■				■				■						■		
Spiraea tomentosa	■	■	■		■	■	■									■			
Staphylea trifolia	■	■	■	■						■							■		
Stewartia ovata			■							■							■		
Symphoricarpos albus	■	■		■					■		■							■	
Symphoricarpos occidentalis	■	■		■				■			■							■	
Symphoricarpos orbiculatus	■	■	■	■					■									■	
Taxus canadensis	■	■								■	■						■		
Vaccinium angustifolium	■	■	■						■	■			■				■		
Vaccinium corymbosum	■	■	■		■					■						■			
Vaccinium macrocarpum	■	■			■										■				
Vaccinium stamineum		■	■						■	■								■	
Viburnum acerifolium	■	■	■							■	■						■		
Viburnum alnifolium	■									■							■		
Viburnum cassinoides	■	■			■					■			■			■			
Viburnum dentatum	■	■	■	■						■				■			■		
Viburnum nudum			■		■					■						■			
Viburnum rafinesquianum	■	■								■	■						■		
Viburnum trilobum	■	■								■				■		■			
Xanthorhiza simplicissima		■	■		■					■						■			
Yucca filamentosa			■						■				■						■
Zenobia pulverulenta			■		■					■						■			

	Floristic Region				Vegetation Formation										Moisture Gradient				
	northern	central	southern	western	bog-swamp	spring-fen	meadow	prairie	savanna-glade-barrens	forest-woodland	cliff-moist/dry	summits-balds	dune	old field-woods edge	wet	wet-mesic	mesic	mesic-dry	dry
Ampelopsis arborea			■	■	■					■				■					
Ampelopsis cordata		■	■	■	■					■				■					
Aristolochia durior		■	■							■	■			■			■		
Berchemia scandens			■	■	■					■				■					
Bignonia capreolata			■	■	■					■				■					
Campsis radicans		■	■	■	■					■				■					
Celastrus scandens	■	■	■	■						■				■					
Clematis verticillaris	■									■	■			■			■		
Clematis virginiana	■	■	■	■			■			■				■					
Cocculus carolinus		■	■		■					■				■					
Lonicera dioica	■	■						■		■				■			■		
Lonicera sempervirens			■	■						■				■					
Menispermum canadense	■	■	■	■						■				■					
Parthenocissus quinquefolia	■	■	■	■						■				■					
Smilax glauca		■	■	■						■			■	■					
Smilax rotundifolia		■	■	■						■				■					
Smilax tamnoides	■	■	■	■						■				■					
Toxicodendron radicans	■	■	■	■						■				■					
Vitis labrusca	■	■	■							■				■					
Vitis riparia	■	■	■	■						■				■					
Wistaria macrostachya			■		■					■				■					

and depressions, sluggish streams (areas of poor internal or surface drainage supporting standing water much of the time), high water tables.

Table III synthesizes the habitat classification format as adapted from Curtis, 1959. By multiplying the five moisture gradient segments (wet to dry) with the ten vegetational formations and the four floristic regions a sum of 200 different habitat situations can be described.

"The environmental designer works with the land, the surface of the earth; his decisions deal with the arrangement of the land and the elements on it for man's use and enjoyment. His challenge is to improve man's relationship with his environment. The disposition of plants is his inescapable responsibility, since plants are integral parts of that physical environment." (Dyas 1970)

Table III provides rapid assessment of the most suitable habitat conditions available to the native shrub and vine species.

FLOOD TOLERANCE:

The observation of natural systems and specific habitats has enabled the professional to confidently extrapolate a more complete picture of the effects of flooding and elevated water table on woody plants. Shrubs and vines vary greatly in their ability to withstand root suffocation by prolonged inundation or by a high water table lying at just below the soil surface.

In wet habitats along rivers and streams, lakes, bogs, and swamps throughout the region, a mosaic of vegetation consistently recurs in a successional pattern that generally parallels the present water margin and maintains a uniform species to species relationship. This pattern correlates directly with the flood/high water table tolerance of each species.

A characteristic feature of many of the small, non-outlet glacial lakes found in Canada and the northern lake states is a band of vegetation that floats over the water along the shore of the lake. This is commonly arranged in a concentric or zonal pattern, with sedges (*Carex spp.*) and sedgelike plants immediately at the waters edge. These are backed by an area of low vegetation made up of a mat of sphagnum moss covered primarily by low ericaceous shrubs including Leatherleaf (*Chamaedaphne calyculata*), Bogrosemary Andromeda (*Andromeda glaucophylla*), Labradortea Ledum (*Ledum groenlandicum*), kalmia (*Kalmia spp.*), many blueberries and cranberries (*Vaccinium spp.*) and Checkerberry Wintergreen (*Gaultheria procumbens*). Farther back on slightly drier ground there is a 20 or 30 meter wide ring of large shrubs including Redosier Dogwood (*Cornus stolonifera*), willow (*Salix spp.*), alder (*Alnus spp.*), the dwarf birches (*Betula pumila* and *Betula glandulosa*), American Elder (*Sambucus canadensis*) and American Black Currant (*Ribes americanum*). Still closer to the original shore a ring of scattered saplings of American Larch (*Larix decidua*), Black Spruce (*Picea mariana*) and Red Maple (*Acer rubrum*) give way to closed spruce-larch forest (Curtis 1959).

Similar hydrosere zonation is also observed in southern, central and midwestern floristic regions.

The following plant lists should assist in the development of a viable vegetation management policy where frequent and prolonged inundation/high water table are a concern. Five classes of tolerance are considered by projecting the survival data for each species against the percent of time flooded or exposed to saturated soils due to high water table during the growing season (Hall and Smith, 1955). Attention is focused on the growing season because periodic winter flooding/high water table is of little significance in the survival of deciduous woody plants. Flooding/high water table during the growing season is mainly responsible for the death and injury observed.

VERY TOLERANT:
generally lowland wet species surviving when flooded or exposed to high water table more than 40

percent of the growing season,
indicator — *Cephalanthus occidentalis* (Common Buttonbush)

Alnus serrulata   (Common Alder)
Amorpha fruticosa   (Indigobush Amorpha)
Andromeda polifolia   (Bogrosemary Andromeda)
Aronia arbutifolia   (Red Chokeberry)
Aronia melanocarpa   (Black Chokeberry)
Aronia prunifolia   (Purplefruit Chokeberry)
Baccharis halimifolia   (Eastern Baccharis)
Betula pumila   (Low Birch)
Cephalanthus occidentalis   (Common Buttonbush)
Chamaedaphne calyculata   (Leatherleaf)
Clethra alnifolia   (Summersweet Clethra)
Cornus amomum   (Silky Dogwood)
Cornus stolonifera   (Redosier Dogwood)
Cyrilla racemiflora   (American Cyrilla)
Gaultheria procumbens   (Checkerberry Wintergreen)
Hamamelis vernalis   (Vernal Witchhazel)
Ilex decidua   (Possumhaw)
Ilex glabra   (Inkberry)
Ilex verticillata   (Common Winterberry)
Itea virginica   (Virginia Sweetspire)

Kalmia angustifolia   (Lambkill Kalmia)
Kalmia latifolia   (Mountainlaurel Kalmia)
Kalmia polifolia   (Bog Kalmia)
Ledum groenlandicum   (Labradortea Ledum)
Lyonia ligustrina   (He-huckleberry)
Magnolia virginiana   (Sweetbay Magnolia)
Myrica pensylvanica   (Northern Bayberry)
Physocarpus opulifolius   (Common Ninebark)
Potentilla fruticosa   (Bush Cinquefoil)
Rhododendron viscosum   (Swamp Azalea)
Ribes americanum   (American Black Currant)
Salix lucida   (Shining Willow)
Sambucus canadensis   (American Elder)
Spiraea alba   (Narrowleaf Meadowsweet Spirea)
Spiraea tomentosa   (Hardhack Spirea)
Vaccinium angustifolium   (Lowbush Blueberry)
Vaccinium corymbosum   (Highbush Blueberry)
Vaccinium macrocarpum   (Cranberry)
Viburnum cassinoides   (Witherod Viburnum)

Ampelopsis arborea   (Peppervine)
Ampelopsis cordata   (Heartleaf Ampelopsis)
Berchemia scandens   (Alabama Supplejack)
Bignonia capreolata   (Crossvine)

Menispermum canadense   (Common Moonseed)
Parthenocissus quinquefolia   (Virginia Creeper)
Toxicodendron radicans   (Common Poisonivy)
Vitis riparia   (Riverbank Grape)

TOLERANT:
generally lowland wet species surviving when flooded or exposed to high water table more than 30
percent of the growing season but less than 40 percent,
indicator — *Viburnum dentatum* (Arrowwood Viburnum)

Calycanthus floridus   (Common Sweetshrub)
Hypericum densiflorum   (Dense Hypericum)
Hypericum kalmianum   (Kalm St.Johnswort)
Rhododendron arborescens   (Sweet Azalea)
Rhododendron nudiflorum   (Pinxterbloom Azalea)
Rhododendron vaseyi   (Pinkshell Azalea)

Viburnum dentatum   (Arrowwood Viburnum)
Viburnum nudum   (Possumhaw Viburnum)
Viburnum trilobum   (American Cranberrybush Viburnum)
Xanthorhiza simplicissima   (Yellowroot)
Zenobia pulverulenta   (Dusty Zenobia)

Clematis virginiana   (Virginsbower)
Cocculus carolinus   (Carolina Snailseed)
Smilax rotundifolia   (Common Greenbrier)

Smilax tamnoides   (Bamboo Greenbrier)
Vitis labrusca   (Fox Grape)
Wistaria macrostachya   (Kentucky Wistaria)

INTERMEDIATE:
generally lowland wet-mesic species surviving occasional inundation or elevated water table between
20 and 30 percent of the growing season,
indicator — *Euonymus americanus* (Brook Euonymus)

Aesculus parviflora   (Bottlebrush Buckeye)
Aesculus pavia   (Red Buckeye)
Cornus racemosa   (Gray Dogwood)
Euonymus americanus   (Brook Euonymus)
Lindera benzoin   (Common Spicebush)
Rhododendron carolinianum   (Carolina Rhododendron)
Ribes cynosbati   (Pasture Gooseberry)
Ribes missouriense   (Missouri Gooseberry)
Rosa setigera   (Prairie Rose)

Rubus allegheniensis   (Allegany Blackberry)
Rubus occidentalis   (Blackcap Raspberry)
Rubus strigosus   (American Red Raspberry)
Salix humilis   (Prairie Willow)
Spiraea corymbosa   (Corymed Spirea)
Staphylea trifolia   (American Bladdernut)
Stewartia ovata   (Mountain Stewartia)
Symphoricarpos orbiculatus   (Indiancurrant Coralberry)

Campsis radicans   (Common Trumpetcreeper)
Celastrus scandens   (American Bittersweet)

Lonicera dioica   (Limber Honeysuckle)
Smilax glauca   (Cat Greenbrier)

INTOLERANT:

generally upland mesic and mesic-dry species rarely inundated or exposed to an elevated water table for periods of short duration, between 5 and 20 percent of the growing season (mesic-dry species commonly dying after 10 percent of growing season),
indicator — *Vaccinium stamineum (Common Deerberry)*

Amelanchier sanguinea   (Roundleaf Serviceberry)
Arctostaphylos uva-ursi   (Bearberry)
Castanea pumila   (Allegany Chinkapin)
Clethra acuminata   (Cinnamon Clethra)
Cornus canadensis   (Bunchberry Dogwood)
Cornus rugosa   (Roundleaf Dogwood)
Corylus americana   (American Filbert)
Corylus cornuta   (Beaked Filbert)
Diervilla lonicera   (Dwarf Bushhoneysuckle)
Euonymus obovatus   (Running Euonymus)
Fothergilla gardeni   (Dwarf Fothergilla)
Fothergilla major   (Large Fothergilla)
Hydrangea arborescens   (Smooth Hydrangea)
Hydrangea quercifolia   (Oakleaf Hydrangea)
Leucothoe catesbaei   (Drooping Leucothoe)
Lonicera canadensis   (American Fly Honeysuckle)

Mahonia aquifolium   (Oregongrape)
Pachistima canbyi   (Canby Pachistima)
Philadelphus grandiflorus   (Big Scentless Mockorange)
Pieris floribunda   (Mountain Pieris)
Rhododendron calendulaceum   (Flame Azalea)
Rhododendron catawbiense   (Catawba Rhododendron)
Rhododendron roseum   (Roseshell Azalea)
Ribes odoratum   (Clove Currant)
Robinia hispida   (Roseacacia Locust)
Robinia viscosa   (Clammy Locust)
Rosa carolina   (Carolina Rose)
Rubus odoratus   (Fragrant Thimbleberry)
Vaccinium stamineum   (Common Deerberry)
Viburnum acerifolium   (Mapleleaf Viburnum)
Viburnum alnifolium   (Hobblebush Viburnum)
Viburnum rafinesquianum   (Rafinesque Viburnum)

Aristolochia durior   (Common Dutchmanspipe)
Clematis verticillaris   (Rock Clematis)

Lonicera sempervirens   (Trumpet Honeysuckle)

VERY INTOLERANT:

generally upland dry species exhibiting immediate and rapid decline frequently culminating in death if inundated or exposed to elevated water table for more than 5 percent of the growing season,
indicator — *Ceanothus americanus* (Jerseytea Ceanothus)

Amorpha canescens   (Leadplant Amorpha)
Ceanothus americanus   (Jerseytea Ceanothus)
Ceanothus ovatus   (Inland Ceanothus)
Comptonia peregrina   (Sweetfern)
Dirca palustris   (Atlantic Leatherwood)
Elaeagnus commutata   (Silverberry)
Epigaea repens   (Trailing-arbutus)
Hypericum frondosum   (Golden St.Johnswort)
Hypericum prolificum   (Shrubby St.Johnswort)
Juniperus communis   (Common Juniper)
Juniperus horizontalis   (Creeping Juniper)
Leiophyllum buxifolium   (Box Sandmyrtle)
Neviusia alabamensis   (Snowwreath)

Pinus aristata   (Bristlecone Pine)
Prunus hortulana   (Hortulan Plum)
Quercus ilicifolia   (Scrub Oak)
Quercus prinoides   (Dwarf Chinkapin Oak)
Rhus aromatica   (Fragrant Sumac)
Sambucus pubens   (Scarlet Elder)
Shepherdia argentea   (Silver Buffaloberry)
Shepherdia canadensis   (Russet Buffaloberry)
Symphoricarpos albus   (Common Snowberry)
Symphoricarpos occidentalis   (Western Snowberry)
Taxus canadensis   (Canada Yew)
Yucca filmentosa   (Adamsneedle Yucca)

SHADE TOLERANCE:

Most plants do well in full sun exposure. Where plants are being considered for shaded or partially shaded site conditions however, it becomes important to know which will perform best and how much shade each will tolerate. An attempt has been made to quantify shade tolerance for native species using a method outlined by Samuel A. Graham, University of Michigan. The method involved rating a sample of each species numerically according to various tolerance indicators. The highest rating any species may have is a 10, the lowest a 0.

Usually the less shade tolerant plant materials of our native hardwood forests have a more open foliage pattern that permit more light to reach the forest floor. Consequently the oak-hickory type, for example, allows a greater amount of light to reach the forest floor that enables somewhat less shade tolerant species

to survive than does a maple-linden forest. The reverse is also true — that the more shade tolerant species require the more stable environment provided by shade of the parent canopy in order to grow, and consequently are not naturally invaders of more open sites. Five classes of shade tolerance have been delineated.

VERY TOLERANT:

shrubs and vines that will grow and survive in a state of health and vigor beneath dense shade; shade tolerance index range (Graham) — 8.0 to 10.0,
indicator — *Dirca palustris* (Atlantic Leatherwood)

Calycanthus floridus (Common Sweetshrub)
Clethra acuminata (Cinnamon Clethra)
Cornus canadensis (Bunchberry Dogwood)
Cornus rugosa (Roundleaf Dogwood)
Diervilla lonicera (Dwarf Bushhoneysuckle)
Dirca palustris (Atlantic Leatherwood)
Euonymus americanus (Brook Euonymus)
Euonymus obovatus (Running Euonymus)
Fothergilla gardeni (Dwarf Fothergilla)
Fothergilla major (Large Fothergilla)
Gaultheria procumbens (Checkerberry Wintergreen)
Hydrangea arborescens (Smooth Hydrangea)
Hydrangea quercifolia (Oakleaf Hydrangea)
Itea virginica (Virginia Sweetspire)
Kalmia angustifolia (Lambkill Kalmia)
Kalmia latifolia (Mountainlaurel Kalmia)
Kalmia polifolia (Bog Kalmia)
Leucothoe catesbaei (Drooping Leucothoe)
Lindera benzoin (Common Spicebush)

Lonicera canadensis (American Fly Honeysuckle)
Mahonia aquifolium (Oregongrape)
Pieris floribunda (Mountain Pieris)
Rhododendron carolinianum (Carolina Rhododendron)
Rhododendron catawbiense (Catawba Rhododendron)
Rhododendron nudiflorum (Pinxterbloom Azalea)
Rhododendron vaseyi (Pinkshell Azalea)
Ribes cynosbati (Pasture Gooseberry)
Ribes missouriense (Missouri Gooseberry)
Rubus odoratus (Fragrant Thimbleberry)
Sambucus canadensis (American Elder)
Sambucus pubens (Scarlet Elder)
Staphylea trifolia (American Bladdernut)
Stewartia ovata (Mountain Stewartia)
Taxus canadensis (Canada Yew)
Viburnum acerifolium (Mapleleaf Viburnum)
Rhododendron alnifolium (Hobblebush Viburnum)
Viburnum trilobum (American Cranberrybush Viburnum)
Xanthorhiza simplicissima (Yellowroot)

Aristolochia durior (Common Dutchmanspipe)
Menispermum canadense (Common Moonseed)
Parthenocissus quinquefolia (Virginia Creeper)
Smilax glauca (Cat Greenbrier)

Smilax rotundifolia (Common Greenbrier)
Smilax tamnoides (Bamboo Greenbrier)
Toxicodendron radicans (Common Poisonivy)

TOLERANT:

shrubs and vines that will grow and survive in a state of health and vigor beneath moderately dense shade, shade tolerance index range 6.0 to 7.9,
indicator — *Clethra alnifolia* (Summersweet Clethra)

Aesculus parviflora (Bottlebrush Buckeye)
Aesculus pavia (Red Buckeye)
Amelanchier sanguinea (Roundleaf Serviceberry)
Andromeda polifolia (Bogrosemary Andromeda)
Clethra alnifolia (Summersweet Clethra)
Comptonia peregrina (Sweetfern)
Cornus racemosa (Gray Dogwood)
Corylus americana (American Filbert)
Corylus cornuta (Beaked Filbert)
Epigaea repens (Trailing-arbutus)
Ilex glabra (Inkberry)
Magnolia virginiana (Sweetbay Magnolia)
Neviusia alabamensis (Snowwreath)
Pachistima canbyi (Canby Pachistima)
Rhododendron arborescens (Sweet Azalea)

Rhododendron calendulaceum (Flame Azalea)
Rhododendron roseum (Roseshell Azalea)
Rubus allegheniensis (Allegany Blackberry)
Rubus occidentalis (Blackcap Raspberry)
Rubus strigosus (American Red Raspberry)
Symphoricarpos albus (Common Snowberry)
Vaccinium angustifolium (Lowbush Blueberry)
Vaccinium corymbosum (Highbush Blueberry)
Vaccinium macrocarpum (Cranberry)
Vaccinium stamineum (Common Deerberry)
Viburnum cassinoides (Witherod Viburnum)
Viburnum dentatum (Arrowwood Viburnum)
Viburnum nudum (Possumhaw Viburnum)
Viburnum rafinesquianum (Rafinesque Viburnum)
Zenobia pulverulenta (Dusty Zenobia)

Celastrus scandens (American Bittersweet)
Clematis verticillaris (Rock Clematis)
Clematis virginiana (Virginsbower)
Lonicera dioica (Limber Honeysuckle)

Lonicera sempervirens (Trumpet Honeysuckle)
Vitis labrusca (Fox Grape)
Vitis riparia (Riverbank Grape)
Wistaria macrostachya (Kentucky Wistaria)

INTERMEDIATE:
shrubs and vines that will grow and survive in a state of health and vigor beneath moderate shade, shade tolerance index range 4.0 to 5.9,
indicator — *Symphoricarpos orbiculatus* (Indiancurrant Coralberry)

Aronia arbutifolia (Red Chokeberry)
Aronia melanocarpa (Black Chokeberry)
Aronia prunifolia (Purplefruit Chokeberry)
Castanea pumila (Allegany Chinkapin)
Ceanothus americanus (Jerseytea Ceanothus)
Ceanothus ovatus (Inland Ceanothus)
Hamamelis vernalis (Vernal Witchhazel)

Ilex decidua (Possumhaw)
Ilex verticillata (Common Winterberry)
Leiophyllum buxifolium (Box Sandmyrtle)
Rhododendron viscosum (Swamp Azalea)
Ribes americanum (American Black Currant)
Symphoricarpos orbiculatus (Indiancurrant Coralberry)

Ampelopsis arborea (Peppervine)
Ampelopsis cordata (Heartleaf Ampelopsis)
Berchemia scandens (Alabama Supplejack)
Bignonia capreolata (Crossvine)

Campsis radicans (Common Trumpetcreeper)
Cocculus carolinus (Carolina Snailseed)
Lonicera sempervirens (Trumpet Honeysuckle)

INTOLERANT:
shrubs and vines that will grow and survive in a state of health and vigor beneath light shade, shade tolerance index range 2.0 to 3.9,
indicator — *Spiraea tomentosa* (Hardhack Spirea)

Amorpha fruticosa (Indigobush Amorpha)
Arctostaphylos uva-ursi (Bearberry)
Chamaedaphne calyculata (Leatherleaf)
Cornus amomum (Silky Dogwood)
Elaeagnus commutata (Silverberry)
Ledum groenlandicum (Labradortea Ledum)
Myrica pensylvanica (Northern Bayberry)
Philadelphus grandiflorus (Big Scentless Mockorange)
Physocarpus opulifolius (Common Ninebark)
Potentilla fruticosa (Bush Cinquefoil)
Prunus hortulana (Hortulan Plum)

Quercus prinoides (Dwarf Chinkapin Oak)
Ribes odoratum (Clove Currant)
Robinia hispida (Roseacacia Locust)
Robinia viscosa (Clammy Locust)
Rosa carolina (Carolina Rose)
Rosa setigera (Prairie Rose)
Spiraea alba (Narrowleaf Meadowsweet Spirea)
Spiraea corymbosa (Corymed Spirea)
Spiraea tomentosa (Hardhack Spirea)
Symphoricarpos occidentalis (Western Snowberry)
Yucca filamentosa (Adamsneedle Yucca)

VERY INTOLERANT:
shrubs and vines that become suppressed in shade and therefore demand full sun exposure for best growth and survival, shade tolerance index range 0. to 1.9,
indicator — *Juniperus communis* (Common Juniper)

Alnus serrulata (Common Alder)
Amorpha canescens (Leadplant Amorpha)
Baccharis halimifolia (Eastern Baccharis)
Betula pumila (Low Birch)
Cephalanthus occidentalis (Common Buttonbush)
Cornus stolonifera (Redosier Dogwood)
Hypericum densiflorum (Dense Hypericum)
Hypericum frondosum (Golden St.Johnswort)
Hypericum kalmianum (Kalm St.Johnswort)
Hypericum prolificum (Shrubby St.Johnswort)

Juniperus communis (Common Juniper)
Juniperus horizontalis (Creeping Juniper)
Lyonia ligustrina (He-huckleberry)
Pinus aristata (Bristlecone Pine)
Quercus ilicifolia (Scrub Oak)
Rhus aromatica (Fragrant Sumac)
Salix humilis (Prairie Willow)
Salix lucida (Shining Willow)
Shepherdia argentea (Silver Buffaloberry)
Shepherdia canadensis (Russet Buffaloberry)

SOIL TEXTURE:

Texture refers to the size of soil particles. These particles are classified in five general categories: coarse - stones and gravels; medium coarse - sands; medium - loams; medium fine - silts; and fine - clays. Soil composition with high percentages of any given particle size determine its overall textural class (Table IV).

Few soils contain only one particle size. Nearly all soils have a certain proportion of sand, silt and clay. Soil texture can be estimated in the field by rubbing a small amount of moist soil between the thumb and forefinger. Sand particles can be seen easily and feel gritty. Silt particles can be seen with a magnifying lens, and when dry they feel like flour. When wet they have a smooth, floury feel with little evidence of stickiness. Clay particles are very fine. Clay is sticky and plastic when wet and can be molded; it will dry into a hard mass.

Textural class for the surface layer is always a part of the soil type name, e.g. Muscatine silty clay loam. Textural class for subsoil and parent material is given in profile descriptions which are a part of all survey reports.

Texture is a permanent soil property that greatly influences root growth and plant health and vigor. Soils with a high proportion of either coarse particles (sandy soils) or fine particles (high clay soils) are often low in productivity. Sandy soils do not hold enough water for good plant growth and they are poor storehouses for plant nutrients. They must receive frequent additions of water and nutrients to be productive. The main problem with high clay soils is their slow permeability and poor internal drainage, which are the result of their large number of very small pores. Soils high in clay will often be so wet that root development is hindered.

The most productive soils are usually medium to moderately fine in texture. Examples are loams, silt loams and silty clay loams. Such soils are good storehouses for plant nutrients and are capable of storing a high proportion of water available to plants. Conditions are generally very favorable for root growth.

COARSE:
Soils containing 35% or more of sand, gravel, or stone particles above 1.0 millimeters in diameter.

MEDIUM COARSE:
Soils containing 35% or more of sand particles of .50 to 1.0 millimeters in diameter.

MEDIUM:
Soils that have evenly divided amounts of sand, silt, and clay particles between .05 and .50 millimeters in diameter.

MEDIUM FINE:
Soils with 30% or more of silt size particles between .002 to .05 millimeters in diameter.

FINE:
Soils with 30% or more of clay particles below .002 millimeters in diameter.

SOIL DRAINAGE:

Drainage refers to the frequency and duration of periods of saturation or partial saturation of the soil. Six classes of natural soil drainage (Table IV) are recognized:

EXCESSIVELY DRAINED:
Water is removed from the soil very rapidly. Excessively drained soils are commonly very coarse textured, rocky, or shallow. Some are on slopes so steep that much of the water they receive is lost as runoff. All are free of mottling due to wetness.

MODERATELY WELL DRAINED:
Water is removed from the soil somewhat slowly during some periods. Moderately well drained soils are wet for only a short time during the growing season. They commonly have a slowly pervious layer within or directly below the solum, or periodically receive high rainfall, or both. Most plants attain their best development on moderate to well-drained sites.

WELL DRAINED:
Water is removed from the soil readily, but not rapidly. It is available to plants throughout most of the growing season, and wetness does not inhibit growth of roots for significant periods during most growing seasons. Well drained soils are commonly medium textured. They are mainly free of mottling.

SOMEWHAT POORLY DRAINED:

Water is removed slowly enough that the soil is wet for significant periods during the growing season. Somewhat poorly drained soils commonly have a slowly pervious layer, a high water table, additional water from seepage, nearly continuous rainfall, or a combination of these.

POORLY DRAINED:

Water is removed so slowly that the soil is saturated periodically during the growing season or remains wet for long periods. Free water is commonly at or near the surface for brief periods during the growing season. The soil is not continuously saturated in layers directly below. Poor drainage results from a high water table, slowly pervious layer within the profile, seepage, nearly continuous rainfall, or a combination of these.

VERY POORLY DRAINED:

Water is removed from the soil so slowly that free water remains at or on the surface during most of the growing season. Very poorly drained soils are commonly level or depressed and are frequently ponded. Yet, where rainfall is high and nearly continuous, they can have moderate or high slope gradients, as for example in "hillpeats" and "climatic moors." Wet sites have cold soils which result in a much shorter growing season.

AVAILABLE SOIL MOISTURE CAPACITY:

Available moisture capacity refers to the capacity of soils to hold water available for use by most plants (Table IV). It is commonly defined as the difference between the amount of soil water at field moisture capacity and the amount at wilting point. Field moisture capacity is the moisture content of a soil held between the soil particles by surface tension after the gravitational, or free water has drained away 2 or 3 days after a soaking rain. It is also called normal field capacity, normal moisture capacity, or capillary capacity. It is commonly expressed as inches of water per given depth of soil. The capacity, in inches, in a 150 centimeter (60-inch) profile or to a limiting layer is expressed as:

VERY HIGH (wet):
More than 30 cm (12 inches)

HIGH: (moist)
22.5 to 30 cm (9 to 12 inches)

MODERATE (average):
15 to 22.5 cm (6 to 9 inches)

LOW (dry):
7.5 to 15 cm (3 to 6 inches)

VERY LOW (droughty):
0 to 7.5 cm (0 to 3 inches)

SOIL REACTION:

Soils can be divided into seven classes based on measurable differences in chemical reaction (Table IV). The degree of acidity or alkalinity of a soil is expressed in pH values. A soil that tests to pH 7.0 is described as precisely neutral in reaction because it is neither acid nor alkaline. The degree of acidity or alkalinity is expressed as:

	Texture					Drainage						Moisture					Reaction-pH				
	coarse	mod. coarse	medium	mod. fine	fine	very poor	poor	mod. poor	mod. well	well	excessive	wet	moist	average	dry	droughty	4.0-5.0	5.1-6.0	6.1-6.5	6.6-7.5	7.6-8.5
Aesculus parviflora		▓	▓	▓			▓	▓	▓				▓	▓				▓	▓		
Aesculus pavia		▓	▓	▓			▓	▓	▓	▓			▓	▓				▓	▓	▓	
Alnus serrulata	▓	▓	▓	▓	▓	▓	▓	▓	▓	▓		▓	▓	▓			▓	▓	▓	▓	▓
Amelanchier sanguinea	▓	▓		▓	▓		▓	▓	▓	▓	▓		▓	▓	▓		▓	▓	▓	▓	▓
Amorpha canescens	▓	▓		▓	▓			▓	▓	▓	▓			▓	▓	▓		▓	▓	▓	▓
Amorpha fruticosa	▓	▓	▓	▓	▓		▓	▓	▓	▓		▓	▓	▓	▓			▓	▓	▓	▓
Andromeda polifolia			▓	▓		▓	▓	▓	▓			▓	▓	▓			▓	▓			
Arctostaphylos uva-ursi	▓	▓	▓	▓	▓				▓	▓	▓		▓	▓	▓	▓	▓	▓	▓		
Aronia arbutifolia	▓	▓	▓	▓	▓		▓	▓	▓	▓		▓	▓	▓			▓	▓	▓	▓	
Aronia melanocarpa	▓	▓	▓	▓	▓		▓	▓	▓	▓		▓	▓	▓			▓	▓	▓	▓	
Aronia prunifolia	▓	▓	▓	▓	▓		▓	▓	▓	▓		▓	▓	▓			▓	▓	▓	▓	
Baccharis halimifolia	▓	▓	▓	▓	▓		▓	▓	▓	▓	▓	▓	▓	▓	▓		▓	▓	▓	▓	▓
Betula pumila	▓	▓	▓	▓		▓	▓	▓				▓	▓	▓			▓	▓	▓	▓	
Calycanthus floridus	▓	▓	▓	▓			▓	▓	▓	▓			▓	▓	▓			▓	▓	▓	
Castanea pumila	▓	▓	▓	▓				▓	▓	▓	▓			▓	▓	▓	▓	▓	▓	▓	
Ceanothus americanus	▓	▓	▓	▓	▓			▓	▓	▓	▓		▓	▓	▓	▓	▓	▓	▓	▓	▓
Ceanothus ovatus	▓	▓		▓	▓			▓	▓	▓	▓			▓	▓	▓	▓	▓	▓	▓	▓
Cephalanthus occidentalis	▓	▓	▓	▓	▓	▓	▓	▓	▓	▓		▓	▓	▓				▓	▓	▓	▓
Chamaedaphne calyculata			▓	▓	▓	▓	▓	▓	▓			▓	▓	▓			▓	▓			
Clethra acuminata	▓	▓	▓	▓			▓	▓	▓	▓		▓	▓	▓			▓	▓	▓		
Clethra alnifolia	▓	▓	▓	▓	▓		▓	▓	▓	▓		▓	▓	▓			▓	▓	▓		
Comptonia peregrina	▓		▓	▓	▓			▓	▓	▓	▓			▓	▓	▓	▓	▓	▓		
Cornus amomum	▓	▓	▓	▓	▓		▓	▓	▓	▓		▓	▓	▓				▓	▓	▓	▓
Cornus canadensis	▓	▓	▓	▓	▓		▓	▓	▓	▓		▓	▓	▓			▓	▓	▓	▓	
Cornus racemosa	▓	▓	▓	▓	▓		▓	▓	▓	▓		▓	▓	▓	▓			▓	▓	▓	▓
Cornus rugosa	▓	▓	▓	▓	▓		▓	▓	▓	▓			▓	▓	▓			▓	▓	▓	▓

Table IV

Soil Correlations: Shrubs

	Texture					Drainage						Moisture					Reaction-pH				
	coarse	mod. coarse	medium	mod. fine	fine	very poor	poor	mod. poor	mod. well	well	excessive	wet	moist	average	dry	droughty	4.0-5.0	5.1-6.0	6.1-6.5	6.6-7.5	7.6-8.5
Cornus stolonifera																					
Corylus americana																					
Corylus cornuta																					
Cyrilla racemiflora																					
Diervilla lonicera																					
Dirca palustris																					
Elaeagnus commutata																					
Epigaea repens																					
Euonymus americanus																					
Euonymus obovatus																					
Fothergilla gardeni																					
Fothergilla major																					
Gaultheria procumbens																					
Hamamelis vernalis																					
Hydrangea arborescens																					
Hydrangea quercifolia																					
Hypericum densiflorum																					
Hypericum frondosum																					
Hypericum kalmianum																					
Hypericum prolificum																					
Ilex decidua																					
Ilex glabra																					
Ilex verticillata																					
Itea virginica																					
Juniperus communis																					
Juniperus horizontalis																					

Soil Correlations: Shrubs — Table IV

	Texture					Drainage						Moisture					Reaction-pH				
	coarse	mod. coarse	medium	mod. fine	fine	very poor	poor	mod. poor	mod. well	well	excessive	wet	moist	average	dry	droughty	4.0-5.0	5.1-6.0	6.1-6.5	6.6-7.5	7.6-8.5
Kalmia angustifolia																					
Kalmia latifolia																					
Kalmia polifolia																					
Ledum groenlandicum																					
Leiophyllum buxifolium																					
Leucothoe catesbaei																					
Lindera benzoin																					
Lonicera canadensis																					
Lyonia ligustrina																					
Magnolia virginiana																					
Mahonia aquifolium																					
Myrica pensylvanica																					
Neviusia alabamensis																					
Pachistima canbyi																					
Philadelphus grandiflorus																					
Physocarpus opulifolius																					
Pieris floribunda																					
Pinus aristata																					
Potentilla fruticosa																					
Prunus hortulana																					
Quercus ilicifolia																					
Quercus prinoides																					
Rhododendron arborescens																					
Rhododendron calendulaceum																					
Rhododendron carolinianum																					
Rhododendron catawbiense																					

	Texture					Drainage						Moisture					Reaction-pH				
	coarse	mod. coarse	medium	mod. fine	fine	very poor	poor	mod. poor	mod. well	well	excessive	wet	moist	average	dry	droughty	4.0-5.0	5.1-6.0	6.1-6.5	6.6-7.5	7.6-8.5
Rhododendron nudiflorum																					
Rhododendron roseum																					
Rhododendron vaseyi																					
Rhododendron viscosum																					
Rhus aromatica																					
Ribes americanum																					
Ribes cynosbati																					
Ribes missouriense																					
Ribes odoratum																					
Robinia hispida																					
Robinia viscosa																					
Rosa carolina																					
Rosa setigera																					
Rubus allegheniensis																					
Rubus occidentalis																					
Rubus odoratus																					
Rubus strigosus																					
Salix humilis																					
Salix lucida																					
Sambucus canadensis																					
Sambucus pubens																					
Shepherdia argentea																					
Shepherdia canadensis																					
Spiraea alba																					
Spiraea corymbosa																					
Spiraea tomentosa																					

	Texture					Drainage						Moisture					Reaction-pH				
	coarse	mod. coarse	medium	mcd. fine	fine	very poor	poor	mod. poor	mod. well	well	excessive	wet	moist	average	dry	droughty	4.0-5.0	5.1-6.0	6.1-6.5	6.6-7.5	7.6-8.5
Staphylea trifolia		▓	▓						▓	▓			▓	▓				▓			▓
Stewartia ovata		▓	▓	▓					▓	▓			▓	▓			▓	▓			
Symphoricarpos albus		▓	▓	▓				▓	▓	▓			▓	▓	▓						
Symphoricarpos occidentalis		▓	▓	▓				▓	▓	▓			▓	▓	▓						
Symphoricarpos orbiculatus		▓	▓	▓				▓	▓	▓			▓	▓	▓					▓	
Taxus canadensis		▓	▓	▓					▓	▓			▓	▓				▓	▓		
Vaccinium angustifolium		▓	▓	▓					▓	▓	▓		▓	▓	▓		▓	▓			
Vaccinium corymbosum		▓	▓	▓			▓	▓	▓	▓		▓	▓	▓			▓	▓			
Vaccinium macrocarpum	▓	▓	▓			▓	▓	▓				▓	▓	▓			▓	▓			
Vaccinium stamineum		▓	▓	▓					▓	▓	▓		▓	▓	▓		▓	▓			
Viburnum acerifolium		▓	▓	▓					▓	▓	▓		▓	▓	▓		▓	▓			
Viburnum alnifolium		▓	▓	▓				▓	▓	▓			▓	▓			▓	▓			
Viburnum cassinoides		▓	▓	▓			▓	▓	▓	▓		▓	▓	▓			▓	▓			
Viburnum dentatum		▓	▓	▓				▓	▓	▓			▓	▓	▓		▓	▓			
Viburnum nudum		▓	▓	▓			▓	▓	▓	▓		▓	▓	▓			▓	▓			
Viburnum rafinesquianum	▓	▓	▓					▓	▓	▓			▓	▓	▓					▓	▓
Viburnum trilobum		▓	▓	▓				▓	▓	▓			▓	▓				▓			
Xanthorhiza simplicissima		▓	▓	▓				▓	▓	▓			▓	▓			▓	▓			
Yucca filamentosa	▓	▓	▓	▓					▓	▓	▓			▓	▓	▓		▓			
Zenobia pulverulenta	▓	▓	▓				▓	▓	▓			▓	▓	▓			▓	▓			

Soil Correlations: Vines — Table IV

	Texture					Drainage						Moisture					Reaction-pH				
	coarse	mod. coarse	medium	mod. fine	fine	very poor	poor	mod. poor	mod. well	well	excessive	wet	moist	average	dry	droughty	4.0-5.0	5.1-6.0	6.1-6.5	6.6-7.5	7.6-8.5
Ampelopsis arborea	▒	▒	▒	▒		▒	▒	▒			▒	▒	▒	▒		▒	▒	▒			
Ampelopsis cordata	▒	▒	▒	▒		▒	▒	▒			▒	▒	▒	▒		▒	▒	▒			
Aristolochia durior		▒	▒		▒		▒	▒	▒		▒	▒	▒	▒	▒	▒	▒	▒			
Berchemia scandens	▒	▒	▒	▒	▒	▒	▒	▒	▒	▒	▒	▒	▒	▒	▒	▒	▒	▒			
Bignonia capreolata	▒	▒	▒	▒	▒	▒	▒	▒	▒	▒	▒	▒	▒	▒	▒	▒	▒	▒			
Campsis radicans	▒	▒	▒	▒	▒	▒			▒	▒	▒	▒	▒	▒	▒	▒	▒	▒			
Celastrus scandens	▒	▒	▒	▒	▒	▒	▒	▒	▒	▒	▒	▒	▒	▒	▒	▒	▒	▒			
Clematis verticillaris	▒	▒	▒	▒	▒	▒	▒	▒	▒	▒	▒	▒	▒	▒	▒	▒	▒	▒			
Clematis virginiana	▒	▒	▒	▒	▒	▒	▒	▒	▒	▒	▒	▒	▒	▒	▒	▒	▒	▒			
Cocculus carolinus	▒	▒	▒	▒	▒	▒	▒	▒	▒	▒	▒	▒	▒	▒	▒	▒	▒	▒			
Lonicera dioica	▒	▒	▒	▒		▒	▒	▒	▒	▒	▒		▒	▒	▒	▒	▒	▒			
Lonicera sempervirens	▒	▒	▒	▒	▒	▒	▒	▒	▒	▒	▒	▒	▒	▒	▒	▒	▒	▒			
Menispermum canadense	▒	▒	▒	▒	▒	▒	▒	▒	▒	▒	▒	▒	▒	▒	▒	▒	▒	▒			
Parthenocissus quinquefolia	▒	▒	▒	▒	▒	▒	▒	▒	▒	▒	▒	▒	▒	▒	▒	▒	▒	▒			
Smilax glauca	▒	▒	▒	▒	▒	▒	▒	▒	▒	▒	▒	▒	▒	▒	▒	▒	▒	▒			
Smilax rotundifolia	▒	▒	▒	▒	▒	▒	▒	▒	▒	▒	▒	▒	▒	▒	▒	▒	▒	▒			
Smilax tamnoides	▒	▒	▒	▒	▒	▒	▒	▒	▒	▒	▒	▒	▒	▒	▒	▒	▒	▒			
Toxicodendron radicans	▒	▒	▒	▒	▒	▒	▒	▒	▒	▒	▒	▒	▒	▒	▒	▒	▒	▒			
Vitis labrusca	▒	▒	▒	▒	▒	▒	▒	▒	▒	▒		▒	▒	▒	▒	▒	▒	▒			
Vitis riparia	▒	▒	▒	▒	▒	▒	▒	▒	▒	▒	▒	▒	▒	▒	▒	▒	▒	▒			
Wistaria macrostachya	▒	▒	▒	▒	▒	▒	▒	▒	▒	▒	▒	▒	▒	▒	▒	▒	▒	▒			

Soil reaction (cont.)

SLIGHTLY ACID: 6.1 to 6.5 ——

MODERATELY ACID: 5.1 to 6.0 ——

STRONGLY ACID: 4.1 to 5.0 ——

EXTREMELY ACID*: Below 4.0 ——

—— NEUTRAL: 6.6 to 7.5

—— ALKALINE: 7.6 to 8.5

—— STRONGLY ALKALINE*: 8.6 and higher

* Plant growth is severely restricted due to hostile soil chemistry. These classes are not included in Table IV and must be modified if plant growth and survival is to be possible. Soil pH can be modified toward neutrality by the introduction of lime to acidic soils. Sulphur, aluminum sulfate or calcium sulfate lowers pH. The most appropriate planting is that which is best suited to local existing conditions. Trees already growing on the site and in surrounding areas should be utilized as a guide in plant selection.

HARDINESS:

Although the combined effects of many environmental factors determine true plant adaptability, winter hardiness is the most important single governing factor according to many contemporary authors. The United States Department of Agriculture publishes a hardiness map which shows the average annual minimum temperatures for most of North America. Each zone delineated on the USDA map includes 10 degree increments and is split into an *a* and *b* area with the lower temperature occurring in the *a* zone. Temperatures of adjacent zones become increasingly similar near their boundaries. A plant species that flourishes in one part of a given zone is likely to be adaptable in other parts of the same zone or in a warmer zone. Other factors of the physical environment must also be relatively comparable.

USDA Hardiness Zones mapped in figure 2:

Zone 2 . . . . -50 to -40F
Zone 3a . . . . -40 to -35F
Zone 3b . . . . -35 to -30F
Zone 4a . . . . -30 to -25F
Zone 4b . . . . -25 to -20F
Zone 5a . . . . -20 to -15F
Zone 5b . . . . -15 to -10F
Zone 6 . . . . -10 to   0F

ZONE 2:

Andromeda polifolia (Bogrosemary Andromeda)
Arctostaphylos uva-ursi (Bearberry)
Betula pumila (Low Birch)
Chamaedaphne calyculata (Leatherleaf)
Comptonia peregrina (Sweetfern)
Cornus canadensis (Bunchberry Dogwood)
Cornus stolonifera (Redosier Dogwood)
Elaeagnus commutata (Silverberry)
Epigaea repens (Trailing-arbutus)
Juniperus communis (Common Juniper)
Juniperus horizontalis (Creeping Juniper)
Kalmia angustifolia (Lambkill Kalmia)
Kalmia polifolia (Bog Kalmia)
Ledum groenlandicum (Labradortea Ledum)

Physocarpus opulifolius (Common Ninebark)
Potentilla fruticosa (Bush Cinquefoil)
Ribes cynosbati (Pasture Gooseberry)
Rubus strigosus (American Red Raspberry)
Salix lucida (Shining Willow)
Shepherdia argentea (Silver Buffaloberry)
Shepherdia canadensis (Russet Buffaloberry)
Symphoricarpos albus (Common Snowberry)
Symphoricarpos occidentalis (Western Snowberry)
Symphoricarpos orbiculatus (Indiancurrant Coralberry)
Taxus canadensis (Canada Yew)
Vaccinium angustifolium (Lowbush Blueberry)
Viburnum cassinoides (Witherod Viburnum)
Viburnum trilobum (American Cranberrybush Viburnum)

Celastrus scandens (American Bittersweet)

Clematis verticillaris (Rock Clematis)

474

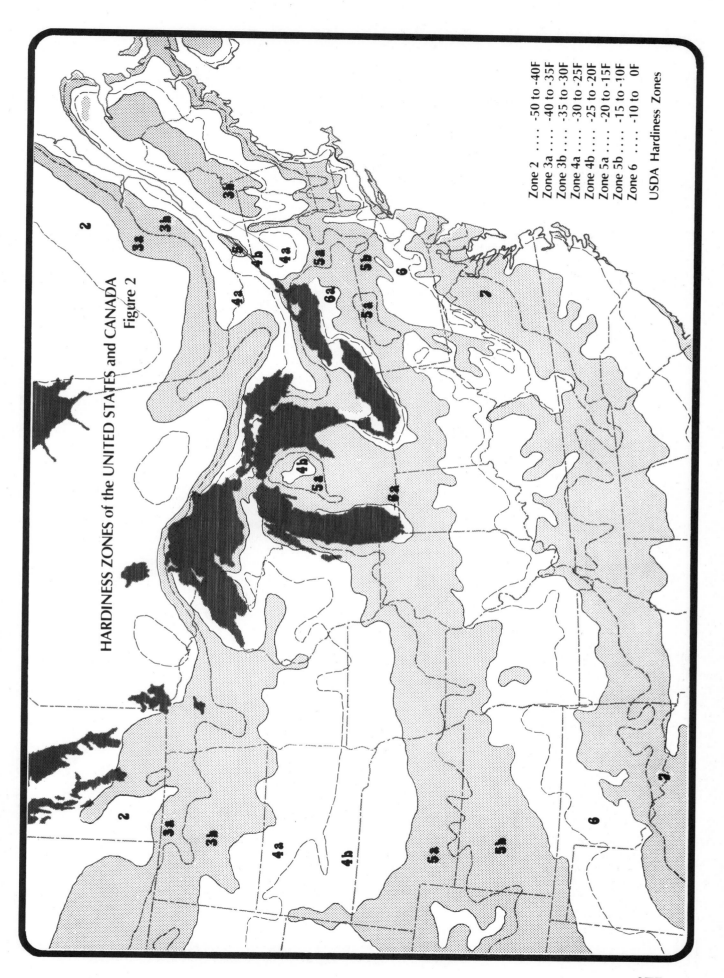

HARDINESS ZONES of the UNITED STATES and CANADA
Figure 2

USDA Hardiness Zones

Zone 2 ..... -50 to -40F
Zone 3a ..... -40 to -35F
Zone 3b ..... -35 to -30F
Zone 4a ..... -30 to -25F
Zone 4b ..... -25 to -20F
Zone 5a ..... -20 to -15F
Zone 5b ..... -15 to -10F
Zone 6 ..... -10 to 0F

Lonicera dioica (Limber Honeysuckle)
Menispermum canadense (Common Moonseed)

Parthenocissus quinquefolia (Virginia Creeper)
Vitis riparia (Riverbank Grape)

ZONE 3a:

Amorpha canescens (Leadplant Amorpha)
Amorpha fruticosa (Indigobush Amorpha)
Aronia melanocarpa (Black Chokeberry)
Cornus racemosa (Gray Dogwood)
Cornus rugosa (Roundleaf Dogwood)
Corylus americana (American Flbert)
Corylus cornuta (Beaked Filbert)
Diervilla lonicera (Dwarf Bushhoneysuckle)
Dirca palustris (Atlantic Leatherwood)
Gaultheria procumbens (Checkerberry Wintergreen)

Lonicera canadensis (American Fly Honeysuckle)
Ribes americanum (American Black Currant)
Salix humilis (Prairie Willow)
Sambucus canadensis (American Elder)
Sambucus pubens (Scarlet Elder)
Spiraea alba (Narrowleaf Meadowsweet Spirea)
Vaccinium macrocarpum (Cranberry)
Viburnum dentatum (Arrowwood Viburnum)
Viburnum rafinesquianum (Rafinesque Viburnum)

Clematis virginiana (Virginsbower)
Smilax tamnoides (Bamboo Greenbrier)

Toxicodendron radicans (Common Poisonivy)

ZONE 3b:

Ceanothus americanus (Jerseytea Ceanothus)
Ceanothus ovatus (Inland Ceanothus)
Euonymus obovatus (Running Euonymus)
Ilex verticillata (Common Winterberry)

Ribes odoratum (Clove Currant)
Rubus allegheniensis (Allegany Blackberry)
Viburnum acerifolium (Mapleleaf Viburnum)
Viburnum alnifolium (Hobblebush Viburnum)

ZONE 4a:

Aronia prunifolia (Purplefruit Chokeberry)
Cephalanthus occidentalis (Common Buttonbush)
Clethra alnifolia (Summersweet Clethra)
Cornus amomum (Silky Dogwood)
Hydrangea arborescens (Smooth Hydrangea)
Hypericum kalmianum (Kalm St.Johnswort)
Hypericum prolificum (Shrubby St.Johnswort)
Ilex glabra (Inkberry)
Rhododendron roseum (Roseshell Azalea)

Rhododendron viscosum (Swamp Azalea)
Rhus aromatica (Fragrant Sumac)
Ribes missouriense (Missouri Gooseberry)
Robinia hispida (Roseacacia Locust)
Rubus occidentalis (Blackcap Raspberry)
Rubus odoratus (Fragrant Thimbleberry)
Spiraea tomentosa (Hardhack Spirea)
Staphylea trifolia (American Bladdernut)

Aristolochia durior (Common Dutchmanspipe)

ZONE 4b:

Aronia arbutifolia (Red Chokeberry)
Myrica pensylvanica (Northern Bayberry)
Pachistima canbyi (Canby Pachistima)
Rhododendron arborescens (Sweet Azalea)

Rhododendron nudiflorum (Pinxterbloom Azalea)
Rosa carolina (Carolina Rose)
Rosa setigera (Prairie Rose)
Vaccinium corymbosum (Highbush Blueberry)

Lonicera sempervirens (Trumpet Honeysuckle)
Vitis labrusca (Fox Grape)

ZONE 5a:

Aesculus parviflora (Bottlebrush Buckeye)
Alnus serrulata (Common Alder)
Amelanchier sanguinea (Roundleaf Serviceberry)
Baccharis halimifolia (Eastern Baccharis)
Calycanthus floridus (Common Sweetshrub)
Hamamelis vernalis (Vernal Witchhazel)
Kalmia latifolia (Mountainlaurel Kalmia)
Lindera benzoin (Common Spicebush)

Mahonia aquifolium (Oregongrape)
Neviusia alabamensis (Snowwreath)
Pinus aristata (Bristlecone Pine)
Prunus hortulana (Hortulan Plum)
Rhododendron vaseyi (Pinkshell Azalea)
Robinia viscosa (Clammy Locust)
Xanthorhiza simplicissima (Yellowroot)
Yucca filamentosa (Adamsneedle Yucca)

Campsis radicans   (Common Trumpetcreeper)
Smilax rotundifolia   (Common Greenbrier)

Wistaria macrostachya   (Kentucky Wistaria)

ZONE 5b:

Castanea pumila   (Allegany Chinkapin)
Ilex decidua   (Possumhaw)
Itea virginica   (Virginia Sweetspire)
Leucothoe catesbaei   (Drooping Leucothoe)
Pieris floribunda   (Mountain Pieris)

Quercus ilicifolia   (Scrub Oak)
Quercus prinoides   (Dwarf Chinkapin Oak)
Rhododendron carolinianum   (Carolina Rhododendron)
Rhododendron catawbiense   (Catawba Rhododendron)
Spiraea corymbosa   (Corymed Spirea)

Ampelopsis cordata   (Heartleaf Ampelopsis)
Smilax glauca   (Cat Greenbrier)

ZONE 6a:

Aesculus pavia   (Red Buckeye)
Clethra acuminata   (Cinnamon Clethra)
Cyrilla racemiflora   (American Cyrilla)
Euonymus americanus   (Brook Euonymus)
Fothergilla gardeni   (Dwarf Fothergilla)
Fothergilla major   (Large Fothergilla)
Hydrangea quercifolia   (Oakleaf Hydrangea)
Hypericum densiflorum   (Dense Hypericum)
Hypericum frondosum   (Golden St.Johnswort)

Leiophyllum buxifolium   (Box Sandmyrtle)
Lyonia ligustrina   (He-huckleberry)
Magnolia virginiana   (Sweetbay Magnolia)
Philadelphus grandiflorus   (Big Scentless Mockorange)
Rhododendron calendulaceum   (Flame Azalea)
Stewartia ovata   (Mountain Stewartia)
Vaccinium stamineum   (Common Deerberry)
Viburnum nudum   (Possumhaw Viburnum)
Zenobia pulverulenta   (Dusty Zenobia)

Ampelopsis arborea   (Peppervine)
Berchemia scandens   (Alabama Supplejack)

Bignonia capreolata   (Crossvine)
Cocculus carolinus   (Carolina Snailseed)

GROWTH RATE:

The measured vertical increase in height during one growing season determines the rate of plant growth. Different species have corresponding varying rates of growth. Rate is also influenced by numerous variables such as age and factors of the plant's physical environment. Generally, young shrubs and vines grow rapidly, adding a great deal of height before slowing with maturity. Three classes are designated.

FAST:
   capable of producing 60 centimeters (24 inches) or more of leader growth annually,
   indicator — Rubus allegheniensis (Allegany Blackberry)

MEDIUM:
   capable of producing between 30 and 60 centimeters (12 to 24 inches) of leader growth per year,
   indicator — Cornus racemosa (Gray Dogwood)

SLOW:
   having an annual leader increment of 30 centimeters (12 inches) or less,
   indicator — Dirca palustris (Atlantic Leatherwood)

Silvical Characteristics: Shrubs   Table V

	Growth			Longevity			Physiol.			Disease			Insect			Wind-Ice		
☐ often longer-lived	slow	medium	fast	very short	short	mod. short	infrequent	occasional	frequent	infrequent	occasional	frequent	infrequent	occasional	frequent	infrequent	occasional	frequent
Aesculus parviflora																		
Aesculus pavia																		
Alnus serrulata																		
Amelanchier sanguinea																		
Amorpha canescens																		
Amorpha fruticosa																		
Andromeda polifolia																		
Arctostaphylos uva-ursi						☐												
Aronia arbutifolia																		
Aronia melanocarpa																		
Aronia prunifolia																		
Baccharis halimifolia																		
Betula pumila																		
Calycanthus floridus																		
Castanea pumila																		
Ceanothus americanus																		
Ceanothus ovatus																		
Cephalanthus occidentalis																		
Chamaedaphne calyculata																		
Clethra acuminata																		
Clethra alnifolia																		
Comptonia peregrina																		
Cornus amomum																		
Cornus canadensis						☐												
Cornus racemosa																		
Cornus rugosa																		

Silvical Characteristics: Shrubs — Table V

☐ often longer-lived

	Growth			Longevity			Physiol.			Disease			Insect			Wind-Ice		
	slow	medium	fast	very short	short	mod. short	infrequent	occasional	frequent	infrequent	occasional	frequent	infrequent	occasional	frequent	infrequent	occasional	frequent
Cornus stolonifera			■	■						■				■		■		
Corylus americana			■			■							■			■		
Corylus cornuta			■			■							■			■		
Cyrilla racemiflora	■					■				■			■			■		
Diervilla lonicera		■			■					■			■			■		
Dirca palustris	■					■				■			■			■		
Elaeagnus commutata			■			☐				■			■			■		
Epigaea repens	■					■				■			■			■		
Euonymus americanus		■				■				■				■		■		
Euonymus obovatus	■					■				■				■		■		
Fothergilla gardeni	■					■				■			■			■		
Fothergilla major	■					■				■			■			■		
Gaultheria procumbens	■					☐				■			■			■		
Hamamelis vernalis	■					■				■			■			■		
Hydrangea arborescens		■				■				■			■			■		
Hydrangea quercifolia		■				■				■			■			■		
Hypericum densiflorum	■	■				■				■			■			■		
Hypericum frondosum	■					■				■			■			■		
Hypericum kalmianum	■					■				■			■			■		
Hypericum prolificum	■					■				■			■					■
Ilex decidua		■				☐				■			■			■		
Ilex glabra	■					☐				■			■			■		
Ilex verticillata		■				■				■			■			■		
Itea virginica		■				■				■			■			■		
Juniperus communis	■					☐				■			■			■		
Juniperus horizontalis	■					☐				■			■			■		

Silvical Characteristics: Shrubs   Table V

	Growth			Longevity			Physiol.			Disease			Insect			Wind-Ice		
☐ often longer-lived	slow	medium	fast	very short	short	mod. short	infrequent	occasional	frequent	infrequent	occasional	frequent	infrequent	occasional	frequent	infrequent	occasional	frequent
Kalmia angustifolia																		
Kalmia latifolia																		
Kalmia polifolia																		
Ledum groenlandicum																		
Leiophyllum buxifolium																		
Leucothoe catesbaei																		
Lindera benzoin																		
Lonicera canadensis																		
Lyonia ligustrina																		
Magnolia virginiana																		
Mahonia aquifolium																		
Myrica pensylvanica																		
Neviusia alabamensis																		
Pachistima canbyi																		
Philadelphus grandiflorus																		
Physocarpus opulifolius																		
Pieris floribunda																		
Pinus aristata						☐												
Potentilla fruticosa																		
Prunus hortulana																		
Quercus ilicifolia						☐												
Quercus prinoides						☐												
Rhododendron arborescens																		
Rhododendron calendulaceum																		
Rhododendron carolinianum																		
Rhododendron catawbiense																		

Silvical Characteristics: Shrubs

Table V

□ often longer-lived

	Growth			Longevity			Physiol.			Disease			Insect			Wind-Ice		
	slow	medium	fast	very short	short	mod. short	infrequent	occasional	frequent	infrequent	occasional	frequent	infrequent	occasional	frequent	infrequent	occasional	frequent
Rhododendron nudiflorum																		
Rhododendron roseum																		
Rhododendron vaseyi																		
Rhododendron viscosum																		
Rhus aromatica																		
Ribes americanum																		
Ribes cynosbati																		
Ribes missouriense																		
Ribes odoratum																		
Robinia hispida																		
Robinia viscosa																		
Rosa carolina																		
Rosa setigera																		
Rubus allegheniensis																		
Rubus occidentalis																		
Rubus odoratus																		
Rubus strigosus																		
Salix humilis																		
Salix lucida																		
Sambucus canadensis																		
Sambucus pubens																		
Shepherdia argentea						□												
Shepherdia canadensis																		
Spiraea alba																		
Spiraea corymbosa																		
Spiraea tomentosa																		

Silvical Characteristics: Shrubs — Table V

☐ often longer-lived

	Growth			Longevity			Physiol.			Disease			Insect			Wind-Ice		
	slow	medium	fast	very short	short	mod. short	infrequent	occasional	frequent	infrequent	occasional	frequent	infrequent	occasional	frequent	infrequent	occasional	frequent
Staphylea trifolia																		
Stewartia ovata																		
Symphoricarpos albus																		
Symphoricarpos occidentalis																		
Symphoricarpos orbiculatus																		
Taxus canadensis						☐												
Vaccinium angustifolium																		
Vaccinium corymbosum																		
Vaccinium macrocarpum																		
Vaccinium stamineum																		
Viburnum acerifolium																		
Viburnum alnifolium																		
Viburnum cassinoides																		
Viburnum dentatum																		
Viburnum nudum																		
Viburnum rafinesquianum																		
Viburnum trilobum																		
Xanthorhiza simplicissima																		
Yucca filamentosa						☐												
Zenobia pulverulenta																		

☐ often longer-lived

	Growth			Longevity			Physiol.			Disease			Insect			Wind-Ice		
	slow	medium	fast	very short	short	mod. short	infrequent	occasional	frequent	infrequent	occasional	frequent	infrequent	occasional	frequent	infrequent	occasional	frequent
Ampelopsis arborea			▓	▓				▓		▓			▓			▓		
Ampelopsis cordata			▓		▓		▓				▓			▓		▓		
Aristolochia durior		▓				☐	▓			▓			▓			▓		
Berchemia scandens		▓				☐	▓			▓			▓			▓		
Bignonia capreolata		▓				☐	▓			▓			▓			▓		
Campsis radicans			▓			☐	▓			▓			▓			▓		
Celastrus scandens			▓			☐	▓			▓				▓			▓	
Clematis verticillaris		▓			▓		▓				▓			▓			▓	
Clematis virginiana			▓	▓			▓				▓			▓			▓	
Cocculus carolinus		▓			▓		▓			▓			▓			▓		
Lonicera dioica		▓			▓		▓			▓			▓			▓		
Lonicera sempervirens		▓				☐	▓			▓			▓			▓		
Menispermum canadense		▓			▓		▓			▓			▓			▓		
Parthenocissus quinquefolia			▓			☐	▓			▓				▓			▓	
Smilax glauca		▓			▓		▓			▓			▓			▓		
Smilax rotundifolia	▓				▓		▓			▓			▓			▓		
Smilax tamnoides		▓			▓		▓			▓			▓			▓		
Toxicodendron radicans			▓			☐	▓			▓				▓			▓	
Vitis labrusca			▓			☐	▓				▓			▓			▓	
Vitis riparia			▓			☐	▓				▓			▓			▓	
Wistaria macrostachya			▓			☐	▓			▓			▓			▓		

LONGEVITY:

Longevity refers to the length of time a selected plant can be expected to live where environmental conditions are favorable and competition with other plants is minimal (Table V). Although the stems and tops of most shrub species are short-lived, the plants often grow for centuries because long-lived root systems continually release new stems and tops that replace old, dying ones.

■□□ VERY SHORT-LIVED:
     20 years or less, original stems/top with extremely short life expectancy,
     indicator — *Rubus occidentalis* (Blackcap Raspberry)

■■□ SHORT-LIVED:
     20 to 50 years,
     indicator — *Cornus stolonifera* (Redosier Dogwood)

■■■ MODERATELY SHORT-LIVED:
     50 to 100 years
     indicator — *Viburnum trilobum* (American Cranberrybush Viburnum)

BIOLOGICAL DISORDERS:

Most kinds of shrubs and vines are subject to one or more biological disorders. Most of these cause little noticeable damage to the plants. Others, by severely injuring leaves, twigs, branches, or roots, cause stunting, decadence and eventual death of the infected plant. Health is affected by the severity of disease, insect, and physiological factors. The most virulent disorders are: chestnut blight, dutch elm disease and oak wilt (disease); gypsy moth and mimosa webworm (insect); and chlorosis (physiological). These usually cause rapid decline. Susceptibility is magnified in species (commonly fast growing pioneer species such as Shining Willow, American Elder, and Common Buttonbush) which suffer frequent breakage as the result of wind and ice storms (Table V).

The value of individual shrubs and vines and plant collections for ornamental purposes on lawns or in recreation areas, for soil erosion control, for wildlife habitat, and for commercial farming purposes can be greatly reduced or destroyed by these disorders. The removal of dead plants and subsequent replacement may be very costly to home owners, park and forest preserve managers, municipal governments and commercial growers (Carter 1964).

Most biological disorders that are of frequent, widespread, or destructive nature are outlined in the master plates section for each species. The reader is referred to county extension service expertise and publications for information on indentification, prevention and control. Three categories of plant susceptibility are presented (Table V).

FREQUENT:
     species whose visual appearance, health and survival are noticeably threatened

OCCASIONAL:
     species hosting only occasional or minor disorders which do not significantly alter visual appearance, threaten health or survival

INFREQUENT:
     species that are rarely afflicted and are generally considered free of disorders

URBAN CONDITIONS:

Where urban vegetation exists it modifies and enhances the urban environment, making it more enjoyable and livable. Nowhere is there a greater need for plant material. Vegetation in parks and plazas, along street and river corridors, or in scattered forest preserves must grow and survive the hostile conditions of environment common to many metropolitan landscapes. The more hostile the environment, the more limited the selection of plants able to withstand it. Limiting factors include air pollution, too little soil moisture, improper drainage, compacted soils, infertile soils, high heat albedos, night lighting, and salt spray. High maintenance costs due to extensive shrub and vine mortality must be avoided in favor of species that are biologically and functionally adapted.

A guide to the selection of suitable native shrubs and vines for the urban environment is included in Table VI. Shrubs and vines are ranked in three general categories (sensitive, intermediate, resistant) according to their tolerance. Table VI is based upon extensive review of popular literature and recent research in some areas. Finally, the designer must use the tolerance data in Table VI with caution; pioneering research in this area is very incomplete with preliminary experimental results often inconclusive.

ATMOSPHERIC POLLUTION TOLERANCE:

Air quality standards are being set that safeguard the health of humans, but not always the most sensitive plants. Plants are ranked in three general categories according to their tolerance of any specific pollutant (Table VI).

SENSITIVE:
   plants injured by low concentrations of a specific pollutant; injury response involves extensive browning and loss of leaves; under severe or continuous conditions these plants will eventually die.

INTERMEDIATE:
   plants displaying moderate sensitivity to a specific pollutant; injury response includes chlorosis or browning of leaves.

RESISTANT:
   plants displaying minimal or no sensitivity to a specific pollutant.

HERBICIDE TOLERANCE:

Selective weed killers have become widely used to control undesirable "weed" plants. Herbicides have long been accepted as environmental pollutants which affect sensitive vegetation. Evidence continues to grow that some herbicide compounds in the ambient atmosphere can reach levels sufficient to cause adverse growth affects on sensitive vegetation. Three classes of plant sensitivity are presented.

SENSITIVE:
   severe foliage and/or growth malformation injury response to low level herbicide drift exposure; under severe or continuous conditions injury will become lethal.

INTERMEDIATE:
   moderate necrosis and chlorosis of leaves and/or growth malformations are injury symptoms of low level exposure to herbicide drift.

RESISTANT:
   plant displaying minimal or no sensitivity to herbicide drift.

NIGHT LIGHTING TOLERANCE:

Research demonstrates that outdoor night lighting from lamps at an intensity of one foot-candle or more, dusk to dawn, has adverse effects on the growth of plants in the landscape that border lighted areas. Outdoor area lighting exerts its greatest effect in photoperiodically extending the growth of many plants and delaying the dormancy of others. Three categories of tolerance are considered.

SENSITIVE:
   extremely photo-responsive plants that continue vegetative growth in response to night vision lighting sources.

INTERMEDIATE:
   plants with moderate vegetative growth response to night vision lighting sources.

RESISTANT:
   plants with no or minimal vegetative growth response to night vision lighting sources.

HEAT/DROUGHT TOLERANCE:

The capacity of most plants to resist the detrimental effects of heat and drought are limited. The ability of plants to survive excessive heat and prolonged drought are presented below.

SENSITIVE:
   plant suffering early heat or drought injury; species with few heat/drought avoidance adaptations.

INTERMEDIATE:
   plants displaying moderate sensitivity and injury to excessive heat or drought, species with some heat/drought avoidance adaptations (high leaf diffusion resistance, abundant leaf waxes, early shedding of leaves during drought, small leaves, deep penetrating and branching roots, root generation potential, etc.)

RESISTANT:
   plants displaying minimal or no sensitivity to excessive heat or prolonged drought; species with many heat/drought avoidance adaptations.

MINE LAND TOLERANCE:

The need for surface mined materials by present-day society continues to increase. Recent reclamation laws of many states demand mining operations to stabilize the soil, to reduce sediment and runoff to adjacent land and downstream areas, to enhance natural beauty, and to return the land to some useful purpose. The major soil limitations for establishing vegetation on mine land sites are droughtiness, coarse textures, claypan soils, wetness, salinity, alkalinity, acidity, shallow depth, toxicity, and severe nutrient imbalance. Slope, stoniness, degree of erosion, and the amount of surface materials available for reclamation are also limiting factors. A general guide to the selection of suitable native plants for common mine land types includes three categories. A more specific suitability can be determined by consulting other tables that present site-specific tolerance data.

SENSITIVE:
   less than 40 percent of 5 year old plantings survive.

INTERMEDIATE:
   between 40 and 60 percent of 5 year old plantings survive.

RESISTANT:
greater than 60 percent of 5 year old plantings survive.

SALT TOLERANCE:

The extensive use of deicing salts in urban environments in northern states has created a synthetic saline environment frequently resulting in significant plant injury. Injury response of intolerant plants in coastal environments is also common. The salts are deposited by aerial drift on dormant buds and twigs of deciduous trees and on twigs, buds, and foliage of evergreen species. Excess accumulations of salts also leach into the root zone. Most authorities attribute the greatest percentage of injury to aerial deposition. Three classes of salt tolerance are presented.

SENSITIVE:
extensive or complete dieback and needle browning of conifers; extensive or complete dieback and inhibition of flowering of deciduous plants; under severe conditions these plants will eventually die.

INTERMEDIATE:
moderate twig dieback or needle browning on conifers; moderate dieback and inhibition of flowering on deciduous plants.

RESISTANT:
minimal or no twig dieback or needle browning on conifers; minimal or no dieback and inhibition of flowering on deciduous plants.

SOIL COMPACTION TOLERANCE:

Pore space, ideally 50 percent, is the portion of the soil matrix that is directly and adversely affected by heavy use. Pore-size distribution (the distribution of macro and micropores) does not remain constant, but is reduced. Soil compaction and anaerobic conditions caused by paving, heavy use, and grade change due to soil addition create an unfavorable environment for most plants. Differences exist in the ability of plant species and of individuals within species to tolerate compacted conditions. Three classes of tolerance are identified.

SENSITIVE:
species most severely injured by anaerobic soil conditions resulting from compaction; under severe or continued conditions these plants will eventually die.

INTERMEDIATE:
species less severely injured by poor soil aeration resulting from compaction.

RESISTANT:
species least injured by poor soil aeration resulting from compaction.

ROOT STRUCTURE:

The roots of a plant perform two primary functions. The vertical taproot and the network of lateral roots branching from it anchor and brace the crown. Root tips and root hairs filter and draw in a steady supply

Plants Suitable for Urban Environments: Shrubs — Table VI

Legend: ● sensitive · ◉ intermediate · ○ resistant

	Atmospheric Pollutants										Other Factors				Root Pattern					
	Sulfur dioxide	Ozone	Oxides of nitrogen	Peroxyacetyl nitrate	Hydrogen fluoride	Hydrogen chloride	Ethylene	Chlorine	Mercury vapor	2,4-D	Light	Heat-drought	Mine spoils	Salt	Soil compaction	Shallow lateral	Deep lateral	Taproot	Stoloniferous	Transplantability
Aesculus parviflora												◉		○	◉					●
Aesculus pavia												◉		○	◉					●
Alnus serrulata		●										○		●	○					○
Amelanchier sanguinea					◉							○		●	●					○
Amorpha canescens												○		○	●					◉
Amorpha fruticosa										●	○	○	○	○						◉
Andromeda polifolia												●	●	○						●
Arctostaphylos uva-ursi												○	○	○	●					●
Aronia arbutifolia												◉		○						◉
Aronia melanocarpa												○		○						◉
Aronia prunifolia												◉		○						◉
Baccharis halimifolia												○		○	○					○
Betula pumila	●				○	○				●	●	◉		◉	○					●
Calycanthus floridus					○							○			◉					○
Castanea pumila												●			●					●
Ceanothus americanus												●		○	●					●
Ceanothus ovatus												●		●	●					●
Cephalanthus occidentalis												○		○	○					◉
Chamaedaphne calyculata												○			○					●
Clethra acuminata												◉		○	●					●
Clethra alnifolia												●		○	○					●
Comptonia peregrina												○		○	●					●
Cornus amomum		●								●	●	○		●	○					○
Cornus canadensis		◉								●	●	●	●	●	○					●
Cornus racemosa		◉								●	●	○	○	●	◉					◉

488

Plants Suitable for Urban Environments: Shrubs   Table VI

Legend: sensitive = ●   intermediate = ◉   resistant = ○

	Atmospheric Pollutants										Other Factors				Root Pattern					
	Sulfur dioxide	Ozone	Oxides of nitrogen	Peroxyacetyl nitrate	Hydrogen fluoride	Hydrogen chloride	Ethylene	Chlorine	Mercury vapor	2,4-D	Light	Heat-drought	Mine spoils	Salt	Soil compaction	Shallow lateral	Deep lateral	Taproot	Stoloniferous	Transplantability
Cornus rugosa		◉								●	●	●	●	●	●					●
Cornus stolonifera	◉	●								●	●	○		●	○					●
Corylus americana						●						◉		●	◉					●
Corylus cornuta						●						◉		●	◉					●
Cyrilla racemiflora												○		○	○					◉
Diervilla lonicera												○			○					◉
Dirca palustris												●	●	○	◉					●
Elaeagnus commutata												○		○	●					○
Epigaea repens												○		○	○					●
Euonymus americanus												●		●	◉					○
Euonymus obovatus												●	●	●	◉					○
Fothergilla gardeni												◉		◉	○					●
Fothergilla major												◉		◉	◉					●
Gaultheria procumbens												◉		○	○					●
Hamamelis vernalis								●				◉		◉	○					●
Hydrangea arborescens									●	●	●	●	○		◉					◉
Hydrangea quercifolia									●	●	●		○	○	◉					◉
Hypericum densiflorum												◉		○	○					◉
Hypericum frondosum												○		○	◉					◉
Hypericum kalmianum												○		○						◉
Hypericum prolificum												○		○						◉
Ilex decidua											◉	○		○	○					◉
Ilex glabra											◉	●		○	○					●
Ilex verticillata											◉	◉		●	○					◉
Itea virginica												○		○	○					○

Plants Suitable for Urban Environments: Shrubs — Table VI

Legend: sensitive ● · intermediate ◉ · resistant ○

	Atmospheric Pollutants										Other Factors				Root Pattern					
	Sulfur dioxide	Ozone	Oxides of nitrogen	Peroxyacetyl nitrate	Hydrogen fluoride	Hydrogen chloride	Ethylene	Chlorine	Mercury vapor	2,4-D	Light	Heat-drought	Mine spoils	Salt	Soil compaction	Shallow lateral	Deep lateral	Taproot	Stoloniferous	Transplantability
Juniperus communis	○				○	○					○	○	○	◉	●					●
Juniperus horizontalis	○				○						○	○	○	◉	●					●
Kalmia angustifolia												○		○	○					●
Kalmia latifolia												◉		◉	○					●
Kalmia polifolia												●		○	○					●
Ledum groenlandicum												◉		○	○					○
Leiophyllum buxifolium												○	○	○	●					●
Leucothoe catesbaei												●		◉	◉					○
Lindera benzoin												●		○	◉					●
Lonicera canadensis										●		○		○	○					◉
Lyonia ligustrina												○		○	○					●
Magnolia virginiana											○	●		○	○					●
Mahonia aquifolium		◉			●							●		○	◉					●
Myrica pensylvanica												○	○	○	○					●
Neviusia alabamensis												◉			●					○
Pachistima canbyi												●			●					●
Philadelphus grandiflorus								○				○		◉	◉					○
Physocarpus opulifolius												○		◉	○					◉
Pieris floribunda												●	●	◉	●					●
Pinus aristata	●	●									○	○	○	◉	●					●
Potentilla fruticosa		◉							●	●	○	○		○	○					○
Prunus hortulana				●	●				●			○		○	◉					○
Quercus ilicifolia					○	○			◉	○	◉	○			●					●
Quercus prinoides					○	○			◉	○	◉	○			●					●
Rhododendron arborescens			●	○	◉		◉	○	○	○	◉	●	●	●	●					◉

Plants Suitable for Urban Environments: Shrubs — Table VI

Legend: ● sensitive ◉ intermediate ○ resistant

	Atmospheric Pollutants										Other Factors				Root Pattern					
	Sulfur dioxide	Ozone	Oxides of nitrogen	Peroxyacetyl nitrate	Hydrogen fluoride	Hydrogen chloride	Ethylene	Chlorine	Mercury vapor	2,4-D	Light	Heat-drought	Mine spoils	Salt	Soil compaction	Shallow lateral	Deep lateral	Taproot	Stoloniferous	Transplantability
Rhododendron calendulaceum		●	◉	○	◉		◉	○	◉	◉	◉	●	●	●	●					◉
Rhododendron carolinianum	◉	●	○	◉			◉	○	◉	◉	◉	●	●	●	●					●
Rhododendron catawbiense		●	◉	○	◉		◉	○	◉	◉	◉	●	●	●	●					●
Rhododendron nudiflorum			●	○	◉		◉	○	◉	◉	◉	◉	●	●	○					◉
Rhododendron roseum		●	●	○	◉		◉	◉	◉	◉	◉	◉	●	●	○					◉
Rhododendron vaseyi		◉	○	◉			◉	○	◉	◉	◉	●	●	●	○					
Rhododendron viscosum		●	○	◉			◉	○	◉	◉	◉	●	●	●	○					
Rhus aromatica		●			◉					●	●	○	○	○	●					○
Ribes americanum					○	◉				●		◉		●	○					◉
Ribes cynosbati					○	◉				●		○			◉					◉
Ribes missouriense					○	◉				●		○			◉					◉
Ribes odoratum					○	◉				●	○	○	○		○					◉
Robinia hispida											○	○		○	●					○
Robinia viscosa											○	○		○	●					○
Rosa carolina			●		◉		●			◉		○		●	◉					○
Rosa setigera			●		◉		●			◉		○	○	●	◉					◉
Rubus allegheniensis					○			●		○		○			◉					◉
Rubus occidentalis					○			●		●		○			◉					◉
Rubus odoratus					○			●		◉		◉			◉					○
Rubus strigosus					◉			●		◉		○								○
Salix humilis	●				○				●	●		○		○	○					○
Salix lucida	●				○				●	●		○		○	○					○
Sambucus canadensis		●			○					●		○		●	○					◉
Sambucus pubens					○					●		●		●	◉					●
Shepherdia argentea												○		○	●					●

491

Plants Suitable for Urban Environments: Shrubs   Table VI

Legend: sensitive = ● , intermediate = ◉ , resistant = ○

	Atmospheric Pollutants										Other Factors				Root Pattern					
	Sulfur dioxide	Ozone	Oxides of nitrogen	Peroxyacetyl nitrate	Hydrogen fluoride	Hydrogen chloride	Ethylene	Chlorine	Mercury vapor	2,4-D	Light	Heat-drought	Mine spoils	Salt	Soil compaction	Shallow lateral	Deep lateral	Taproot	Stoloniferous	Transplantability
Shepherdia canadensis												○		○	●					●
Spiraea alba												○		●	○					○
Spiraea corymbosa												◉		●	◉					○
Spiraea tomentosa												○		●	○					○
Staphylea trifolia												●			◉					◉
Stewartia ovata												●		●	●					●
Symphoricarpos albus		●								●		◉		◉	◉					○
Symphoricarpos occidentalis												○		●	◉					○
Symphoricarpos orbiculatus		●										○		●	◉					○
Taxus canadensis					◉			●	○	◉		●	●	○	●					●
Vaccinium angustifolium					●					◉		○		○	●					◉
Vaccinium corymbosum					●					◉		◉		○	○					◉
Vaccinium macrocarpum					●							●		●	○					●
Vaccinium stamineum					●					○		○		○	◉					◉
Viburnum acerifolium	●				●			◉				◉		●	◉					◉
Viburnum alnifolium	●				●			◉				●		●	◉					◉
Viburnum cassinoides					●			◉				◉		○						◉
Viburnum dentatum					●			◉				○		○	◉					◉
Viburnum nudum					●			◉				○		●	○					◉
Viburnum rafinesquianum	●				●			◉				○		●	◉					◉
Viburnum trilobum	●				●			◉				○		●	○					○
Xanthorhiza simplicissima												◉			◉					◉
Yucca filamentosa												○		○	◉					●
Zenobia pulverulenta												●		○	○					◉

Plants Suitable for Urban Environments: Vines — Table VI

Legend: ● sensitive · ◉ intermediate · ○ resistant

	Sulfur dioxide	Ozone	Oxides of nitrogen	Peroxyacetyl nitrate	Hydrogen fluoride	Hydrogen chloride	Ethylene	Chlorine	Mercury vapor	2,4-D	Light	Heat-drought	Mine spoils	Salt	Soil compaction	Shallow lateral	Deep lateral	Taproot	Stoloniferous	Transplantability
Ampelopsis arborea												○		○	○					○
Ampelopsis cordata												○		○	○					○
Aristolochia durior												●		●	◉					◉
Berchemia scandens												○		○	○					○
Bignonia capreolata												○		○	○					●
Campsis radicans										◉		○		○	○					●
Celastrus scandens		◉								●		○		○	◉					●
Clematis verticillaris												◉			●					●
Clematis virginiana														○						●
Cocculus carolinus												○		○	◉					○
Lonicera dioica										●		○		○	◉					●
Lonicera sempervirens										●		○		○	◉					●
Menispermum canadense												◉		○	○					○
Parthenocissus quinquefolia	●			○				●		◉		○		◉	○					◉
Smilax glauca												○		○	○					●
Smilax rotundifolia												○		○	○					●
Smilax tamnoides												○		○	○					◉
Toxicodendron radicans										◉		○		○	○					○
Vitis labrusca					◉	●		◉		●		◉		○						○
Vitis riparia						●		◉		●		○			○					○
Wistaria macrostachya										●		○		○	○					●

of oxygen, water, and minerals which nourishes the growth of the crown structure overhead. Generally shrubs and vines have a tendency to develop root structure arrangements of four types (Table VI).

SHALLOW LATERAL:
> dividing and redividing, the lateral roots form a fibrous mat up to four feet in depth and from 1½ to 3 times the reach of the crown. In general shallow rooted shrubs and vines are relatively fast growing and easily transplanted. In the midwest, during periods of low precipitation or low available moisture in upper soil layers, shallow rooted plants suffer early injury. Prolonged drought can result in the eventual death of many individuals. Similarly, extensive damage results when soil is compacted forming an impermeable crust which greatly reduces oxygen and moisture in upper soil layers.
> indicator — Sweet Azalea *(Rhododendron arborescens)*

DEEP LATERAL:
> in many species a youthful plant soon develops intermediate to deep penetrating lateral roots.
> indicator — Bottlebrush Buckeye *(Aesculus parviflora)*

TAPROOT:
> shrubs and vines whose deep carrot-like taproot may grow to a depth of 15 feet or more. Plants having deep tap or lateral root systems are considerably more tolerant of drought because root penetration is to a depth where moisture is available from ground water sources. Dieback is not so soon affected by soil compaction or drought. Transplanting of wild shrubs or vines is very difficult and limited to small saplings where sufficient root structure can be retained.
> indicator — Adamsneedle Yucca *(Yucca filamentosa)*

STOLONIFEROUS:
> a horizontal stem, just above or beneath the soil, from the tip of which a plant will sprout (also includes a bent shoot that takes root).
> indicator — Yellowroot *(Xanthorhiza simplicissima)*

ASSOCIATE SPECIES:

Each assemblage of vegetation that is homogeneous and differs from adjacent vegetation assemblages constitutes a stand. All stands in which the dominant species are essentially the same comprise an association (Daubenmire 1968). It is important to recognize that although no two stands grouped into one association are identical, they do exhibit a high degree of similarity. This similarity is quantifiable and can be classified. A plant association then is a kind of plant community of definite composition presenting a uniform appearance and growing in uniform suitable habitat conditions.

The association concept is a useful guide to the environmental planner. After a series of habitat types have been inventoried within the project area, each can be managed in complementary fashion to utilize the landscape resource most efficiently. A habitat type is not equally favorable for all plant associations. Growth and survival vary significantly from one habitat type to another. Similarly plant associations can be used as indicators of potential habitat, since the vegetation community and its environment are inseparable.

As a rule, the random distribution of a single species has little fundamental significance in determining habitat. Where two or more species exhibit similar distribution patterns the designer may suspect intrinsic similarities in environmental tolerance. Optimal management demands recognition of all habitat types in an area. Conscientious land use policy must reflect these unique environmental potentialities. Knowing the correlation between specific associations and their specific habitat tolerances is essential. The common associates are presented for each shrub and vine species catalogued in the master plates.

SIMILAR SPECIES:

The designer, landscape contractor and nurseryman are frequently faced with the task of proposing a comparable substitute when difficulties with nursery availability of the selected plant are incurred. Too often substitutes are suggested whose performance is perceivably incompatible with the original program intent. Such changes in a viable program function are unacceptable to the environmental designer. Substitute species whose genetic or ornamental properties and physiographic requirements most closely resembling those of the selected plant are presented for designer consideration. Critical differences are also reviewed in the Master Plates section.

SPECIES CULTIVARS:

Several of the more contemporary hybrids developed from the native shrubs, and vines are listed and principal variations outlined in the Master Plates section for expanded designer consideration in special performance situations.

SHRUB AND VINE MASTER PLATES

Aesculus parviflora

FORM: globular or mound
Size: **mid-height shrub** - from 2 to 4 m (6 to 12 ft)
Spread: **wide** - 4 to 6 m (12 to 20 ft) or more, typically 2 or more times the height
Mass: **dense**

BRANCHING: **ascending picturesque** candelabra branching, lowest branches **horizontal** often resting on ground; **coarse**
Twig: stout, smooth, buff to **orange brown** or gray brown with raised light brown lenticels
Bud: **large** terminal, 5 mm (⅕ in) long, 4 dry papery scales, **gray brown,** side buds have glittery white cast on scale fringes
Bark: **smooth, red brown to** dark **brown**

FOLIAGE: opposite, **palmately compound,** 5 to 7 leaflets, **oblanceolate to oblong obovate,** fine toothed; **medium coarse**
Surface: **dull,** smooth above, grayish hairy beneath
Color: spring - **light green;** summer - **medium** to dark **green;** autumn - **yellow green**
Season: **deciduous;** emergence - mid **May;** drop - mid **September**

FLOWER: erect cylindrical candle-like **spikes** from 15 to 30 cm (6 to 12 in) tall, long feathery bottlebrush-like stamens
Color: **white** with pinkish white stamens and red anthers
Season: mid **July through** early **August,** after leaves are fully grown
Sex: monoecious   **Fragrant:** slightly perfumed, very attractive to insects

FRUIT: smooth glossy **nut** enclosed by partitioned pitted husk, 3 cm (1⅕ in) diameter, rarely produced in North
Color: husk bright yellow turning light **brown,** nut orange brown
Season: early **September to** late **October**   Human Value: **all parts poisonous** if eaten
Wildlife Value: **very low;** small mammals occasionally

HABITAT: formation - **forest;** region - **Southern;** gradient - **wet-mesic, mesic, and mesic-dry;** rich woods, moist ravine,
          floodplain terrace, protected coves
Shade Tolerance: **tolerant**
Flood Tolerance: **intermediate**

SOIL: Texture: **moderately coarse** loamy sands, loams **to moderately fine** silt loams; shallow soils over limestone
Drainage: **moderately poor to well**
Moisture: **moist to average**
Reaction: **moderately acid to circumneutral;** pH range 5.5 - 7.5

HARDINESS: **zone 5a**
Rate: **slow** on old wood, sucker shoots developing at base are medium to fast with 6 to 12 cm (2 to 4 ft) in one season
Longevity: **short-lived**

SUSCEPTIBILITY: Physiological: **frequent** - leaf scorch
Disease: **infrequent** - none serious
Insect: **infrequent** - none serious
Wind-Ice: **infrequent**

URBAN TOLERANCE: Pollution:
Lighting: **sensitive**   Drought Heat: **intermediate**   Mine Spoils:
Salt: **resistant**   Soil Compaction: **intermediate**
Root Pattern: fibrous, **deep descending,** spreading by underground suckers; **difficult to transplant,** use container or B & B

SPECIES: Associate: trees - Yellow Buckeye, American Beech, Cucumbertree Magnolia, Tuliptree; shrubs - Oakleaf/
          Smooth Hydrangeas, Atlantic Leatherwood, Brook Euonymus, Virginia Stewartia, Common Witchhazel
Similar: Red Buckeye - somewhat larger, red flowers; Shinyleaf Yellowhorn - China, glossy pinnately compound leaves
Cultivars: 'Serotina' - flowers 2 to 3 weeks later; 'Rogers' - large flowers, 2 weeks later, non-suckering habit

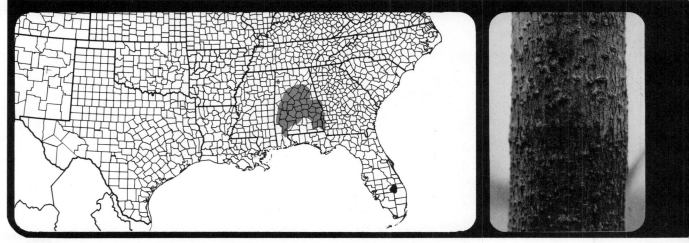

Bottlebrush Buckeye

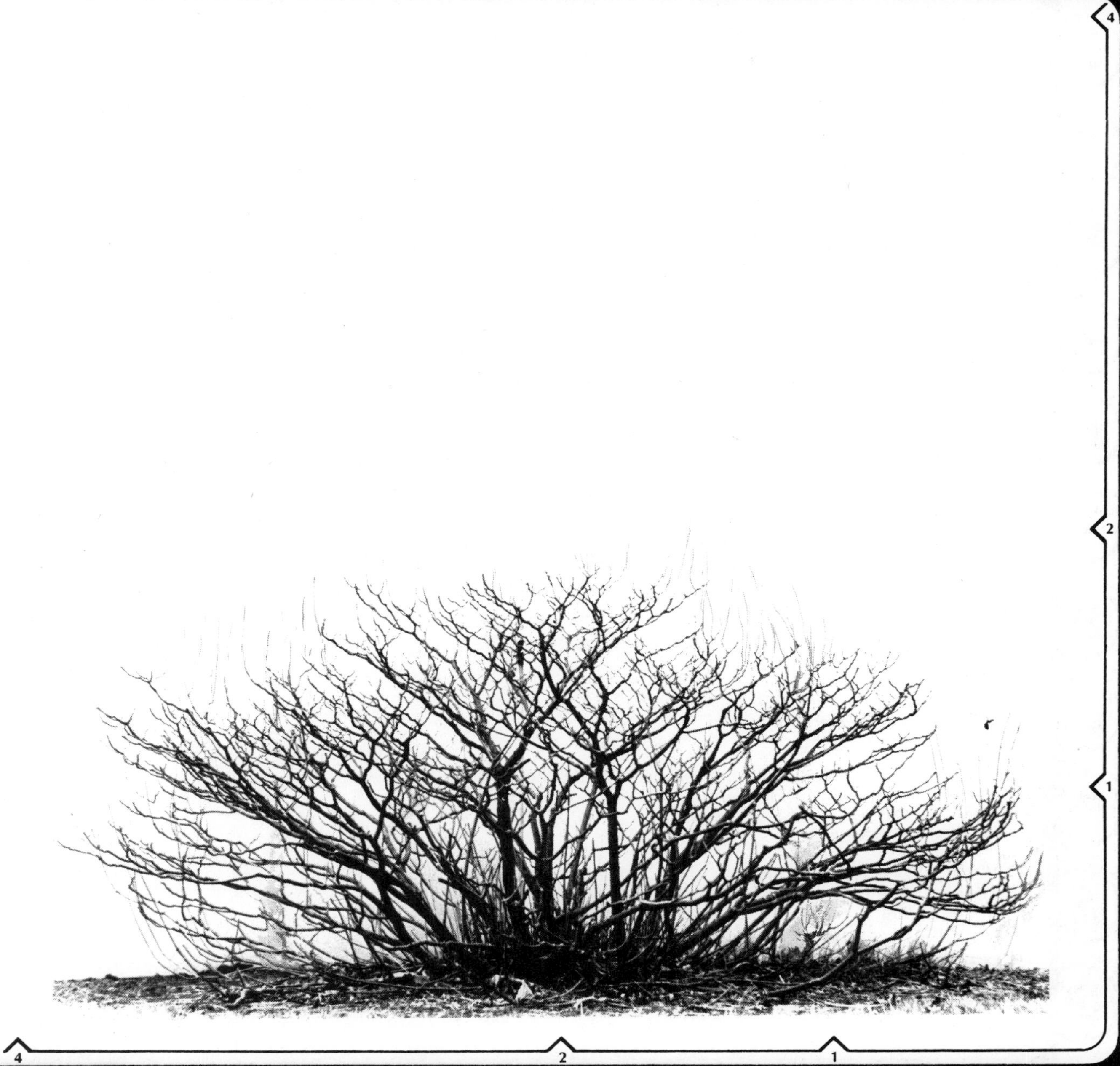

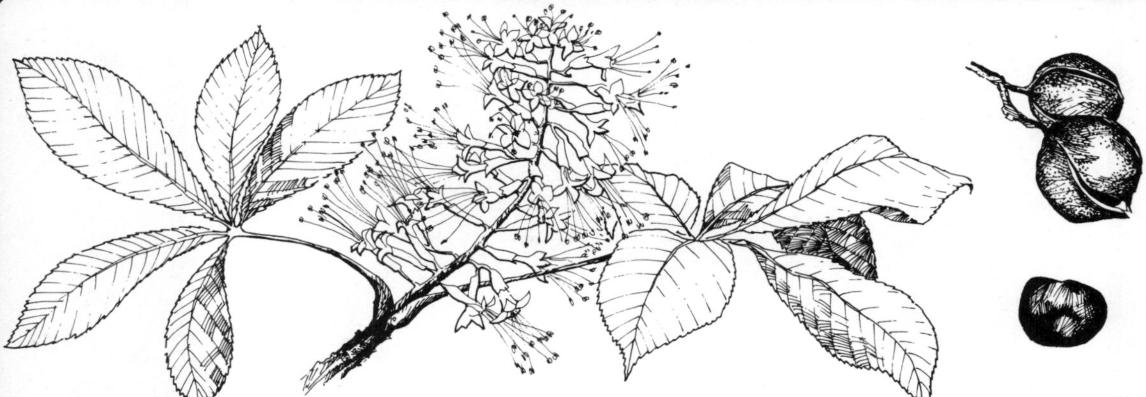

Aesculus pavia

FORM: **obovoid to globular** or mound
Size: **large shrub** - 4 to 6 m (12 to 20 ft) or small tree occasionally to 10 m (35 ft)
Spread: **wide** - 4 to 6 m (12 to 20 ft) or more, usually as broad or broader than high
Mass: **moderate**, large shrubs becoming open and thin

BRANCHING: single or several trunks, large **ascending picturesque** branches; **coarse texture**
Twig: stout, smooth, very crooked, buff to **green brown** with raised light brown lenticels
Bud: **large** terminal, 8 mm (⅓ in) long, smooth dry papery scales, **brown**
Bark: **smooth**, roughened by scattered corky blocks, flaking off in small thin irregular patches, **red brown to dark brown**

FOLIAGE: opposite, **palmately compound,** 5 leaflets, oblong obovate or **oblanceolate,** double toothed; **medium coarse**
Surface: **dull**, smooth, paler beneath
Color: spring - **light green** or coppery; summer - bright **medium green** with long red leafstalks; autumn - **yellow green**
Season: **deciduous;** emergence - early **May,** drop - mid **September**

FLOWER: loose erect cylindric candle-like **spike,** 10 to 15 cm (4 to 6 in) high
Color: bright **red**
Season: mid through late **May,** after leaves, young plants often flowering when not more than 1 m (3 ft) high
Sex: monoecious

FRUIT: smooth **nut** enclosed by partitioned pitted husk, 2.5 to 5 cm (1 to 2 in) diameter, pendulous on slender stems
Color: light **brown**
Season: early **August through** late **September**   Human Value: **all parts poisonous** if eaten
Wildlife Value: **very low;** small mammals occasionally

HABITAT: formation - **swamp, old field, forest;** region - **Southern;** gradient - **wet-mesic, mesic and mesic-dry;** moist or dry
woods, clearings, low rich woods, streamsides, pastures, foothills, swamp margins
Shade Tolerance: **tolerant**
Flood Tolerance: **intermediate**

SOIL: Texture: **moderately coarse** loamy sands **to moderately fine** silt loams; best development on medium loams
Drainage: **moderately poor to well**
Moisture: **moist to average**
Reaction: **moderately acid to circumneutral,** pH 5.5 - 7.5

HARDINESS: zone 6a
Rate: **slow** to medium
Longevity: **moderately short-lived**

SUSCEPTIBILITY: Physiological: **frequent** - leaf scorch
Disease: **infrequent** - none serious, mildew can be a problem
Insect: **infrequent** - none serious
Wind-Ice: **infrequent**

URBAN TOLERANCE: Pollution:
Lighting: **sensitive**   Drought Heat: **intermediate**   Mine Spoils:
Salt: **resistant**   Soil Compaction: **intermediate**
Root Pattern: fibrous, **deep descending; difficult to transplant,** use container or B & B from nursery

SPECIES: Associate: trees - Eastern Redbud, Flowering Dogwood, Black/Scarlet/White Oaks, Loblolly Pine; shrubs -
sumac/hawthorn/dogwood species, Bottlebrush Buckeye, Flame Azalea, Dwarf Fothergilla
Similar: Woolly Buckeye - leaves woolly beneath, flowers red or yellow green; Bottlebrush Buckeye - white flowers
Cultivars: 'Atrosanguinia', 'Rubra' - flowers dark red; 'Humilis' - prostrate form; 'Sublaciniata' - deeply cut leaflets

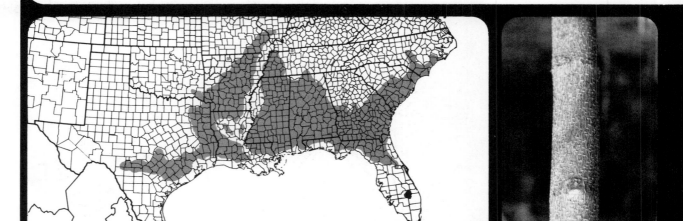

Red Buckeye

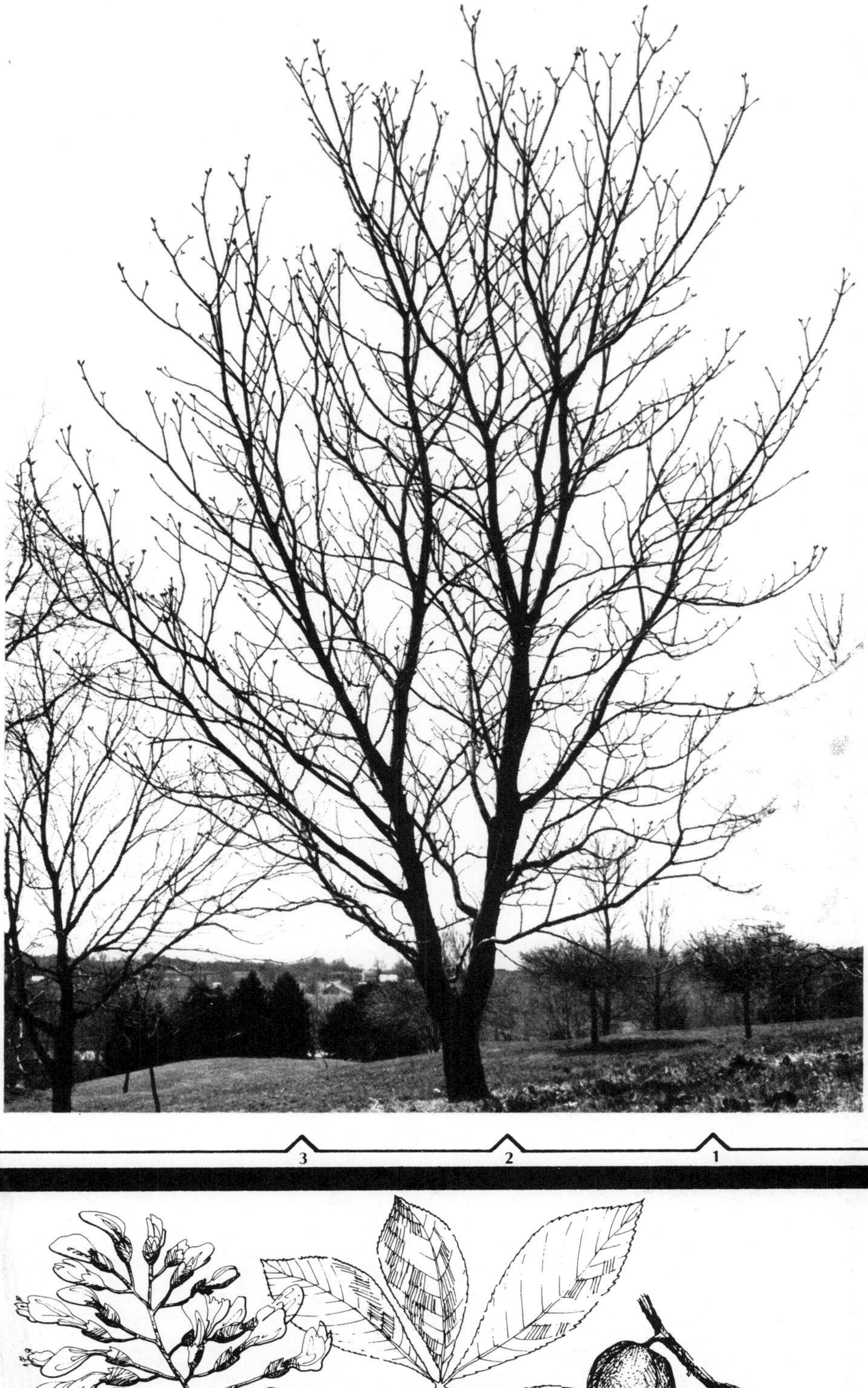

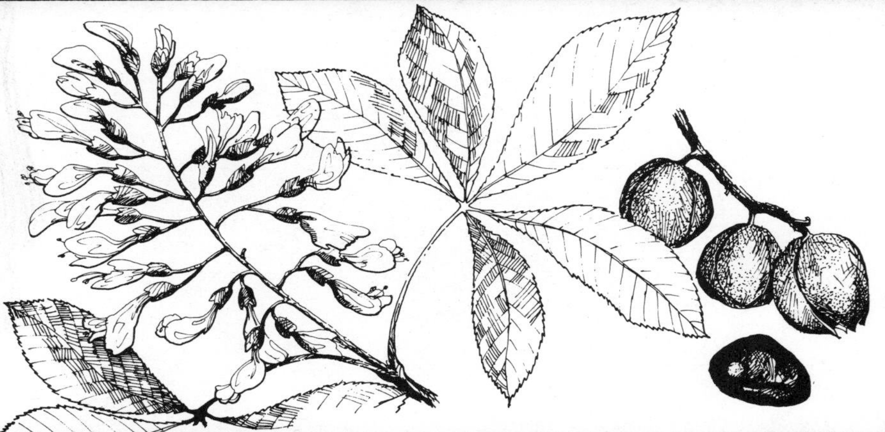

Alnus serrulata

FORM: obvoid to globular
Size: **large shrub** - 4 to 6 m (12 to 20 ft) or rarely small tree to 9 m (30 ft)
Spread: **wide** - 4 to 6 m (12 to 20 ft)
Mass: **open**

BRANCHING: multiple trunks, most branching above middle, **erect, upright spreading picturesque** habit; **medium**
Twig: slender, smooth, flexible, **zigzag, green brown to red brown**
Bud: small, 9.5 mm (⅜ in), distinctly **stalked** with **2 scales, resinous, red to purple or red brown; erect winter catkins**
Bark: **smooth** with corky whitish lenticels, becoming fluted with narrow crack-like verticle fissures, **gray to gray brown**

FOLIAGE: alternate, **simple,** oval to **obovate,** doubly toothed with wavy margin; **medium** texture
Surface: **glossy,** smooth, slightly gummy when young
Color: spring - **light green;** summer - **dark green;** autumn - green late then **yellow** tinged **red**
Season: **deciduous;** emergence - late **April;** drop - mid **October**

FLOWER: slender pencil-like male **catkins** borne in drooping clusters, female catkins ellipsoidal in erect clusters of 3
Color: male **purple** or brown, female deep **purple**
Season: mid through late **March,** before leaves
Sex: monoecious

FRUIT: erect **strobile,** 19 mm (¾ in) long, resembles small woody cone
Color: **brown**
Season: early **August** persisting **through** late February   Human Value: not edible
Wildlife Value: **intermediate;** waterbirds, small mammals, hoofed browsers eat twigs, leaves

HABITAT: formation - **swamp, spring, meadow, forest;** region - **Central, Southern;** gradient - **wet;** forms thickets along
        banks of streams, ponds, lakeshores, boggy swales, sloughs, ditches, swamp borders, wet meadows, springy places
Shade Tolerance: **very intolerant**
Flood Tolerance: **very tolerant**

SOIL: Texture; **coarse** infertile sands, sandy and gravelly loams, stiff clays; prefers **fine** sandy loams, silts, peats, mucks
Drainage: **very poor to well**
Moisture: **wet to moist**
Reaction: **moderately acid to circumneutral;** pH range 5.5 - 7.5

HARDINESS: zone 5a
Rate: **fast**
Longevity: **short-lived**

SUSCEPTIBILITY: Physiological: **infrequent**
Disease: **occasional** - powdery mildew is rarely serious, occasional cankers, leaf rust
Insect: **occasional** - woolly alder aphid, alder flea beetles, alder lace bug, leaf miner, tent catepillar, bagworm
Wind-Ice: **frequent** - weak wooded, breakage often extensive

URBAN TOLERANCE: Pollution: **sensitive** - 0_3
Lighting: Drought Heat: **resistant**   Mine Spoils:
Salt: **sensitive**   Soil Compaction: very **resistant**
Root Pattern: **shallow** coarse **lateral** spreading, suckers freely at base; **transplants easily** B & B or BR spring or fall

SPECIES: Associate: trees - Black/Peachleaf Willows, Pin/Swamp White Oaks, River Birch, Silver Maple; shrubs - Virginia
        Sweetspire, Hardhack Spirea, Swamp Azalea, Common Buttonbush, Silky Dogwood, Yellowroot, Possumhaw
Similar: Hazel Alder - drooping strobiles, speckled bark, Northern; Low Birch - coppery bark, Northern
Cultivars: none available

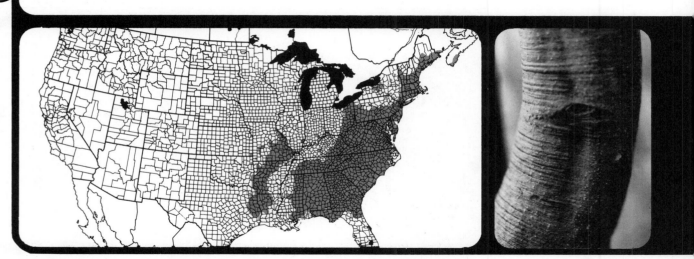

Common Alder

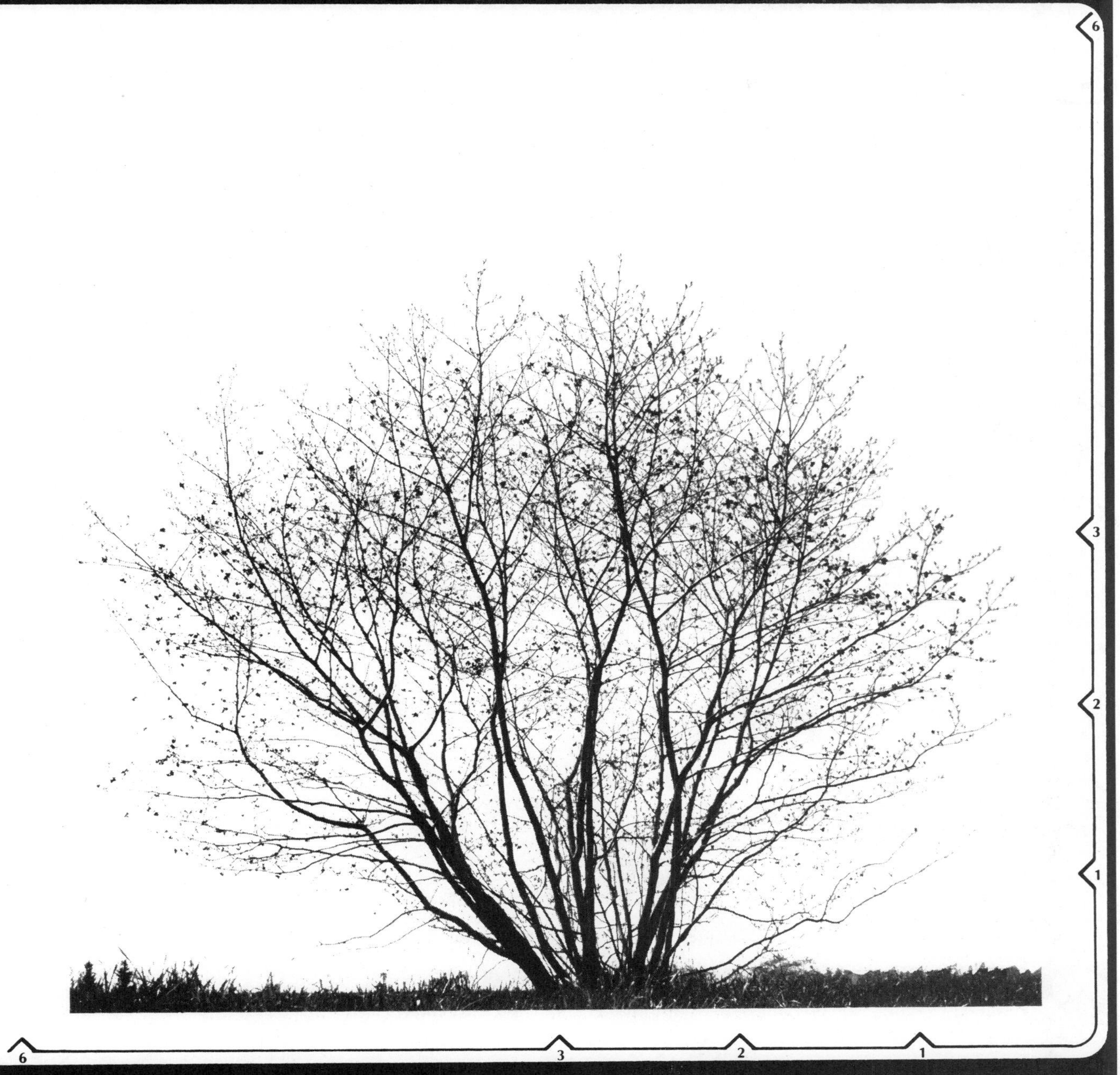

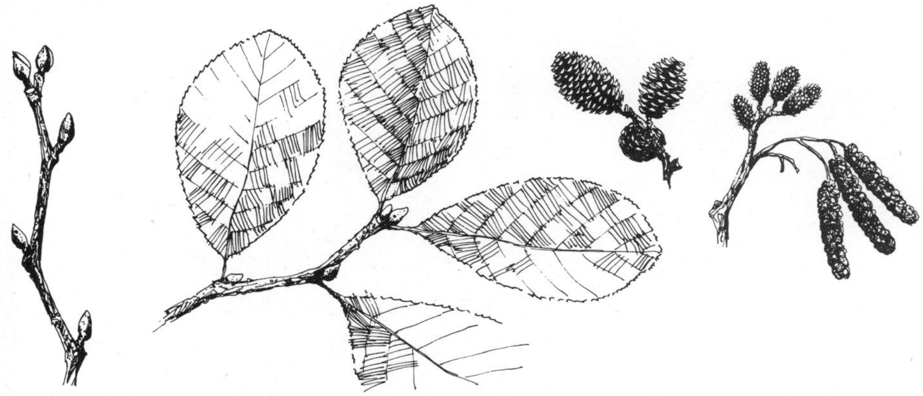

Amelanchier sanguinea

FORM: mound
Size: **small shrub** - from 1 to 2 m (3 to 6 ft)
Spread: **narrow** - 1 to 2 m (3 to 6 ft) plus, typically broader than tall
Mass: **open,** straggling appearance on exposed sites

BRANCHING: solitary or multiple stems, usually branched above middle, **erect or upright spreading to arching; fine** texture
Twig: smooth, very slender, with exfoliating **scales, red to red brown**
Bud: long **pointed,** 4 mm (⅙ in), wine **red to purple or brown**
Bark: **smooth** or with irregular longitudinal splits exposing whitish inner bark, ashy **gray**

FOLIAGE: alternate, **simple, oval to suborbicular,** rather coarsely toothed, entire at base; **medium fine** texture
Surface: **dull,** smooth, paler beneath
Color: spring - **yellow green to red green,** summer - **blue green;** autumn - **orange to red**
Season: **deciduous;** emergence - late **April,** drop - mid **October**

FLOWER: rather loose open ascending or nodding **spikes,** 2.5 to 7.5 cm (1 to 3 in) long
Color: **white,** sometimes pinkish
Season: early through mid **May,** with emerging leaves
Sex: monoecious

FRUIT: globular **berries,** 6 to 9.5 mm (¼ to ⅜ in) diameter, borne in loose ascending or drooping clusters
Color: **red** ripening **to** dark **purple** to nearly black, often **with bluish** bloom
Season: early through late **July**   Human Value: sweet and juicy **edible fruits**
Wildlife Value: **very high;** songbirds, upland gamebirds, large and small mammals; hoofed browsers eat twigs, leaves

HABITAT: formation - **savanna, forest;** region - **Northern;** gradient - **mesic-dry, dry;** open dry woodlands, open brushy
hillsides, rocky slopes and ridges, crevices of open rock faces/cliffs, woods edge, sandy bluffs, sandy places
Shade Tolerance: **tolerant**
Flood Tolerance: **intolerant**

SOIL: Texture: **coarse to medium;** generally on dry sterile rocky, sandy, or gravelly soils, sandy loams, occasionally on clay
Drainage: **well to excessive**
Moisture: **average to dry**
Reaction: **slightly acid to alkaline,** pH 6.1 - 8.5

HARDINESS: zone 5a
Rate: **medium**
Longevity: **short-lived**

SUSCEPTIBILITY: Physiological: **infrequent**
Disease: **occasional** - cedar/serviceberry rust, witches' broom, leaf blight, fire blight, powdery mildews, fruit rot
Insect: **occasional** - leaf miner, borers, pear leaf blister mite, pear slug sawfly, willow scurfy scale
Wind-Ice: **infrequent**

URBAN TOLERANCE: Pollution: **intermediate** - HFI
Lighting: Drought Heat: **resistant**   Mine Spoils:
Salt: **sensitive**   Soil Compaction: **sensitive**
Root Pattern: fibrous, **shallow lateral,** sometimes **stoloniferous** forming thickets; **transplants easily** B & B

SPECIES: Associate: trees - White/Scarlet/Red Oaks, Quaking Aspen, Virginia Pine, American Elm; shrubs - Smooth/
Fragrant Sumacs, American Elder, Common Spicebush, Limber Honeysuckle, Gray Dogwood
Similar: Running/Low/Thicket/Saskatoon Serviceberries; Black/Red Chokeberries - tolerate wet habitats
Cultivars: none available

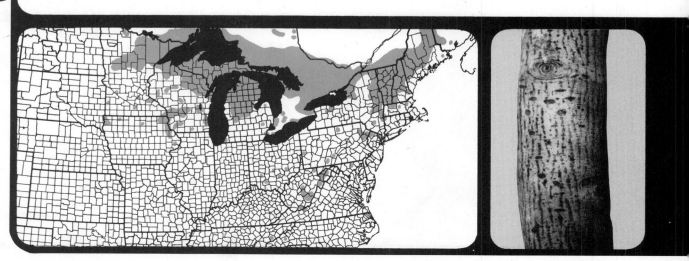

Amorpha canescens

FORM: **globular or mound,** rather flat-topped
Size: **very small shrub** - commonly to 1 m (3 ft), occasionally up to 2 m (6 ft)
Spread: **very narrow** - 1 m (3 ft), occasionally spreading to 2 m (6 ft)
Mass: loose and **open**

BRANCHING: solitary or multiple stems with few stiff **ascending** branches; **coarse** texture
Twig: dense **velvety, angled, gray brown** with white hairs
Bud: small ovoid, **woolly, red brown**
Bark: **smooth, scaly** to exfoliating on very old stems, **gray**

FOLIAGE: alternate, **pinnately compound,** 15 to 45 leaflets, **elliptic oval** to oblong oval, entire margin; **very fine** texture
Surface: both sides **tomentose** with fine white hairs
Color: spring - **silvery gray;** summer - **gray green;** autumn - **gray green or yellowish**
Season: **deciduous;** emergence - early **June,** drop - mid **September**

FLOWER: narrow cylindric terminal **spikes,** 5 to 12.5 cm (2 to 5 in), several spikes crowded together, basal flowers open first
Color: **blue to** deep **purple** with bright orange anthers
Season: mid through late **July,** often into early August, after leaves are fully grown
Sex: monoecious

FRUIT: small one-seeded crescent-shaped **pod,** 8 mm (⅓ in) long, crowded in narrow cylindrical clusters
Color: **brown,** glossy
Season: early **September** persisting **through** late **February**   Human Value: not edible
Wildlife Value: **intermediate;** upland gamebirds, songbirds and small mammals

HABITAT: formation - **prairie, savanna, glade;** region - **Central;** gradient - upland **mesic-dry, dry;** dry prairies, prairie knolls, ridges, bluffs, rocky or sandy open woods, cedar glades, oak barrens
Shade Tolerance: **very intolerant**
Flood Tolerance: **very intolerant**

SOIL: Texture: **coarse to medium;** sandy plains, gravelly and sandy loams, prairie loams
Drainage: **well to excessive**
Moisture: **average to droughty**
Reaction: **neutral to alkaline,** pH 7.0 - 8.5

HARDINESS: zone 3a
Rate: **medium**
Longevity: **very short-lived**

SUSCEPTIBILITY: Physiological: **infrequent** - tops often winterkill
Disease: **infrequent** - rust, twig canker, powdery mildew, leaf spots; none serious
Insect: **infrequent** - none serious
Wind-Ice: **occasional** - weak wooded, twigs broken easily

URBAN TOLERANCE: Pollution:
Lighting: Drought Heat: very **resistant**   Mine Spoils:
Salt: **resistant**   Soil Compacton: **sensitive**
Root Pattern: fibrous, **shallow lateral, stoloniferous** and suckering, nitrogen-fixing; **transplants well**

SPECIES: Associate: grasses and forbs - Purple Prairieclover, Whorled Milkweed, Silky Aster, Sideoats Gramma, Pale Echinacea, Narrowleaved Puccoon, Prairie Dropseed, Little Bluestem, Porcupine Grass, Ohio Spiderwort
Similar: Dwarfindigo Amorpha - dwarf to 0.6 m (2 ft), Northern; Indigobush Amorpha - taller, tolerates wet
Cultivars: 'Glabrata' - branches and leaves sparsely pubescent

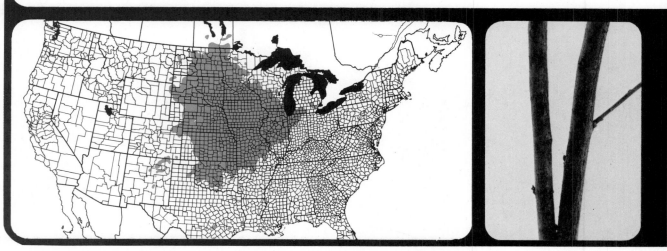

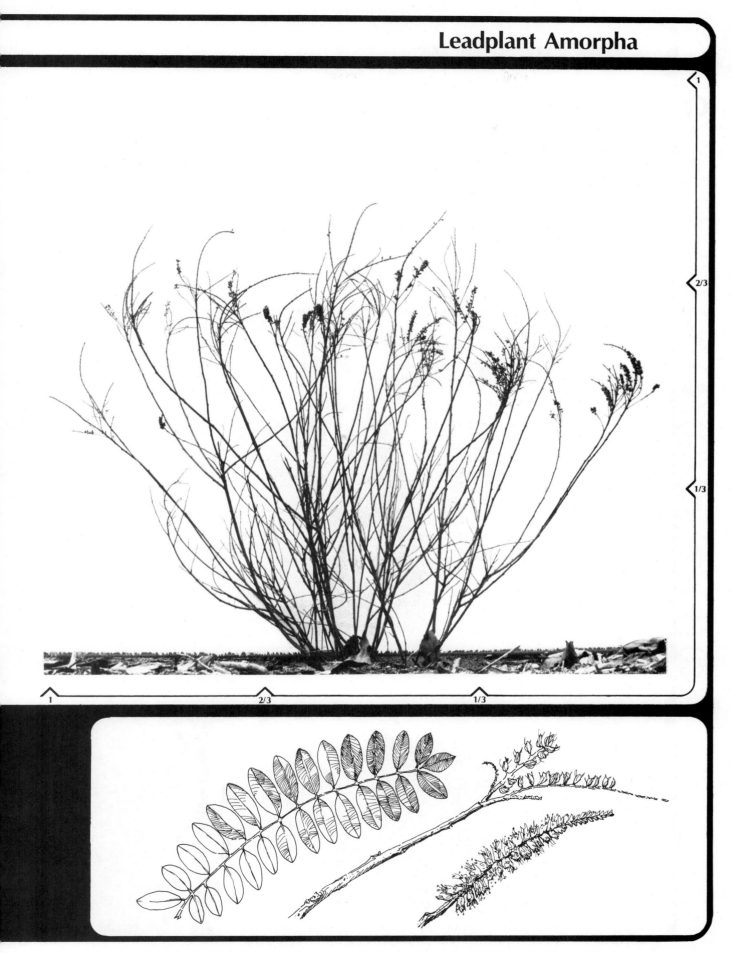

Amorpha fruticosa

FORM: **globular or mound**
Size: **mid-height shrub** - 2 to 4 m (6 to 12 ft), commonly to 6 m (20 ft)
Spread: **wide** - 4 to 6 m (12 to 20 ft), typically up to twice the height
Mass: **open**, bulk of foliage and twigs in upper ⅓ of crown

BRANCHING: multiple stems, lower **horizontal** sweeping ground becoming **ascending** at ends, **leggy** appearance; **medium**
Twig: rigid, slender, round or grooved, **red brown** to gray
Bud: small ovoid, **woolly, red brown**
Bark: **smooth** with prominent transverse lenticels, old trunks **shallow furrowed, gray brown**

FOLIAGE: alternate, **pinnately compound**, 9 to 25 leaflets, **elliptic to oval**, tip slightly indented, entire; **fine texture**
Surface: finely **tomentose** or smooth
Color: spring - **gray green**, summer - bright **medium green**; autumn - **yellow green**
Season: **deciduous**; emergence - early **June**, drop - mid **September**

FLOWER: dense long narrow cylindric terminal **spikes**, 7.5 to 15 cm (3 to 6 in) tall, several tightly clustered upright spikes
Color: deep **purple or bluish** with bright orange anthers
Season: mid through late **June**, after leaves are full grown
Sex: monoecious

FRUIT: small warty kidney-shaped **pods**, 14 mm (½ in) long, with large glandular dots, in crowded cylindric clusters
Color: tan **brown**, glossy
Season: mid **August** persisting **through** winter until late **March**   Human Value: **poisonous fruits**
Wildlife Value: **intermediate;** waterfowl, marshbirds, shorebirds, small mammals

HABITAT: formation - **bog, swamp, dune, meadow, forest**; region - **Central, Southern**; gradient - lowland **wet, wet-mesic**;
stream banks, floodplain depressions, swampy land, hummocks, marshes, wet meadows, wet clearings, lakeshores
Shade Tolerance: **intolerant**
Flood Tolerance: **very tolerant**

SOIL: Texture: **coarse to fine;** infertile sands, sandy loams, stiff clays; best development on sandy loams or silts
Drainage: **very poor to excessive**
Moisture: **wet to droughty**
Reaction: **slightly acid to** circumneutral, tolerates **alkaline**, pH 6.1 - 8.5

HARDINESS: zone 3a
Rate: **medium to fast**
Longevity: **very short-lived**

SUSCEPTIBILITY: Physiological: **occasional** - tip burn damage at branch ends, twigs winterkill in North
Disease: **occasional** - often defoliated by medieval stage of Uropyxis amorphae rust, twig canker, powdery mildew
Insect: **occasional** - inflorescence galls; generally free of insect problems
Wind-Ice: **frequent** - weak wooded, easily broken

URBAN TOLERANCE: Pollution: **sensitive** - 2-4D
Lighting: Drought Heat: **resistant**   Mine Spoils: **resistant**
Salt: **resistant**   Soil Compaction: **resistant**
Root Pattern: fibrous, **shallow lateral,** somewhat suckering, nitrogen-fixing; **transplants well**

SPECIES: Associate: trees - Silver Maple, Red Ash, American Sweetgum; shrubs - Rose Mallow, Silky Dogwood, Common Buttonbush, American Elder; vines - Common Poisonivy, Riverbank Grape, Common Trumpetcreeper
Similar: Leadplant Amorpha - smaller, dry habitat; Hardhack Spirea - erect habit; Roseacacia Locust - armed, dry habitat
Cultivars: 'Albiflora' - white flowers; 'Pendula' - branchlets pendulous; Crispa - leaflets curled; 'Humilis'; others

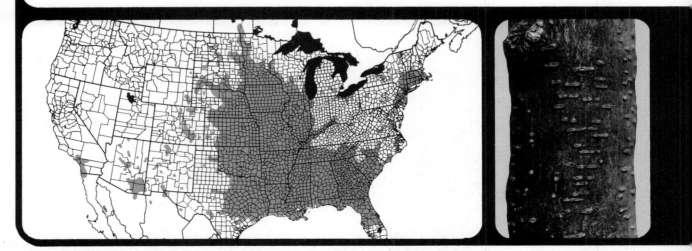

Andromeda polifolia

FORM: low **mat to mound**
Size: **very small shrub** - less than 1 m (3 ft), 20 to 30 cm (8 to 12 in) common
Spread: **very narrow** - less than 1 m (3 ft), typically 0.6 to 1 m (2 to 3 ft)
Mass: **open**

BRANCHING: slender stems elongate and creeping at base, little-branched twigs **erect to upright; fine** texture
Twig: **red brown** to **dark brown**
Bud: small, with 2 outer scales, red brown
Bark: **smooth, gray to brown black**

FOLIAGE: alternate, **simple, linear to oblong linear**, entire with edges rolled under, sharp pointed tip; **fine** texture
Surface: **glossy,** thick leathery, white felty beneath
Color: spring - **silvery gray;** summer, autumn, winter - deep **dark green to blue green**
Season: broadleaf **evergreen**

FLOWER: urn-shaped **bell,** 6 mm (¼ in) long, crowded in small nodding 5 to 6-flowered terminal clusters
Color: **white** to pinkish
Season: early through mid **May**
Sex: monoecious

FRUIT: small dry turban-shaped 5-valved **capsules,** 4 to 5 mm (⅙ to ⅕ in) long
Color: at first bluish, then **brown** with age
Season: early **September through** late **October**   Human Value: **leaves poisonous**
Wildlife Value: **very low;** small mammals occasionally

HABITAT: formation - **bog;** region - **Northern;** gradient - **wet;** cold acid peat bogs, sphagnum bogs, spruce-larch
        swamps
Shade Tolerance: **tolerant** but does best in sunny locations
Flood Tolerance: **very tolerant**

SOIL: Texture: **moderately fine to fine;** organic soils, peats, mucks underlain by calcareous clays, silts, and sands
Drainage: **very poor to moderately poor**
Moisture: **wet to moist**
Reaction: demands **strongly acid or moderately acid,** pH 4.0 - 6.0

HARDINESS: zone 2
Rate: **slow**
Longevity: **moderately short-lived**

SUSCEPTIBILITY: · Physiological: **frequent** - iron chlorosis in lime soils
Disease: **infrequent** - black mildew, powdery mildew, leaf spots, rust; none serious
Insect: **infrequent** - none serious
Wind-Ice: **infrequent**

URBAN TOLERANCE: Pollution:
Lighting: Drought Heat: **sensitive**   Mine Spoils: **sensitive**
Salt: **resistant**   Soil Compaction: **resistant**
Root Pattern: **shallow lateral** creeping rootstocks form large patches; **transplants well,** difficult culture

SPECIES: Associate: trees - Black Spruce, Eastern Arborvitae, American Larch, Black Ash, Red Maple; shrubs -
        Leatherleaf, Bunchberry Dogwood, Checkerberry Wintergreen, Bog Kalmia, Labradortea Ledum, Lowbush Blueberry
Similar: Downy Andromeda - leaves, twigs, fruit whitened with bloom; Lambkill/Bog Kalmias; Cranberry - fine wiry
Cultivars: 'Montana' - more compact, leaves smaller; 'Angustifolia'; 'Compacta'; 'Grandiflora'; 'Major'; 'Nana'; others

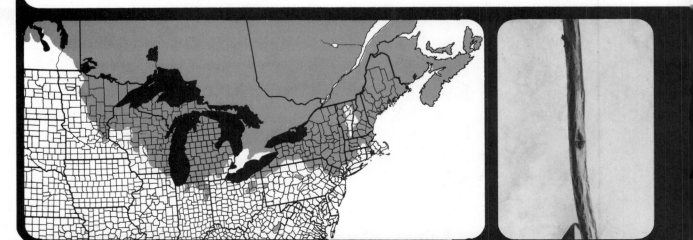

510

Arctostaphylos uva-ursi

FORM: low prostrate **mat**, herb-like
Size: **very small shrub** - less than 1 m (3 ft), typically 5 to 15 cm (2 to 6 in) high
Spread: **very narrow** - commonly to 1 m (3 ft), old established plant may cover area up to 5 m (15 ft) across
Mass: **dense**

BRANCHING: long flexible branches **trailing** flat on ground, flowering branchlets upright; **fine** texture
Twig: white **velvety** at first becoming smooth, **red brown**
Bud: small ovoid, solitary, with 3 scales, dark brown
Bark: **smooth,** older branches with papery **exfoliation, reddish brown** or ashy gray

FOLIAGE: alternate, **simple, obovate to oblong obovate,** entire with edges folded under; **fine** texture
Surface: **glossy,** smooth, thick leathery, lighter beneath
Color: spring - **reddish green;** summer - **dark green;** autumn, winter - **dark green** becoming **reddish green or purplish**
Season: broadleaf **evergreen**

FLOWER: urn-shaped **bell,** 6 to 8 mm (¼ to ⅓ in) long, few in small nodding clusters
Color: **white,** tinged with **pink** on bright red stems
Season: late **April** and early **May**
Sex: monoecious

FRUIT: dry mealy globular **berry,** 6 to 8 mm (¼ to ⅓ in) diameter
Color: bright **red,** glossy
Season: late **July through** late August, often persisting through late **December**   Human Value: **fruits, leaves edible**
Wildlife Value: **low;** upland gamebirds, Mule and White-tailed Deer browse heavily, Black Bear eat fruits

HABITAT: formation - **forest, dune, bald, barrens;** region - **Northern;** gradient - **mesic-dry and dry;** beaches, foredunes
     facing lake, sandy or rocky soils, rock outcroppings, sand barrens, open sandy woods, rocky glades and balds
Shade Tolerance: **intolerant**
Flood Tolerance: **intolerant**

SOIL: Texture: **coarse to moderately coarse;** thin soils over bedrock, infertile sands, loamy sands; intolerant of clay
Drainage: **well to excessive**
Moisture: **average to droughty**
Reaction: **strongly acid to moderately acid,** pH 4.5 - 6.0

HARDINESS: zone 2
Rate: very **slow**
Longevity: **long-lived**

SUSCEPTIBILITY: Physiological: **infrequent**
Disease: **infrequent** - black mildew, rust, leaf galls; none serious
Insect: **infrequent** - none serious
Wind-Ice: **infrequent**

URBAN TOLERANCE: Pollution:
Lighting: Drought Heat: **resistant**   Mine Spoils: **resistant**
Salt: **resistant**   Soil Compaction: **sensitive**
Root Pattern: trailing **shallow**-rooting branches; **difficult to transplant,** use container grown or large mats, mulch heavily

SPECIES: Associate: trees - Jack/Red Pines, Common Chokecherry, Black Oak; shrubs - Common/Creeping Junipers,
     Fragrant Sumac, Pin/Sand Cherries, Bush Cinquefoil, Inland Ceanothus, Kalm St.Johnswort
Similar: Bearberry/Cranberry Cotoneasters; Bearberry Willow; Checkerberry Wintergreen; Lapland Rhododendron
Cultivars: none available

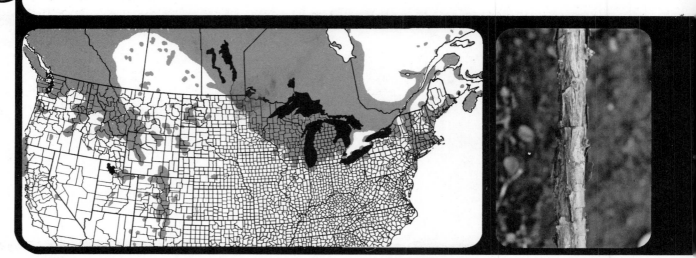

Aronia arbutifolia

FORM: obovoid
Size: **mid-height shrub** - from 2 to 4 m (6 to 12 ft)
Spread: **narrow** - 1 to 2 m (3 to 6 ft), typically ½ to ⅔ the height
Mass: **moderate**

BRANCHING: **erect** multiple stems, **upright spreading** rounded crown, **leggy** with age, foliage in upper ½ to ⅓; **medium**
Twig: slender, dense **velvety, red brown to gray** with exfoliating silvery **scales**
Bud: long **pointed,** 6 to 8 mm (¼ to ⅓ in), **red to purplish**
Bark: **smooth** becoming exfoliated into tight cherry-like curls in cross-check pattern, lenticels conspicuous, **red brown**

FOLIAGE: alternate, **simple,** elliptic to **obovate,** abruptly taper-pointed, finely toothed margin; **medium fine** texture
Surface: **glossy,** thick, grayish tomentose beneath
Color: spring - **red green;** summer - deep **dark green;** autumn - rich **orange to red**
Season: **deciduous;** emergence - early **May,** drop - late **October,** often with premature defoliation in late summer

FLOWER: dense **flat-topped** clusters, 2.5 to 5 cm (1 to 2 in) diameter, 9 to 20 blooms per cluster
Color: **white** with red anthers, petals sometimes tinged reddish or pinkish
Season: mid through late **May,** after leaves
Sex: monoecious

FRUIT: pear-shaped **berry,** 6 mm (¼ in) diameter, borne in dense clusters along stem
Color: bright **red**
Season: early **September through** mid **December**   Human Value: **edible fruits,** bitter
Wildlife Value: **intermediate;** upland gamebirds, songbirds, large and small mammals; hoofed browsers eat twigs, leaves

HABITAT: formation - **bog, swamp, dune, forest, old field;** region - **Central, Southern;** gradient - lowland **wet, wet-mesic;**
boggy places and low pinelands, flatwoods, wet thickets, creek banks, moist rocky ledges, swamps, wet acid sand
Shade Tolerance: **intermediate**
Flood Tolerance: **very tolerant**

SOIL: Texture: **coarse to fine;** peats, mucks, clays, fine sands, fine sandy loams and loams; adapted to coarse soils
Drainage: **very poor to well**
Moisture: **wet to dry**
Reaction: **moderately acid to slightly acid,** pH 5.1 - 6.5

HARDINESS: zone 4b
Rate: **slow**
Longevity: **short-lived**

SUSCEPTIBILITY: Physiological: **infrequent**
Disease: **infrequent** - leafspots, twig and fruit blight, rust; none are serious
Insect: **infrequent** - round-headed apple borer can be locally serious
Wind-Ice: **infrequent**

URBAN TOLERANCE: Pollution:
Lighting: Drought Heat: **intermediate**   Mine Spoils:
Salt: **resistant**   Soil Compaction: **resistant**
Root Pattern: dense, finely fibrous, **shallow lateral,** profuse suckering habit forming colonies; **transplants well**

SPECIES: Associate: trees - River Birch, Common Baldcypress, willow species; shrubs - Sweetgale, Swamp Azalea, Silky
Dogwood, Swamp Rose, He-huckleberry, Inkberry; vines - Alabama Supplejack, Crossvine, Common Poisonivy
Similar: Purple Chokeberry - purple fruit; Low/Thicket/Saskatoon Serviceberries - fruits red turning purple
Cultivars: "Brilliantissima' - fruits glossier and deep red, more profuse; 'Erecta' - narrow upright habit

Aronia melanocarpa

FORM: **globular or mound**
Size: **small shrub** - from 1 to 2 m (3 to 6 ft)
Spread: **narrow** - 1 to 2 m (3 to 6 ft), commonly spreading into broad thickets
Mass: **moderate** to open

BRANCHING: slender multiple stems, stiffly **erect or upright spreading; medium** texture
Twig: slender, smooth, **yellow brown** with exfoliating silvery **scales**
Bud: long sharp **pointed**, smooth, **purplish to red**
Bark: **smooth** with conspicuous lenticels, finally with tight exfoliating curls in cross-check diamond pattern, **red brown**

FOLIAGE: alternate, **simple,** elliptic to **obovate,** finely toothed margin; **medium fine** texture
Surface: **glossy,** smooth
Color: spring - **red green or purplish;** summer - deep **dark green;** autumn - crimson **red**
Season: **deciduous;** emergence - late **April,** drop - early **November**

FLOWER: **flat-topped** terminal 5 to 6-flowered clusters, 2.5 to 5 cm (1 to 2 in) diameter
Color: **white** with pink anthers
Season: early through mid **May,** after leaves
Sex: monoecious

FRUIT: glossy globular **berry,** 6 to 9.5 mm (¼ to ⅜ in) diameter, in loose clusters
Color: **black** or blackish purple
Season: early **September** through late **November,** often falling early   Human Value: **edible fruits**
Wildlife Value: **intermediate;** upland gamebirds, songbirds, large and small mammals; hoofed browsers eat twigs, leaves

HABITAT: formation - **bog, swamp, spring, prairie, dune, bald, cliff, old field;** region - **Northern;** gradient - **wet, wet-mesic, mesic-dry, dry;** wet thickets, creek banks, swampy lands, dry thickets, cliffs, bluffs, clearings, wet acid sand, balds
Shade Tolerance: **intermediate**
Flood Tolerance: **very tolerant**

SOIL: Texture: **coarse** infertile sands and gravels **to fine** mucks, clays, sands, peats; thin soils and rock outcroppings
Drainage: **very poor to excessive**
Moisture: **wet to droughty**
Reacton: **moderately acid to slightly acid,** pH 5.1 - 6.5

HARDINESS: zone 3a
Rate: **slow**
Longevity: **short-lived**

SUSCEPTIBILITY: Physiological: **infrequent**
Disease: **infrequent** - twig and fruit blight cover affected plant parts with powdery mold, leaf spots, rust
Insect: **infrequent** - round-headed apple borer; rarely serious
Wind-Ice: **infrequent**

URBAN TOLERANCE: Pollution:
Lighting: Drought Heat: **resistant**   Mine Spoils: **resistant**
Salt: **resistant**   Soil Compaction: **resistant**
Root Pattern: **shallow** fibrous, fine textured, suckers profusely; **transplants well**

SPECIES: Associate: trees - Pin/Swamp White Oaks, River Birch; shrubs - Common Buttonbush, Hardhack Spirea, Pinkshell Azalea, Virginia Sweetspire, He-huckleberry, Common Winterberry, Common Alder, Shining Willow
Similar: Red Chokeberry - red fruit, taller; Saskatoon/Low/Running Serviceberries - size, form, flower, habitat similar
Cultivars: 'Elata' - taller, less suckering; 'Grandifolia' - glossier leaves, taller

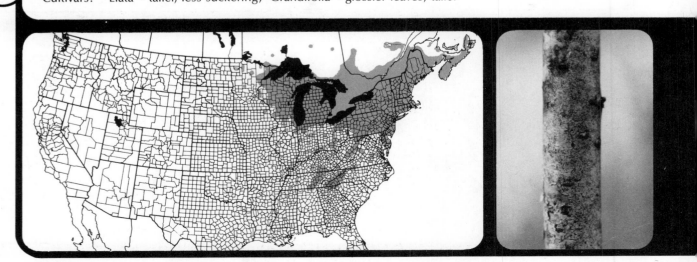

516

Aronia prunifolia

FORM: obovoid to globular
Size: **mid-height shrub** - from 2 to 4 m (6 to 12 ft), tallest of chokeberries
Spread: **narrow** - 1 to 2 m (3 to 6 ft), typically ½ to ⅔ the height
Mass: **moderate**

BRANCHING: slender **erect** stems, **upright spreading** branches, foliage in upper ½ to ⅓ of crown; **medium** texture
Twig: slender, smooth, sometimes velvety, **red brown** with silvery exfoliating **scales**
Bud: oblong ovoid, sharp **pointed, red to brown**
Bark: **smooth** with conspicuous lenticels, finally exfoliating with tight close papery curls in cross-check pattern, **red brown**

FOLIAGE: alternate, **simple,** oval to **obovate,** finely toothed margin; **medium fine** texture
Surface: **glossy,** blackish glands along midrib, tomentose beneath
Color: spring - **red green;** summer - deep **dark green;** autumn - scarlet **red**
Season: **deciduous;** emergence - late **April,** drop - late **October**

FLOWER: in terminal **flat-topped** hawthorn-like clusters, each bloom small, 9.5 mm (⅜ in) diameter, 5 petals
Color: **white** with red anthers, petals often purplish tinged
Season: late **April through** mid **May,** with or after leaves
Sex: monoecious

FRUIT: glossy globular **berry,** 6 to 9.5 mm (¼ to ⅜ in) diameter, in loose clusters
Color: deep **purple**
Season: early **September through** mid **December**　　　　　　　　　　Human Value: **edible fruit**
Wildlife Value: **intermediate;** upland gamebirds, songbirds, large and small mammals; hoofed browsers graze twigs

HABITAT: formation - **bog, swamp, forest, old field;** region - **Northern;** gradient - lowland **wet, wet-mesic;** wet places, invader
of floating bog mats, swamps, wet woods, open seepage slopes
Shade Tolerance: **intermediate**
Flood Tolerance: **very tolerant**

SOIL: Texture: **medium** loams **to fine** sandy loams, sands, heavy clays, peats, and mucks
Drainage: **very poor to well**
Moisture: **wet to dry**
Reaction: **moderately acid to slightly acid,** pH 5.1 - 6.5

HARDINESS: zone 4a
Rate: **slow**
Longevity: **short-lived**

SUSCEPTIBILITY: Physiological: **infrequent**
Disease: **infrequent** - leaf spots, twig and fruit blight, rust; none serious
Insect: **infrequent** - round-headed apple borer; rarely serious
Wind-Ice: **infrequent**

URBAN TOLERANCE: Pollution:
Lighting:　　　　　　　　　　　　　Drought Heat: **intermediate**　　　　　Mine Spoils:
Salt: **resistant**　　　　　　　　　　Soil Compacton: **resistant**
Root Pattern: **shallow** fibrous, profuse suckering habit; **transplants well**

SPECIES: Associate: trees - American Larch, Black Tupelo, Quaking Aspen, Red Maple, Black Ash; shrubs - Low Birch,
Leatherleaf, Highbush Blueberry, Cranberry, Canada Yew, Speckled Alder, Mountain Holly, Witherod Viburnum
Similar: Red Chokeberry - red fruited; Low/Roundleaf/Running Serviceberries - form, flowers, fruit similar, dry habitats
Cultivars: none available

Baccharis halimifolia

FORM: obovoid to globular
Size: **mid-height shrub** - from 2 to 4 m (6 to 12 ft)
Spread: **intermediate** - 2 to 4 m (6 to 12 ft)
Mass: **open**

BRANCHING: numerous small stiff **upright spreading** branches from short trunks, branchlets very dense; **fine** texture
Twig: slender, smooth, rigid, angled with minute longitudinal grooves and ridges, **green**
Bud: small **resinous, red to green**
Bark: **scaly** becoming thin divided by wide **shallow furrows** into flat interlacing and overlapping ridges, dark **gray**

FOLIAGE: alternate, **simple,** broadly **obovate to oblong obovate,** few teeth near tips or somewhat lobed; **medium fine**
Surface: **dull,** firm, resin dotted
Color: spring - **silvery gray;** summer - bright **gray green;** autumn - **gray green** late, **then purple;** winter - **tan brown**
Season: **semi-evergreen,** persistant in North; emergence - early **June,** drop - late **November** or after

FLOWER: **small** dense globular composite **clusters** at branch ends, each bloom 13 mm (½ in) long
Color: **green to white**
Season: autumn, late **August through** mid **September,** after leaves are full grown
Sex: **dioecious**

FRUIT: hairy **achenes** in plume-like clusters, female with paint brush-like appearance
Color: silvery **white**
Season: early **October through** late **November**   Human Value: not edible
Wildlife Value: **very low;** songbirds, waterfowl and shorebirds use occasionally

HABITAT: formation - **bog, swamp, dune, old field;** region - **Southern;** gradient - **wet;** salt marshes, banks of marshes, shores,
     swales, old fields, various disturbed places, sloughs, borders of salt or brackish waters, maritime beaches and dunes
Shade Tolerance: **very intolerant**
Flood Tolerance: **very tolerant**

SOIL: Texture: **coarse** maritime sands and gravels, sandy loams **to fine** peats, mucks, clays and sands
Drainage: **very poor to excessive**
Moisture: **wet to droughty**
Reaction: **neutral to alkaline,** pH 7.0 - 8.5

HARDINESS: zone 4a
Rate: **fast**
Longevity: **moderately short-lived**

SUSCEPTIBILITY: Physiological: **infrequent**
Disease: **infrequent** - black mold, rust; none serious
Insect: **infrequent** - none serious
Wind-Ice: **frequent** - weak wooded, easily broken

URBAN TOLERANCE: Pollution:
Lighting: Drought Heat: **resistant**   Mine Spoils: **resistant**
Salt: **resistant**   Soil Compacton: **resistant**
Root Pattern: **shallow** fibrous, **lateral** spreading; **transplants easily**

SPECIES: Associate: trees - Live Oak; shrubs - Yaupon, Flameleaf Sumac, American Beautyberry, Southern Waxmyrtle,
     Swamp Cyrilla, Herculesclub Pricklyash, Marsh Elder; vines - Yellow Jessamine, Peppervine, greenbrier species
Similar: Common Buttonbush; White Fringetree, American Smoketree - dry habitats; Fivestamen Tamarisk - Asiatic
Cultivars: none available

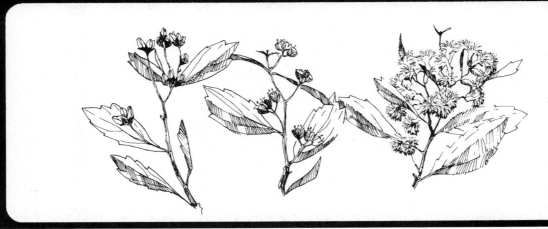

Betula pumila

FORM: **globular or mounded**
Size: **large shrub** - from 4 to 6 m (12 to 20 ft)
Spread: **wide** - 4 to 6 m (12 to 20 ft), typcially 2 times the height
Mass: **open**

BRANCHING: dense multiple stems, **upright spreading** branches, **pendulous** branchlets; **fine** texture
Twig: very slender, wiry, dense **velvety** when young, **orange brown**
Bud: small blunt oblong oval, 3 mm (⅛ in) long, **stalked, clustered,** woolly, **2 to 3 bud scales, brown; winter catkins**
Bark: **smooth** with glandular warty lenticels, coppery **orange brown becoming brown** at base

FOLIAGE: alternate, **simple, suborbicular** to broad elliptic or obovate, coarse dentate teeth; **medium fine** texture
Surface: **dull,** smooth, densely woolly beneath when young
Color: spring - **yellow green;** summer - **medium green;** autumn - golden **yellow**
Season: **deciduous;** emergence - mid **April,** drop - early **October**

FLOWER: female **catkins** cylindric and upright, 13 to 25 mm (½ to 1 in) long
Color: **yellow green**
Season: mid through late **April,** with emerging leaves
Sex: monoecious

FRUIT: cylindric upright cone-like **strobile,** 13 to 25 mm (½ to 1 in) long, stalked
Color: **brown**
Season: mid **August through** late **November**   Human Value: not edible
Wildlife Value: **very high;** songbirds, waterbirds, upland gamebirds, small mammals; hoofed browers graze twigs, leaves

HABITAT: formation - **swamp, meadow, dune, bog;** region - **Northern;** gradient - **wet;** swampy land, marshes, wet meadows,
wet clearings, lakeshores, cold acid peat bogs, sphagnum bogs, moist depressions
Shade Tolerance: **very intolerant**
Flood Tolerance: **very tolerant**

SOIL: Texture: **medium to fine;** primarily organic soils, peats, mucks over mineral soils
Drainage: **very poor to moderately poor**
Moisture: **wet to moist**
Reaction: **moderately acid to** circumneutral, tolerates **alkalines,** pH 5.1 - 8.5

HARDINESS: zone 2
Rate: **medium to fast**
Longevity: **very short-lived**

SUSCEPTIBILITY: Physiological: **occasional** - twig dieback
Disease: **occasional** - leaf spots, leaf blisters, leaf rust, cankers, line pattern mosaic, wood decay, powdery mildews
Insect: **frequent** - aphids, witch-hazel leaf gall aphid, birch leaf miner, birch skeletonizer, bronze birch borer, others
Wind-Ice: **infrequent**

URBAN TOLERANCE: Pollution: **sensitive** - S0₂, 2-4D; **resistant** - HFI, HCl
Lighting: **sensitive**   Drought Heat: **intermediate**   Mine Spoils:
Salt: **intermediate**   Soil Compaction: **resistant**
Root Pattern: **shallow** fibrous; **difficult to transplant**

SPECIES: Associate: trees - American Larch, Black Spruce, Eastern Arborvitae, Black Ash, Red Maple; shrubs - Bog-
rosemary Andromeda, Leatherleaf, Bog Kalmia, Labradortea Ledum, Lowbush Blueberry, Cranberry, Prairie Willow
Similar: Bog Birch, Prairie Willow, Common/Hazel Alders - form, texture, habitat similar
Cultivars: none available

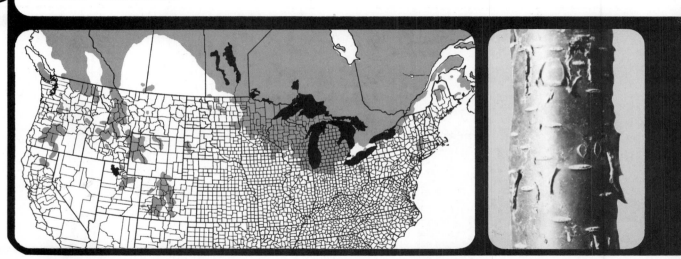

Calycanthus floridus

FORM: globular or mound
Size: **mid-height shrub** - from 2 to 4 m (6 to 12 ft)
Spread: **intermediate** - 2 to 4 m (6 to 12 ft), often forming thickets
Mass: **dense** to moderate

BRANCHING: erect multiple stems with dense **upright spreading or ascending** branches, **pendulous** with fruit; **medium**
Twig: rounded but flattened with **angular** swollen appearance at the nodes, velvety, aromatic when broken, **brown**
Bud: small, round **naked, woolly, brown**
Bark: **smooth** with raised dot-like lenticels, aromatic when bruised, dark **gray brown**

FOLIAGE: opposite, **simple,** ovate to **elliptic** or narrow elliptic, entire margin, **aromatic** when crushed; **medium coarse**
Surface: **glossy,** leathery, dense tomentose beneath
Color: spring - **yellow green;** summer - **yellow green;** autumn - **yellow green** or yellowish
Season: **deciduous;** emergence - early **May,** drop - late **September**

FLOWER: large solitary 5 cm (2 in) diameter, numerous overlapping strap-like petals
Color: maroon **red** to dark reddish **brown**
Season: mid **May,** sporadically **into** late **July,** after leaves
Sex: monoecious   **Fragrant:** fragrance of ripe strawberries

FRUIT: pear or fig-shaped leathery **capsule,** 5 to 6.5 cm (2 to 2½ in) long, fragrant strawberry scent when broken
Color: tan **brown** or red brown   Human Value: not edible
Season: early **September through** late **December**
Wildlife Value: **very low;** rarely used

HABITAT: formation - **forest;** region - **Southern, Central;** gradient - lowland **wet-mesic,** upland **mesic, mesic-dry;** rich woods,
          moist hillsides, banks of quick flowing streams, ravine slopes, footslopes, protected coves
Shade Tolerance: **very tolerant**
Flood Tolerance: **tolerant**

SOIL: Texture: **moderate coarse** loamy sands, sandy loams **to moderately fine** silt loams; best on medium loams
Drainage: **moderately poor to well**
Moisture: **wet to average**
Reaction: **slightly acid to circumneutral,** pH 6.1 - 7.5

HARDINESS: zone 5a
Rate: **slow to medium**
Longevity: **short-lived**

SUSCEPTIBILITY: Physiological: **infrequent**
Disease: **infrequent** - very resistant
Insect: **infrequent** - very resistant
Wind-Ice: **infrequent**

URBAN TOLERANCE: Pollution:
Lighting: Drought Heat: **sensitive**   Mine Spoils:
Salt: Soil Compaction: **intermediate**
Root Pattern: fibrous, **shallow lateral,** prolific suckering habit forming thickets; **easily transplanted**

SPECIES: Associate: trees - Eastern Hemlock, Tuliptree, White Linden, Cucumbertree Magnolia, Northern Red Oak,
          Butternut; shrubs - Pinxterbloom/Flame Azaleas, Mountainlaurel Kalmia, Cinnamon Clethra, Common Spicebush
Similar: Pale Sweetshrub - flowers almost scentless, more fruit set, more Northern
Cultivars: 'Ovatus' - leaves more rounded; 'Purpureus' - leaves purple

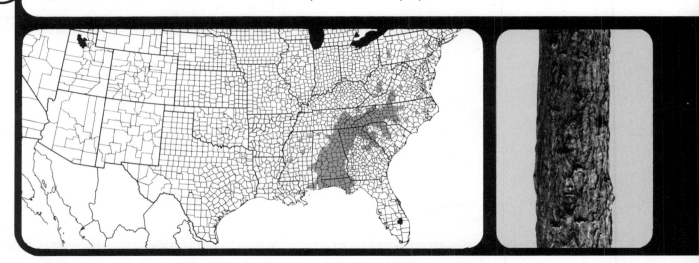

Castanea pumila

FORM: **globular** rounded crown
Size: **large shrub** - from 4 to 6 m (12 to 20 ft) or rarely small tree to 9 m (30 ft)
Spread: **wide** - 4 to 6 m (12 to 20 ft) or more
Mass: **dense**

BRANCHING: single or several trunks, strong **horizontal** lower branches, ascending in upper crown; **medium** texture
Twig: slender, smooth, **red brown to brown**
Bud: small blunt ovoid, 3 mm (⅛ in), **clustered, woolly, reddish to brown**
Bark: smooth at first, becoming **shallow furrowed** with broad flat longitudinal ridges, **brown**

FOLIAGE: alternate, **simple, lanceolate to oblong lanceolate,** coarsely toothed margin with bristle tips; **medium** texture
Surface: **dull,** smooth, white downy beneath
Color: spring - light **red green** or tinged pink; summer - bright **medium green;** autumn - dull golden **yellow or** russet **purple**
Season: **deciduous;** emergence - mid **May,** drop - early **October**

FLOWER: long slender pencil-like ascending **spikes,** 10 to 15 cm (4 to 6 in) long, several spikes crowded together
Color: pale **yellow**
Season: mid to late **June,** after leaves
Sex: monoecious

FRUIT: small glossy ovoid **nut,** 19 mm (¾ in), covered by bur-like husk with needle-sharp prickles, in crowded clusters
Color: dark chestnut **brown**
Season: early **September through** late October   Human Value: sweet **edible fruit**
Wildlife Value: **low;** small mammals occasionally

HABITAT: formation - **swamp, forest, old field;** region - **Central, Southern;** gradient - upland **mesic-dry, dry;** dry rocky slopes, dry woods, steep rocky land, rocky stream banks, sandy ridges, borders of swamps, open woods
Shade Tolerance: **intermediate**
Flood Tolerance: **intolerant**

SOIL: Texture: **coarse** sandy plains, sandy and gravelly loams **to fine** silty clays, sandy clays; dislikes heavy clays
Drainage: **well to excessive**
Moisture: **average to droughty**
Reaction: **moderately acid to slightly acid,** pH 5.1 - 6.5

HARDINESS: **zone 5b**
Rate: **medium**
Longevity: **moderately short-lived**

SUSCEPTIBILITY: Physiological: **infrequent**
Disease: **occasional** - Chestnut blight is lethal, often forming clumps resulting from repeated dieback and sprouting
Insect: **infrequent** - none serious, occasional weevils
Wind-Ice: **infrequent**

URBAN TOLERANCE: Pollution:
Lighting: Drought Heat: **resistant**   Mine Spoils:
Salt: Soil Compaction: **sensitive**
Root Pattern: fibrous, **deep lateral to shallow** spreading, **stoloniferous,** forming expansive thickets; **difficult to transplant**

SPECIES: Associate: trees - Chestnut/White/Black/Post/Blackjack Oaks, Flowering Dogwood, Pignut/Mockernut Hickories, Shortleaf Pine; shrubs - azalea species, Fragrant Sumac, Jerseytea Ceanothus, Common Deerberry
Similar: Ozark Chestnut - taller, hairy leaves; Chinese Chestnut - Asiatic, resistant to blight; Bear/Dwarf Chinkapin Oaks
Cultivars: none available

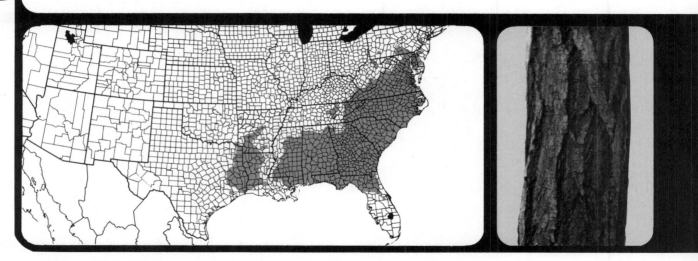

526

Ceanothus americanus

FORM: **globular or mound**
Size: **very small shrub** - to 1 m (3 ft)
Spread: **very narrow** - 1 m (3 ft), up to 2 m (6 ft)
Mass: **dense**

BRANCHING: dense multiple stems, **erect to upright,** unbranched or occasionally branched; **medium** texture
Twig: slender, young twigs somewhat hairy, flexible, yellow brown to **red brown**
Bud: narrow ovoid, somewhat hairy, **red brown** or brown
Bark: **smooth or shallow furrowed** with wide splits showing dark brown inner bark, old stems flaky, **red brown**

FOLIAGE: alternate, **simple, ovate to oblong ovate,** fine toothed, sharp tipped, 3-veined; **medium fine** texture
Surface: **dull to glossy,** smooth, somewhat hairy beneath
Color: spring - bright **medium green;** summer - **medium to dark green;** autumn - remains green late, then **yellow to tan**
Season: **deciduous;** emergence - late **May,** drop - late **November**

FLOWER: short broad dense upright **spikes,** 5 cm (2 in) long, very tiny individual blossoms, unusual claw-like petals
Color: **white**
Season: mid **June through** late **July,** after leaves
Sex: monoecious   **Fragrant:** faintly perfumed

FRUIT: 3-lobed dry triangular **capsule,** saucer-like basal cups persist through winter
Color: **black or brownish,** cups silvery gray
Season: early **September through** late October   Human Value: **edible leaves**
Wildlife Value: **intermediate;** upland gamebirds, songbirds, small mammals; hoofed browsers graze foliage, twigs

HABITAT: formation - **prairie, glade, forest, old field;** region - **Central, Southern;** gradient - upland **mesic-dry and dry;** dry open
woods, upland rocky prairies, woodland borders, mixed deciduous forests, oak and pine barrens, oak openings
Shade Tolerance: **intermediate**
Flood Tolerance: **very intolerant**

SOIL: Texture: **coarse to medium;** sands and gravels, sandy plains, sandy loams, prairie loams, sandy clays
Drainage: **well to excessive**
Moisture: **average to droughty**
Reaction: **strongly acid to moderately acid,** pH 4.5 - 6.0

HARDINESS: zone 3b
Rate: **slow to medium**
Longevity: **very short-lived**

SUSCEPTIBILITY: Physiological: **occasional** - winter dieback
Disease: **infrequent** - leaf spots and powdery mildew are two minor problems
Insect: **infrequent** - none serious
Wind-Ice: **infrequent**

URBAN TOLERANCE: Pollution:
Lighting: Drought Heat: **resistant**   Mine Spoils:
Salt: **resistant**   Soil Compaction: **sensitive**
Root Pattern: **shallow,** large coarse rambling **laterals,** dark red color, nitrogen-fixing; **difficult to transplant**

SPECIES: Associate: trees - Black/Post/Blackjack Oaks, Pignut/Mockernut Hickories, Common Persimmon; shrubs -
Fragrant/Flameleaf Sumacs, Carolina Rose, Common Deerberry, Blackcap Raspberry, Gray Dogwood
Similar: Inland Ceanothus - flowers at branch tips, red fruit; Slender Deutzia - Asiatic; Meadowsweet Spirea
Cultivars: 'Intermedius' - small flower clusters

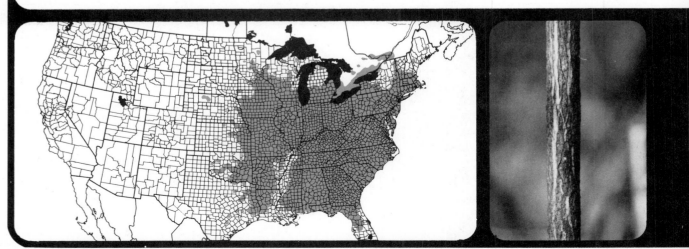

528

Ceanothus ovatus

FORM: globular or **mound,** commonly ovoid
Size: **very small shrub** - less than 1 m (3 ft), typically 0.6 to 1 m (2 to 3 ft) tall
Spread: **very narrow** - less than 1 m (3 ft), often taller than wide
Mass: **very dense**

BRANCHING: multiple stems, **erect to upright** habit, sparingly-branched; **medium** texture
Twig: slender, **velvety, red brown**
Bud: small ovate, slender, **woolly, red brown**
Bark: **smooth,** becoming **shallow furrowed** with wide splits showing dark brown inner bark, old stems flaky, **red brown**

FOLIAGE: alternate, **simple, ovate** to elliptic lanceolate, narrower than Jerseytea Ceanothus, toothed; **medium fine**
Surface: **glossy,** smooth, paler beneath
Color: spring - **medium green;** summer - **medium green;** autumn - **yellow green to brown**
Season: **deciduous;** emergence - late **May,** drop - late **November**

FLOWER: **flat-topped** globular clusters, individual blooms 5 mm (⅕ in) wide, 5 unusual claw-like petals
Color: **white**
Season: early **June through** mid **July,** after leaves
Sex: monoecious

FRUIT: dry 3-lobed **capsule,** splitting into 3 parts, 5 mm (⅕ in) across
Color: **bright red**
Season: mid **July through** early **September**   Human Value: not edible
Wildlife Value: **intermediate;** upland gamebirds, songbirds, small mammals; hoofed browsers graze twigs, leaves

HABITAT: formation - **prairie, glade, forest, dune, old field;** region - **Central, Southern;** gradient - **mesic-dry to dry;** sandy
         woods, open woods, roadside clearings, rocky woods, lake dunes, cedar glade, dry prairie, rocky barrens
Shade Tolerance: **intermediate**
Flood Tolerance: **very tolerant**

SOIL: Texture: **coarse to medium;** sandy plains, pure sands, gravels, sandy loams, loamy sands, prairie loams
Drainage: **well to excessive**
Moisture: **average to droughty**
Reaction: **strongly to moderately acid,** pH range 4.5 - 6.0

HARDINESS: **zone 3b**
Rate: **slow to medium**
Longevity: **very short-lived**

SUSCEPTIBILITY: Physiological: **infrequent**
Disease: **infrequent** - powdery mildew and leaf spots are minor problems
Insect: **infrequent** - none serious
Wind-Ice: **frequent** - flower branches break off in autumn

URBAN TOLERANCE: Pollution:
Lighting: Drought Heat: **resistant**   Mine Spoils:
Salt: **resistant**   Soil Compaction: **sensitive**
Root Pattern: large coarse **shallow laterals,** bright red, nitrogen-fixing nodules on roots; **difficult to transplant**

SPECIES: Associate: trees - Red/Jack Pines, Northern Pin/Bur Oaks, Quaking/Bigtooth Aspens; shrubs - Lowbush
         Blueberry, Checkerberry Wintergreen, American Filbert, rose species, Bearberry, Bush Cinquefoil, St.Johnswort
Similar: Jerseytea Ceanothus - fruits black, leaves broader; Slender Deutzia - Asiatic; Corymed/Japanese White Spireas
Cultivars: none available

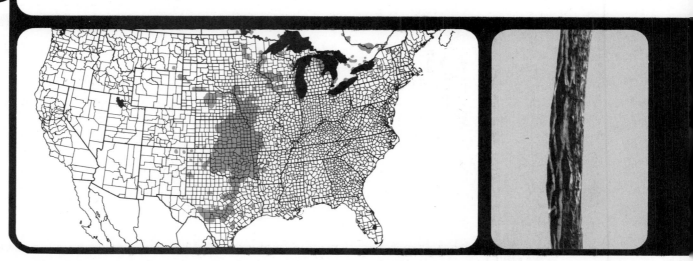

Cephalanthus occidentalis

FORM: **globular or mound**
Size: **mid-height shrub** - from 2 to 4 m (6 to 12 ft) or occasional large shrub, rarely small tree to 9 m (30 ft)
Spread: **wide** - 4 to 6 m (12 to 20 ft) or more, typically equal or 2 times the height
Mass: loosely **open**, lower ⅔ of crown often unbranched

BRANCHING: multi-stemmed, **upright spreading or ascending,** old plants **arching,** spray of twigs at branch tips; **coarse**
Twig: stout, stiff, **velvety,** large lenticels, **red brown or gray brown**
Bud: inconspicuous, imbedded in bark, **brown**
Bark: **shallow furrowed** with long narrow flat-topped ridges, finally shaggy **exfoliating,** dark **gray brown** to nearly black

FOLIAGE: opposite or whorled in 3's and 4's, **simple, lanceolate to oblong lanceolate,** entire margin; **medium coarse** texture
Surface: **glossy,** smooth, prominent depressed veins
Color: spring - **red green** becoming bright green; summer - deep **dark green;** autumn - **yellow green or** dull **yellow**
Season: deciduous; occasionally **persistant;** emergence - early **June,** drop - early **September**

FLOWER: dense **small** ball-like **clusters,** 2.5 to 4 cm (1 to 1½ in) diameter, very long anthers look like pins in pin cushion
Color: creamy **white**
Season: late **July through August,** after leaves
Sex: monoecious   **Fragrant:** arresting sweet fragrance, attracts honeybees

FRUIT: dry hard globular ball-like **multiple,** 2.5 cm (1 in) diameter, in loose upright long stemmed clusters
Color: green tinged with **red,** ultimately **brown**
Season: early **September** persisting **through** late **January**   Human Value: **poisonous leaves**
Wildlife Value: **low;** waterfowl, marshbirds, shorebirds are principal users, small mammals occasionally use

HABITAT: formation - **bog, swamp, meadow, prairie, dune, forest, old field;** region - **Central, Southern;** gradient - lowland **wet, wet-mesic;** marshes, prairie sloughs, low alluvial woods, moist peat, stream banks, shallow ponds, lakeshores, mud
Shade Tolerance: **very intolerant**
Flood Tolerance: **very tolerant**

SOIL: Texture: **coarse to fine;** sands and gravels, loamy sands, silt loams, silty clay loams, stiff clays, peats, mucks
Drainage: **very poor to well**
Moisture: **wet to moist**
Reaction: **slightly acid to** circumneutral, tolerates **alkaline,** pH 6.1 - 8.5

HARDINESS: zone 4a
Rate: **medium**
Longevity: **short-lived**

SUSCEPTIBILITY: Physiological: **infrequent**
Disease: **infrequent** - leaf spots, powdery mildews, rusts; control measures rarely warranted
Insect: **infrequent** - San Jose scale can be troublesome
Wind-Ice: **infrequent**

URBAN TOLERANCE: Pollution:
Lighting: Drought Heat: **sensitive**   Mine Spoils:
Salt: Soil Compaction: **resistant**
Root Pattern: fibrous, **shallow lateral; transplants well**

SPECIES: Associate: trees - Silver Maple, Black Willow, River Birch, Eastern Poplar, American Elm, Pin/Swamp White Oaks; shrubs - American Elder, Common Ninebark, Common Alder, Indigobush Amorpha, Common Winterberry
Similar: American Elder, Common Ninebark, Silky Dogwood - form, flower color, habitat similar
Cultivars: none available

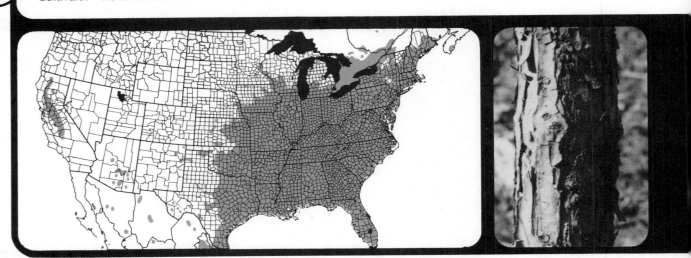

Common Buttonbush

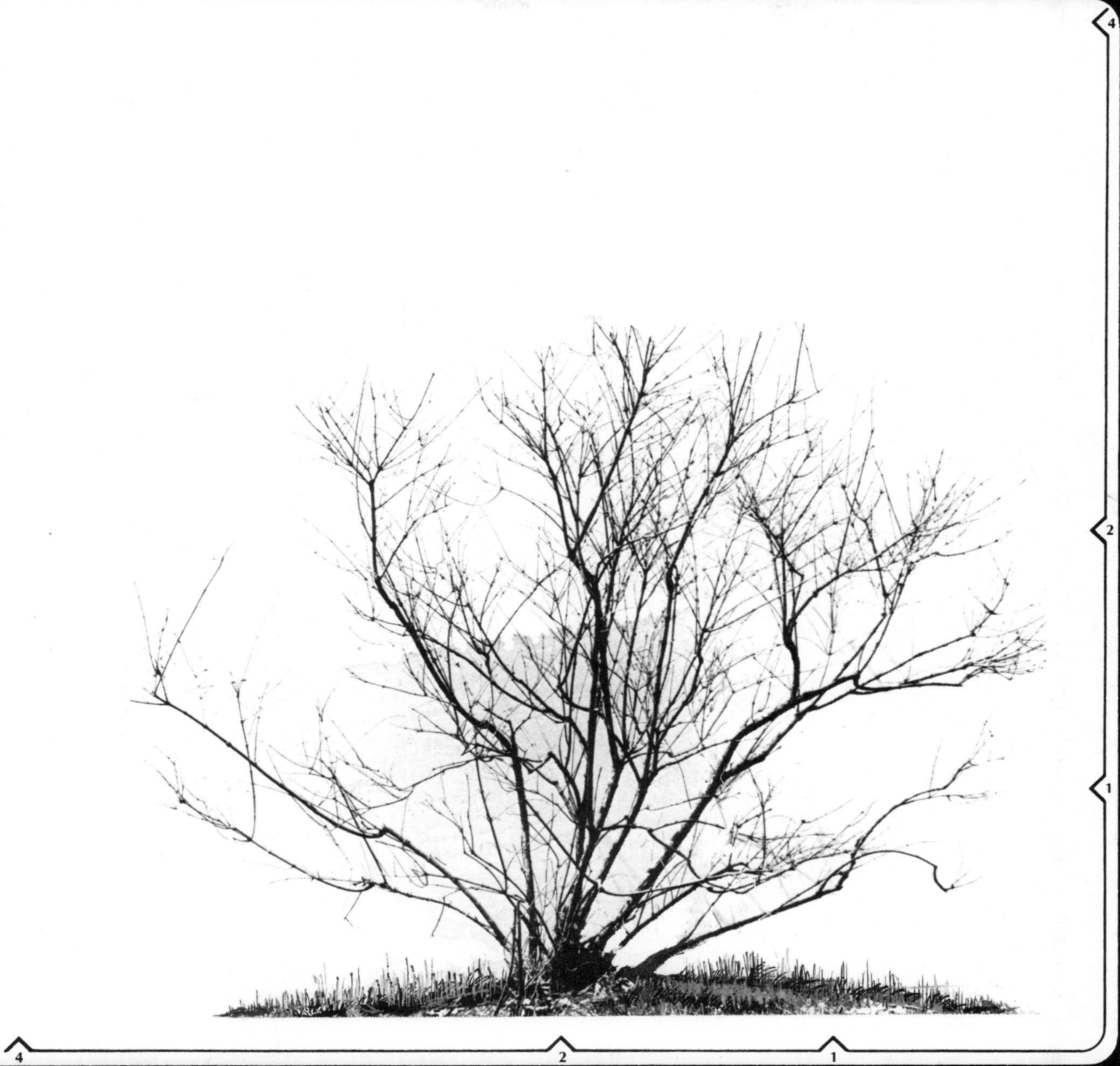

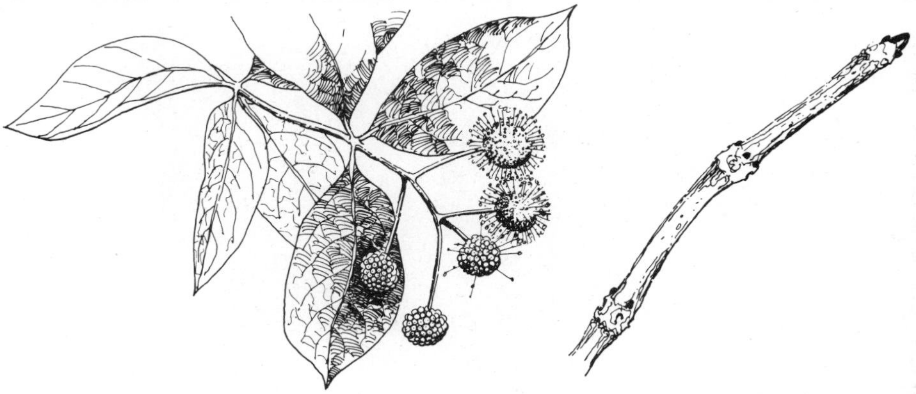

Chamaedaphne calyculata

FORM: globular or **mound**
Size: **very small shrub** - to 1 m (3 ft)
Spread: **very narrow** - 1 m (3 ft) plus, commonly equal or 1½ times height
Mass: very **dense**

BRANCHING: multiple **erect** stems, **upright** spreading, densely branched, forming extensive thickets; **fine** texture
Twig: smooth, slender, **red to red brown or gray brown**
Bud: small, **brown**
Bark: **scaly** or shredding and exposing smooth reddish inner bark, old stems **red brown or gray brown**

FOLIAGE: alternate, **simple, elliptic** to oblong obovate or oblong lanceolate, hug stems, entire, margin rolled; **fine** texture
Surface: **dull,** leathery and thick, slightly scaly above, dense scaly beneath
Color: spring - **dark green;** summer - **dark green,** yellowish beneath; autumn - **dark green** late **then purple;** winter - **purple**
Season: broadleaf **evergreen** with leaves progressively smaller toward twig end

FLOWER: small solitary nodding **bells,** 6 mm (¼ in) long, in angles of upper leaves
Color: **white**
Season: late **April through** mid **May**
Sex: monoecious

FRUIT: globular 10-valved **capsules,** 4 mm (⅙ in) across, with hair-like persistant style
Color: **red** or pink at first, finally **brown**
Season: late **July through** late **September,** persisting several years   Human Value: not edible
Wildlife Value: **low;** infrequent use by songbirds, upland gamebirds; hoofed browsers graze foliage

HABITAT: formation - **bog, swamp;** region - **Northern;** gradient - **wet;** muskeg, acid bogs, peaty swamps, pocosins, peat
bogs, wet meadows, wet shores, low mountain bogs
Shade Tolerance: **intolerant**
Flood Tolerance: **very tolerant**

SOIL: Texture: **moderately fine to fine;** peats and mucks underlain by calcareous lacustrine clays, silts, and sands
Drainage: **very poor to moderately poor**
Moisture: **wet to moist**
Reaction: **strongly to moderately acid;** pH 4.5 - 6.0

HARDINESS: zone 2
Rate: **slow**
Longevity: **short-lived**

SUSCEPTIBILITY: Physiological: **infrequent**
Disease: **infrequent** - none serious
Insect: **infrequent** - rarely affected
Wind-Ice: **infrequent**

URBAN TOLERANCE: Pollution:
Lighting: Drought Heat: **sensitive**   Mine Spoils:
Salt: **resistant**   Soil Compaction: **resistant**
Root Pattern: fibrous, rhizomatous, **shallow lateral; transplants well to difficult**

SPECIES: Associate: trees - Red Maple, Eastern Larch, Black Spruce; shrubs - Bogrosemary Andromeda, Cranberry, Bog
Kalmia, Common Buttonbush, Common Winterberry, Lowbush Blueberry, Bunchberry Dogwood, Labradortea Ledum
Similar: Labradortea Ledum; Dwarf Inkberry - hybrid form; Lambkill Kalmia; Korean Boxwood - demands mesic habitat
Cultivars: 'Nana' - to 0.3 m (1 ft) tall

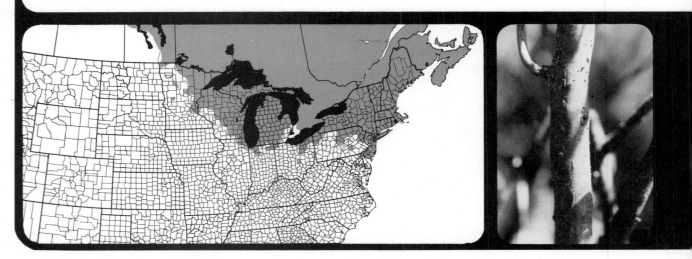

Clethra acuminata

FORM: mound
Size: **large shrub** - from 4 to 6 m (12 to 20 ft)
Spread: **wide** - 4 to 6 m (12 to 20 ft), variable but generally forming broad thickets
Mass: **open**

BRANCHING: **erect** multiple stems with **upright spreading** branches; **medium** texture
Twig: slender, **velvety, gray brown**
Bud: laterals small and obscure, terminal **large** ovoid, 6 mm (¼ in), **woolly, 2 scales, gray to** rosy **red** tinted
Bark: **exfoliating** into thin elongated strips **or** with **scaly** appearance, **red brown**

FOLIAGE: alternate, clustered toward end of branchlets, **simple, oval to** oblong **elliptic,** long sharp fine teeth; **medium**
Surface: **dull,** smooth
Color: spring - bright **medium green;** summer - **medium to dark green;** autumn - **yellow to orange**
Season: **deciduous;** emergence - late **May,** drop - mid **October**

FLOWER: dense often drooping cylindric **spikes,** 8 to 20 cm (3 to 8 in) long, terminal spikes usually solitary
Color: **white**
Season: late **July through** mid **August,** after leaves
Sex: monoecious   **Fragrant:** spicily perfumed

FRUIT: globular to oval nodding **capsules,** 5 mm (⅕) diameter, crowded in erect or drooping spikes
Color: tan **brown**
Season: early **September** persisting **through** late **February**   Human Value: not edible
Wildlife Value: **intermediate;** upland gamebirds, songbirds, small mammals; hoofed browsers graze foliage

HABITAT: formation - **savanna, glade, forest, moist cliff;** region - **Central;** gradient - upland **mesic and mesic-dry;** wooded
    bluffs, steep mesophytic slopes of gorges and ravines, mountain woods, cliffs of non-calcareous rocks
Shade Tolerance: **very tolerant**
Flood Tolerance: **intolerant**

SOIL: Texture: **moderately coarse** stony or sandy loams, loamy sands **to moderately fine** silt loams, loose textured loams
Drainage: **moderately well to well**
Moisture: **moist to average**
Reaction: **strongly acid to slightly acid,** pH 4.5 - 6.5

HARDINESS: **zone 6a**
Rate: **slow**
Longevity: **moderately short-lived**

SUSCEPTIBILITY: Physiological: **infrequent**
Disease: **infrequent - very resistant**
Insect: **infrequent** - tremendously pest free
Wind-Ice: **infrequent**

URBAN TOLERANCE: Pollution:
Lighting: Drought Heat: **intermediate**   Mine Spoils:
Salt: **resistant**   Soil Compaction: **sensitive**
Root Pattern: **shallow lateral** spreading, **stoloniferous** forming thickets; **difficult to transplant**

SPECIES: Associate: trees - Eastern Hemlock, American Beech, linden species, Tuliptree, Sugar/Black Maples; shrubs -
    Common Spicebush, Smooth Hydrangea, Mapleleaf Viburnum, Pasture Gooseberry, Mountain Stewartia
Similar: Summersweet Clethra - smaller; Virginia Sweetspire
Cultivars: none available

Cinnamon Clethra

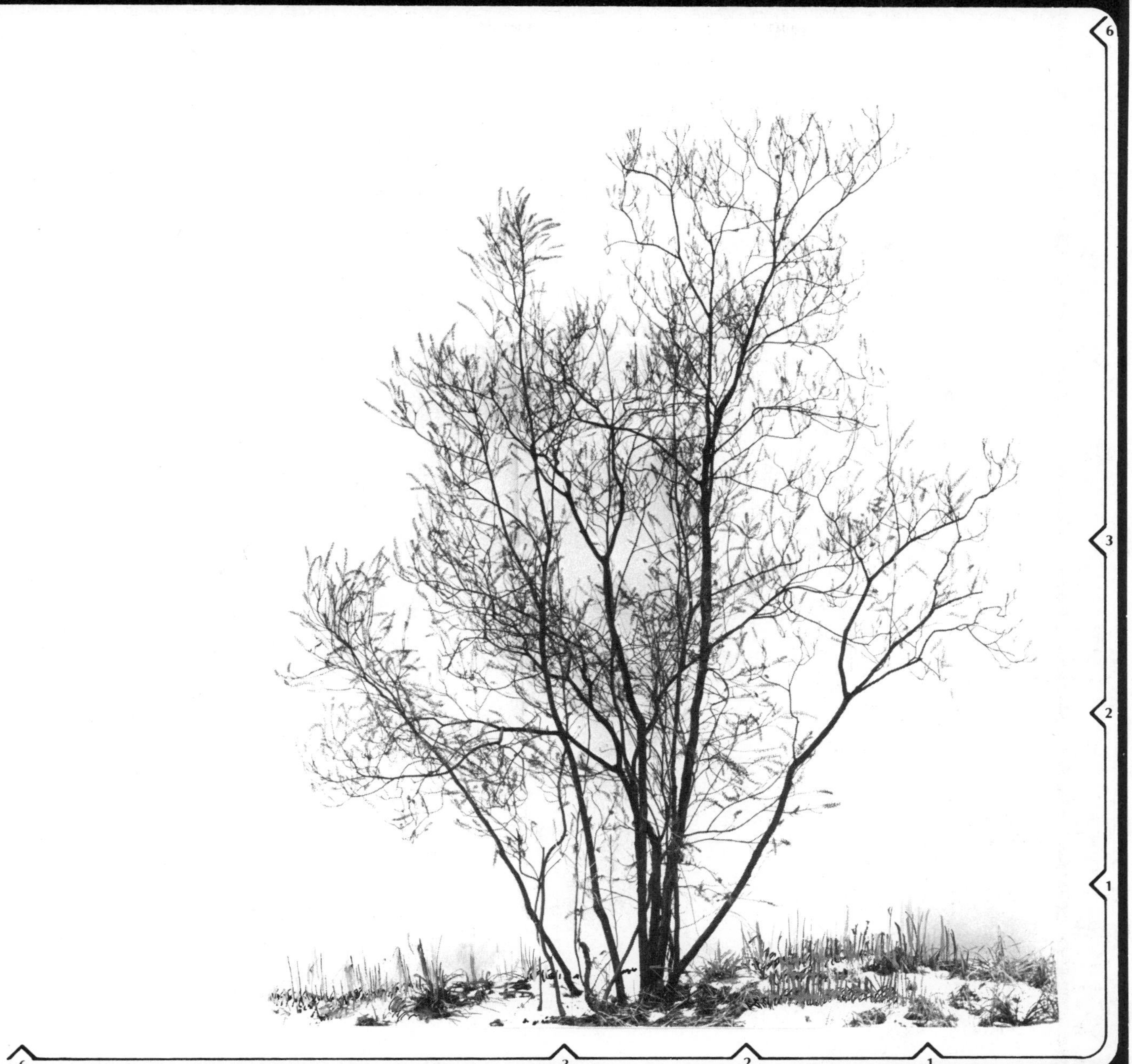

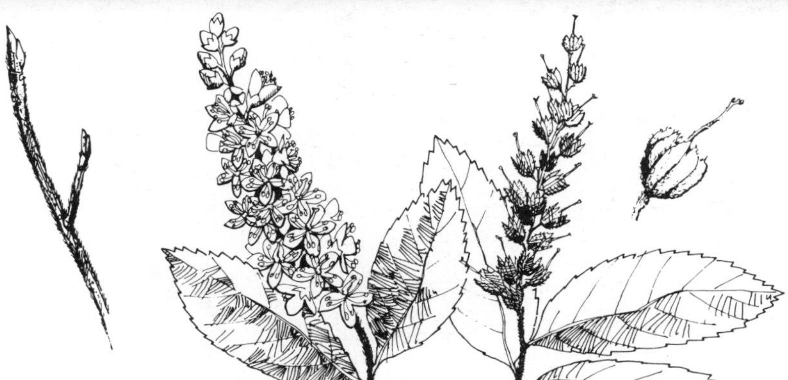

Clethra alnifolia

FORM: obovoid to ovoid
Size: **mid-height shrub** - from 2 to 4 m (6 to 12 ft)
Spread: **narrow** - 1 to 2 m (3 to 6 ft), commonly ½ to ¾ the height, but often spreads into mounded clumps
Mass: **open**

BRANCHING: **erect** multiple stems with upright spreading branches; **medium** texture
Twig: slender, **velvety, gray brown**
Bud: laterals small and obscure, terminal **larger** to 6 mm (¼ in), ovoid, **2** to **3 scales** often shedding, **gray to reddish**
Bark: **scaly** or separating into loose longitudinal **exfoliating** strips, **gray brown to brown black**

FOLIAGE: alternate, **simple, obovate to oblong obovate,** sharp toothed at tip, prominent veination; **medium fine** texture
Surface: **glossy,** smooth to rough
Color: spring - **red green;** summer - **medium to dark green;** autumn - dull **yellow to orange**
Season: **deciduous;** emergence - late **May,** drop - mid **October**

FLOWER: dense upright narrow cylindric **spikes,** 10 to 15 cm (4 to 6 in) long, terminal spikes often clustered together
Color: **white**
Season: early **July** lasting **through** mid **August,** after leaves
Sex: monoecious **Fragrant:** spicily perfumed

FRUIT: globular **capsule,** 3 mm (⅛ in) diameter, crowded in stiff upright spikes
Color: tan **brown** to chocolate brown
Season: early **September** persisting **through** late **February** Human Value: not edible
Wildlife Value: **intermediate;** songbirds, shorebirds, waterfowl, upland gamebirds, small mammals

HABITAT: formation - **bog, swamp, dune, forest;** region - **Southern;** gradient - lowland **wet, wet-mesic;** swampy woodlands,
seashore, stream banks, bay forests, wet marshy land, wet pinelands, flatwoods, pocosins, hillside bogs, lakeshores
Shade Tolerance: **tolerant**
Flood Tolerance: **very tolerant**

SOIL: Texture: **coarse to fine;** sands and gravels, loamy sands, silt loams, peats, mucks, heavy clays
Drainage: **very poor to moderately well**
Moisture: **wet to moist**
Reaction: **strongly acid to slightly acid,** pH 4.5 - 6.5

HARDINESS: zone 4a
Rate: **slow to medium**
Longevity: **short-lived**

SUSCEPTIBILITY: Physiological: **infrequent**
Disease: **infrequent** - remarkably free of problems
Insect: **infrequent** - very resistant, red spider on dry sites can be troublesome
Wind-Ice: **infrequent**

URBAN TOLERANCE: Pollution:
Lighting: Drought Heat: **intermediate** Mine Spoils:
Salt: **resistant** Soil Compaction: **resistant**
Root Pattern: **shallow lateral** spreading, **stoloniferous** stems form extensive clumps; **difficult to transplant**

SPECIES: Associate: trees - Pond/Loblolly Pines, Red Maple, Red Bay Persea; shrubs - Dusty Zenobia, Fetterbush Lyonia,
Summersweet Clethra, Inkberry, Lambkill Kalmia, Virginia Sweetspire, Sweetbay Magnolia, He-huckleberry
Similar: Cinnamon Clethra - leaves larger, taller; Virginia Sweetspire
Cultivars: 'Rosea' - flower buds pink, flowers pinkish at first; 'Paniculata' - large terminal flower spikes

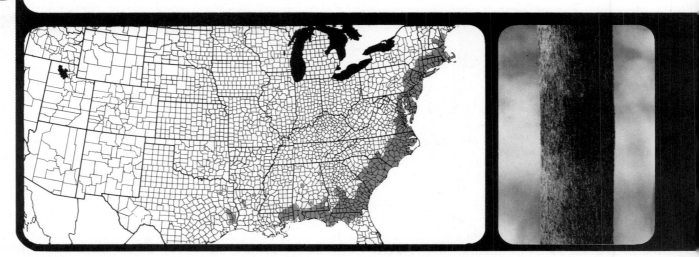

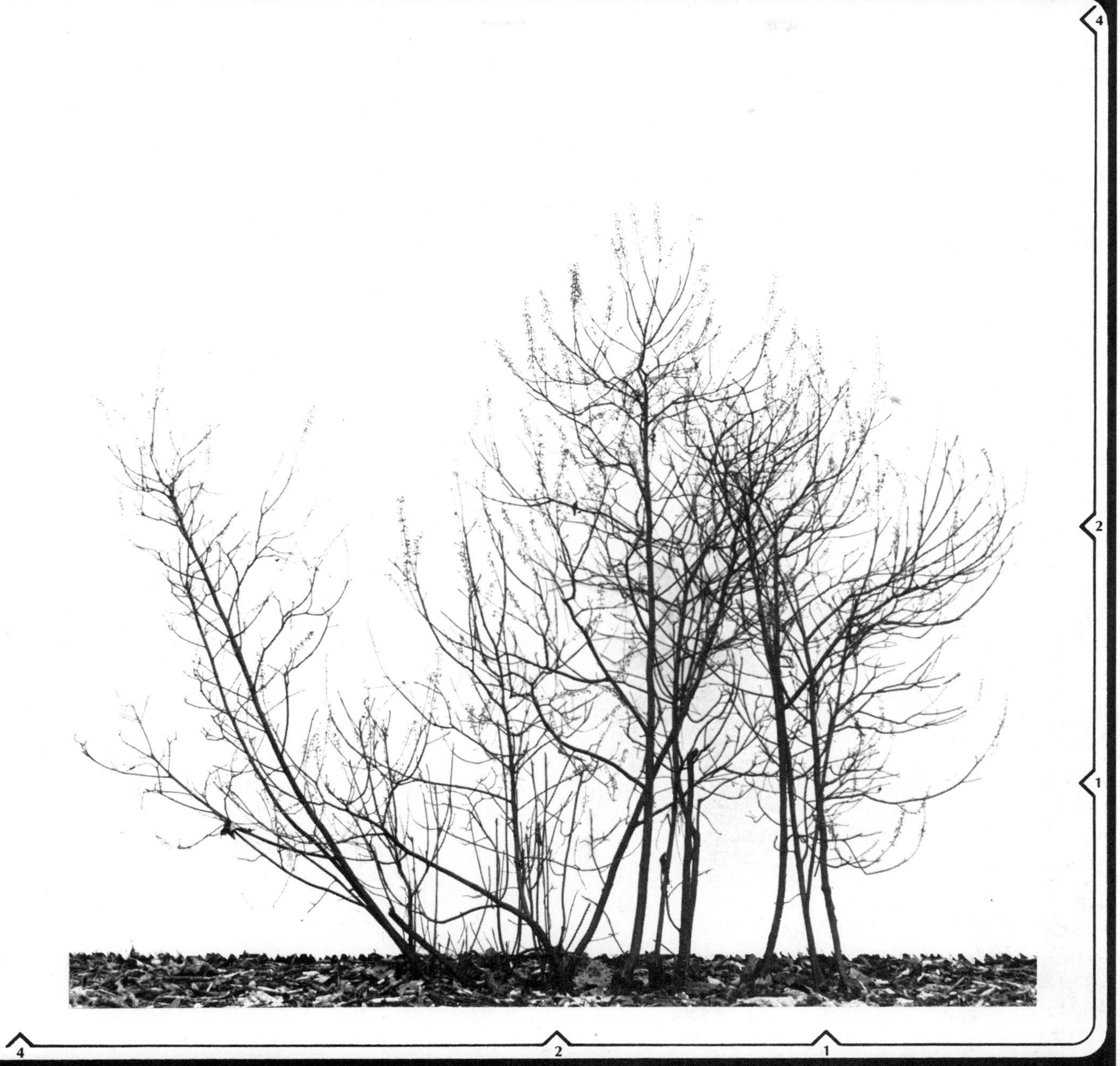
4
2
1
4
2
1

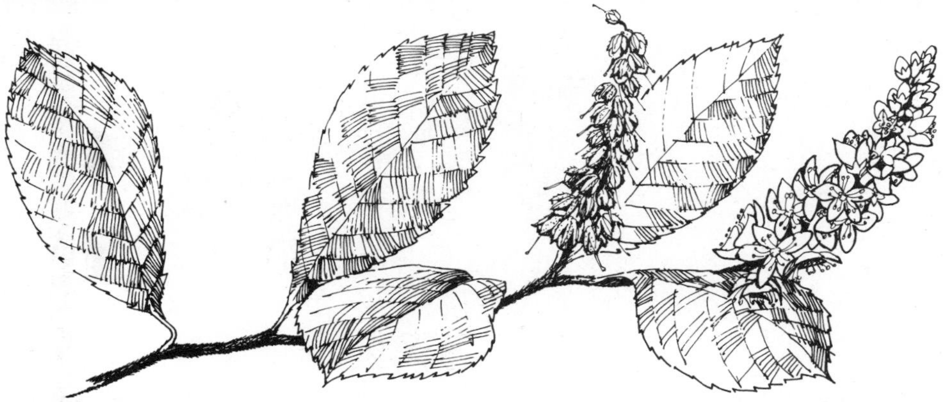

Comptonia peregrina

FORM: globular to mound
Size: **very small shrub** - to 1 m (3 ft)
Spread: **very narrow** - up to 1 m (3 ft), typically equal or 2 times the height, often forming extensive thickets
Mass: **open**

BRANCHING: erect multiple stems with irregular loose **upright spreading** branches; **fine** texture
Twig: **velvety** with tiny **resinous** dots, aromatic when broken, **green brown to brown**
Bud: minute globular, **woolly, resinous, red brown; winter catkins**
Bark: **smooth,** glossy, with conspicious lenticels, color varies from **green,** yellow **to yellow brown, red or purple**

FOLIAGE: alternate, **simple, linear to oblong linear, pinnately lobed,** fern-like, **aromatic** when rubbed; **medium fine** texture
Surface: **glossy,** resinous dot-like glands visible, somewhat hairy beneath
Color: spring - **light green;** summer - **dark green;** autumn - **dark green** late, **becoming tan brown;** winter - **tan brown**
Season: **persistant;** emergence - early **May,** drop - many dried leaves remaining through late **February**

FLOWER: catkins, male cylindric and stiffly erect, 2.5 cm (1 in) long, crowded at twig ends, female roundish, solitary
Color: pale **brown**
Season: late **April through** early or mid **May,** before leaves
Sex: **dioecious,** often monoecious

FRUIT: bur-like **strobiles,** 2.5 cm (1 in) diameter
Color: green brown to **brown**
Season: early **August through** late **October**   Human Value: **edible leaves**
Wildlife Value: **low;** some upland gamebirds, small mammals; browsed heavily by White-tail Deer

HABITAT: formation - **barrens, forest, dry cliff, dune, old field;** region - **Northern;** gradient - upland **mesic-dry, dry;** hillsides
        and openings of woods, sand flats and barrens, marine and lake dunes, on burned areas, abandoned pastures
Shade Tolerance: **tolerant**
Flood Tolerance: **very intolerant**

SOIL: Texture: **coarse to moderately coarse;** sands and gravels, sandy loams; intolerant of clay soils
Drainage: **well to excessive**
Moisture: **dry to droughty**
Reaction: **strongly acid to slightly acid,** pH 4.5 - 6.5

HARDINESS: zone 2
Rate: **slow**
Longevity: **moderately short-lived**

SUSCEPTIBILITY: Physiological: **infrequent**
Disease: **infrequent** - very resistant, occasional blister rust
Insect: **infrequent** - none serious
Wind-Ice: **infrequent**

URBAN TOLERANCE: Pollution:
Lighting: Drought Heat: **resistant**   Mine Spoils: **resistant**
Salt: resistant   Soil Compaction: **sensitive**
Root Pattern: thin stringy long creeping, **shallow lateral,** freely suckers, nitrogen-fixer; **difficult to transplant**/establish

SPECIES: Associate: trees - Bigtooth Aspen, Paper Birch, Sassafras, Scarlet Oak, Red/Jack/Pitch Pines; shrubs - Bear Oak,
        Jerseytea Ceanothus, Mountainlaurel Kalmia, Highbush/Lowbush Blueberries, Trailing-arbutus, Bearberry
Similar: Sweetgale - wet or dry habitats; Northern Bayberry - larger, gray berries, dioecious
Cultivars: asplenifolia - less pubescent leaves, catkins smaller

1

2/3

1/3

1

2/3

1/3

Cornus amomum

FORM: globular or mounded
Size: **mid-height shrub** - from 2 to 4 m (6 to 12 ft)
Spread: **intermediate** - 2 to 4 m (6 to 12 ft), 1½ to 2 times the height
Mass: **moderate** becoming more open with age

BRANCHING: upright multiple stems in youth becoming **arching** at maturity, densely twiggy; **medium** texture
Twig: moderately slender, **velvety, red, green or purple,** pith brown
Bud: small conical, **2 scales,** short **woolly white** hairs, **gray brown**
Bark: **smooth** with tan horizontal lenticels becoming **shallow furrowed, green to** deep reddish **purple,** old bark **gray**

FOLIAGE: opposite, **simple,** elliptic ovate to **elliptic,** often drooping, entire margin, parallel veination; **medium fine**
Surface: **dull,** smooth, pale beneath
Color: spring - deep **red green;** summer - **medium green;** autumn - **purplish** red
Season: **deciduous;** emergence - mid **May,** drop - mid **October**

FLOWER: dense upright **flat-topped** clusters, 4 to 6.5 cm (1½ to 2½ in) diameter
Color: yellowish **white**
Season: mid through late **June,** after leaves
Sex: monoecious

FRUIT: small globular **berry,** 6 to 10 mm (¼ to ⅜ in) diameter, in dense flat-topped clusters
Color: porcelain **blue,** often with white blotches
Season: early through late **August**   Human Value: not edible
Wildlife Value: **very high;** waterfowl, marshbirds, shorebirds, songbirds are major users, large and small mammals

HABITAT: formation - **bog, spring, meadow, forest, dune, old field;** region - **Central, Southern;** gradient - **wet;** floodplain
depressions, ox-bows, swamp borders, low alluvial woods, wet thickets, clearings, pond and lakeshore, calcareous fens
Shade Tolerance: **intolerant**
Flood Tolerance: **very tolerant**

SOIL: Texture: not limiting, ranges from **fine** heavy clay **to coarse** wet sand
Drainage: **very poor to well**
Moisture: **wet to average**
Reaction: **slightly acid to** circumneutral, pH 6.1 - 7.5, tolerates **alkaline** to pH 8.5

HARDINESS: zone 4a
Rate: **fast**
Longevity: **short-lived**

SUSCEPTIBILITY: Physiological: **infrequent**
Disease: **occasional** - crown canker, flower and leaf blight, leaf spots, twig blight, root rots, powdery mildew
Insect: **infrequent** - borers, scales, dogwood club-gall, leaf minor; can be minor problems
Wind-Ice: **infrequent**

URBAN TOLERANCE: Pollution: **sensitive** - 2-4D; **intermediate** - 0_3
Lighting: **sensitive**   Drought Heat: **intermediate**   Mine Spoils:
Salt: **sensitive**   Soil Compaction: **resistant**
Root Pattern: fibrous, **shallow lateral; transplants easily**

SPECIES: Associate: trees - Pin/Swamp White Oaks, River Birch, Common Boxelder, Black/Peachleaf/Shining Willows;
shrubs - American Elder, American Bladdernut, Common Winterberry, Meadowsweet/Hardhack Spireas
Similar: Pale Dogwood - narrow leaf, Southern; Red-osier/Siberian (Asiatic) Dogwoods - stems redder
Cultivars: 'Grandiflorum' - larger flowers; 'Xanthocarpum' - yellow fruit; others

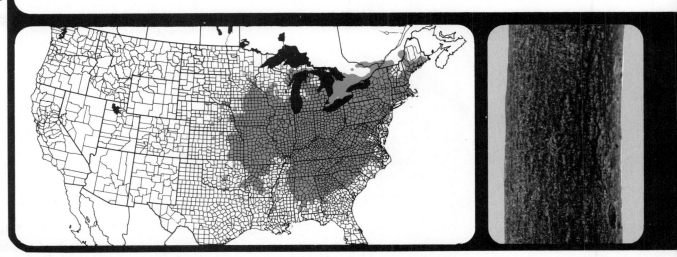

Silky Dogwood

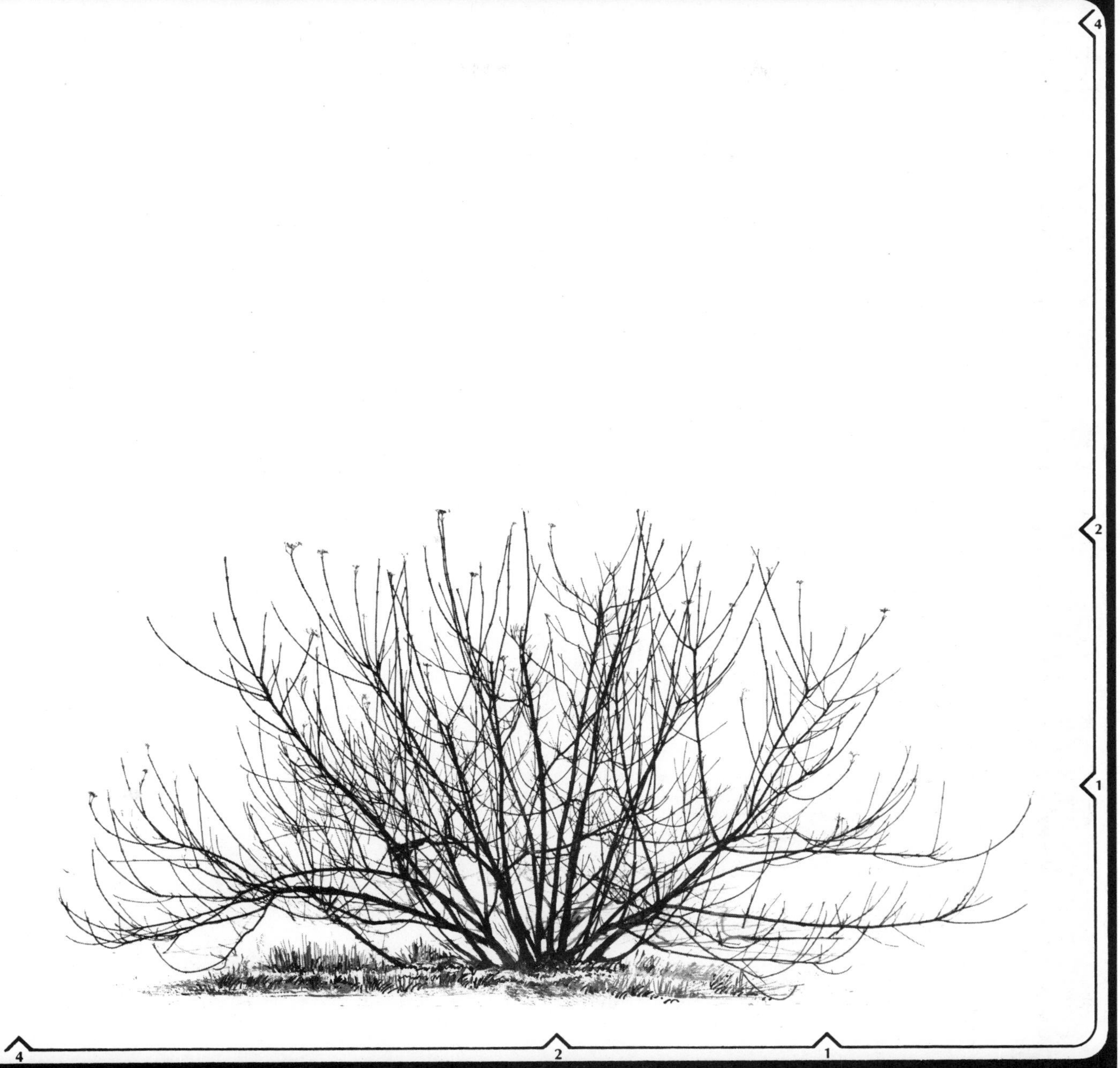

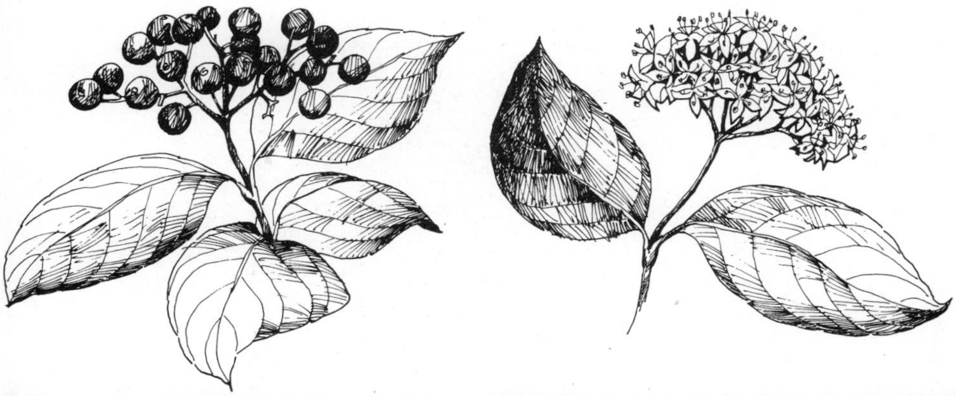

Cornus canadensis

FORM: low prostrate carpet-like **mat,** herb-like
Size: **very small shrub** - less than 1 m (3 ft), commonly 7 to 23 cm (3 to 9 in) tall
Spread: **very narrow** - less than 1 m (3 ft), old colonies are very wide spreading
Mass: **open**

BRANCHING: **trailing** horizontal beneath surface with **erect** unbranched flowering stems; **medium** texture
Twig: slender, smooth, square and **angular,** large leaf scars encircle twig, red to green
Bud: very small, inconspicuous, **2 bud scales**
Bark: **smooth, green to red**

FOLIAGE: whorled leaves borne at top of stem, **simple, elliptic,** entire, parallel veination; **medium fine** texture
Surface: **dull** to glossy, smooth, paler beneath
Color: spring - bright **red green;** summer - **dark green;** autumn - scarlet **red becoming purple;** winter - **purple**
Season: **semi-evergreen;** emergence - early **May,** drop - late **November** or later

FLOWER: **small clusters** surrounded by 4 large bracts, **large solitary** appearance, 2.5 to 4 cm (1 to 1½ in) across
Color: blooms yellow, bracts **white,** similar to those of Flowering Dogwood
Season: mid **May through** late **June,** after leaves
Sex: monoecious

FRUIT: globular **berry,** 6 mm (¼ in) diameter, grouped in terminal round-headed bunches
Color: bright scarlet **red** to orange
Season: early through late **August,** often persisting through late October or after   Human Value: **edible fruit**
Wildlife Value: **low;** primarily songbirds and upland gamebirds

HABITAT: formation - **bog, swamp, forest;** region - **Northern;** gradient - **wet, wet-mesic, mesic, mesic-dry, and dry;** cool damp
    atmosphere, hummocks of bogs, moist to dry coniferous woods, on fallen logs and stumps
Shade Tolerance: **very tolerant**
Flood Tolerance: **intermediate**

SOIL: Texture: **moderately coarse** loamy sands, sandy loams, loams, silt loams **to fine** organic soils, peats and mucks
Drainage: **poor to well**
Moisture: **moist to average**
Reaction: demands **strongly acid or moderately acid,** pH 4.5 - 6.0

HARDINESS: zone 2
Rate: **slow**
Longevity: **long-lived**

SUSCEPTIBILITY: Physiological: **occasional** - chlorosis in neutral or alkaline soils
Disease: **infrequent** - none serious
Insect: **infrequent** - none serious
Wind-Ice: **infrequent**

URBAN TOLERANCE: Pollution: **sensitive** - 2-4D; **intermediate** - 0_3
Lighting: **sensitive**   Drought Heat: **sensitive**   Mine Spoils: **sensitive**
Salt: **sensitive**   Soil Compaction: **resistant**
Root Pattern: extensive **shallow** creeping and forking rhizomes; **difficult to transplant,** difficult culture, use acid peat mulch

SPECIES: Associate: trees - Balsam Fir, White Spruce, Red Pine, Yellow Birch; shrubs - Lowbush Blueberry, Pasture
    Gooseberry, Roundleaf Dogwood, American Fly Honeysuckle, Fragrant Thimbleberry, Beaked Filbert
Similar: Patridgeberry; Checkerberry Wintergreen; Trailing-arbutus; Japanese Spurge - Asiatic, white berries
Cultivars: none available

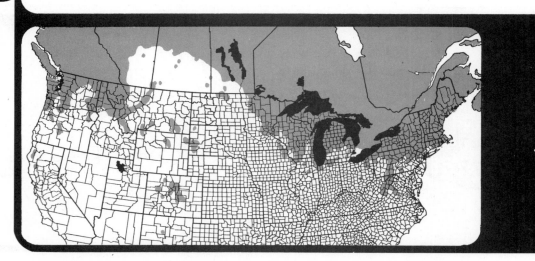

544

Cornus racemosa

FORM: 'obovoid
Size: **mid-height shrub** - from 2 to 4 m (6 to 12 ft)
Spread: **intermediate** - 2 to 4 m (6 to 12 ft), typically ⅔ the height
Mass: **dense**

BRANCHING: multi-stemmed, **upright** and strongly **spreading,** leggy and open base, much-branched crown; **medium**
Twig: slender, smooth, **red brown**
Bud: small ovoid, **2** valvate **scales, reddish to brown**
Bark: smooth but roughened by lenticels, old bark with small thin squarish **scales,** ashy **gray to gray brown**

FOLIAGE: opposite, **simple, ovate lanceolate** to narrow elliptic, entire margin, parallel veination; **medium fine** texture
Surface: **dull,** scattered flattened hairs on both sides or smooth, paler or whitish beneath
Color: spring - **green tinged red;** summer - **gray green;** autumn - maroon **purple**
Season: **deciduous;** emergence - mid **May,** drop - mid **October**

FLOWER: loose upright broad cone-shaped **spike,** 5 cm (2 in) in diameter, profuse
Color: creamy **white**
Season: late **May through** early or mid **June,** after leaves
Sex: monoecious   **Fragrant:** ill-scented

FRUIT: glossy globular **berry,** 6 mm (¼ in) diameter, in broad conical clusters
Color: milky **white** with bright red stems
Season: early **August through** late September   Human Value: not edible
Wildlife Value: **very high;** waterfowl, upland gamebirds, songbirds are major users, large and small mammals

HABITAT: formation - **meadow, savanna, forest, dry cliff, old field;** region - **Central;** gradient - **wet-mesic, mesic-dry, dry;** open
    alluvial woods, rocky wooded hilltops, woods edge, fence row, rocky ledges, limestone outcrops, glades, oak woods
Shade Tolerance: **tolerant**
Flood Tolerance: **intermediate**

SOIL: Texture: **moderately coarse** gravelly and sandy loams, prairie loams to fine silt loams, heavy clays
Drainage: **moderately poor to excessive**
Moisture: **moist to droughty**
Reaction: **slightly acid to** circumneutral, tolerates **alkaline,** pH 6.1 - 8.5

HARDINESS: zone 3a
Rate: **medium,** slow on old wood, shoots developing from roots grow 1 to 2 m (3 to 6 ft) in one season
Longevity: **short-lived**

SUSCEPTIBILITY: Physiological: **infrequent**
Disease: **infrequent** - none serious
Insect: **infrequent** - none serious
Wind-Ice: **infrequent**

URBAN TOLERANCE: Pollution: **sensitive** - 2-4D; **intermediate** - 0_3
Lighting: **sensitive**   Drought Heat: **resistant**   Mine Spoils: **resistant**
Salt: **sensitive**   Soil Compaction: **intermediate**
Root Pattern: fibrous, **shallow lateral,** suckers profusely forming large colonies; **transplants well**

SPECIES: Associate: trees - White Ash, Black Cherry, White/Bur/Red Oaks, Shagbark/Bitternut Hickories, American
    Hophornbeam; shrubs - American Filbert, Rafinesque/Nannyberry Viburnums, Smooth Sumac, Limber Honeysuckle
Similar: Roughleaf Dogwood - rough woolly leaves, twigs; Arrowwood Viburnum
Cultivars: none available

Gray Dogwood

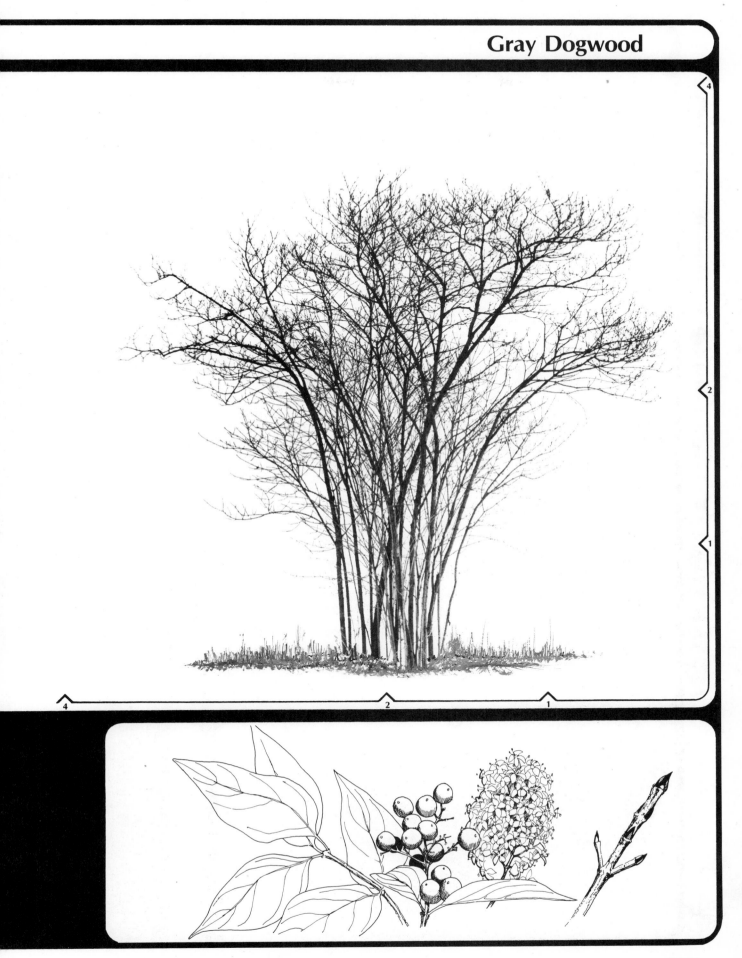

547

Cornus rugosa

FORM: obovoid
Size: **mid-height shrub** - from 2 to 4 m (6 to 12 ft)
Spread: **intermediate** - 2 to 4 m (6 to 12 ft), typically ⅔ the height
Mass: **open**

BRANCHING: few **upright** stems, leggy base, loosely branched and strongly **spreading** umbrella-like crown; **coarse** texture
Twig: smooth, flattened and somewhat **angular**, warty dotted, **green with purple** blotches, purplish or yellowish with age
Bud: oblong with **2** valvate **scales, brown**
Bark: **smooth** but roughened by raised dot-like lenticels, **green or purplish, gray** with age

FOLIAGE: opposite, **simple**, broadly ovate to **suborbicular**, entire margin, parallel veination; **medium coarse** texture
Surface: **dull**, dense woolly beneath
Color: spring - **red green;** summer - **medium green;** autumn - maroon **purple**
Season: **deciduous;** emergence - mid **May,** drop - early **October**

FLOWER: dense **flat-topped** clusters, 5 to 7 cm (2 to 3 in) across
Color: creamy **white**
Season: early through late **June,** after leaves
Sex: monoecious

FRUIT: globular **berry,** 6 mm (¼ in) diameter, borne in flat-topped clusters
Color: light **blue** with red stems
Season: early **August through** early September   Human Value: not edible
Wildlife Value: **very high;** upland gamebirds, songbirds are primary users, large and small mammals; browsers graze

HABITAT: formation - **forest, moist cliff;** region - **Northern;** gradient - upland **mesic, mesic-dry;** shaded rocky or clay slopes,
ravines, coves, stream benches, areas of cool air drainage, in the shadow of rock ledges and cliffs, talus slopes
Shade Tolerance: **very tolerant**
Flood Tolerance: **intolerant**

SOIL: Texture: **moderately coarse** stony or sandy loam **to moderately fine** silt loam and loamy clay; loose textured best
Drainage: **moderatey well to well**
Moisture: **moist to average**
Reaction: **slightly acid to** circumneutral, tolerates **alkaline,** pH 6.1 - 8.5

HARDINESS: zone 3a
Rate: **medium**
Longevity: **short-lived**

SUSCEPTIBILITY: Physiological: **occasional** - winter dieback
Disease: **occasional** - crown canker, flower and leaf blight, leaf spots, powdery mildew, twig blight
Insect: **infrequent** - borers, leaf miner, scales, dogwood club gall midge; none serious
Wind-Ice: **infrequent**

URBAN TOLERANCE: Pollution: **sensitive** - 2-4D; **intermediate** - 0₃
Lighting: **sensitive**   Drought Heat: **sensitive**   Mine Spoils: **sensitive**
Salt: **sensitive**   Soil Compaction: **sensitive**
Root Pattern: fibrous, **shallow lateral; transplants with** moderate **difficulty,** slow to re-establish

SPECIES: Associate: trees - Balsam Fir, White Spruce, Quaking Aspen, Mountain Maple, American Moutainash; shrubs -
Beaked Filbert, Bunchberry Dogwood, Dwarf Bushhoneysuckle, American Fly Honeysuckle, Lowbush Blueberry
Similar: Pagoda Dogwood - larger, tiered appearance; Gray Dogwood - leaves smaller, moderate shade only
Cultivars: none available

548

Roundleaf Dogwood

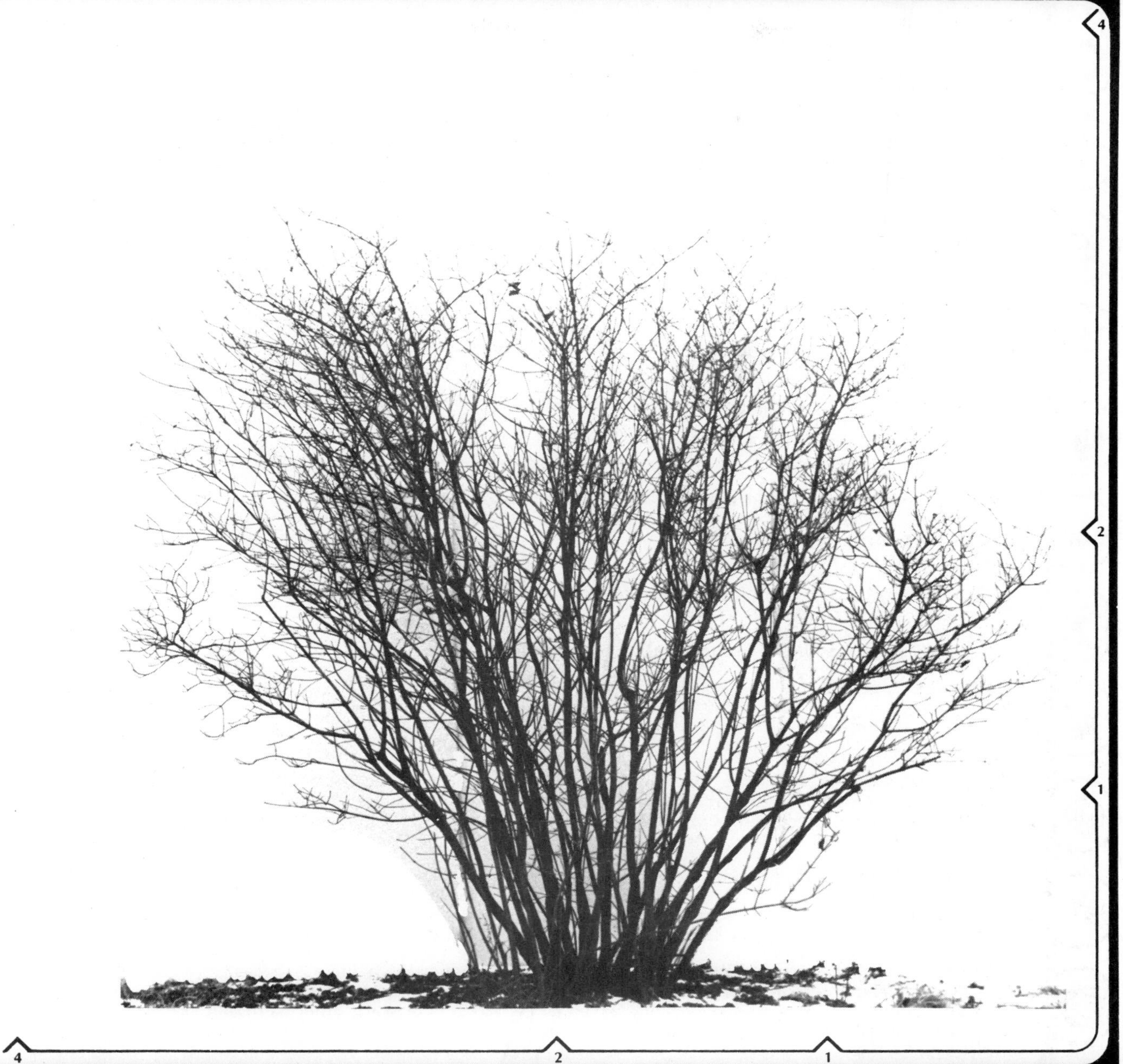

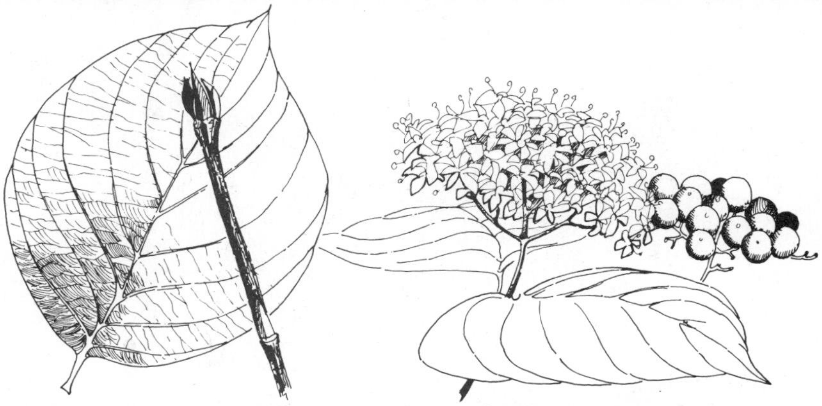

Cornus stolonifera

FORM: **globular or mound**
Size: **mid-height shrub** - from 2 to 4 m (6 to 12 ft)
Spread: **intermediate** - 2 to 4 m (6 to 12 ft), occasionally to 6 m (20 ft)
Mass: **moderate**

BRANCHING: multiple stems, **upright spreading** finally strong **arching** habit, lowest branches horizontal; **medium** texture
Twig: slender, smooth, bright **red** to dark blood red **or purple,** pith large and white
Bud: ovoid, with **2** valvate **scales, brown**
Bark: **smooth** but with obvious horizontal lenticels, bright blood **red to purple,** old stems gray

FOLIAGE: opposite, **simple, ovate to oblong ovate,** entire margin, parallel veination; **medium fine** texture
Surface: **dull,** smooth, somewhat wrinkled above, white bloomy beneath
Color: spring - bright **red green;** summer - **medium green;** autumn - **orange or red** darkening **to** bronze **purple**
Season: **deciduous;** emergence - mid **May,** drop - late **October**

FLOWER: dense upright **flat-topped** clusters, 2.5 - 5 cm (1 to 2 in) diameter
Color: creamy **white**
Season: late **May through** mid **June,** often sporadic occurrence throughout summer, after leaves fully grown
Sex: monoecious

FRUIT: globular pea-size **berry,** 6 mm (¼ in) diameter, in open umbrella-like clusters
Color: dull **white**
Season: early through late **September**   Human Value: not edible
WildlifeValue: **very high;** waterfowl, marshbirds, shorebirds are major users, large and small mammals; hoofed browsers

HABITAT: formation - **meadow, swamp, fen, bog, dune;** region - **Northern;** gradient - lowland **wet;** open marshy ground,
open wet meadow, calcareous fen, lakeshore and dune, river and stream bank, sloughs, sluggish streams, bog thicket
Shade Tolerance: **very intolerant**
Flood Tolerance: **very tolerant**

SOIL: Texture: **coarse** sands and gravels **to fine** silts, peats underlain by calcareous clays, silts, sands
Drainage: **very poor to well**
Moisture: **wet to average**
Reaction: **slightly acid to** circumneutral, tolerates **alkaline,** pH 6.1 - 8.5

HARDINESS: zone 2
Rate: **fast**
Longevity: **short-lived**

SUSCEPTIBILITY: Physiological: **infrequent**
Disease: **occasional** - twig blight and canker may be locally severe, leaf spots, powdery mildew
Insect: **occasional** - scale can be problem, bagworms, other lesser insects
Wind-Ice: **infrequent**

URBAN TOLERANCE: Pollution: **sensitive** - 0₃, 2-4D; **intermediate** - S0₂
Lighting: **sensitive**   Drought Heat: **resistant**   Mine Spoils:
Salt: **sensitive**   Soil Compaction: **resistant**
Root Pattern: fibrous, **shallow lateral, stoloniferous,** forming thickets; **transplants well to difficult,** slow to re-establish

SPECIES: Associate: trees - Eastern Arborvitae, Balsam Fir, Yellow Birch, Black Ash, Eastern Hemlock; shrubs - Common
Winterberry, Common Ninebark, Dwarf Bushhoneysuckle, American Black Currant, Silky Dogwood, willow species
Similar: Stiffcornel/Silky/Siberian (Asiatic)/Bailey Dogwoods - habitat, form, flower color similar
Cultivars: 'Flaviramea' - twigs yellow; Kelseyi - compact, low growing; 'Nitida' - twigs green; others

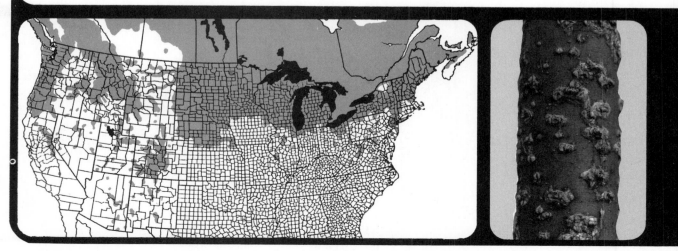

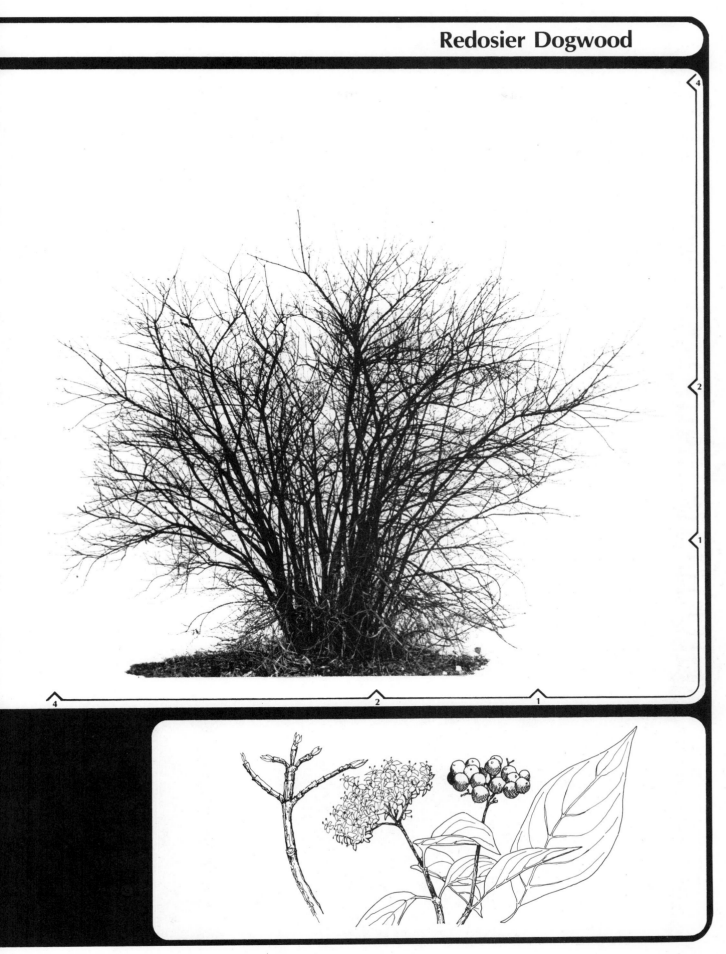

Corylus americana

FORM: **globular or mound**
Size: **mid-height shrub** - from 2 to 4 m (6 to 12 ft)
Spread: **intermediate** - 2 to 4 m (6 to 12 ft), frequently suckers into 6 m (20 ft) thickets
Mass: very **dense**

BRANCHING: multi-stemmed, **erect** with **upright spreading** branches, **leggy** and open base, much-branched crown; **medium**
Twig: **zigzag** appearance, young twigs dense **velvety, red brown**
Bud: small globular, 3 mm (⅛ in), **woolly, red brown to purplish; winter catkins**
Bark: fairly **smooth to shallow furrowed** at base of old stems, **gray brown**

FOLIAGE: alternate, **simple,** broadly **ovate to oblong ovate,** double toothed margin; **medium coarse** texture
Surface: sparingly **tomentose** above, soft tomentose beneath
Color: spring - tawny yellow then **yellow green;** summer - dark **yellow green;** autumn - muddy **yellow to orange**
Season: **deciduous;** emergence - late **May,** drop - late **September**

FLOWER: long drooping pencil-like male **catkins,** 4 to 7.5 cm (1½ to 3 in); female bloom obscure, stringy, 3 mm (⅛ in)
Color: male tawny **brown,** female scarlet **red**
Season: early **March through** early **April,** before leaves
Sex: monoecious

FRUIT: oval **nut** tightly enclosed by 2 leafy irregularly-lobed bracts, nut 13 mm (½ in) diameter, in clusters of 2 to 5
Color: light **brown**
Season: late **August through** late **September**   Human Value: **edible fruit**
Wildlife Value: **intermediate;** upland gamebirds, songbirds, large and small mammals; hoofed browsers graze foliage

HABITAT: formation - **glade, forest, old field;** region - **Central;** gradient - upland **mesic, mesic-dry, dry;** dry woodlands, woods
    edge, rocky wooded or open hillsides, fence rows, wasteland, ravine banks, alluvial woods, brushy pastures
Shade Tolerance: **tolerant**
Flood Tolerance: **intolerant**

SOIL: Texture: **moderately coarse** stony, gravelly, and sandy loams, deep loams **to fine** clay loams, heavy clays
Drainage: **moderately well to well**
Moisture: **moist to dry**
Reaction: **slightly acid to circumneutral,** pH 6.1 - 7.5

HARDINESS: **zone 3a**
Rate: **medium to fast**
Longevity: **moderately short-lived**

SUSCEPTIBILITY: Physiological: **infrequent**
Disease: **infrequent** - blight, black knot, leaf spots, crown gall; rarely serious
Insect: **infrequent** - Japanese leafhopper, scales, caterpillars; none serious
Wind-Ice: **infrequent**

URBAN TOLERANCE: Pollution: **sensitive** - HCl
Lighting: Drought Heat: **intermediate**   Mine Spoils:
Salt: **sensitive**   Soil Compaction: **intermediate**
Root Pattern: fribrous, **shallow lateral,** suckering habit forming broad thickets; **transplants well**

SPECIES: Associate: trees - White/Black/Bur/Chinkapin Oaks, Black Cherry, Shagbark/Bitternut Hickories; shrubs - Gray
    Dogwood, American Elder, Allegany Blackberry, Pasture Gooseberry, Indiancurrant Coralberry, Carolina Rose
Similar: Beaked Filbert - beaked fruits, Northern; European Filbert and hybrids - weeping, contorted, purpleleaf varieties
Cultivars: none available

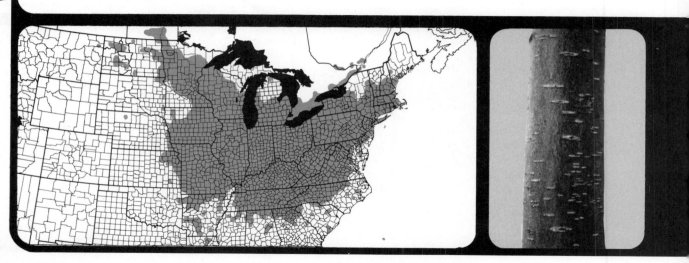

552

American Filbert

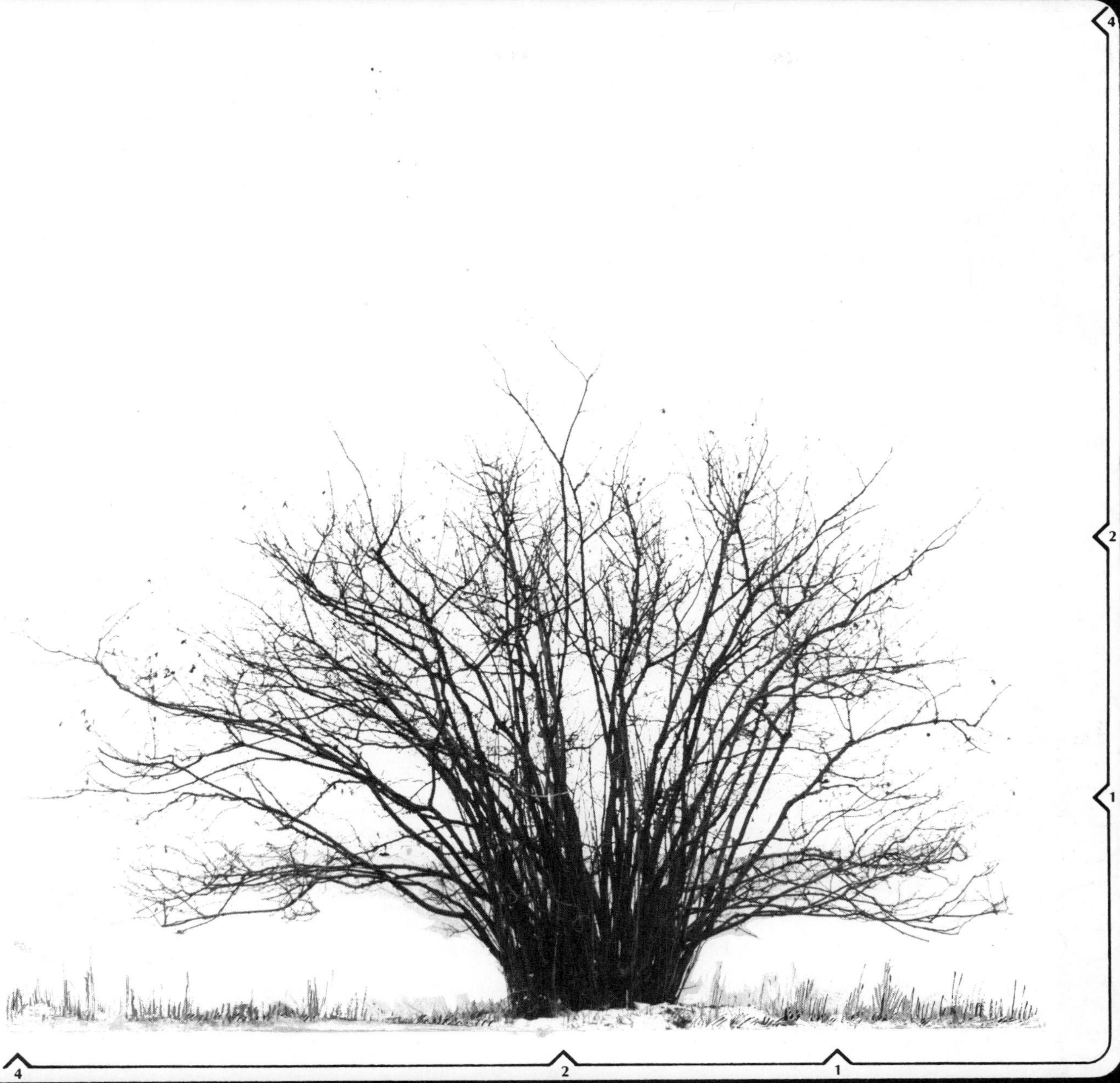

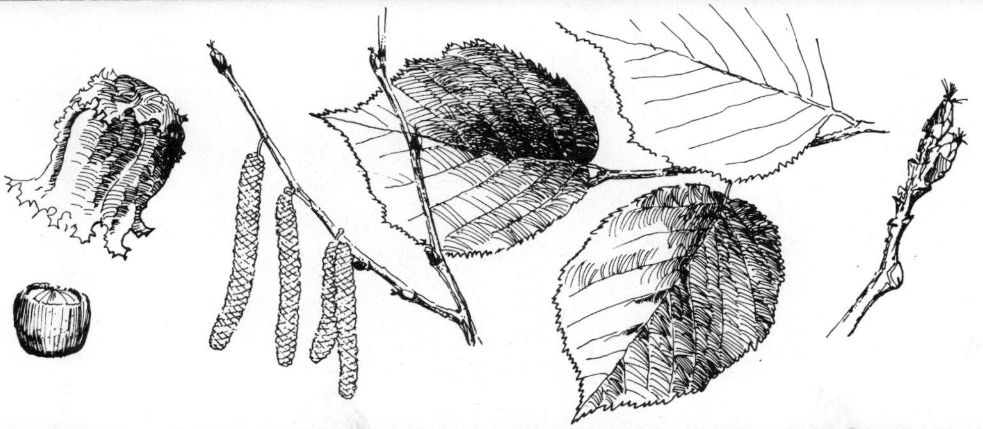

Corylus cornuta

FORM: **globular or mound**
Size: **mid-height shrub** - from 2 to 4 m (6 to 12 ft)
Spread: **intermediate** - 2 to 4 m (6 to 12 ft), frequently suckering into 6 m (20 ft) thickets
Mass: very **dense**

BRANCHING: dense multi-stemmed, **erect** with **leggy upright spreading** branches, open base; **medium** texture
Twig: **zigzag** appearance, young twigs not velvety, **red brown**
Bud: small ovoid, 5 mm (⅕ in), **brown; winter catkins**
Bark: **smooth to** irregularly **shallow furrowed** on very old stems at base, **gray brown**

FOLIAGE: alternate, **simple, ovate** to obovate, double toothed, margin sometimes almost lobed; **medium coarse** texture
Surface: sparingly **tomentose** to dull smooth above, soft tomentose beneath
Color: spring - **yellow green;** summer - bright **medium green;** autumn - **yellow to orange**
Season: **deciduous;** emergence - late **May,** drop - late **September**

FLOWER: long drooping pencil-like male **catkins,** 2.5 to 5 cm (1 to 2 in); female blooms obscure, stringy, 3 mm (⅛ in)
Color: male purplish **brown,** female bright **red**
Season: mid **March through** early **April,** before leaves
Sex: monoecious

FRUIT: oval **nut** tightly enclosed in bristly elongated beak-like husk, nut 13 mm (½ in) diameter, clusters of 1 to 6
Color: **brown**
Season: late **August through** late **September**   Human Value: **edible fruit**
Wildlife Value: **intermediate;** upland gamebirds, songbirds, large and small mammals; hoofed browsers graze twigs

HABITAT: formation - **glade, forest, old field;** region - **Northern;** gradient - **mesic, mesic-dry, dry;** banks of quick flowing
creeks, dry open woods, borders of woods, brushy pastures, fence rows, rocky hillsides
Shade Tolerance: **tolerant**
Flood Tolerance: **intolerant**

SOIL: Texture: **moderately coarse** sandy and gravelly loams, medium loams **to fine** silt loams, heavy clays
Drainage: **moderately well to well**
Moisture: **moist to dry**
Reaction: **slightly acid to circumneutral,** pH 6.1 - 7.5

HARDINESS: **zone 3a**
Rate: **medium**
Longevity: **moderately short-lived**

SUSCEPTIBILITY: Physiological: **infrequent**
Disease: **infrequent** - black knot, crown gall, leaf spots; blight can be locally bothersome
Insect: **infrequent** - scales, caterpillars, Japanese leafhoppers; none serious
Wind-Ice: **infrequent**

URBAN TOLERANCE: Pollution: **sensitive** - HCl
Lighting: Drought Heat: **intermediate**   Mine Spoils:
Salt: **sensitive**   Soil Compaction: **intermediate**
Root Pattern: fibrous, **shallow lateral,** suckering into broad colonies; **transplants well**

SPECIES: Associate: trees - Paper Birch, Quaking/Bigtooth Aspens, Northern Pin Oak, Jack/Red/Eastern White Pines,
Red Maple; shrubs - American Filbert, Dwarf Bushhoneysuckle, Lowbush Blueberry, Mapleleaf Viburnum
Similar: American Filbert - more Southern, taller; European Filbert - taller
Cultivars: none available

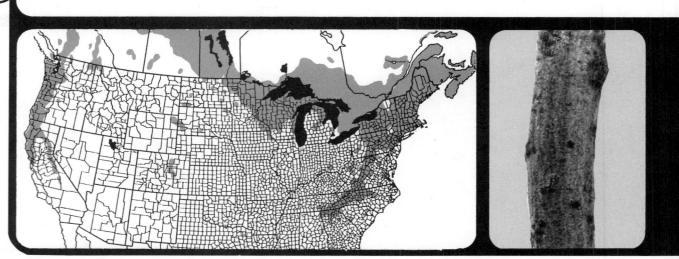

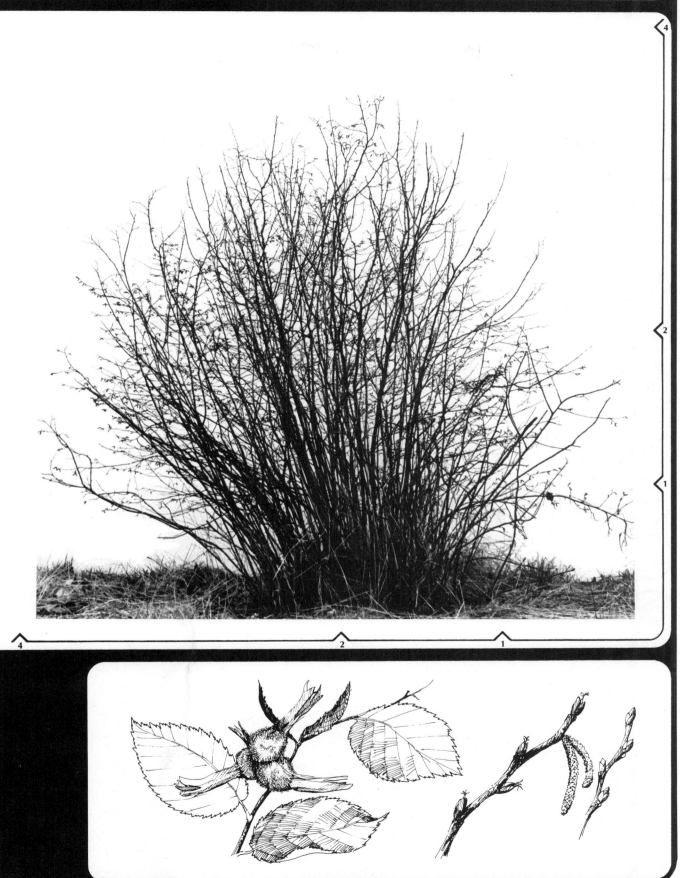

Cyrilla racemiflora

FORM: globular
Size: **large shrub** - 4 to 6 m (12 to 20 ft) or small tree occasionally to 10 m (35 ft)
Spread: **wide** - 4 to 6 m (12 to 20 ft), equal to height
Mass: open to **moderate**

BRANCHING: short trunk, numerous **ascending** symmetrical branches; **fine** texture
Twig: slender, **velvety** then smooth, glossy, often **angular** with 3 sides, **red brown** to ashy gray
Bud: small ovoid, loose overlapping scales, 6 mm (¼ in) long terminal buds, chestnut brown
Bark: smooth or with thin shreddy **scales,** checked at base with small thick shallow furrowed spongy plates, **red brown**

FOLIAGE: alternate, often clustered at tips, **simple,** narrow elliptic to **oblanceolate,** entire wavy margin; **medium** texture
Surface: **glossy,** leathery, paler beneath
Color: spring - **red green;** summer - **dark green;** autumn - turns late, **orange or red;** winter - **purplish green** (evergreen form)
Season: **evergreen or semi-evergreen,** tardily deciduous in North

FLOWER: small bells, in slender drooping **spikes** 10 to 15 cm (4 to 6 in) long, 6 to 10 spikes per cluster at base of new growth
Color: **white** or pinkish
Season: early through mid **July,** after leaves
Sex: monoecious   **Fragrant:** very sweet honey-like perfume, attracts honeybees, insects

FRUIT: dry **capsule,** 3 mm (⅛ in) long, clustered in drooping wand-like spikes
Color: yellow becoming light **brown**
Season: ripens mid **August through** late September, persists to late **April**   Human Value: not edible
Wildlife Value: **low;** a few songbirds, waterbirds, deer browse on tender shoots, leaves

HABITAT: formation - **bog, dune, swamp, forest;** region - **Southern;** gradient - **wet, dry;** high sandy exposed ridges above
          streams, acid bogs, rich shaded alluvial flats, stream banks, bays, dunes, pocosins, cypress swamp, limestone sinks
Shade Tolerance: **intermediate**
Flood Tolerance: **very tolerant,** known to grow in swamps inundated for ¾ of year

SOIL: Texture: **coarse** maritime sands and gravels, sandy loams **to fine** sands, peats, mucks, clays
Drainage: **very poor to moderately poor**
Moisture: **wet to moist,** tolerates dry
Reaction: **moderately acid to** circumneutral, tolerates **alkaline,** pH 5.1 - 8.5

HARDINESS: zone 6a
Rate: **medium**
Longevity: **moderately short-lived**

SUSCEPTIBILITY: Physiological: **infrequent**
Disease: **infrequent** - none serious
Insect: **infrequent** - none serious
Wind-Ice: **infrequent**

URBAN TOLERANCE: Pollution:
Lighting: Drought Heat: **resistant**   Mine Spoils:
Salt: **resistant**   Soil Compaction: **resistant**
Root Pattern: dense fibrous, **shallow to deep laterals, transplants well**

SPECIES: Associate: trees - Swamp/Black Tupelos, Pond Pine, Red Maple, Bald Cypress; shrubs - Inkberry, Dusty
          Zenobia, Summersweet Clethra, Fetterbush Lyonia, Lambkill Kalmia, Virginia Sweetspire, Coast Leucothoe
Similar: Sourwood - small tree
Cultivars: none available

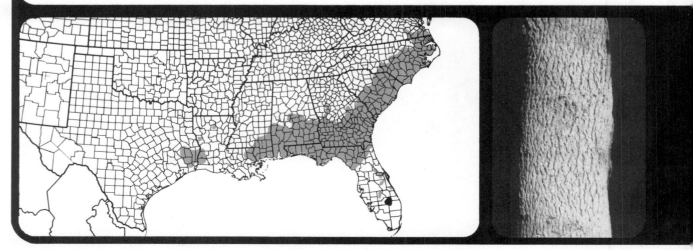

American Cyrilla

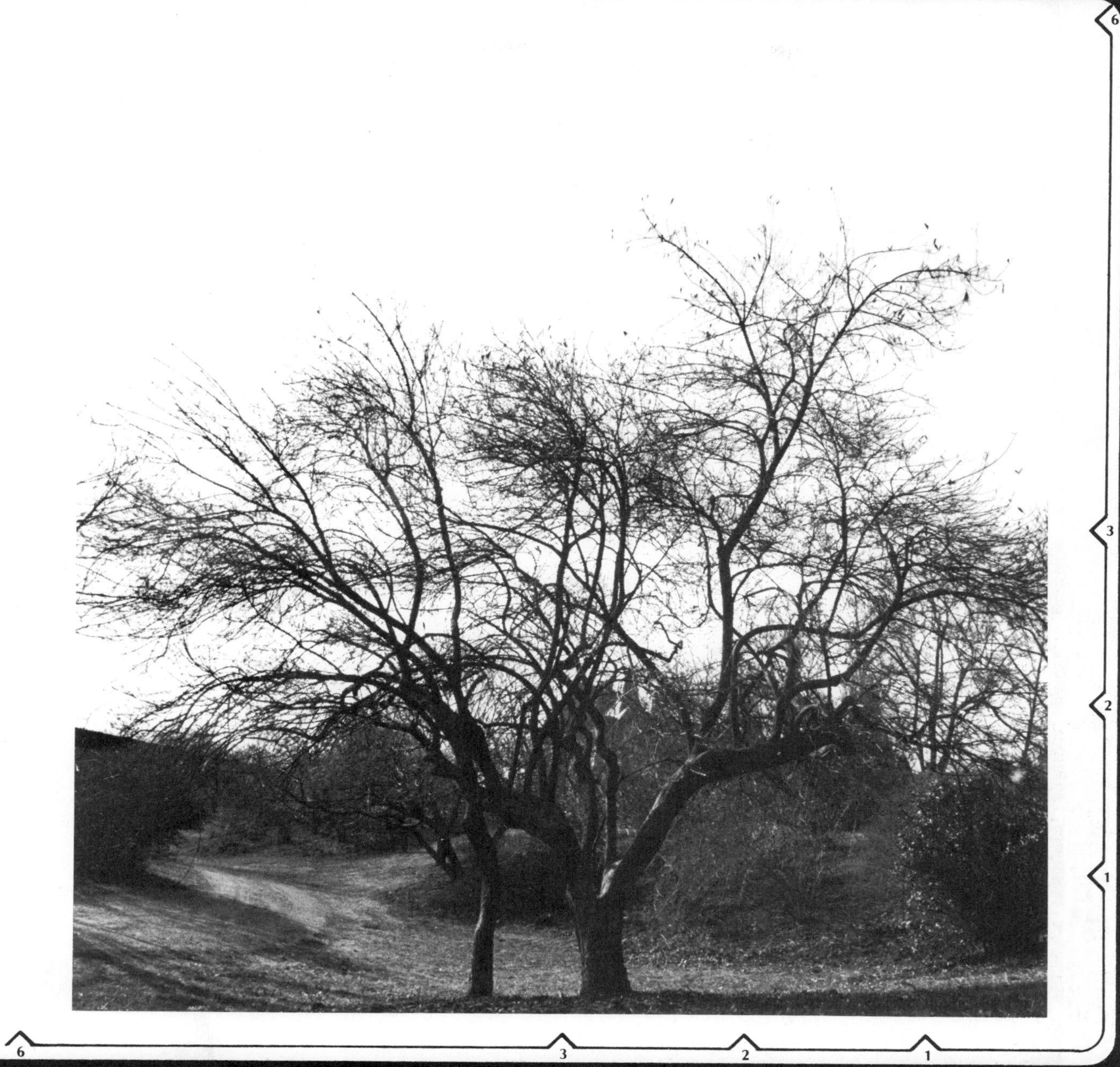

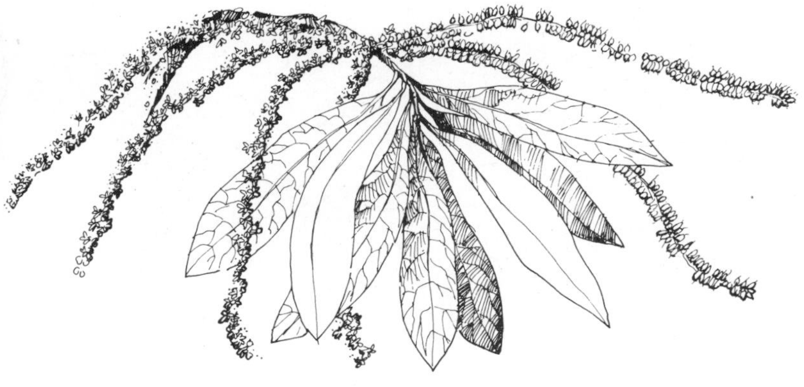

Diervilla lonicera

FORM: **mound**
Size: **very small shrub** - to 1 m (3 ft)
Spread: **very narrow** - commonly less than 1 m (3 ft), often forming broad thickets with age
Mass: **open**

BRANCHING: single/multiple **erect leggy** unbranched/loosely branched stems, **upright spreading or arching** habit; **coarse**
Twig: slender, slightly **angular,** flattened with prominent **ridged** lines beneath leaf scars, **orange brown** resembling straw
Bud: narrow oblong, sharp **pointed,** pale **brown**
Bark: **exfoliating** into long narrow papery ridges, **gray brown** with orange brown inner bark

FOLIAGE: opposite, **simple, ovate to oblong ovate**, margin hairy fringed when young, finely toothed; **medium fine** texture
Surface: **dull,** smooth, pale beneath
Color: spring - **light green**; summer - **dark green**; autumn - **yellow** changing **to orange**, finally **red**
Season: **deciduous**; emergence - mid **May**, drop - mid **October**

FLOWER: small funnel-shaped **bell**, 13 mm (½ in) long, tubes with 5 short spreading lobes, in axillary clusters of 2 to 6
Color: pale yellow at first, turning orange or purplish **red**
Season: early through late **July**, often sporadic through mid August, after leaves
Sex: monoecious

FRUIT: dry long-pointed beaked **capsules**, 16 mm (⅝ in) long, axillary clusters of 2 to 6
Color: **brown**   Human Value: not edible
Season: early through late **September**, often persisting longer
Wildlife Value: **low**; songbirds occasionally

HABITAT: formation - **forest, old field, glade**; region - **Northern**; gradient - upland **mesic, mesic-dry, dry**; woodland borders,
     wayside thickets, rocky places, open sandy or rocky woods, clay or rock slopes, cliffs, sand dunes
Shade Tolerance: **very tolerant**
Flood Tolerance: **intolerant**

SOIL: Texture: **coarse** sands, gravels, loamy sands, sandy loams **to fine** silty clay loams, sandy clay loams, heavy clays
Drainage: **moderately well to excessive**
Moisture: **average to droughty**
Reaction: **slightly acid**, pH 6.1 - 6.5

HARDINESS: zone 3a
Rate: **fast**
Longevity: **very short-lived**

SUSCEPTIBILITY: Physiological: **infrequent**
Disease: **infrequent** - leaf spots, powdery mildew; rarely serious
Insect: **occasional** - lecanium scale may cause considerable damage
Wind-Ice: **infrequent**

URBAN TOLERANCE: Pollution:
Lighting: Drought Heat: **resistant**   Mine Spoils: **resistant**
Salt: Soil Compaction: **resistant**
Root Pattern: fibrous, **shallow lateral, stoloniferous,** suckers freely; **transplants well**

SPECIES: Associate: trees - Balsam Fir, White Spruce, Quaking Aspen, Black Oak, Balsam Poplar, Showy Mountainash;
     shrubs - Bunchberry/Roundleaf Dogwoods, American Fly Honeysuckle, Beaked Filbert, Russet Buffaloberry
Similar: Southern Bushhoneysuckle; Indiancurrant Coralberry - red berries; honeysuckle species
Cultivars: none available

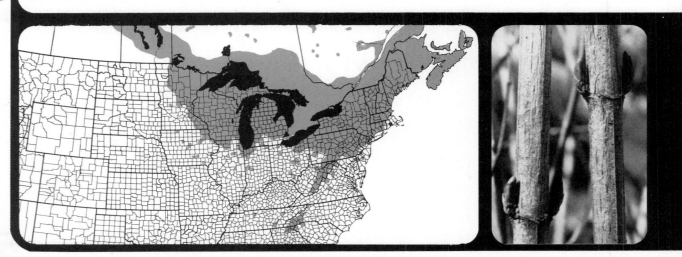

Dwarf Bushhoneysuckle

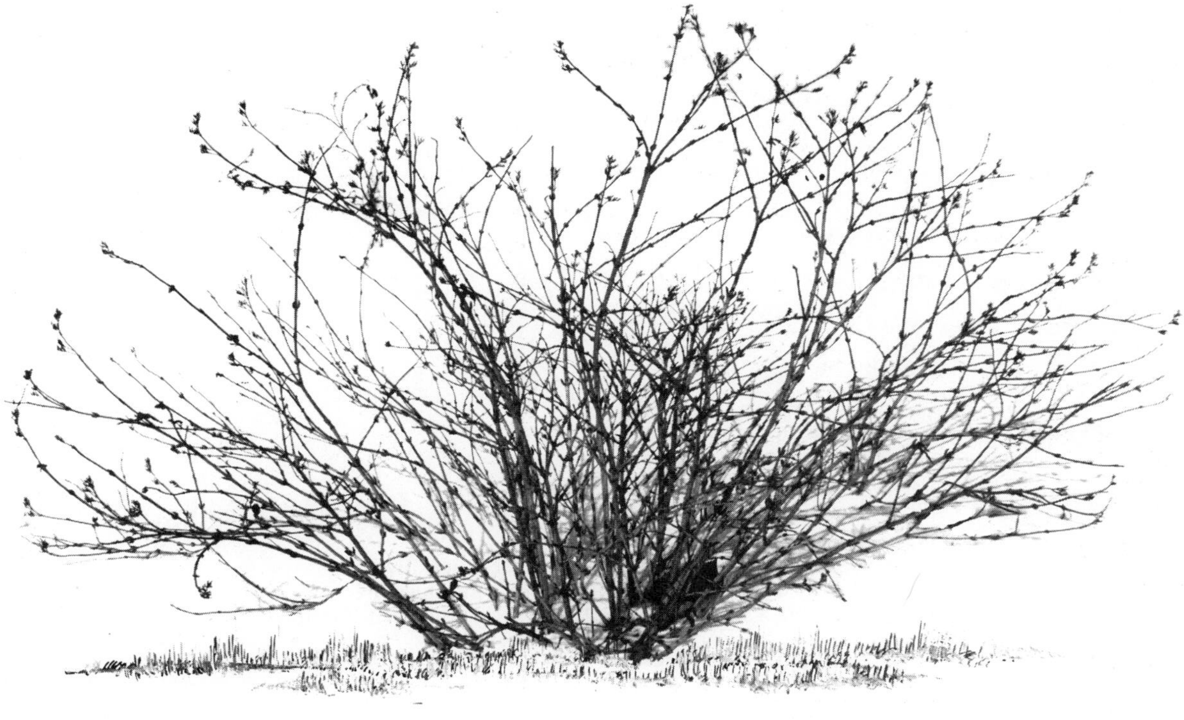

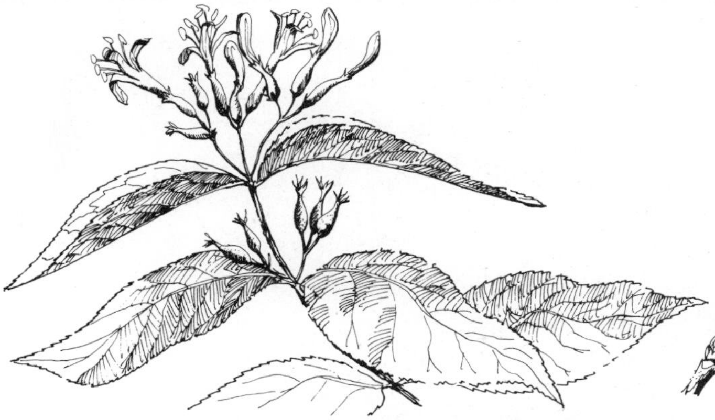

Dirca palustris

FORM: **globular** symmetrical crown
Size: **small shrub** - from 1 to 2 m (3 to 6 ft), occasionally to 3 m (9 ft)
Spread: **narrow** - 1 to 2 m (3 to 6 ft), occasionally to 3 m (9 ft)
Mass: **open** in woods, more dense as specimen

BRANCHING: solitary or few short trunks, **ascending** symmetrical candelabra branching; **medium** texture
Twig: stout, flexible, enlarge upwards appearing socket-jointed or swollen at nodes, **green, green brown or red brown**
Bud: small dome-shaped, **surrounded by leaf scar, woolly, gray to brown**
Bark: **smooth** tough pliable stems, old stems with fine narrow irregular fissures, dark **gray brown to brown black**

FOLIAGE: alternate, **simple, elliptic** to obovate, entire margin, foliage often ranked in flat plain; **medium** texture
Surface: **dull**, smooth, paler beneath
Color: spring - **yellow green**; summer - **medium green**; autumn - dull **yellowish**
Season: **deciduous**; emergence - early **May**, drop - mid **October**

FLOWER: narrow bell-shaped **trumpet**, 6 to 9.5 mm (¼ to ⅜ in) long, 3 to 4 in a pendulous cluster
Color: pale **yellow**
Season: early **March through** early **April**, before leaves
Sex: monoecious

FRUIT: elliptic football-shaped **berry**, 9.5 mm (⅜ in) long
Color: **green late, then reddish**
Season: early **June through** late **July**, soon falling after ripe   Human Value: not edible
Wildlife Value: **low;** upland gamebirds and songbirds occasionally; hoofed browsers eat foliage, twigs

HABITAT: formation - **forest**; region - **Northern, Central**; gradient - **mesic**; rich deep woods, elevated floodplain knobs and
        terraces, sheltered coves, moist ravines and footslopes, cool north and east slopes, base of vertical rock cliff
Shade Tolerance: **very tolerant**
Flood Tolerance: **very intolerant**

SOIL: Texture: **moderately coarse** loamy sands, sandy loams **to moderately fine** silt loams; best on medium loams
Drainage: **moderately well to well**
Moisture: **moist to average**
Reaction: **slightly acid to** circumneutral, tolerates **alkaline**, pH 6.1 - 8.5

HARDINESS: zone 3a
Rate: **slow**
Longevity: **moderately short-lived**

SUSCEPTIBILITY: Physiological: **infrequent**
Disease: **infrequent** - very resistant
Insect: **infrequent** - none serious
Wind-Ice: **infrequent**

URBAN TOLERANCE: Pollution:
Lighting: Drought Heat: very **sensitive**   Mine Spoils: **sensitive**
Salt: **resistant**   Soil Compaction: **intermediate**
Root Pattern: **shallow lateral** with coarse open pattern; very **difficult to transplant**, slow to re-establish

SPECIES: Associate: trees - Sugar Maple, Eastern Hemlock, American Beech, American Linden, American Hornbeam,
        Pagoda Dogwood; shrubs - Scarlet Elder, American Bladdernut, Pasture Gooseberry, Common Witchhazel
Similar: San Francisco Leatherwood - smaller leaves, Western
Cultivars: none available

Elaeagnus commutata

FORM: **globular to obovoid**
Size: **mid-height shrub** - from 2 to 4 m (6 to 12 ft)
Spread: **intermediate** - 2 to 4 m (6 to 12 ft), ⅔ or equal to height, broadest in upper ⅓ of crown
Mass: **open**

BRANCHING: solitary or few short trunks, irregular **ascending** branches, very twiggy; **medium** texture
Twig: covered with **orange brown** scurfy **scales** becoming **silvery gray to gray**; unarmed
Bud: small globular, **silvery gray** scales
Bark: covered with **gray to pale brown scales**

FOLIAGE: alternate, **simple, lanceolate to oblong lanceolate**, entire wavy margin, short petiole; **fine to medium fine**
Surface: **tomentose**, both sides covered with scales, rusty dotted beneath
Color: spring - **silvery gray**; summer - **gray green**; autumn - **gray green**
Season: **deciduous**; emergence - late **May**, drop - late **November**

FLOWER: **small clusters**, bell-like, inconspicuous
Color: **silvery** outside, pale to golden yellow within
Season: mid **June through** early **July**, after leaves
Sex: monoecious   **Fragrant:** spicily perfumed, heavy sweet scent

FRUIT: dry mealy globular **berry**, 1 cm (⅖ in) diameter, covered with scales
Color: **white to silvery gray**
Season: late **August through** late **October**   Human Value: **edible fruit**
Wildlife Value: **low**; some use by upland gamebirds and songbirds; hoofed browsers eat foliage and twigs

HABITAT: formation - **prairie, savanna, old field**; region - **Northern**; gradient - upland **mesic-dry, dry**; dry prairie hillsides and
ridge tops, brushy ravine banks, dry waste areas, river banks, moist hillsides, clearings
Shade Tolerance: **intolerant**
Flood Tolerance: **very intolerant**

SOIL: Texture: **coarse to fine**; sandy plains, infertile sands and gravels, loamy sands, fine clays
Drainage: **well to excessive**
Moisture: **dry to droughty**
Reaction: **slightly acid to alkaline**, pH 6.1 - 8.5

HARDINESS: **zone 2**
Rate: **fast**
Longevity: **long-lived**

SUSCEPTIBILITY: Physiological: **infrequent**
Disease: **infrequent** - leaf spots, cankers, rusts; none serious
Insect: **infrequent** - scales; rarely merit control measures
Wind-ice: **infrequent**

URBAN TOLERANCE: Pollution:
Lighting: Drought Heat: **intermediate**   Mine Spoils:
Salt: **resistant**   Soil Compaction: **sensitive**
Root Pattern: **shallow lateral, stoloniferous** with small tubers, nitrogen-fixing; **transplants well**

SPECIES: Associate: shrubs - Western Snowberry, Indiancurrant Coralberry, Sand Cherry, Common Chokecherry,
American Plum, Russet/Silver Buffaloberries, Prairie Rose
Similar: Autumn/Cherry Eleagnus - Asiatic; Silver/Russet Buffaloberries; Common Seabuckthorn - European
Cultivars: none available

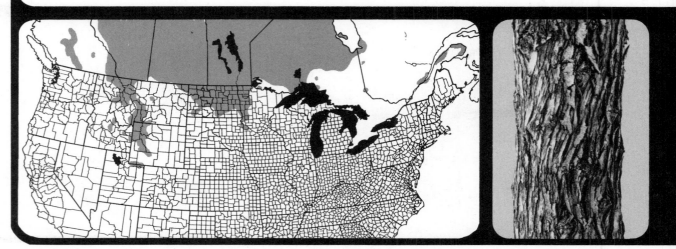

Silverberry

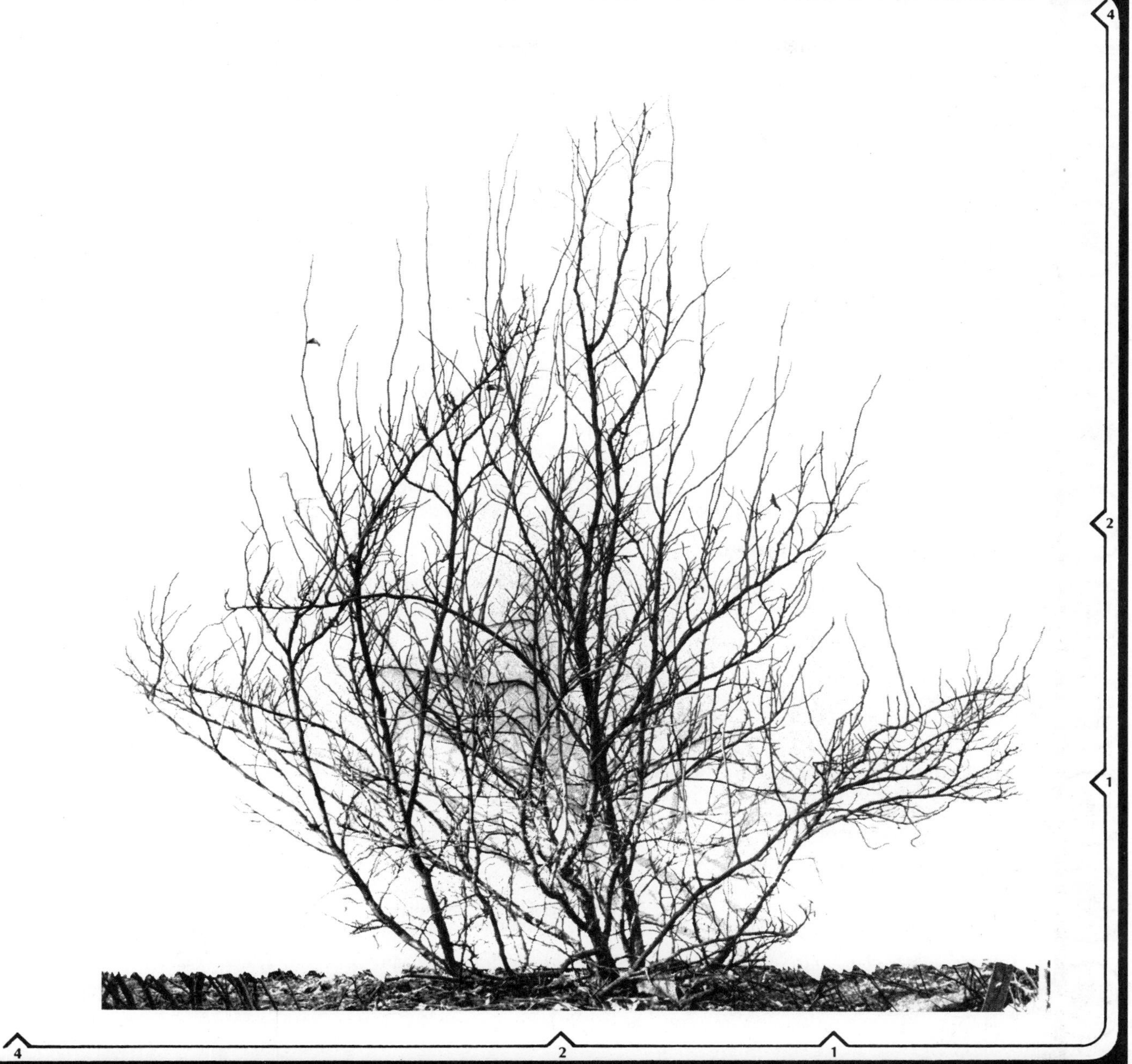

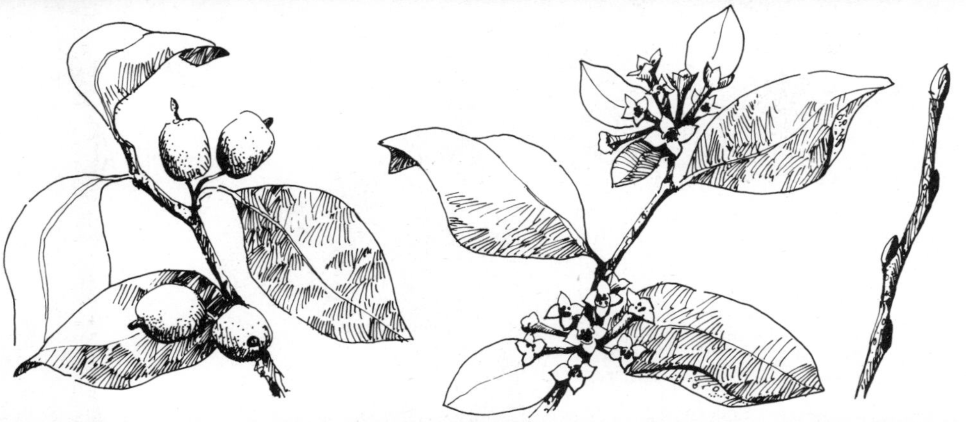

Epigaea repens

FORM: prostrate creeping **mat**
Size: **very small shrub** - less than 1 m (3 ft) commonly 10 to 15 cm (4 to 6 in) high
Spread: **very narrow** - less than 1 m (3 ft), old colonies broader spreading
Mass: **dense** cover

BRANCHING: prostrate **trailing** rooting stems forming patches, sparingly branched; **medium** texture
Twig: slender, **velvety** with rusty **brown** hairs
Bud: inconspicuous
Bark: **smooth, brown**

FOLIAGE: alternate, **simple**, broad **elliptic**, blunt-rounded at tip, entire or hairy fringed, **aromatic; medium fine** texture
Surface: **dull**, leathery, rough on both surfaces with scattered stiff tomentum
Color: spring - **red green to medium green;** summer, autumn, winter - bright **medium green,** slightly bronzed by rusty hairs
Season: broadleaf **evergreen**

FLOWER: slender **trumpet** with 5 broad flared lobes, 13 mm (½ in) wide, in short crowded 4 to 6-flowered clusters
Color: **white to** pale or deep **pink**
Season: mid through late **April**
Sex: **dioecious**   **Fragrant:** exceedingly fragrant, spicy

FRUIT: globular **berry**-like **capsules,** 13 mm (½ in) diameter, resembles raspberry in appearance
Color: **whitish**
Season: early **June through** late **August**   Human Value: **flower** parts **edible**
Wildlife Value: **low,** occasionally by upland gamebirds

HABITAT: formation - **barrens, forest, dune, open field;** region - **Northern;** gradient - **mesic-dry to dry;** dry rocky or sandy
     woods, clearings, rocky ridges, dry banks, pine barrens, dunes
Shade Tolerance: **tolerant**
Flood Tolerance: **very intolerant**

SOIL: Texture: **coarse** sands, sandy plains, loamy sands **to medium** loams; intolerant of clays
Drainage: **well to excessive**
Moisture: **average to droughty**
Reaction: demands **strongly acid to moderately acid,** pH 4.5 - 6.0

HARDINESS: **zone 2**
Rate: very **slow,** 2.5 to 5 cm (1 to 2 in) per year
Longevity: **moderately short-lived**

SUSCEPTIBILITY: Physiological: **frequent** - disturbance by man leads to leaf browning and rot
Disease: **infrequent** - very resistant
Insect: **infrequent** - none serious
Wind-Ice: **infrequent**

URBAN TOLERANCE: Pollution:
Lighting: Drought Heat: **resistant**   Mine Spoils:
Salt: **resistant**   Soil Compaction: **sensitive**
Root Pattern: trailing rooting stems, **deep taproot; difficult to transplant** and perpetuate, roots easily injured, obtain potted

SPECIES: Associate: trees - Red/Eastern White/Loblolly Pines, Bigtooth/Quaking Aspens, oak species; shrubs - Catawba/
     Carolina Rhododendrons, Witherod Viburnum, Mountainlaurel Kalmia, Lowbush/Highbush Blueberries
Similar: Asiatic Trailing-arbutus - zone 5, Japan; Checkerberry Wintergreen; Bunchberry Dogwood - semi-evergreen
Cultivars: 'Plenna' - double-flowering; 'Rosea' - flowers rose red

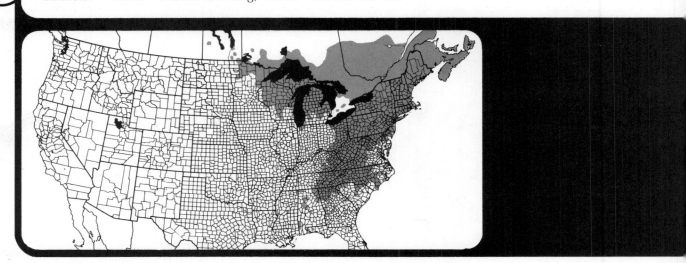

Euonymus americanus

FORM: **obovoid**
Size: **mid-height shrub** - from 2 to 4 m (6 to 12 ft)
Spread: **intermediate** - 2 to 4 m (6 to 12 ft), typically ⅔ the height
Mass: **moderate** to very open

BRANCHING: **erect to upright** spreading, sparingly branched, often irregular, branchlets drooping when in fruit; **fine**
Twig: slender, **angular** with 4 distinct lined **ridges**, smooth, **green, purplish** when exposed to sun
Bud: oblong ovoid, 3 mm (⅛ in), narrow, sharp pointed, loose scales, often streaked, **red to brown** tinged green
Bark: **smooth, green** to brown or gray

FOLIAGE: opposite, **simple,** narrow **ovate to oblong ovate or lanceolate,** fine wavy toothed margin; **medium** texture
Surface: **dull,** thick, smooth above, somewhat downy beneath
Color: spring - bright **medium green;** summer - **medium green;** autumn - dark **red**
Season: **deciduous,** persistent farther south; emergence - mid **May,** drop - mid **November**

FLOWER: **small** 1 to 3-flowered **clusters, 6** mm (¼ in) across, 5 distinct clawed petals
Color: delicate pale **green to** pink with dark **purplish** stamens
Season: late **May through** early **June,** after leaves
Sex: monoecious

FRUIT: 3 to 5-lobed warty strawberry or heart-shaped **capsule,** splitting open exposing pendant seeds - 'hearts a bustin'
Color: **orangish or** crimson **red** capsules with glossy scarlet red pendant seeds
Season: early **September through** early **November**   Human Value: **poisonous fruit**
Wildlife Value: **low;** limited use by songbirds, upland gamebirds, small mammals

HABITAT: formation - **forest, old field;** region - **Central, Southern;** gradient - **wet-mesic, mesic;** deep rich woods, bluffs,
alluvial forests, sheltered coves, stream bottoms and banks, low areas, thickets, borders of woods, moist ravines
Shade Tolerance: **very tolerant**
Flood Tolerance: **intermediate**

SOIL: Texture: **moderately coarse** sandy loams, loamy sands **to moderately fine** silt loams; prefers better aeration
Drainage: **moderately poor to well**
Moisture: **moist to average**
Reaction: **slightly acid to circumneutral,** pH 6.1 - 7.5

HARDINESS: zone 6a, 5b with protection
Rate: **medium**
Longevity: **very short-lived**

SUSCEPTIBILITY: Physiological: **occasional** - extensive dieback in North from severe winters, will kill to ground
Disease: **frequent** - anthracnose, crown gall, leaf spots, powdery mildews are troublesome
Insect: **frequent** - euonymus scale is destructive, other scales, aphids, thrips
Wind-Ice: **frequent** - very weak, often depends on adjacent plants for support

URBAN TOLERANCE: Pollution:
Lighting: Drought Heat: **sensitive**   Mine Spoils:
Salt: **sensitive**   Soil Compaction: **intermediate**
Root Pattern: fibrous, **shallow lateral,** suckers forming colonies; **easily transplanted,** culture easy

SPECIES: Associate: trees - American Beech, Tuliptree, Bitternut Hickory, Sugar Maple, White Ash; shrubs - Common
Spicebush, Smooth Hydrangea, American Elder, American Bladdernut, Running Euonymus, Common Sweetshrub
Similar: Winged Euonymus - leaves and fruits smaller, horizontal habit, Asiatic; Eastern Wahoo - larger
Cultivars: none available

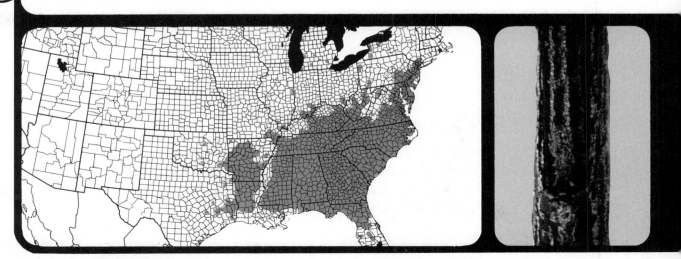

Euonymus obovatus

FORM: prostrate **mat**
Size: **very small shrub** - less than 1 m (3 ft), typically only to 46 cm (18 in) high
Spread: **very narrow** - to 1 m (3 ft), old colonies broader spreading
Mass: **dense**

BRANCHING: procumbent **trailing** rooting stems, ascending at tip forming extensive patches; **medium** texture
Twig: smooth, slender **angled** and squarish with 4 longitudinal lines, bright **green to purple**
Bud: terminal ovoid, 9.5 mm (³⁄₈ in), pointed, green to **reddish or brown**
Bark: **smooth, green** to brownish

FOLIAGE: opposite, **simple, obovate to oblong obovate**, terminal pair largest, finely toothed margin; **medium fine** texture
Surface: **dull**, smooth, paler beneath
Color: spring, summer - **light green;** autumn - **green** late **then** crimson **red**
Season: **deciduous;** emergence - mid **May,** drop - late **November**

FLOWER: **small** 1 to 3-flowered **clusters,** 6 mm (¼ in) across, 5 distinct claw-like petals
Color: **greenish to purple,** stamens bright yellow orange
Season: late **May through** early **June,** after leaves
Sex: monoecious

FRUIT: 3-lobed warty strawberry or heart-shaped **capsule,** 1.5 cm (⁹⁄₁₆ in) across, splitting open exposing pendant seeds
Color: pale **orange to** scarlet **red** capsule, scarlet seeds
Season: early **August through** late **September**   Human Value: **fruits, leaves poisonous**
Wildlife Value: **low;** selective use by upland gamebirds, songbirds, small mammals

HABITAT: formation - **forest;** region - **Central;** gradient - **wet-mesic, mesic;** shaded stream banks and low alluvial ground,
     rich woods, alluvial flats, till plains, occasional rocky slopes, footslopes, north-facing wooded slopes, talus
Shade Tolerance: **very tolerant**
Flood Tolerance: **intermediate**

SOIL: Texture: **moderately coarse** sandy loams, loamy sands **to moderately fine** silt loams
Drainage: **moderately well to well**
Moisture: **moist to average**
Reaction: **slightly acid to circumneutral,** pH 6.1 - 7.5

HARDINESS: **zone 3b**
Rate: **slow to medium**
Longevity: **short-lived**

SUSCEPTIBILITY: Physiological: **infrequent**
Disease: **frequent** - anthracnose, crown gall, leaf spots, powdery mildews are troublesome
Insect: **frequent** - aphids, thrips, scales, euonymus scale is very damaging
Wind-Ice: **infrequent**

URBAN TOLERANCE: Pollution:
Lighting: Drought Heat: **sensitive**   Mine Spoils: **sensitive**
Salt: Soil Compaction: **intermediate**
Root Pattern: creeping stems rooting where they touch moist ground, **deep** fibrous spreading; **easily transplanted**

SPECIES: Associate: trees - Sugar/Black Maples, Northern Red Oak, American Linden, American Beech, Eastern
     Hemlock; shrubs - Mapleleaf Viburnum, Common Spicebush, Smooth Hydrangea, American Bladdernut
Similar: Purpleleaf/Common Wintercreepers - broadleaf evergreens
Cultivars: 'Variegata' - trailing, leaves green and white

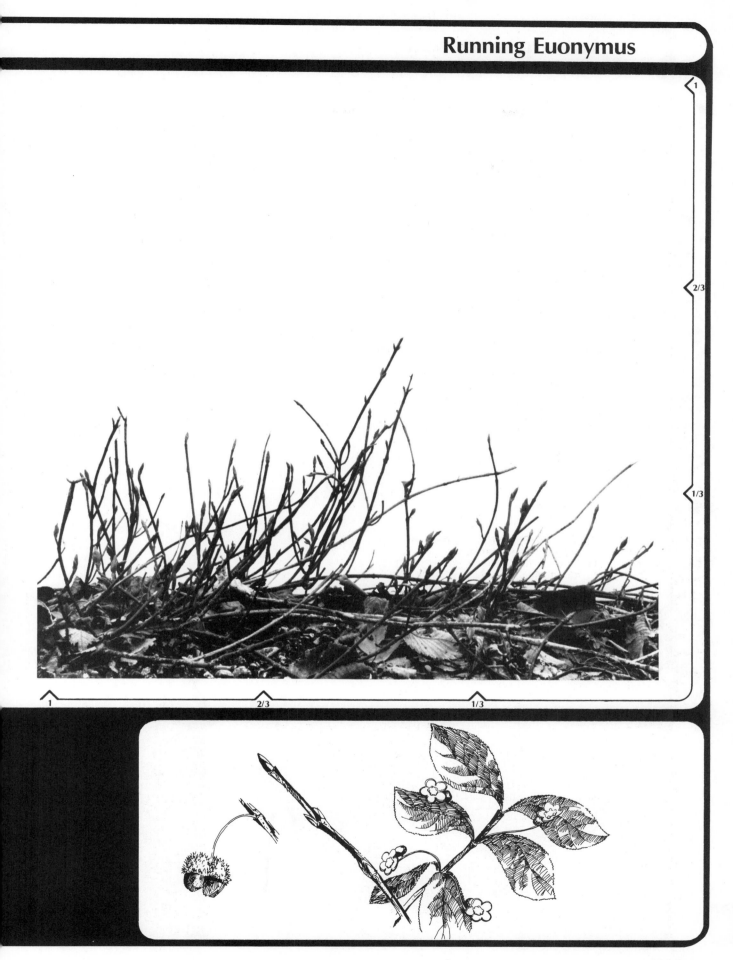

Fothergilla gardeni

FORM: **globular or mound**
Size: **very small shrub** - 1 m (3 ft)
Spread: **very narrow** - 1 m (3 ft) or more, equal or 1½ times height
Mass: **dense**

BRANCHING: **erect** multiple stems, **upright spreading** branches, crooked **picturesque** appearance; **medium** texture
Twig: slender, dense **velvety, angular ridged** appearance, **zigzag, green brown**
Bud: **naked, stalked,** dense **woolly,** green brown
Bark: **smooth,** ashy to dark **gray**

FOLIAGE: alternate, **simple, obovate to oblong obovate,** assymetric base, teeth above middle, **aromatic; medium coarse**
Surface: **dull,** leathery, dense woolly beneath
Color: spring - **light green;** summer - **dark green;** autumn - brilliant **yellow to** scarlet **red**
Season: **deciduous;** emergence - early **May,** drop - late **October**

FLOWER: thimble-like terminal **spikes,** 2.5 to 5 cm (1 to 2 in) long, appearing as a mass of bottlebrush-like stamens
Color: **white**
Season: late **April through** early to mid **May,** before leaves
Sex: monoecious   **Fragrant:** spicily perfumed

FRUIT: woody 2-beaked witchhazel-like ovoid **capsule,** 3 to 13 mm (⅛ to ½ in) long, in broad pyramidal clusters
Color: glossy **brown**
Season: early **July through** late August   Human Value: not edible
Wildlife Value: **low;** upland gamebirds and small mammals occasionally; white-tailed deer eat twigs and foliage

HABITAT: formation - **swamp, forest;** region - **Southern;** gradient - lowland **wet, wet-mesic,** upland **mesic, mesic-dry;** low
    pinelands, boggy shrub thicket, stream banks, sandy swamps, oak woods
Shade Tolerance: **very tolerant**
Flood Tolerance: **intolerant**

SOIL: Texture: **moderately coarse to moderately fine;** sandy and gravelly loams, loams, clay loams, sandy peat
Drainage: **poor to well**
Moisture: **wet to average**
Reaction: **moderately acid to slightly acid,** pH 5.1 - 6.5

HARDINESS: zone 6a
Rate: **slow**
Longevity: **moderately short-lived**

SUSCEPTIBILITY: Physiological: **infrequent**
Disease: **infrequent** - very resistant
Insect: **infrequent** - trouble free
Wind-Ice: **infrequent**

URBAN TOLERANCE: Pollution:
Lighting: Drought Heat: **intermediate**   Mine Spoils:
Salt: Soil Compaction: **resistant**
Root Pattern: **stoloniferous; difficult to transplant**

SPECIES: Associate: trees - White/Post/Blackjack/Chestnut Oaks, Shagbark Hickory, Loblolly/Shortleaf/Virginia Pines;
    shrubs - Trailing-arbutus, Pinxterbloom Azalea, Common Deerberry, American Beautyberry, Flame Azalea
Similar: Large Fothergilla - taller, obovoid form, larger flower spikes
Cultivars: none available

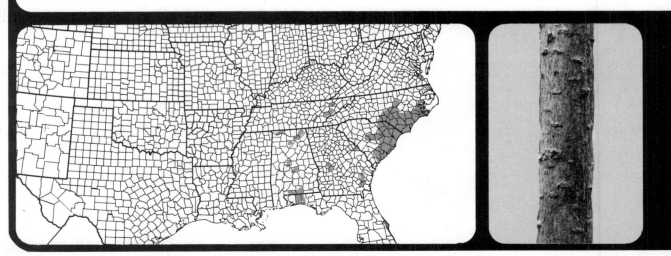

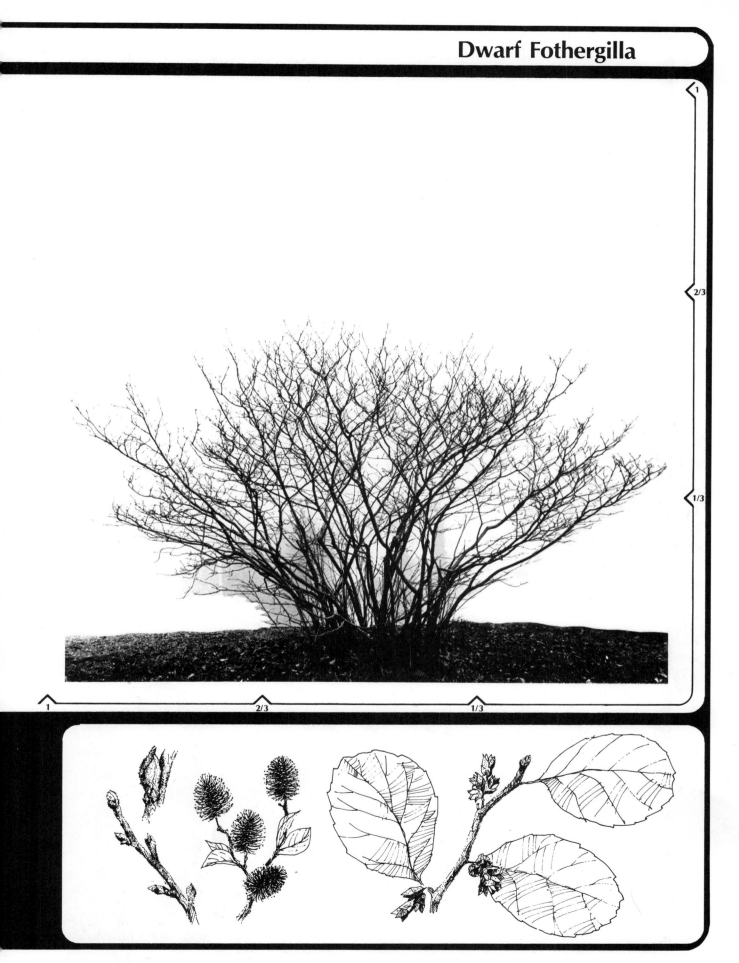

Fothergilla major

FORM: **obovoid** or ovoid
Size: **mid-height shrub** - from 2 to 4 m (6 to 12 ft)
Spread: **intermediate** - 2 to 4 m (6 to 12 ft), slightly taller than wide
Mass: **dense**

BRANCHING: **erect** multiple stems, **upright spreading,** often crooked **picturesque** branches; **medium** texture
Twig: slender, **zigzag** appearance, **velvety**, green brown
Bud: **naked, stalked, woolly, green brown**
Bark: **smooth, gray**

FOLIAGE: alternate, **simple,** suborbicular to **obovate,** coarse toothed at end, assymetric base, **aromatic; medium coarse**
Surface: **dull,** smooth, leathery appearance, dense woolly beneath
Color: spring - **light green;** summer - **dark green to blue green;** autumn - **yellow, orange to** scarlet **red,** often at same time
Season: **deciduous;** emergence - early **May,** drop - late **October**

FLOWER: spire-like terminal **spikes,** 5 to 10 cm (2 to 4 in) tall, masses of long protruding bottlebrush-like stamens
Color: **white**
Season: early through mid **May,** with unfolding leaves
Sex: monoecious   **Fragrant:** spicily perfumed, honey-like

FRUIT: hard beaked **capsules** splitting at top, 13 mm (½ in) long, with two seeds
Color: **brown**
Season: early **September through** late **October**   Human Value: not edible
Wildlife Value: **low;** small mammals, songbirds, upland gamebirds occasionally

HABITAT: formation - **forest;** region - **Southern;** gradient - **mesic-dry to dry;** rich deep mountain woods, rocky ravines and
banks of quick flowing streams
Shade Tolerance: **very tolerant**
Flood Tolerance: **intolerant**

SOIL: Texture: **moderately coarse to moderately fine;** stony, sandy, and gravelly loams, rich loams, silt loams
Drainage: **moderately well to well**
Moisture; **moist to average**
Reaction: **moderately acid to slightly acid,** pH 5.1 - 6.5; intolerant of alkaline soils

HARDINESS: **zone 6a,** 5b with protection
Rate: **slow**
Longevity: **moderately short-lived**

SUSCEPTIBILITY: physiological: **infrequent**
Disease: **infrequent** - very resistant
Insect: **infrequent** - tremendously pest free
Wind-Ice: **infrequent**

URBAN TOLERANCE: Pollution:
Lighting: Drought Heat: **intermediate**   Mine Spoils:
Salt: Soil Compaction: **intermediate**
Root Pattern: fibrous, **deep** coarse **laterals,** suckering habit; **difficult to transplant,** move B & B or container in early spring

SPECIES: Associate: trees - Tuliptree, Carolina Silverbell, Common Pawpaw, Cucumbertree Magnolia, Chestnut Oak,
Sweet Buckeye; shrubs - Common Spicebush, Fragrant Thimbleberry, Common Witchhazel, azalea species
Similar: Dwarf Fothergilla - smaller; Vernal Witchhazel, Buttercup Winterhazel (Asiatic) - yellow flowers
Cultivars: none available

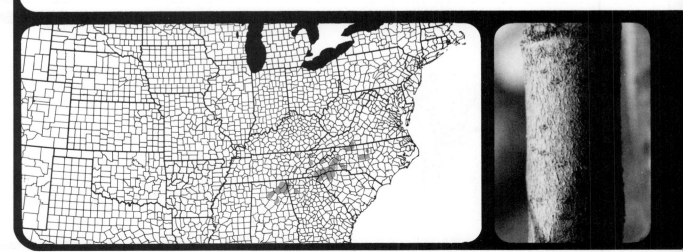

Large Fothergilla

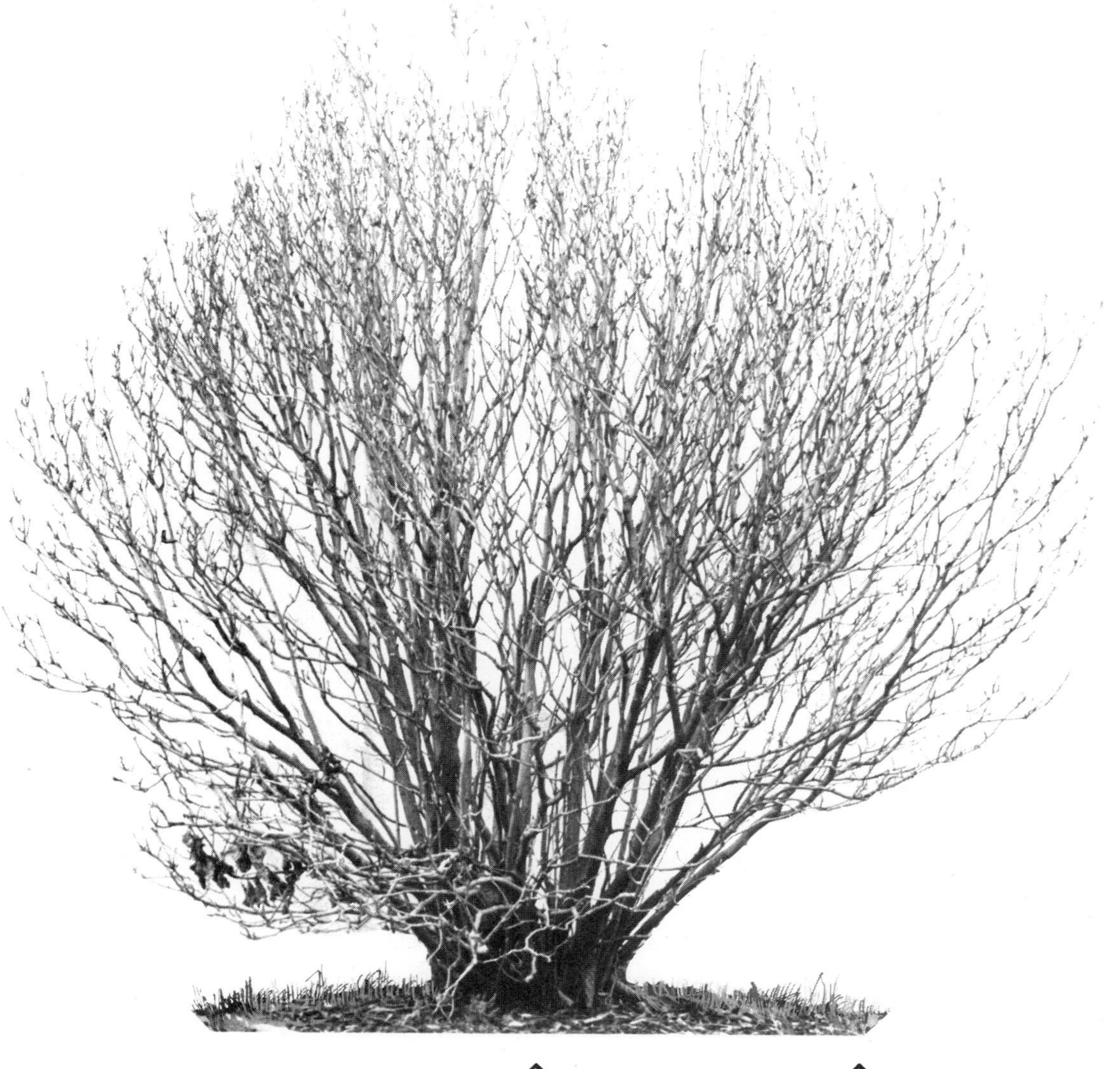

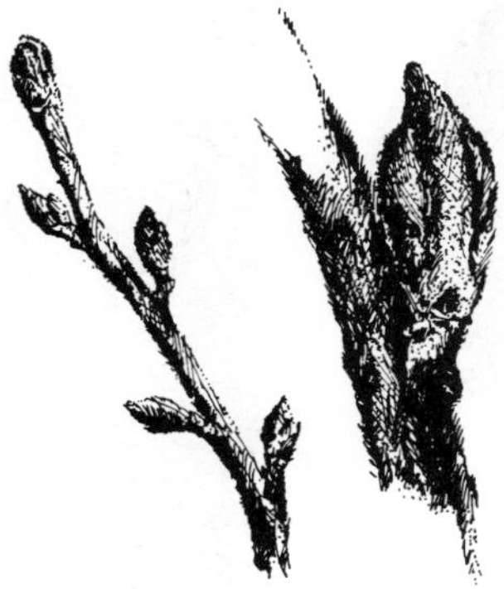

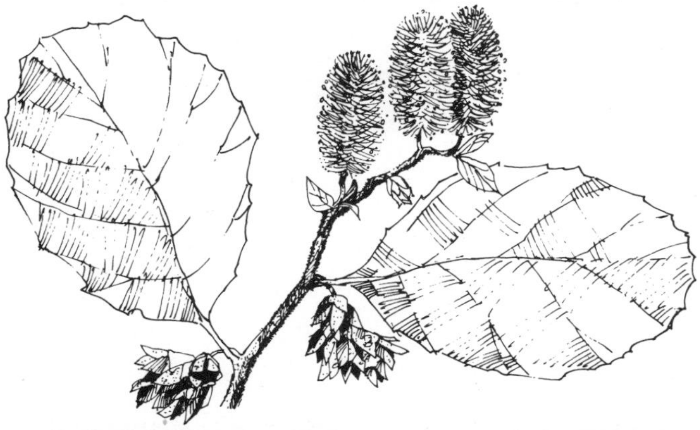

Gaultheria procumbens

FORM: low prostrate **mat,** herb-like
Size: **very small shrub** - less than 1 m (3 ft), commonly 5 to 15 cm (2 to 6 in) high
Spread: **very narrow** - to 1 m (3 ft), established colonies commonly broader
Mass: **dense**

BRANCHING: creeping **trailing** stems mostly underground, upright at ends, minimally branched, leafy at tops; **fine**
Twig: smooth or slightly hairy
Bud: inconspicuous
Bark: downy at first becoming **smooth** and glossy or slightly peeling, burnt-sienna brown

FOLIAGE: alternate, crowded towards tip, **simple, obovate to oblong obovate,** scattered bristle-tip teeth, **aromatic; fine**
Surface: **glossy,** smooth, thick leathery appearance, often variegated with white markings above
Color: spring - **red green to purple;** summer - **dark green,** red petiole; autumn, winter - **dark green** late, **then purplish**
Season: broadleaf **evergreen**

FLOWER: waxy nodding barrel-shaped **bell,** 8 mm (⅓ in) long, usually solitary in leaf axils
Color: **white to pinkish**
Season: mid **May through** mid **August,** occasional blooms through late September
Sex: monoecious

FRUIT: pulpy pea-size **berry-**like capsules, 6 to 9.5 mm (¼ to ⅜ in) across, dry and mealy
Color: bright scarlet **red**
Season: early **July** persisting over winter **through** late **April**   Human Value: **edible fruit, leaves,** wintergreen taste
Wildlife Value: **low;** limited use by large and small mammals, gamebirds, eaten by bears

HABITAT: formation - **bog, swamp, barrens, dune, forest, old field;** region - **Northern;** gradient - **wet, wet-mesic, mesic, mesic-dry to dry;** sandy oak woods, clearings, lake plain, steep rocky open slopes, deep mesic woods, hummocks in bogs
Shade Tolerance: **very tolerant,** demands partial shade
Flood Tolerance: **very tolerant**

SOIL: Texture: **coarse to medium;** in acid humus, light sandy or thin sterile soil, high organic matter
Drainage: **well to excessive**
Moisture: **average to droughty**
Reaction: demands **strongly acid to** moderately acid, pH 4.5 - 6.0, tolerates **slightly acid** pH to 6.5

HARDINESS: zone 3a
Rate: **slow**
Longevity: **long-lived**

SUSCEPTIBILITY: Physiological: **infrequent**
Disease: **infrequent** - very resistant, occasional leaf spots
Insect: **infrequent** - none serious
Wind-Ice: **infrequent**

URBAN TOLERANCE: Pollution:
Lighting: Drought Heat: **intermediate**   Mine Spoils:
Salt: Soil Compaction: **resistant**
Root Pattern: **stoloniferous** with extensive creeping horizontal rhizomes; **difficult to transplant,** start from potted plants

SPECIES: Associate: trees - Eastern White/Red/Jack Pines, Quaking/Bigtooth Aspens, Red Maple, Paper Birch; shrubs - Lowbush/Highbush Blueberries, Black Chokeberry, Trailing-arbutus, Dwarf Bushhoneysuckle, Beaked Filbert
Similar: Bunchberry Dogwood; Creeping Snowberry - white fruit; Bearberry; Partridgeberry; Bog Bilberry
Cultivars: none available

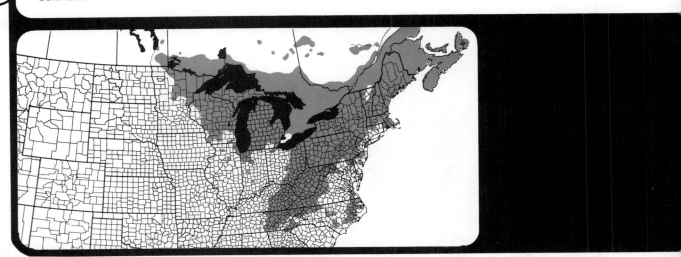

574

Hamamelis vernalis

FORM: obovoid to globular
Size: **mid-height shrub** - from 2 to 4 m (6 to 12 ft)
Spread: **intermediate** - 2 to 4 m (6 to 12 ft), typically ⅔ to ¾ the height
Mass: **dense**

BRANCHING: multiple stems with **ascending or upright spreading** branches; **coarse** texture
Twig: moderately slender, **zigzag, velvety, gray**
Bud: **naked,** dense **woolly,** flower buds **stalked, gray brown**
Bark: **smooth** or with roughened **scaly** patches, often with some stripe-like lenticels, **gray**

FOLIAGE: alternate, **simple, obovate to oblong obovate,** uneven base, double and wavy toothed, **aromatic; medium coarse**
Surface: sparingly **tomentose** and **dull**
Color: spring - **light green;** summer - **medium green;** autumn - golden **yellow;** winter - red brown to **tan brown**
Season: **persistant;** emergence - early **May,** drop - many dried leaves remaining through late **February**

FLOWER: **small** few-flowered **clusters,** petals ribbon-like and crumpled, rolling up in cold weather
Color: **yellow to orange, red** at base
Season: late **January** in mild winters **through** early **March,** before leaves
Sex: monoecious   **Fragrant:** pungently fragrant, attracts honeybees

FRUIT: ovoid fuzzy 2-beaked woody **capsule,** 19 mm (¾ in) long, splitting at maturity catapulting seeds
Color: **yellow green** in first season, weathering to **brown**
Season: **year round,** maturing in summer, persisting 1 to 2 years   Human Value: not edible
Wildlife Value: **low;** minor use by upland gamebirds, small mammals; white-tail deer eat twigs and foliage

HABITAT: formation - **forest, old field;** region - **Central, Southern;** gradient - lowland **wet, wet-mesic;** rocky stream beds,
      gravel bars of swift moving streams, moist woods, inundated stream banks
Shade Tolerance: **intermediate**
Flood Tolerance: **very tolerant**

SOIL: Texture: **coarse to medium;** streamside stones, gravels and sands, sandy and gravelly loams, silt loams, silty clays
Drainage: **very poor to moderately well**
Moisture: **wet to average**
Reaction: **moderately acid to neutral,** pH 5.5 - 7.0

HARDINESS: zone 5a
Rate: **fast to medium**
Longevity: **moderately short-lived**

SUSCEPTIBILITY: Physiological: **infrequent**
Disease: **infrequent** - none serious, occasional leaf spots
Insect: **infrequent** - none serious
Wind-Ice: **infrequent**

URBAN TOLERANCE: Pollution: **intermediate** - SO_2
Lighting: Drought Heat: **intermediate**   Mine Spoils:
Salt: Soil Compaction: **resistant**
Root Pattern: fibrous, **deep** coarse **laterals,** suckering habit; **difficult to transplant,** move B & B or container in early spring

SPECIES: Associate: trees - Willow Oak, American Sweetgum, River Birch, Northern Catalpa, American Planetree,
      Common Boxelder; shrubs - Common Alder, American Elder, Silky/Roughleaf Dogwoods, Arrowwood Viburnum
Similar: Common Witchhazel - blooms fall, Northern, larger; Buttercup Winterhazel - Asiatic; Large Fothergilla
Cultivars: 'Orange Glow' - orangish bronze flowers; 'Rubra' - petals reddish; 'Tomentella' - leaves woolly beneath

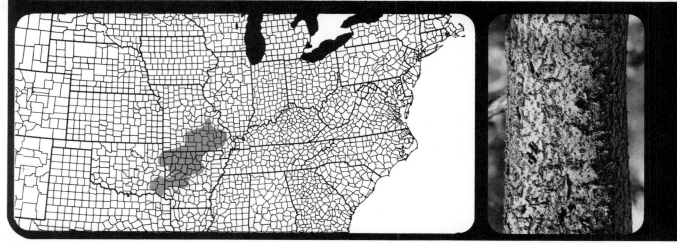

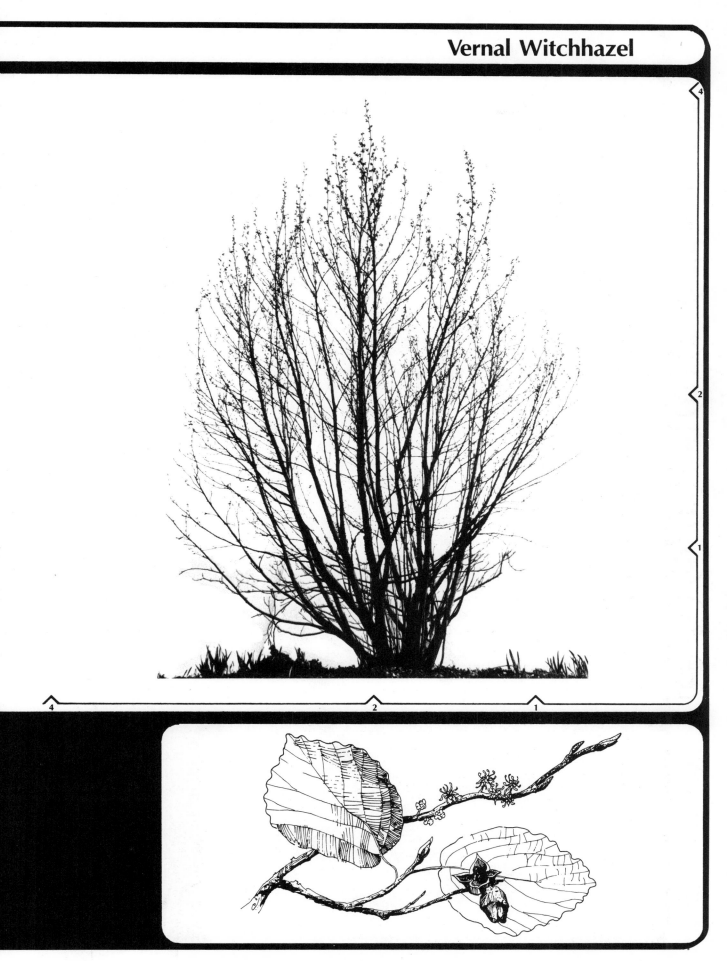

Hydrangea arborescens

FORM: globular or mound
Size: **small shrub** - from 1 to 2 m (3 to 6 ft)
Spread: **narrow** - 1 to 2 m (3 to 6 ft), occasionally to 3 m (9 ft), commonly broader than high
Mass: **dense**

BRANCHING: dense multi-stemmed, **erect to upright spreading** nonbranched or sparingly branched canes; **coarse** texture
Twig: smooth, moderately stout, somewhat herbaceous toward the tips, **red brown to gray brown**
Bud: globular or oblong, 3 mm (⅛ in) smooth, divergent, green brown to pale brown
Bark: **smooth** with older stems **exfoliating** into thin glossy papery strips, **red brown with orange brown** inner bark

FOLIAGE: opposite or in whorls of 3, **simple, elliptic,** broadly ovate, **cordate** or orbicular, coarse toothed; **coarse** texture
Surface: **dull,** upper surface deeply corrugated
Color: spring - light **gray green** becoming **yellow green;** summer - **medium green;** autumn - **yellow to tan**
Season: **deciduous;** emergence - mid **May,** drop - early **October**

FLOWER: **flat-topped** cluster to 15 cm (6 in) across, fertile flowers to 3 mm (⅛ in); larger sterile blooms along edge
Color: greenish changing to dull **white**
Season: late **June through** late **August,** after leaves are fully grown, dried summer blooms persist through winter
Sex: monoecious   **Fragrant:** mildly perfumed

FRUIT: small urn-shaped **capsules** in broad umbrella-like clusters
Color: tan **brown**
Season: early **October** persisting **through** late **January**   Human Value: **poisonous leaves**
Wildlife Value: **low;** limited use

HABITAT: formation - **forest;** region - **Central, Southern;** gradient - **wet-mesic, mesic, mesic-dry;** alluvial forests, sheltered
          mesic coves, deep rich upland forests, bases of bluffs, banks of quick flowing streams
Shade Tolerance: **very tolerant**
Flood Tolerance: **intolerant**

SOIL: Texture: **moderately coarse** sandy loams, loamy sands **to moderately fine** silt loams; best development on loams
Drainage: **moderately poor to well**
Moisture: **moist to average**
Reaction: **slightly acid to** circumneutral, tolerates **alkaline,** pH 6.1 - 8.5

HARDINESS: zone 4a
Rate: **fast**
Longevity: **very short-lived**

SUSCEPTIBILITY: Physiological: **frequent** - sunscald, chlorosis in alkline soils, winter dieback
Disease: **occasional** - bud blight, bacterial wilt, rust, powdery mildew, leaf spots
Insect: **occasional** - aphids, rose chafer, oyster shell scale, two-spotted mite, nematodes, leaf tier, Fur-lined plant bug
Wind-Ice: **frequent** - many weak brittle canes, easily broken

URBAN TOLERANCE: Pollution: **sensitive** - MV, 2-4D
Lighting: Drought Heat: **sensitive**   Mine Spoils: **sensitive**
Salt: **resistant**   Soil Compaction: **intermediate**
Root Pattern: fibrous, **shallow lateral,** suckers freely, creeping over large areas; **transplants well,** easy culture

SPECIES: Associate: trees - American Beech, Sugar/Black Maples, linden species, White/Northern Red Oaks; shrubs -
          Mapleleaf Virburnum, Pasture Gooseberry, Common Spicebush, Brook Euonymus, American Elder
Similar: Panicle Hydrangea - Asiatic
Cultivars: 'Grandiflora' - large sterile florets; 'Annabelle' - very large florets; radiata - white woolly leaves

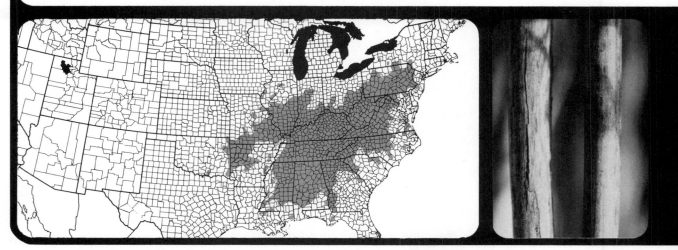

Smooth Hydrangea

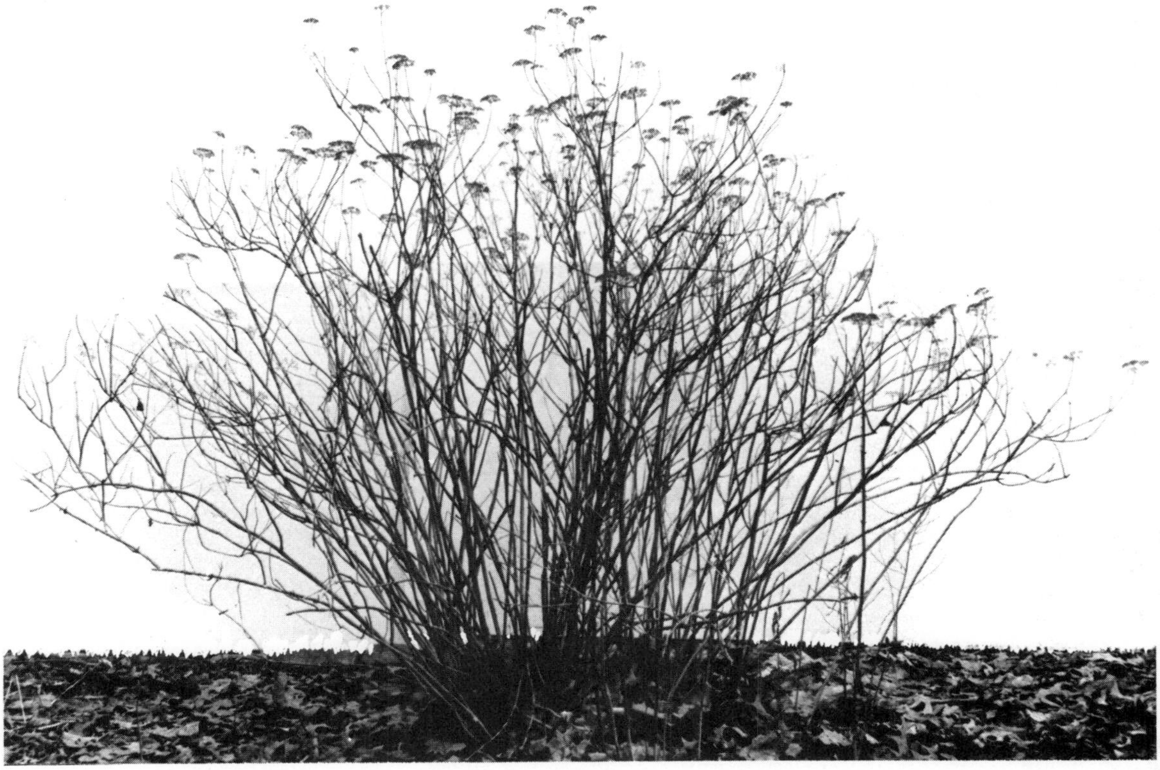

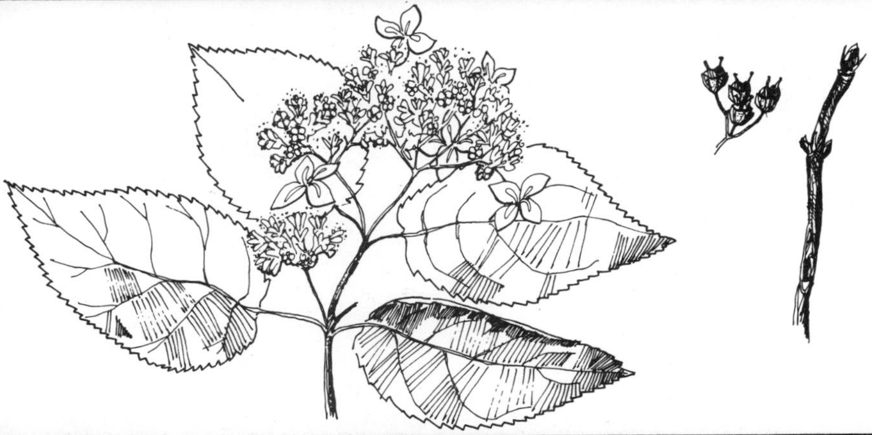

Hydrangea quercifolia

FORM: **globular or mound**
Size: **small shrub** - from 1 to 2 m (3 to 6 ft)
Spread: **narrow** - 1 to 2 m (3 to 6 ft), typically wider than high, spreading into broad colonies
Mass: **open**

BRANCHING: multiple stems, **upright** sparingly branched irregular **picturesque** canes, old canes arching; very **coarse**
Twig: dense **velvety, brown**
Bud: oblong, widely divergent, **brown**
Bark: older stems with heavy shaggy **exfoliation, red brown with orange brown** inner bark

FOLIAGE: opposite, **simple, pinnately** 3 to 7-**lobed**, resembles shape of Red Oak; **coarse** texture
Surface: **dull,** downy felted beneath
Color: spring - **gray green;** summer - **dark green;** autumn - variable, **orange, red to purple or brown**
Season: **deciduous;** emergence - late **May,** drop - mid **November**

FLOWER: erect broad cone-shaped **spikes,** 10 to 30 cm (4 to 12 in) tall, tiny fertile flowers fringed by larger sterile ones
Color: greenish then **white** turning purplish
Season: late **June through** late **July,** after leaves are fully grown, often persisting in dried state into late winter
Sex: monoecious **Fragrant:** delicately perfumed

FRUIT: small urn-shaped **capsules;** 3 mm (⅛ in) diameter, in broad blunt-tipped conical clusters
Color: tan **brown**
Season: early **October** persisting in winter **through** late **March** Human Value: **poisonous leaves**
Wildlife Value: **low;** limited use by songbirds, gamebirds, small mammals

HABITAT: formation - **forest;** region - **Southern;** gradient - lowland **wet-mesic,** upland **mesic, mesic-dry;** river banks, bluffs,
oak woods, shady ravines, damp woods
Shade Tolerance: **very tolerant**
Flood Tolerance: **intolerant**

SOIL: Texture: **moderately coarse** sandy loams, loamy sands **to moderately fine** silt loams; sensitive to heavy clays
Drainage: **moderately well to well**
Moisture: **moist to average**
Reaction: **slightly acid to** circumneutral, tolerates **alklaline,** pH 6.1 - 8.5

HARDINESS: **zone 6a,** top tender
Rate: **medium**
Longevity: **very short-lived**

SUSCEPTIBILITY: Physiological: **frequent** - sunscald, chlorosis caused by alkaline soils, twig dieback in subzero temps.
Disease: **occasional** - powdery mildew, leaf blight are rarely serious, root fungus serious problem on old plants
Insect: **infrequent** - very trouble-free, aphids on new growth occasionally
Wind-Ice: **frequent** - many weak brittle stems, easily broken

URBAN TOLERANCE: Pollution: **sensitive** - MV, 2-4D
Lighting: Drought Heat: **sensitive** Mine Spoils:
Salt: **resistant** Soil Compacton: **intermediate**
Root Pattern: fibrous, **shallow lateral** and **stoloniferous** forming colonies; **transplants well,** easy culture

SPECIES: Associate: trees - Tuliptree, Cucumbertree Magnolia, American Beech, Sugar Maple; shrubs - Carolina
Rhododendron, Leatherwood, Brook Euonymus, Bottlebrush Buckeye, Virginia Stewartia, Common Spicebush
Similar: Bear Oak - solitary/few trunks, taller; leaves similar
Cultivars: 'Harmony' - large flowers, mostly sterile; 'Roanoke' - flowers loose and open; 'Snowflake' - double-flowered

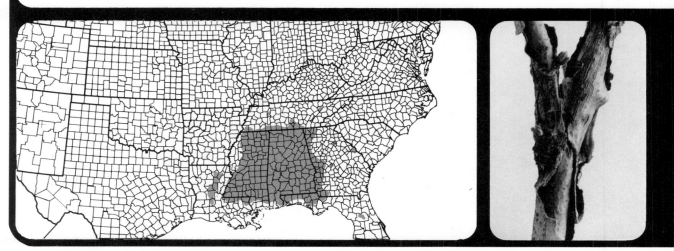

Oakleaf Hydrangea

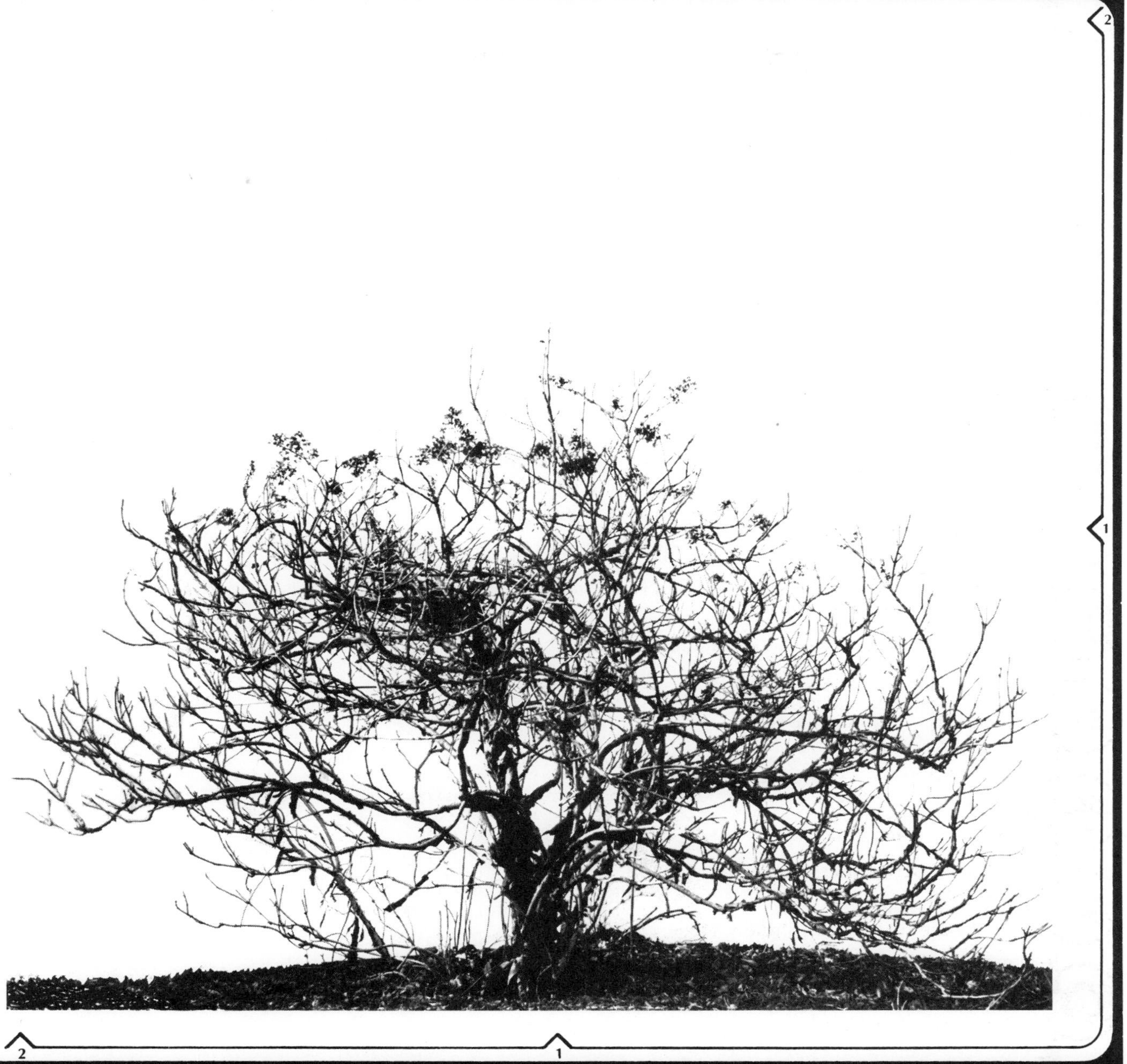

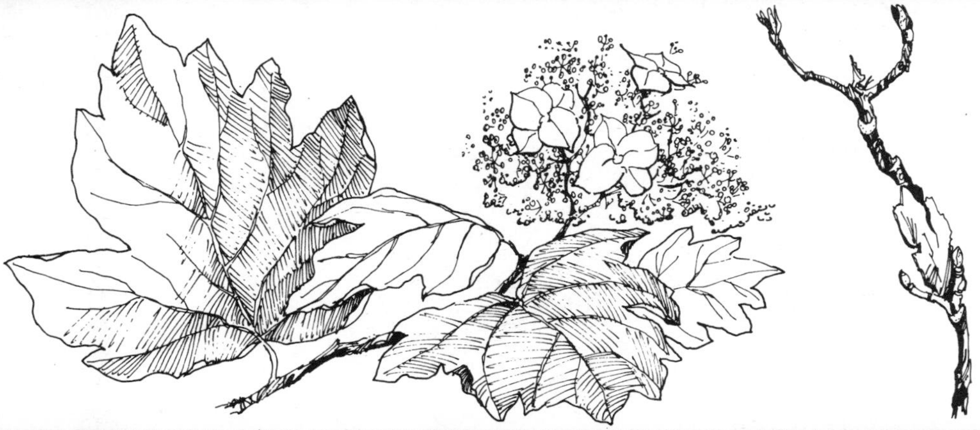

Hypericum densiflorum

FORM: ovoid to obovoid
Size: **small shrub** - from 1 to 2 m (3 to 6 ft)
Spread: **narrow** - 1 to 2 m (3 to 6 ft), typically taller than wide
Mass: **dense**

BRANCHING: **erect** multiple-stems, **upright spreading** branches, densely twiggy; very **fine** texture
Twig: slender, **angular**, flattened with 2 edges, a narrow **ridge** below leaf scars, **yellow brown** becoming **red brown**
Bud: very small, with **2 scales, green brown**
Bark: heavy loose **exfoliating** papery sheets revealing smooth patches, **red brown to** deep **purple**

FOLIAGE: opposite, sometimes crowded, **simple, linear to oblanceolate,** margin rolled down, entire; very **fine** texture
Surface: **dull,** smooth
Color: spring - **medium green;** summer - deep **dark green;** autumn - **yellow green**
Season: **deciduous;** emergence - late **May,** drop - mid **November**

FLOWER: densely crowded in broad **flat-topped** terminal clusters, individual blooms small, 13 mm (½ in) diameter
Color: golden **yellow**
Season: mid **July through** early **September,** after leaves
Sex: monoecious

FRUIT: short slender 3-celled dry ovoid **capsules** with persistant styles, 6 mm (¼ in) long
Color: **red brown to** maroon **purple**
Season: early **October** persisting through winter **to** late **April**   Human Value: not edible
Wildlife Value: **intermediate;** waterbirds, songbirds, upland gamebirds, small mammals major users

HABITAT: formation - **swamp, spring, meadow, forest;** region: - **Central, Southern;** gradient - lowland **wet, wet-mesic;** boggy
    places, seepage slopes, borders of ponds and lakes, wet meadows, stream banks, roadside ditches, moist pinelands
Shade Tolerance: **intolerant**
Flood Tolerance: **very tolerant**

SOIL: Texture: **coarse** sands, gravels, sandy loams **to fine** silts, stiff clays, peats, mucks
Drainage: **very poor to excessive**
Moisture: **wet to droughty**
Reaction: **moderately acid to neutral,** pH 5.5 - 7.0

HARDINESS: zone 6a
Rate: **slow to medium**
Longevity: **very short-lived**

SUSCEPTIBILITY: Physiological: **infrequent**
Disease: **infrequent** - none serious, occasional leaf spots, southern root-knot nematode can be troublesome in south
Insect: **infrequent** - none serious
Wind-Ice: **infrequent**

URBAN TOLERANCE: Pollution:
Lighting: Drought Heat: **intermediate**   Mine Spoils:
Salt: **resistant**   Soil Compaction: **resistant**
Root Pattern: fibrous, **shallow lateral; transplants well**

SPECIES: Associate: trees - American Holly, River Birch, Pin/Swamp White Oaks; shrubs - Common Buttonbush,
    Indigobush Amorpha, Inkberry, Hardhack Spirea, Atlantic St. Peterswort, Swamp Rose, Southern Waxmyrtle
Similar: Shrubby St.Johnswort - more open, dry habitat; Bush Cinquefoil and hybrids
Cultivars: none available

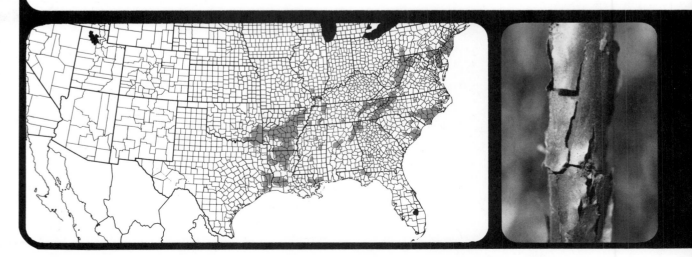

Hypericum frondosum

FORM: **globular**
Size: **very small shrub** - to 1 m (3 ft)
Spread: **very narrow** - to 1 m (3 ft)
Mass: very **dense**

BRANCHING: solitary or few-stemmed, stout **erect or upright spreading** branches; **fine** texture
Twig: slender, **angular** flattened with 2 edges at least near tip, **red brown**
Bud: tiny, with **2 scales, green brown**
Bark: shaggy **exfoliating** papery sheets, **red brown to deep purple**

FOLIAGE: opposite, sometimes crowded, **simple, linear to oblanceolate,** entire irregular margin, apex bristle-tipped; **fine**
Surface: **dull,** glandular dots visible on upper surface, paler or bloomy beneath
Color: spring - bright **medium green;** summer - **blue green;** autumn - **yellow green**
Season: **deciduous;** emergence - late **May,** drop - early **November**

FLOWER: **large solitary** or few clustered together, 2.5 to 4.5 cm (1 to 1¾ in) diameter, terminal, numerous stamens
Color: bright **yellow**
Season: early through late **July,** after leaves
Sex: monoecious

FRUIT: dry 3-celled ovoid **capsules,** 13 mm (½ in) long
Color: **red brown to maroon purple**
Season: early **September** persisting **through** late **April**   Human Value: not edible
Wildlife Value: **intermediate;** primary use by songbirds, occasionally by upland gamebirds, small mammals

HABITAT: formation - **glade, dry cliff;** region - **Southern;** gradient - upland **mesic-dry, dry;** limestone cliffs, rocky hills, glades,
and barrens
Shade Tolerance: **very intolerant**
Flood Tolerance: **very intolerant**

SOIL: Texture: **coarse to moderately coarse;** gravels and sands, shallow soils over limestone or sandstone, loamy sands
Drainage: **well to excessive**
Moisture: **average to droughty**
Reaction: **circumneutral,** tolerates **alkaline;** pH 6.5 - 8.5

HARDINESS: zone 6a
Rate: **slow to medium**
Longevity: **very short-lived**

SUSCEPTIBILITY: Physiological: **infrequent**
Disease: **infrequent** - very resistant, leaf spots, southern root-knot nematode can cause problems
Insect: **infrequent** - none serious
Wind-Ice: **infrequent**

URBAN TOLERANCE: Pollution:
Lighting: Drought Heat: **resistant**   Mine Spoils:
Salt: **resistant**   Soil Compaction: **intermediate**
Root Pattern: fibrous, **shallow lateral; transplants well**

SPECIES: Associate trees - Eastern Red Cedar, Blackjack/Black/Dwarf Chinkapin Oaks, Sassafras, Smooth
Sumac; Shrubs - Fragrant Sumac, Jerseytea Ceanothus, Carolina Rose

Similar: Shrubby St.Johnswort - smaller axillary flowers; Bush Cinquefoil and hybrids
Cultivars: 'Sunburst' - lower growing, 6 to 12 cm (2 to 4 ft)

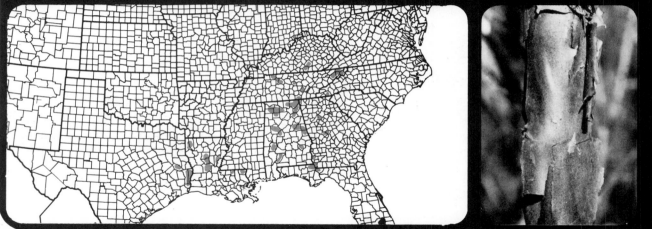

Golden St.Johnswort

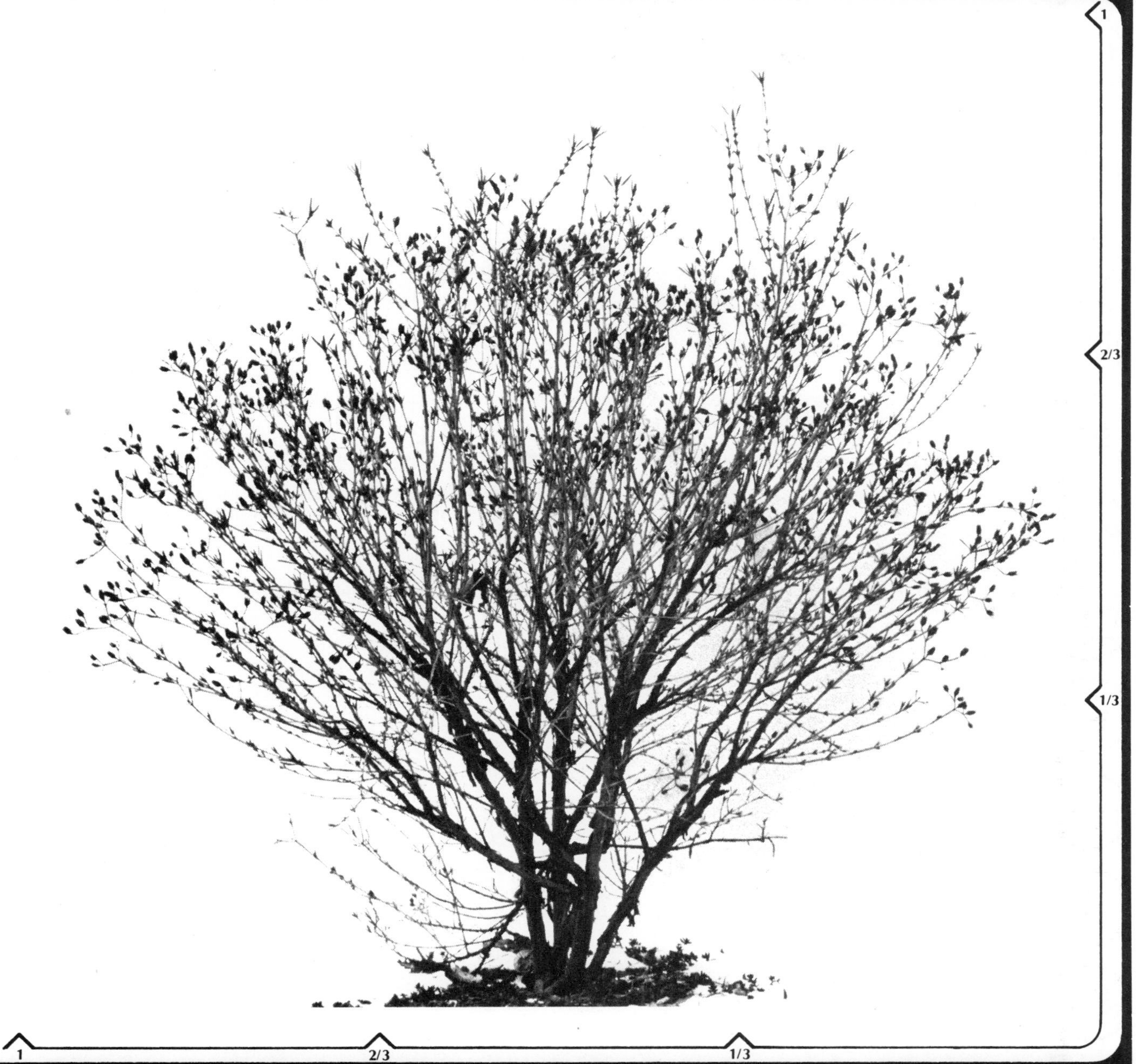

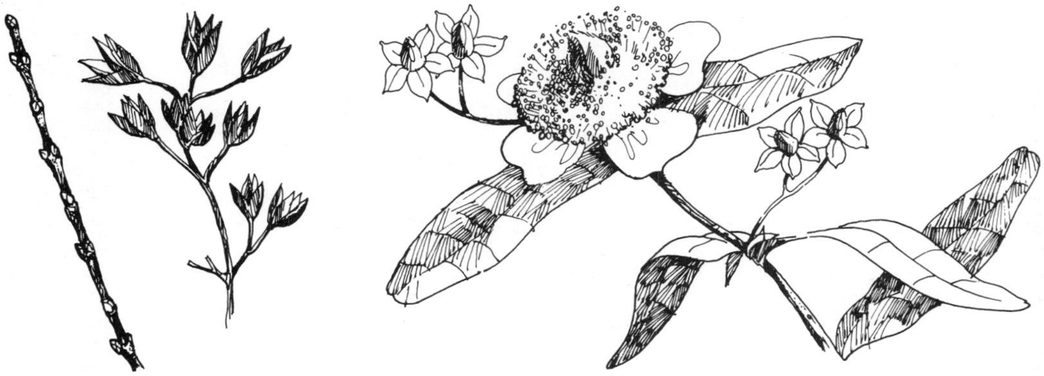

Hypericum kalmianum

FORM: mound
Size: **very small shrub** - to 1 m (3 ft)
Spread: **very narrow** - 1 m (3 ft), typically broader than high but varies
Mass: **dense**

BRANCHING: single or few stems; **erect, upright spreading or** strongly **ascending** symmetrical branches; very **fine** texture
Twig: slender, **angular** below leaf scars with 4-sided branchlets and 2-edged twigs, **red brown**
Bud: very small, **2 scales**, green brown
Bark: flaky with older bark **exfoliating** into thin loose sheets, **red brown to** dark **purple**

FOLIAGE: opposite, **simple, linear** to oblong linear **or oblanceolate,** entire, small leaf tufts in axils of larger; **fine** texture
Surface: **dull,** smooth, white bloomy beneath
Color: spring - bright **medium green;** summer - **blue green;** autumn - **yellow green** to yellowish
Season: **deciduous;** emergence - late **May,** drop - early **November**

FLOWER: large solitary to 3-flowered terminal clusters, 13 to 25 mm (½ to 1 in) diameter, numerous showy stamens
Color: bright golden **yellow,** waxy
Season: early **July through** late **August,** after leaves
Sex: monoecious   **Fragrant:**   somewhat fragrant

FRUIT: small dry 5-parted beaked ovoid **capsules,** 8 to 11 mm (⁵⁄₁₆ to ⁷⁄₁₆ in) long
Color: **red brown to** bronze **purple**
Season: early **September** persisting **through** late **April**   Human Value: not edible
Wildlife Value: **intermediate;** upland gamebirds, songbirds, waterbirds, small mammals; hoofed browsers graze foliage

HABITAT: formation - **bog, dune, cliff;** region: - **Northern;** gradient - **wet, wet-mesic, dry;** cliffs above rivers and lakes, moist
        calcareous sand bordering interdunal ponds, sandy boggy ground, rocky lakeshore, mud
Shade Tolerance: **very intolerant**
Flood Tolerance: **very tolerant**

SOIL: Texture: **coarse** stony, gravelly, and sandy loams, loamy sands **to fine** sands, silts, clays
Drainage: **very poor to excessive**
Moisture: **wet to droughty**
Reaction: **moderately acid to** circumneutral, pH 5.1 - 7.5; tolerates **alkaline** pH to 8.5

HARDINESS: zone 4a
Rate: **slow to medium**
Longevity: **very short-lived**

SUSCEPTIBILITY: Physiological: **infrequent**
Disease: **infrequent** - none serious, leaf spots
Insect: **infrequent** - none serious
Wind-Ice: **infrequent**

URBAN TOLERANCE: Pollution:
Lighting: Drought Heat: **resistant**   Mine Spoils:
Salt: **resistant**   Soil Compaction: **resistant**
Root Pattern: fibrous, **shallow laterals; transplants well**

SPECIES: Associate: trees - Common Boxelder, Silver Maple, American Larch, willow species; shrubs - Narrowleaf
        Meadowsweet/Hardhack Spireas, American Black Currant, Red-osier Dogwood, Bush Cinquefoil, Black Chokeberry
Similar: Shrubby/Golden St.Johnsworts; Dense Hypericum; Bush Cinquefoil and hybrids
Cultivars: none available

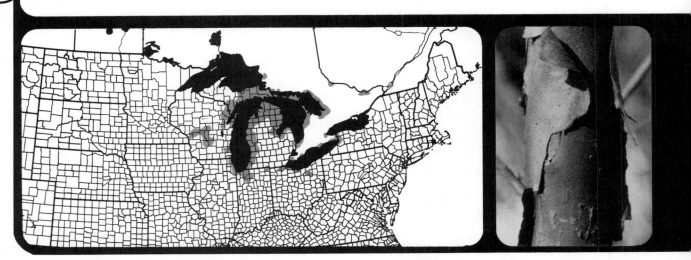

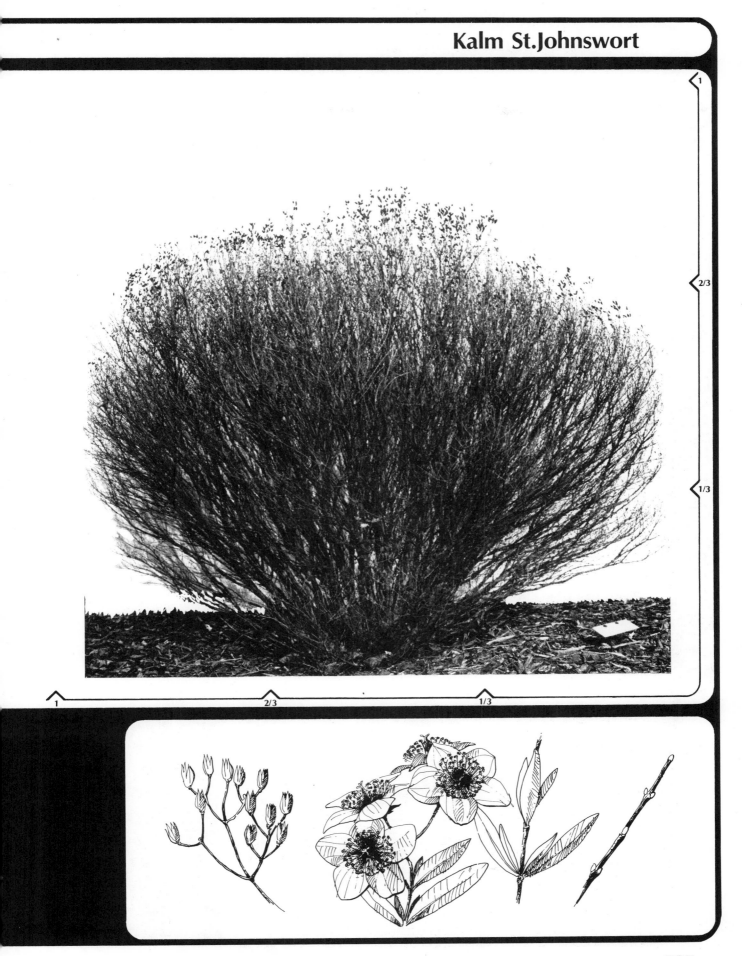

Hypericum prolificum

FORM: mound
Size: **very small shrub** - to 1 m (3 ft)
Spread: **narrow** - from 1 to 2 m (3 to 6 ft), often spreading with age
Mass: **dense**

BRANCHING: solitary or few stems, **upright spreading or ascending,** twiggy, old stems **picturesque** sweeping ground; **fine**
Twig: slender, **angular** and flattened with two wing-like ridges, **red brown**
Bud: very small inconspicuous, **2 scales, green or green brown**
Bark: heavy papery **exfoliation** revealing smooth glossy inner bark, **red brown to dark purple**

FOLIAGE: opposite, sometimes crowded, **simple, oblong linear to oblanceolate,** entire, edges curled down; **fine texture**
Surface: **dull** to glossy, smooth
Color: spring - bright **medium green;** summer - **dark green to blue green;** autumn - **yellow green**
Season: **deciduous;** emergence - late **May,** drop - late **October**

FLOWER: large solitary or few-flowered clusters, 19 mm (¾ in) diameter, conspicuous stamens, 5 petals
Color: bright golden **yellow**
Season: late **June through** late **August,** after leaves
Sex: monoecious

FRUIT: dry 3-celled ovoid **capsules,** 8 mm (⅓ in) long, seeds create rattle-like noise when disturbed or shaken by wind
Color: **red brown to** maroon **purple**
Season: early **October** persisting **through** winter until late **April**   Human Value: not edible
Wildlife Value: **intermediate;** waterbirds, shorebirds, songbirds, upland gamebirds, small mammals; browsers eat foliage

HABITAT: formation - **swamp, cliff, forest, old field;** region - **Central;** gradient - lowland **wet, wet-mesic, mesic-dry, dry;** rocky
        or sandy open woods, abandoned fields, swampy places, banks of streams, gravel bars, calcareous woods, cliffs
Shade Tolerance: **very intolerant**
Flood Tolerance: **very tolerant**

SOIL: Texture: **coarse to moderately fine;** shallow soils over limestone/sandstone, gravels, sands, gravelly/sandy loams
Drainage: **very poor to excessive**
Moisture: **wet to droughty**
Reaction: **slightly acid to** circumneutral, tolerates **alkaline,** pH 6.1 - 8.5

HARDINESS: zone 4a
Rate: **slow to medium**
Longevity: **very short-lived**

SUSCEPTIBILITY: Physiological: **infrequent**
Disease: **infrequent** - none serious, occasional leaf spots
Insect: **infrequent** - none serious
Wind-Ice: **occasional** - old stems cracking at base and sprawling on ground

URBAN TOLERANCE: Pollution:
Lighting: Drought Heat: **resistant**   Mine Spoils: **resistant**
Salt: **resistant**   Soil Compaction: **resistant**
Root Pattern: fibrous, **shallow lateral; transplants well**

SPECIES: Associate: trees - Sugarberry, American Planetree, American Sweetgum, Black Tupelo, Gum Bumelia; shrubs -
        Common Deerberry, He-huckleberry, Roseshell Azalea, American Beautyberry
Similar: Golden St.Johnswort - upright, blue green leaves; Kalm St.Johnswort - Northern, larger flowers
Cultivars: none available

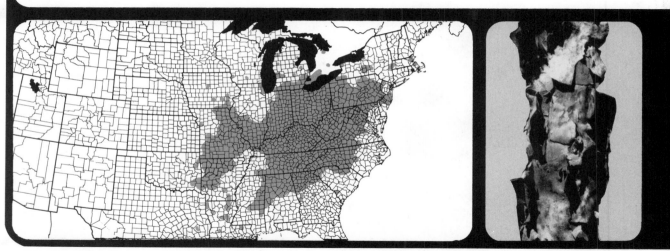

589

Ilex decidua

FORM: obovoid
Size: **large shrub** - from 4 to 6 m (12 to 20 ft), occasionally to 9 m (3 ft)
Spread: **wide** - 4 to 6 m (12 to 20 ft), commonly ⅔ to ¾ the height
Mass: **dense**

BRANCHING: few short trunks; **ascending** becoming strongly **horizontal,** fruited branchlets **pendulous; medium**
Twig: slender, smooth, **zigzag, gray or gray brown; armed** with short stiff thorn-like right angle spur branchlets
Bud: short, **stalked** but inconspicuous, **gray brown**
Bark: generally **smooth** but roughened with small warty lenticels, old trunks **blocky,** light greenish **gray or gray brown**

FOLIAGE: alternate, usually clustered on short spur branchlets, **simple, obovate** to spatulate, toothed; **medium fine** texture
Surface: **glossy,** smooth, paler beneath
Color: spring - **light green;** summer - deep **dark green;** autumn - **dark green,** late; winter - **tan brown**
Season: **deciduous or persistant;** emergence - mid **May,** drop - many dried leaves remaining through late **January**

FLOWER: **small** open **clusters,** inconspicuous
Color: **green to** creamy **white**
Season: late **May through** mid **June,** after leaves
Sex: **dioecious**

FRUIT: glossy globular **berry,** 6 to 9.5 m (¼ to ⅜ in) diameter, single or in clusters of 2 to 5 on short stout stems
Color: **orange to** scarlet **red**
Season: after first frost in **October** persisting in winter **through** late **March**   Human Value: **poisonous fruit**
Wildlife Value: **high;** winter songbirds, upland gamebirds, large and small mammals; hoofed browsers graze occasionally

HABITAT: formation - **swamp, forest, old field;** region - **Central, Southern;** gradient - **wet, wet-mesic, mesic-dry, dry;** floodplain
forests, swamps, pond borders, wet flats, less frequently on dry wooded upland slopes and bluffs, fence rows
Shade Tolerance: **intermediate**
Flood Tolerance: **very tolerant**

SOIL: Texture: **coarse** infertile sands, gravels, loamy sands **to fine** silts, heavy clays, peats, mucks
Drainage: **very poor to excessive**
Moisture: **wet to dry**
Reaction: **strongly acid to** moderately acid, pH 4.0 - 6.0, tolerates **alkaline** to pH 8.5

HARDINESS: zone 5b
Rate: **slow to medium**
Longevity: **long-lived**

SUSCEPTIBILITY: Physiological: **occasional** - spire spot, leaf scorch
Disease: **infrequent** - none serious, occasional tar spot, leaf spots, powdery mildew
Insect: **infrequent** - none serious, leaf minor can be pesky, mulberry whitefly, berry midge
Wind-Ice: **infrequent** - split bark in severe winters, torn or ragged leaves on exposed sites

URBAN TOLERANCE: Pollution:
Lighting: **intermediate**   Drought Heat: **resistant**   Mine Spoils: **resistant**
Salt: **resistant**   Soil Compaction: **resistant**
Root Pattern: fibrous, **shallow lateral; transplants well,** move B & B

SPECIES: Associate: trees - Willow/Water/Nuttal/Laurel Oaks, American Sweetgum, American Planetree, American Elm;
shrubs - Common Buttonbush, Smooth Sumac, dewberry and blackberry species; vines - greenbrier species
Similar: Yaupon, Dahoon - leaves smaller, evergreen, zone 6b
Cultivars: 'Warren's Red' - heavier fruiter; 'Byers Golden' - yellow fruit; 'Oklahoma'; 'Sundance'; 'Fraser's Improved'

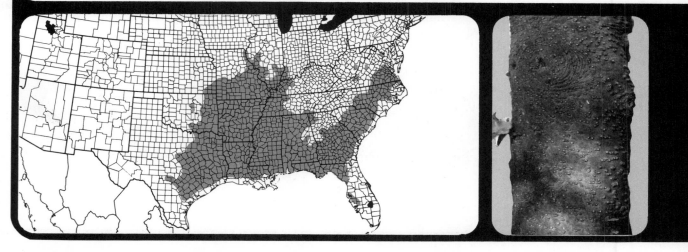

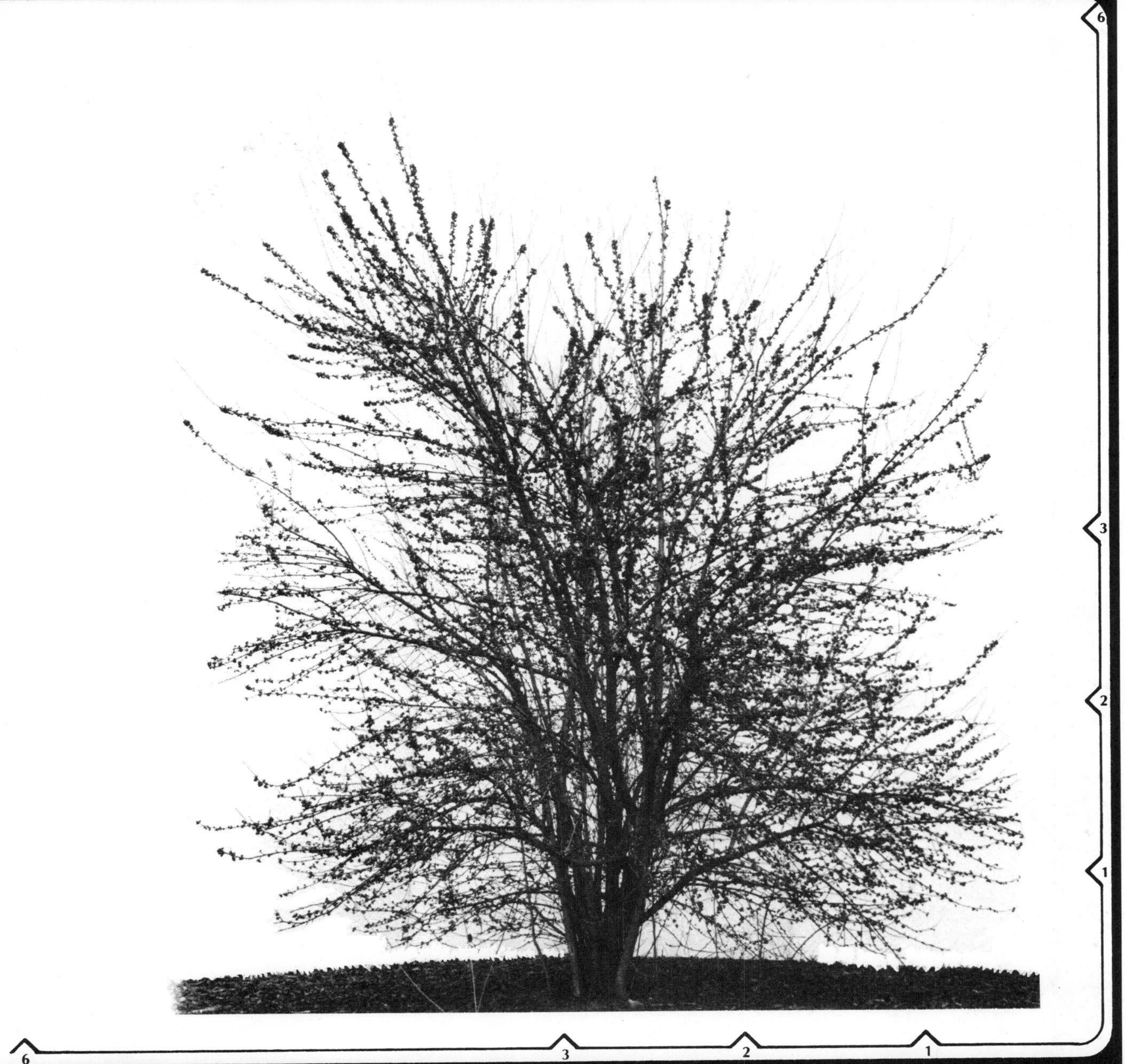
6
3
2
1
6
3
2
1

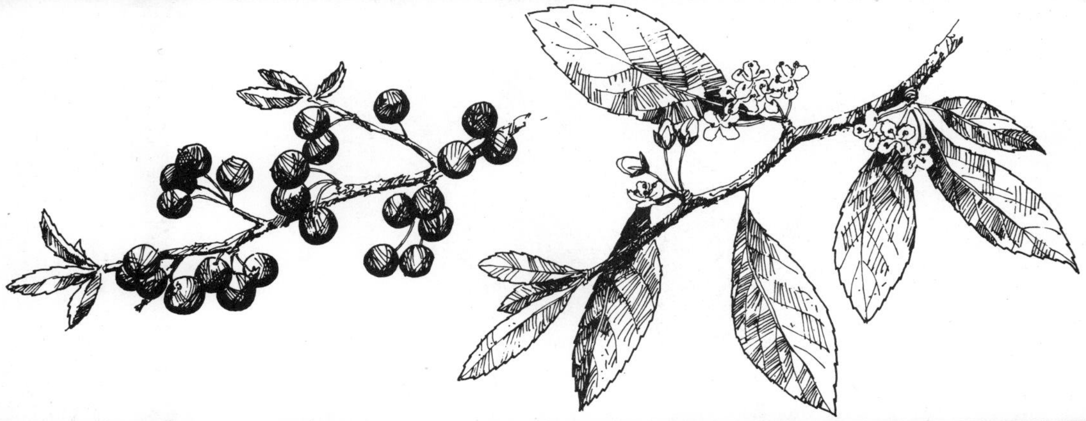

Ilex glabra

FORM: globular or mound
Size: **mid-height shrub** - from 2 to 4 m (6 to 12 ft), but uncommon above 3 m (9 ft)
Spread: **intermediate** - 2 to 4 m (6 to 12 ft)
Mass: somewhat **open** at maturity, dense in youth

BRANCHING: few stems, much-branched, **upright** with numerous **ascending pictureque** branches; **medium** texture
Twig: smooth, slender, **zigzag** appearance, **green** or gray brown
Bud: very tiny, 1.5 mm (¹⁄₁₆ in), gray brown
Bark: **smooth** with conspicuous warty lenticels, old stems with squarish **blocky** pattern, **gray brown**

FOLIAGE: alternate, **simple, oblanceolate,** blunt notched tip, sparingly toothed or entire; **fine** texture
Surface: **dull to glossy,** thick leathery, black dotted beneath
Color: spring - bright **medium green;** summer and autumn - varies, **dark green to** light **yellow green;** winter - **yellow green**
Season: broadleaf **evergreen**

FLOWER: small clusters, inconspicuous, attracts bees
Color: **greenish to white**
Season: early **May through** late **June**
Sex: **dioecious**

FRUIT: mostly solitary globular **berries,** 6 mm (¼ in) diameter, often hidden by foliage
Color: jet **black**
Season: late **September** persisting **through** late **March**   Human Value: **poisonous fruit**
Wildlife Value: **high;** waterfowl and songbirds extensive users, also upland gamebirds, large and small mammals

HABITAT: formation - **prairie, savanna, bog, fen, dune, swamp;** region - **Southern;** gradient - lowland **wet, wet-mesic;** savanna, boggy areas, branch bays, seepage areas in woodlands, wet acid prairies, bordering interdunal ponds
Shade Tolerance: **tolerant**
Flood Tolerance: **very tolerant**

SOIL: Texture: **coarse** infertile sands and gravels **to fine** silty clay loams, heavy clays, organic soils, peats, mucks
Drainage: **very poor to moderately well**
Moisture: **wet to moist**
Reaction: **strongly acid to moderately acid,** pH 4.5 - 6.0

HARDINESS: zone 4a
Rate: **slow**
Longevity: **long-lived**

SUSCEPTIBILITY: Physiological: **occasional** - browning and leaf scorch common in late winter
Disease: **infrequent** - free of problems
Insect: **infrequent** - scales may cause minor damage
Wind-Ice: **occasional** - winter drying, wilt and browning in exposed situations; protect from winter wind, sun

URBAN TOLERANCE: Pollution:
Lighting: **intermediate**   Drought Heat: **sensitive**   Mine Spoils:
Salt: **resistant**   Soil Compacton: **resistant**
Root Pattern: fibrous, **shallow lateral; transplants well**

SPECIES: Associate: trees - Pond Pine, Red Maple, Common Baldcypress; shrubs - Dusty Zenobia, Fetterbush Lyonia, Sweetbay Magnolia, Summersweet Clethra, Common Buttonbush, Common Winterberry
Similar: Large Gallberry (I. coriacea) - also black fruited; Rosemary Barberry - armed twigs
Cultivars: 'Compacta' - dwarf; 'Viridis' - winter leaves green; 'Nigra' - winter leaves purple; 'Ivory Queen' - white fruit

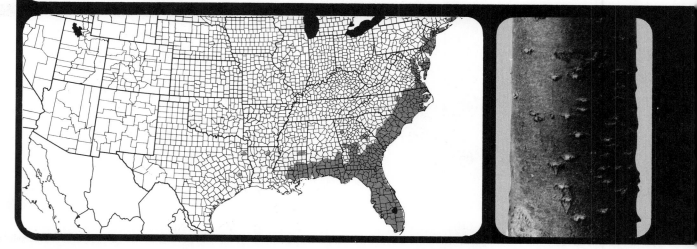

Ilex verticillata

FORM: oval to **obovoid**
Size: **mid-height shrub** - from 2 to 4 m (6 to 12 ft)
Spread: **intermediate** - 2 to 4 m (6 to 12 ft), typically ½ to ¾ the height
Mass: **dense**

BRANCHING: multiple stems, **upright spreading** picturesque branches, densely twiggy; **medium** texture
Twig: slender, smooth, **zigzag** appearance, dark **gray or gray brown**
Bud: extremely minute, 1.5 mm (¹⁄₁₆ in), gray brown
Bark: **smooth** but roughened with small knobby lenticels, dark slate **gray** to blackish

FOLIAGE: alternate, **simple, obovate to oblong obovate** or oblanceolate, sharp often double toothed; **medium fine** texture
Surface: **dull,** smooth
Color: spring - **red green;** summer - deep **dark green;** autumn - dark green late, then **yellow, brown** or black after frost
Season: **deciduous;** emergence - late **May,** drop - mid **October**

FLOWER: **small clusters,** inconspicuous
Color: **greenish to white**
Season: early through late **June,** after leaves
Sex: **dioecious**

FRUIT: globular **berry,** 6 mm (¼ in) diameter, solitary or often in pairs but profusely crowded along twig
Color: scarlet **red** to bright orange
Season: late **August** persisting **through** late **February,** showy at Christmas   Human Value: **poisonous fruit**
Wildlife Value: **high;** winter waterfowl and songbirds major users, also upland gamebirds, small mammals

HABITAT: formation - **forest, meadow, swamp, bog, fen;** region - **Northern, Central;** gradient - **wet, wet-mesic;** swamp forests
and thickets, seepage areas in woodlands, boggy ground, wet meadows, cypress swamps, moist woods at bluff base
Shade Tolerance: **intermediate**
Flood Tolerance: **very tolerant**

SOIL: Texture: **medium to fine;** primarily peats or mucks underlain by calcareous lacustrine clays, silts, and sands
Drainage: **very poor to moderately well**
Moisture: **wet to moist**
Reaction **strongly acid to** moderately acid, pH 4.5 - 6.0, tolerates **alklaline** pH soils to 8.0

HARDINESS: zone 3b
Rate: **slow**
Longevity: **moderately short-lived**

SUSCEPTIBILITY: Physiological: **infrequent**
Disease: **infrequent** - tar spots, leaf spots, powdery mildew; rarely serious
Insect: **infrequent** - scale; not serious
Wind-Ice: **infrequent**

URBAN TOLERANCE: Pollution:
Lighting: **intermediate**   Drought Heat: **intermediate**   Mine Spoils:
Salt: **sensitive**   Soil Compaction: **resistant**
Root Pattern: fine fibrous, **shallow lateral; transplants well**

SPECIES: Associate: trees - Red Maple, River Birch, willow species, Eastern Poplar; shrubs - Red-osier/Silky Dogwoods,
Common Alder, Common Buttonbush, Black Chokeberry, Highbush Blueberry, Common Ninebark, Hardhack Spirea
Similar: Finetooth Holly - Japan; Burkwood Daphne; American Cranberrybush Viburnum
Cultivars: 'Chrysocarpa' - yellow fruits; 'Cacapon', 'Fairfax', 'Shaver' - hardier, good fruiting; 'Nana' - dwarf; others

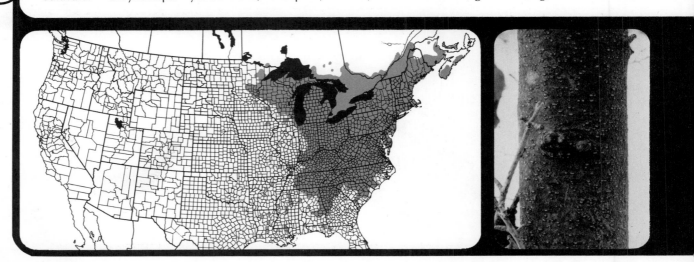

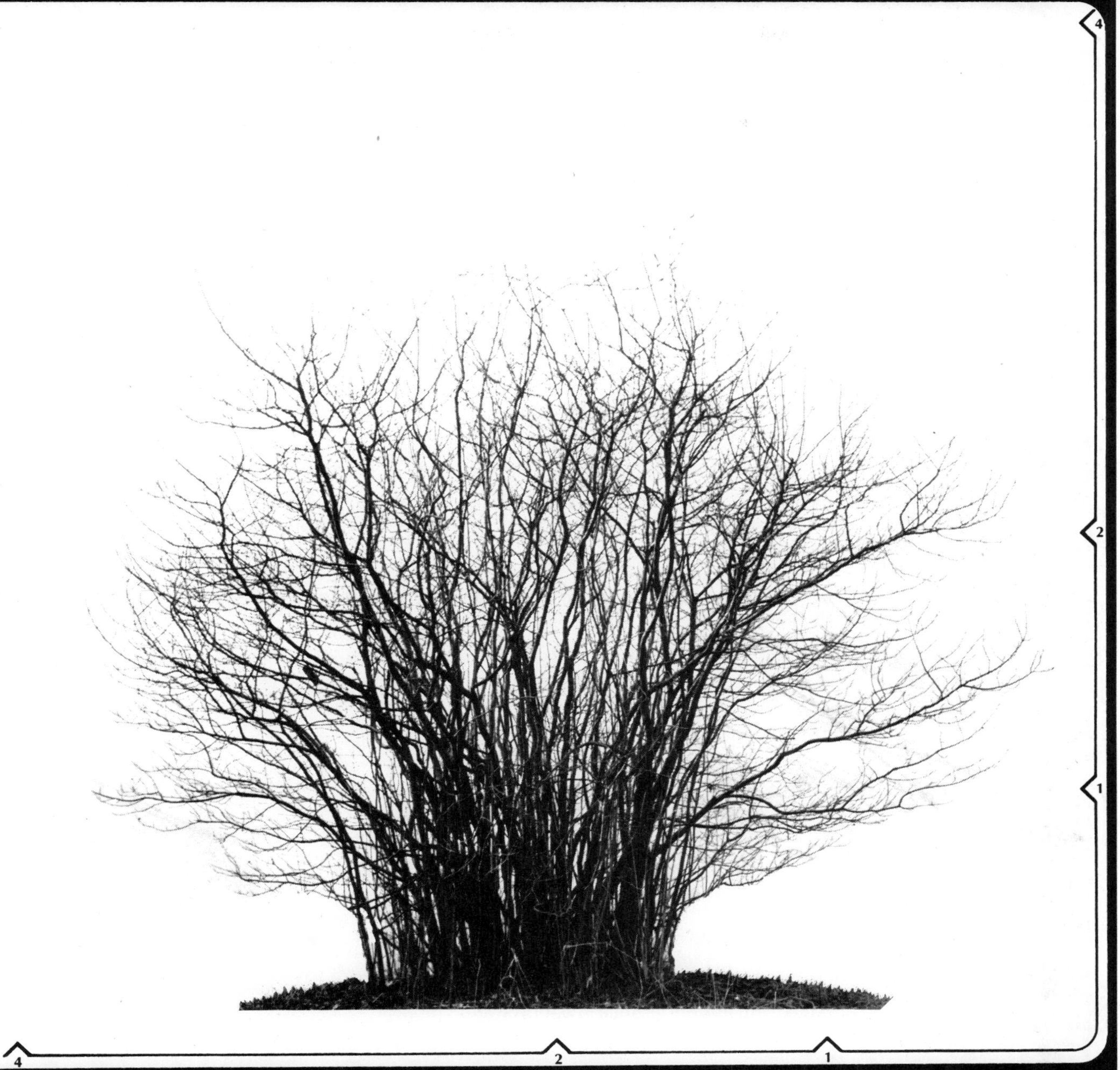
4
2
1
4
2
1

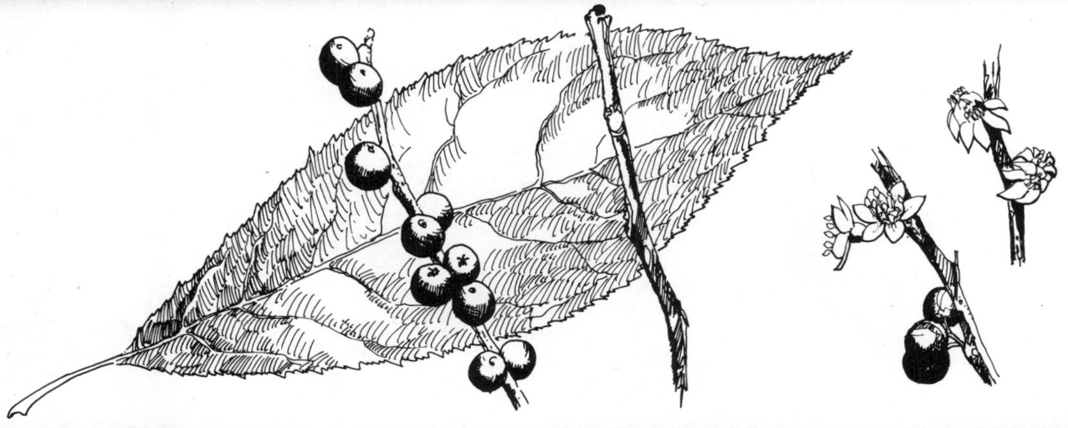

Itea virginica

FORM: **globular or mound**
Size: **mid-height shrub** - from 2 to 4 m (6 to 12 ft)
Spread: **intermediate** - 2 to 4 m (6 to 12 ft), often forming broad thickets
Mass: **open,** loose

BRANCHING: many slender **erect or upright spreading** wand-like stems, branched only towards their tops; **medium** texture
Twig: slender, **velvety** becoming smooth, **green to red**
Bud: small conical, 2 clustered buds above each leaf scar
Bark: smooth with narrow horizontal stripe-like lenticels, old stems with squarish **blocky** segments, **red brown**

FOLIAGE: alternate, **simple, obovate to oblong obovate,** fine bristle-like teeth, **aromatic** when bruised; **medium fine** texture
Surface: **dull,** smooth
Color: spring - **light green;** summer - bright **medium green;** autumn - scarlet **red** and brilliant crimson
Season: **deciduous;** emergence - late **May,** drop - early **November**

FLOWER: dense upright terminal spear-like or tassle-like **spikes,** 5 to 15 cm (2 to 6 in) tall, each bloom small, 6 mm (¼ in)
Color: **white**
Season: late **June through** late **July,** after leaves
Sex: monoecious   **Fragrant:** very strongly perfumed

FRUIT: small elongate 2-grooved downy **capsule,** 6 to 8 mm (¼ to ⅓ in) long, in erect cylindrical clusters
Color: tan **brown** to chocolate brown
Season: late **August** persisting **through** late **March**   Human Value: not edible
Wildlife Value: **low;** infrequent use by waterbirds, songbirds, gamebirds, small mammals

HABITAT: formation - **barrens, forest, bog, dune, swamp;** region - **Southern;** gradient - **wet;** wooded stream banks, swampy
borders, wet woodlands, low pine barrens, pocosins, bay forests, hillside bogs, often growing in shallow water
Shade Tolerance: **very tolerant**
Flood Tolerance: **very tolerant**

SOIL: Texture: **coarse** maritime sands, gravels, loamy sands, **to fine** silt loams, silts, hardpan clays, peats, mucks
Drainage: **very poor to moderately poor**
Moisture: **wet to moist**
Reaction: **moderately acid to neutral,** pH 5.0 - 7.0

HARDINESS: zone 5b
Rate: **slow to medium**
Longevity: **very short-lived**

SUSCEPTIBILITY: Physiological: **infrequent**
Disease: **infrequent** - none serious
Insect: **infrequent** - none serious
Wind-Ice: **infrequent**

URBAN TOLERANCE: Pollution:
Lighting: Drought Heat: **resistant**   Mine Spoils:
Salt: **resistant**   Soil Compaction: **resistant**
Root Pattern: fibrous, **shallow lateral; transplants easily,** best moved B & B

SPECIES: Associate: trees - Black Willow, Common Baldcypress, River Birch, Common Boxelder; shrubs - Common
Alder, Mountainlaurel Kalmia, Yellowroot, Swamp Azalea, Summersweet Clethra, Inkberry, Coast Leucothoe
Similar: Summersweet/Cinnamon Clethras; Meadowsweet Spirea
Cultivars: none available

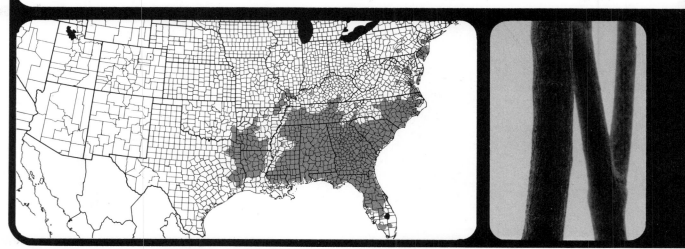

6

3

2

1

6   3   2   1

Juniperus communis

FORM: **mat** or mound
Size: **small shrub** - from 1 to 2 m (3 to 6 ft), frequently to 3 m (9 ft)
Spread: **wide** - 4 to 6 m (12 to 20 ft), old plants often broader
Mass: **dense**

BRANCHING: few stems with **trailing horizontal** branches sweeping ground, stiffly **ascending** at tips; **medium** texture
Twig: smooth, **angular** 3-sided with **ridge**-like **resinous** gland extending below leaf scar, **brown**
Bud: small, **naked**
Bark: very fibrous **exfoliating** into short thin papery shreads, **gray brown,** inner bark **red brown**

FOLIAGE: whorled in sets of 3, **awl**-like needles, concave above with white stripe down middle, **aromatic;** very **fine** texture
Surface: **dull,** bloomy
Color: spring - **gray green to blue green;** summer, autumn - **blue green;** winter - maroon **purple to brownish**
Season: coniferous **evergreen**

FLOWER: male solitary, cylindric, 8 mm (⅓ in), female solitary, 13 mm (½ in), miniature **cone**-like appearance
Color: male yellowish to brown, female green to **yellow green**
Season: late **May through** early **June**
Sex: **dioecious**

FRUIT: globular or egg-shaped **berry**-like cones, 6 mm (¼ in) diameter, ripening in second year, aromatic
Color: dark **blue,** bloomy, weathering **to gray**
Season: early **August** persisting **through** winter until late **April**   Human Value: **edible fruit**
Wildlife Value: **very high;** songbirds, small mammals are major users, also large mammals, upland gamebirds

HABITAT: formation - **glade, prairie, dune, old field, cliff;** region - **Northern;** gradient - **mesic-dry, dry;** open wooded hillsides,
     rocky exposed slopes and ledges, glades, dunes, clay banks, overhanging vertical rock cliffs, goat prairies
Shade Tolerance: **very intolerant**
Flood Tolerance: **very intolerant**

SOIL: Texture: **coarse to moderately coarse;** rock outcroppings, thin soils over rock, sand, sandy and gravelly loams
Drainage: **well to excessive**
Moisture: **average to droughty**
Reaction: **moderately acid to** circumneutral, tolerates **alkaline,** pH 5.0 - 8.5

HARDINESS: zone 2
Rate: **slow**
Longevity: **long-lived** on exposed sites

SUSCEPTIBILITY: Physiological: **infrequent** - gradual stem die-off from center, ice causes twig dieback
Disease: **frequent** - Phomopsis juniper blight is often serious, cedar-apple rust, wilt
Insect: **occasional** - rocky mountain juniper aphid, bagworm, juniper midge, mites, webworm, redcedar bark beetle
Wind-Ice: **infrequent** - decidedly windfirm

URBAN TOLERANCE: Pollution: **resistant** - S0₂, HFI, HCl; **intermediate** - 2-4D
Lighting: **resistant**   Drought Heat: **resistant**   Mine Spoils: **resistant**
Salt: **intermediate**   Soil Compaction: **sensitive**
Root Pattern: deep **taproot;** very **difficult to transplant**

SPECIES: Associate: trees - Jack/Red Pines, Paper Birch, Red Maple, Balsam Poplar; shrubs - Russet Buffaloberry, Sand
     Cherry, Bearberry, Creeping Juniper, rose species; vines - American Bittersweet, Riverbank Grape, Common Poisonivy
Similar: Japagarden Juniper - Asiatic, lower
Cultivars: 'Compressa' - dwarf; 'Mayer' - pyramidal; 'Aurea' - drooping branches, gold tipped; 'Hibermica' - upright

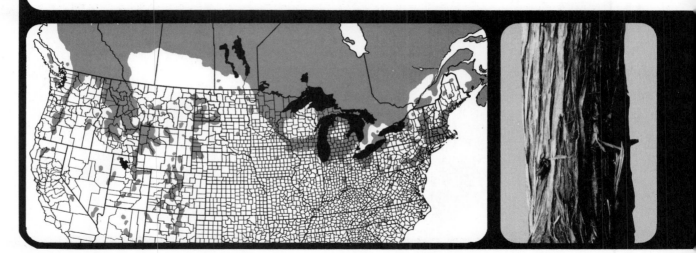

Juniperus horizontalis

FORM: procumbent **mat**
Size: **very small shrub** - less than 1 m (3 ft), typically only 44 cm (18 in)
Spread: **intermediate** - from 2 to 4 m (6 to 12 ft), commonly wide, from 4 to 6 m (12 to 20 ft), forms broad circular mat
Mass: **dense**

BRANCHING: single or few stems, long **horizontal trailing** branches with numerous short branchlets; **fine texture**
Twig: smooth, **brown**
Bud: small, **naked**
Bark: scaly or **exfoliating** into thin flat shaggy strips, **gray brown with red brown** inner bark

FOLIAGE: simple, mostly mature **scale**-type, short prickly juvenile **awl**-type may also be present, **aromatic;** very **fine**
Surface: **dull,** bloomy
Color: spring - **blue green;** summer, autumn - **blue green** to steel blue; winter - maroon **purple to brownish**
Season: coniferous **evergreen**

FLOWER: small cylindrical **cones,** inconspicuous
Color: male - **pale brown,** female - **yellow green**
Season: late **May through** early **June**
Sex: **dioecious**

FRUIT: globular **berry**-like cones, 6 to 10 mm (¼ to ⅖ in) diameter, scales fused, on recurved stems
Color: dark **blue** with heavy bloom, weathering **to gray**
Season: early **August** persisting **through** winter until late **April**   Human Value: **edible fruit**
Wildlife Value: **very high;** songbirds, small mammals and hoofed browsers are major users, also large mammals

HABITAT: formation - **dune, prairie, glade, cliff, old field;** region - **Northern;** gradient - upland **mesic-dry, dry;** sea cliffs, open
           prairie hillsides, eroded areas, rocky ledges, low beach dunes, dry sandy or gravelly hills, old field
Shade Tolerance: **very intolerant**
Flood Tolerance: **very intolerant**

SOIL: Texture: **coarse to moderately coarse;** infertile sands, gravels, sandy loams, rock outcroppings; tolerates clays
Drainage: **moderately well to excessive**
Moisture: **average to droughty**
Reaction: **moderately acid to** circumneutral, tolerates **alkaline,** pH 5.0 - 8.5

HARDINESS: **zone 2**
Rate: **slow** to medium, may grow to 3 m (10 ft) in diameter in 10 years
Longevity: **long-lived** on exposed site

SUSCEPTIBILITY: Physiological: **infrequent**
Disease: **occasional** - Phomopsis juniper blight can be extremely serious, cedar-apple rust, wilt, witches'-broom
Insect: **occasional** - bagworm, scale, webworm, juniper midge, spiders, mites, redcedar bark beetle, juniper aphid
Wind-Ice: **infrequent** - decidedly windfirm, tough

URBAN TOLERANCE: Pollution: **resistant** - S0₂, HFI; **intermediate** - 2-4D
Lighting: **resistant**   Drought Heat: **resistant**   Mine Spoils: **resistant**
Salt: **intermediate**   Soil Compaction: **sensitive**
Root Pattern: deep **taproot** and **stoloniferous; difficult to transplant**

SPECIES: Associate: trees - Jack Pine, Paper Birch, Common Chokecherry, Pin Cherry, Wafer Ash; shrubs - Russet
           Buffaloberry, Common Juniper, Carolina Rose, Bearberry, Sand Cherry, Bush Cinquefoil; vines - American Bittersweet
Similar: Sargent's Chinese Juniper - bright green leaves; Parson's Juniper
Cultivars: many; 'Bar Harbor', 'Douglasi' - trailing, steel blue color; 'Plumosa' - purplish in winter; 'Blue Rug' - dwarf

1

2/3

1/3

1

2/3

1/3

Kalmia angustifolia

FORM: **mat**
Size: **very small shrub** - to 1 m (3 ft)
Spread: **narrow** - 1 to 2 m (3 to 6 ft), typically broader than tall
Mass: variable, **dense** to open

BRANCHING: **trailing** stems spreading on ground with **erect** sparingly-branched tips; **medium** texture
Twig: smooth, **gray brown to brown**
Bud: very small, inconspicuous, **naked**
Bark: **smooth, gray brown**

FOLIAGE: opposite or whorles of 3, clustered at tips, **simple**, narrow **elliptic**, margin entire; **medium fine** texture
Surface: **glossy**, smooth, somewhat leathery, paler beneath
Color: spring - **bright green**; summer, autumn - **dark green**; winter - **dark green, red green to purplish**
Season: broadleaf **evergreen**

FLOWER: small saucer-like **bell**, 13 mm (½ in) diameter, scattered along sides of stem in **small** loose **clusters**
Color: lavender **purple to** crimson **red**
Season: early **June through** early **July**
Sex: monoecious

FRUIT: small downy dry 5-celled depressed globular **capsule**, 3 to 5 mm (⅛ to ⅕ in) diameter, nodding in loose clusters
Color: **brown**
Season: early **September through** late **March**   Human Value: **all parts poisonous**
Wildlife Value: **very low**; infrequent by gamesbirds and small mammals, foliage poisonous to hoofed browsers

HABITAT: formation - **bog, barrens, dune, meadow**; region - **Northern**; gradient - **wet**; wet pasture, sluggish wooded
    streams, barren lands, wet thickets, borders of swamps, pocosins, branch bays, bogs in the coastal plain
Shade Tolerance: **very tolerant**
Flood Tolerance: **very tolerant**

SOIL: Texture: **moderately fine to fine**; organic soils, sandy peats, mucks underlain by calcareous clays, silts, sands
Drainage: **very poor to moderately well**
Moisture: **wet to moist**
Reaction: **strongly acid to moderately acid**, pH 4.5 - 6.0

HARDINESS: **zone 2**
Rate: **slow**
Longevity: **moderately short-lived**

SUSCEPTIBILITY: Physiological: **frequent** - chlorosis caused by iron deficiency on lime soils
Disease: **infrequent** - leaf spots, flower blight; rarely serious
Insect: **infrequent** - none serious
Wind-Ice: **infrequent**

URBAN TOLERANCE: Pollution:
Lighting: Drought Heat: **resistant**   Mine Spoils:
Salt: Soil Compaction: **resistant**
Root Pattern: fibrous, **shallow laterals; transplants well** B & B

SPECIES: Associate: trees - Jack/Red/Eastern White Pines, Black Spruce, Black Oak, Quaking Aspen, Paper Birch; shrubs
    - Lowbush/Highbush Blueberries, Scarlet Elder, Beaked Filbert, Dwarf Bushhoneysuckle, Bunchberry Dogwood
Similar: Bog Kalmia - lower; Labradortea Ledum - flowers white; Leatherleaf; Alpine Azalea
Cultivars: 'Candida' - white flowers; 'Ovata' - leaves ovate to elliptic; 'Rubra' - dark purple flowers

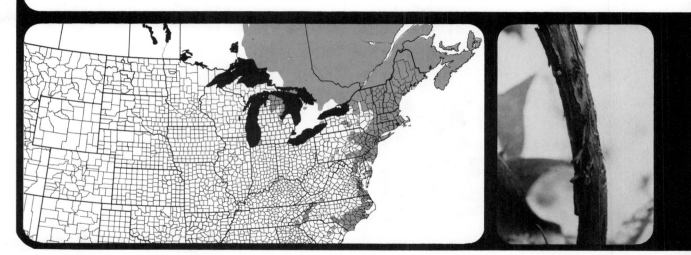

Kalmia latifolia

FORM: **mound**
Size: **large shrub** - from 4 to 6 m (12 to 20 ft), rarely to 9 m (30 ft)
Spread: **wide** - 4 to 6 m (12 to 20 ft), commonly broader than tall
Mass: **dense**

BRANCHING: short gnarled contorted trunks with many rigid **picturesque horizontal and ascending** branches; **medium**
Twig: smooth, **green** at first becoming **red brown**
Bud: laterals small, **naked**, flower buds large, diamond-shaped, fluted and waxy, clustered at tips of twigs
Bark: divided by **shallow** longitudinal **furrows** into narrow ridges separating into long narrow **scales, red brown to gray**

FOLIAGE: alternate, sometimes irregularly whorled in 3's, **simple, ovate lanceolate,** entire margin; **medium coarse** texture
Surface: **glossy,** smooth, leathery, rigid
Color: spring - **light green to yellow green;** summer, autumn - **dark green,** red petiole; winter - **dark green, purplish** in North
Season: broadleaf **evergreen**

FLOWER: large terminal **flat-topped** clusters, 10 to 15 cm (4 to 6 in) across, bowl or **bell**-shaped blooms, 2.5 cm (1 in)
Color: **white to** pale blush **pink** with deep rose spots inside
Season: early through late **June**
Sex: monoecious   **Fragrant:** pleasantly perfumed

FRUIT: depressed globular dry 5-valved **capsules** with persistant style at end, 5 mm (³⁄₁₆ in) diameter
Color: pale **brown**
Season: early **September** persisting **through** late **March**   Human Value: **all parts poisonous**
Wildlife Value: **very low;** minor importance to upland gamebirds, small mammals, foliage poisonous to hoofed browsers

HABITAT: formation - **swamp, meadow, glade, bald, forest, old field;** region - **Central, Southern;** gradient - **wet, wet-mesic,**
mesic, mesic-dry, dry; oak woods, ridge tops, abandoned fields, swamps, cool mountain meadows and slopes
Shade Tolerance: **very tolerant**
Flood Tolerance: **very tolerant**

SOIL: Texture: **coarse to fine;** gravels and sands, loamy sands, loams, silt loams, clay loams, clays, peats
Drainage: **poor to well**
Moisture: **wet to average**
Reaction: **strongly acid to moderately acid,** pH 4.5 - 6.0

HARDINESS: zone 5a
Rate: **slow,** 1.2 to 2.4 m (4 to 8 ft) over 10 year period
Longevity: **moderately short-lived**

SUSCEPTIBILITY: Physiological: **occasional** - chlorosis caused by iron deficiency on lime soils
Disease: **occasional** - leaf spot, flower blight; rarely troublesome
Insect: **occasional** - leaf minor, aphids, lace bug, mulberry whitefly, scale, azalea stem borer, rhododendron borer
Wind-Ice: **infrequent**

URBAN TOLERANCE: Pollution:
Lighting: Drought Heat: **intermediate**   Mine Spoils:
Salt: **intermediate**   Soil Compaction: **resistant**
Root Pattern: fibrous, dense mat, **shallow lateral; transplants well**

SPECIES: Associate: trees - Eastern Hemlock, Yellow/Sweet Birches, American Beech, Rosebay Rhododendron; shrubs -
Cinnamon Clethra, Pinxterbloom/Flame Azaleas, Mapleleaf Viburnum, Common Deerberry, Trailing-arbutus
Similar: Rosebay/Catawba/Carolina Rhododendrons; Mountain/Japanese Pieris - smaller flowers
Cultivars: 'Alba' - white flowers; 'Myrtifolia' - dwarf form; 'Rubra' - deep pink flowers; 'Obtusata'; 'Polypetala'; others

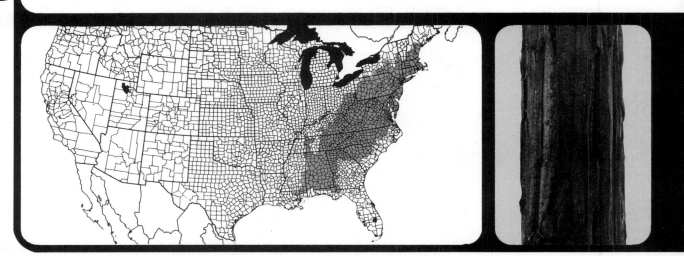

Kalmia polifolia

FORM: low prostrate **mat**
Size: **very small shrub** - less than 1 m (3 ft), commonly from 15 to 60 cm (0.5 to 2 ft) high
Spread: **very narrow** - 1 m (3 ft), established patches often broader
Mass: **moderate**

BRANCHING: **trailing** stems with **erect** sparingly-branched habit; **fine** texture
Twig: smooth, sharp 2-edged **angular** appearance, conspicuous swollen nodes, **yellow brown to** light **brown**
Bud: very small ovoid, **naked**, inconspicuous
Bark: **smooth, gray brown** to dark brown or blackish

FOLIAGE: opposite, rarely whorled, **simple, linear** to lanceolate, entire, margin rolled under; **fine** texture
Surface: **glossy**, smooth, thick leathery, stiff, very fine down beneath and strongly whitened
Color: spring - **silvery gray green;** summer, autumn, and winter - dark **blue green**
Season: broadleaf **evergreen**

FLOWER: small 2 to 5 flowered **clusters** from axils of upper leaves, each bloom **bell**-like, 15 mm (⅗ in) wide
Color: **pink to rose purple**
Season: early through late **June**
Sex: monoecious

FRUIT: 5-valved woody depressed globular **capsule,** 6 mm (¼ in) diameter, persistant style
Color: tan **brown**
Season: early **September** persisting **through** winter to late **March**   Human Value: **all parts poisonous**
Wildlife Value: **very low;** limited use; foliage poisonous to hoofed browsers

HABITAT: formation - **bog, swamp, meadow;** region - **Northern;** gradient - lowland **wet;** cold sphagnum bogs, swampy
          ground, cold wet meadows, low mountain bogs, muskeg
Shade Tolerance: **very tolerant**
Flood Tolerance: **very tolerant**

SOIL: Texture: **moderately fine to fine;** organic soils, sphagnum peats, mucks underlain by calcareous clays, silts, sands
Drainage: **very poor to moderately poor**
Moisture: **wet to moist**
Reaction: **strongly acid to moderately acid,** pH range 4.0 - 5.5

HARDINESS: zone 2
Rate: very **slow**
Longevity: **moderately short-lived**

SUSCEPTIBILITY: Physiological: **frequent** - chlorosis caused by iron deficiency on lime soils
Disease: **occasional** - flower blight, leaf spot
Insect: **occasional** - scale, lace bug, borers
Wind-Ice: **infrequent**

URBAN TOLERANCE: Pollution:
Lighting: Drought Heat: **sensitive**   Mine Spoils:
Salt: Soil Compaction: **resistant**
Root Pattern: fibrous, **shallow lateral; transplants well**

SPECIES: Associate: trees - Black Spruce, American Larch, Red Maple, Balsam Fir; shrubs - American Black Currant, Bog
          Birch, Common Winterberry, Labradortea Ledum, Bogrosemary Andromeda, Leatherleaf, Box Huckleberry
Similar: Lambkill Kalmia - larger; Bogrosemary Andromeda; Cranberry; Box Huckleberry; Rabbiteye Blueberry
Cultivars: 'Leucantha' - white flowers

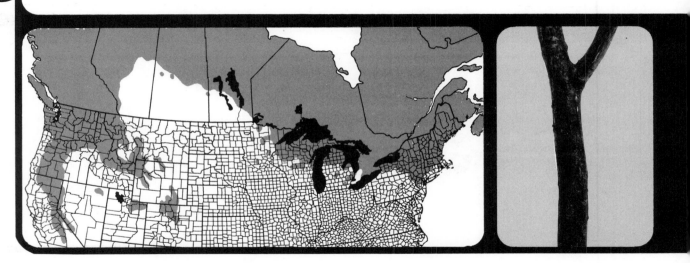

Bog Kalmia

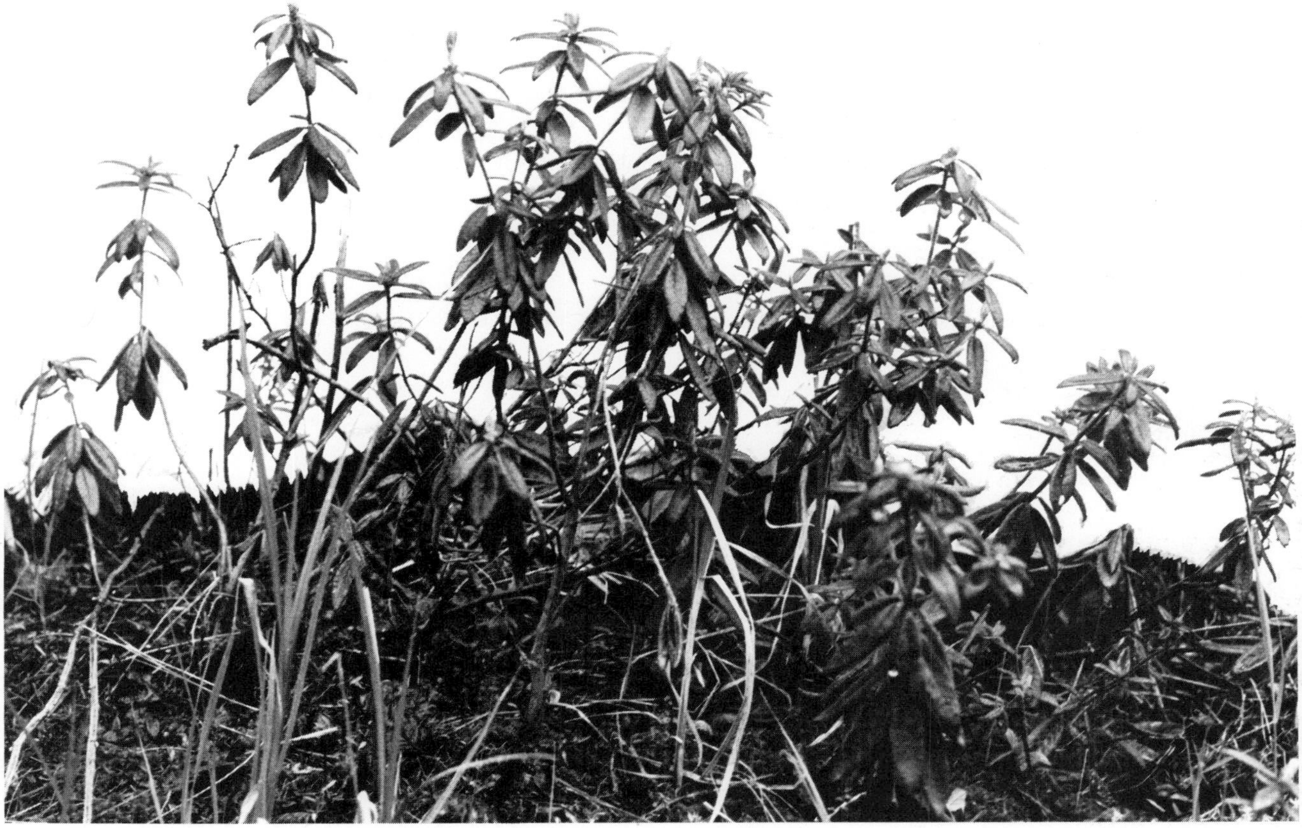

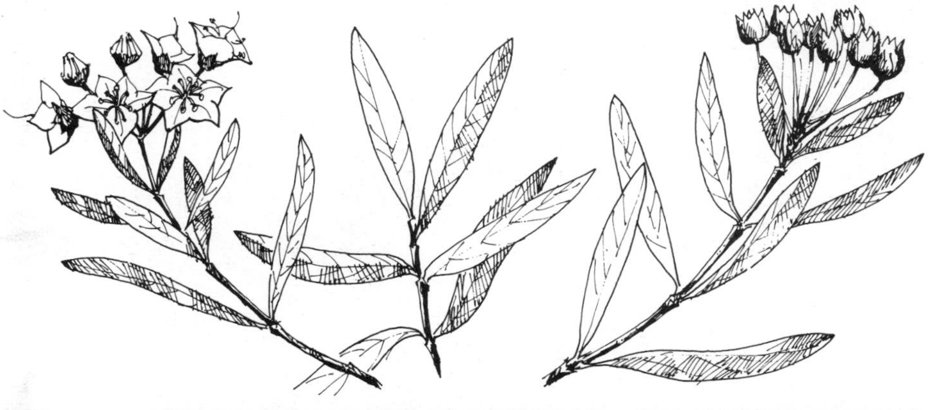

Ledum groenlandicum

FORM: globular
Size: **very small shrub** - up to 1 m (3 ft)
Spread: **very narrow** - to 1 m (3 ft)
Mass: **moderate**

BRANCHING: many **erect** stems with **upright spreading** branches, picturesque habit; **medium** texture
Twig: slender, densely covered with curly **velvety** hair, yellow to **red** becoming **red brown**
Bud: small solitary, 3 exposed scales, terminal flower buds **large,** scales glandular dotted
Bark: **smooth** with fine short hairline cracks, scattered lenticels, coppery **orange brown to red brown**

FOLIAGE: alternate but compressed in tight clusters, **simple,** narrow **elliptic,** entire, rolled edges, **aromatic; fine** texture
Surface: **glossy,** smooth, thick leathery, dense rusty tomentose beneath
Color: spring - **light green;** summer, autumn and winter - deep **dark green**
Season: broadleaf **evergreen**

FLOWER: broad dense terminal **flat-topped** clusters, 5 cm (2 in) wide, individual **bell**-shaped, 9.5 mm (⅜ in) diameter
Color: **white**
Season: early **May through** late **June**
Sex: monoecious

FRUIT: slender oblong 5-valved **capsule,** 5 mm (³⁄₁₆ in) long, splitting from bottom upwards
Color: **brown**
Season: early **September through** late **October,** empty capsules persisting   Human Value: **edible leaves**
Wildlife Value: **low;** infrequent use by songbirds, upland gamebirds

HABITAT: formation - **bog, swamp, forest, dune, glade, meadow;** region - **Northern;** gradient - lowland **wet,** peat bogs, cold
    damp wooded glens, swampy ground, low mountain bogs, wet shores
Shade Tolerance: **intolerant**
Flood Tolerance: **very tolerant**

SOIL: Texture: **moderately coarse to fine;** organic soils, peats, mucks underlain by mineral soils
Drainage: **very poor to moderately poor**
Moisture: **wet to moist**
Reaction: demands **strongly acid to moderately acid,** pH 3.0 - 5.5

HARDINESS: **zone 2**
Rate: **slow**
Longevity: **short-lived**

SUSCEPTIBILITY: Physiological: **infrequent**
Disease: **occasional** - Anthracnose, rusts, leaf galls caused by fungi
Insect: **infrequent** - none serious
Wind-Ice: **infrequent**

URBAN TOLERANCE: Pollution:
Lighting: Drought Heat: **intermediate**   Mine Spoils:
Salt: Soil Compaction: **resistant**
Root Pattern: dense fibrous mass, **shallow lateral; transplants easily**

SPECIES: Associate: trees - Black Spruce, American Larch; shrubs - Bogrosemary Andromeda, Leatherleaf, Bunchberry
    Dogwood, Creeping Snowberry, Lambkill/Bog Kalmias, Lowbush Blueberry, American Black Currant, Sweetgale
Similar: Leatherleaf; Lambkill Kalmia - red flowers; Box Sandmyrtle - Southern to zone 6a
Cultivars: 'Compacta' - dense dwarf to 30 cm (1 ft)

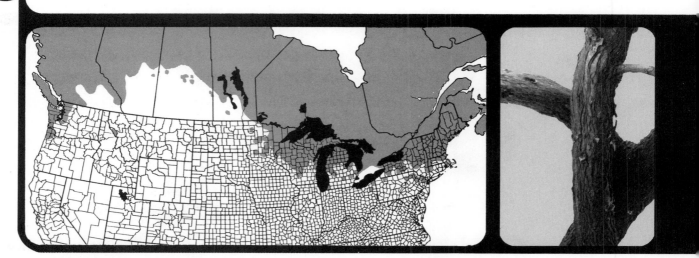

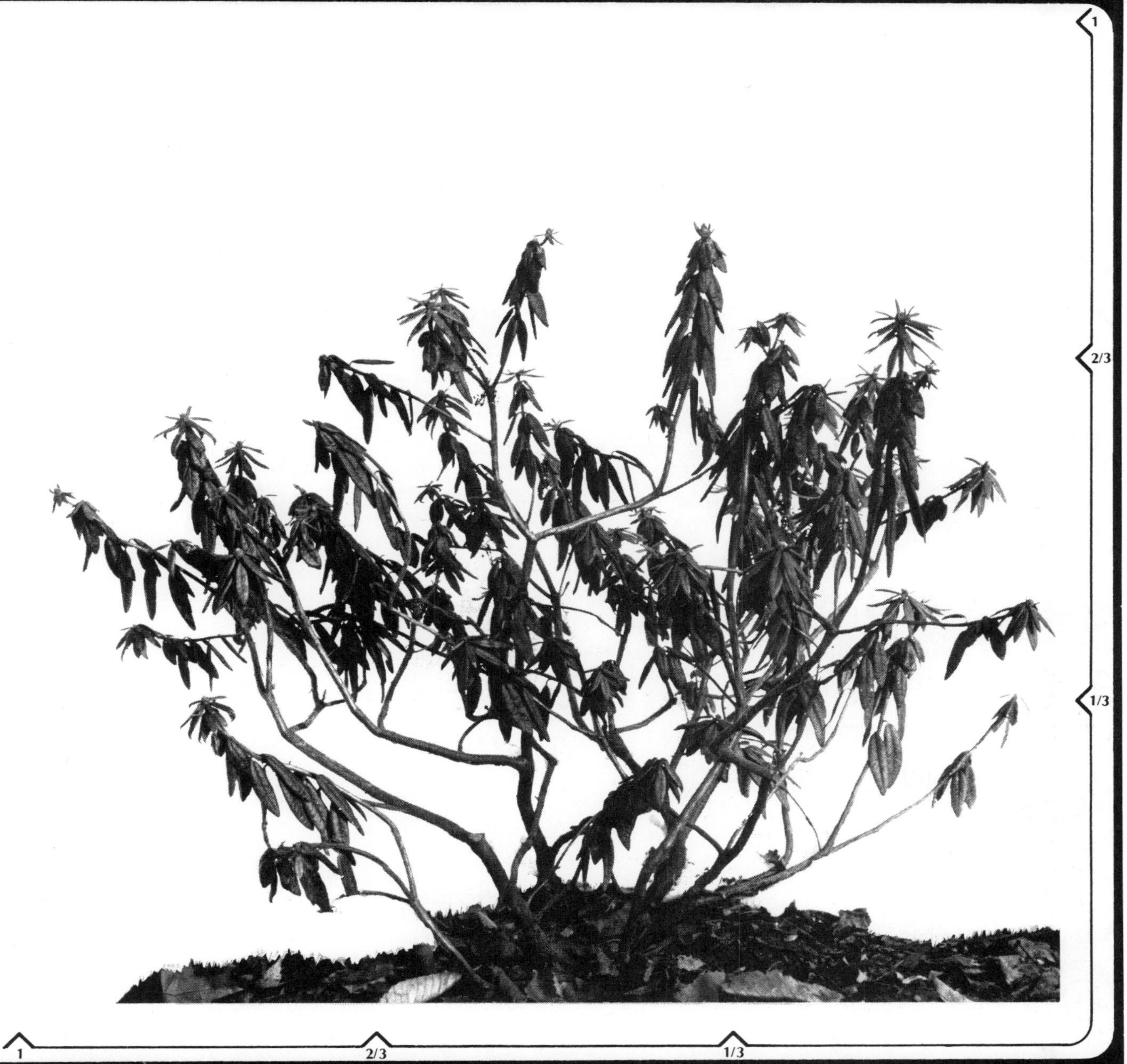
1
2/3
1/3
1
2/3
1/3

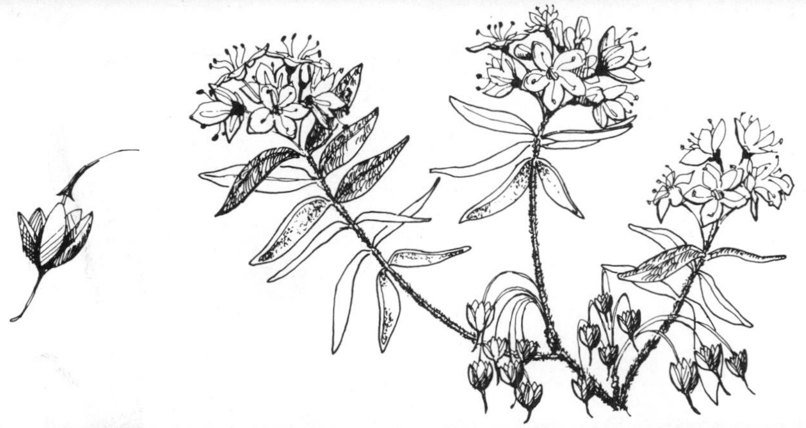

Leiophyllum buxifolium

FORM: billowy **mound**
Size: **very small shrub** - up to 1 m (3 ft)
Spread: **narrow** - 1 to 2 m (3 to 6 ft), 1½ to 2 times the height
Mass: **open**

BRANCHING: many **erect or upright spreading** stems with strong irregular **ascending** branches; **fine** texture
Twig: very slender, smooth, wiry
Bud: small ovoid, solitary, appressed, **2** exposed **scales**
Bark: older bark papery with shreddy **exfoliation**

FOLIAGE: alternate or opposite, crowded, **simple, elliptic,** entire margin, edges somewhat rolled; very **fine** texture
Surface: **glossy,** leathery, black dotted beneath
Color: spring - **light green;** summer, autumn - **dark green;** winter - **red green to** maroon **purple**
Season: broadleaf **evergreen**

FLOWER: dense terminal **flat-topped** clusters, 5 to 7.5 cm (2 to 3 in) across, small waxy bell-shaped blossom
Color: **white,** flower buds pink
Season: early **May through** late **June**
Sex: monoecious

FRUIT: smooth dry 2 to 5-valved ovoid **capsule,** 3 mm (⅛ in) long, grouped in compact terminal clusters
Color: tan **brown**
Season: early **September** persisting **through** winter until late **March**   Human Value: not edible
Wildlife Value: **low;** infrequent use by upland gamebirds, songbirds, small mammals

HABITAT: formation - **forest, barrens;** region - **Southern;** gradient - upland **mesic-dry, dry;** dry sandy pine barrens, oak
  barrens
Shade Tolerance: **intermediate**
Flood Tolerance: **very intolerant**

SOIL: Texture: **coarse to medium;** sands and gravels, sandy loams, loamy sands, deep loams
Drainage: **well to excessive**
Moisture: **average to droughty**
Reaction: demands **strongly acid to moderately acid,** pH 4.0 - 6.0

HARDINESS: zone 6a
Rate: **slow**
Longevity: **moderately short-lived**

SUSCEPTIBILITY: Physiological: **infrequent**
Disease: **infrequent** - free of problems
Insect: **infrequent** - none serious
Wind-Ice: **infrequent**

URBAN TOLERANCE: Pollution:
Lighting: Drought Heat: **resistant**   Mine Spoils: **resistant**
Salt: **resistant**   Soil Compaction: **sensitive**
Root Pattern: **deep** going; **difficult to transplant,** difficult to establish, obtain B & B or container grown

SPECIES: Associate: trees - Pitch/Shortleaf Pines, Blackjack/Post/Black/Scarlet Oaks; shrubs - Bearberry, Scrub/Dwarf
    Chinkapin Oaks, Staggerbush Lyonia, Mountainlaurel/Lambkill Kalmias, Woolly Beachheather, Box Huckleberry
Similar: Canby Pachistima, Lambkill Kalmia, Alpine Azalea, Labradortea Ledum - similar size, form, evergreen
Cultivars: 'Nanum' - much-branched dwarf, pink flowers; prostratum - prostrate, leaves elliptic to orbicular

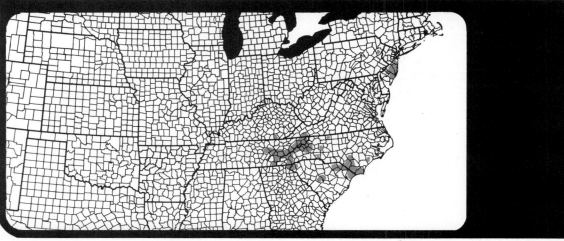

Leucothoe catesbaei

FORM: mound
Size: **small shrub** - from 1 to 2 m (3 to 6 ft)
Spread: **narrow** - 1 to 2 m (3 to 6 ft), typically broader than tall
Mass: **dense**

BRANCHING: multi-stemmed, long graceful fountain-like **arching** habit, little-branched; **medium** texture
Twig: smooth, sparingly downy when young, bright **green or red**
Bud: **large** long cylindric **pointed** flower buds, 13 mm (½ in); **winter catkins**
Bark: rough **scaly** with rectangular flakes, bright **green to red or purple**

FOLIAGE: alternate, **simple, lanceolate to ovate lanceolate,** fine hair-like teeth; **medium** texture
Surface: **glossy,** smooth, leathery
Color: spring - **light green;** summer, autumn - **dark green;** winter - **red green to** maroon **purple**
Season: broadleaf **evergreen**

FLOWER: waxy pitcher-like **bells,** clustered in loose spray-like spikes drooping below the branches, 7.5 cm (3 in) long
Color: **white**
Season: mid **May through** early **June**
Sex: monoecious   **Fragrant:** spicily perfumed like chestnut blossoms

FRUIT: broad globular 5-celled **capsule,** 4 mm (⅙ in) diameter, grouped in loose drooping spike-like clusters
Color: **brown**
Season: early **September through** late **October**   Human Value: **poisonous leaves**
Wildlife Value: **low;** minor use by upland gamebirds, small mammals; hoofed browsers eat twigs, foliage

HABITAT: formation - **forest, bald, meadow;** region - **Central;** gradient - **mesic, mesic-dry;** cool deep mountain woodlands,
        heath thickets, deep wooded ravines, bordering mountain streams, moist protected coves
Shade Tolerance: **very tolerant**
Flood Tolerance: **intolerant**

SOIL: Texture: **moderately coarse** rocky or sandy loams **to moderately fine** silt loams; prefers loose textured soils
Drainage: **moderately poor to well**
Moisture: **moist to average**
Reaction: **strongly acid to moderately acid,** pH 4.5 - 6.0

HARDINESS: zone 5b
Rate: **slow to medium,** 1 to 1.5 m (3 to 5 ft) in 4 to 5 years
Longevity: **short-lived**

SUSCEPTIBILITY: Physiological: **frequent** - sunscald and leaf burn, dieback in severe winters
Disease: **infrequent** - various species of fungi, leaf spots are troublesome; basically none serious
Insect: **infrequent** - very resistant
Wind-Ice: **frequent** - will not tolerate exposure to hot dry winds; protect from winter wind, sun

URBAN TOLERANCE: Pollution:
Lighting: Drought Heat: **sensitive**   Mine Spoils:
Salt: **intermediate**   Soil Compaction: **intermediate**
Root Pattern: dense fibrous, **shallow** spreading by **stoloniferous** stems; **easy to transplant,** requires heavy mulching

SPECIES: Associate: trees - Eastern Hemlock, American Beech, Sweet Buckeye, Sugar Maple, Tuliptree; shrubs -
        Mountain Stewartia, Carolina/Catawba Rhododendrons, Mountainlaurel Kalmia, Common Spicebush, azaleas
Similar: Coast/Redtwig/Sweetbells (deciduous) Leucothoes; Mountain/Japanese Pieris - erect habit
Cultivars: 'Nana' - dwarf form; 'Girards Rainbow' - twigs, leaves various colors; 'Trivar' - multi-colored foliage

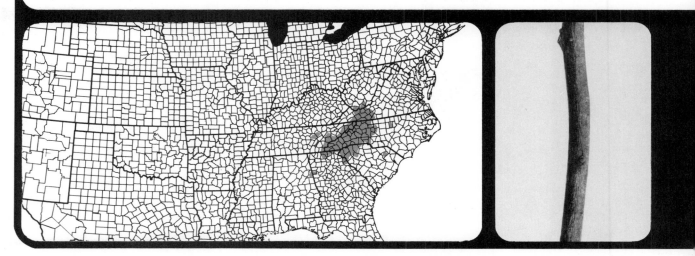

Lindera benzoin

FORM: globular
Size: **mid-height shrub** from 2 to 4 m (6 to 12 ft)
Spread: **intermediate** - 2 to 4 m (6 to 12 ft)
Mass: **moderate**

BRANCHING: solitary or few stems, graceful slender **horizontal and ascending picturesque** branches; **fine** texture
Twig: slender, smooth, graceful **zigzag** appearance, aromatic when crushed; **green to green brown** with pale lenticels
Bud: globular flower buds in **clusters** of 3, **stalked, green** to green brown
Bark: **smooth** with corky lenticels, old stems **shallow furrowed, gray brown**

FOLIAGE: alternate, **simple, obovate to oblong obovate,** entire, short taper-pointed tip, **aromatic** when bruised; **medium**
Surface: **glossy** to dull, smooth
Color: spring - pale yellow then **yellow green;** summer - **light green;** autumn - clear lemon **yellow**
Season: **deciduous;** emergence - mid **May,** drop - often defoliated by mid **September**

FLOWER: delicate **small clusters** along twigs, each blossom 6 to 9.5 mm (¼ to ⅜ in) across, profuse
Color: greenish yellow to pale **yellow**
Season: early through late **April,** before leaves
Sex: **dioecious**   **Fragrant:**   spicy scented

FRUIT: football-shaped **berry,** 10 mm (⅖ in) long, in small dense clusters, showy for brief period after leaves fall
Color: glossy scarlet **red**
Season: early through late **September**   Human Value: **all parts edible,** spicy taste
Wildlife Value: **very high;** quickly devoured by songbirds, upland gamebirds; twig and foliage browsed by White-tail Deer

HABITAT: formation - **forest;** region - **Central;** gradient - **wet-mesic, mesic;** moist rich woodlands, shaded footslopes,
        woodland terraces adjacent small quick-flowing streams, floodplain forests, deep protected coves, shaded dunes
Shade Tolerance: **very tolerant**
Flood Tolerance: **intermediate**

SOIL: Texture: **moderately coarse to moderately fine;** loamy sands, medium loams, silt loams, alluvial soils
Drainage: **moderately poor to well**
Moisture: **wet to average**
Reaction: **strongly acid to slightly acid,** pH 4.5 - 6.5

HARDINESS: zone 5a
Rate: **slow**
Longevity: **moderately short-lived**

SUSCEPTIBILITY: Physiological: **infrequent**
Disease: **infrequent** - none serious
Insect: **infrequent** - none serious
Wind-Ice: **infrequent**

URBAN TOLERANCE: Pollution:
Lighting: Drought Heat: **sensitive**   Mine Spoils:
Salt: **resistant**   Soil Compaction: **intermediate**
Root Pattern: fibrous, coarse **deep laterals; difficult to transplant,** slow to re-establish

SPECIES: Associate: trees - Sugar Maple, Eastern Redbud, American Beech, Northern Red Oak, Flowering Dogwood;
        shrubs - Running/Brook Euonymus, Pasture Gooseberry, Mapleleaf Viburnum, Smooth Hydrangea
Similar: Corneliancherry Dogwood - dense globular form, European
Cultivars: 'Xanthocarpa' - fruit yellow, woolly leaves

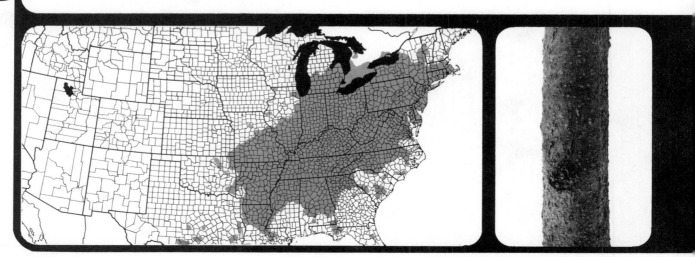

Lonicera canadensis

FORM: **mound**
Size: **small shrub** - from 1 to 2 m (3 to 6 ft)
Spread: **narrow** - 1 to 2 m (3 to 6 ft), commonly broader than tall
Mass: **open** and loose or straggling

BRANCHING: multiple stems, strongly **arching** then **trailing** with irregular sparingly-branched **leggy** habit; **medium** texture
Twig: smooth, longitudinal **ridges** beneath leaf scars, **green** becoming **gray brown or gray**
Bud: small ovoid, 3 to 6 mm (⅛ to ¼ in), widely divergent, green brown
Bark: **exfoliating** with narrow thin loose longitudinal shreds, gray to tan **brown**

FOLIAGE: opposite, **simple, ovate to oblong ovate,** leaf edges fringed with hairs; **medium fine** texture
Surface: **dull,** smooth except for hairy fringed margin
Color: spring - **light green;** summer - bright **medium green;** autumn - green late then dull **yellow green**
Season: **deciduous;** emergence - late **April;** drop - late **November**

FLOWER: long tubular bell-like **trumpet,** 19 mm (¾ in), nodding in pairs on long slender dangling stalks
Color: pale **yellowish to orange**
Season: early through mid **May,** when leaves are still expanding
Sex: monoecious   **Fragrant:**   faintly perfumed

FRUIT: egg-shaped **berries** in pairs on long drooping stems, 6 mm (¼ in) long, often united at base and divergent
Color: light **red**
Season: mid **July through** late **August**   Human Value: **edible fruit**
Wildlife Value: **low;** do not remain long after ripening, minor use by upland gamebirds, songbirds, small mammals

HABITAT: formation - **swamp, forest;** region- **Northern;** gradient - **wet, mesic, mesic-dry;** cool deep moist woods, dry woods,
   swamps, deep ravines, bogs
Shade Tolerance: **very tolerant**
Flood Tolerance: **intolerant**

SOIL: Texture: **moderately coarse to moderately fine;** stony or sandy loams, silt loams, clay loams; less common in clay
Drainage: **moderately well to well**
Moisture: **moist to average**
Reaction: **slightly acid to** circumneutral, tolerates **alkaline,** pH 6.0 - 8.5

HARDINESS: **zone 3a**
Rate: **fast**
Longevity: **short-lived**

SUSCEPTIBILITY: Physiological: **infrequent**
Disease: **occasional** - leaf blight, leaf spots, powdery mildews; rarely serious
Insect: **occasional** - woolly honeysuckle aphid, planthoppers, flea beetle, looper caterpillar, scales, fall webworm
Wind-Ice: **infrequent**

URBAN TOLERANCE: Pollution: **sensitive** - 2-4D
Lighting: Drought Heat: **resistant**   Mine Spoils:
Salt: **resistant**   Soil Compaction: **resistant**
Root Pattern: fibrous, dense, **shallow** spreading; **transplants well**

SPECIES: Associate: trees - Balsam Fir, White Spruce, Mountain Maple, Quaking Aspen, Showy Mountainash, Paper
   Birch; shrubs - Bunchberry/Roundleaf Dogwoods, Beaked Filbert, Dwarf Bushhoneysuckle, Red Raspberry
Similar: Limber Honeysuckle - shrub or low vine; Dwarf/Southern Bushhoneysuckles; other small honeysuckles
Cultivars: none available

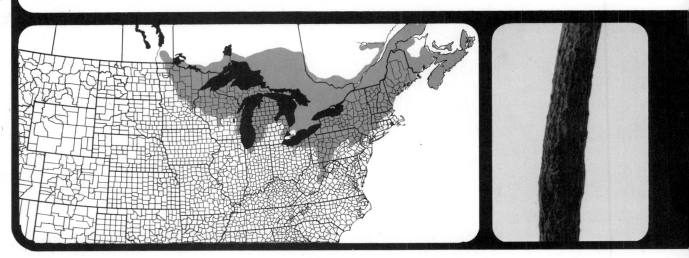

Lyonia ligustrina

FORM: obovoid
Size: **mid-height shrub** - from 2 to 4 m (6 to 12 ft)
Spread: **wide** - 4 to 6 m (12 to 20 ft), up to twice the height
Mass: **open**

BRANCHING: single or multiple stems, **erect** and much-branched; **fine** texture
Twig: slender, smooth, somewhat flattened at each node, **green or yellow brown to brown,** often mottled with **black** spots
Bud: small oblong ovoid, 3 mm (⅛ in) long, **2 scales,** bright **red**
Bark: smooth becoming shaggy and **scaly or shallow furrowed, gray**

FOLIAGE: alternate, **simple, obovate** to oblanceolate, minutely toothed or entire; **medium fine** texture
Surface: **glossy,** smooth or tomentose, paler beneath
Color: spring - **light green;** summer - **medium green;** autumn - **orange to red;** winter - **tan brown**
Season: **deciduous** or persistant; emergence - late **May;** drop -

FLOWER: globe-shaped **bells,** 3 mm (⅛ in) wide, in small crowded nodding one-sided terminal clusters, 15 cm (6 in) long
Color: **white**
Season: early through late **June**
Sex: monoecious

FRUIT: small hard 5-celled globular berry-like **capsules,** 3 mm (⅛ in) diameter, tipped with a persistant sytle
Color: green gray to pale **brown**
Season: persist throughout winter, early **September** to late **March**   Human Value: **poisonous leaves**
Wildlife Value: **low;** occasional use by songbirds, small mammals, leaves poisonous to livestock

HABITAT: formation - **swamp, meadow, dune, forest;** region - **Southern;** gradient - **wet;** low alluvial forests, wet meadows,
borders of sluggish streams, lakeshores, bogs and bays, wet depressions, cypress swamp, tidewater edge
Shade Tolerance: **very intolerant**
Flood Tolerance: **very tolerant**

SOIL: Texture: **medium** loams **to fine** sands, fine sandy loams, heavy clays, organic soils, peats, mucks
Drainage: **very poor to moderately poor**
Moisture: **wet to moist**
Reaction: **strongly acid to moderately acid,** pH 4.0 - 6.0

HARDINESS: zone 6a, possibly zone 4b if available from Michigan Nurseries where northernmost wild populations occur
Rate: **medium**
Longevity: **moderately short-lived**

SUSCEPTIBILITY: Physiological: **infrequent**
Disease: **infrequent** - none serious
Insect: **infrequent** - none serious
Wind-Ice: **infrequent**

URBAN TOLERANCE: Pollution:
Lighting: Drought Heat: **resistant**   Mine Spoils:
Salt: **resistant**   Soil Compaction: **resistant**
Root Pattern: **shallow lateral** spreading, forming rhizomes; **difficult to transplant**

SPECIES: Associate: trees - Water/Willow/Pin/Swamp White Oaks, River Birch, Common Baldcypress; shrubs - Hard-
hack Spirea, Red/Black Chokeberries, Virginia Sweetspire, Pinxterbloom/Swamp Azaleas, Common Winterberry
Similar: Staggerbush Lyonia - smaller, evergreen; Fetterbush Lyonia - larger, semi-evergreen
Cultivars: none available

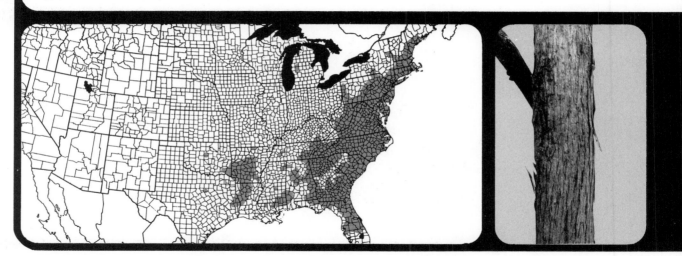

He-huckleberry

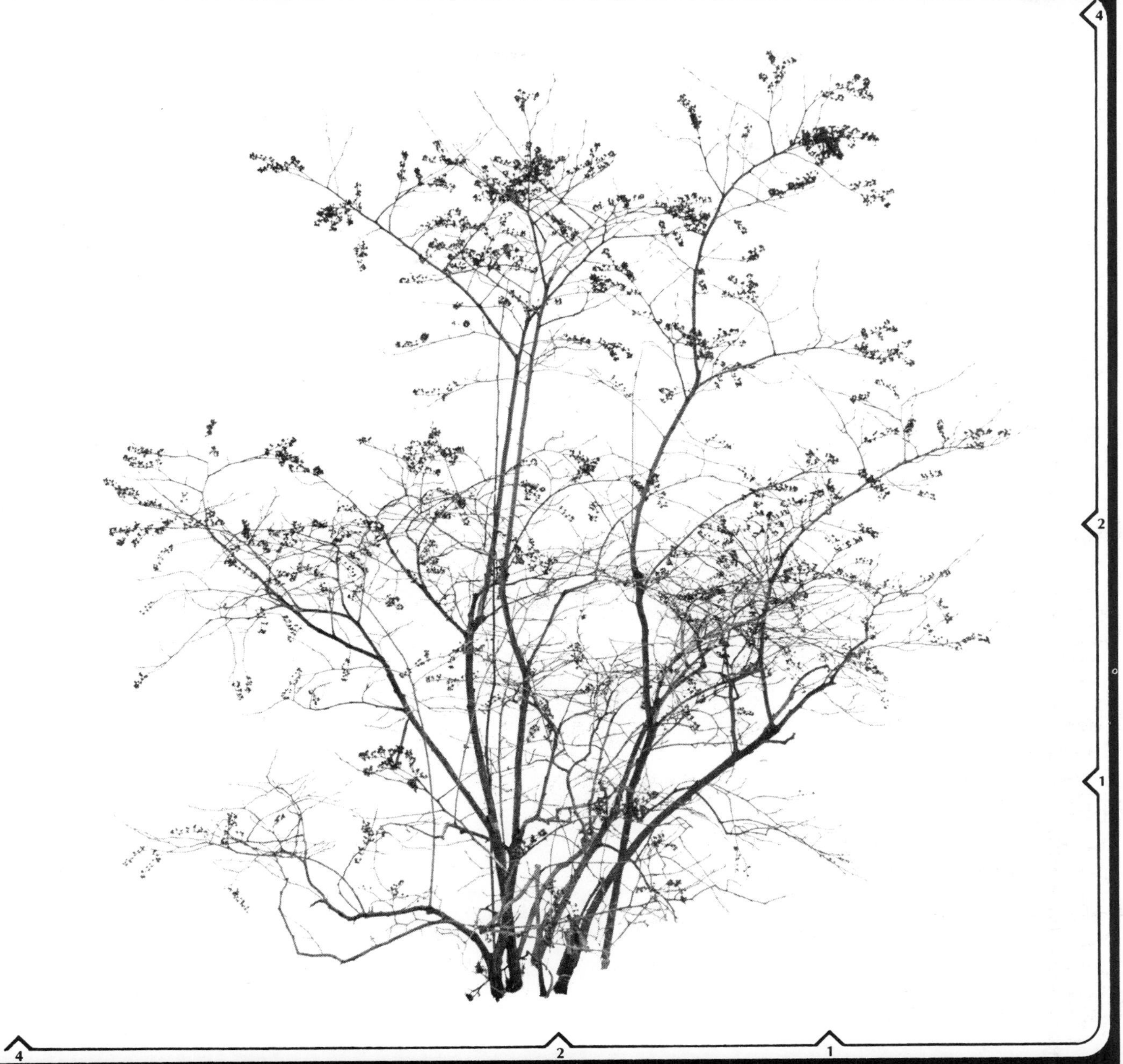

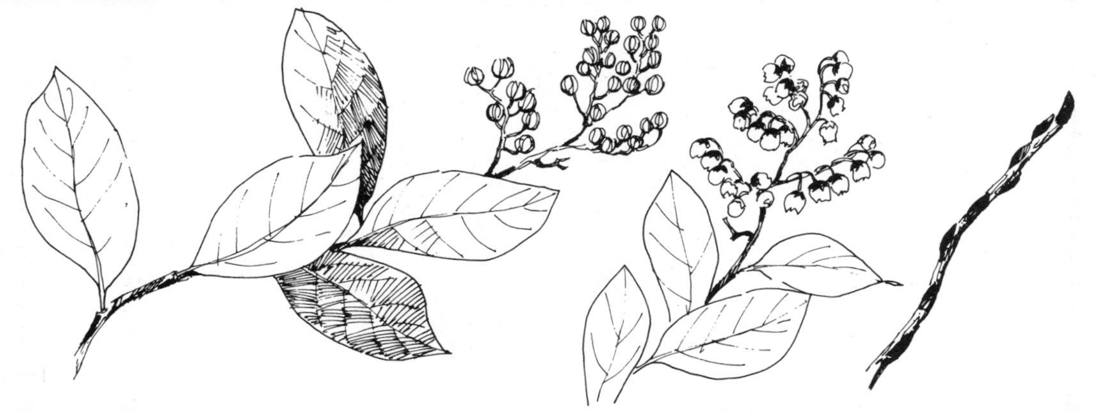

Magnolia virginiana

FORM: irregular, **obovoid**
Size: **large shrub** - from 4 to 6 m (12 to 20 ft) or occasionally to 15 m (50 ft)
Spread: **wide** - 4 to 6 m (12 to 20 ft), typically ½ to ⅔ the height
Mass: loose **open** habit

BRANCHING: 1 to 4 slender mulitple upright trunks, **horizontal picturesque** branches; **medium** texture
Twig: slender, velvety, later smooth with pale lenticels, stipule scars encircle twig, aromatic, bright **green** then red brown
Bud: **large**, long **pointed**, silky **woolly, 2** bud **scales, green to gray**
Bark: **smooth**, becoming broken into very small rectilinear blocks with shallow cracks, pale **gray brown to gray**

FOLIAGE: alternate, **simple, oblong lanceolate,** bluntly rounded at end, entire wavy margin, **aromatic; medium** texture
Surface: **glossy**, smooth, thin leathery, silvery beneath
Color: spring, summer - **dark green;** autumn, winter - **dark green** in South, bronze **purple** until dropped in North
Season: **semi-evergreen** to evergreen in South, tardily deciduous in North; emergence - mid **May**, drop - mid **November**

FLOWER: **large solitary** waxy cup-shaped blooms, 9 to 12 petaled, 5 to 7.5 cm (2 to 3 in) diameter, erect on ends of branches
Color: **white** becoming creamy with age
Season: late **May through** mid **June** and at irregular intervals through August, after leaves, not in great abundance
Sex: monoecious   **Fragrant:** mildly perfumed, lemon scented

FRUIT: erect pickle-like **follicles,** 5 cm (2 in), opening by several small slits, aromatic seeds suspended by silken threads
Color: pink to **red** with scarlet red seeds
Season: mid **September through** late **October**   Human Value: not edible
Wildlife Value: **very low;** limited use by songbirds and small mammals

HABITAT: formation - **bog, spring, dune, swamp, forest;** region - **Southern;** gradient - **wet;** boggy wooded stream courses,
cypress swamps, wet flatwoods, alluvial forests, pocosins, bay forests, springs, seeps, bogs, rich hummocks
Shade Tolerance: **tolerant**
Flood Tolerance: **very tolerant**

SOIL: Texture: **medium** loams **to fine** sands, fine sandy loams, heavy clays, organic soils, peats, mucks
Drainage: **very poor to moderately poor**
Moisture: **wet to moist**
Reaction: **moderately acid to slightly acid,** pH 5.0 - 6.5

HARDINESS: **zone 6a,** sheltered locatons in zone 5b
Rate: **medium**
Longevity: **moderately short-lived**

SUSCEPTIBILITY: Physiological: **frequent** - winter damage browns leaves
Disease: **infrequent** - basically trouble free, black mildew, leaf spots, Nectria canker
Insect: **infrequent** - scales can be bothersome
Wind-Ice: **infrequent**

URBAN TOLERANCE: Pollution:
Lighting: **resistant**   Drought Heat: **sensitive**   Mine Spoils:
Salt: **resistant**   Soil Compaction: **resistant**
Root Pattern: fibrous, **deep** coarse **laterals; difficult to transplant,** slow to re-establish

SPECIES: Associate: trees - Willow/Water/Swamp White Oaks, American Sweetgum, Black Tupelo, American Holly;
shrubs - American Cyrilla, Red Bay, Swamp Privet, Possumhaw, Swamp Rose, Coast Leucothoe, Red Chokeberry
Similar: Umbrella Magnolia - small tree, deciduous; Star/Saucer Magnolias - Asiatic, deciduous
Cultivars: 'Havener' - flowers large, many petals; 'Mayer' - shrubby; 'Australis' - branches hairy, evergreen

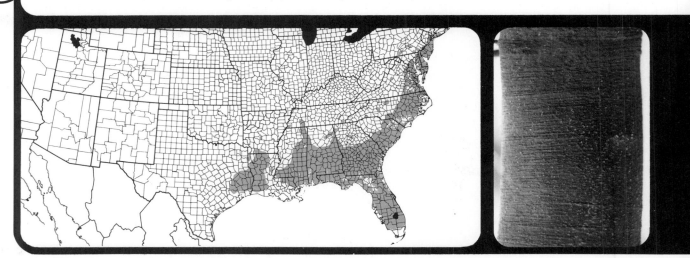

Mahonia aquifolium

FORM: mound
Size: **small shrub** - from 1 to 2 m (3 to 6 ft)
Spread: **very narrow** - from 1 to 2 m (3 to 6 ft), forming broad colonies with age in favorable climates
Mass: **dense**

BRANCHING: stout multiple stems, stiffly **erect** with limited lateral branching; **medium** texture
Twig: smooth, tinged with **purple**
Bud: small ovoid
Bark: numerous **shallow** vertical crack-like **furrows, gray with** bright **yellow brown** fissures

FOLIAGE: alternate, **pinnately compound,** 5 to 9 leaflets, **ovate to oblong ovate,** margin **armed** with spiny teeth; **medium fine**
Surface: **glossy,** smooth, stiff and leathery
Color: spring - bright **yellow green, red green or purple;** summer - **dark green;** autumn, winter - **dark green or purplish** bronze
Season: broadleaf **evergreen**

FLOWER: dense erect pyramidal terminal clusters hug stems, small **bell**-shaped blossoms
Color: golden **yellow**
Season: late **April through** mid May
Sex: monoecious   **Fragrant:** spicy scented

FRUIT: pea-size elliptic **berry,** 8 mm (⅓ in) diameter, in dense grape-like clusters
Color: bloomy **blue,** weathering to **black**
Season: early **August through** late September   Human Value: not edible
Wildlife Value: **high;** relished by upland gamebirds, songbirds, large and small mammals, hoofed browsers graze foliage

HABITAT: formation - **forest;** region - **Western;** gradient - **mesic, mesic-dry;** rich deep coniferous forest, open rocky woods

Shade Tolerance: **very tolerant**
Flood Tolerance: **intolerant**

SOIL: Texture: **moderately coarse to moderately fine;** gravelly or sandy loams, medium loams, silt loams; poor in clay
Drainage: **moderately well to well**
Moisture: **moist to average**
Reaction: **moderately acid to** circumneutral, tolerates **alkaline,** pH 5.0 - 8.5

HARDINESS: zone 5a
Rate: **slow,** 0.6 to 1 m (2 to 3 ft) in 3 to 5 year period
Longevity: **short-lived**

SUSCEPTIBILITY: Physiological: **frequent** - often severe leaf scorch, spire spot
Disease: **infrequent** - leaf rusts, leaf spots; none serious
Insect: **infrequent** - barberry aphid, scale, whitefly; none serious
Wind-Ice: **frequent** - avoid hot dry wind exposure; protect from winter sun, wind

URBAN TOLERANCE: Pollution: **sensitive** - HFI; **intermediate** - 0₃
Lighting: Drought Heat: **sensitive**   Mine Spoils:
Salt: **resistant**   Soil Compaction: **intermediate**
Root Pattern: fibrous, **stoloniferous, shallow lateral,** suckering; **transplants well,** slow to re-establish

SPECIES: Associate: trees - Limber/Ponderosa/Bristlecone Pines, Common Douglasfir, Quaking Aspen, Englemann
        Spruce, Subalpine Fir; shrubs - Creeping Juniper, White Spirea, Grouse Whortleberry, Boxwood Myrtle, Bunchberry
Similar: Leatherleaf Mahonia - taller, Southern; Creeping Mahonia - low carpet, Western; 'Mohoberberis' - simple leaves
Cultivars: 'Compactum' - compact; 'Undulata' - wavy foliage; 'Atropurpureum' - purple in winter; 'Moseri' - pale green

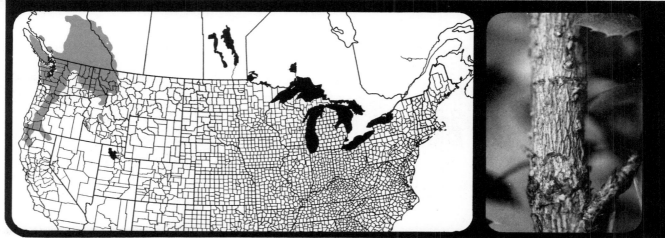

Myrica pensylvanica

FORM: mound
Size: **mid-height shrub** - from 2 to 4 m (6 to 12 ft)
Spread: **intermediate** - 2 to 4 m (6 to 12 ft), commonly broader than tall
Mass: **moderate**

BRANCHING: solitary or few stems branched low to ground, **picturesque horizontal to ascending** habit; **medium** texture
Twig: moderately slender, **velvety, resin** dotted, **reddish or green brown to gray; armed** with short deformed spur branches
Bud: small globular, 3 to 4 mm (⅙ to ⅛ in), with tiny **resinous** glands, **clustered, white**
Bark: **smooth** conspicuous dot-like lenticels, old stems with shallow longitudinal cracks, **gray to gray brown**

FOLIAGE: alternate, crowded, **simple, oblanceolate,** shallowly toothed near tip, **aromatic** when bruised; **medium fine**
Surface: **glossy,** smooth, resin dotted beneath
Color: spring - bright **medium green;** summer and autumn - **dark green;** winter - **tan brown**
Season: **persistant;** emergence - mid **May,** drop - many dried leaves remaining through winter until late **March**

FLOWER: small **catkins,** not showy
Color: **green** with reddish tinge
Season: late **March through** early or mid **April,** before leaves
Sex: **dioecious,** sometimes monoecious

FRUIT: small globular waxy-coated **berry,** 4 mm (⅙ in) diameter, aromatic, in clusters on old wood below leafy tips
Color: **white to gray,** particularly showy after leaves drop　　Human Value: **edible fruits and leaves**
Season: early **September** persisting **through** late **May**
Wildlife Value: **high;** eaten by many winter birds including songbirds, waterfowl, shorebirds, marshbirds

HABITAT: formation - **dune, swamp;** region - **Central;** gradient - lowland **wet;** tidal marshlands, borders of interdunal ponds
and swales, coastal sand flats and dunes, brackish banks, lakeshores, flats, cypress swamps, sluggish stream banks
Shade Tolerance: **intolerant**
Flood Tolerance: **very tolerant**

SOIL: Texture: **coarse to fine;** maritime sands and gravels, sandy loams, fine sands, sandy peats, heavy clays
Drainage: **very poor to excessive**
Moisture: **wet to droughty**
Reaction: **moderately acid to slightly acid,** pH 5.0 - 6.5

HARDINESS: zone 4b
Rate: **medium** from old wood, **fast** from new shoots at base
Longevity: **moderately short-lived**

SUSCEPTIBILITY: Physiological: **occasional** - chlorosis is concern in high pH soils
Disease: **infrequent** - none serious, leaf spots, bayberry yellows virus
Insect: **infrequent** - none serious, red-humped catepillar
Wind-Ice: **infrequent**

URBAN TOLERANCE: Pollution:
Lighting:　　　　　　　　　　　　　　Drought Heat: **resistant**　　　　　　　Mine Spoils: **resistant**
Salt: **resistant**　　　　　　　　　　Soil Compaction: **resistant**
Root Pattern: dense fibrous, **shallow to deep laterals, stoloniferous,** suckers freely, nitrogen-fixing; **transplants well**

SPECIES: Associate: shrubs - Beach Plum, Red/Black Chokeberries, Hardhack Spirea, Sand Cherry, Bear Oak, Sweet-
fern, Marsh Elder, Carolina Rose, Hazel Alder, Eastern Baccharis, Box Sandmyrtle
Similar: Sweetgale - smaller
Cultivars: none available

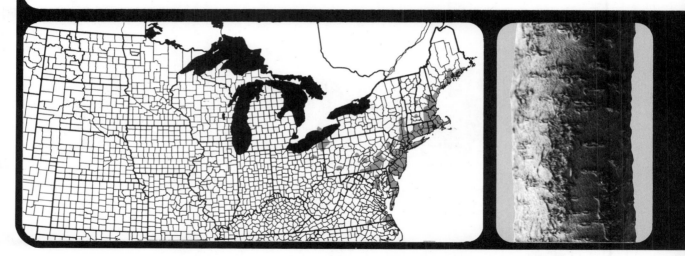

Neviusia alabamensis

FORM: globular
Size: **small shrub** - from 1 to 2 m (3 to 6 ft)
Spread: **narrow** - 1 to 2 m (3 to 6 ft), equal to height
Mass: very **dense** in youth, more open with maturity and on exposed sites

BRANCHING: erect to **upright spreading** stems, becoming strongly arching with advanced age; **medium** texture
Twig: slender, somewhat zigzag, ridges at the nodes, straw-colored golden orange to **yellow brown**
Bud: small ovoid, golden orange brown
Bark: **exfoliating** into thin longitudinal papery shreds, **orange brown** to grayish

FOLIAGE: alternate, **simple, ovate to oblong ovate**, double toothed; **medium fine** texture
Surface: **dull**, somewhat tomentose both sides or nearly hairless
Color: spring - **light green**; summer - **medium green**; autumn - **yellow green**
Season: **deciduous**; emergence - early **May**; drop - early **October**

FLOWER: erect 3 to 8 flowered **spikes**, 2.5 cm (1 in), petals absent with showy feathery stamens, on short lateral branchlets
Color: **white** ✎
Season: early through mid **May**, after leaves
Sex: monoecious

FRUIT: inconspicuous **achenes**, 4 mm (⅙ in) long
Color: **brown**
Season: mid **September through** late **October**   Human Value: not edible
Wildlife Value: **low**; rare plant, little used by wildlife

HABITAT: formation - **moist cliff**; region - **Southern**; gradient - **mesic to mesic-dry**; overhanging shale and limestone cliffs, talus slopes, ridges
Shade Tolerance: **tolerant**
Flood Tolerance: **very intolerant**

SOIL: Texture: **moderately coarse to moderately fine;** shallow soils over limestone or sandstone, sandy and gravelly loams
Drainage: **well to excessive**
Moisture: **dry to droughty**
Reaction: **circumneutral to alkaline,** pH 6.6 - 8.5

HARDINESS: **zone 5a,** in zone 4b with protection
Rate: **medium to slow** on exposed sites
Longevity: **short-lived**

SUSCEPTIBILITY: Physiological: **infrequent**
Disease: **infrequent** - very resistant
Insect: **infrequent** - none serious
Wind-Ice: **infrequent**

URBAN TOLERANCE: Pollution:
Lighting: Drought Heat: **intermediate**   Mine Spoils:
Salt: Soil Compaction: **sensitive**
Root Pattern: fibrous mass, **shallow lateral; easy to transplant,** easy culture

SPECIES: Associate: trees - Red Maple, Blue Ash, White Fringetree, Chestnut Oak; shrubs - Dwarf Chinkapin Oak, blueberry/blackberry/raspberry species, Black Chokeberry, rose species, Mountainlaurel Kalmia
Similar: Meadowsweet spirea; Dwarf Ninebark; Ural False Spirea; Southernplume; Dwarf Fothergilla
Cultivars: none available

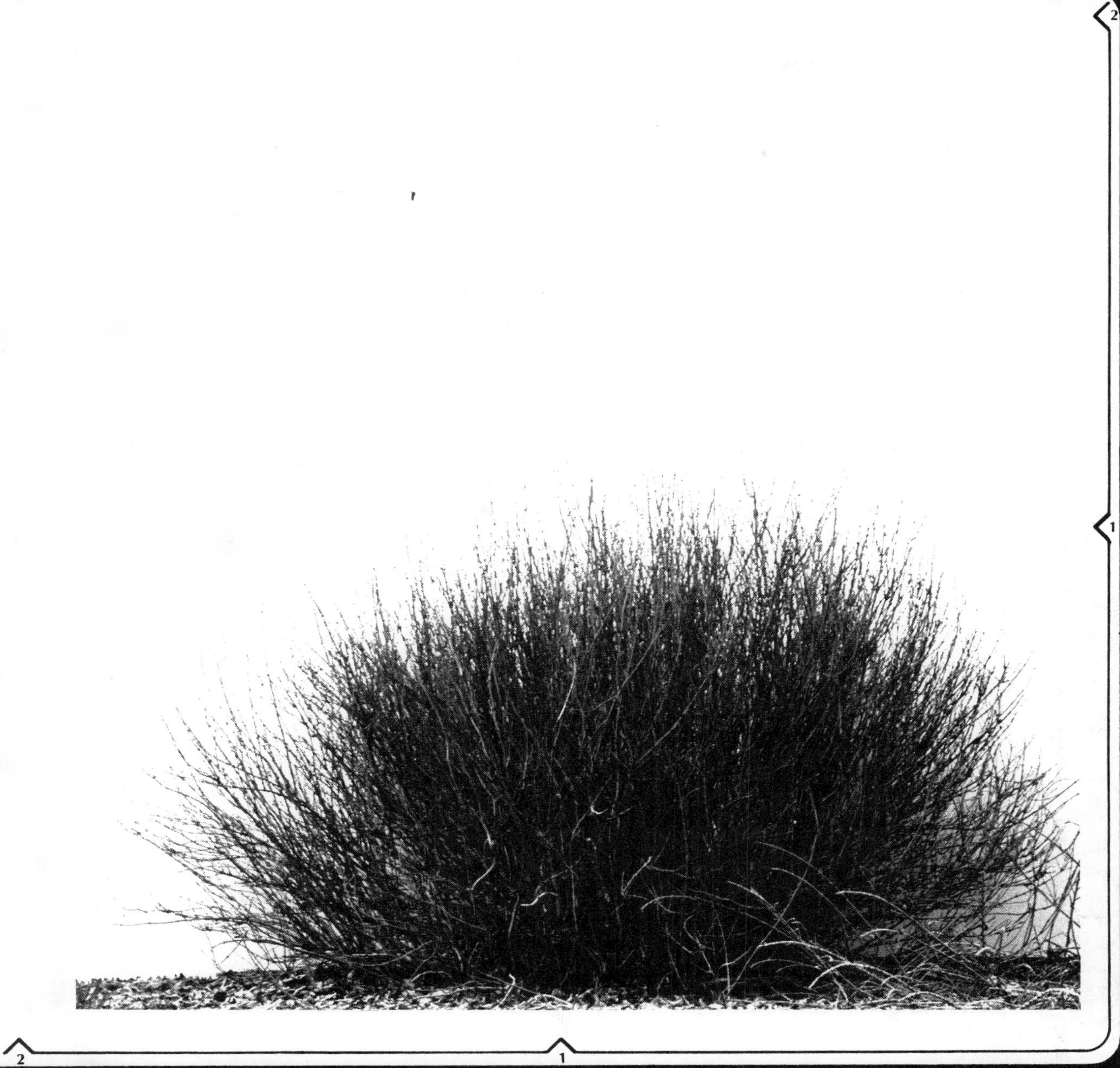
2
1
2
1

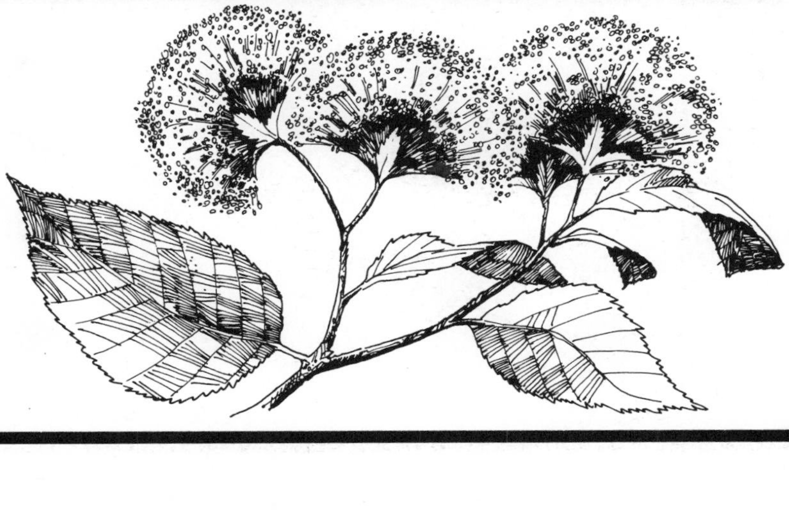

Pachistima canbyi

FORM: mat
Size: **very small shrub** - less than 1 m (3 ft), commonly only to 30 cm (12 in)
Spread: **very narrow** - to 1 m (3 ft), often forming broad colonies with age
Mass: **dense**

BRANCHING: **trailing horizontal** stems and rooting branches with short ascending branchlets; **fine** texture
Twig: smooth, wiry, distinctly **angular** and 4-sided, **red brown**
Bud: very small ovoid, **2 scales**, inconspicuous
Bark: **smooth** becoming thick corky and cross-checked in pattern, **brown**

FOLIAGE: opposite, **simple, linear to oblong linear,** shallow toothed at tip, rolled edges; **fine** texture
Surface: **glossy,** leathery
Color: spring - **light green;** summer - **dark green;** autumn, winter - **dark green to** bronze **purple**
Season: broadleaf **evergreen**

FLOWER: **small clusters,** inconspicuous, in angles of leaves
Color: **green** to brownish
Season: early through mid **May**
Sex: **dioecious**

FRUIT: small leathery 2-valved oblong **capsule,** 3 mm (⅛ in) long
Color: **brown**
Season: early **August through** late **September**   Human Value: not edible
Wildlife Value: **low;** infrequently by songbirds, upland gamebirds

HABITAT: formation - **moist cliff, forest;** region - **Central;** gradient - upland **mesic, mesic-dry;** shaded limestone cliffs and clay
      banks, steep rocky wooded slopes, talus slopes
Shade Tolerance: **tolerant**
Flood Tolerance: **intolerant**

SOIL: Texture: **moderately coarse to moderately fine;** shallow soils over limestone or sandstone, sandy or gravelly loams
Drainage: **moderately well to excessive**
Moisture: **moist to average**
Reaction: **strongly acid to moderately acid,** pH 4.5 - 6.0

HARDINESS: zone 4b
Rate: **slow**
Longevity: **short-lived**

SUSCEPTIBILITY: Physiological: **occasional** - leaf scorch
Disease: **infrequent** - leaf spot; not serious
Insect: **infrequent** - scale can be bothersome
Wind-Ice: **frequent** - protect from winter sun, wind

URBAN TOLERANCE: Pollution:
Lighting: Drought Heat: **sensitive**   Mine Spoils:
Salt: Soil Compaction: **sensitive**
Root Pattern: finely fibrous, creeping rooting branches, **stoloniferous, shallow lateral; transplants well**

SPECIES: Associate: vines - Virginia Creeper, Common Dutchmanspipe; herbs - Alleghany Wild Onion, Glaucous
      Stonecrop, Rocktwist Draba, Moss Pink, Walking Fern, Fragile Rockbrake, Black Spleenwort
Similar: Box Sandmyrtle - taller, shreddy bark; Alpine Azalea - leaves without teeth; Box Huckleberry
Cultivars: none available

Philadelphus grandiflorus

FORM: **obovoid** to globular
Size: **mid-height shrub** - from 2 to 4 m (6 to 12 ft)
Spread: **intermediate** - 2 to 4 m (6 to 12 ft), commonly ⅔ or equal to height
Mass: **dense**

BRANCHING: **stiff erect** multiple stems with **upright spreading** branches, **arching** with age; **coarse** texture
Twig: slender, smooth, leaf scars connected by linear **ridges**, straw-colored **yellow brown or** orange **brown**
Bud: small ovoid, **2 scales**
Bark: older stems **exfoliating** into long fibrous longitudinal papery shreds, **orange brown**, old stems **gray brown**

FOLIAGE: opposite, **simple, ovate**, margin nearly entire or with few widely spaced teeth; **medium fine** texture
Surface: **dull**, smooth
Color: spring - **light green;** summer - **dark green;** autumn - **dark green to yellow green**
Season: **deciduous;** evergreen - late **May,** drop - mid **October**

FLOWER: **large solitary** or usually in clusters of 3, 4.5 cm (1¾ in) diameter, 4 showy cup-shaped petals
Color: pure **white**
Season: mid to late **June,** after leaves
Sex: monoecious

FRUIT: 4-valved angular top-shaped **capsule,** 9.5 mm (⅜ in) long
Color: tan **brown**
Season: early **August** persisting **through** winter until late **April**   Human Value: not edible
Wildlife Value: **low;** some use by songbirds, upland gamebirds

HABITAT: formation - **forest;** region - **Southern;** gradient - **wet-mesic, mesic, mesic-dry, dry;** moist rocky wooded slopes,
     banks of streams, river bluffs, protected coves
Shade Tolerance: **intolerant**
Flood Tolerance: **intermediate**

SOIL: Texture: **moderately coarse to fine;** gravelly and sandy loams, deep loams, silt loams, clay loams, clays
Drainage: **moderately well to excessive**
Moisture: **moist to droughty**
Reaction: **slightly acid to** circumneutral, tolerates **alkaline,** pH 6.1 - 8.5

HARDINESS: **zone 6a**
Rate: **fast**
Longevity: **moderately short-lived**

SUSCEPTIBILITY: Physiological: **infrequent**
Disease: **infrequent** - Nectria canker, leaf spots, powdery mildews, rust; rarely serious
Insect: **infrequent** - aphids, leaf miner, nematodes; none serious
Wind-Ice: **infrequent**

URBAN TOLERANCE: Pollution: **resistant** - 2-4D; **intermediate** - S0$_2$, 0$_3$
Lighting: Drought Heat: **resistant**   Mine Spoils:
Salt: **intermediate**   Soil Compaction: **intermediate**
Root Pattern: fibrous, **shallow lateral,** inclined to sucker; **transplants easily**

SPECIES: Associate: trees - Cucumber tree/Umbrella Magnolias, American Linden, American Beech, Sugar/Red Maples;
     shrubs - Oakleaf/Smooth Hydrangeas, Bottlebrush Buckeye, Mapleleaf Viburnum, Leatherwood, Brook Euonymus
Similar: Scentless/Sweet (European) Mockoranges; Common Ninebark; Amur Privet - China; honeysuckle species
Cultivars: none available

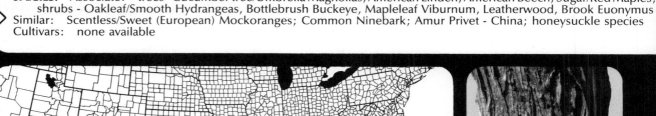
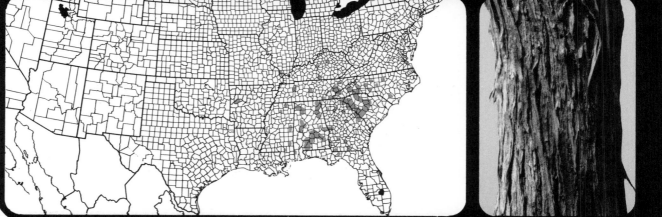

Big Scentless Mockorange

631

Physocarpus opulifolius

FORM: mound
Size: **mid-height shrub** - from 2 to 4 m (6 to 12 ft)
Spread: **intermediate** - 2 to 4 m (6 to 12 ft), typically broader than high
Mass: **dense**

BRANCHING: multiple stems, **upright spreading** with **arching** much-branched habit; **coarse** texture
Twig: slender, smooth, **angular** with 3 distinct linear **ridges** below leaf scars, glossy **red brown**
Bud: small conical, 3 mm (⅛ in), **brown**
Bark: **exfoliating** in thin shreds or large papery sheets, ragged appearance, **brown with orange brown** inner bark

FOLIAGE: alternate, **simple,** ovate, 3 to 5 **palmate lobes,** terminal lobe longer, toothed margin; **medium fine** texture
Surface: **dull,** smooth
Color: spring - bright **yellow green;** summer - **yellow green;** autumn - **yellow to** maroon **purple**
Season: **deciduous;** emergence - early **May,** drop - late **October**

FLOWER: borne in many-flowered **flat-topped** clusters, 2.5 to 5 cm (1 to 2 in) across, each flower 5-petaled, 8 mm (⅓ in)
Color: **white** or with pinkish tinge
Season: late **May through** early **June,** after leaves
Sex: monoecious   **Fragrant:** strongly pungent, unpleasant

FRUIT: small papery 4-parted bladder-like inflated **capsules,** 6 mm (¼ in) diameter, in dense umbrella-like clusters
Color: bright **red** or pinkish at first, **turning brown**
Season: early **July** persisting **through** winter until late **March**   Human Value: not edible
Wildlife Value: **intermediate;** waterfowl, marshbirds, shorebirds, upland gamebirds, small mammals

HABITAT: formation - **bog, spring, dune, cliff, forest;** region - **Northern, Central;** gradient - **wet, wet-mesic, mesic-dry;** rocky or
sandy creek banks, sluggish streams, pond and lakeshore, seepage areas, bogs, moist limestone cliffs
Shade Tolerance: **intolerant**
Flood Tolerance: **very tolerant**

SOIL: Texture: **moderately coarse** gravelly loams, medium loams, **to fine** sandy loams, silt loams, clay loams, clays
Drainage: **very poor to excessive**
Moisture: **wet to droughty**
Reaction: **slightly acid to** circumneutral, tolerates **alkaline,** pH 6.1 - 8.5

HARDINESS: zone 2
Rate: **fast**
Longevity: **moderately short-lived**

SUSCEPTIBILITY: Physiological: **occasional** - iron chlorosis
Disease: **infrequent** - none serious
Insect: **infrequent** - none serious
Wind-Ice: **infrequent**

URBAN TOLERANCE: Pollution:
Lighting: Drought Heat: **resistant**   Mine Spoils:
Salt: **intermediate**   Soil Compaction: **resistant**
Root Pattern: fibrous, **shallow lateral; transplants easily,** easy culture

SPECIES: Associate: trees - Common Chokecherry, Smooth Sumac, Common Hoptree; shrubs - Kalm St.Johnswort,
Russet Buffaloberry, Dwarf Bushhoneysuckle, Lowbush Blueberry, Common Snowberry, Silky Dogwood
Similar: mockorange/privet/honeysuckle species; Vanhoutte Spirea; Common Pearlbush - Asiatic
Cultivars: 'Aureus', 'Luteus' - new leaves yellow, yellow green; 'Nanus', intermedius - dwarf forms with smaller leaves

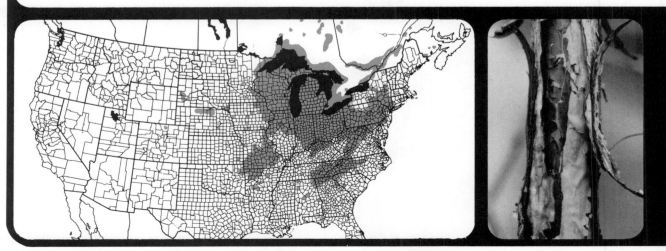

Pieris floribunda

Form: globular or **mound**
Size: **small shrub** - from 1 to 2 m (3 to 6 ft)
Spread: **narrow** - 1 to 2 m (3 to 6 ft), typicaly ¾ the height
Mass: **dense**

BRANCHING: stems stiffly erect, branches **ascending to horizontal**; **medium** texture
Twig: covered with stiff **velvety** hairs
Bud: **large** flower buds formed in fall, greenish white
Bark: **smooth** or with very fine bristle-like fibers, gray brown

FOLIAGE: alternate, crowded in dense clusters, **simple**, elliptic to **oblanceolate**, sparsely toothed; **medium fine** texture
Surface: **glossy**, smooth, lighter and glandular-dotted beneath
Color: spring - **reddish green**; summer, autumn - **dark green**; winter - **purplish green**
Season: broadleaf **evergreen**

FLOWER: small waxy urn-shaped **bell**, erect or nodding terminal clusters, 10 cm (4 in), resembles Lily-of-the-Valley
Color: **white**
Season: mid **April through** early **May**
Sex: moneocious   **Fragrant**: very strong

FRUIT: slightly angled globular **capsule**, 13 cm (½ in) long, in dense nodding clusters
Color: **brown**
Season: early **September** persisting **through late April**   Human Value: not edible
Wildlife Value: **low**; occasional use by songbirds, upland gamebirds, small mammals; hoofed browsers graze leaves

HABITAT: formation - **meadow, bald, forest**; region - **Northern, Central;** gradient - **mesic, mesic-dry;** heath balds, mountain
           woods, cool mountain meadow
Shade Tolerance: **very tolerant**
Flood Tolerance: **intolerant**

SOIL: Texture: **moderately coarse** stony, gravelly, and sandy loams **to medium** loams
Drainage: **moderately well to well**
Moisture: **moist to average**
Reaction: demands **strongly acid to moderately acid**, pH 4.5 - 6.0

HARDINESS: zone 5b
Rate: **slow**, 1 to 2 m (3 to 6 ft) in 5 to 8 years
Longevity: **short-lived**

SUSCEPTIBILITY: Physiological: **frequent** - leaf scorch
Disease: **occasional** - Phytophthora dieback, leaf spots
Insect: **occasional** - lace bug, nematodes, two-spotted mite, Florida wax scale
Wind-Ice: **frequent**- shelter from wind, winter sun

URBAN TOLERANCE: Pollution:
Lighting: Drought Heat: **sensitive**   Mine Spoils: **sensitive**
Salt: **intermediate**   Soil Compaction: **sensitive**
Root Pattern: very slow growing **deep** fibers; **difficult to transplant**, difficult culture, move B & B or container grown plant

SPECIES: Associate:

Similar: Japanese Andromeda; Formosa Andromeda - less hardy; Staggerbush Lyonia; Drooping Leucothoe
Cultivars: 'Grandiflora' - very large flower clusters; 'Brower's Beauty' - dense compact form, new foliage yellow green

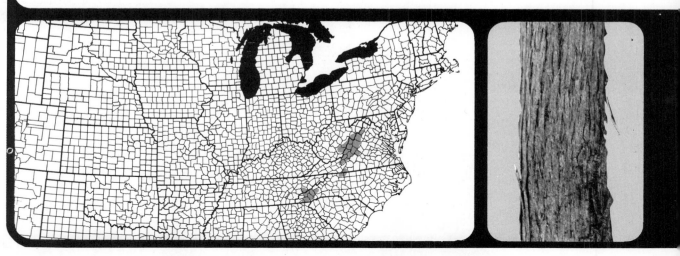

Pinus aristata

FORM: **globular**, in old age growing very **irregular**
Size: **large shrub** - 4 to 6 m (12 to 20 ft), occasionally up to 12 or 15 m (40 to 50 ft) tall
Spread: **wide** - 4 to 6 m (12 to 20 ft)
Mass: dense, **open with age**

BRANCHING: short contorted trunk, upper branches long **ascending**, lower **horizontal**/descending, **picturesque**; medium
Twig: stout, scaly, **gray brown to** coal **black**
Bud: small, 8 mm (⅓ in), **resinous**, brown
Bark: young stems smooth, old trunks **shallow** to deeply **furrowed**, ridges flat with tiny scales, red brown to **black**

FOLIAGE: **simple, acicular**, bundles of 5, stout curved, long tufts at twig ends resembling foxtail, **aromatic**; **medium fine**
Surface: **glossy** on back side, dotted with gummy resin
Color: all seasons - **blue green to gray green**
Season: coniferous **evergreen**

FLOWER: inconspicuous **cone**-like bodies, female 2.5 cm (1 in) long
Color: male - dark orange red, female - dark **purple, yellow**
Season: early through late **June**
Sex: monoecious

FRUIT: short-stalked oblong ovoid cone, 7.5 to 10 cm (3 to 4 in), scales armed with long fragile incurved prickles
Color: **red brown to** dark chocolate **brown**
Season: early **September** persisting **through** winter until late **May**   Human Value: **edible leaves**
Wildlife Value: **very high**; relished by songbirds, upland gamebirds, small mammals; hoofed browsers eat foilage, twigs

HABITAT: formation - **barrens, bald, forest**; region - **Western**; gradient - **mesic-dry, dry**; gravelly mountain slopes, exposed
sites, dry gravelly ridges, rocky foothills
Shade Tolerance: **very intolerant**
Flood Tolerance: **very intolerant**

SOIL: Texture: **coarse to moderately fine**; rock outcroppings, infertile sands, gravels, sandy and gravelly loams
Drainage: **well to excessive**
Moisture: **dry to droughty**
Reaction: **moderately acid to** circumneutral, pH 5.5 - 7.5, tolerates **alkaline** to pH 8.5

HARDINESS: zone 5a
Rate: very **slow**, 16 year old plant only 1.2 m (4 ft) high
Longevity: **long-lived**, maturity reached in 200 to 250 years, attains great age, some over 2,000 years

SUSCEPTIBILITY: Physiological: **occasional** - dieback, tip burn and speckling of leaves in smokey polluted environs
Disease: **occasional** - root rot, stem blister rust, Comandra blister rust, late damping-off, cankers, needle blight, others
Insect: **occasional** - sawflies, pine webworm, pine needle scale, bark beetles, red pine scale, pales weevil, many more
Wind-Ice: **infrequent** - decidedly wind firm

URBAN TOLERANCE: Pollution: **sensitive** - S0₂, O₃, results in tip burn or speckling of leaves
Lighting: **resistant**   Drought Heat: **resistant**   Mine Spoils: **resistant**
Salt: **intermediate**   Soil Compaction: **sensitive**
Root Pattern: deep coarse **taproot**; very **difficult to transplant**

SPECIES: Associate: trees - Limber/Ponderosa/Pinyon Pines, White/Subalpine Firs, Engelmann Spruce, Rocky Mountain
Juniper, Quaking Aspen; shrubs - Common Juniper, Russet Buffaloberry, Mountain Mahagany, Oregongrape
Similar: Mugho Swiss Mountain/Japanese Stone/Japanese Red Pines - European or Asiatic; Waterer Scotch Pine
Cultivars: none available

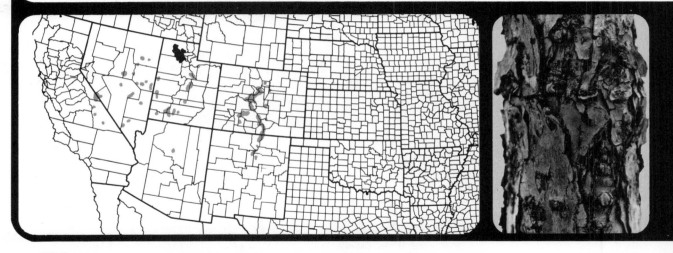

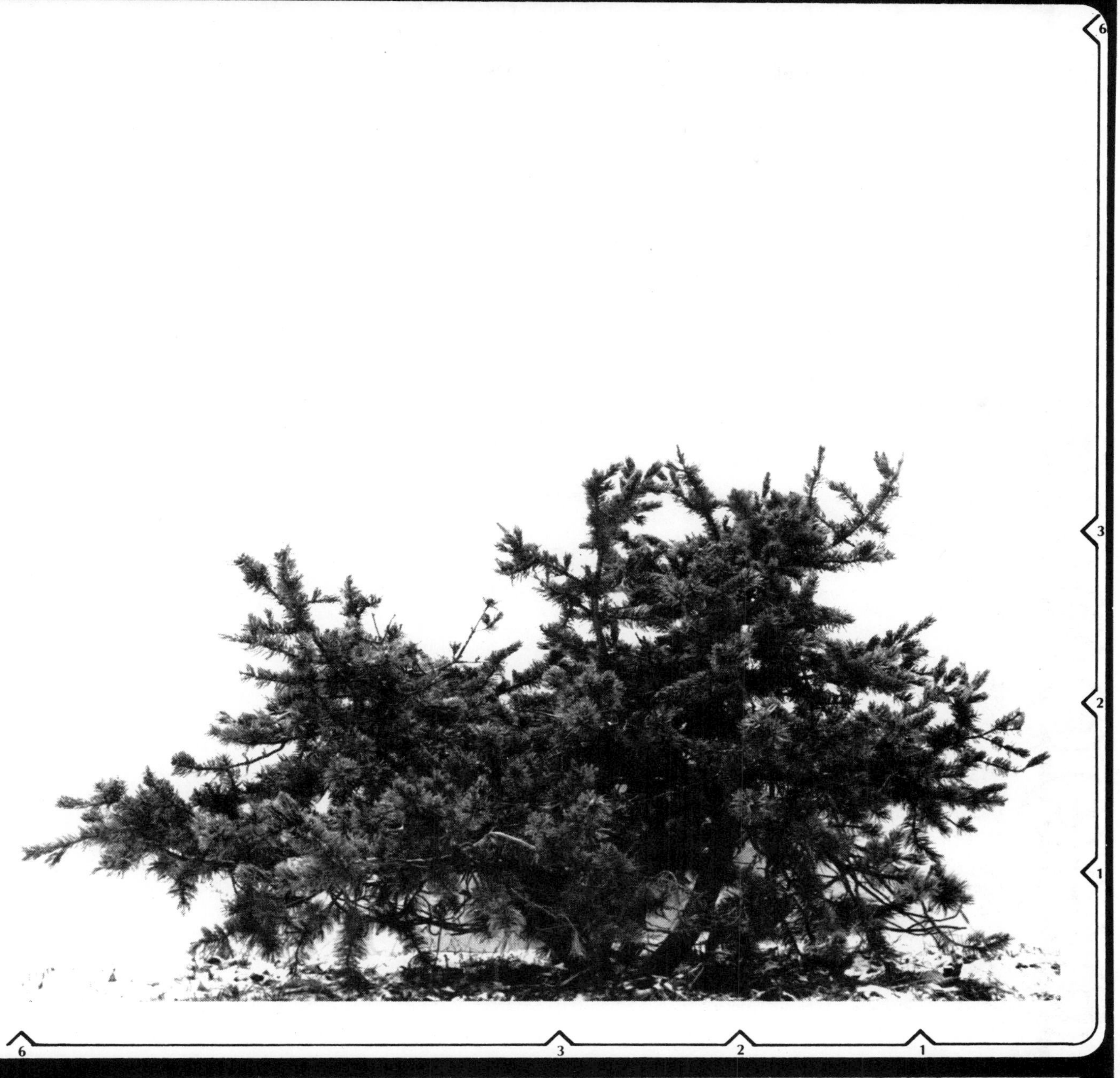
6
3
2
1
6
3
2
1

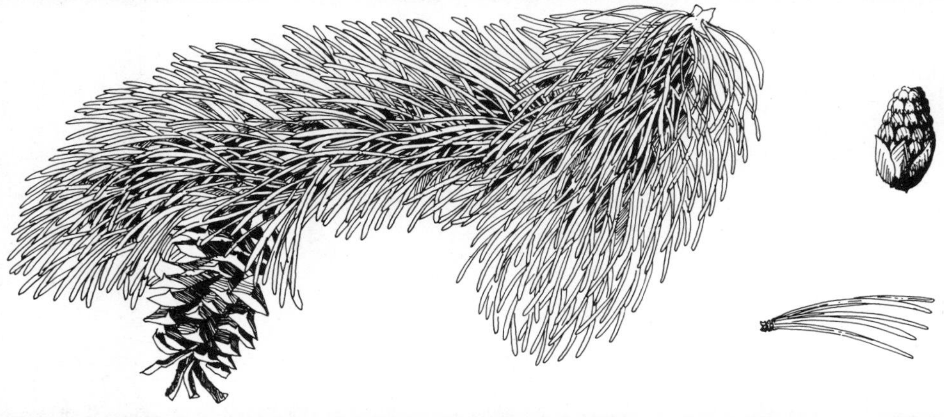

Potentilla fruticosa

FORM: **globular or mound**
Size: **very small shrub** - commonly 1 m (3 ft), up to 1.4 m (4½ ft)
Spread: **very narrow** - up to 1 m (3 ft) plus, equal or 1½ times height
Mass: **dense**

BRANCHING: multi-stemmed, dense branched **upright spreading or arching** habit; **fine** texture
Twig: slender and wispy, smooth, glossy **orange brown** to pale brown with long silky white hairs
Bud: small ovoid, **woolly**, pale **brown**
Bark: **exfoliating** with loose and long wide to thin longitudinal shreds, **gray brown with orange brown** inner bark

FOLIAGE: alternate, **pinnately compound**, 5 to 7 leaflets, **oblanceolate** to elliptic, edges somewhat rolled, entire; **fine**
Surface: **tomentose** with silky hairs both sides
Color: spring - **silvery gray**, summer - **gray green**; autumn - **gray green to yellow brown**
Season: **deciduous**; emergence - mid **May**, drop - mid **November**

FLOWER: **large solitary** or in few-flowered clusters, buttercup-like, 2.5 cm (1 in) diameter, 5 petals
Color: bright **yellow**
Season: early **June** continuing **through** late **September**, after leaves
Sex: monoecious

FRUIT: small dry woolly onion-shaped **capsule** with papery exfoliating appearance
Color: tan **brown**   Human Value: **edible leaves**
Season: early **July** persisting **through** late April
Wildlife Value: **low**; upland gamebirds, songbirds, small mammals; hoofed browsers graze twigs, foliage occasionally

HABITAT: formation - **cliff, prairie, fen, dune, meadow, swamp**; region - **Northern**; gradient - **wet, mesic-dry**, **dry**; moist to dry
rocky areas, dry hill prairies, calcareous cliffs and bluffs, swampy ground, calcareous fens, wet meadows, ledges
Shade Tolerance: **intolerant**
Flood Tolerance: **very tolerant**

SOIL: Texture: **coarse** thin soils over bedrock, rock outcrops, **to fine** organic peats, mucks underlain by mineral soils
Drainage: **poor to excessive**
Moisture: **wet to droughty**
Reaction: **slightly acid to** circumneutral, tolerates **alkaline**, pH 6.1 - 8.5

HARDINESS: zone 2
Rate: **medium**
Longevity: **very short-lived**

SUSCEPTIBILITY: Physiological: **infrequent**
Disease: **infrequent** - leaf spots, downy mildew, powdery mildews; none serious
Insect: **infrequent** - basically pest free
Wind-Ice: **infrequent**

URBAN TOLERANCE: Pollution: **sensitive** - 2-4D, Cl; **intermediate** - O_3
Lighting: Drought Heat: **resistant**   Mine Spoils: **resistant**
Salt: **resistant**   Soil Compaction: **resistant**
Root Pattern: fibrous, **shallow lateral**; **transplants easily**, easy culture

SPECIES: Associate: shrubs - Inland Ceanothus, Bearberry, Kalm St.Johnswort, Common/Creeping Junipers, Sand
Cherry, Leadplant Amorpha
Similar: St.Johnswort species
Cultivars: 'Jackmanni' - larger; 'Veitakii' - white flowers; 'Tangerine' - orange flowers; 'Pyrenaica' - dwarf; many others

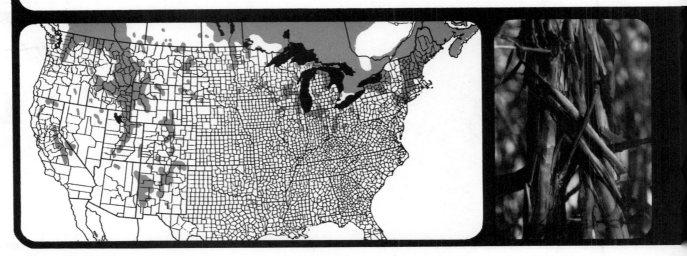

Bush Cinquefoil

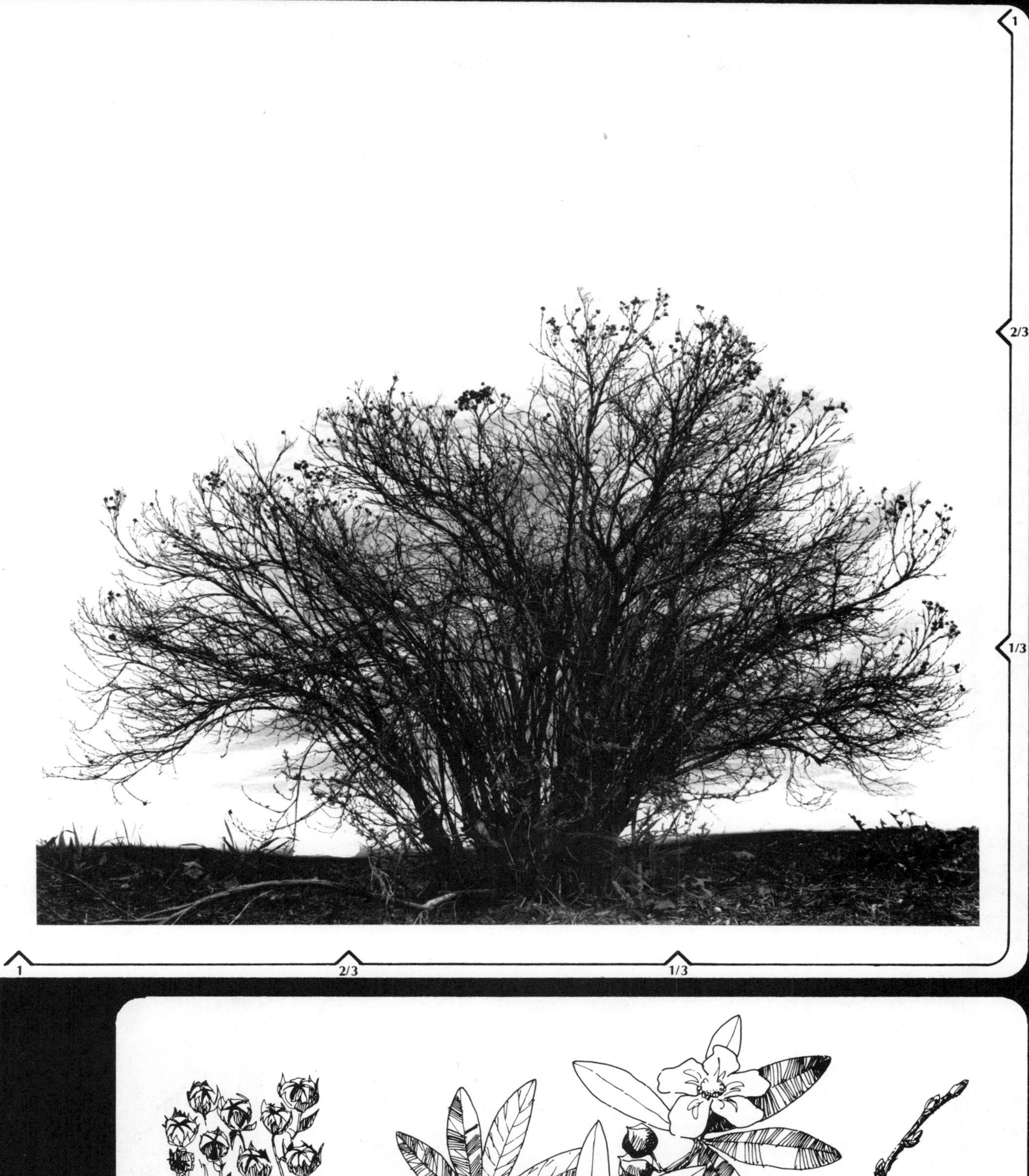

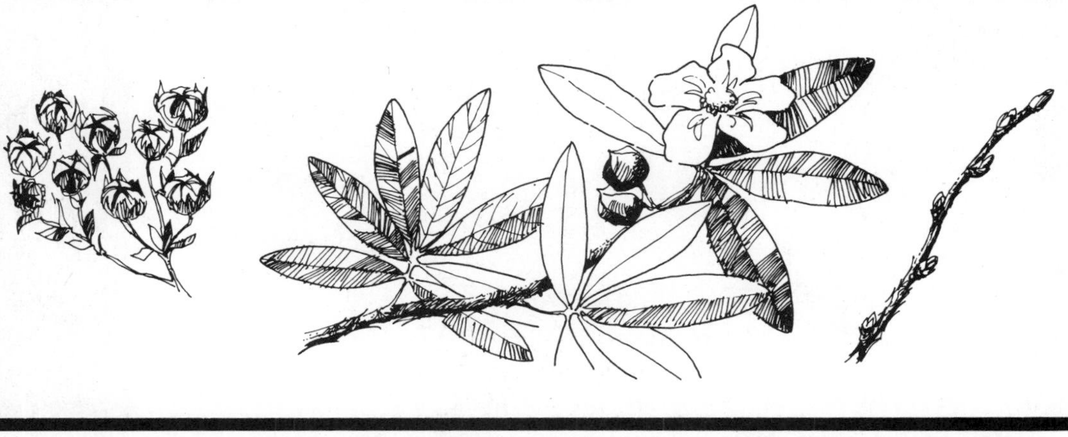

Prunus hortulana

FORM: **globular** rounded crown
Size: **large shrub** - 4 to 6 m (12 to 20 ft), occasionally to 9 m (30 ft)
Spread: **wide** - 4 to 6 m (12 to 20 ft)
Mass: **dense**

BRANCHING: short inclined trunk, thick **ascending** branches, irregular flat-topped crown; **medium** texture
Twig: stout, rigid, **scaly,** flecked with pale lenticels, red brown; **armed** with short sharp modified twigs
Bud: **clustered,** 13 mm (½ in) long, chestnut brown
Bark: **scaly** or with thin tight curls, dark **brown**

FOLIAGE: alternate, **simple, lanceolate to oblong lanceolate**, finely toothed, glandular bumps on petiole; **medium** texture
Surface: **dull** or glossy
Color: spring - **light green**; summer - **medium to dark green**; autumn - golden **yellow**
Season: **deciduous**; emergence - early **May**, drop - late **September**

FLOWER: **small clusters** of 2 to 4, each blossom 15 mm (⅗ in) diameter, profuse
Color: **white**
Season: early through mid **May**, when leaves are ⅓ grown
Sex: monoecious   **Fragrant:** very sweet

FRUIT: glossy globular **berry**, 2.5 cm (1 in) diameter
Color: **red to purple**, sometimes **yellow**
Season: mid **September through** late October   Human Value: **edible fruit**
Wildlife Value: **intermediate**; songbirds, large and small mammals, especially fox

HABITAT: formation - **forest, glade, old field**; region - **Central**; gradient - **wet-mesic, mesic-dry, dry**; rich alluvial forests, low
banks of streams, open woods, edge of woods, thickets, fence rows, open oak woods
Shade Tolerance: **intolerant**
Flood Tolerance: **very intolerant**

SOIL: Texture: **moderately coarse to moderately fine**; loamy sands, sandy loams, silt loams, clay loams
Drainage: **moderately poor to excessive**
Moisture: **moist to droughty**
Reaction: **slightly acid to circumneutral**, pH 6.1 - 7.5

HARDINESS: **zone 5a**
Rate: **fast**
Longevity: **short**, typically 35 to 65 years

SUSCEPTIBILITY: Physiological: **infrequent**
Disease: **occasional** - gum spot, leaf spots, black knot, wood rot; not as susceptible as many cherries
Insect: **occasional** - borers, tent caterpillars
Wind-Ice: **infrequent**

URBAN TOLERANCE: Pollution: **senstive** - HFI, HCI, 2-4D
Lighting: Drought Heat: **resistant**   Mine Spoils: **resistant**
Salt: Soil Compaction: **intermediate**
Root Pattern: **shallow** fibrous; **transplants easily** B & B in early spring or late fall

SPECIES: Associate: trees - Pitch/Shortleaf Pines, Blackjack/Post/Black/Chestnut/Scarlet Oaks, Sourwood, Sassafras;
shrubs - Dwarf Chinkapin Oak, Mountainlaurel Kalmia, Staggerbush Lyonia, Bearberry, Box Sandmyrtle, Sweetfern
Similar: Wildgoose Plum - Southern; American Plum; Beach Plum - smaller
Cultivars: many cultivated varieties; 'Mineri' - thick leaves, fruits later; 'Cumberland'; 'Golden Beauty'; 'Wayland'

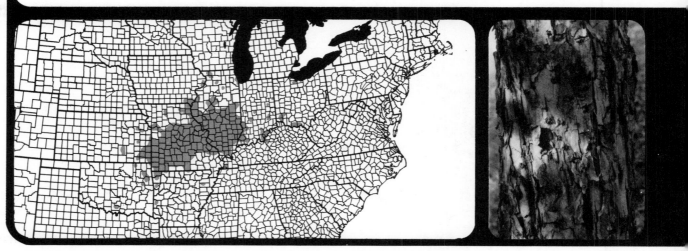

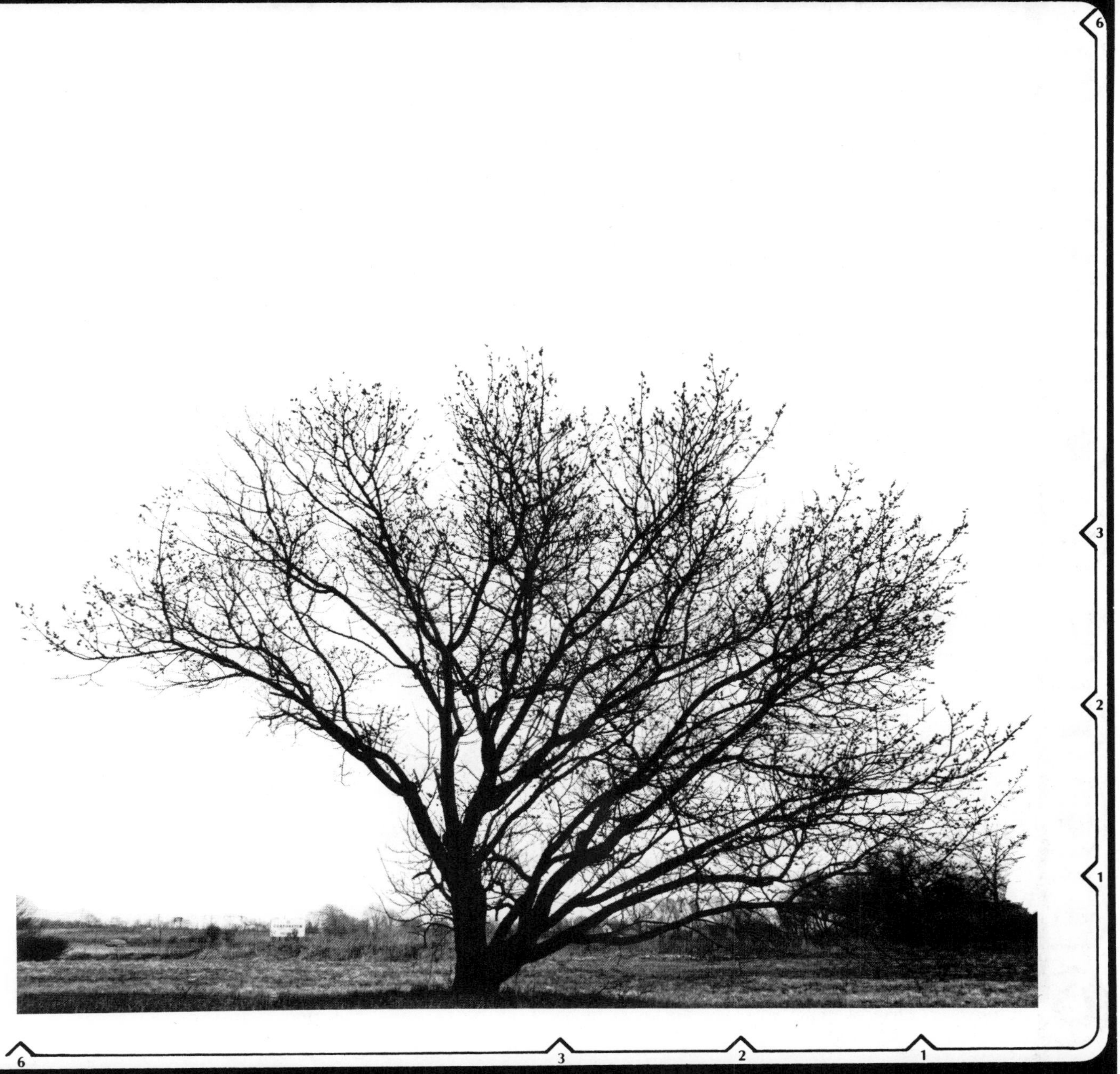
6
3
2
1
6
3
2
1

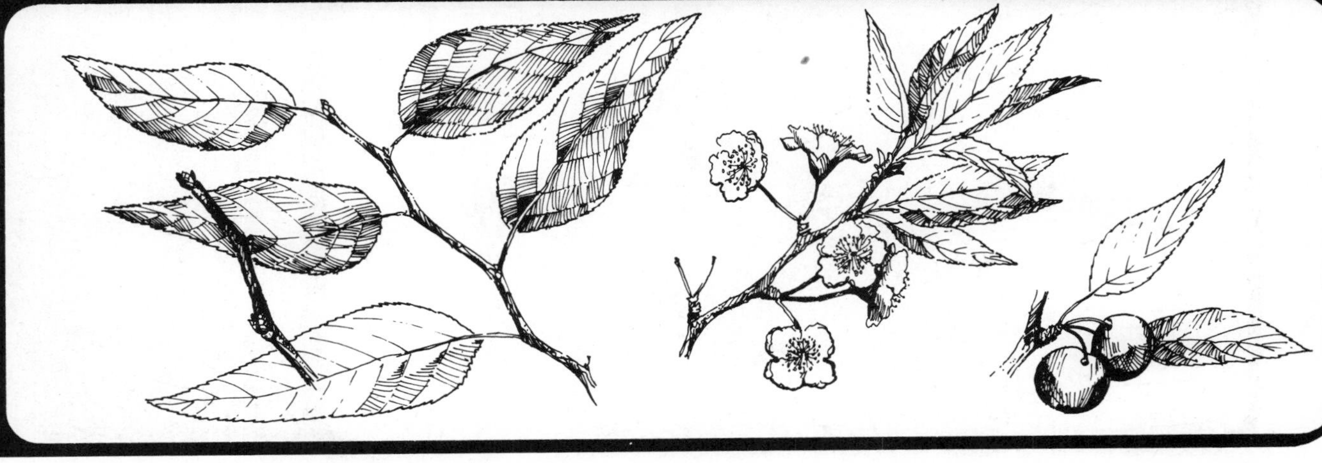

Quercus ilicifolia

FORM: **globular**
Size: **large shrub** - from 4 to 6 m (12 to 20 ft)
Spread: **wide** - 4 to 6 m (12 to 20 ft), forms dense thickets in burned over areas
Mass: **dense**

BRANCHING: contorted trunks divided near ground, **horizontal picturesque** intertwined branches; **medium** texture
Twig: slender, smooth or **velvety, green, green brown to red brown**
Bud: bluntly conical, 3mm (⅛ in) long, **clustered** end buds, dark chestnut **brown**
Bark: smooth becoming **scaly** on older stems, **gray brown** to dark brown

FOLIAGE: alternate, **simple, pinnately lobed**, 3 to 7 (usually 5) bristle-tipped lobes, shallow sinuses; **medium** texture
Surface: **glossy**, thick leathery, dense white pubescence beneath
Color: spring - **red green**; summer - **dark green**; autumn - **yellow**, scarlet **red to purplish**; winter - **tan brown**
Season: **persistant**; emergence - mid **May**, drop - most leaves persisting until mid **April** or later

FLOWER: **catkin,** 10 to 12.5 cm (4 to 5 in) long, cling to twigs through mid summer
Color: **yellow green** or reddish
Season: late **May through** early **June**, when leaves are ½ developed
Sex: monoecious

FRUIT: small **acorn**, 12 mm (½ in) long, in pairs, very abundant; nut broadly ovoid, glossy, striped, half enclosed by cup
Color: light **brown**
Season: early **September** persisting **through** late **January**   Human Value: **edible fruits**
Wildlife Value: **very high**; at top of wildlife food list, songbirds, gamebirds, waterbirds, large and small mammals

HABITAT: formation - **barrens, bald, forest, dune, old field**; region - **Central**; gradient - **dry**; pine barrens, rocky ridges,
    mountaintops, rocky hillsides, openings of woods, sand flats, marine/lake dunes, burned areas, abandoned pastures
Shade Tolerance: **very intolerant**
Flood Tolerance: **very intolerant**

SOIL: Texture: **coarse** infertile sands, rock outcrops, sandy and gravelly loams, sandy plains **to fine** clay loams, clays
Drainage: **well to excessive**
Moisture: **dry to droughty**
Reaction: **strongly acid to circumneutral**, pH 4.0 - 7.5

HARDINESS: zone 5b
Rate: **medium**
Longevity: **long-lived**

SUSCEPTIBILITY: Physiological: **occasional** - chlorosis due to absence of soil nutrients
Disease: **occasional** - leaf blister, leaf spots, powdery mildew, rust, twig blight, anthracnose, basal canker; others
Insect: **occasional** - various galls, scales, oak skeletonizer, two-lined chestnut borer, oak mite, oak lace bug; none serious
Wind-Ice: **infrequent** - decidedly windform

URBAN TOLERANCE: Pollution: **intermediate** - CI; **resistant** - HFI, HCI, 2-4D
Lighting: **intermediate**   Drought Heat: **resistant**   Mine Spoils: **resistant**
Salt: **resistant**   Soil Compaction: **sensitive**
Root Pattern: fibrous **deep laterals, stoloniferous**, freely suckering; **difficult to transplant**

SPECIES: Associate: trees - Pitch/Shortleaf Pines, Blackjack/Chestnut/Scarlet/Black/Post Oaks, Sourwood, Sassafras;
    shrubs - pure stands, Sweetfern, Dwarf Chinkapin Oak, Mountainlaurel Kalmia, Staggerbush Lyonia, Bearberry
Similar: Dwarf Chinkapin Oak; Allegany/Chinese Chestnuts - larger fruit, prickly husk
Cultivars: none available

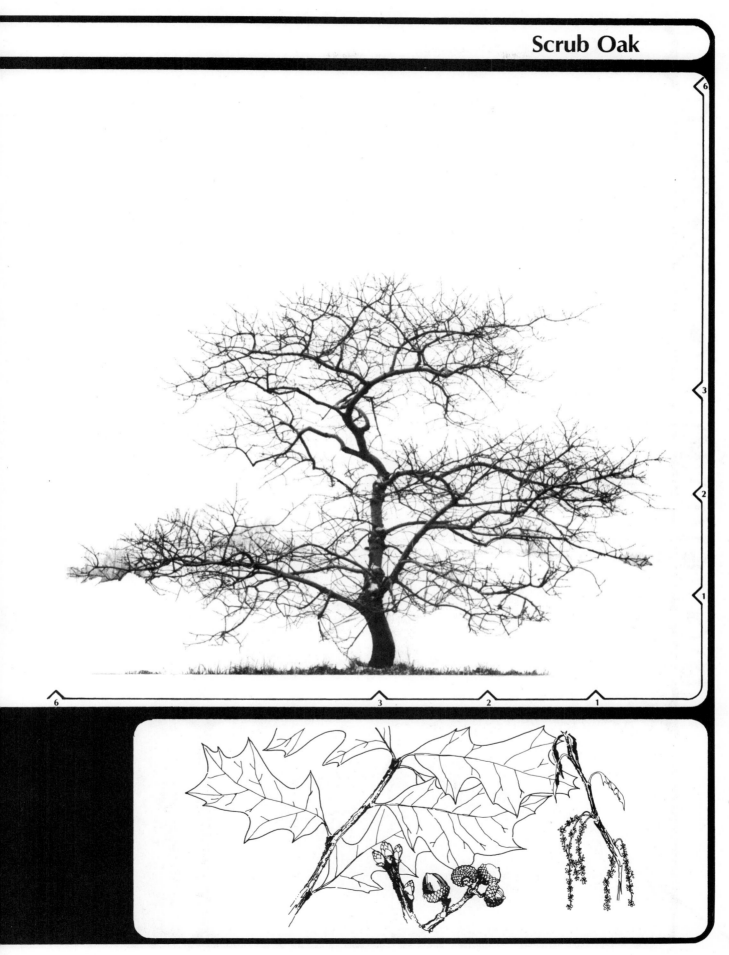

Quercus prinoides

FORM: **globular**
Size: **large shrub** - from 4 to 6 m (12 to 20 ft), commonly to only 4 m (12 ft)
Spread: **wide** - 4 to 6 m (12 to 20 ft)
Mass: **moderate**

BRANCHING: solitary or few clustered trunks, **horizontal picturesque** crooked branches; **medium** texture
Twig: smooth or sparingly hairy, **orange brown** becoming **gray to brown**
Bud: ovoid, blunt rounded at tip, 1.5 to 3 mm (¹⁄₁₆ to ⅛ in), **clustered, brown**
Bark: smooth at first becoming **scaly** with small narrow rectangular flakes, **gray brown**

FOLIAGE: alternate, **simple, ovate to oblong ovate**, coarse rounded sharp saw-like teeth, wavy margin; **medium coarse**
Surface: **glossy,** smooth, white hairs beneath
Color: spring - **red green** or pink, then **light green**; summer - **medium green**; autumn - rich **orange to red**; winter - **tan brown**
Season: **persistant;** emergence - mid **May,** drop - many dried leaves remaining through winter until late **March**

FLOWER: elongated pencil-like **catkins**, male 3 to 5 cm (1 to 2 in) long, in drooping clusters
Color: **yellow green**
Season: mid through late **May**, with leaves
Sex: monoecious

FRUIT: nut-like ovoid **acorn**, 10 to 22 mm (⅜ to ⅞ in) long, ½ covered by knobby cup, with tight scales
Color: light **brown**
Season: early **September through** late **October**
Wildlife Value: **very high**; at top of wildlife food list, songbirds, upland gamebirds, large and small mammals

HABITAT: formation - **forest, barrens, dry cliff, old field**; region - **Central**; gradient - upland **dry**; dry rocky or clayey ridges
    and banks, pasture hilltops, sandy barrens, borders of woods, rocky river bluffs, dry banks of streams, glades
Shade Tolerance: **intolerant**
Flood Tolerance: **very intolerant**

SOIL: Texture: **coarse to fine**; sands and gravels, thin soils over exposed bedrock, sandy loams, heavy loams, clays
Drainage: **well to excessive**
Moisture: **dry to droughty**
Reaction: **moderately acid to** circumneutral, tolerates **alkaline**, pH 5.1 - 8.5

HARDINESS: zone 5b
Rate: **slow**
Longevity: **long-lived**

SUSCEPTIBILITY: Physiological: **occasional** - chlorosis due to lack of soil nutrients
Disease: **occasional** - anthracnose, basal canker, leaf blister, leaf spots, mildews, rust, twig blight; none serious
Insect: **occasional** - oak lace bug, leaf miner, flatheaded borer, two-lined chestnut borer, oak skeletonizer; none serious
Wind-Ice: **infrequent** - decidedly wind firm

URBAN TOLERANCE: Pollution: **intermediate** - CI; **resistant** - HCl, HFI, 2-4D
Lighting: **intermediate**   Drought Heat: **resistant**   Mine Spoils:
Salt: Soil Compaction: **sensitive**
Root Pattern: fibrous, **deep laterals, stoloniferous** suckering habit; **transplants with difficulty**

SPECIES: Associate: trees - Chinkapin/Scarlet/Black Oaks, hawthorn species, Black Locust, Sassafras, Pitch/Shortleaf
    Pines; shrubs - blackberry/blueberry species, Bear Oak, Mountainlaurel Kalmia, Sweetfern, Allegany Chinkapin
Similar: Chinkapin Oak - small tree; Bear Oak; Allegany/Chinese Chestnuts - larger nuts, prickly husk
Cultivars: none available

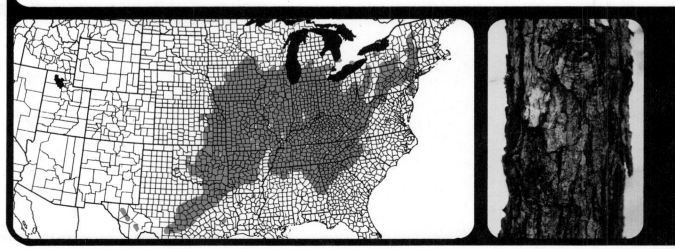

Dwarf Chinkapin Oak

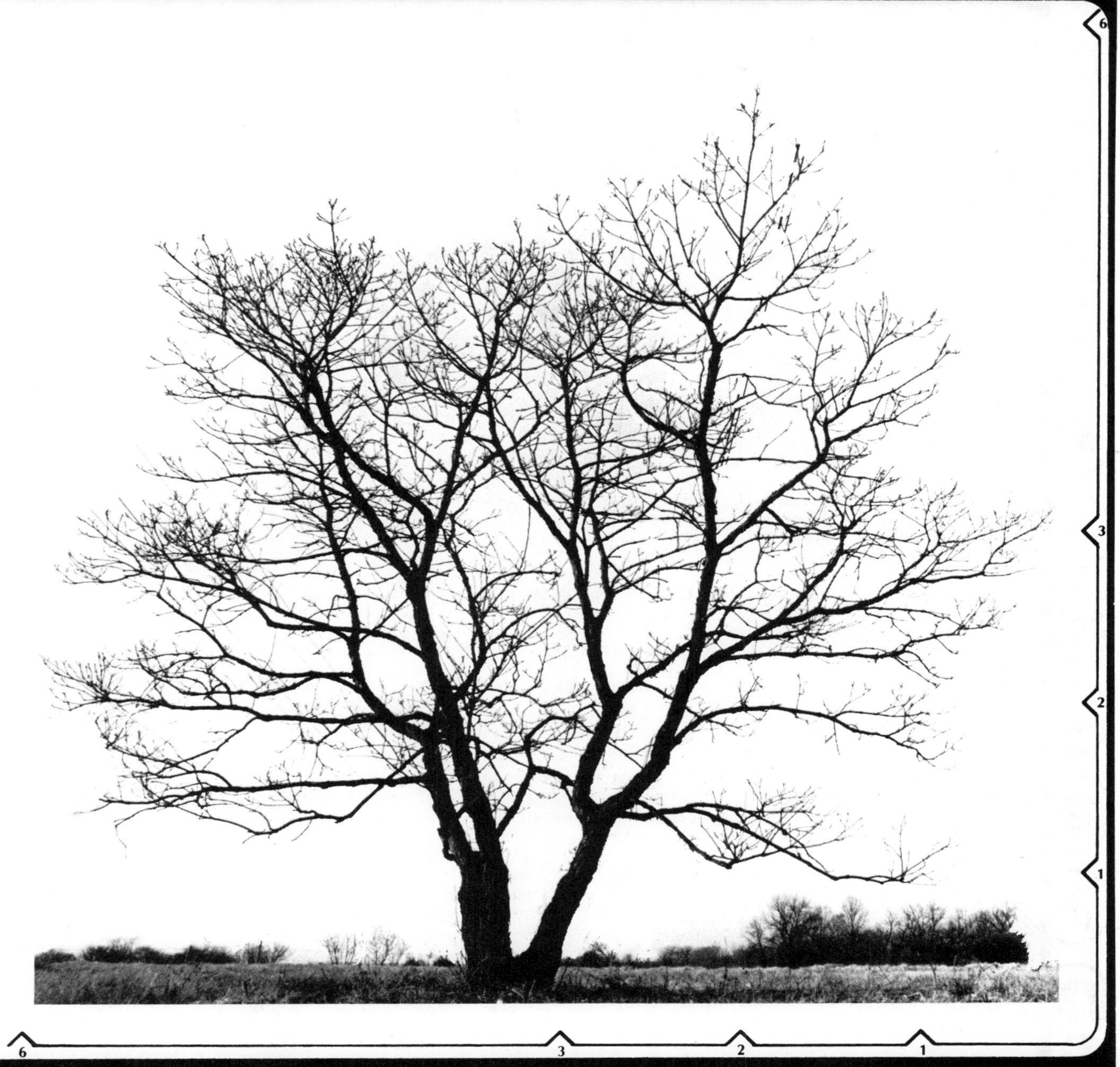

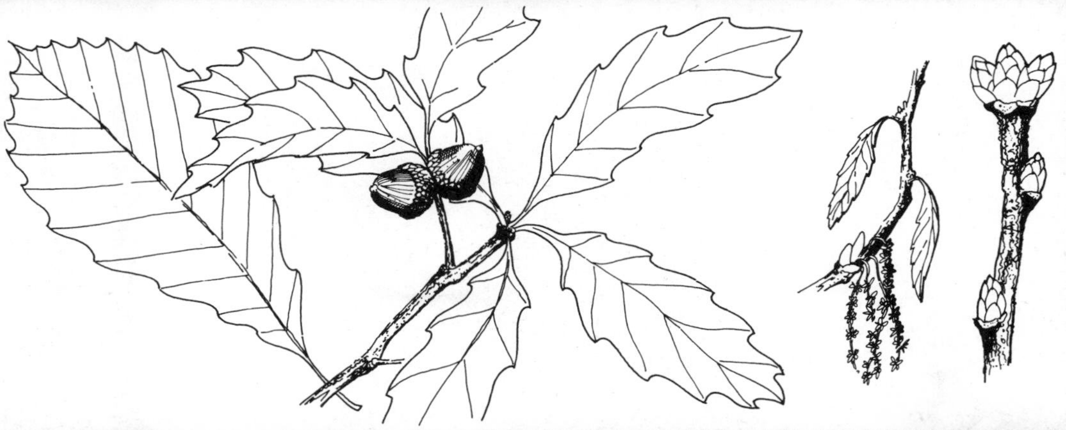

Rhododendron arborescens

FORM: **globular or mound**
Size: **large shrub** - from 4 to 6 m (12 to 20 ft)
Spread: **wide** - 4 to 6 m (12 to 20 ft), typically broader than high
Mass: **moderate**

BRANCHING: solitary or few erect clustered stems, loose **picturesque** irregular **ascending** branches; **medium** texture
Twig: smooth, usually with **powdery bloom, yellow brown to reddish**
Bud: **large clustered, yellow brown to red brown**
Bark: **smooth,** very old stems **scaly** with fine thin flakes, **gray**

FOLIAGE: alternate, crowded at twig tips, **simple, obovate,** entire or hairy fringed, **aromatic** when crushed; **medium fine**
Surface: **glossy,** smooth, lacks hairs beneath unlike other native azaleas
Color: spring - **light green;** summer - **medium green;** autumn - deep **red to** rich **purple**
Season: **deciduous;** emergence - late **May,** drop - mid **October**

FLOWER: funnel-shaped **bell,** 4 to 5 cm (1½ to 2 in) diameter, very long filaments, in **large** terminal **clusters** of 3 to 6
Color: pure **white** or tinged pink, filaments purplish red
Season: **early** through late **June,** after leaves, one of last azaleas to bloom
Sex: monoecious   **Fragrant:** strong fragrance of Heliotrope

FRUIT: dense hairy oblong ovoid **capsule,** 13 mm (½ in) long, opening down from the top
Color: **brown**
Season: early **August** persisting **through** late **March**   Human Value: **all parts poisonous**
Wildlife Value: **low;** minor use by upland gamebirds, songbirds, small mammals; hoofed browsers eat foliage, twigs

HABITAT: formation - **swamp, glade, meadow, forest;** region - **Northern, Central;** gradient - lowland **wet, wet-mesic,** upland
mesic; banks of quick flowing mountain streams, cool mountain meadows, upland rocky woods, swampy ground
Shade Tolerance: **tolerant**
Flood Tolerance: **tolerant**

SOIL: Texture: **moderately coarse to fine;** sandy or stony loams, deep loams, silt loams
Drainage: **poor to well**
Moisture: **wet to moist**
Reaction: demands **strongly acid to moderately acid,** pH 4.5 - 6.0

HARDINESS: **zone 4b,** hardiest native white azalea in North
Rate: **slow**
Longevity: **moderately short-lived**

SUSCEPTIBILITY: Physiological: **frequent** - iron chlorosis, leaf scorch
Disease: **frequent** - Botrytis blotch, bud and twig blight, Botryesphaeria canker, crown rot, dampening off, others
Insect: **frequent** - azalea stem borer, black vine and strawberry weevils, azalea leaf tier, rhododendron aphid, mealy bugs
Wind-Ice: **occasional** - requires winter sun, wind protection

URBAN TOLERANCE: Pollution: **sensitive** - N0$_x$; **intermediate** - HFI, 2-4D, MV, C$_2$H$_6$; **resistant** - CI, PAN
Lighting: **intermediate**   Drought Heat: **sensitive**   Mine Spoils: **sensitive**
Salt: **sensitive**   Soil Compaction: **sensitive**
Root Pattern: finely fibrous, very **shallow laterals; transplants well**

SPECIES: Associate: trees - Fraser Fir, Red Spruce, Quaking Aspen, Mountain Maple, American Mountainash; shrubs -
Large Fothergilla, Catawba Rhododendron, Hobblebush Viburnum, Cinnamon Clethra, Northern Dewberry
Similar: Swamp Azalea - wet to dry habitat; Snow Azalea - Japan, semi-evergreen, gray green leaves
Cultivars: 'Rubescens' - flowers tinged purplish pink, rare; richardsoni - dwarf to 1.5 m (5 ft)

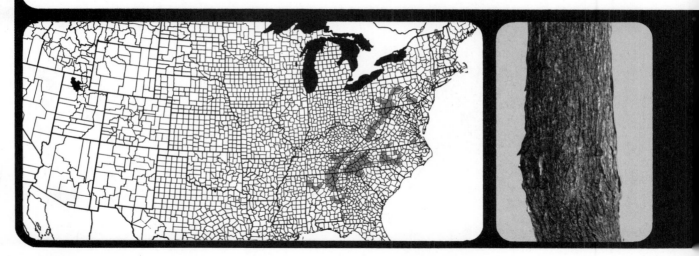

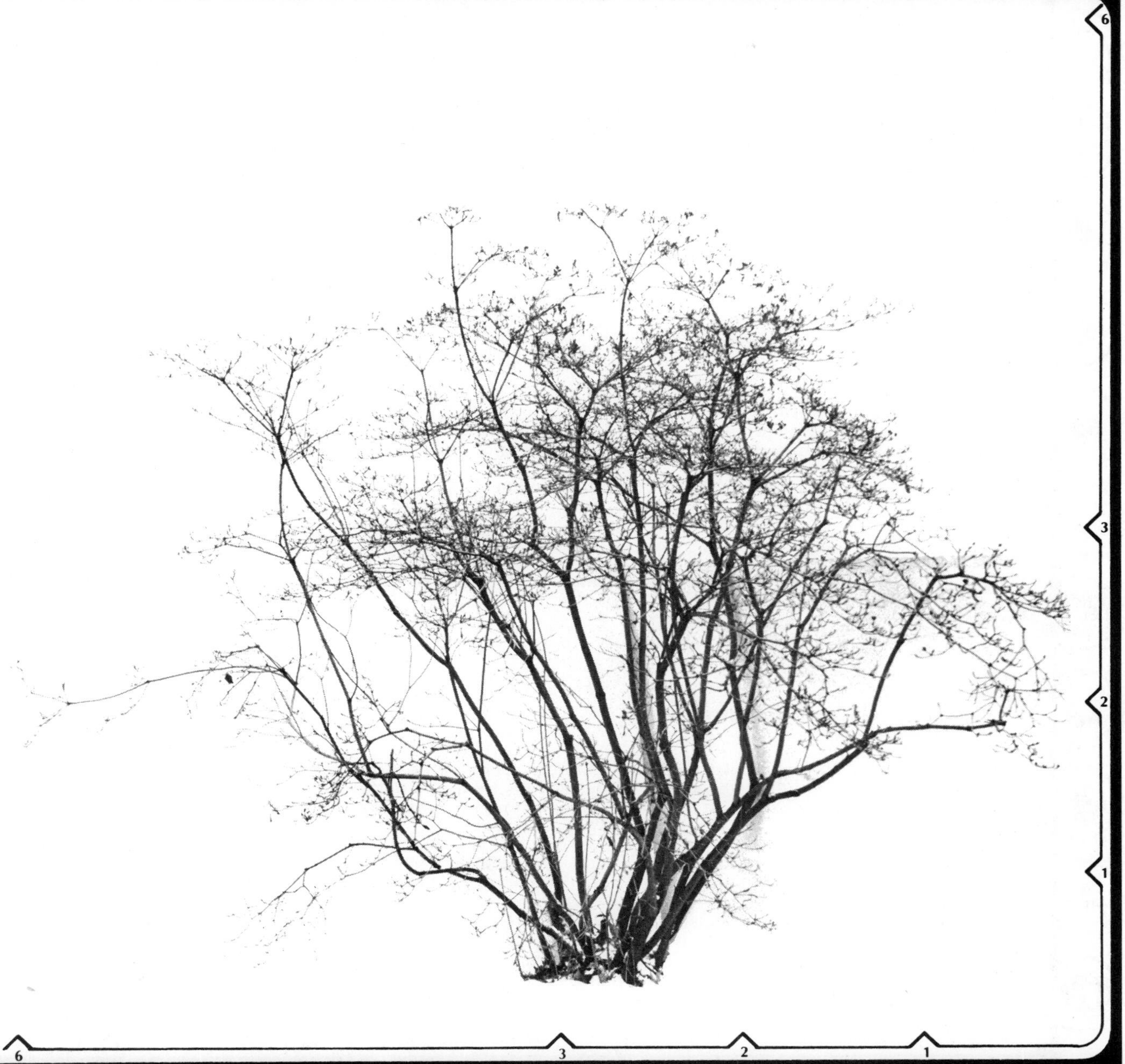
6
3
2
1
6
3
2
1

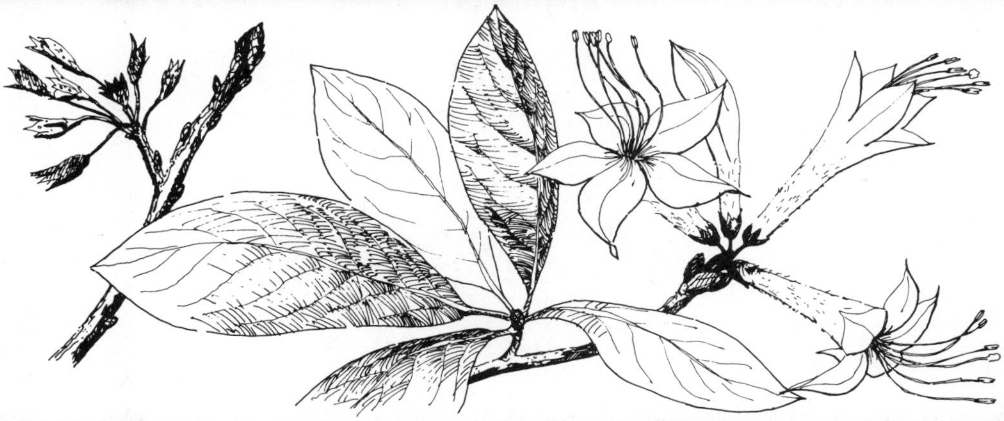

Rhododendron calendulaceum

FORM: **globular**
Size: **mid-height shrub** - 2 to 4 m (6 to 12 ft)
Spread: **intermediate** - 2 to 4 m (6 to 12 ft)
Mass: **moderate** to loosely open

BRANCHING: short clustered trunks with stout rugged **picturesque** irregularly **ascending** branches; **medium** texture
Twig: **velvety, orange brown to gray brown**
Bud: **large,** broad ovoid, **clustered** at branch tips, **green to yellow brown**
Bark: **smooth or** with fine thin **scaly** plates, **gray**

FOLIAGE: alternate, **simple,** broad **elliptic** to narrow obovate, entire and hairy fringed, tip pointed; **medium** texture
Surface: finely tomentose above when young, then **dull,** smooth, pale hairy beneath
Color: spring - **light green;** summer - **medium green;** autumn - **yellow green**
Season: **deciduous;** emergence - mid **May,** drop - mid **October**

FLOWER: funnel-shaped **bell** in large terminal **clusters** of 5 or more, each 5 cm (2 in) in diameter
Color: highly variable; **yellow, orange,** orange red, **and** scarlet **red**
Season: early through mid **June,** about with or shortly after leaves
Sex: monoecious

FRUIT: dry hairy ovoid **capsule,** 19 mm (¾ in) long, splitting down from top like peeled banana
Color: chocolate **brown**
Season: early **August** persisting to late **February**   Human Value: **all parts poisonous**
Wildlife Value: **low;** occasional use by songbirds, upland gamebirds, small mammals; deer browse leaves and twigs

HABITAT: formation - **forest, bald;** region - **Central, Southern;** gradient - upland **mesic-dry, dry;** open oak woods, dry rocky
woodlands, damp slopes, rocky banks of mountain streams, ridges, heath balds, mountain summits
Shade Tolerance: **tolerant**
Flood Tolerance: **intolerant**

SOIL: Texture: **moderately coarse to fine;** sandy or gravelly loams, loams, silt loams, heavy clays
Drainage: **moderately well to well**
Moisture: **moist to** average, tolerates **dry**
Reaction: **moderately acid,** pH 5.1 - 6.0

HARDINESS: **zone 6a**
Rate: medium to **slow**
Longevity: **moderately short-lived**

SUSCEPTIBILITY: Physiological: **frequent** - chlorosis from high pH soils, leaf scorch, dieback
Disease: **frequent** - shoot blight, gray blight, leaf spots, powdery mildew, shoestring root rot, crown rot, many others
Insect: **frequent** - rhododendron tip midge, pitted ambrosia beetle, scales, thrips, rhododendron whitefly, many more
Wind-Ice: **infrequent**

URBAN TOLERANCE: Pollution: **sensitive** N0$_x$; **intermediate** - HFI, 2-4D, C$_2$H$_6$, MV; **resistant** - CI, PAN
Lighting: **intermediate**   Drought Heat: **sensitive**   Mine Spoils: **sensitive**
Salt: **sensitive**   Soil Compaction: **sensitive**
Root Pattern: fibrous, **shallow lateral; transplants well**

SPECIES: Associate: trees - Rosebay Rhododendron, Red/Black/Chestnut/Scarlet Oaks, Sourwood; shrubs - Common
Deerberry, Mapleleaf Viburnum, Mountainlaurel Kalmia, Common Spicebush, Mountain Stewartia, Bear Oak
Similar: Cumberland Azalea - blooms after leaves; Keisk/Chinese Azaleas - Asiatic, yellow blooms; Torch Azalea
Cultivars: 'Aurantcum' - flowers 5 cm (2 in), orange to scarlet; 'Croceum' - flowers 5 cm (2 in), orange; 'Luteum'; 'Roseum'

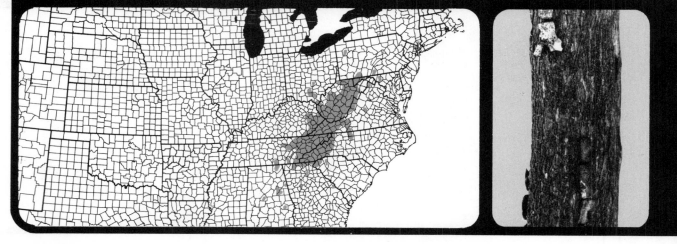

Rhododendron carolinianum

FORM: **globular** or mound
Size: **small shrub** - generally from 1 to 2 m (3 to 6 ft)
Spread: **narrow** - 1 to 2 m (3 to 6 ft), typically equal or greater than height
Mass: **moderate**

BRANCHING: upright stems, **picturesque** irregular **ascending** branches; **medium** texture
Twig: smooth, **gray brown**
Bud: **large, clustered**
Bark: **smooth,** becoming **scaly** with fibrous flakes, **gray**

FOLIAGE: alternate, **simple, elliptic** to narrow elliptic, entire margin, **aromatic** when bruised; **medium** texture
Surface: **dull,** smooth, thick leathery, rusty scales beneath
Color: spring - **light green;** summer and autumn - **dark green;** winter - **dark green, purplish** in North
Season: broadleaf **evergreen**

FLOWER: broad funnel-shaped **bell,** 4 cm (1½ in) diameter, not or slightly spotted, in **large** terminal **clusters** of 5 to 10
Color: pure white to pale blush **pink or** rosy **purple**
Season: mid through late **May,** first rhododendron to bloom, before or with the leaves
Sex: monoecious   **Fragrant:** mildly scented

FRUIT: dry **capsule,** 13 mm (½ in) long, splitting from top and peeling
Color: **brown**
Season: early **August** persisting **through** late **February**   Human Value: **all parts poisonous**
Wildlife Value: **low;** quite limited use by upland gamebirds, songbirds, small mammals; greater use by hoofed browsers

HABITAT: formation - **forest, bald, meadow;** region - **Central;** gradient - **wet-mesic, mesic, mesic-dry;** rocky woodlands,
        mountain summits, cool meadows, heath balds, damp slopes, rocky banks of mountain streams
Shade Tolerance: **very tolerant**
Flood Tolerance: **intermediate**

SOIL: Texture: **moderately coarse to moderately fine;** rocky, gravelly, or sandy loams, shallow loams, silt loams, clay loams
Drainage: **moderately poor to well**
Moisture: **moist to average**
Reaction: demands **strongly acid to** moderately acid, pH 4.5 - 6.0, tolerates **slightly acid** pH to 6.5

HARDINESS: zone 5b
Rate: medium to **slow,** 1 to 1.5 m (3 to 5 ft) over 10 year period
Longevity: **moderately short-lived**

SUSCEPTIBILITY: Physiological: **frequent** - leaf scorch, clorosis from high pH soils, dieback
Disease: **frequent** - gray blight, leaf spots, crown rot, shoestring root rot, powdery mildew, shoot blight, others
Insect: **frequent** - nematodes, rhododendron whitefly, thrips, scales, pitted ambrosia beetle, rhododendron tip midge
Wind-Ice: **frequent** - protect from winter wind and sun

URBAN TOLERANCE: Pollution: **sensitive** - $N0_x$; **intermediate** - 0_3, HFI, C_2H_6, MV, 2-4D; **resistant** - CI, PAN
Lighting: **intermediate**   Drought Heat: **sensitive**   Mine Spoils:
Salt: **sensitive**   Soil Compaction: **sensitive**
Root Pattern: **shallow** fibrous; **transplants well**

SPECIES: Associate: trees - Fraser Fir, Carolina Hemlock, Red Maple, Rosebay Rhododendron; shrubs - Pinxterbloom/
        Flame Azaleas, Mountainlaurel Kalmia, Painted Buckeye, Common Sweetshrub, Common Spicebush
Similar: Catawba Rhododendron - larger leaves; Korean Rhododendron; PJM Rhododendron; Mountainlaurel Kalmia
Cultivars: 'Album' - white flowers, later; 'Luteum' - flowers mimosa yellow; 'Foliatum' - loose habit, spotted flowers

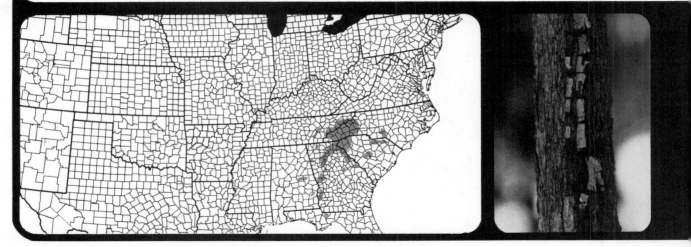

Rhododendron catawbiense

FORM: **globular or mound**
Size: **mid-height shrub** - from 2 to 4 m (6 to 12 ft), rarely to 6 m (20 ft)
Spread: **intermediate** - 2 to 4 m (6 to 12 ft), typically broader than high
Mass: **moderate** foliage to ground, becoming more open in age

BRANCHING: short clustered trunks, stout rugged **picturesque** often leggy irregularly **ascending** branches; **coarse** texture
Twig: smooth or sparingly hairy, **gray brown**
Bud: **large** oval, 13 mm (½ in), terminal bud 19 mm (¾ in), pointed, **clustered, green** to yellow green
Bark: **smooth** with older stems becoming **scaly** to fibrous, **gray**

FOLIAGE: alternate, crowded at twig ends, **simple, elliptic** to oblong, entire, tip blunt bristle-tipped; **medium coarse**
Surface: **glossy,** smooth, thick leathery, pale to whitish beneath
Color: spring - **light green;** summer, autumn and winter - deep **dark green,** yellow green in exposed locations
Season: broadleaf **evergreen**

FLOWER: broad **bell**-shaped, 5 to 6.5 cm (2 to 2½ in) diameter, funnel spotted, in **large** compact terminal **clusters**
Color: rosy lilac to magenta **purple** with green or yellow brown spots inside funnel
Season: mid to late **May or** early **June**
Sex: monoecious

FRUIT: dry hairy oblong ovoid **capsule,** 13 mm (½ in) long, splitting down from the top
Color: dark **brown**
Season: early **August** persisting **through** late **February**   Human Value: **all parts poisonous**
Wildlife Value: **low;** limited use by songbirds, upland gamebirds, small mammals; greater use by hoofed browsers

HABITAT: formation - **cliff, bald, meadow, forest;** region - **Central;** gradient - **mesic, mesic-dry, dry;** rocky mountain slopes, summits, bluffs and cliffs, cool damp slopes, rocky banks of mountain streams, flat rock outcrops, heath balds
Shade Tolerance: **very tolerant**
Flood Tolerance: **intolerant**

SOIL: Texture: **moderately coarse to fine;** thin soils over rock, rocky or sandy loams, rich loams, silt loams, heavy clays
Drainage: **moderately well to well**
Moisture: constantly **moist to average**
Reaction: demands **strongly acid to moderately acid,** pH 4.5 - 6.0

HARDINESS: **zone 5b;** hardy to −30°F, one of hardiest Rhododendron species
Rate: **slow**
Longevity: **moderately short-lived**

SUSCEPTIBILITY: Physiological: **frequent** - leaf scorch, chlorosis in high pH soils
Disease: **frequent** - Botrytis blotch, gray blight, crown rot, shoestring rot, shoot blight, powdery mildew, leaf spots, others
Insect: **frequent** - giant hornet, Japanese beetle, asiatic garden beetle, red-banded leafhopper, azalea leaf miner, many
Wind-Ice: **frequent** - shelter from winter wind and sun

URBAN TOLERANCE: Pollution: **sensitive** - O_3, NO_x; **intermediate** - HFl, C_2H_6, MV, 2-4D; **resistant** - Cl, PAN
Lighting: **intermediate**   Drought Heat: **sensitive**   Mine Spoils: **sensitive**
Salt: **sensitive**   Soil Compaction: **sensitive**
Root Pattern: fine fibrous **shallow** surface roots, never far reaching nor very deep; **transplants well**

SPECIES: Associate: trees - Carolina Hemlock, Fraser Fir, Red Spruce, Red Maple, White Fringetree, Rosebay Rhododendron; shrubs - Black Chokeberry, Mountainlaurel Kalmia, Carolina Rhododendron, Drooping Leucothoe
Similar: Rosebay Rhododendron - taller; Mountainlaurel Kalmia - smaller leaves; Fortune Rhododendron - Asiatic
Cultivars: 'Album' - white flowers; Compactum - less than 1 m (3 ft); 'Roseum Elegans'; 'Nova Zembla'; 'America'; many

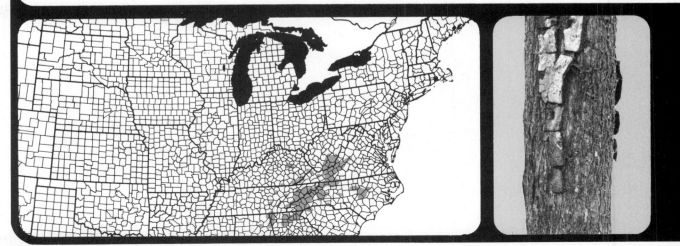

Rhododendron nudiflorum

FORM: **globular**
Size: **mid-height shrub** - 2 to 4 m (6 to 12 ft), but typically only to 3 m (9 ft)
Spread: **intermediate** - 2 to 4 m (6 to 12 ft)
Mass: **moderate**

BRANCHING: stems unbranched below, much-branched above; **horizontal to ascending picturesque** branches; **medium**
Twig: slender, **velvety** becoming smooth, **gray brown**
Bud: **large** oval, pointed, **clustered, red to greenish**
Bark: **smooth** becoming fine **flaky** to fibrous, **gray**

FOLIAGE: alternate, crowded at twig ends, **simple, oblanceolate,** entire and hairy-fringed, **medium fine** texture
Surface: **dull**, smooth, finely hairy beneath
Color: spring - light **red green** to pink, then **light green;** summer - bright **medium green;** autumn - dull **yellow**
Season: **deciduous;** emergence - mid **May,** drop - mid **November**

FLOWER: funnel-shaped **bell,** 4 cm (1½ in) diameter, two-lipped with hairy corolla, in 6 to 12 **large**-flowered **clusters**
Color: light pink or **purplish,** rarely white
Season: late **April through** early **May,** before or with leaves
Sex: monoecious   **Fragrant:** faintly perfumed

FRUIT: dry erect linear oblong 5-celled **capsule,** 19 mm (¾ in) long, splitting and recurving from the top like peeled banana
Color: dark **brown**
Season: early **August** persisting **through** late **March**   Human Value: **all parts poisonous**
Wildlife Value: **low;** minor use by upland gamebirds, songbirds, small mammals

HABITAT: formation - **forest, swamp, cliff;** region - **Central, Southern;** gradient - **wet, wet-mesic, mesic, mesic-dry, dry;** moist to
 dry rocky woods, low swampy areas, overhanging vertical limestone cliffs, rich cove forests
Shade Tolerance: **very tolerant**
Flood Tolerant: **tolerant**

SOIL: Texture: **coarse,** gravelly or sandy loams, thin soils over bedrock **to fine** silt loams, sandy clay loams, sandy peat
Drainage: **very poor to well**
Moisture: **wet to** average, tolerates **dry**
Reaction: demands **strongly acid to moderately acid,** pH 4.5 - 5.5

HARDINESS: zone 4b
Rate: **slow**
Longevity: **short-lived**

SUSCEPTIBILITY: Physiological: **frequent** - chlorosis in high pH soils, leaf scorch, dieback
Disease: **frequent** - leaf spots, crown rot, shoestring root rot, powdery mildew, shoot blight, gray blight, others
Insect: **frequent** - nematodes, rhododendron whitefly, scales, rhododendron tip midge, pitted ambrosia beetle, others
Wind-Ice: **infrequent**

URBAN TOLERANCE: Pollution: **sensitive** - NO_x; **intermediate** - HFl, C_2H_6, MV, 2-4D; **resistant** - Cl, PAN
Lighting: **intermediate**   Drought Heat: **intermediate**   Mine Spoils: **sensitive**
Salt: **sensitive**   Soil Compaction: **resistant**
Root Pattern: finely fibrous, very **shallow,** somewhat **stoloniferous; transplants well**

SPECIES: Associate: trees - Tuliptree, American Beech, Northern Red/White Oaks, Sugar Maple, Flowering Dogwood;
 shrubs - Mountainlaurel Kalmia, Carolina Rhododendron, Common Spicebush, Common Sweetshrub
Similar: Roseshell Azalea - deep pink, fragrant, tolerates alkaline soil, Northern; Pinkshell Azalea
Cultivars: 'Pinxterbloom' - hardier, flowers white to pink; 'Roseum' - darker pink flowers; 'Album' - white flowers

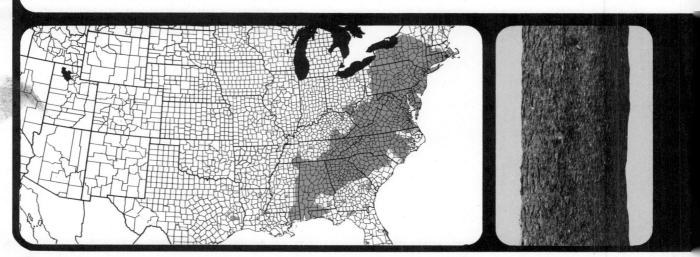

Rhododendron roseum

FORM: **globular**
Size: **mid-height shrub** - 2 to 4 m (6 to 12 ft), but typically only to 3 m (9 ft)
Spread: **intermediate** - 2 to 4 m (6 to 12 ft), typically comparable to height
Mass: **moderate**

BRANCHING: several stems with numerous **picturesque ascending** branches; **medium** texture
Twig: dense **velvety, gray brown**
Bud: **large** oval, **woolly, clustered** toward branch tips, **gray**
Bark: thin squarish **scaly plates or smooth, gray**

FOLIAGE: alternate, **simple,** obovate to **oblanceolate,** entire margin; **medium** texture
Surface: **dull,** smooth, woolly beneath
Color: spring - **red green** to pink, **then light green;** summer - **medium green to blue green;** autumn - **dark green to purplish**
Season: **deciduous;** emergence - late **May,** drop - mid **October**

FLOWER: funnel-shaped **bell,** 5 cm (2 in) diameter, stamens 3 times length of floral tube, in 5 to 9 **large-**flowered **clusters**
Color: bright rosy **pink or purple** with pink stamens
Season: mid through late **May,** before or with leaves
Sex: monoecious   **Fragrant:** spicily fragrant, like cloves

FRUIT: dry erect oblong **capsules,** 19 mm (¾ in) long, peeling back from the top like peeled banana
Color: **brown**
Season: early **August** persisting **through** late **March**   Human Value: **all parts poisonous**
Wildlife Value: **low;** limited use by upland gamebirds, songbirds, small mammals; hoofed browsers graze twigs, foliage

HABITAT: formation - **forest, cliff;** region - **Central;** gradient - upland **mesic, mesic-dry, dry;** open oak woods, steep wooded
    slopes, rocky woods, bluffs, overhanging cliffs
Shade Tolerance: **tolerant**
Flood Tolerance: **intolerant**

SOIL: Texture: **moderately coarse** rocky or sandy loams **to fine** sandy loams, clay loams; thin soils and bare rock
Drainage: **well**
Moisture: **moist to dry**
Reaction: best in **moderately acid to** slightly acid, pH 5.1 - 6.5, tolerates circumneutral and **alkaline** 6.6 - 8.0

HARDINESS: zone 4a
Rate: **slow**
Longevity: **short-lived**

SUSCEPTIBILITY: Physiological: **occasional** - leaf scorch
Disease: **frequent** - Botrytis blotch, bud and twig blight, azalea petal blight, Botryosphaerna canker, many more
Insect: **frequent** - rhododendron aphid, azalea leaf tier, strawberry weevil, azalea stem borer, azalea leaf minor, others
Wind-Ice: **infrequent**

URBAN TOLERANCE: Pollution: **sensitive** - O_3, NO_x; **intermediate** - HFI, C_2H_6, MV, 2-4D; **resistant** - CI, PAN
Lighting: **intermediate**   Drought Heat: **intermediate**   Mine Spoils: **sensitive**
Salt: **sensitive**   Soil Compaction: **sensitive**
Root Pattern: finely fibrous, very **shallow,** occasionally **stoloniferous; transplants well**

SPECIES: Associate: trees - Rosebay Rhododendron, Flowering Dogwood, American Sweetgum, Sugarberry; shrubs -
    Common Deerberry, American Beautyberry, Mountainlaurel Kalmia, Highbush/Lowbush Blueberries
Similar: Pinxterbloom Azalea - pink flower; Pinkshell Azalea - red fall color; Piedmont Azalea - more Southern
Cultivars: none available

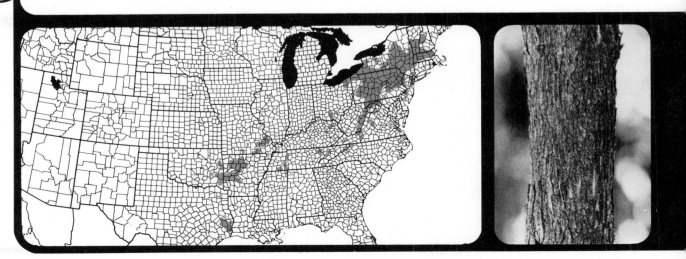

Roseshell Azalea

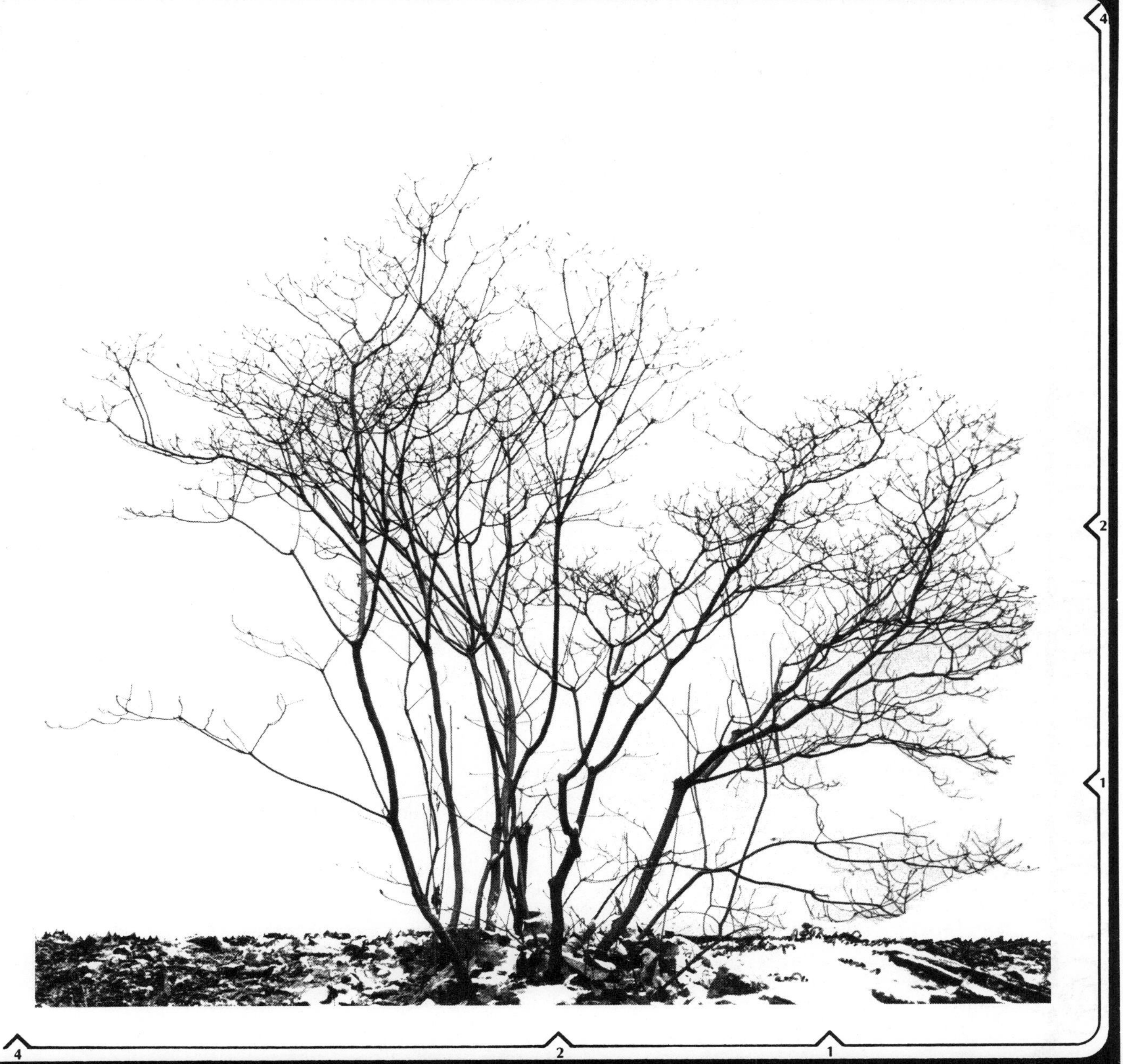

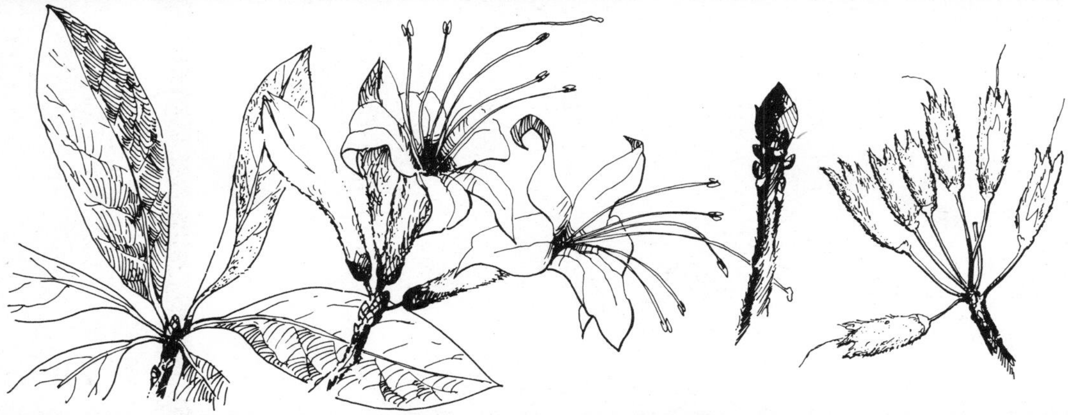

Rhododendron vaseyi

FORM: ovoid to obovoid or globular
Size: **mid-height shrub** - from 2 to 4 m (6 to 12 ft), typically to 3 m (9 ft)
Spread: **intermediate** - between 2 to 4 m (6 to 12 ft), narrow species commonly taller than broad
Mass: **moderate,** open with advanced age

BRANCHING: multiple stems, slender **picturesque** irregular **upright** branches; **medium** texture
Twig: smooth, **red brown**
Bud: **large** broad ovoid, **clustered** toward branch tips, **red brown to gray brown**
Bark: **smooth,** older stems with thin irregular **scales, gray**

FOLIAGE: alternate, clustered at twig ends, **simple, elliptic** to oblong elliptic, entire and hairy-fringed; **medium** texture
Surface: **glossy,** smooth
Color: spring - pale **red green, then light green;** summer - **dark green to red green;** autumn - pale crimson **red to purple**
Season: **deciduous;** emergence - late **May,** drop - mid **November**

FLOWER: funnel-shaped **bell,** 3 cm (1½ in) diameter, in 5 to 8 **large**-flowered terminal **clusters,** on long unbranched twigs
Color: clear rose **red,** spotted with orange
Season: mid through late **May,** before leaves
Sex: monoecious

FRUIT: dry woody oblong **capsule,** 19 mm (¾ in) long, opening from top
Color: **brown**
Season: early **August** persisting **through** late **February**   Human Value: **all parts poisonous**
Wildlife Value: **low;** very limited use by songbirds, upland gamebirds, small mammals

HABITAT: formation - **meadow, swamp, bald;** region - **Central;** gradient - **wet, wet-mesic, mesic;** rocky mountain slopes,
        summits, cool heath meadows, pond borders, heath balds
Shade Tolerance: **very tolerant**
Flood Tolerance: **tolerant**

SOIL: Texture: **moderately coarse to fine;** thin gravelly loams over bedrock, sandy loams, loams, clay loams, sands, peats
Drainage: **poor to well**
Moisture: **wet to moist**
Reaction: demands **strongly acid to moderately acid,** pH 4.5 - 6.0

HARDINESS: zone 5a
Rate: **medium**
Longevity: **short-lived**

SUSCEPTIBILITY: Physiological: **frequent** - leaf scorch
Disease: **frequent** - shoestring root rot, Botrytis blotch, crown rot, shoot blight, powdery mildew, azalea petal blight
Insect: **frequent** - Japanese beetle, Asiatic garden beetle, red-banded leafhopper, azalea leaf minor, giant hornet, others
Wind-Ice: **infrequent**

URBAN TOLERANCE: Pollution: **sensitive** - NO_x; **intermediate** - HFI, MV, 2-4D, C_2H_6; **resistant** - CI, PAN
Lighting: **intermediate**   Drought Heat: **sensitive**   Mine Spoils: **sensitive**
Salt: **sensitive**   Soil Compaction: **resistant**
Root Pattern: fine fibrous **shallow laterals,** never far reaching nor deep; **transplants well**

SPECIES: Associate: trees - Rosebay Rhododendron, Flowering Dogwood, Sourwood, White Fringetree; shrubs - Black
        Chokeberry, Mountainlaurel Kalmia, Carolina/Catawba Rhododendrons, Cinnamon Clethra, Drooping Leucothoe
Similar: Pinxterbloom/Roseshell Azaleas; Royal Azalea - taller, fragrant; Korean/Yodogawa Azaleas - Asiatic
Cultivars: Album, 'White Find' - white flowers

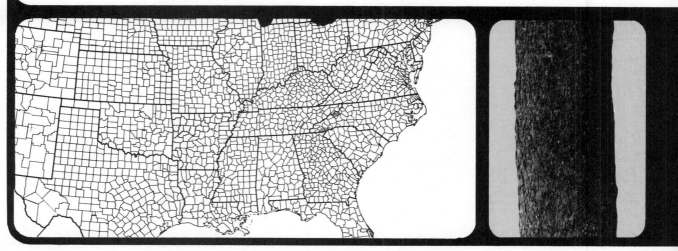

Rhododendron viscosum

FORM: **globular**
Size: **mid-height shrub** from 2 to 4 m (6 to 12 ft)
Spread: **intermediate** - between 2 to 4 m (6 to 12 ft)
Mass: **moderate** becoming loose and open with age

BRANCHING: multi-stemmed, straight **upright spreading** loose-branched habit, somewhat picturesque; **medium**
Twig: dense **velvety, brown**
Bud: **large** ovoid, dense **woolly, clustered** at branch tip, **red brown**
Bark: **smooth** or with fine thin **scaly** plates, **gray**

FOLIAGE: alternate, clustered at twig ends, **simple, obovate to oblong ovate,** entire with wispy hairs; **medium fine** texture
Surface: **glossy,** smooth, bloomy
Color: spring - **light green;** summer - **dark green;** autumn - **yellowish, orange to** maroon **purple**
Season: **deciduous;** emergence - late **May,** drop - mid **November**

FLOWER: tubular funnel-shaped **bell,** 2.5 cm (1 in) diameter, funnel hairy, in 4 to 9 **large**-flowered **clusters**
Color: pink in bud, opening **white** or rarely with pink stripes
Season: early through mid **July,** after leaves, last native azalea to bloom
Sex: monoecious   **Fragrant:** very spicy clove scent

FRUIT: short erect hairy oblong ovoid **capsules,** 1 to 2.5 cm (⅖ to 1 in) long, opens from top like partially peeled banana
Color: dark **brown**
Season: early **August** persisting **through** late **March**   Human Value: **all parts poisonous**
Wildlife Value: **low;** limited use by waterfowl, marshbirds, shorebirds, small mammals

HABITAT: formation - **forest, dune, swamp, bog;** region - **Southern;** gradient - lowland **wet;** low alluvial woodlands
floodplain depressions, wet pine flatlands, bays, sluggish stream banks, swamp borders, pocosins, hillside bogs
Shade Tolerance: **intermediate**
Flood Tolerance: **very tolerant**

SOIL: Texture: **coarse** wet sands and gravels, loamy sands, **to fine** sands, clay loams, stiff clays, peats, mucks
Drainage: **very poor to moderately poor**
Moisture: **wet to moist**
Reaction: demands **strongly acid to moderately acid,** pH 4.0 - 6.0

HARDINESS: **zone 4a**
Rate: **medium**
Longevity: **short-lived**

SUSCEPTIBILITY: Physiological: **occasional** - leaf scorch
Disease: **frequent** - Botrytis blotch, bud and twig blight, Botryosphaerna canker, azalea petal blight, many more
Insect: **frequent** - rhododendron aphid, azalea stem borer, azalea leaf tier, strawberry weevil, azalea leaf minor, others
Wind-Ice: **infrequent**

URBAN TOLERANCE: Pollution: **sensitive** - NO_x; **intermediate** - HFl, C_2H_6, MV, 2-4D; **resistant** - Cl, PAN
Lighting: **intermediate**   Drought Heat: **intermediate**   Mine Spoils: **sensitive**
Salt: **sensitive**   Soil Compaction: **resistant**
Root Pattern: very **shallow,** fine fibrous; **transplants well**

SPECIES: Associate: trees - American Sweetgum, Black/Swamp Tupelos, Eastern Arborvitae, Red Maple, Pond Pine
shrubs - Common Alder, Virginia Sweetspire, Summersweet Clethra, Swamp Cyrilla, Yellowroot
Similar: Sweet Azalea - unusually fragrant; Dwarf Azalea - low clump form, pink flowers, less hardy
Cultivars: 'Rhodanthum', 'Nitidum' - flowers bright pink; 'Glaucum' - blue green leaves; 'Montanum' - dwarf

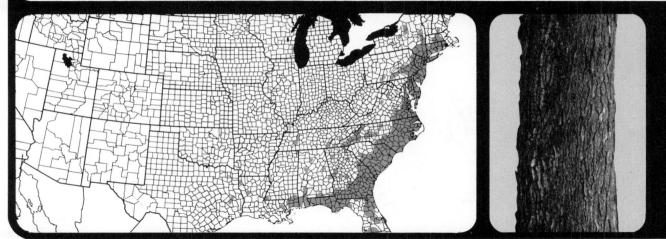

Rhus aromatica

FORM: mound
Size: **mid-height shrub** - from 2 to 4 m (6 to 12 ft)
Spread: **wide** - from 4 to 6 m (12 to 20 ft) plus, many mid-age specimens on Iowa State Campus exceed 9 m (30 ft)
Mass: **dense** tangle of stems and leaves

BRANCHING: dense multi-stemmed, lower branches spreading **horizontal** on ground, **ascending** at tips; **coarse** texture
Twig: slender, dense **velvety**, strong aromatic odor when broken, somewhat zigzag, prominent nodes, **red brown**
Bud: very small, hidden, **dome-shaped surrounded by leaf scar, woolly,** yellow to **yellow brown; winter catkins**
Bark: **smooth or scaly** with conspicuous transverse lenticels, **shallow furrowed** on old stems, **red brown**

FOLIAGE: alternate, **trifoliate, ovate,** terminal leaflet larger, coarsely toothed above middle, **aromatic; medium fine** texture
Surface: **tomentose** both sides, often glossy and smooth above at maturity
Color: spring - bright **yellow green or red green;** summer - **dark green to red green;** autumn - **orange,** scarlet **red,** then **purple**
Season: **deciduous;** emergence - mid **May,** drop - late **November**

FLOWER: numerous **small** lemon drop-like female **clusters** at branch tips, male catkins to 2.5 cm (1 in) long
Color: female light **yellow,** male brownish
Season: mid **March through** early **April,** before leaves
Sex: **dioecious**

FRUIT: small downy globular **berries,** 6 mm (¼ in) diameter, in dense terminal masses, often produced sparingly
Color: dark wine **red**
Season: mid **July** persisting **through** winter to mid **March**   Human Value: **edible fruit**
Wildlife Value: **very high;** winter food for many upland gamebirds, songbirds, large and small mammals, hoofed browsers

HABITAT: formation - **prairie, cliff, old field, barrens, dune;** region - **Central;** gradient - upland **dry;** limestone cliffs, dry open
          upland woods, open rocky bluffs, oak barrens, oak opening, foredunes, sandy or rocky goat prairies, barren rock
Shade Tolerance: **very intolerant**
Flood Tolerance: **very intolerant**

SOIL: Texture: **coarse to moderately coarse;** rock outcrops, sandy plains, infertile sands/gravels, sandy/gravelly loams
Drainage: **well to excessive**
Moisture: **average to droughty**
Reaction: **slightly acid to** circumneutral, tolerates **alkaline,** pH 6.1 - 8.5

HARDINESS: zone 4a
Rate: slow to **medium**
Longevity: **short-lived**

SUSCEPTIBILITY: Physiological: **infrequent**
Disease: **occasional** - leaf spots, rusts, powdery mildews, Verticillium wilt, cankers; none serious
Insect: **occasional** - sumac aphid, mites, scales, currant borer, potato flea beatle, sumac psyllid; none serious
Wind-Ice: **infrequent**

URBAN TOLERANCE: Pollution: **sensitive** - 0₃, 2-4D; **intermediate** - HFl
Lighting: **sensitive**   Drought Heat: **resistant**   Mine Spoils: **resistant**
Salt: **resistant**   Soil Compaction: **sensitive**
Root Pattern: **shallow** fibrous, trailing stems often rooting upon soil contact, prolific suckering habit; **easily transplanted**

SPECIES: Associate: trees - Common Hoptree, Common Chokecherry, Black Oak, Jack Pine; shrubs - Carolina Rose,
          Leadplant Amorpha, Red-osier Dogwood, Silverberry, Russet Buffaloberry; vines - American Bittersweet
Similar: Skunkbush Sumac - Western, upright to 3 m (6 ft) high; Common Poisonivy - vine, trifoliate leaves similar
Cultivars: 'Laciniata' - leaves narrow, deeply lobed; 'Green Globe', 'Grolow' - low spreading, glossy leaves

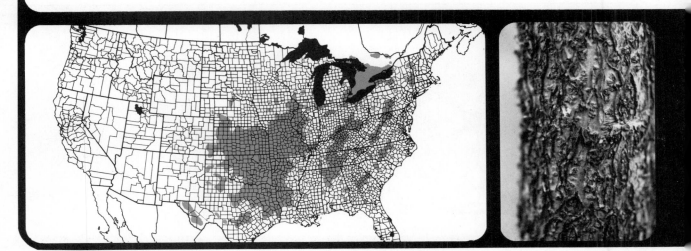

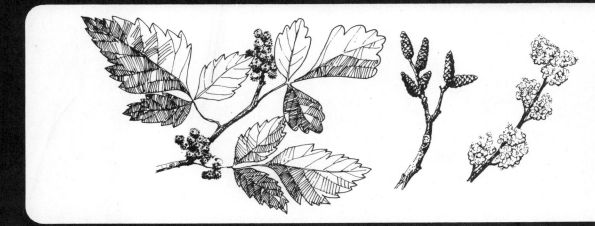

Ribes americanum

FORM: globular
Size: **small shrub** - from 1 to 2 m (3 to 6 ft)
Spread: **narrow** - between 1 to 2 m (3 to 6 ft)
Mass: **moderate**

BRANCHING: slender multiple stems, graceful **erect to upright spreading**, canes little-branched; **medium** texture
Twig: slender, smooth, **angular**, longitudinal lines beneath leaf scar, dotted with **resinous** glands, **orange brown to gray**
Bud: small ovoid, 6 mm (¼ in), dotted with tiny yellow **resin** glands, **stalked, clustered, purplish to brown**
Bark: **smooth** with small oval light colored lenticels, deep red or **purple**, finally dark **brown black**

FOLIAGE: alternate, clustered on spur-like twigs, **simple**, 3-5 **palmate lobes**, coarse dentate teeth, **aromatic; medium fine**
Surface: **dull**, smooth, with plainly visible yellow resinous dots
Color: spring - **light green;** summer - **medium green;** autumn - **yellow,** crimson **red to** deep maroon **purple;** winter - **tan brown**
Season: **persistant;** emergence - mid **April**, drop - some dried leaves remaining through **December** or later

FLOWER: **bell**-shaped, 6 to 8 mm (¼ to ⅓ in) long, in loose drooping 2 to 12 small-flowered axillary clusters
Color: creamy **white** to pale yellow
Season: late **April through** mid **May,** after leaves
Sex: **dioecious**

FRUIT: smooth glossy globular **berry**, 10 mm (⅜ in) diameter, with crooked terminal wisker, in open drooping clusters
Color: deep **purple to** coal **black**
Season: early **July through** late August   Human Value: **edible fruit**
Wildlife Value: **high;** songbirds and small mammals major users, large mammals, waterfowl and hoofed browsers also use

HABITAT: formation - **bog, cliff, spring;** region - **Northern;** gradient - **wet, wet-mesic, mesic-dry;** margin of bogs, boggy
borders of sluggish streams, steep rocky cliffs, calcareous springy woods, floodplains, rock ledges
Shade Tolerance: **intermediate**
Flood Tolerance: **very tolerant**

SOIL: Texture: **medium to fine;** thin soils over bedrock, clay loams, heavy clay, well decomposed peat over mineral soils
Drainage: **very poor to well**
Moisture: **wet to average**
Reaction: **slightly acid to** circumneutral, pH 6.1 - 7.5, tolerates **alkaline** pH to 8.5

HARDINESS: zone 3a
Rate: **medium**
Longevity: **very short-lived**

SUSCEPTIBILITY: Physiological: **infrequent**
Disease: **occasional** - anthracnose, cane blight, leaf spots, rust can be locally severe
Insect: **occasional** - currant aphid, imported currant worm, scales, currant bud mite
Wind-Ice: **infrequent**

URBAN TOLERANCE: Pollution: **sensitive** - 2-4D; **intermediate** - HCl; **resistant** - HFl
Lighting: Drought Heat: **intermediate**   Mine Spoils:
Salt: **sensitive**   Soil Compaction: **resistant**
Root Pattern: dense, finely fibrous, **shallow** spreading, suckers freely; **transplants well**

SPECIES: Associate: trees - Black Ash, Eastern Arborvitae, American Larch; shrubs - Hazel Alder, Meadowsweet Spirea,
American Cranberrybush Viburnum, Bunchberry/Redosier Dogwoods, Common Winterberry, Canada Yew
Similar: European Black Currant - garden species, hardier; Hudsonbay Currant - more Northern/Western, white flowers
Cultivars: none available

664

Ribes cynosbati

FORM: **globular**
Size: **small shrub** - from 1 to 2 m (3 to 6 ft)
Spread: **narrow** - between 1 to 2 m (3 to 6 ft), equal or slightly wider than height
Mass: **dense**

BRANCHING: many tightly clustered **upright spreading or arching** stems, branched toward their tips; **fine** texture
Twig: slender, smooth, dark **brown; armed** with 2 to 3 slender dark red spines per node
Bud: narrow ovoid, 5 mm (³⁄₁₆ in), **red brown**
Bark: **shallow furrowed or exfoliating** into thin papery shreds, light **tan brown to gray; armed** with dense prickles to base

FOLIAGE: alternate, clustered on short spur-like twigs, **simple, palmately** 3-**lobed,** irregularly toothed; **medium fine** texture
Surface: both sides **tomentose**
Color: spring - **light green;** summer - **medium green;** autumn - golden **yellow** tinged **orange to red, then purple**
Season: **deciduous;** emergence - late **April,** drop - mid **October**

FLOWER: small trumpet-shaped **bell** with 5 flaired petals, 13 mm (½ in) long, solitary or groups of 2 to 3
Color: **greenish to white**
Season: late **April through** mid **May,** with leaves
Sex: **dioecious**   **Fragrant:** delicately perfumed

FRUIT: prickly globular to elliptic **berry,** 3 to 13 mm (⅛ to ½ in) long, solitary or clusters of 2 to 3
Color: deep **purple** with faint pale **black** lines
Season: early **July through** late August   Human Value: **fruit edible** but prickly
Wildlife Value: **high;** songbirds and small mammals major users, upland gamebirds, large mammals; hoofed browsers use

HABITAT: formation - **forest, spring, old field;** region - **Northern, Central;** gradient - **wet-mesic, mesic, mesic-dry, dry;** dry rocky
          woodlands, open alluvial forests, old clearings, rocky wooded slopes above creeks, deep mesic forests, talus slopes
Shade Tolerance: **very tolerant**
Flood Tolerance: **intermediate**

SOIL: Texture: **coarse to fine;** most soils, best development in deep loam; tolerates heavy clay, light sands
Drainage: **moderately poor to excessive**
Moisture: **moist to droughty**
Reaction: **slightly acid to** circumneutral, tolerates **alkaline,** pH 6.1 - 8.5

HARDINESS: zone 2
Rate: **medium to fast**
Longevity: **very short-lived**

SUSCEPTIBILITY: Physiological: **infrequent**
Disease: **occasional** - anthracnose, cane blight, leaf spots, rust
Insect: **occasional** - currant aphid, imported currant worm, scales, currant bud mite
Wind-Ice: **infrequent**

URBAN TOLERANCE: Pollution: **sensitive** - 2-4D; **intermediate;** HCl; **resistant** - HFl
Lighting: Drought Heat: **resistant**   Mine Spoils:
Salt: Soil Compaction: **intermediate**
Root Pattern: very dense, fine fibrous **shallow** spreading, prolific suckering habit; **transplants well**

SPECIES: Associate: trees - Black/Sugar Maples, American Hornbeam, Flowering/Pagoda Dogwoods, American Beech;
          shrubs - Running Euonymus, Common Spicebush, American Elder, Atlantic Leatherwood, Indiancurrant Coralberry
Similar: Missouri/Hairystem Gooseberries - fruits smooth, edible
Cultivars: none available

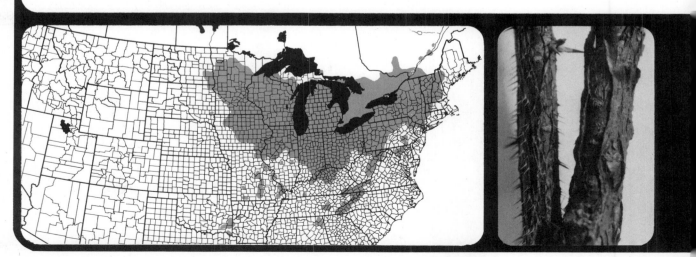

Ribes missouriense

FORM: **globular**
Size: **small shrub** - from 1 to 2 m (3 to 6 ft)
Spread: **narrow** - between 1 to 2 m (3 to 6 ft), equal or somewhat wider than height
Mass: **dense**

BRANCHING: many tightly clustered **upright spreading or arching** stems, branched near their tips; **fine** texture
Twig: smooth, dark red brown to **brown; armed** with infrequent spines
Bud: narrow ovoid, 4 to 6 mm (⅙ to ¼ in), scales spreading at tip, **red brown**
Bark: **shallow furrowed or exfoliating** into thin papery lateral peeling curls, **red brown to gray; armed** with stout red prickle.

FOLIAGE: alternate, **simple, palmately lobed,** 3 to 5 lobes, shallow rounded sinuses, coarse teeth; **medium fine texture**
Surface: **dull**, smooth
Color: spring - **light green;** summer - **medium green;** autumn - **yellow** tinged **orange to red** then deep **purple**
Season: **deciduous;** emergence - late **April,** drop - late **October**

FLOWER: small trumpet-shaped **bell** with recurved petals at tip, 2 to 2.5 cm (¾ to 1 in) long, solitary or 2 to 3 togethe
Color: **greenish to whitish**
Season: late **April through** mid **May,** with leaves
Sex: **dioecious** **Fragrant:** delicately perfumed

FRUIT: smooth globular to elliptic **berry,** 8 to 15 mm (⅓ to ⅗ in) long, with faint watermelon-like longitudinal stripe
Color: green becoming dark **purple to black**
Season: early **July through** late **August** **Human Value:** tart **edible fruit**
Wildlife Value: **high;** songbirds, upland gamebirds, large and small mammals; hoofed browsers graze twigs, leaves

HABITAT: formation - **forest, old field;** region - **Central;** gradient - **wet-mesic, mesic, mesic-dry, dry;** open woods, strear
banks, borders of woods, grazed or cutover pastures, rocky wooded creek banks, grazed woods, alluvial wood
Shade Tolerance: **very tolerant**
Flood Tolerance: **intermediate**

SOIL: Texture: **coarse to fine;** most soils, tolerates infertile sands and gravels, heavy silt loams, silts, clays
Drainage: **moderately poor to excessive**
Moisture: **moist to** dry, tolerates **droughty**
Reaction: **slightly acid to** circumneutral, tolerates **alkaline,** pH 6.1 - 8.5

HARDINESS: zone 4a
Rate: **medium to fast**
Longevity: **very short-lived**

SUSCEPTIBILITY: Physiological: **infrequent**
Disease: **occasional** - leaf spots, rust, cane blight, anthracnose, white pine blister rust
Insect: **occasional** - currant bud mite, currant aphid, scales, imported currant worm
Wind-Ice: **infrequent**

URBAN TOLERANCE: Pollution: **sensitive** - 2-4D; **intermediate** - HCl; **resistant** - HFl
Lighting: Drought Heat: **resistant**
Salt: Soil Compaction: **intermediate** Mine Spoils:
Root Pattern: dense, fine fibrous, **shallow lateral** spreading, prolific suckering habit; **transplants well**

SPECIES: Associate: trees - White Ash, Black Cherry, White Oak, Common Chokecherry, Slippery Elm; shrubs
American Elder, Allegany Blackberry, Gray Dogwood, American Filbert, Limber Honeysuckle; vines - Virginia Creepe
Similar: Snow Gooseberry- flowers smaller; Pasture Gooseberry - prickly fruit
Cultivars: none available

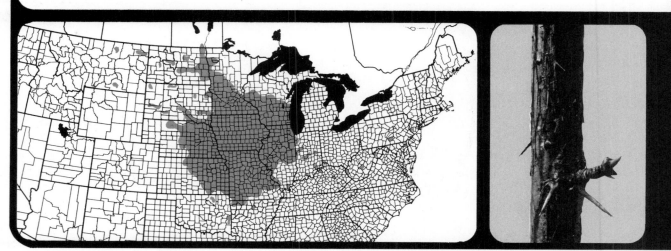

Missouri Gooseberry

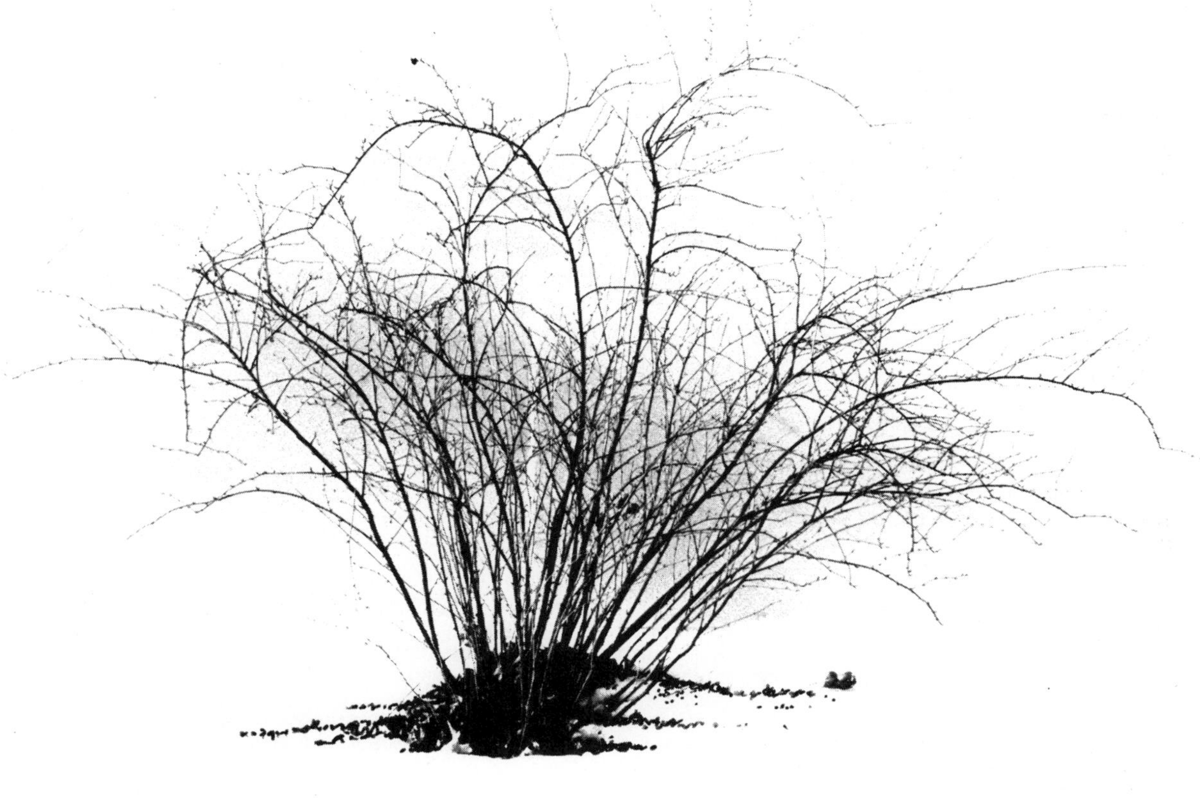

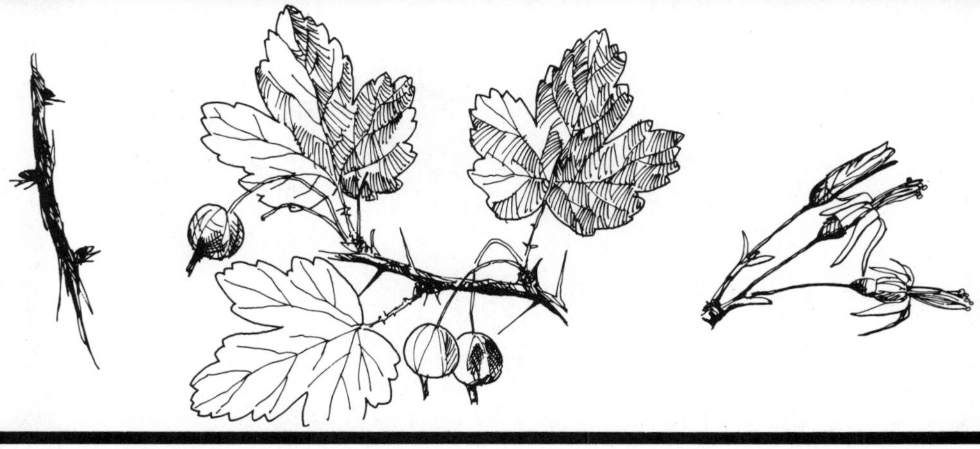

Ribes odoratum

FORM: globular
Size: **mid-height shrub** - from 2 to 4 m (6 to 12 ft), commonly to 3 m (9 ft)
Spread: **intermediate** - between 2 to 4 m (6 to 12 ft), will sucker into large colony if released
Mass: **moderate** becoming open with age

BRANCHING: multiple stems, stiffly **erect to upright spreading** finally **arching** habit; **medium** texture
Twig: **velvety,** somewhat ridged with light longitudinal stripes, spur-like, **red brown**
Bud: narrow ovate, 3 to 5 mm (⅛ to ⅕ in) long, **woolly, stalked, clustered,** red brown
Bark: **smooth or exfoliating** into scurfy thin sheets curling laterally, **red brown to purplish gray or black**

FOLIAGE: alternate, **simple,** 3 to 5 deep **palmate lobes,** coarsely toothed at lobe tips; **medium fine** texture
Surface: **dull,** smooth
Color: spring - bright **medium green;** summer - bright **medium green;** autumn - scarlet **red then** deep **purple**
Season: **deciduous;** emergence - mid **April,** drop - mid **October**

FLOWER: small elongated tubular **trumpet,** 2.5 cm (1 in) long, closing with age, in nodding clusters of 5 to 10
Color: golden **yellow** with red center
Season: late **April through** early **May,** after leaves
Sex: **dioecious**   **Fragrant:**   very strong odor of cloves

FRUIT: smooth globular to elliptic **berry,** 8 to 10 mm (⅓ to ⅖ in) long
Color: jet **black**
Season: early June through late July   Human Value: **edible fruit**
Wildlife Value: **high;** songbirds, small mammals major users, large mammals, upland gamebirds, hoofed browsers

HABITAT: formation - **prairie, savanna, old field;** region - **Central;** gradient - upland **mesic-dry, dry;** borders of open woods,
        ravines, fence rows, exposed rock ledges, limestone or dolomite bluffs, rocky prairie, old fields, railroad rights-of-way
Shade Tolerance: **intolerant**
Flood Tolerance: **intolerant**

SOIL: Texture: **coarse to medium;** sandy plain, thin soils over limestone/sandstone, gravelly/sandy loam, prairie loam
Drainage: **well to excessive**
Moisture: **average to droughty**
Reaction: **slightly acid to alkaline,** pH 6.1 - 8.5

HARDINESS: zone 3b
Rate: **medium to fast**
Longevity: **very short-lived**

SUSCEPTIBILITY: Physiological: **infrequent**
Disease: **occasional** - white pine blister rust, anthracnose is serious, cane blight, leaf spots, powdery mildew
Insect: **occasional** - scales, currant aphid, imported currant worm, currant bud mite
Wind-Ice: **infrequent**

URBAN TOLERANCE: Pollution: **sensitive** - 2-4D; **intermediate** - HCl; **resistant** - HFl
Lighting: Drought Heat: **resistant**   Mine Spoils: **resistant**
Salt: **resistant**   Soil Compaction: **intermediate**
Root Pattern: dense, finely fibrous, **shallow** spreading, freely suckering; **transplants well**

SPECIES: Associate: trees - Bur/Black Oaks, Black Cherry, Prairie Crabapple, sumac/hawthorn species; shrubs - Blackcap
        Raspberry, Common Chokecherry, Missouri Gooseberry, Fragrant Sumac, Silverberry, Western Snowberry
Similar: Alpine Currant - European, red fruit; Golden Currant - Western; Winter Currant - red flowers, Western
Cultivars: 'Crandall' - larger edible fruit

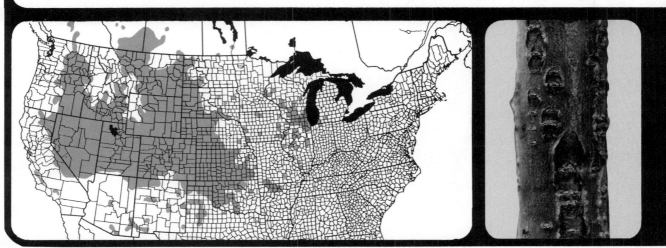

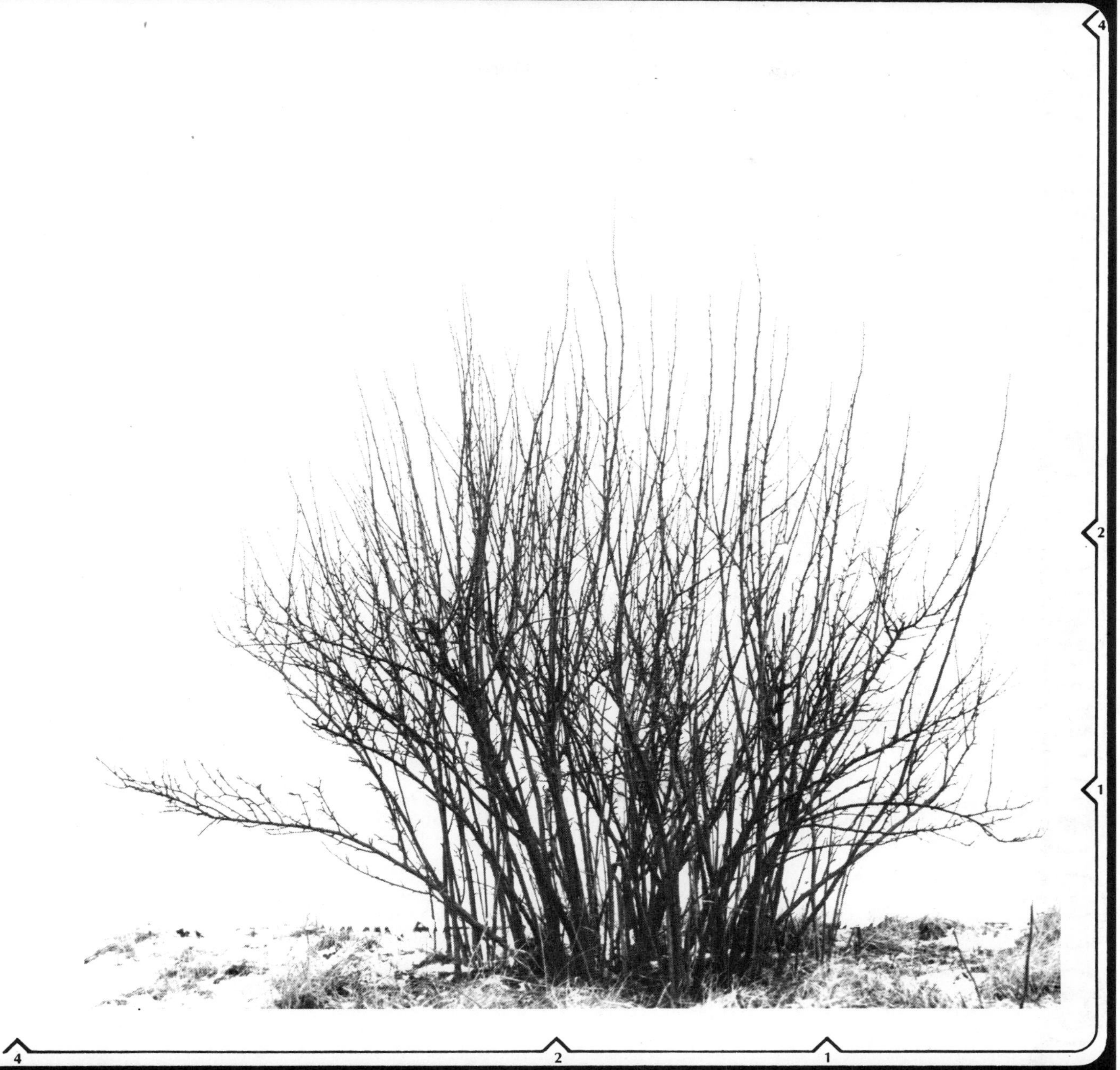
4
2
1
4
2
1

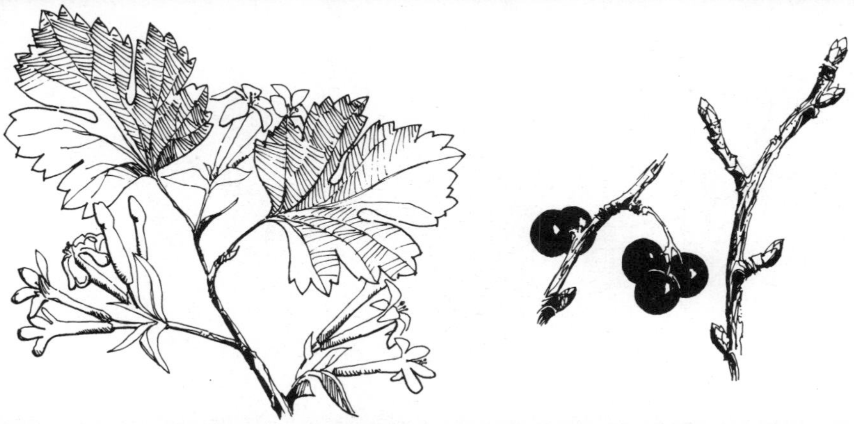

Robinia hispida

FORM: **irregular to obovoid**
Size: **mid-height shrub** - from 2 to 4 m (6 to 12 ft), commonly less than 3 m (9 ft)
Spread: **narrow** - 1 to 2 m (3 to 6 ft) plus, typically ½ the height, but freely suckers into colonies
Mass: **open**

BRANCHING: solitary **erect** trunk, **leggy** with tortuous **picturesque arching** habit; **coarse** texture
Twig: **velvety** with thick bristly hairs, **red to red brown; armed** with scattered spines
Bud: inconspicuous, imbedded in bark, **brown**
Bark: generally smooth and marked with short horizontal streaks or roughened into **scaly** plates, **gray brown**

FOLIAGE: alternate, **pinnately compound,** 7 to 13 **elliptic** leaflets, entire but bristle-tipped, rachis bristly; **fine** texture
Surface: **dull,** smooth
Color: spring - **red green;** summer - **blue green;** autumn - **blue green, then yellow green**
Season: **deciduous;** emergence - late **May** to early **June,** drop - mid **September**

FLOWER: long pendulous 3 to 7-flowered **spikes,** pea-like appearance, 2.5 cm (1 in) diameter, stalks bristly
Color: rosy **red or** pale **purple**
Season: peak from early through late **June,** often sporadically through late July, after leaves ½ grown
Sex: monoecious

FRUIT: dense bristly bean-like **pods,** 5 to 7.5 cm (2 to 3 in) long, pendant in few-fruited clusters, sets fruit sparingly
Color: **brown to** dark **red brown**
Season: early **August through** late **September,** often persisting through winter   Human Value: **all parts poisonous**
Wildlife Value: **very low;** few upland gamebirds and small animals

HABITAT: formation - **forest, barrens, old field;** region - **Southern;** gradient - upland **mesic-dry, dry;** oak barrens, open
     mountain slopes, woods edge, steep rocky land, open wooded slopes, waste places, abandoned fields
Shade Tolerance: **intolerant**
Flood Tolerance: **intolerant**

SOIL: Texture: **coarse to moderately coarse;** shallow soils over bedrock, rock outcrops, sands, gravels, sandy loams
Drainage: **moderately well to excessive**
Moisture: **average to** dry, tolerates **droughty**
Reaction: best in **slightly acid to** neutral, pH 6.1 - 7.0, tolerant of **alkaline** pH to 8.5

HARDINESS: **zone 4a**
Rate: **fast**
Longevity: **short-lived**

SUSCEPTIBILITY: Physiological: **infrequent**
Disease: **frequent** - canker, leaf spots, dampening-off, powdery mildews, wood decay, witches' broom, rot
Insect: **frequent** - locust borer can be severe, locust leaf minor, locust twig borer, carpenter worm, scales, aphids
Wind-Ice: **frequent** - weak brittle wood, easily broken, shelter from wind

URBAN TOLERANCE: Pollution:
Lighting: Drought Heat: very **resistant**   Mine Spoils: **resistant**
Salt: **resistant**   Soil Compaction: **sensitive**
Root Pattern: rhizomes **shallow** spreading, **stoloniferous,** suckering into thickets, nitrogen-fixing; **transplants easily**

SPECIES: Associate: trees - Longleaf Pine, Common Persimmon, Black Cherry, Black Tupelo, Turkey Oak; shrubs -
     Common Deerberry, Box Sandmyrtle, Sparkleberry, Flameleaf Sumac, Adamsneedle Yucca
Similar: Clammy/Hartwig Locusts - large shrubs; Fertile Locust; Bristly Aralia; Common Pricklyash; Indigobush Amorpha
Cultivars: 'Macrophylla' - nearly free from prickles; 'Monument' - dwarf to 3 m (10 ft); 'Superba'; rosea

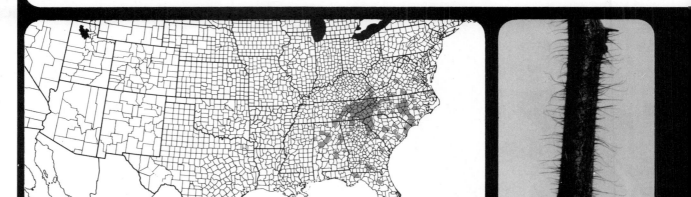

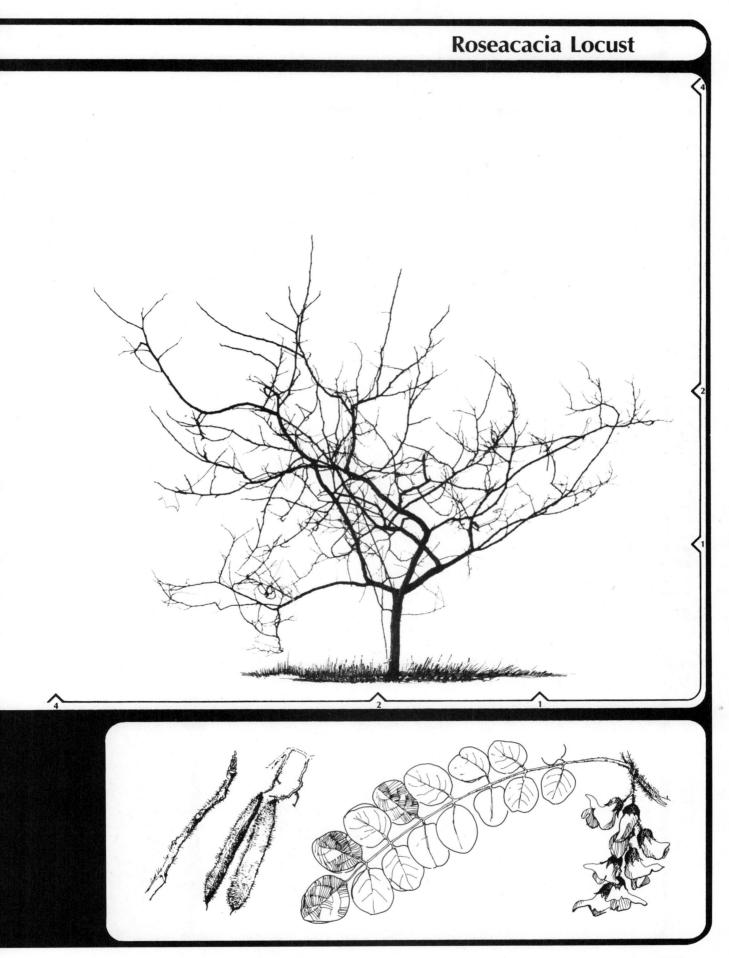

Robinia viscosa

FORM: **irregular to obovoid**
Size: **mid-height shrub** - from 2 to 4 m (6 to 12 ft), commonly to 6 m (20 ft) or more
Spread: **narrow** - between 1 to 2 m (3 to 6 ft), typically ⅓ to ½ the height but forms broad colonies
Mass: **open**

BRANCHING: solitary stem, several **erect** limbs, **leggy** with tortuous picturesque habit, suckers freely; **coarse** texture
Twig: sticky warty glands, without long velvety hairs, **red or red brown;** occasionally **armed** with paired weak stipular spines
Bud: tiny, imbedded in bark, conspicuous dark **woolly** hairs, **brown**
Bark: **smooth** or roughened with short horizontal lenticels, **gray brown** often tinged red; **armed** with or without spines

FOLIAGE: alternate, **pinnately compound,** 13 to 21 leaflets, **elliptic** to ovate, entire margin, bristle-tipped; **fine** texture
Surface: **dull,** smooth
Color: spring - **red green;** summer - dark **blue green;** autumn - **blue green, then yellow green**
Season: **deciduous;** emergence - early **June,** drop - mid **September**

FLOWER: short crowded drooping **spikes,** pea-like appearance, 17 mm (⅔ in) diameter, minute hairs on stems
Color: pale **pink or purplish**
Season: mid **June through** early **July,** after leaves
Sex: monoecious

FRUIT: bean-like **pods,** 5 to 9 cm (⅔ to ½ in) long, smooth or sparingly bristly, in loose open pendant clusters
Color: dark **red brown to brown**
Season: early **August through** late **September,** often persisting in winter   Human Value: **all parts poisonous**
Wildlife Value: **very low;** occasional use by small mammals, upland gamebirds

HABITAT: formation - **forest, barrens, old field;** region - **Southern;** gradient - upland **mesic-dry, dry;** steep rocky land, along
          borders of mountain streams, open upland forests, dry steep wooded slopes, ridge tops
Shade Tolerance: **intolerant**
Flood Tolerance: **intolerant**

SOIL: Texture: **coarse to moderately coarse;** infertile sands and gravels, rock outcroppings, thin soils over bedrock
Drainage: **moderately well to excessive**
Moisture: **average to dry,** tolerates **droughty**
Reaction: **slightly acid to** circumneutral, tolerates **alkaline,** pH 6.1 - 8.5

HARDINESS: zone 5a
Rate: **fast**
Longevity: **short-lived**

SUSCEPTIBILITY: Physiological: **infrequent**
Disease: **frequent** - witches' broom, wood decay, powdery mildews, leaf spots, dampening-off, cankers
Insect: **frequent** - scales, locust twig borer, locust leaf minor, carpenter worm, locust borer is often severe
Wind-Ice: **frequent** - weak wooded, brittle, suffers breakage in exposed area

URBAN TOLERANCE: Pollution:
Lighting: Drought Heat: very **resistant**   Mine Spoils: **resistant**
Salt: **resistant**   Soil Compaction: **sensitive**
Root Patterns: numerous **shallow** suckering fibers, **stoloniferous,** nitrogen-fixing; **transplants well**

SPECIES: Associate: Chestnut/Scarlet Oaks, Sourwood, Black Tupelo, Virginia/Pitch Pines; shrubs - Mountainlaurel
          Kalmia, rhododendron species, Smooth Hydrangea, blueberry/blackberry/raspberry species
Similar: Hartwig Locust - to 4.5 m (15 ft); Roseacacia Locust - small shrub; Devils-Walkingstick; Herculesclub Pricklyash
Cultivars: none available

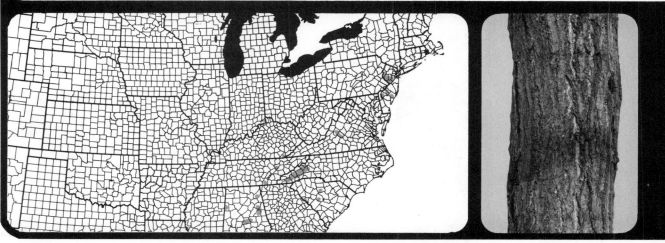

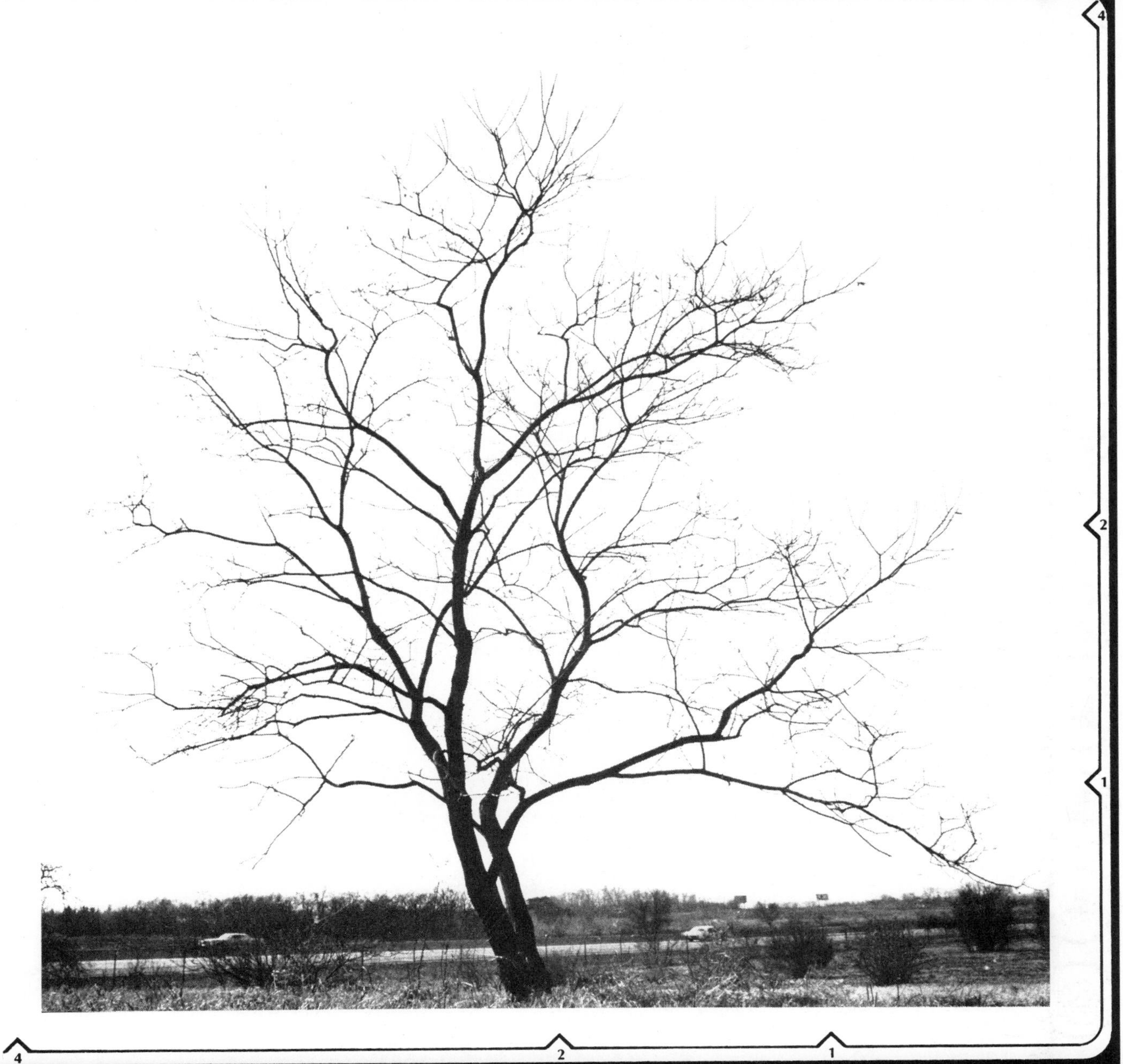

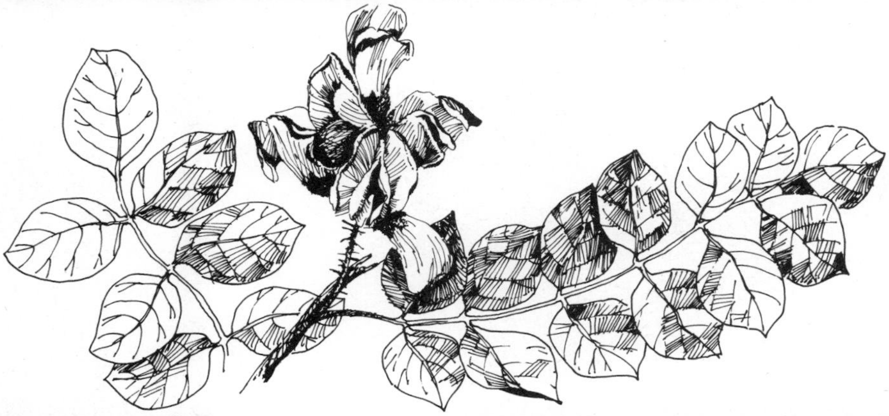

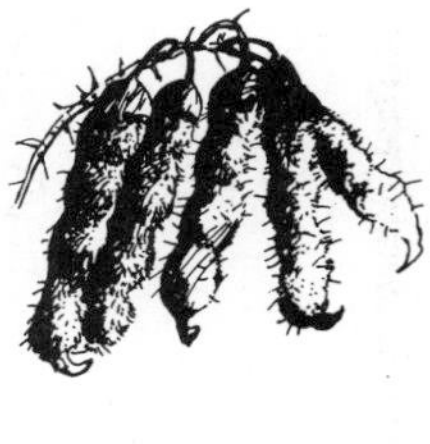

Rosa carolina

FORM: mound
Size: **very small shrub** - up to 1 m (3 ft), occasionally to 1.5 m (4.5 ft)
Spread: **intermediate** - from 2 to 4 m (6 to 12 ft), broader colonies common
Mass: **dense**

BRANCHING: dense stemmed, stiff **erect** little-branched canes, forms broad **leggy** thickets; **medium** texture
Twig: stout, smooth, **zigzag** appearance, **green or red; armed** with scattered or paired prickles
Bud: small ovoid, 3 mm (⅛ in), **reddish**
Bark: **smooth,** dull **red or green;** densely **armed** with slender straight bristle-like prickles at stem base

FOLIAGE: alternate, **pinnately compound,** 5 to 7 narrow **elliptic** leaflets, sharply toothed, petiole prickly and winged; **fine**
Surface: **dull,** smooth
Color: spring - **red green becoming light green;** summer - **light to medium green;** autumn - **yellowish to orange and** dull **red**
Season: **deciduous;** emergence - late **May,** drop - mid **October**

FLOWER: **large solitary** or 2 to 3 together, 5 to 6.5 cm (2 to 2½ in) diameter, 5 showy petals
Color: deep **pink** with bright yellow stamens
Season: late **June through** mid **July,** after leaves
Sex: monoecious   **Fragrant:** sweet perfumed

FRUIT: globular or pear-shaped **berries** - 'hips', 13 mm (½ in) wide, more or less bristly, in clusters of 1 to 3
Color: bright **red**
Season: late **August** persisting in winter **through** late **March**   Human Value: **edible fruits and flowers**
Wildlife Value: **intermediate;** upland gamebirds major users, large and small mammals minor users

HABITAT: formation - **swamp, prairie, old field, forest, glade;** region - **Central;** gradient - upland **mesic-dry, dry;** dry prairie,
sandy open woods, old fields, fence rows, roadsides, swamp and stream borders, woods edge, steep rocky slopes
Shade Tolerance: **intolerant**
Flood Tolerance: **intolerant**

SOIL: Texture: **coarse to fine;** sandy plains, infertile sands and gravels, sandy or gravelly loams, prairie loams, clays
Drainage: **poor to excessive**
Moisture: **wet to droughty**
Reaction: **slightly acid to** circumneutral, tolerates **alkaline,** pH 6.1 - 8.5

HARDINESS: zone 4b
Rate: **fast**
Longevity: **short-lived**

SUSCEPTIBILITY: Physiological: **occasional** - cold winter causes dieback
Disease: **occasional** - black spot, powdery mildew are most serious, various cankers, virus diseases, crown gall, rusts
Insect: **occasional** - aphids, beatles, borers, leafhopper, scales, rose slug, thrips, mites, rose midge, nematodes, many
Wind-Ice: **infrequent**

URBAN TOLERANCE: Pollution: **sensitive** - N0$_x$, C$_2$H$_6$; **intermediate** - HFI, 2-4D
Lighting: Drought Heat: **resistant**   Mine Spoils:
Salt: **sensitive**   Soil Compaction: **intermediate**
Root Pattern: **shallow** fibrous, freely suckering into broad thickets; **transplants easily**

SPECIES: Associate: trees - Eastern Red Cedar, Black/Bur Oaks, Shagbark Hickory, Prairie Crabapple, American Plum;
shrubs - Jerseytea Ceanothus, Leadplant Amorpha, Smooth Sumac, Gray Dogwood, American Filbert, Clove Currant
Similar: Virginia/Meadow/Arkansas/Rugosa Roses; raspberry/blackberry/thimbleberry species
Cultivars: 'Alba' - white flowers

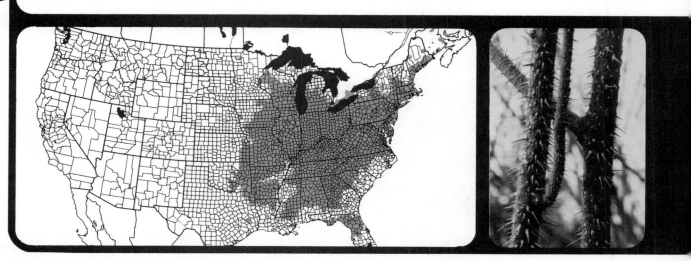

1

2/3

1/3

1

2/3

1/3

Rosa setigera

FORM: **mound** or climbing vine
Size: **mid-height shrub** - from 2 to 4 m (6 to 12 ft) **or** occasionally **low vine** to 6 m (20 ft) high
Spread: **wide** - from 4 to 6 m (12 to 20 ft) plus, often to 9 m (30 ft) or more, typically 2 to 3 times the height
Mass: **dense**

BRANCHING: **arching** mostly unbranched canes forming fountain-like clump, also scrambling or climbing vine; **coarse**
Twig: stout, smooth, with **powdery bloom, zigzag** appearance, **green or red**
Bud: very small ovoid, 1.5 to 1.8 mm (1/32 to 1/16 in), **red**
Bark: **smooth,** glossy to dull, **green to red,** old **red brown** stems split into narrow slits; **armed** with scattered hooked prickles

FOLIAGE: alternate, **pinnately compound,** 3 to 5 leaflets, ovate, base coarsely toothed, winged prickly petiole; **medium fine**
Surface: **glossy,** smooth
Color: spring - **light green;** summer - **dark green;** autumn - various, **yellow, orange,** pink, scarlet **red, then purple**
Season: **deciduous;** emergence - late **May,** drop - mid **October**

FLOWER: **large solitary** or few-flowered clusters, 6.5 to 7.5 cm (2½ to 3 in) diameter, 5 deeply notched petals
Color: deep to pale **pink** fading to whitish, bright yellow stamens
Season: early through late **July,** after leaves, one of latest native roses to bloom
Sex: monoecious   **Fragrant:** slightly perfumed

FRUIT: elliptic football-shaped **berry,** 10 mm (3/8 in) long, more or less bristly, in open clusters of 1 to 8
Color: pale **red** or orangish
Season: early **September** persisting in winter **through** late **March**   Human Value: **edible fruits and flowers**
Wildlife Value: **intermediate;** upland gamebirds major users, large and small mammals; hoofed browsers minor use

HABITAT: formation - **forest, prairie, glade, old field;** region - **Central;** gradient - **wet-mesic, mesic-dry, dry;** open alluvial
forest, abandoned pasture, roadsides, fence rows, clearings, rock ledges along creeks, prairie thickets, grazed woods
Shade Tolerance: **intolerant**
Flood Tolerant: **intermediate**

SOIL: Texture: **coarse to moderately fine;** thin soils over bedrock, sandy or gravelly loams, prairie loams, silt loams
Drainage: **moderately poor to excessive**
Moisture: **moist to droughty**
Reaction: **slightly acid to** circumneutral, tolerates **alkaline,** pH 6.1 - 8.5

HARDINESS: zone 4b
Rate: very **fast,** rambling canes may extend 4.5 m (15 ft) in one season
Longevity: **short-lived**

SUSCEPTIBILITY: Physiological: **infrequent**
Disease: **occasional** - powdery mildew, black spot can be serious, rusts, rose anthracnose, cankers, black mold; minor
Insect: **occasional** - aphids, beetles, leafhopper, scales, slugs, thrips, mites, webworms, nematodes, rose budworm
Wind-Ice: **infrequent**

URBAN TOLERANCE: Pollution: **sensitive** - $N0_x$, C_2H_6; **intermediate** - HFI, 2-4D
Lighting: Drought Heat: **resistant**   Mine Spoils: **resistant**
Salt: **sensitive**   Soil Compaction: **intermediate**
Root Pattern: **shallow,** fibrous, suckering; **transplants well**

SPECIES: Associate: trees - Bur Oak, American Plum, Black Cherry, Prairie Crabapple, Eastern Red Cedar, hawthorn
species; shrubs - Fragrant/Smooth Sumacs, Allegany Blackberry, Indiancurrant Coralberry, Missouri Gooseberry
Similar: Multiflora Rose; Fiveleaved Aralia; Japanese Kerria - yellow flowers; Black Jetbead; Japanese Barberry
Cultivars: parent of many cultivated climbing roses; Tomentosa - leaflets dull above, woolly beneath

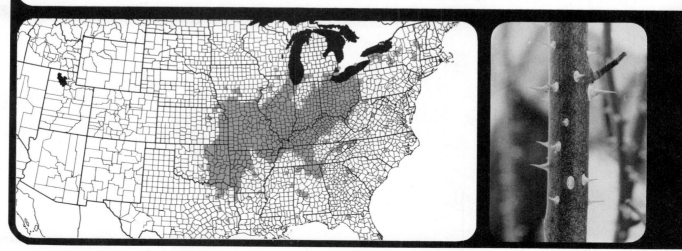

Rubus alleghaniensis

FORM: **mound**
Size: **small shrub** - from 1 to 2 m (3 to 6 ft)
Spread: **intermediate** - between 2 to 4 m (6 to 12 ft), commonly forming broad colonies
Mass: **open**

BRANCHING: multi-stemmed, little-branched **leggy** canes at first stiffly **erect,** finally high **arching; coarse** texture
Twig: stout, smooth, somewhat **angular** ribbed, **zigzag** appearance, **green** becoming **red to purplish**
Bud: narrow ovoid, 3 to 4 mm (⅛ to ⅙ in), **red**
Bark: **smooth,** without bloom, green becoming **purplish red; armed** with numerous stout recurved claw-like prickles

FOLIAGE: alternate, **palmately or pinnately compound,** 3-5 leaflets, **ovate,** double toothed, petioles prickly; **medium fine**
Surface: **glossy,** smooth, woolly beneath
Color: spring - bright **red green;** summer - **dark green;** autumn - **orange to red becoming** maroon **purple**
Season: **deciduous;** emergence - mid **May,** drop - late **September** or sooner

FLOWER: loose conical 14 to 18-flowered, terminal **spikes,** each 2.5 cm (1 in) wide, 5 petals, tendency to double-flower
Color: **white**
Season: early through late **June,** after leaves
Sex: monoecious

FRUIT: glossy thimble-shaped **berry,** multiple aggregate resembling a mulberry, 13 to 25 mm (½ to 1 in) long
Color: coal **black**
Season: early **July through** late **August**   Human Value: sweet spicy **edible fruits**
Wildlife Value: **very high;** ranks at top for summer food, upland gamebirds, songbirds, large and small mammals

HABITAT: formation - **forest, old field, glade;** region - **Central;** gradient - upland **mesic-dry, dry;** woodland edges, disturbed
   woods, clearings, roadsides, fence rows, old fields, dry rocky slopes, dry thickets
Shade Tolerance: **tolerant**
Flood Tolerance: **intermediate**

SOIL: Texture: **moderately coarse to moderately fine;** sandy or gravelly loams, medium loams, silt loams, sandy clays
Drainage: **moderately well to excessive**
Moisture: **average to droughty**
Reaction: **strongly acid to circumneutral,** pH 4.5 to 7.5

HARDINESS: zone **3b**
Rate: **fast**
Longevity: **very short,** 5 to 10 years, roots attain greater age than tops

SUSCEPTIBILITY: Physiological: **infrequent**
Disease: **occasional** - powdery mildew, rust, leaf spot, mosaic, anthracnose, systemic orange rust is damaging
Insect: **infrequent** - crown gall; minor problem
Wind-Ice: **infrequent**

URBAN TOLERANCE: Pollution: **resistant** - HFl, 2-4D
Lighting: Drought Heat: **resistant**   Mine Spoils:
Salt: Soil Compaction: **intermediate**
Root Pattern: **shallow** fibrous, suckering; **transplants well**

SPECIES: Associate: trees - White Ash, Black Cherry, Paper Birch, Eastern White Pine, Common Chokecherry, Red
   Maple; shrubs - Gray Dogwood, Dwarf Bushhoneysuckle, Rafinesque/Mapleleaf Virburnums, Pasture Gooseberry
Similar: rose/blackberry/raspberry/barberry species - similar habitat, form, fruit, armed
Cultivars: several garden varieties; 'Eldorado', 'Bailey', 'Darrow', 'Smoothstem', 'Midnite' - larger fruit at different times

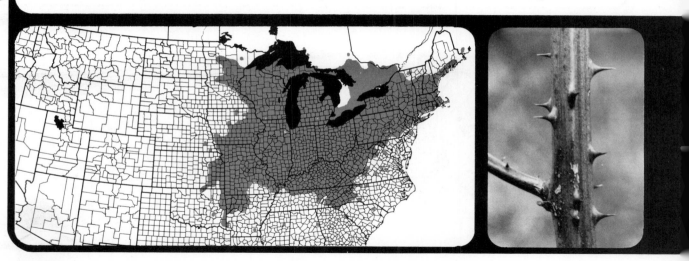

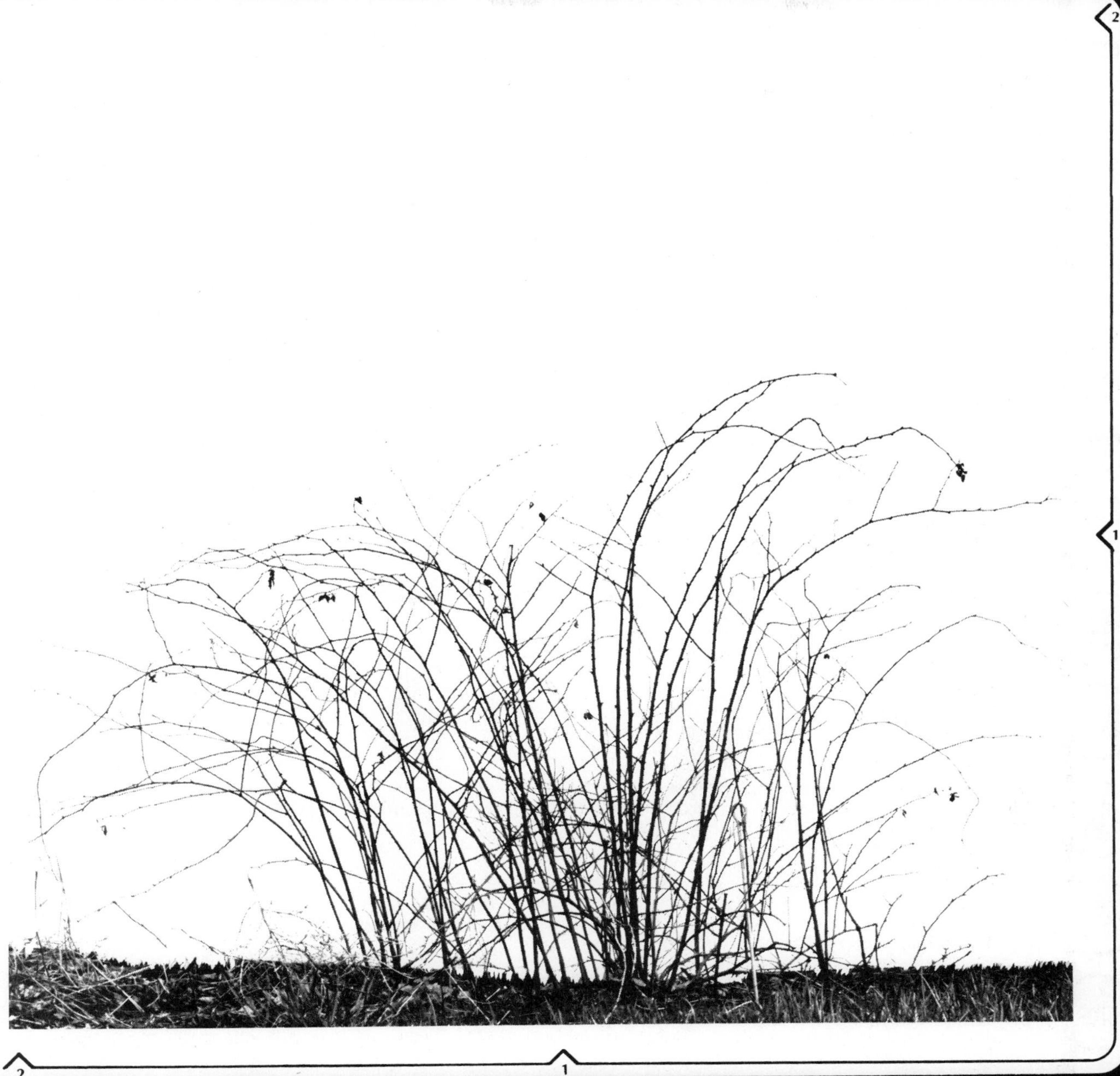
2
1
2
1

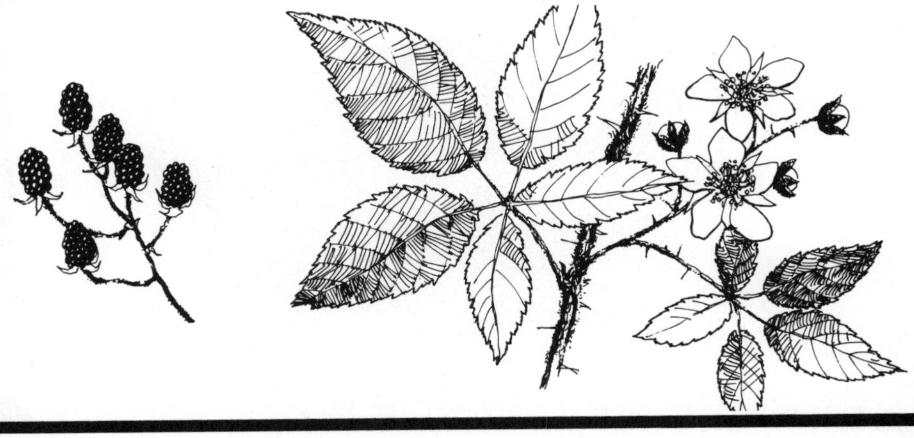

Rubus occidentalis

FORM: **mound**
Size: **small shrub** - from 1 to 2 m (3 to 6 ft)
Spread: **intermediate** - 2 to 4 m (6 to 12 ft), broader patches common
Mass: **open**

BRANCHING: **erect leggy** sparse-branched habit, finally graceful long slender **arching** canes, rooting at tips; **coarse**
Twig: smooth, **zigzag** appearance, **green** becoming **red to purple or black, white powdery bloom** on first year twigs
Bud: narrow ovoid, 3 to 6 mm (⅛ to ¼ in), partially hidden, **red brown**
Bark: **smooth,** white bloomy first year canes, old stems **red, purple to red brown; armed** with strong hooked prickles

FOLIAGE: alternate, **palmately or pinnately compound,** 3-5 leaflets, broadly **ovate,** coarse irregular teeth; **medium fine**
Surface: **dull,** smooth, white downy beneath
Color: spring - pale **yellow green;** summer - **blue green;** autumn - **blue green to yellowish**
Season: **deciduous;** emergence - mid **May,** drop - late **September** or earlier

FLOWER: **flat-topped** clusters, each blossom 13 mm (½ in) diameter, 5 petals, conspicuous green sepals twice petal size
Color: **white**
Season: late **May through** mid **June,** after leaves
Sex: monoecious

FRUIT: glossy hemispheric **berry,** multiple aggregate of drupes, 9.5 to 16 mm (⅜ to ⅝ in) diameter
Color: red at first maturing to coal **black** or deep purplish black
Season: early **July through** late **August**   Human Value: sweet **edible fruit**
Wildlife Value: **very high;** relished by songbirds, upland gamebirds, large and small mammals; browsers eat foliage

HABITAT: formation - **forest, glade, old field;** region - **Central;** gradient - upland **mesic-dry, dry;** disturbed woodlands, open
        bluffs, pastures, fence rows, roadsides, edges of woods, ravine thickets, abandoned fields
Shade Tolerance: **tolerant**
Flood Tolerance: **intermediate**

SOIL: Texture: **moderately coarse** gravelly or sandy loams **to moderately fine** silt loams, sandy clay loams, clay loams
Drainage: **moderately poor to excessive**
Moisture: **moist to droughty**
Reaction: **strongly acid to slightly acid,** pH 4.5 - 6.5

HARDINESS: zone 4a
Rate: **fast**
Longevity: **very short,** biennial, roots longer-lived

SUSCEPTIBILITY: Physiological: **infrequent**
Disease: **occasional** - mosaic, powdery mildew, rust, systemic orange rust is damaging
Insect: **infrequent**
Wind-Ice: **infrequent**

URBAN TOLERANCE: Pollution: **sensitive** - 2-4D; **resistant** - HFl
Lighting: Drought Heat: **resistant**   Mine Spoils:
Salt: Soil Compaction: **intermediate**
Root Pattern: **shallow** fibrous; **transplants well**

SPECIES: Associate: trees - Sassafras, hawthorn/serviceberry species, White/Chinkapin Oaks, Flowering Dogwood,
        Mockernut/Bitternut Hickories; shrubs - Gray Dogwood, Jerseytea Ceanothus, Carolina Rose, Fragrant Sumac
Similar: blackberry/raspberry/rose/barberry species - armament, fruit, flower, habitat, form similar
Cultivars: many garden varieties; 'Palidus' - yellow fruit; 'Allen', 'Bristol', 'Huron', 'Dundee', 'Jewel' - larger fruits

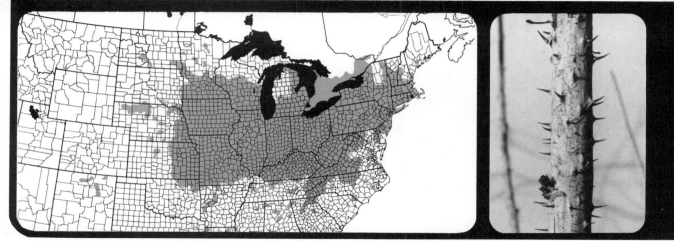

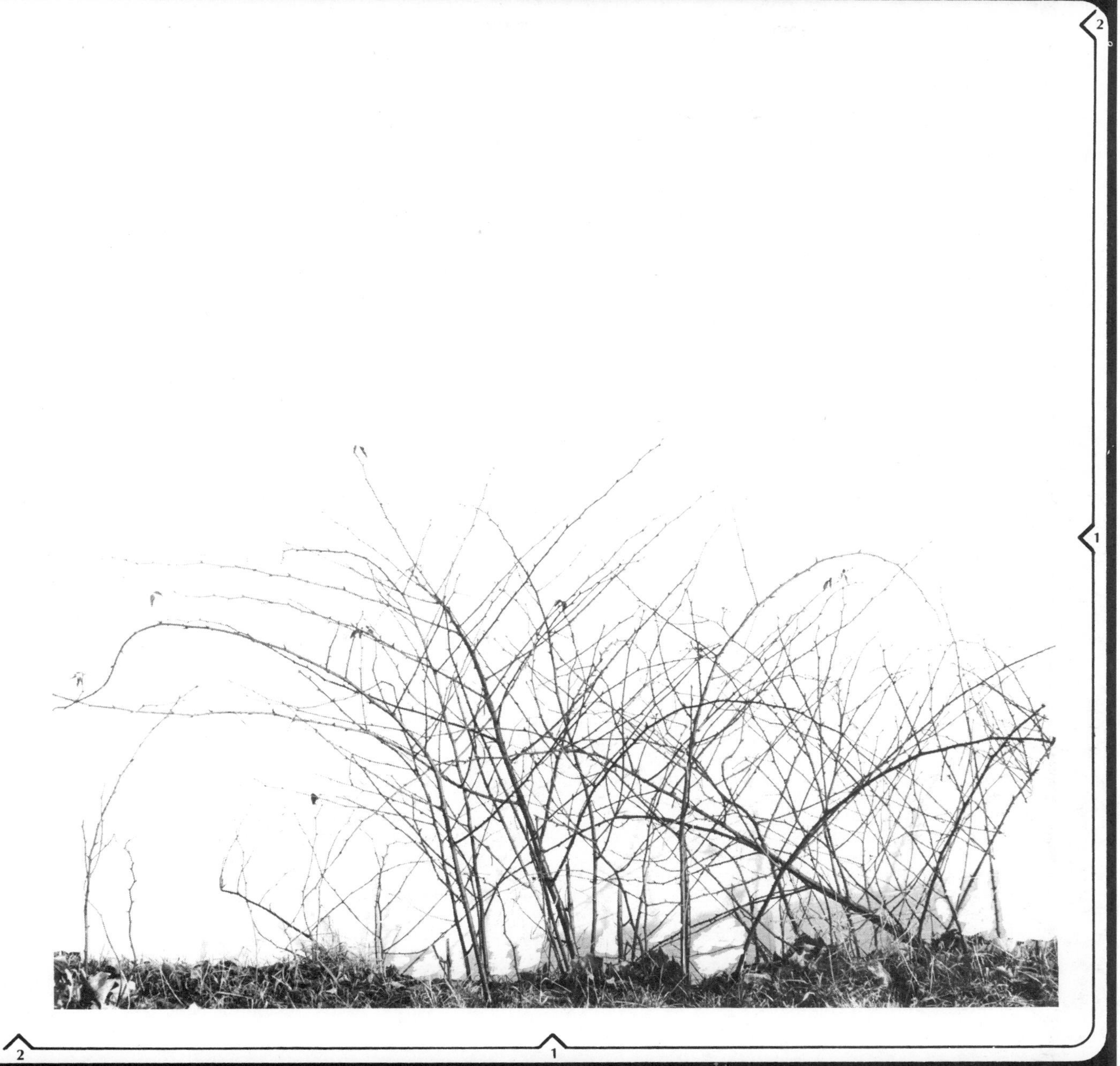
2
1
2
1

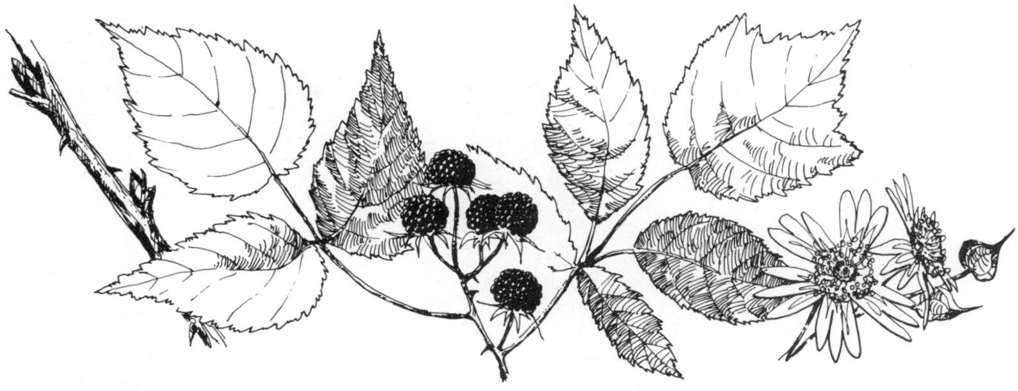

Rubus odoratus

FORM: mound
Size: **small shrub** - from 1 to 2 m (3 to 6 ft)
Spread: **intermediate** - 2 to 4 m (6 to 12 ft), often forming broad patches
Mass: **open**

BRANCHING: erect suckering **leggy** form with **arching** stems at maturity; **coarse** texture
Twig: **velvety** with stiff bristly hairs, **zigzag** appearance, **yellow brown**
Bud: ovate, woolly, pale **yellow brown**
Bark: **smooth** unarmed canes, heavy shaggy papery **exfoliation**, pale **yellow brown to orange brown**, old canes **gray**

FOLIAGE: alternate, **simple, palmately 5-lobed**, maple-like, irregularly toothed, bristly petioles; **coarse** texture
Surface: more or less **tomentose**, both sides
Color: spring - **yellow green to red green**; summer - **medium green**, petioles purplish red; autumn - pale **yellow**
Season: **deciduous**; emergence - late **May**, drop - late **September**

FLOWER: **large solitary** or open-branched few-flowered clusters, 5 petals, 4 to 5 cm (1½ to 2 in) across, resembles rose
Color: rose **purple**
Season: early **July through** late **August,** after leaves
Sex: monoecious   **Fragrant:** spicily perfumed or not noticeable

FRUIT: broad flat hemispheric **berry,** to 8 to 16 mm (⁵⁄₁₆ to ⅝ in) diameter
Color: pale dull **red to purplish**
Season: late **August through** late **September**   Human Value: scarcely **edible fruit,** dry & mealy, acid
Wildlife Value: **very high;** very popular with songbirds, upland gamebirds, large and small mammals, hoofed browsers

HABITAT: formation - **forest, bald, savanna, old field;** region - **Northern, Central;** gradient - **mesic, mesic-dry;** cool shaded
ravines, rocky woodlands, deep coves, woods edge, banks of quick flowing mountain streams, mountain summits
Shade Tolerance: **very tolerant**
Flood Tolerance: **intolerant**

SOIL: Texture: **moderately coarse to medium;** rocky, gravelly or sandy loams, deep forest loams, silt loams
Drainage: **moderately well to excessive**
Moisture: **moist to average**
Reaction: **moderately acid,** pH 5.1 - 6.0

HARDINESS: zone 4a
Rate: **fast**
Longevity: **very short-lived**

SUSCEPTIBILITY: Physiological: **occasional** - twig dieback in winter, several inches from tips
Disease: **infrequent** - none serious
Insect: **infrequent** - none serious
Wind-Ice: **frequent** - soft, scarcely woody stems, breakage in exposed areas

URBAN TOLERANCE: Pollution: **resistant** - HFI, 2-4D
Lighting: Drought Heat: **intermediate**   Mine Spoils:
Salt: Soil Compaction: **intermediate**
Root Pattern: **shallow** fibrous, freely suckering; **easily transplanted**

SPECIES: Associate: trees - White Ash, White Mulberry, American Beech, Sugar Maple, Yellow/Sweet Birches; shrubs -
American Elder, Mapleleaf Viburnum, Common Witchhazel, Brook Euonymus, Hobblebush Viburnum
Similar: Western Thimbleberry - flowers white; Rose of Sharon - larger, Asiatic; Common Ninebark - form, bark similar
Cultivars: none available

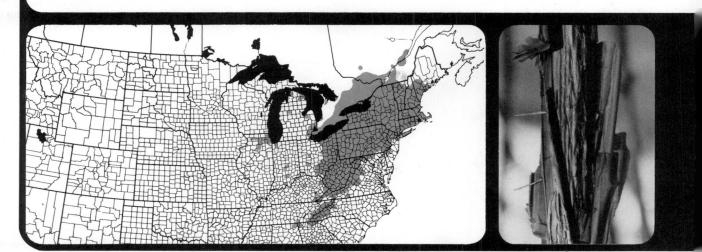

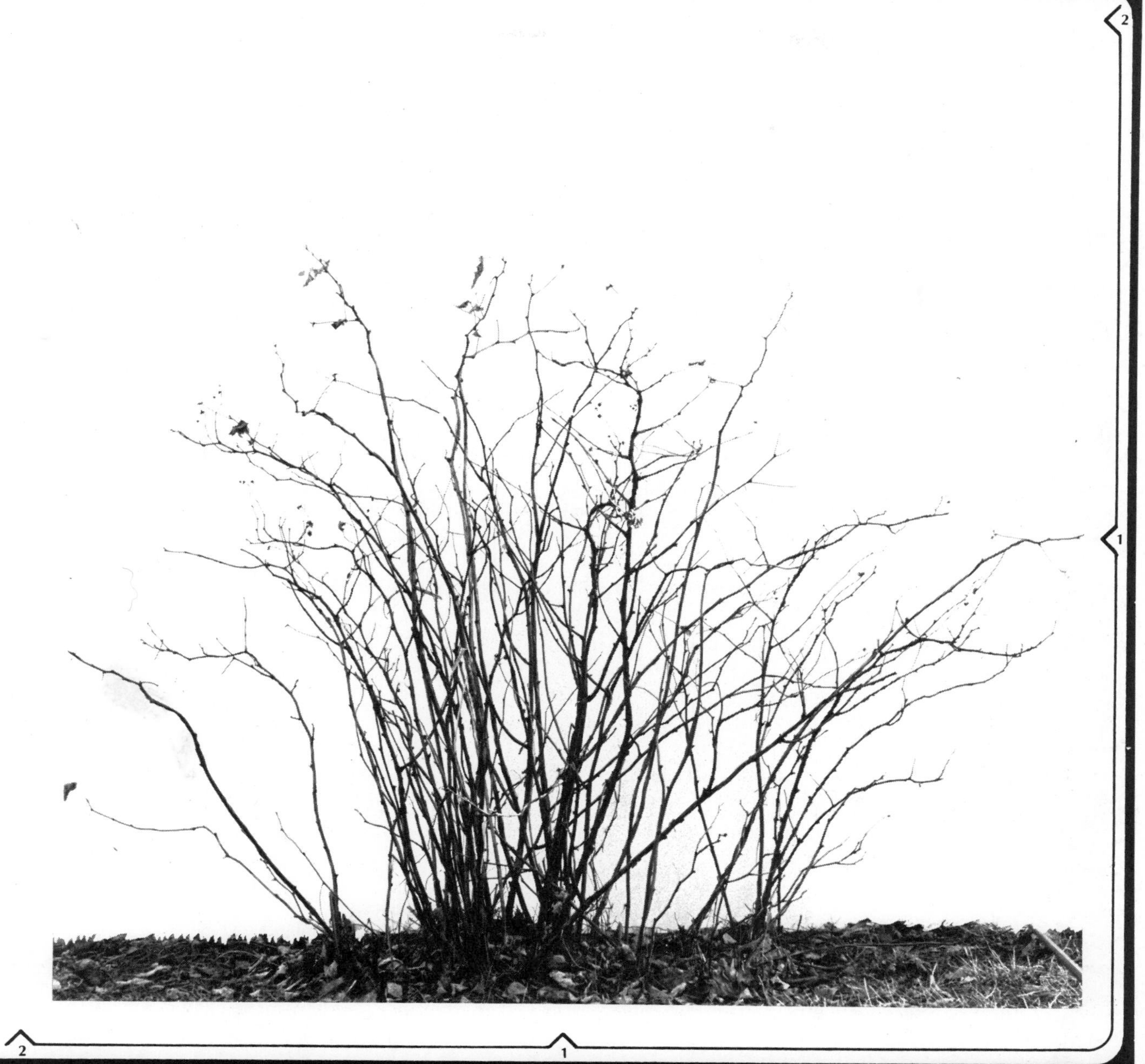
2
1
2
1

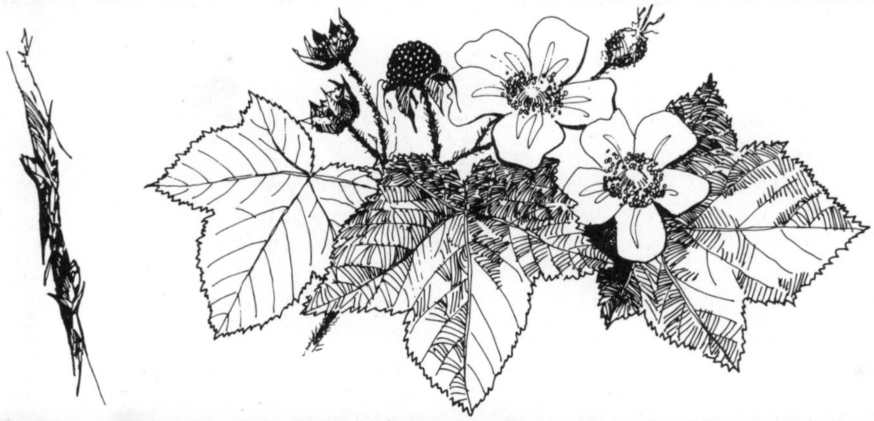

Rubus strigosus

FORM: mound
Size: **small shrub** - from 1 to 2 m (3 to 6 ft)
Spread: **intermediate** - 2 to 4 m (6 to 12 ft), often forming broader thickets
Mass: **open**

BRANCHING: multiple stems, stiffly **erect** little-branched **leggy** canes nodding at tips, finally **arching; coarse** texture
Twig: moderately slender, dense bristly, **zigzag,** first year twigs with **white powdery bloom,** then **red to purple or black**
Bud: small ovoid, 3 to 6 mm (⅛ to ¼ in), downy, **brown**
Bark: **smooth** with whitened bloom, older canes **red purple or red brown;** flowering shoots **armed** with stiff prickles

FOLIAGE: alternate, **pinnately compound,** 3 to 5 leaflets, **ovate,** sharp double toothed, petioles prickly; **medium fine** texture
Surface: **dull,** smooth, dense tomentose beneath
Color: spring - **red green;** summer - bright **medium green;** autumn - deep wine **red to** maroon **purple**
Season: **deciduous;** emergence - mid **May,** drop - mid **October** or later

FLOWER: open scattered **flat-topped** clusters, each bloom 13 mm (½ in) diameter, 5 petals, rose-like appearance
Color: **white**
Season: late **May through** mid **July,** after leaves
Sex: monoecious

FRUIT: hemispheric **berry,** aggregate of drupes, somewhat downy, 13 to 17 mm (½ to ⅔ in) diameter
Color: bright **red**
Season: early **July through** late **August**   Human Value: spicily flavored **edible fruit**
Wildlife Value: **very high;** quickly eaten by songbirds, upland gamebirds, large and small mammals; browsers graze

HABITAT: formation - **bog, cliff, forest, old field;** region - **Northern;** gradient - lowland **wet,** upland **mesic-dry, dry;** swampy
woods, peaty or boggy sites, ravine banks, talus slopes, open or wooded hillsides, clearings, rocky slopes, burns
Shade Tolerance: **tolerant**
Flood Tolerance: **intermediate**

SOIL: Texture: **moderately coarse** rocky, gravelly, or sandy loams **to fine** sandy clay loams, silt loams, sandy peats
Drainge: **very poor to excessive**
Moisture: **wet to droughty**
Reaction: **moderately acid to neutral,** pH 5.5 - 7.0

HARDINESS: zone 2
Rate: **fast**
Longevity: **very short,** biennial, roots longer-lived

SUSCEPTIBILITY: Physiological: **infrequent**
Disease: **occasional** - mosaic, anthracnose, systemic orange rust is damaging
Insect: **infrequent**
Wind-Ice: **infrequent**

URBAN TOLERANCE: Pollution: **intermediate** - HFI, 2-4D
Lighting: Drought Heat: **resistant**   Mine Spoils:
Salt: Soil Compaction: **resistant**
Root Pattern: **shallow** fibrous, **stoloniferous,** suckering freely; **transplants easily**

SPECIES: Associate: Red/Striped/Mountain/Sugar Maples, Jack/Red/Eastern White Pines; shrubs - American Fly
Honeysuckle, Beaked Filbert, Scarlet Elder, Lowbush Blueberry; Western Thimbleberry, Pasture Gooseberry
Similar: many raspberry/blackberry/thimbleberry/rose/barberry species - fruits, form, habitat, fall color similar
Cultivars: progenitor of all the cultivated garden varieties; 'Amber'; 'Milton'; 'Taylor'; 'September'; 'Scepter'; many

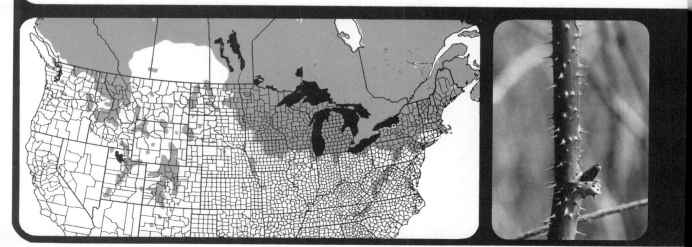

American Red Raspberry

687

Salix humilis

FORM: **globular or mound**
Size: **mid-height shrub** - from 2 to 4 m (6 to 12 ft)
Spread: **intermediate** - between 2 to 4 m (6 to 12 ft), typically up to twice the height
Mass: **open**

BRANCHING: clustered multiple stems, **upright spreading or ascending** wand-like branches; **medium** texture
Twig: dull, slender, densely covered with **velvety** grayish down, **yellow brown** in summer varying **to red** in winter
Bud: small blunt oval, 4 to 6 mm (⅙ to ¼ in), **1 bud scale, woolly, yellow brown, brown to red; winter catkins**
Bark: smooth with conspicuous lenticels, old stems **shallow furrowed** with irregular crack-like fissures, **orange brown**

FOLIAGE: alternate, crowded at branch tips, **simple,** narrow **oblanceolate,** nearly entire, edges wavy, rolled; **medium fine**
Surface: **dull,** smooth, wrinkled veiny appearance, whitened and soft downy beneath
Color: spring - **light green;** summer - **gray green to blue green;** autumn - dull **yellow**
Season: **deciduous;** emergence - mid **May,** drop - mid **October**

FLOWER: slender pencil-like drooping **catkins,** 16 to 32 mm (⅝ to 1¼ in) long
Color: **greenish to yellow green**
Season: mid **April through** early **May,** before leaves
Sex: **dioecious**

FRUIT: small slender long-beaked **capsules;** 6 mm (¼ in) long, releasing cottony wind-disseminated seeds
Color: **brown**
Season: late **May through** mid **June**   Human Value: **edible leaves**
Wildlife Value: **high;** early season harvest for songbirds, waterbirds, marshbirds, small mammals; hoofed browsers graze

HABITAT: formation - **bog, meadow, prairie, bald, barrens, old field;** region - **Northern, Central;** gradient - **wet, mesic-dry, dry;**
boggy swales, mountain balds, rocky mountain ridges, barrens, dry upland prairies, dry rock outcrops, roadsides
Shade Tolerance: **very intolerant**
Flood Tolerance: **tolerant**

SOIL: Texture: **coarse to fine;** thin soils over bedrock, infertile sands, gravels, silts, clays, well decomposed peats
Drainage: **very poor to excessive**
Moisture: **wet to droughty**
Reaction: **slightly acid to circumneutral,** pH 6.1 - 7.5

HARDINESS: **zone 3a**
Rate: **slow to medium**
Longevity: **short-lived**

SUSCEPTIBILITY: Physiological: **infrequent**
Disease: **occasional** - crown gall, leaf blight, black canker, cytospora canker, leafspots, rust, powdery mildew, tar spot
Insect: **occasional** - willow lace bug, poplar borer, mottled willow borer, willow shoot sawfly, willow scurfy scale, others
Wind-Ice: **frequent** - weak wooded, stems often damaged or broken

URBAN TOLERANCE: Pollution: **sensitive** - 2-4D, S0₂, MV; **resistant** - HFI
Lighting: Drought Heat: **resistant**   Mine Spoils:
Salt: **resistant**   Soil Compaction: **resistant**
Root Pattern: **shallow fibrous; transplants easily**

SPECIES: Associate: trees - Quaking Aspen, Black/Northern Pin/Bur Oaks, Eastern Red Cedar, Staghorn/Smooth
Sumacs; shrubs - Meadowsweet Spirea, Fragrant Sumac, American Filbert, Roundleaf/Gray Dogwoods
Similar: Dwarf Prairie Willow, other willows; Low/Bog Birches - coppery bark; Hazel/Common Alders
Cultivars: none available

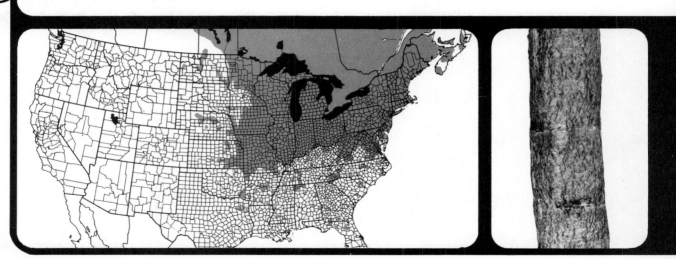

Prairie Willow

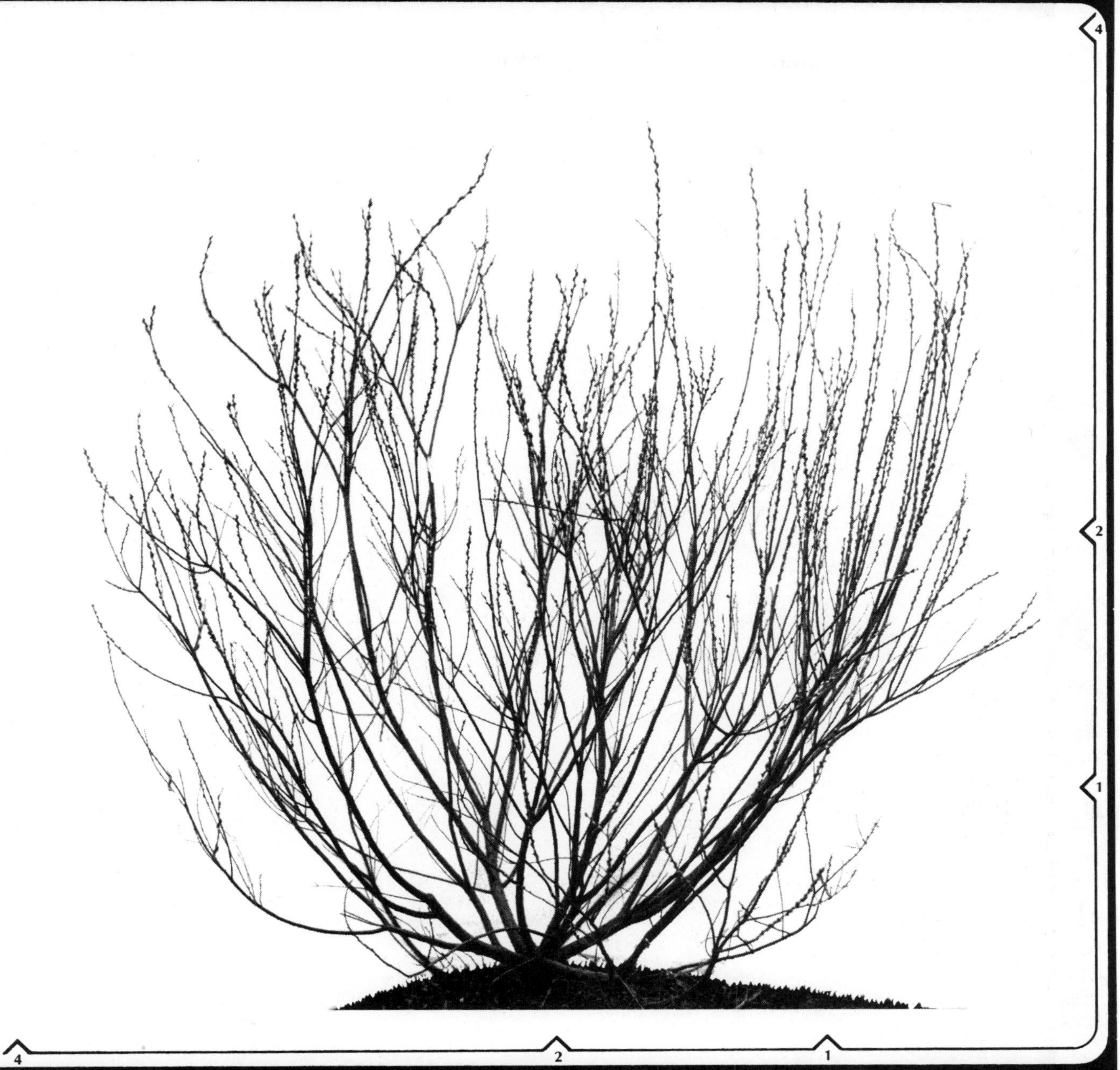

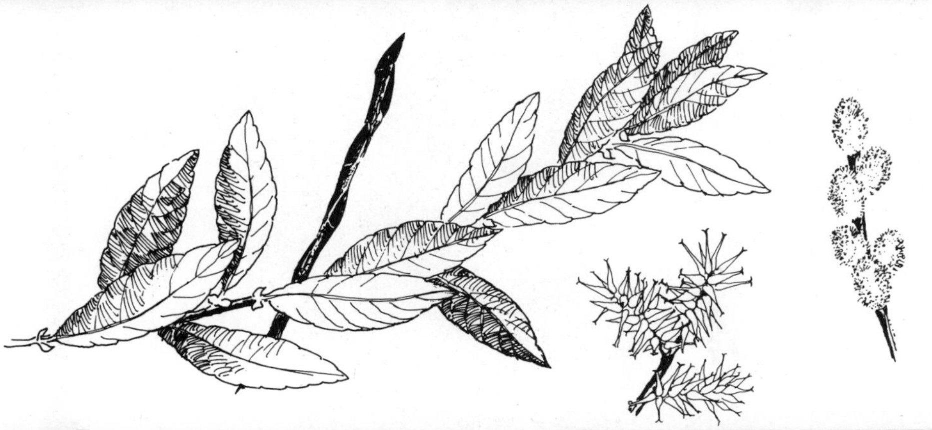

Salix lucida

FORM: broad **globular or mounded** crown
Size: **large shrub** - from 4 to 6 m (12 to 20 ft)
Spread: **wide** - 4 to 6 m (12 to 20 ft), occasionally to 8 m (26 ft)
Mass: **open**

BRANCHING: short trunk, **upright spreading** habit; **fine** texture
Twig: slender and wiry, glossy, **orange brown** or tinged with red becoming **brown**
Bud: narrow ovoid, 6 mm (¼ in) long, glossy, **1 bud scale, orange brown or brown; winter catkins**
Bark: **smooth,** thin, dark **red brown**

FOLIAGE: alternate, **simple,** narrow lanceolate to **ovate lanceolate,** fine toothed, petiole winged at base; **fine** texture
Surface: **glossy** on both surfaces, smooth
Color: spring - bright **yellow green;** summer - **yellow green to medium green;** autumn - **yellowish green** late, **then purplish**
Season: **deciduous;** emergence - late **April,** drop - mid **October**

FLOWER: erect cylindric **catkin,** 4 to 5 cm (1½ to 2 in) long, densely flowered
Color: light **green to yellow green**
Season: late **April through** mid **May,** with leaves
Sex: **dioecious**

FRUIT: glossy cylindric cluster of **capsules,** releasing cottony wind-disseminated seed
Color: **brown**
Season: early **June through** early **July**   Human Value: **edible leaves**
Wildlife Value: **high;** early season popularity with songbirds, marshbirds, waterbirds, small mammals

HABITAT: formation - **bog, spring, meadow, forest, dune;** region - **Northern;** gradient - lowland **wet;** banks of streams and
    swamps, islands, calcareous fens, springy places, lake dunes, beaches, wet meadows, ditches, mud flats
Shade Tolerance: **very intolerant**
Flood Tolerance: **very tolerant**

SOIL: Texture: almost any soil; **coarse** sands and gravels, loamy sands **to fine** silt loams, silty clay loams
Drainage: **very poor to moderately poor**
Moisture: **wet to moist**
Reaction: **slightly acid to circumneutral,** pH 6.1 - 7.5

HARDINESS: zone 2
Rate: **fast**
Longevity: **short-lived**

SUSCEPTIBILITY: Physiological: **infrequent**
Disease: **occasional** - witches' broom, tar spot, rust, powdery mildew, leaf spots, gray scab, cytospora canker, others
Insect: **occasional** - bagworm, hemlock looper, thrips, willow shoot sawfly, willow scurfy scale, poplar borer, many more
Wind-Ice: **frequent** - weak wood, easily broken

URBAN TOLERANCE: Pollution: **sensitive** - S0₂, MV, 2-4D; **resistant** - HFI
Lighting: Drought Heat: **resistant**   Mine Spoils:
Salt: **resistant**   Soil Compaction: **resistant**
Root Pattern: **shallow lateral; easily transplanted**

SPECIES: Associate: trees - Balsam Poplar, American Larch, Balsam Fir, Hazel Alder, willow species; shrubs - pure stands,
    Black Chokeberry, Hardhack Spirea, Silky/Red-osier Dogwoods, blueberry species, Common Buttonbush
Similar: many shrub forms of willow/alder/birch species
Cultivars: none available

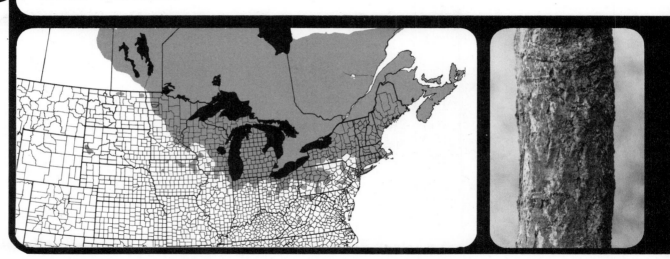

Sambucus canadensis

FORM: obovoid to globular
Size: **mid-height shrub** - from 2 to 4 m (6 to 12 ft)
Spread: **intermediate** - between 2 to 4 m (6 to 12 ft), typically ⅔ or equal to height
Mass: **open**

BRANCHING: tightly clustered stems at base, **leggy upright spreading** finally **arching** branches; **coarse** texture
Twig: stout, smooth, large warty lenticels, **large leaf scars** connected by linear **ridges,** joints swollen; **yellow brown**
Bud: small ovoid, 1.5 to 2 mm (¹⁄₁₆ to ⅛ in), divergent, solitary or **clustered, red brown to brown or purplish** tinged
Bark: **smooth** with rough prominent wart-like lenticels, aromatic when bruised, pale **yellow brown to gray brown**

FOLIAGE: opposite, **pinnately compound,** 5 to 11 usually 7 leaflets, **lanceolate,** coarsely toothed; **medium** texture
Surface: **dull,** smooth
Color: spring - bright **medium green;** summer - **medium green;** autumn - green late, then **yellow green**
Season: **deciduous;** emergence - early **May,** drop - early **November** or later

FLOWER: small star-shaped flowers in very large **flat-topped** clusters, 15 to 25 cm (6 to 10 in) across, profuse
Color: **white**
Season: late **June through** mid **July,** often intermittently through fall, after leaves
Sex: monoecious   **Fragrant:** slightly or heavily scented

FRUIT: smooth globular **berry,** 5 mm (³⁄₁₆ in) diameter, in broad usually drooping flat-topped clusters
Color: deep **purple to black,** stems red to purple
Season: early **August through** late **September**   Human Value: **edible fruit and flowers**
Wildlife Value: **very high;** relished by 48 species of birds, also large and small mammals; hoofed browsers eat twigs, leaves

HABITAT: formation - **forest, old field, bog, spring, meadow;** region - **Central, Southern;** gradient - **wet, wet-mesic, mesic,**
   mesic-dry; bogs, ditches, banks of canals, bayous, disturbed sites, alluvial forests, marshes, fence rows, deep woods
Shade Tolerance: **very tolerant**
Flood Tolerance: **very tolerant**

SOIL: Texture: almost any soil, **coarse** sands and gravels, deep loams **to fine** silts, heavy clays, peats, mucks
Drainage: **very poor to excessive**
Moisture: **wet to dry,** tolerates **droughty**
Reaction: **slightly acid to circumneutral,** pH 6.1 - 7.5

HARDINESS: zone 3a
Rate: **fast**
Longevity: **very short-lived,** however root masses producing new shoots longer-lived

SUSCEPTIBILITY: Physiological: **frequent** - tips of twigs die back regularly
Disease: **occasional** - cankers, leaf spots, powdery mildews, root rots, thread blight, Verticillium wilt, others
Insect: **infrequent** - none serious, borers, San Jose scale, grape mealybug, green stink bug, thrips, potato flea beetle
Wind-Ice: **frequent** - pith large (white coloration), scarcely woody, broken with light hand pressure

URBAN TOLERANCE: Pollution: **sensitive** - 0₃, 2-4D; **intermediate** - HFI
Lighting: Drought Heat: **resistant**   Mine Spoils:
Salt: **sensitive**   Soil Compaction: **resistant**
Root Pattern: amply fibrous, **shallow lateral, stoloniferous,** suckers freely forming thickets; **transplants well,** culture easy

SPECIES: Associate: trees - Black/Peachleaf Willows, River Birch, American Planetree, Common Hackberry, Black
   Walnut; shrubs - Possumhaw, Common Alder, Common Ninebark, Indiancurrant Coralberry, Common Winterberry
Similar: Scarlet Elder - red fruit, mesic habitat; European Elder - taller; Arrowwood Viburnum
Cultivars: 'Aurea' - golden yellow leaves; 'Rubra' - red fruit; 'Maxima' - large flower cluster; 'Adams'; 'Acutiloba'; others

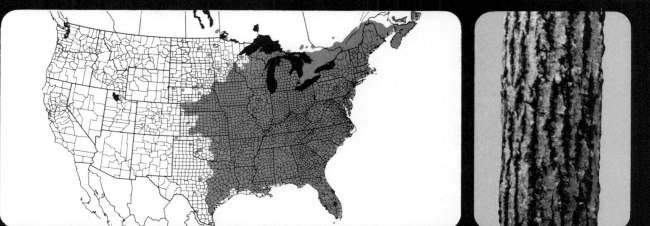

Sambucus pubens

FORM: **obovoid to globular**
Size: **mid-height shrub** - from 2 to 4 m (6 to 12 ft), occasionally to 5 m (16 ft)
Spread: **intermediate** - between 2 to 4 m (6 to 12 ft), commonly ⅔ or equal to height
Mass: **open**

BRANCHING: tightly clustered basal stems with **leggy upright spreading** branches, finally arching with age; **coarse** texture
Twig: stout, smooth with many brown warty lenticels, **large leaf scars** with **ridged** lines between, **gray brown to purplish**
Bud: **large** ovoid to obovoid, 13 mm (½ in), short **stalked**, dark **purple** to red
Bark: **smooth** with rough warty raised lenticels, old stems with squarish **blocky** pattern, **purplish** becoming **gray**

FOLIAGE: opposite, **pinnately compound,** 5 to 7 leaflets, **lanceolate to oblong lanceolate,** sharply toothed; **medium** texture
Surface: **dull,** smooth, somewhat downy beneath
Color: spring - **medium green;** summer - bright **medium green;** autumn - green late, then **yellow green**
Season: **deciduous;** emergence - late **April,** drop - early **November** or later

FLOWER: small flower in loose upright broadly conical **spikes,** 10 cm (4 in) tall, terminal spikes solitary or compound
Color: **white**
Season: early through late **May,** after leaves, one of earliest native shrubs in bloom
Sex: monoecious   **Fragrant:** very heavy odor

FRUIT: globular pea-size **berry,** 5 to 6 cm (⅕ to ¼ in) diameter, in broad conical upright clusters
Color: **brilliant red**
Season: late **June through** late **July**   Human Value: **all parts poisonous**
Wildlife Value: **very high;** important summer food, songbirds, upland gamebirds, large and small mammals

HABITAT: formation - **forest, moist cliff;** region - **Northern;** gradient - upland **mesic, mesic-dry;** deep rich woods, cool talus
slopes, dry rocky woods, lining quick flowing creeks, moist rock crevices, sheltered coves and ravines
Shade Tolerance: **very tolerant**
Flood Tolerance: **very intolerant**

SOIL: Texture: shallow **moderately coarse** rocky or sandy loams over bedrock, medium loams **to moderately fine** silt loams
Drainage: **moderately well to well**
Moisture: **moist to average**
Reaction: **slightly acid to** circumneutral, tolerates **alkaline,** pH 6.1 - 8.5

HARDINESS: **zone 3a**
Rate: **fast**
Longevity: **very short-lived**

SUSCEPTIBILITY: Physiological: **infrequent**
Disease: **infrequent** - various cankers, leaf spot, powdery mildew, root rot, thread blight, Verticillium wilt; rarely serious
Insect: **infrequent** - borers; rarely serious
Wind-Ice: **frequent** - pith large (orange or brown color), weak wooded, easily broken

URBAN TOLERANCE: Pollution: **sensitive** - 2-4D; **resistant** - HFI, S0$_2$
Lighting: Drought Heat: **sensitive**   Mine Spoils:
Salt: **sensitive**   Soil Compaction: **intermediate**
Root Pattern: fibrous, **deep laterals; transplants with difficulty**

SPECIES: Associate: trees - Sugar Maple, American Beech, Bitternut Hickory, Yellow Birch, Black Ash; shrubs - Running
Euonymus, Common Spicebush, Mapleleaf Viburnum, Leatherwood, Beaked Filbert, Roundleaf Dogwood
Similar: American Elder - fruit purple; American Cranberrybush/Wright Viburnums, Common Winterberry - red berries
Cultivars: 'Dissecta' - deeply divided leaflets; 'Leucocarpa' - white fruits; 'Xanthocarpa' - yellow fruit; others

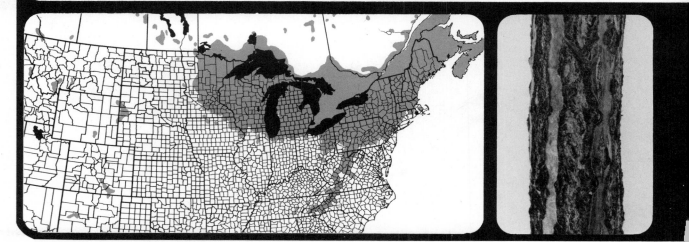

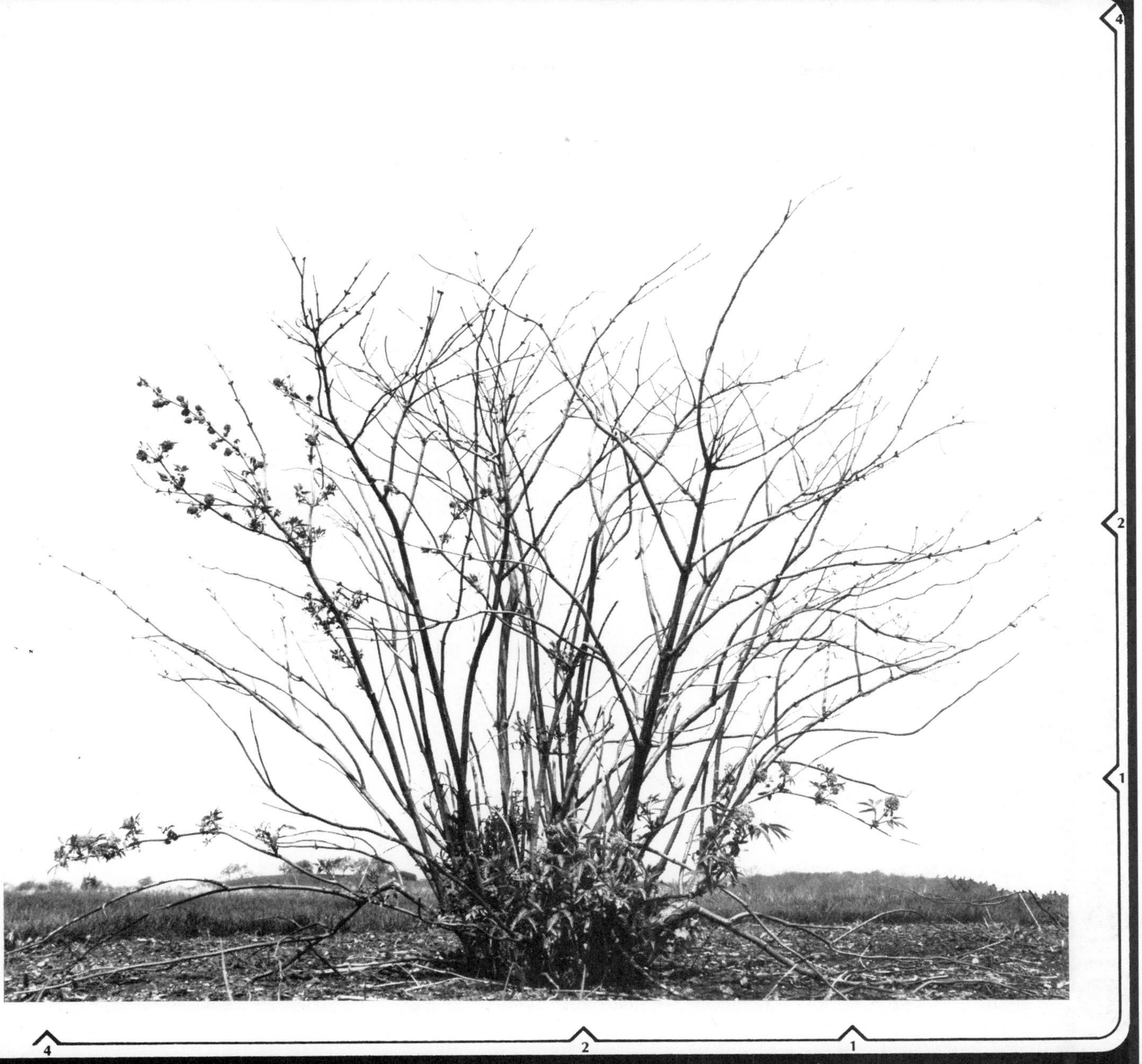
4
2
1
4
2
1

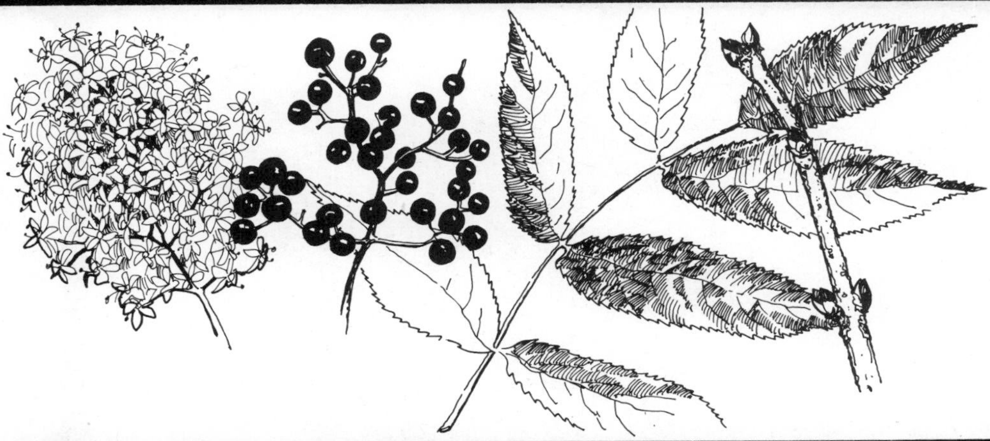

Shepherdia argentea

FORM: **mound to globular**
Size: **mid-height shrub** - from 2 to 4 m (6 to 12 ft), occasionally to 6 m (20 ft)
Spread: **intermediate** - between 2 to 4 m (6 to 12 ft), often to 6 m (20 ft)
Mass: **open**

BRANCHING: solitary or few short-trunked stems, dense twiggy **ascending** branches; **medium** texture
Twig: covered with fine **white** velvety hairs and **silvery gray or gray** bran-like **scales; armed** with sharp-pointed spiny twigs
Bud: **naked,** silvery **gray or whitish**
Bark: **scaly** becoming **shallow furrowed; gray to gray brown**

FOLIAGE: opposite, **simple, elliptic to oval,** entire; **fine** texture
Surface: **dull,** with fine scurfy tomentum and/or scales on both sides
Color: spring - light **silvery gray** to white; summer, autumn - **silvery gray green**
Season: **deciduous;** emergence - mid **May,** drop - mid **October**

FLOWER: male in **small clusters** at joints of previous years growth, female often solitary, bell-shaped, inconspicuous
Color: female - **yellow**
Season: mid **April through** early **May,** before leaves
Sex: **dioecious**

FRUIT: cherry-like football-shaped **berry,** 4 to 6 mm (⅙ to ¼ in) long, single or in clusters of 2 to 5
Color: scarlet **red, yellow or orange**
Season: mid **July through** late **August**   Human Value: sour **edible fruit**
Wildlife Value: **low;** limited use by song and game birds, small mammals

HABITAT: formation - **glade, barrens, prairie, old field;** region - **Northern;** gradient - **mesic-dry to dry;** calcareous clay ridges
and slopes, glades, stream banks
Shade Tolerance: **very intolerant**
Flood Tolerance: **very intolerant**

SOIL: Texture: **coarse to moderately coarse;** pure sands, gravels, sandy plains, sandy or gravelly loams
Drainage: **well to excessive**
Moisture: **dry to droughty**
Reaction: **slightly acid to** circumneutral, tolerates **alkaline,** pH 6.1 - 8.5

HARDINESS: zone 2
Rate: **medium**
Longevity: **long-lived**

SUSCEPTIBILITY: Physiological: **infrequent**
Disease: **infrequent** - leaf spots, powdery mildew, rust; unimportant
Insect: **infrequent** - very resistant
Wind-Ice: **infrequent**

URBAN TOLERANCE: Pollution:
Lighting: Drought Heat: very **resistant**   Mine Spoils:
Salt: **resistant**   Soil Compaction: **sensitive**
Root Pattern: **deep** coarse **laterals,** nitrogen-fixing; very **difficult to transplant**

SPECIES: Associate: shrubs - Indiancurrant Coralberry, Western Snowberry, Leadplant Amorpha, Prairie Rose, Silver-
berry, Russet Buffaloberry, Fragrant Sumac, Clove Currant
Similar: Silverberry; Autumn Eleagnus; Russet Buffaloberry; Common Seabuckthorn - taller, European
Cultivars: 'Xanthocarpa' - yellow fruit

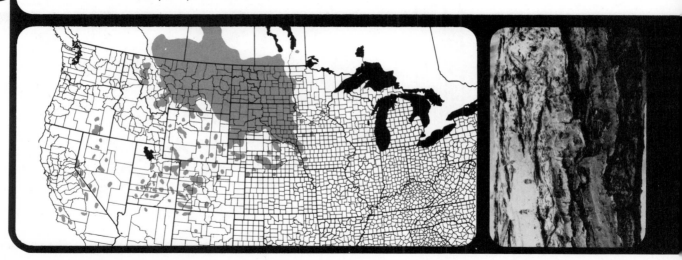

Silver Buffaloberry

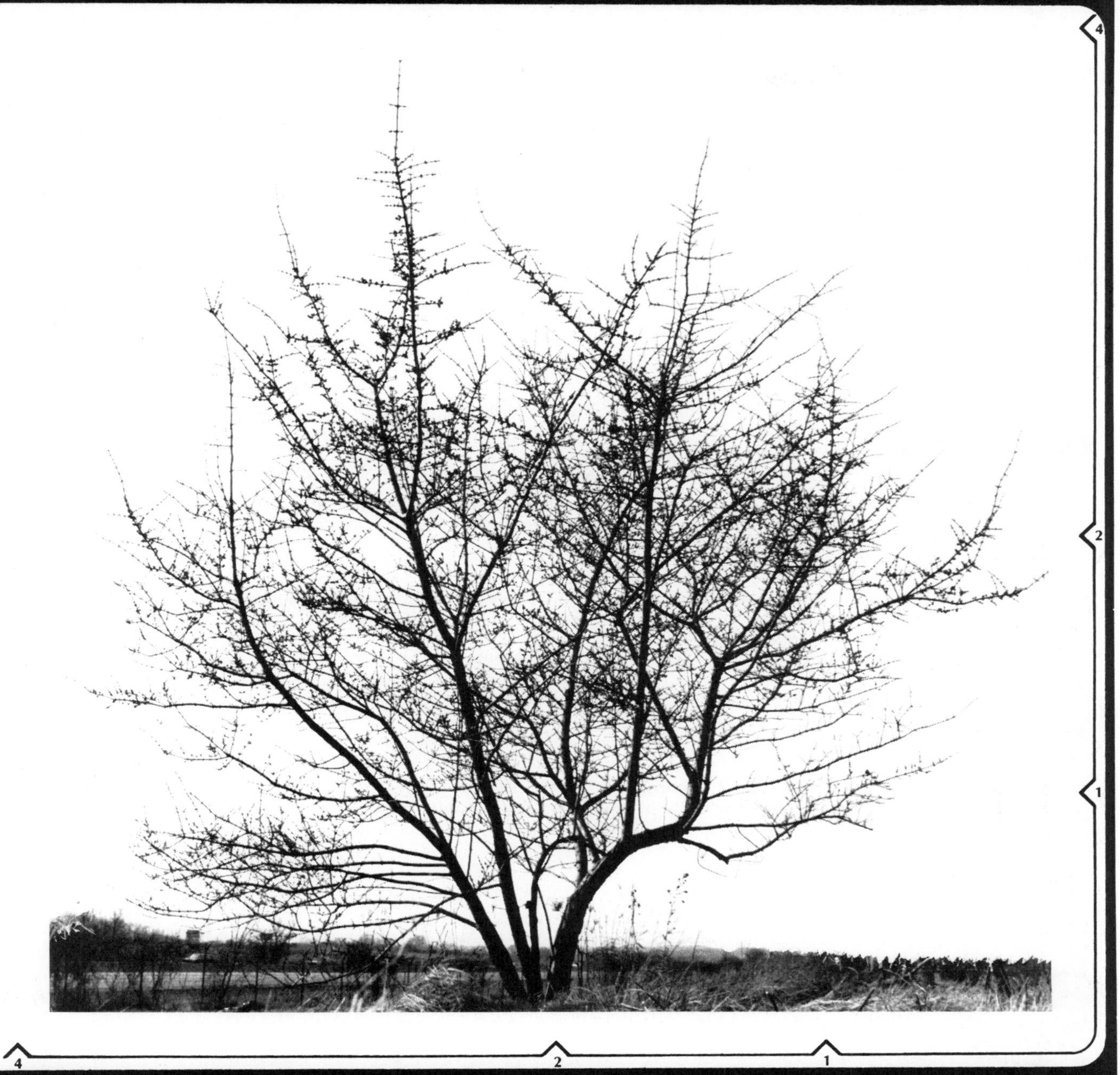

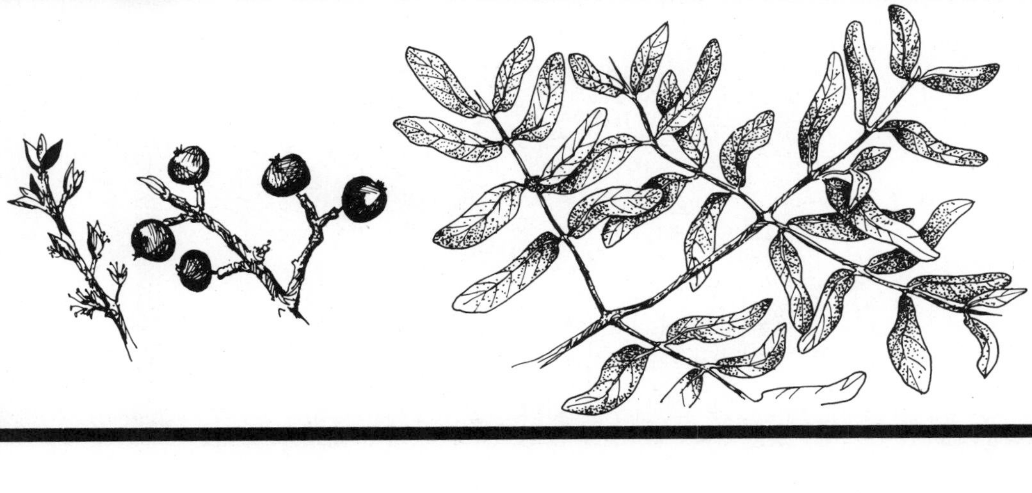

Shepherdia canadensis

FORM: **obovoid to globular,** typically broadest at crown apex and somewhat flattened
Size: **mid-height shrub** - from 2 to 4 m (6 to 12 ft), occasionally to 6 m (20 ft), but commonly to only 3 m (9 ft)
Spread: **intermediate** - between 2 to 4 m (6 to 12 ft), typically ⅔ or equal to height
Mass: **open**

BRANCHING: solitary or few-clustered stems, twiggy **ascending** branches; **medium** texture
Twig: slender, covered with rusty red **brown** flaky bran-like **scales;** not spiny
Bud: small, **naked,** solitary or clustered, 5 mm (³⁄₁₆ in), distinctly **stalked, red brown**
Bark: **scaly or shallow furrowed** with minute horizontal lenticels, dark **gray brown to gray**

FOLIAGE: opposite, **simple, elliptic,** entire margin, small leaves commonly crowded at base of petiole; **fine** texture
Surface: **dull,** smooth above, silvery and scurfy with rusty scales beneath
Color: spring - **silvery gray;** summer - **gray green;** autumn - **gray green becoming** rusty **purple**
Season: **deciduous;** emergence - mid **May,** drop - mid **October**

FLOWER: **small** solitary or few-flowered **clusters, bell**-shaped, 4 mm (⅙ in) diameter, generally inconspicuous
Color: greenish yellow or pale **yellow**
Season: mid **April through** early **May,** before leaves
Sex: **dioecious**

FRUIT: translucent ovoid cherry-like **berry,** 8 mm (⅓ in) long, single or clusters of 2 to 5
Color: **yellow to red**
Season: late **June through** mid **August**   Human Value: **edible fruit**
Wildlife Value: **low;** limited use by upland gamebirds, songbirds, small mammals

HABITAT: formation - **savanna, forest, old field;** region - **Northern;** gradient - upland **mesic-dry, dry;** dry open rocky or sandy
     hill slopes, ridge tops, woods edge, banks of streams, limestone outcrops
Shade Tolerance: **very intolerant**
Flood Tolerance: **very intolerant**

SOIL: Texture: **coarse** gravels and sands **to moderately coarse** thin rocky or sandy loams over bedrock
Drainage: **well to excessive**
Moisture: **dry to droughty**
Reaction: **slightly acid to** circumneutral, tolerates **alkaline,** pH 6.1 - 8.5

HARDINESS: **zone 2**
Rate: slow to **medium**
Longevity: **moderately short-lived**

SUSCEPTIBILITY: Physiological: **infrequent**
Disease: **infrequent** - powdery mildew, rust, several leaf spots; none are serious
Insect: **infrequent** - often afflicted by aphids, leafrollers; rarely serious
Wind-Ice: **infrequent**

URBAN TOLERANCE: Pollution:
Lighting: Drought Heat: **very resistant**   Mine Spoils:
Salt: **resistant**   Soil Compaction: **sensitive**
Root Pattern: **deep** fibrous **laterals,** nitrogen-fixing; very **difficult to transplant**

SPECIES: Associate: trees - Paper Birch, Flameleaf Sumac, Nannyberry Viburnum, Pin Cherry; shrubs - Kalm
     St.Johnswort, Common Ninebark, Roundleaf Dogwood, Common Juniper, Limber Honeysuckle, Beaked Filbert
Similar: Silver Buffaloberry - silvery leaves, thorny, larger; Silverberry; Autumn Eleagnus; Common Seabuckthorn
Cultivars: 'Xanthocarpa' - yellow fruits; 'Rubra' - red fruits

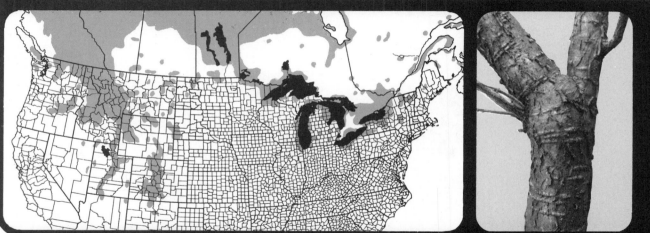

Spiraea alba

FORM: **mound**
Size: **small shrub** - from 1 to 2 m (3 to 6 ft)
Spread: **narrow** - between 1 to 2 m (3 to 6 ft), commonly broader
Mass: **dense**

BRANCHING: numerous **erect** stems, wand-like and seldom branched; **fine** texture
Twig: slender, smooth or slightly velvety, somewhat angular, golden **yellow brown to** light **red brown**
Bud: small ovoid, numerous, 1.5 mm (¹⁄₁₆ in) long, silky **woolly**, pale **brown**
Bark: smooth or **exfoliating** into shaggy papery sheets, **orange brown to brown**

FOLIAGE: alternate, **simple**, narrow elliptic to **oblong obovate**, finely and sharply toothed; **medium fine** texture
Surface: **dull**, stiff, smooth on both sides
Color: spring - bright **yellow green to red green**; summer - **yellow green**; autumn - golden **yellow**
Season: **deciduous;** emergence - mid **May;** drop - early **October**

FLOWER: broad conical erect terminal **spikes,** 5 to 15 cm (2 to 6 in) high, stamens longer than petals
Color: **white**
Season: late **June through** mid **August;** after leaves   **Fragrant:** slightly
Sex: monoecious

FRUIT: small dry **capsules,** arranged in clusters of 5 and borne in broad conical terminal clusters
Color: pale **brown to red brown**
Season: early **September** persisting **through** winter until late **March**   Human Value: not edible
Wildlife Value: **intermediate;** upland gamebirds; hoofed browsers graze leaves, twigs

HABITAT: formation - **bog, savanna, spring, dune, old field, meadow;** region - **Northern;** gradient - **wet;** stream banks, wet
thickets, bogs, pond and lakeshores, pastures, wet sedge meadows, forest openings, roadside ditches
Shade Tolerance: **intolerant**
Flood Tolerance: **very tolerant**

SOIL: Texture: **medium** loams **to fine** silt loams, silty clay loams, wet clays, peats and mucks
Drainage: **very poor to moderately poor**
Moisture: **wet to moist**
Reaction: **circumneutral,** pH 6.6 - 7.5

HARDINESS: zone 3a
Rate: **fast**
Longevity: **very short-lived**

SUSCEPTIBILITY: Physiological: **infrequent**
Disease: **occasional** - fire blight, bacterial hairy root, leaf spots, powdery mildews, root rot
Insect: **occasional** - spirea aphid, oblique-banded leaf roller, scales
Wind-Ice: **infrequent**

URBAN TOLERANCE: Pollution:
Lighting: Drought Heat: **resistant**   Mine Spoils:
Salt: **sensitive**   Soil Compaction: **resistant**
Root Pattern: dense, fibrous, **shallow lateral** spreading, freely suckering; **transplants well**

SPECIES: Associate: trees - Black Tupelo, Bebb/Pussy Willows, Quaking Aspen; shrubs - Red-osier Dogwood, Hardhack
Spirea, Black Chokeberry, Common Winterberry, Swamp Blackberry, Purple Chokeberry, alder species
Similar: Meadowsweet Spirea - broader leaves; Ural False Spirea; Summersweet Clethra; Virginia Sweetspire
Cultivars: none available

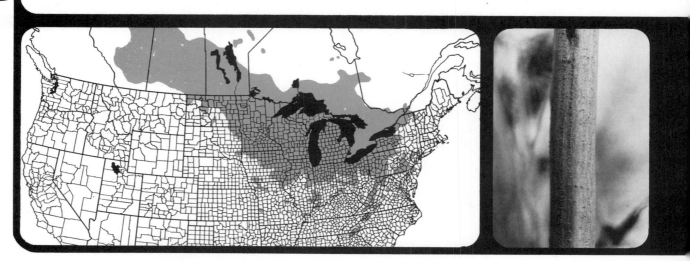

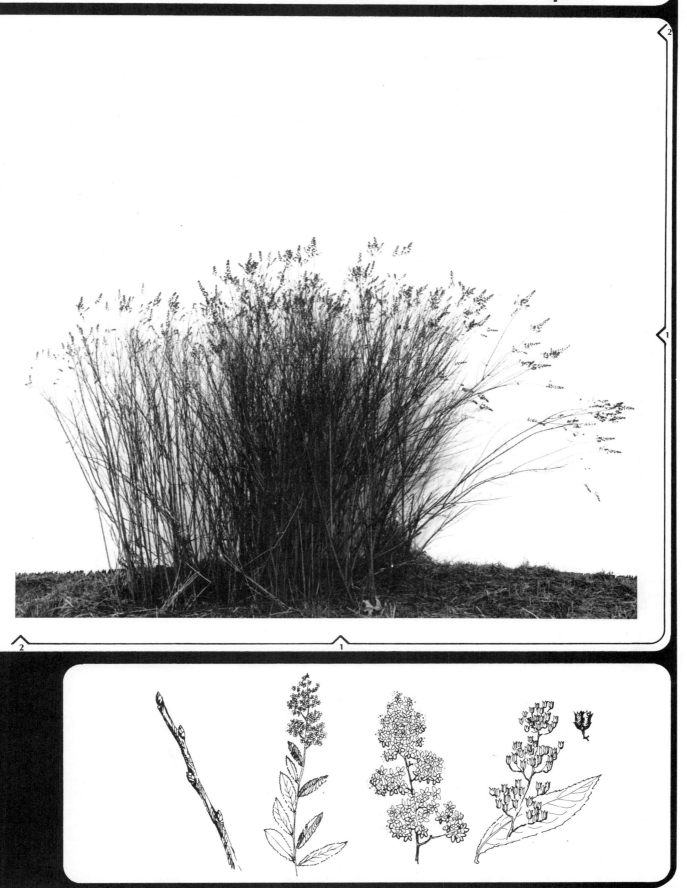

Spiraea corymbosa

FORM: mound
Size: **small shrub** - from 1 to 2 m (3 to 6 ft), typically to 1.5 m (4.5 ft)
Spread: **narrow** - between 1 to 2 m (3 to 6 ft), 1½ times the height or more
Mass: **open**

BRANCHING: numerous **erect** stems, sparingly branched; **fine** texture
Twig: slender, smooth, **red to purple or red brown**
Bud: small ovoid, hairless, **brown**
Bark: smooth, often with thin papery **exfoliation**; bright purplish brown to **orange brown**

FOLIAGE: alternate, **simple, obovate to oblong obovate,** entire below middle, coarse irregular teeth above; **medium fine**
Surface: **dull,** stiff, smooth
Color: spring - **yellow green;** summer - **medium green;** autumn - bright **yellow**
Season: **deciduous;** emergence - early **May,** drop - early **October**

FLOWER: flat-topped terminal clusters, 5 to 10 cm (2 to 4 in) across
Color: **white**
Season: mid **May through** late **June;** just after leaves
Sex: monoecious

FRUIT: small dry **capsule,** arranged in broad flat terminal clusters
Color: pale **brown to red brown**
Season: early **August** persisting **through** late **March**   Human Value: not edible
Wildlife Value: **intermediate;** songbirds, upland gamebirds, small mammals; hoofed browsers graze foliage

HABITAT: formation - **meadow, glade;** region - **Northern;** gradient - **mesic and mesic-dry;** rocky mountain meadows,
        barrens, open mountain slopes
Shade Tolerance: **intolerant**
Flood Tolerance: **intermediate**

SOIL: Texture: **moderately coarse to moderately fine;** sandy or gravelly loams, thin soils over bedrock, clay loam
Drainage: **moderately well to excessive**
Moisture: **average to dry**
Reaction: **slightly acid to** circumneutral, tolerates **alkaline,** pH 6.1 - 8.5

HARDNESS: zone 5b
Rate: **medium**
Longevity: **very short-lived**

SUSCEPTIBILITY: Physiological: **infrequent**
Disease: **occasional** - fire blight, root rot, powdery mildews, leaf spot, bacterial hairy root
Insect: **occasional** - spirea aphid, scales, saddled prominent caterpillar, oblique-banded leaf roller
Wind-Ice: **infrequent**

URBAN TOLERANCE: Pollution:
Lighting: Drought Heat: **intermediate**   Mine Spoils:
Salt: **sensitive**   Soil Compaction: **intermediate**
Root Pattern: densely fibrous, **shallow** spreading, prolific suckering habit; **transplants easily**

SPECIES: Associate: trees - Red Maple, Eastern White/Red/Virginia Pines, Yellow/Gray/Paper Birches, aspen species,
        Black/Pin Cherries; shrubs - Highbush/Lowbush Blueberries, Canada Yew, Checkerberry Wintergreen
Similar: Japanese White Spirea; Japanese/Striped Spireas - flowers white to pale pink; Dwarf Ninebark
Cultivars: none available

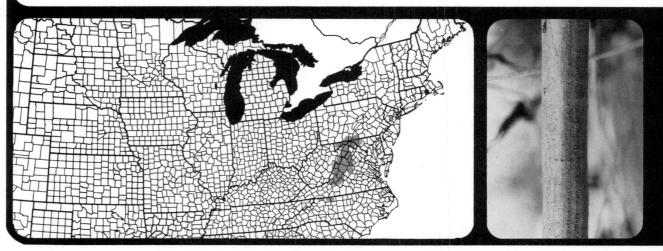

Corymed Spirea

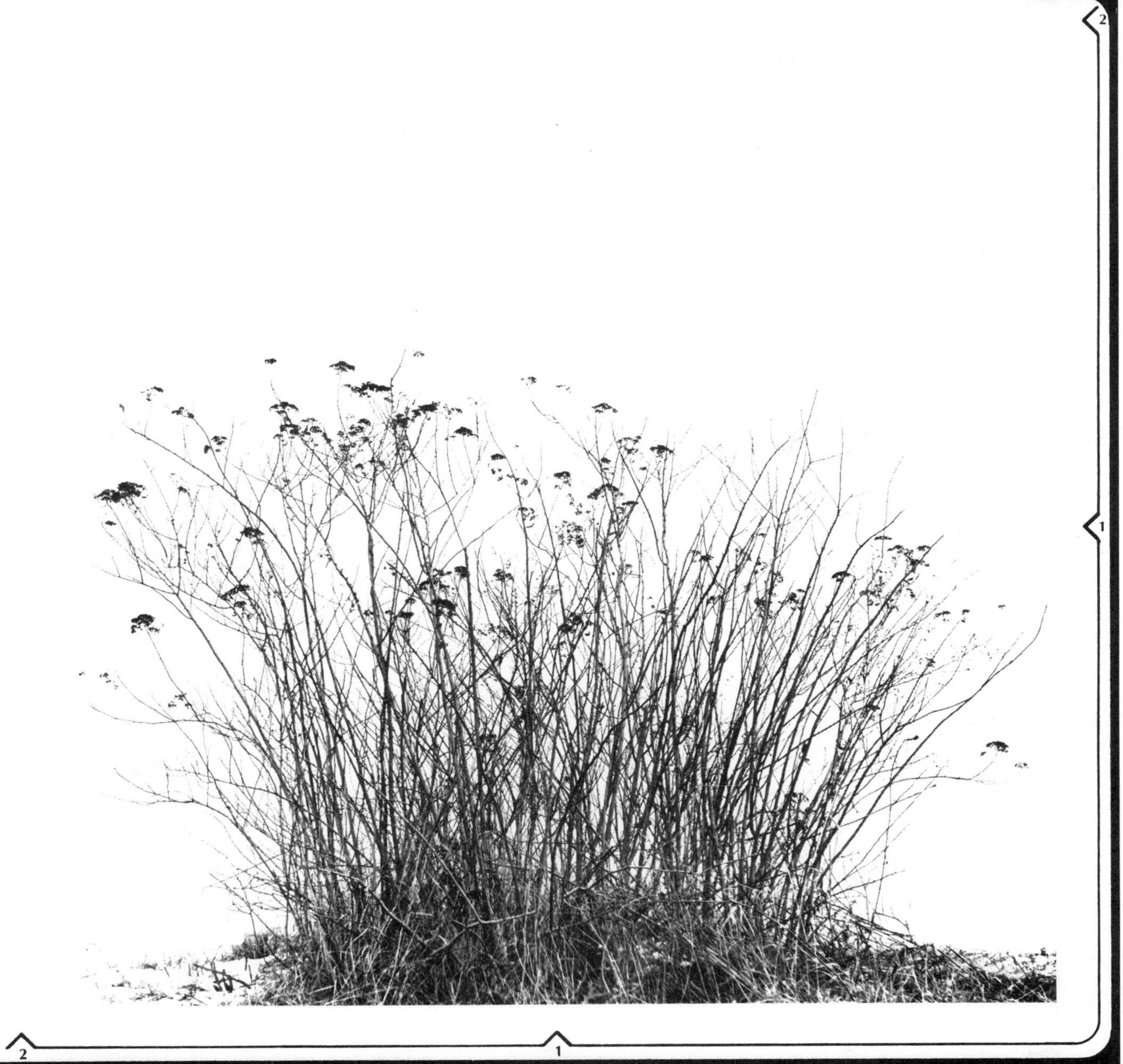

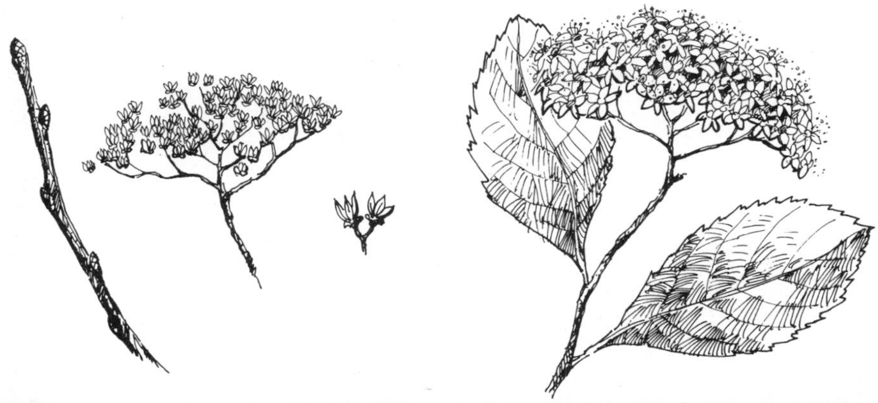

Spiraea tomentosa

FORM: **mound**
Size: **small shrub** - from 1 to 2 m (3 to 6 ft)
Spread: **narrow** - between 1 to 2 m (3 to 6 ft), commonly much broader
Mass: **open** to dense

BRANCHING: forms a thicket of **erect** slender wand-like stems, unbranched or occasionally branched; **fine** texture
Twig: slender, dense **velvety,** brown or red brown
Bud: small blunt ovoid, 1.5 mm (¹⁄₁₆ in), dense **woolly, brown**
Bark: smooth or **exfoliating** into shaggy papery sheets, **orange brown to red brown**

FOLIAGE: alternate, **simple, ovate or oblong ovate,** coarsely toothed, often double toothed; **medium fine** texture
Surface: **dull,** wrinkled above, smooth or slightly **tomentose,** densely tomentose beneath
Color: spring - **light green;** summer - **medium green;** autumn - **yellow green or yellowish**
Season: **deciduous;** emergence - mid **May,** drop - mid **October**

FLOWER: dense erect spire-like or steeple-shaped terminal **spikes,** 10 to 17.5 cm (4 to 7 in) tall, bloom from top to bottom
Color: bright **pink to** deep rose or rose **purple**
Season: mid **July through** early **September,** after leaves
Sex: monoecious

FRUIT: small dry felty **capsules,** arranged in groups of 5, borne in narrow conical terminal clusters
Color: dark **red brown to** chocolate **brown**
Season: mid **September** persisting **through** winter until late **March**   Human Value: not edible
Wildlife Value: **intermediate;** songbirds, upland gamebirds, waterbirds, marshbirds, small mammals

HABITAT: formation - **meadow, bog, spring, dune, prairie, old field;** region - **Northern, Central;** gradient - **wet;** wet meadows,
wet pastures, boggy or springy areas, roadside swales, dunes, marshes, abandoned fields, wet prairies, lake margins
Shade Tolerance: **intolerant**
Flood Tolerance: **very tolerant**

SOIL: Texture: **medium** loams **to fine** sands, silt loams, wet clays, organic peats and mucks
Drainage: **very poor to moderately poor**
Moisture: **wet to average**
Reaction: usually **moderately acid,** pH 5.1 - 6.0

HARDINESS: zone 4a
Rate: **fast**
Longevity: **very short-lived**

SUSCEPTIBILITY: Physiological: **infrequent**
Disease: **occasional** - bacterial hairy root, fireblight, leaf spot, powdery mildews, other problems that afflict rose family
Insect: **occasional** - root-knot nematode, caterpillars, scales, oblique-banded leaf roller, spirea aphid
Wind-Ice: **infrequent**

URBAN TOLERANCE: Pollution:
Lighting: Drought Heat: **resistant**   Mine Spoils:
Salt: **sensitive**   Soil Compaction: **resistant**
Root Pattern: dense, **shallow** fibrous and suckering; **transplants easily**

SPECIES: Associate: trees - Pin/Swamp White/Shingle Oaks, Red Maple, American Sweetgum, willow species, Common
Boxelder; shrubs - Narrowleaf Meadowsweet Spirea, Common Alder, Common Winterberry, Red-osier Dogwood
Similar: Douglas/Billiard/Willowleaf Spireas; Indigobush Amorpha; Bumalda/Margarita/Japanese Spireas
Cultivars: 'Alba' - white flowers; 'Rosea' - red flowers

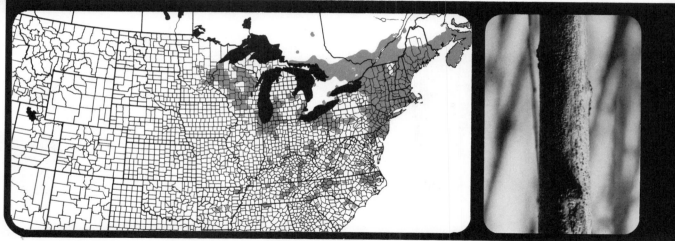

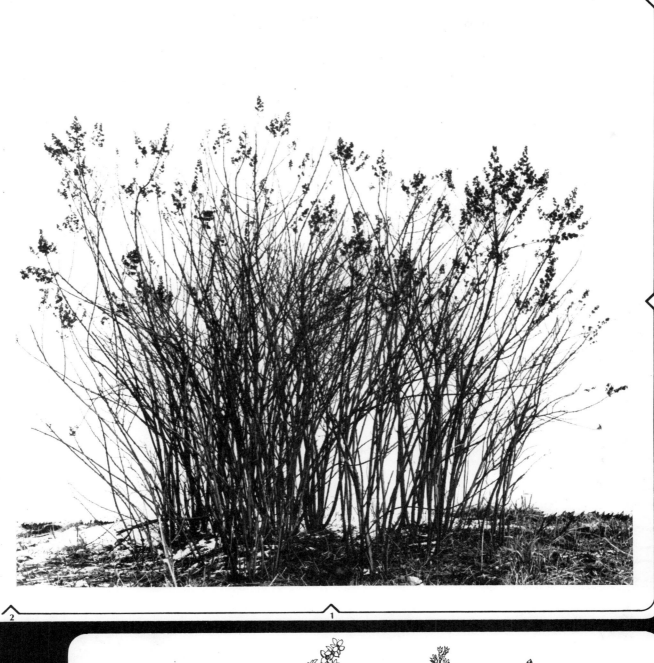

Staphylea trifolia

FORM: obovoid
Size: **mid-height shrub** - from 2 to 4 m (6 to 12 ft)
Spread: **intermediate** - between 2 to 4 m (6 to 12 ft), typically ⅔ the height, much narrower in youth
Mass: **open**

BRANCHING: multiple stems, stout stiff **upright spreading** twiggy branches; **medium** texture
Twig: moderately slender, smooth with few warty lenticels or none, dark olive **green to green brown**
Bud: small oblong, 3 to 4 mm (⅛ to ³⁄₁₆ in), **2 scales, red brown to** coal **black**
Bark: **smooth,** lenticel dotted, older stems **scaly or shallow furrowed** with longitudinal **white** stripes; **red brown or gray**

FOLIAGE: opposite, **pinnately compound, trifoliate,** broadly **elliptic,** finely toothed; **medium fine** texture
Surface: **dull,** smooth
Color: spring - **light green;** summer - **light green;** autumn - **yellow green to** pale lemon **yellow**
Season: **deciduous;** emergence - mid **May,** drop - early **October**

FLOWER: small **bells,** 9.5 mm (⅜ in) across, in loose drooping clusters to 10 cm (4 in) long
Color: greenish white to creamy **white**
Season: mid through late **May,** with leaves
Sex: monoecious

FRUIT: smooth elliptic 3-lobed papery inflated bladder-like **capsule,** 4 to 7.5 cm (1½ to 3 in) long, profusely produced
Color: deep **red brown to brown**
Season: early **August** persisting **through** late **December**   Human Value: not edible
Wildlife Value: **low;** negligible use

HABITAT: formation - **forest;** region - **Central;** gradient - **wet-mesic, mesic;** deep rich woods, floodplain forests, moist
    ravines, shores of lakes and ponds, rocky wooded streambanks, footslopes, talus slopes, shaded dunes
Shade Tolerance: **very tolerant**
Flood Tolerance: **intermediate**

SOIL: Texture: **moderately coarse** sandy or gravelly loams, medium loams **to moderately fine** silt loams
Drainage: **moderately poor to well**
Moisture: **moist to average**
Reaction: **slightly acid to** circumneutral, tolerates **alkaline,** pH 6.1 - 8.0

HARDINESS: zone 4a
Rate: **medium**
Longevity: **moderately short-lived**

SUSCEPTIBILITY: Physiological: **infrequent**
Disease: **infrequent** - very resistant, occasional twig blight, leaf spots
Insect: **infrequent** - oyster scale; not serious
Wind-Ice: **infrequent**

URBAN TOLERANCE: Pollution:
Lighting: Drought Heat: **sensitive**   Mine Spoils:
Salt: Soil Compaction: **intermediate**
Root Pattern: **shallow** fibrous; **transplants well**

SPECIES: Associate: trees - American Beech, Tuliptree, Cucumbertree Magnolia, Sugar Maple, Butternut, Yellow Birch;
    shrubs - Smooth Hydrangea, Brook Euonymus, American Elder, Common Spicebush, Pasture Gooseberry
Similar: Colchis Bladdernut - 5 leaflets, Asiatic; Common Hoptree - fruit wafer-like
Cultivars: 'Pauciflora' - low, suckering form

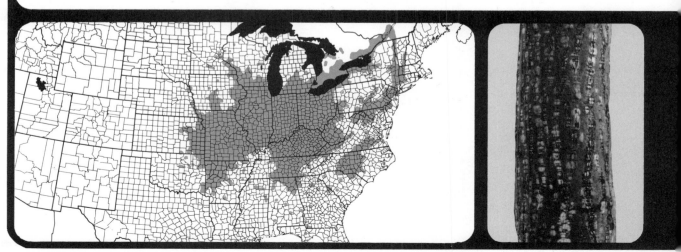

American Bladdernut

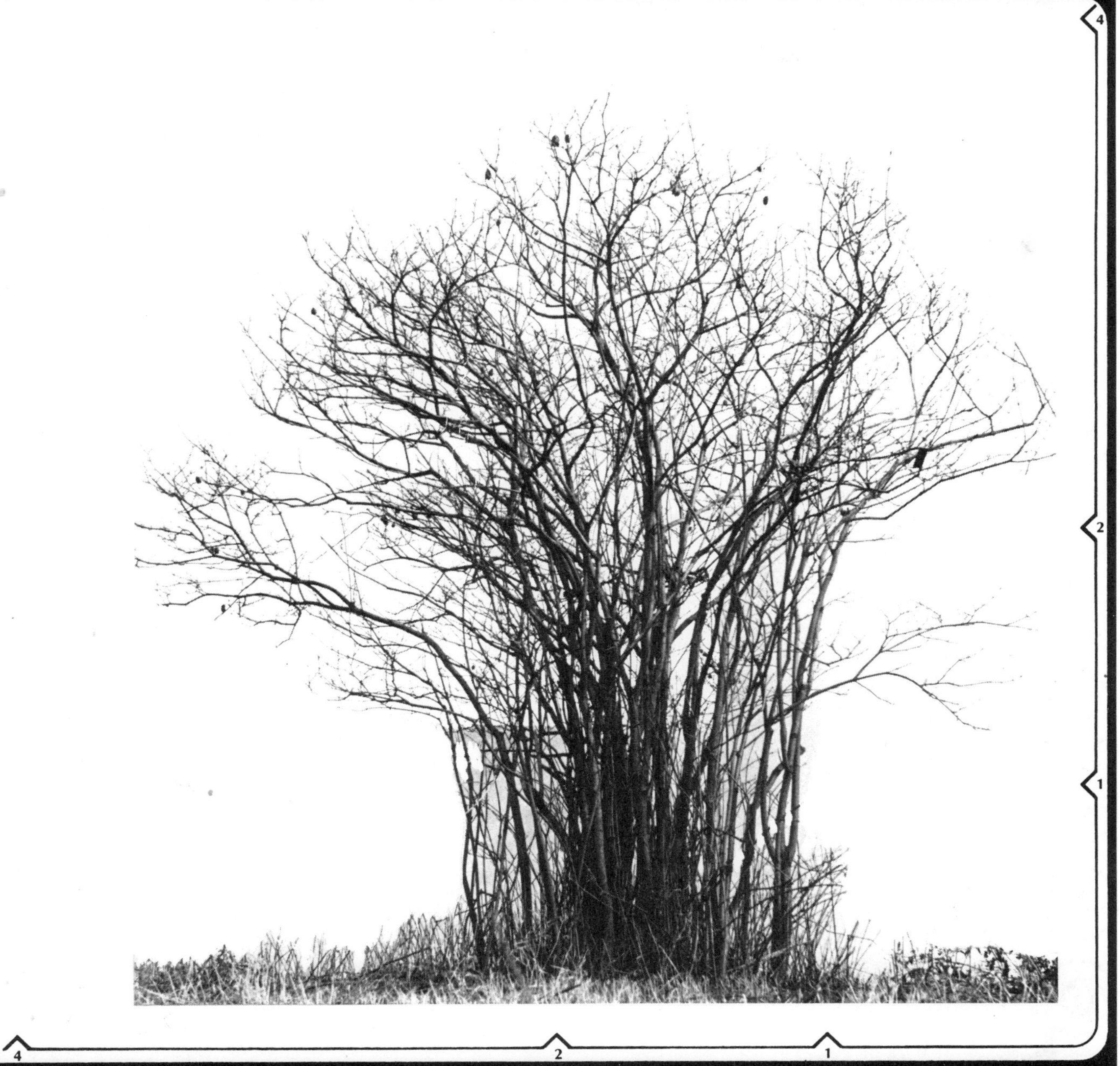

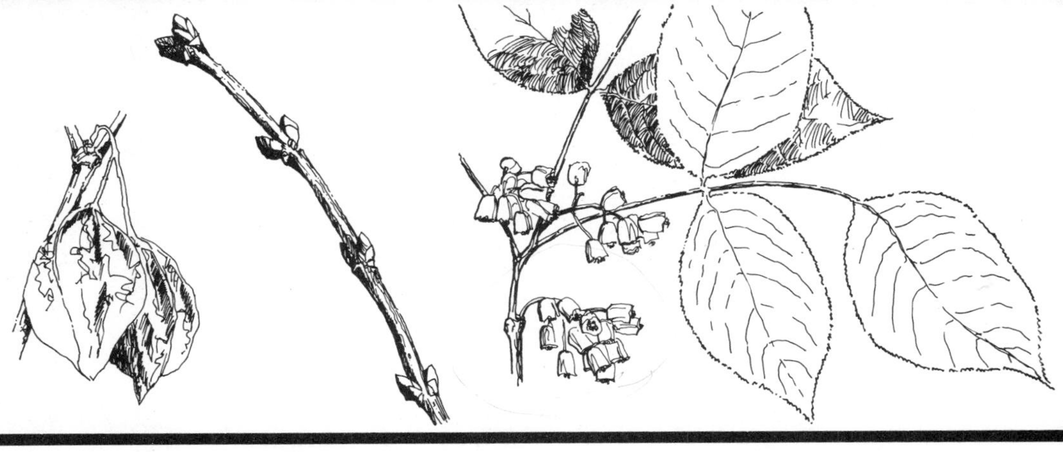

Stewartia ovata

FORM: ovoid
Size: **large shrub** - from 4 to 6 m (12 to 20 ft)
Spread: **wide** - 4 to 6 m (12 to 20 ft), typically ¾ the height
Mass: open

BRANCHING: solitary or few-clustered stems, strongly **ascending** branches; **medium** texture
Twig: slender, smooth, **red brown**
Bud: small, 3 mm (⅛ in), **2** to **3 scales, woolly, pointed,** flower buds **large,** 2.5 cm (1 in)
Bark: **smooth** with mottled patchy **exfoliating** sheets, dark **brown** with light green and **orange brown** inner bark

FOLIAGE: alternate, **simple, elliptic** to ovate, finely or sparingly toothed, tip taper-pointed; **medium** texture
Surface: **dull,** smooth, paler and hairy below
Color: spring - **medium green;** summer - **dark green;** autumn - **orange to** scarlet **red**
Season: **deciduous;** emergence- mid **May,** drop - early **October**

FLOWER: **large solitary,** 10 cm (4 in) diameter, shallow cup-shaped, 5-6 petals with crimped scalloped edges, exotic
Color: **white** with numerous purple stamens
Season: early through mid or late **July,** after leaves
Sex: monoecious

FRUIT: woolly sharply 5-angled ovoid woody **capsule,** 2.5 cm (1 in) long, splitting along 5 lines of suture
Color: tan **brown**
Season: early **September through** late **December**   Human Value: not edible
Wildlife Value: **low;** very limited use

HABITAT: formation - **forest;** region - **Central;** gradient - **wet-mesic, mesic, mesic-dry;** steep wooded gorges, sheltered mesic
coves, rich wooded ravines, mountain slopes, bluffs, spring-fed streams
Shade Tolerance: **very tolerant**
Flood Tolerance: **intermediate**

SOIL: Texture: **moderately coarse** rocky or sandy loams **to moderately fine** sandy loams, silt loams; will not tolerate clay
Drainage: **moderately poor to well**
Moisture: **moist to average**
Reaction: **strongly acid to moderately acid,** pH 4.5 - 6.0

HARDINESS: **zone 6a**
Rate; **slow**
Longevity: **moderately short-lived**

SUSCEPTIBILITY: Physiological: **infrequent**
Disease: **infrequent** - very resistant
Insect: **infrequent** - basically pest free
Wind-Ice: **infrequent**

URBAN TOLERANCE: Pollution:
Lighting: Drought Heat: **sensitive**   Mine Spoils:
Salt: **sensitive**   Soil Compaction: **sensitive**
Root Pattern: **deep laterals; very difficult to transplant,** difficult culture, move small sapling B & B or container in spring

SPECIES: Associate: trees - Flowering/Pagoda Dogwoods, American Beech, Tuliptree, American Holly, Sweet Buckeye;
shrubs - Common Spicebush, Common Witchhazel, Smooth Hydrangea, Mapleleaf Viburnum, Cinnamon Clethra
Similar: Virginia Stewartia - zone 6b; Korean/Japanese Stewartias - zone 5b, Asiatic, taller; Franklinia - zone 6a
Cultivars: Grandiflora - larger flowers to 10 cm (4 in), purple stamens

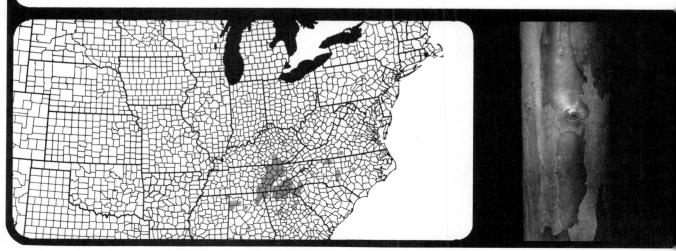

Mountain Stewartia

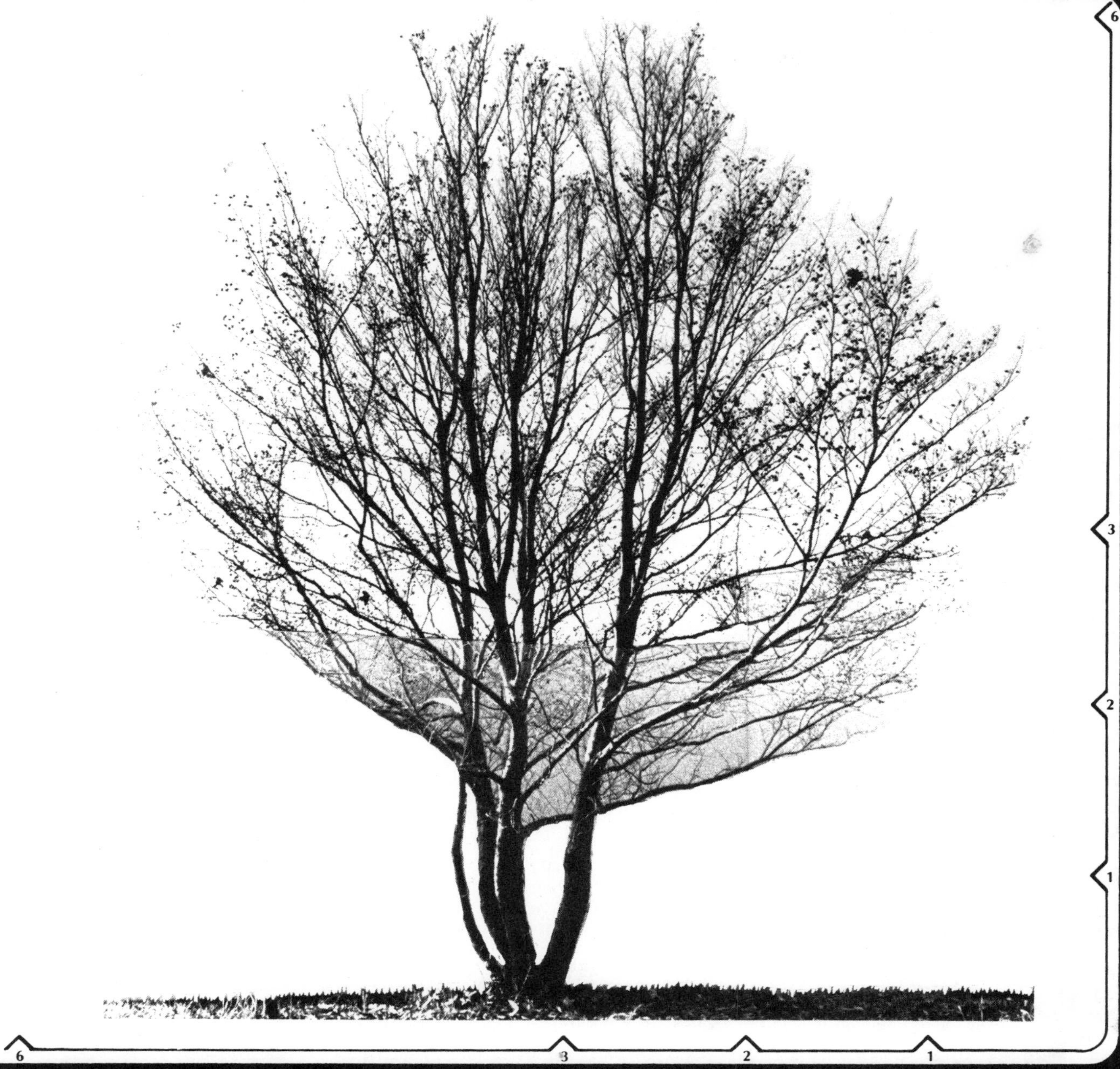

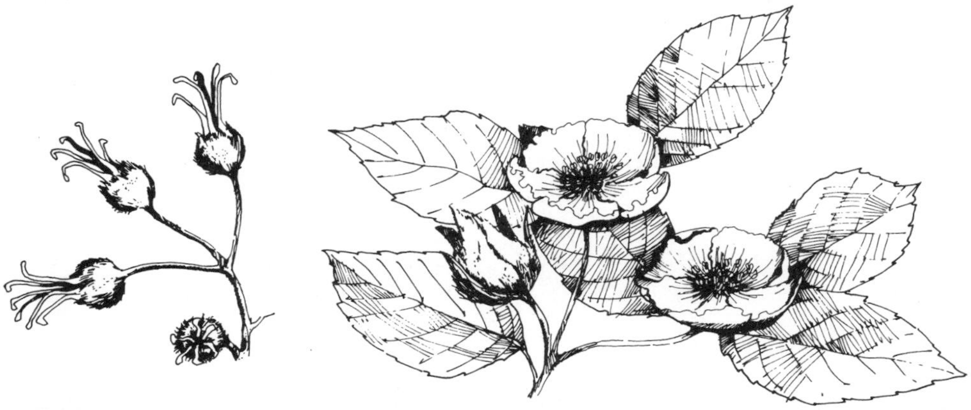

Symphoricarpos albus

FORM: **globular or mound**
Size: **small shrub** - 1 to 2 m (3 to 6 ft), commonly 1 to 1.3 m (3 to 4 ft)
Spread: **narrow** - 1 to 2 m (3 to 6 ft); suckers into drifts
Mass: **dense**

BRANCHING: slender **erect** stems, sparsely branched, **upright spreading** habit, fruited branchlets **pendulous; fine**
Twig: very slender and wiry, smooth, **gray brown**
Bud: minute ovoid, **brown**
Bark: shredding vertically into long narrow threads at base, upper stems with thin lateral **exfoliation, gray brown**

FOLIAGE: opposite, **simple,** broadly oval to **orbicular,** entire or shallow-lobed margin on vigorous stems; **medium fine**
Surface: **dull,** smooth, paler beneath
Color: spring - light **blue green;** summer - **blue green;** autumn - **blue green,** no effective coloring
Season: **deciduous;** emergence - early **May,** drop - late **October**

FLOWER: **small** terminal **clusters, bell**-shaped, basically inconspicuous
Color: **pink** or whitish
Season: early **June through** early **July,** often continuously until September, after leaves
Sex: monoecious

FRUIT: large globular spongy **berry,** 16 mm (⅝ in) diameter, in open pendant terminal clusters or solitary
Colors: snow **white** with a dark end spot, turning brown
Season: early **September through** late **November**   Human Value: not edible
Wildlife value: **high;** important cover and food, songbirds, upland gamebirds, large and small mammals

HABITAT: formation - **cliff, dune, forest;** region - **Northern;** gradient - upland **mesic, mesic-dry, dry;** open rocky slopes, shady
limestone cliffs, dry wooded hillsides, talus slopes, dry rocky clay banks, pine woods, shaded sand dunes, ridges
Shade Tolerance: **tolerant**
Flood Tolerance: **very intolerant**

SOIL: Texture: **coarse to fine;** infertile sands and gravels, thin soils over bedrock, sandy loams, clay loams, clays
Drainage: **moderately well to well**
Moisture: **moist to dry**
Reaction: **slightly acid to** circumneutral, tolerates **alkaline,** pH 6.1 - 8.5

HARDINESS: zone 2
Rate: **fast**
Longevity: **very short-lived**

SUSCEPTIBILITY: Physiological: **infrequent**
Disease: **frequent** - authracnose, rusts, powdery mildews, leaf spots, stem gall, berry rot is often severe
Insect: **occasional** - glacial whitefly, San Jose scale, snowberry clearwing, aphids
Wind-Ice: **infrequent**

URBAN TOLERANCE: Pollution: **sensitive** - 03, 2-4D
Lighting: Drought Heat: **intermediate**   Mine Soils:
Salt: **intermediate**   Soil Compaction: **intermediate**
Root Pattern: **shallow** fibrous, profuse suckers form extensive colonies; **transplants easily**

SPECIES: Associate: trees - American Hophornbeam, Northern Red Oak, American Linden; shrubs - American
Bladdernut, Leatherwood, Limber Honeysuckle, Pasture Gooseberry; vines - American Bittersweet, Riverbank Grape
Similar: Western Snowberry - fruites smaller, more prolific, larger leathery leaves; Symphoricarpos hybrids - white fruit
Cultivars: 'Laevigatus' - larger fruit, taller; 'Mother of Pearl' - pink fruited

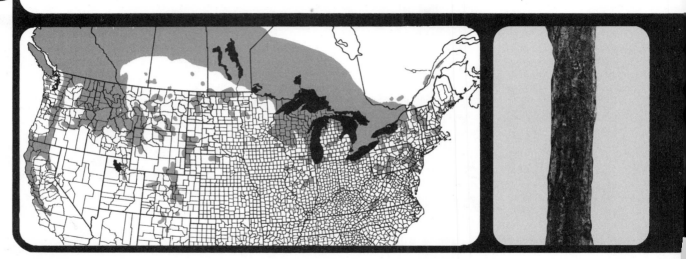

710

711

Symphoricarpos occidentalis

FORM: globular or **mound**
Size: **small shrub** - from 1 to 2 m (3 to 6 ft), commonly 1 to 1.3 m (3 to 4 ft)
Spread: **narrow** - between 1 to 2 m (3 to 6 ft), spreads into large circular patches if released
Mass: **dense** to moderate

BRANCHING: numerous **erect or upright spreading** finally **arching** stems, little-branched, **pendulous** with fruit; **fine texture**
Twig: slender, wiry, **velvety** becoming smooth, flexible, **large leaf scars, gray brown**
Bud: **small ovoid, 3 mm (⅛ in), brown**
Bark: **exfoliating** into wide often ridged sheets attached at one edge and curling outward, shaggy, **gray brown**

FOLIAGE: opposite, **simple,** broadly ovate to **orbicular,** entire, often with shallow wavy lobes; **medium fine** texture
Surface: **dull,** smooth, thick leathery, pale beneath
Color: spring - **yellow green;** summer - **blue green;** autumn - **blue green** late, **then yellow green;** winter - **tan brown**
Season: **persistant;** emergence - mid **May,** drop - most dried leaves remaining through late **February**

FLOWER: **small** terminal or axillary **clusters** of 10 to 20 flowers, **bell**-shaped, somewhat inconspicuous
Color: **pink**
Season: mid **June through** mid **July,** after leaves
Sex: monoecious

FRUIT: globular spongy **berry,** 6 to 9 mm (¼ to ⅜ in) diameter, in globular or cylindric clusters of 10 to 20, 5 cm (2 in) wide
Color: **green to** dull **white,** soon discoloring to brown or blackish
Season: early **September through** late **December**   Human Value: not edible
Wildlife Value: **high;** songbirds, upland gamebirds, large and small mammals; hoofed browsers graze extensively

HABITAT: formation - **prairie, glade, forest, old field;** region - **Northern, Central, Western;** gradient - **mesic-dry, dry;** dry rocky
hillsides, ravine banks, dry prairies, sandy flats, open oak woods, railroad rights-of-way, loess bluffs, sand plains
Shade Tolerance: **intolerant**
Flood Tolerance: **very intolerant**

SOIL: Texture: **coarse to fine;** infertile sands and gravels, sandy loams, deep prairie loams, fine sandy loams
Drainage: **well to excessive**
Moisture: **average to droughty**
Reaction: **moderately acid to** circumneutral, tolerates **alkaline,** pH 5.5 - 8.5

HARDINESS: zone 2
Rate: **fast**
Longevity: **very short-lived**

SUSCEPTIBILITY: Physiological: **infrequent**
Disease: **occasional** - anthracnose and berry rot cause damage, leaf spots, powdery mildews, rust, stem gall
Insect: **occasional** - aphids, San Jose scale, snowberry clearwing, glacial whitefly
Wind-Ice: **infrequent**

URBAN TOLERANCE: Pollution:
Lighting: Drought Heat: **resistant**   Mine Spoils: **resistant**
Salt: **sensitive**   Soil Compaction: **intermediate**
Root Pattern: **shallow** fibrous, vigorous suckering habit forming broad circular colonies; **easily transplanted,** easy culture

SPECIES: Associate: trees - Slippery Elm, Bur Oak, Eastern Red Cedar; shrubs - Smooth Sumac, Leadplant Amorpha,
Jerseytea Ceanothus, Gray Dogwood, American Filbert, rose species; vines - Thicket Creeper, Common Poisonivy
Similar: Common Snowberry - leaves smaller, not leathery; Indiancurrant Coralberry - red fruits
Cultivars: none available

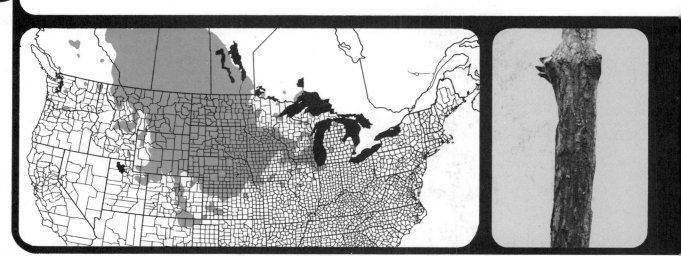

Symphoricarpos orbiculatus

FORM: globular or **mound**
Size: **small shrub** - from 1 to 2 m (3 to 6 ft), typically 1 to 1.3 m (3 to 4 ft) tall
Spread: **narrow** - between 1 to 2 m (3 to 6 ft), forms broad circular colonies if released
Mass: **dense**

BRANCHING: numerous slender **erect to upright spreading or arching** little-branched stems, **pendulous** in fruit; **fine** texture
Twig: very slender, dense minute **velvety** hairs when young, **gray brown**
Bud: inconspicuous, **brown**
Bark: **exfoliating** into small short flakes or long thin strips, **brown or gray brown**

FOLIAGE: opposite, **simple,** broadly oval to nearly **orbicular,** entire margin, occasionally wavy edged; **fine** texture
Surface: **dull,** smooth, lighter beneath
Color: spring - **red green;** summer - **blue green;** autumn - **blue green** late; **then yellow green**
Season: **deciduous;** emergence - mid **May,** drop - late **November**

FLOWER: **small** tight **clusters** in leaf axils, **bell**-shaped, not showy
Color: **green** to pinkish
Season: late **June through** late **July,** after leaves
Sex: monoecious

FRUIT: small globular **berry,** 4 to 6 mm (⅙ to ¼ in) across, in dense axillary clumps along arching stems
Color: coral **red to** magenta **purple**
Season: early **October** persisting **through** late **January**   Human Value: not edible
Wildlife Value: **high;** occasional winter use by songbirds, gamebirds, large and small mammals; browsers graze

HABITAT: formation - **forest, savanna, old field;** region - **Central;** gradient - **wet-mesic, mesic-dry, dry;** disturbed floodplain
forests, old field, stream banks, rocky upland woods, oak woods, fence rows, dry sandy plains, woods edge
Shade Tolerance: **intermediate**
Flood Tolerance: **intermediate**

SOIL: Texture: **coarse to fine;** interfile sands, sandy and gravelly loams, forest or prairie loams, silt loams, clays
Drainage: **moderately poor to excessive**
Moisture: **moist to droughty**
Reaction: **moderately acid to** circumneutral, tolerates **alkaline,** pH 5.5 - 8.5

HARDINESS: zone 2
Rate: **fast**
Longevity: **very short-lived**

SUSCEPTIBILITY: Physiological: **infrequent**
Disease: **occasional** - rusts, powdery mildews, leaf spots, anthracnose, berry rot, stem gall
Insect: **occasional** - aphids, snowberry clearwing, San Jose scale, glacial whitefly
Wind-Ice: **infrequent**

URBAN TOLERANCE: Pollution: **sensitive** - O_3
Lighting: Drought Heat: **resistant**   Mine Spoils:
Salt: **sensitive**   Soil Compaction: **intermediate**
Root Pattern: **shallow** fibrous, freely suckering into broad thickets; **easily transplanted**

SPECIES: Associate: trees - Black Walnut, Common Hackberry, White Oak, Shagbark/Bitternut Hickories, Common
Honeylocust; shrubs - American Elder, Missouri Gooseberry, Western Snowberry, Gray Dogwood, Filbert
Similar: Cheanalt Coralberry - hybrid; American/Japanese Beautyberries - less hardy; Western Snowberry - fruits white
Cultivars: 'Leucocarpus' - fruit white; 'Variegatus' - foliage varigated with yellow; Hancock - low grower to 0.6 m (2 ft)

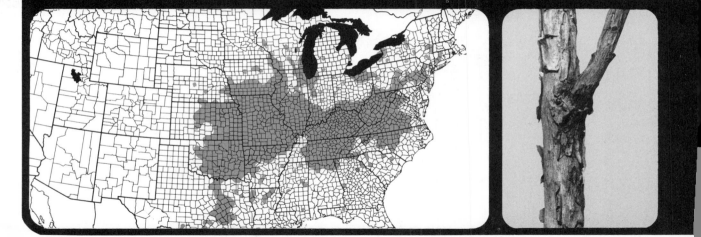

714

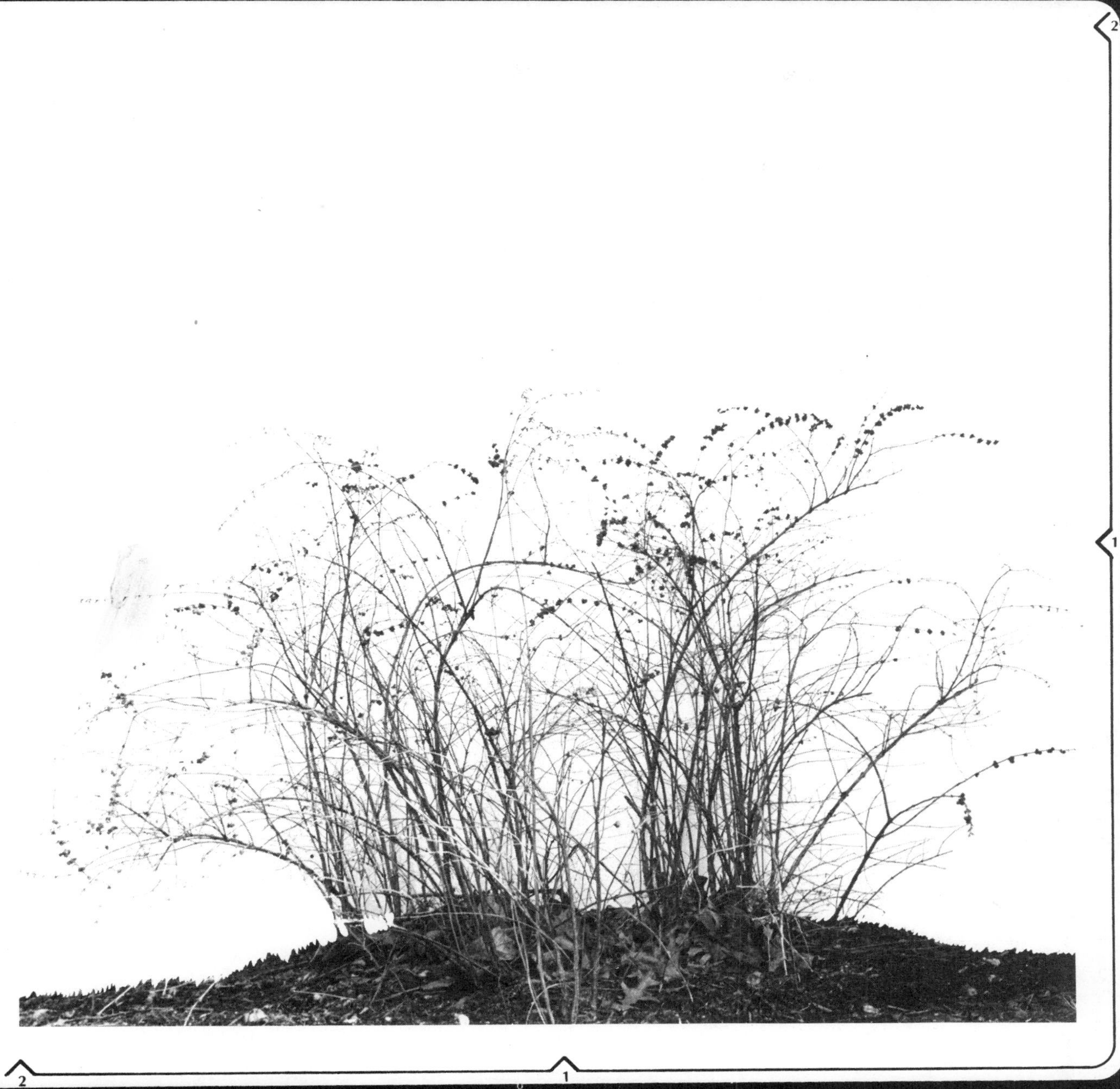

2
1
2
1

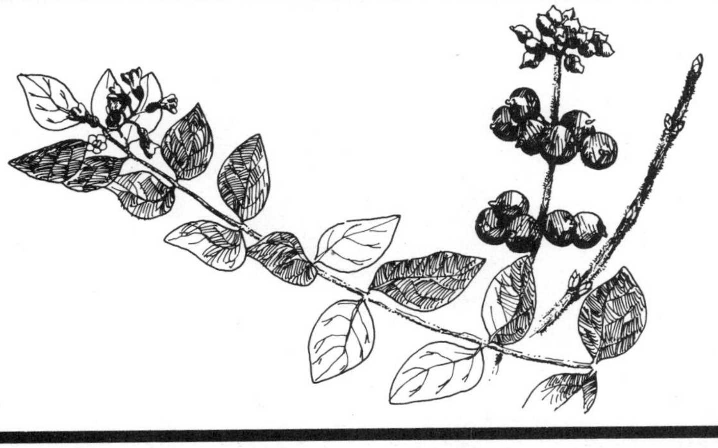

Taxus canadensis

FORM: low mound or **mat**
Size: **small shrub** - from 1 to 2 m (3 to 6 ft)
Spread: **intermediate** - between 2 to 4 m (6 to 12 ft), typically 2 to 3 times the height or more
Mass: dense to **open** in poorer habitat

BRANCHING: prostrate multiple stems, **trailing** horizontal hugging ground, **ascending** at tips; **fine** texture
Twig: smooth, **green** becoming yellow **brown**
Bud: small blunt globular, yellow green
Bark: **scaly** loose rectilinear strips **or exfoliating** into thin shaggy plates, **red brown** with **reddish** inner bark

FOLIAGE: spirally arranged but appears 2-ranked, **simple, linear,** flattened, rigid, sharp-tipped, **aromatic; fine** texture
Surface: **glossy,** smooth, yellowish beneath
Color: spring - **light green;** summer, autumn - deep **dark green;** winter - **dark green** or with reddish tint
Season: coniferous **evergreen**

FLOWER: small cylindrical **cones,** inconspicuous
Color: **yellow green**
Season: late **May and** early **June**
Sex: **dioecious,** sometimes monoecious

FRUIT: translucent fleshy **berry**-like cone, 6 mm (¼ in) diameter, bony-coated cone surrounded by cup-like pulpy disc
Color: **orange to** bright **red**
Season: early **September through** late **November**   Human Value: **all parts poisonous**
Wildlife Value: **low;** limited use by songbirds, upland gamebirds

HABITAT: formation - **forest, cliff, dune;** region - **Northern;** gradient - upland **mesic;** moist coniferous forest, cool moist
      gorge, steep moist ravine, overhanging shaded limestone cliffs, cool talus slopes, shaded dune slopes
Shade Tolerance: **very tolerant,** requires shade
Flood Tolerance: **very intolerant**

SOIL: Texture: **moderately coarse** moist sands, gravelly and sandy loams, medium loams **to moderately fine** sandy loams
Drainage: **moderately well to well**
Moisture: demands moist
Reaction: **moderately acid to circumneutral,** pH 5.1 - 7.5

HARDINESS: **zone 2,** hardiest yew
Rate: **slow**
Longevity: **long-lived**

SUSCEPTIBILITY: Physiological: **frequent** - winter twig dieback and leaf browning in exposed sunny winter location
Disease: **infrequent** - very resistant but needle blight, root rot reported
Insect: **infrequent** - none serious, black vine weevil, Taxus mealybug, scales, nematodes, ants and termites
Wind-Ice: **frequent** - winter injuries from too much sun, wind exposure

URBAN TOLERANCE: Pollution: **sensitive** - Cl; **intermediate** - HFI, 2-4D, MV
Lighting: **Drought Heat: sensitive**   Mine Spoils:
Salt: **resistant**   Soil Compaction: **sensitive**
Root Pattern: deep **taproot or** several **deep** spreading **laterals;** very **difficult to transplant,** move B & B

SPECIES: Associate: trees - Sugar/Striped/Red/Mountain Maples, Yellow Birch, American Beech, White Ash, Downy
      Serviceberry; shrubs - Scarlet Elder, Hobblebush Viburnum, Common Winterberry, Flame/Roseshell Azaleas
Similar: Dwarf Japanese Yew; 'Denseformis' Japanese Yew; Canby Pachistima - leaves, form similar
Cultivars: 'Fastigiata', 'Stricta' - branches stiffly upright; 'Aurea' - leaves slightly varigated; 'Compacta' - very dense

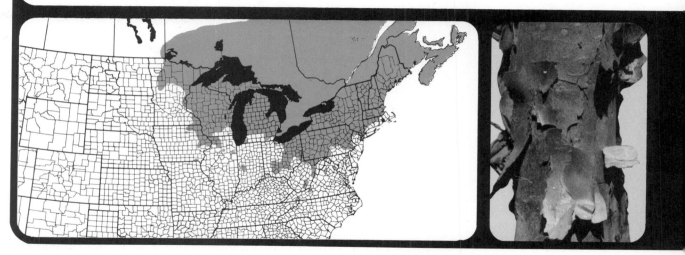

Vaccinium angustifolium

FORM: **globular**
Size: **very small shrub** - less than 1 m (3 ft), typically to 0.6 m (2 ft)
Spread: **very narrow** - less than 1 m (3 ft), generally equal to height
Mass: **open**

BRANCHING: multiple stems, **upright spreading** twiggy branches; **medium** texture
Twig: **velvety, zigzag** appearance, slightly **angular** and grooved, warty, **green to reddish** becoming brown
Bud: small, **red brown to bright red**
Bark: thin **scaly** flakes separated by fine shallow fissures, **gray brown to** dark **gray or blackish**

FOLIAGE: alternate, **simple,** narrow **elliptic,** finely toothed, each tooth bristle-tipped; **fine** texture
Surface: **glossy,** smooth
Color: spring - **red green;** summer - **blue green;** autumn - scarlet **red to** maroon **purple**
Season: **deciduous;** emergence - mid **May,** drop - mid to late **September**

FLOWER: small cylindric urn-shaped **bells,** 6 mm (¼ in) diameter, waxy appearance, in few-flowered clusters
Color: milky **white** or tinged with pink
Season: early through late **May,** before or with leaves
Sex: monoecious

FRUIT: globular **berry,** 6 to 13 mm (¼ in to ½ in) diameter
Color: bloomy **blue,** weathering **to black**
Season: early **July through** mid **August**   Human Value: sweet spicy **edible fruit**
Wildlife Value: **very high;** relished by songbirds, waterfowl, upland gamebirds, marshbirds, large and small mammals

HABITAT: formation - **bald, old field, glade;** region - **Northern;** gradient - upland **mesic-dry, dry;** old burns, old field, open
rocky or sandy ground
Shade Tolerance: **tolerant**
Flood Tolerance: **very tolerant.**

SOIL: Texture: rock outcroppings, **coarse** sands and gravels, sandy or gravelly loams **to fine** clay loams, clays
Drainage: **well to excessive**
Moisture: **moist to droughty**
Reaction: demands **strongly acid to moderately acid,** pH 4.0 - 6.0

HARDINESS: **zone 2**
Rate: **slow**
Longevity: **short-lived**

SUSCEPTIBILITY: Physiological: **occasional** - iron chlorosis in lime soils or near cement walls where lime leaches
Disease: **occasional** - cultivated varieties have many diseases; species treatment rarely warranted
Insect: **occasional** - stem gall wasp, azalea stem borer, forest tent caterpillar, scales, fall webworm; rarely serious
Wind-Ice: **infrequent**

URBAN TOLERANCE: Pollution: **sensitive** - HFI; **intermediate** - 2-4D
Lighting: Drought Heat: **resistant**   Mine Spoils:
Salt: **resistant**   Soil Compaction: **sensitive**
Root Pattern: **shallow** spreading and fibrous, **stoloniferous; transplants well**

SPECIES: Associate: trees - Jack/Pitch/Red Pines, Paper Birch, Bigtooth/Quaking Aspens; shrubs - Red/Flame Azaleas,
Highbush Blueberry, Mountainlaurel Kalmia, Checkerberry Wintergreen, Black/Purple Chokeberries
Similiar: Blueridge Blueberry - Southern, larger leaves and fruits
Cultivars: 'Album' - white fruit; Laevifolium - smooth leaf surface; 'Leucocarpum'

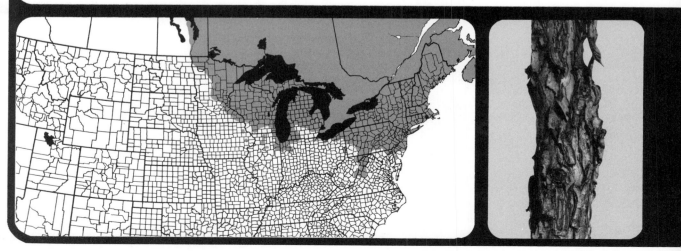

Vaccinium corymbosum

FORM: **globular**
Size: **mid-height shrub** - from 2 to 4 m (6 to 12 ft)
Spread: **intermediate** - between 2 to 4 m (6 to 12 ft)
Mass: **dense,** compact

BRANCHING: **upright spreading** multiple stems with numerous **ascending** dense twiggy branches; **medium** texture
Twig: slender, **velvety,** with minute warty dots, **zigzag** appearance, bright **green to** bright **red** in winter
Bud: small ovoid, 3 mm (⅛ in), **green or red**
Bark: separating into thin irregular **scales,** dark **gray brown** to brown black

FOLIAGE: alternate, **simple, lanceolate to oblong lanceolate,** entire margin; **medium fine** texture
Surface: **dull,** smooth, paler beneath
Color: spring - **red green;** summer - **dark green to blue green;** autumn - various, **yellow, orange, red to** maroon **purple**
Season: **deciduous;** emergence - mid **May,** drop - mid **November**

FLOWER: small urn-shaped **bell,** 8 mm (⅓ in) diameter, in dense drooping clusters, often from leafless old wood, prolific
Color: **white or pinkish**
Season: mid **May through** early **June,** with leaves but before they unfold
Sex: monoecious

FRUIT: globular **berry,** 6 to 13 mm (¼ to ½ in) diameter
Color: heavy **bluish** bloom, weathering **to black**
Season: early **July through** late **August**   Human Value: sweet juicy **edible fruit,** pleasantly acid
Wildlife Value: **very high;** waterfowl, songbirds, upland gamebirds, large and small mammals; browsers eat foliage

HABITAT: formation - **forest, bog, meadow, barrens, old field;** region - **Southern;** gradient - lowland **wet, wet-mesic,** upland
    mesic-dry, dry; bogs, pocosins, pine barrens, oak woods
Shade Tolerance: **tolerant**
Flood Tolerance: **very tolerant**

SOIL: Texture: rock outcroppings, **coarse** gravelly or sandy loams **to fine** loamy sand, organic peats
Drainage: **very poor to well**
Moisture: **wet to dry**
Reaction: demands **strongly acid to** moderately acid, pH 3.5 - 6.0, tolerates **slightly acid** to pH 6.5

HARDINESS: zone 4b
Rate: **slow**
Longevity: **short-lived**

SUSCEPTIBILITY: Physiological: **frequent** - chlorosis caused by iron deficiency in lime soil or near cement walls
Disease: **occasional** - leaf and stem fleck, leaf spots, root rot, crown rot, red ringspot; rarely warrant treatment
Insect: **occasional** - stem gall wasp, fall webworm, scales, forest tent caterpillar, azalea stem borer; rarely serious
Wind-Ice: **infrequent**

URBAN TOLERANCE: Pollution: **sensitive** - HFI; **intermediate** - 2-4D
Lighting: Drought Heat: **intermediate**   Mine Spoils:
Salt: **resistant**   Soil Compaction: **resistant**
Root Pattern: **shallow** fibrous, very close to surface, freely suckering; **transplants well** B & B or container grown

SPECIES: Associate: trees - oak/hickory species, Pond Pine, Red Maple; shrubs - Dusty Zenobia, Fetterbush Lyonia,
    Summersweet Clethra, Inkberry, Virginia Sweetspire, Common Deerberry, rhododendron/leucothoe/azalea species
Similar: Elliott Blueberry - Southern, glossy leaves; Common Deerberry - Southern, fruits greenish
Cultivars: over 40 commercial varieties; 'Berkeley' - largest fruit; 'Cabot' - long fruiting; 'Jersey'; 'Katherine'; 'Atlantic'

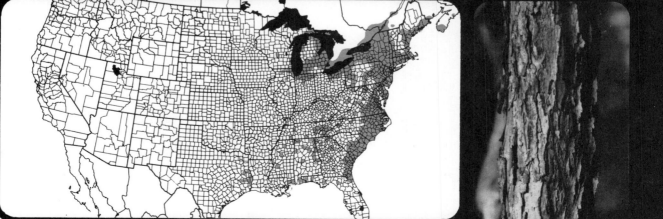

Vaccinium macrocarpum

FORM: low prostrate **mat**
Size: **very small shrub** - less than 1 m (3 ft), typically to 30 cm (1 ft) or less
Spread: **very narrow** - up to 1 m (3 ft), spread is indefinite for established plants
Mass: **open**

BRANCHING: low horizontal **trailing** forked stems, rooting at nodes, with **erect** flowering intertwined branchlets; **fine**
Twig: slender, wiry, smooth, obscurely or distinctly angled, **brown**
Bud: minute, 2 scales or more, inconspicuous
Bark: separating into thin flaky **scales,** dark **brown**

FOLIAGE: alternate, **simple, elliptic,** entire margin, flat or with slightly rolled edges; **fine** texture
Surface: **glossy,** smooth, leathery, whitened beneath
Color: spring - **light green to red green;** summer - **dark green;** autumn - **dark green** late, **then purple;** winter - **purple to red**
Season: broadleaf **evergreen**

FLOWER: small tube-shaped **trumpet,** 6 to 19 mm (¼ to ¾ in) long, petals reflexed, in 1 to 10-flowered nodding clusters
Color: **white to pink,** shooting star appearance
Season: mid **June through** late **July**
Sex: monoecious

FRUIT: slender-stalked globular or oblong **berry,** 10 to 19 mm (⅜ to ¾ in) diameter
Color: dark **red**
Season: early **September through** late November   Human Value: very acid **edible fruit**
Wildlife Value: **very low;** waterbirds, marsh and shorebirds, upland gamebirds infrequent users

HABITAT: formation - **bog, swamp;** region - **Northern;** gradient - lowland **wet;** cool sphagnum bogs, low mountain bogs,
cool wet swampy ground
Shade Tolerance: **intermediate**
Flood Tolerance: **very tolerant**

SOIL: Texture: **moderately fine to fine;** well decomposed organic soils, peats, mucks
Drainage: **very poor to poor**
Moisture: demands **wet**
Reaction: demands **strongly acid to moderately acid,** pH 4.0 - 6.0

HARDINESS: zone 3a
Rate: **slow**
Longevity: **moderately short-lived**

SUSCEPTIBILITY: Physiological: **frequent** - chlorosis due to soil alkalinity
Disease: **occasional** - leaf and stem fleck, cankers, leaf spots, crown rot, red ringspot; rarely serious
Insect: **occasional** - stem gall wasp, scales, fall webworm; rarely serious
Wind-Ice: **infrequent**

URBAN TOLERANCE: Pollution: **sensitive** - HFl
Lighting: Drought Heat: **sensitive**   Mine Spoils:
Salt: **sensitive**   Soil Compaction: **resistant**
Root Pattern: **stoloniferous** with extensive creeping horizontal rhizomes; **difficult to transplant,** start from potted plants

SPECIES: Associate: trees - American Larch, Black Spruce, Red Maple; shrubs - Creeping Snowberry, Bogrosemary
Andromeda, Skunk Currant, Small Cranberry, Leatherleaf, Purple Chokeberry, Highbush Blueberry, Bunchberry
Similar: Mountain Cranberry - smaller leaves, fruit; Box Huckleberry; Tundra Bilberry; Crowberry; Patridgeberry
Cultivars: several commercial varieties developed; 'Early Black', 'Howes', 'Scarlet Jumbo'

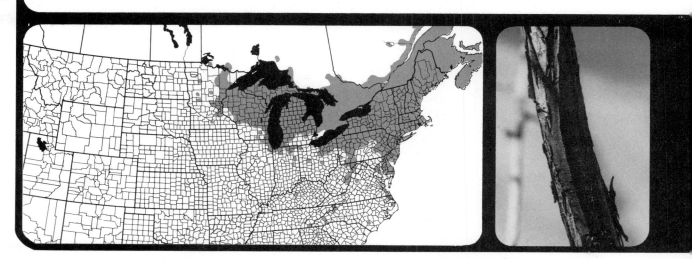

1

2/3

1/3

1

2/3

1/3

Vaccinium stamineum

FORM: **globular**
Size: **mid-height shrub** - from 2 to 4 m (6 to 12 ft)
Spread: **intermediate** - between 2 to 4 m (6 to 12 ft)
Mass: **moderate**

BRANCHING: **upright spreading** multiple stems with diffuse arching branchlets, very twiggy; **medium** texture
Twig: slender, **velvety** becoming scaly, zigzag appearance, **red to purple** or brown, often with whitened bloom
Bud: small ovoid, diverge at 45 degree angle from twig, **red brown to** bright **red**
Bark: thin regular papery **scales** separated by fine shallow fissures, **gray to gray brown or brown black**

FOLIAGE: alternate, **simple,** oval to **oblong obovate,** entire margin, downy petiole; **medium fine** texture
Surface: **dull,** smooth, thin, whitened beneath and woolly
Color: spring - **light green to red green;** summer - **medium green;** autumn - scarlet **red to** maroon **purple**
Season: **deciduous;** emergence - mid **May,** drop - mid **November**

FLOWER: graceful nodding broad cup-shaped **bells,** 6 to 8 mm (¼ to ⅓ in) wide, on short divergent twigs
Color: greenish **white, often pink** tinged
Season: late **May through** early **June,** after leaves
Sex: monoecious

FRUIT: globular or slightly pear-shaped **berries,** 13 mm (½ in) diameter, in loose dangling clusters
Color: pale **greenish to** pale **bluish black,** often with whitish bloom
Season: mid **September through** mid **October,** soon dropping   Human Value: sour **fruit, edible** if sweetened
Wildlife Value: **very high;** relished by upland gamebirds, songbirds, large and small mammals

HABITAT: formation - **forest, barrens, old field;** region - **Central, Southern;** gradient - **wet-mesic, mesic-dry, dry;** dry upland
oak woods, ridge tops, floodplain forests, clearings and thickets, pine woods and barrens
Shade Tolerance: **tolerant**
Flood Tolerance: **intolerant**

SOIL: Texture: **coarse to fine;** rock outcroppings, infertile sands and gravels, sandy loams, silt loams, heavy clays
Drainage: **well to excessive**
Moisture: **moist to droughty**
Reaction: **strongly to slightly acid,** pH 4.0 - 6.5

HARDINESS: zone 6a
Rate: **slow**
Longevity: **short-lived**

SUSCEPTIBILITY: Physiological: **frequent** - iron chlorosis in alkaline soils, twig dieback
Disease: **occasional** - leaf and stem fleck, leafspots, root rot; rarely serious
Insect: **occasional** - azalea stem borer, fall webworm, several scales, forest tent caterpillar, stem-gall wasp
Wind-Ice: **infrequent**

URBAN TOLERANCE: Pollution: **sensitive** - HFl; **resistant** - 2-4D
Lighting: Drought Heat: **resistant**   Mine Spoils:
Salt: **resistant**   Soil Compaction: **intermediate**
Root Pattern: dense fibrous, **shallow lateral** spreading; **transplants well** B & B or container grown

SPECIES: Associate: trees - Pitch/Virginia Pines, Scarlet/Chestnut/White Oaks, Pignut/Mockernut Hickories, Tuliptree,
Flameleaf Sumac; shrubs - Mountainlaurel Kalmia, Buffalonut, Blueridge Blueberry, Sweetfern, Trailing-arbutus
Similar: Highbush Blueberry; Wilson Snowbell - China, zone 6b; White Enkianthus - Japan; Carolina Silverbell - larger
Cultivars: Neglectum - branchlets, leaves glossy

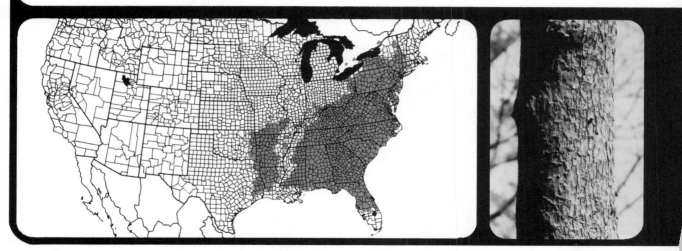

724

Common Deerberry

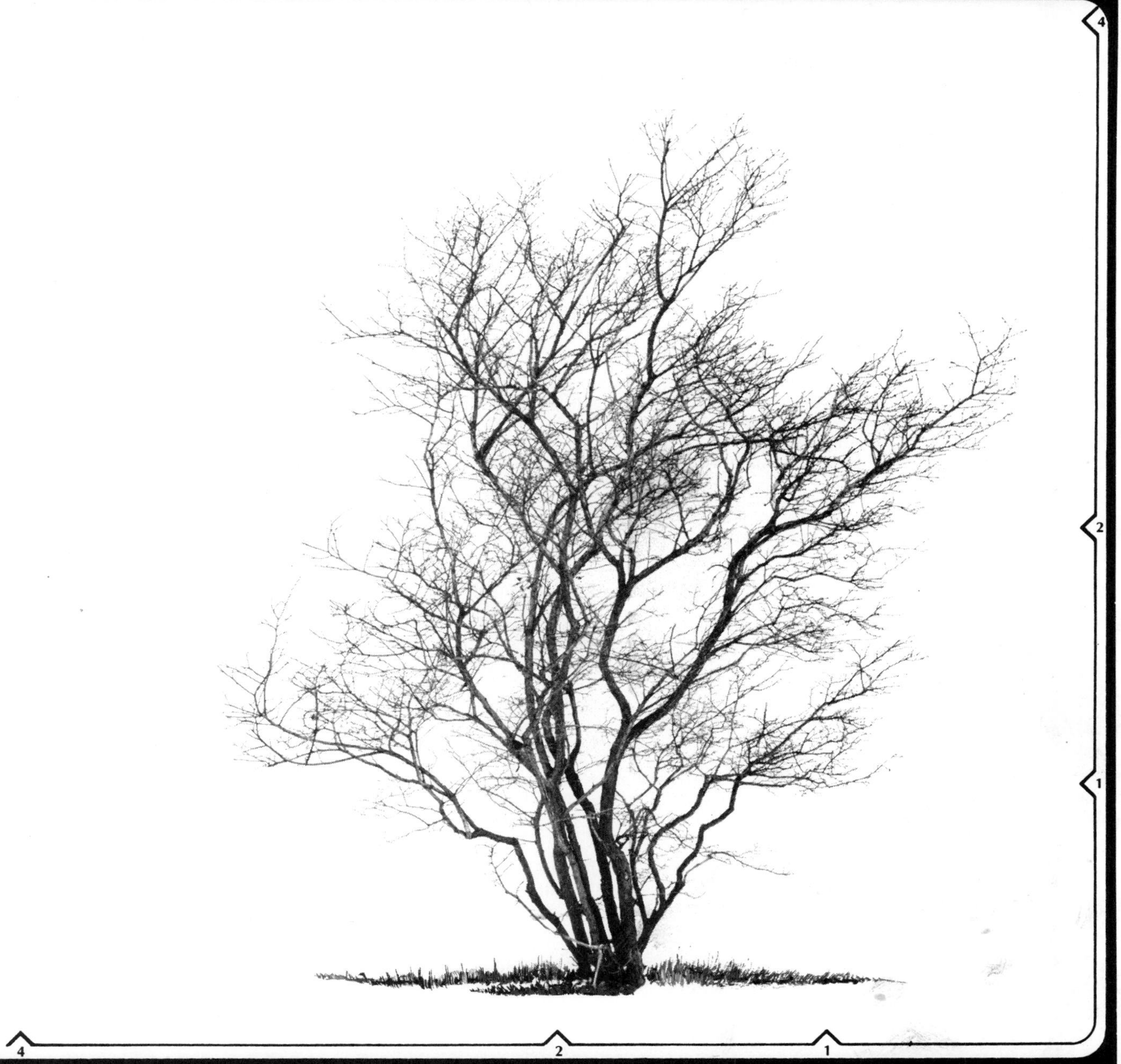

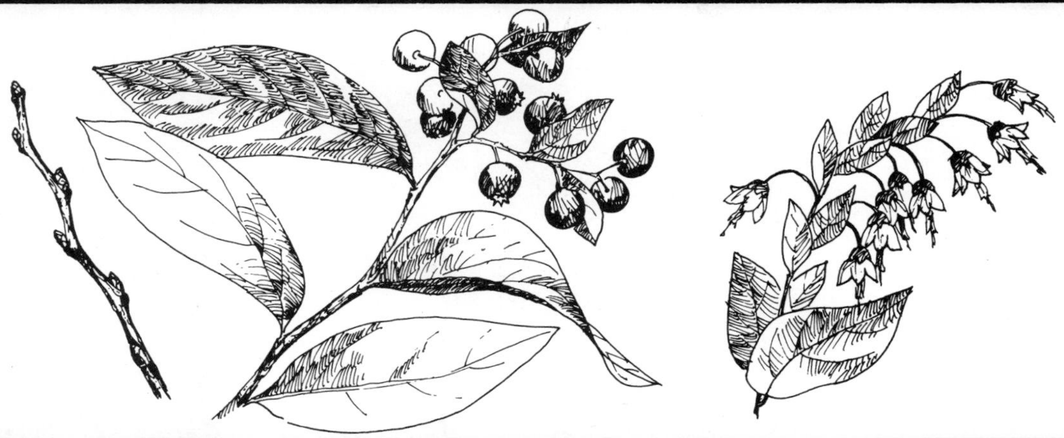

Viburnum acerifolium

FORM: obovoid to globular
Size: **small shrub** - from 1 to 2 m (3 to 6 ft)
Spread: **narrow** - between 1 to 2 m (3 to 6 ft), typically somewhat taller than broad
Mass: **dense**

BRANCHING: multiple stems, slender **upright spreading** with strong forking v-shaped branches; **medium** texture
Twig: slender, **velvety, gray brown**
Bud: small narrow ovoid, smooth, **green** tinged **with red**
Bark: **smooth** with prominent lenticels, old stems **scaly, purplish to gray brown**

FOLIAGE: opposite, **simple, palmately lobed,** 3 shallow lobes, commonly coarse toothed, maple-like appearance; **medium**
Surface: scattered **tomentose** or smooth above, dense woolly beneath, small dark dots beneath
Color: spring - **yellow green;** summer - bright **medium green;** autumn - various, **yellow,** pinkish **to crimson red, then purple**
Season: **deciduous;** emergence - mid **May,** drop - mid **October**

FLOWER: small, in long-stalked terminal **flat-topped** clusters, 7.5 cm (3 in) across, small fertile flower type only
Color: creamy **white**
Season: mid through late **June,** after leaves
Sex: monoecious

FRUIT: oval **berries,** 8 mm (⅓ in) long, in broad flattened clusters
Color: red ripening to bloomy **blue,** weathering **to black**
Season: mid **August through** mid **December**   Human Value: dry **edible fruit**
Wildlife Value: **high;** upland gamebirds, songbirds, large and small mammals; hoofed browsers graze leaves, twigs

HABITAT: formation - **forest, moist cliff;** region - **Northern, Central;** lowland **wet-mesic,** upland **mesic, mesic-dry, dry;**
floodplain forests, dry wooded slopes, mixed deciduous forests, talus slopes, rock outcrops, wooded ravines
Shade Tolerance: **very tolerant**
Flood Tolerance: **intolerant**

SOIL: Texture: **moderately coarse to fine;** sandy and gravelly loams, loams, silt loams, fine sandy loams, clays
Drainage: **moderately poor to well**
Moisture: **moist to dry**
Reaction: **moderately acid,** pH 5.1 - 6.0

HARDINESS: zone 3b
Rate: **slow to medium**
Longevity: **short-lived**

SUSCEPTIBILITY: Physiological: **occasional** - leaf burn resulting from sulphur sprays commonly used on roses
Disease: **occasional** - bacterial leaf spot, crown gall, leaf spots, powdery mildew, rusts, spot anthracnose
Insect: **occasional** - snowball aphid, viburnum shoot sawfly, viburnum aphid, scales, thrips, dogwood twig borer
Wind-Ice: **infrequent**

URBAN TOLERANCE: Pollution: **sensitive** - SO_2, HFl; **intermediate** - Cl
Lighting: Drought Heat: **intermediate**   Mine Spoils:
Salt: **sensitive**   Soil Compaction: **intermediate**
Root Pattern: fibrous, **shallow laterals; transplants well**

SPECIES: Associate: trees - Butternut, White Ash, Tuliptree, Slippery Elm, Cucumbertree Magnolia, Sweet Birch,
Northern Red/White Oaks; shrubs - Common Spicebush, American Bladdernut, Common Deerberry
Similar: Rafinesque/Arrowwood Viburnums; American Cranberrybush Viburnum - taller, red fruit
Cultivars: not commercially available

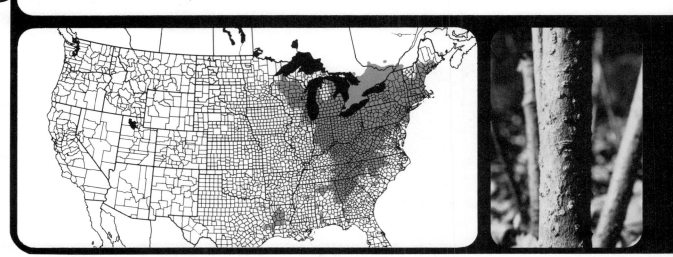

Mapleleaf Viburnum

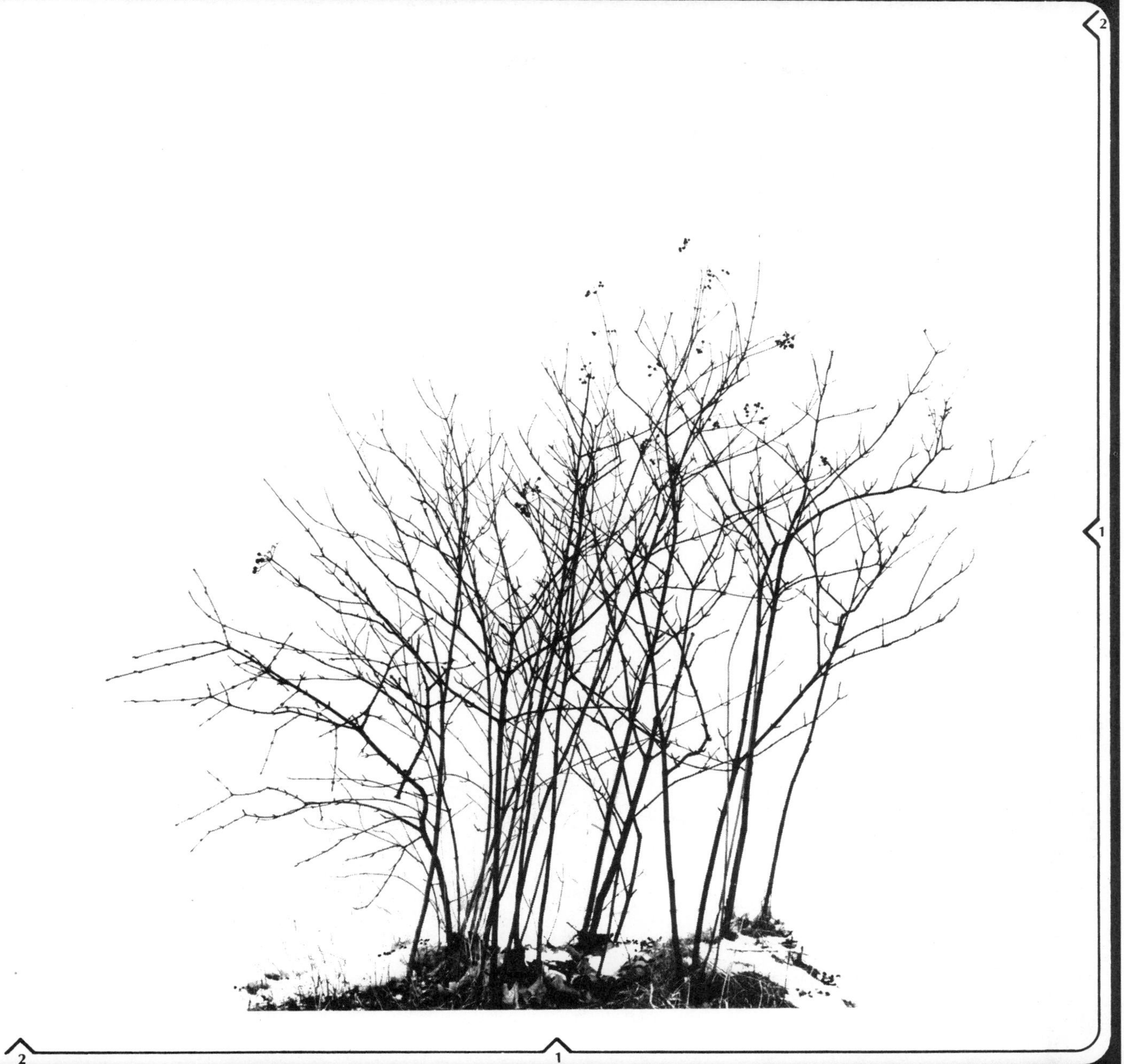

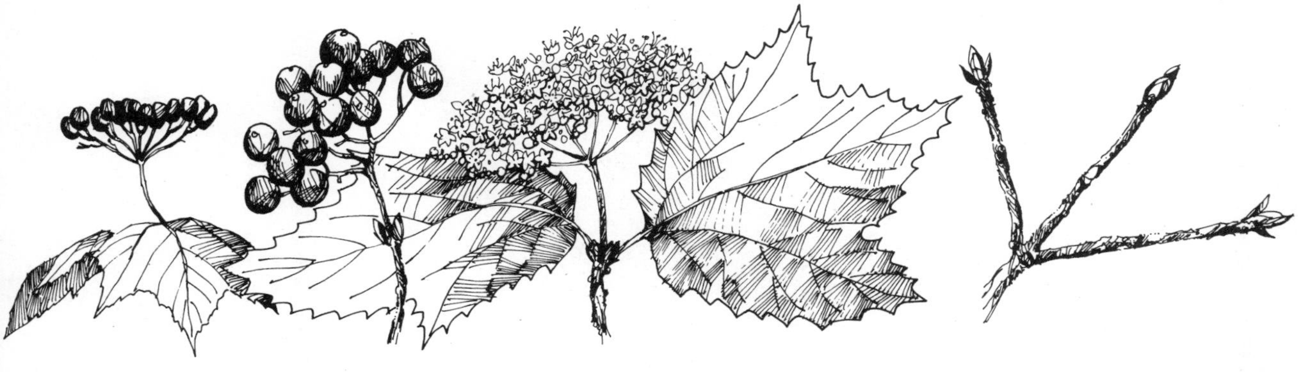

Viburnum alnifolium

FORM: obovoid to globular
Size: **mid-height shrub** - from 2 to 4 m (6 to 12 ft)
Spread: **intermediate** - between 2 to 4 m (6 to 12 ft), typically ⅔ or equal to height
Mass: **open** and loose, sprawling

BRANCHING: **erect** multiple stems, **upright spreading** forked branches, outer branches arching, rooting at tips; **coarse**
Twig: stout, dense **velvety, green brown** with **reddish to purple** woolly hairs
Bud: **large**, 13 to 19 mm (½ to ¾ in), dense **woolly, naked,** protected by embryonic leaves, **yellow brown to red brown**
Bark: smooth or becoming **scaly** on old stems, **brown**

FOLIAGE: opposite, **simple,** broadly **ovate, cordate to orbicular,** finely toothed, veins deep set; **coarse** texture
Surface: rusty **tomentose** becoming smooth, paler woolly beneath
Color: spring - **red green to purple;** summer - **medium green;** autumn - **orange to** claret **red, then** maroon **purple**
Season: **deciduous;** emergence - early **May;** drop - mid **November**

FLOWER: small, in large **flat-topped** clusters, 7.5 to 12.5 cm (3 to 5 in) across, fringed by larger 5-petaled sterile blooms
Color: creamy **white**
Season;   early or mid **May,** after leaves
Sex: monoecious

FRUIT: elliptic **berry,** 9.5 mm (⅜ in) long, in broad umbrella-like clusters
Color: brilliant red ripening to bloomy **blue,** weathering **to black**
Season: early **August through** late **September** or later   Human Value: sweet **edible fruit**
Wildlife Value: **high;** upland gamebirds, songbirds, large and small mammals; hoofed browsers eat leaves, twigs

HABITAT: formation - **forest, bald;** region - **Northern, Central;** gradient - upland **mesic, mesic-dry;** cool moist woodlands,
          wooded coves, cool rocky stream banks, cool rocky mountain summits, heath balds
Shade Tolerance: **very tolerant**
Flood Tolerance: **intolerant**

SOIL: Texture: **moderately coarse to moderately fine,** rock outcroppings, gravelly and sandy loams, loams, silt loams
Drainage: **moderately well to well**
Moisture: **moist to average**
Reaction: **strongly acid to slightly acid,** pH 5.5 - 6.5

HARDINESS: zone 3b
Rate: **medium**
Longevity: **short-lived**

SUSCEPTIBILITY: Physiological: **occasional** - cannot tolerate sulphur sprays often used on roses
Disease: **occasional** - bacterial leaf spot, shoot blight, powdery mildew, leaf spots, crown gall
Insect: **occasional** - asiatic garden beetle, citris flatid planthopper, tarnished plant bug, scales, thrips
Wind-Ice: **infrequent**

URBAN TOLERANCE: Pollution: **sensitive** - S0$_2$, HFI; **intermediate** - CI
Lighting: Drought Heat: **sensitive**   Mine Spoils:
Salt: **sensitive**   Soil Compaction: **intermediate**
Root Pattern: fibrous, **shallow laterals,** arching branches often rooting at tips; **transplants well**

SPECIES: Associate: trees - Sugar/Mountain/Striped Maples, American Beech, Yellow/Sweet Birches, Red Spruce,
          Eastern Hemlock, Cucumbertree Magnolia; shrubs - Scarlet Elder, Flame/Rose/Pinxterbloom Azaleas, Mountainlaurel
Similar: Wayfaringtree Viburnum - European; Doublefile Viburnum - horizontal habit, leaves bright green
Cultivars: 'Praecox' - blooms 3 weeks earlier

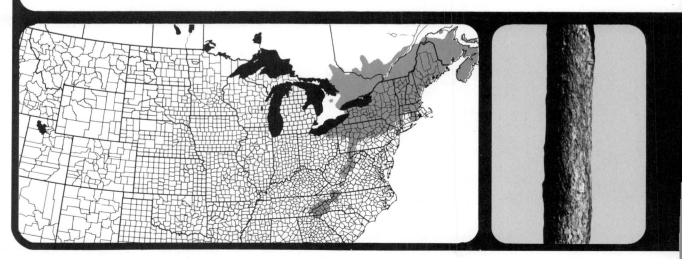

Hobblebush Viburnum

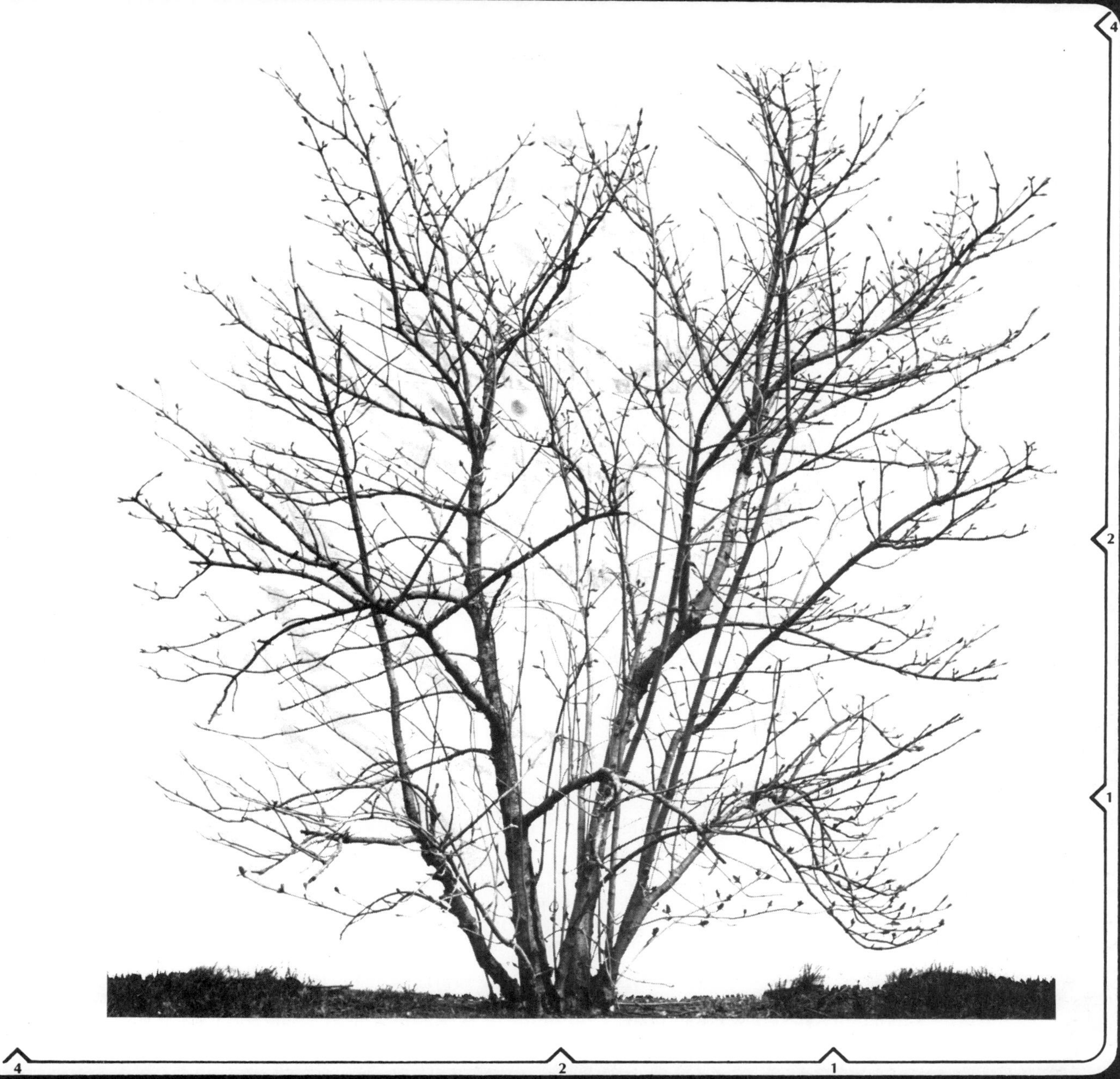

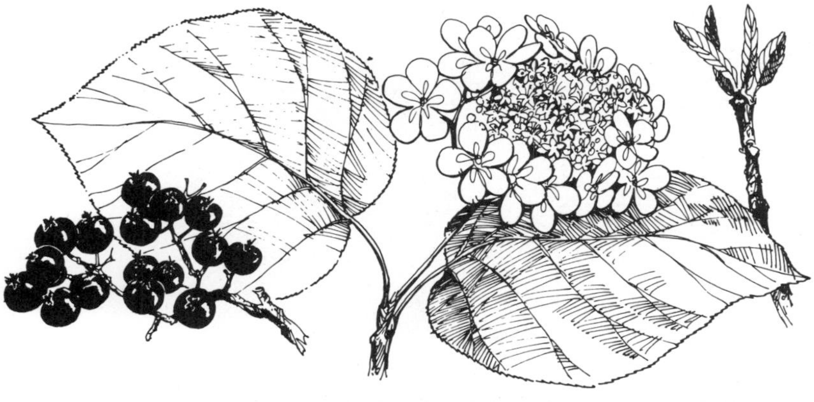

Viburnum cassinoides

FORM: obovoid to globular
Size: **mid-height shrub** - from 2 to 4 m (6 to 12 ft)
Spread: **intermediate** - between 2 to 4 m (6 to 12 ft), commonly ⅔ or equal to height
Mass: **dense**

BRANCHING: **upright spreading** stems and branches, becoming **arching** with age; **medium** texture
Twig: slender, **velvety, gray brown** with silvery gray exfoliating scurfy **scales**
Bud: **large,** long sharp-**pointed,** 9.5 to 13 mm (⅜ to ½ in), flower bud with **2 scales,** base swollen, **yellow brown**
Bark: **smooth** and dotted with numerous light lenticels, old stems **scaly, gray brown**

FOLIAGE: opposite, **simple, ovate,** irregularly toothed above middle or entire, wavy margin, petiole winged; **medium**
Surface: **glossy** to dull, smooth, thick and firm
Color: spring - **red green;** summer - bright **medium green;** autumn - **orange to** crimson **red, then** maroon **purple**
Season: **deciduous;** emergence - early **May,** drop - mid **October**

FLOWER: small, in terminal **flat-topped** clusters, 5 to 10 cm (2 to 4 in) across, small fertile flowers only
Color: creamy **white**
Season: early through mid **June,** after leaves
Sex: monoecious   **Fragrant:** pungently scented, disagreeable

FRUIT: spherical or oblong **berry,** 10 mm (⅜ in) long, in heavy drooping clusters
Color: often multiple colors at same time; first **yellow,** then pink **to red** ripening to bloomy **blue,** weathering **to black**
Season: mid **August through** mid October   Human Value: raisin-like **edible fruit**
Wildlife Value: **high;** upland gamebirds, songbirds, marsh and shorebirds, large and small mammals

HABITAT: formation - **bog, swamp, dune, old field, forest;** region - **Northern, Central;** gradient - **wet, wet-mesic, mesic-dry;**
moist rocky woods, clearings, swamps, bog thickets, low wet sandy woods
Shade Tolerance: **tolerant**
Flood Tolerance: **very tolerant**

SOIL: Texture: **moderately coarse to fine;** gravelly and sandy loams, fine sandy loams, silt loams, peats and mucks
Drainage: **very poor to well**
Moisture: **wet to dry**
Reaction: **moderately acid to slightly acid,** pH 5.1 - 6.5

HARDINESS: zone 2
Rate: **medium**
Longevity: **moderately short-lived**

SUSCEPTIBILITY: Physiological: **infrequent**
Disease: **infrequent** - spot anthracnose, downy leaf spot, powdery mildew, shoot blight; none serious
Insect: **infrequent** - southern root-knot nematode, scales, borers, thrips, viburnum aphid; none serious
Wind-Ice: **infrequent**

URBAN TOLERANCE: Pollution: **sensitive** - HFI; **intermediate** - CI
Lighting: Drought Heat: **intermediate**   Mine Spoils:
Salt: **resistant**   Soil Compaction: **resistant**
Root Pattern: fibrous, **shallow lateral; transplants well**

SPECIES: Associate: trees - Black Willow, River Birch, American Planetree, Water/Willow/Swamp White Oaks; shrubs
Common Alder, Silky Dogwood, Common Buttonbush, American Elder, Possumhaw, Purple Chokeberry, Inkberry
Similar: Nannyberry/Blackhaw/Possumhaw Viburnums - naked buds, habit, fruit, and habitat similar, all larger
Cultivars: 'Nanum' - dense dwarf form

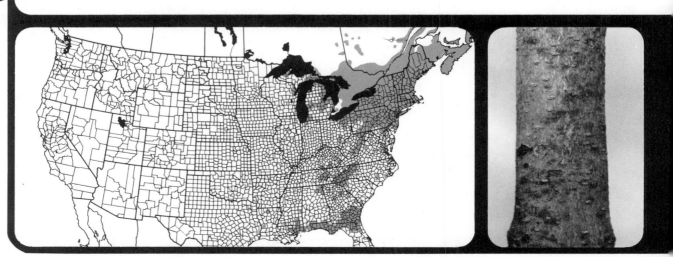

Viburnum dentatum

FORM: obovoid to globular
Size: **mid-height shrub** - 2 to 4 m (6 to 12 ft)
Spread: **intermediate** - between 2 to 4 m (6 to 12 ft), typically ⅔ or equal to height
Mass: **moderate** to dense

BRANCHING: slender straight **upright spreading** stems and branches, finally **arching** to ground with age; **medium** texture
Twig: **velvety** to smooth, often **angular** with 6 **ridged** sides; **gray brown**
Bud: small ovoid, pressed against twig, several scales, **red brown**
Bark: **smooth,** old stems **scaly** or with **shallow** cross checked **furrows, gray brown**

FOLIAGE: opposite, **simple,** broadly **ovate,** coarse dentate teeth, conspicuous veins; **medium fine** texture
Surface: **glossy,** smooth above
Color: spring - **red green;** summer - **medium green;** autumn - **dark green** late, **then** maroon **purple**
Season: **deciduous;** emergence - mid **May,** drop - early **November**

FLOWER: **flat-topped** clusters, 5 to 10 cm (2 to 4 in) across, small fertile flowers only
Color: creamy **white**
Season: late **May through** early **June,** after leaves
Sex: monoecious

FRUIT: small globular pea-size **berries,** 6 mm (¼ in) diameter, in stiff much-branched drooping flat-topped clusters
Color: porcelain **blue** weathering **to** bluish **black,** on bright yellow or reddish stems
Season: early **September through** late **November**
Wildlife Value: **high;** upland gamebirds, songbirds, and small mammals in small quantities

HABITAT: formation - **forest, old field, bog;** region - **Central, Southern;** gradient - lowland **wet, wet-mesic;** floodplain forests,
stream banks, wet woodlands, bogs, low wet acid-sand habitats
Shade Tolerance: **tolerant**
Flood Tolerance: **tolerant**

SOIL: Texture: **moderately coarse to fine;** gravelly and sandy loams, fine loamy sands, silt loams, silts, peats
Drainage: **very poor to well**
Moisture: **wet to average**
Reaction: **moderately acid to slightly acid,** pH 5.1 - 6.5

HARDINESS: zone 3a
Rate: **medium**
Longevity: **short-lived**

SUSCEPTIBILITY: Physiological: **infrequent**
Disease: **infrequent** - none serious
Insect: **infrequent** - none serious
Wind-Ice: **infrequent**

URBAN TOLERANCE: Pollution: **sensitive** - HFI; **intermediate** - CI
Lighting: Drought heat: **resistant** Mine Spoils:
Salt: **resistant** Soil Compaction: **intermediate**
Root Pattern: **shallow** fibrous, suckers freely from base; **transplants well**

SPECIES: Associate: trees - Red Maple, Water Hickory, Overcup/Swamp Chestnut Oaks, Swamp Tupelo; shrubs -
Inkberry, Common Winterberry, He-huckleberry, Sweetbay Magnolia, Common Buttonbush, Virginia Sweetspire
Similar: Rafinesque Viburnum - smaller, open, Northern; Mapleleaf/Missouri Viburnums
Cultivars: none available

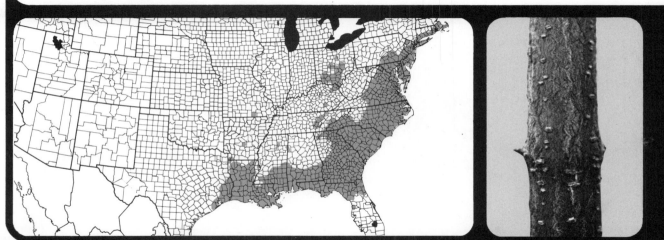

733

Viburnum nudum

FORM: obovoid to globular
Size: **large shrub** - from 4 to 6 m (12 to 20 ft)
Spread: **wide** - between 4 to 6 m (12 to 20 ft), commonly ⅔ to ¾ or equal to height
Mass: **moderate**

BRANCHING: multiple stems with **upright spreading** to nearly horizontal branches, strongly arching with age; **coarse**
Twig: **glossy**, slightly scurfy, greenish brown to **red brown**
Bud: **large**, long sharp-**pointed**, finger-like, 13 mm (½ in), flower bud only partially covered by **2 scales, red brown**
Bark: smooth with prominent lenticels, old stems with scurfy rough blocky **scales, gray brown**

FOLIAGE: opposite, **simple, lanceolate to oblong lanceolate,** entire or obscurely toothed, wavy rolled edge; **medium** texture
Surface: **glossy**, smooth, thick, paler beneath
Color: spring - light **yellow green** or reddish; summer - **dark green to blue green;** autumn - **dark green** late, **then red to purple**
Season: **deciduous;** emergence - mid **May,** drop - mid **October**

FLOWER: small, in broad terminal **flat-topped** clusters on long stalks, 7.5 to 12.5 cm (3 to 5 in) across, fertile flowers only
Color: creamy **white**
Season: late **June through** early **July,** after leaves
Sex: monoecious   **Fragrant:** strong odor

FRUIT: football-shaped **berry,** 6 to 10 mm (¼ to ⅜ in) long, in heavy broad flattened terminal clusters
Color: white, pinkish to red ripening to heavy bloomy **blue,** finally **black** on rusty red brown stems
Season: early **September through** late **October**   Human Value: highly acid **edible fruit**
Wildlife Value: **high;** songbirds, waterbirds, marsh and shorebirds, small mammals

HABITAT: formation - **swamp, spring, bog, forest, old field;** region - **Southern;** gradient - lowland **wet, wet-mesic,** upland
  mesic; swamps, flatwoods, heath bogs, deep rich upland forests, creek bottoms, wet sandy woods, springheads
Shade Tolerance: **tolerant**
Flood Tolerance: **tolerant**

SOIL: Texture: **moderately coarse to fine;** gravelly and sandy loams, fine sands, silt loams, silts, peats, mud flats
Drainage: **very poor to well**
Moisture: **wet to average**
Reaction: **moderately acid,** pH 5.1 - 6.0

HARDINESS: zone 6a
Rate: **medium**
Longevity: **moderately short-lived**

SUSCEPTIBILITY: Physiological: **infrequent**
Disease: **infrequent** - none serious
Insect: **infrequent;** - none serious
Wind-Ice: **infrequent**

URBAN TOLERANCE: Pollution: **sensitive** - HFl; **intermediate** - Cl
Lighting: Drought Heat: **resistant**   Mine Spoils:
Salt: **sensitive**   Soil Compaction: **resistant**
Root Pattern: **shallow** fibrous; **transplants well**

SPECIES: Associate: trees - Swamp Tupelo, Red Maple, Water Hickory, Overcup/Swamp Chestnut Oaks, Black Willow;
  shrubs - Sweetbay Magnolia, Arrowwood Viburnum, Common Winterberry, Inkberry, Virginia Sweetspire
Similar: Witherod/Nannyberry/Blackhaw/Rusty Blackhaw Viburnums - buds, form, flower, fruit similar
Cultivars: none available

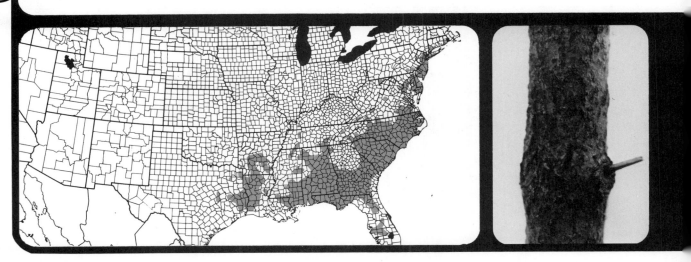

Viburnum rafinesquianum

FORM: obovoid to globular
Size: **small shrub** - from 1 to 2 m (3 to 6 ft), occasionally to 3 m (10 ft)
Spread: **narrow** - between 1 to 2 m (3 to 6 ft), typically somewhat taller than broad
Mass: **open** and loose

BRANCHING: multi-stemmed, slender **upright spreading** branches, loose habit; **medium** texture
Twig: slender, rigid, smooth, not ridged, **gray brown**
Bud: small ovoid, 3 to 6 mm (⅛ to ¼ in), smooth, **gray brown**
Bark: **smooth** with conspicuous lenticels, old stems with **shallow** cross-checked **furrows, gray brown**

FOLIAGE: opposite, **simple, ovate or oblong ovate,** coarse dentate teeth; **medium fine** texture
Surface: **dull,** smooth, hairy beneath
Color: spring - **red green;** summer - **medium green;** autumn - deep maroon **purple**
Season: **deciduous;** emergence - mid **May,** drop - late **October**

FLOWER: **flat-topped** terminal clusters, 3 to 6 cm (⅛ to ¼ in) across, small fertile type only
Color: creamy **white**
Season; late **May through** early **June,** after leaves
Sex: monoecious

FRUIT: smooth glossy oval-shaped **berry,** 8 to 10 mm (⅓ to ⅖ in) long, in flat 2 to 15-fruited clusters
Color: dark **bluish black**
Season; early **September through** late **November**   Human Value: not edible
Wildlife Value: **high;** upland gamebirds, songbirds and small mammals; also grazed by hoofed browsers

HABITAT: formation - **forest, barrens, old field;** region - **Central;** gradient - upland **mesic-dry, dry;** dry oak woods, stony slopes, rocky stream banks, barrens, bluffs, fence rows, clearings, rocky or sandy ravine slopes, calcareous ledges
Shade Tolerance; **tolerant**
Flood Tolerance: **intolerant**

SOIL: Texture: **medium to fine;** loams, sandy and gravelly loams, clay loams, heavy clay
Drainage: **moderately well to excessive**
Moisture: **average to droughty**
Reaction: **slightly acid to** circumneutral, tolerates **alkaline,** pH 6.1 - 8.5

HARDINESS: zone 3a
Rate: **medium**
Longevity: **short-lived**

SUSCEPTIBILITY: Physiological: **infrequent** - burn caused by sulphur sprays used on roses can be extensive
Disease: **infrequent** - none serious
Insect: **infrequent** - none serious
Wind-Ice: **infrequent**

URBAN TOLERANCE: Pollution: **sensitive** - S0$_2$, HFl; **intermediate** - Cl
Lighting: Drought Heat: **resistant**   Mine Spoils:
Salt: **intermediate**   Soil Compaction: **intermediate**
Root Pattern: fibrous, **shallow laterals; transplants well**

SPECIES: Associate: trees - White Ash, Black Walnut, Black Cherry, White Oak, Shagbark/Bitternut Hickories; shrubs - Gray Dogwood, Missouri Gooseberry, American Filbert, Allegany Blackberry, Indiancurrant Coralberry
Similar: Arrowwood/Missouri Viburnums - taller, more dense; Mapleleaf Viburnum - dense shade, lobed leaves
Cultivars: none available

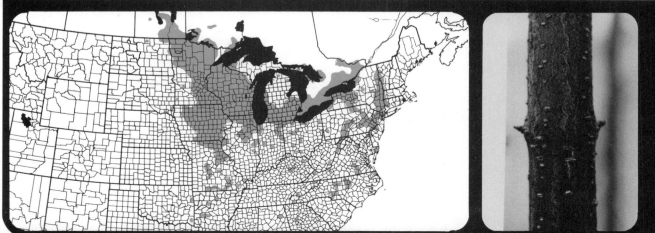

Viburnum trilobum

FORM: obovoid to globular
Size: **mid-height shrub** - from 2 to 4 m (6 to 12 ft), occasionally to 5 m (16 ft)
Spread: **intermediate** - between 2 to 4 m (6 to 12 ft), typically taller than wide
Mass: **dense**

BRANCHING: tightly clustered stems, **upright** spreading **or arching** branches, fruited branchlets **pendulous; coarse** texture
Twig: slender, smooth, rigid, with a waxy appearance, light tan or dull **yellow brown** becoming **gray**
Bud: plump ovate, 6 to 10 mm (¼ to ⅜ in), **2 scales,** sometimes **resinous, green or** bright **red** in winter
Bark: **smooth,** old stems with irregular longitudinal cracks, light tan becoming **gray brown**

FOLIAGE: opposite, **simple, palmately lobed,** 3 seldom-toothed lobes, maple-like, petioles with small glands; **medium**
Surface: **dull,** smooth, thick
Color: spring - **yellow green;** summer - **medium green;** autumn - **dark green** late, **then red to** maroon **purple**
Season: **decidous;** emergence - mid **May,** drop - late **November**

FLOWER: **flat-topped** terminal clusters, 7.5 to 10 cm (3 to 4 in) across, small fertile flowers fringed by larger sterile
Color: **white**
Season: late **May through** early **June,** after leaves
Sex: monoecious

FRUIT: firm glossy translucent globular **berries,** 6 to 10 mm (¼ to ⅜ in) diameter, heavy drooping clusters
Color: scarlet **red to orange**
Season: early **September** persisting **through** late **February**   Human Value: sharply acid **edible fruit**
Wildlife Value: **high;** consumed in small winter quantities by songbirds, gamebirds, small mammals, waxwings devour

HABITAT: formation - **moist cliff, bog, old field, forest;** region - **Northern;** gradient - **wet, wet-mesic, mesic, mesic-dry;** talus
     slopes, peat bogs, swampy woods, alder thickets, wet pastures, lake banks, footslopes, mesic ravines, bluffs
Shade Tolerance: **very tolerant**
Flood Tolerance: **tolerant**

SOIL: Texture: **moderately coarse to fine;** rock outcrops, sandy/gravelly loams, silt loams, clay loams, organic peats
Drainage: **very poor to well**
Moisture: **wet to average**
Reaction: most abundant on basic or **circumneutral,** pH 6.6 - 7.5

HARDINESS: zone 2
Rate: **medium**
Longevity: **moderately short-lived**

SUSCEPTIBILITY: Physiological: **occasional** - leaf burn from sulphur base sprays
Disease: **infrequent** - none serious
Insect: **infrequent** - none serious, susceptable to aphids but less so than European Cranberrybush Viburnum
Wind-Ice: **infrequent**

URBAN TOLERANCE: Pollution: **sensitive** - S0₂, HFl; **intermediate** - Cl
Lighting: Drought Heat: **resistant**   Mine Spoils:
Salt: **sensitive**   Soil Compaction: **resistant**
Root Pattern: **shallow** fibrous; **transplants easily**

SPECIES: Associate: trees - Black Ash, American Larch, Balsam Fir, Red Maple, Black Tupelo; shrubs - Glossy Buckthorn,
     Bunchberry/Red-osier Dogwoods, Common Winterberry, American Fly Honeysuckle, Canada Yew, Hazel Alder
Similar: European Cranberrybush Viburnum; Wright/Linden Viburnums - unlobed leaves, Asiatic
Cultivars: 'Compactum' - compact dwarf; 'Andrews', 'Halis', 'Wentworth' - all with large fruits, used in preserves

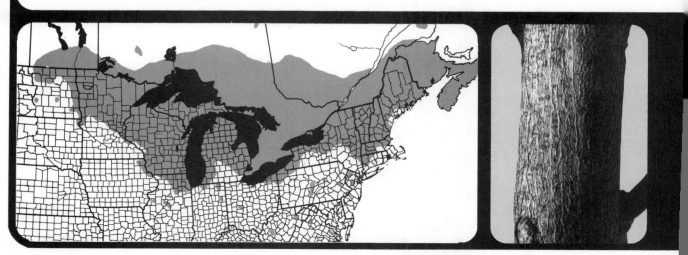

American Cranberrybush Viburnum

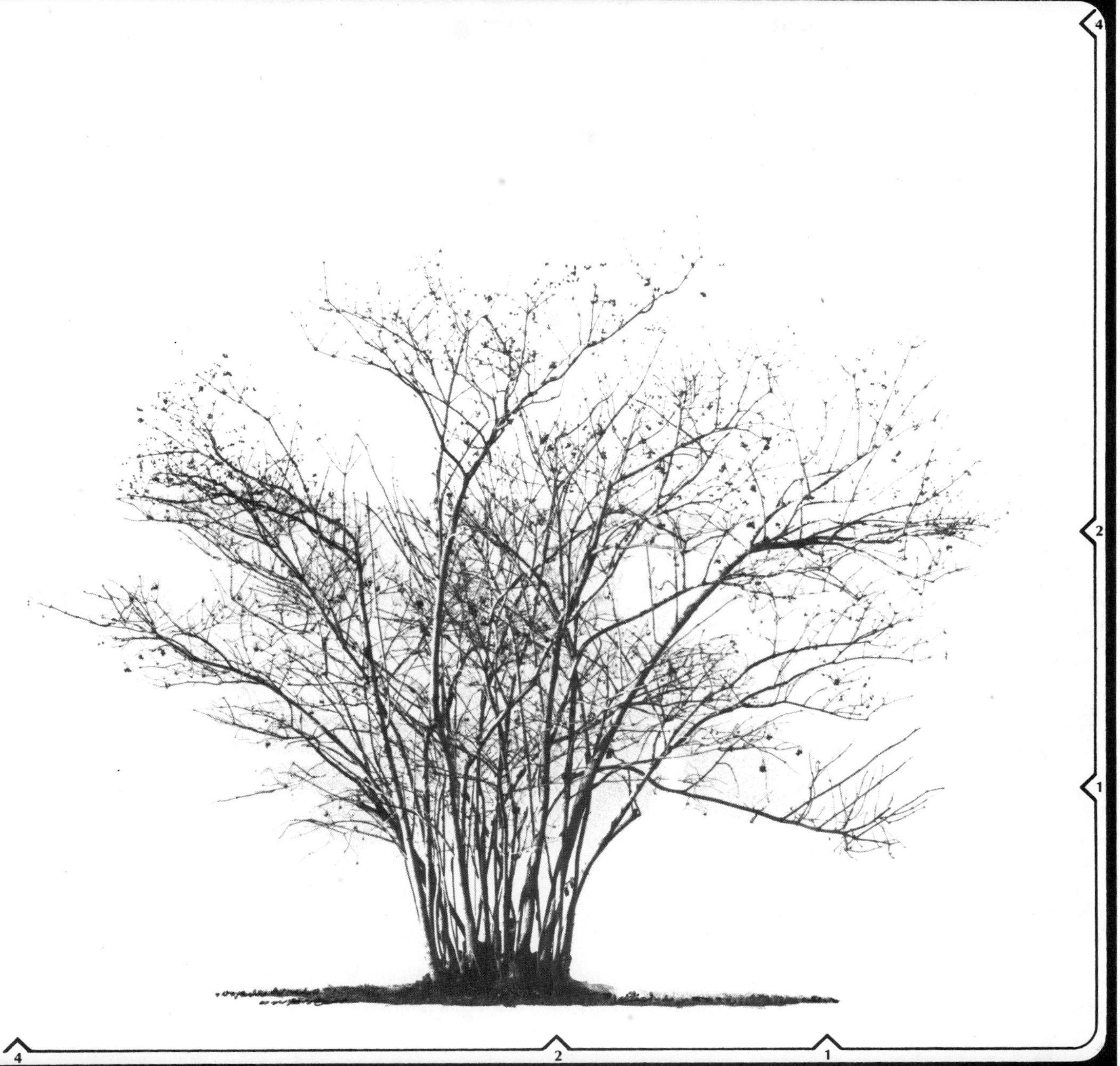

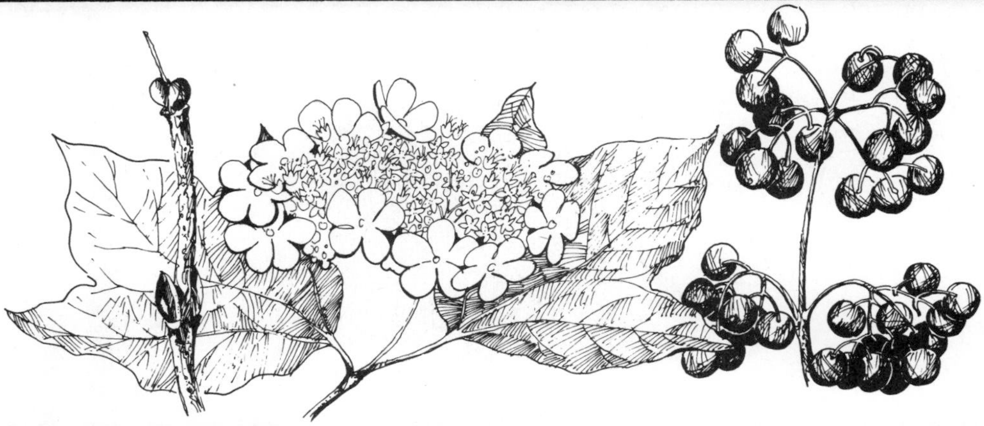

Xanthorhiza simplicissima

FORM: **mat**
Size: **very small shrub** - up to 1 m (3 ft)
Spread: **intermediate** - from 2 to 4 m (3 to 6 ft), spreading into large colonies
Mass: **open**

BRANCHING: spreading underground with stout little-branched **erect** stems, **leggy** appearance; **coarse** texture
Twig: stout, smooth, leaf scar encircling twig giving a segmented appearance, **green** becoming **gray brown**
Bud: end bud very **large,** 25 mm (1 in), **red brown**
Bark: **smooth** or separating into fine thin **scaly** flakes, **gray brown**

FOLIAGE: alternate, clustered at twig ends, **pinnate/bi-pinnate compound,** 5 leaflets, **ovate,** coarse teeth; **medium fine**
Surface: **glossy,** smooth, thin, pale beneath
Color: spring - **light green;** summer - **medium green;** autumn - green late, then **yellow to red, or purple;** winter - **tan brown**
Season: **deciduous or persistant;** emergence - late **April,** drop - many dried leaves remaining through **December**

FLOWER: in **small** drooping star-like **clusters,** 5 to 15 cm (2 to 6 in) long, crowded at ends of stems
Color: plum **purple** shading **to** chocolate **brown**
Season: late **April or** early **May,** with leaves
Sex: monoecious

FRUIT: small dry inflated **follicle,** in drooping clusters of 4 to 8, inconspicuous
Color: light **yellowish**
Season: early **August through** late **September**   Human value: not edible
Wildlife Value: **high;** upland gamebirds, songbirds, and small mammals

HABITAT: formation - **spring, swamp, forest;** region - **Southern;** gradient - lowland **wet, wet-mesic;** river and stream banks,
springy places, rich moist shady woodlands, alluvial forest, wet depressions
Shade Tolerance: **very tolerant**
Flood Tolerance: **tolerant**

SOIL: Texture: **coarse to moderately fine;** infertile sands and gravels, silt loams, heavy silts
Drainage: **poor to well**
Moisture: **wet to average**
Reaction: **strongly acid to slightly acid,** pH 4.0 - 6.5

HARDINESS: zone 5a
Rate: **medium**
Longevity: **moderately short-lived**

SUSCEPTIBILITY: Physiological: **infrequent**
Disease: **infrequent** - very resistant
Insect: **infrequent** - none serious
Wind-Ice: **occasional** - brittle stems may suffer breakage with heavy ice glaze

URBAN TOLERANCE: Pollution:
Lighting: Drought Heat: **intermediate**   Mine Spoils:
Salt: Soil Compaction: **intermediate**
Root Pattern: **shallow** fibrous, **stoloniferous** forming broad patches, bright yellow roots; **transplants well** in spring or fall

SPECIES: Associate: trees - Black Willow, American Sweetgum, American Planetree, Black Tupelo, River Birch, Common
Boxelder; shrubs - Virginia Sweetspire, Swamp Azalea, Common Alder, Summersweet Clethra, Common Buttonbush
Similar: Fragrant Sumac - especially dwarf varieties, dry habitats
Cultivars: none available

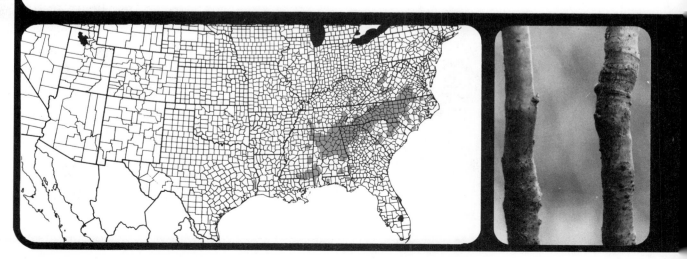

Yellowroot

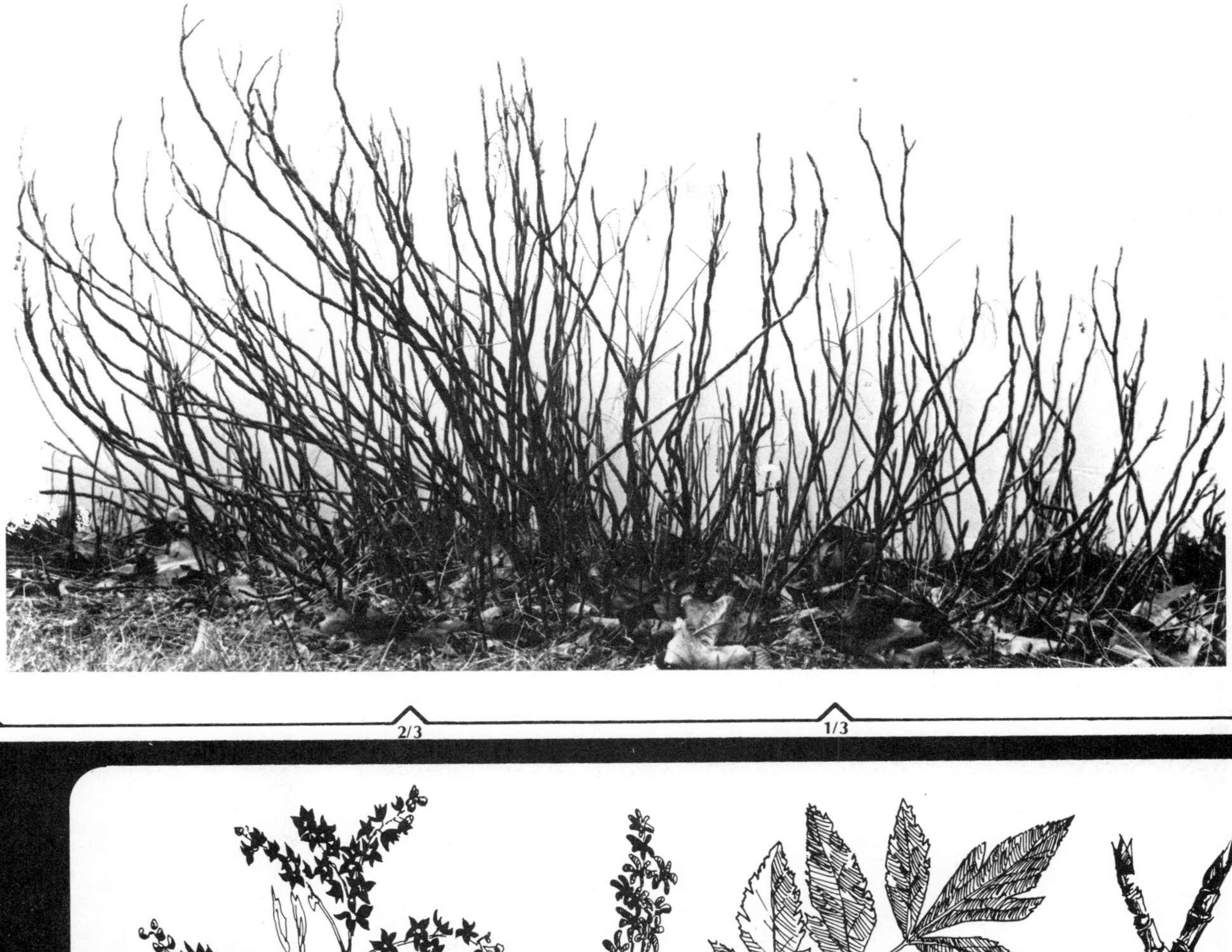

1 2/3 1/3

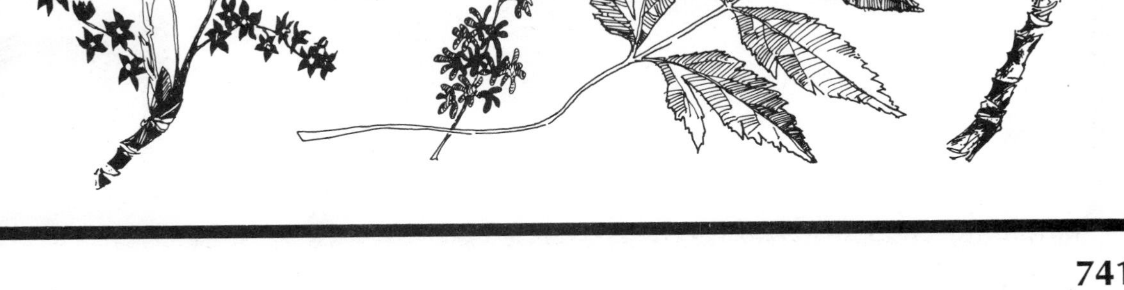

Yucca filamentosa

FORM: **globular** cluster of leaves
Size: **very small shrub** - up to 1 m (3 ft), flower stalks to 2 m (6 ft)
Spread: **very narrow** - up to 1 m (3 ft)
Mass: **dense**

BRANCHING: a rosette of **erect** leaves with stem rarely exposed above ground; **coarse** texture
Twig: none visible
Bud: none visible
Bark: **smooth**, not generally visible above ground

FOLIAGE: clump-like cluster, **simple**, long **linear**, dagger-like, margin entire with curly fibers, spiny **armed** tip; **coarse**
Surface: **dull**, smooth, stiff thick woody appearance
Color: all seasons - **blue green**
Season: **evergreen**

FLOWER: saucer-shaped **bell**, 5 to 7.5 cm (2 to 3 in) diameter, in **large** pendulous **clusters** on vertical stalks above leaves
Color: creamy **white**
Season: late **June** through late **July**
Sex: monoecious   **Fragrant:** somewhat perfumed, flowers visited by hummingbirds

FRUIT: dry woody elliptic 6-sided pod-like **capsule**, 2.5 to 4 cm (1 to 1½ in) long
Color: dark **brown**
Season: early **September** persisting **through** winter until late **March**   Human Value: **edible flowers**
Wildlife Value: **very low;** fruits occasionally used by small mammals

HABITAT: formation - **dune, prairie, barrens, old field, glade;** region - **Southern;** gradient - upland **dry;** roadsides, waste
areas, beach and dune, sandy areas, abandoned pasture, glades, rocky slopes, dry sandy prairies, sandy pine barrens
Shade Tolerance: **intolerant**
Flood Tolerance: **very intolerant**

SOIL: Texture: **coarse** sands and gravels, loamy sands **to medium** loams; sandy loams best
Drainage: **well to excessive**, requires good drainage
Moisture: **dry to droughty**
Reaction: **moderately acid to circumneutral**, pH 5.5 - 7.5

HARDINESS: zone 5a
Rate: **medium to slow**
Longevity: **long-lived**

SUSCEPTIBILITY: Physiological: **infrequent**
Disease: **infrequent** - leaf spot and blight during rainy growing seasons; rarely serious
Insect: **infrequent** - scale problem in humid poor air-drainage situations; rarely serious
Wind-Ice: **infrequent** - decidedly wind firm, tough

URBAN TOLERANCE: Pollution:
Lighting   Drought Heat: **resistant**   Mine Spoils: **resistant**
Salt: **resistant**   Soil Compaction: **intermediate**
Root Pattern: deep **taproot** to 6 m (20 ft) or **deep lateral** side shoots; very **difficult to transplant**, purchase container grown

SPECIES: Associate: trees - Turkey/Scarlet/Black/Blackjack/Post/Bluejack Oaks, Longleaf/Pitch/Shortlead Pines; shrubs -
Box Sandmyrtle, Common Deerberry, Bristly Locust, Bear Oak, Bearberry, Box Huckleberry, Blueridge Blueberry
Similar: Small Soapweed - Western; other yucca species
Cultivars: 'Concava' - spoonlike leaves are broader; also variegated form in trade, but very rare

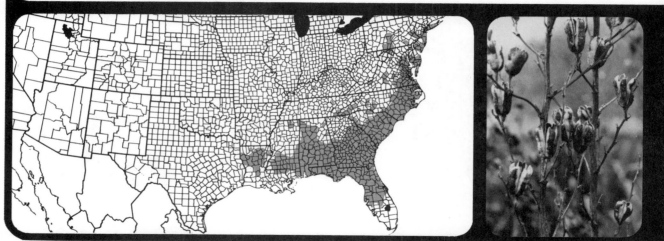

Adamsneedle Yucca

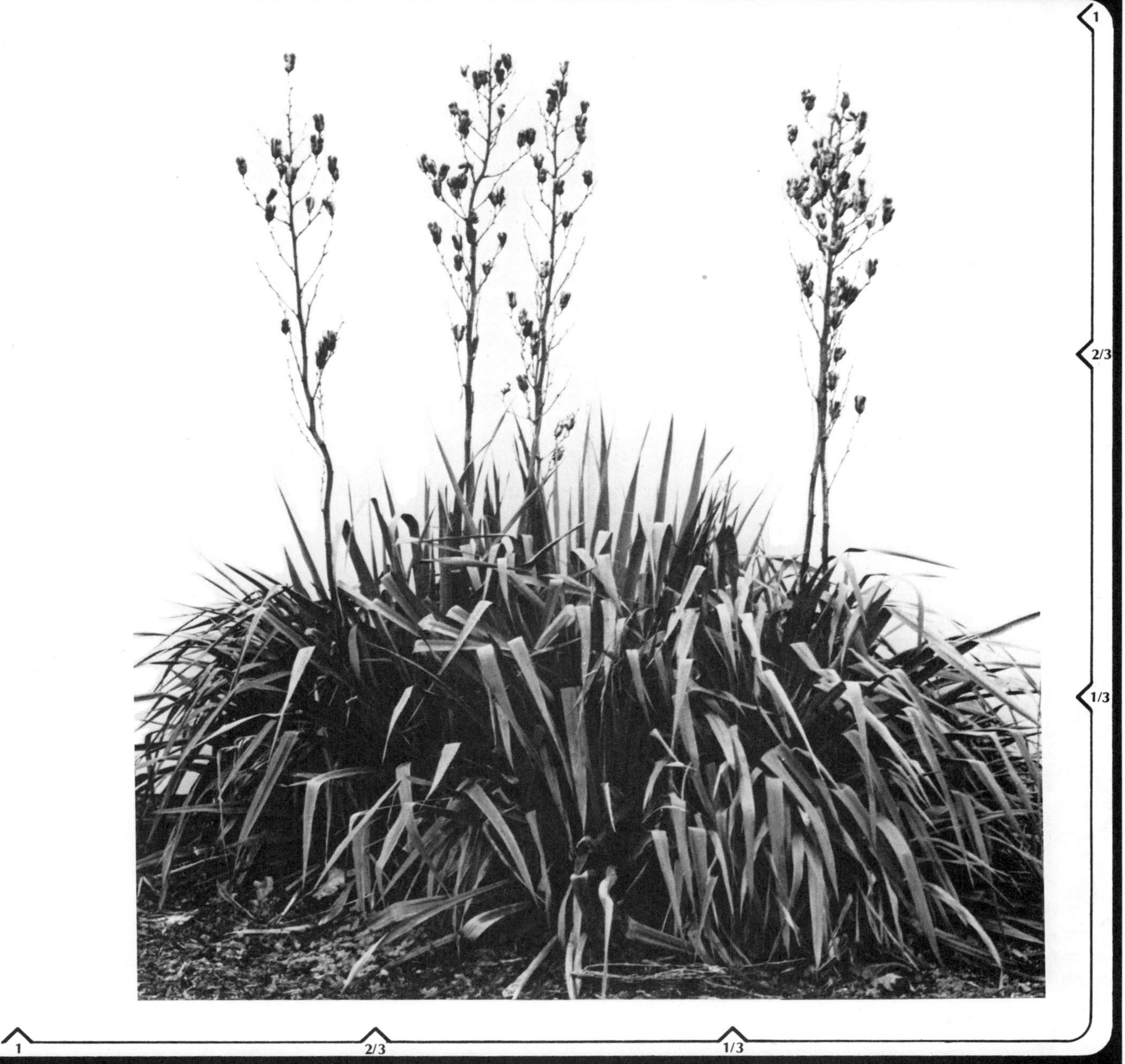

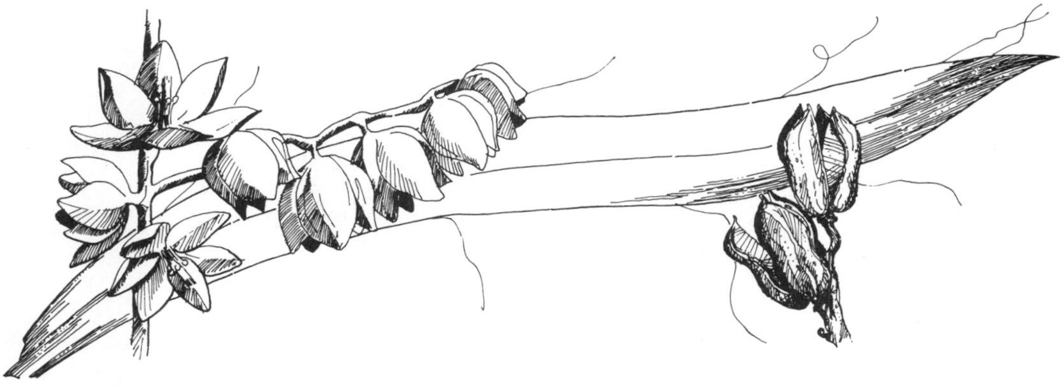

Zenobia pulverulenta

FORM: globular or mound
Size: **small shrub** - from 1 to 2 m (3 to 6 ft), occasionally to 3 m (10 ft)
Spread: **narrow** - between 1 to 2 m (3 to 6 ft)
Mass: **dense**

BRANCHING: multiple stems, **upright spreading** or arching habit; **medium** texture
Twig: smooth with whitened powdery bloom, **reddish** becoming **red brown**
Bud: small broad conical, **2 to 3 scales**
Bark: **exfoliating** into heavy papery sheets, **red brown to brown**

FOLIAGE: alternate, **simple**, **elliptic** to elliptic ovate, entire wavy edge; **medium fine** texture
Surface: **dull**, smooth, leathery, **powdery bloom,** bluish white beneath
Color: spring, summer - **silver gray**; autumn - **gray green** late, **then** dull **red to** deep **purple**
Season: tardily deciduous or **semi-evergreen**; emergence - late **May**, drop - late **November** or after

FLOWER: **small** nodding one-sided axillary **clusters**, bell-like blossoms, 6 to 8 mm (¼ to ⅓ in) across
Color: **white**
Season: mid through late **June**, after leaves
Sex: monoecious

FRUIT: dry ball-shaped 5-parted **capsule**, 2 to 3 mm (¹⁄₁₀ to ⅛ in) long
Color: **brown**
Season: early **September** persisting **through** winter until late **April**   Human Value: not edible
Wildlife Value: **low**; limited use by upland gamebirds, songbirds, small mammals

HABITAT: formation - **bog, swamp, spring, dune, barrens, glade**; region - **Southern**; gradient - lowland **wet**; shrub bogs and
          bays, pine savannas, borders of swamps, pocosins, bay forests, hillside bogs
Shade Tolerance: **tolerant**
Flood Tolerance: **very tolerant**

SOIL: Texture: **coarse** sands and gravels **to fine** sandy and gravelly loams, organic peats and mucks
Drainage: **very poor to moderately poor**
Moisture: **wet to average**
Reaction: **moderately acid to slightly acid**, pH 5.1 - 6.5

HARDINESS: zone 6a
Rate: **medium**
Longevity: **short-lived**

SUSCEPTIBILITY: Physiological: **infrequent**
Disease: **infrequent** - none serious
Insect: **infrequent** - none serious
Wind-Ice: **infrequent**

URBAN TOLERANCE: Pollution:
Lighting: Drought Heat: **resistant**   Mine Spoils:
Salt: **resistant**   Soil Compaction: **resistant**
Root Pattern: rhizomatous, forming colonies by **shallow stoloniferous** stems; **transplants well**

SPECIES: Associate: trees - Pond/Longleaf/Slash Pines, Sassafras; shrubs - Inkberry, Coast Leucothoe, Summersweet
          Clethra, Sweetbay Magnolia, Southern Waxmyrtle, Common Sweetleaf, Staggerbush Lyonia, Sawpalmetto
Similar:
Cultivars: Nitida - leaves green and without bloom

744

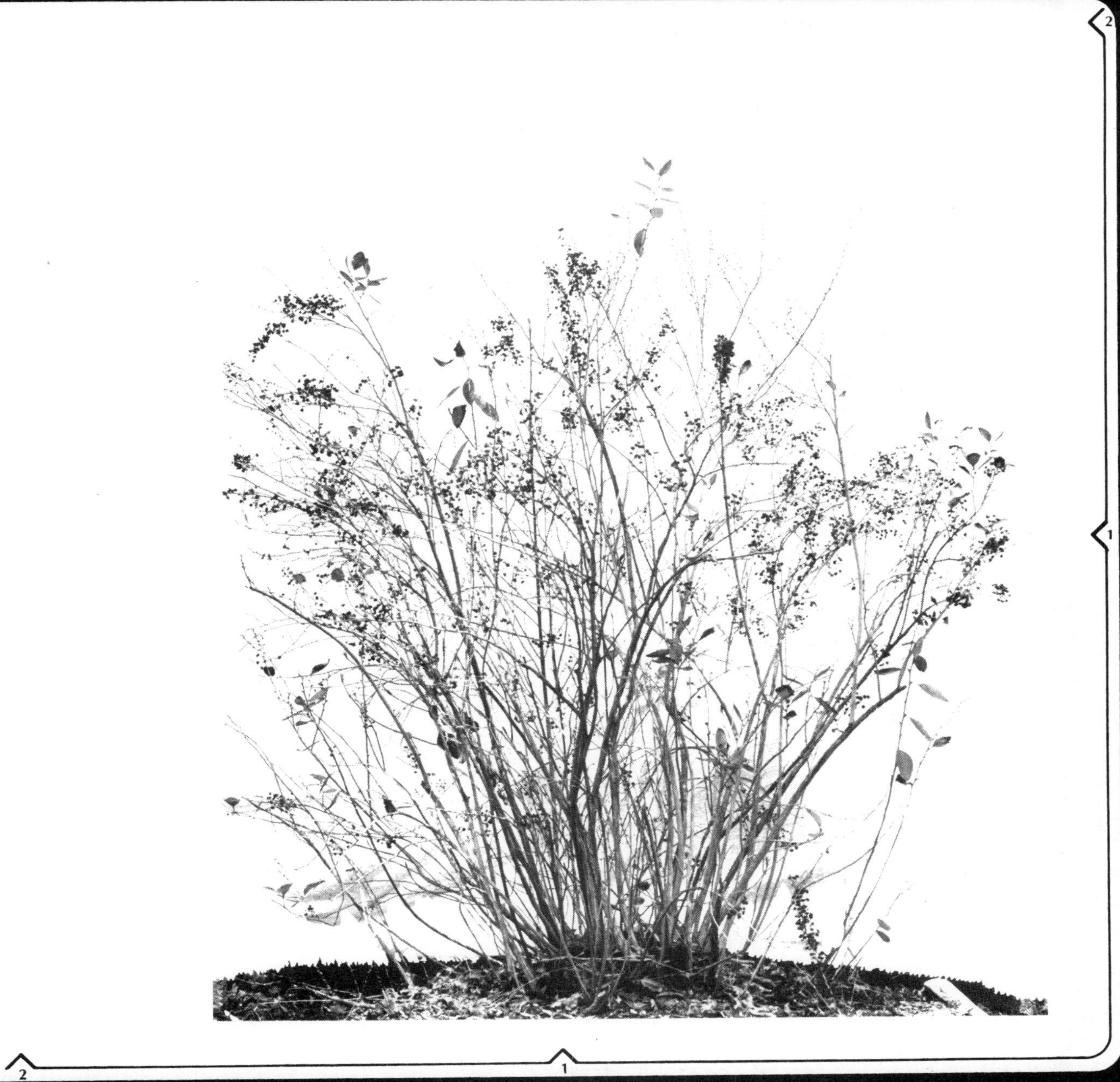

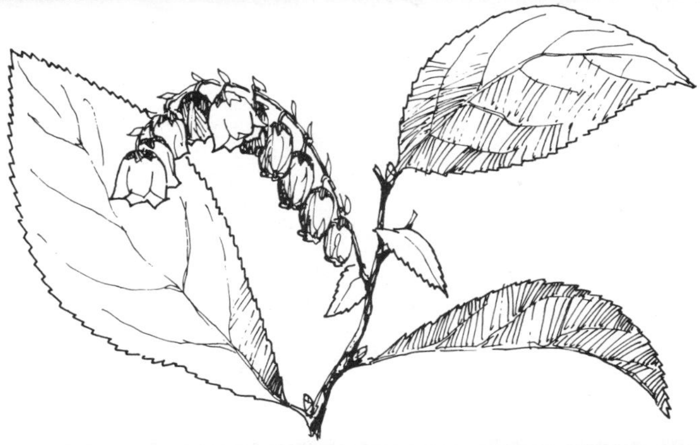

Ampelopsis arborea

FORM: variable - **groundcover-like, shrub-like or climbing**
Size: **tall vine** - 10 m (35 ft) or more
Spread: **wide** - from 6 to 10 m (20 to 35 ft)
Mass: **open**

BRANCHING: climbing with few smooth forked **tendrils, leggy** appearance, commonly bushy and upright; **medium**
Twig: slender, conspicuously **zigzag,** smooth with warty lenticels, **brown**
Bud: small, inconspicuous, **red brown**
Bark: **smooth, brown**

FOLIAGE: alternate, **bi-pinnately** or tri-pinnately **compound, ovate to oblong ovate,** coarse dentate teeth; **medium fine**
Surface: **dull or glossy,** smooth or finely tomentose, lighter beneath
Color: spring - **red green to purple green;** summer - **dark green;** autumn - pale **yellow**
Season: deciduous, **semi-evergreen** in South; emergence - late **May;** drop - mid **October**

FLOWER: small **flat-topped** clusters, 1 to 7.5 cm (⅖ to 3 in) wide, individual blooms tiny, inconspicuous
Color: **green**
Season: early through mid **June,** after leaves
Sex: monoecious or **dioecious**

FRUIT: glossy globular **berry,** 8 mm (⅓ in) in diameter, often warty-dotted
Color: dark **bluish to purple** or jet black
Season: late **August through** late **November**   Human Value: not generally edible with bitter, peppery taste
Wildlife Value: **intermediate;** popular with songbirds and upland gamebirds, large and small mammals

HABITAT: formation - **swamp, savanna, dune, old field, forest;** region - **Southern;** gradients - **wet, wet-mesic, mesic-dry, dry;**
alluvial woods, marshes, swamp margin, sand and gravel bars, stream banks, woodland borders
Shade Tolerance: **intermediate**
Flood Tolerance: **very tolerant**

SOIL: Texture: **coarse** sands and gravels, sandy loams **to fine** silt loams, heavy silts, silty clay loams, stiff clays
Drainage: **very poor to moderately well**
Moisture: **wet to dry**
Reaction: **slightly acid to circumneutral,** pH range 6.1 - 7.5

HARDINESS: **zone 6a,** roots hardy in zone 5a with good growth each year
Rate: **very fast** - up to 5 m (15 ft) in first year
Longevity: **very short-lived**

SUSCEPTIBILITY: Physiological: **occasional** - twig dieback, to ground in North
Disease: **infrequent** - stem canker, downy mildew, leaf spots, powdery mildew, wilt; none serious
Insect: **infrequent** - Japanese beetle, grape flea beetle, rose chafer, scales, eight-spotted forester; rarely serious
Wind-Ice: **infrequent**

URBAN TOLERANCE: Pollution:
Lighting: Drought Heat: **resistant**   Mine Spoils:
Salt: **resistant**   Soil Compaction: **resistant**
Root Pattern: fibrous, **shallow lateral** spreading; **transplants easily,** culture easy

SPECIES: Associate: trees - American Holly, Winged/Water Elms, Sugarberry, Black Willow, Swamp Poplar, Black Tupelo;
shrubs - He-huckleberry, Fetterbush Lyonia, Virginia Sweetspire, Common Winterberry, Common Buttonbush
Similar: Oriental Ampelopsis - Asiatic, zone 6a; Heartleaf/Porcelain (Asiatic) Ampelopsis - simple leaves
Cultivars: none available

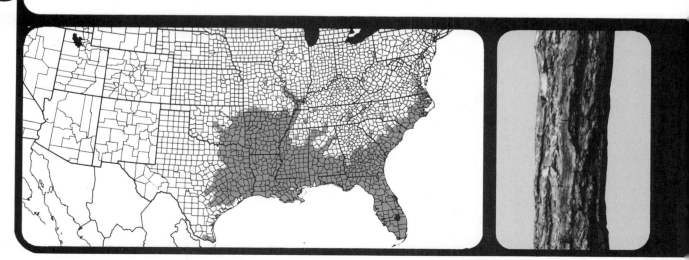

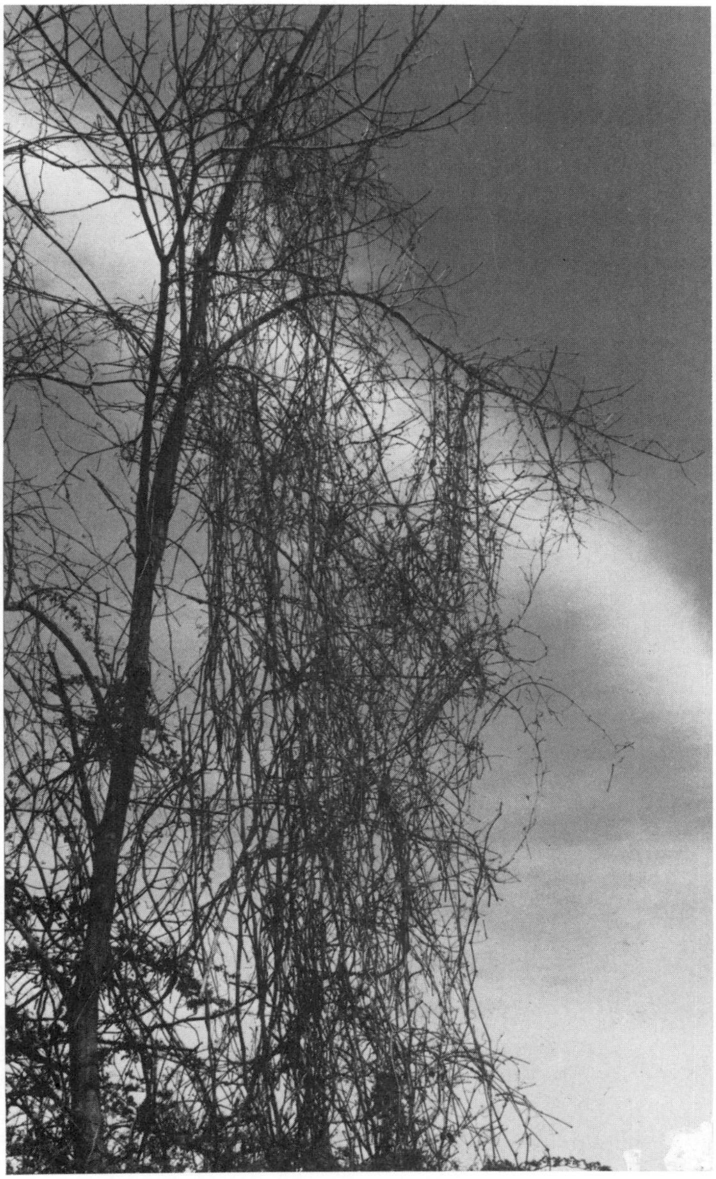

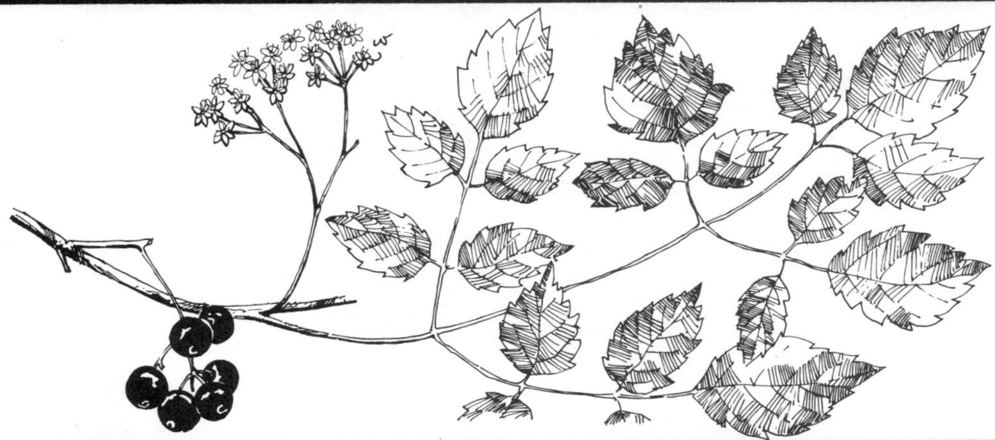

Ampelopsis cordata

FORM: variable - groundcover-like, **shrub-like or climbing**
Size: **tall vine** - 10 m (35 ft) or more, typically not high-climbing
Spread: **wide** - from 6 to 10 m (20 to 35 ft)
Mass: **open**

BRANCHING: scrambling prostrate habit, climbs by few-forked **tendrils,** often lacking tendrils, **leggy** appearance; **medium**
Twig: smooth, slightly angular with longitudinal ridges, flexible, warty raised lenticels, **yellow brown to** light brown
Bud: concealed beneath bark
Bark: smooth with numerous oval warty lenticels, becoming **deep furrowed** with long flat-topped ridges, dark **brown**

FOLIAGE: alternate, **simple,** broadly ovate or **cordate,** coarse dentate teeth, palmately veined; **coarse** texture
Surface: **dull,** smooth above, paler beneath
Color: spring - **red green;** summer - dark **yellow green or dark** olive green; autumn - pale **yellow**
Season: **deciduous;** emergence - late **May,** drop - mid **October**

FLOWER: small loose **flat-topped** cluster, 2.5 to 7.5 cm (1 to 3 in) across
Color: **greenish** to whitish
Season: early through mid **June,** after leaves
Sex: **dioecious**

FRUIT: dry depressed globular pea-size **berry,** 6 to 9 mm (¼ to ⅜ in) diameter, in drooping rounded clusters of 8 to 15
Color: changes from green to orange to rose **purple,** finally turquoise **blue** with brownish spots
Season: maturing late **August through** late **November**   Human Value: not edible, dry
Wildlife Value: **intermediate;** a favorite of many songbirds, also eaten by large and small mammals, upland gamebirds

HABITAT: formation - **swamp, barrens, old field, dune, forest;** region - **Central, Southern;** gradients - **wet, wet-mesic, mesic,**
mesic-dry, dry; stream banks, rocky open hillsides, fence rows, moist woods, rich bottomlands, sand and gravel bars
Shade Tolerance: **intermediate**
Flood Tolerance: **very tolerant**

SOIL: Texture: **coarse to fine;** sands, gravels, rocks, sandy loams, silt loams, clays
Drainage: **very poor to moderately well**
Moisture: **wet to average**
Reaction: **slightly acid to circumneutral,** pH range 6.1 - 7.5

HARDINESS: **zone 5b**
Rate: **fast** - up to 5 m (15 ft) in one year
Longevity: **short-lived**

SUSCEPTIBILITY: Physiological: **occasional** - twig dieback, to ground in North
Disease: **infrequent** - powdery mildew, leaf spots, downy mildew, wilt, stem canker, root rot
Insect: **infrequent** - scales, leaf hoppers, eight-spotted forester, Japanese beetle, grape flea beetle
Wind-Ice: **occasional** - wood soft, pith large, breakage common

URBAN TOLERANCE: Pollution:
Lighting: Drought Heat: **resistant**   Mine Spoils:
Salt: **resistant**   Soil Compaction: **resistant**
Root Pattern: **shallow** fibrous, **lateral** spreading; **transplants easily,** easy culture

SPECIES: Associate: trees - Eastern Poplar, Black/Water Tupelo, American Planetree, River Birch, Silver Maple, Red
Mulberry; shrubs - Eastern Wahoo, American Bladdernut, Arrowwood Viburnum, Dense Hypericum, Silky Dogwood
Similar: Porcelain/Hop Ampelopsis - Asiatic; Muscadine Grape; other grape species
Cultivars: none available

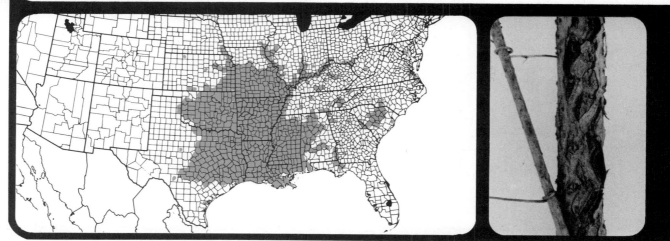

Aristolochia durior

FORM: climbing
Size: **mid-height vine** - from 6 to 10 m (20 to 35 ft)
Spread: **intermediate** - from 4 to 6 m (12 to 20 ft), typically taller than broad
Mass: **dense**

BRANCHING: climbs by vigorous **twining** stems, **picturesque;** very **coarse** texture
Twig: slender, smooth, **large leaf scars,** flexible, enlarged at nodes, aromatic when broken, dull **green or purplish**
Bud: small, **woolly, clustered, gray**
Bark: **smooth** becoming **scaly** or somewhat cracked with short-rounded ridges, **gray**

FOLIAGE: alternate, overlapping layered appearance, **simple, cordate,** entire, **aromatic** when crushed; very **coarse** texture
Surface: **dull,** smooth, pale grayish beneath
Color: spring - **light green;** summer - **dark green;** autumn - **dark green** late, **then yellow green** or with little change
Season: **deciduous;** emergence - mid **May;** drop - mid **October**

FLOWER: **large solitary** or 2 to 3 in clusters, 3 to 4 cm (1 to 1½ in), sharply curved **trumpet**-like blooms resemble Dutch pipe
Color: chocolate **brown** with yellow tube
Season: late **May through** early **June,** after leaves and hidden among them
Sex: monoecious   **Fragrant:**   strong scented, like ginger

FRUIT: dry pendant 6-ribbed cylindric pod-like **capsule,** 4 to 8 cm (1½ to 3 in) long
Color: **green becoming brown**
Season: early **September through** late **October**   Human Value: not edible
Wildlife Value: **very low;** insignificant use, but valued for cover and nesting

HABITAT: formation - **forest;** region - **Central;** gradients - **mesic, mesic-dry;** streamsides, mesic calcareous woods, fertile
         Appalachian forests, bases of bluffs, moist coves and ravines, rich mountain woodlands
Shade Tolerance: **very tolerant**
Flood Tolerance: **intolerant**

SOIL: Texture: **moderately coarse** gravelly or sandy loams **to moderately fine** silt loams; best in deep loams
Drainage: **moderately well to well**
Moisture: **moist to average**
Reaction: **slightly acid to alkaline,** pH range 6.1 - 8.5

HARDINESS: zone 4a
Rate: **medium** after transplanting **then fast** and rank growing, from 1.2 to 2 m (4 to 6 ft) in one year
Longevity: **moderately short-lived**

SUSCEPTIBILITY: Physiological: **infrequent**
Disease: **infrequent** - very resistant
Insect: **infrequent** - none serious
Wind-Ice: **occasional** - soft porous weak wood with large pith, occasional breakage

URBAN TOLERANCE: Pollution:
Lighting: .   Drought Heat: **sensitive**   Mine Spoils:
Salt: Soil Compaction: **intermediate**
Root Pattern: fibrous, **shallow lateral,** odor of camphor when broken; **transplants well**

SPECIES: Associate: trees - American Hophornbeam, White Oak, American Linden, American Beech, Eastern Hemlock,
         shrubs - Pasture Gooseberry, Leatherwood, Common Witchhazel, Common Spicebush, Fragrant Thimbleberry
Similar: Virginia Snakeroot Dutchmanspipe; Manchurian Dutchmanspipe - zone 5a; Common Greenbrier - armed
Cultivars: none available

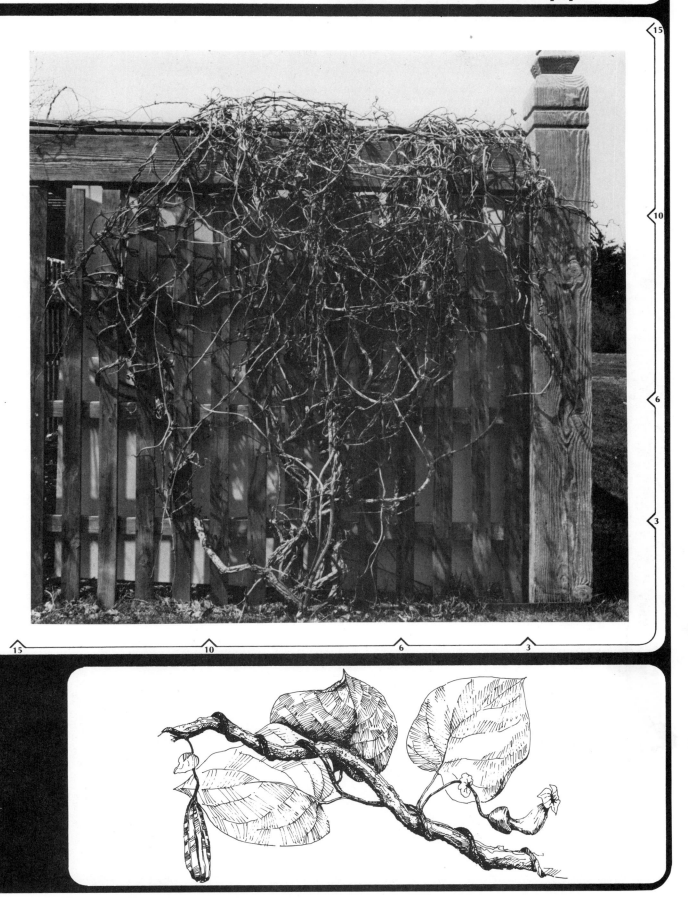

Berchemia scandens

FORM: **climbing** or shrub-like on drier sites
Size: **low vine** - from 1 to 6 m (3 to 20 ft) in North or tall vine from 18 to 30 m (60 to 100 ft) in South
Spread: **narrow** - from 2 to 4 m (6 to 12 ft)
Mass: **open**

BRANCHING: climbs by **twining picturesque** stems, leggy appearance, branch mass at top, naked at base; **medium**
Twig: smooth, flexible, **green**
Bud: **naked,** long **pointed,** hug twigs
Bark: **smooth, reddish brown** to black

FOLIAGE: alternate, **simple, elliptic** to oblong ovate, entire or fine toothed, distinctive straight veins; **medium** texture
Surface: **glossy,** smooth, leathery, paler beneath
Color: spring - **light green;** summer - **dark green;** autumn - golden **yellow**
Season: **deciduous;** emergence - mid **May,** drop - mid **October**

FLOWER: small lose terminal **spikes,** 6 to 10 cm (2 to 4 in) long, each blossom 3 mm (⅛ in) across
Color: **greenish white**
Season: late **May through** early **June**
Sex: monoecious

FRUIT: football-shaped **berry,** 5 to 8 mm (⅕ to ⅓ in) long, in large loose clusters, showy
Color: **blue to black** with powdery bloom
Season: late **July through** late October   Human Value: not edible
Wildlife Value: **intermediate;** eaten by numerous gamebirds, songbirds, large and small mammals

HABITAT: formation - **swamp, savanna, old field, forest;** region - **Southern;** gradient - **wet, wet-mesic, mesic-dry, dry;** moist
bottomlands, moist or dry woods, swamps, thickets, glades, bluffs, pine flatwoods
Shade Tolerance: **intermediate**
Flood Tolerance: **very tolerant**

SOIL: Texture: **coarse** sands and gravels, sandy loams **to fine** silt loams, heavy silts, silty clay loams, stiff clays, peats
Drainage: **very poor to excessive**
Moisture: **wet to droughty**
Reaction: **slightly acid to circumneutral,** pH 6.1 - 7.5

HARDINESS: **zone 6a**
Rate: **medium**
Longevity: **long-lived**

SUSCEPTIBILITY: Physiological: **infrequent**
Disease: **infrequent** - none serious
Insect: **infrequent** - very resistant
Wind-Ice: **infrequent** - very strong stems often girdle and kill large trees

URBAN TOLERANCE: Pollution:
Lighting: Drought Heat: **resistant**   Mine Spoils:
Salt: Soil Compaction: **resistant**
Root Pattern: **shallow** fibrous, **lateral** spreading; **transplants easily,** easy culture

SPECIES: Associate: trees - American Sweetgum, Green Ash, American Planetree, River Birch, Loblolly Pine, Shumard/
Laurel/Overcup Oaks; shrubs - Virginia Sweetspire, Common Spicebush, Brook Euonymus, Possumhaw
Similar: Japanese Supplejack - Asiatic, seldom available
Cultivars: none available

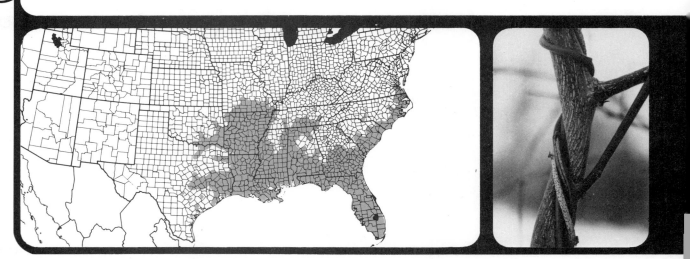

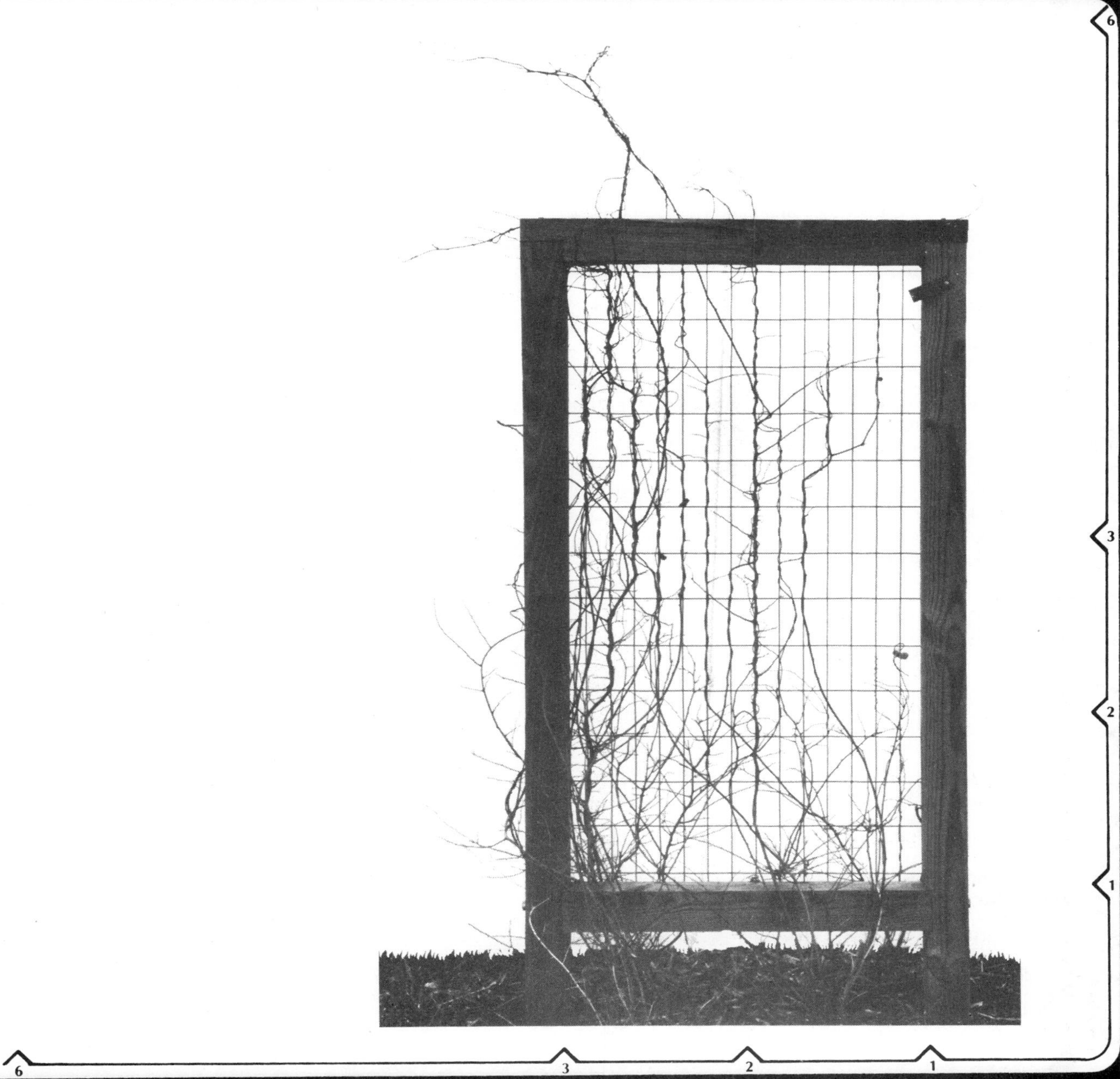
6
3
2
1

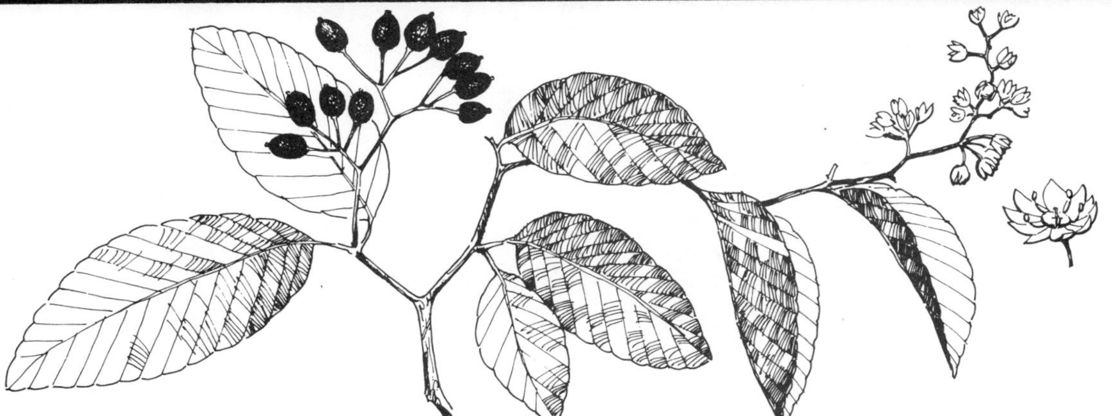

Bignonia capreolata

FORM: climbing
Size: **tall vine** - 10 m (35 ft) or more, to tops of tallest trees and buildings in South
Spread: **wide** - from 6 to 10 m (20 to 35 ft)
Mass: **dense**

BRANCHING: climbs by twining branched **tendrils** with sticky **suction disks** at tips; **coarse** texture
Twig: slender, green to **gray**
Bud: small, wider than long, **2 scales**
Bark: rough curled papery **exfoliation, gray**

FOLIAGE: opposite, **compound, bifoliate** with 2 leaflets, **lanceolate to oblong lanceolate,** entire; **medium** texture
Surface: **dull,** smooth, stiff, paler beneath
Color: spring - **light green;** summer - **dark green;** autumn and winter - **purple green or purple**
Season: broadleaf **evergreen,** semi-evergreen in North

FLOWER: large **trumpet,** 5 to 8 cm (2 to 3 in) long, in 2 to 5-flowered axillary clusters
Color: **red to orange** with bright yellow tubes, visited by hummingbirds
Season: late **May through** early **June**
Sex: monoecious

FRUIT: dry flattened leathery linear pod-like **capsule,** 10 to 18 cm (4 to 7 in) long, in clusters, splits releasing winged seeds
Color: **brown**
Season: late **August through** late **October**   Human Value: not edible
Wildlife Value: **low;** occasional use by small mammals

HABITAT: formation - **bog, barrens, cliff, old field, forest;** region - **Central, Southern;** gradients - **wet, wet-mesic, mesic-dry, dry;**
    alluvial woods, swampy forests, calcareous soils on river banks, cliffs in ravines, open dry woods, bogs, fence rows
Shade Tolerance: **intermediate**
Flood Tolerance: **very tolerant**

SOIL: Texture: rock outcrops, **coarse** sands and gravels, sandy loams **to fine** silt loams, heavy silts, stiff clays
Drainage: **very poor to well**
Moisture: **wet to dry**
Reaction: **slightly acid to alkaline,** pH range 6.1 - 8.5

HARDINESS: in **zone 6a** as scrambling groundcover, kills to ground in extreme cold but readily sprouts in spring
Rate: **very fast** - between 5 to 6 m (15 to 20 ft) in single season
Longevity: **long-lived**

SUSCEPTIBILITY: Physiological: **infrequent**
Disease: **infrequent** - leaf spot, blight, black mildew, mealy bugs; none serious
Insect: **infrequent** - none serious
Wind-Ice: **infrequent**

URBAN TOLERANCE: Pollution:
Lighting: Drought Heat: **resistant**   Mine Spoils:
Salt: Soil Compaction: **resistant**
Root Pattern: fibrous, **deep** descending; **difficult to transplant**

SPECIES: Associate: trees - Baldcypress, Black Willow, Black Tupelo, River Birch, Eastern Poplar, Black Walnut; shrubs -
    Common Alder, Swamp Azalea, Summersweet Clethra, Inkberry, He-Huckleberry, Southern Waxmyrtle, Swamp Rose
Similar: Common Trumpetcreeper - pinnately compound, deciduous; Trumpet Honeysuckle - semi-evergreen
Cultivars: 'Atrosanguinea' - flowers dark purple, leaves longer and narrower

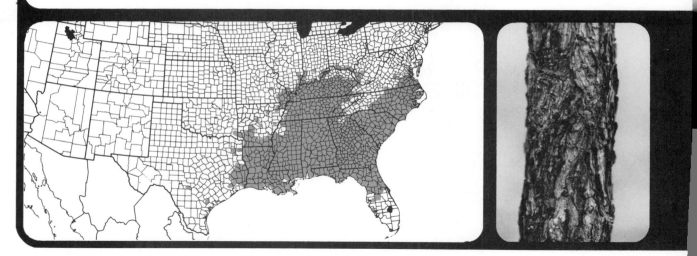

Campsis radicans

FORM: **groundcover-like or climbing**
Size: **tall vine** - 10 m (35 ft) or more, commonly from 6 to 9 m (20 to 30 ft) in North
Spread: **wide** - from 6 to 10 m (20 to 35 ft)
Mass: **open**

BRANCHING: climbing by **aerial rootlets,** leggy appearance with mass of branches at top, naked stems at base; **coarse**
Twig: smooth, flexible, long internodes, **large leaf scars,** warty lenticels, pale **yellow brown to orange brown**
Bud: small, 2 mm (1/10 in), wider than long, smooth, **yellowish**
Bark: shreddy, **exfoliating** into thin long strips, straw-like **orange brown** color **to gray brown**

FOLIAGE: opposite, **pinnately compound,** 7-13 leaflets, **ovate to oblong ovate,** coarse toothed, petioles winged; **medium fine**
Surface: **dull or glossy,** smooth, more or less hairy beneath
Color: spring - **red green or purplish;** summer - **medium** olive **green to yellow green;** autumn - **yellow green**
Season: **deciduous;** emergence - late **May,** drop - mid to late **October**

FLOWER: large **trumpet,** 5 to 8 cm (2 to 3 in) long, in large 2 to 9-flowered terminal clusters
Color: **orange to scarlet red,** attracts hummingbirds
Season: mid **July through** mid **September,** over a long season
Sex: monoecious

FRUIT: dry cigar-shaped pod-like **capsule,** 10 to 20 cm (4 to 8 in) long, leathery, 2-ridged, slightly flattened, bulging sides
Color: tan to **brown**
Season: late **August** persisting **through** winter until late **March**　　　Human Value: **leaves/flowers poisonous** to touch
Wildlife Value: **very low;** little used

HABITAT: formation - **savanna, old field, forest;** region - **Central, Southern;** gradient - **wet-mesic, mesic-dry, dry;** moist
　　　woodlands, fence rows, roadside thickets, floodplain forests, rock hillsides, open woods, stream banks, old fields
Shade Tolerance: **intermediate**
Flood Tolerance: **intermediate**

SOIL: Texture: **coarse** sands and gravels, sandy loams **to fine** silt loams, heavy silts, silty clay loams, stiff clays
Drainage: **moderately poor to excessive**
Moisture: **moist to droughty**
Reaction: **slightly acid to circumneutral,** pH range 6.1 - 7.5

HARDINESS: **zone 5a**
Rate: **very fast** - up to 3 m (10 ft) in one year
Longevity: **long-lived**

SUSCEPTIBILITY: Physiological: **occasional** - stem dieback to ground in severe winters
Disease: **infrequent** - none serious, powdery mildew, blight, leaf spots; rarely warrant control measures
Insect: **infrequent** - none serious
Wind-Ice: **occasional** - porous soft wood, suffers breakage caused by heavy ice glaze

URBAN TOLERANCE: Pollution: **intermediate** - 2-4D
Lighting:　　　　　　　　　　　　　　Drought Heat: **resistant**　　　　　　Mine Spoils:
Salt:　　　　　　　　　　　　　　　　Soil Compaction: **resistant**
Root Pattern: fibrous, long underground runners, **deep** going; **difficult to transplant**

SPECIES: Associate: trees - River Birch, Green Ash, American/Winged Elms, Black Willow, Common Boxelder, American
　　　Sweetgum; shrubs - Common Deerberry, Common Buttonbush, Common Alder, Brook Euonymus
Similar: Crossvine - evergreen, Southern; Trumpet Honeysuckle - smaller, orange berries; Chinese Trumpetcreeper
Cultivars: 'Flava' - yellowish flowers; 'Praecox' - blooms June, scarlet flowers; 'Speciosa' - scarcely climbing, shrubby

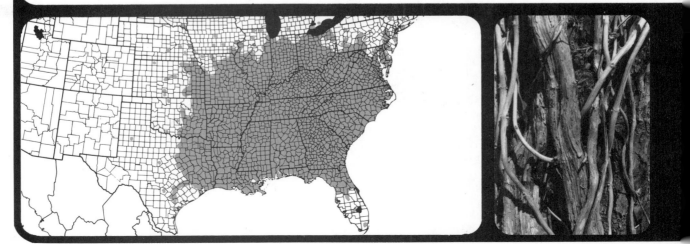

Celastrus scandens

FORM: **climbing,** sometimes groundcover-like or shrub-like
Size: **low vine** - from 1 to 6 m (3 to 20 ft), commonly **mid-height vine** up to 10 m (35 ft)
Spread: **intermediate** - from 4 to 6 m (12 to 20 ft), often narrow from 2 to 4 m (6 to 12 ft)
Mass: **dense**

BRANCHING: tangled trailing habit or climbing by **twining** stems, often twining on itself, **picturesque; medium**
Twig: slender, glossy, smooth, flexible with prominent lenticels, buff yellow to **brown** or gray brown
Bud: small conical, projecting like small knobs at right angles to twigs, **red brown**
Bark: **smooth,** old trunks with flake-like **scales, gray to brown**

FOLIAGE: alternate, **simple, elliptic to ovate,** fine toothed, wavy margin; **medium coarse** texture
Surface: **glossy** or dull, smooth, paler beneath
Color: spring - light **yellow green;** summer - dark **yellow green;** autumn - lemon **yellow**
Season: **deciduous;** emergence - mid **May,** drop - mid **October**

FLOWER: **small** in few-flowered terminal **clusters,** 3 to 9 mm (⅛ to ⅜ in) wide, inconspicuous
Color: yellow green to **green**
Season: late **May through** mid **June,** after leaves
Sex: **dioecious**

FRUIT: 3-sectioned pea-size **capsules,** 3 to 12 mm (⅛ to ½ in) diameter, in loose drooping terminal clusters of 6 to 20
Color: bright **orange** capsule with scarlet **red** seeds
Season: late **September** persisting **through** late **December** or longer   Human Value: **all parts poisonous**
Wildlife Value: **low;** songbirds, gamebirds, small mammals use to limited extent, provides important cover

HABITAT: formation - **glade, forest, dune, old field;** region - **Northern, Central;** gradients - **mesic, mesic-dry, dry;** roadsides,
        woods edge, fence rows, abandoned pastures, hedges, rocky streams, bluffs, rocky slopes, dunes, sandy oak woods
Shade Tolerance: **tolerant**
Flood Tolerance: **intermediate**

SOIL: Texture: **coarse to fine;** rocky soil, infertile sands and gravels, gravelly or sandy loams, clay loams, heavy clays
Drainage: **moderately poor to excessive**
Moisture: **average to droughty**
Reaction: **slightly acid to circumneutral,** pH range 6.1 - 7.5

HARDINESS: zone 2
Rate: **very fast** - up to 3 m (10 ft) in single season
Longevity: **long-lived**

SUSCEPTIBILITY: Physiological: **infrequent**
Disease: **infrequent** - leaf spot, powdery mildew, crown gall, stem canker; minor problems
Insect: **occasional** - euonymus scale is often serious, aphids, two-marked treehopper
Wind-Ice: **infrequent** - very strong twining stems often kill sapling trees

URBAN TOLERANCE: Pollution: **sensitive** - 2-4D; **intermediate** - O_3
Lighting: Drought Heat: **resistant**   Mine Spoils:
Salt: **resistant**   Soil Compaction: **intermediate**
Root Pattern: sparsely fibrous, **deep** going and long spreading, suckering; **difficult to transplant**

SPECIES: Associate: trees - Black Cherry, Wafer Ash, Black/Blackjack/Post Oaks, Common Persimmon, Sassafras; shrubs
        - Fragrant/Smooth Sumacs, Common Pricklyash, Gray Dogwood, Carolina Rose, blackberry/raspberry species
Similar: Running Euonymus - smaller; Oriental Bittersweet - yellow capsules, China; Bigleaf Wintercreeper - evergreen
Cultivars: none available

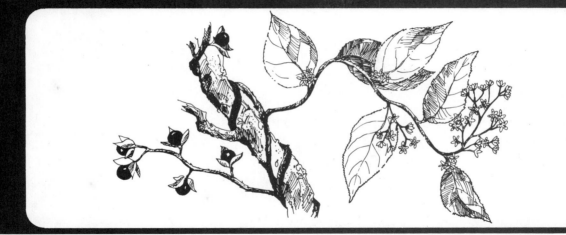

Clematis verticillaris

FORM: **climbing** or groundcover-like
Size: **low vine** - from 1 to 6 m (3 to 20 ft)
Spread: **narrow** - from 2 to 4 m (6 to 12 ft)
Mass: **open**

BRANCHING: trailing and scrambling or climbing by **twisting leafstalks; fine** texture
Twig: slender, smooth, **angular** ribbed with 6-12 **ridged** sides, large often swollen nodes, light **brown**
Bud: small ovoid
Bark: old wood **shallow furrowed** and **exfoliating, red brown to brown** or purplish

FOLIAGE: opposite, occasionally whorled, **trifoliate, ovate to oblong ovate,** entire or few coarse teeth; **medium fine** texture
Surface: **dull,** smooth, thin
Color: spring - **light green;** summer - **medium green;** autumn - **yellow green**
Season: **deciduous;** emergence - late **May,** drop - mid **November**

FLOWER: **large solitary,** 5 to 7.5 cm (2 to 3 in) wide when expanded, 4 petal-like sepals, axillary on old branches
Color: lavendar **purple or bluish**
Season: early through mid **June**
Sex: **dioecious**

FRUIT: feathery plume-like clusters of **achenes** on long stalks, the silky tails 5 cm (2 in) long
Color: silvery **gray**
Season: mid **July through** late **September**   Human Value: **poisonous leaves**
Wildlife Value: **very low;** some songbirds

HABITAT: formation - **glade, forest, old field;** region - **Northern;** gradients - **mesic-dry, dry;** rocky woods, open rocky slopes,
abandoned rocky pastures, talus slopes, cliffs, rocky stream banks
Shade Tolerance: **tolerant**
Flood Tolerance: **intolerant**

SOIL: Texture: **coarse to moderately fine;** rocks, gravels and sands, gravelly or sandy loams, clay loams
Drainage: **well to excessive**
Moisture: **average to dry**
Reaction: **slightly acid to circumneutral,** pH range 6.1 - 7.5, tolerates **alkaline**

HARDINESS: **zone 2**
Rate: **medium to fast** - 0.6 to 3 m (2 to 10 ft) in one season depending on site
Longevity: **very short-lived**

SUSCEPTIBILITY: Physiological: **infrequent**
Disease: **occasional** - leaf spot and stem rot can cause damage, powdery mildew, smut, and leaf blights; rarely serious
Insect: **infrequent** - black blister beetle, clematis borer, root-knot nematodes can kill, mites, whiteflies; rarely serious
Wind-Ice: **infrequent**

URBAN TOLERANCE: Pollution:
Lighting: Drought Heat: **intermediate**   Mine Spoils:
Salt: Soil Compaction: **sensitive**
Root Pattern: sparse, coarsely fibrous, **deep** spreading **laterals; difficult to transplant**

SPECIES: Associate: trees - Jack/Red Pines, Bigtooth/Quaking Aspens, Showy Mountainash; shrubs - Roundleaf
Dogwood, Checkerberry Wintergreen, Allegany Blackberry, American Red Raspberry, Rafinesque Viburnum
Similar: Curly Clematis - petals curled, blue; Italian Clematis; Oriental Clematis - dissected leaves, yellow flowers
Cultivars: dissecta - leaflets deeply dissected, violet blue flowers, Western

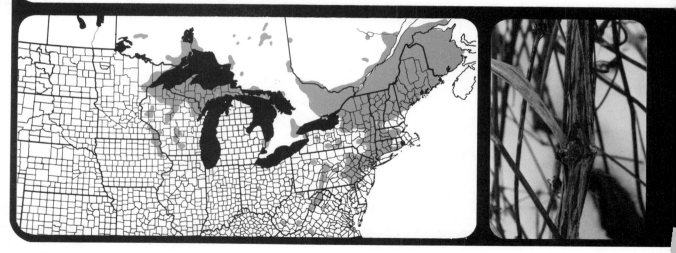

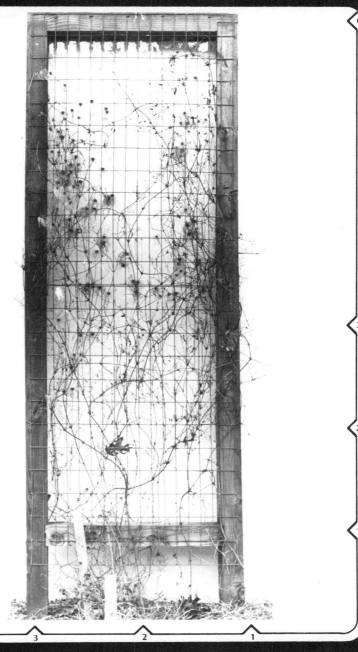

Clematis virginiana

FORM: **climbing**
Size: **low vine** - from 1 to 6 m (3 to 20 ft), typically from 4 to 5 m (12 to 15 ft)
Spread: **narrow** - from 2 to 4 m (6 to 12 ft)
Mass: **open** and loose

BRANCHING: climbs by **twisting leafstalks,** heavy branched at top, thin leggy unbranched stems at base; **fine** texture
Twig: slender, wiry, smooth, young growth **angular** ribbed with 6-12 **ridged** sides, dull **red or purple** becoming **gray brown**
Bud: small ovoid, **woolly** scales, **brown**
Bark: wood **shallow furrowed** and **exfoliating,** yellowish **gray to reddish purple**

FOLIAGE: opposite, **pinnately compound, trifoliate, ovate to oblong ovate,** coarse unequal teeth or 3-lobed; **medium fine**
Surface: **dull,** smooth, thin, paler beneath
Color: spring - **light green;** summer - **medium green;** autumn - dull **yellow green or purplish**
Season: **deciduous;** emergence - late **May;** drop - mid **November**

FLOWER: **small** leafy axillary **clusters,** each bloom 13 to 19 mm (½ to ¾ in) wide, profuse
Color: dull **white**
Season: mid **July** to late **September,** over a long season
Sex: **dioecious**   **Fragrant:** very sweet

FRUIT: cluster of feathery plume-like hairy **achenes,** 4 to 5 cm (1½ to 2 in) diameter
Color: silvery **gray**
Season: late **August** persisting **through** late November   Human Value: **poisonous leaves**
Wildlife Value: **very low;** some use by songbirds

HABITAT: formation - **swamp, glade, old field, cliff, forest;** region - **Northern, Central, Southern;** gradients - **wet, wet-mesic,**
mesic-dry, dry; river banks, low calcareous thickets, woods edge, roadside swales, swamps, overhanging cliffs
Shade Tolerance: **tolerant**
Flood Tolerance: **tolerant**

SOIL: Texture: **coarse** sands and gravels **to fine** silt loams, heavy silts, silty clay loams, stiff clays, peats
Drainage: **poor to excessive**
Moisture: **wet to droughty**
Reaction: **slightly acid to** circumneutral, pH range 6.1 - 7.5, tolerates **alkaline** pH to 8.5

HARDINESS: zone 3a
Rate: **very fast** - up to 6 m (20 ft) in one year
Longevity: **very short**

SUSCEPTIBILITY: Physiological: **frequent** - twig and stem dieback in severe winters
Disease: **occasional** - powdery mildew, leaf blight, rusts, leaf spot, stem rot can cause damage
Insect: **infrequent** - root-knot nematodes can kill plants, mites, whiteflies, clematis borer, black blister beetle; few serious
Wind-Ice: **occasional** - hardly woody, stems easily broken

URBAN TOLERANCE: Pollution:
Lighting: Drought Heat: **resistant**   Mine Spoils:
Salt: Soil Compaction: **resistant**
Root Pattern: long fibrous, sparse and **deep** reaching; **difficult to transplant,** easy culture

SPECIES: Associate: trees - Green Ash, American/Slippery/Winged Elms, Common Boxelder, Red Mulberry; shrubs -
Silky/Gray Dogwoods, Common Ninebark, Meadowsweet/Hardhack Spireas, Summersweet Clethra
Similar: Sweetautumn Clematis - taller, flowers in late August, semi-evergreen, Japan
Cultivars: Missouriensis - leaflets usually 5, silky underneath

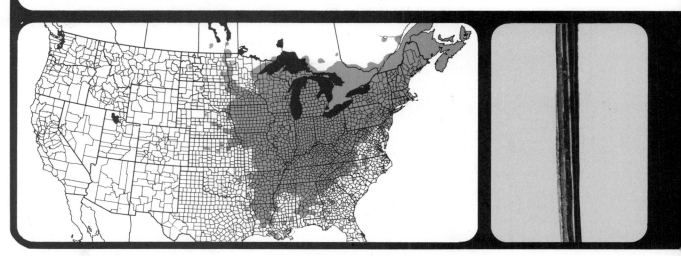

Cocculus carolinus

FORM: **climbing**
Size: **low vine** - from 1 to 6 m (3 to 20 ft)
Spread: **narrow** - from 2 to 4 m (6 to 12 ft), commonly to 5 m (16 ft)
Mass: **dense**

BRANCHING: scrambling little-branched habit or climbing by **twining** stems and petioles, **picturesque; medium** textur
Twig: slender, flexible, **velvety,** finely ridged, with long internodes, gray green to **gray brown**
Bud: hidden
Bark: smooth becoming **blocky** with warty bumps or corky ridges, old stems **shallow furrowed,** dark **brown to gray brown**

FOLIAGE: alternate, **simple,** broadly **ovate to cordate or orbicular,** entire or 3 to 5 shallow **palmate lobes; coarse** texture
Surface: smooth or finely **tomentose** above, paler dense woolly below
Color: spring - very **light green;** summer - **medium green or yellow green;** autumn - **yellowish**
Season: tardily deciduous or **persistant,** semi-evergreen in South; emergence - mid **May,** drop - mid **November**

FLOWER: very small in loose axillary **spikes,** 12 to 15 cm (5 to 6 in) long
Color: greenish **white**
Season: early **July through** late **August**
Sex: **dioecious**

FRUIT: glossy flattened pea-size **berry,** 6 mm (¼ in) wide, in loose drooping grape-like clusters, 5 to 15 cm (2 to 6 in) long
Color: brilliant **red,** takes 3 to 5 years before fruiting, seeds snail-shaped, hence common name
Season: late **September to** late **October** or longer   Human Value: **poisonous fruits**
Wildlife Value: **intermediate;** songbirds, upland gamebirds, large and small mammals major users

HABITAT: formation - **glade, cliff, forest, old field;** region - **Central, Southern;** gradients - **wet, wet-mesic, mesic-dry, dry;** mois
woods, fence rows, unattended hedge rows, roadside thickets, woods edge, brushy rocky hillsides, limestone cliff
Shade Tolerance: **intermediate**
Flood Tolerance: **tolerant**

SOIL: Texture: **coarse to fine;** pure sands, gravels, loamy sands, organic soils, peats, mucks, fine sands, silt loams, silts
Drainage: **poor to excessive**
Moisture: **wet to droughty**
Reaction: **slightly acid to** circumneutral, tolerates **alkaline,** pH range 6.1 - 8.5

HARDINESS: **zone 6a**
Rate: **very fast,** from 2 to 3 m (6 to 10 ft) in one year
Longevity: **very short-lived**

SUSCEPTIBILITY: Physiological: **infrequent**
Disease: **infrequent** - very resistant
Insect: **infrequent** - none serious
Wind-Ice: **occasional** - soft porous, not very woody, stems easily broken

URBAN TOLERANCE: Pollution:
Lighting: Drought Heat: **resistant**   Mine Spoils:
Salt: Soil Compaction: **sensitive**
Root Pattern: fibrous, **shallow lateral** and suckering; **transplants easily,** easy culture

SPECIES: Associate: trees - Pond Pine, Red Maple, Black Tupelo, Sugarberry, Winged/American Elms, Water Ash, Black
Willow; shrubs - Fetterbush Lyonia, Sweetbay Magnolia, Swamp Azalea, Highbush Blueberry, Coast Leucothoe
Similar: Common Moonseed - Northern, black fruit; Coral Greenbrier - armed, Southern to zone 6b
Cultivars: none available

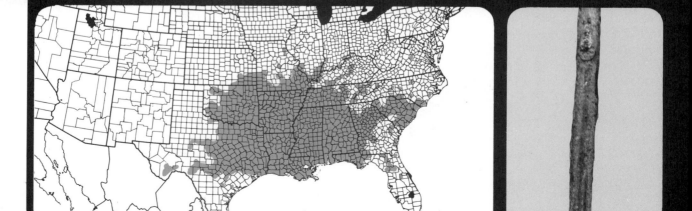

Lonicera dioica

FORM: shrub-like or climbing
Size: **very low vine** or very small shrub - 1 m (3 ft), climbing form often up to 3 m (9 ft)
Spread: **very narrow** - up to 2 m (6 ft)
Mass: **open,** straggly

BRANCHING: climbs by **twining, picturesque** habit, shrub form strongly arching, then trailing across ground; **mediu**
Twig: smooth, **gray,** often with whitish bloom
Bud: small ovoid, 6 mm (¼ in) long, divergent, loose scales, **brown**
Bark: **exfoliating** in thin longitudinal fibrous strips on old stems, **gray brown**

FOLIAGE: opposite, **simple,** narrow **elliptic or oval,** upper pairs united at base encircling stem, entire; **medium fine textur**
Surface: **dull,** smooth, pale downy whitened beneath
Color: spring - **medium green;** summer - **dark green;** autumn - **yellow green**
Season: **deciduous;** emergence - mid **May,** drop - late **November**

FLOWER: small 2-lobed **trumpet,** 13 to 25 mm (½ to 1 in) long, in dense crowded head-like whorls
Color: bright **yellow** often fading **to orangish or purplish** with bright yellow stamens
Season: late **May through** mid **June,** after leaves
Sex: monoecious **Fragrant:** strongly perfumed

FRUIT: globular **berry,** 10 mm (⅜ in) diameter, in whorled terminal clusters
Color: salmon **red to orange**
Season: mid **July through** late **August** Human Value: not edible
Wildlife Value: **intermediate;** primary use by songbirds, occasionally by upland gamebirds, small mammals

HABITAT: formation - **swamp, forest, dry cliff, old field;** region - **Northern, Central;** gradients - **mesic-dry, dry;** rocky wood
bluffs, calcareous springy woods, calcareous clay banks, overhanging limestone or sandstone cliffs, ridges
Shade Tolerance: **tolerant**
Flood Tolerance: **intermediate**

SOIL: Texture: **coarse to moderately fine;** rock covered with humus, gravels and sands, fine sandy loams, clay loam
Drainage: **moderately well to excessive**
Moisture: **moist to dry**
Reaction: **slightly acid to** circumneutral, pH range 6.1 - 7.5, tolerates **alkaline** to pH 8.5

HARDINESS: zone 2
Rate: **medium to fast,** very robust after established
Longevity: **short-lived**

SUSCEPTIBILITY: Physiological: **infrequent**
Disease: **infrequent** - leaf blight, leaf spots, powdery mildews, rust, twig blight, crown gall, hairy root; none seriou
Insect: **occasional** - woolly honeysuckle aphid, honeysuckle sawfly, four-lined plant bug, scales, greenhouse whitef
Wind-Ice: **infrequent**

URBAN TOLERANCE: Pollution: **sensitive** - 2-4D
Lighting: Drought Heat: **resistant** Mine Spoils:
Salt: **resistant** Soil Compaction: **intermediate**
Root Pattern: fibrous, sparse and long, **deep lateral** spreading; **difficult to move,** slow to re-establish

SPECIES: Associate: trees - Bigtooth Aspen, White/Northern Red Oaks, Black/White Ashes; shrubs - Gray Dogwoo
American Filbert, Allegany Blackberry, Pasture/Missouri Gooseberries, Rafinesque Viburnum, Russett Buffaloberr
Similar: Hall's Japanese Honeysuckle - black berries, vigorous; Canada Fly Honeysuckle, Dwarf Bushhoneysuckle - shrub
Cultivars: none available

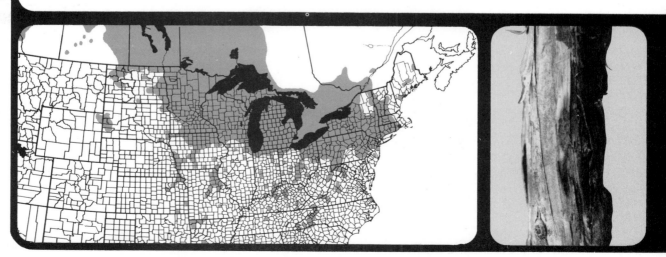

Limber Honeysuckle

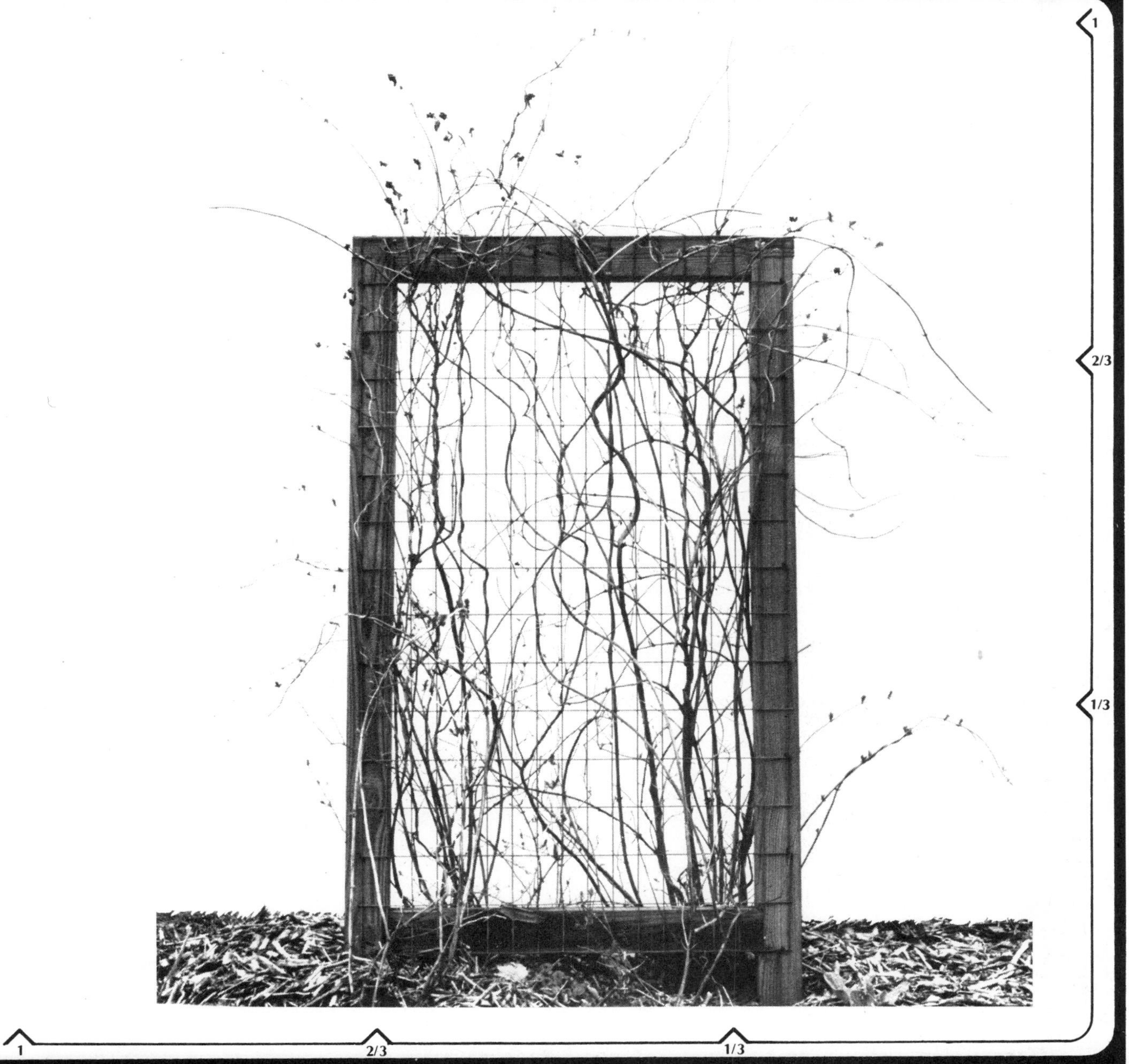

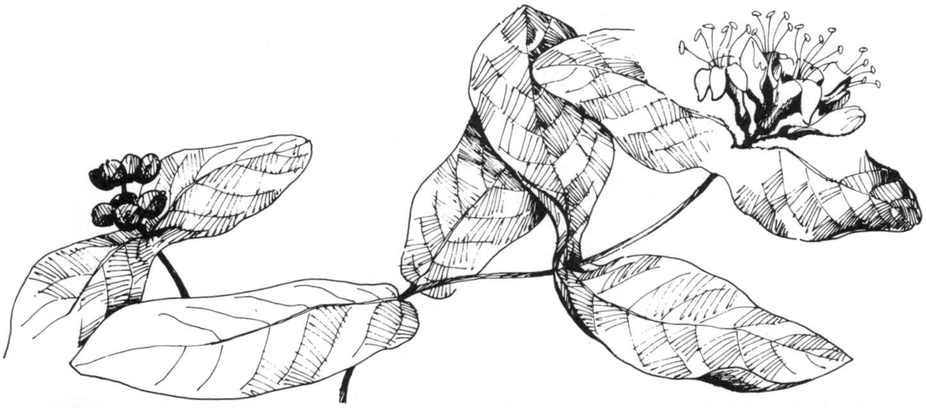

Lonicera sempervirens

FORM: **climbing**
Size: **low vine** - from 1 to 6 m (3 to 20 ft)
Spread: **narrow** - from 2 to 4 m (6 to 12 ft)
Mass: **open**

BRANCHING: climbs by **twining** stems, **picturesque** habit; **coarse** texture
Twig: moderately slender, smooth, dull yellow to yellow brown becoming **gray brown** with numerous small black lenticels
Bud: small narrow ovoid, 3 to 6 mm (⅛ to ¼ in) long, **brown**
Bark;   papery **exfoliation** into long fibrous longitudinal strips, straw-like **orange brown** color

FOLIAGE: opposite, **simple,** ovate to **elliptic,** entire, upper pairs united together at base forming disk; **medium fine** texture
Surface: **dull,** leathery, whitened bloom heavy to slight or absent above, heavy beneath
Color: spring - **gray green;** summer - dark **blue green;** autumn - **blue green** until frost, sometimes dingy yellow gray
Season: persistant in North, **semi-evergreen or evergreen** in South; emergence - late **May,** drop - early **November** or later

FLOWER: long slender **trumpet,** 5 cm (2 in) long, grouped in terminal whorled clusters
Color: **orange to scarlet red,** bright yellow tubes, attracts hummingbirds
Season: late **June through** late **July,** often in intervals until severe October frost, overlaps with fruiting season
Sex: monoecious

FRUIT: translucent ovoid **berries,** 8 to 10 mm (⅓ to ⅖ in) diameter, in terminal whorls of 3 to 6
Color: **red to orange**
Season: mid **August through** late **October**   Human Value: not edible
Wildlife Value: **intermediate;** songbirds, upland gamebirds, small mammals

HABITAT: formation - **glade, forest, dry cliff, old field;** region - **Central, Southern;** gradients - **mesic dry, dry;** roadside thickets,
   old farmsteads, fence rows, open woods, dry stony woods, edge of woods, overhanging limestone or sandstone cliffs
Shade Tolerance: **tolerant**
Flood Tolerance: **intolerant**

SOIL: Texture: **moderately coarse to fine;** rocky, gravelly or sandy loams, heavy clays
Drainage: **moderately well to excessive**
Moisture: **moist to droughty**
Reaction: **slighty acid to circumneutral,** pH range 6.1 - 7.5

HARDINESS: zone **4b**
Rate: **medium** to slow in North, very fast in South, from 3 to 4.5 m (10 to 15 ft) in single season
Longevity: **long-lived**

SUSCEPTIBILITY: Physiological: **infrequent**
Disease: **infrequent** - powdery mildew, leaf spot, leaf blight, twig blight; rarely serious
Insect: **occasional** - woolly honeysuckle aphid, leaf rollers, honeysuckle sawfly, planthopper, long-tailed mealy bug
Wind-Ice: **infrequent**

URBAN TOLERANCE: Pollution: **sensitive** - 2-4D
Lighting: Drought Heat: **resistant**   Mine Spoils:
Salt: Soil Compaction: **intermediate**
Root Pattern: sparse, long fibrous, **deep lateral** spreading; **difficult to transplant,** slow to re-establish

SPECIES: Associate: trees - Post Oak, Tuliptree, Flowering Dogwood, White Fringetree, Shortneedle/Loblolly Pines,
   Eastern Red Cedar, sumac, Sourwood, Persimmon; shrubs - Possumhaw/Blackhaw Viburnums, Gray Dogwood
Similar: Yellow Honeysuckle - flowers yellow; Everblooming Honeysuckle; Common Trumpetcreeper - compound leaf
Cultivars: 'Magnifica' - late scarlet flower; 'Sulphurea' - yellow flowers; 'Superba' - bright scarlet flowers; others

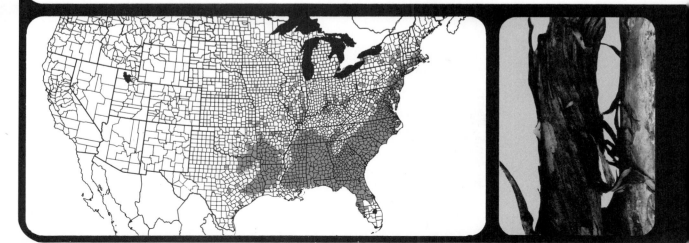

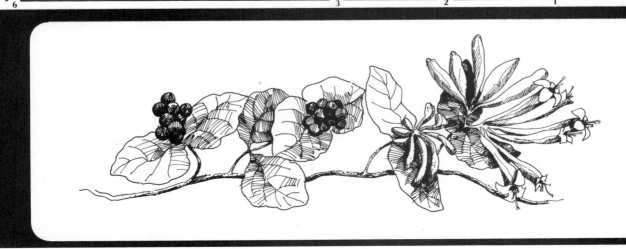

Menispermum canadense

FORM: **groundcover-like or climbing**
Size: **low vine** - from 1 to 6 m (3 to 6 ft), commonly 2 to 4 m (6 to 12 ft)
Spread: **narrow** - from 2 to 4 m (6 to 12 ft)
Mass: **dense**

BRANCHING: climbing by **twining** stems or scrambling and trailing on ground, **picturesque; medium** texture
Twig: slender, flexible, glossy, finely **ridged, large leaf scars**, dark **brown or green**
Bud: hidden, embedded in bark
Bark: **smooth** becoming warty **or blocky** on old stems with short corky ridges, brown or **red brown**

FOLIAGE: alternate, **simple, orbicular to cordate**, entire or 3 to 7 **palmate lobes**, petiole attached to leaf underside; **coarse**
Surface: **dull**, smooth, paler beneath
Color: spring - **light green;** summer - **medium green;** autumn - **yellow**
Season: **deciduous;** emergence - mid **May**, drop - mid **October**

FLOWER: **small** loose drooping axillary **clusters**, 4 to 5 cm (1½ to 2 in) long, clusters with 15 to 40 blooms
Color: greenish **white or yellow green**
Season: early **June through** early **July**
Sex: **dioecious**

FRUIT: globular **berry**, 6 to 9 mm (¼ to ⅜ in) diameter, in loose open grape-like clusters on long stems
Color: **bluish black,** seeds crescent or moon-shaped, hence common name
Season: early through late **September,** often persisting **to** late **December**   Human Value: very **poisonous fruit**
Wildlife Value: **high;** quickly devoured by songbirds, upland gamebirds, large and small mammals

HABITAT: formation - **swamp, glade, forest, old field;** region - **Northern, Central;** gradients - **wet, wet-mesic, mesic, mesic-dry;**
fence rows, woods edge, shaded alluvial woods, rocky bluffs, roadside thickets, ravines, streambanks, bluff base
Shade Tolerance: **very tolerant**
Flood Tolerance: **very tolerant**

SOIL: Texture: **coarse** rocky sandy and gravelly loams **to fine** silt loams, heavy silts, silty clay loams, stiff clays
Drainage: **poor to well**
Moisture: **wet to dry**
Reaction: **moderately acid to circumneutral,** pH range 5.1 - 7.5

HARDINESS: zone 2
Rate: **very fast** - from 2 to 3 m (6 to 10 ft) in a year
Longevity: **very short-lived**

SUSCEPTIBILITY: Physiological: **frequent** - twigs and stems die back to ground in severe winters
Disease: **infrequent** - none serious
Insect: **infrequent** - none serious
Wind-Ice: **frequent** - soft, hardly woody, easily broken

URBAN TOLERANCE: Pollution:
Lighting: Drought Heat: **intermediate**.   Mine Spoils:
Salt: Soil Compaction: **resistant**
Root Pattern: **shallow** fibrous, suckering; **transplants easily,** easy culture

SPECIES: Associate: trees - White/Green Ashes, Black Cherry, Common Hackberry, oak/hickory/hawthorn/elm species;
shrubs - Gray Dogwood, Smooth/Fragrant Sumacs, American Filbert, Jerseytea Ceanothus
Similar: Carolina Snailseed - Southern, red fruit, zone 6a; Cupseed - Southern; wild grape species - tall vines
Cultivars: none available

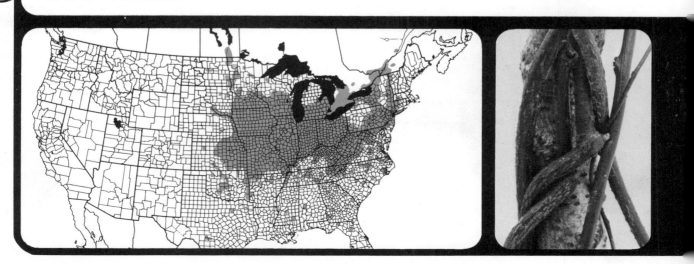

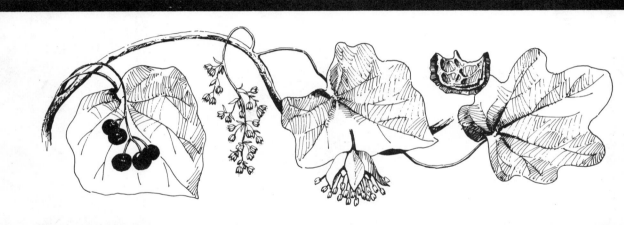

Parthenocissus quinquefolia

FORM: **groundcover-like or climbing,** very closely clinging when growing on walls
Size: **tall vine** - 10 m (35 ft) or more
Spread: **wide** - from 6 to 10 m (20 to 35 ft) or more
Mass: **moderate**

BRANCHING: prostrate trailing habit or climbs by aerial rootlets and tendrils that end in a circular **suction disc; medium**
Twig: slender, flexible, **large leaf scars,** light gray to **brown** with tan lenticels
Bud: small conical, 2 to 3 mm (¹⁄₁₀ to ¹⁄₈ in) long, sharp pointed, **red to brown**
Bark: roughened and **scaly** becoming **shallow or deep furrowed,** ridges broad and rounded, dark **brown**

FOLIAGE: alternate, **palmately compound,** 5 leaflets, **oblanceolate** to obovate, coarsely toothed, long petiole; **medium**
Surface: **glossy or dull,** smooth, paler below
Color: spring - pinkish or **red green;** summer - **dark green;** autumn - crimson or rose **red,** one of earliest vines to color
Season: **deciduous;** emergence - mid **May,** drop - late **October**

FLOWER: small inconspicuous **flat-topped** clusters, 5 to 13 cm (2 to 5 in) long, rather loose
Color: whitish **green** or purplish green
Season: mid **June through** early **July**
Sex: monoecious

FRUIT: globular **berry,** 5 to 8 mm (¹⁄₅ to ¹⁄₃ in) diameter, in clusters of 1 to 5
Color: bloomy **bluish black** on bright red stems
Season: late **September through** October, often persisting through late **February**   Human Value: **poisonous fruit**
Wildlife Value: **high;** eagerly consumed by primarily songbirds, occasional use by upland gamebirds, small mammals

HABITAT: formation - **savanna, forest, cliff, old field;** region - **Northern, Central, Southern;** gradients - **wet, wet-mesic, mesic, mesic-dry, dry;** fence rows, woodland edges, open woods, alluvial woods, ravines and bluffs, rich deep woods, cliffs
Shade Tolerance: **very tolerant**
Flood Tolerance: **very tolerant**

SOIL: Texture: **coarse** sands and gravels, sandy loams **to fine** silt loams, heavy silts, silty clay loams, stiff clays
Drainage: **poor to excessive**
Moisture: **wet to droughty**
Reaction: **moderately acid to circumneutral,** pH 5.1 - 7.5

HARDINESS: zone 2
Rate: **very fast** when well established, between 2 to 3 m (6 to 10 ft) in single season
Longevity: **long-lived**

SUSCEPTIBILITY: Physiological: **infrequent**
Disease: **occasional** - stem canker, downy mildew, leaf spot, powdery mildew, anthracnose, thread blight, root rot
Insect: **occasional** - Japanese beetle, rose chafer, eight-spotted forester, leaf hoppers, scales, rusty plum aphid, mites
Wind-Ice: **infrequent**

URBAN TOLERANCE: Pollution: **sensitive** - O_3, Cl; **intermediate** - 2-4D; **resistant** - HFl
Lighting: Drought Heat: **resistant**   Mine Spoils:
Salt: **intermediate**   Soil Compaction: **resistant**
Root Pattern: fibrous, **shallow lateral** stems spreading and rooting at nodes; **transplants well,** slow to re-establish

SPECIES: Associate: trees - Black/Sugar Maples, White/Green Ashes, White/Red Oaks, American Linden, American Beech, Black Cherry, American Elm; shrubs - Gray Dogwood, Missouri/Pasture Gooseberries, American Filbert
Similar: Thicket Creeper - lacks suction discs; Japanese Creeper - maple-like leaves; Common Poisonivy - 3 leaflets
Cultivars: 'Engelmannii' - small leaflets; 'Saint-Paulii' - small leaflets, aerial rootlets; 'Hirsuta' - leaves woolly beneath

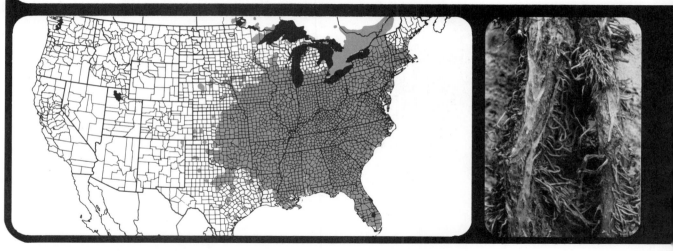

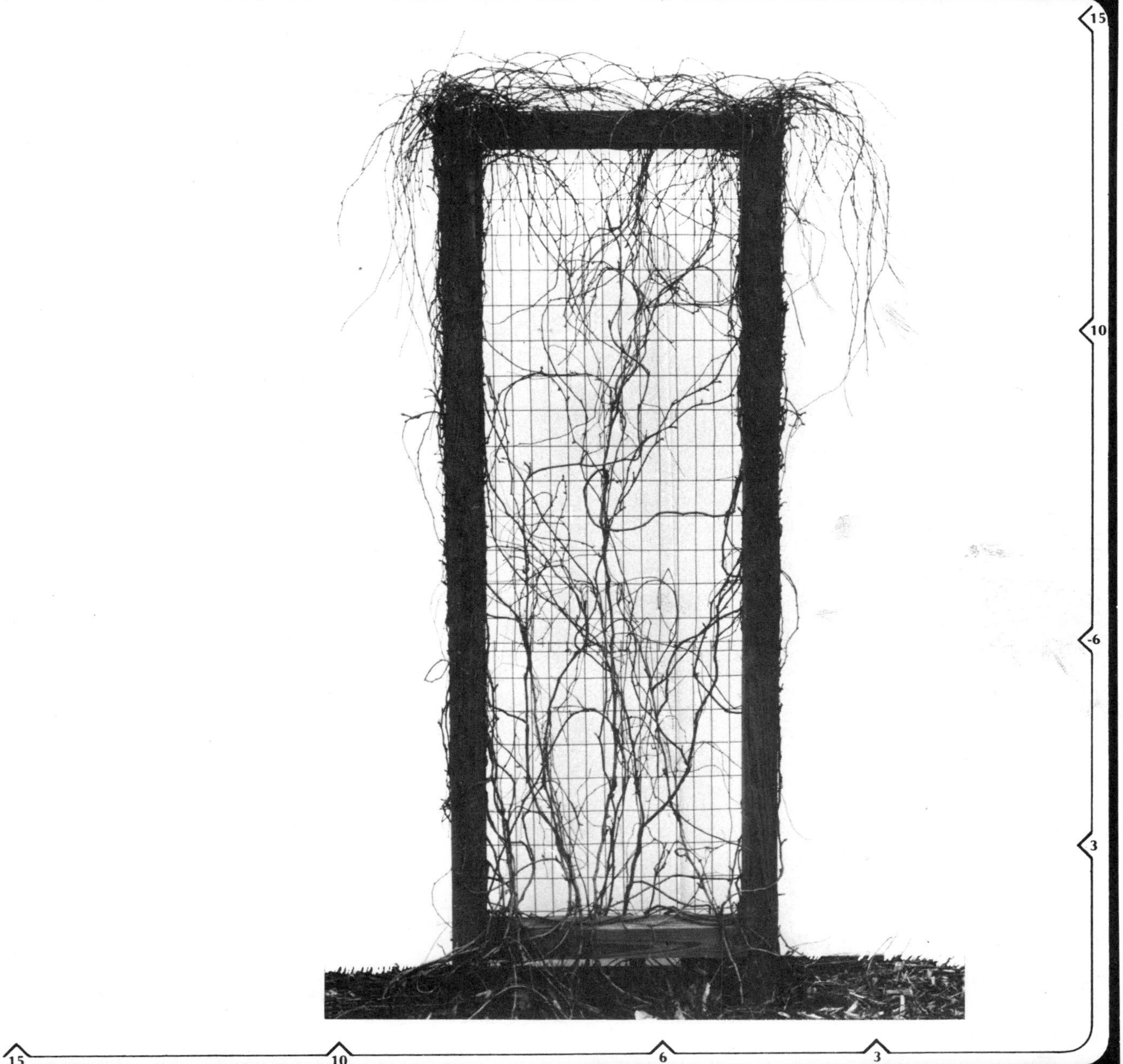
15
10
6
3
15
10
6
3

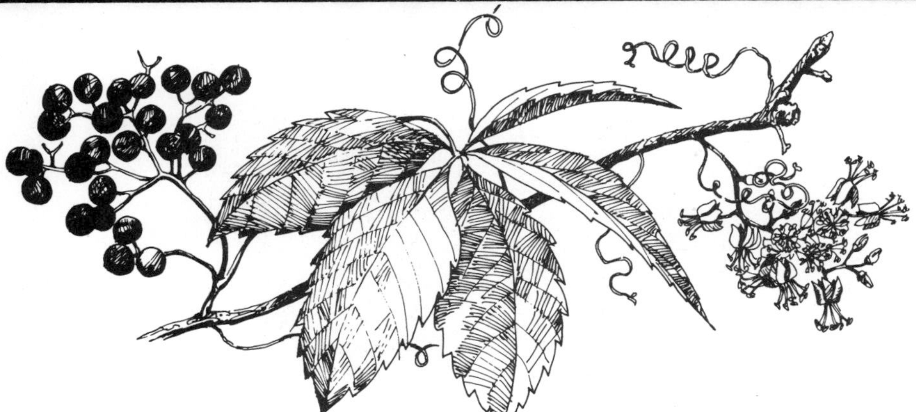

Smilax glauca

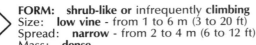

FORM: shrub-like **or** infrequently **climbing**
Size: **low vine** - from 1 to 6 m (3 to 20 ft)
Spread: **narrow** - from 2 to 4 m (6 to 12 ft)
Mass: **dense**

BRANCHING: climbs by use of scattered **tendrils,** shrub-like form with arched scrambling habit; **coarse** texture
Twig: slender, smooth, wiry and tough, **green with white powdery bloom;** unarmed or **armed** with scattered weak prickles
Bud: small ovoid, divergent, 1 scale, hidden by remnants of leaf base
Bark: **smooth, green** becoming dark brown; older stems **armed** with scattered broad-based prickles resembling cat claws

FOLIAGE: alternate, **simple, elliptic or oval** to cordate, entire, parallel veination, 3 to 5 veined; **coarse** texture
Surface: **dull,** smooth, thin, distinctly whitened below
Color: spring, summer - **medium green;** autumn - **medium green or** golden **yellow brown**
Season: tardily **deciduous or semi-evergreen;** emergence - mid or late **May,** drop - late **November** or after

FLOWER: **small** ball-like 6 to 12-flowered axillary **clusters,** profuse but inconspicuous
Color: **green**
Season: mid through late **May,** with leaves
Sex: monoecious or **dioecious**

FRUIT: **globular berry,** 6 to 8 mm (¼ to ⅓ in) diameter, in dense globular clusters arranged like spokes on a wheel
Color: **black** with **bluish** powdery bloom
Season: early **September to** late October, persisting through late **January**   Human Value: **roots and leaves edible**
Wildlife Value: **intermediate;** important winter food for songbirds, upland gamebirds, large and small mammals

HABITAT: formation - **glade, forest, old field;** region - **Central, Southern;** gradient - **wet, wet-mesic, mesic, mesic-dry, dry;** mois
to dry woods, roadside thickets, abandoned fields, clearings, alluvial woods, calcareous leached eroded ground
Shade Tolerance: **very tolerant**
Flood Tolerance: **intermediate**

SOIL: Texture: **coarse** sands and gravels, sandy loams **to fine** silt loams, heavy silts, silty clay loams, stiff clays
Drainage: **poor to excessive**
Moisture: **moist to droughty**
Reaction: **slightly acid to** circumneutral, tolerates **alkaline,** pH 6.1 - 8.5

HARDINESS: zone 5b
Rate: **fast**
Longevity: **short-lived**

SUSCEPTIBILITY: Physiological: **infrequent**
Disease: **infrequent** - leaf spots, rusts; unimportant
Insect: **infrequent** - various scales; none serious
Wind-Ice: **infrequent**

URBAN TOLERANCE: Pollution:
Lighting: Drought Heat: **resistant**   Mine Spoils:
Salt: **resistant**   Soil Compaction: **resistant**
Root Pattern: long slender **deep lateral** roots with coarse thick **tubers** in masses; **transplants with difficulty**

SPECIES: Associate: trees - Common Persimmon, Flowering Dogwood, Pitch/Shortleaf Pines, White/Scarlet/Post/Black
jack Oaks, Sassafras; shrubs - Jerseytea Ceanothus, Box Huckleberry, Mountainlaurel Kalmia, Common Deerberry
Similar: Lanceleaf Greenbrier - Southern; Redbead Greenbrier - Southern, zone 6b, red fruit
Cultivars: none available

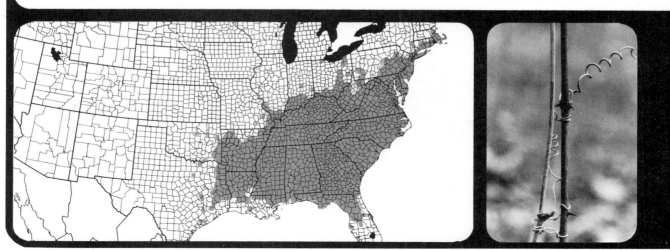

Cat Greenbrier

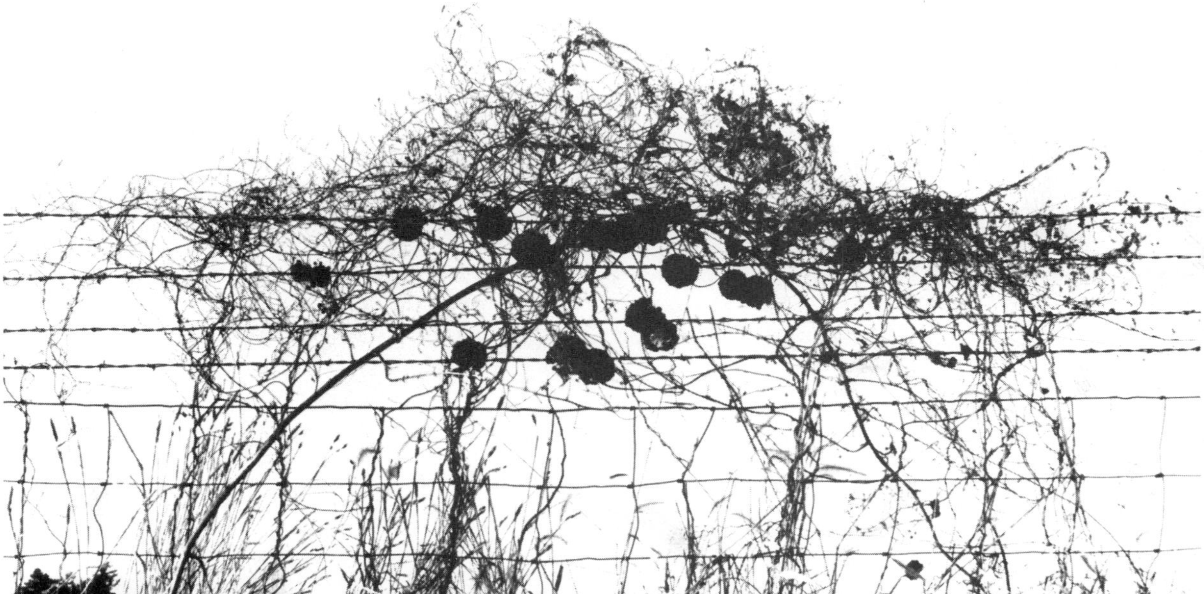

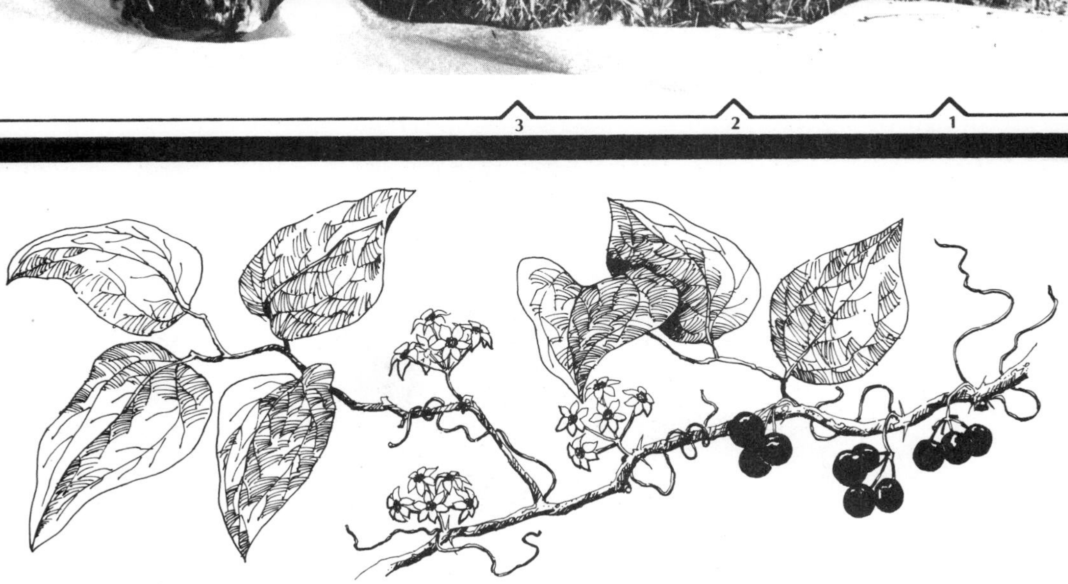

Smilax rotundifolia

FORM: **climbing**
Size: **mid-height vine** - from 6 to 10 m (20 to 35 ft)
Spread: **intermediate** - from 4 to 6 m (12 to 20 ft)
Mass: **dense**

BRANCHING: climbs by **tendrils** at base of petioles, strong; **medium** texture
Twig: quadrangular with fine **ridges**, often zigzag, **green**
Bud: hidden, covered by remnants of leaf base, if visible then small ovoid, 3-sided, divergent, 1 bud scale, **green**
Bark: **smooth, green** to yellow green; **armed** with scattered straight or hooked black-tipped prickles, not numerous

FOLIAGE: alternate, **simple**, variable - **orbicular to cordate;** entire, parallel veination, usually 3-veined; **coarse** texture
Surface: **glossy** on both sides, smooth, leathery
Color: spring - **light green;** summer - **medium to dark green;** autumn - **dark green** late, **then** golden **yellow brown**
Season: tardily deciduous or **persistant;** emergence - late **May,** drop - mid **December,** later in mild winters

FLOWER: **small** ball-like axillary **clusters,** profuse but inconspicuous
Color: **yellowish green to green purple**
Season: late **May through** early **June,** with leaves
Sex: monoecious or **dioecious**

FRUIT: globular **berry,** 6 mm (¼ in) diameter, in small ball-like clusters arranged like spokes on a wheel, 6 to 12 per group
Color: **black** with **bluish** bloom
Season: early **September** often persisting **through** late **March**   Human Value: **roots, leaves,** young stems **edible**
Wildlife Value: **intermediate;** important winter food for waterfowl, gamebirds, songbirds, large/small mammals

HABITAT: formation - **swamp, glade, bald, dune, old field, forest;** region - **Northern, Central, Southern;** gradient - **wet, wet-**
    mesic, mesic, mesic-dry, dry; low woods, clearings, thickets, dune slopes, deep woods, swampy ground, ridges
Shade Tolerance: **very tolerant**
Flood Tolerance: **tolerant**

SOIL: Texture: **coarse** sands and gravels, sandy loams **to fine** silt loams, heavy silts, silty clay loams, stiff clays, mucks
Drainage: **poor to well**
Moisture: **wet to dry**
Reaction: **moderately acid to** circumneutral, tolerates **alkaline,** pH 5.1 - 8.5

HARDINESS: zone 5a
Rate: **slow to medium**
Longevity: **short-lived**

SUSCEPTIBILITY: Physiological: **infrequent**
Disease: **infrequent** - rusts, leaf spots; rarely merit treatment
Insect: **infrequent** - scales; rarely serious
Wind-Ice: **infrequent**

URBAN TOLERANCE: Pollution:
Lighting: Drought Heat: **resistant**   Mine Spoils:
Salt: **resistant**   Soil Compaction: **resistant**
Root Pattern: **shallow** underground stems running for long distances, few **tubers,** form thickets; **difficult to transplant**

SPECIES: Associate: trees - Sugar Maple, Flowering Dogwood, Red/White Oaks, American Beech, White Ash, Shadblow
    Serviceberry; shrubs - Running Euonymus, Pasture Gooseberry, Gray/Silky Dogwoods, Indiancurrant Coralberry
Similar: Bristly Greenbrier - mass of prickles at stem base; Saw Greenbrier - variable-shaped leaf
Cultivars: none available

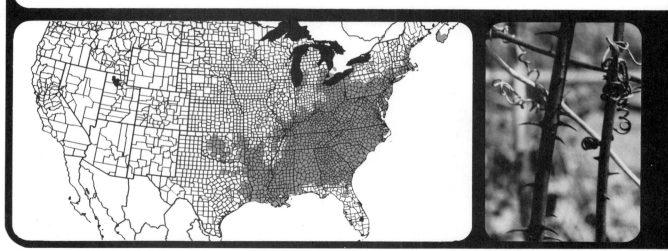

Smilax tamnoides

FORM: climbing
Size: **mid-height vine** - from 6 to 10 m (20 to 35 ft), occasionally up to 12 m (40 ft)
Spread: **intermediate** - from 4 to 6 m (12 to 20 ft)
Mass: **dense**

BRANCHING: stems climbing by means of paired **tendrils** at base of petioles; **coarse** texture
Twig: **angular** with fine lines or **ridges, green; armed** with few or no prickles
Bud: hidden by old leaf bases, if visible then small ovoid, 3-sided, divergent, 1 bud scale, **green**
Bark: **smooth, green** to brown; **armed** with dense needle-straight black to dark purple prickles

FOLIAGE: alternate, **simple,** broadly **ovate** or cordate to oblanceolate, entire, mostly 5 parallel veins; **coarse** texture
Surface: both sides **glossy,** smooth, thick leathery, paler green beneath
Color: spring - **light green;** summer - **medium to dark green;** autumn - **green** late, sometimes golden **yellow brown**
Season: **deciduous, often persistant;** emergence - late **May,** drop - mid **December** or persisting longer

FLOWER: **small** ball-like 10 to 20 flowered axillary **clusters,** spoke-like arrangement, each bloom star-shaped, inconspicuous
Color: **green or yellowish green**
Season: late **May** and early **June,** with leaves
Sex: **dioecious**

FRUIT: globular **berry,** 8 mm (⅓ in) diameter, in drooping spherical clusters on long stalks
Color: **bluish black**
Season: early **October through** late **November,** often persisting longer   Human Value: **roots,** young **leaves edible**
Wildlife Value: **intermediate;** relished by winter songbirds, upland gamebirds, wood ducks, large and small mammals

HABITAT: formation - **forest, old field;** region - **Central, Southern;** gradient - **wet-mesic, mesic, mesic-dry;** moist woods, fence
rows, streambanks, rich deep woods, wooded pastures, second growth woods and thickets, shady alluvial woods
Shade Tolerance: **very tolerant**
Flood Tolerance: **intermediate**

SOIL: Texture: **moderately coarse to moderately fine;** gravelly or sandy loams, loams, silt loams, clay loams, clays
Drainage: **moderately poor to well**
Moisture: **moist to average**
Reaction: **slightly acid to** circumneutral, tolerates **alkaline,** pH 6.1 - 8.5

HARDINESS: zone 3a
Rate: **slow**
Longevity: **short-lived**

SUSCEPTIBILITY: Physiological: **infrequent**
Disease: **infrequent** - leaf spot, several rusts; rarely treated
Insect: **infrequent** - none serious, occasional scale
Wind-Ice: **infrequent** - strong hard wood

URBAN TOLERANCE: Pollution:
Lighting: Drought Heat: **resistant**   Mine Spoils:
Salt: **resistant**   Soil Compaction: **resistant**
Root Pattern: short, **shallow** never spreading far, woody, slow growing; **transplants** moderately **well**

SPECIES: Associate: trees - Black/Sugar Maples, American Linden, Common Honeylocust, Silver Maple, Common
Hackberry, American Elm; shrubs - Running Euonymus, American Elder, Pasture/Missouri Gooseberries, raspberry
Similar: Saw Greenbrier - dense; Common Greenbrier - more Southern; Common Dutchmanspipe - leaf similar
Cultivars: none available.

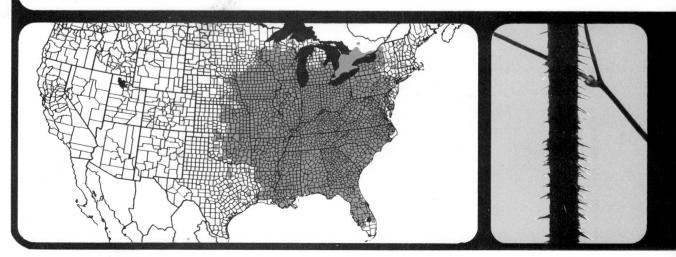

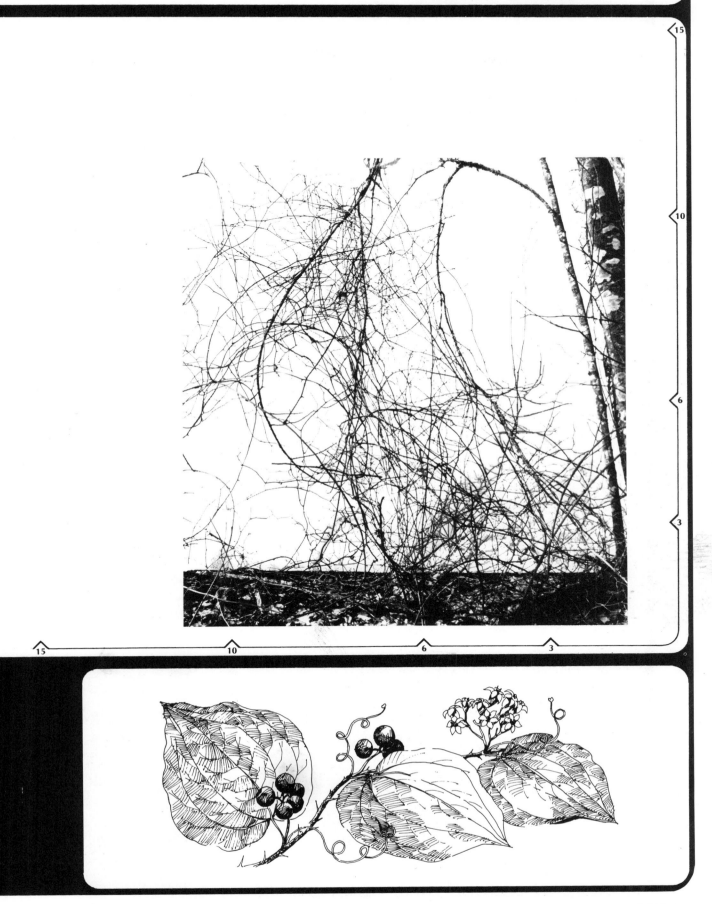

Toxicodendron radicans

FORM: variable - **groundcover-like, often shrub-like or climbing**
Size: **tall vine** - 10 m (35 ft) or more, often climbing the tallest trees
Spread: **wide** - from 6 to 10 m (20 to 35 ft)
Mass: **moderate**

BRANCHING: trailing underground with erect little-/much-branched stems or climbing by **aerial rootlets; leggy; coarse**
Twig: moderately slender, flexible, **velvety, large leaf scars,** conspicuous lenticels, **green brown to** tan **brown**
Bud: **naked,** long pointed, **woolly,** end bud 4 to 5 mm (⅙ to ⅕ in) long, **stalked, reddish** to orange
Bark: **smooth,** roughened with tiny raised lenticels becoming deeply furrowed with fibrous **exfoliation, red brown to gray**

FOLIAGE: alternate, **trifoliate, ovate lanceolate,** side leaflets assymetric, margins entire, toothed, or lobed; **medium coarse**
Surface: glossy or **dull,** smooth, paler beneath
Color: spring - **red green or purple;** summer - dark **yellow green;** autumn - dull **orange to red**
Season: **deciduous;** emergence - mid **May,** drop - early **October**

FLOWER: small axillary **spikes,** 3 to 10 cm (1 to 4 in) long, generally inconspicuous
Color: greenish **white**
Season: late **May through** mid **June,** after leaves
Sex: **dioecious**   **Fragrant:**   sweet perfumed

FRUIT: globular **berry,** 5 mm (⅕ in) diameter, with longitudinal pumpkin-like creases, loose drooping grape-like clusters
Color: waxy **white** or ivory
Season: late **September through** late November, often persisting to late **January**   Human Value: **all parts poisonous**
Wildlife Value: **high;** eagerly consumed by songbirds, upland gamebirds, large and small mammals

HABITAT: formation - **dune, glade, forest, old field;** region - **Northern, Central, Southern;** gradient - **wet, wet-mesic, mesic,**
  mesic-dry, dry; roadsides, open or dense woods, pastures, fence rows, dunes, wooded floodplains, river banks
Shade Tolerance: **very tolerant**
Flood Tolerance: **very tolerant**

SOIL: Texture: **coarse** rocks, sands and gravels, sandy loams **to fine** silt loams, heavy silts, silty clay loams, stiff clays
Drainage: **very poor to excessive**
Moisture: **wet to droughty**
Reaction: **moderately to slightly acid,** pH range 5.1 - 6.5

HARDINESS: **zone 3a**
Rate: **fast**
Longevity: **long-lived**

SUSCEPTIBILITY: Physiological: **infrequent**
Disease: **infrequent** - none serious
Insect: **infrequent** - rarely afflicted
Wind-Ice: **infrequent**

URBAN TOLERANCE: Pollution: **intermediate** - 2-4D
Lighting: Drought Heat: **resistant**   Mine Spoils:
Salt: Soil Compaction: **resistant**
Root Pattern: **shallow** underground rhizomes form thickets; **easily transplanted** - often unwanted with other plants

SPECIES: Associate: trees - Common Boxelder, Common Honeylocust, Silver Maple, Black/Post/Scarlet/White/
  Chinkapin/Red Oaks; shrubs - American Elder, Silky/Gray Dogwoods, Arrowwood/Rafinesque Viburnums
Similar: Fragrant Sumac - similar leaves, shrub; Virginia Creeper - 5 leaflets, blue black fruit
Cultivars: none available

Vitis labrusca

FORM: climbing
Size: **tall vine** - 10 m (35 ft) or more to the tops of the tallest trees
Spread: **wide** - from 6 to 10 m (20 to 35 ft) plus
Mass: **dense**

BRANCHING: climbs with slender forked **tendrils** at every joint, dense-branched at top, **leggy** unbranched base; **coarse**
Twig: slender, **velvety**, finely ridged, red **brown**
Bud: small, **2 bud scales**, brown
Bark: loose and **exfoliating** into thin longitudinal shaggy strips, **red brown**

FOLIAGE: alternate, **simple, palmately** 3-**lobed**, sinuses usually shallow, sometimes deep, coarse broad teeth; **coarse**
Surface: **dull**, smooth, wrinkled above, somewhat leathery, rusty woolly beneath
Color: spring - **reddish green;** summer - **light to medium green;** autumn - green late then **yellow green**
Season: **deciduous;** emergence - mid **May**, drop - late September or early **October**

FLOWER: small **spike**-like clusters, 6 to 10 cm (2 to 4 in) long, inconspicuous
Color: **green** to creamy white
Season: late **May through** mid **June,** after leaves
Sex: **dioecious**   **Fragrant:** very perfumed

FRUIT: globular **berry**, 10 to 15 mm (⅖ to ⅗ in) diameter, in drooping compact bunches of usually less than 15
Color: dull red or amber to purple or **black,** sometimes light bloomy **blue**
Season: mid **August through** late **September**   Human Value: sweet musky scented **edible fruits**
Wildlife Value: **very high;** preferred food of many songbirds, waterfowl, upland gamebirds, large and small mammals

HABITAT: formation - **glade, forest, old field;** region - **Northern, Central;** gradients - **wet, wet-mesic, mesic-dry, dry;** woodland
     borders, fence rows, hedge rows, stream banks, alluvial woods, rocky open hillsides, wet ravines
Shade Tolerance: **tolerant**
Flood Tolerance: **tolerant**

SOIL: Texture: **coarse** sands and gravels, sandy loams **to fine** silt loams, heavy silts, silty clay loams, stiff clays
Drainage: **very poor to well**
Moisture: **wet to dry**
Reaction: **moderately acid to circumneutral,** pH range 5.5 - 7.5

HARDINESS: zone 4b
Rate: **very fast,** up to 6 m (20 ft) in one season
Longevity: **long-lived**

SUSCEPTIBILITY: Physiological: **infrequent**
Disease: **infrequent** - none serious
Insect: **infrequent** - none serious
Wind-Ice: **infrequent**

URBAN TOLERANCE: Pollution: **sensitive** - 2-4D, HCl; **intermediate** HFI, CI
Lighting: Drought Heat: **intermediate**   Mine Spoils:
Salt: **resistant**   Soil Compaction: **resistant**
Root Pattern: **shallow lateral** and fibrous; **easily transplanted**

SPECIES: Associate: trees - American Sweetgum, American Holly, American Planetree, Water Oak; shrubs - Pinxter-
     bloom Azalea, Common Spicebush, Southern Waxmyrtle, Lambkill/Mountainlaurel Kalmias, Sweetbay Magnolia
Similar: Muscadine Grape; Summer Grape
Cultivars: several - 'Concord', 'Worden', 'Hartford'; dominant parent of others - 'Niagara', 'Catawba', 'Iona', 'Brighton'

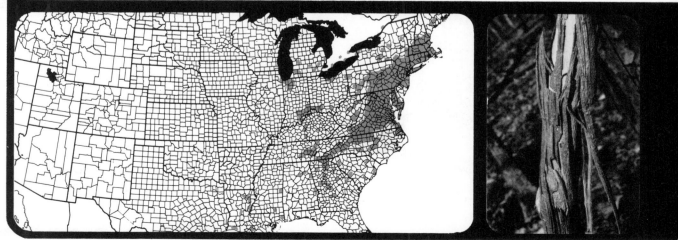

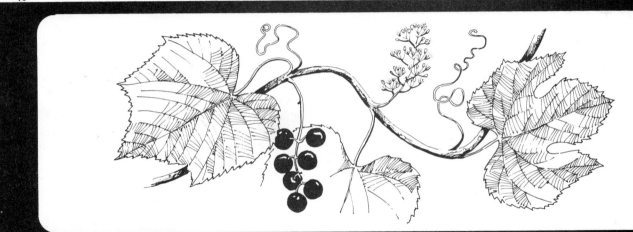

Vitis riparia

FORM: trailing or **climbing**
Size: **tall vine** - 10 m (35 ft) or more, commonly reaching to tops of tallest trees
Spread: **wide** - from 6 to 10 m (20 to 35 ft) plus
Mass: **dense**

BRANCHING: stems climb by forked **tendrils, leggy; coarse** texture
Twig: slender, flexible, minutely **ridged, red and green becoming** tan **brown**
Bud: small conical, 2 to 3 mm (1/10 to 1/8 in), **2 scales, red brown**
Bark: shreddy loose **exfoliation** in long thin longitudinal papery strips, dark **red brown**

FOLIAGE: alternate, **simple,** cordate, **palmately** 3-**lobed,** maple-like, deep sinuses, coarse long-pointed teeth; **coarse**
Surface: glossy or **dull,** smooth, thin, shiny beneath
Color: spring - orangish or **reddish green;** summer - **medium green;** autumn - **yellow green or** bright **yellow**
Season: **deciduous;** emergence - mid **May,** drop - mid **October**

FLOWER: small in loose many-flowered **spikes,** 8 to 12 cm (3 to 5 in) long
Color: yellowish **green**
Season: late **May through** mid **June,** after leaves
Sex: **dioecious**   **Fragrant:** very perfumed

FRUIT: globular **berry,** 6 to 10 mm (1/4 to 2/5 in) diameter, in compact loose conical clusters, usually more than 15
Color: **black or** with dense **bluish** bloom
Season: mid **July through** early **September**   Human Value: juicy **fruit** is **edible** but acid sour
Wildlife Value: **very high;** favorite food of songbirds, upland gamebirds, waterfowl, large and small mammals

HABITAT: formation - **swamp, glade, old field, forest;** region - **Northern, Central;** gradient - **wet, wet-mesic, mesic-dry, dry;**
river banks, low wooded bottomlands, rocky open hillsides, fence rows, wet ravines, woods edge, hedge rows
Shade Tolerance: **tolerant**
Flood Tolerance: **very tolerant**

SOIL: Texture: **coarse** sands and gravels, sandy loams **to fine** silt loams, heavy silts, silty clay loams, stiff clays
Drainage: **very poor to excessive**
Moisture: **wet to droughty**
Reaction: **slightly acid to** circumneutral, tolerates **alkaline,** pH range 6.1 - 8.5

HARDINESS: zone 2
Rate: **very fast,** between 6 to 9 m (20 to 30 ft) in one year
Longevity: **long-lived**

SUSCEPTIBILITY: Physiological: **infrequent**
Disease: **infrequent** - none serious
Insect: **infrequent** - none serious
Wind-Ice: **occasional** - soft porous wood, pith brown and large, breakage in heavy wind or ice not uncommon

URBAN TOLERANCE: Pollution: **sensitive** - 2-4D, HCl; **intermediate** - Cl
Lighting: Drought Heat: **resistant**   Mine Spoils:
Salt: Soil Compaction: **resistant**
Root Pattern: fibrous, **shallow** spreading **laterals; easily transplanted**

SPECIES: Associate: trees - Silver Maple, Common Boxelder, Green Ash, Ohio Buckeye, Kentucky Coffeetree; shrubs -
Hardhack Spirea, Missouri Gooseberry, Silky/Gray Dogwoods, American Elder, Indigobush Amorpha
Similar: Frost Grape - sweet edible fruit after frost; Heartleaf Ampelopsis - fruit bitter; Japanese Creeper - red fall color
Cultivars: 'Praecox' - June fruiting; parent of 'Clinton' and other cultivated grapes

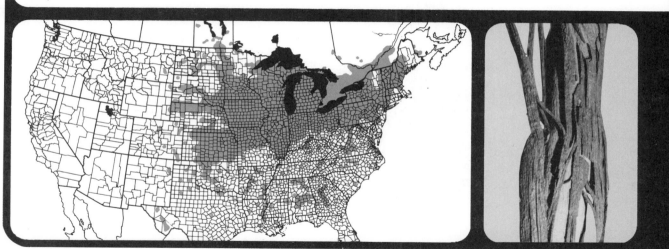

Wistaria macrostachya

FORM: climbing
Size: **mid-height vine** - from 6 to 10 m (20 to 35 ft)
Spread: **intermediate** - from 4 to 6 m (12 to 20 ft)
Mass: **dense**

BRANCHING: stems climb by **twining** branches, **picturesque; medium** texture
Twig: **velvety,** sometimes slightly ridged, **green brown** with white hairs
Bud: **woolly,** long **pointed, 2 bud scales, brown**
Bark: **smooth, gray** to red brown

FOLIAGE: alternate, **pinnately compound,** 5 to 11 leaflets, **lanceolate to oblong lanceolate,** entire, rolled under; **medium fine**
Surface: **dull,** smooth, paler beneath
Color: spring - **reddish green;** summer - **medium green;** autumn - **yellow**
Season: **deciduous;** emergence - early **June,** drop - mid **October**

FLOWER: dense terminal drooping **spikes,** 15 to 30 cm (6 to 12 in) long
Color: **blue to** lavender **purple**
Season: early and mid **June,** with leaves
Sex: monoecious   **Fragrant:** sweet perfumed

FRUIT: linear knobby bean-like **pod,** 5 to 13 cm (2 to 5 in) long
Color: red **brown**
Season: early **September through** late **February**   Human Value: **poisonous fruits**
Wildlife Value: **very low;** of little use

HABITAT: formation - **swamp, dune, old field, forest;** region - **Central;** gradients - **wet, wet-mesic;** low wet woods, swamp
margins, floodplain forests, stream banks, pond and lake margins, bayous
Shade Tolerance: **tolerant**
Flood Tolerance: **tolerant**

SOIL: Texture: **coarse to fine;** sands, gravels, sandy loams, loamy sands, fine sandy loams, silt loam, clay loam, heavy clay
Drainage: **very poor to well**
Moisture: **wet to average**
Reaction: **slightly acid to circumneutral,** pH range 6.1 - 7.5

HARDINESS: **zone 5a**
Rate: **fast,** between 1.5 to 2 m (5 to 7 ft) in single season
Longevity: **long-lived**

SUSCEPTIBILITY: Physiological: **infrequent**
Disease: **infrequent** - bacterial crown gall, leaf spots, stem canker, powdery mildew, root rot, tobacco mosaic virus
Insect: **infrequent** - sweet-potatoe leaf beetle, silver-spotted skipper, fall webworm, black vine weevil; rarely serious
Wind-Ice: **infrequent**

URBAN TOLERANCE: Pollution: **sensitive** - 2-4D
Lighting: Drought Heat: **resistant**   Mine Spoils:
Salt: **resistant**   Soil Compaction: **resistant**
Root Pattern: fibrous, **deep** descending; **difficult to transplant**

SPECIES: Associate: trees - River Birch, Green Ash, Common Boxelder, elm species, Willow/Water/Swamp White Oaks;
shrubs - alder species, Eastern Baccharis, Possumhaw, Witherod/Possumhaw Viburnums, Dense Hypericum, Inkberry
Similar: American Wisteria - smaller flowers; Japanese/Chinese/Formosa Wisterias - hardy exotics to zone 5a
Cultivars: 'Nivea' - flowers white

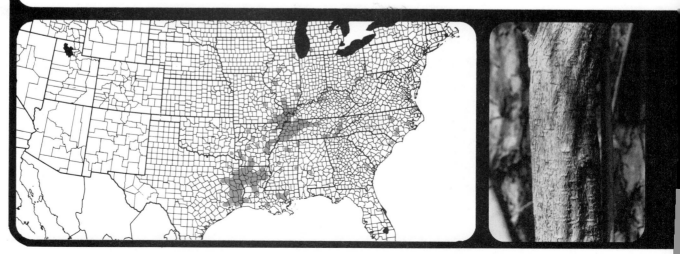

GLOSSARY

Achene—Small, dry, one-seeded fruit; as in a sunflower. The achene does not open at maturity.

Acicular—Slender needle-shaped leaf.

Acorn—A thick-walled nut with a woody cup-like base; the fruit of the oaks.

Aeration—To supply or impregnate with air; as with soil or liquid.

Aerial Rootlets—Small root-like organs along stems of some climbing vines, used for support.

Aerobic—The presence of free oxygen.

Aesthetic—Appreciative of or responsive to the basic principles of nature and its environmental beauty.

Aggregate—Collected together; as a fruit formed by the coherence of many pistils that were distinct in the flower; a multiple fruit.

Alluvial—Soils deposited by running water, generally along rivers and streams.

Alternate—Arrangement of leaves or other plant parts not opposite or whorled; parts situated one at a node, as leaves on a twig.

Ambient—Moving around, encompassing on all sides.

Anaerobic—The absence of free oxygen.

Angled—With obvious longitudinal angles or ridges.

Annual—Maturing and living one season only.

Anther—The terminal part of a stamen in which pollen is formed.

Apex—Tip or terminal end.

Appressed—Flattened against another part of the plant.

Arching—Curving gracefully, upright spreading, becoming descending; umbrella-like.

Armament—Provided with sharp defenses; thorns, spines, barbs, prickles, or sharply modified twigs.

Aromatic—Fragrantly scented, when broken or crushed; especially twigs, foliage.

Ascending—Main primary branches diverging at near 45-degree angle from the vertical.

Association—A kind of plant community of definite composition presenting a uniform appearance and growing in uniform habitat conditions.

Awl-shaped—Tapering from the base to a slender and stiff point.

Bark—Dead outer protective tissue of a woody root or stem; varying in appearance and texture.

Barrens—A major vegetation formation with either a low total woody coverage or with stunted individuals of species that elsewhere reach considerable size.

Basal—Situated at the base of the stem.

Bell—Flower shape; bell- or trumpet-like.

Berry—Fruits with soft fleshy covering over the seed.

Biennial—A plant lasting two seasons, flowering the second year.

Biome—A major vegetation formation; such as grassland, prairie, or forest.

Biotic—Of or relating to life; referring to biota, the flora and fauna of a region.

Bipinnately Compound—Leaf structure that is twice compound.

Bladder-like—Inflated, empty sack with thin walls.

Blade—The expanded part of a leaf, usually flat, thin, and attached to the stem by a little stalk.

Blocky—Bark having knobby, warty, flat-topped squarish plates or ridges.

Bloom—A powdery or waxy grayish coating, easily removed by rubbing; found on stems, leaves, flowers, and fruits.

Bole—Stem or trunk of a tree.

Boreal—Northern biogeographical region.

Bract—A modified leaf usually beneath a flower and sometimes colored and petal-like.

Branch—A secondary limb from a main stem.

Branchlet—Smaller or secondary divisions of a main branch.

Bristle—A stiff hair.

Broadleaf Evergreen—Trees whose leaves remain throughout the year, continually dropping and being replaced by new springtime growth.

Bud—A structure of embryonic tissues that become a leaf, flower, or both, or a new shoot; naked or enclosed with scales.

Bud Scale—A modified leaf or stipule covering the embryonic tissue of the bud.

Bulk Density—The weight of the soil solids per unit volume of total soil.

Calcareous—Impregnated with lime or containing calcium carbonate; as calcareous soils.

Canopy—Tree crown greater than 15 meters (50 feet) in height at maturity.

Capillary Water—Water held as a film around soil particles and in tiny spaces between particles.

Capsule—Fruit of more than one chamber usually splitting lengthwise along multiple seams from one end.

Catkin—Flowers in the form of a slender elongated pencil-like cluster of linear scaly bracts.

Clay—A fine-grained, firm, natural material, plastic when wet, that consists primarily of silicates of aluminum; as clay soils.

Climax—The final result of succession; a self-perpetuating plant community with no further development possible under existing climatic or physiographic conditions.

Climbing—Tall growing vines that use other plants or objects for vertical support.

Clustered—Leaves or buds crowded so as not to be clearly opposite, alternate, or whorled.

Coarse (texture)—Consisting of large or rough parts.

Columnar—Cylindrical, vertical axis much exceeding horizontal.

Community—An aggregation of living organisms having a mutual relationship among themselves and to their environment.

Compound Leaf—A leaf composed of two or more blades; called leaflets.

Cone—Woody fruit having stiff overlapping scales that support naked seeds; or small staminate and pistillate flowers clustered into tight cylindrical cones, primarily of coniferous plants.

Conical—Approaching triangular in outline, broadest at base, three dimensional.

Coniferous—Pertaining to cone-bearing plants, or the order of coniferales, such as pine, fir, juniper, or yew.

Cordate—Heart-shaped, frequently employed to designate a structure of ovate outline and heart-shaped base.

Corky Ridges—Elongated warts or strips of soft spongy wood.

Crown—The upper mass or head of a tree, shrub, or vine, including branches with foliage.

Cultivar—A cultivated variety that is given a name by the originator. For example, *Rhododendron calendulaceum Roseum* is a cultivar of Flame Azalea.

Cylindric—Shaped like a cylinder.

Deciduous—Shedding or losing foliage at the end of the growing season.

Deltoid—Delta-shaped, triangular.

Dense (mass)—Extremely well developed branching system, heavily clothed with foliage, negative space minimal or absent.

Dentate—Coarse-toothed leaf margin with teeth directed outward.

Descending—Main primary branches diverging from the bole or stem at an angle below the horizontal.

Dioecious—Having male and female flowers on separate plants.

Disc—The central flat "button" in daisy-type (composite) flowers.

Dissemination—The spread by biological or physiological factors of ripe seeds away from the parent plant.

Divergent—Spreading broadly or apart; pointing away.

Divided—Separated to the base into divisions.

Doubly Compound—See bipinnately compound.

Doubly Serrate—Major serrations bearing minute teeth on margins.

Doubly Toothed—Major serrations bearing minute teeth on leaf margins.

Downy—Pubescent, clothed with a coat of soft, fine hairs.

Drooping—Hanging from the base, suggesting wilting.

Dry—A habitat with low soil water content and often with high evaporation rate.

Dull—Lacking luster, absorbing light.

Ecosystem—An ecological community together with its physical environment, considered as a unit.

Edible Plant—Plant parts edible by humans and nutritious.

Ellipsoid—Three-dimensional shape of an ellipse; football shape.

Elliptical—Having the outline of an ellipse, broadest at middle and narrower at each end.

Elongate—Lengthened.

Endangered Species—Those plant or animal species in danger of becoming extinct throughout all or a significant portion of their natural range.

Entire—Leaf margin without divisions, lobes, or teeth.

Environment—The sum of all external forces or influences that affect an organism, or community of organisms.

Ephemeral—Persisting for one day only, of short duration.

Erect—Upright habit of growth.

Evergreen—Holding green leaves, either broadleaf or needle-shaped, throughout the year.

Exfoliating—Peeling or flaking away; usually referring to bark character.

Exotic—From another part of the world, not indigenous, foreign.

Extinct Species—Plant or animal species no longer living on earth in their natural habitat.

Fibrous—Bark having long narrow shreds or flakes; roots having no prominent central axis or prominent lateral branches.

Filament—The stalk of a stamen that supports the anther.

Filamentous—Thread-like.

Fine Texture—Consisting of small, rather delicate parts.

Fissure—Narrow openings or cracks of considerable length and depth, occurring from breaking or parting of bark tissue.

Flaky—Shreddy, with short rectangular fragments.

Flat-Top—Small flowers in rounded or flattened clusters mostly at the ends of twigs.

Fleshy—Applied to a fruit somewhat pulpy or juicy at maturity, as opposed to a dry, hard, or papery fruit.

Floodplain—A plain bordering a river, subject to flooding.

Flora—All plants of a region.

Foliage—The sum of all leaves of a plant that function primarily in food manufacture and photosynthesis.

Follicle—Aggregate of small fleshy pods on stout, short, erect stem.

Form—Characteristic shapes of tree, shrub, or vine species referring to the outline of the crown as perceived in silhouette, grown in the open field under favorable environmental conditions.

Fragrant—Agreeable or sweet scented, specific reference to flower.

Fruit—A matured ovary containing seed or seeds.

Furrowed—Having longitudinal channels or grooves; as describing bark characteristics.

Genus—A category of biological classification ranking between the family and the species, comprising structurally or genetically related species. The generic name comes first and is capitalized, and the specific name, second. For example, *Cornus racemosa* is the gray dogwood.

Globular—Rounded circular form, vertical and horizontal axis about equal.

Glossy—Shining, reflecting light.

Grassland—An area, such as prairie or meadow, of indigenous grass or grasslike vegetation.

Groundcover-like—Low-growing woody plants that trail on the ground resembling groundcover.

Growth Rate—The measured vertical increase in height during one growing season.

Gummy—Consisting of or containing a sticky, adhesive resin substance.

Habit—The general aspect or mode of growth of a plant.

Habitat—The place or type of site where a plant or animal normally lives.

Hair—Superficial outgrowth.

Hairy—Pubescence with long hairs.

Height—Vertical plant dimension at maturity.

Herb—Plant, either annual, perennial, or biennial, of which the parts above the ground are not woody.

Horizontal—Possessed of main primary branches predominately oriented at near 90-degree angles to the trunk.

Hue—The attribute of colors that permits them to be classed as red, yellow, green, blue, or an intermediate between a contiguous pair of colors.

Humus—A brown or black organic substance consisting of partially or wholly decayed vegetable matter that provides nutrients for plants and increases the ability of soil to retain water.

Impervious—A soil layer through which water, air, or roots penetrate slowly.

Inflated—Bladder-like, loose, and membranous about the seed.

Internode—Portion of the stem between two nodes.

Intolerant—Unable to grow and survive in a state of health and vigor.

Inundation—To cover over with water or flooding.

Irregular—Asymmetrical, uneven outline.

Juvenile—An early phase of plant growth, usually characterized by non-flowering.

Key—A small indehiscent fruit with a wing, a samara.

Lanceolate—Much longer than wide, widest near stem; lance-shaped.

Landscape—The landforms of a region including its vegetation, wildlife, hydrology, geology, and physical and biological characteristics of form.

Lateral—Borne at or on the side, as flowers, buds, branches, or roots; not at the apex.

Lateral Bud—A bud borne in the axil of a previous season's leaf.

Leader—The primary trunk of a tree.

Leaf—A lateral outgrowth from a stem that constitutes a unit of the foliage of a plant that functions primarily in food manufacture by photosynthesis.

Leaflet—A foliar element of a compound leaf.

Leaf Scar—A mark on a twig indicating the point where a leaf was once attached.

Leggy—Tall-stemmed, devoid of foliage.

Lenticel—Corky growth on young bark that admits air to the interior of a twig or branch.

Limb—The primary branch of a tree.

Linear—Much longer than wide, with nearly parallel margins.

Loam—Consisting of about equal proportions of sand, clay, silt, and organic matter; a type of soil.

Lobe—A projecting part or segments of a leaf margin divided with sinuses that do not reach the midrib.

Longevity—The length of time a selected plant can be expected to live when environmental conditions are favorable.

Lustrous—Glossy or shiny.

Margin—The edge of a leaf.

Mass—Degree of density and measurement of foliage and branching parts as controlled by species genetic code.

Mat—Prostrate, low, widespreading form; horizontal axis greatly exceeds vertical, 10 to 1 ratio is common.

Mature—The later phase of growth characterized by flowering, fruiting, and a reduced rate of size increase.

Medium Texture—Consisting of intermediate diameter and spacing of plant parts.

Mesic—A habitat with moderate soil water content and well drained.

Midrib—The primary rib or mid-vein of a leaf or leaflet.

Modified Twig—A dwarf, stiff branch.

Monoecious—Species having both sexes on the same plant.

Mound—Broad elliptic plant form, horizontal axis exceeding vertical by 2 to 1 ratio.

Multiple Fruit—One formed from several flowers into a single structure having a common axis or point, as in planetree, sweetgum, or common buttonbush.

Naked Bud—One without scales.

Native—Inherent and original to a geographic area.

Needle—The slender leaf of many conifers.

Node—A joint on a stem represented by the point of origin of a leaf or bud; sometimes represented by a distinct leaf scar.

Nut—Fruit structure partially or wholly enclosed in a husk that may be papery, woody, leafy, or spiny in character.

Oblanceolate—About four times as wide as long, widest at tip end, inversely lanceolate.

Oblong-lanceolate—About four times as long as wide, widest at base and middle, rectangular or nearly parallel at the base.

Oblong-obovate—Egg-shaped, widest near the base and middle.

Obovate—Egg-shaped, widest above the middle, inversely ovate.

Obovoid—Three-dimensional egg-shaped, broadest at crown apex.

Olfactory—Of, relating to, or connected with the sense of smell.

Onion (bud)—Having shape characteristics similar to those of the genus onion.

Opacity—Possessing structural qualities that are impervious to the rays of light.

Opposite—An arrangement in which two leaves or buds grow on the opposite sides of a twig at a single node.

Orbicular—Circular leaf shape, round in overall outline.

Ornamental—Relating to a plant cultivated for its beauty rather than for its natural use.

Oval—Twice as long as broad, widest at the middle, both ends rounded.

Ovate—Egg-shaped in outline, widest near stem end.

Ovoid—Three-dimensionally egg-shaped, broadest below middle.

Paired—Occurring in two's.

Palmate—Radiating fan-like from a common point, as leaflets of a palmately compound leaf or lobes of a palmately lobed leaf.

Papery—resembling paper in thinness, usually dry and brittle.

Parallel—Veins running side by side paralleling leaf margin from base of leaf to apex.

Particle Density—Average density of soil particles.

Peat—Partially carbonized vegetable matter; usually mosses, found in bogs.

Pendulous—Hanging or drooping habit.

Permeable—The quality that enables a soil to transmit water or air through the soil; measured as the number of meters per hour that water moves.

Persistent—Leaves losing summer color in autumn but with a significant percentage remaining into winter or early spring.

Petal—Unit of the floral envelope; usually showy.

Petiole—Leaf stem or stalk.

pH—A measure of the acidity or alkalinity of a solution, numerically equal to 7 for neutral solutions, increasing with increasing alkalinity and decreasing with increasing acidity.

Phenology—The science that studies the timing of biological events and observations of life cycle phases of species or communities throughout the year.

Phenological Events—See phenophase.

Phenophase—Different plants, having different timing in development, maturity, reproductive cycles, and leaf drop.

Photoperiod—Alternating periods of lightness and darkness as they affect the growth and maturity of plant material.

Photosynthesis—Formation of carbohydrates in the chlorophyll-containing tissues of plants exposed to light.

Physiological—The vital biological process of an organism.

Physiological Disorders—Physiological damage to plants often caused by unfavorable environmental conditions.

Picturesque—Naturally irregular or contorted, especially said of branching.

Pinnate—Arranged like a feather; with leaflets on opposite sides of a common axis or veins on opposite sides of a leaf midrib.

Pistillate—Female flowers.

Pith—The spongy or hollow center of twigs or stems.

Plume—A much branched silky feather-like cluster of seeds.

Pod—A dry linear leguminous fruit.

Pointed—Having a pointed, sharp tip.

Poisonous Plant—Plant whose parts are toxic if ingested and/or touched by humans.

Pore Space—Voids around solid particles, usually water and air sharing the void in variable proportion; as in soils.

Prickle—A small spine-like growth from the bark or epidermis.

Primary—Of first rank, importance, or size; as said of main branches.

Procumbent—Lying on the ground; usually describes growing habit.

Prostrate—Lying on the ground, also horizontal or flat.

Pyramidal—Having the form of a pyramid, narrowing gradually to a point.

Rachis—Axis of a compound leaf bearing leaflets.

Radial—Diverging in all directions from a central point.

Ranked—Foliage arranged in a flattened horizontal plane around a stem.

Recurving—Main primary branches arching at near 45-degree angle from the bole, becoming descending to recurving, ascending at the branch tips.

Resinous—Secreting a sticky, gummy substance.

Rhizome—A thick, fleshy, horizontal subterranean stem that is usually near the soil surface.

Ridges—Raised portion of bark.

Root—The descending underground axis of the plant.

Rosette—A radiating arrangement of leaves close to the ground.

Samara—Seeds with a thin membranous wing.

Sand—Loose, granular, gritty particles of worn or disintegrated rock, finer than gravel and coarser than dust.

Savanna—Transitional zone between grasslands and forests, on which there are scattered individual trees and/or clumps of trees and shrubs.

Scales—Small modified leaves, usually thin, seen in buds and cones; the flakes into which the outer bark often divides.

Scaly (bud)—Covered with or compised of small modified leaf scales or bracts.

Season—Refers to the period of time during which the flowers, fruits, or foliage remain ornamentally effective.

Secondary—Of second rank, importance, or size; as said of branches.

Semi-Evergreen—Many leaves remain green throughout autumn and occasionally early winter before turning brown.

Serrate—Saw-toothed, teeth pointing forward.

Shrub—A woody perennial, usually having several stems.

Shrub-like—Multiple-branched vines that resemble a woody shrub in appearance and structure.

Silt—A sedimentary soil consisting of fine mineral particles intermediate in size between sand and clay.

Simple—Leaves having only one blade in which the midrib is unbranched and is continuously united along the blade margin.

Sinus—The space or recess between two lobes.

Smooth—Having a continuous even surface with minimal fissures.

Soil Moisture—Water held in the soil by capillary and hydroscopic forces, as plants only utilize capillary soil moisture for growth processes.

Spatial—Relating to, occupying, or having the character of space.

Species—A category of biological classification ranking immediately below the genus. Species is both singular and plural. The specific name, often descriptive, follows the generic name, is not capitalized, and can be followed by a varietal name. For example, *Comptonia peregrina* is the sweetfern.

Sphagnum—Any of various pale or ashy mosses, the decomposed remains of which form peat.

Spike—Usually an unbranched elongated cylindrical inflorescence; the flowers may be congested or widely spaced.

Spine—A sharp mostly woody outgrowth from a branch or stem.

Spread—Horizontal plant dimension at maturity.

Spreading—Branching structure commonly erect or upright through the lower and middle crown diverging to a 45-degree angle in the upper crown.

Spur—A short-projecting, sharp-pointed root or branch of a twig.

Stalk—A short, slender, peg-like supporting structure of a leaf, flower, fruit, or other organ.

Stalked—Bud positioned above short slender peg-like stem along twig.

Stamen—The pollen-bearing organ of the male flower.

Staminate—Male flowers; provided with stamens but without pistils.

Stem—The main axis of a plant that grows upward and bears leaves and flowers.

Stolon—A shoot that runs along the ground, underground, or bends to the ground and roots.

Stoloniferous—Bearing stolons.

Stoma—An orifice in the epidermis of a leaf used to connect internal cavities with air.

Stomata—Plural of stoma.

Strata—A part, or series, representing a period or stage of development.

Strobile—Slender pendant or erect cone-like fruit with papery overlapping seeds.

Sucker—A shoot that springs from a parent stem underground, where it makes a root of its own.

Suction Discs—An adhesive cup-like organ by which some climbing vines fasten to an object for support.

Surface Tension—The adhesive force that holds capillary water in the soil.

Tapering—Gradually decreasing toward the end.

Taproot—The primary descending root, usually very large in most species.

Tendrils—A coiling thread-like organ by which certain vines grasp an object for support.

Terminal—At the end, summit, or tip.

Tertiary—Of third rank, importance, or value; as said of branchlets.

Texture—Refers to size and spacing, especially said of branching, foliage, and bark.

Thicket—A dense colony of one species, commonly spreading by underground roots.

Thorn—A sharp unbranched or branched outgrowth in the position of a lateral branch.

Threatened Species—Plant or animal species that are not presently endangered but are likely to become so within the immediate or foreseeable future throughout all or a significant portion of their natural range.

Tolerant—Capable of enduring.

Tomentose—Covered with dense, woolly, matted hairs.

Toothed—Leaf margins broken into small, sharp, pointed divisions.

Topographic Gradient—Lowland or upland landscape position.

Trailing—Horizontal orientation but with most branches hugging the ground.

Translucent—Transmitting light but diffused enough to distort images.

Transpiration—The passage or movement of water vapor from living tissues through a membrane or pores (stomates).

Tree—A woody plant at least 6 meters (20 feet) tall with one main stem usually and unbranched at or near base.

Trifoliate—Compound leaf with three leaflets.

Trunk—The main stem of a tree apart from limbs and roots; bole.

Tuber—A swollen, usually underground, root-like storage organ that bears buds or "eyes."

Turgid—Stiff and firm.

Twig—The shoot of a woody plant representing the growth of the current season.

Twining—Clasping method by which certain climbing vines wind stems around an object for support.

Twisting Leafstalk—Clasping method by which certain climbing vines wind leafstalks around an object for support.

Understory—Tree crown greater than 6 meters (20 feet) but less than 15 meters (50 feet) in height at maturity.

Upright—Main primary branches stiffly vertical or diverging at a slight angle from vertical.

Variegated—Leaves that are striped, margined, or mottled with a color other than green.

Variety—A category of biological classification ranking below the species. The varietal name follows the species name and is usually capitalized. For example, *Hydrangea quercifolia Snowflake* is a double-flowered variety of oakleaf hydrangea.

Vegetation Formation—The broad vegetation cover differences as expressed by their growth form characteristics. Bog, desert, prairie and forest are representative.

Vein—Vascular channels of a leaf.

Venation—Pattern of the veins of a leaf; three common types—parallel, pinnate, and palmate.

Velvety—Having long, stiff, densely erect hairs.

Vine—A plant that trails on the ground or climbs by twining, tendrils, aerial roots, or other means of vertical support.

Wavy—Undulate margin of a leaf.

Weed—Plant that grows spontaneously in a habitat that has been greatly modified by man, especially a species confined chiefly or exclusively to such habitats; correctly applied to some exotic species only.

Weeping—Secondary branchlets hanging or drooping.

Wet—Pertaining to, characterized by, or requiring considerable moisture; poorly drained.

Whorled—An arrangement in which three or more leaves circle a twig at a single node.

Wilt—To become limp and lose turgor resulting from deficiency of water as accelerated during drought conditions.

Wing—Thin membranous appendage.

Witches'-broom—Tufts of shoots or stems resulting from an infection by fungi or an infestation by insects.

Wooly—Having long, flat, densely appressed hairs.

Xeric—A habitat with low soil water content and often with high evaporation rate.

Zigzag—Bent back and forth.

Zone—An area restricted by a range of annual average minimum temperature used in determining plant hardiness and adaptability.

BIBLIOGRAPHY

Ahlgren, Clifford E. "Some Effects of Temporary Flooding on Coniferous Trees." *Jour. For.* 55:647–50.

——. 1957. "Phenological Observations of 19 Native Tree Species in Northwestern Minnesota." *Ecol.* 3:622–28.

Aiken, George D. 1968. *Pioneering with Wildflowers.* Englewood Cliffs, New Jersey: Prentice-Hall.

Aikman, John M. 1948. *Native Shrubs and Vines of Iowa.* Ames, Iowa: Iowa State University Press.

Ajilvsgi, Geyata. 1979. *Wild Flowers of the Big Thicket.* College Station, Texas: Texas A & M University Press.

Andresen, John W. 1976. Selection of Trees for Endurance of High Temperatures and Artificial Lights in Urban Areas. Better Trees for Metropolitan Landscapes Symp. Proc., U.S.D.A. For. Serv. Gen. Tech. Rep. N.E. Expt. Sta. 22:67–77.

Angier, Bradford. 1972. *Feasting Free on Wild Edibles.* Harrisburg, Pennsylvania: Stackpole Books.

——. 1974. *Field Guide to Edible Wild Plants.* Harrisburg, Pennsylvania: Stackpole Books.

Anonymous. 1974. "Urban Plants vs. Pollution." *Agric. Res.* 23(2):3–5.

Arend, John L. 1955. Tolerance of Conifers to Foliage Sprays of 2,4-D and 2,3,5-T in Lower Michigan. U.S. For. Serv., Lake States Expt. Sta., Tech. Note 437, 2 p.

Ashby, W. C. 1964. Vegetational Development on a Strip-Mined Area in Southern Illinois. Trans. Ill. State Acad. Sci. 57:78–83.

Bailey, Liberty Hyde, Ethel Zoe Bailey, and staff of L. H. Bailey Hortorium. 1976. *Hortus Third.* New York: Macmillan Publishing Co., Inc.

Bailey, Ralph, ed. 1972. *Plant Finder Index.* The Good Housekeeping Illustrated Encyclopedia of Gardening, Vol. 16. New York: Book Division, Hearst Magazines.

Baker, Frederick S. 1949. "A Revised Tolerance Table." *Jour. For.* 47:179–81.

Balyea, R. M., D. A. Fraser and A. H. Rose. 1951. "Seasonal Growth of Some Trees in Ontario." *For. Chron.* 27:300–305.

Barrington, Rupert. 1972. *A Garden for Your Birds.* New York: Grosset & Dunlap.

Beckerson, D. W., Nancy Cain, Gerry Hofstra, D. P. Ormond, and Patricia A. Campbell. 1980. "A Guide To: Plant Sensitivity to Environmental Stress." *Landsc. Arch.,* 299–303.

Bell, D. J. 1974. Flood Caused Tree Mortality Around Illinois Reservoirs (forests). Ill State Acad. Sci. Trans. 67(1):29–37.

Benson, Lyman, and Robert A. Darrow. 1954. *The Trees and Shrubs of the Southwestern Deserts.* Albuquerque, New Mexico: The University of New Mexico Press.

Bernstein, L. 1964. Salt Tolerance of Plants. U.S.D.A. Inf. Bull. 283.

Bernstein, L., L. E. Francois, and R. A. Clark. 1972. "Salt Tolerance of Ornamental Shrubs and Ground Covers." *Jour. Amer. Soc. Hort. Sci.* 97:550–56.

Billard, Ruth Sawyer. 1972. Birdscaping Your Yard. State of Connecticut, Department of Environmental Protection.

Billings, W. D. 1970. *Plants, Man and the Ecosystem.* 2nd ed. Belmont, California: Wadsworth Publishing Co., Inc.

Billington, Cecil. 1949. *Shrubs of Michigan.* 2nd ed. Bloomfield Hills, Michigan: Cranbrook Institute of Science.

Birdseye, Clarence, and Eleanor G. Birdseye. 1972. *Growing Woodland Plants.* New York: Dover Publications.

Blakeslee, Albert F., and Chester D. Jones. 1972. *Northeastern Trees in Winter.* New York: Dover Publications.

Booth, W. E. and J. C. Wright. 1966. *Flora of Montana Part II Dicotelydons.* Bozeman, Montana: Montana State College.

Brainerd, John W. 1973. *Working with Nature: A Practical Guide.* New York: Oxford University Press.

Bramble, W. C. 1952. "Reforestation of Strip-Mined Bituminous Coal Land in Pennsylvania." *Jour. For.* 50:308–14.

Braun, Lucy E. 1961. *The Woody Plants of Ohio.* Columbus, Ohio: Ohio State University Press.

———. 1967. *Deciduous Forests of Eastern North America.* New York: Hafner Press.

Bray, J. R. 1958. "The Distribution of Savanna Species in Relation to Light Intensity." *Can. Jour. Bot.* 36:671–81.

———. 1960. "The Composition of Savanna Vegetation in Wisconsin." *Ecol.* 41:721–32.

Bray, W. L. 1906. Distribution and Adaptation of the Vegatation of Texas. Bul. of Univ. of Texas No. 82, Scientific Series No. 10. University of Texas, Austin, Texas.

Brennan, E., and I. A. Leone. 1968. "Responses of plants to sulphur dioxide or ozone-polluted air supplied at varying flow rates." *Phytopath.* 58:1161–1664.

Briggs, Shirley A. 1973. *Landscaping for Birds.* Washington, D.C.: Audubon Naturalist Society of the Central Atlantic States Inc.

Britton, N. L. 1889. *Catalogue of Plants found in New Jersey.* Trenton, New Jersey: John L. Murphy Publishing Co.

Brockman, C. F. 1968. *Trees of North America.* New York: Western Publishing Co., Inc.

Brooklyn Botanic Garden. *Natural Gardening.* Number 77, Brooklyn Botanic Garden Handbooks. Brooklyn, New York: Brooklyn Botanic Garden.

Brown, C. A. 1972. *Wildflowers of Louisiana and Adjoining States.* Baton Rouge, Louisiana: Louisiana State University Press.

Brown, James H. 1962. Success of Tree Plantings on Strip-Mined Areas in West Virginia. W. Va. Agr. Exp. Sta. Bul. 473:1–35.

Bruce, Hal. 1976. *How to Grow Wildflowers and Wild Shrubs and Trees in Your Own Garden.* New York: Alfred A. Knopf.

Bruning, Walter F. 1971. *Minimum Maintenance Gardening Handbook.* New York: Harper & Row Publishers.

Campana, Richard J. 1976. "Air Pollution Effects on Urban Trees." *Trees* 35(2):35–38.

Carleton, R. Milton. 1961. *Your Garden Soil: How to Make the Most of It.* Princeton, New Jersey: D. Van Nostrand Company.

Carpenter, E. D. 1970. "Salt Tolerance of Ornamental Plants." *Amer. Nurseryman* 131(2):12, 54–71.

Carson, Rachel. 1962. *Silent Spring.* Boston, Massachusetts: Houghton Mifflin Co.

Carter, Cedric J. 1970. *Illinois Trees: Selection, Planting and Care.* Urbana, Illinois: Illinois National History Survey.

———. 1964. *Illinois Trees: Their Diseases.* Urbana, Illinois: Illinois National History Survey.

Cathey, Henry M., and Lowell E. Campbell. 1975. "Effectiveness of Five Vision Lighting Sources on Photo-Regulation of 22 Species of Ornamental Plants." *Jour. Amer. Soc. Hort. Sci.* 199 (1):65–71.

Clark, Ross C. 1971. "The Woody Plants of Alabama." *Ann. Mo. Bot. Gard.* 58:99–242.

———. 1969. A Distributional Study of the Woody Plants of Alabama. Unpublished PhD. thesis, University of North Carolina, Chapel Hill, North Carolina.

Cline, Van. 1979. Ecological Health of Agriculture Landscape. Unpublished MLA thesis, Iowa State University, Ames, Iowa.

Cloud, Katherine Mallet Prevost. 1927. *The Cultivation of Shrubs.* New York: Dodd, Mead & Co.

———. 1957. *Evergreen and Flowering Shrubs for Your House.* New York: Publisher Greensburg.

Coffin, Marian C. 1948. *Trees and Shrubs for Landscape Effects.* New York: Charles Scribner's Sons.

Collingwood, G. H., and Warren D. Brush. 1964. *Knowing Your Trees.* Washington, D.C.: American Forestry Association.

Cooper, Tom C., ed. 1982. *Iowa's Natural Heritage.* Des Moines, Iowa: Iowa Natural Heritage Foundation and the Iowa Academy of Science.

Core, Earl L. 1966. *Vegetation of West Virginia.* Parsons, West Virginia: McClain Printing Company.

Cornwall, S. M. 1971. "Anthracite Mining Spoils in Pennsylvania: I. Spoil Classification and Plant Cover Studies." *Jour. Appl. Ecol.* 3:401–9.

Correll, Donovan S., and Marshall C. Johnston. 1970. *Manual of the Vascular Plants of Texas.* Renner, Texas: Texas Research Foundation.

Correll, D. S., and H.B. Correll. 1972. *Aquatic and Wetland Plants of the Southwestern United States.* Washington, D.C.: Environmental Protection Agency.

Crockett, James Underwood. 1971. *Evergreens.* New York: Time-Life Books.

———. 1972. *Trees.* New York: Time-Life Books.

Crockett, James Underwood, and O. Allen. 1977. *Wildflower Gardening.* Alexandria, Virginia: Time-Life Books.

Croxton, W. C. 1928. "Revegetation of Illinois Coal-Stripped Lands." *Ecol.* 9:155–75.

Curtis, John T. 1971. *Vegetation of Wisconsin: An Ordination of Plant Communities.* Madison, Wisconsin: University of Wisconsin Press.

Daubenmire, Rexford. 1968. *Plant Communities—A Textbook of Plant Autecology.* New York: Harper & Row Publishers.

———. 1974. *Plants and Environment: A Texbook of Autecology.* New York: John Wiley and Sons, Inc.

Daubenmire, Rexford, and Jean B. Daubenmire. 1968. Forest Vegetation of Eastern Washington and Northern Idaho. Tech. Bull. 60. Wash. Agric. Exp. Sta. Pullman, Washington: Washington State University.

Davidson, Robert Austin. 1957. The Flora of Southeastern Iowa. Unpublished Ph.D. thesis, State University of Iowa Botany Library, Iowa City, Iowa.

Davis, D. D., and J. B. Coppolino. 1974. "Relative Ozone Susceptibility of Selected Woody Ornamentals." *Hort. Sci.* 9:537–39.

Davis, D. D., and Henry D. Gerhold. 1976. Selection of Trees for Tolerance of Air Pollutants. Better Trees for Metropolitan Landscapes Symp. Proc. U.S.D.A. Forest Service Gen. Tech. Rep. N.E. Expt. Sta. 22:61–67.

Davis, D. D., and R. G. Wilhour. 1976. Susceptibility of Woody Plants to Sulfur Dioxide and Photochemical Oxidants. A Literature Review. Corvallis, Oregon: Corvallis Environmental Research Laboratory, Office of Research and Development, U.S. EPA.

Davis, D. D., and F. A. Wood. 1972. "The Relative Susceptibility of Eighteen Coniferous Species to Ozone." *Phytopath.* 62:14–19.

Davison, Verne E. 1967. *Attracting Birds from the Prairies to the Atlantic.* New York: Thomas Y. Crowell Co.

Deam, Charles C. 1924. *Shrubs of Indiana.* Indianapolis,Indiana: William B. Bunford Printing Co.

———. 1932. *Trees of Indiana.* 4th ed. Indianapolis, Indiana: Indiana Department of Conservation, Division of Forestry.

———. 1940. *Flora of Indiana.* Indianapolis, Indiana: Department of Conservation, Division of Forestry, William B. Bunford Printing Co.

Degraff, Richard M., and Gretchen H. Witmen. 1979. *Trees, Shrubs and Vines for Attracting Birds.* Amherst, Massachusetts: University of Massachusetts Press.

De Wolfe, Gordon P., Jr. 1974. "Guide to Potentially Dangerous Plants." *Arnoldia* 34(2), March/April.

Dennis, John V. 1975. *A Complete Guide to Bird Feeding.* New York: Alfred A. Knopf.

Diekelman, John, and Robert Schuster. 1982. *Natural Landscaping: Designing with Native Plant Communities.* New York: McGraw-Hill Book Co.

Dirr, Michael A. 1976. Salts and Woody-Plant Interactions in the Urban Environment. Better Trees for Metropolitan Landscapes Symp. Proc., U.S.D.A. For. Serv., Gen. Tech., Rep., N.E. Expt. Sta. 22:103–13.

———. 1976. "Selection of Trees for Tolerance to Salt Injury." *Jour. Arboric.* 2:209–16.

———. 1977. *Manual of Woody Landscape Plants: Their Identification, Ornamental Characteristics, Culture, Propagation, and Use.* Champaign, Illinois: Stipes Publishing Company.

Dowden, Anne O. 1972. *Wild Green Things in the City: A Book of Weeds.* New York: Thomas Y. Crowell Co.

Downs, Robert J., and H. A. Borthwick. 1956. "Effect of Photoperiod on Growth of Trees." *Bot. Gaz.* 117:310–26.

Duncan, Wilber H. 1975. *Woody Vines of the Southeastern United States.* Athens, Georgia: The University of Georgia Press.

Duncan, Wilbur H., and John T. Kartesz. 1981. *Vascular Flora of Georgia.* Athens, Georgia: The University of Georgia Press.

Du Pont, Elizabeth N. 1978. *Landscaping with Native Plants in the Mid-Atlantic Region.* Chadds Ford, Pennsylvania: Brandywine Conservancy.

Dyas, Robert W. 1972. The Spirit of the Savanna. Traveling Photographic Exhibit, Iowa State University, Ames, Iowa.

————. 1976. A Designer Looks at the Garden. The Longwood Program Seminars, Vol. 8, University of Delaware, Newark, New Jersey.

Eaton, Leonard K. 1964. *Landscape Artist in America: The Life and Work of Jens Jensen.* Chicago: University of Chicago Press.

Eckbo, Garrett. 1950. *Landscape for Living.* New York: McGraw-Hill Book Co.

————. 1978. *Home Landscape: The Art of Home Landscaping.* Rev. ed. New York: McGraw-Hill Book Co.

Edgecombe, Samual. 1944. Ornamental Shrubs for the Canadian Prairies. Bull. No. 4. Winnepeg, Manitoba, Canada: Line Elevators Farm Service.

Editors of Organic Gardening. 1970. *Lawn Beauty the Organic Way.* Emmaus, Pennsylvania: Rodale Books.

Edminster, Frank C., and Richard M. May. 1957. *Shrub Plantings for Soil Conservation and Wildlife Cover in the Northeast.* Washington, D.C.: U.S. Department of Agriculture.

Eilers, Lawrence J. 1964. The Flora and Phytogeography of the Iowa Lobe of the Wisconsin Glaciation. Unpublished thesis. State University of Iowa Botany Library, Iowa City, Iowa.

Einspahr, Dean W. 1955. Coal Spoil-Bank Materials as a Medium for Plant Growth. Unpublished Ph.D. Thesis, Iowa State College, Ames, Iowa.

Fairbrother, Nan. 1970. *New Lives, New Landscapes.* London, England: The Architectural Press.

Faircloth, Wayne R. 1971. The Vascular Flora of Central South Georgia. Unpublished Ph.D. thesis, University of Georgia, Athens, Georgia.

Fassett, Norman C. 1976. *Spring Flora of Wisconsin.* Madison, Wisconsin: The University of Wisconsin Press.

Fay, Marcus Joseph. 1953. The Flora of Southwestern Iowa. Unpublished thesis, State University of Iowa Botany Library, Iowa City, Iowa.

Fein, Albert. 1972. *Frederick Law Olmstead and the American Environmental Tradition.* New York: George Braziller, Inc.

Finn, Raymond F. 1958. Ten Years of Strip-Mine Forestation Research in Ohio. U.S.D.A. For. Serv. Cent. States For. Expt. Sta., Tech. Paper 153.

Flawn, Peter T. 1970. *Environmental Geology: Conservation, Land Use Planning and Resource Management.* New York: Harper & Row Publishers.

Flemer, William. 1972. *Nature's Guide to Successful Gardening and Landscaping.* New York: Thomas Y. Crowell Co.

Foley, Daniel J. 1961. *Ground Covers for Easier Gardening.* New York: Dover Publications, Inc.

Fox, W. Sherwood, and James H. Soper. 1952–54. The Distribution of Some Trees and Shrubs of the Carolinian Zone of Southern Ontario. Trans. R. Ca. Inst. 29:65–84, maps, 1952; 30:3–32, maps, 1953; 30:99–130, maps, 1954.

Freitus, Joe. 1975. *160 Edible Plants (Commonly Found in the United States and Canada).* Iowa City, Iowa: Stone Wall Press.

Geiger, Rudolf. 1966. *The Climate Near the Ground.* Cambridge, Massachusetts: Harvard University Press.

Gibbons, Boyd. 1982. "Aldo Leopold: A Durable Scale of Values." *National Geographic* 160(5):682–708.

Gilbert, E. F. 1961. "Phenology of Sumacs." *Amer. Midland Naturalist* 66:286–300.

Gill, Don, and Penelope Bonnett. 1973. *Nature in the Urban Landscape: A Study of City Ecosystems.* Baltimore, Maryland: York Press.

Gleason, Henry A. 1952. *The New Britton and Brown Illustrated Flora of the Northeastern United States and Adjacent Canada.* 3 vols. New York: Hafner Press.

Gleason, Henry A., and Arthur Cronquist. 1964. *The Natural Geography of Plants.* New York: Columbia University Press.

Goff, F. G., and Cottom, G. 1967. "Gradient Analysis: The Use of Species and Synthetic Indices." *Ecol.* 48(5):793–806.

Gottehrer, Dean M. 1978. *Natural Landscaping.* New York: E. P. Dutton.

Graham, Samuel A. 1954. Scoring Tolerance of Forest Trees. University of Michigan School of Natural Resources. Michigan For. 4.

Graves, Arthur Harmount. 1956. *Illustrated Guide to Trees and Shrubs.* Rev. ed. New York: Harper and Brothers.

Graves, George. 1945. *Trees, Shrubs and Vines for the Northeastern United States.* New York: Oxford University Press.

Green, George Rex. 1933. *Trees of North America (Exclusive of Mexico).* Ann Arbor, Michigan: Edwards Bros. Inc.

Green, William E. 1947. "Effect of Water Impoundment on Tree Mortality and Growth." *Jour. For.* 45:118–20.

Grimm, William C. 1952. *The Shrubs of Pennsylvania.* Harrisburg, Pennsylvania: Stackpole Books.

———. 1966. *Recognizing Native Shrubs.* Harrisburg, Pennsylvania: Stackpole Books.

Guillet, Alma C. 1962. *Make Friends of Trees and Shrubs.* Garden City, New York: Doubleday.

Gunter, A. Y. 1972. *The Big Thicket.* Austin, Texas: Jenkins Publishing Co.

Hall, T. F., and G. E. Smith. 1955. "Effects of Flooding on Woody Plants, West Sandy Dewatering Project, Kentucky Reservoir." *Jour. For.* 53:281–85.

Hamblin, Stephen Francis. 1923. *List of Plant Types for Landscape Planting.* Cambridge, Massachusetts: Harvard University Press.

Harlow, William M. 1946. *Fruit Key and Twig Key.* New York: Dover Publications, Inc.

———. 1957. *Trees of the Eastern and Central United States and Canada.* New York: Dover Publications, Inc.

Harper, Roland M. 1907–8. "Georgia's Forest Resources." *Southern Woodlands* 1(3):4–23, illus. (maps); 1(4):1–19, illus. (maps); 1(5):3–19, illus. (maps); 1(6):15–32, illus. (maps).

Harrar, Elwood S., and J. George Harrar. 1962. *Guide to Southern Trees.* 2nd ed. New York: Dover Publications, Inc.

Harrison, Thieron P. 1974. *A Floristic Study of the Woody Vegetation of the Cross Timbers.* Denton, Texas: North Texas State University.

Hart, G. E., and W. R. Byrnes. 1960. Trees for Strip-Mined Lands. N.E. For. Expt. Sta. Paper 136.

Hartley, Thomas G. 1962. The Flora ot the Driftless Area. Unpublished Ph.D. thesis, State University of Iowa Botany Library, Iowa City, Iowa.

Harvill, A.M., Jr. 1977. *Atlas of the Virginia Flora.* Farmville, VA: Virginia Botanical Associates.

Haworth-Booth, Michael. 1962. *Effective Flowering Shrubs.* London, England: Collins.

Hayward, H. E., and L. Bernstein. 1958. "Plant-Growth Relationships on Salt-Affected Soils." *Bot. Rev.* 24:584–629.

Heckscher, A. 1968. "Nature and the City." *Nat. Hist.* 77:6–10.

Hepting, George H. 1971. *Diseases of Forest and Shade Trees of the United States.* Agr. Handbook No. 386. U.S.D.A. For. Serv. Washington, D.C.: Supt. of Doc., U.S. Gov. Printing Office.

Hicks, Ray R., Jr., and George K. Stephenson. 1978. *Woody Plants of the Western Gulf Region.* Dubuque, Iowa: Kendall/Hunt Publishing Co.

Hightshoe, Gary L. 1978. *Native Trees for Urban & Rural America: A Planting Design Manual for Environmental Designers.* Ames, Iowa: Iowa State University Research Foundation.

———. 1981. "The Natural Forest Communities of Iowa, A Resource in Trouble." *Iowa Sci. Teachers Jour.* 18(1):2–15.

———. 1984. "Computer-Assisted Program for Forest Preservation/Conservation/Restoration: Upper Midwest Region." *Landsc. Jour.* 3(1):45–60.

———. 1985. "Natural Landscaping: Selecting Plants Attuned to a Site and to Each Other." *Amer. Nurseryman.* 162(3):61–72.

Hightshoe, Gary L., and S. R. Brower. 1971. *Plant Forms and Facts.* Ames, Iowa: Iowa State University Press.

Hightshoe, Gary L., and Ronald S. Niemann. 1981. *PLTSEL: A Computer-Assisted Plant Selection System for Environmental Designers.* Ames, Iowa: Iowa State University Research Foundation.

———. 1982. "Plant Selection System (PLTSEL): Midwestern and Eastern Floristic Regions." *Landsc. Jour.* 1(1):23–30.

Himelick, E. B. 1981. *Transplanting Manual for Trees and Shrubs.* Urbana, Illinois: International Society of Arboriculture.

Holt, Joseph Bixby. 1962. *Man and the Earth.* Englewood Cliffs, New Jersey: Prentice-Hall.

Hosie, R. C. 1973. *Native Trees of Canada.* Ottawa, Canada: Information Canada.

Hosner, J. F. 1960. "Relative Tolerance to Complete Inundation of Fourteen Bottomland Tree Species." *For. Sci.* 6:246–51.

Hottes, Alfred. 1947. *The Book of Shrubs.* New York: A.T. De La Mare Co., Inc.

Hough, R. B. 1947. *Handbook of the Trees of the Northeastern States and Canada (East of the Rocky Mountains).* New York: MacMillan Company.

Howard, Francis. 1959. *Landscaping with Vines.* New York: Macmillan Company.

Howe, V. K. 1974. "Site Changes and Root Damage (trees)." *Arbor. News* 39(1):25–28.

Hudler, G. "Salt Injury to Roadside Plants." *Grounds Maint.* 16(2):80–84.

Hyland, Fay, and Ferdinand H. Steinmetz. 1944. *The Woody Plants of Maine, Their Occurrence and Distribution; an Annotated Catalog of the Woody Spermatophytes.* Univ. Maine Stud. 2d Ser. 59. Orono, Maine: University of Maine.

Ibrahim, Joseph Hindawi. 1970. Air Pollution Injury to Vegetation. Air Pollution Control Administration Publication No. AP-71. Washington, D.C.: U.S. Government Printing Office.

Iowa State University of Science and Technology. 1975. Landscape Plants for Iowa. Coop. Ext. Serv., Pm 212 (Rev.).

Ireys, Alica. 1975. *How to Plan and Plant Your Own Property.* New York: William Morrow and Co.

Jacobson, J. S., and A. C. Hill, eds. 1970. Recognition of Air Pollution Injury to Vegetation: A Pictorial Atlas. Agr. Committee, Air Pollution Control Assn. Inf. Report 1, TR-7.

James, Frederick C. 1969. The Woody Flora of Virginia. Unpublished Ph.D. thesis, University of North Carolina, Chapel Hill, North Carolina.

Jaques, H. E. 1972. *How to Know the Trees.* 2nd ed. Dubuque, Iowa: W.C. Brown Co.

Jenkins, Robert. 1972. Ecosystem Restoration; Third Midwest Prairie Conference Proceedings. Kansas State University, Manhattan, Kansas.

Jensen, Jens. 1956. *Siftings, The Major Portion of the Clearing and Collected Writings.* Chicago: Ralph Fletcher Seymour Publisher.

Kaufman, Edgar, ed. 1955. *An American Architecture: Frank Lloyd Wright.* New York: Horizon Press.

Keeler, Harriet. 1969. *Our Northern Shrubs.* New York: Dover Publications.

Kellman, Martin C. 1980. *Plant Geography.* 2nd ed. New York: St. Martin's Press.

Kellogg, Charles E. 1952. *Our Garden Soils.* New York: Macmillan Co.

Kelsey, Harlan P., and William A. Dayton. 1942. *Standardized Plant Names.* 2nd ed. Harrisburg, Pennsylvania: J. Horace McFarland Co.

Kindilien, Carlin. 1977. *Natural Landscaping: An Energy-Saving Alternative.* Lyme, Connecticut: Weathervane Books.

Kirscht, David Allen. 1967. Visual, Cultural and Ecological Aspects of Trees for Landscape Use In Iowa and Southern Minnesota. Unpublished MLA thesis, Iowa State University, Ames, Iowa.

Kobuski, C. E. 1951. "Studies in the Theaceae, XXI, The Species of Theaceae Indigenous to the United States. *Jour. Arnold Aboric.* 32:123–38.

Korling, Torkel. 1972. *The Prairie: Swell and Swale.* Dundee, Illinois: Korling.

Korling, Torkel, and Robert O. Petty. 1974. *Eastern Deciduous Forest.* Evanston, Illinois: Korling.

Kozlowski, T. T. 1976. Drought and Transplantability of Trees. Better Trees for Metropolitan Landscapes Symp. Proc., U.S.D.A. For. Serv. Gen. Tech. Rep. N.E. Expt. Sta. 22:77–90.

Kozlowski, T. T., and R. C. Ward. 1957. "Seasonal Height Growth of Deciduous Trees." *For. Sci.* 3:168–174.

Kraenzel, Carl Frederick. 1955. *The Great Plains in Transition.* Norman, Oklahoma: University of Oklahoma Press.

Kramer, Jack. 1972. *The Natural Way to Pest-Free Gardening.* New York: Charles Scribner's Sons.

Küchler, August Wilhelm. 1964. *Potential Natural Vegetation of the Coterminous United States.* New York: American Geographic Society.

Kvaalen, R. 1979. Roadside De-Icing Salts and Ornamental Plants. Yard and Garden HO-142, Hort. Dept., Purdue University, West Lafayette, Indiana.

Lamb, George N. 1915. A Calendar of the Leafing, Flowering and Seeding of the Common Trees of the Eastern United States, U.S. Monthly Weather Rev., Sup. 2, Pt. 1.

Lane, Robert Lee. 1976. The Vascular Flora of the West Central Coastal Plain of Georgia. Unpublished Ph.D. thesis, University of Georgia, Athens, Georgia.

Leedy, Daniel L., Robert M. Maestro, and Thomas M. Franklin. 1978. *Planning for Wildlife in Cities and Suburbs.* Washington, D.C.: American Planning Association.

Leone, L. A., et al. 1977. "Damage to Woody Species by Anaerobic Landfill Gases." *Jour. Arboric.* 3(12):221–25.

Leopold, Aldo. 1949. *A Sand County Almanac.* New York: Oxford University Press.

Levitt, J. 1972. *Responses of Plants to Environmental Stresses.* New York: Academic Press.

Limstrom, G. A. 1960. *Forestation of Strip-Mined Land in the Central States.* U.S.D.A. Handbook 166. Washington, D.C.: U.S. Government Printing Office.

Little, Elbert L., Jr. 1971. *Atlas of United States Trees, Volume 1, Conifers and Important Hardwoods.* U.S.D.A. For. Serv. Misc. Publ. 1146. Washington, D.C.: U.S. Government Printing Office.

————. 1976. *Atlas of United States Trees, Volume 3, Minor Western Hardwoods.* U.S.D.A. For. Serv. Misc. Publ. 1314. Washington, D.C.: U.S. Government Printing Office.

————. 1977. *Atlas of United States Trees, Volume 4, Minor Eastern Hardwoods.* U.S.D.A. For. Serv. Misc. Publ. 1342. Washington, D.C.: U.S. Government Printing Office.

Looman, J., and K. F. Best. 1979. *Budd's Flora of the Canadian Prairie Provinces.* Research Branch Agriculture Canada Pub. #1662. Quebec, Canada: Canadian Government Publishing Centre.

Lorenz, R.W. 1939. High Temperature Tolerance of Forest Trees. Univ. Minn. Agric. Exp. Sta. Tech. Bul. 141.

Lorio, P. L. Jr., G E. Gatherund, and W. D. Shrader. 1964. Tree Survival and Growth on Iowa Coal Spoil Materials. Spec. Report No. 39, Ag. and Home Econ. Expt. Sta. Iowa State University, Ames, Iowa.

Lumis, G. P., G. Hofstra, and R. Hall. 1973. "Sensivitivity of Roadside Trees and Shrubs to Aerial Drift of Deicing Salts." *Hort. Sci.* 8:475–77.

————. 1976. "Roadside Woody Plant Susceptibility to Sodium and Chloride Accumulation During Winter and Spring." *Can. Jour. Plant Sci.* 56:853–59.

————. 1977. Salt Damage to Roadside Plants. Ontario Dept. Agric. and Food, Agdex 275.

Lundell, Longworth C. 1961. *Flora of Texas.* 3 vols. Renner, Texas: Texas Research Foundation.

Lunt, O. R., H. C. Kohl, and A. M. Kofranek. 1957. "Tolerance of Azaleas and Gardenias to Salinity Conditions and Boron." *Proc. Amer. Soc. Hort. Sci.* 69:543–48.

McCurdy, D. R., W. G. Spangenberg, and C. P. Doty. 1972. *How to Choose Your Tree.* Carbondale, Illinois: Southern Illinois University Press.

McElroy, Thomas P., Jr. 1974. *The Habitat Guide to Birding.* New York: Alfred A. Knopf.

McFarland, Julian E. 1969. *The Pioneer Era on the Iowa Prairies.* Lake Mills, Iowa: Graphic Publishing Co.

McGourty, Frederick, ed. 1979. *Nursery Source Guide.* Rep. New York: Brooklyn Botanic Garden.

———. 1980. *The Environment and the Home Gardener.* Rep. New York: Brooklyn Botanic Garden.

McHarg, Ian L. 1971. *Design with Nature.* Garden City, New York: Natural History Press.

Margolin, Malcolm. 1975. *The Earth Manual.* Boston, Massachusetts: Houghton Mifflin Co.

Martin, Alexander C., with Herbert S. Zim and Arnold L. Nelson. 1951. *American Wildlife and Plants: A Guide to Wildlife Food Habits.* New York: Dover Publications.

Means, Francis H., Jr. 1969. The Vascular Plants of Southeast Oklahoma from the Saus Bois to the Kiamiche Mountains. Unpublished Ph.D. thesis. Oklahoma State University, Stillwater, Oklahoma.

Menninger, E. A. 1964. *Seaside Plants of the World.* New York: Hearthside Press.

Medsger, O. P. 1942. *Edible Wild Plants.* New York: Macmillan Co.

Middleton, J. T., E. F. Darley, and R. F. Brewer. "Damage to Vegetation from Polluted Atmosphere." *Jour. Air Poll. Cont. Assn.* 8:7–15.

Mohlenbrock, Robert H., and Douglas M. Ladd. 1978. *Distribution of Illinois Vascular Plants.* Carbondale, Illinois: Southern Illinois University Press.

Monk, R. W., and H. B. Peterson. 1962. "Tolerance of Some Trees and Shrubs to Saline Conditions." *Proc. Amer. Soc. Hort. Sci.* 81:556–61.

Monk, R.W., and H. H. Wiebe. 1981. "Salt Tolerance and Protoplastic Salt Hardiness of Various Woody and Herbaceous Ornamental Plants. *Plant Physol.* 36:478–82.

Mooberry, F. M., and Jane H. Scott. 1980. *Grow Native Shrubs in Your Garden.* Chadds Ford, Pennsylvania: Brandywine Conservancy.

Morley, Thomas. 1969. *Spring Flora of Minnesota.* Minneapolis, Minnesota: The University of Minnesota Press.

Moxley, L., and H. Davidson. 1973. Salt Tolerance of Various Woody and Herbaceous Plants. Michigan State Univ. Hort. Rep. 23, Ann Arbor, Michigan.

Mudd, J. B., and T. T. Kozlowski. 1975. *Responses of Plants to Air Pollution.* New York: Academic Press.

National Wildlife Federation. 1974. *Gardening With Wildlife.* Vienna, Virginia: National Wildlife Federation.

Natural Woodland Nursery, Ltd. 1979. *A Guide to Natural Woodland and Prairie Gardening.* Waterloo, Ontario, Canada: Natural Woodland Nursery, Ltd.

Nehrling, Arno, and Irene Nehrling. 1975. *Easy Gardening with Drought-Resistant Plants.* New York: Dover Publications.

Niering, William A., and Richard H. Goodwin. 1975. Energy Conservation on the Home Grounds: The Role of Naturalistic Landscaping. Conn. Arbor. Bul. Ser. no. 21. New London, Connecticut: The Connecticut Arboretum.

Nitsch, J. D. 1957. "Growth Responses of Woody Plants to Photoperiodic Stimuli." *Amer. Soc. Hort. Sci. Proc.* 70:512–25.

Noble, W., and W. Terry. 1969. *A Partial List of Smog Resistant Plants.* Arcadia, California: Los Angeles State and County Arboretum.

Norris, C. Ann. 1983. "Native Plants in the Landscape blend regional distinctiveness with low maintenance." *Amer. Nurseryman* 157(6):99–122.

Odenwald, Neil G., and James R. Turner. 1977. *Plants for Designers, A Handbook for Plants of the South.* Baton Rouge, Louisiana: Claitor's Publishing Division.

Oosting, Henry J. 1956. *The Study of Plant Communities.* 2nd ed. San Francisco, California: W.H. Freeman and Co.

Ormrod, D. P., and G. P. Lumis. 1976. Security Lighting Effects on Landscape Plants. OMAF Factsheet 76-025.

Pammel, L. H., J. F. Ford, Joseph Kelso, and R. R. Harlan. 1919. Iowa Parks. Conservation of Iowa Historic Scenic and Scientific Areas. Rep. State Bd. of Conserv. Des Moines, Iowa.

Parker, Johnson. 1950. "The Effects of Flooding on the Transportation and Survival of Some Southeastern Forest Tree Species." *Plant Physiol.* 25:453–60.

Patterson, James C, 1976. Soil Compaction and its Effects Upon Urban Vegetation. Better Trees for Metropolitan Landscapes Symp. Proc. U.S.D.A. For. Ser. Gen. Tech. Rep. N.E. Expt. Sta. 22:91–103.

Peattie, Donald C. 1950. *Natural History of Trees of Eastern and Central North America.* Boston, Massachusetts: Houghton Mifflin Co.

Pellett, Frank C. 1931. *Flowers of the Wild, Their Culture and Requirements.* New York: A. T. De La Mare Co.

Pellett, N.E. 1972. Salt Tolerance of Trees and Shrubs. Univ. Ver. Ext. Serv., Brieflet 1212.

Penn, Cordelia. 1982. *Landscaping with Native Plants.* Winston-Salem, North Carolina: John F. Blair, Publisher.

Perkins, Harold Oliver. 1942. Woody Plant Material and Landscape Architecture. Unpublished MLA thesis, Iowa State College, Ames, Iowa.

Peterson, Lee. 1978. *A Field Guide to Edible Plants of Eastern and Central North America.* Boston, Massachuetts: Houghton Mifflin Co.

Peterson, Rogert T., et al. 1974. *Gardening with Wildlife.* Vienna, Virginia: National Wildlife Federation.

Petrides, George A. 1972. *A Field Guide to Trees and Shrubs.* 2nd ed. Boston, Massachusetts: Houghton Mifflin Co.

Philbrick, Helen, and Richard Gregg. 1966. *Companion Plants and How to Use Them.* New York: Devin Adair Co.

Phillips, W. Louis, and Ronald L. Stuckey. 1976. *Index to Plant Distribution Maps in North American Periodicals through 1972.* Boston, Massachusetts: G.K. Hall & Co.

Phipps, H. M. 1963. "The Role of 2,4-D in the Appearance of Leaf Blight of Some Plains Tree Species." *For. Sci.* 9:283–88.

Pirone, Pascal P. 1970. *Diseases and Pests of Ornamental Plants.* 4th ed. New York: Ronald Press Co.

Porsild, A. E., and W. J. Cody. 1980. *Vascular Plants of the Continental Northwest Territories Canada.* Ottawa, Ontario, Canada: National Museum of Natural Sciences, National Museum of Canada.

Preston, Richard J. 1961. *North American Trees.* Cambridge, Massachusetts: The M.I.T. Press.

Radford, Albert E., Harry E. Ahles, and C. Ritchie Bell. 1964. *Manual of the Vascular Flora of the Carolinas.* Chapel Hill, North Carolina: The University of North Carolina Press.

————. 1965. Atlas of the Vascular Flora of the Carolinas. N.C. Univ. Dep. Bot. Tech. Bul. 165.

Ramseur, George S. 1959. The Vascular Flora of High Mountain Communities of the Southern Appalacians. Unpublished Ph.D. thesis, University of North Carolina, Chapel Hill, North Carolina.

Reeves, R. G. 1972. *The Flora of Central Texas.* Fort Worth, Texas: Prestige Press.

Rehder, Alfred. 1940. *Manual of Cultivated Trees and Shrubs.* 2nd ed. New York: Macmillan Co.

Reisch, Kenneth W., Phillip C. Kozel, and Gayle A. Weinstein. 1975. *Woody Ornamentals for the Midwest (deciduous).* Dubuque, Iowa: Kendall/Hunt Publishing Co.

Rich, A. E. 1972. "Effects of Salt on Eastern Highway Trees." *Amer. Nurseryman* 135:36–39.

Richards, Charles Davis. 1953. Phytogeographical Studies in the Northern Peninsula of Michigan. Unpublished Ph.D. thesis, University of Michigan, Ann Arbor, Michigan.

Rickett, Harold W. 1973. *Wildflowers of the United States.* New York: McGraw-Hill Book Co.

Riley, John L., and S. M. McKay. 1980. *The Vegetation of Phytogeography of Coastal SW James Bay.* Toronto, Ontario, Canada: Royal Ontario Museum.

Roberts, Edith Adelaide, and Elsa Rehmann. 1929. *American Plants for American Gardens: Plant Ecology—The Study of Plants in Relation to Their Environment.* New York: MacMillan Co.

Robichaud, Beryl, and Murray F. Buell. 1973. *Vegetation of New Jersey: A Study of Landscape Diversity.* New Brunswick, New Jersey: Rutgers University Press.

Robinette, Gary O. 1977. *Landscape Planning for Energy Conservation.* Reston, Virginia: Environmental Design Press.

————. 1977. *Plants, People and Environmental Quality.* Portland, Oregon: National Book Co.

Robinson, Florence Bell. 1941. *Tabular Keys for the Identification of Woody Plants.* Madison, Wisconsin: American Printing and Publishing Inc.

————. 1960. *Useful Trees and Shrubs: A Card File of Data on Approximately 500 Hardy Woody Plants.* Champaign, Illinois: Garrard Press.

Roland, A. E., and E. C. Smith. 1969. *The Flora of Nova Scotia.* Halifax, Nova Scotia, Canada: The Nova Scotia Museum.

Rosendahl, Carl O. 1928. *Trees and Shrubs of Minnesota.* Minneapolis, Minnesota: University of Minnesota Press.

————. 1955. *Trees and Shrubs of the Upper Midwest.* Minneapolis, Minnesota: University of Minnesota Press.

Rousseau, Camille. 1974. *Geographic floristique de Quebec-Labrador, distribution des principales especes vasculaires.* Laval, Quebec, Canada: Les Presses de L'Univ.

Rowell, Chester M. 1967. Vascular Plants of the Texas Panhandle and South Plains. Unpublished Ph.D. thesis, Okalahoma State University, Stillwater, Oklahoma.

Rudd, Robert L. 1964. *Pesticides and the Living Landscape.* Madison, Wisconsin: University of Wisconsin Press.

Sargent, Charles Sprague. 1891–1902. *The Silva of North America: A Description of the Trees Which Grow Naturally in North America (Exclusive of Mexico).* 14 vols. Boston, Massachusetts, and New York: Houghton, Mifflin and Co.

————. 1961. *Manual of the Trees of North America (Exclusive of Mexico).* 2nd ed., Rep. in 2 vols. New York: Dover Publications.

Schoeneweiss, P. F. 1973. "Diagnosis of Physiological Disorders of Woody Ornamentals." *Proc. Intl. Shade Tree Conf.* 49:33a–38a.

Scoggan, H. J. 1978. *The Flora of Canada.* Ottawa, Ontario, Canada: National Museum of Canada.

Scott, D. H. 1973. *Air Pollution Injury to Plant Life.* Washington, D.C.: National Landscape Association.

Settergran, Carl, and R. E. McDermitt. 1969. Trees of Missouri. Univ. of Missouri Agr. Expt. Sta.

Seymour, Frank C. 1969. *The Flora of New England.* Rutland, Vermont: The Charles E. Tuttle Co.

Sharp, W. Curtis. 1977. Conservation Plants for the Northwest. U.S.D.A. Soil Cons. Serv. Prog. Aid No. 1154. Washington, D.C.: U.S. Government Printing Office.

Shaw, Charles Gardener. 1952. Injury to Trees and Shrubs in the State of Washington as a Result of Air Pollution. Univ. Wash. Arboretum Bul. 15:22–23.

Silker, T. H. 1948. "Planting of Water Tolerant Trees along the Margins of Fluctuating Level Reservoirs. *Iowa State College Jour. Sci.* 22:431–47.

Simonds, John O. 1986. *Earthscape: A Manual of Environmental Planning.* New York: Van Nostrand Reinhold Co.

Small, J. K. 1933. *Manual of the Southeastern Flora.* New York: Science Press.

Smith, Alice Upham. 1969. *Trees in a Winter Landscape.* New York: Holt, Rinehart, and Winston.

Smith, E. M., and T. A. Fretz. 1979. Chemical Weed Control in Commercial Nursery and Landscape Plantings. Ohio Coop. Ext. Serv. MM-297.

Smith, William H., and Leon S. Dochinger. 1976. Capability of Metropolitan Trees to Reduce Atmospheric Contaminants. Better Trees for Metropolitan Landscapes Symp. Proc. U.S.D.A. For. Serv. Gen. Tech. Rep. N.E. Expt. Sta. 22:49–61.

Smithsonian Institution. 1978. *Endangered and Threatened Plants of the United States.* Washington, D.C.: Smithsonian Institution Press.

Smyser, Carol A., and the Editors of Rodale Press Books. 1982. *Nature's Design.* Emmaus, Pennsylvania: Rodale Press.

Snyder, Leon C. 1980. *Trees and Shrubs for Northern Gardens.* Minneapolis, Minnesota: University of Minnesota Press.

Society of American Foresters. 1954. *Forest Cover Types of North America (Exclusive of Mexico)*. Washington, D.C.: Society of American Foresters.

———. 1980. *Forest Cover Types of the United States and Canada*. F. H. Eyre, ed. Washington, D.C.: Society of American Foresters.

Soil Conservation Society of America. 1982. *Sources of Native Seed and Plants*. Ankeny, Iowa: Soil Conservation Society of America.

Soper, James H. 1949. *The Vascular Plants of Southern Ontario*. Toronto, Canada: University of Toronto and the Federation of Ontario Naturalists.

Soper, James H., and Margaret L. Heimberger. 1982. *Shrubs of Ontario*. Toronto, Canada: The Royal Ontario Museum Publications in Life Sciences.

Spangler, Ronald S., and Jerry Ripperda. 1977. *Landscape Plants for Central and Northeastern United States*. East Lansing, Michigan: Michigan State University.

Spurr, Stephen H., and Burton V. Barnes. 1980. *Forest Ecology.* 3rd ed. New York: John Wiley & Sons.

Stephens, H. A. 1967. *Trees, Shrubs and Woody Vines in Kansas*. Lawrence, Kansas: University Press of Kansas.

———. 1973. *Woody Plants of the North Central Plains*. Lawrence, Kansas: University Press of Kansas.

———. 1980. *Poisonous Plants of the Central United States*. Lawrence, Kansas: The Regents Press of Kansas.

Steyermark, Julian A. 1963. *Flora of Missouri*. Ames, Iowa: The Iowa State University Press.

Stone, Wilmer. 1911. "The Plants of Southern New Jersey, with Especial Reference to the Flora of the Pine Barrens and the Geographic Distribution of the Species." *Ann. Rep. N.J. State Mus.,* 1910:23-823.

Strausbaugh, P. D., and Earl L. Core. 1952. Flora of West Virginia. W. Va. Univ. Bul. Series 52 No. 12-2; 1952 Part I, Morgantown, West Virginia.

Swink, Floyd, and Gerould Wilhelm. 1976. *Plants of the Chicago Region*. Lisle, Illinois: The Morton Arboretum.

Symonds, George. 1958. *The Tree Identification Book*. New York: William Morrow and Co., Inc.

———. 1963. *The Shrub Identification Book*. New York: M. Barrows.

Tatnall, Robert R. 1946. *Flora of Delaware and the Eastern Shore*. Lancaster, Pennsylvania: The Society of Natural History of Delaware.

Taylor, Albert D. 1921. *The Complete Garden*. New York: Garden City Publishing Co., Inc.

Taylor, Fred G., Jr. 1972. *Phenodynamics of Production in a Mesic Deciduous Forest*. Oak Ridge, Tennessee: Oak Ridge National Laboratory, U.S. Atomic Energy Commission.

Taylor, Kathryn S. 1949. *A Traveler's Guide to Roadside Flowers, Shrubs and Trees*. New York: Farrar, Straus.

Taylor, Kathryn S., and Stephen F. Hamblin. 1962. *Handbook of Wild Flower Cultivation*. New York: MacMillan Publishing Co.

Taylor, Norman. 1961. *Taylor's Encyclopedia of Gardening*. Boston, Massachusetts: Houghton Mifflin Co.

Tenebaum, Frances. 1973. *Gardening with Wildflowers*. New York: Charles Scribner's Sons.

Thomas, Moyer D. 1961. Effects of Air Pollution on Plants. World Health Organization monograph series (Geneva) 46:233–79.

Thorne, Robert F. 1950. The Flora of Southwest Georgia. Unpublished Ph.D. thesis, Cornell University, Ithaca, New York.

Treshow, M., and D. Stewart. 1973. "Ozone Sensitivity of Plants in Natural Communities." *Biol. Cons.* 5:209–14.

Tryon, E. H., and Rudolfs Markus. 1953. Development of Vegetation on Century-Old Iron Ore Spoil Banks. W. Va. Agr. Expt. Sta. Bul. 360.

Tucker, Gary E. 1976. A Guide to the Woody Flora of Arkansas. Unpublished Ph.D. thesis, University of Arkansas, Fayetteville, Arkansas.

U.S.D.A. Forest Service. 1965. *Silvics of Forest Trees of the United States.* U.S.D.A. Handbook, No. 271. Washington, D.C.: U.S. Government Printing Office.

U.S.D.A. Forest Service. 1971. Atlas of United States Trees. Vol. 1, Conifers and Important Hardwoods. Misc. publication No. 1146. Washington, D.C.: U.S. Government Printing Office.

U.S.D.A. Forest Service. 1973. *Air Pollution Damage to Trees.* Northeast Area, Upper Darby, Pennsylvania.

U.S.D.A. Forest Service. 1973. Trees for Polluted Air. Misc. publication No. 1230. Washington, D.C.: U.S. Government Printing Office.

U.S.D.A. Forest Service. 1976. Atlas of United States Trees. Vol. 3, Minor Western Hardwoods. Misc. publication No. 1314. Washington, D.C.: U.S. Government Printing Office.

U.S. E.P.A. 1972. *Diagnosing Vegetation Injury Caused by Air Pollution.* Washington, D.C.: U.S. Government Printing Office.

Van Bruggen, Theodore. 1958. The Flora of Southcentral Iowa. Unpublished thesis, State University of Iowa Botany Library, Iowa City, Iowa.

Van Dersal, William. 1938. *Native Woody Plants of the U.S.: Their Erosion Control and Wildlife Values.* Washington, D.C.: U.S. Government Printing Office.

Vines, R. A. 1960. *Trees and Shrubs and Woody Vines of the Southwest.* Austin, Texas: University of Texas Press.

Voight, John W., and Robert H. Mohlenbrock. 1964. *Plant Communities of Southern Illinois.* Carbondale, Illinois: Southern Illinois University Press.

Vosburgh, John. 1968. *Living with Your Land.* New York: Charles Scribner's Sons.

Voss, Edward G. 1972. *Michigan Flora, a Guide to the ID and Occurrence of Native Seed Plants of the State.* Bloomfield Hills, Michigan: Cranebrook Institute of Science.

Wali, Mohan K., ed. 1974. *Prairie: A Multiple View—Proceedings of the 4th Midwest Prairie Conference.* Grand Forks, North Dakota: University of North Dakota Press.

Wareing, P. F. 1956. "Photoperiodism in Woody Plants." *Annu. Rev. Plant Physiol.* 7:191–214.

Watts, May T. 1975. *Reading the Landscape.* Rev. ed. New York: Macmillan Publishing Co.

Waxman, Sidney. 1957. "The Development of Woody Plants as Affected by Photoperiodic Treatment." *Diss. Abs.* 17(2):23–72.

Wharton, M.E., and R.W. Barbour. 1973. *Trees and Shrubs of Kentucky.* Lexington, Kentucky: University Press of Kentucky.

Wherry, E. T., J. M. Fogg, and H. A. Wahl. 1979. *Atlas of the Flora of Pennsylvania.* Philadelphia, Pennsylvania: The Morris Arboretum of the University of Pennsylvania.

Whitcomb, Carl E. 1975. *Know It and Grow It*. Stillwater, Oklahoma: Oklahoma State University Press.

White, John. 1978. Illinois Natural Areas Inventory, Survey Methods and Results. Tech. Rep. I performed under contract to Illinois Department of Conservation. Urbana, Champaign: The Department of Landscape Architecture, University of Illinois and the Natural Land Institute at Rockford.

White, William H. 1968. *The Last Landscape*. Garden City, New York: Doubleday and Co.

Whitlow, T. H., and R. W. Harris. 1979. *Flood Tolerance in Plants: A State-of-the-Art Review*. U.S. Army Eng. Waterways Exp. Sta. Tech Report E-79-2, Vicksburg, Mississippi.

Whittaker, Robert H. 1975. *Communities and Ecosystems*. New York: Macmillan Publishing Co.

Williston, H. L. 1959. Inundation Damage to Upland Hardwoods. U.S. For. Serv. South. For. Expt. Sta., South. For. Notes No. 123.

Williams, John E. 1973. *Atlas of the Woody Plants of Oklahoma*. Norman, Oklahoma: Oklahoma Biological Survey.

Wisconsin Department of Agriculture. 1968. Pests and Diseases of Trees and Shrubs. Wisc. State Dept. of Agr. Bul. 700-65.

Wood, F. A., and J. B. Coppolini. 1971. "The Influence of Ozone on Selected Woody Ornamentals." *Phytopath*. 61:133.

Workmam, Richard. 1980. *Growing Native-Native Plants for Landscape Use in Coastal South Florida*. Sanibel, Florida: The Sanibel Captive Conservation Foundation Inc.

Wyman, Donald. 1965. Trees for American Gardens. New York: Macmillan Publishing Co.

———. 1969. *Shrubs and Vines for American Gardens*. New York: Macmillan Publishing Co.

———. 1974. *Dwarf Shrubs*. New York: Macmillan Publishing Co.

Yeager, A. F. 1935. "Root Systems of Certain Trees and Shrubs Growing on Prairie Soils." *Jour. Agr. Red*. 51:1085–92.

———. 1953. Notes on Flowering and Fruiting of Northeastern Trees. U.S. For. Serv., N.E. For. Expt. Sta. Pap. 56.

Yeager, L. E. 1949. Effect of Permanent Flooding on a River-Bottom Timber Area. *Ill. Nat. Hist. Survey Bul.*, vol. 25, Art, 2:29–65.

Yelonosky, G. 1964. Tolerance of Trees to Deficiencies of Soil Aeration. Int. Shade Tree Conf. Proc. 40:127–247.

Zelasney, L. W. 1968. "Salt Tolerance of Roadside Vegetation" in *Proceedings Symposium: Pollutants in the Roadside Environment*, ed. E. D. Carpenter. Storrs, Connecticut: Plant Science Dept., University of Connecticut.

Zimmerman, P. W. 1955. Chemicals Involved in Air Pollution and Their Effects on Vegetation. Boyce Thompson Institute professional paper 21(4):124–45.

Zimmerman, P. W., and William Crocker. 1934. Toxicity of Air Containing Sulphur Dioxide Gas. Contrib. Boyce Thompson Institute 6(4):455-70.

Zimmerman, P. W., and A. E. Hitchcock. 1956. Susceptibility of Plants to Hydroflouric Acid and Sulphur Dioxide Gases. Contrib. Boyce Thompson Institute 18:263–79.

Zion, Robert L. 1968. *Trees for Architecture and the Landscape*. New York: Reinhold Book Corp.

Zucker, Isabel. 1966. *Flowering Shrubs*. Princeton, New Jersey: M.S. Van Nostrand.

INDEX